T0122900

Advanced Algorithms and Data Structures

MARCELLO LA ROCCA

MANNING
SHELTER ISLAND

For online information and ordering of this and other Manning books, please visit www.manning.com. The publisher offers discounts on this book when ordered in quantity. For more information, please contact

Special Sales Department
Manning Publications Co.
20 Baldwin Road
PO Box 761
Shelter Island, NY 11964
Email: orders@manning.com

Manning Publications Co.
20 Baldwin Road

PO Box 761
Shelter Island, NY 11964

Development editor: Jenny Stout
Technical development editor: Arthur Zubarev and Aurelio De Rosa
Review editor: Aleksandar Dragosavljevic
Production editor: Deirdre Hiam
Copy editor: Katie Petito
Proofreader: Melody Dolab
Technical proofreader: German Gonzalez-Morris
Typesetter: Gordan Salinovic
Cover designer: Marija Tudor

ISBN 9781617295485
Printed in the United States of America

Don't let fear get in the way and don't be afraid to say "I don't know" or "I don't understand" – no question is a dumb question.

—*Margaret H. Hamilton*

Simplicity is a great virtue but it requires hard work to achieve it and education to appreciate it. And to make matters worse: complexity sells better.

—*Edsger Dijkstra*

Cu `un fa nenti `un sbagghia nenti.
(Only those who try make mistakes)

—*Sicilian proverb*

contents

foreword

Algorithms and data structures lie at the very heart of the intersection between the beauty of theory and the excitement of cutting-edge technology. One can say that if the body of the advancements in computation is hardware, then the mind is certainly the study of algorithms and data structures. Many of the recent advances in technology have come to life thanks to the effective use of computing resources to solve problems, and this is often due to the effective development and implementation of algorithms and clever use of data structures.

A computer scientist, a software developer, a data scientist, or anyone whose work is dependent on the power of computation needs to be fluent in the language of algorithms and data structures. It is for this reason that problems in this field are some of the most common in interviews for companies in Silicon Valley or similar technology sectors.

It is quite difficult, even for experts, to learn and remember all the details of all the algorithms in existence. However, it is important to have a good intuition about them in such a way that one can use them as building blocks to create larger projects or to solve problems. In order to master this intuition, one must develop a rigid theoretical and mathematical base, solid programming knowledge, and a strong understanding of the core concepts.

Building this intuition is precisely what *Advanced Algorithms and Data Structures* does so well. In this book, Marcello combines the rigidity of the theory with the versatility of the practical application, painted with the strokes of a colorful narrative full of enjoyable stories and real-life examples.

Marcello also uses his extensive experience as a developer at some of the most prominent technology companies and as a researcher in machine learning to give the reader a very clear, concise, and thorough picture of some of the most important algorithms and data structures used across industries and research fields.

With a one-size-fits-all approach, a friendly language, and fun analogies, Marcello manages to lift the curtain and demystify complicated topics such as map reduce, genetic algorithms, and simulated annealing, with the same ease as he exposes the basics of trees and heaps. Certainly a must-read for anyone who wants to get a solid understanding of the building principles of computer science. The only question in my head after reading *Advanced Algorithms and Data Structures* was, "Where was this book when I was preparing for my first Silicon Valley interview?"

LUIS SERRANO, PHD

RESEARCH SCIENTIST IN QUANTUM ARTIFICIAL INTELLIGENCE

ZAPATA COMPUTING

preface

Welcome to Advanced Algorithms and Data Structures

It's great to have you on board for this journey into the world of data structures and algorithms. I hope this will be as exciting a journey for you as it was for us.

The topics discussed in this book have contributed to advancing software engineering and have changed the world around us. They still do make a difference, and on average, you likely come in contact every day with dozens of devices and services using these algorithms.

The study of algorithms far predates the dawn of computer science: think about the Euler algorithm and the whole field of graph theory, which are three centuries old. But that's nothing compared to the two millennia since the sieve of Eratosthenes (used to make tables of prime numbers) was first conceived.

And yet, for a long time in the computer era, algorithms were mostly relegated to academia, with a few notable exceptions like Bell Labs, where between the 1950s and the 1990s their R&D teams produced great advancements in the field, such as (to name a few) dynamic programming, the Bellman-Ford algorithm, and convolutional neural networks for image recognition.

Luckily, many things have changed since those days. In the new millennium, mathematicians and computer scientists are increasingly sought by the largest software companies, new fields like machine learning have emerged, others like Artificial Intelligence (AI) and neural networks have regained interest after a long winter, and top experts in these fields are now among the best paid positions in the entire software engineering industry.

Personally, I became fascinated by algorithms in college—I had already studied search and sorting algorithms in high school—but it wasn't until I learned about trees and graphs that I became aware of the difference they can make and how much I liked these topics.

It was the first time I had a feeling that writing code that worked was not the only goal, nor the main goal. How it works, how efficiently it runs, and how clean it is can be just as important, if not more so. (Unfortunately, I still had to wait a couple more years to have the same epiphany about testing.)

Writing this book was a lot of work, far more than I anticipated four years ago when I first pitched the idea to an editor. The story of how it came to be published is quite funny (well, at least in retrospect!), but I won't bother you with it here. Just know that while writing this book I went through four years, three jobs (and a half!), two countries, and five different apartments!

It took a great (team) effort, for sure, but it was also rewarding. First and foremost, writing a book means starting a growth path, because it doesn't matter how long you've worked on a topic and how well you think you know it. To write about any topic, you'll be forced to question all you know about it, delve into details you might have overlooked when you previously applied it, and spend a lot of time researching, digesting, and processing the concepts until you are confident enough to explain them to someone who doesn't know anything about the subject. Usually a good test is getting someone in your family who doesn't work in that field and forcing them to listen to you while you unravel your lecture. Just make sure you choose someone very patient.

acknowledgments

There are quite a few people I'd like to thank for helping me along the way.

I'd like to acknowledge my editors at Manning: Helen Stergius, who had the unenviable task of helping me transition my manuscript from its original draft to Manning's standards, and Jennifer Stout, who worked on this project for the last couple of years. Without their help, it would have been impossible to get this to the goal. It was a pleasure working with you both. Thank you for your help, your invaluable advice, and your patience! I feel that by working with you, I learned a lot about the best way to write about a topic, teach, and address readers, and you have made this book better for everyone who reads it.

Next, I'd like to thank both the technical editors who worked on this book.

A huge thank you to Arthur Zubarev, who joined the team a couple of years ago, providing a ton of great feedback and always giving voice to my critical conscience. Working with you has been a pleasure and an honor.

A special shout-out goes to my friend Aurelio De Rosa. I had the privilege to have him as an editor on a JavaScript blog, on which we both wrote long before this book got started. Besides teaching me so much about technical writing, his contribution to this book is huge. He was its first technical editor and set the course for the whole book, discussed the topics to include, and reviewed the code. In addition to that, he also introduced me to Manning when I was looking for a publisher for my draft.

Thanks as well to all the other folks at Manning who worked with me on the production and promotion of the book: Deirdre Hiam, my project editor; Katie Petito, my copyeditor; Melody Dolab, my page proofer; and Aleksandar Dragosavljevic, my reviewing editor. It was truly a team effort. And thanks to the reviewers: Andrei Formiga, Christoffer Fink, Christopher Haupt, David T. Kerns, Eddu Melendez, George Thomas, Jim Amrhein, John Montgomery, Lucas Gerardo Tettamanti, Maciej Jurkowski, Matteo Gildone, Michael Jensen, Michael Kumm, Michelle Williamson, Rasmus Kirkeby Strøbæk, Riccardo Noviello, Rich Ward, Richard Vaughan, Timmy Jose, Tom Jenice, Ursula Cervantes, Vincent Zaballa, and Zachary Fleischmann who took the time to read my manuscript at various stages during its development and who provided invaluable feedback.

I couldn't wrap this up without thanking my family and friends, as they have all been supportive and patient during these years. I'm not sure if I've mentioned this already (have I?), but writing this book was quite an effort! If you ever try the experience, you'll see it will mean giving up many evenings, holidays, and weekends, where instead of going to the lake or having a beer with friends—or just doing your chores—you need to focus and work on the manuscript. I couldn't have done this without the help and patience of my closest ones—and now I'll have to make up for all the time together that we missed (and for all those chores I skipped)!

Finally, I need two special mentions, to special people who allowed me to be the computer scientist I am today.

First, I'd like to thank my former professors at the University of Catania. For the sake of brevity, I can only individually thank my mentors, Prof. Gallo, Prof. Cutello, and Prof. Pappalardo, but I have a really long list of names, and I'd probably still leave someone out. I feel that, in a time where the usefulness of college degrees is being questioned in favor of quicker, more practical alternatives, it's important to give recognition to the outstanding job carried out by my former instructors and by my alma mater over the years. MOOCs and code camps are great alternatives, and they are a step in the direction of a more affordable and democratic education regardless of location and status, but one thing that I feel I would have missed without my college experience is the development of a critical attitude, a scientist mentality of learning how to reason on problems and getting a broader skillset than just the bare minimum needed to land a job.

I must admit that I, too, was skeptical about some of the courses in my curriculum, like the one on linear algebra, because I couldn't see how to apply them as a developer. A few years after my graduation, I started studying machine learning and then all that math came in handy and gave me an advantage.

The last mention has to be for the one who supported me through my early life and my studies: my mother who, at the price of many sacrifices, raised me and sustained me through the years of my education, allowing me to follow my passion. Her support enabled me to reach all the goals in my career, including writing this book, and so, in a way, she shares the credit for all its good parts.

about this book

I can give you at least three good reasons to invest your time in learning algorithms:

1. *Performance*—Choosing the right algorithm can speed your application up dramatically. Just limiting to something as simple as search, we'll see that there is a huge gain going from linear search to binary search.
2. *Security*—If you choose the wrong algorithm, an attacker can use it to crash your server, node, or application. Consider, for instance, the hash DoS attack,[1] where the use of a hash table as a dictionary to store variables sent with *POST* requests was leveraged to overload it with a sequence causing a huge number of collisions. This in turn would make a server unresponsive. Another interesting example was how flawed random number generators[2] allowed the hacking of online poker sites.
3. *Efficiency in designing code*—If you already know that there are building blocks for whatever you'd like to accomplish, you will be faster in developing it, and the result will be cleaner (especially if you reuse code).

That said, why should you read *this* book? I believe one great reason is that we are striving to select and present in the same book a strategic pool of advanced algorithms that will help developers improve their code and face some of the challenges of modern systems.

---

1 See http://ocert.org/advisories/ocert-2011-003.html.

2 See, for instance, Arkin, Brad, et al. "How we learned to cheat at online poker: A study in software security." The developer.com journal (1999), http://www.bluffnakedpoker.com/PDF/developer_gambling.pdf.

Moreover, we are trying to use a different approach than the usual college textbook. Like those books, we will explain the theory behind algorithms, but at the same time, we will also try to give you some context about real-world applications that leverage each algorithm we describe and situations where it is advisable to use them.

In your daily work, you'll often have to deal with small, specific parts of larger (possibly legacy) software. However, in your career, there will be moments in which those large software applications need to be designed. That is the moment where you'll need most of the content discussed here, and we will try to provide you with insight about how to write clean, fast code to solve some of the most relevant problems you could face.

By using a fresh approach, where for each chapter we enumerate problems that a given data structure can help solve, we will offer a handbook, a helper tool that you can refer to any time you need a suggestion on the best way to improve your application's performance.

Last but not least, if you happened to have read *Grokking Algorithms*, by Aditya. Y. Bhargava (Manning Publications, 2016), and you enjoyed it, then this book represents the natural next step if you'd like to continue on your path of learning about algorithms. If you haven't read it yet, I warmly encourage you to take a look at that book: it's a great choice to get an introduction to these topics, explained clearly to all audiences. It's not by chance that it turned out to be a wildly popular book. We hope to have made this book as enjoyable and clear.

Who should read this book?

Most of the chapters in this book are written for an audience that has already some basic understanding of algorithms, programming, and math, but we also provide a crash course in the appendices, if you need a refresher or a quick intro to these topics.

Reading this book will be much easier if you are already familiar (or make yourself familiar) with the following concepts:

- Good foundations in math and algebra will help you understand the theory sections, but we will nonetheless include a short introduction to big-O notation and asymptotic analysis in appendix B.
- Likewise, if you have taken an introductory class in computer science, or even algorithms, it's likely you are already familiar with the basic data structures that will be the basis for what we will build throughout the book.
- The data structures discussed in this book require some basic prior knowledge to be fully understood:
  - Basic storage structures such as arrays and linked lists
  - Hash tables and hashing
  - Trees
  - Containers (queues and stacks)
  - The basics of recursion
- If you need a refresher, we do provide a quick review of these structures in appendix C.

How this book is organized: a roadmap

The book starts in chapter 1, with a gentle introduction to the way topics are discussed in this book, a preview of what you'll find in the typical chapter.

Starting from chapter 2, the rest of the book will be divided into three parts, plus the appendices. Each part is focused on a theme that can be either an abstract goal or a class of problems we aim to solve.

Part 1 focuses on discovering advanced data structures that allow you to improve some basic operations, for example, keeping track of things or groups of things. The key point is to become accustomed to the idea that there are many ways to perform operations on data, and the best way depends on the context and requirements.

Chapter 1 defines algorithms and data structures, explains the differences between them, and, through an example, explains the process of exploring different algorithms to solve a problem and how they can be leveraged to find better solutions.

Chapter 2 introduces an advanced variant of binary heaps, the *d-way heap*. It also describes the structure we use in each chapter in this part to explain topics.

Chapter 3 further explores advanced use of heaps with *treap*, a hybrid between a binary search tree and a heap that can also help in different contexts.

Chapter 4 switches to *Bloom filters*, an advanced form of hash table that can help save memory while maintaining amortized constant-time search.

Chapter 5 introduces a few alternative data structures used to keep track of *disjoint sets*, a cornerstone needed to build countless advanced algorithms and used in several practical real-world applications.

Chapter 6 presents two data structures that outperform general-purpose containers when it comes to storing and searching strings: *tries* and *radix tries*, also known as compact prefix trees.

Chapter 7 leverages the data structures presented so far to build a composed data structure, the *LRU-cache*, to efficiently handle caching. The *LFU-cache* variant is also discussed at length, as well as the issues with synchronizing shared containers in multithread environments.

Part 2 introduces another special case in search: dealing with multi-dimensional data, indexing this data and performing spatial queries. We will once again show how ad-hoc data structures can provide drastic improvements over using basic search algorithms. But this part also describes other important topics: clustering, heavily leveraging spatial queries, and distributed computing, in particular with the MapReduce programming model.

Chapter 8 introduces the *nearest neighbor* problem.

Chapter 9 describes *k-d trees*, a solution for efficient search in multi-dimensional data sets.

Chapter 10 presents more advanced versions of these trees, *ss-trees* and *r-trees*.

Chapter 11 focuses on the applications of *nearest neighbor search*, with a use case described in depth (finding the closest warehouse from which goods should be shipped to customers).

Chapter 12 presents another real-world use case leveraging the efficient nearest neighbor search algorithms presented so far: three clustering algorithms, *k-means*, *DBSCAN* and *OPTICS*.

Chapter 13 concludes this part by introducing *MapReduce*, a powerful computational model for distributed computing, and applying it to the clustering algorithms discussed in chapter 12.

Part 3 focuses on a single data structure, *graphs*, that will be the common thread in introducing a few optimization techniques that drive today's AI and big data efforts.

Chapter 14 is a short introduction to *graphs*, condensing the basics for this fundamental data structure, needed to understand part 3. It also illustrates *DFS*, *BFS*, *Dijkstra's* and the *A** algorithms, and describes how to use them to solve the "minimum-distance path" problem.

Chapter 15 introduces graph *embeddings*, planarity, and a couple of problems we will try to solve in the remaining chapters: finding the minimum crossing number (*MCN*) embedding of a graph and drawing a graph nicely.

Chapter 16 describes a fundamental algorithm in machine learning, *gradient descent*, and shows how it can be applied to graphs and embeddings.

Chapter 17 builds on the previous chapter and presents *simulated annealing*, a more powerful optimization technique that tries to overcome gradient descent shortcomings when we have to deal with non-differentiable functions or functions with multiple local minima.

Chapter 18, finally, describes *genetic algorithms*, an even more advanced optimization technique that helps with faster convergence.

Chapters follow a specific structure, guiding you on a path from a problem to designing a data structure for its solution, to implementing that solution, and understanding its running time and memory needs.

But enough for now; you'll learn more about this structure in chapter 2.

At the end of the book, there is an extra section for appendices, covering crucial topics that are needed to navigate through the topics of this book. Appendices have a different structure than chapters because they are not built around examples, but rather present a summary of material that the reader should be familiar with before embarking on the journey through the chapters. Most of the topics in the appendices are covered in basic algorithm classes, and chapters have several references to the appendices to help readers leverage them at the right time, but our suggestion is for you to at least skim through them before going to chapter 2.

Appendix A introduces the notation we use for our *pseudo-code* to describe algorithms.

Appendix B provides an overview of *big-O notation* and time-space analysis.

Appendix C and appendix D offer a summary of the *core data structures* that are used as building blocks of the advanced ones in this book.

Appendix E explains *recursion*, a challenging programming technique that often allows for clearer and more concise definitions of algorithms—with some tradeoffs, as we will see.

Appendix F gives the definition of *randomized algorithms*, both *Monte Carlo* and *Las Vegas* types, and introduces classification problems and metrics for randomized solutions.

About the code

The algorithms in this book will be explained using pseudo-code, so you are not required to have any prior knowledge of any specific programming language.

It is, however, assumed that you have a certain familiarity with basic, language-agnostic, programming concepts such as loops and conditionals, not to mention Boolean operators and the concepts of variables and assignments.

To help you go through the pseudo-code in this book, we provide a short guide in appendix A describing the syntax (or rather, pseudo-syntax) that we'll use throughout the chapters. You might want to take a look at appendix A before starting with chapter 1, or if you feel more confident, you can start looking at code snippets and refer to appendix A if or when you feel the syntax used is not immediately clear.

Besides pseudo-code, if you do have knowledge of or an interest in a specific programming language, or if you'd like to see these concepts implemented in real, executable, code, we provide a repository on GitHub[3] with implementations in a few languages (starting with Java, Python, and JavaScript) for the data structures described.

liveBook discussion forum

Purchase of *Advanced Algorithms and Data Structures* includes free access to a private web forum run by Manning Publications where you can make comments about the book, ask technical questions, and receive help from the author and from other users. To access the forum, go to https://livebook.manning.com/book/algorithms-and-data-structures-in-action/welcome/v-14. You can also learn more about Manning's forums and the rules of conduct at https://livebook.manning.com/#!/discussion.

Manning's commitment to our readers is to provide a venue where a meaningful dialogue between individual readers and between readers and the author can take place. It is not a commitment to any specific amount of participation on the part of the author, whose contribution to the forum remains voluntary (and unpaid). We suggest you try asking the author some challenging questions lest his interest stray! The forum and the archives of previous discussions will be accessible from the publisher's website as long as the book is in print.

[3] See https://github.com/mlarocca/AlgorithmsAndDataStructuresInAction.

about the author

MARCELLO LA ROCCA is a senior software engineer at Tundra.com. His work and interests focus on graphs, optimization algorithms, genetic algorithms, machine learning, and quantum computing. He has contributed to large-scale web applications and data infrastructure at companies like Twitter, Microsoft, and Apple, undertaken applied research in both academia and industry, and authored the NeatSort adaptive sorting algorithm.

about the cover illustration

The figure on the cover of *Advanced Algorithms and Data Structures* is captioned "Femme de Fiume," or "Woman from Rijeka." The illustration is taken from a collection of dress costumes from various countries by Jacques Grasset de Saint-Sauveur (1757-1810), titled *Costumes de Différents Pays,* published in France in 1797. Each illustration is finely drawn and colored by hand. The rich variety of Grasset de Saint-Sauveur's collection reminds us vividly of how culturally apart the world's towns and regions were just 200 years ago. Isolated from each other, people spoke different dialects and languages. In the streets or in the countryside, it was easy to identify where they lived and what their trade or station in life was just by their dress.

The way we dress has changed since then and the diversity by region, so rich at the time, has faded away. It is now hard to tell apart the inhabitants of different continents, let alone different towns, regions, or countries. Perhaps we have traded cultural diversity for a more varied personal life—certainly for a more varied and fast-paced technological life.

At a time when it is hard to tell one computer book from another, Manning celebrates the inventiveness and initiative of the computer business with book covers based on the rich diversity of regional life of two centuries ago, brought back to life by Grasset de Saint-Sauveur's pictures.

1 Introducing data structures

This chapter covers

- Explaining why you should learn about data structures and algorithms
- Understanding the difference between algorithms and data structures
- Abstracting a problem
- Moving from problems to solutions

So, you want to learn about algorithms and data structures: excellent decision!

If you are still deciding whether this is for you, I hope this introductory chapter can dispel your doubts and spark your interest in this great topic.

Why should you learn about algorithms? The short answer is to try to become a better software developer. Knowing about data structures and algorithms is like adding a tool to your tool belt.

Have you ever heard of Maslow's hammer, aka the law of the instrument? It's a conjecture, driven by observation, about how people who only know one way to do things tend to apply what they know to all kinds of different situations.

If your tool belt only has a hammer, you will be tempted to treat everything as a nail. If you only know how to sort a list, you will be tempted to sort your tasks list every time you add a new task or have to pick the next one to tackle, and you will never be able to leverage the context to find more efficient solutions.

The purpose of this book is to give you many tools you can use when approaching a problem. We will build upon the basic algorithms normally presented in a computer science 101 course (or the like) and introduce you to more advanced material.

After reading this book, you should be able to recognize situations where you could improve the performance of your code by using a specific data structure and/or algorithm.

Obviously, your goal should not be to remember by heart all the details of all the data structures we will discuss. Rather, we will try to show you how to reason about issues, and where to find ideas about algorithms that might help you in solving problems. This book will also serve as a handbook, sort of like a recipe collection, with indications about some common scenarios that could be used to categorize those problems and the best structures you could use to attack them.

Keep in mind that some topics are quite advanced and, when we delve into the details, it might require a few reads to understand everything. The book is structured in such a way as to provide many levels of in-depth analysis, with advanced sections generally grouped together toward the end of each chapter, so if you'd like to only get an understanding of the topics, you are not required to delve into the theory.

1.1 Data structures

To start with our journey, we first need to agree on a common language to describe and evaluate algorithms.

Describing them is pretty much a standard process: algorithms are described in terms of the input they take and the output they provide. Their details can be illustrated with pseudo-code (ignoring implementation details of programming languages) or actual code.

Data structures (DS) follow the same conventions, but they also go slightly beyond. We also have to describe the actions you can perform on a data structure. Usually each action is described in term of an algorithm, with an input and an output, but in addition to those, for DSs we also need to describe *side effects*, the changes an action might cause to the data structure itself.

To fully understand what this means, we first need to properly define data structures.

1.1.1 Defining a data structure

A data structure is a specific solution for organizing data that provides storage for items and capabilities[1] for storing and retrieving them.

[1] Specifically, at least one method to add a new element to the DS, and one method either to retrieve a specific element or to query the DS.

The simplest example of a DS is an array. For instance, an array of characters provides storage for a finite number of characters and methods to retrieve each character in the array based on its position. Figure 1.1 shows how `array = ['C', 'A', 'R']` is stored: an array of characters storing the characters `C`, `A`, and `R`, such that, for instance, `array[1]` corresponds to the value `'A'`.

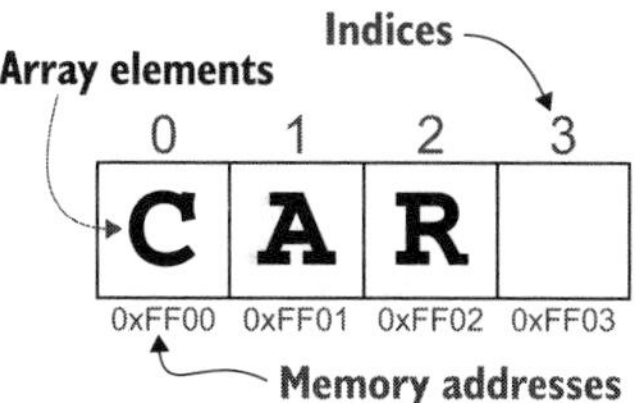
Indices
Array elements
0 1 2 3
C A R
0xFF00 0xFF01 0xFF02 0xFF03
Memory addresses

Figure 1.1 The (simplified) internal representation of an array. Each element of the array in the picture corresponds to a byte of memory,[2] whose address is shown below it. Each element's index is shown above it. An array is stored as a contiguous block of memory, and each element's address can be obtained by adding its index within the array to the offset of the first element. For instance, the fourth character of the array (array[3], empty in the figure), has address 0xFF00 + 3 = 0xFF03.

Data structures can be abstract or concrete:

- An abstract data type (ADT) specifies the operations that can be performed on some data and the computational complexity of those operations. No details are provided on how data is stored or how physical memory is used.
- A data structure (DS) is a concrete implementation of the specification provided by an ADT.

What is an ADT?

You can think about an ADT as the blueprint, while a DS is the translation of those specifications into real code.

An ADT is defined from the point of view of the one who uses it, by describing its behavior in terms of possible values, possible operations on it, and the output and side effects of these operations.

A more formal definition would describe an ADT as a set of types, a designated type from that type set, a set of functions, and a set of axioms.

In contrast, a data structure, which is a concrete representation of data, is described from the point of view of an implementer, not a user.

Back to our array example, a possible ADT for a static array is, for example, a container that can store a fixed number of elements, each associated with an index (the position of the element within the array), and access any element by its position (random access).

Its implementation, however, needs to take care of details such as

- Will the array size be fixed at creation or can it be modified?
- Will the array be allocated statically or dynamically?

[2] In modern architectures/languages, it is possible that an array element corresponds to a *word* of memory rather than a byte, but for the sake of simplicity, let's just assume an array of char is stored as an array of bytes.

- Will the array host only elements of a single type or of any type?
- Is it going to be implemented as a raw chunk of memory or as an object? And what attributes will it hold?

Even for such a basic data structure as arrays, different programming languages make different choices with respect to the previous questions. But all of them make sure their version of arrays abides by the array's ADT we described earlier.

Another good example to help understand the difference might be a stack. We will describe stacks in appendices C and D, but I assume you have likely heard of stacks before.

A possible description of a stack as an ADT is the following: a container that can store an indefinite number of elements, and can remove elements one at a time, starting from the most recent, according to the inverse order of insertion.

An alternative description could break down the actions that can be performed on the container. A stack is a container that supports two main methods:

1. Insertion of an element.
2. Removal of an element. If the stack is not empty, the element that was added most recently will be removed from the stack and returned.

It's still a high-level description, but it's clearer and more modular than the previous one.

Either description is abstract enough to make it easily generalizable, allowing you to implement a stack in a wide range of programming languages, paradigms, and systems.[3]

At some point, however, we will have to move to a concrete implementation and will need to discuss details such as

- Where are the elements stored?
  - An array?
  - A linked list?
  - A B-tree on disk?
- How do we keep track of the order of insertion? (Connected to the previous question.)
- Will the max size of the stack be known and fixed in advance?
- Can the stack contain elements of any type or must all be the same type?
- What happens if removal is called on an empty stack? (For instance, returning `null` versus throwing an error.)

And we could keep on going with questions, but hopefully you get the idea.

[3] In principle, it doesn't need to be anything related to computer science. For instance, you could describe as a system a stack of files to be examined, or—a common example in computer science classes—a pile of dishes to be washed.

1.1.2 Describing a data structure

The crucial part of an ADT definition is to list the set operations that it allows. This is equivalent to defining an API,[4] a contract with its clients.

Every time you need to describe a data structure, you can follow a few simple steps to provide a comprehensive and unambiguous specification:

- Specifying its API first, with a focus on the methods' input and output
- Describing its high-level behavior
- Describing in detail the behavior of its concrete implementation
- Analyzing the performance of its methods

We will use the same workflow for the data structures presented in this book after describing a concrete scenario in which each data structure is actually used.

Starting in chapter 2, with the description of the first data structure presented, we will also explain in further detail the conventions we use for the API description.

1.1.3 Algorithms and data structures: Is there a difference?

No, they are not exactly the same thing; technically they are not equivalent. Nevertheless, we might sometimes use the two terms interchangeably and, for the sake of brevity, use the term *data structure* to mean a DS and all its relevant methods.

There are many ways to point out the difference between the two terms, but I particularly like this metaphor: data structures are like *nouns*, while algorithms are like *verbs*.

I like this angle because, besides hinting at their different behavior, it implicitly reveals the mutual dependency between them. For instance, in English, to build a meaningful phrase, we need both nouns and verbs, a subject (or object), and an action performed (or endured).

Data structures and algorithms are interconnected; they need each other:

- Data structures are the substrate, a way to organize an area of memory to represent data.
- Algorithms are procedures, a sequence of instructions aimed to transform data.

Without algorithms to transform them, data structures would just be bits stored on a memory chip; without data structures to operate on, most algorithms wouldn't even exist.

Every data structure, moreover, implicitly defines algorithms that can be performed on it—for instance, methods to add, retrieve, and remove elements to/from the data structure.

Some data structures are actually defined exactly with the purpose of enabling one or more algorithms to run efficiently on them. Think of hash tables and search by key.[5]

---

[4] Application programming interface.

[5] You can find more on this topic in appendix C.

So, when we use algorithm and data structure as synonyms, it's just because in that particular context one implies the other. For instance, when we describe a DS, for that description to be meaningful and accurate, we necessarily need to describe its methods (that is, algorithms).

1.2 Setting goals: Your expectations after reading this book

One question you might have by now is, "Will I ever need to write my own data structures?"

There is a good chance that you will rarely find yourself in a situation where you don't have any alternative to writing a data structure from scratch. Today it isn't difficult to find libraries implementing the most common data structures in most programming languages, and usually these libraries are written by experts who know how to optimize performance or take care of security concerns.

The main goal of this book, in fact, is to give you familiarity with a broad range of tools and train you to recognize opportunities to use them to improve your code. Understanding how these tools work internally, at least at a high level, is an important part of the learning process. But nevertheless, there are still certain situations in which you might need to get your hands dirty with code; for example, if you are using a brand new programming language for which there aren't many libraries available, or if you need to customize a data structure to solve a special case.

In the end, whether you are going to write your own implementation of data structures really depends on many factors.

First and foremost, how advanced is the data structure you need, and how mainstream is the language you use?

To illustrate this point, let's take clustering as an example.

If you are working with a mainstream language—for instance, Java or Python—it's very likely that you can find many trusted libraries for k-means, one of the simplest clustering algorithms.

If you are using a niche language, maybe experimenting with a recently created one such as *Nim* or *Rust*, then it might be harder to find an open-source library implemented by a team that has thoroughly tested the code and will maintain the library.

Likewise, if you need an advanced clustering algorithm, like *DeLiClu*, it will be hard to find even Java or Python implementations that can be trusted to run as part of your application in production.

Another situation in which you might need to understand the internals of these algorithms is when you need to customize one of them; maybe because you need to optimize it for a real-time environment, or you need some specific property (for example, tweaking it to run concurrently and be thread-safe), or even because you need a slightly different behavior.

That said, even focusing on the first part, understanding when and how to use the data structures we present will be a game changer, letting you step up your coding skills to a new level. Let's use an example to show the importance of algorithms in the real world and introduce our path in describing algorithms.

1.3 Packing your knapsack: Data structures meet the real world

Congrats, you have been selected to populate the first Mars colony! Grocery stores on Mars are still a bit short of goods . . . and hard to find. So, you will have to eventually grow your own food. In the meantime, for the first few months, you will have goods shipped to sustain you.

1.3.1 Abstracting the problem away

The problem is, your crates can't weight more than 1000 kilograms, and that's a hard limit.

To make things harder, you can choose only from a limited set of things, already packed in boxes:

- Potatoes, 800 kgs
- Rice, 300 kgs
- Wheat flour, 400 kgs
- Peanut butter, 20 kgs
- Tomato cans, 300 kgs
- Beans, 300 kgs
- Strawberry jam, 50 kgs

You'll get water for free, so no worries about that, but you can either take a whole crate or not take it. You'd certainly like to have some choice, and not a ton of potatoes (aka *The Martian* experience).

But, at the same time, the expedition's main concern is keeping you well sustained and energetic throughout your stay, so the main discriminant to choose what goes with you will be the nutritional values. Let's say the total calories will be a good indicator. Table 1.1 sheds a different light on the list of available goods.

Table 1.1 A recap of the available goods, with their weight and calories

Food	Weight (kgs)	Total calories
Potatoes	800	1,501,600
Wheat flour	400	1,444,000
Rice	300	1,122,000
Beans (can)	300	690,000
Tomatoes (can)	300	237,000
Strawberry jam	50	130,000
Peanut butter	20	117,800

Since the actual content is irrelevant for the decision (despite your understandable protests, mission control is very firm on that point), the only things that matter are the weight and total calories provided for each of the boxes.

Hence, our problem can be abstracted as "choose any number of items from a set, *without the chance to take a fraction of any item*, such that their total weight won't be over 1000 kgs, and in such a way that the total amount of calories is maximized."

1.3.2 Looking for solutions

Now that we have stated our problem, we can start looking for solutions. You might be tempted to start packing your crate with boxes starting from the one with the highest calories value. That would be the potatoes box weighing 800 kgs.

But if you do so, neither rice nor wheat flour will fit in the crate, and their combined calorie count exceeds, by far, any other combination you can create within the remaining 200 kgs left. The best value you get with this strategy is 1,749,400 calories, picking potatoes, strawberry jam, and peanut butter.

So, what would have looked like the most natural approach, a *greedy*[6] algorithm that at each step chooses the best immediate option, does not work. This problem needs to be carefully thought through.

Time for brainstorming. You gather your logistics team and together look for a solution.

Soon enough, someone suggests that, rather than the total calories, you should look at the calories per kg. So you update table 1.1 with a new column, and sort it accordingly. The result is shown in table 1.2.

Table 1.2 The list in table 1.1, sorted by calories per kg

Food	Weight (kgs)	Total calories	Calories per kg
Peanut butter	20	117,800	5,890
Rice	300	1,122,000	3,740
Wheat flour	400	1,444,000	3,610
Strawberry jam	50	130,000	2,600
Beans (can)	300	690,000	2,300
Potatoes	800	1,501,600	1,877
Tomatoes (can)	300	237,000	790

Then you try to go top to bottom, picking up the food with the highest ratio of calories per unit of weight, ending up with peanut butter, rice, wheat flour, and strawberry jam, for a total of 2,813,800 calories.

That's much better than our first result. It's clear that this was a step in the right direction. But looking closely, it's apparent that adding peanut butter prevented us from taking beans, which would have allowed us to increase the total value of the crate

[6] A greedy algorithm is a strategy to solve problems that finds the optimal solution by making the locally optimal choice at each step. It can only find the best solution on a small subclass of problems, but it can also be used as a heuristic to find approximate (sub-optimal) solutions.

even more. The good news is that at least you won't be forced to follow *The Martian's* diet anymore; no potatoes go on Mars this time.

After a few more hours of brainstorming, you are all pretty much ready to give up: the only way you can solve this is to check, for each item, if you can get a better solution by including it or leaving it out. And the only way you know of doing so is enumerating all possible solutions, filtering out the ones that are above the weight threshold, and picking the best of the remaining ones. This is what's called a *brute force* algorithm, and we know from math that it's a very expensive one.

Since for each item you can either pack it or leave it, the possible solutions are 2^7=128. You guys are not too keen on going through a hundred solutions, but after a few hours, despite understanding why it's called brute force, you are totally exhausted but almost done with it.

Then the news breaks: someone called from mission control, and following complaints from some settlers-to-be, 25 new food items have been added to the list, including sugar, oranges, soy, and marmite (don't ask . . .).

After checking your numbers everyone is in dismay: now you'd have approximately 4 billion different combinations to check.

1.3.3 Algorithms to the rescue

At that point, it's clear that you need a computer program to crunch the numbers and make the best decision.

You write one yourself in the next few hours, but even that takes a long time to run, another couple of hours. Now, as much as you'd like to apply the same diet to all the colonists, it turns out some of them have allergies: a quarter of them can't eat gluten, and apparently many swear they are allergic to marmite. So you'll have to run the algorithm again a few times, each time taking into account individual allergies. To make thing worse, mission control is considering adding 30 more items to the list to make up for what people with allergies will miss. If that happens, we will end up with 62 total possible items, and the program will have to go over several billions of billions of possible combinations. You try that, and after a day the program is still running, nowhere close to termination.

The whole team is ready to give up and go back to the potatoes diet, when someone remembers there is a person on the launch team who had an algorithms book on his desk.

You call them in, and they immediately see the problem for what it is: the 0-1 knapsack problem. The bad news is that it is an NP-complete[7] problem, and this means it is hard to solve, as there is no "quick" (as in polynomial with respect to the number of items) known algorithm that computes the optimal solution.

---

[7] NP-complete problems are a set of problems for which any given solution can be verified quickly (in polynomial time), but there is no known efficient way to locate a solution in the first place. NP-complete problems, by definition, can't currently be solved in polynomial time on a classical deterministic machine (for instance, the RAM model we'll define in the next chapter).

There is, however, also good news: there exist a pseudo-polynomial[8] solution, a solution using *dynamic programming*[9] that takes time proportional to the max capacity of the knapsack. Luckily, the capacity of the crate is limited: so the solution takes takes a number of steps equal to the number of possible values for the capacity filled multiplied by the number of items, so assuming the smallest unit is 1kg, it only takes 1000×62 steps. Wow, that's much better than 2^{62}! And, in fact, once you rewrite the algorithm, it finds the best solution in a matter of seconds.

At this time, you are willing to take the algorithm as a black box and plug it in without too many questions. Still, this decision is crucial to your survival . . . it seems like a situation where you could use some deep knowledge of how an algorithm works.

For our initial example, it turns out that the best possible combination we can find is rice, wheat flour, and beans, for a total of 3,256,000 calories. That would be quite a good result compared to our first attempt, right?

You probably had already guessed the best combination, but if it seems too easy in the initial example, where we only have seven items, try the same with hundreds of different products, in a setup closer to the real scenario, and see how many years it takes you to find the best solution by hand!

We could be happy with this solution; it's the best we can find given the constraint.

1.3.4 Thinking (literally) outside of the box

But in our narration, this is the point when the real expert in algorithms comes in. For instance, imagine that a distinguished academic is visiting our facilities while preparing the mission, and has been invited to help with computing the best route to save fuel. During lunch break someone proudly tells her about how you brilliantly solved the problem with packing goods. And then she asks an apparently naïve question: Why can't you change the size of the boxes?

The answer will likely be either that "this is the way it has always been," or that "items come already packed from vendors, and it would cost time and money to change this."

And that's when the expert will explain that if we remove the constraint on the box size, the 0-1 knapsack problem, which is an NP-complete problem, becomes the unbounded knapsack problem, for which we have a linear-time[10] greedy solution that is usually better than the best solution for the 0-1 version.

---

[8] For a pseudo-polynomial algorithm, the worst-case running time depends (polynomially) on the *value* of some inputs, not just the number of inputs. For instance, for the 0-1 knapsack, the inputs are `n` elements (with weight and value), and the capacity `C` of the knapsack: a polynomial algorithm depends only on the number `n`, while a pseudo-polynomial also (or only) depends on the *value* `C`.

[9] Dynamic programming is a strategy for solving complex problems with certain characteristics: a recursive structure of subproblems, with the result of each subproblem needed multiple times in the computation of the final solution. The final solution is computed by breaking the problem down into a collection of simpler subproblems, solving each of those subproblems just once, and storing their solutions.

[10] Linear-time, assuming the list of goods is already sorted. Linearithmic, otherwise.

Translated into human-understandable language, we can turn this problem into one that's easier to solve and that will allow us to pack the crates with the largest possible total of calories. The problem statement now becomes this:

Given a set of items, choose any subset of items *or fraction* of items from it, such that their total weight won't be over 1000 kgs, and in such a way that the total amount of calories is maximized.

And yes, it is worth the time to go through the overhead of repacking everything, because we get a nice improvement.

Specifically, if we can take any fraction of the original weights for each product, we can simply pack products starting from the one with the highest ratio of calories per kg (peanut butter, in this example), and when we get to one box that would not fit in the remaining available space, we take a fraction of it to fill the gap, and repack it. So, in the end we wouldn't even have to repack all the goods, just one.

The best solution would then be peanut butter, rice, wheat flour, strawberry jam, and 230 kilograms of beans, for a total of 3,342,800 calories.

1.3.5 Happy ending

So, in our story, the future Mars settlers will have greater chances of survival and won't go into depression because of a diet comprising only potatoes with a peanut butter and strawberry dip.

From a computational point of view, we moved from incorrect algorithms (the greedy solutions taking the highest total, or highest ratio first), to a correct but unfeasible algorithm (the brute force solution enumerating all the possible combinations) to, finally, a smart solution which would organize the computation in a more efficient fashion.

The next step, as important or even more so, brought us to thinking outside of the box to simplify our problem, by removing some constraints, and thus finding an easier algorithm and a better solution. This is actually another golden rule: always study your requirements thoroughly, question them, and when possible, try to remove them if that brings you a solution that is at least as valuable, or a slightly less valuable one that can be reached with a much lower cost. Of course, in this process, other concerns (such as laws and security, at all levels) must be taken into consideration, so some constraints can't be removed.

In the process of describing algorithms, as we explained in the previous section, we would next describe our solution in detail and provide implementation guidelines.

We will skip these steps for the 0-1 knapsack dynamic programming algorithm, both because it's an algorithm, not a data structure, and it is thoroughly described in literature. Not to mention that in this chapter its purpose was just illustrating the following:

- How important it is to avoid bad choices for the algorithms and data structures we use
- The process we will follow in the next chapters when it comes to introducing a problem and its solutions

Summary

- Algorithms should be defined in terms of their input, their output, and a sequence of instructions that will process the input and produce the expected output.
- A data structure is the concrete implementation of an abstract data type, and it is made of a structure to hold the data and a set of algorithms that manipulate it.
- Abstracting a problem means creating a clear problem statement and then discussing the solution to the problem.
- Packing your knapsack efficiently can be tough (especially if you plan to go to Mars!), but with algorithms and the right data structure, (almost) nothing is impossible!

Part 1

Improving over basic data structures

The first part of this book lays the foundations for the more advanced sections that we'll discuss later. It focuses on discovering advanced data structures that provide an improvement over other more basic structures; for example, how we can improve binary heaps or make trees balanced, and how we can solve problems such as keeping track of things or groups of things?

Through these examples, we'll show that there are many ways to perform operations on data, and as developers we need to get accustomed to the fact that the best way we can choose depends on the context and requirements. We thus need to look at requirements, examine the context, and learn to question our knowledge when we solve a problem, in order to spot the best solution for the specifics we are facing.

Chapter 2 introduces an advanced variant of binary heaps, the *d-way heap*. It also describes the structure we use, in each chapter in this part, to explain topics.

Chapter 3 further explores the advanced use of heaps with *treap*, a hybrid between a binary search tree and a heap that can also help in different contexts.

Chapter 4 switches to *Bloom filters*, an advanced form of hash table that can help save memory while maintaining amortized constant-time search.

Chapter 5 introduces a few alternative data structures used to keep track of *disjoint sets*, a cornerstone needed to build countless advanced algorithms and that is used in several practical real-world applications.

Chapter 6 presents two data structures that out-perform general-purpose containers when it comes to storing and searching strings: *tries* and *radix tries*, also known as compact prefix trees.

Chapter 7 leverages the data structures presented in the first six chapters to build a composed data structure, the *LRU-cache*, to efficiently handle caching. The *LFU-cache* variant is also discussed at length, as well as the issues with synchronizing shared containers in multi-thread environments.

2 Improving priority queues: d-way heaps

This chapter covers

- Solving the problem of serving tasks based on priority
- Using priority queues to solve our problem
- Implementing a priority queue with a heap
- Introducing and analyzing d-way heaps
- Recognizing use cases where heaps improve performance

In the previous chapter we introduced some basic concepts about data structures and programming techniques, described the structure of this book, and hopefully raised your interest. You should now be aware of *why* developers need to know about data structures.

In this chapter, we will further develop those ideas and refine our narration. This chapter is meant to be a soft introduction to what is presented in this book; we have chosen a topic that should be familiar to readers with some background in algorithms, while providing a review of heaps along with some new insight on branching factors.

To this end, however, we assume that the reader is familiar with some basic concepts traditionally taught in CS 101 courses: big-O notation, the RAM model, and simple data structures such as arrays, lists, and trees. These building blocks will be leveraged throughout the book to build increasingly complex structures and algorithms, and it's important that you familiarize yourself with such concepts in order to be able to go through the next chapters. This is why we provided a recap of these fundamental topics in the appendices at the end of the book; feel free to take a look or skim through them in order to make sure you have a good understanding of the material.

Now that we have settled the basics, we will start with the core focus of this book, and in section 2.1 we describe the structure that we will use for each of the remaining chapters.

Section 2.2 introduces the problem we are going to use in this chapter (how to efficiently handle events with priority), while section 2.3 outlines possible solutions, including priority queues, and explains why the latter are better than more basic data structures.

Next, in section 2.4 we describe the priority queue API,[1] and we show an example of how to use it as a black box, before delving into its internals in sections 2.5 and 2.6. In the former we analyze in detail how a d-ary heap works, describing the functioning of its methods. In section 2.6 we delve into the implementation of a d-way heap.

Sections 2.7 and 2.8 describe use cases where heaps and priority queues make a difference and allow speeding up applications or other algorithms.

Finally, the focus of section 2.9 is understanding the optimal branching factor for a heap. Although it can be considered optional, I suggest you at least try to read it through to gain a deeper understanding of how a heap works and why you might want to choose a ternary heap instead of a binary heap, or vice versa.

This is a long chapter, and it might look intimidating, but hang in there; we are going to cover a lot of ground and lay the foundations for the whole book.

2.1 Structure of this chapter

Starting with the current chapter, we will embrace a schematic way to present our data structures.

Each chapter will be driven by a practical use case for its main topic, a real-world problem showing how the data structure is used in practice, but also a step-by-step explanation of how operations are performed. We also provide code samples showing how to use the algorithms we will focus on next.

So, first we are going to introduce a problem, one that is typically solved using the main topic of the chapter.

Then we present one or more ways to solve it. There might be several possible solutions to the same problem, and if that's the case, we explain when and why using a

[1] **A**pplication **P**rogramming **I**nterface (API).

particular data structure is a good idea. At this point, usually, we still treat our data structure as a black box: we focus on how to use it and ignore the details of its implementation.

Only in the next section do we start discussing how a data structure works. We focus on describing the mechanism, using figures and pseudo-code examples to clarify how it works.

After the code section, we are going to discuss advanced theory topics such as performance or mathematical proofs for the algorithms.

Usually we also provide a list of additional applications that use the algorithms presented, although for most of these further examples we have to omit coding for the sake of space.

2.2 The problem: Handling priority

The first problem we are going to tackle is handling tasks based on priority. This is something all of us are familiar with in some way.

The problem can be described in these terms: given a collection of tasks with different priorities, determine which task should be executed next.

We can find many examples in the real world where we apply, consciously or not, techniques that help us decide what to do next. Our daily lives are full of tasks; usually the order in which we run them is a result of time constraints and the importance we assign to those tasks.

A common example of an environment where tasks are executed by priority is an emergency room, where patients are seen, not according to the order in which they arrived, but instead depending on how urgent their conditions are. If we move closer to our IT domain, there are many tools and systems that have the same behavior. Think, for instance, about your operating system scheduler. Or maybe you are using a mobile app to take a to-do list.

2.2.1 Priority in practice: Bug tracking

The example I'd like to use in this chapter, though, is a bug-tracking suite. You are probably already familiar with such a tool. When you work in teams, you need a way to track bugs and tasks so that no two people work on the same issue and duplicate effort, while making sure issues are tackled in the right order (whatever that is, depending on your business model).

To simplify our example, let's restrict it to the case of a bug-tracking tool where each bug is associated with a priority, expressed as the number of days within which it needs to be solved (lower numbers mean higher priority). Also, let's assume that bugs are independent, so no bug requires solving another bug as a prerequisite.

For our example, let's consider the following list of bugs (in sparse order) for a single-page web application.

Each bug will look like a tuple:

```
<task description, importance of missing the deadline>
```

So, for instance we could have this.

Task description	Severity (1-10)
Page loads take 2+ seconds	7
UI breaks on browser X	9
Optional form field blocked when using browser X on Friday the 13th	1
CSS style causes misalignment	8
CSS style causes 1px misalignment on browser X	5

Whenever resources (for example, developers) are limited, there comes the need to prioritize bugs. Therefore, some bugs are more urgent than others: that's why we associate priorities to them.

Now, suppose a developer on our team completes her current task. She asks our suite for the next bug that needs to be solved. If this list were static, our suite's software could just sort the bugs once, and return them in order.[2]

Task description	Severity (1-10)
UI breaks on browser X	9
CSS style causes misalignment	8
Page loads take 2+ seconds	7
CSS style causes 1px misalignment on browser X	5
Optional form field blocked when using browser X on Friday the 13th	1

As you can imagine, though, this is not the case. First, new bugs are discovered all the time, and so new items will be added to the list. Say a nasty encryption bug is found—you'd need to have it solved by yesterday! Moreover, priority for bugs can change over time. For instance, your CEO might decide that you are going after the market share that's mostly using browser X, and you have a big feature launch next Friday, the 13th, so you really need to solve that bug at the bottom within a couple of days.

Task description	Severity (1-10)
Unencrypted password on DB	10
UI breaks on browser X	9

[2] Often bug-tracking suites associate lower numbers with higher priority. To keep things simple in our discussion, we will instead assume higher numbers mean higher priority.

Task description	Severity (1-10)
Optional form field blocked when using browser X on Friday the 13th	8
CSS style causes misalignment	8
Page loads take 2+ seconds	7
CSS style causes 1px misalignment on browser X	5

2.3 Solutions at hand: Keeping a sorted list

We could, obviously, update our sorted list every time we have an item inserted, removed, or modified. This can work well if these operations are infrequent and the size of our list is small.

Any of these operations, in fact, would require a linear number of elements changing position, both in worst cases and in the average case.[3]

For this use case, it could probably work. But if our list had millions or billions of elements, then we would most likely be in trouble.

2.3.1 From sorted lists to priority queues

Luckily for us, there is a better solution. This is the perfect use case for one of the core data structures. A priority queue will keep a partial ordering of the elements, with the guarantee that the next element returned from the queue will hold the highest priority.

By giving up the requirement of a total ordering (which we wouldn't need in this case, because we only consume tasks one by one), we gain in performance: each of the operations on the queue can now require only logarithmic time.

As a side note, this reminds us how important it is to get our requirements right before implementing any solution. We need to make sure we don't overcomplicate our work and requirements: for example, keeping a list of elements sorted when all we need is a partial ordering wastes resources and complicates our code, making it harder to maintain and scale.

2.4 Describing the data structure API: Priority queues

Before delving into the topic of the chapter, let's take a step back.

As explained in appendix C, each data structure can be broken down into a few lower-level components:

- *API*—The API is the contract that a data structure *(DS)* makes with external clients. It includes method definitions, as well as some guarantees about the methods' behavior that are provided in the DS's specification. For example, a priority queue *(PQ)* (see table 2.1) provides these methods and guarantees:

[3] With an array implementation, we could find the right position for our item in logarithmic time, using binary search. But then we would need to move all the elements on the right of the insertion point to make room for it, and this requires linear time on average.

  - `top()`—Returns and extracts the element with the highest priority.
  - `peek()`—Like `top` it returns the element with the highest priority, but without extracting it from the queue.
  - `insert(e, p)`—Adds a new element `e` with priority `p` to the PQ.
  - `remove(e)`—Removes element `e` from the queue.
  - `update(e, p)`—Changes the priority for element `e` and sets it to `p`.
- *Invariants*—(Optional) internal properties that always hold true throughout the life of the data structure. For instance, a sorted list would have one invariant: every element is not greater than its successor. The purpose of invariants is making sure the conditions necessary to live up to the contract with the external clients are always met. They are the internal counterparts of the guarantees in the API.
- *Data model*—To host the data. This can be a raw chunk of memory, a list, a tree, etc.
- *Algorithms*—The internal logic that is used to update the data structure while making sure that the invariants are not violated.

Table 2.1 API and contract for priority queue

Abstract data structure: Priority queue	

API	`class PriorityQueue {`
	`  top() → element`
	`  peek() → element`
	`  insert(element, priority)`
	`  remove(element)`
	`  update(element, newPriority)`
	`  size() → int`
	`}`

Contract with client	The top element returned by the queue is always the element with highest priority currently stored in the queue

In appendix C we also clarify how there is a difference between an *abstract data structure* and *concrete data structures.* The former includes the API and invariants, describing at a high level how clients will interact with it and the results and performance of operations. The latter builds on the principles and API expressed by the abstract description, adding a concrete implementation for its structure and algorithms (data model and algorithms).

This is exactly the relationship between *priority queues* and *heaps.* A priority queue is an abstract data structure that can be implemented in many ways (including as a sorted list). A heap is a concrete implementation of the priority queue using an array to hold elements and specific algorithms to enforce invariants.

2.4.1 Priority queue at work

Imagine you are provided with a priority queue. It can come from a third-party library or from a standard library (many languages, such as C++ or Scala, provide an implementation for priority queues in their standard container lib).

You don't need to know the internals of the library at this point; you just need to follow its public API and use it, confident it's properly implemented. This is the black box approach (figure 2.1).

For instance, let's suppose we add our bugs to our PQ in the same order we have seen before.

Task description	Severity (1-10)
Page loads take 2+ seconds	7
UI breaks on browser X	9
Optional form field blocked when using browser X on Friday the 13th	1
CSS style causes misalignment	8
CSS style causes 1px misalignment on browser X	5

If we returned the tasks in the same order as we inserted them, we would just implement as a plain queue (see figure 2.2 for a quick glance at how a queue works, and appendix C for a description of basic containers). Instead, let's assume that now we have our priority queue containing those five elements; we still don't know the internals of the PQ, but we can query it through its API.

?
5
Priority
Queue
top
peek
insert
remove
update

Figure 2.1 Representation of a priority queue as a black box. If we employ an implementation of a priority queue provided by a third-party library (or from standard libraries), and we trust this implementation to be correct, we can use it as a black box. In other words, we can ignore its internals, and just interact with it through its API.

For instance, we can check how many elements it contains and even take a peek at the one at the top (figure 2.1). Or we can directly ask it to return us the top element (the one with the highest priority) and remove it from the queue.

If, after inserting the five elements in figure 2.1, we call `top`, the element returned will be "UI breaks on browser X" and the size of the queue will become 4. If we call `top` again, the next element will be "CSS style causes misalignment" and the size will become 3.

As long as the priority queue is implemented correctly and given the priorities in our examples, we can be sure those two elements will be the ones returned first, independently of the order in which they are inserted.

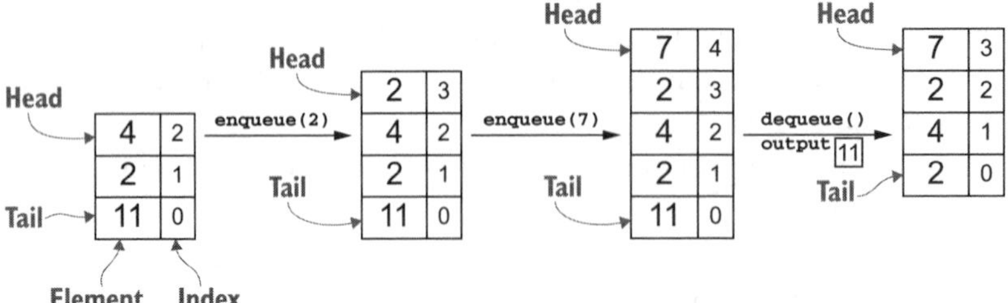
Head
Tail
Element
Index
enqueue(2)
enqueue(7)
dequeue()
output 11

Figure 2.2 Operations on a queue: elements are generic integers, but they could be any value here, because in plain queues priority is only given by the order of insertion (see appendix D). Insertion (enqueue) adds an element to the front of the queue. Deletion (dequeue) removes the last element in the queue and returns it. With some caution, both operations can be performed in constant time.

2.4.2 Priority matters: Generalize FIFO

Now the question is how we choose the priority of an element. Often, the natural ordering given by how much time an element waits in a line can be considered the fairest. Sometimes, however, there is something special about some elements that might suggest they should be served sooner than others that waited longer. For instance, you don't always read your emails in the order you received them, but often you skip newsletters or "funny" jokes from friends to read work-related messages first. Likewise, in an emergency room, the next case treated is not necessarily going to be one that has been waiting for the longest time. Rather, every case is evaluated at arrival and assigned a priority, and the highest priority one is going to be called in when a doctor becomes available.

That's the idea behind priority queues: they behave like regular, plain queues, except that the front of the queue is dynamically determined based on some kind of priority. The differences caused to the implementation by the introduction of priority are profound, enough to deserve a special kind of data structure.

But that's not all: we can even define basic containers as *bag* or *stack* as special cases of priority queues; appendix D explores how this is possible. This is an interesting topic to help you gain a deeper understanding of how priority queues work, although in practice those containers are usually implemented ad hoc, because we can achieve better performance by leveraging their specific characteristics.

2.5 Concrete data structures

Let's now move from abstract to concrete data structures. Knowing how the API of a priority queue works is good enough to use it, but often it is not enough to use it well. Especially on time-critical components or in data-intensive applications, we often need to understand the internals of the data structures and the details of its implementation to make sure we can integrate it in our solution without introducing a bottleneck.[4]

Every abstraction needs to be implemented using a concrete data structure. For example, a stack can be implemented using a list, an array, or in theory even a heap (although this would be silly, as will be clear in a few sections). The choice of the underlying data structure used to implement a container will only influence the container's performance. Choosing the best implementation is usually a tradeoff: some data structures speed up some operations but will make other operations slower.

2.5.1 Comparing performance

For the implementation of a priority queue, we will initially consider three naïve alternatives using core data structures discussed in appendix C: an unsorted array, where we just add elements to its end; a sorted array, where we make sure the ordering is reinstated every time we add a new element; and balanced trees, of which heaps are a special case. Let's compare, in table 2.2, the running times[5] for basic operations implemented with these data structures.

2.5.2 What's the right concrete data structure?

From table 2.2 we can see that naïve choices would lead to a linear time requirement for at least one of the core operations, while a balanced tree would always guarantee a logarithmic worst case. Although linear time is usually regarded as "feasible," there is still a tremendous difference between logarithmic and linear: for a billion elements, the difference is between 1 billion operations and a few dozens. If each operation takes 1 millisecond, that means going from 11 days to less than a second.

Table 2.2 Performance for operations provided by PQs, broken bown by underlying data structure

Operation	Unsorted array	Sorted array	Balanced tree
`Insert`	O(1)	O(n)	O(log n)
`Find-Minimum`	O(1) [a]	O(1)	O(1) [a]
`Delete-Minimum`	O(n) [b]	O(1) [c]	O(log n)

[a]By saving an extra value with the minimum and charging the cost of maintaining its value on insert and delete.

[b]If we use a buffer to speed up find-minimum, then we need to find the next minimum on delete. Unfortunately, nothing comes for free. Alternatively, we could have constant-time delete by giving up the buffer and swapping the deleted element with the last in the array, and linear time find-minimum.

[c]Storing the array in reverse order, deleting the last element might just be a matter of shrinking the size of the array, or somehow keeping track of what's the last element in the array.

---

[4] Besides performance, there are other aspects we might need to check, depending on our context. For instance, in a distributed environment, we must make sure our implementation is thread-safe, or we will incur race conditions, the nastiest possible bugs that could afflict our applications.

[5] You can find an introduction to algorithm analysis and big-O notation in appendix B.

Moreover, consider that most of the times containers, and priority queues in particular, are used as support structures, meaning that they are part of more complex algorithms/data structures and each cycle of the main algorithm can call operations on the PQ several times. For example, for a sorting algorithm, this could mean going from `O(n²)`, which usually means unfeasible for `n` as large as 1 million, or even less, to `O(n*log(n))`, which is still tractable for inputs of size 1 billion or more.[6] However, this would come at a cost, because the implementation of balanced binary trees is usually not trivial.

Next, we present a way to efficiently implement a generic priority queue.

2.5.3 Heap

A binary heap is the most used version of priority queues. It allows elements to be inserted and retrieved in either ascending or descending order, one at a time.

While in reality an underlying array is used to store heap's elements, it can conceptually be represented as a particular kind of binary tree, abiding by three invariants:

- Every node has at most two children.
- The heap tree is complete and left-adjusted. Complete (see figure 2.3) means that if the heap has height `H`, every leaf node is either at level `H` or `H-1`. All the levels are left-adjusted, which means that no right sub-tree has a height greater than its left sibling. So, if a leaf is at the same height as an internal node,[7] the leaf can't be on the left of that node. Invariant numbers 1 and 2 are the structural invariants for heaps.
- Every node holds the highest priority in the subtree rooted at that node.

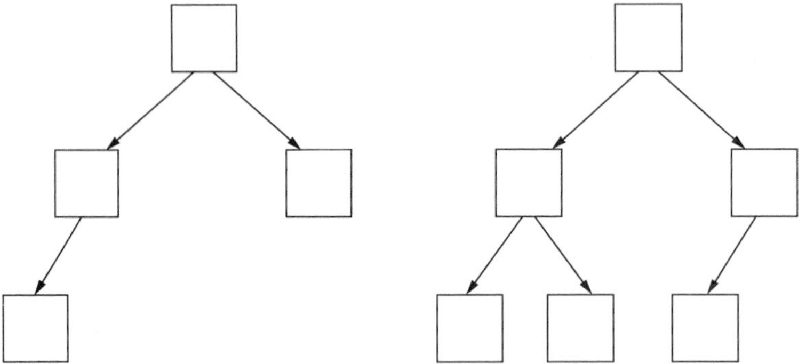

Figure 2.3 Two examples of complete binary trees. All levels in the tree have the maximum possible number of nodes, except (possibly) the last one. All leaves in the last level are left-adjusted; at the previous level, no right subtree has more nodes than its left sibling.

[6] Whether a problem is really tractable or not for a certain size of the input also depends on the kind of operations performed and on the time they take. But even if each operation takes as little as 1 nanosecond, if the input has 1 million elements, a quadratic algorithm will take more than 16 minutes, while a linearithmic algorithm would require less than 10 milliseconds.

[7] A leaf is a tree node that doesn't have any children. An internal node is a node that has at least one child or, equivalently, a node that is not a leaf.

Properties (1) and (2) allow for the array representation of the heap. Supposing we need to store `N` elements, the tree structure is directly and compactly represented using an array of `N` elements, without pointers to children or parents. Figure 2.4 shows how the tree and array representation of a heap are equivalent.

In the array representation, if we are starting to count indices from `0`, the children of the `i`-th node are stored in the positions[8] `(2 * i) + 1` and `2 * (i + 1)`, while the parent of node `i` is at index `(i - 1) / 2` (except for the root, which has no parent). For example, looking at figure 2.4, the node at index `1` (whose priority is `3`) has two children at indices `3` and `4`, and its parent is at index `0`; if we consider a node at position `5`, its parent is the element at index `2` and its children (not shown in the picture) would be at indices `11` and `12`.

It might seem counterintuitive that we use an array to represent a tree. After all, trees were invented to overcome array limitations. This is generally true, and trees have a number of advantages: they are more flexible and, if balanced, allow for better performance, with worst-case logarithmic search, insertion, and delete.

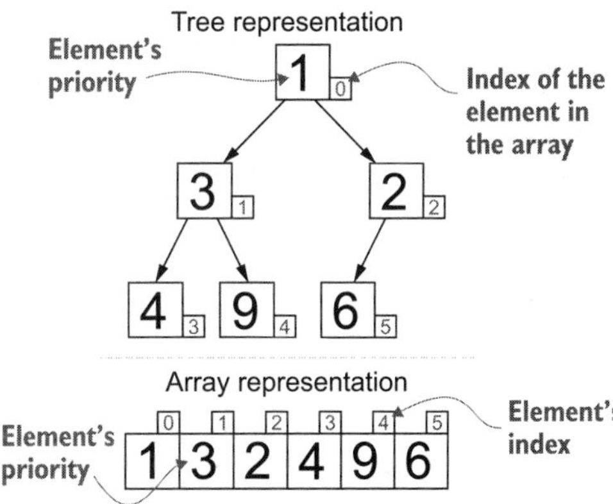
Tree representation
Element's priority
1
0
Index of the element in the array
3
1
2
2
4
3
9
4
6
5
Array representation
Element's priority
0 1 2 3 4 5
1 3 2 4 9 6
Element's index

Figure 2.4 A binary heap. Only priorities are shown for the nodes (elements are irrelevant here).The numbers inside the small squares show the indices of the heap elements in the array. Nodes are matched into array elements top to bottom, left to right. Top: the tree representation for the heap. Notice how every parent is smaller than (or at most equal to) its children and, in turn, all elements in its subtree. Bottom: the same heap in its array representation.

But the improvement we get with trees comes with a price, of course. First, as with any data structure that uses pointers (lists, graphs, trees, and so on) we have a memory overhead in comparison to arrays. While with the latter we just need to reserve space for the data (plus maybe, depending on the implementation details, some constant space for pointers and the node structure itself), every tree node requires extra space for the pointers to its children and possibly to its parent.

Without getting into too much detail, arrays also tend to be better at exploiting *memory locality*: all the elements in the array are contiguous in memory, and this means lower latency when reading them.

Table 2.3 shows how a heap matches a priority queue for its abstract part, and what its concrete data model and invariants are.

---

[8] We use explicit parenthesis for the following expressions. In the rest of the book, we will generally omit redundant parentheses, so that, for instance, we will write `2*i + 1`.

Table 2.3 Underlying components for a heap

Concrete data structure: Heap	

API	`Heap {`
	`  top() → element`
	`  peek()→ element`
	`  insert(element, priority)`
	`  remove(element)`
	`  update(element, newPriority)`
	`}`

Contract with client	The top element returned by the queue is always the element with highest priority currently stored in the queue.
Data model	An array whose elements are the items stored in the heap.
Invariants	Every element has two "children." For the element at position *i*, its children are located at indices 2*i+1 and 2*(i+1). Every element has higher priority than its children.

2.5.4 Priority, min-heap, and max-heap

When we stated the three heap's properties, we used the wording "highest priority." In a heap, we can always say that the highest priority element will be at the top, without raising any ambiguity.

Then when it comes to practice, we will have to define what priority means, but if we implement a general-purpose heap, we can safely parameterize it with a custom priority function, taking an element and returning its priority. As long as our implementation abides by the three laws as stated in section 2.5.3, we will be sure our heap works as expected.

Sometimes, however, it's better to have specialized implementations that leverage the domain knowledge and avoid the overhead of a custom priority function. For instance, if we store tasks in a heap, we can use tuples `(priority, task)` as elements, and rely on the natural ordering of tuples.[9]

Either way, we still need to define what highest priority means. If we assume that highest priority means a larger number, that is, if $p_1 > p_2$ means p_1 is the highest priority, then we call our heap a *max-heap*.

At other times we need to return smallest numbers first, so we assume instead that $p_1 > p_2$ means p_2 is the highest priority. In this case, we are using a *min-heap*. In the rest of the book, and in particular in the coding section, assume we are implementing a max-heap.

The implementation of a min-heap differs only slightly from a max-heap, the code is pretty much symmetric, and you just need to exchange all occurrences of $<$ and $\leq$ to $>$ and $\geq$ respectively, and swap `min` with `max`.

Or, alternatively, it's even easier if you have an implementation of one to get the other by simply taking the reciprocal of priorities (either in your priority function or when you pass priority explicitly).

---

[9] $(a_1, b_1, c_1,\ldots) < (a_2, b_2, c_2,\ldots)$ if and only if $a_1 < a_2$ or $(a_1 == a_2$ and $(b_1, c_1,\ldots) < (b_2, c_2,\ldots))$.

To give you a concrete example, suppose you have a min-heap that you use to store `(age, task)` pairs: a min-heap will return the task with smallest ages first. Because we might instead be interested in having the oldest task returned first, we would rather need a max-heap; it turns out we can get the same result without changing any code for out heap! We just need to store elements as tuples `(-age, task)` instead. If `x.age < y.age`, in fact, then `-x.age > -y.age`, and thus the min-heap will return first the tasks whose age have the largest absolute value.

For instance, if we have task `A` with age 2 (days) and task `B` with age 3, then we create the tuples `(-2, A)` and `(-3, B)`; when extracting them from a min-heap, we can check that `(-3, B) < (-2, A)` and so the former will be returned before the latter.

2.5.5 *Advanced variant: d-ary heap*

One could think that heaps needs to be binary trees. After all, binary search trees are the most common kind of trees, intrinsically associated with ordering. It turns out that there is no reason to keep our branching factor[10] fixed and equal to 2. On the contrary, we can use any value greater than 2, and use the same array representation for the heap.

For a branching factor 3, the children of the i-th node are at indices `3*i + 1`, `3*i + 2` and `3*(i + 1)`, while the parent of node `i` is at position `(i - 1)/3`.

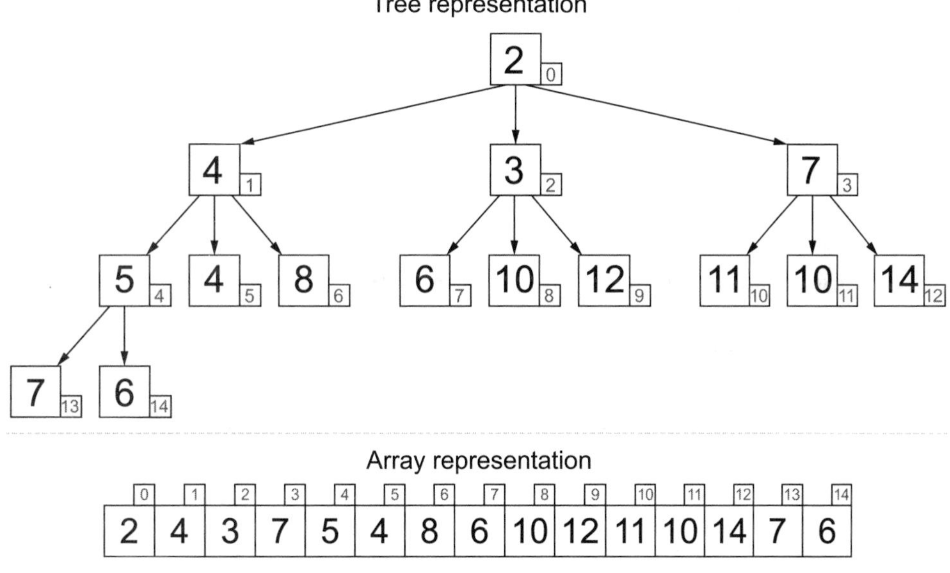
Tree representation
2 0
4 1
3 2
7 3
5 4
4 5
8 6
6 7
10 8
12 9
11 10
10 11
14 12
7 13
6 14
Array representation
0 1 2 3 4 5 6 7 8 9 10 11 12 13 14
2 4 3 7 5 4 8 6 10 12 11 10 14 7 6

Figure 2.5 A three-way heap. Only priorities are shown for the nodes (values are irrelevant here). The smaller squares next to the elements show the indices of the heap elements in the array. Top: the tree representation for a min-heap. Notice how every parent is smaller than (or at most equal to) its children and, in turn, all elements in its subtree. Bottom: the same heap in its array representation.

[10] The branching factor of a tree is the maximum number of children a node can have. For example, a binary heap, which in turn is a binary tree, has a branching factor of 2. See appendix C for more details.

Figure 2.5 shows both the tree and array representation of a 3-ary heap. The same idea holds for branching factors 4, 5, and so on.

For a *d-ary* heap, where the branching factor is the integer `D > 1`, our three heap invariants become

- Every node has at most `D` children.
- The heap tree is complete, with all the levels that are left-adjusted. That is, the `i`-th sub-tree has a height at most equal to its siblings on its left (from `0` to `i-1`, `1 < i <= D`).
- Every node holds the highest priority in the subtree rooted at that node.

FUN FACT It's worth noting that for `D = 1`, the heap becomes a sorted array (or a sorted doubly linked list in its tree representation). The heap construction will be the insertion sort algorithm and requires quadratic time. Every other operation requires linear time.

2.6 How to implement a heap

At this point we have a good idea of how a priority queue should be used and its internal representation. It's about time we delve into the details of the implementation for a heap.

Before we go, let's once again take a look at our API:

```
class Heap {
  top()
  peek()
  insert(element, priority)
  remove(element)
  update(element, newPriority)
}
```

These are just the public methods defining the API of our class.

But first things first. We will assume, hereafter, that we store all the `(element, priority)` tuples added to the heap in an array named `pairs`, as shown in listing 2.1.

Listing 2.1 The DHeap class properties

```
class DHeap
  #type Array[Pair]
  pairs
  function DHeap(pairs=[])
```

This is the first time we see a code snippet in this book. It might be a good chance for you to review appendix A, where we explain the syntax used. For instance, if we have a variable `p` holding such a tuple, we embrace a specific syntax for destructured assignment of its fields into two variables:

```
(element, priority) ← p
```

We also assume that the tuple's fields are named, so that we can access, in turn, `p.element` and `p.priority`, or create a tuple `p` with this syntax:

```
p ← (element='x', priority=1)
```

In many figures in this section, we will only show an element's priorities or, to see it in another way, we assume that elements and priorities are the same. This is just for the sake of space and clarity in diagrams, but it also highlights an important characteristic of heaps: in all their methods, we only need to access and move priorities. This can be important when elements are large objects, especially if they are so large that they won't fit in cache/memory or for any reason they are stored on disk; then the concrete implementation can just store and access a reference to the elements and its priority.

Now, before delving into the API methods, we need to define two helper functions that will be used to reinstate the heap properties whenever a change is performed. The possible changes for a heap are

- Adding a new element to the heap
- Removing the top element of the heap
- Updating an element's priority

Any of these operations can cause a heap element to have higher priority than its parent or a lower priority than (one of) its children.

2.6.1 BubbleUp

When an element has a higher priority than its parent, it is necessary to call the `bubbleUp` method, as shown in listing 2.2. Figure 2.6 shows an example based on our task management tool: the priority of the element at index 7 is higher than its parent (at index 2) and thus these two elements need to be swapped.

Listing 2.2 The `bubbleUp` method

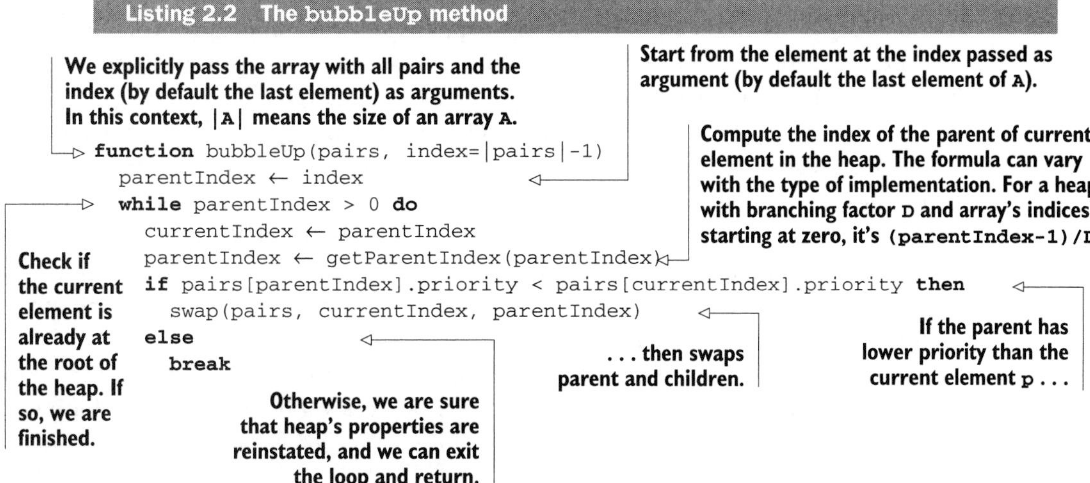

```
function bubbleUp(pairs, index=|pairs|-1)
  parentIndex ← index
  while parentIndex > 0 do
    currentIndex ← parentIndex
    parentIndex ← getParentIndex(parentIndex)
    if pairs[parentIndex].priority < pairs[currentIndex].priority then
      swap(pairs, currentIndex, parentIndex)
    else
      break
```


We explicitly pass the array with all pairs and the index (by default the last element) as arguments. In this context, |A| means the size of an array A.
Start from the element at the index passed as argument (by default the last element of A).
Compute the index of the parent of current element in the heap. The formula can vary with the type of implementation. For a heap with branching factor D and array's indices starting at zero, it's (parentIndex-1)/D.
Check if the current element is already at the root of the heap. If so, we are finished.
If the parent has lower priority than the current element p . . .
. . . then swaps parent and children.
Otherwise, we are sure that heap's properties are reinstated, and we can exit the loop and return.

As listing 2.2 shows, we keep swapping elements until either current element gets assigned to the root (line #3), or its priority is lower than its next ancestor (line #6-#9). This means that each call to this method can involve at most `log`$_D$`(n)` comparisons and exchanges, because it's upper-bounded by the height of the heap.

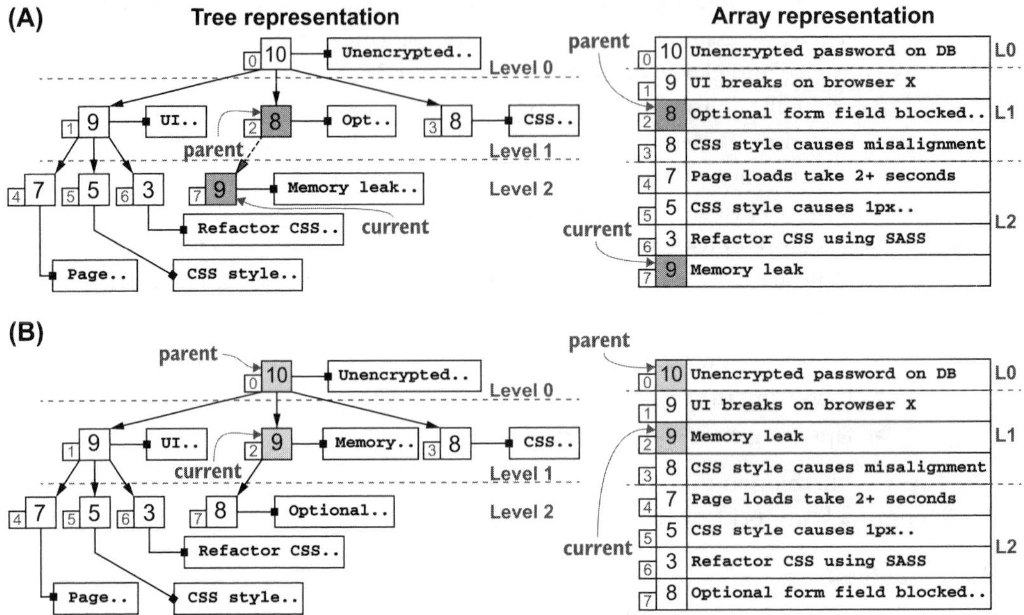
(A)
Tree representation
Array representation
parent
Unencrypted..
Level 0
UI..
Opt..
CSS..
parent
Level 1
Memory leak..
Level 2
Refactor CSS..
current
current
Page..
CSS style..
Unencrypted password on DB
UI breaks on browser X
Optional form field blocked..
CSS style causes misalignment
Page loads take 2+ seconds
CSS style causes 1px..
Refactor CSS using SASS
Memory leak
L0
L1
L2
(B)
parent
parent
Unencrypted..
Level 0
UI..
Memory..
CSS..
current
Level 1
Optional..
Level 2
Refactor CSS..
current
Page..
CSS style..
Unencrypted password on DB
UI breaks on browser X
Memory leak
CSS style causes misalignment
Page loads take 2+ seconds
CSS style causes 1px..
Refactor CSS using SASS
Optional form field blocked..
L0
L1
L2

Figure 2.6 The bubbleUp method in action on a ternary max-heap. (A) The element at index 7 has a higher priority (9) than its parent (whose priority is 8). (B) We swap element at index 7 with its parent at index 2. The element now at index 7 has certainly found its final position, while the one bubbled up needs to be compared to its new parent. In this case, the root has a higher priority, so bubbling up stops.

Remember we are implementing a max-heap, so higher numbers mean higher priority. Then, as shown in figure 2.6 (A), the element at index [7] is out of place, because its parent, "Optional form field blocked . . . " at index [2], has priority 8 < 9.

At this point, to fix things we need to call `bubbleUp(pairs, 7)`. We enter the loop at line #3, because `parentIndex` is `7 > 0`, compute the new parent's index, which is 2, and hence the condition at line #6 is also `true`, so at line #7 the two elements will be swapped. After the update, the heap's array will look like figure 2.6 (B).

At the next iteration of the loop (`parentIndex` is still `2 > 0`, so the loop will be entered at least once more), the new values for `currentIndex` and `parentIndex` will evaluate, at lines #4-5, to 2 and 0, respectively.

Since elements' priorities are now, in turn, 9 and 10 for child and parent, the condition at line #6 is not met anymore, and the function will break out of the loop and return.

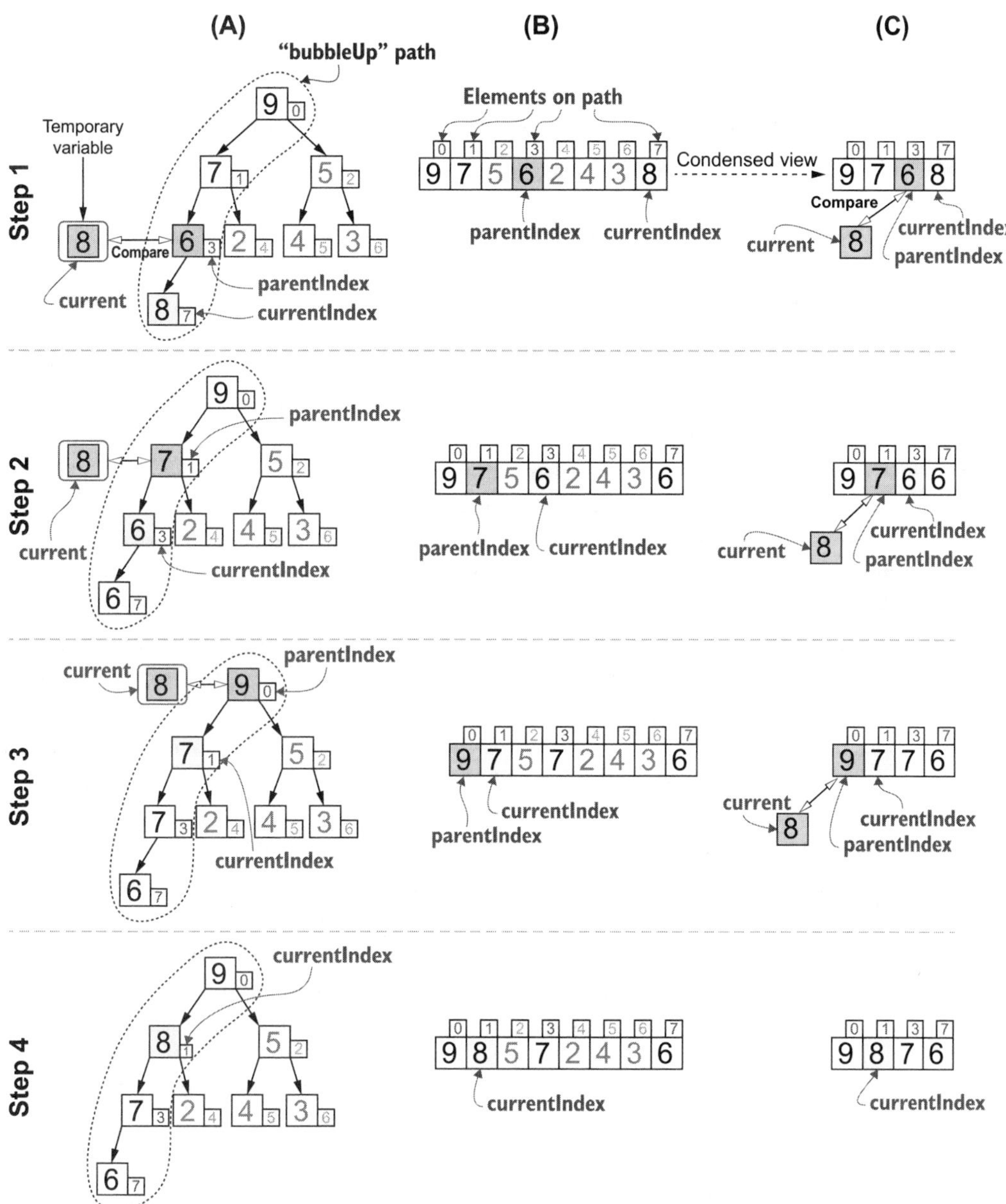
(A)
(B)
(C)
"bubbleUp" path
Elements on path
Temporary variable
Condensed view
Compare
current
parentIndex
currentIndex
Step 1
Step 2
Step 3
Step 4

Figure 2.7 Bubbling up of an element in a max-heap, using the method that reduces the number of assignments to one-third. The figure shows a call to `bubbleUp(pairs, 7)` displaying the tree representation (A) and the array representation (B) for a max-heap, and filtered elements (C) in the path `P` from the element to the root.

Notice that this method, if the height of the tree is `H`, requires at most `H` swaps, because each time we swap two elements, we move one level up in the tree, toward its root.

This result is an important result, as we will see in section 2.7. Because heaps are balanced binary trees, their height is logarithmic in the number of elements.

But we can add a further improvement with just a small change. If you notice, we are repeatedly swapping the same element with its current parent; this element, the one on which `bubbleUp` is initially called, keeps moving toward the root. You can see in figure 2.6 that it "bubbles up," like a soap bubble floating toward the top of the heap. Each swap requires three assignments (and the use of a temporary variable), so the naïve implementation in listing 2.2 would require (at most) `3*H` assignments.

While both indices, the current and the parent node's, change at each iteration, the value of the current element is always the same.

Figure 2.7 highlights the path that such an element has to travel. In the worst case it travels up to the root, as shown in the picture, but possibly bubbling up could stop at an intermediate node. It turns out that bubbling up an element in the path `P` to the heap's root is equivalent to inserting that element in the (sub)array obtained by only considering those elements in `P` (see figure 2.7 (B)).

Referring to figure 2.7, the first action needed is saving to a temporary variable the element `X` that will move up (step 1). Then, starting with its parent, we compare all elements in the path to the temporary variable and copy them over in case they have lower priority (steps 1–3). At each time, we copy the parent element over its one child that is on the path `P`. It's like we filter out all the elements in the heap's array that are not part of `P:` this is highlighted in 2.7 (C).

Finally, when we find an element `Y` along `P` that has higher priority than our temporary, we can copy element `X` from the temporary variable to the one child of `Y` that belongs to `P` (step 4).

Now, this can be done efficiently, in the same way each iteration of the insertion sort algorithm works. We initially save in a temporary variable a copy of the element to bubble up (call it `X`), and then check the elements on its left in the array. We "move" the elements to their right (check figure 2.7 (C)) by copying them to the next position on their left, until we find an element with a priority higher than `X`'s. This can be done with just (at most) `H+1` assignments for a path of length `H`, thus saving about 66% of the assignments.

Listing 2.3 shows the improved version of the `bubbleUp` method. Notice how, at some point, there will momentarily be two copies of the element originally at index [3] (and later, of the element at index [1]). This is because rather than actually swapping elements, we can just overwrite the current element with its parent at each iteration (line #6) and write the element bubbling up just once at the end as the last action in the method. This works because bubbling up an element is conceptually equivalent to the inner loop of *insertion sort*, where we are looking for the right position to insert the current element into the path connecting it to heap's root.

Listing 2.3 An optimization of the bubbleUp method

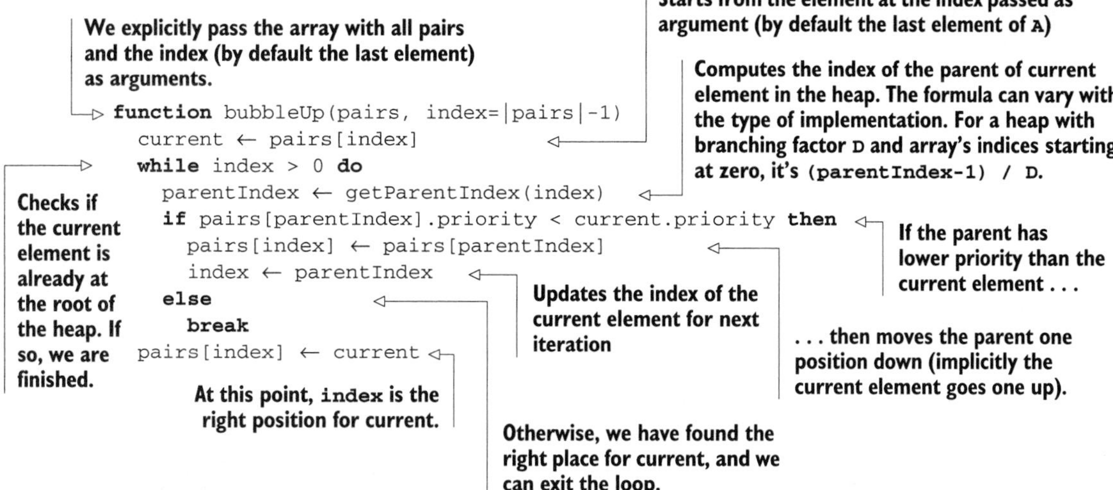

```
function bubbleUp(pairs, index=|pairs|-1)
  current ← pairs[index]
  while index > 0 do
    parentIndex ← getParentIndex(index)
    if pairs[parentIndex].priority < current.priority then
      pairs[index] ← pairs[parentIndex]
      index ← parentIndex
    else
      break
  pairs[index] ← current
```


We explicitly pass the array with all pairs and the index (by default the last element) as arguments.
Starts from the element at the index passed as argument (by default the last element of A)
Computes the index of the parent of current element in the heap. The formula can vary with the type of implementation. For a heap with branching factor D and array's indices starting at zero, it's (parentIndex-1) / D.
Checks if the current element is already at the root of the heap. If so, we are finished.
If the parent has lower priority than the current element . . .
Updates the index of the current element for next iteration
. . . then moves the parent one position down (implicitly the current element goes one up).
At this point, index is the right position for current.
Otherwise, we have found the right place for current, and we can exit the loop.

2.6.2 PushDown

The pushDown method handles the symmetric case where we need to move an element down toward the leaves of the heap, because it might be larger than (at least) one of its children. An implementation is shown in listing 2.4.

There are two differences with the "bubble up" case:

- *The triggering condition*—In this case, the altered node doesn't violate invariant 3 with respect to its parent but might violate it when compared to its children. This would happen, for instance, when the root is extracted from the heap and replaced with the last leaf in the array, or when a node priority is changed by assigning it a lower priority.
- *The algorithm*—For every level the element we are pushing down goes through, we need to find its highest-priority child, in order to find where the element could land without violating any property.

Listing 2.4 The pushDown method

```
function pushDown(pairs, index=0)
  currentIndex ← index
  while currentIndex < firstLeafIndex(pairs) do
    (child, childIndex) ← highestPriorityChild(currentIndex)
    if child.priority > pairs[currentIndex].priority then
      swap(pairs, currentIndex, childIndex)
```

Starts at the index passed as argument (by default at the first element of the array A)

Leaves have no children, so can't be pushed down anymore. `firstLeafIndex` returns the index of the first leaf in the heap. If D is the branching factor, and array's indices starting at zero, then it's `(|pairs| - 2) / D + 1`.

We need to identify the current node's children with the highest priority, because that will be the only element that is safe to move up without breaking heap properties.

If the highest priority child has higher priority than the current element p . . .

. . . then swaps the current element with the one among its children with highest priority.

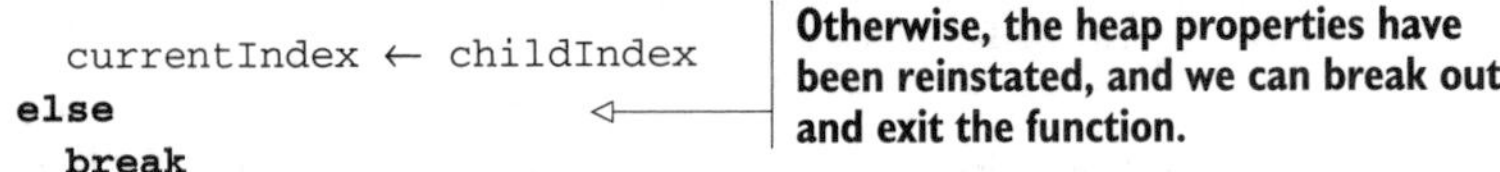

```
    currentIndex ← childIndex
  else
    break
```

Otherwise, the heap properties have been reinstated, and we can break out and exit the function.

This method's running time, while asymptotically equivalent to `bubbleUp`'s, requires a slightly larger number of comparisons. In the worst case, `D * log`$_D$`(n)`, for a heap with branching factor `D` and containing `n` elements. This is also the reason why increasing the branching factor (the max number of children for each node) indefinitely is not a good idea: we'll see this in section 2.10.

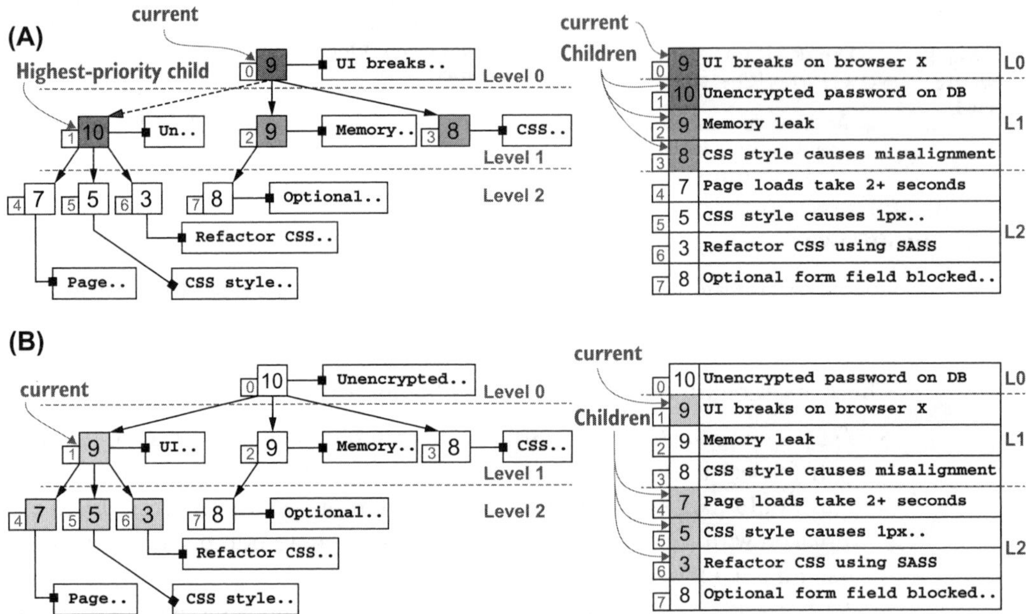

(A)
current
Highest-priority child
9
UI breaks..
Level 0
10
Un..
9
Memory..
8
CSS..
Level 1
7
5
3
8
Optional..
Level 2
Refactor CSS..
Page..
CSS style..
current
Children
9 UI breaks on browser X
10 Unencrypted password on DB
9 Memory leak
8 CSS style causes misalignment
7 Page loads take 2+ seconds
5 CSS style causes 1px..
3 Refactor CSS using SASS
8 Optional form field blocked..
L0
L1
L2
(B)
current
10
Unencrypted..
Level 0
9
UI..
9
Memory..
8
CSS..
Level 1
7
5
3
8
Optional..
Level 2
Refactor CSS..
Page..
CSS style..
current
Children
10 Unencrypted password on DB
9 UI breaks on browser X
9 Memory leak
8 CSS style causes misalignment
7 Page loads take 2+ seconds
5 CSS style causes 1px..
3 Refactor CSS using SASS
8 Optional form field blocked..
L0
L1
L2

Figure 2.8 An example of applying the `pushDown` method to the root of a ternary heap. (A) The root of the tree violates heap's properties, being smaller than one of its children. The algorithm finds the child with the highest priority, and then compares it to current node (the root, in this example). (B) We swapped the root with its highest-priority children: the node at index 1. Now, in turn, we compare the updated child with its children: since none of them has a higher priority than current node, we can stop.

To stick to our tasks example, let's consider the case where the root's priority is lower than its children, shown in figure 2.8. Working on a ternary Heap, its first leaf is stored at index 4.

We call `pushDown(pairs, 0)` to fix the third heap's property; helper function `firstLeafIndex` at line #3 will return 3 (because the element at index [7], the last one in the array, is a child of the node at index [2], which is the last internal node), and so we will enter the loop.

The children of element [0] are at positions [1], [2], and [3], and among them we'll choose the highest priority child of the root, at line #4. It turns out to be the element

<Unencrypted password on DB, 10>. Its priority is higher than current element's, so at line #6 we will swap it with current element.

Overall, after one iteration of the while loop, we have the situation illustrated by sub-figure 2.8.B, and currentIndex is set to 1.

Therefore, when we enter the loop for the second time, at line #3 currentIndex evaluates to 1, which is still less than 3, the index of the first leaf. The children of the element at index [1] are at indices [4], [5], and [6]. Among those elements we look for the node with highest priority among the current node's children, at line #4 in listing 2.4; it turns out it is the element at index [4], <Page loads take 2+ seconds, 7>.

Therefore, at line #5, we find out that this time, all children's priorities are lower than the current element's, and we break out of the loop and return without any further change.

Similar to bubbleUp, pushDown can be improved by simply keeping the current element in a temporary variable and avoiding swaps at each iteration.

Listing 2.5 shows the final improved version of the method. We encourage the reader to work our example out line by line, similar to what we have done in the previous section for bubbleUp, to have a better grasp of how it works.

Listing 2.5 Optimizing the pushDown method

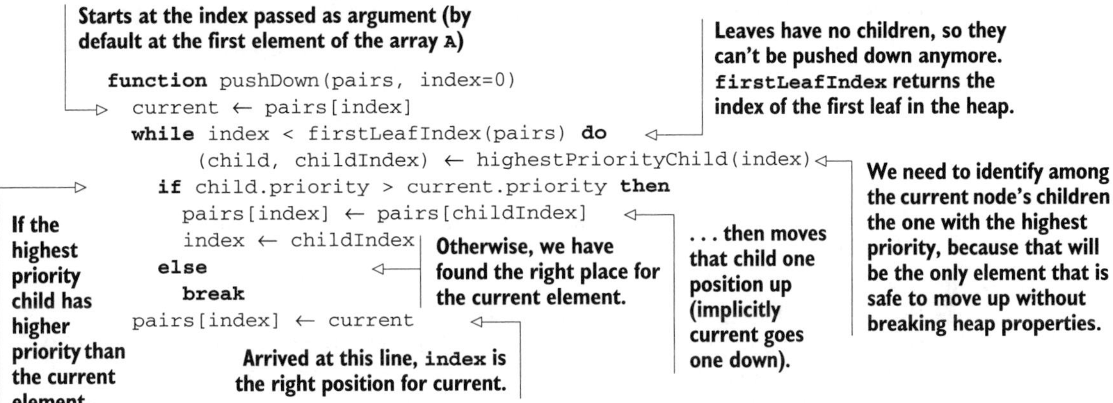

```
function pushDown(pairs, index=0)
  current ← pairs[index]
  while index < firstLeafIndex(pairs) do
      (child, childIndex) ← highestPriorityChild(index)
    if child.priority > current.priority then
      pairs[index] ← pairs[childIndex]
      index ← childIndex
    else
      break
  pairs[index] ← current
```

Starts at the index passed as argument (by default at the first element of the array A)
Leaves have no children, so they can't be pushed down anymore. firstLeafIndex returns the index of the first leaf in the heap.
We need to identify among the current node's children the one with the highest priority, because that will be the only element that is safe to move up without breaking heap properties.
If the highest priority child has higher priority than the current element . . .
. . . then moves that child one position up (implicitly current goes one down).
Otherwise, we have found the right place for the current element.
Arrived at this line, index is the right position for current.

Now that we have defined all the helper methods we need, we can finally implement the API methods. As a spoiler, you will notice how all the logic about priority and max-heap vs min-heap is encapsulated into bubbleUp and pushDown, so by defining these two helper methods, we greatly simplify our life whenever it comes to adapting our code to different situations.

2.6.3 Insert

Let's start with insertion. Listing 2.6 describes the pseudocode for inserting a new (element, priority) pair into a heap.

As mentioned at the end of the previous section, the insert method can be written by leveraging our helper methods, and as such its code is valid independent of whether we use a min-heap or a max-heap and of the definition of priority.

Listing 2.6 The insert method

```
function insert(element, priority)
  p ← Pair(element, priority)
  pairs.append(p)
  bubbleUp(pairs, |pairs| - 1)
```

Creates a new pair holding our new element and priority

Adds the newly created pair at the end of our heap's array, incrementing the array's size

After adding the new element, we need to make sure that the heap's properties are reinstated.

The first two steps in listing 2.6 are self-explanatory: we are just performing some maintenance on our data model, creating a pair from the two arguments and appending it to the tail of our array. Depending on the programming language and the type of container used for pairs, we might have to manually resize it (statically dimensioned arrays) or just add the element (dynamic arrays or lists).[11]

The last step is needed because the new pair might violate the heap's properties we defined in section 2.5.3. In particular, its priority could be higher than its parent's. To reinstate heap properties, we then need to "bubble it up" toward the root of the heap, until we find the right spot in the tree structure.

Insert operations, just like delete or update, or even heap's construction, will have to make sure the heaps properties holds on completion.

Because of the compact array implementation there will be no pointers to redirect, and the structure will be guaranteed to be consistent with properties 1 (by construction) and 2 (unless you have bugs in your code, of course).

So, we have to guarantee property 3, or in other words that each node is larger (for a max-heap) than each one of its `D` children. To do so, as we mentioned in previous sections, we might have to push it down (on deletes, and possibly updates), or bubble it up toward the root (on insert, and updates as well), whenever heap invariants are violated.

What's the running time for insertion?

How many swaps will we need to perform in order to reinstate the heap properties? That depends on the concrete case, but since we move one level up at each swap, it can't be more than the heap's height. And since a heap is a balanced complete tree, that means no more than $\log_D(n)$ swaps for a D-way heap with `n` elements.

The caveat here is that in any concrete implementation we need to expand the array beyond its current size. If we use a fixed-size static array, we will need to allocate it when the heap is created and set the max number of elements it can hold. In this case, however, the method is logarithmic in the worst case.

If we use a dynamic array, then the logarithmic bound becomes amortized and not worst-case, because we will periodically need to resize the array (see appendix C to check out more on dynamic arrays performance).

---

[11] As we explain in appendix C, this doesn't change the asymptotic analysis, because it can be proven that inserting `n` elements in a dynamic array requires at most `2n` assignments, so each insertion requires an *amortized* constant time.

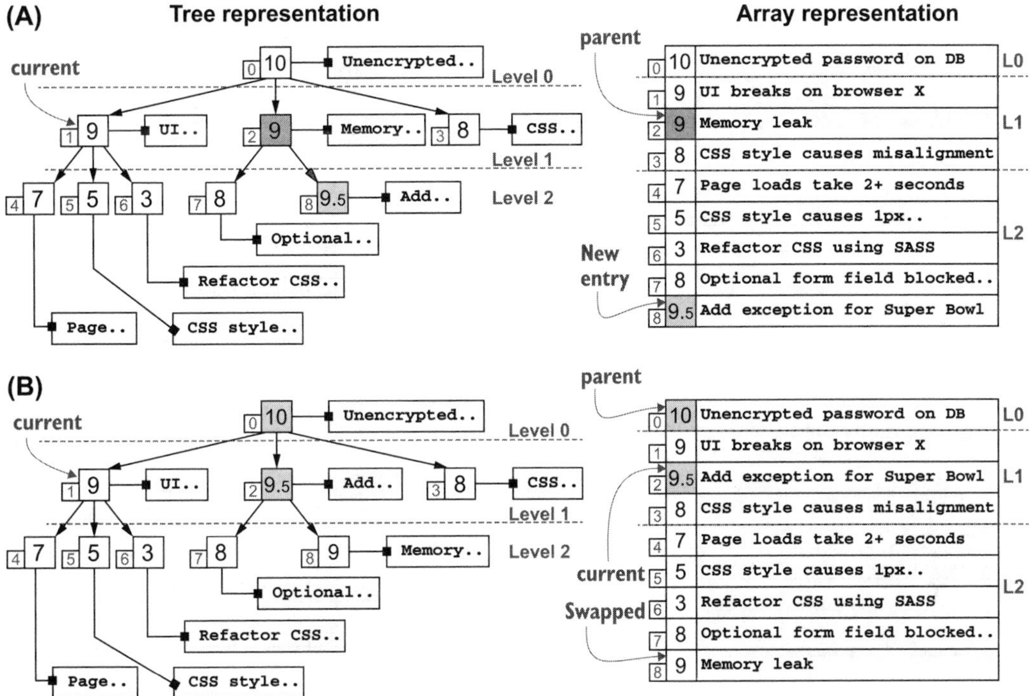
(A)
Tree representation
Array representation
current
parent
Level 0
Level 1
Level 2
Unencrypted..
UI..
Memory..
CSS..
Add..
Optional..
Refactor CSS..
Page..
CSS style..
10 Unencrypted password on DB
9 UI breaks on browser X
9 Memory leak
8 CSS style causes misalignment
7 Page loads take 2+ seconds
5 CSS style causes 1px..
3 Refactor CSS using SASS
8 Optional form field blocked..
9.5 Add exception for Super Bowl
L0
L1
L2
New entry
(B)
current
parent
10 Unencrypted password on DB
9 UI breaks on browser X
9.5 Add exception for Super Bowl
8 CSS style causes misalignment
7 Page loads take 2+ seconds
5 CSS style causes 1px..
3 Refactor CSS using SASS
8 Optional form field blocked..
9 Memory leak
Swapped

Figure 2.9 Adding a new element to a ternary max-heap. (A) The initial state of the heap; we first add the new element, with priority 9.5 at the end of the heap's array. (B) Then we bubble it up until we find the right spot for it; that is, the first spot where it does not violate the heap's properties.

If we go back to our task management example, we can see how insert works on a ternary max-heap. Suppose we have the initial state shown in figure 2.9 (A), describing the heap right after a call to `insert("Add exception for Superbowl", 9.5)` to add a particularly urgent task that marketing is pushing to have fixed by the end of the day. (And yes, they do cheat using fractional numbers for priority! But that's probably not the first time you've seen someone changing requirements after you've pulled up a lot of work, is it?). After executing line #3 in listing 2.6, in fact, the list would be in this intermediate state (where heap properties are still violated).

Line #4 is then executed to reinstate heap property number 3, as we saw in section 2.6.2, and the final result is shown in figure 2.9 (B). Notice the order in which the children of the root appear in the array: siblings are not ordered, and in fact a heap doesn't keep a total ordering on its elements like a BST would.

2.6.4 Top

Now that we have seen how to insert a new element, let's define the `top` method that will extract the heap's root and return it to the caller.

Figure 2.10 shows an example of a max-heap, highlighting the steps that are performed in listing 2.7.

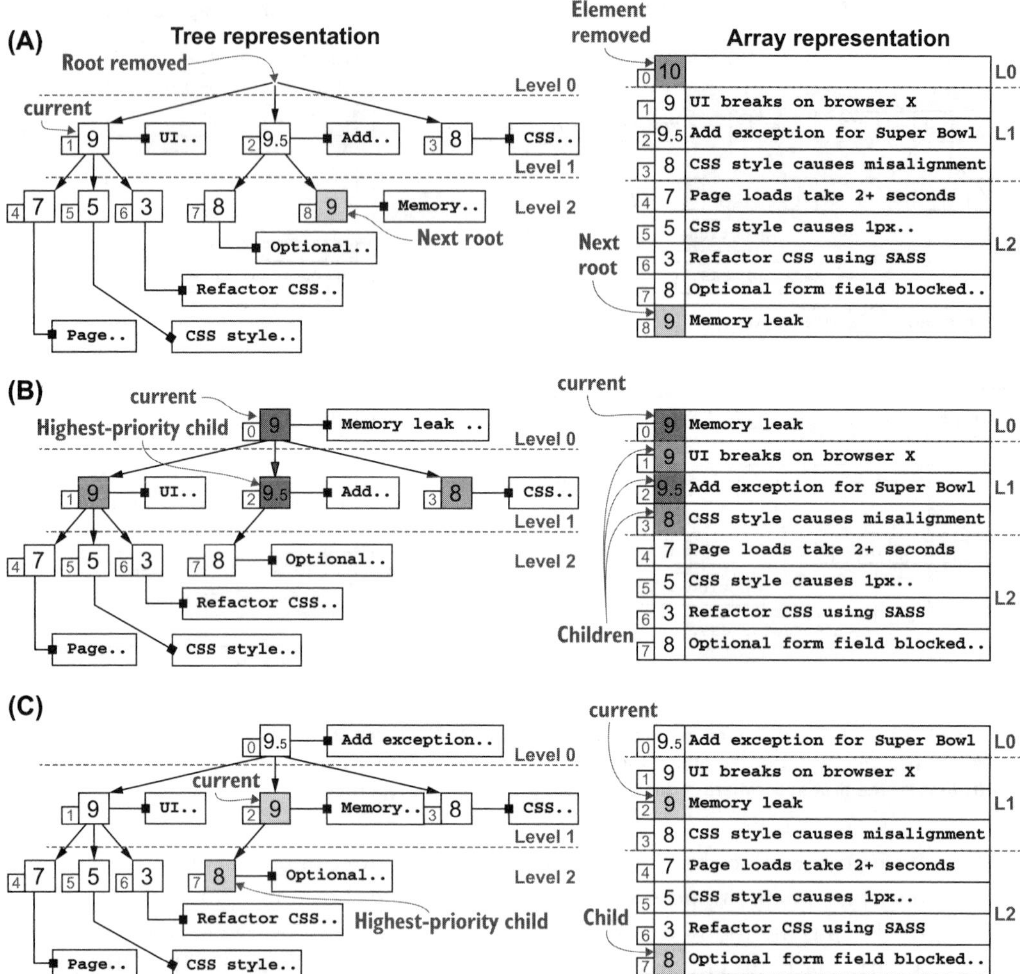
(A)
Tree representation
Root removed
current
Level 0
Level 1
Level 2
UI..
Add..
CSS..
Memory..
Next root
Optional..
Refactor CSS..
Page..
CSS style..
Element removed
Array representation
UI breaks on browser X
Add exception for Super Bowl
CSS style causes misalignment
Page loads take 2+ seconds
CSS style causes 1px..
Refactor CSS using SASS
Optional form field blocked..
Memory leak
Next root
L0
L1
L2
(B)
current
Highest-priority child
Memory leak ..
Children
(C)
Add exception..
Highest-priority child
Child

Figure 2.10 Removing the top element from a binary heap. (A) From a valid ternary heap, we remove the root of the heap (storing it in a temporary location, in order to return it at the end). (B) We replace the old root with the last element in the array (which is also removed from its tail). The new root might violate heap's properties (and it does, in this example), so we need to push it down, comparing it to its children to check that the heap's properties are not violated. (C) We move the new root down toward the heap's leaves, until we find a valid spot for it (that is, the first one that does not violate the heap's properties).

The first thing we do is check that the heap is not empty. If it is, we certainly can't extract the top element, so we need to issue an error.

The idea is that since we will remove the root of the heap, and by doing so we leave a "hole" in the array, we need to replace it with another element.

We could "promote" one of its children as the new root, as shown in listing 2.7. (One of them will certainly be the next-highest priority element; try to prove it as an exercise.)

Listing 2.7 The `top` method

```
function top()
  if pairs.isEmpty() then error()
  p ← pairs.removeLast()
  if pairs.isEmpty() then
    return p.element
  else
   (element, priority) ← pairs[0]
    pairs[0] ← p
    pushDown(pairs, 0)
    return element
```

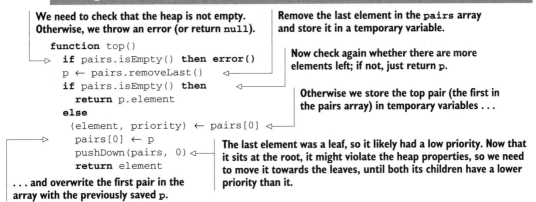

We need to check that the heap is not empty. Otherwise, we throw an error (or return `null`).

Remove the last element in the `pairs` array and store it in a temporary variable.

Now check again whether there are more elements left; if not, just return `p`.

Otherwise we store the top pair (the first in the pairs array) in temporary variables . . .

. . . and overwrite the first pair in the array with the previously saved `p`.

The last element was a leaf, so it likely had a low priority. Now that it sits at the root, it might violate the heap properties, so we need to move it towards the leaves, until both its children have a lower priority than it.

However, we would then only move the problem to the subtree rooted at this node that we moved to the root, and then to the next level, and so on.

Instead, since we also have to shrink the array, and since it's easier to add or remove the array's elements from its tail, we can simply pop the last element in the array and use it to replace the root.

The caveat is that this new root might violate heap's properties. As a matter of fact, being a leaf, the probability is pretty high that there is a violation. Therefore, we need to reinstate them using a utility method, `pushDown`.

> **Running time for `top()`**
>
> Similar to what happens for insertion, the nature of the heap and the fact that we move one step toward the leaves at every swap guarantee that no more than a logarithmic number of swaps is required, in the worst case.
>
> In this case as well, concrete implementations have to deal with array sizing, and we can only guarantee an *amortized* logarithmic upper bound (if we need a worst-case logarithmic bound, we need to use static arrays with all the disadvantages they carry).

Back to our task management example. Let's see what happens when calling `top()` on the ternary heap shown at the end of figure 2.9 (B).

First, at line #3 we remove the last element of the heap, at index [8], and save it to a temporary variable; at line #4 we check whether the remaining array is empty. If that had been the case, the last element in the array would also have been the top of the heap (its only element!) and we could have just returned it.

But this is clearly not the case in this example, so we move on to line #7, where we store the first element of the heap, `<Unencrypted password on DB, 10>`, to a temporary variable, which will be returned by the method. At this point, we can imagine the heap to be like what's shown in figure 2.10 (A), three disconnected branches without a root. To sew them together, we add a new root, using the element we had saved at line #3, the one entry that used to be the last in the array, at index `[8]`. Figure 2.10 (B) shows the situation at this point.

This new root, however, is violating heap's properties, so we need to call `pushDown` at line #8 to reinstate them by swapping it with its second children, whose priority is `9.5`, and producing the heap shown in figure 2.10 (C); the `pushDown` method will handle this phase, stopping when the right position for element `<Memory Leak, 9>` is found.

To conclude this sub-section, it's worth noting that the `peek` method returns the top element in the heap, but it just returns it without any side effects on the data structure. Its logic is therefore trivial, so we will skip its implementation.

2.6.5 *Update*

This is arguably the most interesting of heap's public methods, even if it's not always directly provided in implementations.[12]

When we change an element, its priority could stay unchanged, and in that case, we don't need any further action. See listing 2.8. But it could also become lower or higher. If an element's priority becomes higher, we need to check that it doesn't violate the third invariant for its parents; if it becomes lower, it could violate the same invariant for its children.

Listing 2.8 The `update` method

```
function update(oldValue, newPriority)
  index ← pairs.find(oldValue)
  if index ≥ 0 then
    oldPriority ← pairs[index].priority
    pairs[index] ← Pair(oldValue, newPriority)
    if (newPriority < oldPriority) then
      bubbleUp(pairs, index)
    elsif (newPriority > oldPriority) then
      pushDown(pairs, index)
```

- Get the position of the element to update.
- Check whether the element is actually stored in the heap, and update it with the new value/priority.
- Check whether the new priority is higher than the old one.
- If so, bubble up the element towards the root.
- Otherwise, push it down toward the leaves.

In the former situation, we need to bubble up the modified element until we find a higher-priority ancestor or until we reach the root. In the latter, we instead push it down until all its children are lower priority, or we reach a leaf.

As we saw, the first case can always be implemented more efficiently[13] and luckily for us, most algorithms only require us to reduce elements' priority.

---

[12] For instance, in Java's `PriorityQueue`, a class provided in standard library, you need to remove an element and then insert the new one to perform the same operation. This is far from ideal, especially because the removal of a random element is implemented inefficiently, requiring linear time.

[13] Using Fibonacci heaps, it could be implemented even in amortized constant time, at least in theory.

> **Running time for `update`**
>
> From a performance point of view, the challenge of this method is in line #2: the search for the old element can take linear time in the worst case, because on a failed search (when the element is not actually in the heap), we will have to search the whole heap.
>
> To improve this worst-case scenario, it is possible to use auxiliary data structures that will help us in performing searches more efficiently. For instance, we can store a `map` associating each element in the heap with its index. If implemented with a hash table, the lookup would only need an amortized `O(1)` time.
>
> We will see this in further detail when describing the `contains` method. For now, let's just remember that if the `find` operation takes at most logarithmic time, the whole method is also logarithmic.

2.6.6 *Dealing with duplicates*

So far, we've also assumed that our heap doesn't hold duplicates. We will have to tackle further challenges if this assumption doesn't hold true. In particular, we will need to figure out the order we use in case there are duplicates. To show why this is important, we will abandon our example for an easier configuration, illustrated in figure 2.11. For the sake of space we will only show priorities in nodes.

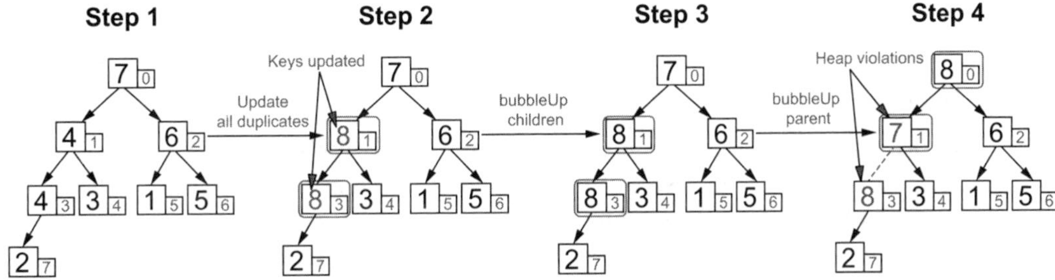

Step 1
Step 2
Step 3
Step 4
Keys updated
Update
all duplicates
bubbleUp
children
bubbleUp
parent
Heap violations

Figure 2.11 Updating an element in a binary max-heap with duplicates.

We could have two duplicates—call them `X` and `Y`—one being the child of the other. Let's consider the case where `X` is a child of `Y`, and we call update to change their priority to a higher one. Inside `update`, after updating the two elements' priorities, there would have to be two calls to `bubbleUp`, one for `X`, and one for `Y`. The catch is that if we run them in the wrong order, we will end with an inconsistent heap, which violates the heap's properties.

Suppose we bubble up `X`, the children, first: then it will immediately find its parent (which is `Y`) and stop (because it has the same value). When we call `bubbleUp(Y)`, we will discover that its parent now has lower priority, so we do need to move it toward the root. Unfortunately, we will never check `X` again, so it will never be moved up together with `Y` and heap's property won't be correctly reinstated.

Figure 2.11 provides a step-by-step description of how the `update` method could violate heap's constraints if it's not implemented in such a way to avoid duplicates:

- In step 1, we can see the initial max-heap.
- In step 2, all occurrences are changed from 4 to 8.
- In step 3, you see bubbling up the deepest node updated at index `3`. It will stop immediately because its parent has the same priority (it just updated together with current node). The nodes involved in the call to `bubbleUp` are highlighted with a red outline.
- In step 4, you see bubbling up the other node that was updated at index `1`. This time some swaps are actually performed as the node's new priority, `8`, is higher than its parent's (just `7`). The node that was bubbled up first, at step 3, will never be updated again, and so the heap's properties will be violated.

How can we solve this issue? Following a left-to-right order for the calls to `bubbleUp` will guarantee that the heap properties are properly reinstated.

As an alternative, we could change the conditions in `bubbleUp` and `pushDown`, and only stop when we find a strictly higher-priority parent and strictly lower-priority children, respectively. Yet another alternative could be bubbling up (or pushing down) the nodes as we update them. Both these solutions, however, would be far from ideal for many reasons, not least performance-wise, because they would require a larger bound for the worst-case number of swaps (the proof is easy enough if you count the worst-case possible number of swaps in a path where all elements are the same—details are left to the reader).

2.6.7 Heapify

Priority queues can be created empty, but they are also often initialized with a set of elements. If that's the case, and if we need to initialize the heap with `n` elements, we can still obviously create an empty heap and add those elements one by one.

To do so, we will need at most `O(n)` time to allocate the heap array, and then repeat `n` insertions. Every insertion is logarithmic, so we have an upper bound of `O(n log n)`.

Is this the best we can do? Turns out that we can do better. Suppose that we initialize the heap with the whole sets of `n` elements, in any order.

As we have seen, each position of the array can be seen as the root of a sub-heap. So, leaves, for example, are trivial sub-heaps, containing only one element. Being singletons, they are valid heaps.

How many leaves are there in a heap? That depends on the branching factor. In a binary heap, half the nodes are leaves. In a 4-way heap, the last three-fourths of the array contain leaves.

Let's stick to the case of a binary heap, for the sake of simplicity. We can see an example of a min-heap in figure 2.12, where we can follow step by step how `heapify` works.

If we start at the last internal node for the heap—let's call it `X`—it will have at most two children, both leaves, and hence both valid heaps.

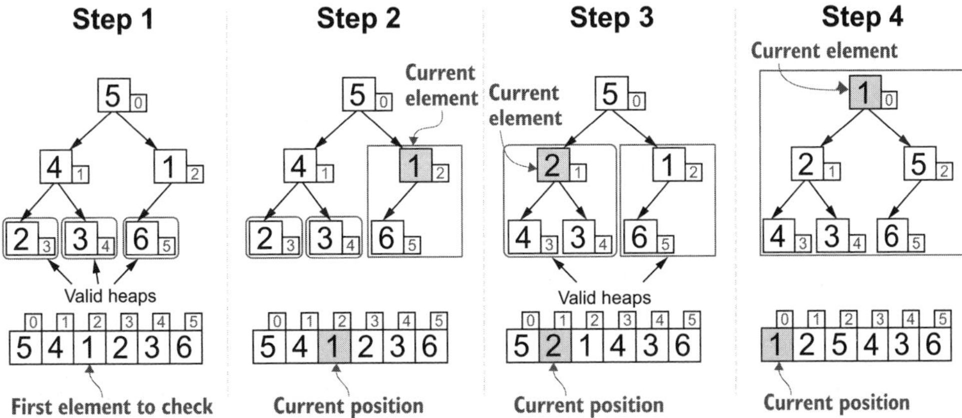
Step 1
Step 2
Step 3
Step 4
Current element
Current element
Current element
Valid heaps
Valid heaps
First element to check
Current position
Current position
Current position

Figure 2.12 Heapification of a small array. The boxes with rounded corners surround valid sub-heaps; that is, portions of the tree for which we have verified that they abide by the heap properties. Step 1: Initially, only leaves are valid min-heap; here, smaller numbers mean higher priority. Step 2: The element from which we start our iteration is the first internal node in the heap, at index 2 in our array. In the bottom part of the leftmost figure, it is pointed at by an arrow. We repair the heap properties for the sub-heap rooted at this node by swapping its content with its child's. Step 3: We move the arrow pointing to the current element one position to the left and repeat the operation for the sub-heap rooted at index 1. Step 4: Finally, the whole array is *heapified*, by pushing down the temporary root (with priority 5) until we find its right place.

We can't say yet if `X` is the root of a valid heap, but we can try to push it down and possibly swap it with the smallest of its children. Once we have done that, we are sure that the sub-heap rooted at `X` is a valid heap. This happens because `pushDown`, by construction, reinstates the heap properties on a sub-heap where all children are valid heaps, and only the root might be misplaced.

If we now move one position left in the array, we can repeat the procedure, and get another valid sub-heap. Continuing on, at some point we visit all internal nodes that only have leaves as their children. And after that, we'll start with the first internal node that's the root of a sub-heap with height 2. Let's name it `Y`. If we tackle elements in a right-to-left order in the array, we have the guarantee that `Y`'s children are sub-heaps that

- Have at most height 1 and
- Whose properties have already been fixed

Once again, we can use `pushDown` and be sure the sub-heap rooted at `Y` will be a valid heap afterward.

If we repeat these steps for all nodes until we reach the root of our heap, we have the guarantee that we will end up with a valid heap, as shown in listing 2.9.

Listing 2.9 The `heapify` method

```
function heapify(pairs)
  for index in {(|pairs|-1)/D .. 0} do
    pushDown(pairs, index)
```

We start at the first internal node of the heap (D is the branching factor) and iterate until the root.

Ensures the sub-heap rooted at index is a valid heap

Running time for `heapify`

In total, in a binary heap, we will call `pushDown` `n/2` times, with an initial estimate of the upper bound of `O(n*log(n))`.

However, notice that the sub-heaps that only have leaves as children have a height equal to 1, so they only need at most one swap to be fixed. And there is `n/2` of them. Likewise, sub-heaps with height 2 only need at most two swaps, and we have `n/4` of them.

Going up toward the root, the number of swaps increases but the number of calls to `pushDown` decreases at the same rate. Finally, we'll have only two calls for `pushDown` that requires at most $\log_2(n)-1$ swaps, and only one call, the one on the root, that requires $\log_2(n)$ swaps in the worst case.

Putting all these together, we see that the total number of swaps is given by

$$\sum_{h=0}^{\lfloor \log n \rfloor} \left\lceil \frac{n}{2^{h+1}} \right\rceil \cdot O(h) = O\left(n \sum_{h=0}^{\lfloor \log n \rfloor} \left\lceil \frac{h}{2^h} \right\rceil \right)$$

Since the last summation is limited by geometric series with seed 2, we have

$$\sum_{h=0}^{\lfloor \log n \rfloor} \left\lceil \frac{h}{2^h} \right\rceil \le \sum_{h=0}^{\infty} \left\lceil \frac{h}{2^h} \right\rceil = 2$$

and therefore, the total number of swaps is linear in the worst case (at most `2n`).

So, our final analysis is that heapify's complexity is `O(n)`.

We leave the computation for a d-ary heap as an exercise. It is similar to the previous one, replacing the branching factor.

2.6.8 Beyond API methods: Contains

One thing that heaps are definitely not good for is checking whether or not an element is stored in them. We have no other choice than going through all the elements until we find the one we were looking for, or we get to the end of the array. This means a linear time algorithm. Compare it with a hash table's optimal average constant time, or even `O(log(n))` for binary search trees (average) or balanced binary search trees (worst case).

However, we also would like to support priority increment/decrement. As we saw in section 2.6.5, it's paramount for these operations to efficiently retrieve the element whose priority needs to be changed. Therefore, when implementing heaps, we might add an auxiliary field, a HashMap from elements to positions, that allows us to check whether an element is in the heap (or get its position) in constant time, on average. See a possible implementation of contains in listing 2.10.

Listing 2.10 The contains method

```
function contains(elem)
  index ← elementToIndex[elem]
  return index >= 0
```

The function uses an extra field elementToIndex we can add to our heap. This is possible under two assumptions:

- That elementToIndex[elem] by default returns -1 if elem is not stored in the heap.
- That we don't allow duplicate keys in the heap; otherwise, we will need to store a list of indices for each key.

2.6.9 Performance recap

With the description of the contains method, we have concluded our overview of this data structure.

We have presented several operations on heaps, so it feels like the right time to order and recap their running time (table 2.4), and as importantly, show the amount of extra memory they need.

Table 2.4 Operations provided by heaps, and their cost on a heap with n elements

Operation	Running time	Extra space
Insert	O(log(n))	O(1)
Top	O(log(n))	O(1)
Remove	O(log(n))[a]	O(n)[a]
Peek	O(1)	O(1)
Contains (naïve)	O(n)	O(1)
Contains	O(1)[a]	O(n)[a]
UpdatePriority	O(log(n))[a]	O(n)[a]
Heapify	O(n)	O(1)

[a]Using the advanced version of contains and maintaining an extra map from elements to indices

As with most things in computer science, time versus space is often a tradeoff. Nevertheless, sometimes there is a tendency to neglect the extra memory factor in informal analysis. With the volumes we've operated since the dawn of the era of big data, however, our data structures need to hold and process billions of elements, or even more. Therefore, a fast algorithm that consumes quadratic space could be the best choice for small volumes of data, but it becomes impractical for some real case scenarios where you need to scale out. And so a slower algorithm using constant or logarithmic space could be the choice of election as our dataset grows.

The takeaway is that it's even more important to take the memory factor into account as early as possible when we design a system that needs to scale.

For heaps, consider that we naturally need constant extra space per element, and linear extra space in total, to host a map from elements to indices.

We have closely examined all operations. Yet, it's worth spending a few more words on a couple of things.

For `insert` and `top`, the running time guarantee is amortized, not worst case. If a dynamic array is used to provide a flexible size, some calls will require linear time to resize the array. It can be proven that to fill a dynamic array with `n` elements, at most `2n` swaps are needed. However, the worst-case logarithmic guarantee can be offered only if the heap size is set from the beginning. For this reason, and for allocation/garbage collection efficiency, in some languages (for instance, Java), it is advisable to initialize your heaps to their expected size, if you have a reasonable estimate that will remain true for most of the container's life.

The performance for `remove` and `updatePriority` relies on the efficient implementation of `contains`, in order to provide a logarithmic guarantee. To have efficient search, however, we need to keep a second data structure besides the array for fast indirection. The choice is between a hash table or a bloom filter (see chapter 4).

In case either is used, the running time for contains is assumed to be constant, with a caveat: the hash for each element needs to be computable in constant time. Otherwise, we will need to take that cost into account in our analysis.

2.6.10 From pseudo-code to implementation

We have seen how a d-way heap works in a language-agnostic way. Pseudo-code provides a good way to outline and explain a data structure, without worrying about the implementation details so you can focus on its behavior.

At the same time, however, pseudo-code is of little practical use. To be able to move from theory to practice, we need to choose a programming language and implement our d-way heap. Independently of what platform we choose, language-specific concerns will arise and different problematics need to be taken into consideration.

We'll provide implementations of the algorithms in this book, in an effort to give readers a way to experiment and get their hands dirty with these data structures.

The full code, including tests, can be found in our book's repo on GitHub.[14]

---

[14]See https://github.com/mlarocca/AlgorithmsAndDataStructuresInAction#d-ary-heap.

2.7 Use case: Find the k largest elements

In this section we are going to describe how we can use a priority queue to keep track of the k largest elements of a set.

If we have the full set of n elements in advance, we have a few alternatives that don't need any auxiliary data structure:

- We could sort the input and take the last k elements. This naïve approach requires O(n*log(n)) comparisons and swaps and, depending on the algorithm, might require additional memory.
- We could find the largest element from the set and move it to the end of the array, then look at the remaining n-1 elements and find the second to last and move it to position n-2, and so on. Basically, this algorithm runs the inner cycle of Selection Sort algorithm k times, requiring O(k) swaps and O(n*k) comparisons. No additional memory would be needed.

In this section we will see that by using a heap, we can achieve our goal using O(n+k*log(k)) comparisons and swaps, and O(k) extra memory. This is a game-changing improvement if k is much smaller than n. In a typical situation, n could be on the order of millions or billions of elements, and k between a hundred and a few thousand.

Moreover, by using an auxiliary heap, the algorithm can naturally be adapted to work on dynamic streams of data and also to allow consuming elements from the heap.

2.7.1 The right data structure . . .

When your problem involves finding a subset of largest/smallest elements, priority queues seem like a natural solution.

In programming, choosing the right data structure can make a difference.[15] That's not always enough, because you also need to use it correctly.

Suppose, for instance, that we have a static set of elements available from the beginning. We could use a max-heap, insert all n elements, and then extract the largest k of them.

We would need O(n) extra space for the heap, and then use heapify to create it from the full set in linear time, O(n). Then we would call top k times, with a cost of O(log(n)) for each call. The total cost for this solution would be O(n+k*log(n)) comparisons and swaps.

That's already better than the naïve solutions, but, if you think about it, if[16] n>>k, we are creating a huge heap just to extract a few elements. That certainly sounds wasteful.

[15]Usually, though, the greatest concern is to avoid choosing the wrong data structure.

[16]n>>k is normally interpreted as "n is much larger than k."

2.7.2 . . . and the right use

So our goal should be having a small heap with k elements. Using a max-heap doesn't really work anymore. Let's see why with an example.

Suppose we want to find the largest three of the following numbers: 2, 4, 1, 3, 7, 6. We add the first three and we have the following max-heap: [4, 2, 1]. Now we proceed to the next number in the list, and it's 3. It's larger than two out of three elements currently in the heap, but we have no way of knowing this, because we can only peek at the top of the heap. Then we can insert 3 into the heap, and we obtain [4, 3, 1, 2]. Now, if we want to keep the size of the heap at k elements, we need to remove one, which is the minimum. How do we know where it is inside the heap? We only know where the maximum is (at the top of the max-heap), and so the search for the min could take up to linear time (even noting that the minimum will be in one of the leaves, there are unfortunately a linear number of them, n/D).

You can verify that even by inserting the elements in a different order, we often find a similar situation.

The catch is that when we want the k largest elements, at each step we are interested in understanding if the next number we evaluate is larger than the smallest of the k elements we already have. Hence, rather than a max-heap, we can use a min-heap bound to k elements where we store the largest elements found so far.

For each new element, we compare it to the top of the heap, and if the new one is smaller, we are sure it's not one of the k largest elements. If our new element is larger than the heap's top (that is, the *smallest* of our k elements), then we extract the top from the heap and then add our newly arrived. This way, updating the heap at each iteration costs us only constant time,[17] instead of the linear time bound if we used a max-heap.

2.7.3 Coding it up

That's neat, right? And simple to implement. Since code is worth a thousand words, let's see our heap in action in listing 2.11.

Listing 2.11 Top k elements of a list

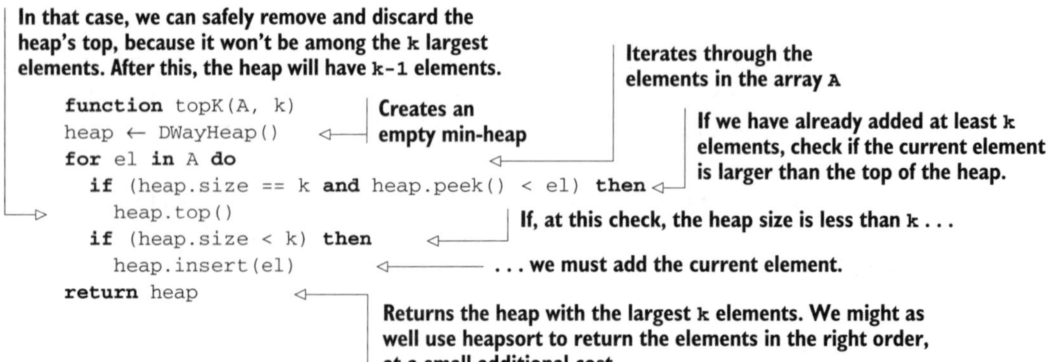
```
function topK(A, k)
  heap ← DWayHeap()
  for el in A do
    if (heap.size == k and heap.peek() < el) then
      heap.top()
    if (heap.size < k) then
      heap.insert(el)
  return heap
```
In that case, we can safely remove and discard the heap's top, because it won't be among the k largest elements. After this, the heap will have k-1 elements.
Creates an empty min-heap
Iterates through the elements in the array A
If we have already added at least k elements, check if the current element is larger than the top of the heap.
If, at this check, the heap size is less than k . . .
. . . we must add the current element.
Returns the heap with the largest k elements. We might as well use heapsort to return the elements in the right order, at a small additional cost.

[17] O(log(k)) to be precise, but since k in this context is a constant (much smaller than, and not depending on n), then O(log(k))==O(1).

2.8 More use cases

The heap is one of the most universally used data structures. Together with stack and queue, it is the basis of almost every algorithm that needs to process the input in a specific order.

Replacing a binary heap with a d-ary heap can improve virtually any piece of code that uses a priority queue. Before delving into a few algorithms that can benefit from the use of a heap, make sure you are familiar with graphs, because most of these algorithms will concern this data structure. To that end, chapter 14 provides a quick introduction to graphs.

Let's now discuss some algorithms that can benefit from the use of a heap.

2.8.1 Minimum distance in graphs: Dijkstra

Priority queues are crucial to implementing Dijkstra and A* algorithms, described in detail in chapter 14, sections 14.4 and 14.5. Figure 2.13 shows a minimal example of a graph, illustrating the concept of shortest path between two vertices. As we will discuss in chapter 14, the running time of these fundamental algorithms on graphs (which compute the minimum distance to a target) heavily depends on the implementation chosen for the priority queue, and upgrading from a binary to a d-ary heap can provide a consistent speedup.

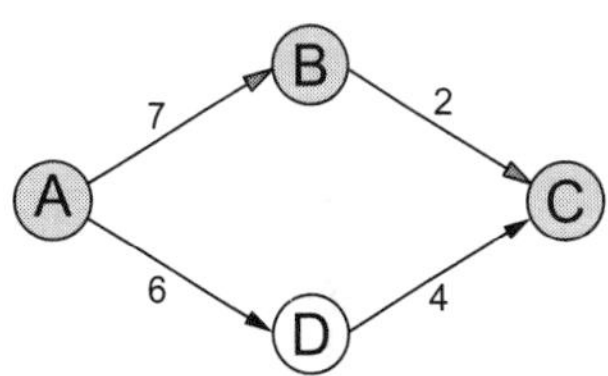
A
B
C
D
7
2
6
4
Figure 2.13 A directed graph showing the shortest path between vertices `A` and `C`

2.8.2 More graphs: Prim's algorithm

Prim's algorithm computes the minimum spanning tree (MST) of an undirected, connected graph `G`.

Suppose `G` has `n` vertices. The minimum spanning tree of `G` is

1. A tree (a connected, undirected, acyclic graph)
2. That is a subgraph of `G` with `n` vertices and
3. Whose sum of edges' weights is the least possible among all of the subgraphs of `G` that are also trees and span over all `n` vertices

Considering the graph in the example shown in section 2.8.1, its minimum spanning tree would be the one in figure 2.14.

Prim's algorithm works exactly as Dijkstra's, except

- Without keeping track of the distance from the source.
- Storing the edge that connected the front of the visited vertices to the next closest vertex.
- The vertex used as "source" for Prim's algorithm is going to be the root of the MST.

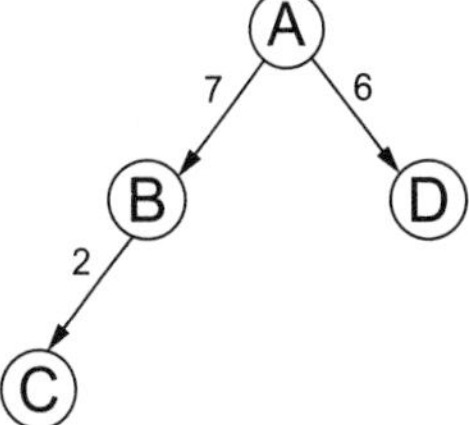
A
7
6
B
D
2
C
Figure 2.14 A spanning tree for the graph in figure 2.13

It should be no surprise that its running time is similar to Dijkstra's:

- `O(V²)` using arrays (sorted or unsorted) for the priority queue
- `O(V*log(V) + E*log(V))` using binary or d-ary heap
- `O(V*log(V) + E)` using Fibonacci heap

2.8.3 Data compression: Huffman codes

Huffman's algorithm is probably the most famous data compression algorithm, and you have likely already heard of it if you took an "introduction to CS" course. It is a simple, brilliant, *greedy* algorithm that, despite not being the state of the art for compression anymore, was a major breakthrough in the '50s.

A Huffman code is a tree, built bottom-up, starting with the list of different characters appearing in a text and their frequency. The algorithm iteratively

1. Selects and removes the two elements in the list with the smallest frequency
2. Then creates a new node by combining them (summing the two frequencies)
3. And finally adds back the new node to the list

While the tree itself is not a heap, a key step of the algorithm is based on efficiently retrieving the smallest elements in the list, as well as efficiently adding new elements to the list. You probably have guessed by now that, once again, that's where heaps come to the rescue.

Let's take a look at the algorithm itself in listing 2.12.

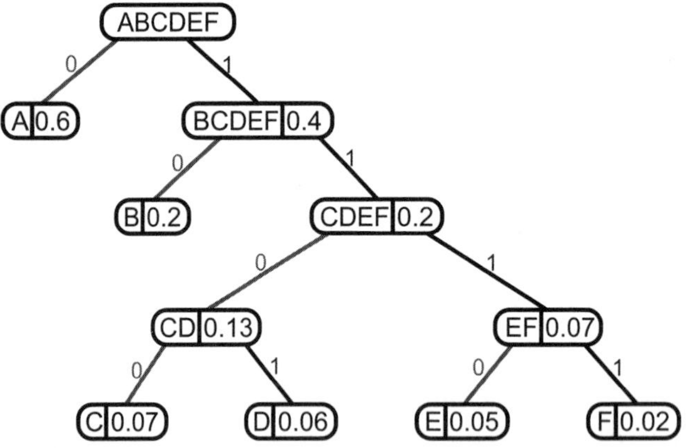
ABCDEF
0
1
A 0.6
BCDEF 0.4
0
1
B 0.2
CDEF 0.2
0
1
CD 0.13
EF 0.07
0
1
0
1
C 0.07
D 0.06
E 0.05
F 0.02

Figure 2.15 A Huffman coding tree built from this character frequency table: A=0.6, B=0.2, C=0.07, D=0.06, E=0.05, and F=0.02

We assume the input for the algorithm is a text, stored in a string (of course, the actual text might be stored in a file or stream, but we can always have a way to convert it to a string[18]), and the output is a map from characters to binary sequences.

---

[18] Additional challenges can occur if the text is so large that either it can't be contained in memory, or a map-reduce approach is advisable: we encapsulate all that complexity in the `ComputeFrequencies` method.

The first sub-task that we need to perform is to transform the text: we want to compute some statistics on it to identify the most used and least used characters in it. To that end, we compute the frequency of characters in the text.[19]

The details of the `ComputeFrequencies` method at line #2 are both out of scope and (at least in its basic version) simple enough, and there is no need to delve into that helper method here.

Once we have computed the frequency map, we create a new priority queue and then at lines #4 and #5 we iterate over the frequency map, creating a new `TreeNode` for each character and then adding it to the priority queue, as in listing 2.12. Obviously, considering the subject of this chapter, for the queue we use a heap, and in particular a min-heap, where the element at the top is the one with the smallest value for the priority field. And in this case the priority field is (not surprisingly) the frequency field of the `TreeNode`.

Listing 2.12 The Huffman coding algorithm

```
function huffman(text)
  charFrequenciesMap ← ComputeFrequencies(text)
  priorityQueue ← MinHeap()
  for (char, frequency) in charFrequenciesMap do
    priorityQueue.insert(TreeNode([char], frequency))
  while priorityQueue.size > 1 do
    left ← priorityQueue.top()
    right ← priorityQueue.top()
    parent ← TreeNode(left.chars + right.chars,
                      left.frequency + right.frequency)
    parent.left ← left
    parent.right ← right
    priorityQueue.insert(parent)
  return buildTable(priorityQueue.top(), [], Map())
```

Each `TreeNode`, in fact, contains two fields (besides the pointers to its children): a set of characters and the frequency of those characters in the text, computed as the sum of the frequencies of individual characters.

If you look at figure 2.15, you can see that the root of the final tree is the set of all characters in our example text, and hence the total frequency is 1.

This set is split into two groups, each of which is assigned to one of the root's children, and so each internal node is similarly split until we get to leaves, each of which contains just one character.

Back to our algorithm, you can see how the tree in figure 2.15 is constructed bottom-up, and lines #2 to #5 in listing 2.12 take care of the first step, creating the leaves of the tree and adding them to the priority queue.

---

[19] Instead of the actual frequency it might be easier, and equivalent for the algorithm, just counting the number of occurrences of each character.

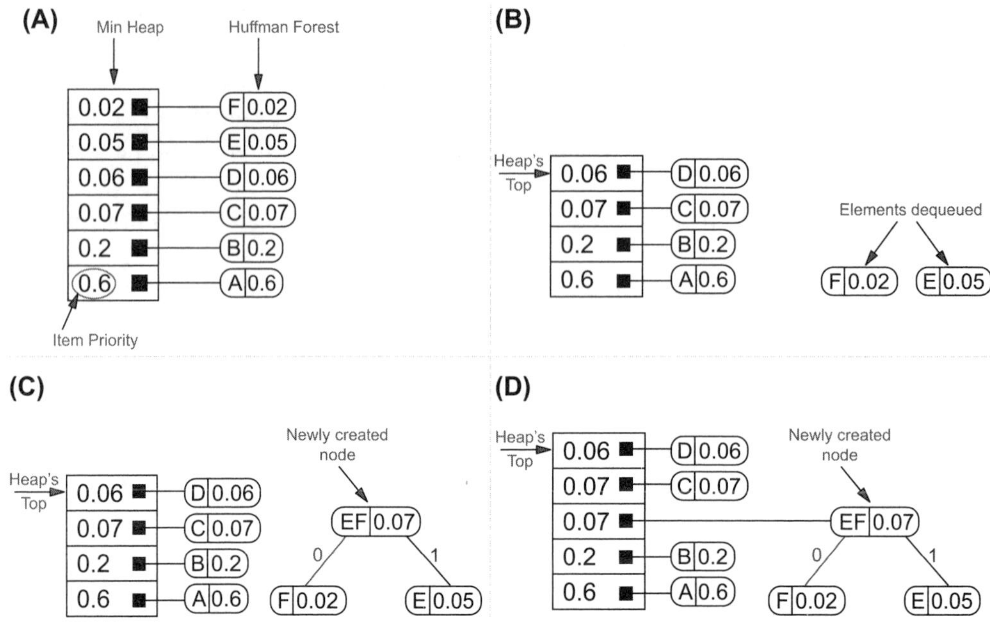
(A)
Min Heap
Huffman Forest
0.02
0.05
0.06
0.07
0.2
0.6
F 0.02
E 0.05
D 0.06
C 0.07
B 0.2
A 0.6
Item Priority
(B)
Heap's Top
0.06
0.07
0.2
0.6
D 0.06
C 0.07
B 0.2
A 0.6
Elements dequeued
F 0.02
E 0.05
(C)
Newly created node
Heap's Top
0.06
0.07
0.2
0.6
D 0.06
C 0.07
B 0.2
A 0.6
EF 0.07
0
1
F 0.02
E 0.05
(D)
Heap's Top
0.06
0.07
0.07
0.2
0.6
D 0.06
C 0.07
B 0.2
A 0.6
Newly created node
EF 0.07
0
1
F 0.02
E 0.05

Figure 2.16 The first step in the Huffman coding algorithm. As mentioned in the text, the algorithm will use two auxiliary data structures, a priority queue and a binary tree. Each tree node will have a value, a set of characters in the text, and a priority, the sum of the frequencies of those characters in the text. (A) Initially, we create one tree node for each character, associated with its frequency in the text. We also add each node into a priority queue, using the frequency as its priority (smaller frequency means higher priority hence we would use a min-heap). (B) We extract two elements from the top of the priority queue. (C) We create a new tree node to which we add the two nodes extracted at step (B) as its children. By convention, we assume that the smallest node will be added as left child and the second-smallest as right child (but any consistent convention works here). The newly created node will hold the union of the set of characters in its children as value, and the sum of the two priorities as priority. (D) Finally, we can add the new root for this subtree back to the priority queue. Note that the nodes in the heap are showed in sorted order, but for the sake of simplicity the order in which nodes are stored inside a priority queue is an implementation detail, the contract for PQ's API only guarantees that when we dequeue two elements, those will be the ones with the smallest frequencies.

Now, from line #6 we enter the core of the algorithm: until there is only one element left in the queue, we extract the top `TreeNode` entries, in lines #7 and #8. As you can see in figure 2.16 (B), those two elements will be the subtrees with the lowest frequencies so far.

Let's call these subtrees `L` and `R` (the reason for these names will be apparent soon).

Figure 2.16 (C) shows the actions performed in lines #9 to #11 of our pseudocode: a new `TreeNode` is created (let's call it `P`) by merging the two entries' character sets and setting its frequency as the sum of the old subtrees' frequencies. Then the new node and two subtrees are combined in a new subtree, where the new node `P` is the root and the subtrees `L` and `R` are its children.

Finally, at line #12 we add this new subtree back into the queue. As it's shown in figure 2.16 (D), it can sometimes be placed at the top of the queue, but that's not always the case; the priority queue will take care of this detail for us (notice that here the priority queue is used as a black box, as we discussed in section 2.4).

Listing 2.13 The Huffman coding algorithm (building a table from the tree)

```
function buildTable(node, sequence, charactersToSequenceMap)
  if node.characters.size == 1 then
    charactersToSequenceMap[node.characters[0]] ← sequence
  else
    if node.left <> null then
      buildTable(node.left, 0 + sequence, charactersToSequenceMap)
    if node.right <> null then
      buildTable(node.right, 1 + sequence, charactersToSequenceMap)
  return charactersToSequenceMap
```

These steps are repeated until there is only one element left in the queue (figure 2.17 shows a few more steps), and that last element will be the `TreeNode` that is the root of the final tree.

We can then use it in line #13 to create a compression table, which will be the final output of the `huffman` method. In turn, the compression table can be used to perform the compression of the text by translating each one of its characters into a sequence of bits.

While we won't show this last step,[20] we provide listing 2.13 with the steps needed to create a compression table from the tree in figure 2.15. And even if this goes beyond the scope of this chapter (because the method doesn't use a priority queue), providing a brief explanation should help those readers interested in writing an implementation of Huffman coding.

We wrote the `buildTable` method using recursive form. As explained in appendix E, this allows us to provide cleaner and more easily understandable code, but in some languages concrete implementations can be more performant when implemented using explicit iterations.

We pass three arguments to the method: a `TreeNode node` that is the current node in the traversal of the tree, a sequence that is the path from the root to current node (where we add a 0 for a "left turn" and a 1 for a "right turn"), and the `Map` that will hold the associations between characters and bit sequences.

At line #2, we check if the set of characters in the node has only one character. If it does, it means we have reached a leaf, and so the recursion can stop. The bit sequence that is associated with the character in the node is the path from root to current node, stored in the `sequence` variable.

Otherwise, we check whether the node has left and right children (it will have at least one, because it's not a leaf) and traverse them. The crucial point here is how we build the `sequence` argument in the recursive calls: if we traverse the left child of current node, we add a 0 at the start of the sequence, while if we traverse the right child, we add a 1.

[20]It's simply going to be a 1:1 mapping over the characters in the text, with extra attention needed to efficiently construct the bits encoding in output.

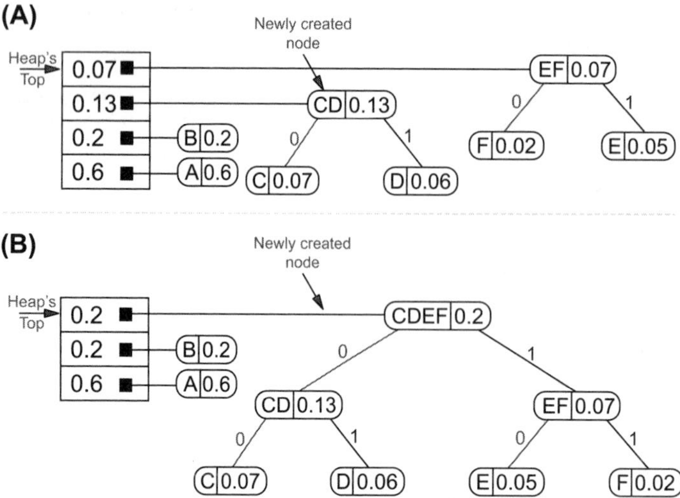
(A)
Newly created node
Heap's Top
0.07
0.13
0.2
0.6
B 0.2
A 0.6
CD 0.13
C 0.07
D 0.06
EF 0.07
F 0.02
E 0.05
0
1
(B)
Newly created node
Heap's Top
0.2
0.2
0.6
B 0.2
A 0.6
CDEF 0.2
CD 0.13
EF 0.07
C 0.07
D 0.06
E 0.05
F 0.02
0
1

Figure 2.17 The result of the next couple of steps in the Huffman coding algorithm. (A) We dequeue and merge the top two nodes on the heap, C and D. At the end of this step, EF and CD become the two smallest nodes in the heap. (B) Now we merge those two nodes into CDEF, and we add it back to the heap. Which node between CDEF and B will be kept at the top of the priority queue is an implementation detail, and it's irrelevant for the Huffman coding algorithm (the code will change slightly depending on which one is extracted first, but its compression ratio will remain unchanged). The next steps are easy to figure, also using figure 2.15 as a reference.

Table 2.5 shows the compression table produced starting from the tree shown in figure 2.15; the last column would not be part of the actual compression table, but it's useful to understand how the most used characters end up translated into shorter sequences (which is the key to an efficient compression).

Table 2.5 The compression table created from the Huffman tree in figure 2.15

Character	Bit sequence	Frequency
A	0	0.6
B	10	0.2
C	1100	0.07
D	1101	0.06
E	1110	0.05
F	1111	0.02

Looking at the sequences, the most important property is that they form a prefix code: no sequence is the prefix of another sequence in the code.

This property is the key point for the decoding: iterating on the compressed text, we immediately know how to break it into characters.

For instance, in the compressed text `1001101`, if we start from the first character, we can immediately see that sequence `10` matches `B`, then the next `0` matches `A`, and finally `1101` matches `D`, so the compressed bit sequence is translated into `"BAD"`.

2.9 Analysis of branching factor[21]

Now that we know how d-way heaps work, the next question we need to ask is this: Wouldn't we be just fine with a regular, binary heap? Is there an advantage in a higher branching factor?

2.9.1 Do we need d-ary heaps?

Usually binary heaps are enough for all our programming needs. The main advantage of this data structure is that it guarantees a logarithmic running time for each one of the common operations. In particular, being a binary balanced tree, the main operations are guaranteed to require a number of comparisons proportional, in the worst case, to $\log_2(N)$. As we discuss in appendix B, this guarantees that we can run these methods on much larger containers than if the running time was linear. Consider that even with a billion elements, $\log_2(N)$ just evaluates to about 30.

As we have seen in the introduction, constant factors are irrelevant for the running time, that is, `O(c*N) = O(N)`, and we know from algebra that two logarithms with different bases only differ by a constant factor, in particular

$$\log_b(N) = \log_2(N) / \log_2(b)$$

So, in conclusion, we have

$$O(\log_2(N)) = O(\log_3(N)) = O(\log(N))$$

When we move to the implementation, however, constant factors matter. They matter so much that, in some edge cases, algorithms that would be better according to the running time analysis actually are slower than a simpler algorithm with worse running time, at least for any practical input (for instance, if you compare 2^n and $n*100^{100000}$, then for the constant factor not to matter anymore, the input should be huge).

A prominent example of this behavior is given by Fibonacci heap[22]: in theory they provide amortized constant time for some crucial operations such as insert or priority update, but in practice they are both complicated to implement and slow for any viable input size.

---

[21] This section includes advanced concepts.

[22] The Fibonacci heap is an advanced version of priority queue that is implemented with a set of heaps. For a Fibonacci heap, find-minimum, insert, and update priority operations take constant amortized time, `O(1)`, while deleting an element (including the minimum) requires `O(log n)` amortized time, where `n` is the size of the heap. So, in theory, Fibonacci heaps are faster than any other heap, although in practice, being overly complicated, their implementations end up being slower than simple binary heaps.

The constant factors, in general, are due to several different reasons that include

- Lag for reading/writing to memory (scattered vs localized readings)
- The cost of maintaining counters or to iterate loops
- The cost of recursion
- Nitty/gritty coding details that in the asymptotic analysis are abstracted away (for instance, as we have seen, static vs dynamic arrays)

So, at this point it should be clear that in any implementation we should strive to keep this constant multiplicators as small as possible.

Consider this formula:

$$\log_b(N) = \log_2(N) / \log_2(b)$$

If $b > 2$, it's apparent that $\log_b(N) < \log_2(N)$, and therefore if we have a logarithmic factor in our algorithm's running time, and we manage to provide an implementation that instead of $\log_2(N)$ steps will require $\log_b(N)$, while all other factors stay unchanged, then we will have provided a (constant-time) speed-up.

In section 2.10 we will further investigate how this applies to d-ary heaps.

2.9.2 Running time

So the answer is yes, there is an advantage in tuning the heap's branching factor, but compromise is the key.

The insertion will always be quicker with larger branching factors, as we at most need to bubble up the new element to the root, with $O(\log_D(n))$ comparisons and swaps at most.

Instead, the branching factor will affect deletion and priority update. If you recall the algorithms for popping elements, for each node we need to first find the highest priority among all its children, then compare it to the element we are pushing down.

The larger the branch factor, the smaller the height of the tree (it shrinks logarithmically with the branching factor). But, on the other hand, the number of children to compare at each level also grows linearly with the branch factor. As you can imagine, a branching factor of 1000 wouldn't work very well (and it would translate into a linear search for less than 1001 elements!).

In practice, through profiling and performance tests, the conclusion has been reached that in most situations, `D=4` is the best compromise.

2.9.3 Finding the optimal branching factor

If you are looking for an optimal value for `D` that works in every situation, then you are going to be disappointed. To a certain extent, theory comes to the rescue by showing us a range of optimal values. It can be shown that the optimal value can't be greater than `5`. Or, to put it another way, it can be mathematically proven that

- The tradeoff between insert and delete is best balanced with `2 <= D <= 5`.
- A 3-way heap is in theory faster than a 2-way heap.
- 4-way heaps and 3-way heaps have similar performance.
- 5-way heaps are a bit slower.

In practice, the best value for `D` depends on the details of the implementation and of the data you are going to store in the heap. The optimal branching factor for a heap can only be determined empirically, case by case. There is no overall optimal branching factor, and it depends on the actual data and on the ratio of insertions/deletions, or, for instance, how expensive it is to compute priority versus copying elements, among other things.

In common experience, binary heaps are never the fastest, 5-way heaps are seldom faster (for narrow domains), and the best choice usually falls between 3 and 4, depending on nuances.

So while I feel safe suggesting starting with a branching factor of 4, if this data structure is used in a key section of your application and small performance improvement can make a relevant difference, then you need to tune the branching factor as a parameter.

2.9.4 Branching factor vs memory

Notice that I suggested the larger branching factor among the two best performing ones for a reason. It turns out there is, in fact, another consideration to be made when looking for the optimal branching factor for heaps: locality of reference.

When the size of the heap is larger than available cache or than the available memory, or in any case where caching and multiple levels of storage are involved, then on average a binary heap requires more cache misses or page faults than a d-ary heap. Intuitively, this is due to the fact that children are stored in clusters, and that on update or deletion, for every node reached, all its children will have to be examined. The larger the branching factor becomes, the more the heap becomes short and wide, and the more the principle of locality applies.

D-way heap appears to be the best traditional data structure for reducing page faults.[23] New alternatives focused on reducing cache misses and page swaps have been proposed over the years; for instance, you can check out *splay trees*.

While these alternatives aren't in general able to have the same balance between practical and theoretical performance as heaps, when the cost of page faults or disk access dominates, it might be better to resort to a linearithmic[24] algorithm with higher locality rather than sticking with a linear algorithm with poor locality.

---

[23] See http://comjnl.oxfordjournals.org/content/34/5/428.

[24] `O(n*log(n))`, for an input of size `n`.

2.10 Performance analysis: Finding the best branching factor

We've discussed the theory. Now let's try to apply it to a real case and describe how to profile the implementation of a data structure and an application.

We have seen that priority queues are a key component in the Huffman compression pipeline. If we measure the performance of our heap's methods as the number of swaps performed, we have shown that we have at most h swaps per method call, if h is the height of the heap. In section 2.5 we also showed that because the heap is a complete balanced tree, the height of a d-ary heap is exactly $\log_D(n)$.[25]

Therefore, for both methods insert and top, it would seem that the larger the branching factor, the smaller the height, and in turn the better heap performance should be.

But just limiting to swaps doesn't tell us the whole story. In section 2.9 we delve into the performance analysis of these two methods and take into consideration also the number of array accesses, or equivalently the number of comparisons on heap elements that are needed for each method. While insert accesses only one element per heap's level, method top traverses the tree from root to leaves, and at each level it needs to go through the list of children of a node. Therefore, it needs approximately up to $D*\log_D(n)$ accesses on a heap with branching factor D and containing n elements.

Tables 2.6 and 2.7 summarize the performance analysis for the three main methods in heaps' API.

Table 2.6 Main operations provided by a d-ary heap, and the number of swaps (assuming n elements)

Operation	Number of swaps	Extra space
Insert	$\sim\log_D(n)$	O(1)
Top	$\sim\log_D(n)$	O(1)
Heapify	~n	O(1)

For method top, a larger branching factor doesn't always improve performance, because while $\log_D(n)$ becomes smaller, D becomes larger. Bringing it to an extreme, if we choose D > n-1, then the heap becomes a root with a list of n-1 children, and so while insert will require just 1 comparison and 1 swap, top method will need n comparisons and 1 swap (in practice, as bad as keeping an unsorted list of elements).

There is no easy[26] way to find a value for D that minimizes function $f(n) = D*\log_D(n)$ for all values of n, and besides, this formula gives us just an estimate of the maximum number of accesses/swaps performed. The exact number of comparisons and swaps actually performed depends on the sequence of operations and on the order in which elements are added.

[25] Where D is the branching factor for the d-ary heap under analysis.

[26] It is, obviously, possible to find a formula for f(D)'s minima using calculus, and in particular computing the first and second order derivatives of the function.

Table 2.7 Cost of main operations provided by heaps as a number of comparisons (assuming `n` elements)

Operation	Number of comparisons	Extra space
Insert	$\sim\log_D(n)$	O(1)
Top	$\sim D*\log_D(n)$	O(1)
Heapify	~n	O(1)

Then the question arises: How do we choose the best value for the branching factor?

The best we can do here is profile our applications to choose the best value for this parameter. In theory, applications with more calls to `insert` than to `top` will perform better with larger branching factors, while when the ratio of calls between the two methods approaches 1.0, a more balanced choice will be best.

2.10.1 Please welcome profiling

And so we are stuck with *profiling*. If you are asking yourself "What's profiling?" or "Where do I start?", here are a few tips:

- Profiling means measuring the running time and possibly the memory consumption of different parts of your code.
- It can be done at a high level (measuring the calls to high level functions) or a lower level, for each instruction, and although you can set it up manually (measuring the time before and after a call), there are great tools to aid you—usually guaranteeing an error-free measurement.
- Profiling can't give you general-purpose answers: it can measure the performance of *your* code on the input you provide.
- In turn, this means that the result of profiling is as good as the input you use, meaning that if you only use a very specific input, you might tune your code for an edge case, and it could perform poorly on different inputs. Also, another key factor is the data volume: to be statistically significant, it can be nice to collect profiling results on many runs over (pseudo)random inputs.
- It also means that results are not generalizable to different programming languages, or even different implementations in the same language.
- Profiling requires time. The more in depth you go with tuning, the more time it requires. Remember Donald Knuth's advice: "premature optimization is the root of all evil." Meaning you should only get into profiling to optimize critical code paths. Spending two days to shave 5 milliseconds on an application that takes 1 minute is frankly a waste of time (and possibly, if you end up making your code more complicated to tune your app, it will also make your code worse).

If, in spite all of these disclaimers, you realize that your application actually needs some tuning, then brace yourself and choose the best profiling tool available for your framework.

To perform profiling, obviously we will have to abandon pseudocode and choose an actual implementation; in our example, we will profile a `Python` implementation of Huffman encoding and d-ary heap. You can check out the implementation on our repo[27] on GitHub.

Code and tests are written in Python 3, specifically using version 3.7.4, the latest stable version at the time of writing. We are going to use a few libraries and tools to make sense of the profiling stats we collect:

- Pandas
- Matplotlib
- Jupyter Notebook

To make your life easier, if you'd like to try out the code I suggest you install the Anaconda distribution, which already includes the latest Python distribution and all the packages listed.

To do the actual profiling, we use `cProfile` package, which is already included in the basic `Python` distro.

We won't explain in detail how to use `cProfile` (lots of free material online covers this, starting from the Python docs linked previously), but to sum it up, `cProfile` allows running a method or function and records the per-call, total, and cumulative time taken by every method involved.

```
   ncalls  tottime  percall  cumtime  percall filename:lineno(function)
        1    0.000    0.000    0.002    0.002 {built-in method builtins.exec}
        1    0.000    0.000    0.002    0.002 <string>:1(<module>)
        1    0.000    0.000    0.002    0.002 huffman_profile.py:24(run_test)
        1    0.000    0.000    0.002    0.002 huffman.py:116(create_encoding)
        1    0.000    0.000    0.001    0.001 huffman.py:92(_heap_to_tree)
       37    0.000    0.000    0.001    0.000 dway_heap.py:190(top)
       44    0.000    0.000    0.001    0.000 dway_heap.py:71(_push_down)
       95    0.000    0.000    0.001    0.000 dway_heap.py:141(_highest_priority_child_index)
  780/452    0.000    0.000    0.000    0.000 {built-in method builtins.len}
        1    0.000    0.000    0.000    0.000 huffman_profile.py:11(read_text)
        1    0.000    0.000    0.000    0.000 huffman.py:72(_frequency_table_to_heap)
     37/1    0.000    0.000    0.000    0.000 huffman.py:49(tree_encoding)
        1    0.000    0.000    0.000    0.000 {built-in method io.open}
        1    0.000    0.000    0.000    0.000 dway_heap.py:18(__init__)
        1    0.000    0.000    0.000    0.000 dway_heap.py:169(_heapify)
      328    0.000    0.000    0.000    0.000 dway_heap.py:44(__len__)
       18    0.000    0.000    0.000    0.000 dway_heap.py:217(insert)
       45    0.000    0.000    0.000    0.000 dway_heap.py:166(first_leaf_index)
        1    0.000    0.000    0.000    0.000 {method 'read' of '_io.TextIOWrapper' objects}
        1    0.000    0.000    0.000    0.000 huffman.py:67(_create_frequency_table)
```

Figure 2.18 Printing `Stats` after profiling Huffman encoding function.

[27] See https://github.com/mlarocca/AlgorithmsAndDataStructuresInAction#huffman-compression.

Using `pStats.Stats`, we can retrieve and print (or process) those stats; the output of profiling looks something like what's shown in figure 2.18.

Now, to reduce the noise, we are only interested in a few methods, specifically the functions that use a heap: in particular `_frequency_table_to_heap`, which takes the dictionary with the frequency (or number of occurrences) of each character in the input text and creates a heap with one entry per character, and `_heap_to_tree`, which in turn takes the heap created by the former function and uses it to create the Huffman encoding tree.

We also want to track down the calls to the heap methods used: `_heapify`, `top`, and `insert`. Instead of just printing those stats, we can read them as a dictionary, and filter the entries corresponding to those five functions.

To have meaningful, reliable results, we also need to profile several calls to the method `huffman.create_encoding`, and so processing the stats and saving the result to a CSV file seems the best choice anyway.

To see the profiling in action, check out our example[28] on GitHub. The example profiles several calls to the method creating a Huffman encoding over an ensemble of large text files[29] and a bitmap image. The bitmap needs to be duly pre-processed in order to make it processable as text. The details of this pre-processing are not particularly interesting, but for the curious reader we encode image bytes in base64 to have valid characters.

2.10.2 Interpreting results

Now that we've stored the results of profiling in a CSV file, we just need to interpret them to understand what's the best choice of branching factor for our Huffman encoding app. At this point it should look like a piece of cake, right?

We can do it in many ways, but my personal favorite is displaying some plots in a Jupyter Notebook: take a look here at an example.[30] Isn't it great that GitHub lets you already display the Notebook without having to run it locally?

Before delving into the results, though, we need to take a step back: because we will use a boxplot[31] to display our data, let's make sure we know how to interpret these plots first. If you feel you could use a hint, figure 2.19 comes to the rescue!

To make sense of the data our example notebook uses *Pandas* library, with which we read the CSV file with the stats and transform it into a `DataFrame`, an internal Pandas representation. You can think about it as a SQL table on steroids. In fact, using this `DataFrame` we can partition data by test case (*image* versus *text*), then group it by method, and finally process each method separately and display results, for each

---

[28] https://github.com/mlarocca/AlgorithmsAndDataStructuresInAction/blob/master/Python/mlarocca/tests/huffman_profile.py.

[29] We used copyright-free novels downloaded from Project Gutenberg, http://www.gutenberg.org (worth checking out!).

[30] Disclaimer: There are many possible ways to do this, and possibly better ways too. This is just one of the possible ways. https://github.com/mlarocca/AlgorithmsAndDataStructuresInAction/blob/master/Python/mlarocca/notebooks/Huffman_profiling.ipynb.

[31] https://matplotlib.org/3.1.1/api/_as_gen/matplotlib.pyplot.boxplot.html.

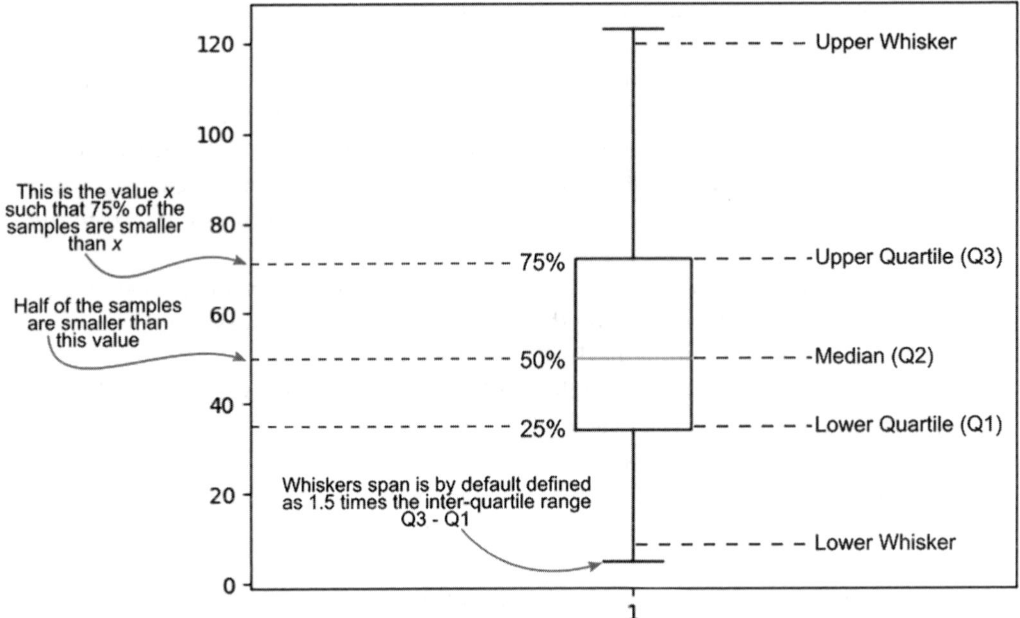

120
100
80
60
40
20
0
1
Upper Whisker
This is the value x such that 75% of the samples are smaller than x
75%
-Upper Quartile (Q3)
Half of the samples are smaller than this value
50%
-Median (Q2)
25%
-Lower Quartile (Q1)
Whiskers span is by default defined as 1.5 times the inter-quartile range Q3 - Q1
Lower Whisker

Figure 2.19 Explaining how to read an example boxplot. Boxplots show the distribution of samples using a nice and effective chart. The main idea is that the most relevant samples are those whose values lie between the first and third quartile. That is, we find three values, Q1, Q2 (aka the median), and Q3 such that 25% of the samples are smaller than Q1; 50% of the samples are smaller than Q2 (which is the very definition of median, by the way); and 75% of the samples are smaller than Q3. The box in the boxplot is meant to clearly visualize the values for Q1 and Q3. Whiskers, instead, shows how far from the median the data extends. To that end, we could also display outliers, that is, samples that are outside the whiskers' span. Sometimes outliers, though, end up being more confusing than useful, so in this example we will not use them.

method, grouped by branching factor. Figure 2.20 shows these results for encoding a large text, comparing the two main functions in Huffman encoding that use a heap.

If we look at those results, we can confirm a few points we mentioned in section 2.9:

- 2 is never the best choice for a branching factor.
- A branching factor of 4 or 5 seems a good compromise.
- There is a consistent difference (even -50% for `_frequency_table_to_heap`) between a binary heap and the d-ary heap with best branching factor.

There is, however, also something that might look surprising: `_frequency_table_to_heap` seems to improve with larger branching factors, while `_heap_to_tree` has a minimum for branching factors around 9 and 10.

As explained in section 2.6, which shows the pseudocode implementation of heap methods (and as you can see from the code on GitHub), the former method only calls the `_push_down` helper method, while the latter uses both `top` (which in turn calls `_push_down`) and `insert` (relying on `_bubble_up` instead), so we would expect to see the opposite result. Anyway, it is true that even `_heap_to_tree` has a ratio of two calls to `top` per `insert`.

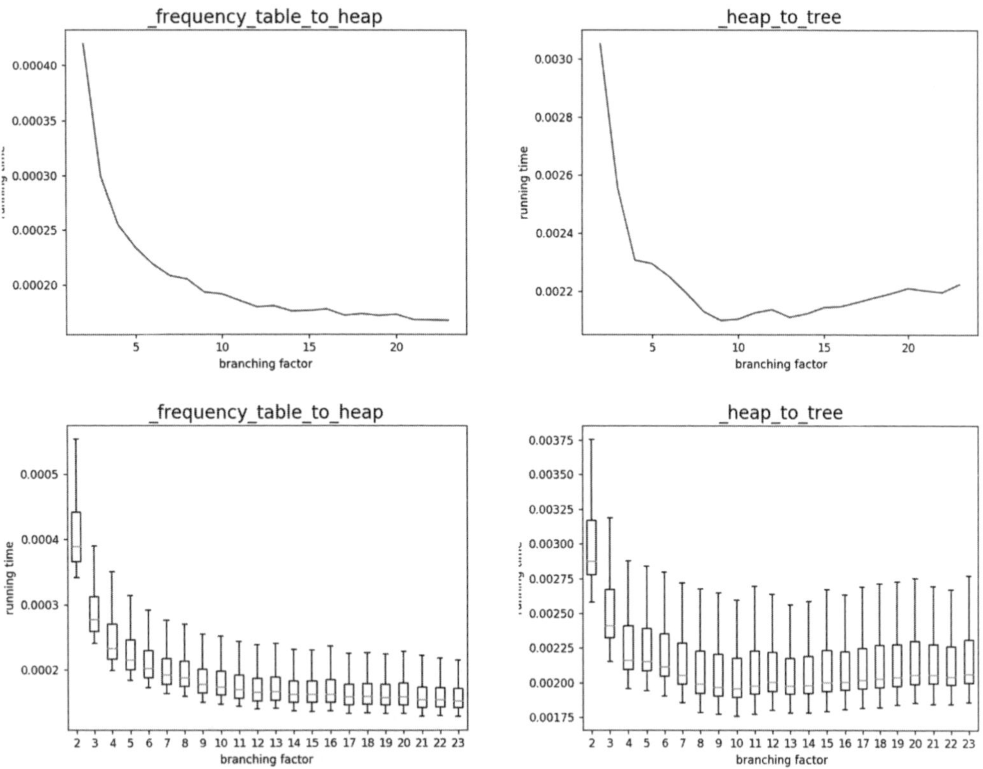
_frequency_table_to_heap
_heap_to_tree
running time
branching factor
_frequency_table_to_heap
_heap_to_tree
running time
branching factor

Figure 2.20 The distribution of running times for the two high-level functions in Huffman.py using a heap. (Top) Mean running time by branching factor. (Bottom) Boxplots for the distribution of running times for each branching factor. All charts are created using data about the running time per single call for the compression of an ensemble of text files.

Let's now delve into the internals of these high-level methods, and see the running time per call of heap's internal method `_heapify` (figure 2.22), and of API's methods `top` and `insert` and their helper methods `_push_down` and `_bubble_up` (figures 2.21 and 2.23).

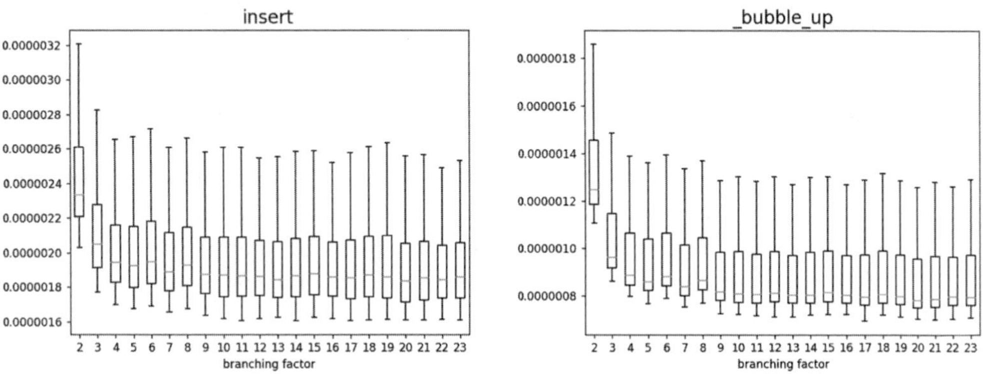
insert
_bubble_up
branching factor
branching factor

Figure 2.21 The distribution of recorded running times per call for `insert` and `_bubble_up`

Before digging into the most interesting part, let's quickly check out the insert method. Figure 2.21 shows there are no surprises here; the method tends to improve with larger branching factors, as does _bubble_up, its main helper.

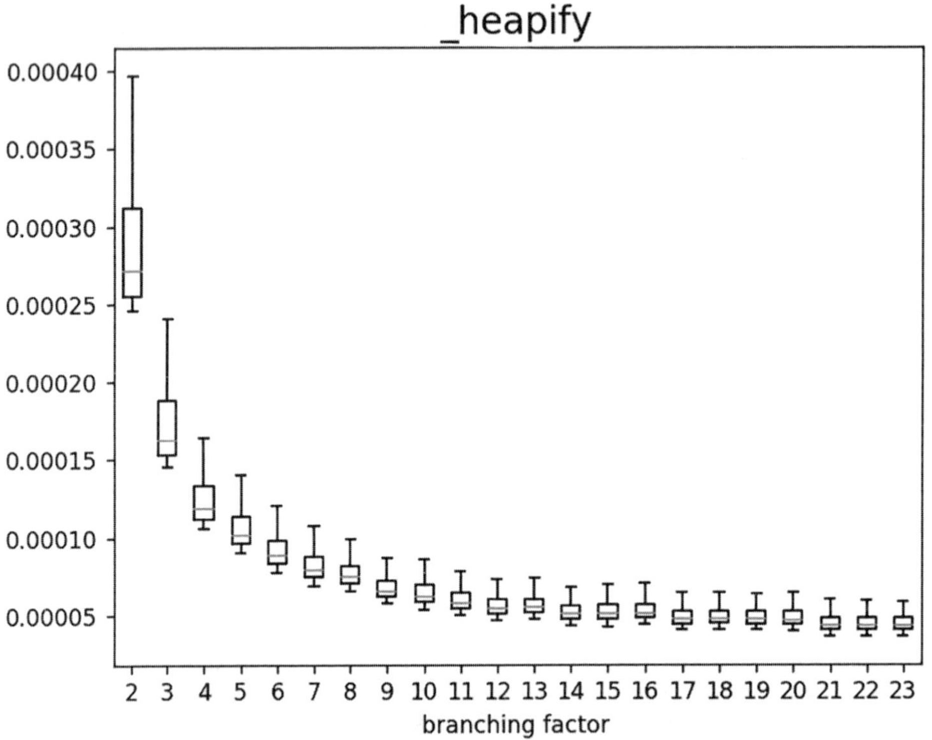
_heapify
0.00040
0.00035
0.00030
0.00025
0.00020
0.00015
0.00010
0.00005
2 3 4 5 6 7 8 9 10 11 12 13 14 15 16 17 18 19 20 21 22 23
branching factor

Figure 2.22 The distribution of recorded running times per call for heapify.

The _heapify method, as expected, shows a trend similar to _frequency_table_to_heap, because all this method does is create a heap from the frequency table. Still, is it a bit surprising that _heapify's running time doesn't degrade with larger branching factors?

Now to the juicy part. Let's take a look at top in figure 2.23. If we look at the running time per call, the median and distribution clearly show a local minimum (around D==9), as we would have expected, considering that the method's running time is $O(D*\log_D(n))$, confirming what we have previously discussed and summarized in table 2.7. Not surprisingly, the _push_down helper method has an identical distribution.

If we look at listings 2.7 and 2.4 and sections 2.6.2 and 2.6.4, it's clear how pushDown is the heart of the top method, and in turn the largest chunk of work for pushDown is the method that at each heap's level retrieves the child of current node. We called it highestPriorityChild.[32]

[32] In our Python implementation, the names become respectively _push_down and _highest_priority_child, to follow Python naming conventions.

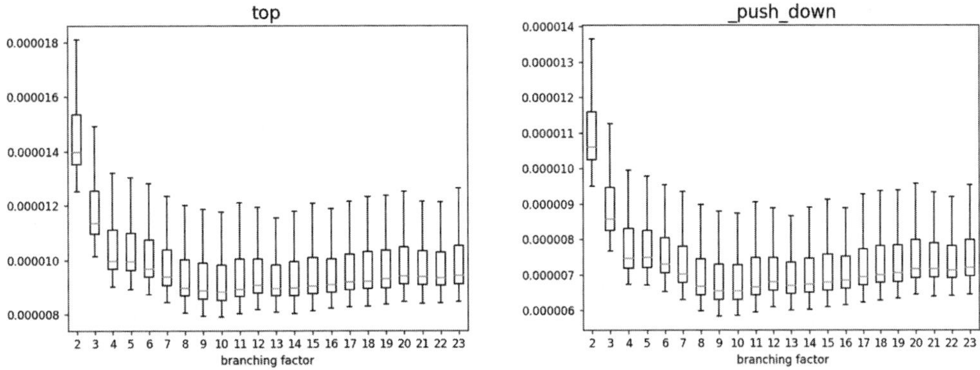
top
_push_down
branching factor
branching factor

Figure 2.23 The distribution of recorded running times per call for `top` and `_push_down`

And if then we look at the running time per call for `_highest_priority_child` (figure 2.24 (A)), we have a confirmation that our profiling does make sense, because the running time per call increases with the branching factor. The larger `D` is, the longer the list of children for each node, which this method needs to traverse entirely in order to find which tree branch should be traversed next.

You might then wonder why `_push_down` doesn't have the same trend. Remember that while the running time for `_highest_priority_child` is `O(D)`, in particular with `D` comparisons, `_push_down` performs (at most) $\log_D(n)$ swap sand $D*\log_D(n)$ comparisons, because it calls `_highest_priority_child` at most $\log_D(n)$ times.

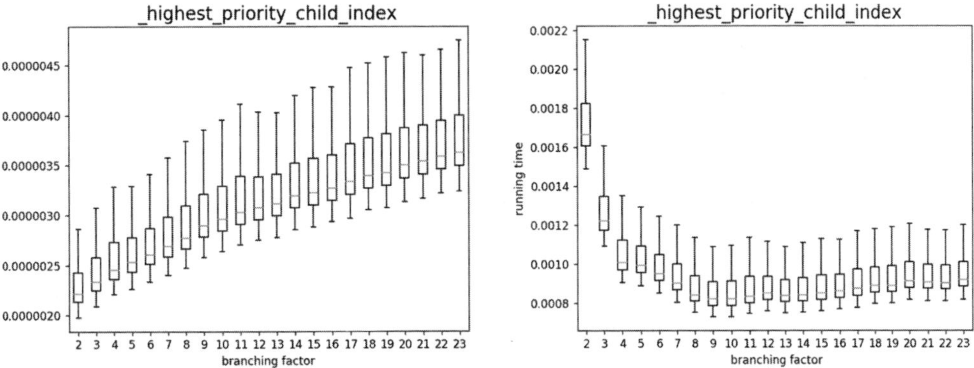
_highest_priority_child_index
_highest_priority_child_index
running time
branching factor
branching factor

Figure 2.24 (A) The distribution of recorded running times per-call for `_highest_priority_child`. (B) The distribution of cumulative running times for `_highest_priority_child`.

The larger the branching factor `D`, the fewer calls are made to `_highest_priority_child`. This becomes apparent if, instead of plotting the running time per-call for `_highest_priority_child`, we use the total cumulative time (the sum of all calls to each method), as shown in figure 2.24 (B). There we can see again how this composite function, $f(D) = D*\log_D(n)$, has a minimum at `D==9`.

2.10.3 The mystery with heapify

Summing up, `_heapify` keeps improving even at larger branching factors, although we can also say it practically plateaus after `D==13`, but this behavior is not caused by the methods `top` and `_push_down`, which do behave as expected.

There could be a few explanations for how the `_heapify` running time grows:

1. It's possible that, checking larger branching factors, we discover that there is a minimum (we just haven't found it yet).
2. The performance of this method heavily depends on the order of insertions: with sorted data it performs way better than with random data.
3. Implementation-specific details make the contribution of calls to `_push_down` less relevant over the total running time.

But . . . are we sure that this is in contrast with theory? You should know by now that I like rhetorical questions; this means it is time to get into some math.

And indeed, if we take a closer look at section 2.6.7, we can find out that the number of swaps performed by `_heapify` is limited by:

$$\frac{n}{D} \cdot \sum_{h=0}^{\lfloor log_D(n) \rfloor} \left\lceil \frac{h}{D^h} \right\rceil$$

As you can imagine, analyzing this function is not straightforward. But, and here is the fun part, now you can certainly plot the function using your (possibly newly acquired) Jupyter Notebook skills. It turns out that, indeed, plotting this function of `D` for a few values of `n`, we get the charts in figure 2.25, showing that, despite the fact that the single calls to `_push_down` will be slower with a higher branching factor, the total number of swaps is expected to decrease.

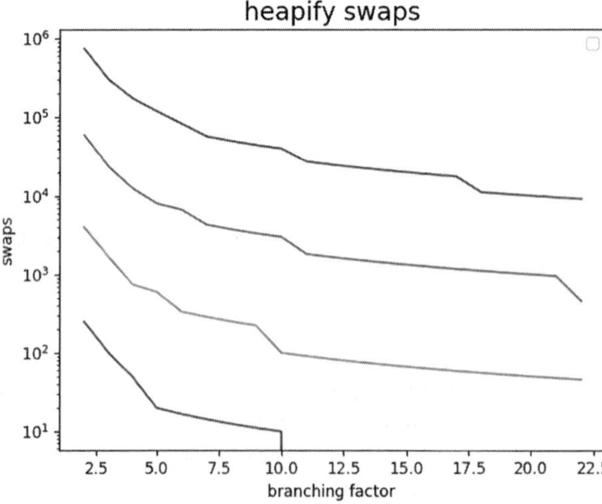
heapify swaps
swaps
10⁶
10⁵
10⁴
10³
10²
10¹
2.5
5.0
7.5
10.0
12.5
15.0
17.5
20.0
22.5
branching factor

Figure 2.25 The upper bound for the number of swaps needed by the `heapify` method, as a function of the branching factor `D`. Each line is a different value of `n`. Notice that the `y` axis uses a logarithmic scale.

So, mystery solved; `_heapify` does behave as expected. And good news, too: it gets faster as we increase the branching factor.

2.10.4 Choosing the best branching factor

For a mystery solved, there is still a big question standing: What is the best branching factor to speed up our Huffman encoding method? We digressed, delving into the details of the analysis of heaps and somehow left the most important question behind.

To answer this question, there is only one way: looking at figure 2.26, showing the running time for the main method of our Huffman encoding library.

It shows three interesting facts:

- The best choice seems to be `D==9`.
- Choosing any value larger than 7 will likely be as good.
- While the max gain for `_frequency_table_to_heap` is 50%, and for `_heapify` even up to 80%, we merely get to a 5% here.

Notice how the chart for `create_encoding` looks more similar to the method `_heap_to_tree` than to `_frequency_table_to_heap`. Also, considering the third point, the explanation is that the operation on the heap only contributes to a fraction of the running time, while the most demanding methods needs to be searched elsewhere. (Hint: for `create_frequency_table`, the running time depends on the length of the input file, while for the other methods it only depends on the size of the alphabet.)

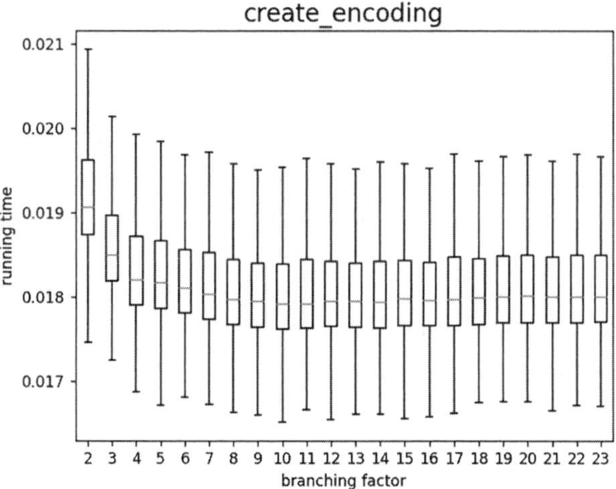
create_encoding
running time
0.021
0.020
0.019
0.018
0.017
2 3 4 5 6 7 8 9 10 11 12 13 14 15 16 17 18 19 20 21 22 23
branching factor

Figure 2.26 Distribution of per-call running time for the method `huffman.create_encoding`

You can check out the full results, including the other examples, on the notebook on GitHub. Keep in mind that this analysis uses a limited input, and as such is likely to be biased. This is just a starting point, and I highly encourage you to try running a more thorough profiling using more runs on different inputs.

You can also pull the full profiling and visualization code and delve even deeper into the analysis.

To wrap up, I'd like to highlight a few takeaways:

- D-ary heaps are faster than binary ones.
- If you have parametric code, profiling is the way to tune your parameter. The best choice depends on your implementation as well as on input.
- Be sure to run your profiling on a representative sample of your domain. If you use a limited subset, you will likely optimize for an edge case, and your results will be biased.

As a general rule, make sure to optimize the right thing: only profile critical code, and perform high-level profiling first to spot the critical section of code whose optimization would give you the largest improvement, and verify that this improvement is worth the time you'll spend on it.

Summary

- The theory behind the functioning and analysis of d-way heaps makes heavy use of the basic structures and tools we describe in appendices A to F.
- There is a difference between concrete and abstract data structures, where the latter are better served to be used as black boxes, during the design of an application or algorithm using them.
- When we move from abstract data structures to their concrete implementations in a programming language, we need to pay attention to those nitty-gritty details that are specific to the language we chose, and make sure we don't slow down our methods by choosing the wrong implementation.
- A heap is conceptually a tree, but it's implemented using an array for the sake of efficiency.
- Changing the branching factor of a heap won't affect asymptotic running time for its methods, but will still provide a constant factor improvement that matters when we move from pure theory to applications with a massive amount of data to manage.
- For several advanced algorithms we make use of priority queues to improve their performance: BFS, Dijkstra, and Huffman codes are just some examples.
- When high performance is paramount, and the data structures we use allow parameters (such as *branching factor* for heaps), the only way to find the best parameters for our implementation is profiling our code.

Treaps: Using randomization to balance binary search trees

This chapter covers

- Solving the problem of indexing data according to multiple criteria
- Understanding the treap data structure
- Keeping a binary search tree balanced
- Using treaps to implement balanced binary search trees (BST)
- Working with Randomized Treaps (RT)
- Comparing plain BSTs and RTs

In chapter 2 we saw how it is possible to store elements and retrieve them based on their priorities by using heaps, and how we can improve over binary heaps by using a larger branching factor.

Priority queues are especially useful when we need to consume elements in a certain order from a dynamically changing list (such as the list of tasks to run on a

CPU), so that at any time we can get the next element (according to a certain criterion), remove it from the list, and (usually) stop worrying about fixing anything for the other elements. The difference with a sorted list is that we only go through elements in a priority queue once, and the elements already removed from the list won't matter for the ordering anymore.

Instead, if we need to keep track of the ordering of elements and to possibly go through them more than once (such as a list of objects to render on a web page), priority queues might not be the best choice. Moreover, there are other kinds of operations that we might need to perform; for example, efficiently retrieving the minimum or maximum element of our collection, accessing the `i`-th element (without removing all elements before it), or finding the predecessor or successor of an element in our ordering.

In appendix C we discuss how trees are the best compromise when we care about all these operations, in addition to insertion and removal. If a tree is balanced, we can perform any of these actions in logarithmic time.

The issue is that trees in general and binary trees in particular are not guaranteed to be balanced. Figure 3.1 shows how, depending on the order of insertion, we might have very balanced or very skewed trees.

In this chapter, we are going to explore a way to use heaps' properties to be (reasonably) sure we have balanced binary trees.

To explain how this works we will introduce *treaps*, a hybrid between trees and heaps; however, we are going to take a different approach to treaps that is somewhat unusual in the literature on this data structure.

But first, as always, let's start by introducing a problem that we would like to solve.

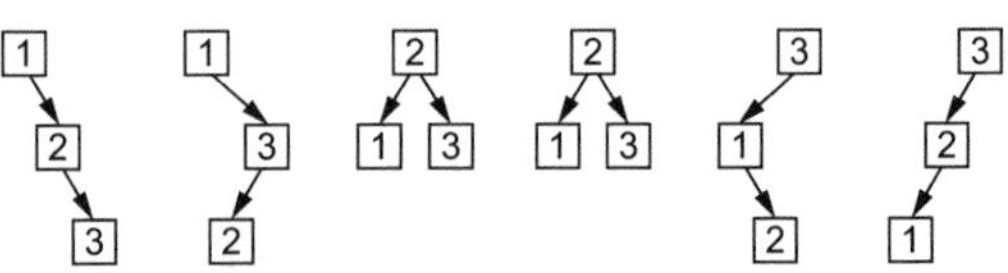

Figure 3.1 All possible layouts for BSTs of size 3. The layout depends on the order in which elements are inserted. Notice how two of the sequences produce identical layouts: for `[2, 1, 3]` and `[2, 3, 1]` we get the same final result.

3.1 Problem: Multi-indexing

Your family runs a small grocery shop, and you'd like to help your parents keep up with the inventory. To impress your family and show everyone those computer science classes are worth the effort, you embark on the task of designing a digital inventory management tool, an archive for stock keeping, with two requirements:

- Be able to (efficiently) search products by name so you can update the stock.
- Get, at any time, the product with the lowest items in stock, so that you are able to plan your next order.

Of course, you could just buy an off-the-shelf spreadsheet, but where would the fun be in that? Moreover, would anybody be really impressed with that? So, here we go, designing an in-memory data structure that can be queried according to two different criteria.

Clearly, real-world scenarios are more complex than this. You can imagine that each product requires a different time to be shipped to you, that some products are ordered from the same vendors (and therefore you might want to group them in the same order to save on shipment costs), that a product's price may and will vary with time (so you can choose the cheapest brand for, say, brakes or suspensions), and even that some products might be unavailable sometimes.

All this complexity, however, can be captured in a heuristic function, a score that is computed keeping in mind all the nuances of your business. Conceptually, you can handle that score in the same exact way as the simple inventory count, so you can keep things simple in our example and just use that.

One way to handle these requirements could be by using two different data structures: one for efficient search by name, for instance a hash table, and a priority queue to get the item which most urgently needs to be resupplied.

We will see in chapter 7 that sometimes combining two data structures for a goal is the best choice. This is not the time yet; for now you need to keep in mind the issues in coordinating two such containers, and also that you will likely need more than twice the memory.

Both considerations are kind of worrying; wouldn't it be nice if there was a single data structure that could handle both aspects natively and efficiently?

3.1.1 The gist of the solution

Let's be clear about what we are seeking here: it's not just a matter of optimizing all the operations on a container, like we discuss in appendix C. Here each bit of data, each entry in the container, is made of two separate parts, and both can be "measured" in some way. There are the names of each product, which can be sorted alphabetically, and the number of items we have in stock, that's also associated with each product: quantities that can be compared to each other to determine which products are scarcer and most urgent to resupply.

Now, if we sort the list of entries according to one criterion—for example, the name—we need to scan the whole list to find a given value for the other criterion, in this case the quantity in stock.

And if we use a min-heap with the scarcer products at its top, then (as we learned in chapter 2) we will also need linear time to scan the whole heap looking for a product to update.

Long story short, none of the basic data structures we describe in appendix C, nor a priority queue, can single-handedly solve our problem.

3.2 Solution: Description and API

Now that we have an idea of what our ideal container should do (but we still don't know how it should do it), we can define an abstract data structure (*ADT*) with the appropriate API. As long as our implementations will abide by this API, we can use any of them seamlessly in an application, or as part of a more complex algorithm, without having to worry about breaking anything (see table 3.1).

Table 3.1 API and contract for `SortedPriorityQueue`

Abstract data structure: `SortedPriorityQueue`	

API	`class SortedPriorityQueue {`
	`  top() → element`
	`  peek() → element`
	`  insert(element, priority)`
	`  remove(element)`
	`  update(element, newPriority)`
	`  contains(element)`
	`  min()`
	`  max()`
	`}`

Contract with client	Entries are kept sorted by element (aka key), but at any time the `top()` and `peek()` methods can return the element with the highest priority.

To that end, we can imagine an extension of priority queues that also keeps its elements sorted. In the rest of the chapter, we will use the term *key* to refer to elements, and associate a priority to each element.

With respect to the `PriorityQueue` ADT that we introduced in chapter 2, this `SortedPriorityQueue` class has a few new methods: a search method to find a given key in the container and two methods returning the minimum and maximum key stored.

If you look at appendix C, you can see that these three operations are usually implemented by many basic data structures, such as linked lists, arrays, or trees (some of them in linear time and others with better performance, offering logarithmic methods).

Thus, we can think about our `SortedPriorityQueue` as a melting pot between two different containers, integrating both data structures' characteristics and providing methods from both of them. For instance, it could be thought of as a fusion between heaps and linked lists, or . . .

3.3 Treap

. . . between a tree and a heap!

Treap[1] is just the *portmanteau*[2] of tree and heap. Binary search trees, in fact, offer the best average performance across all standard operations: `insert`, `remove`, and `search` (and also `min` and `max`).

Heaps, on the other hand, allow us to efficiently keep track of priorities using a tree-like structure. Since binary heaps are also binary trees, the two structures seem compatible; we only need to find a way to make them co-exist in the same structure, and we could get the best of both.

[1] Treaps were introduced in the paper "Randomized search trees," by Cecilia R. Aragon and Raimund C. Seidel, 30th Annual Symposium on Foundations of Computer Science. IEEE, 1989. Although the title of the paper might be misleading, we will see later in this chapter how treaps are related to randomized search trees.

[2] A portmanteau is a blend of two or more words, where parts of each word are combined into a new word.

It's easier said than done, however! If we have a set of unidimensional data, we can't enforce BST's and heap's invariants at the same time:

- Either we add a "horizontal" constraint (given a node `N`, with two children `L`, its left child, and `R`, its right child, then all keys in the left subtree—rooted at `L`—must be smaller than `N`'s key, and all keys in the right subtree—rooted at `R`—must be larger than `N`'s key).
- Or we add a "vertical" constraint: the key in the root of any subtree must be the smallest of the subtree.

Anyway, we are in luck, because each of our entries has two values: its name and the stock inventory. The idea, therefore, is to enforce BST's constraints on the names, and heap's constraint on the quantities, obtaining something like figure 3.2.

In this example, product names are treated as the keys of a binary search tree, so they define a total ordering (from left to right in the figure).

The inventory quantities, instead, are treated as priorities of a heap, so they define a partial ordering from top to bottom. For priorities, like all heaps, we have a partial ordering, meaning that only nodes on the same path from root to leaves are ordered with respect to their priority. In figure 3.2 you can see that children nodes always have a higher stock count than their parents, but there is no ordering between siblings.

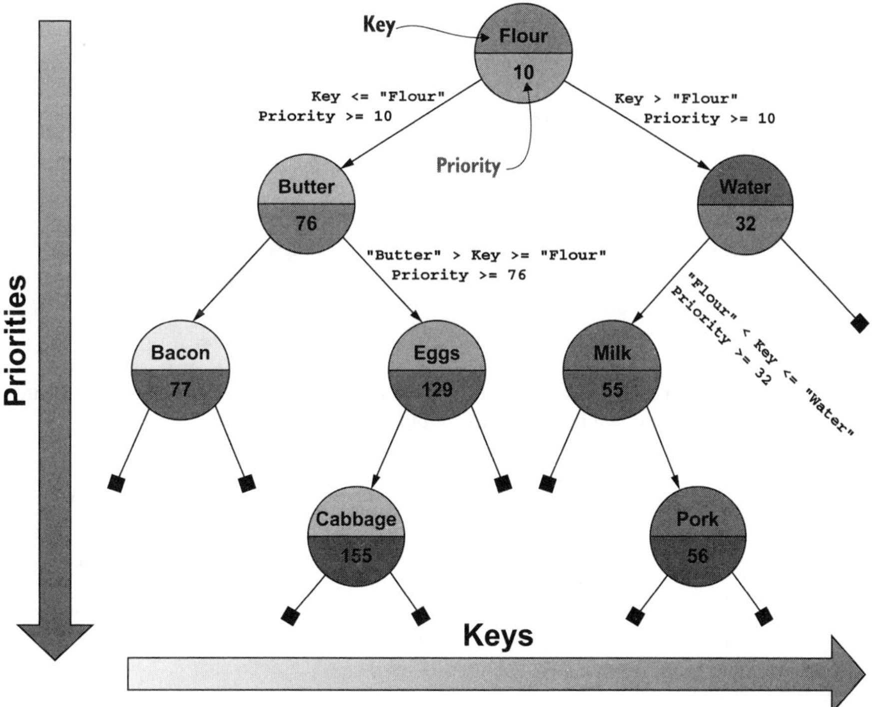
Key
Flour
10
Key <= "Flour"
Priority >= 10
Key > "Flour"
Priority >= 10
Priority
Butter
76
Water
32
"Butter" > Key >= "Flour"
Priority >= 76
"Flour" < Key <= "Water"
Priority >= 32
Bacon
77
Eggs
129
Milk
55
Cabbage
155
Pork
56
Priorities
Keys

Figure 3.2 An example of a treap, with strings as BST keys and integers as heap priorities. Note that the heap, in this case, is a min-heap, so smaller numbers go on top. For a few links close to the root, we also show the range of keys that can be hosted in the tree's branch rooted at the node they point to.

This kind of tree offers an easy way to query entries by key (by the product names, in the example). While we can't easily run a query on priorities, we can efficiently locate the element with the highest priority.[3] It will always be at the root of the tree!

Extracting the top element however . . . it's going to be more complicated than with heaps! We can't just replace it with a heap's leaf and push it down, because we need to take into account the BST's constraints as well.

Likewise, when we insert (or delete) a node, we can't just use the simple BST algorithm. If we just search for the position that the new key would hold in the tree and add it as a leaf, as shown in figure 3.3, the BST constraint will still be abided by, but the new node's priority might violate the heap's invariants.

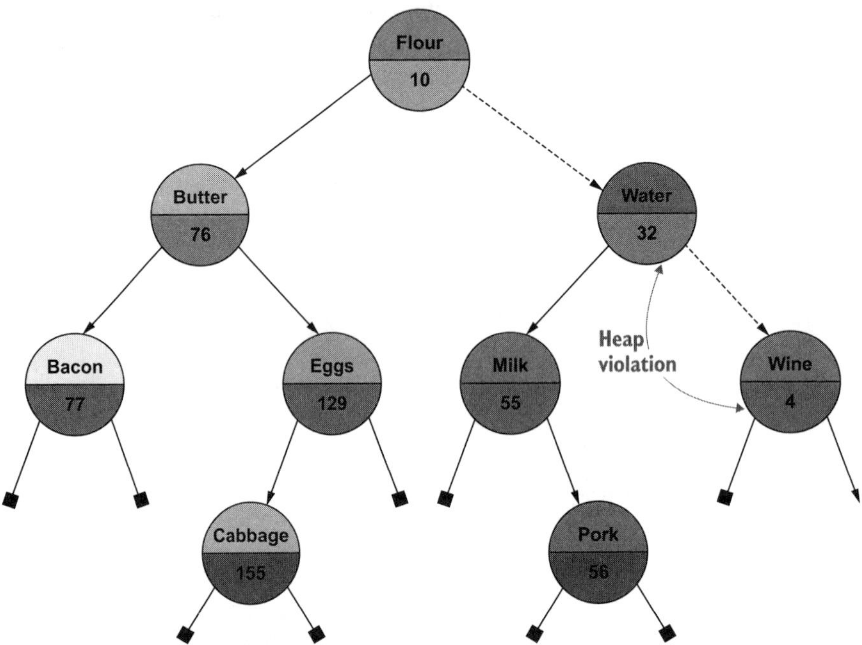
Flour
10
Butter
76
Water
32
Bacon
77
Eggs
129
Milk
55
Heap violation
Wine
4
Cabbage
155
Pork
56

Figure 3.3 An example of the insertion of a node in a treap, based on the keys ordering only. The priority of the new node, however, violates the heap constraints.

Listing 3.1 introduces a possible implementation for the treap's main structure. We will use an auxiliary class to model the tree's nodes, and this will be instrumental in our implementation. You might have noticed we are using explicit links to the node's children, differently from what we did with heaps in chapter 2. We'll go back to discussing this choice in more detail in section 3.3.2.

[3] As we discussed in chapter 2, "higher priority" is an abstraction that can mean lower or higher values, depending on the type of heap we are using. Here we are dealing with a min-heap, and higher priority means "lower inventory count," so smaller values go to the top. The code also assumes we are implementing a min-heap.

Listing 3.1 Class Treap

```
class Node
  key
  #type double
  priority

  #type Node
  left
  #type Node
  right
  #type Node
  parent

  function Node(key, priority)
    (this.key, this.priority) ← (key, priority)
    this.left ← null
    this.right ← null
    this.parent ← null

  function setLeft(node)
    this.left ← node
    if node != null then
      node.parent ← this

class Treap
  #type Node
  root

  function Treap()
    root ← null
```

The constructor for the class Node sets the key and priority to the arguments and null for all links.

Updates the left child of a Node. This also takes care of updating the parent reference for the children. Method setRight, not shown for the sake of space, works symmetrically.

In this implementation, the `Treap` class is mostly a wrapper for the root of the actual tree; each node of the tree holds two attributes for a `key` (that can be of any type, as long as there is a total ordering defined on the possible values) and a `priority`, that we'll assume to be a double precision number in this case. (An integer or any type with a total ordering could work too, but we'll see in the next section that a double works better.)

Moreover, nodes will hold pointers (or references) to two children, left and right, and their parent.

The constructor for a node will just set the key and priority attributes from its arguments, and initialize left and right pointers to `null`, effectively creating a leaf. The two branches can then be set after construction, or, alternatively, an overloaded version of the constructor also taking the two children can be provided.

3.3.1 Rotations

How do we get out of the impasse? There is one operation on binary search trees that can help us: rotations. Figure 3.4 illustrates how rotations can heal (or break!) the constraints on a treap. Rotations are common operations on many versions of BSTs, such as red-black trees or 2-3 trees.[4]

[4] Red-black and 2-3 trees are fancy versions of balanced BSTs. We'll talk more about them in a few sections.

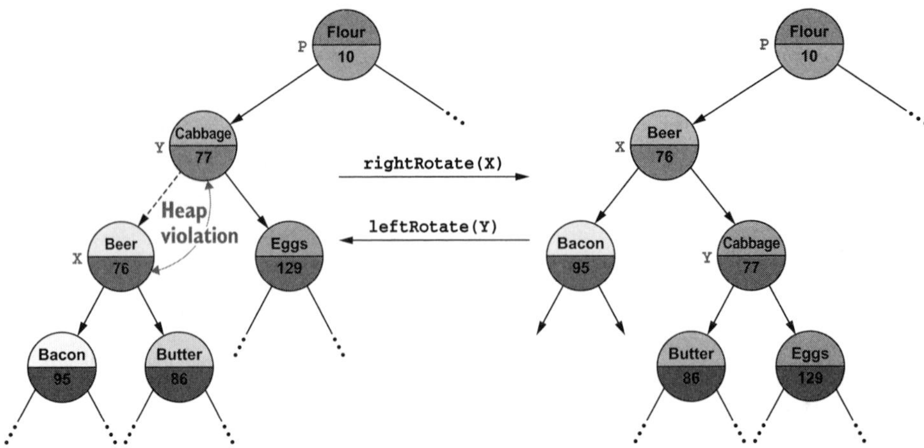
P
Flour
10
Y
Cabbage
77
Heap
violation
X
Beer
76
Eggs
129
Bacon
95
Butter
86
rightRotate(X)
leftRotate(Y)
P
Flour
10
X
Beer
76
Bacon
95
Y
Cabbage
77
Butter
86
Eggs
129

Figure 3.4 Left and right rotations illustrated on an example. The treap on the left violates heap's invariants, and a right rotation on the node marked as X can fix it. Conversely, if we apply a left rotation to the node marked with Y in the heap on the right, the result will break heap's constraints. Notice how right rotation is always applied to left children, and left rotation to right children.

A rotation, in a binary search tree, is a transformation whose goal is inverting the parent-child relation between two nodes of the tree, `Y` and `X` in figure 3.4. We want the child node to become the parent node and vice versa, but we can't just swap those two nodes: otherwise, in the general case where the keys of the two nodes are different, we would end up violating the ordering of keys.

Instead, what we need to do is remove the whole subtree rooted at the parent, replace it with the (smaller) subtree rooted at the child, and then find a way to plug back in the removed nodes in this new subtree.

How are we going to do that? As you can see in figure 3.4, first we need to distinguish two cases, depending on whether the child node is a left or a right child. The two cases are symmetrical, so we'll mainly focus on the former.

Listings 3.2 and 3.3 show the pseudocode for right and left rotations, explicating the details of the operations we described a few lines prior. Figure 3.5 illustrates the steps needed for right rotations, where the child node `X`, the pivot of the rotation, is the left child of its parent `Y`.

We need to remove `Y` from the tree, update `Y`'s parent `P` (lines #4–11), replacing `Y` with node `X` as its child (either left or right, see lines #8-#11); at this point, `Y` is disconnected from the tree, and with `Y` its whole right subtree.

Listing 3.2 Right rotation

Method `rightRotate` takes a `Treap` node `x` and performs a right rotation. It returns nothing, but it has side effects on the treap.

```
function rightRotate(treap, x)
  if x == null or isRoot(x) then
    throw
```

Checks if `x` is `null` or the root of the tree. If it is, there is an error. Arguably, we can just return instead of throwing, but swallowing exceptions is usually not a good idea. Method `isRoot` is left to the reader to implement. (It's easy, since the root is the only node in a tree without a parent.)

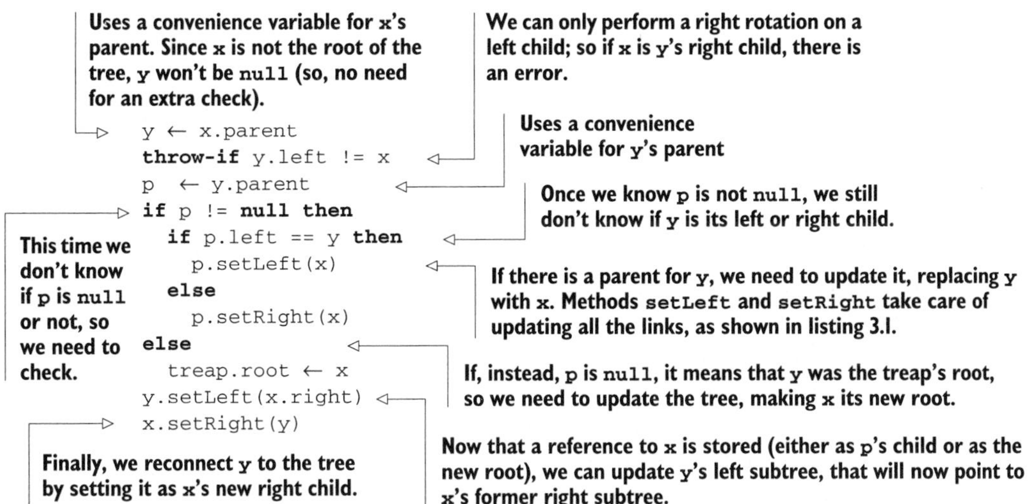
Uses a convenience variable for x's parent. Since x is not the root of the tree, y won't be null (so, no need for an extra check).
We can only perform a right rotation on a left child; so if x is y's right child, there is an error.
Uses a convenience variable for y's parent
Once we know p is not null, we still don't know if y is its left or right child.
This time we don't know if p is null or not, so we need to check.
If there is a parent for y, we need to update it, replacing y with x. Methods setLeft and setRight take care of updating all the links, as shown in listing 3.1.
If, instead, p is null, it means that y was the treap's root, so we need to update the tree, making x its new root.
Now that a reference to x is stored (either as p's child or as the new root), we can update y's left subtree, that will now point to x's former right subtree.
Finally, we reconnect y to the tree by setting it as x's new right child.

```
y ← x.parent
throw-if y.left != x
p ← y.parent
if p != null then
  if p.left == y then
    p.setLeft(x)
  else
    p.setRight(x)
else
  treap.root ← x
y.setLeft(x.right)
x.setRight(y)
```

Y's left subtree, instead, is empty because we disconnected X and moved it. We can then move X's right subtree and assign it to Y's left child (line #14), as shown in the lower-left section of figure 3.5. This certainly doesn't violate the key ordering, because

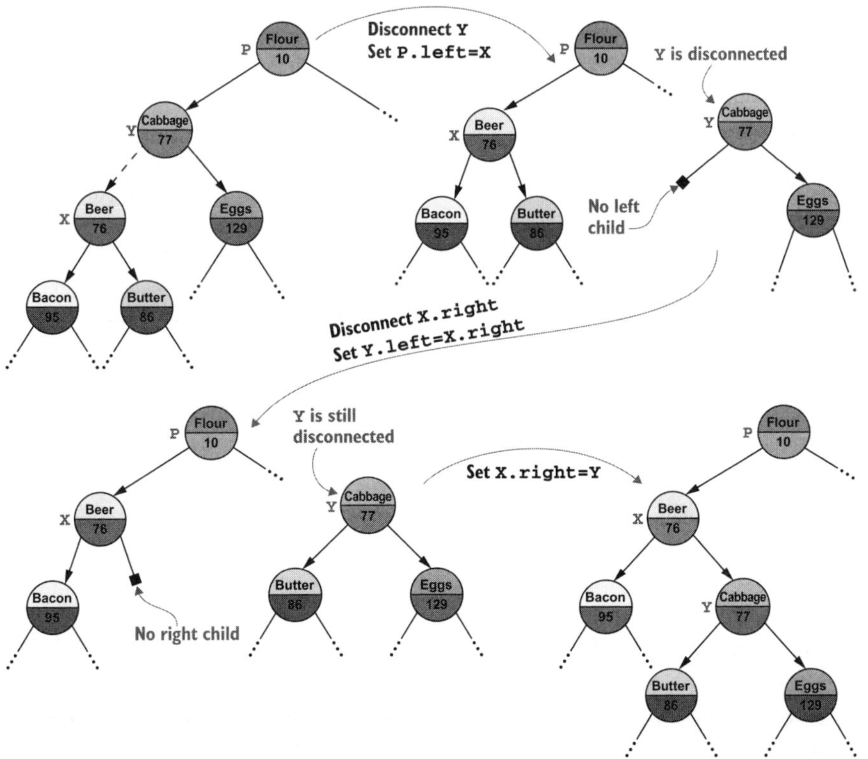
Disconnect Y
Set P.left=X
Y is disconnected
P
Flour
10
Y
Cabbage
77
X
Beer
76
Eggs
129
Bacon
95
Butter
86
No left child
Disconnect X.right
Set Y.left=X.right
Y is still disconnected
No right child
Set X.right=Y

Figure 3.5 The algorithm for performing a right rotation on a BST illustrated

(assuming there was no violation *before* the rotation) `key[Y]>=key[Y.left]` and `key[Y]>=key[Y.left.right]`. In other words, since X was the left child of node Y, then the right subtree of node X is still in Y's left subtree, and all keys in a node's left subtree are smaller, or at most equal, to the node's own key. You can also use figure 3.2 as a reference.

All that's left to do now is reconnect Y to the main tree: we can assign it to X's right child (line #15), and we won't have any violation. In fact, we already know that Y (and its right sub-tree) have larger keys than X's, and for what concerns Y's left subtree, it was constructed using the former right subtree of X, and by definition all those keys too are larger than X's.

We saw how to perform a rotation. It's nothing fancy; it's just about updating a few links in the tree. The only mystery at this point might be, why is it called a rotation?

Figure 3.6 tries to answer this question, interpreting the steps we saw in listing 3.2 and figure 3.5 from a different point of view. Let me remark that this is just an informal way to illustrate how a rotation works. When you are going to implement this method, you'd better refer to listing 3.2 and figure 3.5.

Listing 3.3 Left rotation

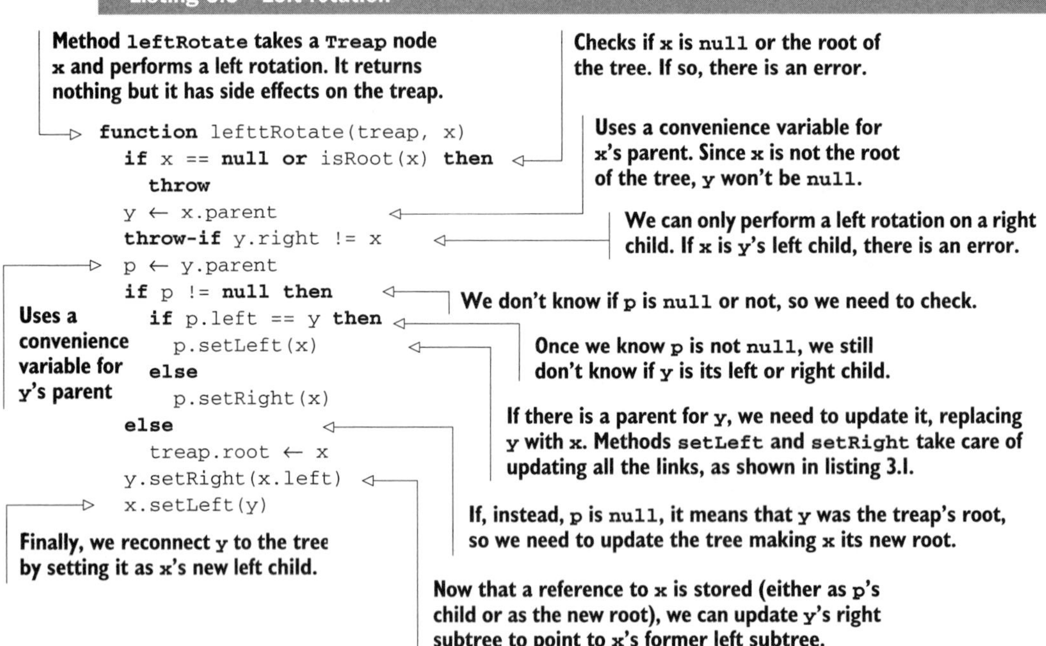
Method leftRotate takes a Treap node x and performs a left rotation. It returns nothing but it has side effects on the treap.
Checks if x is null or the root of the tree. If so, there is an error.
function lefttRotate(treap, x)
if x == null or isRoot(x) then
throw
y ← x.parent
throw-if y.right != x
p ← y.parent
if p != null then
if p.left == y then
p.setLeft(x)
else
p.setRight(x)
else
treap.root ← x
y.setRight(x.left)
x.setLeft(y)
Uses a convenience variable for x's parent. Since x is not the root of the tree, y won't be null.
We can only perform a left rotation on a right child. If x is y's left child, there is an error.
Uses a convenience variable for y's parent
We don't know if p is null or not, so we need to check.
Once we know p is not null, we still don't know if y is its left or right child.
If there is a parent for y, we need to update it, replacing y with x. Methods setLeft and setRight take care of updating all the links, as shown in listing 3.1.
If, instead, p is null, it means that y was the treap's root, so we need to update the tree making x its new root.
Finally, we reconnect y to the tree by setting it as x's new left child.
Now that a reference to x is stored (either as p's child or as the new root), we can update y's right subtree to point to x's former left subtree.

First, let's assume we call rotate on node X, and node Y is X's parent. Once again, we analyze right rotation, so X is a left child of Y.

If we consider the subtree rooted at Y, we can visually "rotate" it clockwise (hence "right rotation"), pivoting on node X, until X looks like the root of this tree; hence, all other nodes appear to be below X, as shown in figure 3.6.

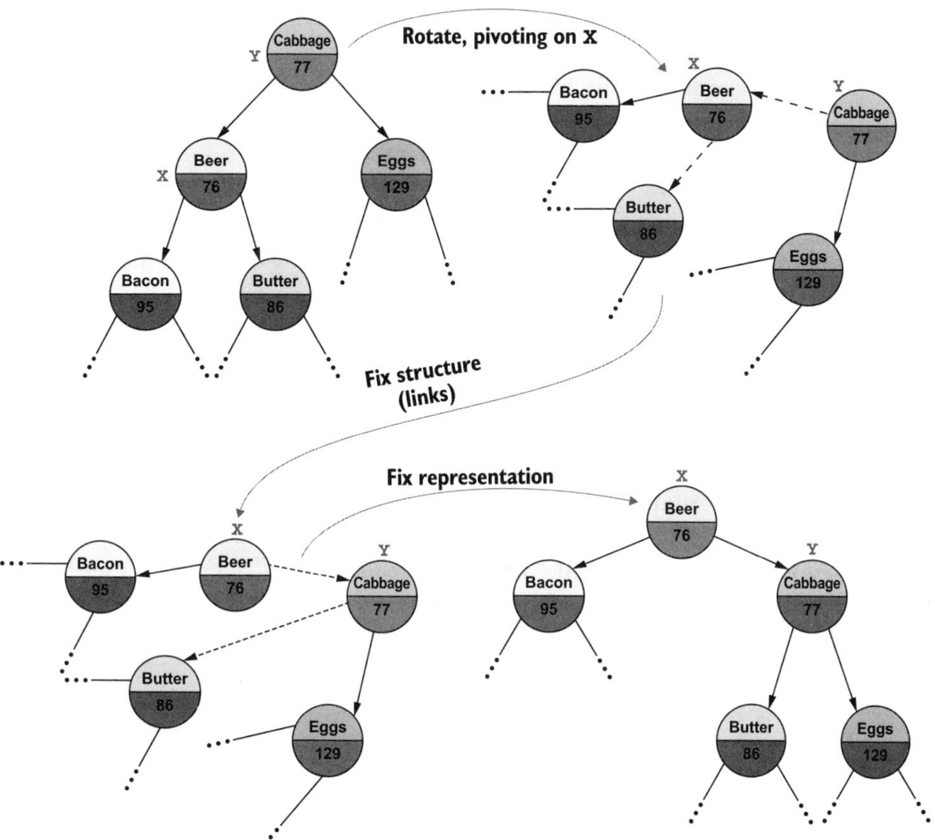
Rotate, pivoting on X
Fix structure (links)
Fix representation
X
Y
Cabbage
77
Beer
76
Eggs
129
Bacon
95
Butter
86

Figure 3.6 A more intuitive interpretation of the `rightRotate` operation that helps explain its name and also helps with memorizing its steps

The result should look something like the top-right quadrant of figure 3.6. Of course, in order for this to be a valid BST rooted at node `X`, we need to make a few changes. For instance, there seems to be an edge from a child to its parent, from `Y` to `X`: but that's not allowed in trees, so we need to revert the direction of the edge. If we just did that, though, `X` would end up with three children, and that's also not allowed in a binary tree; to fix it, we can transfer the link between `X` and its right child to `Y`. Both changes are shown in the bottom-left portion of figure 3.6.

At this point, the subtree is structurally fixed, and as a last step we can just enhance its visual representation to make it also look a little better.

You can imagine the tree structure like some kind of bolt and strings dangling structure, and then the whole operation can be described as grabbing the tree by node `X` and letting all the other nodes dangle from it, with the caveat that we need to also move `X`'s right child to node `Y`.

Before closing the discussion on rotations, it's important to note that rotations always preserve BST constraints, but they do not preserve heap's invariants. Rotations, in fact, can be used to fix broken treaps, but if applied to a valid tree, they will break the priority constraints on the node to which they are applied.

3.3.2 A few design questions

Treaps are heaps, which in turn are special trees with a dual array representation. As we saw in chapter 2, we can implement a heap using an array, a more space-efficient representation that also exploits locality of reference.

Can we also implement a treap using an array? I encourage you to take a minute and think about this question, before moving on and reading the answer. What would be the pros and cons of using an array versus a tree, and what could be the pain points of using a tree?

The issue with the array representation is that it's not particularly flexible. It works well if we only swap random elements and remove/add only from the array's tail; if, instead, we need to move elements around, it's a disaster! For instance, even inserting a new element in the middle of the array causes all the elements after it to be moved, for an average `O(n)` swaps (see figure 3.7).

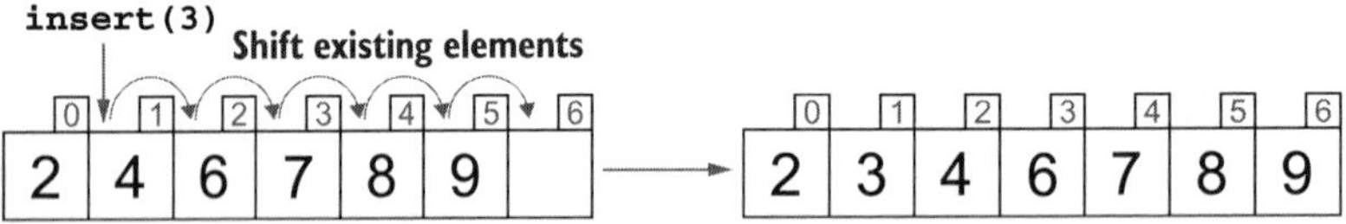
insert(3)
Shift existing elements
0 1 2 3 4 5 6
2 4 6 7 8 9
0 1 2 3 4 5 6
2 3 4 6 7 8 9

Figure 3.7 When a new element is inserted in an ordered array, all the elements larger than the new one must be shifted one position toward the tail of the array (provided there is still room). This means that if the array has `n` elements and the new value will be stored at index `k` (that is, it will be the `(k+1)`-th element in the array), then `n-k` assignments will be needed to complete the insertion.

The key point with heaps is that they are complete, balanced, and left-aligned trees, which is possible because heaps don't keep a total ordering on keys, so we can add and remove elements from the tail of the array, and then bubble up/push down a single element of the heap to reinstate the heap's properties (see chapter 2).

Treaps, on the other hand, are also binary search trees, which do keep a total ordering on keys. That's why we need rotations when we insert or delete new elements from a treap. As we described in section 3.2.1, a rotation implies moving a whole subtree from the right subtree of a node `X` to the left subtree of its parent `Y` (or vice versa). As you can imagine, this is the kind of operation that is easily performed in constant time when using pointers on a tree's nodes, but it can become excruciatingly painful on arrays (like, linear-time painful).

And that's why the array representation is not used for treaps (or for BSTs).

Another design question you might ask (and also *should* ask) before getting on with the implementation concerns the branching factor for the heap. We saw in chapter 2 that heaps can have branching factors other than 2, and in section 2.10 we also saw that a heap with a branching factor of 4 or higher sensibly outperforms a binary heap (at least in our example application). Can we also implement a treap with a generic branching factor greater than 2?

Unfortunately, it's not that simple. First and foremost, we are using binary search trees, so a tree with a branching factor of 2: if the heap's branching factor didn't match the BST's, it would be a mess!

Then you might suggest using ternary search trees, or their generalization; however, that would make the rotation operations much more complicated, which means the code of the implementation would become terribly complicated and unclean (which likely also means slower!). Moreover, we would have a harder time keeping the tree balanced, unless we use something like a 2-3 tree, but that's already guaranteed to be a balanced tree in the first place.

3.3.3 Implementing search

Now that we have a better idea of how a treap is going to be represented in memory and how rotations work, we can move to the implementation of the main API's methods. You can also find a Java implementation of treaps in the book's repo on GitHub.[5]

We can start from the search method that's the easiest to describe. In fact, it's just the plain search method implemented in binary search trees: we traverse the tree from the root until we find the key we are looking for or reach a leaf without finding it.

As with plain BSTs, we only traverse one branch of each subtree, going left or right depending on how the target key compares to the current node's key.

Listing 3.4 shows the implementation of the internal method taking a node as input and traversing its subtree; this version uses recursion (a technique described in appendix E). It's worth repeating that although recursion often results in cleaner code when applied to iterative data structures such as trees, recursive methods can cause stack overflow if the depth of the recursion is significant. In this particular case, some programming languages' compilers will be able to apply tail call optimization and transform recursion into an explicit loop, while translating the code into machine language.[6] Generally, however, it might be worth considering directly writing the explicit loop equivalent even in the higher level language, especially if you are not sure about your compiler support for tail recursion optimization, or the conditions where it can be applied.

---

[5] See https://github.com/mlarocca/AlgorithmsAndDataStructuresInAction#treap.

[6] You can read more about the issue with stack overflow and tail call optimization in appendix E.

Listing 3.4 Method search

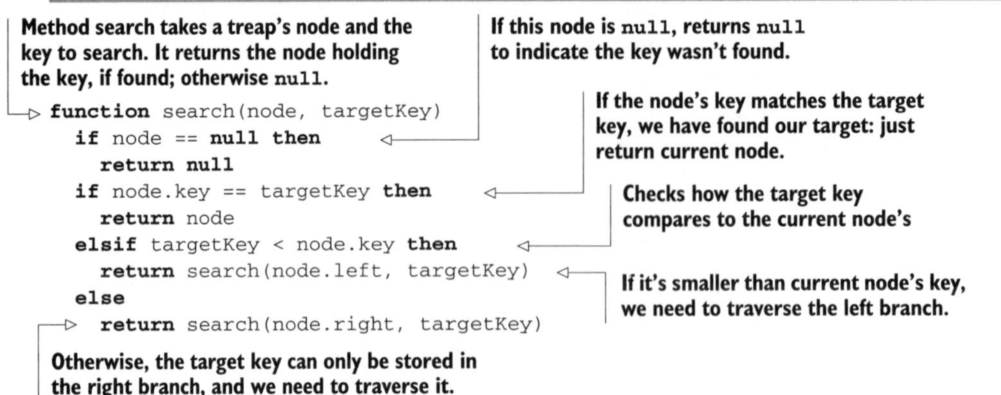
Method search takes a treap's node and the key to search. It returns the node holding the key, if found; otherwise null.
If this node is null, returns null to indicate the key wasn't found.
If the node's key matches the target key, we have found our target: just return current node.
Checks how the target key compares to the current node's
If it's smaller than current node's key, we need to traverse the left branch.
Otherwise, the target key can only be stored in the right branch, and we need to traverse it.

```
function search(node, targetKey)
  if node == null then
    return null
  if node.key == targetKey then
    return node
  elsif targetKey < node.key then
    return search(node.left, targetKey)
  else
    return search(node.right, targetKey)
```

The API method `contains` for the `Treap` class just calls method search on the root and returns `false` or `true` depending on whether the result is `null` or not.

3.3.4 Insert

While searching a key in a treap is relatively easy, inserting a new entry is a completely different story. As we mentioned in section 3.3.1, using BST insertion won't work in the general case, because while the new entry's key would end up in the right place in the tree, its priority might violate the heap's invariants, being larger than its parent (figure 3.8).

There is no reason to despair, though! We have a way to fix the heap's invariants, and we have actually already seen the solution: performing a rotation on the node violating the priority constraints.

At a high level, the `insert` method has just two steps: insert the new node as a leaf, and then check if its priority is higher than its parent. If that's the case, we need to bubble the new node up, but we can't just swap it with its parent, like we would in a heap.

Using figure 3.6 as a reference, we need to take the subtree rooted in the new node's parent and then rotate it so that the new node becomes the root of this subtree (because it's certainly going to be the node with the highest priority).

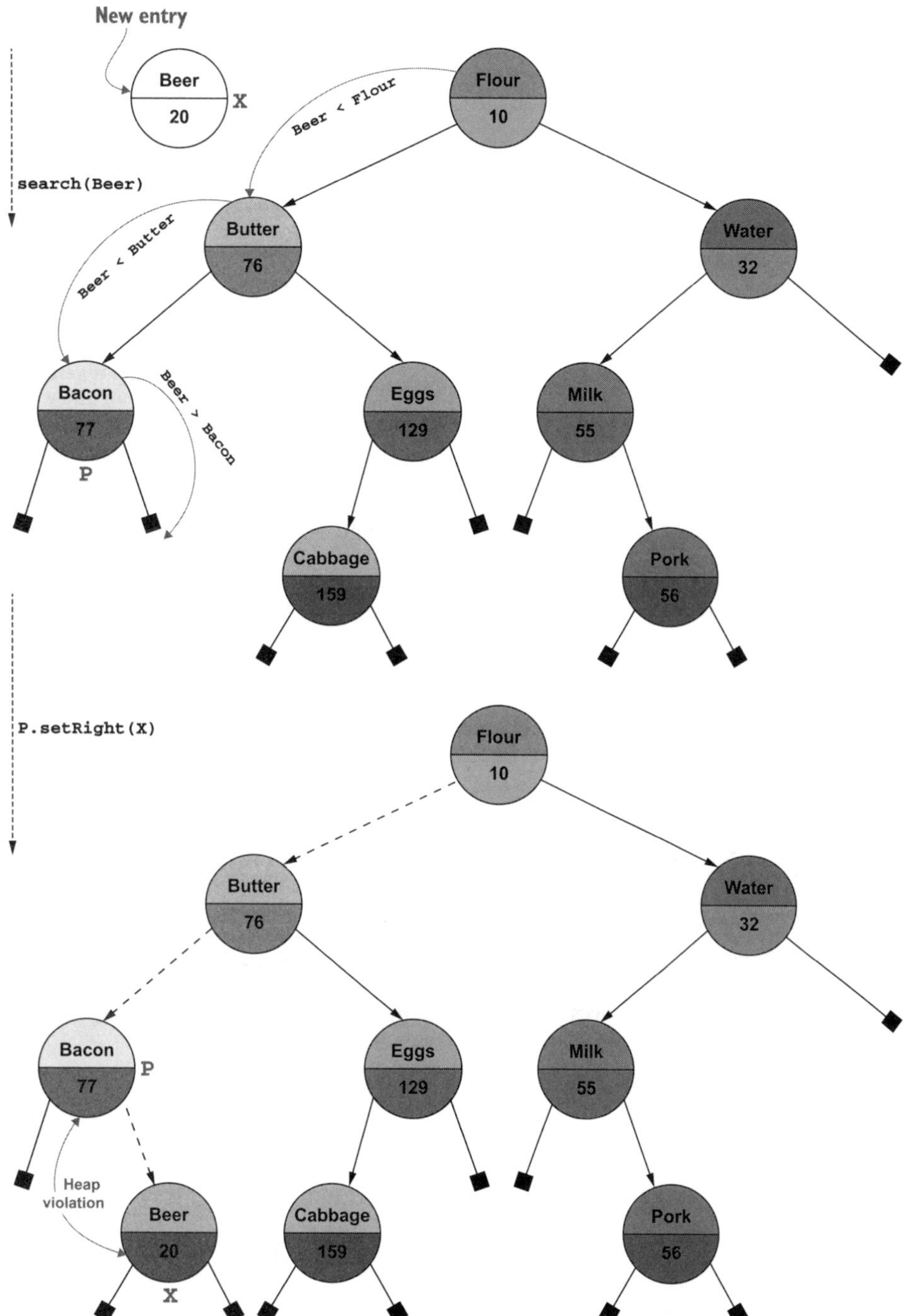
New entry
Beer
20
X
Flour
10
Beer < Flour
search(Beer)
Butter
76
Beer < Butter
Water
32
Bacon
77
P
Beer > Bacon
Eggs
129
Milk
55
Cabbage
159
Pork
56
P.setRight(X)
Flour
10
Butter
76
Water
32
Bacon
77
P
Eggs
129
Milk
55
Heap
violation
Beer
20
X
Cabbage
159
Pork
56

Figure 3.8 First steps of inserting a new entry. We search the new entry's key to spot the right place to add a new leaf in the tree. Now we must check if the new node violates the heap's invariants. Unfortunately, in this example it does, so we need to correct the situation by performing a left rotation (shown in figure 3.9).

Listing 3.5 describes the pseudocode for the insertion method, while figures 3.8 and 3.9 illustrate an example of inserting a new entry to add "Beer" to the inventory with 20 units in stock.

Listing 3.5 Method `Node::insert`

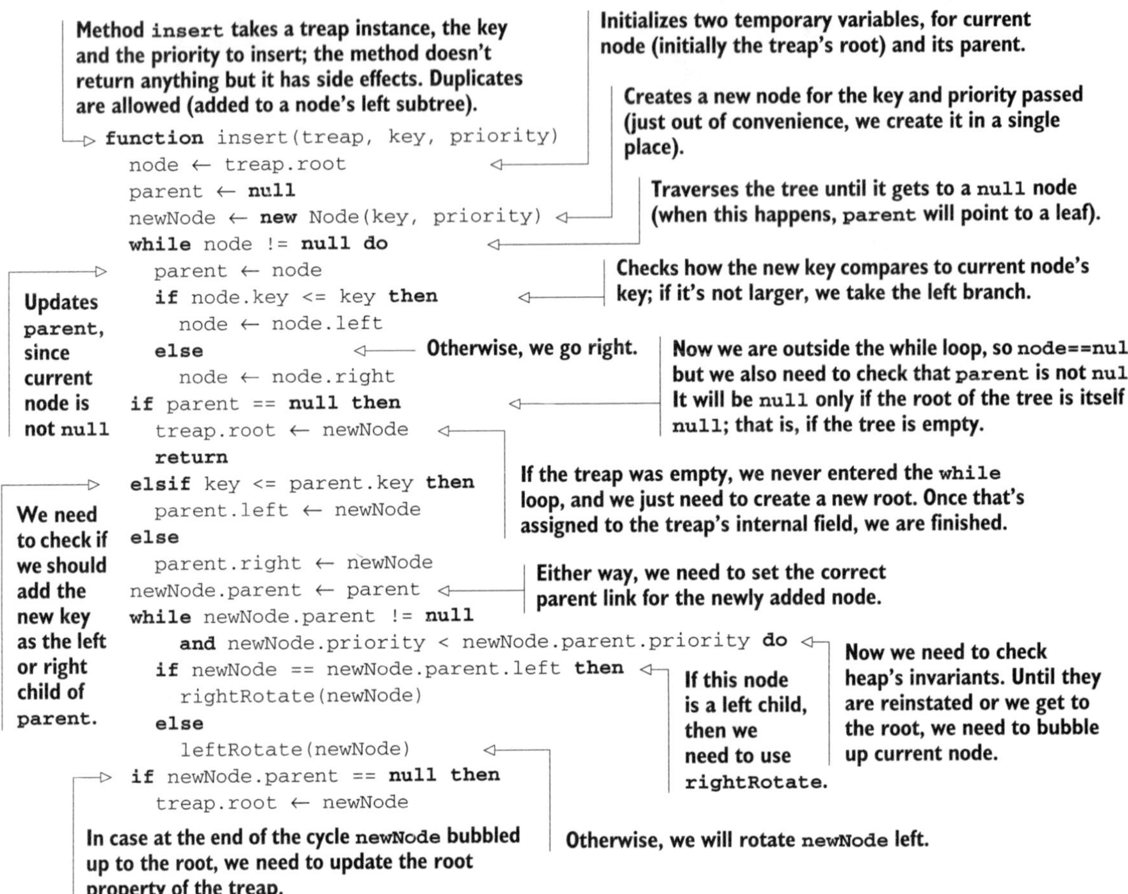

```
function insert(treap, key, priority)
  node ← treap.root
  parent ← null
  newNode ← new Node(key, priority)
  while node != null do
    parent ← node
    if node.key <= key then
      node ← node.left
    else
      node ← node.right
  if parent == null then
    treap.root ← newNode
    return
  elsif key <= parent.key then
    parent.left ← newNode
  else
    parent.right ← newNode
  newNode.parent ← parent
  while newNode.parent != null
      and newNode.priority < newNode.parent.priority do
    if newNode == newNode.parent.left then
      rightRotate(newNode)
    else
      leftRotate(newNode)
  if newNode.parent == null then
    treap.root ← newNode
```

Method insert takes a treap instance, the key and the priority to insert; the method doesn't return anything but it has side effects. Duplicates are allowed (added to a node's left subtree).
Initializes two temporary variables, for current node (initially the treap's root) and its parent.
Creates a new node for the key and priority passed (just out of convenience, we create it in a single place).
Traverses the tree until it gets to a null node (when this happens, parent will point to a leaf).
Updates parent, since current node is not null
Checks how the new key compares to current node's key; if it's not larger, we take the left branch.
Otherwise, we go right.
Now we are outside the while loop, so node==null, but we also need to check that parent is not null. It will be null only if the root of the tree is itself null; that is, if the tree is empty.
If the treap was empty, we never entered the while loop, and we just need to create a new root. Once that's assigned to the treap's internal field, we are finished.
We need to check if we should add the new key as the left or right child of parent.
Either way, we need to set the correct parent link for the newly added node.
Now we need to check heap's invariants. Until they are reinstated or we get to the root, we need to bubble up current node.
If this node is a left child, then we need to use rightRotate.
Otherwise, we will rotate newNode left.
In case at the end of the cycle newNode bubbled up to the root, we need to update the root property of the treap.

First, we need to find the right place to insert the new entry in our existing inventory. This is done with a traversal of the tree, exactly like what happens with search, only keeping track of the parent of the current node in order to be able to add the new leaf. Notice that we implemented this traversal using an explicit loop here, instead of recursion, to show to our readers how this approach works.

As we can see in the top half of figure 3.8, the first step is traversing the tree to search the right spot where we can add the new node as a leaf. We go left when we traverse "Flour" and "Butter," then right at "Bacon" (lines #5–10 of listing 3.5).

Notice that for brevity we used a contracted naming notation in the figure. The newly added node, corresponding to variable `newNode` in listing 3.5, is denoted as `X` in the figures, and its parent with `P`.

At this point, when we exit the while loop, the temporary variable `parent` points to the node with key "Bacon"; therefore the conditions at lines #11 and #14 are false, and we add the new node as a right child of `parent`, as shown in the bottom half of figure 3.8.

Looking at the example, we can also notice how the new node has a higher priority (a lower number of units in stock) than its parent; therefore, we enter the loop at line #19, and perform a left rotation. After the first iteration of the loop and the left rotation, the "Beer" node still has higher priority than its new parent, "Butter," as shown in the top half of figure 3.9. Therefore, we enter a second iteration of the loop, this time performing a right rotation, because node `X` is now a left child of `P`.

Since now (bottom half of figure 3.9) no invariant is violated anymore, we can exit the loop. And since the new node wasn't bubbled up all the way to the root, the check at line #24 fails, and we don't need to do anything else.

What's the running time for insert? Adding a new leaf requires `O(h)`, because we need to traverse the tree from its root to a leaf. Then we can bubble up the new node at most to the root, and at each rotation we move the node one level up, so we can perform at most `h` rotations. Each rotation requires a constant number of pointers to be updated, so that bubbling up the new node and the whole method finally requires `O(h)` steps.

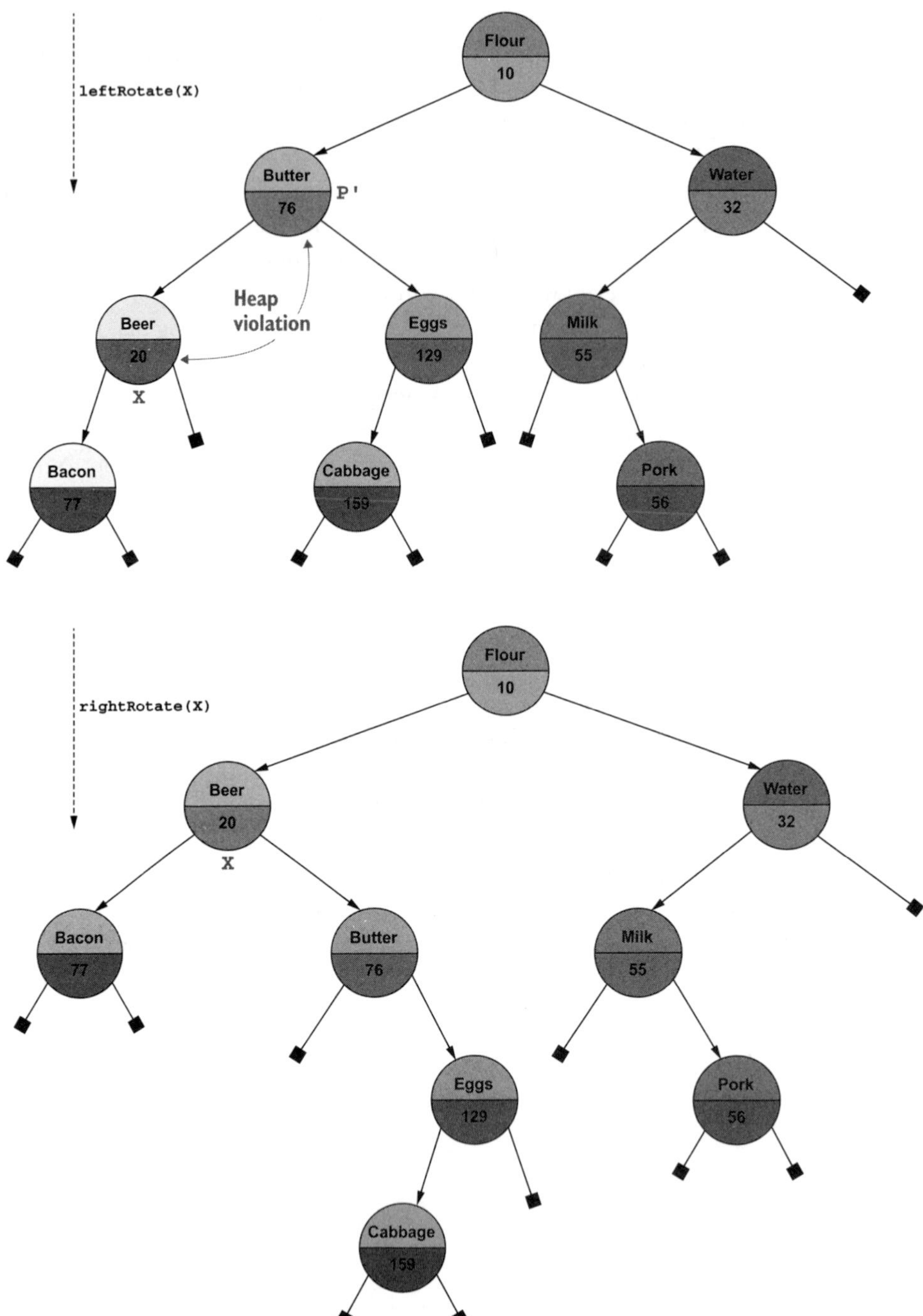
leftRotate(X)
Flour
10
Butter
76
P'
Water
32
Heap
violation
Beer
20
X
Eggs
129
Milk
55
Bacon
77
Cabbage
159
Pork
56
rightRotate(X)
Flour
10
Beer
20
X
Water
32
Bacon
77
Butter
76
Milk
55
Eggs
129
Pork
56
Cabbage
159

Figure 3.9 Insertion (continued). To fix the heap's invariants, we needed to perform a right rotation on the treap at the end of figure 3.8. This action bubbles up the new node one level, and the result is shown at the top of this figure. The heap's invariants are still violated, so we need to perform a further rotation (left, this time).

3.3.5 Delete

Deleting a key from a treap is a conceptually simpler operation, although it requires a completely different approach with respect to BSTs. In binary search trees, we replace the removed node with its successor (or predecessor), but this approach wouldn't work in treaps, because this replacement could have a smaller priority than its new children, and in that case, it would need to be pushed down. Moreover, in the general case for BSTs, the successor of a node is not a leaf, and so it needs to be recursively removed.

A simpler approach consists of preemptively pushing down the node to be removed, all the way until it reaches a leaf. As a leaf, it can then be disconnected from the tree without any effect.

Conceptually, it's like assigning the lowest possible priority to the node to be removed, and fixing the heap's invariants by pushing down the node. The operation won't stop until the node with an infinite (negative) priority reaches a leaf.

This is illustrated in figure 3.10 and described in listing 3.6.

Listing 3.6 Method `Treap::remove`

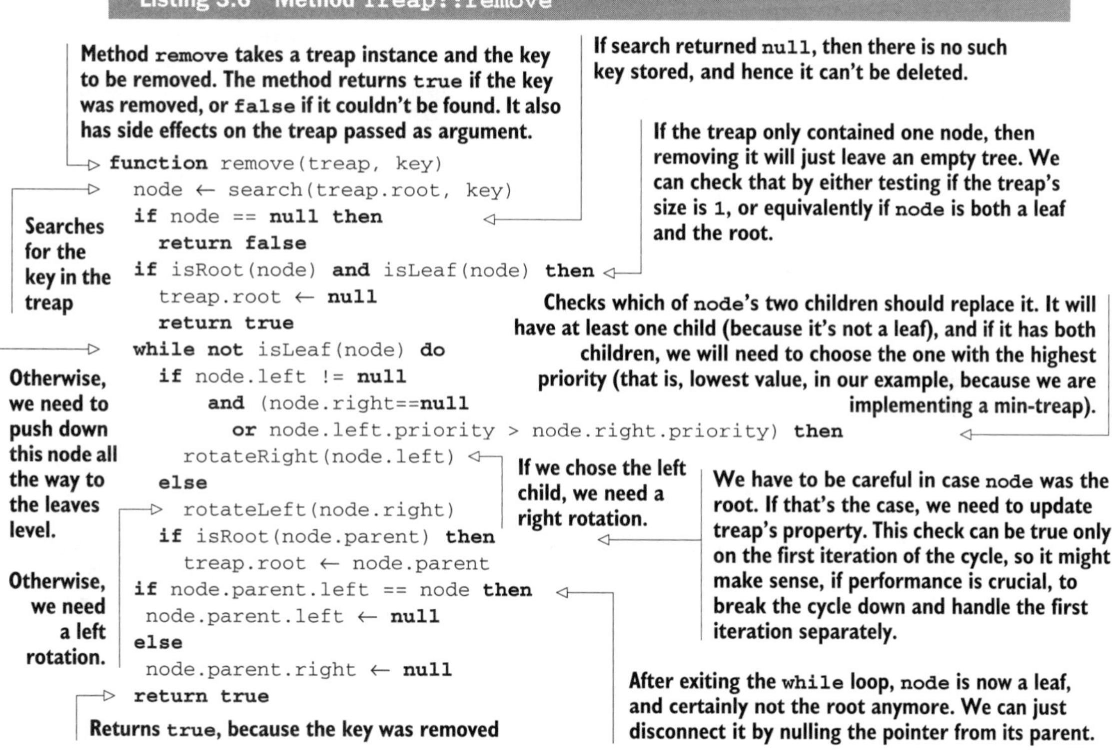
Method remove takes a treap instance and the key to be removed. The method returns true if the key was removed, or false if it couldn't be found. It also has side effects on the treap passed as argument.
If search returned null, then there is no such key stored, and hence it can't be deleted.
If the treap only contained one node, then removing it will just leave an empty tree. We can check that by either testing if the treap's size is 1, or equivalently if node is both a leaf and the root.
Searches for the key in the treap
Checks which of node's two children should replace it. It will have at least one child (because it's not a leaf), and if it has both children, we will need to choose the one with the highest priority (that is, lowest value, in our example, because we are implementing a min-treap).
Otherwise, we need to push down this node all the way to the leaves level.
If we chose the left child, we need a right rotation.
We have to be careful in case node was the root. If that's the case, we need to update treap's property. This check can be true only on the first iteration of the cycle, so it might make sense, if performance is crucial, to break the cycle down and handle the first iteration separately.
Otherwise, we need a left rotation.
After exiting the while loop, node is now a leaf, and certainly not the root anymore. We can just disconnect it by nulling the pointer from its parent.
Returns true, because the key was removed

```
function remove(treap, key)
  node ← search(treap.root, key)
  if node == null then
    return false
  if isRoot(node) and isLeaf(node) then
    treap.root ← null
    return true
  while not isLeaf(node) do
    if node.left != null
        and (node.right==null
          or node.left.priority > node.right.priority) then
      rotateRight(node.left)
    else
      rotateLeft(node.right)
    if isRoot(node.parent) then
      treap.root ← node.parent
  if node.parent.left == node then
   node.parent.left ← null
  else
   node.parent.right ← null
  return true
```

In listing 3.6, in particular, we see why it was useful to have method `search` return the node where the key was found. We can reuse it now to write the `remove` method, whose first step is indeed searching the key to remove and then, if it was found, this method will take over from the node that needs to be pushed down.

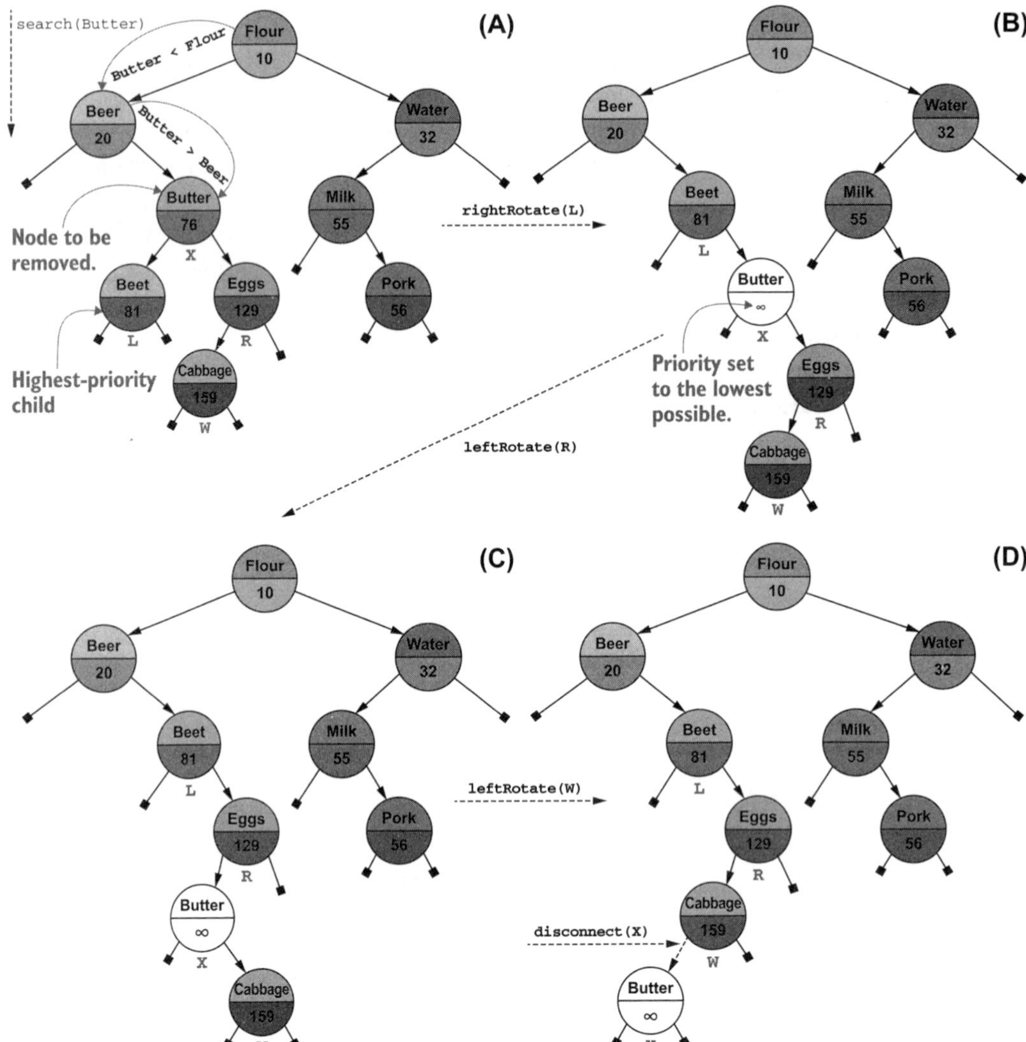
search(Butter)
Butter < Flour
Butter > Beer
(A)
Flour
10
Beer
20
Water
32
Butter
76
X
Node to be removed.
Beet
81
L
Eggs
129
R
Milk
55
Pork
56
Cabbage
159
W
Highest-priority child
rightRotate(L)
(B)
Butter
∞
Priority set to the lowest possible.
leftRotate(R)
(C)
(D)
leftRotate(W)
disconnect(X)

Figure 3.10 Deleting the key `Butter` from our example treap. The first step is finding the node holding the key to remove. Then, we set its priority to the lowest possible priority and push it down to a leaf. To do so, we need to find out which one of its children has the highest priority and rotate it. Finally, once the node reaches a leaf, we can just unplug it from the tree without violating any invariant.

Special care, as always, needs to be paid to be sure we remove the root.

Let's follow how the algorithm works using our example. Suppose we want to remove "Butter" from our inventory (for instance, because we won't sell it anymore or we sold all of it).

The first step, shown in figure 3.10 (A), is searching for the key `"Butter"` in the tree (line #2 in listing 3.6). Once we find the node (that's obviously not `null`, line #3), as usual marked with X in the figures, we verify that it's neither the root nor a leaf (hence, the check at line #5 returns `false`), so we can enter the `while` loop at line #8.

At line #9, we choose X's left child, denoted with L in the figure, as its highest-priority child, so we perform a right rotation (line #10), which produces the tree shown in figure 3.10 (B).

Here in the figure we changed the priority of the node being pushed down to $+\infty$,[7] but in the code we don't actually need to do that; we can just push down the node without checking priorities, until it becomes a leaf.

At this point X is not yet a leaf, although it just has one child, its (also former) right child R; therefore, we will enter another iteration of the `while` loop, and this time perform a left rotation, producing the tree shown in figure 3.10 (C). One more left rotation, and X finally becomes a leaf.

At this point we exit the `while` loop, and at line #15 we are sure that `node` is not the root (otherwise, we would have caught this case at line #5), so it will have a non-null parent. We still need to disconnect the node from the tree by removing the pointer from its parent, and to do so we need to check whether it was a left or right child.

Once the right link has been set to `null`, we are done and the key was successfully removed.

If we compare this method with the plain BST's version, the positive aspect is that we don't have to call `remove` recursively on the successor (or predecessor) of the node that will be removed. We just perform one removal, although possibly with several rotations. And that's actually one negative aspect: if we delete a node close to the root, we will need to push it down for several layers until it reaches a leaf.

The worst-case running time for the `remove` algorithm is, in other words, `O(h)`, where `h` is the height of the treap. As a consequence, it becomes particularly important, as you can imagine, that the height of the tree is kept as small as possible.

As you can see from our examples, using the treap for storing both keys and meaningful priorities might tend to produce an unbalanced tree, and removing a node might make the tree even more unbalanced, because of the many rotations starting from an already bad situation.

3.3.6 Top, peek, and update

The remaining methods in class `Treap`'s API are easier to implement. Method `peek` is trivial to implement; it's exactly the same as for regular heaps, the only difference being in how we access the heap's root.

If we also need to implement method `top`, to make sure our treap can seamlessly replace a heap, we can leverage the `remove` method and write almost a one-liner, as shown in listing 3.7.

[7] In our example, the lowest priority corresponds to the highest availability in stock, and so $+\infty$ is the highest possible value for the units in stock.

Listing 3.7 Method `Treap::top`

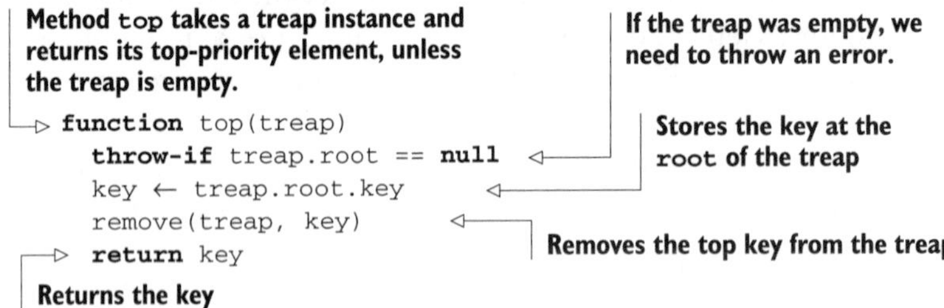
Method top takes a treap instance and returns its top-priority element, unless the treap is empty.
If the treap was empty, we need to throw an error.
Stores the key at the root of the treap
Removes the top key from the treap
Returns the key

```
function top(treap)
  throw-if treap.root == null
  key ← treap.root.key
  remove(treap, key)
  return key
```

Besides validating the treap's status, checking that it's not empty, we just need to retrieve the key stored in the root and then remove it from the treap.

Similarly, if we need to update the priority associated with a key, we can follow the same logic as for plain heaps, bubbling up the updated node (when increasing priority, or pushing down, when we lower priority). The only difference is that instead of just swapping nodes we need to perform rotations to move the updated node. Implementation of this method is left as an exercise (or you can check it out on the book's repo).

3.3.7 Min, max

The last methods left to implement in our API are `min` and `max`, returning the minimum and maximum key stored in the treap.

These keys are stored respectively in the left-most and right-most nodes of the tree. Be careful, though; these nodes are not necessarily going to be leaves, as shown in figure 3.11.

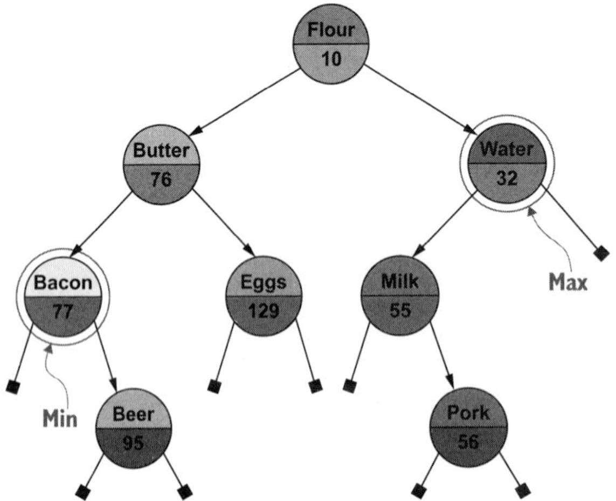
Flour
10
Butter
76
Water
32
Bacon
77
Eggs
129
Milk
55
Max
Min
Beer
95
Pork
56

Figure 3.11 How to find minimum and maximum keys in a treap (or, in general, in a binary search tree): the minimum is stored in the left-most node, and the maximum in the right-most node. Notice how these nodes aren't necessarily tree leaves.

Listing 3.8 shows a possible implementation of method `min`. Exactly as in BSTs, we just traverse the tree, always taking the left branch until we reach a node whose left child is `null`. Method `max` is symmetric; you just need to replace `node.left` with `node.right`.

Listing 3.8 Method `Treap::min`

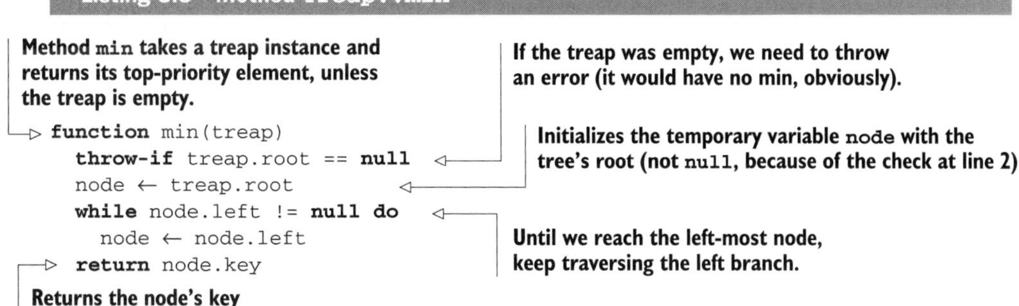
Method min takes a treap instance and returns its top-priority element, unless the treap is empty.
If the treap was empty, we need to throw an error (it would have no min, obviously).
Initializes the temporary variable node with the tree's root (not null, because of the check at line 2)
Until we reach the left-most node, keep traversing the left branch.
Returns the node's key

```
function min(treap)
  throw-if treap.root == null
  node ← treap.root
  while node.left != null do
    node ← node.left
  return node.key
```

3.3.8 *Performance recap*

This concludes our discussion on the implementation of treaps. In the next sections, we'll discuss applications of treaps and analyze them in more detail.

For now, let's recap the running time of the treap's methods, shown in table 3.2. Notice that

- All operations only depend on the height of the tree, rather than on the number of elements. Of course, in the worst case, `O(h)=O(n)` for skewed trees.
- We omitted the space analysis, because all these methods only require constant extra space.

Table 3.2 Operations provided by treaps, and their cost for a tree with `n` keys and height `h`

Operation	Running time	Worst case
`Insert`	`O(h)`	`O(n)`
`Top`	`O(h)`	`O(n)`
`Remove`	`O(h)`	`O(n)`
`Peek`	`O(1)`	`O(1)`
`Contains`	`O(h)`	`O(n)`
`UpdatePriority`	`O(h)`	`O(n)`
`Min/Max`	`O(h)`	`O(n)`

3.4 *Applications: Randomized treaps*

So, we are now able to implement our inventory, keep track of the products in stock, and extract the ones closest to running out of stock. That would certainly impress everyone at the next family reunion!

Hopefully, our example helped you understand how treaps work, but . . . I have a confession to make: treaps are not really used as a way to index multidimensional data.

We'll see in the next chapters, and in particular in chapter 7, when we talk about cache, that there are better ways to address problems equivalent to the example we presented in this chapter.

Let me be clear: using treaps as both trees and heaps is possible, perfectly legal, and can even offer decent performance, under certain conditions, although in the general case we have seen that keeping data organized by both criteria will likely produce an unbalanced tree (which means linear-time operations).

But that's not why treaps were invented, nor is it the main way they are used today. In the end, the point is that there are better ways to index multidimensional data and better ways to use treaps. Instead, we'll see that we can use treaps as a building block to implement a different, and efficient, data structure.

3.4.1 Balanced trees

One aspect that we stressed is that unbalanced treaps tend to have long paths, whose length can be, in the worst-case scenario, in the order of `O(n)` nodes.

Conversely, when discussing heaps, we saw that balanced trees, like heaps, have logarithmic height, making all operations particularly convenient to run.

With heaps, however, the catch is that we trade the benefit of balanced trees in exchange for restricting to a limited set of operations. We can't efficiently search a heap for an element's key, or retrieve the maximum or minimum key,[8] or delete or update a random element (without knowing beforehand its position in the heap) in sublinear running time.

Nevertheless, there are, in algorithm literature, many other examples of balanced trees, data structures that guarantee that the height of the tree will be logarithmic, even in the worst case. Some examples that we mentioned in section 3.2 are 2-3 trees[9] (shown in figure 3.12) and red-black trees[10] (figure 3.13).

The algorithms to maintain the constraints for these trees, however, tend to be quite complicated, so much so that many textbooks on algorithms, for instance, omit the `delete` method altogether.

Turns out, quite surprisingly, that we can use treaps, which seems quite unbalanced, to obtain tendentially balanced[11] binary search trees using a set of easier and cleaner algorithms (in comparison to red-black trees and the like).

[8] Remember that in a heap, elements are partially ordered by priority, but not ordered at all by key. We can get the element with the highest priority, but to get the smallest (or largest) key, we need to check all elements.

[9] Aho, Alfred V., and John E. Hopcroft. *The design and analysis of computer algorithms.* Pearson Education India, 1974.

[10] Guibas, Leo J., and Robert Sedgewick. "A dichromatic framework for balanced trees." 19th Annual Symposium on Foundations of Computer Science (sfcs 1978). IEEE, 1978.

[11] Meant as balanced, with a high probability.

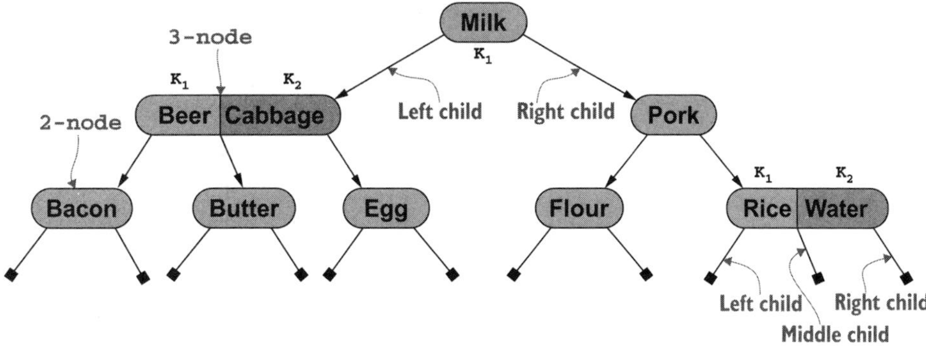
Milk
K_1
3-node
K_1
K_2
2-node
Beer
Cabbage
Left child
Right child
Pork
K_1
K_2
Bacon
Butter
Egg
Flour
Rice
Water
Left child
Right child
Middle child

Figure 3.12 A 2-3 tree containing the keys we used in our grocery store example. Nodes in 2-3 trees can contain one or two keys, sorted ascendingly, and respectively 2 or 3 links. Besides left and right children, 3-nodes also have a middle child. All keys `K` in the subtree pointed to by a middle link must obey this condition: $K_1 > K >= K_2$, where K_1 and K_2 are the first and second key, respectively, of the 3-node. 2-3 trees are guaranteed to be balanced by the way insertion is performed: keys are added to the leaves, and when a leaf grows to three elements, it's split and the middle element is bubbled up to the parent node (which is also possibly recursively split). It is guaranteed that the height of a 2-3 tree with `n` keys is between $\log_2(n)$ and $\log_3(n)$.

As we saw in the introduction to this chapter, plain BSTs also suffer this same problem, having their structure depend on the order in which elements are inserted.

And if we go back to the last section, we saw treaps can be skewed if the particular combination of keys and priorities, and the order in which elements are inserted, is particularly unlucky, because rotations can cause the tree to get even more unbalanced (see figure 3.9).

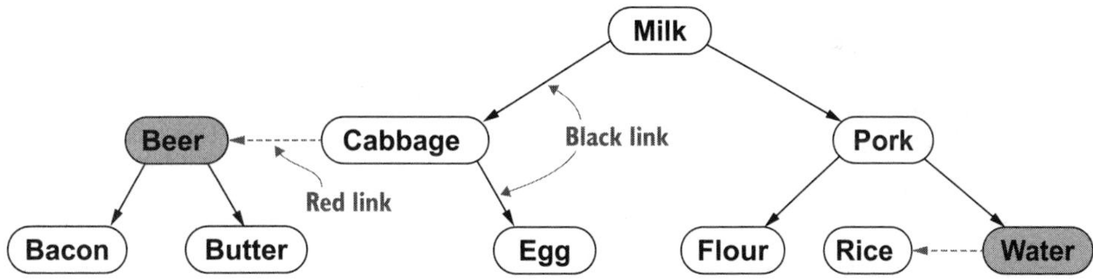
Milk
Beer
Cabbage
Black link
Pork
Red link
Bacon
Butter
Egg
Flour
Rice
Water

Figure 3.13 Red-black containing the same keys of our example. Red-black trees are one of the simplest implementations of 2-3 trees. A red-black BST is like a regular BST, except that the links between nodes can be of two different kinds: red links (dashed lines), and black links (solid lines). Red links connect keys that, in the corresponding 2-3 tree, would belong to the same 3-node. Black links, instead, would be the actual links of a 2-3 tree. There are two constraints: (1) No node has two red links connected to it (either in- or out-going); this encodes the fact that in a 2-3 tree there are only 2-nodes and 3-nodes. (2) All paths from the root to a leaf have the same number of black links. Equivalently, nodes can be marked as red or black. Here, we used red (shaded) and white (unshaded) for clarity. There can't be two consecutive red nodes in any path. Together, these constraints guarantee that the longest possible path in a red-black BST, alternating red and black links, can at most be twice as long as the shortest possible path in the tree, containing only black links. In turn, this guarantees that the height of the tree is logarithmic. These invariants are maintained by appropriately using rotations, after insertions and deletions.

So here is the idea: we can use rotations to rebalance the tree. If we strip priorities from their meaning (in our example, forget about the units in stock for each product), we can, in theory, update the priority value of each node so that fixing the heap's invariants will produce a more balanced tree.

Figure 3.14 illustrates the process. The right branch of the tree is not balanced, and by updating the second-to-last-level node, we can force a right rotation that will bring it up one level, rebalancing its subtree, and in this simple example, the whole tree.

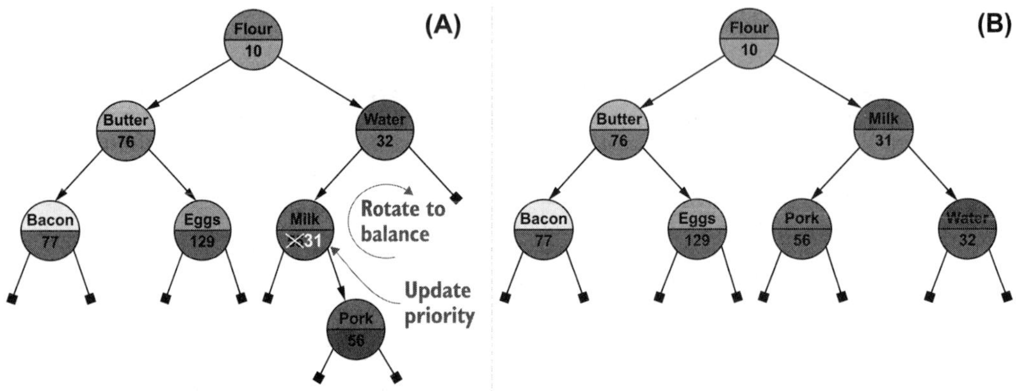
(A)
Flour 10
Butter 76
Water 32
Bacon 77
Eggs 129
Milk 31
Pork 56
Rotate to balance
Update priority
(B)
Flour 10
Butter 76
Milk 31
Bacon 77
Eggs 129
Pork 56
Water 32

Figure 3.14 Rebalancing a treap by carefully updating its priorities. If we change the priority of the node with key "Milk" to a value smaller than its parent (but larger than the root, in this case), we can fix the heap invariants with a right rotation. Incidentally, by doing so we will get a perfectly balanced tree.

We need to be clear now: By discarding the meaning of the priority field, we are implementing something different than what we had in section 3.3. In particular, this new data structure will no longer adhere to the priority queue public interface, and it will not offer any `top` or `peek` method. Instead, it will just be a binary search tree that *internally* uses the concepts we developed for treaps to maintain its structure balanced. Table 3.3 shows the methods and contract for BSTs. The data structure we are about to introduce will adhere to this API.

Table 3.3 API and Contract for BinarySearchTree (BST)

Abstract data structure: Binary search tree	

API	`class BST {`
	`  insert(element)`
	`  remove(element)`
	`  contains(element)`
	`  min()`
	`  max()`
	`}`

Contract with client	Entries are kept sorted by element (*aka* key).

3.4.2 *Introducing randomization*

If getting better results using simpler algorithms sounds too good to be true to you . . . well, you might be partially right, meaning that there is a price to pay for simplicity.

Updating priorities to keep the tree balanced seemed easy on our small example, but doing it systematically on a large tree becomes difficult and expensive.

Difficult because it becomes like solving a puzzle: every time we rotate an internal node, we potentially cause lower levels in the subtrees pushed down to become more unbalanced, so it's not trivial to come up with the right order of rotations to obtain the best possible tree structure.

Expensive, because we need to keep track of the height of each subtree, and because coming up with a sequence of rotations requires extra work.

In the previous section, we used the term *tendentially balanced* to describe the result we can get. This has probably already revealed a key point to the eyes of the most observant readers: we are talking about introducing a randomized element in our data structures.

Randomness will be a constant factor in this first part of the book. We'll see several data structures leveraging it, including Bloom filters. To help all readers be comfortable with the topic, we prepared a short introduction to randomized algorithms in appendix F; feel free to take a look before delving into this section.

In the original work by Aragon and Raimund, treaps were introduced as a means to obtain "randomized balanced search trees." They used the same idea we described in section 3.4.1, leveraging priorities to force a balanced tree structure, but they avoided all the complexity of manually setting these values by using a uniform random numbers generator to choose the values for the nodes' priorities.

Figure 3.15 shows a more balanced version of the tree produced at the end of figure 3.9, by replacing those priorities with randomly generated real numbers. It's also possible to use random integers for priorities, but using real numbers reduces the possibility of ties and improves the final result.

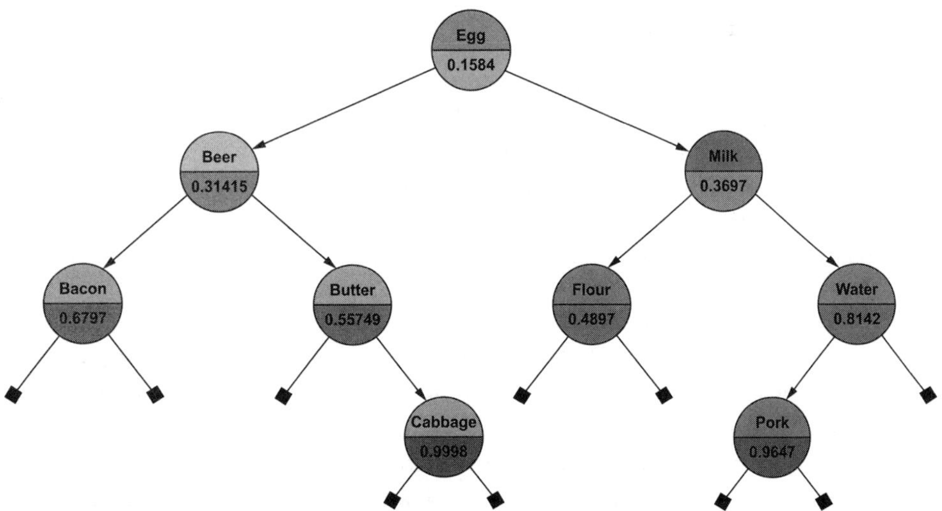
Egg
0.1584
Beer
0.31415
Milk
0.3697
Bacon
0.6797
Butter
0.55749
Flour
0.4897
Water
0.8142
Cabbage
0.9998
Pork
0.9647

Figure 3.15 An example of a Randomized Treap (RT) for the keys in the treap shown in figure 3.9 (after inserting the key "Beer"). Priorities are random numbers between 0 and 1. This is just one possible structure for the keys, corresponding to one random choice of the priorities.

We will see in section 3.5 that, if the priorities are drawn from a uniform distribution, the expected height of the tree is logarithmic in the number of nodes.

The best part is that we have already written almost all the code needed to implement this new data structure. We can internally use a treap (listing 3.9) and all its API methods will just be wrappers for treap's methods, except for `insert`; that's the only one for which we need to write an extra line of code.

Listing 3.9 Class `RandomizedTreap`

```
class RandomizedTreap
  #type Treap
  treap

  #type RandomNumberGenerator
  randomGenerator

  function RandomizedTreap()
    this.treap ← new Treap
```

As it's shown in listing 3.10, all we need to do is generate a random priority when we insert a new key in our Randomized Treap.

You can find a Java implementation for RTs on the book's repo on GitHub.[12]

Listing 3.10 Method `RandomizedTreap::insert`

Method `insert` takes the key to insert into the tree. It doesn't return anything but has side effects on the tree.

We insert a new entry in the treap: the key will be the method's argument, while the priority will be a random real number.

```
function insert(key)
  return this.treap.insert(key, this.randomGenerator.next())
```

3.4.3 Applications of Randomized Treaps

As we saw in the last section, Randomized Treaps are the main application for treaps. Now the question is, what are the most common applications for Randomized Treaps?

In general, we can use a Randomized Treap everywhere we would use a BST. In particular, they are indicated for situations where we need a balanced tree, but we are fine with having guarantees on the average case only, not on the worst case.

Another aspect to consider is that, as always when randomization and "average case" bounds are involved, the guarantees are more likely to hold when the number of entries is larger, while for smaller trees, it's easier to obtain skewed structures. (For small trees, however, the performance difference between slightly skewed and balanced trees will also be less relevant, obviously.)

BSTs, in turn, are often used to implement dictionaries and sets. We will see more about these structures in chapter 4.

[12] See https://github.com/mlarocca/AlgorithmsAndDataStructuresInAction#treap.

Other examples include keeping data read from a stream sorted, counting the number of elements smaller (larger) than any given element of a dynamic set, and in general all applications where we need to keep a dynamic set of elements in sorted order, while supporting fast search, insertion, and removal.

Practical examples of real-world code using BSTs are, for instance, managing a set of virtual memory areas (VMAs) in operating system kernels and keeping track of packet IP verification IDs. For the latter, a hash table would be faster, but it would also be vulnerable to worst-case input attacks, where an attacker could send packets from IPs hashing to the same value: this would degenerate the hash table into an unsorted list (if concatenation[13] is used), transforming the hash table in a bottleneck and possibly slowing down packet resolution or the whole kernel.

3.5 Performance analysis and profiling

As we saw in section 3.3, all API methods on Randomized Treaps require time proportional to the height of a tree. As we know (see the introduction to this chapter and appendix C), in the worst case the height of a binary tree can be linear in the number of elements and, in fact, one of the problems with BSTs is that there are specific sequences of insertions that will certainly cause a tree to be skewed. This issue makes binary search trees particularly vulnerable to attacks when used as dictionaries, because all an attacker needs to degrade the data structure's performance is to send an ordered sequence, which will cause the tree to degenerate into a linked list, having a single path from the root to a leaf containing all the elements.

Randomized Treaps offer a two-fold improvement. First and foremost, introducing randomness in the assignment of priorities prevents[14] attackers from being able to exploit known sequences. But also, as we promised in section 3.4, it will give us on average a more balanced tree than plain binary search trees.

What does "on average" mean? And how much of an improvement can we get? There are two ways to answer these questions. From a theoretical point of view, we can analyze the expected height of a Randomized Treap, and mathematically prove that, on average, the height will be logarithmic.

But also, from a practical angle, we can just run a simulation to verify that what we expect is true and compare the height of a BST versus a Randomized Treap with the same elements.

3.5.1 Theory: Expected height

To analyze the expected height of a random data structure, we need to introduce some concepts about statistics.

First and foremost, we will need to use the concept of expected value for a *random variable* V. We can informally define it as the mean value (not the most likely value) that variable will assume over a large set of occurrences.

---

[13]See appendix C for a recap on hashing.

[14]It goes without saying that this holds if the pseudo-random generators are implemented properly and within the limits caused by the fact that a classic computer can't offer true randomness. Either way, we make the attackers' job a little harder.

More formally, if `V` can assume values in a finite, countable set `{`v_1`,` v_2`, . . .` v_M`}`, each with probability `{`p_1`,` p_2`, . . . ,` p_M`}`, then we define the expected value of `V` as

$$E[V] = \sum_{i=1}^{M} v_i \cdot p_i$$

For our Randomized Treap, we will define a random variable D_k for the depth of a given node N_k, where the index `k ∊ {0, . . . n-1}` denotes the index of the node's key in the sorted set: N_k has the `k`-th smallest key in the tree.

In simple terms, D_k counts how many ancestors there are for the node holding the `k`-th smallest key, N_k. Yet another way to see this number is the following: How many nodes are in the path from the tree's root to N_k?

Formally:

$$D_k = \sum_{i=0}^{n-1} N_i \text{ is an ancestor of } N_k$$

We can denote the event "N_i is an ancestor of N_k" with the indicator (a binary variable) A_k^i: this way, given any pairs of nodes `Ni` and N_k, A_k^i `== 1` means that N_i is in the path between N_k and the root, while A_k^i `== 0` means that either they are in different branches or, at most, N_i is a descendent of N_k.

Then the expected value for D_k becomes

$$E[D_k] = \sum_{i=0}^{n-1} 1 \cdot P(N_i \text{ is an ancestor of } N_k) = \sum_{i=0}^{n-1} P(A_k^i)$$

To compute the probability $P(A_k^i)$, we need to introduce a new variable, and a lemma (an intermediate result).

We define `N(i,k) = N(k,i) = {`N_i`,` N_{i+1}`, . . .` N_{k-1}`,` N_k`}` as the subset of treap nodes whose keys are between the `i`-th and `k`-th smallest[15] of the whole tree.

Obviously, `N(0,n-1) = N(n-1,0)` contains all the nodes in the treap. Figure 3.16 shows a few examples of these subsets to help you visualize them.

Notice that the successor and predecessor of any node `N` are always on a path between `N` and the root, or `N` and a leaf. In other words, to find the predecessor—or successor—of a node, you only need to look either in the subtree rooted at `N`, where this node will be the left-most, or right-most for successors, or in the path between `N` and the root.

[15] Assuming `i < k`; otherwise, if `i > k`, we refer the subset `{`N_k`,` N_{k+1}`, ...` N_{i-1}`,` N_i`}`.

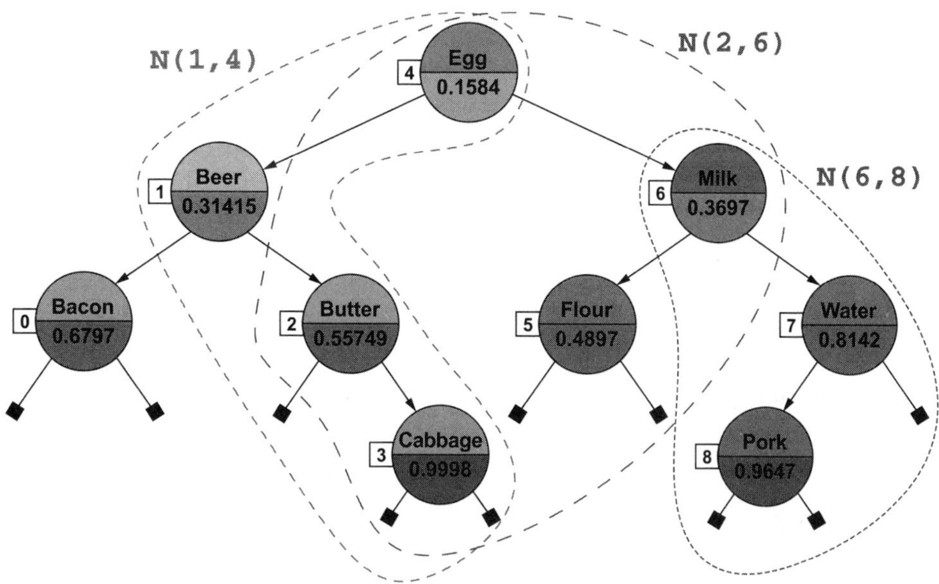
N(1,4)
N(2,6)
N(6,8)
4
Egg
0.1584
1
Beer
0.31415
6
Milk
0.3697
0
Bacon
0.6797
2
Butter
0.55749
5
Flour
0.4897
7
Water
0.8142
3
Cabbage
0.9998
8
Pork
0.9647

Figure 3.16 A few examples of the subsets of nodes `N(i,k)` defined in this section.

It can be proved that the following lemma holds:

> *For all* `i≠k, 0≤i,k≤n-1,` N_i *is an ancestor of* N_k *if and only if* N_i *has the smallest priority among all nodes in* `N(i,k)`.

We will not prove this lemma here. If you'd like to take the challenge, it can be easily proven by induction.

So, armed with the lemma, we can compute the probability that the node with the `i`-th smallest key becomes an ancestor of the node with the `k`-th smallest key. Since we assume that the priorities are drawn from a uniform continuous set, as with all real numbers between 0 and 1, then each node in a subset of nodes is equally likely to hold the smallest priority.

Therefore, for each `i≠k` we can write the probability of `i` being an ancestor of `k` as

$$P(A_k^i)_{i \neq k} = \frac{1}{|N(i,\,k)|} = \frac{1}{|k-i|+1}$$

while for `i=k`, instead, the probability is simply 0 (a node can't be its own ancestor).

Replacing these values in the formula for the expected value of D_k, we get

$$E[D_k] = \sum_{i=0}^{n-1} P(A_k^i) = \sum_{i=0}^{k-1} \frac{1}{k-i+1} + \sum_{i=k}^{k} 0 + \sum_{i=k+1}^{n-1} \frac{1}{i-k+1}$$

The middle term of the sum obviously evaluates to `0`, while for the first term of the sum, we notice that when `i=0`, the denominator becomes equal to `k-1`, and it diminishes of `1` unit as `i` increases until, for `i=k-1`, it becomes equal to `2`.

Similar considerations can be made for the last term of the formula, giving us:

$$E[D_k] = \sum_{j=2}^{k-1}\frac{1}{j} + \sum_{j=2}^{n-k}\frac{1}{j} = \sum_{j=1}^{k-1}\frac{1}{j} - 1 + \sum_{j=1}^{n-k}\frac{1}{j} - 1 = H_{k-1} - 1 + H_{n-k} - 1$$

The two summations in the previous formula are, in fact, both partial sums of the harmonic series, denoted as H_n; $H_n < \ln(n)$, where `ln` is the natural logarithm. We finally obtain

$$E[D_k] = H_{k-1} + H_{n-k} - 2 < ln\ (k-1) + ln\ (n-k) - 2 < 2 \cdot ln(n) - 2$$

This result guarantees that, over a large number of attempts, the mean value for the height of a Randomized Treap is `O(log(n))`, logarithmic in the number of keys stored (independently of the order keys are added or removed, and on the distribution of keys).

3.5.2 *Profiling height*

You could object that it's just a guarantee on the average among several attempts. What if we get really unlucky on a crucial run? To get better insight into the actual performance of this data structure, we can run a little profiling, just like we did in section 2.10 for d-heaps. This time, we'll use a profiling tool for Java, JProfiler.[16]

We could even omit using a profiling tool, because our tests are going to compare an implementation of a plain BST versus a Randomized Treap, and after performing the same sequence of operations on two instances of those two containers, they'll check how the heights of the two trees compare.

This measure will give us the gist of the asymptotic improvement of balanced trees over BSTs, because, as we discussed, operations on binary trees (balanced or not) require a number of steps proportional to the height of the tree.

We also know, however, that asymptotic analysis discards the constant coefficients, hiding the code complexity that usually comes with more advanced algorithms; therefore, having an indication of the actual running time will provide more thorough information that can help us choose the best implementation for our applications.

In the tests that you can find on the book's GitHub repo,[17] we try three different scenarios:

- We create large trees of increasing (random) size, whose keys are random integers, with an initial sequence of insertions, followed by random removals and insertions (with a rate of 1:1).
- We proceed similarly to the previous step, but the possible key values are limited to a small subset (for instance, just 0 . . . 100, forcing several duplicates in the tree).
- We insert an ordered sequence of numbers into the trees.

---

[16] JProfiler is a commercial tool. You can find open-source alternatives that will also get the job done.

[17] https://github.com/mlarocca/AlgorithmsAndDataStructuresInAction/blob/master/Java/tests/org/mlarocca/containers/treap/RandomizedTreapProfiling.java.

The results of the first test we ran are shown in figure 3.17. You can see that the height of both trees is growing logarithmically. At first this seems rather discouraging, as there seems to be no improvement given by using Randomized Treaps over plain BSTs.

We need, however, to make a couple of considerations.

First, let's clarify the rules of the game: given a target size for the tree, `n`, then we add (to both containers) the same `n` integers, chosen at random, without any limit. After these insertions, we perform another `n` operations. Each of them can remove an existing key (randomly chosen) or add a new random integer to it. Obviously, we repeat this test for growing sizes.

We used an efficient implementation of BSTs (you can find it on the book's repo[18]) that limits the skewing effect of removing elements.[19] This expedient already improves the balance of BSTs and reduces the gap with balanced trees.

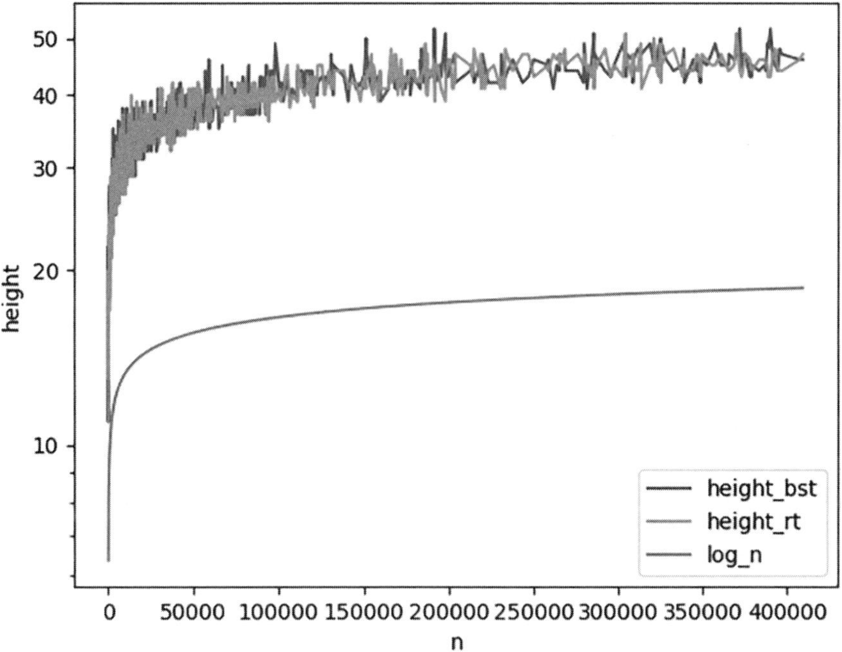

height
50
40
30
20
10
0
50000
100000
150000
200000
250000
300000
350000
400000
n
height_bst
height_rt
log_n

Figure 3.17 The height of a Randomized Treap versus a BST. On both data structures the same operations were performed, and the keys are random integers. Notice that the `y` axis uses a logarithmic scale.

[18]https://github.com/mlarocca/AlgorithmsAndDataStructuresInAction/blob/master/Java/src/org/mlarocca/containers/tree/BST.java.

[19]The standard implementation of the `remove` method in BSTs, when the node `N` to remove has both children, uses the node's successor to replace the key to delete (and then recursively delete this successor). Over a long number of removals, this causes the tree to become skewed, left-leaning. A solution to mitigate this effect is randomly deciding, with a 50% probability, to use the predecessor of a key instead of its successor.

Finally, there is one consideration to make. In our experiment, we add completely random keys since the range of values is so large compared to the number of elements in the container. The expected number of duplicates is negligible, and we can assume that all sequences of keys to insert will be drawn with the same probability. In this scenario, it's unlikely that an adversarial sequence, causing the height to be super-logarithmic, will be chosen (the chances are beyond slim already for `n ~= 100`).

Basically, we are using the same concept of Randomized Treaps, moving the randomness into the generator of the sequences of keys to insert; unfortunately, however, we don't always get to choose the data to add to our containers!

And so, in order to verify this hypothesis, we can run a different experiment, reducing the influence of the random generator by limiting the set of possible keys. The results of limiting the keys to values in the range 0 . . . 1000 are shown in figure 3.18. Now we can immediately notice a difference between the two data structures: the BST grows linearly, with a slope of approximately 10^{-3}, while the Randomized Treap still shows logarithmic height.

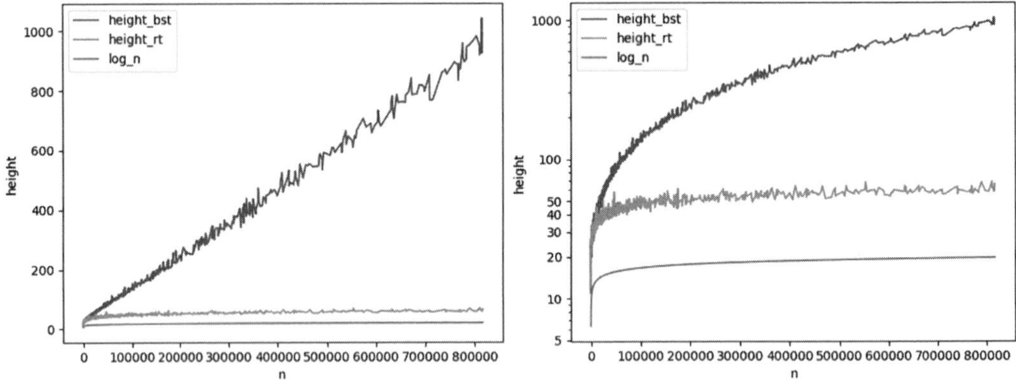
height_bst
height_rt
log_n
height
n
1000
800
600
400
200
0
0
100000 200000 300000 400000 500000 600000 700000 800000
height_bst
height_rt
log_n
height
n
1000
100
50
40
30
20
10
5
0
100000 200000 300000 400000 500000 600000 700000 800000

Figure 3.18 The height of a Randomized Treap versus a BST, when possible keys are randomly extracted from the set of integers between 0 and 1000. The charts show the same data, on the left with linear scale and on the right using logarithmic scale for heights.

There are two reasons for this difference:

- Having a high duplicates rate (larger and larger as `n` is growing) produces sequences of insertions with longer streaks of sorted data.
- BSTs are naturally left-leaning when duplicates are allowed. As you can also see in listing 3.5, we need to break ties when inserting new keys, and we decided to go left every time we find a duplicate. Unfortunately, in this case we need a deterministic decision. We can't use the same workaround as for deletions, and so when input sequences contain a large number of duplicates, as in this test, BSTs become tangibly skewed.

This is already a nice result for treaps, because real-world inputs can easily contain several duplicates in many applications.

But what about those applications that don't allow duplicates? Are we safe from adversarial sequences in those situations? Truth to be told, we haven't clarified how important the role of ordering is. What better way to do it than trying the worst possible case—a totally ordered sequence? Figure 3.19 shows the results for this test. Here we stripped out all randomness and just added to the containers all integers from `0` to `n-1`, no calls to remove performed.

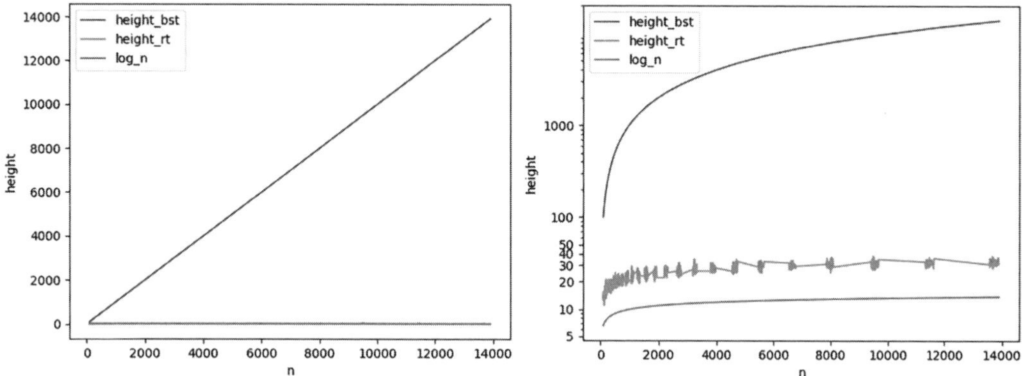
height_bst
height_rt
log_n
height
n
14000
12000
10000
8000
6000
4000
2000
0
1000
100
50
40
30
20
10
5

Figure 3.19 The height of a Randomized Treap versus a BST, after inserting the sequence `0, 1, . . . , n-1`. The charts show the same data, on the left with linear scale and on the right using logarithmic scale for heights.

As expected, for BSTs the height is always not just linear in the number of nodes, but equal to the number of nodes (this time the slope is exactly 1), because the tree degenerates to a linked list, as expected.

Randomized Treaps, instead, keep performing well with logarithmic height, just like for the other tests, even in the most unfavorable case.

We can then conclude that if the parameter to improve is the height of the tree, Randomized Treaps do have an advantage in comparison to BSTs, and it is true that they keep a logarithmic height in all situations; therefore, their performance is comparable to more complex data structures such as red-black trees.

Dangers of recursion

The degeneration of BSTs in this test caused the recursive implementation of the `add` method, provided on our repo, to crash with a stack overflow[18] for `n~=15K` elements.

This should remind you, once again, how important it is to be careful when writing recursive methods and, at the same time, how important it is to use the right data structure. In theory, while treaps could also cause stack overflows, since their height is logarithmic, we would need to add $\sim 2^{15000} = 10^{5000}$ elements to cause a stack overflow (which is way more than it's possible to allocate on any computer's RAM anyway, so it's unlikely you'll ever get a crash from a recursive treap).

[20]Stack overflow, its relation with recursion, and how to avoid such crashes is explained in appendix E.

3.5.3 *Profiling running time*

The height of the tree, however, is not the only criteria we are interested in. We want to know if there is a catch, and what's the price we have to pay in terms of running time and memory usage (figure 3.20).

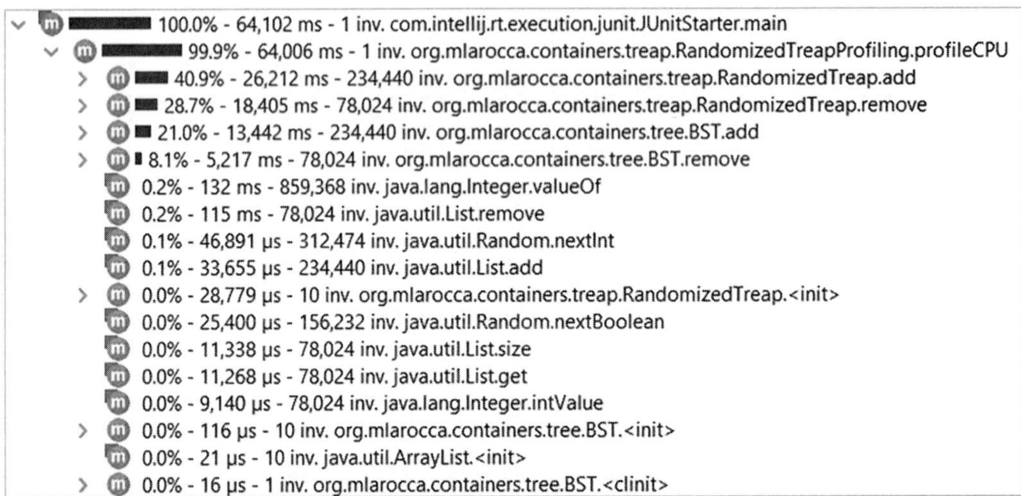
100.0% - 64,102 ms - 1 inv. com.intellij.rt.execution.junit.JUnitStarter.main
99.9% - 64,006 ms - 1 inv. org.mlarocca.containers.treap.RandomizedTreapProfiling.profileCPU
40.9% - 26,212 ms - 234,440 inv. org.mlarocca.containers.treap.RandomizedTreap.add
28.7% - 18,405 ms - 78,024 inv. org.mlarocca.containers.treap.RandomizedTreap.remove
21.0% - 13,442 ms - 234,440 inv. org.mlarocca.containers.tree.BST.add
8.1% - 5,217 ms - 78,024 inv. org.mlarocca.containers.tree.BST.remove
0.2% - 132 ms - 859,368 inv. java.lang.Integer.valueOf
0.2% - 115 ms - 78,024 inv. java.util.List.remove
0.1% - 46,891 µs - 312,474 inv. java.util.Random.nextInt
0.1% - 33,655 µs - 234,440 inv. java.util.List.add
0.0% - 28,779 µs - 10 inv. org.mlarocca.containers.treap.RandomizedTreap.<init>
0.0% - 25,400 µs - 156,232 inv. java.util.Random.nextBoolean
0.0% - 11,338 µs - 78,024 inv. java.util.List.size
0.0% - 11,268 µs - 78,024 inv. java.util.List.get
0.0% - 9,140 µs - 78,024 inv. java.lang.Integer.intValue
0.0% - 116 µs - 10 inv. org.mlarocca.containers.tree.BST.<init>
0.0% - 21 µs - 10 inv. java.util.ArrayList.<init>
0.0% - 16 µs - 1 inv. org.mlarocca.containers.tree.BST.<clinit>

Figure 3.20 Profiling CPU usage when inserting/removing random unbounded integers in a BST and Randomized Treap

To find out this, we run a proper profiling of the first test (with unbounded integers as keys, so with low or no duplicates) using JProfiler and recording the CPU time. The profiling used the implementations of BSTs and Randomized Treaps provided in the book's repo. It's worth noting that this profiling only gives us information on the implementations we examine, but we could get different results on optimized or differently designed software.

The results for our profiling run are shown in figure 3.20, where we can see that for insertion (method `add`) the cumulative running time spent for `Randomized-Treap` is almost twice as much as for `BST::add`; for method `remove;` instead, the ratio becomes 3.5 times.

From this first test, it seems that we pay a high price, in the general case, for the overhead due to the greater complexity of Randomized Treaps. This result is somehow expected, because when the height of the trees is approximately the same, the code for treaps is substantially more complex than for BSTs.

Should we just throw away our `RandomizedTreap` class? Well, not so fast. Let's see what happens when we profile the second test case introduced in section 3.5.2, the one where we still add random integers to the containers, but limited to the range [0, 1000].

In the previous section, we saw that, in this case, BST's height grows linearly, while for Randomized Treaps we still have a logarithmic growth.

Figure 3.21 shows the result of this profiling. We can immediately see that the situation has radically changed, and BSTs perform tremendously worse now. So much worse that `BST::add` takes 8-fold the running time of `RandomizedTreap::add`. For the method `remove` the ratio is even worse; we are talking about almost a 15-fold speed-up using Randomized Treaps—that's exactly the situation where we would want to use our new, fancy, balanced data structure!

100.0% - 191 s - 1 inv. com.intellij.rt.execution.junit.JUnitStarter.main
100.0% - 191 s - 1 inv. org.mlarocca.containers.treap.RandomizedTreapProfiling.profileCPU
67.3% - 129 s - 77,252 inv. org.mlarocca.containers.tree.BST.remove
24.5% - 46,919 ms - 232,460 inv. org.mlarocca.containers.tree.BST.add
4.6% - 8,770 ms - 77,252 inv. org.mlarocca.containers.treap.RandomizedTreap.remove
3.3% - 6,235 ms - 232,460 inv. org.mlarocca.containers.treap.RandomizedTreap.add
0.1% - 126 ms - 77,252 inv. java.util.List.remove
0.1% - 117 ms - 851,884 inv. java.lang.Integer.valueOf
0.0% - 42,899 µs - 309,722 inv. java.util.Random.nextInt
0.0% - 30,716 µs - 232,460 inv. java.util.List.add
0.0% - 23,381 µs - 154,856 inv. java.util.Random.nextBoolean
0.0% - 10,548 µs - 77,252 inv. java.util.List.get
0.0% - 9,713 µs - 77,252 inv. java.util.List.size
0.0% - 8,046 µs - 77,252 inv. java.lang.Integer.intValue
0.0% - 4,859 µs - 10 inv. org.mlarocca.containers.treap.RandomizedTreap.<init>
0.0% - 63 µs - 10 inv. org.mlarocca.containers.tree.BST.<init>
0.0% - 26 µs - 10 inv. java.util.ArrayList.<init>
0.0% - 12 µs - 1 inv. org.mlarocca.containers.tree.BST.<clinit>

Figure 3.21 Profiling CPU usage when inserting/removing random integers between 0 and 1000 in a BST and Randomized Treap

For the sake of completeness, let's also take a look at the worst-case scenario for BSTs. Figure 3.22 shows the profiling of the last test case introduced in section 3.5.2, where we insert an ordered sequence in our containers. In this case, I believe that the results don't even need to be commented, because we are talking about thousands of seconds versus microseconds (we had to test on a smaller set because BSTs performance was so degraded as to be unbearably slow).

All things considered, these results would suggest that if we are not sure about how uniform and duplicates-free the data we have to hold are, we should consider using Randomized Treaps. Instead, if we are sure the data will have lots of duplicates or

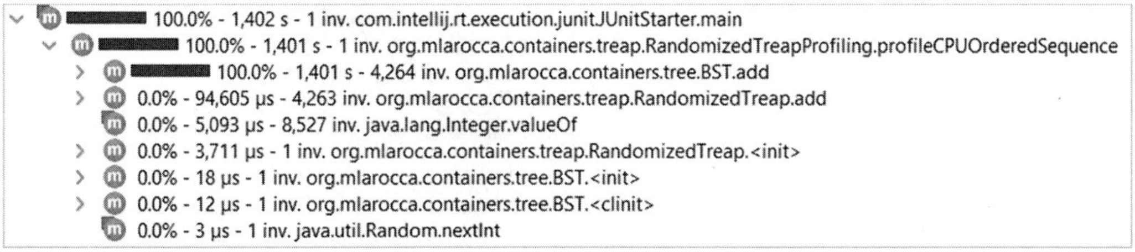

100.0% - 1,402 s - 1 inv. com.intellij.rt.execution.junit.JUnitStarter.main
100.0% - 1,401 s - 1 inv. org.mlarocca.containers.treap.RandomizedTreapProfiling.profileCPUOrderedSequence
100.0% - 1,401 s - 4,264 inv. org.mlarocca.containers.tree.BST.add
0.0% - 94,605 µs - 4,263 inv. org.mlarocca.containers.treap.RandomizedTreap.add
0.0% - 5,093 µs - 8,527 inv. java.lang.Integer.valueOf
0.0% - 3,711 µs - 1 inv. org.mlarocca.containers.treap.RandomizedTreap.<init>
0.0% - 18 µs - 1 inv. org.mlarocca.containers.tree.BST.<init>
0.0% - 12 µs - 1 inv. org.mlarocca.containers.tree.BST.<clinit>
0.0% - 3 µs - 1 inv. java.util.Random.nextInt

Figure 3.22 Profiling CPU usage when adding ordered sequences to a BST and Randomized Treap

possibly be close to sorted, then we definitely want to avoid using plain BSTs and resort to a balanced tree.

3.5.4 Profiling memory usage

So much for CPU usage, you might say, but what about memory usage? Because maybe Randomized Treaps are faster in some situations, but they require so much space that you won't be able to store them in memory for large datasets.

First, we make a consideration: memory usage will be approximately the same for all the test cases we have introduced in the previous sections (when comparing containers of the same size, of course). This is because the number of nodes in both trees won't change with their height; these trees do not support compression, and balanced and skewed trees will always need `n` nodes to store `n` keys.

Once we have established that, we can therefore be happy by profiling memory allocation for the most generic case, where the two trees are both approximately balanced. Figure 3.23 shows the cumulative memory allocated for the whole test for instances of the two classes.

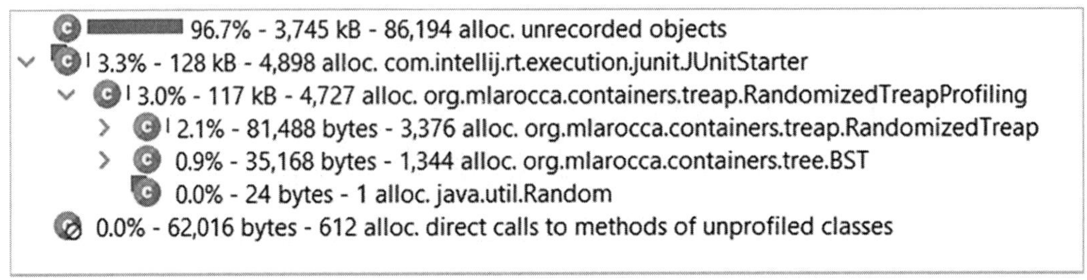
96.7% - 3,745 kB - 86,194 alloc. unrecorded objects
3.3% - 128 kB - 4,898 alloc. com.intellij.rt.execution.junit.JUnitStarter
3.0% - 117 kB - 4,727 alloc. org.mlarocca.containers.treap.RandomizedTreapProfiling
2.1% - 81,488 bytes - 3,376 alloc. org.mlarocca.containers.treap.RandomizedTreap
0.9% - 35,168 bytes - 1,344 alloc. org.mlarocca.containers.tree.BST
0.0% - 24 bytes - 1 alloc. java.util.Random
0.0% - 62,016 bytes - 612 alloc. direct calls to methods of unprofiled classes

Figure 3.23 Cumulative memory allocation for `BST` and `RandomizedTreap`, in the most generic case, with random insertions and removals

We can see that `RandomizedTreap` requires slightly more than twice the memory of `BST`. This is obviously not ideal, but is to be expected, considering that each node of a treap will hold a key (an `Integer`, in this test), plus a `Double` for the priority.

If we try a different kind of data for the keys—for instance, `String`—we can see that the difference becomes much smaller, as shown in figure 3.24. It's just a ratio of 1.25 when storing strings between four and ten characters as keys.

Hot Spot	Total Allocated Memory	Allocations
com.intellij.rt.execution.junit.JUnitStarter	6,813 kB (100 %)	350,907
org.mlarocca.containers.treap.RandomizedTreapProfiling	6,803 kB (99 %)	350,691
org.mlarocca.containers.treap.RandomizedTreap	3,558 kB (52 %)	183,372
org.mlarocca.containers.treap.Treap	3,425 kB (50 %)	177,832
org.mlarocca.containers.treap.Treap$TreapNode	3,351 kB (49 %)	174,139
org.mlarocca.containers.tree.BST	2,836 kB (41 %)	149,718
org.mlarocca.containers.tree.BST$BSTNode	2,765 kB (40 %)	146,201
java.lang.Integer	200 kB (2 %)	8,937
java.lang.Double	88,152 bytes (1 %)	3,673
org.mlarocca.containers.treap.Treap$TreapEntry	44,688 bytes (0 %)	1,862
java.util.concurrent.locks.ReentrantReadWriteLock$WriteLock	64 bytes (0 %)	2
java.util.concurrent.locks.ReentrantReadWriteLock	48 bytes (0 %)	3

Figure 3.24 Cumulative memory allocation for `BST` and `RandomizedTreap` when storing strings between 4 and 10 characters.

3.5.5 Conclusions

The analysis of the comparative performance and height of BSTs and Randomized Treaps suggests that, while the latter requires slightly more memory and can be slower in the generic case, when we don't have any guarantee on the uniform distribution of keys or on the order of the operations, using BSTs carries a far greater risk of becoming a bottleneck.

If you remember, when we introduced data structures in chapter 1 we made it clear: knowing the right data structure to use is more about avoiding the wrong choices than finding the perfect data structure. This is exactly the same case. We (as developers) need to be aware of the situations where we need to use a balanced tree to avoid attacks or just degraded performance.

It's worth reiterating that the first part of the analysis, focusing on the height of the trees, has general value[21] and is independent of the programming language used. The analysis of running time and memory usage, instead, only has value for this implementation, programming language, design choices, and so on. All these aspects can, in theory, be optimized for your application's specific requirements.

My advice, as always, is to carefully analyze requirements, understand what's critical in your software and where you need certain guarantees about time and memory, and then test and profile the critical sections. Avoid wasting time on non-critical sections; usually you'll find that the Pareto principle holds for software, and you can get an 80% performance gain by optimizing 20% of your code. Although the exact ratio may vary, the overall principle that you can get a significant improvement by optimizing the most critical parts of your application will likely hold.

Try to get a balance between clean code, time used to develop it, and efficiency. "Premature optimization is the root of all evil," as stated by Donald Knuth,[22] because trying to optimize all of your code will likely distract your team from finding the critical issues, and produce less-clean, less-readable, and less-maintainable code.

Always make sure to try to write clean code first, and then optimize the bottlenecks and the critical sections, especially those on which you have a service-level agreement, with requirements about time/memory used.

To give you a concrete example, the Java implementation we provide on the book's repo makes heavy use of the `Optional` class (to avoid using `null`, and provide a nicer interface and a better way to handle unsuccessful searches/operations), and consequently also a lot of lambda functions.

If we profile in more detail the memory usage, disabling the filter on the package (to speed-up profiling, you usually want to avoid recording standard libraries, etc.), the final result is quite surprising, as we can see in figure 3.25.

---

[21] Assuming the algorithms are implemented verbatim, it's also not dependent on the specific implementation.

[22] "The real problem is that programmers have spent far too much time worrying about efficiency in the wrong places and at the wrong times. Premature optimization is the root of all evil (or at least most of it) in programming." Knuth, Donald Ervin. *The art of computer programming*. Pearson Education, 1997.

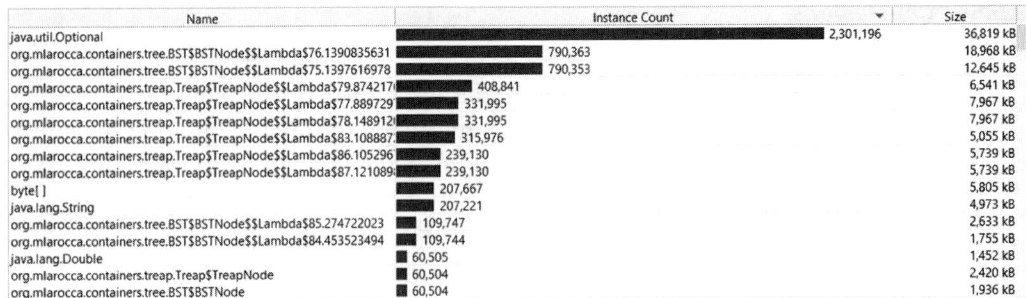

Name	Instance Count	Size
java.util.Optional	2,301,196	36,819 kB
org.mlarocca.containers.tree.BST$BSTNode$$Lambda$76.1390835631	790,363	18,968 kB
org.mlarocca.containers.tree.BST$BSTNode$$Lambda$75.1397616978	790,353	12,645 kB
org.mlarocca.containers.treap.Treap$TreapNode$$Lambda$79.874217	408,841	6,541 kB
org.mlarocca.containers.treap.Treap$TreapNode$$Lambda$77.889729	331,995	7,967 kB
org.mlarocca.containers.treap.Treap$TreapNode$$Lambda$78.148912	331,995	7,967 kB
org.mlarocca.containers.treap.Treap$TreapNode$$Lambda$83.108887	315,976	5,055 kB
org.mlarocca.containers.treap.Treap$TreapNode$$Lambda$86.105296	239,130	5,739 kB
org.mlarocca.containers.treap.Treap$TreapNode$$Lambda$87.121089	239,130	5,739 kB
byte[ ]	207,667	5,805 kB
java.lang.String	207,221	4,973 kB
org.mlarocca.containers.tree.BST$BSTNode$$Lambda$85.274722023	109,747	2,633 kB
org.mlarocca.containers.tree.BST$BSTNode$$Lambda$84.453523494	109,744	1,755 kB
java.lang.Double	60,505	1,452 kB
org.mlarocca.containers.treap.Treap$TreapNode	60,504	2,420 kB
org.mlarocca.containers.tree.BST$BSTNode	60,504	1,936 kB

Figure 3.25 Memory allocation by class for our test, without any filtering on the package

You can see that most space is used by instances of `Optional` and lambdas (implicitly created in `Optional::map`, etc.).

A complementary example for performance could be supporting multi-threading. If your application does not involve (ever) sharing these containers among different threads, you can avoid making your implementation thread-safe and save the overhead needed to create and synchronize locks.

> **Clean or optimized code?**
>
> If performance and memory usage are critical for your application, you will probably want to write a different, optimized version of this code where these fancy language features are not used. You will also likely want to avoid using recursion and write explicit loops instead.
>
> But if low-level optimization is not critical, you might prefer sticking with cleaner and more maintainable code, using better interfaces and APIs, because in the long run having readable code will make your life (and the job of future team members) much easier.

Summary

- Binary search trees offer good performance on all the typical container's methods, but only if they're kept balanced. Depending on the order of insertion of its keys, however, a BST can become skewed.
- The edge case is when an ordered sequence is added to a BST, that will then contain a single path of length `n`, de facto degenerating in a linked list.
- Treaps are a hybrid between BSTs and heaps, abiding by BST's invariants for keys, and heap's invariants for priorities.
- If we randomly assign priorities, drawing them from a uniform continuous set (such as, but not limited to, all real numbers between 0 and 1), we can mathematically guarantee that for large enough values of `n`, the tree will store `n` elements and maintain a height not greater than `2*log(n)`.

- Besides the theoretical guarantees, it's possible to verify (as we did with Java implementations) that Randomized Treaps will keep a logarithmic height even in the worst-case scenarios for BSTs.
- Moreover, the performance in term of CPU running time and memory usage is comparable for both data structures in the general case, and much better for Randomized Treaps in the edge cases where BSTs struggle.

4 Bloom filters: Reducing the memory for tracking content

This chapter covers

- Describing and analyzing Bloom filters
- Keeping track of large documents using little memory
- Showing why dictionaries are an imperfect solution
- Improving the memory print by using Bloom filters
- Recognizing use cases where Bloom filters improve performance
- Using metrics to tune the quality of Bloom filters' solutions

Starting with this chapter we'll be reviewing less common data structures that solve, as strange as it might seem, common problems. *Bloom filters* are one of the most prominent examples; they are widely used in most industries, but not as widely known as you would expect for such a cornerstone.

In section 4.1 we introduce the problem that will be our North Star in this chapter: we need to keep track of large entities with the smallest memory print possible.

In section 4.2 we continue our narration by discussing a few increasingly complex solutions, showing their strengths and weaknesses; the latter, in particular, ought to be considered chances for improvement and fertile ground for algorithms designers.

As part of this discussion, we introduce the *dictionary*, an abstract data type that we discuss in depth in section 4.3, while section 4.4 switches to concrete data structures that implement dictionaries: hash tables, binary search trees, and Bloom filters.

You have probably guessed that we are particularly interested in the latter, because it is the topic of this chapter. We describe in section 4.5 the principles governing how a Bloom filter works; then we delve into each of its methods in section 4.6, showing the pseudo-code for the crucial parts.

Section 4.7 closes the first part of the chapter with a discussion of some typical use cases for Bloom filters: from distributed databases and file systems to rooters, this technology is pervasive.

In order to reach this goal, we keep a practical approach with an emphasis on enabling readers to recognize opportunities to use Bloom filters and giving them the instruments to do so.

Starting with section 4.8, the focus shifts to theory, providing a background for the interested reader who wants to understand not just how, but why, Bloom filters work. To facilitate understanding of these sections, readers can go through appendix F (as well as appendices B and C, if needed) to review randomized algorithms, big-O notation, and basic data structures prior to starting with section 4.8.

The next few sections will then closely examine the performance of our data structure, including running time and memory print (section 4.9), as well as the accuracy of the algorithm (section 4.10).

Finally, section 4.11 describes some of the most advanced variants of Bloom filters used to provide new features or lower the false-positive rate.

4.1 The dictionary problem: Keeping track of things

Let's go over a hypothetical scenario: you work for a company that is large enough to maintain its own email service. This is a legacy service, providing basic features only. After the last reorganization, the new CTO[1] decides that you need to reinvent the email service to be aggressive on the market segment, and she puts your new manager in charge of the product redesign.

They want a brand-new, modern client with features like a contacts list and cool tricks. For instance, when you add a new recipient to an email, your application should check whether it's already in the contacts list, and if it's not, a popup (like the one shown in figure 4.1) should appear asking you if you'd like to add the new recipient.

And, needless to say, you are the lucky one who gets to be responsible for implementing this feature.

[1] Chief Technology Officer.

Of course, the resources allocated for the project are scarce, so you are only going to do a refactoring of the client, while on the server side you'll have to make do with legacy code and legacy services running on proprietary machines.

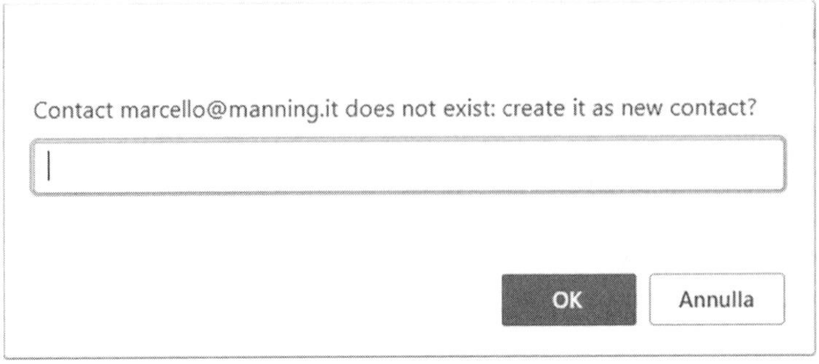

Contact marcello@manning.it does not exist: create it as new contact?
OK
Annulla

Figure 4.1 Our email application prompting the user to add a new contact after an unsuccessful search

Calling the database every time you need to check an email address against your contacts list is out of the question: you are stuck with this legacy machine that can't scale up, and you didn't get funds for refactoring and scaling it out.[2] Your DB could not support more than a few calls per second, and your management's projection is in the hundreds of emails written per second (they are very optimistic, and a bit reckless, but let's not worry about that for now!). Your first instinct would be to ask for a remote distributed cache, like Memcached, Cassandra, or Redis. A roundtrip to the cache server alone would take in the range of a hundred milliseconds, best case scenario, which would be good. But neither spinning up a new server for the cache, nor buying it as a cloud service is feasible for you, budget-wise.

In the end, you decide you only have one way to solve this: asynchronously get your contacts list when you log in (or, more lazily, the first time you click on *Compose* during the current browser session), save the contacts list in your web page's session storage space, and check the local copy of that data every time you look for existing contacts.

So far for the application design, figure 4.2 shows a possible architecture for our minimum viable product. Now you just need an efficient way to browse a contacts list and check if an email belongs to it.

Looking through a list for a certain entry is a common problem in computer science, known as the *dictionary problem*.

[2] *Scale up* means moving your application to a more powerful, more expensive machine, while with *scale out* we usually refer to redesigning an application to run in a distributed architecture over several cheaper machines. While there is an upper limit to the possibility of scaling up (the most powerful machine that can be bought by your company—and price grows exponentially in the higher end), with proper design it is possible, in theory, to scale out indefinitely.

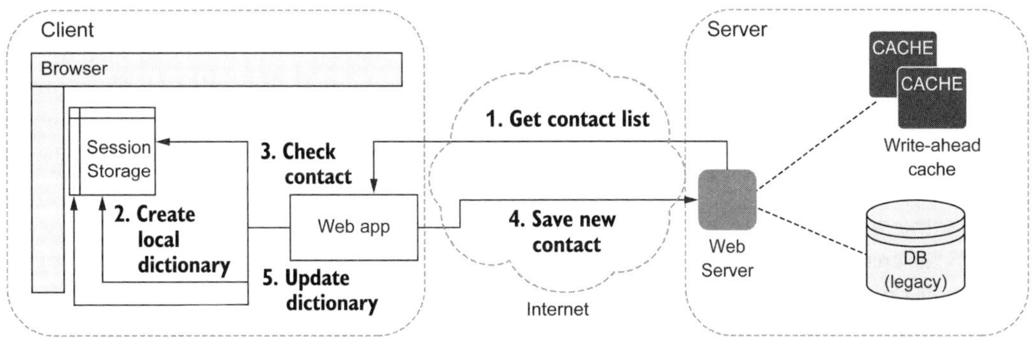
Client
Browser
Session Storage
3. Check contact
2. Create local dictionary
Web app
5. Update dictionary
1. Get contact list
4. Save new contact
Internet
Server
CACHE
CACHE
Write-ahead cache
Web Server
DB (legacy)

Figure 4.2 A possible architecture for the "save new contact (with suggestion)" feature. On the client side, the web app receives the contacts list from the web server, and with those data creates a dictionary on the session storage. Whenever the user adds a recipient on an email, the web app checks the dictionary. If the contact is not in the list, a popup is shown to the user, who can then decide to save it. In that scenario, to save the new contact another HTTP call is made to the web server, and at the same time the dictionary is updated with the new value (although without going through the server).

4.2 Alternatives to implementing a dictionary

The name shouldn't be surprising; it's exactly like when you need to look up a word in a dictionary (and by dictionary I mean one of those old gigantic paper books that have been almost entirely replaced by online dictionaries and search engines) or even in a phone book (which had no better luck after the third computer revolution).

To recap, our contacts web app needs to

- Download the list of contacts from a server
- Create a local copy for fast lookup/storage
- Allow looking up for a contact
- Provide the option to add a new contact if lookup is unsuccessful
- Sync with the server when a new contact is added (or an existing one modified)

What we really need is a data structure that is specialized in these kinds of operations; we need it to support fast insertion, and at the same time it needs to provide a way to look up an entry by value.

To be clear, when we use a plain array, we don't have an efficient array's method that tells us the index of an element `X`, nor an efficient (as in *sublinear*) method to tell us if an element is in the array or not. The only way we have to tell if an element is in the array is by going through all the array's elements, although in a sorted array we could use *binary search* to speed up the search.

For example, we could store the strings `["the", "lazy", "fox"]` in an array, and to search for `"lazy"`, we would skim through the whole array, element by element.

An associative array, instead, by definition has a native method that efficiently accesses the stored entries with a lookup by value. Usually this structure allows storing (key, value) pairs. For instance, we would have a list like `<("the", article), ("lazy",` `adjective), ("fox", noun)>`. We could search for `"lazy"` and the associative array would return `adjective`.

Another difference with regular arrays would be that the order of insertion in an associative array doesn't matter; it's not even well defined. That's the price you pay to speed up lookup by value.

To really understand how efficiently we can solve this problem, we need to get into the details of implementations. Using the dictionary abstraction, however, allows us to discuss how to solve a problem (for instance, finding whether an email belongs to a list of contacts) without having to deal with the details of the data structure's representation, hence leaving us free to focus on the task itself.

4.3 Describing the data structure API: Associative array

An associative array (also referred to as *dictionary*,[3] *symbol table*, or just *map*), is composed of a collection of (key, value) pairs, such that

- Each possible key appears at most once in the collection.
- Each value can be retrieved directly through the corresponding key.

The easiest way to grasp the essence of associative arrays is to think about regular arrays as a special case: the keys are just the set of indices between `0` and the size of the array minus `1`, and we can always retrieve a value by providing its index, so that the (plain) array `["the", "lazy", "fox"]` can be interpreted as a dictionary storing the associations `(0, "the")`, `(1, "lazy")` and `(2, "fox")`.

Associative arrays generalize this concept, allowing keys to be drawn from virtually any possible domain.

Abstract data structure: Associative array (aka dictionary)	

API	`class Dictionary {`
	`  insert(key, value)`
	`  remove(key) → value`
	`  contains(key) → value`
	`}`

Contract with client	A dictionary permanently stores all the pairs added by the client(s). If a pair `(K,V)` was added to the dictionary (and not removed afterward), then `contains(K)` will return `V`.

With this API defined, we can sketch a solution for our initial problem.

When users log in to their email, our client receives a list of contacts from the server and stores them in a dictionary that we can keep in memory (having so many contacts that it won't fit the browser's session storage would be an exceptional situation even for an Instagram rock star!). If the user adds a new contact to our address

[3] We used the term associative array here to avoid confusion between the *dictionary problem* and the *dictionary* abstract data type. Though the two terms are connected, they are not the same thing.

book, we perform a call to `insert` on the dictionary; likewise, if users remove an existing contact, we just keep the dictionary in sync by calling `remove`. Whenever a user writes an email and inserts a recipient, we first check the dictionary, and only if the contact is not in the address book do we show a popup asking users if they would like to save the new contact.

This way, we never do an HTTP call to our server (and in turn to the DB) to check whether a contact is on our address book, and we only read from the DB once on startup (or the first time during a session that we write an email).

4.4 Concrete data structures

So far, so good with the theory, but of course, implementing associative arrays to be used on real systems is a completely different thing.

In theory, if the domain (the set of possible keys) is small enough, we can still use arrays by defining a total ordering on the keys and using their position in the order as the index for a real array. For instance, if our domain is made of the words `{"a", "terrible", "choice"}`, we could sort keys lexicographically, and then we would store the values in a plain string array; for instance, `{"article", "noun", "adjective"}`. If we need to represent a dictionary that only contains a value for key `"choice"`, we could do that by setting the values corresponding to missing keys to `null`: `{null, "noun", null}`.

Usually, however, this is not the case, and the set of possible values for the keys is large enough to make it impractical to use an array with an element for any possible key's value; it would just require too much memory, which would remain largely unused.

To overcome this issue with the memory, we present two naïve implementations, and three of the most widely used alternatives.

4.4.1 Unsorted array: Fast insertion, slow search

Even if you have never seen one of those paper dinosaurs (a dictionary), you ought to at least be familiar with print books, like this one (unless, of course, you bought the e-book version!).

Suppose you need to look for a specific word in this book—maybe a name—like Bloom, and note all the places where it occurs. One option you have is to go through the book starting from the first page, word by word, until you encounter it. If you need to find all the occurrences of the word Bloom, you will have to go through the book from cover to cover.

A book taken as a collection of words, in the order they are printed, is like an unsorted array. Table 4.1 summarizes the performance of the main operations needed using this approach with unsorted arrays.

Unsorted arrays have the advantage of no extra work needed on creation, and adding a new entry is pretty easy, provided you have enough capacity.

Table 4.1 Using unsorted arrays as dictionaries

Operation	Running time	Extra memory
`Creating the structure`	O(1)	No
`Looking up an entry`	O(n)	No
`Insert a new entry`	O(1) [a]	No
`Remove an entry`	O(1)	No

[a]Amortized time.

4.4.2 Sorted arrays and binary search: Slow insertion, fast(-ish) search

That's not exactly practical, as you can imagine. If, after going through the whole book, you need to search a second word, like "filter," you would have to start all over and do a second pass through the hundreds of thousands of words in the book. That's why most books have what's called an index, usually toward the end of the book; there you can find an alphabetically ordered list of the most *uncommon* words (and names) used in the book. Common words don't make it onto this list because they are used too frequently (articles like "the" and "a" are probably used on every single page) to be worth being listed, since the value of finding places where they are used would be minimal. Conversely, the rarer a word is in English (and names are the perfect example here), the greater importance it has when it's used in your text.[4]

So, you can check the index and look for the name Bloom. Being in lexicographical order, you could go through it from the start until you catch the word you are looking for; it shouldn't be too long with Bloom. You wouldn't be that lucky with terms like hashing or, even worse, tree, which will be toward the end of the index.

That's why, naturally, we do lookups in sorted lists by subconsciously using binary search:[5] with a phone book, you open it at a random page around the middle (or closer to the beginning or end, if you have an idea where the name you are looking for might be), then look at the first letter of the first word on that page, and jump either before or after the current page depending on what you are looking for. For example, if you are still looking for Bloom, and you open a phone book to a page where the first surname is Kurtz, then you know you can discard every page after that, and look only at the pages before. You randomly open another page (to the left of the

[4] This reasoning is also the basis for the TF-IDF metric used in text search and text analysis. Short for *term frequency–inverse document frequency*, TF-IDF is computed as the ratio of raw occurrences of a term in a document (TF), over the logarithm of another fraction, the total number of documents in a *corpus* divided by the number of corpus documents in which the term appears (IDF). This means that TF-IDF will be large when a term appears often in a document but rarely in the corpus, and small when, conversely, the term is used frequently in many documents.

[5] Binary search takes its name from the fact that you always search the middle of a list, splitting it into two parts: one before the search location, and one after it. Depending on how the element you are looking for compares to the one in the search location, you then might recursively check the first half or the second half of your list (or neither, if you just found what you were looking for).

one with Kurtz) and the last name on that page is Barrow; then you know Bloom will be on a page after the one with Barrow and before the one with Kurtz.

Going back to our problem with the contact list, one approach could be sorting your contacts and searching them using binary search.

As you can see from table 4.2, in terms of running time, both the initial cost (to sort the list) and the cost for adding a new entry are pretty high. Also, linear extra memory might be needed if we need to make a copy of the original list, to preserve the original order.

Table 4.2 Using sorted arrays as dictionaries

Operation	Running time	Extra memory
`Creating the structure`	O(n*log(n))	O(n)
`Looking up an entry`	O(log(n))	No
`Add a new entry`	O(n)	No
`Remove an entry`	O(n)	No

4.4.3 Hash table: Constant-time on average, unless you need ordering

We introduced hash tables and hashing in appendix C. The main take away for hash tables is that they are used to implement associative arrays where the possible values to store come from a very large set (for instance, all possible strings or all integers), but normally we only need to store a limited number of them. If that's the case, then we use a hashing function to map the set of possible values (the *domain*, or source set) to a smaller set of `M` elements (the *codomain*, or target set), the indices of a plain array where we store the values associated to each key. (As we explained in appendix C, we get to decide how big `M` is depending on some considerations on the expected performance.) Typically, the set of values in the domain is referred to as *keys*, and the values in the codomain are indices from `0` to `M-1`.

Since the target set of a hashing function is typically smaller than the source set, there will be collisions: at least two values will be mapped to the same index. Hash tables, as we have seen in chapter 2, use a few strategies to resolve conflicts, such as *chaining* or *open addressing*.

The other important thing to keep in mind is that we distinguish hash maps and hash sets. The former allows us to associate a value[6] to a key; the latter only to record the presence or absence of a key in a set. Hash sets implement a special case of dictionary, the `Set`. With respect to our definition of dictionary as an abstract data structure, given at the beginning of this section, a *set* is a specialization of a dictionary, where the `value` type is set to `Boolean`; the second parameter to `insert` becomes redundant, as the value associated with a key in the hash set will be implicitly assumed to be `true`.

[6] Not to be confused with the index generated by the hashing function.

Abstract data structure: Set	

API	`class Set {`
	`  insert(key)`
	`  remove(key)`
	`  contains(key) → true/ false`
	`}`

Contract with client	A set maintains a set of keys. If a key K was added to the set (and not removed afterward), then `contains(K)` will return `true`; otherwise it will return `false`.

As we explain in appendix C, all operations in a hash table (and hash set) can be performed in amortized `O(1)` time.

4.4.4 Binary search tree: Every operation is logarithmic

Binary search trees (*BSTs*) are another old acquaintance of ours; we met them in chapters 2 and 3, and they are also discussed in appendix C.

A BST is a special kind of binary tree that can store keys on which it defined a total ordering: this means that for each pair of keys, it must be possible to compare them and decide which one is smaller, or if they are equal. A total ordering benefits from *reflexive, symmetric,* and *transitive* properties.

> **Ordering relations**
>
> Given a set `S` on which we defined an ordering relation ≤, this relation is a total ordering if, for any three keys `x, y, z`, the following properties hold:
>
> Reflexive: `x ≤ x`
>
> Symmetric: if `x ≤ y`, then `y ≤ x`
>
> Transitive: if `x ≤ y` and `y ≤ z` then `x ≤ z`

BSTs use these properties to make sure that the position of a key in the tree can be determined just by looking at a single path from the root to a leaf.

When we insert a new key, in fact, we compare it to the tree's root. If it's smaller, we take a left turn, traversing the root's left subtree; otherwise, we go on the right subtree. At the next step, we repeat the comparison with the subtree's root, and so on until we get to a leaf, and that's exactly the position where we need to insert the key.

If you remember what we saw in chapter 2 regarding heaps (or if you had a chance to refresh your memory, in appendix C), all operations in a BST take time proportional to the height of the tree (the longest path from root to a leaf). In particular for balanced BSTs, all operations take `O(ln(n))` time, where `n` is the number of keys added to the tree.

Of course, compared to the `O(1)` amortized running time of hash tables, even balanced BSTs don't seem like a good choice for implementing an associative array. The catch is that while their performance on the core methods is *slightly* slower, BSTs allow a substantial improvement for methods like finding the predecessor and successor `o` key, and finding minimum and maximum: they all run in `O(ln(n))` asymptotic time for BSTs, while the same operations on a hash table all require `O(n)` time.

Moreover, BSTs can return all keys (or values) stored, sorted by key, in linear time, while for hash tables you need to sort the set of keys after retrieving it, so it takes `O(M + n*ln(n))` comparisons.

Now that we have described the basic data structures most commonly used to implement dictionaries, it feels like a good time to recap what we have described so far. Table 4.3 gathers the running times of the main operations on the possible implementations of dictionaries we mentioned.

Table 4.3 Running time of operations on dictionaries for different implementations

Operation	Unsorted arrays	Sorted arrays	BST	Hash table
`Create the DS`	O(1)	O(n*log(n))	O(n*log(n))	O(n)
`Look-up an entry`	O(n)	O(log(n))	O(log(n))	O(n/M) [a]
`Add a new entry`	O(1) [a]	O(n)	O(log(n))	O(n/M) [a]
`Remove an entry`	O(1)	O(n)	O(log(n))	O(n/M) [a]
`Sorted List`	O(n*log(n)	O(n)	O(n)	O(M+n*log(n))
`Min/Max`	O(n)	O(1)	O(1) [b]	O(M+n)
`Prev/Next`	O(n)	O(1)	O(log(n))	O(M+n)

[a]Amortized time.
[b]By storing max/min separately and amortizing the time to replace them on insert/delete.

Looking at table 4.3, it's evident that if we don't have to worry about any operation that involves the order of the element, or the order they were inserted, then the amortized time of hash tables is the best. If `n~=M` (and there are approximately as many buckets as elements), then a hash table can perform insertion, removal, and look-up in amortized constant time.

4.4.5 Bloom filter: As fast as hash tables, but saves memory (with a catch)

We haven't officially met this data structure yet in the book, but there is a good chance you have already heard of *Bloom filters*. They are a data structure named after Burton Howard Bloom, who invented them in the 1970s.

There are three notable differences between hash tables and Bloom filters:

- Basic Bloom filters don't store data; they just answer the question, is a *datum* in the set? In other words, they implement a *hash set*'s API, not a *hash table's* API.
- Bloom filters require less memory in comparison to hash tables; this is the main reason for their use.
- While a negative answer is 100% accurate, there might be false positives. We will explain this in detail in a few sections. For now, just keep in mind that sometimes a Bloom filter might answer that a value was added to it when it was not.
- It is not possible to delete a value from a Bloom filter.[7]

There is a tradeoff between the accuracy of a Bloom filter and the memory it uses. The less memory, the more false positives it returns. Luckily, there is an exact formula that, given the number of values we need to store, can output the amount of memory needed to keep the rate of false positives within a certain threshold. We'll go into the details for this formula in the advanced sections toward the end of the chapter.

4.5 Under the hood: How do Bloom filters work?

Let's now delve into the details of Bloom filter implementation. A Bloom filter is made of two elements:

- An array of `m` elements
- A set of `k` hash functions

The array is (conceptually) an array of bits, each of which is initially set to `0`; each hash function outputs an index between `0` and `m-1`.

It is crucial to clarify as soon as possible that there is not a 1-to-1 correspondence between the elements of the array and the keys we add to the Bloom filter. Rather, we will use `k` bits (and so `k` array's elements) to store each entry for the Bloom filter; `k` here is typically much smaller than `m`.

Note that `k` is a constant that we pick when we create the data structure, so each and every entry we add is stored using the same amount of memory, exactly `k` bits. With string values, this is pretty amazing, because it means we can add arbitrarily long strings to our filter using a constant amount of memory, just `k` bits.

When we insert a new element key into the filter, we compute `k` indices for the array, given by the values h_0`(key)` up to $h_{(k-1)}$`(key)`, and set those bits to `1`.

When we look up an entry, we also need to compute the `k` hashes for it as described for `insert`, but this time we check the `k` bits at the indices returned by the hash functions and return `true` if and only if all bits at those positions are set to `1`.

Figure 4.3 shows both operations in action.

[7] At least not from their basic version, but we'll see that some variants have been developed to also handle element removal.

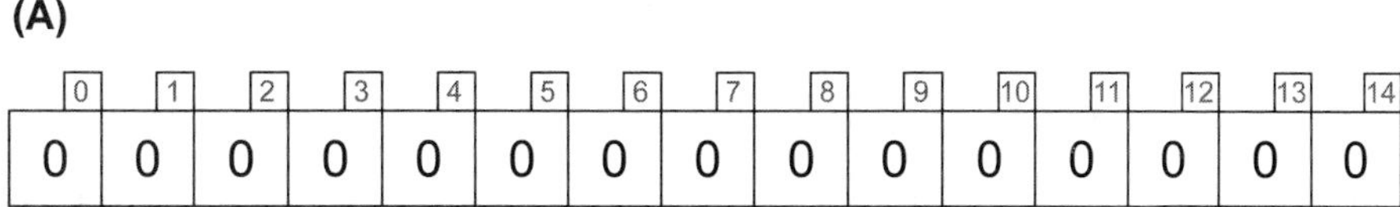
(A)
0 1 2 3 4 5 6 7 8 9 10 11 12 13 14
0 0 0 0 0 0 0 0 0 0 0 0 0 0 0

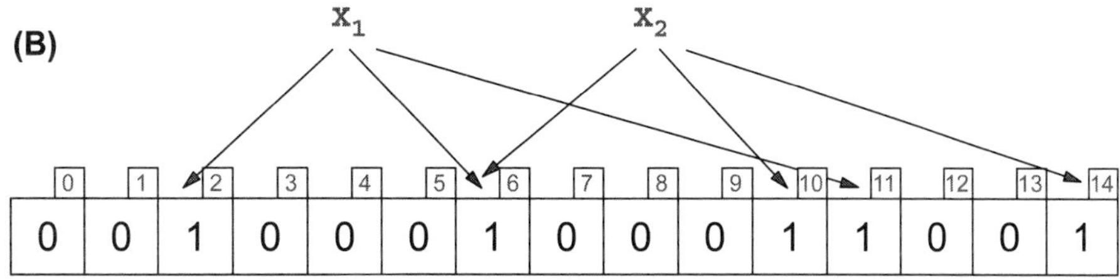
(B)
X1
X2
0 1 2 3 4 5 6 7 8 9 10 11 12 13 14
0 0 1 0 0 0 1 0 0 0 1 1 0 0 1

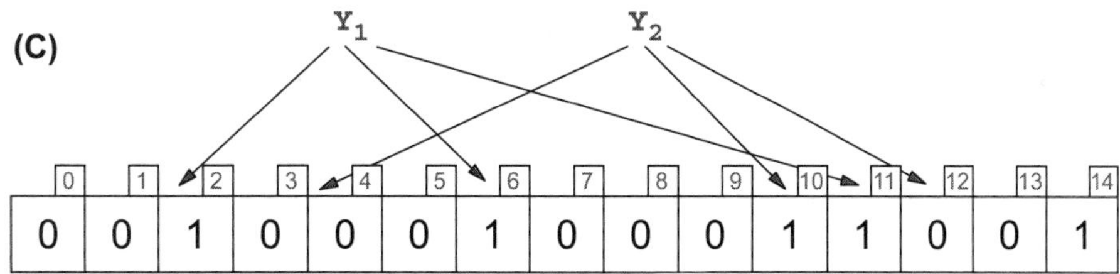
(C)
Y1
Y2
0 1 2 3 4 5 6 7 8 9 10 11 12 13 14
0 0 1 0 0 0 1 0 0 0 1 1 0 0 1

Figure 4.3 An example of a Bloom filter. (A) Initially the filter is an array of zeroes. (B) To store an item X_i, it is hashed `k` times (in the example, `k=3`), with each hash yielding the index of a bit; then these `k` bits are all set to `1`. Notice how the two triplets of indices generated by X_1 and X_2 partially overlap (they both point to the sixth element). For a more detailed example of how insertion works, see figure 4.5. (C) Likewise, to check if an element Y_i is in the set, it's hashed `k` times, obtaining just as many indices; then we read the corresponding bits, and if and only if all of them are set to `1`, we return `true`. In the bottom drawing, element Y_1 appears to be in the set (but we can't exclude that the filter is returning a false positive), while element Y_2 can't be in the set because one of the indices generated from its hashing holds a `0`. Check figure 4.4 for further insight into how lookup works.

Ideally, we would need `k` different independent hash functions, so that no two indices are duplicated for the same value. It is not easy to design a large number of independent hash functions, but we can get good approximations. There are a few solutions commonly used:

- Use a parametric hash function `H(i)`. This meta-function, which is a generator of hash functions, takes in as input an initial value `i` and outputs a hash function H_i`=H(i)`. During the Bloom filter's initialization, we can create `k` of this functions, H_0 to H_{k-1}, by calling the generator `H` on `k` different (and usually random) values.
- Use a single hash `H` function but initialize a list `L` of `k` random (and unique) values. For each entry `key` that is inserted/searched, create `k` values by adding or appending `L[i]` to `key`, and then hash them using `H`. (Remember that

well-designed hash functions will produce very different results for small changes in the input.)

- Use double or triple hashing.[8]

While the latter won't guarantee independence among the hash functions generated, it has been proven[9] that we can relax this constraint with a minimal increase in the false positive rate. To keep things simple, in our implementation we use double hashing with two independent hash functions: *Murmur hashing*[10] and *Fowler-Noll-Vo*[11] (fnv1) *hashing*.

The general format of our `i-th` hash function, for `i` between `0` and `k-1`, will be

```
hᵢ(key) = murmurhash(key) + i * fnv1(key) + i * i
```

4.6 Implementation

Enough with the theory; now it's time to once again get our hands dirty! As usual, in the next sections we'll show pseudo-code snippets and comment the key sections. Trivial methods will be omitted. On the book's repo on GitHub,[12] you can also find an implementation with the full code along with unit tests.

4.6.1 Using a Bloom filter

Back to our contacts application: How would we use a Bloom filter to make it faster? Well, as mentioned, we need to use it as a dictionary, so we are going to create a new Bloom filter when our email application starts, retrieve all the contacts from the server, and add them to the Bloom filter. Listing 4.1 summarizes this initialization process.

Listing 4.1 Starting up an email application

```
function initBloomFilter(server, minSize)
  contactsList ← server.loadContacts()
  size ← max(2 * |contactsList|, minSize)
  bloomFilter ← new BloomFilter(size)
  for contact in contactsList do
    bloomFilter.insert(contact)
  return bloomFilter
```

Method `initBloomFilter` takes an interface to a server (a façade object) and the minimum size that should be used to initialize the Bloom filter; it returns the newly created Bloom filter.

On startup, it optionally loads the list of contacts from a server that takes care of durable storage.

The size of the Bloom filter should be at least twice the current contact list's, but at least equal to `minSize`, a minimum value that can be passed as an argument.

Creates an empty Bloom filter with the right size

Cycles through the list of contacts

For each contact, adds it to the Bloom filter

---

[8] Double hashing is a technique used to resolve hash collisions (see appendix C, sections C.2.2-C.2.3). When a collision occurs, it adds an offset to the initial position computed by using a secondary hash of the key. Triple hashing computes the offset by using a linear combination of two auxiliary hash functions.

[9] Dillinger, Peter C., and Panagiotis Manolios. "Fast and accurate bitstate verification for SPIN." International SPIN Workshop on Model Checking of Software. Springer, Berlin, Heidelberg, 2004.

[10] See https://sites.google.com/site/murmurhash/.

[11] See http://www.isthe.com/chongo/tech/comp/fnv/index.html.

[12] See https://github.com/mlarocca/AlgorithmsAndDataStructuresInAction#bloom-filter.

Once we set up our directory application, we have two operations that we are mainly interested in: checking if a contact is on the list and adding a new contact to the directory.

For the former operation, shown in listing 4.2, we can check the Bloom filter, and if it says the contact has never been added, then we have our answer; the contact is not in the system. If, however, the Bloom filter returns `true`, then it might be a false positive, so we need to contact the server to double-check.

Listing 4.2 Checking an email

Method `checkContact` verifies if an email contact is stored in the application. It takes a Bloom filter, a server façade, and the contact to check. It returns `true` if `contact` is already in our contacts book.

```
function checkContact(bloomFilter, server, contact)
  if bloomFilter.contains(contact) then
    return server.contains(contact)
  else
    return false
```

Checks the Bloom filter for the contact passed to the method

If the Bloom filter returned `true`, we need to check if the server actually stores the contact, because it could be a false positive.

Otherwise, since Bloom filters don't have false negatives (but only false positives), we can return `false`.

For adding new contacts, we always have to sync to our permanent storage,[13] as shown in listing 4.3. Since this likely implies a remote connection through a network, there is a non-negligible probability that the call to the server fails; therefore, we need to handle possible failures and make sure the remote call succeeds before also updating the Bloom filter.

To be thorough, in real implementations we should also synchronize the access to the server and Bloom filter, using a locking mechanism (see chapter 7), and using a try-catch around the whole operation, rolling back (or retrying) if the call on the Bloom filter fails.

Listing 4.3 Adding a new contact

Method `addContact` adds a new contact to the system; it takes a Bloom filter and a server object, in addition to the new contact to add. It returns `true` if and only if the operation succeeds.

```
function addContact(bloomFilter, server, contact)
  if server.storeContact(contact) then
    bloomFilter.insert(contact)
    return true
  else
    return false
```

Try to add the contact to the server, and if it succeeds . . .

. . . then add it to the Bloom filter as well...

. . . and return `true`.

Otherwise, the insertion failed, so return `false`.

[13] We could, of course, check our local Bloom filter for the contact, but even when it returns `true`, without checking the server we have no way to know if it's a false positive!

4.6.2 *Reading and writing bits*

Now, let's move to the implementation of a Bloom filter, starting, as usual, with the helper methods that will give us the basic blocks to build the implementation of our API.

In particular, we need

- Some way to read and write bits at any location in our filter's buffer
- A mapping between a key in input and the bits' indices in the buffer
- A set of deterministically generated hash functions that will be used to transform keys into a list of indices

If we are using Bloom filters to save memory, it wouldn't make sense to store bits inefficiently. We will need to pack bits into the smallest integer type available in the programming language we choose; therefore, both reading and writing a bit forces us to map the index of the bit to be accessed into a couple of integers.

In modern programming languages, in fact, you can typically speed up these operations by using fixed-size numerical arrays of primitive types and vector algebra. The price to pay is that when we get a request to access the i-th bit in the filter, we need to extract two coordinates from index i: the array element that is storing the i-th bit and the offset of the bit we need to extract with respect to that element.

Listing 4.4 shows what this means and how it can be computed.

Listing 4.4 findBitCoordinates

Function findBitCoordinates is a utility method that, given the index of a bit in a bit array, returns the index of the array and the offset of the bit with respect to the array's element at that index.

```
function findBitCoordinates(index)
  byteIndex ← floor(index / BITS_PER_INT)
  bitOffset ← index mod BITS_PER_INT
  return (byteIndex, bitOffset)
```

Given the index of the bit to retrieve, we extract the byte index; that is, which element of the array buffer contains the bit to extract. BITS_PER_INT is a (system) constant whose value is the number of bits used to store an int in the programming language used (for most languages it's 32).

Extract the bit offset inside the buffer's byte. In other words, to extract the local index of the bit by performing a modulo operation, we need the rest of the division performed at line #2.

Returns the byte index and bit offset as a couple of values. Note that some programming languages allow native structures for tuples; in other languages, you can make do by returning an array with two elements.

Once we have those two indices, we can easily read or write any bit; it just becomes a matter of bitwise arithmetic. For instance, listing 4.5 shows the readBit method taking care of the reading part.

Listing 4.5 Method readBit

```
function readBit(bitsArray, index)
  (element, bit) ← findBitCoordinates(bitsArray, index)
  return (bitsArray[element] & (1 << bit)) >> bit
```

Method `readBit` extracts the index-th bit from the bits array passed as first argument. It returns the value of the bit, so either 0 or 1.

Retrieves the element index and offset for the bit in the bits array

Some bitwise algebra to return the value. First retrieve the buffer element, then put it in AND with a mask that extracts a single bit (at the right position); finally, it shifts the extracted value back so that the result will either be a 0 or a 1. We could save a left shift by preparing a constant array of `BITS_PER_INT` masks, and use `bit` as an index to decide which mask should be applied.

Listing 4.6 shows the writing counterpart, method `writeBit`. You might be surprised to see that we don't pass the value to write, but since (this version of) Bloom filter doesn't support deleting elements, we can only write a 1; we never write zeros.

Listing 4.6 Method writeBit

```
function writeBit(bitsArray, index)
  (element, bit) ← findBitCoordinates(bitsArray, index)
  bitsArray[element] ← bitsArray[element] | (1 << bit)
  return bitsArray
```

Method `writeBit` takes the bits arrays and the index of the bit where a 1 should be written; it returns the bits array after modifying it.

Retrieves the element index and offset for the bit in the bits array

Some more bitwise algebra to store the value. Put the current buffer's byte in OR with a mask having a single 1 in the position where we need to write, and then store the result back on the buffer. If the buffer already had a 1 at the index-th bit, then it won't change; otherwise, only that bit will be updated. We are assuming, here, that we only write ones, never zeroes (because our version of Bloom filter does not support the delete operation).

Let's go through an example for `readBit` and `writeBit`. Suppose we have this buffer: `B=[157, 25, 44, 204]`, with `BITS_PER_INT=8`.

We call `readBit(B, 19)`; then we have: `element==2, bit==3`.

Therefore

- `bitsArray[element]` `(evaluates to 44)`
- `(1 << bit)` `(8)`
- `bitsArray[element] & (1 << bit)` `(8)`

And the returned value will be `1`.

If, instead, we call `writeBit(B, 15)`, then we have: `(element==1, bit==7)`.

Therefore

- `bitsArray[element]` `(evaluates to 25)`
- `(1 << bit)` `(128)`
- `bitsArray[element] | (1 << bit)` `(153)`

And the buffer will be updated to `B=[157, 153, 44, 204]`.

4.6.3 Find where a key is stored

To generate all the indices for the bits used to store a key, we go through a two-step process, described in listing 4.7.

Keep in mind that our ultimate goal is to transform a string into `k` positions, between `0` and `m - 1`.

First, we use two hash functions on strings very different from each other: *murmur hashing* and *fnv1 hashing*. The chances that, for a given string, both of them produce the same result are beyond slim.

Then, for each of the `k` bits we have to store, we retrieve the corresponding hash function in our pool. For each position `i` between `0` and `k-1` we have generated (on initialization) a double hashing function h_i. The `i`-th bit will therefore be returned by $h_i(h_M, h_F)$, where h_M is the result of murmur hashing on the input key and h_F the result of fnv1 hashing.

Although the highest level of randomization would be obtained with a random seed for each run, we need to have a way to force a deterministic behavior both for tests and to recreate a Bloom filter that can make sense of a given buffer, in case the filter is serialized, or to support quick restart over failure. Therefore, we should also leave the option to pass the seed to the Bloom filter's constructor.

Listing 4.7 Method `key2Positions`

Method `key2Positions` takes an array of hash functions as input, together with a seed to initialize these functions and the key that will be hashed. It returns the set of bit indices that needs to be updated in the Bloom filter to read/write key.

```
function key2Positions(hashFunctions, seed, key)
  hM ← murmurHash32(key, seed)
  hF ← fnv1Hash32(key)
  return hashFunctions.map(h => h(hM, hF))
```

Applies murmur hashing to the key, with a given seed

Applies fnvl hashing to the key

We use a functional programming notation here. We create a lambda function taking a hash function `h` as input and applying `h` to the two values generated by murmur and fnvl hashing. Then we map this lambda function to every element of the `hashFunctions` array. This operation transforms an array of hash functions (taking two integers as arguments and producing an integer as result) into an array of integers.

4.6.4 Generating hash functions

In listing 4.7 we described how, in the `key2Positions` method, we pass an array of hash functions and use it to transform a key into a list of indices: the positions in the filter's bits array where we store the key. Now it's time to see in listing 4.8 how we initialize these `k` hash functions needed to map each key (already transformed into a string) into a set of `k` indices, pointing to the bits that will hold the information about a key (stored vs not stored).

The set of functions will be created by using double hashing to combine the two arguments in `k` different ways. With respect to linear or quadratic hashing, double hashing will increase the number of possible hashing functions that we can obtain, from O(k) to O(k²). Still, this is far from the ideal O(k!) guaranteed by uniform hashing, but in practice it is close enough to have good performance (meaning a low collision rate).

Listing 4.8 Method initHashFunctions

Method `initHashFunctions` takes the number of desired functions and the number of bits held by the Bloom filter and creates and returns a list of double hashing functions, taking two values and returning their hash.

We again use functional notation, applying a lambda function to an array. For convenience, we map from integers 0 to `numHashes-1` (included) into a list of equally many double hashing functions.

```
function initHashFunctions(numHashFunctions, numBits)
  return range(0, numHashFunctions).map(i => ((h1, h2)
  ➥ => (h1 + i * h2 + i * i) mod numBits))
```

4.6.5 Constructor

Let's move on to the public API, which will mirror the API for set that we defined in section 4.3.3. Let's start from the constructor method.

As it happens most of the times, the task for our constructor is mostly boilerplate code to set up all the internal state of a Bloom filter. In this case, however, there is also some non-trivial math to work out in order to compute the resources to allocate in order for the container to live up to the accuracy required by the client.

Listing 4.9 describes the code for a possible constructor. Notice, in particular, at lines #5 and #8 how we compute respectively the number of bits and the number of hash functions needed to have a ratio of false positives within the tolerance specified by maxTolerance (and consequently, at line #9, the number of array elements needed to store the filter). Here we assume that we use an array whose elements are integers, and BITS_PER_INT is a system variable that gives us the size, in bits, of integers. Clearly, for those languages supporting multiple numerical types, we can also choose to have arrays of bytes, when available.

Listing 4.9 Bloom filter's constructor

Signature of the constructor method. Argument `maxTolerance` has a default value of 0.01; `seed` is by default initialized to a random integer. Not all programming languages provide an explicit syntax for default values in function signatures, but there are workarounds to cope with those that don't.

Initially no element is stored in the filter, so the size is initialized to 0.

```
function BloomFilter(maxSize, maxTolerance=0.01, seed=random())
  this.size ← 0
  this.maxSize ← maxSize
  this.seed ← seed
  this.numBits ← -ceil(maxS * ln(maxTolerance) / ln(2) / ln(2))
  if numBits > MAX_SIZE then
    throw new Error("Overflow")
  this.numHashFunctions ← -ceil(ln(maxTolerance) / ln(2))
```

We store in class variables the (local) arguments for the constructor.

Computes the optimal number of bits needed: `m = - n * ln(p) / ln(2)2; ceil(x)` is the standard ceiling function returning the smallest integer larger or equal to `x`

Checks that the size will fit in memory without issues

We throw an error that can be handled by the client.

Computes the optimal number of hash functions needed. Equivalently, as we'll see, this can be written in terms of size of the array versus the maximum size of the Bloom filter as: `k = m/n * ln(2)`.

The number of elements for the (integer) buffer is computed by dividing the number of total bits needed by the number of bits per int. Notice how we use the ceiling function here.

Creates the buffer that will store the filter's bits, all initialized to 0

```
numElements ← ceil(numBits / BITS_PER_INT)
this.bitsArray ← 0 (∀ i ∈ {0, …, numElements-1})
this.hashFunctions ← initHashFunctions(numHashFunctions, maxSize)
```

Creates and stores the hash functions that will be used to get the bit indices for a key

On creation, we need to provide only the maximum number of elements that the filter will be expected to contain. If at any time we realize that we stored in the filter more than `maxSize` elements, the good news is that we won't run out of space, but the bad news is that we can no longer guarantee the expected precision.

Speaking of which, we can pass an optional second parameter to set the expected accuracy. By default, the threshold for the probability of a false positive (`maxTolerance`) is set to 1%, but we can aim for better accuracy by passing a smaller value, or settle for worse accuracy as a tradeoff for a lower amount of memory needed by passing a higher value.

The last optional parameter is needed, as explained in the previous section, to force a deterministic behavior for the filter. When omitted by the caller, a random value is generated for the seed.

After validating the arguments received (omitted in listing 4.9), we can start setting a few base fields. Then comes the trickiest part; given the number of elements and the expected precision, compute how large our buffer needs to be. We use the formula described in section 4.10, but we need to verify that the size of the buffer is still safe to be held in memory.

Once we have the size of the buffer, we can compute the optimal number of hashes needed to keep the rate of false positives as low as possible.

4.6.6 Checking a key

We can now start composing the helper methods presented so far to build the Bloom filter's API methods. One note of caution: we assume keys are going to be strings, but they can also be serializable objects. If that's the case, you will need a consistent serialization function that turns equivalent objects (for instance, two sets containing the same elements) into the same string; otherwise, no matter how good your implementation of the Bloom filter (or any other dictionary you might use) is, your application won't work properly.

> **NOTE** Data massaging and preprocessing are often as important, or more important, than the actual algorithms run on it.

With all the helper functions we already defined, checking the Bloom filter for a key becomes a piece of cake. We just need to retrieve the positions where the bits for the

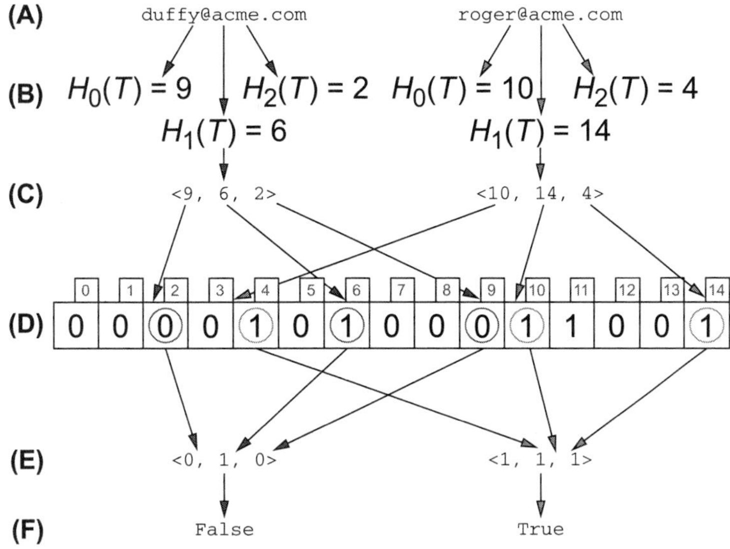
(A)
duffy@acme.com
roger@acme.com
(B)
$H_0(T) = 9$
$H_2(T) = 2$
$H_1(T) = 6$
$H_0(T) = 10$
$H_2(T) = 4$
$H_1(T) = 14$
(C)
<9, 6, 2>
<10, 14, 4>
(D)
0 1 2 3 4 5 6 7 8 9 10 11 12 13 14
0 0 0 0 1 0 1 0 0 0 1 1 0 0 1
(E)
<0, 1, 0>
<1, 1, 1>
(F)
False
True

Figure 4.4 Checking if an entry is in a Bloom filter, step by step. (A) We start with the email we would like to check, "duffy@acme.com". (B) The key (our email) is processed through our set of hash functions. In our example, we assume k=3, so we'll have three different hash functions, H_0, H_1, and H_2. (C) Each hash function produces an index for our binary array. In this case, the three indices might be, for instance, <9, 6, 2>. (D) We access the elements of the binary array at those indices. (E) The first element, at index 2, is 0. The other bits are 0 and 1 respectively. (F) Since not all the bits we checked were equal to 1, it means that "duffy@acme.com" is not stored in the Bloom filter, and we will return false. The same workflow is followed for "roger@acme.com", on the right. Because all three bits checked are set to 1, we return true: this means that "roger@acme.com" *might* have been stored in the Bloom filter, with a certain degree of confidence.

key would be stored, and check that those bits are all 1. To review the whole process, you can take a look at figure 4.4, and find the pseudo-code for the method in listing 4.10.

Listing 4.10 Method contains

Function contains takes a key and returns true if and only if all bits corresponding to the key are set to I. It is possible to pass explicitly the array of positions. Some operations on the filter require multiple accesses to a location, and this allows saving some computations. In languages allowing private methods and overloading, passing the second parameter should only be allowed for internal methods.

Checks if the array of positions has been passed. If so, avoids computing it again.

Retrieves the bit indices corresponding to current key

```
function contains(key, positions=null)
  if positions == null then
    positions ← key2Positions(this.hashFunctions, this.seed, key)
  return positions.all((i) => readBit(this.bitsArray, i) != 0)
```

Returns true if and only if all bits read are not 0. This line also uses a functional notation, with the all method that is similar to map, except it takes a predicate (a particular lambda function that returns a Boolean), applies it to every element in the list, and its result is true only if the predicate is true for all elements.

You might have noticed that in `contains` we check that the value returned by `readBit` isn't `0`. While it would technically suffice to check that the bit we read is equal to `1`, this would force us to use an extra right-shift bitwise operation. If our bit is stored in the `i`-th element of the array as its `j`-th bit (from the right), in fact, we should in theory shift the result of our bitwise extraction process `j` bits to the right, or compare it with a mask made of a single `1` shifted `j` positions to the left. This way we don't need to, and we can trim off a few milliseconds (per operation) from our implementation.

Also notice that the method takes an optional second parameter. The reason will become clear in the next section.

4.6.7 Storing a key

Storing a key is pretty similar to checking it, only we need a little extra effort to keep track of the number of elements added to the filter and to use `write` instead of `read`. Figure 4.5 shows a step-by-step example, putting together all the little pieces we have coded so far.

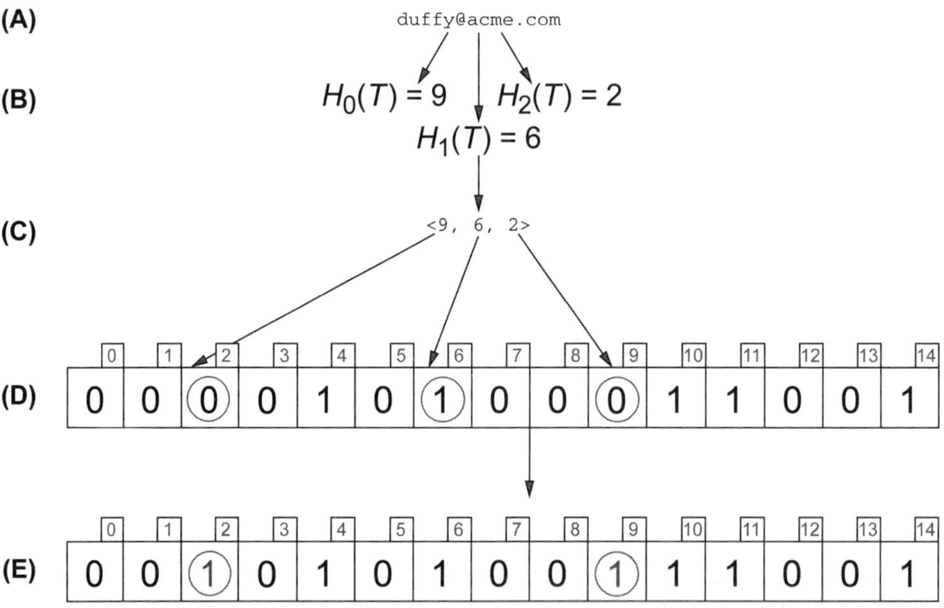
(A)
duffy@acme.com
(B)
$H_0(T) = 9$
$H_2(T) = 2$
$H_1(T) = 6$
(C)
<9, 6, 2>
(D)
0 1 2 3 4 5 6 7 8 9 10 11 12 13 14
0 0 0 0 1 0 1 0 0 0 1 1 0 0 1
(E)
0 1 2 3 4 5 6 7 8 9 10 11 12 13 14
0 0 1 0 1 0 1 0 0 1 1 1 0 0 1

Figure 4.5 Adding a new entry to a Bloom filter, step by step. (A) We start with the email we would like to store, "`duffy@acme.com`". (B) The key (our email) is processed through our set of hash functions: in our example we assume `k=3`, so we'll have three different hash functions, H_0, H_1, and H_2. (C) Each hash function produces an index for our binary array. In this case the three indices might be, for instance, `<9, 6, 2>`. Notice how these indices are the same as in figure 4.4: hash functions are deterministic, though their results might seem random. (D) We access the elements of the binary array at those indices. The first element, at index `2`, is `0`. The other bits are `0` and `1` respectively. (E) We flip the bits that were still set to `0`: (in this example, the ones at indices `2` and `9`). Now all the bits to which "`duffy@acme.com`" hashes to are set to `1`, so any future lookup will return `true`.

Note that in this implementation for `insert`, shown in listing 4.11, when we compute the size of the filter, we keep track of the number of unique elements added to the filter, rather than the total number of times the `add` method is called.

Listing 4.11 Method `insert`

```
function insert(key)
  positions ← key2Positions(key)
  if not contains(key, positions) then
    this.size ← this.size + 1
    positions.map((i) => writeBit(this.bitsArray, i));
```

Function `insert` takes a key and stores it in the Bloom filter

Transforms the string representation of the key to add into a sequence of `k` bit indices

For each index, we need to write a I in our buffer (here, using functional notation, we can leverage `map`, just ignoring its result, or use a more appropriate functional operator like `reduce` or `forEach`).

Before incrementing the size of the filter and storing I in each of the bits corresponding to the bits, we check that the key is not already contained by the filter. This is more than just optimization: `size` is crucial to estimating the filter's false positive ratio, so we need to accurately count the elements actually stored. Notice how we pass the `positions` array as a second argument to `contains`. As mentioned in the previous section, this allows us to avoid computing it again in `contains`, and to perform this expensive operation only once for each call to `insert`.

This is because the precision of the filter would not be altered by adding the same key twice, thrice, or an infinite number of times. To all extents, it would count as if the key was added once.

There is a twist, though. If we add a new unique key x for which all bits' indices clash with locations already set to `1`, it will be treated as a duplicate key and the data structure's size won't be incremented. Again, this makes perfect sense if you consider that in that situation and before actually adding the new colliding key, a call to `contains(x)` would have returned a false positive anyway.

In listing 4.11 you can see the reason why, when we wrote method `contains`, we added the possibility to pass it an array with the pre-computed bit indices for the current key. Inside `insert`, we perform a read closely followed by a write. The operation to compute all the indices for the bits of a key can be expensive, so to avoid repeating this operation twice at a short distance, we need a way to pass its result to `contains`. At the same time, we don't want to add this option to our API, since this is internal magic that clients don't need to know about. If your programming language supports polymorphism and private methods, restricting the optional parameter to a private version of `contains` (internally called by the public one) would be wise.

Another possible approach to save this duplicated effort could be having `writeBit` check whether the bit overridden was already set to `1` and return a Boolean to state if the bit's value has changed. Then `insert` could check to see if at least one bit was flipped. This alternative implementation will be provided in our repo.[14] It's up to you to decide which one you consider the cleanest.

Either way, striving to count unique keys added to the filter is going to be costly. Will the overhead be justified? That depends: if you don't expect many duplicate keys added to your filter, then it's probably not worth it. But just know that you need it to have an accurate estimate of the current probability to get a false positive.

4.6.8 Estimating accuracy

In fact, our last task is to provide a method to estimate the probability of a false positive based on the current status of the filter; that is, on the number of elements currently stored in the filter, compared to its maximum capacity.

As we will see in section 4.10, this probability is roughly[15]

$$p = \left(1 - e^{-\frac{numHashes \cdot size}{numBits}}\right)^{numHashes}$$

Listing 4.12 briefly illustrates the pseudo-code that computes this method.

Listing 4.12 Method falsePositiveProbability

```
function falsePositiveProbability()
    return pow((1 - pow(E, this.numHashes * this.size / this.numBits)),
    ➥ this.numHashes)
```

This concludes the current section about how to implement a Bloom filter. Before we delve into the theoretical part explaining the mathematical basis of this data structure, let's first review some of the many applications for Bloom filters.

4.7 Applications

I'd like to let you think about this consideration: it is pretty likely that some software you are using right now is leveraging Bloom filters. In fact, if you are reading the digital version of this book, then it's 100% sure that its download leveraged Bloom filters, because it's common for internet nodes to use them for their routing tables.[16]

4.7.1 Cache

With *caching* we refer to the process of storing some information retrieved on a fast storage system A, in order to have it ready in case we need to read it again in the near

---

[14] https://github.com/mlarocca/AlgorithmsAndDataStructuresInAction/blob/master/JavaScript/src/bloom_filter/bloom_filter.js

[15] Here e is Euler's number; we'll see it again in section 4.10.

[16] Bloom filters also are or have been used for a long time in browsers for "safe browsing," basically keeping a blacklist of malicious sites. Chromium engine, for instance, replaced it with compressed PrefixSets only a few years ago.

future. The data might have been previously retrieved from a slow(er) storage system B or be the result of a CPU-intensive computation.

For web applications, scalability is a major concern, probably the one aspect that is most debated in design reviews for any product that aspires to become viral.

One of my favorite books tackling design and scalability, *Scalability Rules* (by Martin L. Abbot and Michael T. Fisher, Addison-Wesley Professional, 2016), has a chapter titled "Use Caching Aggressively," where it is shown how caching at all levels of a web app is fundamental to allowing its scaling.

Cache is often the only thing saving databases from literally catching fire—or at least crashing. But even your laptop has several levels of caching, from fast L1-cache inside its CPU to in-memory cache used to process big files. Your very operating system caches memory pages in and out of RAM, swapping them to disk, in order to have a larger virtual address space and give you the impression that it has more memory available than is actually installed on your machine.

In other words, caches are one of the foundations of modern IT systems. Of course, since fast storage is costlier, there is only a limited amount of it, and the majority of the data will have to be left out of the cache.

The algorithm used to decide what data stays in the cache determines the behavior of the cache and the rate of cache hit (when the data searched for is already in the cache) and miss. Some of the most used algorithms are *LRU* (Least Recently Used), *MRU* (Most Recently Used), and *LFU* (Least Frequently Used). Chapter 7 gets into the details of these algorithms, but for now it is enough to note that they, as well as many other cache replacement policies, all suffer from "one-hit wonders." In other words, they struggle with objects, memory locations, or web pages requested just once, and never again (in the average lifetime of the cache). This is particularly common for routers and *Content Delivery Networks* (CDNs), where an average of 75% of the requests for a node are one-hit wonders.

Using a dictionary to keep track of requests allows us to only store an object in cache when it's requested for the second time, filtering out one-hit wonders and improving the cache *hit ratio*. Bloom filters allow performing such lookups using amortized constant time operations and with limited space, at the cost of accepting some painless false positives. For this application, the only result of false positives, however, would be a tiny reduction of the cache performance gain we get by using the Bloom filter in the first place (so, no harm done).

4.7.2 Routers

Modern routers have limited space and, with the volume of packets they process per second, they need extremely fast algorithms. They are thus the perfect recipient for Bloom filters, for all those operations that can cope with a small rate of errors.

Besides caching, routers often employ Bloom filters to keep track of forbidden IPs and to maintain statistics that will be used to reveal *DoS* (Denial of Service) attacks.[17]

[17] "Utilizing Bloom filters for detecting flooding attacks against SIP based services.", Geneiatakis, Dimitris, Nikos Vrakas, and Costas Lambrinoudakis, *Computers & Security* 28.7 (2009): 578-591.

4.7.3 Crawler

Crawlers are automated software agents scanning a network (or even the entire web) and looking for content, parsing, and indexing anything they find.

When a crawler finds links in a page or document, it is usually programmed to follow them and recursively crawl the link's destination. There are some exceptions: for instance, most file types will be ignored by crawlers, as will links created using `<a>` tags with an attribute `rel="nofollow"`.

> **TIP** It is actually recommended that you mark in this way any anchor with a link to an action having side effects. Otherwise, search engines' crawlers, even if they respect this policy, will cause unpredictable behavior.

What can happen is that if you write your own crawler and you are not careful, it might end up in an endless loop between two or more pages with mutual links (or chain of links) to each other.

To avoid such loops, crawlers need to keep track of pages they already visited. Bloom filters, again, are the best way to do so, because they can store URLs in a compact way and perform checking and saving of the URLs in constant time.

The price you pay here for false positives is a bit higher than for the previous examples, because the immediate result will be that the crawler will never visit a URL that caused a false positive.

To overcome this issue, it is possible to keep a complete list of the URLs visited in a proper dictionary (or another kind of collection) stored on disk, and if and only if the Bloom filter returns `true`, double-check the answer in the dictionary. This approach doesn't allow any space saving, but it provides some savings on the execution time if there is a high percentage of one-hit wonders among the URLs.

4.7.4 IO fetcher

Another area where Bloom filter-based caching helps is reducing the unnecessary fetching/storage of expensive IO resources. The mechanism is the same as with crawling: the operation is only performed when we have a "miss," while "hits" usually trigger a more in-depth comparison (for instance, on a hit, retrieving from disk just the first few lines or the first block of a document, and comparing them).

4.7.5 Spell checker

Simpler versions of spell checkers used to employ Bloom filters as dictionaries. For every word of the text examined, a lookup on a Bloom filter would validate the word as correct or mark it as a spelling error. Of course, the false positive occurrences would cause some spelling error to go undetected, but the odds of this happening could be controlled in advance. Today, however, spell checkers mostly take advantage of *tries*: these data structures provide good performance on text searches without the false positives.

4.7.6 *Distributed databases and file systems*

Cassandra uses Bloom filters for index scans to determine whether an SSTable has data for a particular row.

Likewise, Apache HBase uses Bloom filters as an efficient mechanism to test whether a StoreFile contains a specific row or row-col cell. This in turn boosts the overall read speed, by filtering out unnecessary disk reads of HFile blocks that don't contain a particular row or row-column.

We are at the end of our excursus on practical ways to use Bloom filters. It's worth mentioning that other applications of Bloom filters include rate limiters, blacklists, synchronization speedup, and estimating the size of joins in DBs.

4.8 *Why Bloom filters work*[18]

So far, we have asked you to take for granted that Bloom filters do work as we described. Now it's time to look more closely and explain why a Bloom filter actually works. Although this section is not strictly needed to implement or use Bloom filters, reading it might help you understand this data structure in more depth.

As already mentioned, Bloom filters are a tradeoff between memory and accuracy. If you are going to create an instance of a Bloom filter with a storage capacity of 8 bits and then try to store 1 million objects in it, chances are that you won't get great performance. On the contrary, considering a Bloom filter with an 8-bit buffer, its whole buffer would be set to `1` after approximately 10-20 hashes. At that point, all calls to `contains` will just return `true`, and you will not be able to understand whether or not an object was actually stored in the container. Figure 4.6 shows an example of such a situation.

If, instead, we allocate sufficient space and choose our hash functions well, then the indices generated for each key won't clash, and for any two different keys the overlap between the lists of indices generated will be minimal, if any.

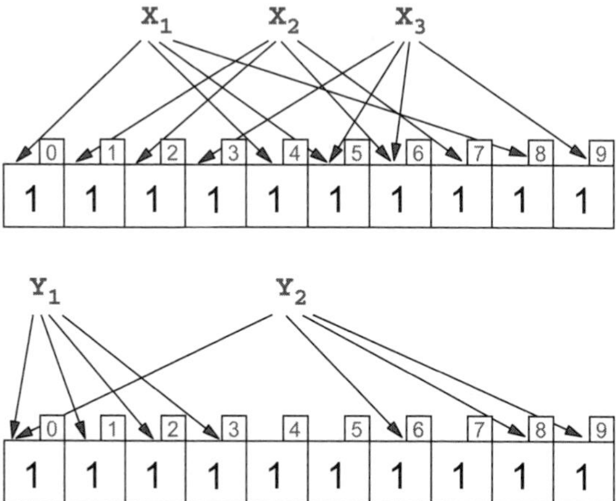
X1
X2
X3
0 1 2 3 4 5 6 7 8 9
1 1 1 1 1 1 1 1 1 1
Y1
Y2
0 1 2 3 4 5 6 7 8 9
1 1 1 1 1 1 1 1 1 1

Figure 4.6 Bloom filter saturation. In the example, `m=10`, so the bloom filter has 10 bits, and `k=4`, so each element is stored with 4 bits. We can saturate the filter by adding three elements, setting all bits to 1. Then even if we look up Y_1 and Y_2, which were not added to the filter, we still get a false positive. Although the example is an extremization (with `k` unrealistically too large for the value of `m`), it illustrates the mechanism that leads to saturation or to degraded precision.

[18] This section, as well as the following ones, are theory-intensive and feature advanced concepts.

But how much space is sufficient? Internally a Bloom filter translates each key into a sequence of k indices chosen out of m possible alternatives:[19] the trick is that we store keys efficiently by flipping these k bits in the filter's buffer, a bit-array.

If you have brushed up on your school algebra recently, you might have guessed that we can only represent m^k different sequences of k elements drawn from m values; we need, however, to make two considerations:

1. We actually can't even use all these sequences. We would like all indices associated to a key to be different (otherwise, we would actually store less than k bits per key), so we strive for all lists of k indices to be duplicate-free.
2. We are not really interested in the order of these k indices. It's completely irrelevant if we first write the bit at index 0 and then the bit at index 3, or vice versa. We can thus consider sets instead of sequences.

All considered, we only (at least in theory) allow a fraction of all the possible sets of exactly k (distinct) indices drawn from the range 0..m-1, and the number of all these possible (valid) sets is given by

$$\binom{m}{k} = \frac{m!}{k! \cdot (m-k)!}$$

The binomial coefficient[20] in this formula expresses the number of ways we can extract k (unique) elements from a set of size m, and hence it tells us how many sets with exactly k distinct indices our k hash functions can return.

If we want each key to map to a different set of k indices, then given k and n, the number of keys to store, we can compute a lower bound for m, the size of the buffer, by using the formula above.

Another way to look at the question is that given a sequence of m bits (the buffer), we can only represent 2^m different values, so at a given time the Bloom filter can only be in one of 2^m possible states; however, this only gives us a loose (although easier to compute) bound on n, because we would not take into consideration that we will store k bits per key (2^m becomes an exact bound only for k==1).

We'll see in section 4.10 how to choose the number of hash functions and the size of the array in order to optimize the ratio of false positives for a Bloom filter capable of storing a given number of keys.

4.8.1 *Why there are no false negatives . . .*

In the simplest version of Bloom filters, deletion is not allowed. This means that if a bit is flipped when a key is stored, it will never ever be set to 0 again.

At the same time, the output of the hash functions is deterministic and constant in time.

---

[19]Assuming m is the size of the filter's buffer.

[20]m *choose* k is a binomial coefficient; see https://en.wikipedia.org/wiki/Binomial_coefficient.

TIP Remember to pay attention and abide by these properties in your implementation if you need to serialize Bloom filters and deserialize them later.

So, if a lookup finds out that one of the bits associated with a key `X` is set to `0`, then we know for sure that `X` was never added to the filter; otherwise, all the bits to which `X` is hashed would be `1`.

4.8.2 . . . But there are false positives

The reverse, though, doesn't hold up, unfortunately! An example will help you understand why. Suppose we have a simple Bloom filter with 4 bits and 2 hash functions. Initially our buffer is empty:

```
B = [0, 0, 0, 0]
```

First, we insert the value `1` into the Bloom filter. Assume we had chosen our hash functions such that h_0`(1) = 0` and h_1`(1) = 2`, so the key `1` maps to indices `{0,2}`. After updating it, our buffer now looks like this:

```
B = [1, 0, 1, 0]
```

Now we insert the value `2`, and it turns out that h_0`(2) = 1` and h_1`(2) = 2`. Therefore, we now have:

```
B = [1, 1, 1, 0]
```

Finally, suppose that h_0`(3) = 1` and h_1`(3) = 0`. If we perform a lookup for the value `3` after those two insertions, both bits at indices `1` and `0` will have been set to `1` even if we never stored `3` in our instance of the filter! Therefore, `3` would give us a false positive.

On the other hand, if we had a different mapping from the hash functions, for instance, h_0`(3) = 3` and h_1`(3) = 0`, since the fourth bit hadn't been set yet `(B[0]==0)`, a lookup would have returned `false`.

Of course, this is a simplistic example intentionally crafted to prove a point: false positives are possible, and they are more likely to happen if we don't choose the parameters of our Bloom filter carefully. In section 4.10, we'll learn how to tune these parameters, based on the number of elements we anticipate we will store and on the precision we need.

4.8.3 Bloom filters as randomized algorithms

Appendix F introduces the taxonomy of randomized algorithms, and in particular the dichotomy between *Las Vegas* and *Monte Carlo* algorithms.

If you don't have a clear idea of the difference between these two classes or what randomized algorithms are, this would be a good time to check appendix F.

Once those definitions are clear to you, it should not be hard to make an educated guess: Which category do our Bloom filters belong to?

As you might have already figured out, Bloom filters are an example of a Monte Carlo data structure. Method `contains`, the algorithm that checks if a key is stored in a Bloom filter, in particular, is a *false-biased* algorithm. In fact, it might return `true` for some keys never added to the filter, but it always correctly returns `true` when a key was previously added, so there are no false-negatives (that is, every time it answers `false`, we are sure the answer is correct).

> **NOTE** Bloom filters are also a tradeoff between memory and accuracy. The deterministic version of a Bloom filter is a *hash set.*

4.9 Performance analysis

Before starting on Bloom filter analysis, I suggest a deep dive into metrics for classification algorithms in appendix F.

We have seen how and why Bloom filters work; now let's see how efficient they are. First, we'll examine the running time for the most important operations provided by a Bloom filter. Next, in section 4.10, we will tackle the challenge of predicting the precision of method `contains`, given a Bloom filter with a certain structure (in particular, its size and the number of hash functions used will matter).

4.9.1 Running time

We have already hinted at the fact that Bloom filters can store and look up a key in constant time. Technically, this is only true for constant-length inputs; here we will examine the most generic case, when keys stored are strings of arbitrary length.[21]

But let's start from the beginning: the very construction of a Bloom filter. Afterwards we'll examine in detail `insert` and `contains`.

4.9.2 Constructor

Construction of a Bloom filter is pretty easy; we just have to initialize an array of bits, with all its elements set to `0`, and generate the set of `k` hash functions. We have seen that the implementation also involves some computation, but it's safe to mark that part as constant time.

Creating and initializing the array requires, obviously, `O(m)` time, while generating each of the hash functions typically requires constant time; hence `O(k)` time overall is needed to generate the whole set.

The whole construction can be ultimately finished in `O(m+k)` steps.

4.9.3 Storing an element

For each key to store, we need to produce `k` hash values, and flip a bit in each of the elements of the array indexed by those results.

We'll make the following assumptions:

[21] Any object or value can be serialized to a string (for instance, a binary string).

- Storing a single bit requires constant time (possibly including the time needed for bitwise operations in case we use compressed buffers to save space).
- Hashing a key `X` requires `T(X)` time.
- The number of bits used to store a key doesn't depend on the key's size, or on the number of elements already added to the container.

Given these assumptions, the running time for `insert(X)` is `O(k*T(|X|))`. For each of the `k` hash functions we need, in fact, to generate a hash value from the key and store a single bit. If keys are numbers—for instance, integers or doubles—then `|X|=1` and `T(|X|) = O(1)`, meaning that we can typically generate a hash value in constant time.

If, however, our keys are of variable length—for example, strings—then computing each hash value requires linear time in the length of the string. In this case, `T(|X|) = O(|X|)`, and the running time will depend on the length of the keys we add.

Now, suppose we know that the longest key will have at most `z` characters, where `z` is a constant. Remembering our assumption about the length of keys being independent of anything else, we can then still argue that running time for `insert(X)` is `O(k*(1+z)) = O(k)`. Thus, this is a constant time operation, no matter how many elements have been already added to the container.

4.9.4 *Looking up an element*

The same considerations hold true for the lookup of a key: we need to transform keys into a set of indices (done in time `O(z*k)`), and then check each bit at those indices (`O(k)` time for all of them). So, lookup is also a constant time operation, under the assumption that keys' lengths are bounded by a constant.

4.10 *Estimating Bloom filter precision*[22]

Before we start, we need to fix some notations and make a few more assumptions:

- `m` is the number of bits in our array.
- `k` is the number of hash functions we use to map a key to `k` different positions in the array.
- Each of the `k` hash functions we use is independent from the others.
- The pool of hash functions from which we extract our `k` functions is a universal hashing set.

If these assumptions hold, then it can be proven that a good approximation for the false positive probability after `n` insertions is given by

$$p(n, m, k) = \left(1 - e^{-\frac{k \cdot n}{m}}\right)^k$$

where `e` is Euler's number, the base of natural logarithms.

[22]This section includes advanced, math-intensive content.

Now we have a formula to estimate the probability of a false positive! That's nice per se, but what's even better is that it allows us to tune `m` and `k`, our Bloom filter parameters. This way we can decide the size of the Bloom filter's buffer and the number of hash functions needed to have optimal precision.

There are three variables in the formula for `p(n, m, k)`:

- `m`, the number of bits in the buffer
- `n`, the number of elements that will be stored in the container
- `k`, the number of hash functions

Of those three, `k` is the one that seems less meaningful to us. Or, from another point of view, it is the one less coupled with our problem. In fact, `n` is probably going to be a variable that can we can estimate, but we can't fully control. We might need to store as many elements as we get requests for, but most of the time we can anticipate the volume of requests and make estimates pessimistic, to be on the safe side.

We might be limited in the choice of `m` as well, since we could have memory constraints; maybe we can't use more than `m` bits.

For `k`, instead, we have no constraint on it, and we can tune it to get optimal precision, meaning, as we explained in appendix F, minimal probability of false positives.

Luckily finding the optimal value for `k`, given `m` and `n`, isn't even that hard—it's just a matter of finding the minimum for the function:

$$f(k) = \left(1 - e^{-\frac{k \cdot n}{m}}\right)^k$$

Note that `n` and `m` are constants in the formula.

We will go into the details of finding the minimum for `f(k)` in the next section; for now (or if you are more interested in the result), just know that the optimal value is

$$k^* = \frac{m}{n} \cdot \ln(2)$$

Now that we have a formula for `k*`, we can substitute it in our previous formula, the one for `p(n, m, k)`, and after a some algebraic manipulation, we obtain an expression for the optimal value for `m` (let's call it `m*`):

$$m^* = -n \cdot \frac{ln(p)}{ln(2)^2}$$

This means that if we know in advance the total number `n` of unique elements that we will insert in the container, and we set the probability `p` of a false positive to the largest value that is acceptable, then we can compute the optimal size of the buffer (and the number of bits per key we need to use) in order to guarantee the desired precision.

Two aspects are significant when looking at the formulas we derived:

- The size of the Bloom filter's buffer is proportional to the number of elements being inserted.
- At the same time, the required number of hash functions only depends on the target false positive probability p (you can see this by substituting m^* into the formula for k^*, but don't worry, we'll discuss the math in the next section).

4.10.1 Explanation of the false-positive ratio formula

In this section we'll explain in more detail how the formulas to estimate a Bloom filter's precision are derived; first, let's see how we obtain the estimate for the false probability ratio.

After a single bit has been stored in a Bloom filter with a capacity of m bits, the probability that a specific bit is set to 1 is 1/m; then the probability that the same bit is set to 0 after all k bits used to store an element have been flipped (assuming the hash functions will always output k different values for the same input[23]) is therefore

$$\left(1 - \frac{1}{m}\right)^k$$

If we consider the events of flipping any specific bit to 1 as independent events, then after inserting n elements, for each individual bit in the buffer the probability that the bit is still 0 is given by

$$p_{bit} = \left(1 - \frac{1}{m}\right)^{k \cdot n} \approx e^{-\frac{k \cdot n}{m}}$$

To have a false positive, all the k bits corresponding to an element V must have been set to 1 independently, and the probability that all of those k bits are 1 is given by

$$p(n, m, k) = (1 - p_{bit})^k = \left(1 - \left(1 - \frac{1}{m}\right)^{k \cdot n}\right)^k \approx \left(1 - e^{-\frac{k \cdot n}{m}}\right)^k$$

Which is, lo and behold, the probability formula we gave at the beginning of this section.

At this stage, as we mentioned in the last section, we can consider n and m as constants. It makes sense because in many cases we know how many elements we need to add to the Bloom filter (n) and how many bits of storage we can afford (m); what we would like to do is trade performance for accuracy by tuning k, the number of (universal) hash functions we use.

---

[23]In other words, as we have seen in the previous sections, we assume the hash functions are drawn from a set of universal hash functions.

This is equivalent to finding the global minimum of function `f`, defined as

$$f(k) = \left(1 - e^{-\frac{k \cdot n}{m}}\right)^k$$

If you know some calculus, you probably have already guessed that we need to compute the derivatives of `f` with respect to `k`. (If you don't know calculus, don't worry; you can skip the next few lines and resume on the next page, where we will be using the result of this computation.)

To make our job easier, we can rewrite `f` by applying natural logarithm and exponentiation,[24] so that we get

$$f(k) = \left(1 - e^{-\frac{k \cdot n}{m}}\right)^k = e^{k \cdot \ln\left(1 - e^{-\frac{k \cdot n}{m}}\right)}$$

This function is minimal when its exponent is minimal, so we can define function `g`

$$g(k) = k \cdot \ln\left(1 - e^{-\frac{k \cdot n}{m}}\right)$$

and compute the derivatives of `g` instead, which is easier to work with.

The first order derivative of `g(k)` is

$$g'(k) = \frac{\partial g}{\partial k} = \ln\left(1 - e^{-\frac{k \cdot n}{m}}\right) + \frac{k \cdot n}{m} \cdot \frac{-e^{-\frac{k \cdot n}{m}}}{1 - e^{-\frac{k \cdot n}{m}}}$$

and it becomes equal to `0` for `k=ln(2)*m/n`.

To make sure this is a minimum for the function, we still need to compute the second order derivative and check that it returns a negative value when computed on the *zero* of `g'`:

$$g''\left(\ln(2) \cdot \frac{m}{n}\right) < 0$$

We'll skip this step for the sake of space, but you can double check that it's indeed true.

It's worth noting that

- The formula for `k` gives us a single, exact value for the optimal choice of the number of hash functions.
- `k` must obviously be an integer, so the result needs to be rounded.

[24] e^x and `ln(x)` are inverse functions, so that for `x>0`, `ln(e^x) = e^ln(x) = x`; that holds true even if `x` is a function (as long as it's always positive).

- Larger values for `k` mean worst performance for insert and lookup (because more hash functions need to be computed for each element), so a compromise with slightly smaller values of `k` can be preferred.

If we use the best value for `k` as computed previously, this means that the rate of false positives `f` becomes

$$f = \left(\frac{1}{2}\right)^k = (0.6185)^{\frac{m}{n}}$$

By replacing the value `k` in the formula for `p(n,m,k)`, we can get a new formula that links the number of storage bits to the (maximum) number of elements that can be stored, independently of `k` (the value for `k` can be computed later) to guarantee a false-positive probability smaller than a certain value `p`:

$$p = p(n, m) = \left(1 - e^{-\left(\frac{m}{n} \cdot \ln(2) \cdot \frac{n}{m}\right)}\right)^{\frac{m}{n} \cdot \ln(2)} = (1 - e^{-\ln(2)})^{\frac{m}{n} \cdot \ln(2)} = \left(\frac{1}{2}\right)^{\frac{m}{n} \cdot \ln(2)}$$

Taking the base 2 logarithm of both sides

$$\log_2(p) = \log_2\left[\left(\frac{1}{2}\right)^{\frac{m}{n} \cdot \ln(2)}\right] = -\frac{m}{n} \cdot \ln(2)$$

and then solving for `m` finally gives us

$$m^* = -n \cdot \frac{\log_2(p)}{\ln(2)} = -n \cdot \frac{\ln(p)}{\ln(2)^2}$$

This means that if we know in advance the total number `n` of unique elements that we will insert in the Bloom filter, and we set the false positive probability `p` to the largest value that is acceptable, then we can compute the optimal size of the buffer that guarantees the desired precision. We will also have to set `k` accordingly, using the formula we derived for it:

$$k^* = \ln(2) \cdot \frac{m^*}{n} = -\ln(2) \cdot n \cdot \frac{\ln(p)}{\ln(2)^2} \cdot \frac{1}{n} = -\frac{\ln(p)}{\ln(2)}$$

For instance, if we would like to have a precision of 90%, and so at most 10% false positives, we can plug in the numbers and get

$$k = -\frac{\ln(0.1)}{\ln(2)} = -\frac{-2{,}3025}{0{,}6931} = 3{,}32$$

$$m = -n \cdot \frac{\ln(p)}{\ln(2)^2} = 4{,}792 \cdot n$$

4.11 Improved variants

Bloom filters have been around for almost 50 years, so it's natural that many variations and improvements have been proposed in the meantime. Let's examine some of them, with a focus on those that improve accuracy.

4.11.1 Bloomier filter

As we hinted at, Bloom filters corresponds to faster, lighter versions of HashSets, since they can only store whether a key is present/absent.

The leaner counterpart of HashTables has been introduced only recently: *Bloomier filters*[25] allow associating values to keys. When the key/value pair has actually been stored in the Bloomier filter, then the value returned is always correct. There are still false positives; that is, keys that were not actually stored in the data structure but for which a value is returned.

4.11.2 Combining Bloom filters

By storing the same key in two or more different Bloom filters, possibly with different buffer sizes, but most importantly with a different set of hash functions for each one, we can arbitrarily lower the probability of false positives.

Of course, this is not for free, so the space needed grows proportionally, and the time needed to store or check for a key in theory would double as well.

At least for the running time, though, there is a silver lining: each of the component filters can actually be queried in parallel on a multicore hardware! So, besides maintaining the `O(k)` constant time bound, even actual implementations could possibly be as fast as regular Bloom filters (in other words, the constant factor remains approximately the same).

The way this structure works is the following: for `insert`, each of the components stores the key independently. For calls to `contains`, the answer is the combination of all answers: `true` is returned only if all the components return `true`.

What's the accuracy of such an array of filters? It can be proven that the precision of a single Bloom filter using `m` bits is the same as the precision of `j` Bloom filters using `m/j` bits each.

However, when using a parallel version of the ensemble algorithm, the running time can be just a fraction of the original one, `1/j`.

4.11.3 Layered Bloom filter

A layered Bloom filter[26] (*LBF*) also uses multiple Bloom filters, but organized in layers. Each layer is updated for a key only after the previous layer has already stored the same

[25]Chazelle, Bernard; Kilian, Joe; Rubinfeld, Ronitt; Tal, Ayellet (2004), "The Bloomier filter: An efficient data structure for static support lookup tables," Proceedings of the Fifteenth Annual ACM-SIAM Symposium on Discrete Algorithms (PDF), pp. 30–39.

[26]Zhiwang, Cen; Jungang, Xu; Jian, Sun (2010), "A multi-layer Bloom filter for duplicated URL detection", Proc. 3rd International Conference on Advanced Computer Theory and Engineering (ICACTE 2010), 1, pp. V1–586–V1–591, doi:10.1109/ICACTE.2010.5578947

key. Layered Bloom filters are normally used to implement a counting filter: an LBF with `R` levels can count up to `R` insertions of the same key. Often deletion is also supported.

Each call to `contains` starts by checking the layers, from the closest to the deepest, and returns the index of the last layer where the key was found, or `-1` (or, equivalently, `false`) if the key is not stored in the first layer.

When storing a key, the `insert` method stores it in the first layer for which `contains` returns `false`.

Assuming that each layer has a false-positive ratio equal to P_F, and that all layers use different sets of hash functions, then if an element has been stored `c` times on the filter

- The probability that `contains` returns `c+1`, a counter 1 unit larger than the real number of times a key was stored, is approximately P_F.
- The probability of returning `c+2` is P_F^2.
- Similarly, for `c+d`, the probability becomes P_F^d.

Those, however, are approximate (optimistic) estimates, because the assumptions about the universality and independence of the hash functions are hard to guarantee. To compute the exact probabilities, we would need to take into account the depth and the number of layers.

On an LBF with `L` layers, each using `k` bits per key, the running time for both `insert` and `contains` becomes `O(L*k)`, but since both `L` and `k` are predetermined constants, it's still equivalent to `O(1)` and independent of the number of items added to the container.

4.11.4 Compressed Bloom filter

When used in web caches, the main issue with Bloom filters is not with the RAM they use, but rather, since these filters need to be transferred between proxies, it's the size of data transmitted on the network.

While at first you might think that's a moot point, if we plan to compress the Bloom filters before transmitting them through a network, then it does actually have practical relevance. It turns out we can optimize the values of the filter's parameters, which in turn regulate the size of the bit array, and as a result get a larger uncompressed Bloom filter that could be compressed more efficiently.

That's the idea behind compressed Bloom filters,[27] where the number of hash functions `k` is chosen in such a way that the number of bits with value `1` in the bits array is kept below `m/3`, where `m` is the size of the array. As a consequence, at least `2/3` of the buffer's bits will always be set to `0`, and we can take advantage of this fact to compress the bit array more efficiently.

Each proxy would then have to decompress the Bloom filter before looking up elements. Clearly now we have another target to optimize. We need to find a compromise between the uncompressed size of the bits array, `m`, and its compressed size, which we want to keep as small as possible.

---

[27] Mitzenmacher, Michael. "Compressed Bloom filters." IEEE/ACM Transactions on Networking (TON) 10.5 (2002): 604-612.

The uncompressed size, in fact, determines the running time of lookups (through the formulas we developed in section 4.10), while the compressed size determines the transfer ratio.

Since router tables will be updated periodically, decompressing the whole filter could be a heavy overhead for nodes. A good compromise is breaking the filter into pieces and compressing each piece independently. This makes the overall compression rates slightly worse, but when updates are frequent (compared to lookups), it reduces the overhead for decompression even more, since each proxy, between two updates, won't decompress the whole bits array, but only the chunks it needs.

4.11.5 Scalable Bloom filter

A scalable Bloom filter is yet another combination of several Bloom filters, working similarly to a layered Bloom filter. Only this time the different layers have increasing capacity (and hence smaller false positives ratio). This allows the container to adapt dynamically to the number of elements stored and keeps the probability of false positives low.

Summary

- We can choose the best abstract data structure (ADT) to perform certain operations, but we can also choose among different implementations, or concrete data structures (CDT) of an ADT, and that choice also makes a difference.
- Many common problems in computer science revolve around keeping track of values. It might be URLs browsed by a crawler, documents examined by an indexer, or values to store in a cache, just to name a few.
- Depending on the context, there are different additional constraints for the implementation of a *set* that we might want to use.
- Randomized algorithms are a subset of algorithms whose execution might depend on randomization, and therefore running a randomized algorithm twice on the same input does not always return the same result.
- Randomized algorithms are divided into Monte Carlo and Las Vegas algorithms, depending on where the uncertainty lies.
- For Bloom filters, we use the *precision metric* to estimate the ratio of false positives.
- If we know in advance the maximum number of items that will be stored in a Bloom filter at the same time, we have an exact formula for computing the total amount of memory needed to achieve an arbitrarily low ratio of false positives.

5 Disjoint sets: Sub-linear time processing

This chapter covers

- Solving the problem of keeping a set partitioned into disjoint sets and merging partitions dynamically
- Describing an API for a data structure for disjoint sets
- Providing a simple linear-time solution for all methods
- Improving the running time by using the right underlying data structure
- Adding easy-to-implement heuristics to get quasi-constant running time
- Recognizing use cases where the best solution is needed for performance

In this chapter we are going to introduce a problem that seems quite trivial—so trivial that many developers wouldn't even consider it worth a performance analysis, so they'd just implement the obvious solution to it. Nevertheless, if the expression "wolf in sheep's clothing" was applied to data structures, this would be the best heading for this chapter.

We will use a disjoint set every time that we would like to account for the partitioning of an initial set of objects into disjoint groups (that is, subsets without any element in common between them). For instance, we might start with a list of wines, which would be the initial set, and partition those wines depending on their flavor, creating a disjoint set where wines with a similar flavor are grouped together, and groups have no intersections with each other. Or we could group foods based on their nature and properties, grouping vegetables, fruit, processed food, and so on. This would be a trivial example of a disjoint set, shown in figure 5.1.

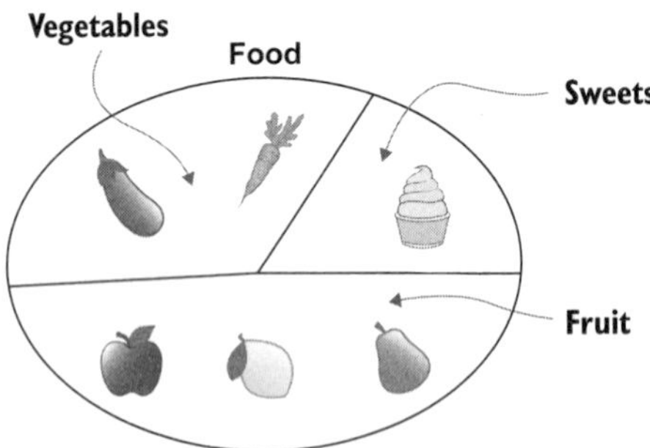
Vegetables
Food
Sweets
Fruit

Figure 5.1 An example of a disjoint set. The whole set, the so-called Universe, is the set of "Food." Three partitions are shown: Fruit, Vegetables, and Sweets. The key point is that these subsets have no intersections with each other.

We will tackle this problem starting with its definition, then cover the most basic (and naïve) algorithms, to give readers an understanding of what an actual solution looks like. Once that's clear, we will be ready to delve into making our solutions more efficient, and show how to use them as part of more complex algorithms. By the end of the chapter you will be able to code the best possible solution for disjoint sets and employ it to improve the performance of higher-level applications.

5.1 The distinct subsets problem

For instance, imagine this: you are running a new, recently created, e-commerce website, and for your launch, you'd like to provide non-personalized recommendations to your users. If it helps you feel like this is a real situation, you might imagine owning a time-machine and being back in 1999. Or more realistically, you can think about opening a geographically localized website with stronger ties to your country's retailers; or maybe you open a specialized retail website focusing on niche products. Either way, this can be a very interesting exercise.

So, non-personalized recommendations, we were saying. You might ask what that's about. Allow me to take a short detour to explain this: personalized recommendations are targeted on individual customers, based on the data we have about them (past purchases or metadata that shows similarity with other users). But sometimes we don't have this data at all: for instance, when we start a new website, or even when we get a new customer about which we know nothing at all. That's why many websites, such as

Twitter, Pinterest, Netflix, and MovieLens, ask you questions on sign-up to understand your tastes and be able to provide some rough personalized recommendations based on users with similar profiles.

Non-personalized recommendations, on the other hand, are not targeted to you, the customer, and are the same for all customers. They might be hardcoded associations, if you have no data at all, or based on purchases made by all other customers, for example.

And that's exactly what we are going to do: whenever customers add something to their cart, we would like to provide them with a recommendation about something else they might want to buy along with it. Our goal is finding products that are frequently bought together; sometimes we are going to find reasonable associations, such as milk and bread bought together. Other times, the result might be more surprising: you probably have already heard about the research performed at Walmart linking the purchase of diapers and beer, since it's one of the most quoted data science anecdotes.

Figure 5.2 illustrates what we would like to achieve. Initially, since we have no data at all, we consider every product as a group of its own, or if you prefer, no two products will have an association.

When customers frequently buy two products together, we then establish a link between them, considering both to be part of the same group. To keep things simple, imagine that the rule set by the data science team is that if item `X` and item `Y` are bought together more than a fixed threshold during the last hour, then their two categories are merged.

For instance, it might be that if, during the last hour, phones and tablets are bought together more than 500 times (or for more than 1% of total purchases), then they should be in the same group, so we merge their groups.

Then if a customer buys a product `X`, we can suggest to them a random item from the same group.

This process described is pretty common in data science. Some of you might have recognized that it's nothing less than hierarchical clustering. If that doesn't ring a bell, do not worry; we will expand on clustering in section 5.7.3.

This is, obviously, an extreme simplification. In a real non-personalized recommender system, we would track associations between products, measuring the strength of the link as the confidence that when `X` is bought, `Y` is also. For that, we may compute the number of purchases where both appear, divided by the total number of purchases where at least `Y` appears. That would give us better insight about what goes with what, we could define a threshold on the confidence for merging groups, and instead of picking a random item in the same group, show the top five strongest associations.

Nevertheless, clustering items in groups will probably be a smart move, because it will help performance, allowing us to run some algorithms on each group of items separately rather than on the whole catalog.

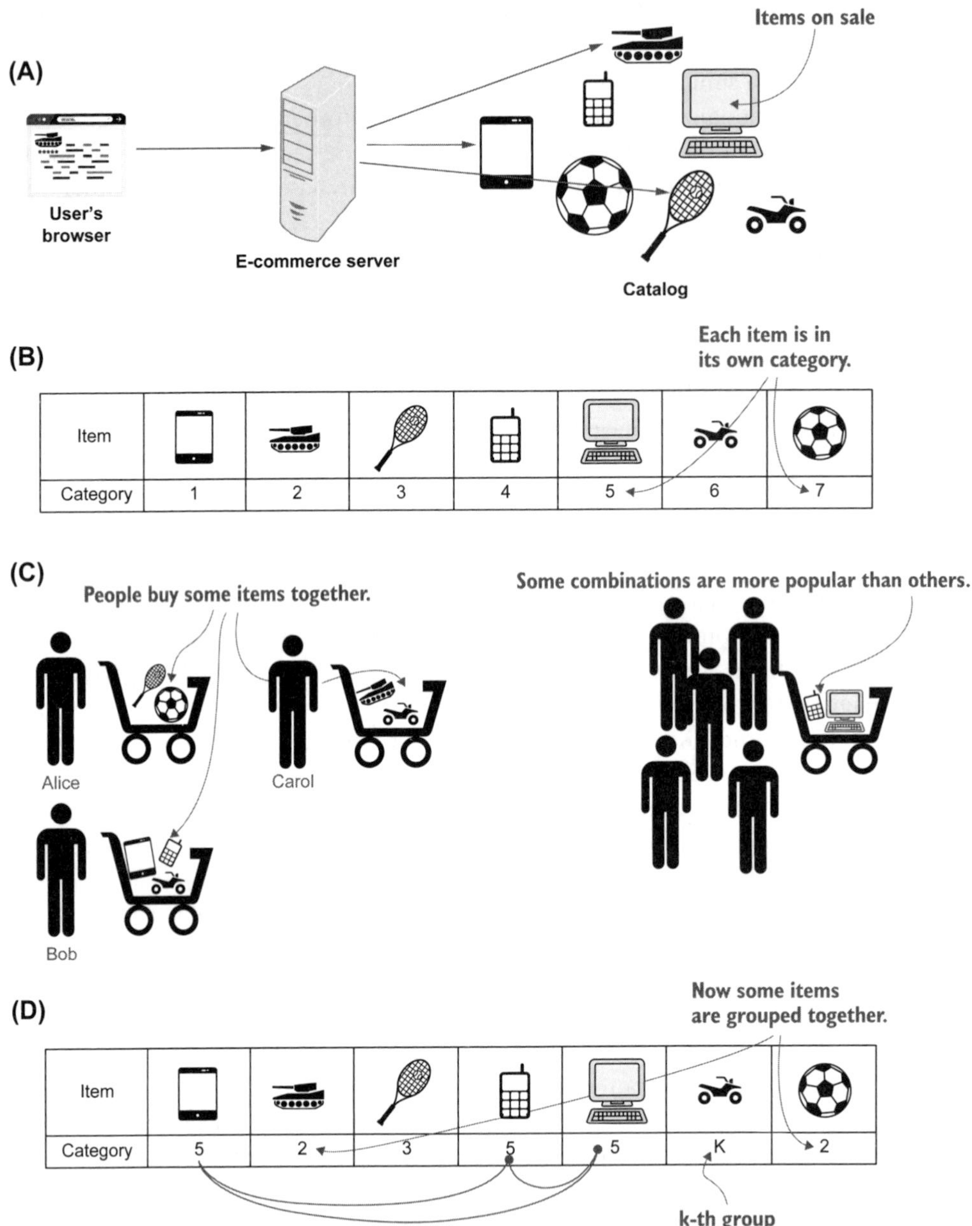

(A)
Items on sale
User's browser
E-commerce server
Catalog
(B)
Each item is in its own category.
Item
Category
1
2
3
4
5
6
7
(C)
People buy some items together.
Some combinations are more popular than others.
Alice
Carol
Bob
(D)
Now some items are grouped together.
Item
Category
5
2
3
5
5
K
2
k-th group

Figure 5.2 An example of an application of a disjoint set. (A) In this scenario, an e-commerce website is trying to understand what products sell well together in order to provide better recommendations to its customers. (B) Initially, each item on sale is in a different category. (This would also work if we started from already predefined categories, such as SSD disks or blenders, and grouped categories of objects selling together. But for the sake of simplicity, bear with me and imagine there is only one product of each category on sale.) (C) Items frequently bought together, such as laptops and external disks, or tennis rackets and tennis balls, are grouped together. (D) After a while, things tend to stabilize and steady groups are formed. Now, the next time a customer adds a football to her cart, we can suggest a pair of skis as a follow-up purchase.

If you are interested in knowing more about non-personalized (and personalized) recommender systems, we suggest you look at *Practical Recommender Systems* (by Kim Falk, Manning Publications, 2019), a fine and thorough guide to the topic.

Back to our example: the gist is that we would need to start from this huge set of items and partition them into disjoint groups. And of course, new items are added to the catalog all the time, and relations are dynamic, so we would need to be able to update both the list of items and the groups.

5.2 Reasoning on solutions

In this and the following sections, we will mainly use the term *partition* to refer to disjoint groups. However, *group* and *set* can also appear as synonyms.

We will also restrict to the aggregative case; in other words, two partitions can be merged in a single, bigger set; the opposite, however, is not allowed. That is, a partition can't be split into two subsets.

Now imagine that there was a design discussion between your data science team and your support engineering team, and one engineer fiercely stood up and exclaimed, "Well, that's easy! You keep an array (a dynamic array or a vector) for each subset."

You don't want to be that person, believe me, and one of the goals of this book is making sure you don't find yourself in that situation. Because the next thing to happen, hopefully, is that somebody else points out how, by using arrays, understanding whether two elements are in the same set could potentially require going over all the elements of all the subsets. Likewise, just understanding which subset an element belongs to could require the same number of element checks; that is, search could be linear in the total number of elements.

This would be a real performance concern, and it seems obvious we should be able to do better.

The next idea in this brainstorming could involve adding a map from elements to subsets, together with the list of subsets explained previously. This is a slightly better improvement for some operations; although, as we will see, it still forces operations such as merging two sets to potentially require `O(n)` assignments.

Performance, however, is not the main concern with that design. Using two independent data structures is a terrible idea, because you will have to manually sync them every time you face this problem in your application. This is very error-prone.

An already better solution is to provide a wrapper class that internally uses those two structures: it gives you encapsulation and isolation and as a result, you are able to write only once the code that syncs both structures on, say, add or merge (and so you gain reusability). Even more important, you are able to unit test your class in isolation and hence have a reasonable guarantee that it's going to do its job without experiencing bugs every time you use it in your application (that is, provided you do write good and thorough unit tests, acing the edge cases and challenging the behavior of your class in all possible contexts).

So, let's assume we agree on the need to write a class that takes care of the whole problem, keeping track of which (disjoint) subset an element belongs to, and encapsulating all the logic in it. We are going to delay the discussion on implementation for now: before focusing on the details, let's discuss its public API and behavior.

Depending on the size of the catalog, we could even fit such a data structure in memory, but let's instead assume that we set up a REST service (illustrated in figure 5.3) based on a persisted Memcached-like storage,[1] something like Redis. Durability of the data is important in this case, because in our example, the monitoring activity over the items will last for years, and we don't want to recompute the whole disjoint set structure every time there is a change or a new product is added.

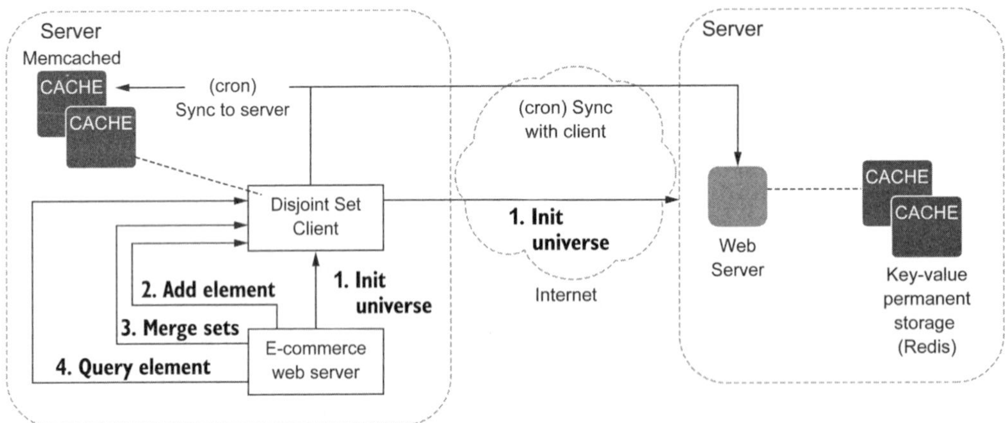
Server
Memcached
CACHE
CACHE
(cron)
Sync to server
Disjoint Set
Client
2. Add element
3. Merge sets
4. Query element
1. Init
universe
E-commerce
web server
(cron) Sync
with client
1. Init
universe
Internet
Server
Web
Server
CACHE
CACHE
Key-value
permanent
storage
(Redis)

Figure 5.3 A possible design for an application using disjoint set. The disjoint set client can be anything ranging from a library to a REST client. The purpose of the (thin) client here is to be an interface between the in-memory storage (the Memcached node in the picture) and the server, which has persistent storage. The server can be a web server, but it could also just be another native application storing data on a disk. The disjoint set client will run on the same intranet, possibly even on the same machine, as the e-commerce server. It will have a cron job to keep the persistent storage in sync with the in-memory version (this could happen every few seconds or asynchronously after each operation). Moreover, it will respond to calls from the e-commerce site, querying the in-memory storage or, when needed, calling the web server (and, in case not all the data will fit in memory, it will also take care of swaps).

Alternatively, if the size of the universe[2] is small enough to fit in memory, it could be possible to imagine a synchronization mechanism that periodically serializes our in-memory data structure into a persistent database.

[1] A (no-SQL) key-value store used as a distributed object caching system.

[2] The set of all possible items—traditionally denoted as Universe (U) in set theory.

5.3 Describing the data structure API: Disjoint set

In our design, our data structure needs to offer only a few, though crucial, operations.

Abstract data structure: `DisjointSet`	

API	`class DisjointSet {`
	`  init(U);`
	`  findPartition(x);`
	`  merge(x, y);`
	`  areDisjoint(x,y);`
	`}`

Contract with client	A disjoint set keeps track of the mutual relations between elements in a universe U. The relation is not explicitly defined by the data structure; it is left to the client to define it. However, it is assumed that such a relation ® has the reflexive, symmetric and transitive properties; this means that given x, y, z elements of U ▪ x® x ▪ if x® y, then y® x ▪ if x® y and y® z then x® z The guarantees provided by the class are ▪ It's possible to add a relation between any two elements. ▪ If two elements at any point are merged (that is, a relation between them is added), they will be part of the same disjoint set. ▪ If there is a chain of elements x_1, x_2, …, x_n such that x_1 has been merged to x_2, x_2 has been merged with x_3 and so on, then x_1 and x_n will be in the same partition. ▪ If two elements are not in the same partition, then there is no other element belonging to both elements' disjoint sets.

First, we'd like, obviously, to initialize our instance on construction. Without any loss of generality, we can restrict to the case where the Universe `U`, that is, the set of all possible elements, is known in advance and static. We also assume that initially every element is in its own partition. Workarounds to support violations to these assumptions are easily achievable by making wise use of dynamic arrays and the class's very own methods.

Finally, throughout this chapter we assume the elements of our Universe `U` are the integers between `0` and `n-1`. This is not a real restriction, because we can easily associate an index to each of the actual elements of `U`.

Initialization, therefore, just takes care of allocation of the basic fields needed by the class and assigns each element into its own partition.

The `findPartition` method, when called on an element `x` of `U`, will return the partition to which `x` belongs. This output might not be meaningful outside of the instance of our data structure: think of this method mostly as a *protected method*[3] for the class, or even consider restricting its visibility to *private.*

[3] Definition of protected visibility varies depending on the programming language. Here, we assume a protected method or attribute is only visible to the class declaring it and its sub-classes. A private method, conversely, is not visible to any classes inheriting from the one in which it is declared.

The two main operations that we'd like to perform are

- Given two elements `x` and `y`, both belonging to `U`, we'd like to check if they belong to different partitions (`areDisjoint`).
- Given two elements `x` and `y`, we'd like to merge their partitions into a single one (`merge`).

5.4 Naïve solution[4]

The most immediate solution for our problem is to represent each partition with a list (or array), as illustrated in figure 5.4. For each element, we need to keep track of the pointer to the head of the list.

To find out if two elements are in the same partition, we need to retrieve the list for one element, and check if it is the same list as for the other.[5]

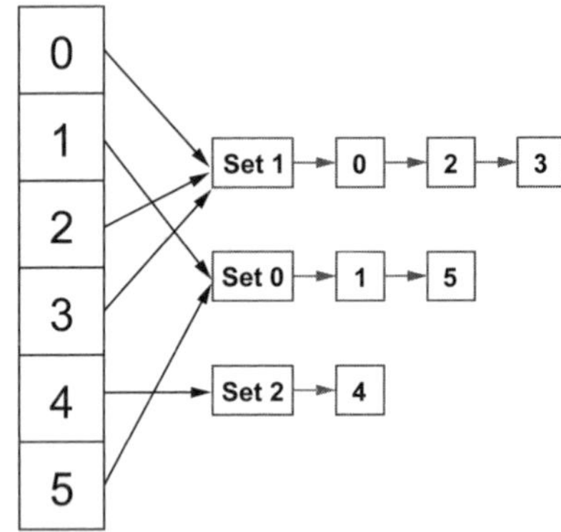
0
1
2
3
4
5
Set 1
0
2
3
Set 0
1
5
Set 2
4

Figure 5.4 Representing a disjoint set with lists. Each array element stores a pointer to the head of a linked list. Each linked list, in turn, represents a set. Here sets are numbered arbitrarily, as the index doesn't really provide any information on the set (nor can it be retrieved).

To merge two partitions, P_1 and P_2, modeled with two lists, L_1 and L_2, we need to update the `next` pointer[6] of the last element in L_1 so that it points to the head of L_2 (or vice versa, with the last element of L_2 pointing to the head of L_1). This operation, which is shown in figure 5.5, can be done in constant time by keeping an extra (constant space) pointer to the tail of each list. Unfortunately, though, we aren't done just yet: for every element in L_2, we also need to update its list pointer in our map to point to the head of the new merged list.

This operation requires linear time in the worst case, because we might have to update up to `n-1` elements (where `n` is the total number of elements in the Universe `U`).

There is one way to slightly improve the expected number of assignments we have to perform: by always appending the shortest of the two lists, we will make sure that we won't have to update more than `n/2` elements' pointers. Unfortunately, this does not improve the asymptotic execution time.[7]

Let's delve into code to better explain how this works.

---

[4] This is a theory-intensive section.

[5] As an implementation detail, we likely need to use referential equality here when comparing lists.

[6] For a refresher on linked lists, or if you are not sure what the `next` pointer is, check out appendix C.

[7] Remember that constant factors are irrelevant in big-O analysis, so `O(n/2) = O(n)`.

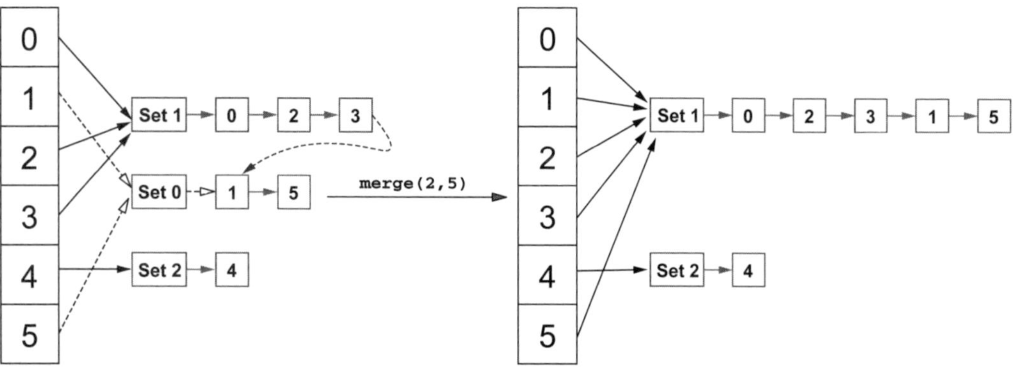
0
1
2
3
4
5
Set 1
0
2
3
Set 0
1
5
Set 2
4
merge(2,5)
0
1
2
3
4
5
Set 1
0
2
3
1
5
Set 2
4

Figure 5.5 Merging two partitions. On the left: one of the two lists is appended to the other by adding a new edge tail-to-head and removing links from the array to the second list. On the right is shown the result after the merge, with all head-pointers for array elements belonging to the appended list (elements 1 and 5 in the example) updated.

5.4.1 Implementing naïve solution

Let's start with the pseudo-code for the constructor, and the class definition (see listing 5.1). All methods in the next sections will be assumed to be class methods for `DisjointSet`.

Listing 5.1 Naïve solution, `constructor`

```
class DisjointSet
  #type HashMap[Element, List[Element]]
  partitionsMap

function DisjointSet(initialSet=[])
    this.partitionsMap ← new HashMap()
    for elem in initialSet do
      throw-if (elem == null or partitionsMap.has(elem)))
      partitionsMap[elem] ← new Set(elem)
```

The constructor takes a list of elements as argument, but by default initializes the disjoint set with an empty set.

Creates a new map from elements to sets

Goes over each element in the argument list

Throws an exception if the element is `null` or a duplicate

Adds a mapping between current element and a new singleton set containing current element only

Initialization is simple: we will check that the list passed as argument contains no duplicates and initialize the disjoint set with its elements.

In a real implementation, you should worry about how elements are compared. Depending on the programming language, it can use referential equality, an equality operator, or a method defined on the elements' class. The following code is only meant to illustrate how a basic solution works, so we won't worry about the details.

First, we initialize the associative array that is going to index the elements and map them to the partition they belong to (line #2).

Next, we just go through `initialSet`'s elements, one by one, check they are defined and that there is no duplicate, and then initialize their partition to the singleton containing the element itself (initially each element is disjoint from every other element).

Now that we have taken care of initializing our disjoint set, we can provide a couple of useful methods. For example, we can add a `size` public property, simply defined as the number of entries stored in the local partitions map.

You can find examples of such methods implemented in our repo. Here, instead, we will focus on the main API methods, starting with the `add` method, illustrated in figure 5.6, whose pseudo-code is shown in listing 5.2.

Listing 5.2 Naïve solution, add

```
function add(elem)
  throw-if elem == null
  if partitionsMap.has(elem) then
    return false
  partitionsMap[elem] ← new Set(elem)
  return true
```

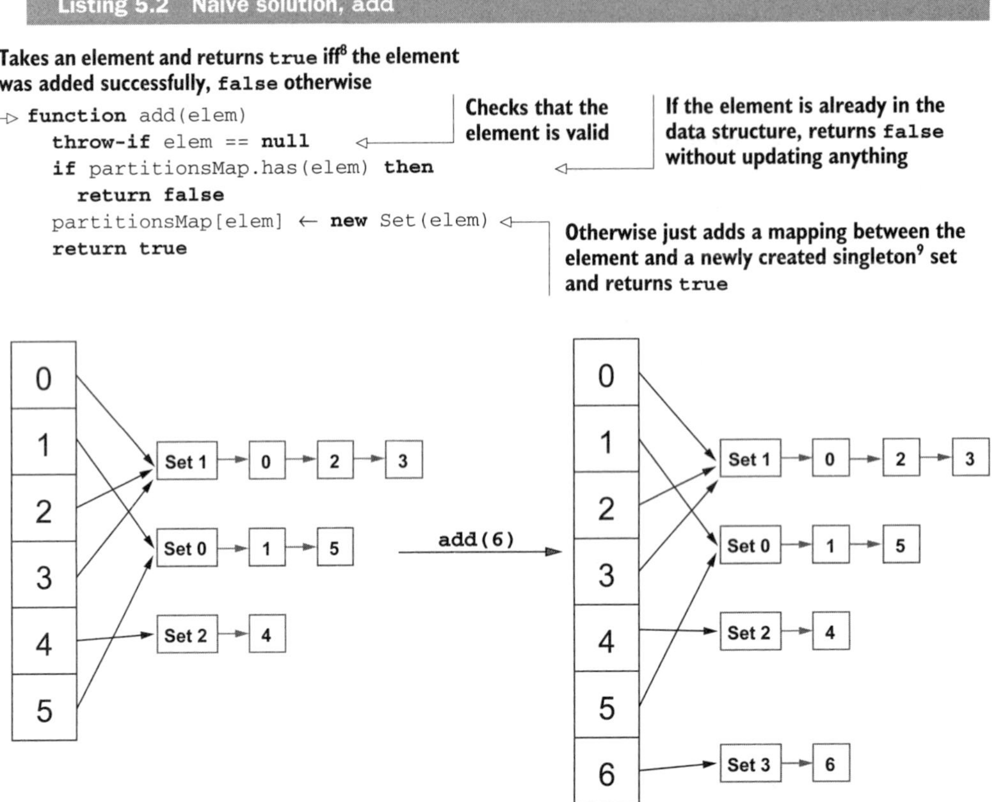
Takes an element and returns true iff[8] the element was added successfully, false otherwise
Checks that the element is valid
If the element is already in the data structure, returns false without updating anything
Otherwise just adds a mapping between the element and a newly created singleton[9] set and returns true
0
1
2
3
4
5
Set 1
0
2
3
Set 0
1
5
Set 2
4
add(6)
0
1
2
3
4
5
6
Set 1
0
2
3
Set 0
1
5
Set 2
4
Set 3
6

Figure 5.6 Adding a new element to the container. Provided the new element is not a duplicate of any element currently in our container, we can add it by creating a new singleton partition, which will only contain the newly added element.

This method is used to allow the Universe to grow, with new (unique) elements that can be added at any time. Every time we add a new element, we just add a brand-new partition containing that element alone. But, of course, we need to check that the argument passed to `add` is well-defined, so that it's not `null` and not a duplicate of another element already in our Universe.

[8] Abbreviation for "if and only if."

[9] A singleton is a set with exactly one element.

Now we get to the really interesting stuff: first and foremost, the `findPartition` method, shown in listing 5.3.

Listing 5.3 Naïve solution, `findPartition`

```
function findPartition(elem)
  throw-if (elem == null or not partitionsMap.has(elem))
  return partitionsMap[elem]
```

Takes an element and returns a `Set`, the partition (aka disjoint set) to which the element belongs

Checks that the element is valid

Returns the `Set` containing the argument

In this basic implementation, the method is particularly trivial: after the usual validation (including checking that the element is actually stored in the disjoint set), we just need to return the partition containing `elem`.

As we mentioned, this implementation of the `findPartition` method only requires constant time (assuming that the hash for `elem` can be computed in constant time).

Another easy-to-implement method, shown in listing 5.4, is the one checking if two elements belong to the same partition.

Listing 5.4 Naïve solution, `areDisjoint`

```
function areDisjoint(elem1, elem2)
  p1 ← this.findPartition(elem1)
  p2 ← this.findPartition(elem2)
  return p1 != p2
```

Takes two elements and returns `true` iff the elements are valid but don't belong to the same partition, `false` iff the elements are valid but do belong to the same partition. Notice that if either element is `null` or hasn't been added to this container, then this method will throw an error (because in turn `findPartition` will throw an error).

Retrieves the disjoint set to which `elem1` belongs. If the argument is invalid or not found, this call will throw an error.

Repeats the same operation for `elem2`

Compares the two sets, and checks if they are the same, and hence if the elements belong to the same partition

We just need to reuse `findPartition`, call it for both elements, and check whether both calls return the same partition. Note that by reusing `findPartition`, we can make sure that the implementation of `areDisjoint` won't need to change, no matter how our elements are stored or `findPartition` is implemented (as long as its interface remains the same, and partitions can be compared with the inequality operator).

Moreover, we decided to implement a check for elements belonging to different partitions rather than for elements belonging to the same one: this is because of how disjoint sets are normally used. We are normally interested in checking whether two elements don't belong to the same partition, and if that's the case, we merge the two partitions. But depending on the way you are going to use this container, it is possible that the other way around is more convenient, and there is nothing preventing you from defining a samePartition method instead.

All the methods we have seen so far run in constant time with respect to the size of the container. Now, it's time to implement the method merging two partitions, shown in listing 5.5 (and illustrated in figure 5.5). As we have seen, the merge method requires O(n) assignments in the worst case.

Listing 5.5 Naïve solution, merge

```
function merge(elem1, elem2)
  p1 ← this.findPartition(elem1)
  p2 ← this.findPartition(elem2)
  if p1 == p2 then
    return false
  for elem in p1 do
    p2.add(elem)
    this.partitions[elem] ← p2
  return true
```

- Takes two elements, merges their partitions, and returns true iff the two elements were in two different partitions that now are merged, or false if they were already in the same partition
- Retrieves the partitions to which elem1 and elem2 belong. If the argument is invalid or not found, these calls will throw.
- Compares p1 and p2, and if they are the same, there is nothing left to do. The elements are already in the same partition, and so no merge happens: false is returned.
- Loops over the elements in the first partition. For each element in p1 do:
- . . . add the element to p2 . . .
- . . . then update the mapping for that element, which now belongs to p2.

This method is more complex than the previous ones. And yet, by reusing findPartition, it still looks quite simple.

We first check if elements belong to the same partition by calling findPartition on both and checking the result. Those calls also take care of validating the input.

Once we've established that we actually need to perform an action, we proceed and merge the two sets, correcting the pointers in the partitions map when needed. If the partitions were implemented with linked lists instead of Set, we could have just appended the head of a list to the tail of the other. Sets, instead, force us to actually add elements one by one. An extra linear number of assignments is needed (worst case), but this doesn't change the order of the function's runtime; we still need to update the references for elements of one of the two lists (that is, sets) anyway.

Here, we show the simplest code, always pouring the first partition's elements into the second one. On our repo on GitHub[10] you can find a slightly better version that checks which set is smaller and adds its elements to the larger sets; however, this is just a constant-time improvement on the simplest version and the running time remains linear in the minimum of the sets' sizes.

[10] See https://github.com/mlarocca/AlgorithmsAndDataStructuresInAction#disjoint-set.

5.5 Using a tree-like structure[11]

To recap what we attained with our basic implementation, we managed to write a constant-time `findPartition` method and a worst-case linear-time `merge` method.

Now, can we do any better than linear, not just for `findPartition`, but for all the operations on a disjoint set? Well, turns out that yes, we can!

5.5.1 From list to trees

The idea is simple: instead of using lists to represent each partition, we will use trees, as shown in figure 5.7. Each partition is then uniquely identified by the root of the tree associated with the partition. The advantage of trees over lists is that if the tree is balanced, any operation on the tree is logarithmic (instead of linear, as for a list).

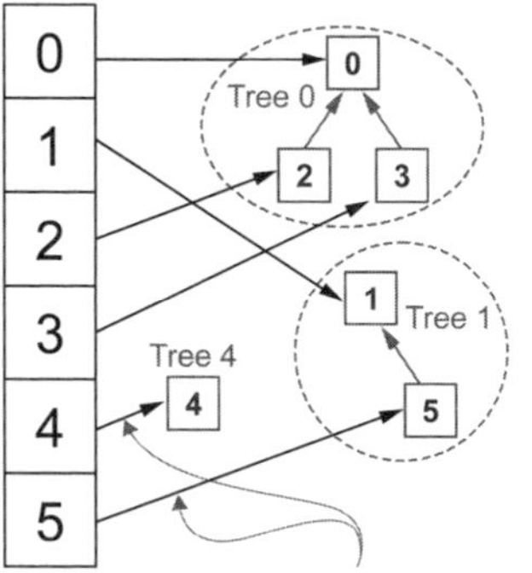
0
1
2
3
4
5
Tree 0
0
2
3
Tree 1
1
5
Tree 4
4
1:1 Element - Tree node

Figure 5.7 Representing a disjoint set with trees. Trees are named after their root, because we use the tree root as a unique identifier for the partition (we can do so under the assumption that elements are unique). Each element in the array points to a tree node: in the naïve implementation there is a 1:1 mapping between elements and tree nodes. This means that to get to the root of the tree, we might need to climb up the whole tree (and, on average, half of the height of the tree).

When we merge two partitions, we will set one tree root as the child of the root of the other tree; see figure 5.8 to see an example.

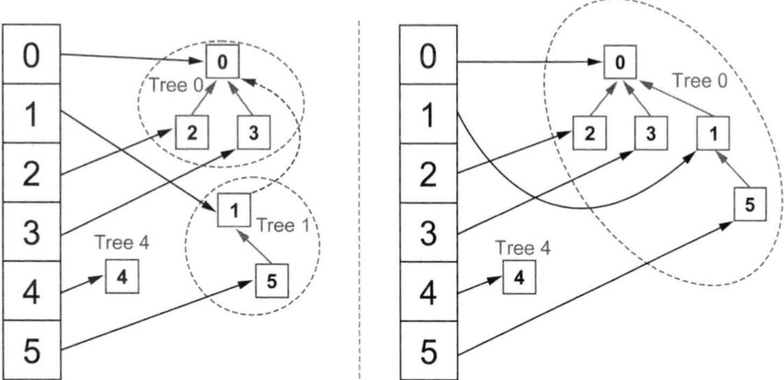
0
1
2
3
4
5
Tree 0
Tree 1
Tree 4
Tree 0
Tree 4

Figure 5.8 Merging two sets when using the tree representation. It only requires creating one new link (plus some tree traversing). In the figure on the left, we add one edge from the root tree of Tree 1 to the root of Tree 0, to merge them. On the right, we show how this changes the data structure: now we only have two trees, but the height of tree 0 is now larger than before the merge.

[11]This section is theory-intensive and features advanced concepts.

This is a huge improvement over the naïve solution, because we won't have to update the partition map for any of the other elements in the partitions merged. Instead, each node in the tree will maintain a link to its parent (we don't need to save links to children, because they are of no use in this case).

The roots of the tree, as mentioned, uniquely identify each partition. So, when we need to find out which partition an element belongs to, we just retrieve the tree node it's pointing to and walk up to the root of its tree. In method `areDisjoint`, if we do the same for both elements and then compare the roots found, we can easily see if two elements belong to the same partition (if and only if the two roots are equal).

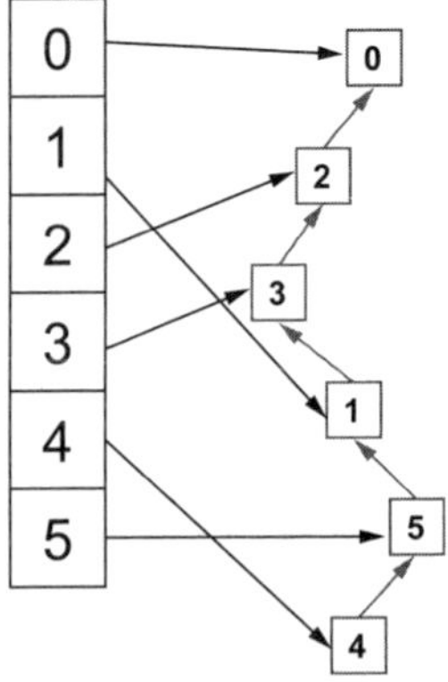
0
1
2
3
4
5
0
2
3
1
5
4

Figure 5.9 Worst case scenario for naive tree implementation: the height of the final tree is equal to n, the total number of elements, because the tree degenerated into a list.

So, merging two partitions now requires a constant number of changes, plus the number of look-ups needed to find the two roots. Finding the set to which an element belongs (or seeing if two elements belong to the same partition) requires logarithmic time on average (remember when we introduced trees?[12]) but linear time in the worst case. That's because when merging partitions, we might get unlucky with the choice of which tree's root we set as child of the other. By randomly choosing each time which root is going to be used as a child of the other, we can make this worst-case scenario unlikely . . . but it would still be possible (although extremely unlucky) to find ourselves in an edge situation such as the one depicted in figure 5.9. This means that our worst-case scenario for `merge` still requires `O(n)` lookups and, what's worst, now even `findPartition` has linear running time.

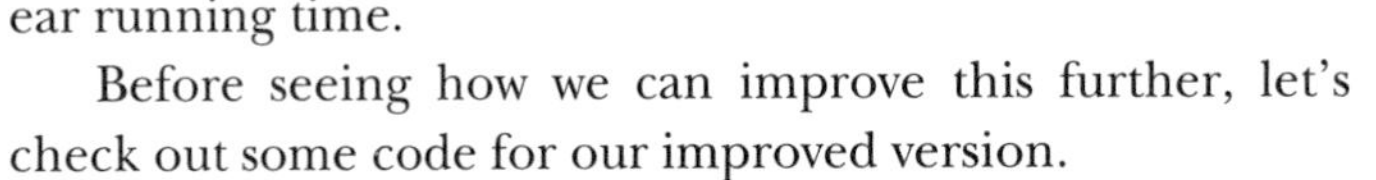

Before seeing how we can improve this further, let's check out some code for our improved version.

5.5.2 *Implementing the tree version*

Let's see in detail how this improved implementation works. Most code remains unchanged from the previous section, so we won't show it here. In the methods that have changes with respect to the naïve version, we will underline those changes to help readers quickly compare the two versions.

Instead of mapping to an actual set, elements in the partition map point to each element's parent in the tree. That's why, as you can see in the book's repo, we can rename our `partitionsMap` to `parentsMap` to make its purpose explicit.

At initialization, we conveniently set each element as its own parent. Trust me on that one; we'll see why later.

The same change applies to the `add` method, which otherwise stays unchanged.

---

[12]Check out appendix C, section C.1.3.

The findPartition method (described in listing 5.6) needs quite a bit of tuning to work properly. Two notes on its implementation:

- With respect to the basic implementation, in this case we won't return a list anymore, but rather the element at the root of the partition's tree.
- The return value of findPartition might not immediately make sense to an external caller, and in fact this method will mostly be used internally when called by merge and areDisjoint methods.

Listing 5.6 Tree-based solution, findPartition

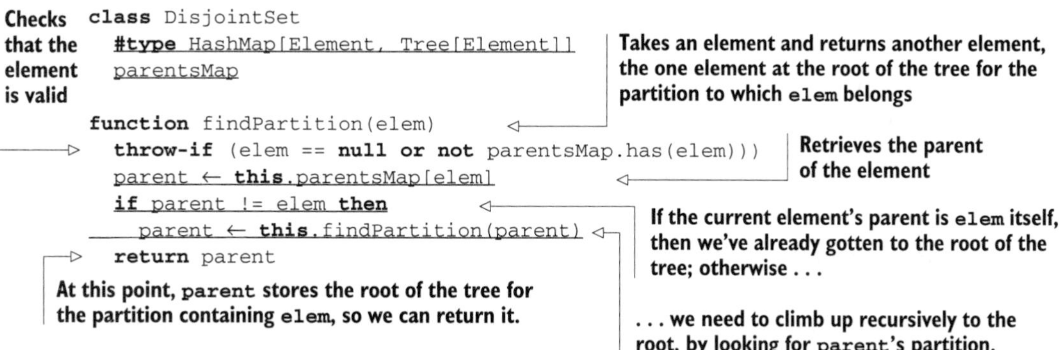
Checks that the element is valid
Takes an element and returns another element, the one element at the root of the tree for the partition to which elem belongs
Retrieves the parent of the element
If the current element's parent is elem itself, then we've already gotten to the root of the tree; otherwise . . .
. . . we need to climb up recursively to the root, by looking for parent's partition.
At this point, parent stores the root of the tree for the partition containing elem, so we can return it.

```
class DisjointSet
  #type HashMap[Element, Tree[Element]]
  parentsMap

function findPartition(elem)
  throw-if (elem == null or not parentsMap.has(elem)))
  parent ← this.parentsMap[elem]
  if parent != elem then
    parent ← this.findPartition(parent)
  return parent
```

After getting the element's parent, we check to see if it's the element itself. If an element is its own parent, then we know this means we've reached the root of the partition's tree, because of the way we initialize this field, and because, in merge, we never change a root's parent.

Otherwise, if the current element does have a parent, we walk up the tree toward its root and perform a recursive call to findPartition, returning its result (line #5).

This new implementation of findPartition, as we already mentioned, is not running in constant time anymore. We will have as many recursive calls as the height of the partition's tree. Since we can't make any assumption about the trees so far, this means that we possibly have a number of calls proportional to the number of elements in the Universe U, although this is the worst case and, on average, we can expect far better performance.

It might seem so far that we have only made our data structure's performance worse. We need to define our new implementation of the merge operation, shown in listing 5.7, to see the advantage of using trees.

Listing 5.7 Tree-based solution, merge

Takes two elements, merges their partitions, and returns true iff the two elements were in two different partitions that now are merged, false if they were already in the same partition

Retrieves the partitions to which elem1 and elem2 belong to. If the argument is invalid or not found, this call will throw.

```
function merge(elem1, elem2)
  p1 ← this.findPartition(elem1)
  p2 ← this.findPartition(elem2)
```

Compares `p1` and `p2`, and if they are the same there is nothing left to do. The elements are already in the same partition, and so no merge happens: `false` is returned.

```
if p1 == p2 then
  return false
this.parentsMap[p2] ← p1
return true
```

Sets the parent of `p2` to be equal to `p1`, so that now both `p1` and `p2` have the same parent, but also all elements in `p2` will ultimately share `p1` as the root of their tree

By comparing the two implementations you can immediately see that this is simpler, although only the last few lines changed. The good news is that we no longer need to iterate through a list of elements! To merge two partitions, we simply need to get to both trees' roots, and then set one root as the parent of the other. We still need to find those tree roots, though.

The new line we added only requires constant time, so the method runtime is dominated by the two calls to `findPartition`. As we have seen, they require time proportional to the height of the tree they are called on, and in the worst case this can still be linear. However, in the average case, and especially in the early stages after initialization, we know the height of the trees will be much smaller.

So, in summary, with this implementation we have a disjoint set for which all the operations still require linear time in the worst case, but on average will only need logarithmic time—even for those operations that were constant-time in the naïve implementation. Admittedly, that doesn't sound like a great result if we focus on worst cases. Nevertheless, if you look at it from a different perspective, we've already managed to have a more balanced set of operations on our disjoint set, which is especially nice in those contexts where `merge` is a common operation (while in read-intensive applications, where `merge` is only executed rarely, the naïve implementation could overall be preferable).

Just read through the next section before dismissing the tree solution; it will be worth it.

5.6 Heuristics to improve the running time[13]

The next step in our quest for optimal performance is to make sure `findPartition` is logarithmic even in the worst-case scenario. Luckily, this is pretty easy! We discussed balanced trees in appendix C; feel free to check it out if you feel you could use a refresher.

Long story short, here we can easily keep track of the *rank* (aka size) of each tree, using linear extra space and performing constant-time extra operations in method `merge`, where we will update rank only for trees' roots.

When we merge two trees, we will make sure to set as child the tree with the smallest number of nodes, as shown in figure 5.10.

[13]This section is theory-intensive and features advanced concepts.

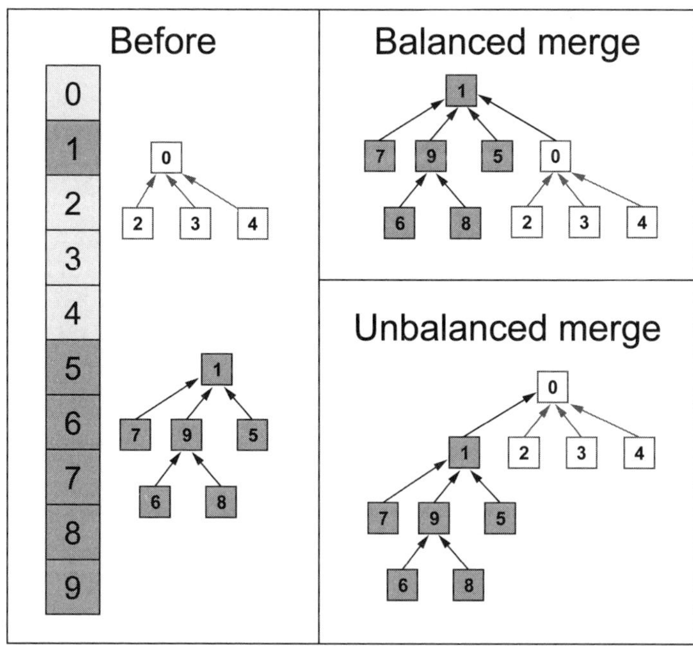
Before
Balanced merge
Unbalanced merge
0
1
2
3
4
5
6
7
8
9

Figure 5.10 Merging two set trees: examples of balanced vs unbalanced merges. Arrows from the array are omitted for convenience, because each array element points to the corresponding tree element (so all light red elements point to the red [light] tree, and so on).

It can be proven by induction that this tree will also be the one with the smallest height: this means the new tree will either have the same height as the old one, or just have its height increased by 1. It is also provable that the height of a tree can't be increased more than a logarithmic number of times.

As a logarithm grows really slowly (for instance `ln(1000) ~= 10, ln(1000000) ~= 20`), this is, in practice, already a good result, sufficient for most applications.

However, if you are writing some really critical core code, such as a kernel or firmware code, you might want to do even better.

Why? Well, because you can. And sometimes also because you need to. If you shave 0.001ms over an operation you will repeat a billion times, you've already saved 16 minutes of computation.

NOTE Most of the time, in our job as developers, performance isn't the only metric to consider regarding this kind of improvement. First, it depends on whether you are saving those 16 minutes over a computation taking an hour or a day (needless to say, in the latter situation the gain would be irrelevant). But it also depends at what price you get the savings. If it makes your code terribly more fragile, more complicated, and harder to maintain, or just requires weeks of development time, you will have to weigh the pros and cons before going down this path. Luckily for disjoint sets, this is not the case, and path compression is easy to implement, while it gives a big gain.

Let's see how we could have this further improvement before delving into code.

5.6.1 *Path compression*

As hinted in the previous section, we can do even better than just having balanced trees and logarithmic-time methods.

To improve our results further, we can use a heuristic called *path compression*. The idea, shown in figure 5.11, is even simpler: for each node in the trees, instead of storing a link to its parent, we can store one to the root of the tree. After all, we don't really need to keep track of the history of the merges we performed; we just need to know at the current time what the root is for an element's partition—and find that out as quickly as we can.

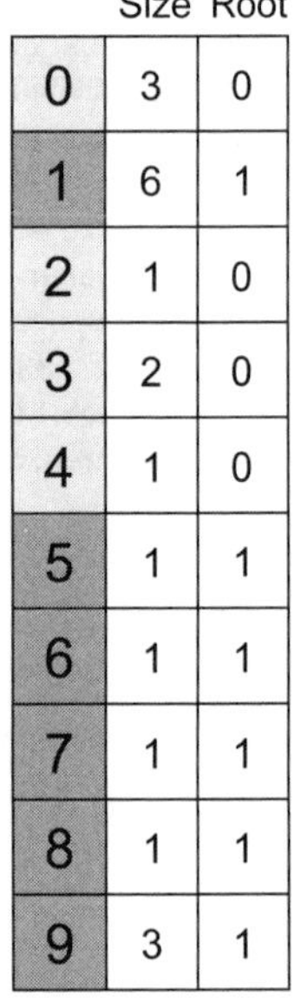

	Size	Root
0	3	0
1	6	1
2	1	0
3	2	0
4	1	0
5	1	1
6	1	1
7	1	1
8	1	1
9	3	1

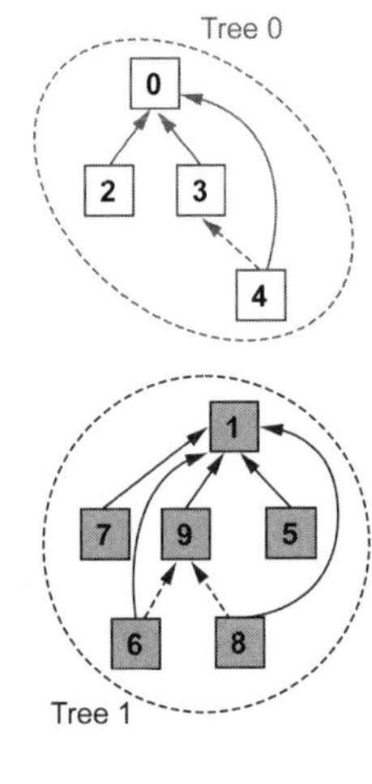
Tree 0
0
2
3
4
1
7
9
5
6
8
Tree 1

Figure 5.11 Disjoint set represented using a tree with path compression. Internal representation is shown next to the elements' array. In tree representation, dashed arrows are parent links, while solid arrows are pointers to the set's root. The structure initially holds two sets, colored in light red and dark blue and whose roots are respectively 0 and 1.

Now, if you were to update all the root pointers as part of merge, it wouldn't be a logarithmic method anymore; we would need linear time to update each node in the tree.

But let's see—what happens if we don't update immediately the parent pointers in the nodes of the tree set as child? Simply put, next time we run `findPartition` on one of the elements in that tree—call it `x`—we need to walk the tree from `x` up to its old root x_R, and then from x_R to the new root `R`.

Keep in mind that the pointers for the elements in the old tree could have been in sync before the merge (and then we would just need two hops to get to the new root; see figure 5.12), or they might have never been updated.

Because we will have to walk up the tree anyway, we can then retrace our steps from the top, `R`, down to `x` and update the root pointers for all those elements. This won't influence our asymptotic performance for `findPartition`, since by retracing the same path we just double the number of steps (and constant factors are irrelevant in asymptotic analysis; see appendix B).

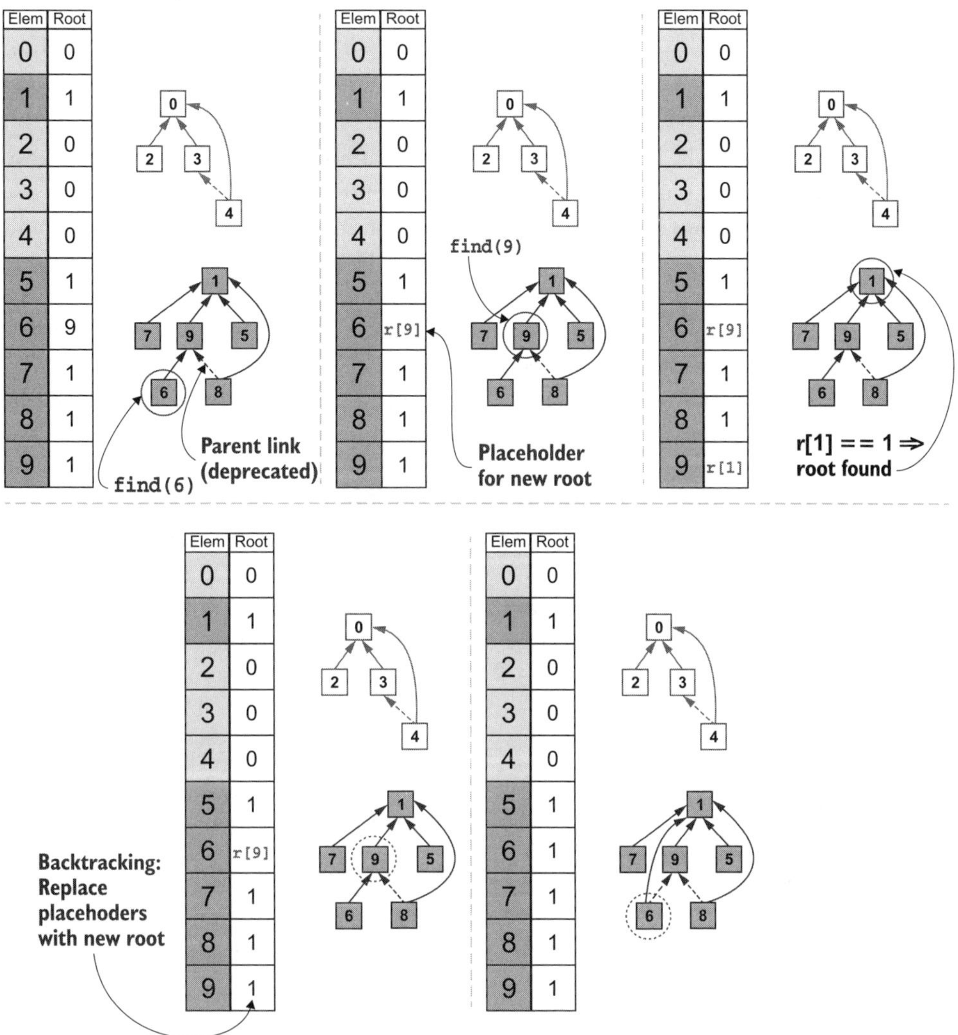

Elem Root
find(6)
Parent link (deprecated)
find(9)
Placeholder for new root
r[9]
r[1]
r[1] == 1 ⇒ root found
Backtracking: Replace placehoders with new root

Figure 5.12 Call to `find` on the same disjoint set of figure 5.11. Notice that the dark blue tree is out of sync. If we call `find` on the element `6`, the algorithm starts slowly crawling up the blue tree, until it finds its root (third diagram). Then (bottom diagrams), the algorithm backtracks, updating the root for the intermediate elements `9` and `6`.

But as a consequence of these extra steps that we take, next time we call `findPartition` on any elements in the path from `x` to `root(x)`, we know for sure that those pointers will be up to date and we will just need one single step to find their root.

At this point, we would like to understand how many times we will need to update the root pointers, on average, for a single operation or, in amortized analysis, over a certain number `k` of operations. This is where the analysis of the algorithm gets a bit complicated.

We won't go into its details. Just know that it is proven that the running amortized time for m calls to `findPartition` and `merge` on a set of n elements will require `O(m * Ack(n))` array accesses.

Here `Ack(n)` is an approximation of the *inverse Ackermann* function, a function growing so slowly that it can be considered a constant (its value will be lower than 5 for any integer that can be stored on a computer).

So, we managed to obtain an amortized constant bound for all the operations on this data structure! If you are not impressed by this result . . . you should be!

It is not yet known if this is the lowest bound for the Union-Find data structure. It has been proven,[14] though, that `O(m * InvAck(m, n))` is a strict lower bound, where `InvAck(m, n)` is the true inverse Ackermann function.

I know, this is a lot to take in. But do not despair; it turns out that we only need a few small changes to implement the path compression heuristic.

5.6.2 Implementing balancing and path compression

We will now discuss the final implementation of our disjoint set structure, including both the "tree balancing by rank" and "path compression" heuristics.

For each element, we'll have to store some information about its subtree. Therefore, we'll use a helper (private) class `Info` to gather all the info together, as shown in listing 5.8.

Listing 5.8 Class Info

```
class Info
  function Info(elem)
    throw-if elem == null
    this.root ← elem
    this.rank ← 1

class DisjointSet
  #type HashMap[Element, Info]
  parentsMap
```

- The constructor for the `Info` class just takes an element of the disjoint set.
- Validates the argument
- Initially, an element is assigned to the singleton tree rooted at the element itself.
- The rank of the subtree is initially 1, because it only contains one element.

This `Info` class models (the info associated with) a node of the partitions' tree. It is, to all purposes, just a container for two values: the root of the tree and the rank (that is, size) of the tree rooted at the current element.

In the root property, we won't store references to other nodes. Instead, we will directly store the (index of) the element itself, that we then use as a key to a `HashMap`, exactly as we have shown in the previous sections.

[14] It is possible to find plenty of literature on the subject. Be aware, though, that it's very interesting reading, but challenging.

If we were actually modeling a tree data structure, this design would result in imperfect encapsulation. But we are just using the `Info` class as a tuple to gather all the properties associated with an element.

Most implementations for disjoint set would use two arrays for this. Since our implementation does not restrict keys to integers and we are using hash maps, we could define two `Maps` for the element's roots and ranks. In doing so, however, we would store each element three times: twice as a key of each map and once as a root of some tree (this last entry could store, of course, some keys several times and some others not once).

By using this extra wrapper and a single "info" map, we make sure to store elements only once as keys.

While objects would be stored as reference, with minimal overhead, immutable values, and especially strings, would be stored by value. Therefore, even avoiding storeing each element once more can lead to consistent memory saving.

We could, in theory, do even better by storing each element in object wrappers and using those wrappers as keys. This way, we would only store each key once, and use wrappers' references all the time, both as keys for our map(s) and as values.

Is the overhead and increased complexity of the wrapper solution worth it? This depends on the assumptions you can make on the type and size of the keys. In most cases, it is probably not, so be sure to properly profile your application and analyze your input before embarking on such optimizations.

To go back to our implementation: once again, changes are minimal. In both constructor and `add`, we just need to update the very last line:

```
parentsMap[elem] = new Info(elem)
```

We use the constructor for `Info` and create a new instance associated with each element.

Things definitely get more interesting when we move to `findPartition`, implemented in listing 5.9.

Listing 5.9 Tree-with-heuristics solution, `findPartition`

```
function findPartition(elem)
  throw-if (elem == null or not parentsMap.has(elem)))
  info ← this.parentsMap[elem]
  if (info.root == elem) then
    return elem
  info.root ← this.findPartition(info.root)
  return info.root
```

Annotations:

- Takes an element and `return` another element, the one element at the root of the tree for the partition to which elem belongs
- Checks that the element is valid
- Retrieves the info node stored for current element
- If the element's root is the element itself, then we already got to the root of the tree, and we can return it.
- Otherwise, we need to climb up recursively to the root, but meanwhile we can update the root link for the current element so that it points to the actual root of the tree.

As described at the beginning of the section, when using the path compression heuristic, we don't update the root of all elements on merge, but we do update it on findPartition. So, the main difference from the older version is that we save the result of the recursive calls to findPartition at line #6, and we use it to update the current element's root. Everything else remains exactly the same.

It goes without saying that the largest portion of changes will be implemented in the merge method, as shown in listing 5.10.

Listing 5.10 Tree-with-heuristics solution, merge

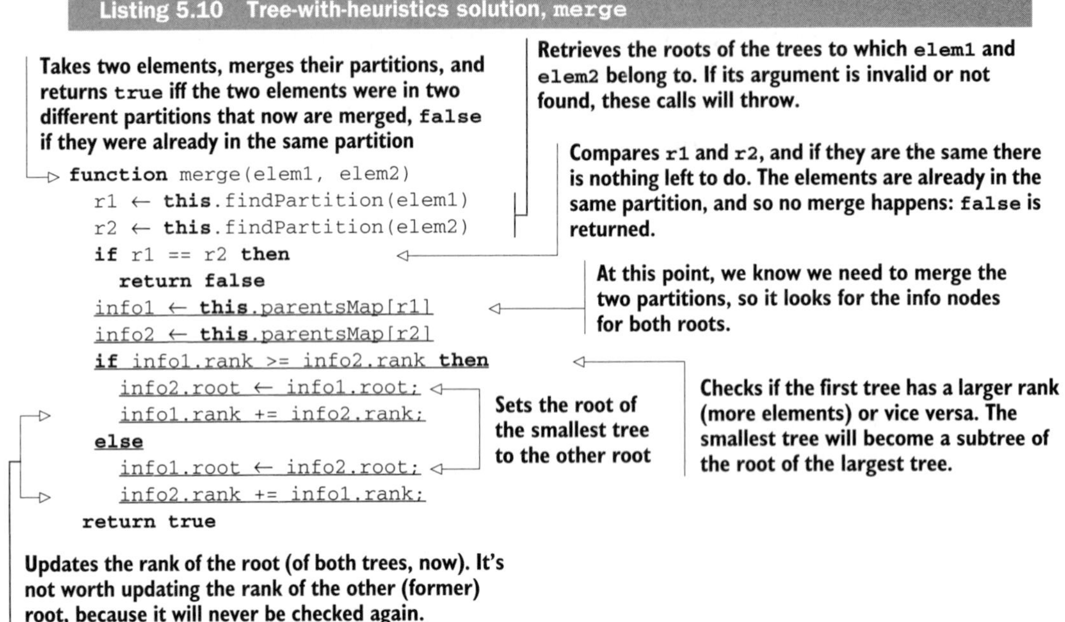
Takes two elements, merges their partitions, and returns true iff the two elements were in two different partitions that now are merged, false if they were already in the same partition
Retrieves the roots of the trees to which elem1 and elem2 belong to. If its argument is invalid or not found, these calls will throw.
Compares r1 and r2, and if they are the same there is nothing left to do. The elements are already in the same partition, and so no merge happens: false is returned.
At this point, we know we need to merge the two partitions, so it looks for the info nodes for both roots.
Sets the root of the smallest tree to the other root
Checks if the first tree has a larger rank (more elements) or vice versa. The smallest tree will become a subtree of the root of the largest tree.
Updates the rank of the root (of both trees, now). It's not worth updating the rank of the other (former) root, because it will never be checked again.

```
function merge(elem1, elem2)
  r1 ← this.findPartition(elem1)
  r2 ← this.findPartition(elem2)
  if r1 == r2 then
    return false
  info1 ← this.parentsMap[r1]
  info2 ← this.parentsMap[r2]
  if info1.rank >= info2.rank then
    info2.root ← info1.root;
    info1.rank += info2.rank;
  else
    info1.root ← info2.root;
    info2.rank += info1.rank;
  return true
```

We still retrieve the elements at the roots of the trees as before, and still check that they are not the same.

But after that, we actually have to retrieve the info for both roots, and we check which tree is larger: the smaller one will end up as the child, and we will reassign its root. Moreover, we need to update the rank for the larger tree's root; its subtree will now also contain all the elements in its new child.

If you'd like to look at some code for the heuristics implementation, we have an example on GitHub.

This is all we need to change in order to achieve a tremendous boost in performance. The simplicity of the code shows you how clever this solution is, and in the next sections we will also see why it is so important to get it right.

5.7 Applications

Applications for disjoint set are ubiquitous, and the reason they have been studied at length is exactly due to the number of cases where they prove useful.

5.7.1 Graphs: Connected components

For *undirected graphs*, there is a simple algorithm that uses disjoint sets to keep track of their *connected components*, that is, areas of the graph that are interconnected.

While connected components are usually computed using Depth First Search (*DFS*), we can use a disjoint set to keep track of the components while we scan all the graph's edges. An example is shown in listing 5.11.

Listing 5.11 Computing connected components of a graph with a disjoint set

```
disjointSet = new DisjointSet(graph.vertices)
for edge in graph.edges do
  disjointSet.merge(edge.source, edge.destination)
```

- **Creates a new disjoint set where each vertex of the graph is initially in a different partition** (line 1)
- **Loops over each edge in the graph** (line 2)
- **Merges the partitions to which source and destination vertices belong to** (line 3)

At the end, each partition of vertices in `disjointSet` will be a connected component.

It's worth noting that this algorithm can not be used for directed graphs and strongly connected components.

5.7.2 Graphs:[15] Kruskal's algorithm for minimum spanning tree

A spanning tree for a connected undirected *graph* `G` is a tree whose nodes are the vertex of the graphs, and whose edges are a subset of `G`'s edges. If `G` is connected, then it certainly has at least one spanning tree—possibly many, if it also has cycles (see figure 5.13).

Among all possible spanning trees, a *minimum spanning tree* (*MST*) is the one for which the sum of edges' weights is minimal.

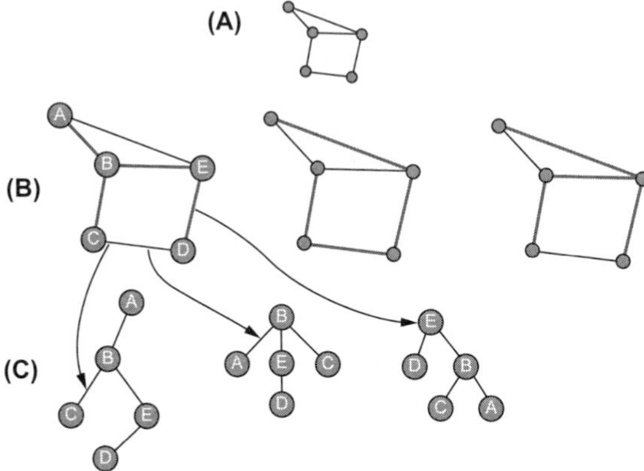

(A)
(B)
(C)
A
B
C
D
E

Figure 5.13 An example of a graph with several spanning trees. (A) An undirected, connected graph, containing cycles. (B) Since the graph has cycles, there are several spanning trees covering all nodes. A few examples are shown, each of them selecting only the smallest set of edges (the thick ones) that "span" all vertices. (C) For each set of edges, several trees can be obtained, depending on the root of the tree and the order of the children. (Only a few examples are shown. Notice, though, how they are not limited to binary trees.)

[15] For an introduction to graphs, see appendix G.

Kruskal's algorithm is beyond the scope of this book. Here it suffices to say that it constructs the MST for a graph by

1. Starting with each vertex in a difference set.
2. Keeping a disjoint set of the graph vertices.
3. Going through the graph's edges in order of increasing weight.
4. For each edge, if its extremes are not in the same partition, merge their components.
5. If all vertices belong to the same component, stop.

The MST will be defined by the list of edges that triggers, at point (4), merge calls for the disjoint set.

5.7.3 Clustering

Clustering is the most-used unsupervised learning[16] algorithm. The problem here is that we would like to get a partitioning of a set of points into a few, usually disjoint subsets, as shown in figure 5.14.

There are several types of clustering algorithms. Although a taxonomy of clustering is beyond the scope of this chapter (we will devote chapter 12 to this topic), here we will mention one particular class of these algorithms.

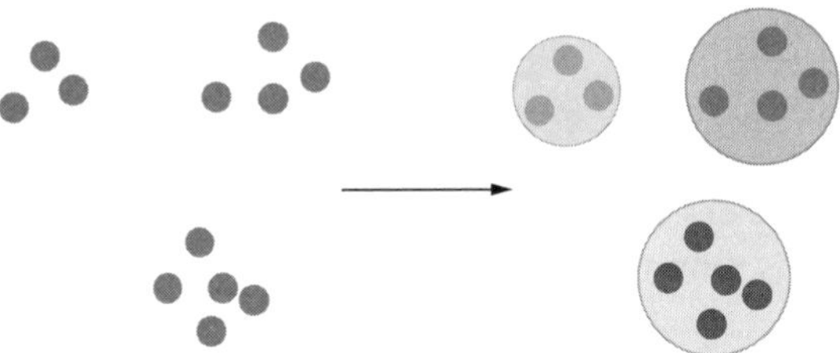

Figure 5.14 An example of clustering. On the left, we have a raw dataset of 2-D points. We have no extra information about the points or the relationships between them. After clustering the dataset, on the right we can see that we have inferred some relationships between the points, and in particular we grouped them in three subsets whose points seem to show higher correlation.

Agglomerative hierarchical clustering starts with each point in its own *cluster* (partition) and continuously merges two points (and their clusters) until all clusters are merged into one; figure 5.15 shows an example of how it works. The algorithm keeps a history of this process, and it is possible to get a snapshot of the clusters created at any of the steps. The exact point where this snapshot is taken is controlled by a few parameters and determines the result of the algorithm.

The description of the algorithm should ring a bell: at each step we need to find two points belonging to two different clusters. You can easily imagine what the best

[16]Unsupervised machine learning deals with making sense of "unlabeled" data (that is, data that has not been classified or categorized), with the goal of finding a structure in the raw data.

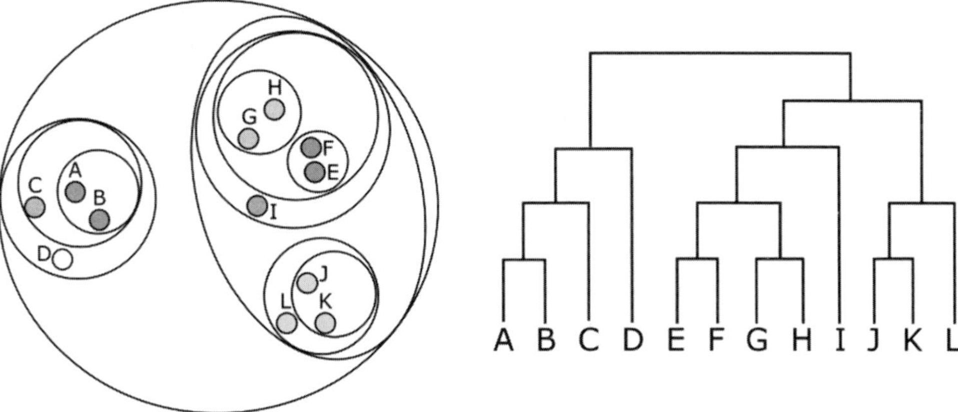
A
B
C
D
E
F
G
H
I
J
K
L
A B C D E F G H I J K L

Figure 5.15 An example of hierarchical clustering. On the left, the dataset (a collection of 2-D points) is shown with progressive grouping shown as ellipses. From the figure, it can be inferred that, for instance, A and B are grouped together before C is added to the two of them to form a larger cluster. Hence, the relationship between A and B is inferred to be stronger than the one between A and C or B and C. On the right, the same process is shown using a *dendrogram*.[17] Note that both figures could be the result either of agglomerative or divisive clustering: the former produces the dendrogram starting from the bottom, the latter starting from the top.

data structure is to compute and find that information. In chapter 13, we'll see a practical application of disjoint set as part of a distributed clustering algorithm.

5.7.4 Unification

Unification is the process of solving equations between symbolic expressions. One of the ways of solving such an equation is finding terms on both sides that are equivalent, and removing them from the equation.

Of course, solution strategies depend on which expressions (terms) can appear in the equation and how you can compare them or when they are considered to be equal. For instance, they might be evaluated and considered equal if they have the same value, or they might be symbolic and considered equal if they are equivalent, possibly net of some variable substitution.

As you can imagine, the disjoint set data structure is perfect for high-performance algorithms solving this problem.

Summary

- The beauty of a disjoint set is that we can build increasingly complex and efficient solutions to solve it, just adding small incremental changes.
- We can sometimes settle for a sub-optimal implementation if that's efficient enough and performance is not critical.

[17] A dendrogram (from Greek dendro "tree" and gramma "drawing") is a tree diagram specifically used to illustrate the arrangement of the clusters produced by hierarchical clustering.

- Probably we could settle for the naïve linear time solution, but it is such a fundamental part of many graph algorithms that we just need to optimize it as much as possible.
- We do know a theoretical lower bound for the running time of operations of a disjoint set, but we don't know if there exists an algorithm that runs with that bound, or even any other algorithm faster than the ones we know.
- The *inverse Ackermann function*, whose value won't be greater than 5 for any integer that could fit on a computer, models the order of magnitude of the running time for the `merge` operation on disjoint sets. Merging two subsets will, on average, only require at most five swaps.

6 Trie, radix trie: Efficient string search

This chapter covers

- Understanding why working with strings is different
- Introducing trie[1] for efficient string search and indexing
- Introducing radix tree[2] as a memory-efficient evolution of trie
- Using prefix trees to solve string-related problems
- Leveraging tries to implement an efficient spell-checker

How many times have you sent a text or an email or tweeted in a hurry, only to realize a second later that you made a typo? For me, it was too many times! Lately, however, we've had a precious ally on our side in email clients and browsers in general: spell-checkers! If you'd like to know more about how they work and how to implement them efficiently, this chapter is the right place to start.

[1] Also known as prefix tree.

[2] Also known as radix trie or compact prefix tree.

In chapter 3 we described balanced trees, which offer the best compromise when it comes to containers and are ideal for efficiently storing dynamically changing data on which we need to perform frequent searches. In appendix C we discussed and compared the options we have for containers providing fast lookup, fast insertion, or fast removal, and trees offer the best tradeoff between all the operations.

Balanced trees, in particular, guarantee logarithmic running time in the worst-case for all the main operations. In the general case, when we don't know anything about the data we need to store and (later) search, this is really the best we can hope.

But what happens when we know that we will only store certain types of data in a container? Turns out there are several cases where if we have more information on the kind of data we need to handle, we can leverage better algorithms than the general-purpose ones.

Take, for instance, sorting: if we know that keys are integers in a limited range, we can use *RadixSort*, which means achieving better-than-linearithmic performance, defying the lower bound for sorting by comparison.[3]

Likewise, if we know that we need to sort strings, there are several specialized algorithms, such as the *3-way string quicksort*, that are optimized for this kind of data and perform better than plain, general-purpose quicksort (or any comparison-based sorting algorithm).

In this chapter, we will analyze a particular sub-class of containers, string containers, and investigate how we can optimize them both with respect to memory and running time by introducing new, specialized data structures: tries and radix tries. Then we'll use those containers to implement an efficient spell-checker.

6.1 Spell-check

But first, let's introduce the problem that we will solve in this chapter: spell-checking.

Not that the problem really needs any introduction, right? We would like to have a piece of software that can take words as inputs and return `true` or `false`, respectively, whether the input is a valid English word[4] or not.

That's a bit of a vague description that leaves the door open to many possible (and possibly inefficient) solutions; we need more context to clarify our requirements. Let's assume that we are developing a new client for a social network on a client with low resources (for instance, on a mobile OS) and we need to add a live spell-checker that produces the classic red wavy underline below a misspelled word. Every time we type a word (and every time we type a word separator, like a space, commas, and so on) we need to check whether there is a typo.

---

[3] It has been proven that it's not possible to sort a list of `n` elements with less than `O(n*log(n))` operations if the method used is exclusively based on comparisons. RadixSort can get as low as `O(n * log(k))` for sorting `n` integers that can take any of `k` possible values. For large values of `k`, when `k~=n`, the algorithm behaves no better than the generic linearithmic bound.

[4] Obviously, it's possible to write spell checkers for any language; choosing English is just a matter of convenience.

Due to scarce resources, we need our spell-checker to be fast and lightweight; we need to reduce its impact as much as possible, both in terms of CPU and memory usage.

But we would also like our spell-checker to be able to learn—for instance, so users can add their names or the name of their town/club/favorite artists and so on.

6.1.1 A prncess, a Damon, and an elf walkz into a bar

Have you noticed the typos in this section's title?[5] Typos are always around the corner when you need to send a message in a hurry (regardless of the medium used) and unfortunately, once these messages are sent out, there is no going back—you can't edit them anymore.[6]

That's why a spell-checker that clearly highlights typos comes in handy, and today it's often included natively in browsers.

In the end, the design of our spell-checker is pretty simple: it is a wrapper around a *dictionary*,[7] and the client's method that checks spelling just calls the container `contains` method, and if the result is a miss, adds the visual feedback to show the error.

In turn, the design of our container's API is also simple. It's a generic container supporting search, like the API of binary search trees or Randomized Treaps (described in section 3.4).

We can already think about how to implement this container with the tools that we learned. For instance, if we knew that we had to support fast lookups on a static set, then we would have chosen a hash table or, if we could trade saving some memory for a certain loss of precision, we could even resort to a Bloom filter. Since the requirement is maintaining an open, dynamic set, however, the one data structure providing the best compromise for all the operations would be a tree.

A simple binary tree could, of course, be enough to support all the operations provided by dictionaries. Figure 6.1 shows a possible representation of what these trees could look like, where we chose to show only a small part of the subtree containing a few similar words (we'll see why this is relevant in a few lines).

How fast can operations on such a tree be? Assuming the tree is balanced, its height will be logarithmic in the number of words it contains, so for each call to `contains`, `insert`, `remove`, and so on, we'll need to traverse on average (and at most) `O(log(n))` nodes.

So far, however, when we've analyzed trees, we've assumed their keys were either integers or could be checked in constant time and require a constant space.

---

[5] Ring a bell? It should . . .

[6] With tweets, of course, you can now delete them—if you are fast enough—even before someone notices.

[7] Here the term refers to the abstract data structure called a dictionary that, incidentally but not surprisingly, is used to model the digital equivalent of actual dictionaries. See appendix C and chapter 4 for more details.

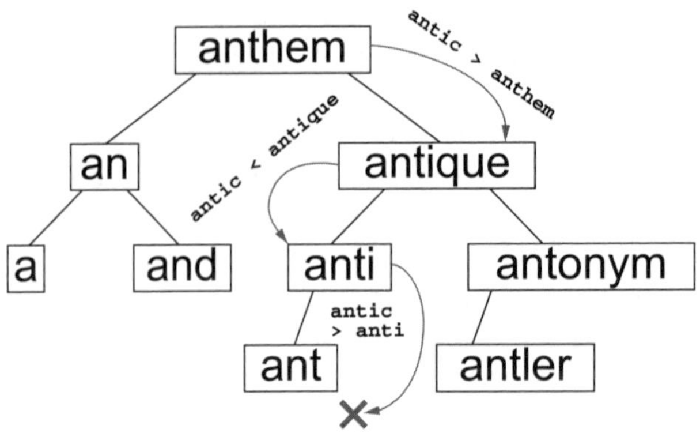
anthem
antic > anthem
an
antic < antique
antique
a
and
anti
antonym
antic
> anti
ant
antler

Figure 6.1 A BST storing (part of) a dictionary, and the steps to search the word "antic". In this example, it's a miss because the word was not stored in the tree shown.

For generic strings, this assumption is not realistic anymore. Each node will need to store a string of unbounded length, so the total memory needed to store the tree will be the sum, for each node, of all the keys' lengths:

$$E[S(n)] = E\left[\sum_{i=0}^{n-1} |k_i|\right] = \sum_{i=0}^{n-1} E\,[k_i] \approx \sum_{i=0}^{n-1} L = n \cdot L$$

If we assume that the average length of the strings held by the tree is `L`, the expected value for `S(n)`, the space needed to store the tree, is proportional to `n*L`. If the maximum length for strings is denoted with `m`, then `S(n) = O(n*m)` is a strict upper bound for the worst case.

Likewise, if we look at the running time of the `search` method, we see that we can't ignore the strings' lengths anymore. For instance, a call to `search("antic")` on the tree in figure 6.1 would start from the root and compare `"antic"` to `"anthem"`, which would require at least four characters to be compared before verifying the two words are not the same. Then we would move to the right branch and again compare the two strings, `"antic"` and `"antique"` (five more character-to-character comparisons), and since they don't match, traverse the left subtree now, and so on.

Therefore, a call to search would require, worst case, `T(n) = O(log(n)*m)` comparisons.

6.1.2 Compression is the key

This quick analysis shows that using a tree is not ideal, either space-wise or performance-wise. If we look more closely at the tree in figure 6.1, we can see that there seems to be a lot of overhead: all words start with the character `"a"`, but this is stored once for every node of the subtree in the illustration, and for each step in the traversal of the tree, it will be compared with the text that is being searched (or inserted).

Looking at the path to search for the word `"antic"`, all the four nodes shown and traversed share the same prefix, `"ant"`. Wouldn't it be nice if we could somehow compress these nodes and only store the common prefix once with the deltas for each node?

6.1.3 Description and API

The data structure that we are going to introduce in the next section was created to answer these needs, and also to offer an efficient way to solve another operation: find all the keys in the container that start with the same prefix.

From our example in the previous sub-section, you can already see that if we were able to somehow store the common prefixes of strings only once, we should be able to quickly access all strings starting with those prefixes.

Table 6.1 shows the public API for an abstract data structure (ADT) that supports the usual container basic operations, plus two new ones: retrieving all the strings starting with a certain prefix and finding the longest prefix of a string stored in the container.

From what we saw in the previous example, `PrefixTree` could be a good name for this data structure, although `StringContainer` is more generic (as an abstract data structure, we don't care if it's implemented using a tree or some other concrete counterpart.) It conveys the gist of this container: being specific for strings. The fact that prefix search is supported is almost a natural consequence of designing a container for strings.

Table 6.1 API and contract for `StringContainer`

Abstract Data Structure: `StringContainer`	

API	`class StringContainer {`
	`  insert(key)`
	`  remove(key)`
	`  contains(key)`
	`  longestPrefix(key)`
	`  keysStartingWith(prefix)`
	`}`

Contract with client	Besides all the operations of a regular, plain container, this structure allows us to search for the longest prefix of a string that is stored in it and return all the stored strings that start with a certain prefix.

Now that we have fixed an API and described the ADT that we will use to solve our spell-check problem, we are ready to delve into more details and see a few concrete data structures that could implement this ADT.

6.2 Trie

The first implementation of `StringContainer` that we will illustrate is the *trie*; incidentally, all the other data structures that we will show in the next sections are based on tries, so we couldn't choose to start anywhere else.

The first thing you should know about trie is that it's actually pronounced "try." Its author,[8] René de la Briandais, chose this term because it was similar to tree, but also

[8] De La Briandais, Rene. "File searching using variable length keys." Papers presented at the March 3-5, 1959, western joint computer conference. ACM, 1959.

because it's part of the word re*trie*val, which is the main purpose of this container; its peculiar pronunciation is partly meant as an indented pun, and partly meant to avoid confusion with "tree."

Tries were originally developed as a compact, efficient way to search strings in files; the idea behind this data structure is, as we saw in the previous section, providing a way to reduce redundancy by storing common prefixes of strings just once.

This couldn't be achieved using a plain binary search tree, or with just a binary tree, so a paradigm shift was needed: de la Briandais then used n-ary trees, where edges are marked with all the characters in an alphabet, and nodes just connect paths.

Nodes also have a small but crucial function: they store a tiny bit of information stating if the path from root to current node corresponds to a key stored in the trie.

Let's take a look at figure 6.2 before moving to a more formal description. It shows the structure of a typical trie, containing the words `"a"`, `"an"`, `"at"`, and `"I"`.

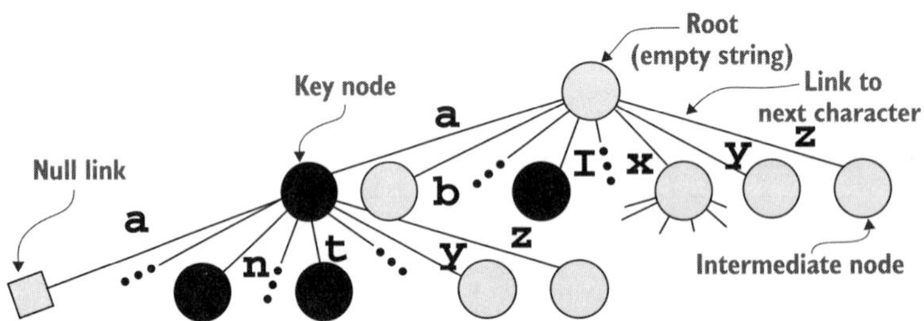
Root
(empty string)
Link to
next character
Key node
Null link
Intermediate node
a
b
I
x
y
z
a
n
t
y
z

Figure 6.2 The structure of a trie. Words are encoded in the tree using edges, each edge corresponds to a single character, and each node `n` is associated with a single word, the one obtained by joining the characters associated with the edges in the path from the root to `n`. The root node corresponds to the empty string (because no edge is traversed), the leftmost leaf corresponds to `"aa"`, and so on. Not all the paths make meaningful words, and not all the nodes store the word associated with them. Only filled, black nodes (called "key nodes") mark words stored in the trie, while hollow nodes, aka "intermediate nodes," correspond to prefixes of words stored in the trie. Notice that all leaves should be key nodes.

If you feel that figure 6.2 is a bit confusing, you are right. In their classic implementation, a trie's nodes have one edge for each possible character in the alphabet used: some of these edges point to other nodes, but most of them (especially in the lower levels of the tree) are `null` references.[9]

Nevertheless, this specific representation of tries looks terrible on paper: too many links and too many nodes that result in chaos.

That's why we will use an alternative representation, shown in figure 6.3. We'll only show links to actual trie nodes, omitting links to `null`.

[9] As we'll shortly see, this happens for all characters `c` for which there is no suffix of the current node whose next character is `c`.

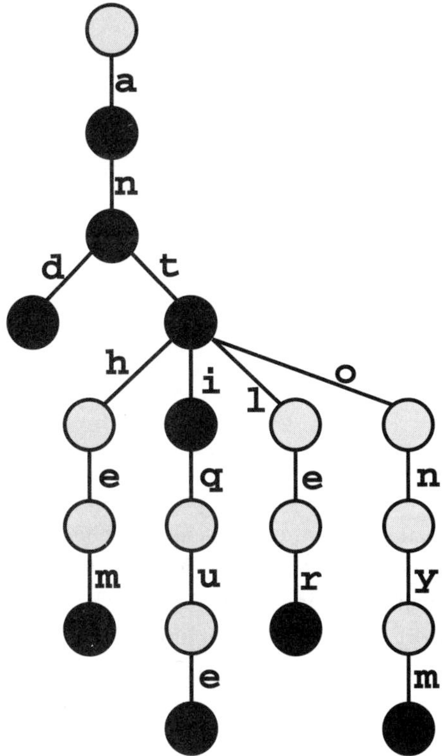
a
n
d
t
h
i
l
o
e
q
e
n
m
u
r
y
e
m

Figure 6.3 A more compact representation of a trie. This example trie contains the same elements as the binary search tree in figure 6.1.

Formally, given an alphabet Σ with `|Σ|=k` symbols, a trie is a `k`-ary[10] tree where each node has (at most) `k` children, each one marked with a different character in Σ; links to children can point to another node, or to `null`.

Unlike `k`-ary search trees, though, no node in the tree actually stores the key associated with it. Instead, the characters held in the trie are actually stored in the edges between a node and its children.

Listing 6.1 illustrates a possible implementation of a `Trie` class (in object-oriented pseudo-code); you can also take a look at a full implementation on the book's repo on GitHub.[11]

Listing 6.1 Class Trie

```
#type Char[]
Alphabet

class Node
```

[10]Although we'd usually talk about n-ary trees, we also usually reserve `n` to denote the number of entries in a container (or, in general, the input size for a problem). To avoid confusion, then, we will use `k` for the size of the alphabet and, consequently, the term k-ary.

[11]See https://github.com/mlarocca/AlgorithmsAndDataStructuresInAction#trie.

```
    #type boolean
    keyNode

    #type HashMap<Char, Node>
    children

    function Node(storesKey)
      for char in Alphabet do
        this.children[char] ← null
      this.keyNode ← storesKey

class Trie
    #type Node
    root

    function Trie()
      root ← new Node(false)
```

In the simplest version, trie's nodes can only hold a tiny piece of information, just `true` or `false`. When marked with `true`, a node `N` is called a *key node* because it means that the sequence of characters in the edges of the path from the root to `N` corresponds to a word that is actually stored in the trie. Nodes holding `false` are called *intermediate nodes* because they correspond to intermediate characters of one or more words stored in the trie.

As you can see, tries go beyond the usual duality between leaves and inner nodes, introducing another (orthogonal) distinction. It turns out, though, that all leaves in a well-formed, minimal trie are key nodes: a leaf would make no sense as an intermediate node, as we will see.

The fact that words are stored in paths means that all the descendants of a node share a common prefix: the path from the root to their common parent. For instance, if we look at figure 6.3, we can see that all nodes share the prefix `"an"`, and all but one node share `"ant"`. These two words, incidentally, are also stored in the trie, because the nodes at the end of their path are key nodes.

The root is, to all extents, an intermediate node associated with the empty string; it would be a key node only if the empty string belonged to the corpus contained in the trie.

While for spell checkers storing a Boolean in each node could be enough (after all, we only need to know whether a word is in a dictionary), tries are often used to store or index words in texts. If that's the case, we often need to know either how many occurrences of a word appear in the text or the positions where they appear. In the former situation we can store a counter in each node and only key nodes will have a positive value. In the latter we will instead use a list of positions, storing the index in the text where each occurrence starts.

6.2.1 Why is it better again?

Let's address space first: why is the trie in figure 6.3 better than the binary search tree in figure 6.1?

Let's do some quick math! But first, we need to make some assumptions:

- We only consider ASCII strings and characters, so we have to account for 1 byte for each char (Unicode wouldn't change much; rather, it would make the savings obtained by using the cheapest option even greater) plus, in BSTs, 1 byte for each string's terminator.
- We only explicitly store links to actual nodes in tries and account for a fixed number of bytes for null-pointers in BSTs (the same space taken by non-null references).
- As we mentioned, each node in a trie has $|\Sigma|$ links, where $|\Sigma|$ is the alphabet size. This means that in tries, and especially in nodes in the lower levels, most links are `null`, and indeed in listing 6.1 it's also possible to see how all those links are initialized in `Node's` constructor.
- For each node in a trie, we account for a fixed amount of space to store the children list (we can imagine that we use a hash table to store the link to children), plus a variable amount depending on the number of actual children.
- Each link in a tree will require 8 bytes (64 bit references), and each link in a trie will require 9 bytes (8 for the reference plus 1 for the character to which it's associated).
- Each node in the BST will require as many bytes as the number of characters in its key, plus 4 bytes[12] for the Node object itself.
- Each node in the trie requires 1 bit (to hold the Boolean) plus the same constant amount as for the BST; let's round up to 5 bytes.

Given these premises, we note that the BST in figure 6.1 has 9 nodes (whose keys are strings) and consequently `2*9=18` links, while the trie in figure 6.3 has 19 nodes and 18 links. For the BST, the root node contains the key `"anthem"` and requires 27 bytes (4 for the Node itself, 7 for the string, 2*8 for the links). Likewise, its left child, with key `"an"`, requires 23 bytes. You see how it's computed; it's 21 bytes per node, plus the length of the string. For the whole tree, considering it has 9 nodes and requires a total of 47 bytes for the keys, we need 227 bytes.

Let's now check the trie: each node requires 5 bytes, and each link 9 bytes—a total of 257 bytes.

So, in practice, this trie might require a little more memory than the corresponding BST. These quantities depend on many factors; first of all, the overhead for objects. Since this trie has more nodes, the more this overhead is, the larger the delta will be.

Obviously, however, the shape of the tree and the actual number of nodes also play a big role. In the example in figure 6.3, only a short prefix is shared among the keys. It turns out that tries are more efficient when holding keys with a large shared prefix. The example in figure 6.4 shows how the balance can be in favor of tries in these cases. As

---

[12]This quantity is completely arbitrary; real objects in programming languages have an overhead, which can be way larger than 4 bytes (for instance, usually between 8 and 16 bytes in Java or C++).

you can see, in figure 6.4 most trie nodes are black (key nodes), and when the ratio of key nodes versus intermediate nodes is higher, intuitively it means that the efficiency of the trie is also higher, because when a path has more than one key node, we are storing at least two words in a single path (one of which is a prefix of the other). In a BST they would require two BST nodes storing both of the strings separately.

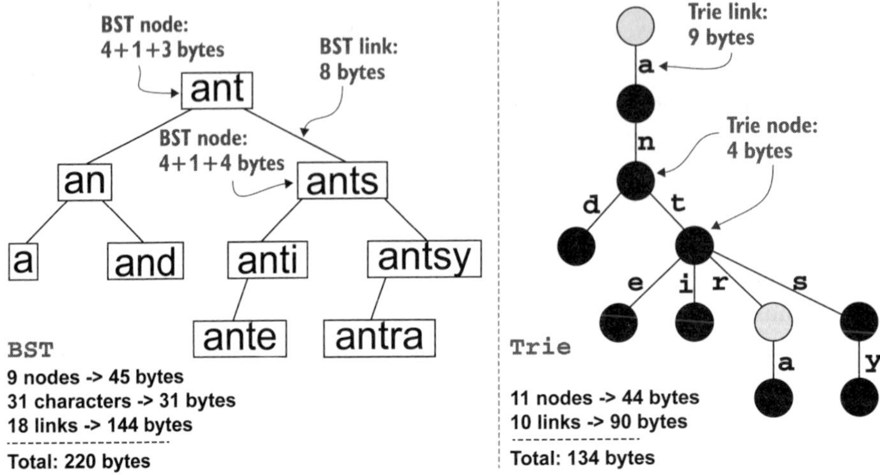
BST node:
4+1+3 bytes
BST link:
8 bytes
ant
BST node:
4+1+4 bytes
an
ants
a
and
anti
antsy
ante
antra
BST
9 nodes -> 45 bytes
31 characters -> 31 bytes
18 links -> 144 bytes
Total: 220 bytes
Trie link:
9 bytes
Trie node:
4 bytes
a
n
d
t
e
i
r
s
a
y
Trie
11 nodes -> 44 bytes
10 links -> 90 bytes
Total: 134 bytes

Figure 6.4 Comparing BST and trie approaches on a different example. When the keys in the trie have a larger ratio of shared characters (that is, a longer common prefix), tries are more efficient in storing strings

Another sign of more-efficient storage is when there are deep nodes branching out. In that case, the trie is "compressing" the space needed for two strings with a common prefix by storing the common prefix only once.

In the end, with just nine words stored in this second example, using the same assumptions as shown previously, the difference becomes 220 bytes versus 134 bytes, with tries saving almost 40% of the space. If we consider an 8-byte overhead for nodes, the difference would be 256 versus 178 bytes, and the savings would be around 30%, which is still impressive. For large trees containing dictionaries or indexing large texts, we would be talking about hundreds of megabytes.

Figure 6.4 shows the best-case scenario for tries, but obviously things are not always looking this good. Figure 6.5 shows a different edge case, close to the worst-case scenario, where the longest prefix in a (degenerate) trie is the empty string. In cases like this, information

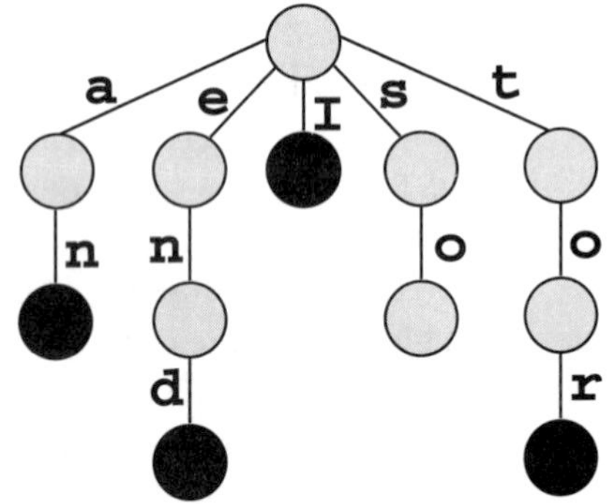
a
e
I
s
t
n
n
o
o
d
r

Figure 6.5 A degenerate trie, where no string shares a prefix with another string

ends up being stored very inefficiently; luckily, however, these edge cases are incredibly unlikely in real-world applications.

So much for space consumption. At worst, tries can be considered comparable to binary search trees. What about their running time? We will answer this question while looking at the individual methods in order to develop an understanding of how these results are derived.

6.2.2 Search

Let's start with search. Assuming we have built a proper trie, how do we check whether it contains a certain key?

Turns out, it's not too difficult, compared to a BST. The main difference is that we need to walk the tree one character (of the searched key) at a time, following the link that is marked precisely with that character.

Both strings and tries are recursive structures, whose unit of iteration is the single character; each string, in fact, can be described as either

- The empty string, `""`
- The concatenation of a character `c` and a string `s'`: `s=c+s'`, where `s'` is a string one character shorter than `s` and can possibly be the empty string

NOTE In most programming languages single quote characters wouldn't be allowed in variable names, so we use `tail` in listing 6.2 as a substitute name for `s'`, which denotes the tail of current string `s` in the figures.

For instance, the string `"home"` is made of the character `'h'` concatenated to the string `"ome"`, which in turn is `'o' + "me"`, and so on, until we get to `"e"`, which can be written as the character `'e'` concatenated to the empty string `""`.

A trie, on the other end, stores strings as paths from the root to key nodes. We can describe a trie `T` as a root node connected to (at most) $|\Sigma|$ shorter tries. If a sub-trie `T'` is connected to the root by an edge marked with character `c` ($c \in \Sigma$), then for all strings s in `T', c + s` belongs to `T`.

For instance, in figure 6.3, the root has only one outgoing edge, marked with `'a'`; considering `T'` as the only sub-trie of the root, `T'` contains the word `"n"`, and this means that `T` contains `'a' + "n" = "an"`.

Since both strings and tries are recursive, it's natural to define the search method recursively. We can consider just the case where we search the first character of a string `s=c+s'` starting from the root `R` of the trie `T`. If `c`, the first character of `s`, matches an outgoing of `R`, then we can search `s'` in the (sub)trie `T'`. We assume the root of the sub-trie is not `null` (as we'll see shortly, it's a reasonable assumption).

If at any point `s` is the empty string, then we have traversed the whole path in the trie corresponding to `s`. We then need to check the current node to verify whether our string `s` is stored in the tree.

If, instead, at some point the current node doesn't have an outgoing edge matching current character `c`, then we are sure string `s` is not stored in the trie.

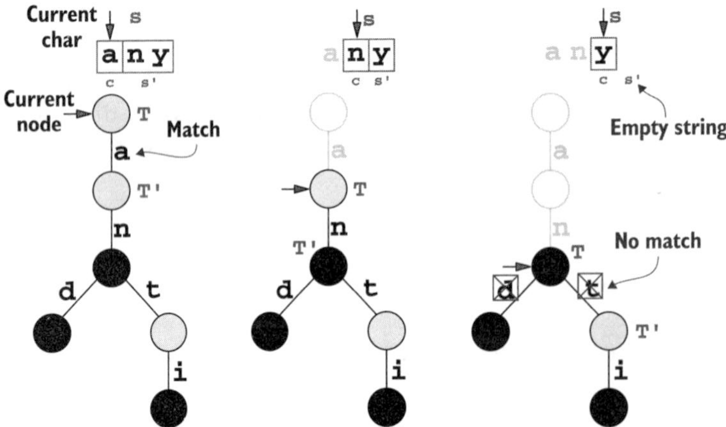
Current char
s
any
c s'
Current node
T
Match
a
T'
n
d
t
i
Empty string
No match

Figure 6.6 An unsuccessful search in a trie. At each step, we break the key to search, the string `s`, into `c+s'`: the concatenation of its first character and the rest of the string. Then we compare `c` to the current node's outgoing edges, and if we find a match, we go ahead traversing the tree. In this example, the search fails because the last character in the string doesn't match any outgoing edge.

We'll illustrate these examples in figures 6.6 and 6.7, but first, let's take a look at the implementation of the search method that we will then use as a reference while describing these examples.

In listing 6.2 we show a recursive implementation of the search method. At each call, we need to check if the first character in the substring searched matches an outgoing edge of the current node, and then recursively search the tail of the current string in the subtree referenced by that edge. Figures 6.6 and 6.7 shows the parallel between moving "right" in the string searched and traversing down the trie.

The same method can obviously be implemented using explicit loops. This implementation of the search method is likely suitable for a compiler's tail-call optimization,[13] but as discussed in appendix E and chapter 3, if you are not comfortable with recursion or are not sure that your compiler will apply tail-call optimization, my advice is to write the iterative version of these methods to avoid stack overflow.

Listing 6.2 Method search

Method `search`, a standalone function, takes a trie node and the string key `s` to be searched. It returns `true` if `s` is stored in the trie, and `false` otherwise. We assume that node is never `null`, which is a reasonable assumption if this method is implemented as a private method internally called by the trie's API search method.

Checks if the string searched is empty. If it is, since this method is implemented using recursion, we know it has traversed the whole path in the trie.

We are at the target node for the target key; the trie stores it only if the current node is a key node.

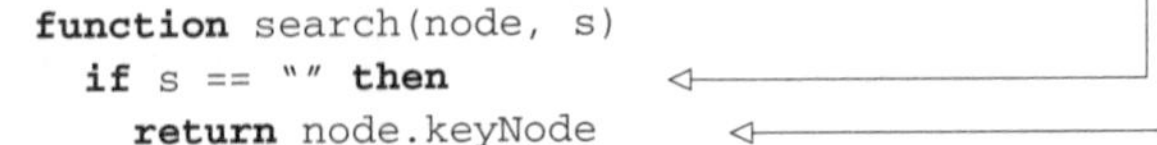

```
function search(node, s)
  if s == "" then
    return node.keyNode
```

[13]As explained in appendix E, whenever in a method defined using recursion the recursive call is limited to the very last operation, compilers can optimize the target machine code by rewriting code using explicit loops instead of function calls. The caveat is that not all compilers provide this optimization.

Since s is not the empty string, it can be broken into a *head* character, c (the first character of s) and a *tail*, the rest of the string.

If there is no outgoing edge in node for the character c, it means that we cannot traverse the trie any further, so that s is not stored in the subtree rooted at node.

Otherwise, we recursively search tail into the subtree referenced by children[c].

```
c, tail ← s.splitAt(0)
if node.children[c] == null then
  return false
else
  return search(node.children[c], tail)
```

Listing 6.3 shows the trie's API counterpart, which in turn will call the method in listing 6.2. We will omit these wrapper methods for the other operations when they are as trivial as for search.

Listing 6.3 Method Trie::search

Method search (for class Trie) takes a string key s to be searched; it returns true if s is stored in the trie, and false otherwise.

Checks if the trie's root is null. If so, no string is stored in the trie, and we can return false.

Otherwise, we forward the call to the root's search method.

```
function Trie::search(s)
  if this.root == null then
    return false
  else
    return search(this.root, s)
```

As already mentioned, there are two possible cases of unsuccessful search in tries: in the first one, shown in figure 6.6, we traverse the trie until we get to a node that doesn't have an outgoing edge for the next character. In the example, a call to trie.search("any"), this happens when we get to the key's last character, 'y' (as shown in the right diagram in figure 6.6). In listing 6.2, this corresponds to the condition in the if at line #5 returning true.

The other possible case for an unsuccessful search is that we always find a suitable outgoing edge until we recursively call search on the empty string. When this happens, it means we've reached the trie's node whose path from the root spells out the searched key. For instance, in figure 6.7 we traverse the tree link by link and check the string key character by character, until the condition at line #2 of listing 6.2 returns true and we go to line #3.

The result of line #3 is the only difference between a successful and an unsuccessful search. Looking at the example in figure 6.7, a successful search for the word "ant" would follow the exact same steps, with the only difference being that the final node (denoted with T in the rightmost diagram) would have to be a key node.

Notice that in listing 6.3, we can avoid checking for empty tries or handling the root as a special case, because in the trie constructor in listing 6.1, we create the root as an empty node. This (together with careful implementation of all the methods) will also support our assumption that the node argument in search (and all the other methods) is never null.

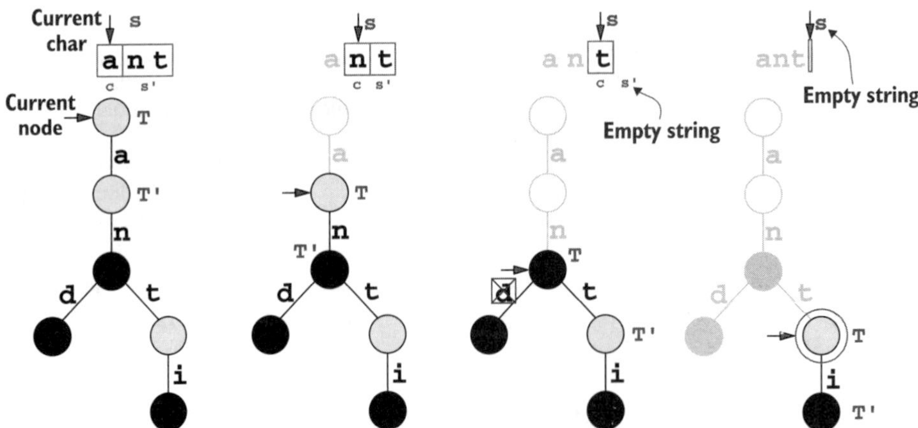
Current char
s
ant
c s'
Current node
T
a
T'
n
d
t
i
Empty string
Empty string

Figure 6.7 Another example of an unsuccessful search in a trie. In this example, the search fails because the path corresponding to the string searched ends in an *intermediate node*.

The `search` method is the most important method for tries, because all the other methods will be based on it. Search is so crucial to those implementations that we provide (in listing 6.4) a variant, `searchNode`, that returns the node found, rather than just `true` or `false`. We'll see in the next sections how this can be used to implement `remove`.

Listing 6.4 Method searchNode

```
function searchNode(node, s)
  if s == "" then
      return node
  c, tail ← s.splitAt(0)
  if node.children[c] == null then
    return null
  else
    return search(node.children[c], tail)
```

Performance-wise, how fast is `search`? The number of recursive calls we make is limited by the smaller of two values: the maximum height of the trie and the length of the search string. The latter is usually shorter than the former, but either way, for a string of length `m` we can be sure that no more than `O(m)` calls are going to be made, regardless of the number of keys stored in the trie.

The key is, then, how long each step takes. It turns out there are three factors influencing this cost:

- The cost of comparing two characters: this can be assumed to be `O(1)`.
- The cost of finding the next node: for an alphabet Σ of size `k`, this can be, depending on the implementation:

  - Constant (amortized or worst-case[14]), `O(1)`, using hash tables for edges
  - Logarithmic worst-case `O(log(k))`, using a balanced tree
  - Linear worst-case `O(k)`, using plain arrays

  Amortized constant time can reasonably be assumed in most cases.

- The cost of following a link and of splitting a string into `head+tail`. This point is the one where we need to be really careful. The naïve approach of extracting a substring for each node would be a performance disaster in most programming languages. Strings are usually implemented as immutable objects, so extracting a substring would require linear time and extra space, `O(m)`, for each call. Luckily, the solution is simple: we can pass to the recursive call a reference to the beginning of the string and the index of the next character. This way, even this operation can be considered `O(1)`.

Since each call can be implemented in such a way as to require amortized constant time, the whole search takes `O(m)` amortized running time.

6.2.3 *Insert*

Like `search`, `insert` can be better defined recursively. We can identify two different scenarios for this method:

- The trie already has a path corresponding to the key to be inserted. If that's the case, we only have to change the last node in the path, making it a key node (or, if we are indexing a text, adding a new entry to the list of indices for the word).
- The trie only has a path for a substring of the key. In this case, we will have to add new nodes to the trie.

Figure 6.8 illustrates an example of the former situation, where a call to `insert("anthem")` on the trie in figure 6.7 will result in adding a new branch to one of the leaves of the tree.

The method, as shown in listing 6.5, mainly consists of two steps. In the first step, we traverse the tree, following links corresponding to the next character in the key to add, until we either have consumed the whole input string, or we get to a node where there is no outgoing edge matching the key's next character.

Using listing 6.5 as a reference, we can see that the first step of the algorithm is implemented in lines #1 to #7, where we keep traversing the tree using the characters in the key to insert to choose the next branch to traverse. This is exactly the same as for `search`, with one difference: if we consume all characters in the input string (meaning that we traversed the whole path from the root, and reached the target trie node) we just have to set the node at the end of the path to a key node. This corresponds to the first scenario described at the beginning of the section (not shown in figure 6.8).

---

[14]Since the set of keys for the hash table, that is, the alphabet, is static and known in advance, it is possible to use perfect hashing and obtain worst-case constant time lookup. See appendix C for more details.

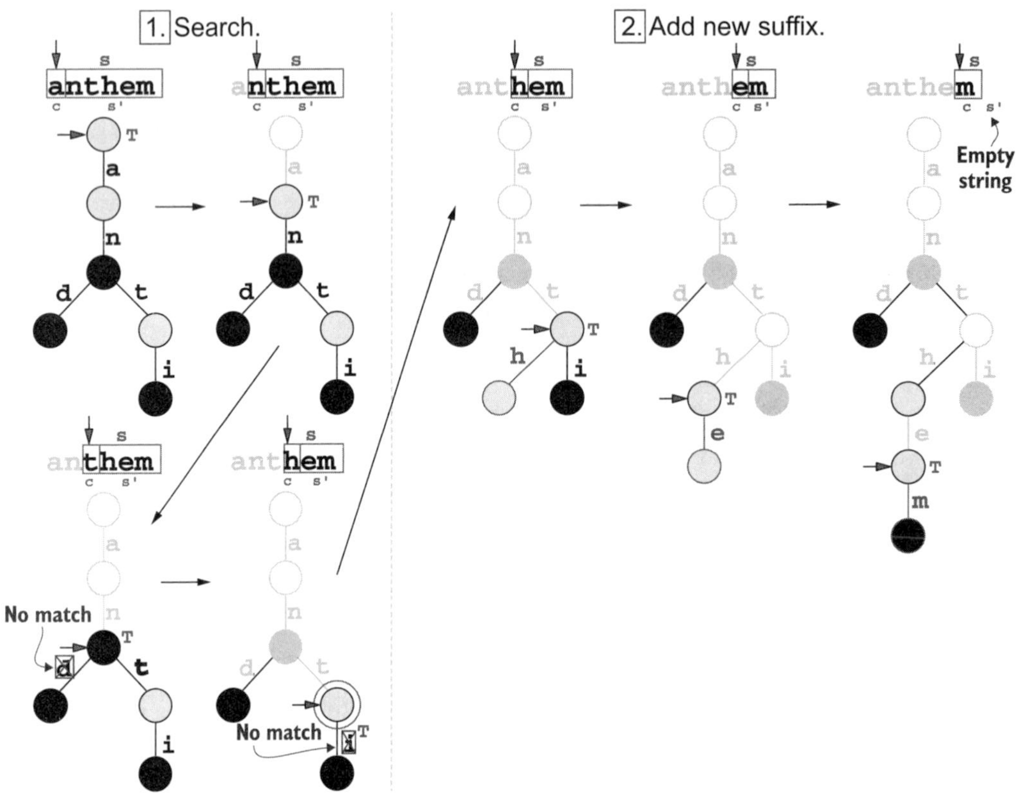

1. Search.
2. Add new suffix.
anthem
No match
No match
Empty string

Figure 6.8 An example of method `insert`. In a call to `trie.insert("anthem")`, we first search the longest prefix of `s` in the trie (`"ant"`); then, as a second step, from the node corresponding to the longest common prefix we add a new path for the remainder of `s` (`"hem"`).

When we reach the status shown in the last diagram of the left half of figure 6.8, it means that the condition at line #6 of listing 6.5 has become `false`. If that's the case, we need to jump to line #9 and add a brand new branch to the tree for the remaining characters in the string: by doing so, we are adding a suffix to the string matching the path from root to current node (in the example, we will add the suffix `"hem"` to the string `"ant"` already in the trie).

Listing 6.5 Method insert

Method `insert` takes a trie node and the string key `s` to be inserted. It returns nothing but has side effects on the trie. Again, we assume that `node` is never `null`: this is a reasonable assumption if this method is implemented as a private method, internally called by the trie's API `insert` method.

Checks if the string searched is empty. If it is, since this method is implemented using recursion, we know it has traversed the whole path in the trie.

We are at the target node for the target key. We set current node to a key node to ensure it will store s.

```
function insert(node, s)
  if s == "" then
    node.keyNode ← true
    return
```

Since s is not the empty string, it can be broken into a *head* character, c (the first character of s) and a *tail*, the rest of the string.

If there is an outgoing edge in node for the character c, we can keep recursively traversing the tree.

Following the recursive definition of this method, we need to insert tail in the subtree referenced by the edge marked with character c.

```
c, tail ← s.splitAt(0)
if node.children[c] != null then
  return insert(node.children[c], tail)
else
  return addNewBranch(node, s)
```

Otherwise, it means that we cannot traverse the trie any further: now we have to add the remaining characters in s as a new branch. (Be careful: not just the ones in tail! We also need to include character c.)

This last operation is implemented in a different utility method that is shown in listing 6.6 using (surprise!) recursion.

The definition of the method is quite straightforward. As shown in the right half of figure 6.8, we just consume one character of the remaining string, create a new edge marked with this character and a brand new, empty node N at the other side of the edge, and then recursively add the tail of the string to the tree T rooted at N.[15]

Listing 6.6 Method addNewBranch

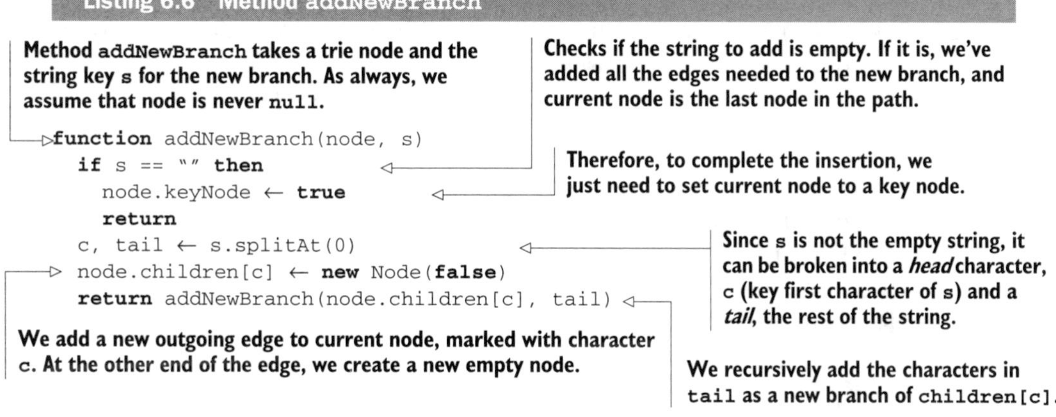
Method addNewBranch takes a trie node and the string key s for the new branch. As always, we assume that node is never null.
Checks if the string to add is empty. If it is, we've added all the edges needed to the new branch, and current node is the last node in the path.
Therefore, to complete the insertion, we just need to set current node to a key node.
Since s is not the empty string, it can be broken into a *head* character, c (key first character of s) and a *tail*, the rest of the string.
We add a new outgoing edge to current node, marked with character c. At the other end of the edge, we create a new empty node.
We recursively add the characters in tail as a new branch of children[c].

```
function addNewBranch(node, s)
  if s == "" then
    node.keyNode ← true
    return
  c, tail ← s.splitAt(0)
  node.children[c] ← new Node(false)
  return addNewBranch(node.children[c], tail)
```

Similarly to what we did for search, we can prove that insert also takes O(m) amortized time, if the creation of a new node can be performed in constant time (which is the case if we use hash tables for edges, but not if we use plain arrays).

6.2.4 Remove

When it comes to removing a key from a trie, we are in the position to choose. We can go for an easier, cheaper algorithm that will cause the tree to grow beyond what's necessary, or we can implement the full method, more complicated and possibly slower in practice, but with the lowest impact on memory.

[15]Notice that, since we just created this node N, it will be the only node in its subtree.

The difference between the two alternatives is that the first one simply unmarks a key node, making it an intermediate node, and doesn't worry about the tree structure. This can be easily implemented reusing the `searchNode` method in listing 6.4, shown in listing 6.7.

Listing 6.7 Method `Trie::remove` (no pruning)

```
function Trie::remove(s)
  node ← searchNode(this.root, s)
  if node == null or node.keyNode == false then
    return false
  else
    node.keyNode ← false
    return true
```

- Method `remove` (for class `Trie`) can be implemented naively for the `Trie` class using `search`. Here it takes the key to remove and returns a `Boolean` conveying the information about whether the key has been found and deleted.
- Performs a search on the trie and gets the node for `s` (if present)
- If `node` is `null`, or it's not a key node, it means that the key was not stored in the trie, so we return `false`.
- Otherwise, we mark the node as an intermediate node, and return `true`.

What's the issue with this method? Take a look at figure 6.8. If we just transform a key node N into an intermediate node, we can have two possible situations:

- N is an inner node, so it will have children storing keys that can only be reached by passing through N itself.
- N is a leaf, which means that there is no key stored in the trie that can only be reached through N.

The case where N is a leaf is illustrated in figure 6.9. After "unmarking" the key node at the end of the path, we can see that the trie has a "dangling" branch that contains no key. While it is perfectly fine to leave such a branch, because all the methods for manipulating tries will still work, if data is dynamic and there is a large ratio of deletions on the trie, the amount of memory wasted in dangling branches can become significant.

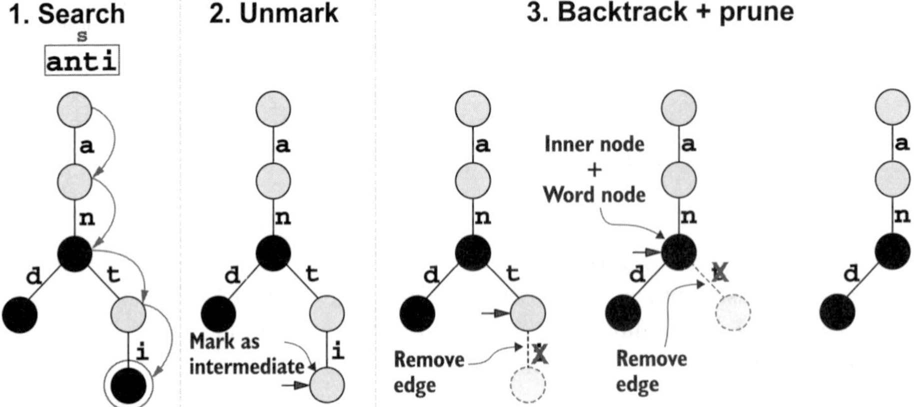
1. Search
s
anti
a
n
d
t
i
2. Unmark
Mark as intermediate
3. Backtrack + prune
Inner node + Word node
Remove edge
Remove edge

Figure 6.9 An example of method delete. (1) Find the key to delete. (2) Mark the node at the end of the path as "intermediate node." (3) Prune the tree to remove dangling branches.

The solution, in these cases, is implementing a pruning method that will remove dangling nodes while backtracking the path traversed during search. If we have the guarantee that the trie is "clean," meaning there were no dangling branches before removing the current node, there are just two conditions for which we would stop pruning while backtracking:

- We reach a key node. Obviously, we can't remove a node holding a key.
- We reach an inner intermediate node. After removing the last edge in the path being backtracked, if the current node becomes a leaf, it can be removed; otherwise, if this node has other children, then all its sub-branches will hold at least a key (because of our premise) and therefore the current node corresponds to an intermediate character in one or more strings stored in the trie, and it can't be deleted.

Listing 6.8 shows the implementation of this method performing deletion + pruning. Using figure 6.9 as a reference, you can see that, after turning it to an intermediate node (line #4), the node at the end of the path `"anti"` becomes a worthless leaf. We backtrack to its parent and remove the edge marked with `'i'` (lines #9 to #12 in listing 6.8), and then the node at the end of the path for `"ant"`, which also is an intermediate node, becomes a leaf too, and can thus be removed.

When we backtrack once more, we can see that its parent is both a key node, and has another child, so we can't prune the tree anymore.

Listing 6.8 Method `remove` (with pruning)

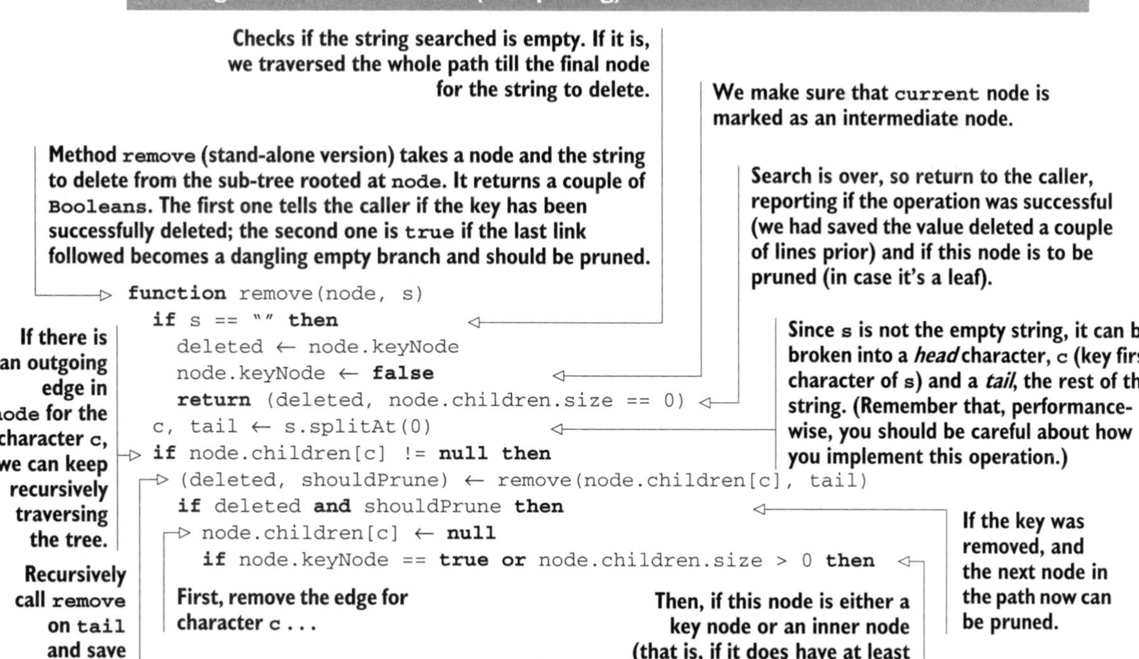

```
function remove(node, s)
  if s == "" then
    deleted ← node.keyNode
    node.keyNode ← false
    return (deleted, node.children.size == 0)
  c, tail ← s.splitAt(0)
  if node.children[c] != null then
    (deleted, shouldPrune) ← remove(node.children[c], tail)
    if deleted and shouldPrune then
      node.children[c] ← null
      if node.keyNode == true or node.children.size > 0 then
```

Checks if the string searched is empty. If it is, we traversed the whole path till the final node for the string to delete.
We make sure that current node is marked as an intermediate node.
Method remove (stand-alone version) takes a node and the string to delete from the sub-tree rooted at node. It returns a couple of Booleans. The first one tells the caller if the key has been successfully deleted; the second one is true if the last link followed becomes a dangling empty branch and should be pruned.
Search is over, so return to the caller, reporting if the operation was successful (we had saved the value deleted a couple of lines prior) and if this node is to be pruned (in case it's a leaf).
If there is an outgoing edge in node for the character c, we can keep recursively traversing the tree.
Since s is not the empty string, it can be broken into a *head* character, c (key first character of s) and a *tail*, the rest of the string. (Remember that, performance-wise, you should be careful about how you implement this operation.)
If the key was removed, and the next node in the path now can be pruned.
Recursively call remove on tail and save the result.
First, remove the edge for character c . . .
Then, if this node is either a key node or an inner node (that is, if it does have at least one other child left) . . .

```
            shouldPrune ← false
      return (deleted, shouldPrune)
    else
      return (false, false)
```

... it means that this node can't be pruned anymore, so we update the flag before returning.

If execution gets here, it means we haven't found the key in the trie, so it can't be deleted.

This version of removal obviously needs a different implementation of the trie method than the naïve one shown in listing 6.7. In this case, though, the API method is even simpler than the one shown in listing 6.7; basically, it just becomes a wrapper.

Performance-wise, the same considerations made for `search` and `insert` apply for `remove`. If we implement the method with pruning, the number of operations on the tree is at worst `2*m`, twice as much as for the naïve version without pruning, for which at most `m` edges are traversed. Execution time is also probably going to be more than two-fold, because, as you can see from the code, the delta in code complexity is relevant.

The tradeoff for faster running time, however, is that the tree can grow significantly if we don't prune dangling branches; the best choice depends on your requirements and context. If you have a dynamic set and expect many calls to delete, you'd better use pruning. If, instead, the ratio of insertion/removal is low, or you expect to have to add back deleted strings frequently or shortly after, then you are better off with the faster (though messier) removal shown in listing 6.7.

6.2.5 Longest prefix

With remove, we completed our overview of the classic operations on containers. As we mentioned, though, tries can also provide two new kind of operations, which are the most exciting parts of this data structure.

In this section we'll focus on the method that returns the longest prefix of the searched string; given an input string `s`, we traverse the trie following the path corresponding to characters in `s` (as long as we can), and return the longest key we found.

Sometimes, even if a key wasn't stored in our trie, we are just interested in getting its longest prefix. We'll see an example in the applications section.

The search for the longest prefix is almost entirely the same as the `search` method. The only difference is that in a recursive implementation, when we backtrack we need to check whether we have already found a key, and if we haven't and the current node is a key node, we'll have to return the current node's key. This also means that we have to return a string, not just `true` or `false`, and at each call keep track of the path traversed, because we need to know what we can return. Since backtracking walks the path backward, the first key node we find while backtracking will hold the longest prefix.

Listing 6.9 clarifies these concepts by showing the implementation of this method. If you recall how `insert` works, it can be rethought as a two-step operation: finding the longest common prefix of the key to be inserted already in the trie, and then adding a branch with the remaining characters. As an exercise, try to rewrite the pseudocode for `insert` by leveraging method `longestPrefix`.

Listing 6.9 Method longestPrefix

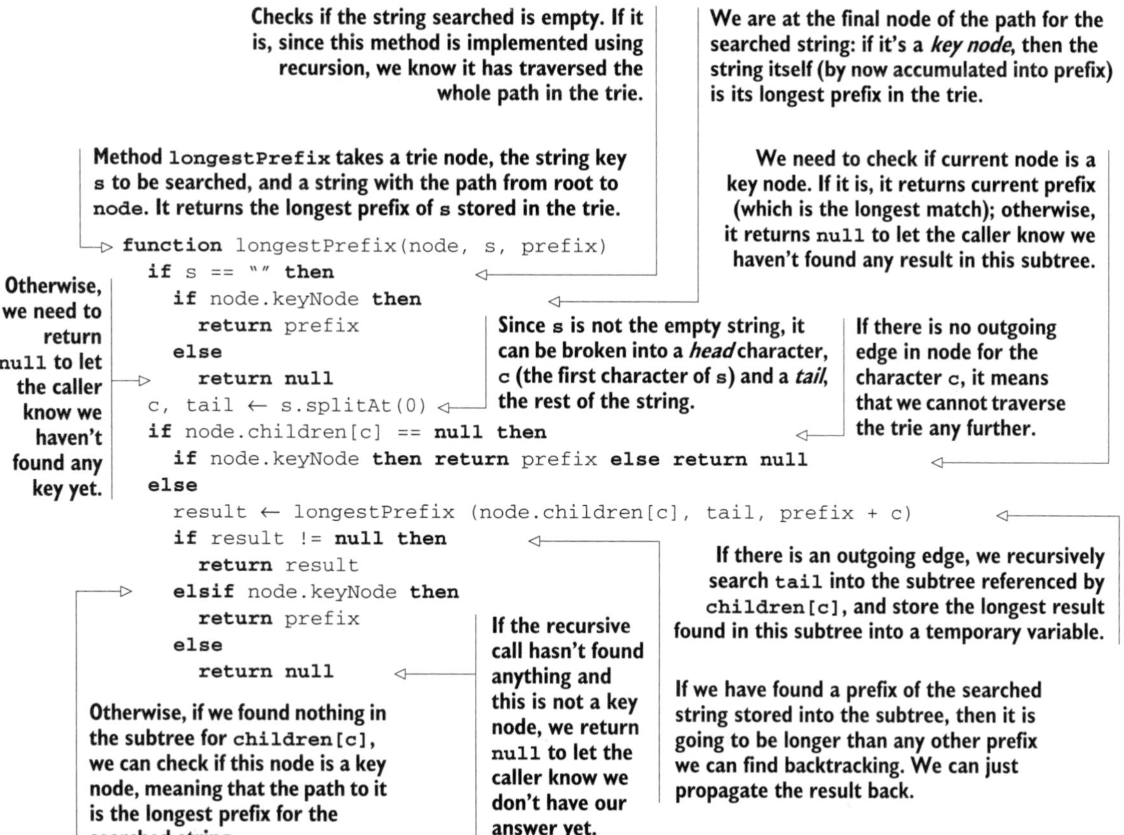

Checks if the string searched is empty. If it is, since this method is implemented using recursion, we know it has traversed the whole path in the trie.
We are at the final node of the path for the searched string: if it's a key node, then the string itself (by now accumulated into prefix) is its longest prefix in the trie.
Method longestPrefix takes a trie node, the string key s to be searched, and a string with the path from root to node. It returns the longest prefix of s stored in the trie.
We need to check if current node is a key node. If it is, it returns current prefix (which is the longest match); otherwise, it returns null to let the caller know we haven't found any result in this subtree.
Otherwise, we need to return null to let the caller know we haven't found any key yet.
Since s is not the empty string, it can be broken into a head character, c (the first character of s) and a tail, the rest of the string.
If there is no outgoing edge in node for the character c, it means that we cannot traverse the trie any further.
If there is an outgoing edge, we recursively search tail into the subtree referenced by children[c], and store the longest result found in this subtree into a temporary variable.
If the recursive call hasn't found anything and this is not a key node, we return null to let the caller know we don't have our answer yet.
If we have found a prefix of the searched string stored into the subtree, then it is going to be longer than any other prefix we can find backtracking. We can just propagate the result back.
Otherwise, if we found nothing in the subtree for children[c], we can check if this node is a key node, meaning that the path to it is the longest prefix for the searched string.


```
function longestPrefix(node, s, prefix)
  if s == "" then
    if node.keyNode then
      return prefix
    else
      return null
  c, tail ← s.splitAt(0)
  if node.children[c] == null then
    if node.keyNode then return prefix else return null
  else
    result ← longestPrefix (node.children[c], tail, prefix + c)
    if result != null then
      return result
    elsif node.keyNode then
      return prefix
    else
      return null
```

As with the other methods we have described so far, this operation is also linear in the length of the searched string: `O(m)`, if `|s|==m`.

6.2.6 Keys matching a prefix

The last method we are going to describe returns all the keys matching a certain prefix.

If you stop and think about the definition of a trie, the implementation for this method will flow almost naturally. Even the alias for this data structure, *prefix tree*, suggests a solution. We have seen, in fact, that tries compactly store strings sharing the same prefix, because each string is translated in a path from the root to a key node, and strings sharing the same prefix will result in sharing the same path in the trie.

For instance, in figure 6.3, all the strings `"and"`, `"ant"`, `"anthem"` share a portion of their path, corresponding to the common prefix `"an"`.

Listing 6.10 shows the implementation of this method. Not surprisingly, it's one more method that leverages the `searchNode` method defined in listing 6.4.

Listing 6.10 Method Trie:: keysStartingWith

Method `keysStartingWith` for the `Trie` class takes a string `prefix`, and returns the list of all keys stored in the trie that starts with this prefix.

Performs a search on the trie and gets the node for `prefix` (if present). Remember that `searchNode` will return the node at the end of the path, even if it's an intermediate node, or `null` if there isn't any such path.

```
function Trie::keysStartingWith(prefix)
  node ← searchNode(this.root, prefix)
  if node == null then
    return []
  else
    return allKeys(node, prefix)
```

If node is `null`, it means that there is no key stored in the trie that starts with `prefix`, so we return an empty list.

Otherwise, we have to return all keys stored in the sub-tree rooted at node.

Clearly, there is a new method that we still need to define: `allKeys`, the method that traverses a (sub)trie and collect all its keys; this method, shown in listing 6.11, is a traversal of the whole subtree. We traverse all branches for each node, and we only stop following a path when we reach a leaf. We also need to pass the (string corresponding to the) path traversed so far, up to `node`, as the second argument, because we will need that to know which key we should return.

Listing 6.11 Method allKeys

Method `allKeys` takes a trie node and the string `prefix` corresponding to the path from the trie's root to `node`. It returns the list of strings s_k=prefix+suffix$_k$, where suffix$_k$ is the `k`-th string contained in this subtree.

If current node is a key node, then we need to add `prefix` to the list of strings contained in the subtree rooted at `node`—assuming `prefix` is the correct string for the path from root to current node.

Iterate over `node`'s outgoing edges; in particular, we need the characters marking each edge.

```
function allKeys(node, prefix)
  keys ← []
  if node.keyNode then
    keys.insert(prefix)
  for c in node.children.keys() do
    keys ← keys + allKeys(node.children[c], prefix + c)
  return keys
```

Initializes the list of strings to return

Returns all keys gathered

Add to the list of keys for the subtree rooted at `node` all the keys in the subtree referenced by the edge. For this subtree, the path from the root will be made by `prefix + c`. Be careful about the implementation of this operation; it can be costly if not implemented properly.

When we run the asymptotic analysis for this method, we need to be especially careful with line #6. Depending on the programming language and data type used, concatenating lists can be quite expensive, if it's not done right.

The most efficient way to accumulate the keys found would be to pass a third parameter to the method, an accumulator, to which we would add each key only once and in one place, line #4.

Under this assumption, the running time for method `allKeys` is `O(j)`, for a trie with `j` nodes, and therefore the worst-case upper bound for the method `keysStartingWith` is `O(m+j)`, for a trie with `j` nodes and a prefix with `m` characters.

The caveat is that it's hard to know or even estimate how many nodes a trie will have based on the number of keys it stores. If, however, we know it contains `n` keys whose maximum length is `M`, then the worst-case (loose) bound for a non-empty string is `O(m + n*(M-m))`, corresponding to a degenerate trie where all words share exactly the prefix searched, and no further character.

In the example shown in figure 6.10, we search for all keys matching prefix `"ant"`, so `n=6, m=3` and `M=8` (the length of the longest key, `"antidote"`).

If, instead, we search all keys starting whose prefixes include the empty string, this will return all keys in the tree, and the running time will be `O(n*M)`, which would also be the worst-case upper bound for the method.

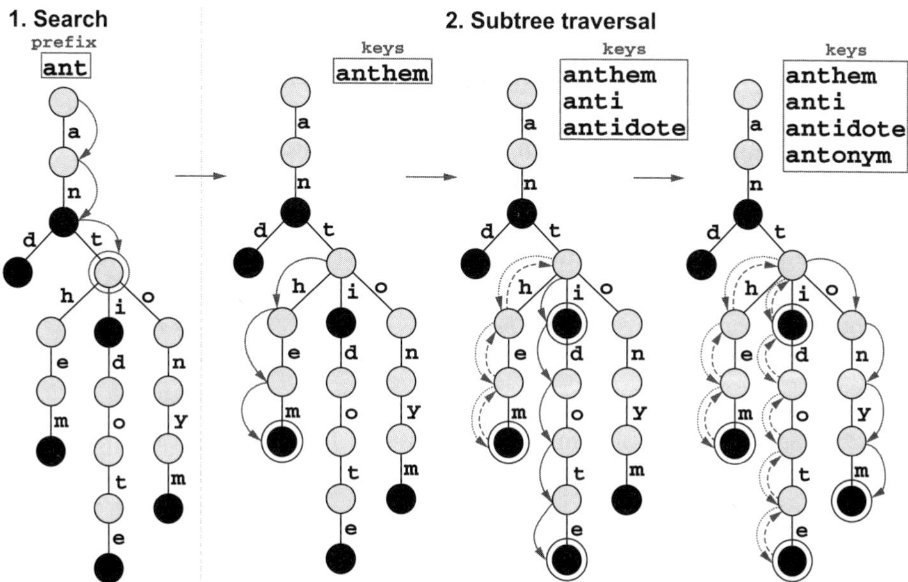
1. Search
prefix
ant
2. Subtree traversal
keys
anthem
keys
anthem
anti
antidote
keys
anthem
anti
antidote
antonym

Figure 6.10 An example of method `keysWithPrefix`. (1) Traverse the path corresponding to the common prefix. (2) Collect all keys found traversing the subtree at the end of the path for `prefix`.

6.2.7 *When should we use tries?*

Now that we have described all the main methods on tries, it feels like taking a moment to recap would be a good idea. Table 6.2 shows the performance of tries on these methods, compared to the equivalent methods for balanced BSTs.

Table 6.2 helps answer the question about performance that we put on hold in section 6.2.1. We saw when a trie would require less memory than a BST; now we also know that it would almost always be faster.

Remember that while in general we express the running time for BSTs in terms of `n`, the number of entries stored, in this case we can't assume that the cost to compare two keys is `O(1)`, but it's rather `O(m)`, depending on the length `m` of the shortest of the two keys.

Table 6.2 Running time for operations on tries vs balanced BSTs, assuming n keys with average length `m`; finally, as a simplification we assume for the size of the input keys `m`, that `m ∈ O(M)`

Method	BST	BST + hash	Trie
`Search`	O(m*log(n))	O(m+log(n))	O(m)
`insert`	O(m*log(n))	O(m+log(n))	O(m)
`remove`	O(m*log(n))	O(m+log(n))	O(m)
`longestPrefix`	O(m*n)	O(m+n)	O(m)
`keysWithPrefix`	O(m*n)	O(m+n)	O(n+m)[a]

[a]average

The third column in table 6.2 shows the results for a particular variant of BSTs where we store a hash of the string, together with the key itself, in each node. This approach, which requires an extra `O(n)` memory to store these fields, allows for a fast two-pass comparison. Given a search string `w`, we compute `h(w)` before starting the search. Then for each node we first check whether `h(w)` matches the node's hash (which requires constant time), and only when it does do we perform a proper strings comparison.

Before moving on, let's also recap the pros and cons of using tries, and when we should prefer a trie over a BST.

On the pros side, compared to using BSTs or hash tables

- The search time only depends on the length of the searched string.
- Search misses only involve examining a few characters (in particular, just the longest common prefix between the search string and the corpus stored in the tree).
- There are no collisions of unique keys in a trie.
- There is no need to provide a hash function or to change hash functions as more keys are added to a trie.
- A trie can provide an alphabetical ordering of the entries by key.

As appalling as this list looks, as we have repeated many times, unfortunately there is no perfect data structure. So even tries do have some downsides:

- Tries can be slower than hash tables at looking up data whenever a container is too big to fit in memory. Hash tables would need fewer disk accesses, even down to a single access, while a trie would require `O(m)` disk reads for a string of length `m`.
- Hash tables are usually allocated in a single big and contiguous chunk of memory, while trie nodes can span the whole heap. So, the former would better exploit the principle of locality.
- A trie's ideal use case is storing text strings. We could, in theory, stringify any value, from numbers to objects, and store it. Yet, if we were to store floating

point numbers, for instance, there are some edge cases that can produce long meaningless paths,[16] such as periodic or transcendent numbers, or results of certain floating points operations such as 0.1+0.2, due to issues with double precision representation.[17]

- Tries have memory overhead for nodes and references. As we have seen, some implementations require each node to store an array of $|\Sigma|$ edges, where Σ is the alphabet used—even if the node has few or no children at all.

In summary, the advice could be to use tries when you have to frequently perform prefix searches (`longestPrefix` or `keysWithPrefix`). Use hash tables when data is stored on slow supports like disk or whenever memory locality is important. In all intermediate cases, profiling can help you make the best decision.

Tries offer extremely good performance for many string-based operations. Due to their structure, though, they are meant to store an array of children for each node. This can quickly become expensive. The total number of edges for a trie with `n` elements can swing anywhere between `|Σ|*n` and `|Σ|*n*m`, where `m` is the average word length, depending on the degree of overlap of common prefixes.

We have seen that we can use associative arrays, dictionaries in particular, to implement nodes, only storing edges that are not `null`. Of course, this solution comes at a cost: not only the cost to access each edge (that can be the cost of hashing the character plus the cost of resolving key conflicts), but also the cost of resizing the dictionary when new edges are added.

6.3 Radix tries

To overcome these issues with tries, a few alternatives have been developed: the *ternary search trie* (TST), which trades off lower memory usage for worse running time, or the *radix trie,* just to name a few.

While TSTs improve the space requirements to store links, and free us from worrying about platform-specific implementations to optimize how we store edges, the number of nodes we need to create is still on the order of magnitude of the number of characters contained in the whole corpus stored, `O(n*m)` for `n` words of average length `m`.

In tries, most of the nodes don't store keys and are just hops on a path between a key and the ones that extend it. Most of these hops are necessary, but when we store long words, they tend to produce long chains of internal nodes, each with just one child. As we saw in section 6.2.1, this is the main reason tries need too much space, sometimes more than BSTs.

Figure 6.11 shows an example of a trie. Nothing special, just a small, regular trie. We can see that intermediate nodes always have children (assuming we prune dangling branches after deleting keys); sometimes just one child, sometimes more.

---

[16]See http://stackoverflow.com/questions/588004/is-floating-point-math-broken/27030789#27030789.

[17]See https://en.wikipedia.org/wiki/IEEE_floating_point#Basic_formats.

When an intermediate node has more than one child, we have several branches that we can traverse from it. When, instead, there is just one child, those two nodes begin to resemble a linked list. For example, take the first three nodes from the root of figure 6.11: they encode the prefix "an", and the search of any other string starting with 'a' but not followed by an 'n' couldn't get anywhere in the tree.

In fact, it turns out that an intermediate node is a branching point if it has more than one child: it means that the trie stores at least two keys sharing the common prefix corresponding to that node. If that's the case, the node carries valuable information that we can't compress in any way.

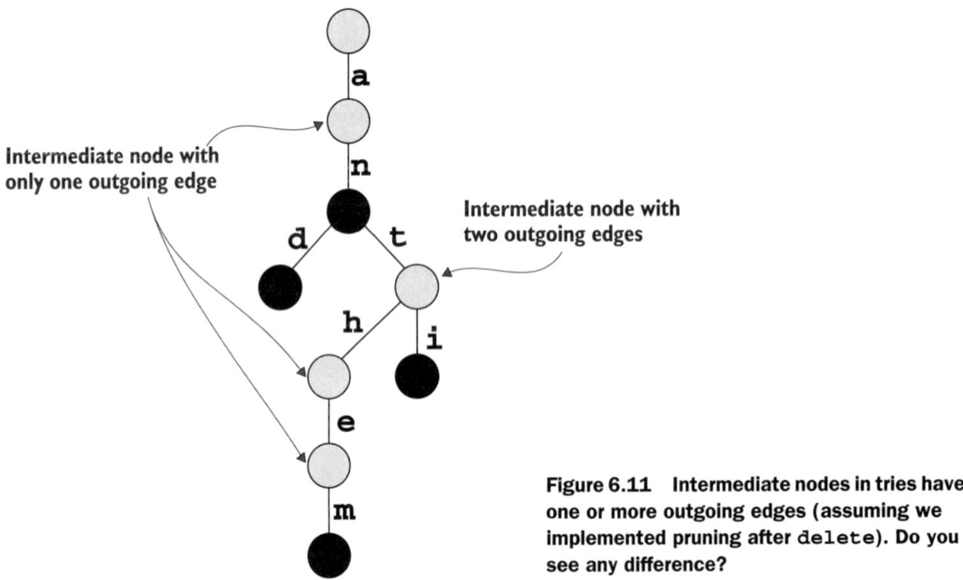
a
Intermediate node with
only one outgoing edge
n
Intermediate node with
two outgoing edges
d
t
h
i
e
m

Figure 6.11 Intermediate nodes in tries have one or more outgoing edges (assuming we implemented pruning after `delete`). Do you see any difference?

Key nodes also store information, regardless of the number of children they have. They tell us that the path to reach them composes a string that is stored in the trie.

If, however, an intermediate node stores no key and only has one child, then it carries no relevant information; it's only a forced step in the path.

Radix tries (aka *radix trees*, aka *Patricia trees*[18]) are based on the idea that we can somehow compress the path that leads to this kind of nodes, that are called *pass-through nodes.*

How? Figure 6.12 gives a hint about the process to compress these paths. Every time a path has a pass-through node, we can squash the section of the path hinging on these nodes into a single edge, which will be labeled with the string made concatenating the labels of the original edges.

[18] The original name for this DS, Patricia tree, is an acronym. Morrison, Donald R. "PATRICIA—practical algorithm to retrieve information coded in alphanumeric." Journal of the ACM (JACM) 15.4 (1968): 514-534.

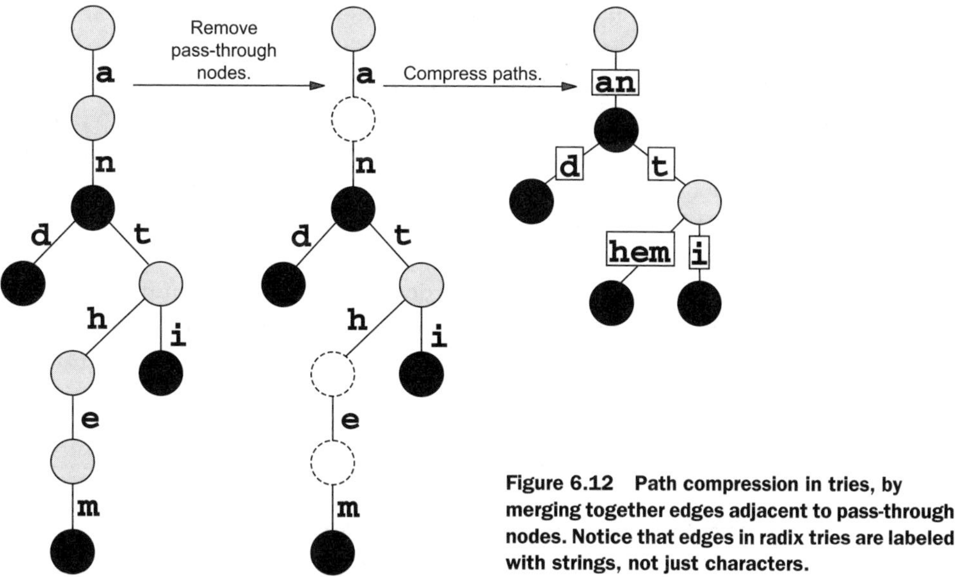
Remove pass-through nodes.
Compress paths.
a
n
d
t
h
i
e
m
an
hem

Figure 6.12 Path compression in tries, by merging together edges adjacent to pass-through nodes. Notice that edges in radix tries are labeled with strings, not just characters.

How much can we save with this change? Let's look at the two trees in figure 6.12 to get an idea.

The original trie has 9 nodes and 8 edges, and with the assumptions made in section 6.2.1, with a 4-byte overhead per node, this means 9 * 4 + 8 * 9 = 108 bytes.

The compressed trie on the right has 6 nodes and 5 edges, but in this case each edge carries a string, not just a character; however, we can simplify the operation by accounting for edge references and string labels separately. This way, we would still count 9 bytes per edge (because we would include the string terminator byte in the edge cost), but we could add the sum of string lengths as a third term in the final expression; the total number of bytes needed is given by 6 * 4 + 5 * 9 + 8 * 1 = 77 bytes.

In other words, for this simple trie, the compressed version requires 30% less memory.

6.3.1 *Nodes and edges*

All the operations that we have described for tries can be similarly implemented for radix trees, but instead of edges labeled by chars, we need to store and follow edges labeled by strings.

While at a high level the logic of the methods is almost the same as for trie, to check which branch we should traverse, we can't just check the next character in the key, because edges could be labeled with a substring that matches more than one character of our argument `s`.

One important property in these trees is that no two outgoing edges of the same node share a common prefix. This is crucial and allows us to store and check edges more efficiently.

A first solution is keeping edges in sorted order and using binary search to look for a link that starts with the next character `c` in the key. Because there can't be two edges starting with `c`, if we find one, we can compare the rest of the characters in its label to the next characters in the string. Moreover, binary search allows us to find this edge in logarithmic time in the number of edges, and because there can't be more than `k=|Σ|` edges per node (because there can be at most one starting with each character in our alphabet Σ), we know that the worst case running time for performing binary search and finding a candidate edge is `O(log(k))`.

Because `k` is a constant that doesn't depend either on the number of keys stored in the trie or on the length of the words searched/inserted/etc., we can consider `O(log(k))=O(1)` as far as asymptotic analysis is concerned. Moreover, no extra space[19] is required to store edges with this solution.

This solution is illustrated in figure 6.13, where we also show how binary search works to find the possible edge matching.

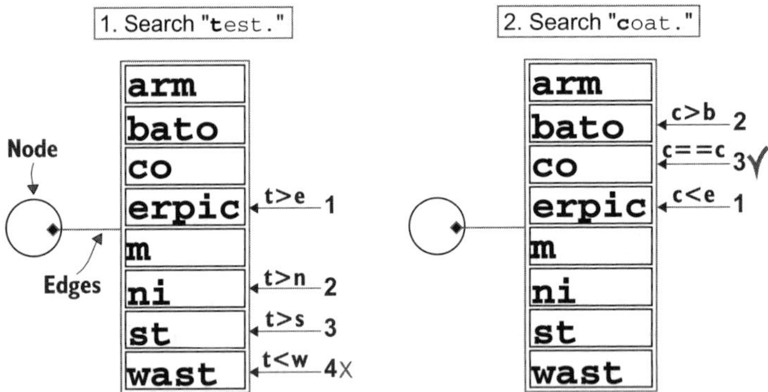
1. Search "test."
2. Search "coat."
Node
Edges
arm
bato
co
erpic
m
ni
st
wast
t>e 1
t>n 2
t>s 3
t<w 4X
c>b 2
c==c 3
c<e 1

Figure 6.13 An example of a radix trie node with edges stored as in sorted array. (Left) A failed binary search. (Right) A successful search. Comparisons are performed only on the first character of each string: in the successful search, though, the edge's label is a prefix of the searched string.

Notice that the match between the string searched and an edge's label doesn't have (and usually isn't) full; we'll see in a moment what this means for our algorithms and how to handle these situations.

Of course, using sorted arrays, as we discussed in chapter 4 and appendix C, means logarithmic search, but linear (translated: slow!) insertion. Although the number of elements can be considered a constant, in asymptotic analysis, from a practical point of view this implementation can significantly slow down insertion of new keys in large tries.

The alternative solutions to implement this dictionary for edges are the usual: balanced search trees, which would guarantee logarithm search *and* insertion, or hash

[19] Except a constant overhead for the array object, in most languages.

tables. The latter is illustrated in figure 6.14. We can keep a dictionary whose keys are characters and whose values are the full string labels of the node's edges, together with a reference to the children linked by the edge. This solution requires `O(k)` additional space for a node with `k` children, and worst-case it will require `O(|Σ|)` extra space per node.

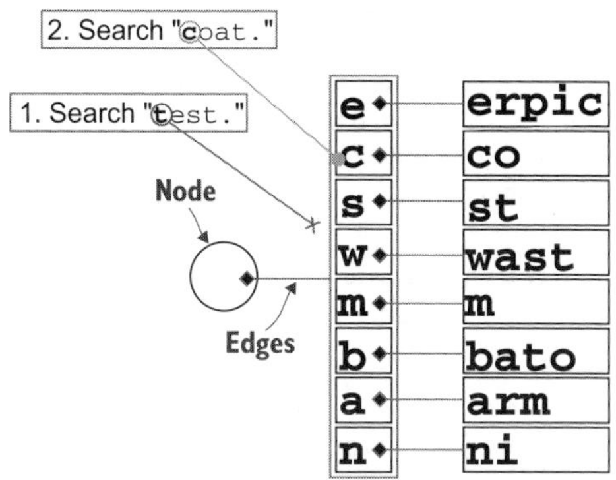
2. Search "coat."
1. Search "test."
Node
Edges
e
c
s
w
m
b
a
n
erpic
co
st
wast
m
bato
arm
ni

Figure 6.14 An example of a node where edges to children are stored in a dictionary. Dictionary's keys are characters, the first letter of each label, while values contain the full labels and the references to the destination node of the edge. The figure shows a simplification of the same searches in figure 6.13. As before, comparisons are based on the first character of the searched strings.

Despite requiring more space and a little bookkeeping on insertion and deletion to update the hash table, this solution allows amortized constant-time lookup when searching the path for a key.

Independently of the implementation, the first step will be comparing the first character of the input string to the first character of the edges' label.

Overall, we have four possible cases, illustrated in figure 6.15:

1. The string s_E labeling an edge perfectly matches a substring of `s`, the input the string. This means `s` starts with s_E, so we can break it up as $s=s_E+s'$. In this case, we can traverse the edge to the children, and recurse on the input string `s'`.
2. There is an edge starting with the first character in `s`, but s_E is not a prefix of `s`; however, they must have a common prefix s_P (at least one character long). The action here depends on the operation we are running. For search, it's a failure because it means there isn't a path to the searched key. For insert, as we'll see, it means we have to decompress that edge, breaking down s_E.
3. The input string `s` is a prefix of the edge's label s_E. This is a special case of point #2 and can be handled similarly.
4. Finally, if we don't find a match for the first character, then we are sure we can't traverse the trie any longer.

Now that we have clarified the high-level structure of radix trie's nodes, let's delve into the algorithms. Keeping in mind the considerations we just discussed, their behavior will flow naturally from trie's methods.

Listing 6.12 shows the pseudo-code for the `RadixTrie` and `RTNode` classes, used to model this new data structure. We also added a class to model edges, to make code

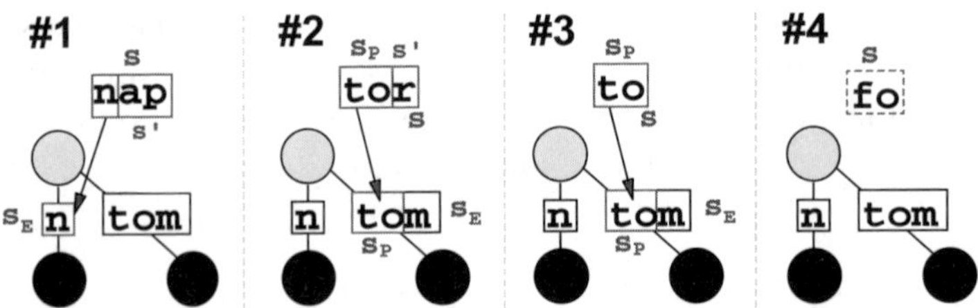
#1
s
nap
s'
sE n tom
#2
sP s'
tor
s
n tom sE
sP
#3
sP
to
s
n tom sE
sP
#4
s
fo
n tom

Figure 6.15 Possible cases comparing a search string to a node's links. (1) An edge's label completely matches part of the string. (2) An edge's label and the search string have a common prefix that is shorter than both strings. (3) The search string is a prefix of one of the edge's labels. (4) The search string has no common prefix with any of the edges.

cleaner. I wonder if you have you noticed a tiny, but meaningful, detail: we don't need to define a fixed alphabet beforehand, like for tries!

You can also take a look at a full implementation on the book's repo on GitHub.[20]

Listing 6.12 Class RadixTrie

```
class RTEdge
  #type RTNode
  destination

  #type string
  label

class RTNode
  #type boolean
  keyNode

  #type HashMap<Char, RTEdge>
  children

  function RTNode(storesKey)
    children ← new HashMap()
    this.keyNode ← storesKey

class RadixTrie
  #type RTNode
  root

  function RadixTrie()
    root ← new RTNode(false)
```

6.3.2 Search

The search method, shown in listing 6.13, is almost identical to the trie's counterpart; the only difference is the way we get the next edge to traverse. Because we are going to

[20] See https://github.com/mlarocca/AlgorithmsAndDataStructuresInAction#radix-trie-aka-patricia-tree.

reuse this operation over and again for the other methods, we extract its logic into a utility method, shown in listing 6.14.

Listing 6.13 Method `search` for radix tries

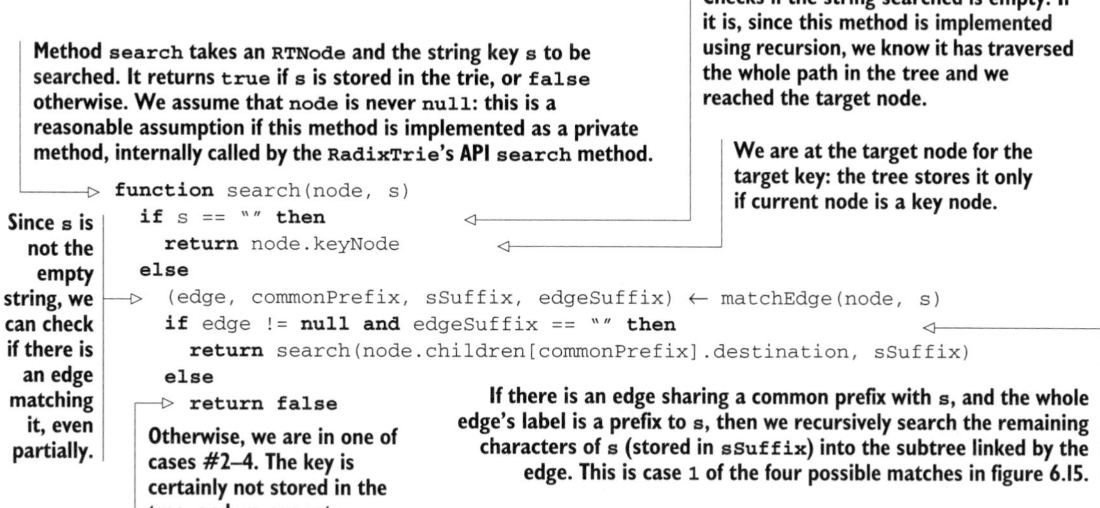

Method search takes an RTNode and the string key s to be searched. It returns true if s is stored in the trie, or false otherwise. We assume that node is never null: this is a reasonable assumption if this method is implemented as a private method, internally called by the RadixTrie's API search method.
Checks if the string searched is empty. If it is, since this method is implemented using recursion, we know it has traversed the whole path in the tree and we reached the target node.
We are at the target node for the target key: the tree stores it only if current node is a key node.
Since s is not the empty string, we can check if there is an edge matching it, even partially.
If there is an edge sharing a common prefix with s, and the whole edge's label is a prefix to s, then we recursively search the remaining characters of s (stored in sSuffix) into the subtree linked by the edge. This is case 1 of the four possible matches in figure 6.15.
Otherwise, we are in one of cases #2–4. The key is certainly not stored in the tree, and we can return.


```
function search(node, s)
  if s == "" then
    return node.keyNode
  else
    (edge, commonPrefix, sSuffix, edgeSuffix) ← matchEdge(node, s)
    if edge != null and edgeSuffix == "" then
      return search(node.children[commonPrefix].destination, sSuffix)
    else
      return false
```

This method just looks for an edge with a common prefix with the target string s, if any. Remember that all edges can't have any prefix in common, so there can be at most one starting with the same character as s.

It returns some useful information that the caller can use to decide the action to take: the longest common prefix between searched string and edge's label, and the suffixes of these two strings (with respect to their common prefix).

Listing 6.14 Method `matchEdge` for Radix Tries

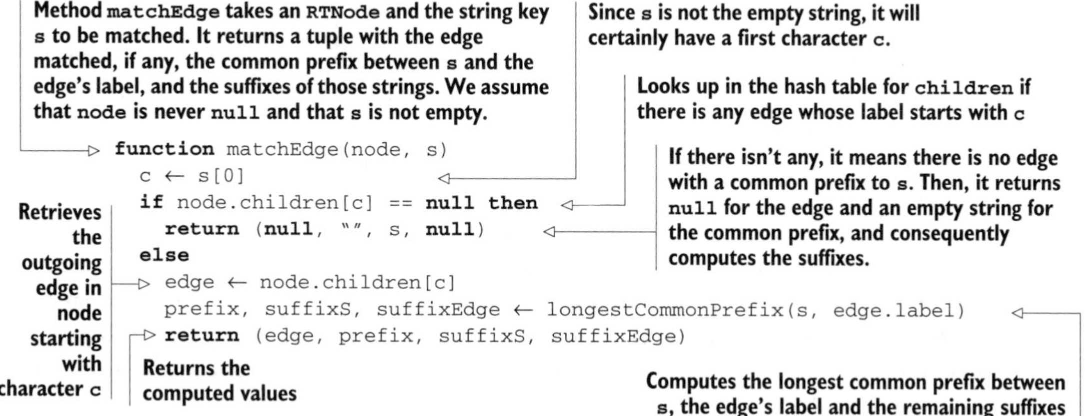

Method matchEdge takes an RTNode and the string key s to be matched. It returns a tuple with the edge matched, if any, the common prefix between s and the edge's label, and the suffixes of those strings. We assume that node is never null and that s is not empty.
Since s is not the empty string, it will certainly have a first character c.
Looks up in the hash table for children if there is any edge whose label starts with c
If there isn't any, it means there is no edge with a common prefix to s. Then, it returns null for the edge and an empty string for the common prefix, and consequently computes the suffixes.
Retrieves the outgoing edge in node starting with character c
Returns the computed values
Computes the longest common prefix between s, the edge's label and the remaining suffixes


```
function matchEdge(node, s)
  c ← s[0]
  if node.children[c] == null then
    return (null, "", s, null)
  else
    edge ← node.children[c]
    prefix, suffixS, suffixEdge ← longestCommonPrefix(s, edge.label)
    return (edge, prefix, suffixS, suffixEdge)
```

At line #6 of listing 6.13, we use this information to distinguish between the four match cases illustrated in figure 6.15. The only positive case for `search` is the first one, so we need to check that there is an edge whose label is a prefix of `s`.

The implementation of the utility method is straightforward, assuming we have a way to extract the longest common prefix of two strings. This can be done by comparing the characters at the same indices in the two strings, one by one, until we find a mismatch.

We assume that this method is given, and it also returns the suffixes of the two strings, meaning two strings made of the remaining characters in each of the input strings, once stripped of their common prefix.

Figure 6.16 shows an example of the search method on the radix tree resulting from compressing the trie in figure 6.3.

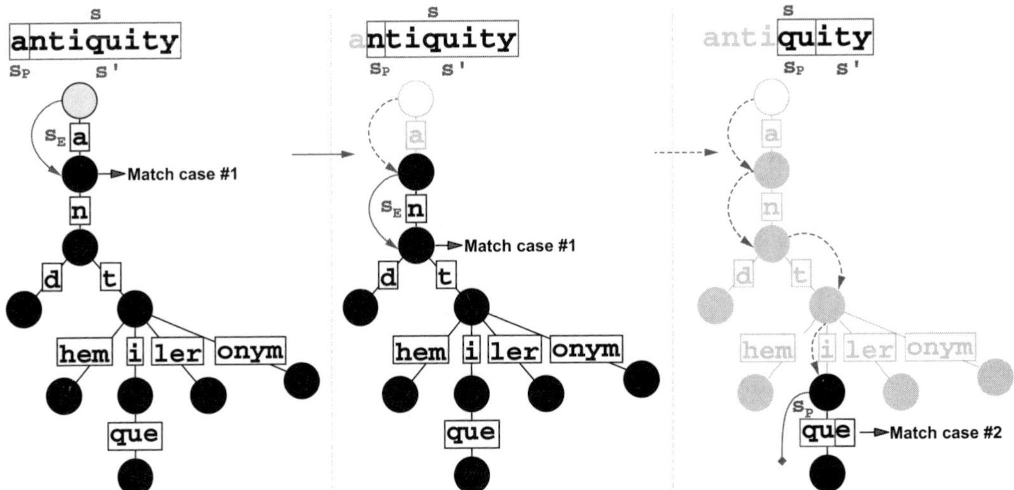
s
antiquity
sP
s'
sE
a
Match case #1
n
d
t
hem
i
ler
onym
que
s
antiquity
sP
s'
sE
n
Match case #1
s
antiquity
sP
s'
sP
que
Match case #2

Figure 6.16 Unsuccessful search for the string "antiquity" in the radix tree corresponding to the trie in figure 6.3. The first two diagrams show the initial steps in the search; then we fast forward to the final step.

6.3.3 Insert

As mentioned, cases #2 and #3 are the most complicated to handle, especially for method `insert`. When we find a partial match between a key and an edge, we will need to break the edge's label down, split the edge into two new edges, and add a new node in the middle, corresponding to the longest common prefix s_P.

This is illustrated in figure 6.17. Once the common prefix has been found, we need to add a new node in order to split the edge partially matching the string to insert, and then we can add a new branch to this new node.

This node we add is called a *bridge node*, because it will be a bridge between the existing node corresponding to the common prefix of the two strings, and the paths leading to the final nodes for these strings. Bridge nodes are, obviously, bifurcation points, where the path from root branches out.

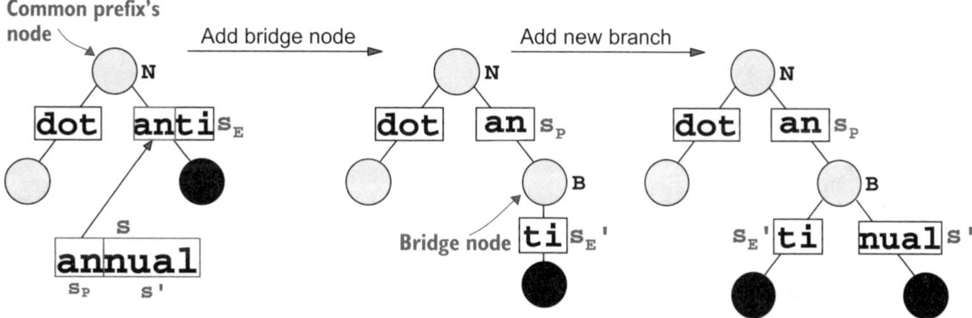
Common prefix's node
N
Add bridge node
Add new branch
dot
anti
s_E
s
annual
s_P
s'
an
s_P
B
Bridge node
ti
s_E'
nual
s'

Figure 6.17 Handling case #2 in edge matching while performing an insertion. In this example, we add the word "annual" to a node containing an edge labeled with "anti". To do so, we insert a bridge node B, linked to N by an edge labeled with the common prefix "an", and then two new edges leaving B.

To better understand this operation, it might help you to imagine that we decompress the edge to the child into a path, going back to the trie representation with one char per link. Then we traverse this path until we get to the end of the common prefix (to, say, a node B), we add a new branch as a child of B, and finally we compress again the two sub-paths on the two sides of B.

Listing 6.15 Method insert for radix tries

```
function insert(node, s)
  if s == "" then
    node.keyNode ← true
  else
    (edge, commonPrefix, sSuffix, edgeSuffix) ← matchEdge(node, s)
    if edge == null then
      this.children[s[0]] ← new RTEdge(s, new Node(true))
    elif edgeSuffix == "" then
      insert(edge.destination, sSuffix)
    else
      bridge ← new Node(false)
      this.children[s[0]] ← new RTEdge(commonPrefix, bridge)
      bridge.children[edgeSuffix[0]] ←
          new RTEdge(edgeSuffix, edge.destination)
      insert(bridge, sSuffix)
```

Method insert takes a RTNode and the string key s to be inserted. It returns nothing but has side effects on the trie. Again, we assume that node is never null. This is a reasonable assumption if this method is implemented as a private method, internally called by the trie's API insert method.

Checks if the string searched is empty. If it is, since this method is implemented using recursion, we know it has traversed the whole path in the trie.

We are at the target node for the target key. We set the current node to a key node to ensure it will store s.

Since s is not the empty string, we can see if there is an edge matching it, even partially.

Match case #4 (figure 6.15). If there isn't any edge sharing a common prefix, not even the first character, with s, then we need to add a new edge, with label s, to a new key node.

Match case #1. There is an edge whose label is a prefix to s; we just need to traverse the edge.

Updates the outgoing edge for this node, with an edge pointing to the bridge node, and labeled with the common prefix

Adds an edge from the bridge node to the former children of the current node: the label will be the original edge's label, stripped of commonPrefix.

Otherwise, we are in match case #2 or #3. There is a common prefix between the edge's label and s, but there are also characters in the edge's label not matching s. Therefore, we need to break down the edge and create a bridge node.

Finally, we still need to recursively add the remaining part of the key to the bridge node. If sSuffix is the empty string, this corresponds to match case #3, otherwise to match case #2.

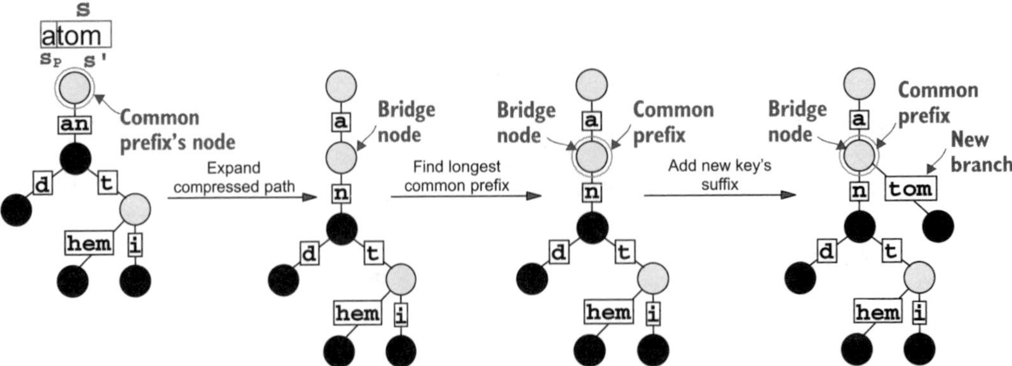
s
atom
sp s'
an
Common prefix's node
d
t
hem
i
Expand compressed path
a
Bridge node
n
Find longest common prefix
Bridge node
Common prefix
Add new key's suffix
Common prefix
New branch
tom

Figure 6.18 An example of method `insert`

Listing 6.15 describes the pseudo-code for the `insert` method, and figures 6.18 and 6.19 show two examples of how this method works on a simplified tree.

The method follows the same high-level logic as the trie's version we saw in listing 6.5. We traverse the tree as far as we can (following the longest path covering a prefix of the string to insert), and then add a new branch for the new key.

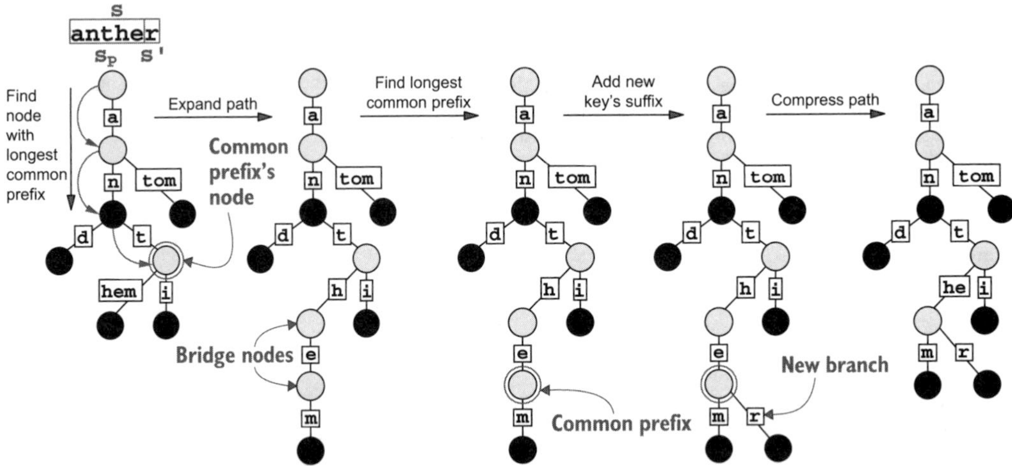
s
anther
sp s'
Find node with longest common prefix
Expand path
Common prefix's node
Find longest common prefix
Add new key's suffix
Compress path
a
n
tom
d
t
hem
i
h
e
m
he
r
Bridge nodes
Common prefix
New branch

Figure 6.19 Another example of method `insert` with path decompression explained step by step

Traversing the tree becomes more complicated because at each node we need to distinguish between the four different possible results of the edge label matching, and this complexity is reflected in the length of the method. Moreover, when we bump into case #2 or #3, we need to break down an edge and add a bridge node. Adding a new branch, however, becomes easier, because we just need to add a new edge and a single node.

6.3.4 Remove

Like for search, the only changes to the `remove` method, with respect to tries, revolve around the extraction of the common prefix. This is not surprising, because deleting a key can be thought of as a successful search followed by a clean-up of the deleted node.

With `remove`, we don't have to worry about splitting edges or adding bridge nodes. Because we need to find the key first, there must be a path perfectly matching the key to be deleted, in order to be able to complete the operation. We might, however, have the chance to compact the final part of the deleted path, because turning an existing key node into an intermediate node can change the tree structure, introducing a pass-through node (see 6.3.1).

Figure 6.20 shows an example of `remove` in action on a radix tree.

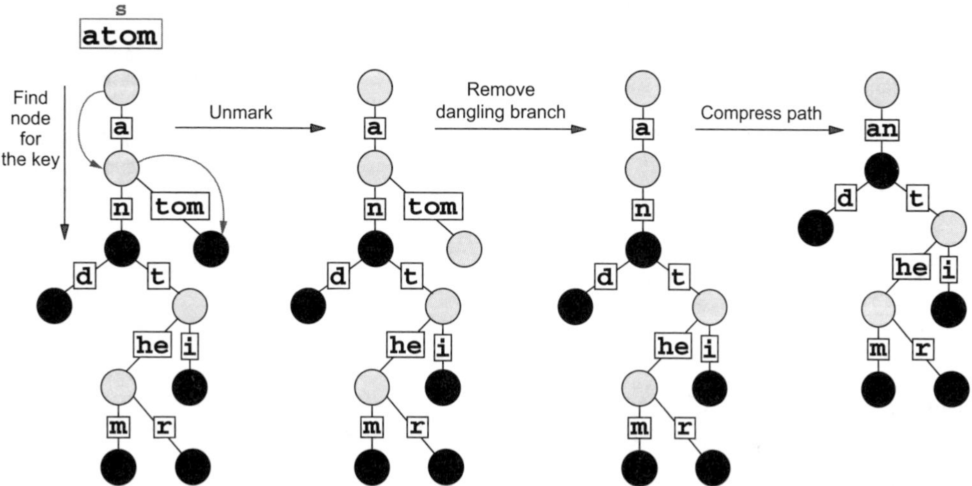
s
atom
Find node for the key
Unmark
Remove dangling branch
Compress path
a
n
tom
d
t
he
i
m
r
an

Figure 6.20 Removing the word "atom" from an example radix trie. (1) Find the node at the end of the path for the key to delete. The path must entirely match the key. (2) Unmark the node, making it an intermediate node. If the node is a leaf, it will create a dangling branch. (3) Remove the dangling branch. If the parent of the node removed had only two children, it now became a pass-through node. (4) Compress the path by removing the pass-through node and merging edges.

Besides that, we might have to perform the usual pruning when deleting a key in a leaf. The difference with tries, in this case, is that we will only have to remove a single edge in radix trees.

The example in figure 6.20 shows both cases where we have to correct a node's parent. We first remove the key from a leaf, and then, once the node is removed from the tree, its parent becomes a pass-through node, and hence can be removed, allowing us to compress the path from its parent to its only child.

Listing 6.16 shows the pseudo-code for this method, where we use two utility functions.

isPassThrough checks if a node is a pass-through node. This only happens when a node is not a key node, it has only one outgoing edge, and even its parent only has one outgoing edge (hence we need to pass the parent too). Implementation is left as an exercise.

Since a pass-through node only has one outgoing edge, its children field will have exactly one entry; getPassThroughEdge is a wrapper for retrieving this entry.

Listing 6.16 Method remove for radix tries

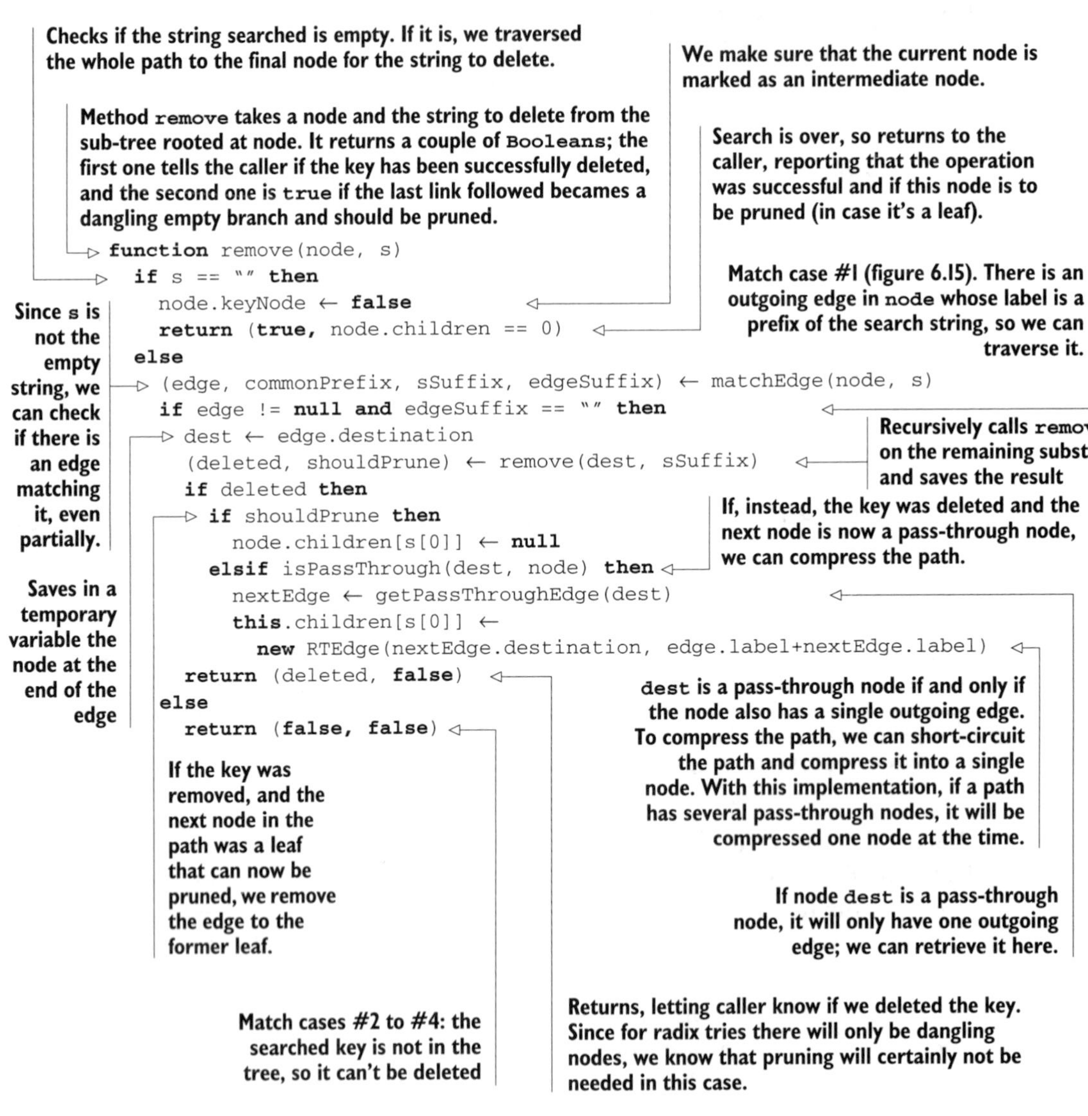

```
function remove(node, s)
  if s == "" then
    node.keyNode ← false
    return (true, node.children == 0)
  else
    (edge, commonPrefix, sSuffix, edgeSuffix) ← matchEdge(node, s)
    if edge != null and edgeSuffix == "" then
      dest ← edge.destination
      (deleted, shouldPrune) ← remove(dest, sSuffix)
      if deleted then
        if shouldPrune then
          node.children[s[0]] ← null
        elsif isPassThrough(dest, node) then
          nextEdge ← getPassThroughEdge(dest)
          this.children[s[0]] ←
            new RTEdge(nextEdge.destination, edge.label+nextEdge.label)
      return (deleted, false)
    else
      return (false, false)
```


Checks if the string searched is empty. If it is, we traversed the whole path to the final node for the string to delete.
Method remove takes a node and the string to delete from the sub-tree rooted at node. It returns a couple of Booleans; the first one tells the caller if the key has been successfully deleted, and the second one is true if the last link followed becames a dangling empty branch and should be pruned.
We make sure that the current node is marked as an intermediate node.
Search is over, so returns to the caller, reporting that the operation was successful and if this node is to be pruned (in case it's a leaf).
Match case #1 (figure 6.15). There is an outgoing edge in node whose label is a prefix of the search string, so we can traverse it.
Since s is not the empty string, we can check if there is an edge matching it, even partially.
Recursively calls remove on the remaining substring and saves the result
If, instead, the key was deleted and the next node is now a pass-through node, we can compress the path.
Saves in a temporary variable the node at the end of the edge
dest is a pass-through node if and only if the node also has a single outgoing edge. To compress the path, we can short-circuit the path and compress it into a single node. With this implementation, if a path has several pass-through nodes, it will be compressed one node at the time.
If the key was removed, and the next node in the path was a leaf that can now be pruned, we remove the edge to the former leaf.
If node dest is a pass-through node, it will only have one outgoing edge; we can retrieve it here.
Match cases #2 to #4: the searched key is not in the tree, so it can't be deleted
Returns, letting caller know if we deleted the key. Since for radix tries there will only be dangling nodes, we know that pruning will certainly not be needed in this case.

6.3.5 Longest common prefix

Porting this method from the trie's version is straightforward. It's just a matter of slightly modifying the search algorithm to take into account the different way we do edge matching. Listing 6.17 describes the pseudo-code for the radix trie's version.

Listing 6.17 Method `longestPrefix` for radix trie

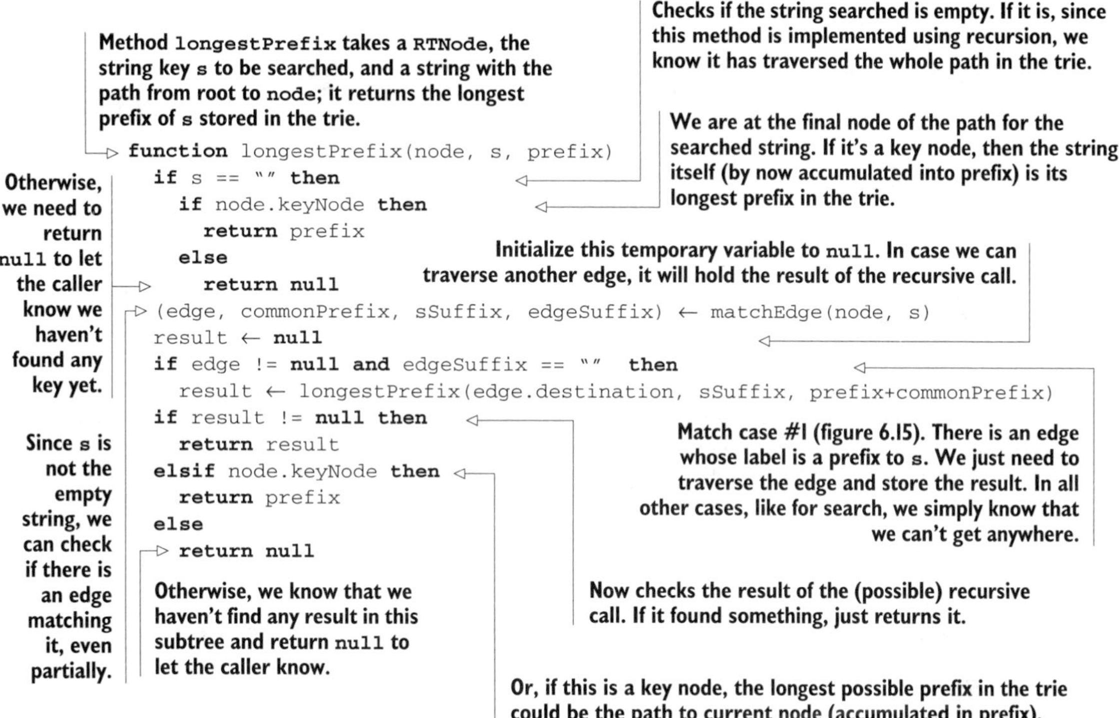

```
function longestPrefix(node, s, prefix)
  if s == "" then
    if node.keyNode then
      return prefix
    else
      return null
  (edge, commonPrefix, sSuffix, edgeSuffix) ← matchEdge(node, s)
  result ← null
  if edge != null and edgeSuffix == "" then
    result ← longestPrefix(edge.destination, sSuffix, prefix+commonPrefix)
  if result != null then
    return result
  elsif node.keyNode then
    return prefix
  else
    return null
```

Method longestPrefix takes a RTNode, the string key s to be searched, and a string with the path from root to node; it returns the longest prefix of s stored in the trie.
Checks if the string searched is empty. If it is, since this method is implemented using recursion, we know it has traversed the whole path in the trie.
We are at the final node of the path for the searched string. If it's a key node, then the string itself (by now accumulated into prefix) is its longest prefix in the trie.
Otherwise, we need to return null to let the caller know we haven't found any key yet.
Initialize this temporary variable to null. In case we can traverse another edge, it will hold the result of the recursive call.
Since s is not the empty string, we can check if there is an edge matching it, even partially.
Match case #1 (figure 6.15). There is an edge whose label is a prefix to s. We just need to traverse the edge and store the result. In all other cases, like for search, we simply know that we can't get anywhere.
Otherwise, we know that we haven't find any result in this subtree and return null to let the caller know.
Now checks the result of the (possible) recursive call. If it found something, just returns it.
Or, if this is a key node, the longest possible prefix in the trie could be the path to current node (accumulated in prefix).

6.3.6 Keys starting with a prefix

For tries, this method leverages `search` to find the starting point of a full-fledged traversal, retrieving all keys in the subtree rooted at the prefix.

Unfortunately for radix tries, the situation is a bit more complicated, because prefixes that are not stored in the tree can partially match edges. Take, for instance, the tree in figure 6.20, where prefixes such as `"a"` or `"anth"` are not stored in the tree. The latter doesn't even have a node at the end of the corresponding path, but still the radix trie contains several words starting with those prefixes.

If we were just looking for nodes that lie at the end of the path for those strings, we would miss all those legit results. We need, instead, to rewrite a special version of the search method for this operation, where we distinguish the edge match case #2, where we have a no-go, and case #3, where, instead, since the string fragment searched is a proper prefix of the last edge in the path, the subtree referenced by the edge will

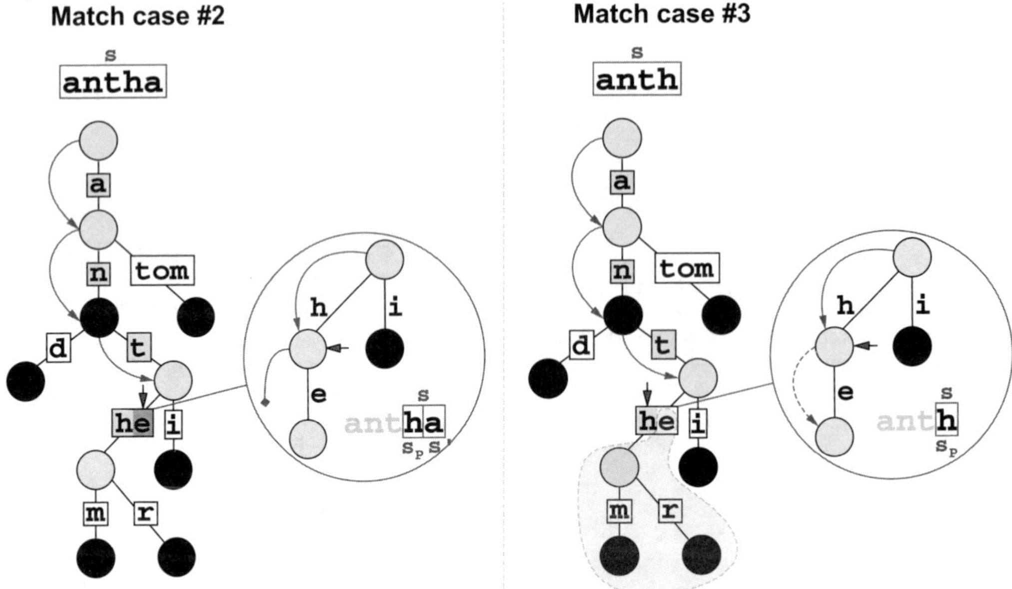
Match case #2
s
antha
a
n
tom
d
t
he
i
m
r
h
i
e
s
antha
s_P s
Match case #3
s
anth
a
n
tom
d
t
he
i
m
r
h
i
e
s
anth
s_P

Figure 6.21 The difference in facing match cases #2 and #3 while looking for the node matching the shorter string including a prefix. (Left) When we face case #2, it means that the next edge doesn't match all the characters in the string fragment left; therefore, in the corresponding trie, `searchNode(s)` would return `null`. (Right) With case #3, we have a full match of the string fragment that ends in the middle of an edge. In the corresponding trie, the search would return an intermediate node, in particular a pass-through node; therefore, since no keys are stored in pass-through nodes, we can equivalently start enumerating keys from the first non-pass-through among its descendants.

indeed contain strings that match the searched prefix. The difference between the two cases is illustrated in figure 6.21.

Listing 6.18 illustrates this new method, called `searchNodeWithPrefix`, to distinguish it from an exact match search. The API method `keysStartingWith` and the utility method `allKeysInBranch` are, instead, basically identical to the equivalent method in tries, so we leave its pseudo-code as a useful exercise for the reader.

Listing 6.18 Method `searchNodeWithPrefix` for radix trie

```
function searchNodeWithPrefix(node, s)
  if s == "" then
    return node
  (edge, commonPrefix, sSuffix, edgeSuffix) ← matchEdge(node, s)
  if edge == null then
    return null
```

- Method `searchNodeWithPrefix` takes an `RTNode` and a string key `s` to be searched; returns the root of the subtree containing all the keys stored that have `s` as a prefix.
- Checks if the string searched is empty. If it is, since this method is implemented using recursion, we know it has traversed the whole path in the trie: this is the node exactly matching `s`.
- Because `s` is not the empty string, we can check if there is an edge matching it, even partially.
- Match case #4 (figure 6.15). The searched prefix is not stored in the tree.

Match case #3. Although there is no node storing a key at the end of the path for the searched prefix, there would be a pass-through node for it in the uncompressed trie. This means that all prefixes stored in the subtree rooted at `node` will start with `s+edgeSuffix`, and those will be the only strings stored having `s` as a prefix.

Match case #1. There is an edge whose label is a prefix to `s`. We just need to traverse the edge and recurse on the remaining characters in the string.

```
  elsif edgeSuffix == "" then
    return searchNodeWithPrefix(edge.destination, sSuffix)
  elsif sSuffix == null then
    return edge.destination
  else
    return null
```

Match case #4. There is no path starting with `s` in the (sub)trie rooted at `node`.

This concludes our rundown of the main methods for radix tries, and the discussion on data structures for efficient strings search. To the interested reader who would like to delve further into this subject, we suggest taking a look at suffix trees and suffix arrays, two interesting data structures that are fundamental to fields like bioinformatics, and that are unfortunately out of scope for this chapter.

6.4 Applications

Now that we know two concrete data structures for implementing the ADT `String-Container`, we can confidently look at applications where they make a difference.

As is usual with data structures, the difference is not about new things that couldn't be done without tries, but rather about doing some operations better or faster than with other DSs.

This is particularly true for tries, as they were specifically designed to improve the running time of string-based queries. As one of the main uses for tries is to implement text-based dictionaries, the touchstone will often be hash tables.

6.4.1 Spell-checker

Time to go back to our main example! We saw in chapter 4 that Bloom filters were used for the first versions of spell-checkers, but after a while they were replaced with more efficient alternatives, such as tries.

The first step to build a spell-checker is, obviously, inserting all the keys from our dictionary (here meant as "English dictionary," not the data structure!) in a trie.

Then, using the trie for spell check when the feedback we want is just highlighting typos is simple. We just need to perform a search, and if it's a miss, we have a typo.

But suppose, instead, that we would like to also provide suggestions about how we could correct the typo—how can we do that with a trie?

Let's say that the word `w` we are checking has `m` characters, and we can accept suggestions differing by at most `k` characters from `w`: in other words, we want words whose *Levenshtein distance* (also known as edit distance) is at most `k`.

To find those words in a trie, we start traversing the tree from the root, and while traversing it we keep an array of `m` elements, where the `i`-th element of this array is the smallest edit distance necessary to match the key corresponding to the current node to the first `i` characters in our search string.

For each node `N`, we check the array holding the edit distances:

- If all distances in the array are greater than out maximum tolerance, then we can stop; there's no need to traverse its subtree any further (because the distances can only grow).
- Otherwise, we keep track of the last edit distance (the one for the whole search string), and if it's the best we have found so far, we pair it with current node's key and store it.

When we finish traversing, we will have saved the closest key to our search string and its distance.

Figure 6.22 shows how the algorithm works on a simplified example. It uses a trie, but the same algorithm, with minor changes, can easily be shown and implemented on radix trees. In fact, for this algorithm we are mostly interested in key nodes, not intermediate ones.

The algorithm starts at the root that corresponds to the empty string (because the path that leads to it is also empty). At each step, we have to compare the target word `s` (`"amt"`, in the example) to the word corresponding to the current node; in particular, we compute the distance between each prefix of s and the word associated to the current node.

So, for the root, the distance between the empty string and the empty prefix of `"amt"` (which also is the empty string, obviously) is `0` (because they match). The distance between `""` and `"a"` is `1`, because we need to add one character to the former to make the latter, and so on.

After computing our vector of distances, we traverse any outgoing edge and repeat the process for the next nodes. In this case, there is only one, associated with the string `"a"`, the concatenation of the labels leading to it. We can build the next row in the table using only the previous row, and compare the last character (the one marking the last edge traversed) to each character in `s` (note that for the empty string column, the distance will always be the length of the path).

Therefore, the second row in our table will start with a `1`, then have 0 in cell [1,1], because both strings start with an `'a'`. For the next character in `s`, there isn't a corresponding char in the node's key (because it's shorter), so we need to add 1 to have its distance, and the same for the last character. In fact, as a double-check, if we consider the prefix `"am"`, the distance to `"a"` is 1, while for `"amt"` is 2.

Notice that the cost to compare two strings is always contained in the bottom-right cell, so for `"a"` and `"amt"` this distance is 2.

The algorithm goes on traversing all branches, until we get to a point where the cost can't decrease any more (when the path is already as long as the string `s` or longer, there is no point in going down a branch as soon as we find a key node) or all the

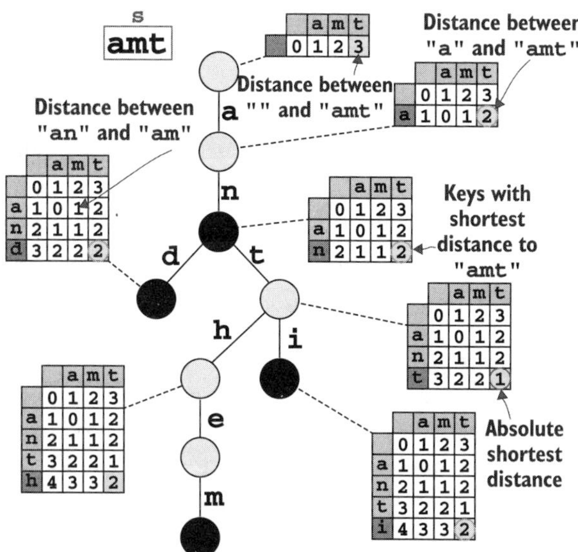
s
amt
Distance between "a" and "amt"
Distance between "" and "amt"
Distance between "an" and "am"
Keys with shortest distance to "amt"
Absolute shortest distance
a
n
d
t
h
i
e
m

Figure 6.22 Searching spell suggestions for the word s="amt" using a trie. Notice that for each node, we only compute the last row of each table, based on the previous row (from the node's parent). While the path with the closest distance to "amt" would spell "ant", in this trie the corresponding node is not a key node, so "ant" is not stored in the trie and can't be returned as a result! Instead, there are three keys at distance 2: "an", "and", "anti". They can all be returned.

distances in the last row are larger than a user-defined threshold, the max meaningful distance. This is particularly useful when searching long strings that would otherwise cause most of the tree to be traversed (while words within a distance of 2-3 characters are the most likely anyway).

As you saw in figure 6.22, the smallest distance is obtained for the path `"ant"`; however, there is a catch! This trie, in fact, doesn't contain `"ant"` as a key, and therefore we can't take this value into consideration.

Instead, there are several keys at distance 2, and any of them, or all of them, can be returned as a suggestion.

How fast can we find a suggestion? As we know at this point, after the discussion in section 6.1, searching a string in a trie has a better worst-case running time than the alternatives: `O(m)` comparisons for a string of length `m`, while for hash tables or binary search trees it would be `O(m + log(n))` at best.

6.4.2 *String similarity*

The similarity between two strings is a measure of the distance that separates them. Usually, it's some function of the number of changes needed to transform one string into the other.

Two examples of these distances are

- The *Levenshtein distance*, the number of single-character edits
- The *Hamming distance*, the number of positions in which the strings are different

As we have seen in the previous sub-section, string similarity is used by spell-checkers to decide the best suggestions to correct typos.

But recently another even more important use case has become popular: bioinformatics, matching sequences of DNA. This is a computationally intensive task, so using the wrong data structures can make it impossible to solve.

When we have to compare just two strings, directly computing the Levenshtein distance is the most effective way to go; however, if we have to compare a single string to `n` other strings to find the best match, computing `n` times the Levenshtein distance becomes impractical. The running time would be `O(n * m * M)`, where `m` is the length of our search string and `O(M)` is the average length of the `n` strings in the corpus.

Turns out, we can do much better using a trie. By using the same algorithm shown for spell-checkers (without the threshold-based pruning), computing all the distances will only take time `O(m * N)`, where `N` is the total number of nodes in the trie, and while the trie construction could take up to `O(n * M)`, it would only happen once at the beginning, and if the rate of lookups is high enough, its cost would be amortized.

In theory `N` can be `O(n * M)`, as we saw in section 6.2, if no two strings in the corpus share the same prefix. In practice, however, it is likely that `N` is order of magnitudes smaller than `n * M`, and closer to `O(M)`. Moreover, as we saw in the last sub-section, if we set a threshold for the max tolerance, that is, for the largest difference between two strings, and keep track of the best result we have found, we can prune even more the number of nodes we traverse during search.

6.4.3 String sorting

Burstsort[21] is a cache-efficient sort algorithm that works similarly to MSD (Most Significant Digit) radix sort. However, *burstsort* is cache-efficient and even faster than radix sort!

They both have the same asymptotic running time, `O(n * M)`, which is a theoretical lower bound for sorting `n` strings of length `M`, but burstsort creates results twice as fast by exploiting locality of reference and better memory distribution.

Going into the details of this algorithm is out of the scope of this chapter, but to give you an idea of how burstsort works, it dynamically constructs a trie while the strings are sorted, and uses it to partition them by assigning each string to a bucket (similar to radix sort). The asymptotic cost, as mentioned, is the same as MSD's, because leading characters of each string are inspected once only. The pattern of memory accesses, however, makes better use of cache.

While MSD, prior to the bucket-sorting phase, accesses each string once for each character, burstsort accesses each string only once overall. The trie nodes, instead, are accessed randomly.

However, the set of trie nodes is much smaller than the set of strings, so cache is used more wisely.

If the set of string exceeds cache size, burstsort becomes considerably faster than any other string sorting algorithms.

[21] Sinha, Ranjan, and Justin Zobel. "Efficient trie-based sorting of large sets of strings." Proceedings of the 26th Australasian computer science conference-Volume 16. Australian Computer Society, Inc., 2003.

6.4.4 T9

T9 was such a big milestone in mobile history that we still (mistakenly) address new mobiles' spell-checkers as T9—though it was abandoned long ago with the advent of smartphones.

The name comes as an abbreviation of "Text on 9 keys," as the alphabet was (long before mobile phones) divided into groups of three to four characters that would fit into a digital phone numpad.

In the original design for landline phones, every number had to be pressed one to four times to choose every single letter. For instance, 2 had to be pressed once for `'a'`, twice for `'b'`, and thrice for `'c'`.

Instead, the idea with T9 was that the user would press each key once for each letter in the word, to state that the `i`-th letter belonged to the group of the `k`-th button. Then T9 would offer suggestions for possible words made out of those combinations of letters, or even directly provide the right word, if only one possible match was found.

For instance, typing 2-6-3 would select all three letters combinations to form the Cartesian product `[a,b,c]x[m,n,o]x[d,e,f]`, and T9 would provide valid English words such as `[and, cod, con,...]`.

This was made possible by keeping a trie, and for each key pressed refining the search:

1 When keypad button 2 is pressed, we would start traversing the trie, going, in parallel, to the subtrees linked by edges marked with `'a'`, `'b'`, `'c'` (all three of them would likely be in the trie for any language using the Latin alphabet).
2 When the second keypad button is pressed, for each of the three paths that we are currently traversing, T9 checks to see if they have children labeled with `'m'`, `'n'` and `'o'`, and keeps track of the nodes reached at this second level. Each combination represents a path from the root to a level-2 node. Most likely, not all of the 9 combinations would have a path in the trie: for example, it's unlikely any word will start with `"bn"`.
3 The process continues with the next buttons pressed, until there is no node reachable through the possible paths traversed.

For this specific task, the trie nodes would likely store more than just a Boolean for each key. They would rather store the corpus frequency of that word (for instance, how likely it is that a word is used in English). This way, the most likely result would be returned when more than one result is available: for instance, you would somehow expect that `and` would be preferred over `cod`.

6.4.5 Autocomplete

In the last 10 years or so, we have all become familiar with the autocomplete feature of search boxes. Today we even expect search boxes to provide it by default.

The usual autocomplete workflow is the following: A user on the client side (typically a browser) starts typing in a few letters, and the autocomplete search box shows a few options that start with the characters already typed (Does this ring a bell? Sounds like "all keys with prefix"?). If the set of possible values that could be inserted in the search box was static and small, then it could be transmitted to the client together with the page, cached, and used directly on the client.

This, however, is usually not the case, since the sets of possible values are normally large, and they might change over time, or even be dynamically queried.

So, in real-world applications the client usually sends (asynchronously) a REST request to the server with the characters typed so far.

The application server keeps a trie (or more likely a Patricia tree) with the valid entries, searches for the strings starting with what was inserted so far and a valid prefix, and returns a certain number of entries in this string's subtree.

When the response comes back to the client, it simply shows the list of results from the server as suggestions.

Autocomplete across the Net

It's not strictly required that the request is performed through a REST endpoint or that it is sent asynchronously. However, the former indicates a clean design, and without the latter the autocomplete feature would make little sense.

To avoid wasting net bandwidth and server computations, usually the requests to autocomplete are sent every few seconds or when a user stops typing. When a response comes back, the page updates the list of entries shown.

This is still not ideal, because with HTTP/1.1 it is not possible to cancel requests that have already been sent and have reached the server. Moreover, we have no guarantee of the order in which responses come back. Therefore, if more characters are typed or erased before the previous response comes back, we'll have to keep some kind of versioning for the responses and never replace the results shown if a stale response arrives.

This will be mitigated with HTTP/2, since it introduces cancellable requests, among other cool things.

Summary

- There is a fundamental difference between working with primitive data types like integers or floats and working with strings: while all integers will require the same amount of memory to be stored,[22] strings can be of arbitrary length, and hence require arbitrarily many bytes.

[22]With exceptions; for instance, the *bignum* integer type in Python can represent arbitrarily large numbers, using a variable number of bytes.

- The length of the string on which a data structure works is an important factor in its asymptotic analysis; this leaves space for further optimizations that are not possible with the simplest data types.
- Tries allow us to more efficiently store and query large sets of strings, assuming many of them share some common prefixes.
- String prefixes are a key factor for this new data structure, which in turn allows us to efficiently perform queries to find strings with a common prefix or, vice versa, given a string find its longest prefix in the dataset.
- Radix tries compress paths, whenever possible, to provide a more compact representation of tries, without having to compromise in terms of complexity or performance.
- From spell-checkers to bioinformatics, many applications and fields manipulating strings can benefit from using tries.

7 Use case: LRU cache

This chapter covers

- Avoiding computing things twice
- Introducing caching as a solution
- Describing different types of caches
- Designing an efficient solution for LRU cache
- Discussing MFU and other choices for handling priority
- Discussing caching strategies
- Reasoning about concurrency and synchronization
- Describing how caches can be applied in a sentiment analyzer's pipeline

This chapter is going to be different from what you have seen so far in this book. We are not going to introduce a new data structure, but instead we will use the ones described in chapters 2–5 to create a more complex data structure. By using lists, queues, hash tables, and so on as building blocks, we will be able to create an advanced data structure that can be used to quickly access values and computed results that were recently accessed—although one could argue that a cache is more than just a data structure; it's a sophisticated component with several moving parts.

In its simplest form, a cache can be implemented as an associative array, but we will see during the course of this chapter that it can become as complex as a web service.

In this chapter, we'll delve into the details of how caches of increasing complexity work, so after reading it, you should be able to articulate an informed opinion on the topic.

7.1 Don't compute things twice

In our daily job as software developers, we write applications, most of which perform really simple tasks. Adding two numbers, or even dividing them, or adding two vectors (with modern GPUs[1]) are trivial operations, fast enough that we don't need to bother with optimizing them. (Of course, this wasn't always the case, but if you happen to be young enough, you've never had to deal with x86 processors.)

Yet, no matter how fast and optimized multicore processors or server clusters become, there will always be some kind of computations, some complex operations for which it will just be too expensive for us to ignore how wasteful it would be to perform them multiple times when we don't need to.

Back to the previous vector sum. If our vectors have billions of elements (or too many to fit in a GPU's memory at once), then even this operation becomes quite expensive. The same is true if we are going to repeat the same divisions billions of times when we could have gotten away with a few hundred of them: the impact on our applications' running time will be sensible.

Number crunching is not the only context in which optimizing your computation matters. If we move to web applications, for example, one of the costliest operations is certainly accessing a database, and even more so if it involves iterating through a cursor to count or compute something.

It's not just terribly expensive (in terms of resources) and slow. Database cursors[2] might involve extensive (possibly even table- or DB-wide) locks[3] if they are not read-only, but even writing single rows can, in some DBs, require locking a page or a whole table.

Every time we lock some data, all read operations on that data have to wait until the lock is released. If this is not handled carefully, a big load of write operations to the DB can put it on fire,[4] slowing your application down and producing an inconvenient lag

---

[1] Graphics Processing Units were originally designed to speed up image processing and buffering for display devices. With the turn of the century they became increasingly used as general (parallel) computation devices, so much so that they actually are the election choice, instead of CPUs (Central Processing Unit), for algebraic-intensive tasks such as machine learning.

[2] Cursors are control structures that allow traversing a set of rows in a DB table; as a simplification, they can be thought of as pointers to the next row to read in a portion of the table, and they are used to subsequently process rows (either reading data or modifying it) one by one, as opposed to a batch read/write where a group of records is read/written at once.

[3] Locks are another DB construct that prevents all reads/writes on a raw/table/DB while data is being modified. They are needed for consistency, but they can have a dramatic impact on availability. In general, using cursors that allow updating the data is not advised because they might hold locks for a long time.

[4] Not literally! Just jargon.

for your users, or even grinding your DB to a halt, which in turn will cause all your HTTP calls to time out and thus an outage of your website/application.

Wow, that's scary, isn't it? Now, if there only was a way to avoid it!

Many companies, even tech giants, in their early days (and at the dawn of the internet age), had to experience first-hand the troubles of running and growing a website smoothly. That is, until they found ways to adapt and cope with it.

One of the best ways to ease the load on a database is to avoid computing expensive results twice in a short time. There are many other strategies orthogonal to this, from *sharding*[5] to loosening the consistency constraint (moving to *eventual consistency*[6]), that are needed or at least helpful in order to achieve good, stable performance on a web application. This is obviously not the right place to present them, but the literature on scalability is rich, and if you are going to work in the field, we definitely recommend you look at some of the amazing books or web guides that have been published.[7]

In this chapter we are going to focus, instead, on caching. To narrow our scope a bit, and hopefully make our example clearer, let's consider a plausible situation where you could actually use some caching.

Imagine you have this aggregator service that gathers news about companies from social networks, and provides some sort of insight on them; for example, if people are talking about a company in a positive or negative way (what's called *sentiment analysis*[8] in data science). Figure 7.1 shows a possible simplified architecture for such a service.

You will need to call external APIs to gather posts from the major social networks and then analyze them and assign a sentiment to each post. Once they are all labeled, each with a certain degree of confidence, you need to decide if overall the sentiment about the company is positive or negative. For instance, you can decide that a tweet spoke positively about company X, with a degree of confidence of 70%, while for another tweet you have a degree of confidence of 95% that the sentiment is negative. Then you'll have to weigh the two of them, taking that confidence into consideration (among many other things).

You will likely have to subscribe to, pay for, and connect to different services for the different social networks and write adapters that cope with the different formats.

Each external service requires an HTTP call outside your intranet, and each call will have some latency that's different for the various services. You can call each service in

---

[5] Sharding consists in breaking down data, users or transactions (or all of them) in groups, each of which is assigned to a different machine/cluster/data-center. This balances the loads and allows us to use smaller, cheaper servers and databases for each group, ultimately allowing applications to scale better and in a cheaper way.

[6] Relaxing the temporal requirement on consistency. We'll explain a bit more later in the chapter.

[7] For instance, https://www.manning.com/books/principles-of-cloud-design or https://www.manning.com/books/progressive-web-apps, which also has a nice chapter on caching.

[8] Using techniques such as natural language processing, text analysis, and computational linguistics to automatically identify the attitude of one or more subjects with respect to some topic.

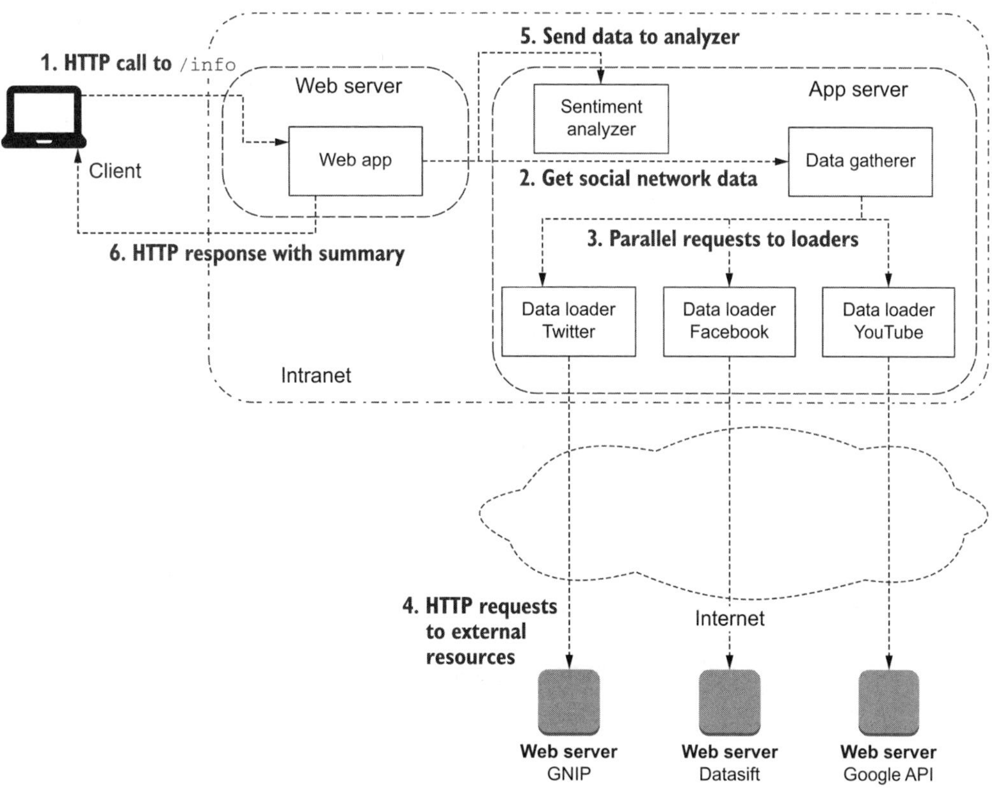
1. HTTP call to /info
Web server
Web app
Client
6. HTTP response with summary
5. Send data to analyzer
Sentiment analyzer
App server
Data gatherer
2. Get social network data
3. Parallel requests to loaders
Data loader Twitter
Data loader Facebook
Data loader YouTube
Intranet
4. HTTP requests to external resources
Internet
Web server GNIP
Web server Datasift
Web server Google API

Figure 7.1 A possible architecture for the "Get social networks daily summary" application. (1) The client sends an HTTP call to the web server asking for the daily summary (for a specific company). (2) The web server contacts the app server to get the data from the major social networks (here the list is just meant as an example). The app server might be physically and logically on the same machine as the web server (in which case the call is a method call), or physically hosted on the same machine but in a different process, or even hosted in a different machine, such that the call ends up being an actual HTTP call. (3) The data gatherer starts one new thread for each loader/social network. All these calls are asynchronous. (4) Each loader sends an HTTP call to an external API over the internet. Once it's done, it returns the loaded data to the gatherer. Once all the loaders are finished, the gatherer returns all the collected data to its caller (the web server, in this case). (5) The web server synchronously calls the sentiment analyzer, passing the raw data, and expecting the summary in return. Alternatively, the web server could have called an orchestrator or the sentiment analyzer directly at point 2, and this step would be delegated. (6) Once the sentiment has been computed and passed back to the web server, it builds an HTTP response around it and sends it back to the client.

parallel, but even then, if you do need all the data to make a decision, your latency will be at least as high as the slowest of those services.

Latency can really be a problem; say you offered your customer a *service-level agreement* (SLA) where you committed to return 95% of your monthly calls within 750ms, but unfortunately, during peaks of traffic, a couple of those external services can take as long as 3s to answer.

To make things worse, your timeout for HTTP responses is set to 3.5s, meaning that you have to return an answer to the client within 3.5 seconds; otherwise your load balancer will kill the call. I can imagine you are thinking it would be enough to adjust the timeout, but suppose you can't change this timeout, because otherwise you couldn't support the traffic load, given the resources you have available. So, assuming you take around 250ms to process data for a single source, if it takes 3 seconds to get that data, considering the time to handle the incoming call, do some post-processing, and send the response back, you risk having a lot of 503[9] errors. And guess what? That also goes against your SLA.

At this point it is worth noting that if you are a paid service and you violate your SLA, you might have to give some money back to your customers. So, you definitely would like to avoid that.

Let's say, in order to keep things simple for our example, that you'd like to provide this sentiment analysis for one company at a time (one company per HTTP call), per day, and always only based on the day before. Imagine that people will use the information gathered yesterday before the stock market opens to decide whether or not it's a good idea to invest in a company. Also, let's assume we only provide our prediction service to the Fortune 100 top companies.

7.2 First attempt: Remembering values

At this point, we know that we can't afford to compute each intermediate result over and again every time we receive a call; that would be too expensive. So, the most natural thing to do is store these intermediate results once we compute them and look them up when we need the results again.

We are obviously in luck because the function to produce the summary takes only one argument, the name (or internal ID) of the company and its domain[10] is relatively small.[11] And thus we can easily identify the intermediate results we need, and we can expect to reuse them several times. If our application runs for long enough without restarting, after an initial warm-up period when we have to actually compute values (and hence latency will be high during this warm-up), we will have computed enough intermediate results to respond to calls quickly, without the extra latency due to the external HTTP calls.

Take a look at how these assumptions change our architecture in figure 7.2, and meet the cache, our knight in shining armor that will save us from failing our SLA and going out of business.

To get rid of all the nitty-gritty HTTP related details that are not particularly important for our analysis, let's abstract them out in a magic function that can be called by our sentiment analyzer and just return all the data we need for all the social

[9] HTTP status code for "Service unavailable."

[10] The set of possible inputs for the function.

[11] As we said, we are restricting ourselves to only top Fortune 100 companies in this example.

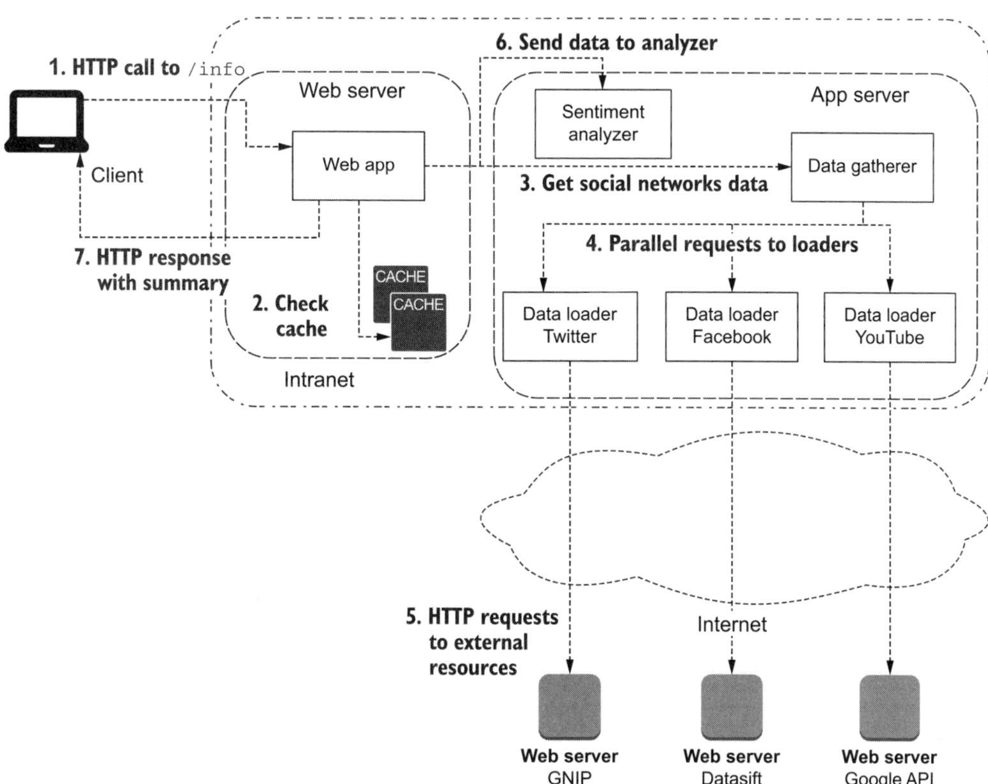

1. HTTP call to /info
Client
Web server
Web app
2. Check cache
CACHE
CACHE
7. HTTP response with summary
Intranet
6. Send data to analyzer
Sentiment analyzer
App server
Data gatherer
3. Get social networks data
4. Parallel requests to loaders
Data loader Twitter
Data loader Facebook
Data loader YouTube
5. HTTP requests to external resources
Internet
Web server GNIP
Web server Datasift
Web server Google API

Figure 7.2 With the introduction of cache, before issuing a call to the app server, the web server checks if the results have already been computed, and in that case skips steps 3–6 in this figure. Note that cache can be added also for the single loaders, in case we allow partial results (for instance, if one of the external services is down). In theory, it can also be added to the "data cruncher" instead of the web server, delegating the interface with the data gatherer to the data cruncher, so that the web server directly calls only the data cruncher. Having cache on the web server (physically on the same machine), however, has several advantages.

networks we draw our posts from. Figure 7.3 shows the simplified architecture for the sentiment analyzer.

It looks much cleaner now, right? Remember, we are hiding all complexity in the "sentiment generator" because we want to focus on the caching mechanism, and we are not interested in the details of how this sentiment is computed. Nonetheless, this doesn't mean that you can only use caching in-memory or for standalone applications; on the contrary, web applications are probably one of the best places to add some caching layers: the detailed example from which we started should have made this clear.

Moreover, it is important to remember that simplifying complex things by abstracting low-level details is a paramount technique in algorithm analysis. For instance, we often assume that some containers will store integers instead of worrying about every possible type of entry that could be stored, and even the RAM model itself, that we

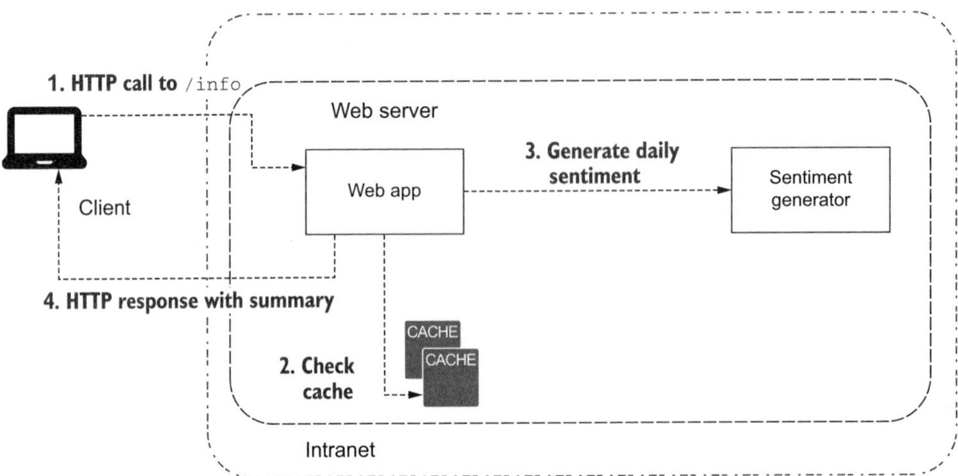
1. HTTP call to /info
Web server
3. Generate daily sentiment
Web app
Sentiment generator
Client
4. HTTP response with summary
CACHE
CACHE
2. Check cache
Intranet

Figure 7.3 The architecture of our example application, after abstracting out all details relative to the generation of the summary into an ad hoc component, the "sentiment generator", that we can imagine is hosted on the web server, and is called synchronously from the web app.

introduced in appendix B, is a simplification to hide the details of the myriad of different configurations that real computers can have.

7.2.1 *Description and API*

As always, let's draft an API and a contract that our data structure should adhere to.

Abstract data structure: Cache	

API	`class Cache {`
	`  init(maxSize);`
	`  get(key);`
	`  set(key, value);`
	`  getSize();`
	`}`

Contract with client	A cache stores a certain number of entries (the `maxSize` argument for the constructor, in the API), always allows you to set new entries, and retains elements based on the concrete cache's implementation of the eviction policy.[a] When `set` is called, if an entry with the same key already exists on the cache, the new value will overwrite the old one.

[a] A cache's eviction policy is used to decide which element should be purged from a full cache to make room for a new entry.

7.2.2 *Fresh data, please*

Now that we have a first solution for our specific example, we could ask if these conclusions apply also to the general case. To that end, we need to discuss some concerns that we've swept under the proverbial rug so far. We need to question if the computation is static, isolated, and time-independent. Think, for instance, of a matrix product or numerically computing a complex integral. If that's the case, we are in luck, because we can compute the results once (for each input), and they will be valid forever.

It might happen, instead, that we have to deal with some computation that can vary depending on time (for instance, on day of the week or month) or on any other external factor (for instance, an aggregate of daily orders that will change when new orders are placed and when the date changes). In this case, we would have to be careful when reusing values we have already computed, because they can go *stale;* meaning that under some conditions, the value once computed and stored in our cache might not be the most up to date, or even relevant, anymore.

How we deal with stale cache depends heavily on the context. In some cases, even stale values can provide an acceptable approximation when a certain margin of error is acceptable. For instance, if we do compute aggregates on daily sales and show them in a live chart, we might be OK with having data synched every minute or every 10 minutes. This would avoid recomputing all the aggregates (possibly grouped by product or store) every time the chart is displayed in our reporting tool, which could be used by tens of employees at the same time.

Probably the best example explaining why this "controlled staleness" can be acceptable is provided by web caches. HTTP standards allow the server (the provider of the content) to add headers[12] to resources (web pages, but also images, files, and so on) to let the client (usually the browser) know when it is allowed to read a certain resource from cache, and also to let intermediate cache nodes know if[13] and for how long the response provided by the server to an HTTP (GET, usually) call can be cached.

Vice versa, if we have a time-critical, safety-critical application, such as a monitoring application for a nuclear power plant (for some reason, this example works well in communicating a sense of criticality . . .), then we can't afford approximations and stale data (certainly not for more than a few seconds).

The other open questions are these: What makes data stale and do we have a quick way to know when that happens? If data simply ages, we can store a timestamp when we write it to cache and check it when we read it. If it's too old to still be relevant, we can recompute and update the cache. If there are other external conditions—for instance, a change in configuration or some event, such as a new order made or a change of the required precision for calculus—we are still fine as long as we can check these conditions, and the check is relatively inexpensive with respect to computing the value again from scratch.

---

[12]Ideally, all http responses should add `Cache-Control`, `Expires`, and `Last-Modified` headers to make sure the resources are taken from cache as much as possible.

[13]Not all data can be shared without limits. That's why there are private caches where data is shared with a single user/IP, and public caches (used, for example, for static, anonymous content) shared with anyone interested in the resource.

In the rest of the chapter we simplify the problem by assuming that cached content doesn't go stale. Handling stale content can be seen as an orthogonal task that can enhance the base caching mechanism we built, for the most part independently of the choices we made for this mechanism.

7.2.3 Handling asynchronous calls

Acknowledging the existence of stale data and discussing workarounds was a good starting point toward generalizing caching solutions to more than just our carefully crafted example. The next step is generalizing the computation model. So far, we have assumed we are in a single-threaded environment, so calls are handled by a synchronous queue and are executed one after the other. This is not only unrealistic; this is also wasteful. Real-world applications can't afford the latency that would result in leaving clients waiting while previous calls are being processed. We can run many copies of this pipeline, as shown in figure 7.4, but each of them will have its own cache and will be able to handle one call at a time. Caching would not be as effective as possible, because if two threads get the same request, neither will be able to read the result from cache. But even worse, assuming the sentiment generator works synchronously, handling one request at a time slows us down even more.

Consider any of the threads depicted in figure 7.4 and suppose the cache has already stored the intermediate results for Twitter and Facebook when the sentiment generator receives four more requests for Google, Twitter, Facebook, and Google. For the first request, we'll have to compute everything from scratch, but for the next two, we already have all we need in cache, and we could output the result immediately. In a synchronous architecture, however, we would be forced to wait for the first call to

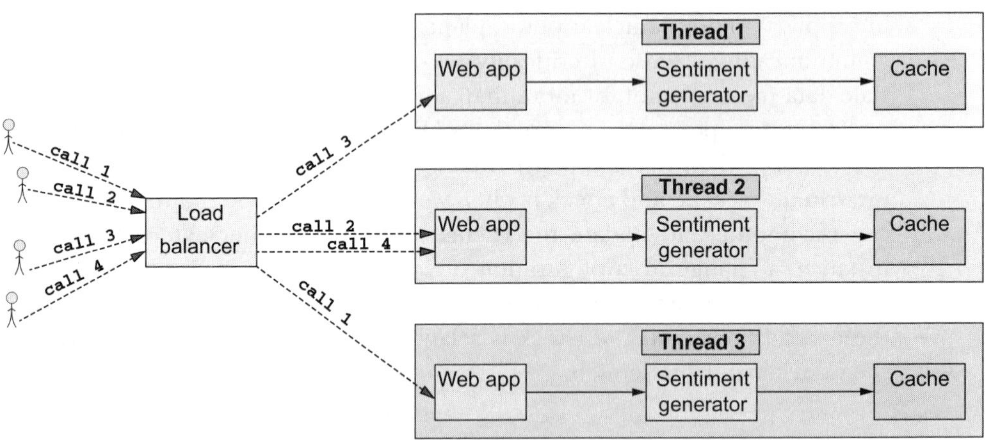
Thread 1
Web app
Sentiment generator
Cache
Thread 2
Web app
Sentiment generator
Cache
Thread 3
Web app
Sentiment generator
Cache
call 1
call 2
call 3
call 4
Load balancer
call 3
call 2
call 4
call 1

Figure 7.4 A possible configuration for the app running with one cache per thread. Each thread hosts a full pipeline (web server, sentiment generator, and cache) and handles one call at a time, running synchronously. A load balancer makes sure to distribute the calls to the many threads running, waiting for each web server to answer before forwarding the next call (in the figure, the web app in thread 2 would have returned the response for call #2 before the load balancer could forward call #4).

complete before the next two (and all the others that would possibly pile up in the meantime) could be processed by the sentiment generator and returned. In an asynchronous configuration, however, the web app can call the sentiment generator asynchronously for each sentiment analysis request, "join" on the responses containing the intermediate results, and return as soon as all the information for a call is gathered, and it can compute the final result. What happens, though, if in the figure's example sequence the second request for Google is processed while the first one is still computing the intermediate results?

If the first call hasn't finished yet, no value is added to the cache for Google. So, when the second call comes, the web app sees a cache miss and calls the sentiment generator to retrieve all the data from social networks and compute the sentiment again.

Then, the result of whichever call that finishes first will be stored in the cache. And when the other call finally produces a result, it will also try to store that result in the cache. Depending on the implementation of the cache, this can simply overwrite the old result (they could be different for a lot of reasons), discard the new result, or in the worst-case scenario, produce a duplicate.[14]

But regardless of how the collision is handled, the worst part is that we twice compute a result that we could have retrieved from cache. This in turn means unnecessarily high latency, and in some cases extra costs. For instance, in our example, data providers do charge for data from social networks.

7.2.4 *Marking cache values as "Loading"*

Finding a perfect solution for race conditions is not easy. In some cases, it is impossible. Here, for example, if we consider the fully detailed architecture of figure 7.2, we have several HTTP calls that can have a variable latency or fail altogether. So, we can't be sure which one of the two calls to retrieve Google sentiment would return first. Assuming the first call finishes first can be reasonable, but it can also lead to inefficiency, if for any reason the first call to the data gatherer[15] lasts more than the average. That's not the worst-case scenario, though: if we decide that the second call to our `/sentiment` endpoint will wait and reuse the result computed for the first one, and then the calls to the data gatherer fail for some reason, the net result will be that both web calls to our web server will fail.

That said, we can and need to try to do better and avoid wasting resources. To handle the situation described in the last sub-section, one thing we could do is certainly add a "loading" state for cache values, used to mark entries in the cache that are currently being computed. When the first call to `/sentiment/Google` checks the cache and finds a miss, it will create an entry for Google and mark it as "in progress."

When the second call checks the cache, it will be aware that the value is being computed. Then we can either do some time-based polling of the cache, checking

[14]We'll pick this example up again in section 7.7. Figure 7.12 illustrates it.

[15]A software component shown in figures 7.1 and 7.2.

every few hundreds of milliseconds until a value is stored for that entry, or implement a publisher-subscriber mechanism, with the web app subscribing to the cache to let it know it's interested in the entry "Google," and the cache notifying all subscribers for that entry once its value is finally computed.

Either way, we can't completely solve the problems with the race conditions mentioned here, but risking a little extra delay and a few more 500s responses is in many cases worth the savings we earn by avoiding re-computing values that are in progress.

7.3 Memory is not enough (literally)

Let's stop for a minute and recap what we have discussed so far:

- We have a complex problem which has a lot of intermediate results that can internally be reused frequently.
- To exploit this fact, we need a mechanism to remember the intermediate results so that we compute them only once (or at least as few times as possible).

That seems straightforward, right? For our example, it probably is: we have a very small number of possible entries (at most 100), and for each one we only store the sentiment computed. It seems likely that we would be OK with a very small amount of memory to store our cache.

What do you think would happen, however, if we needed to create a cache for the data gatherer in figure 7.2, storing all the messages across the major social networks mentioning a company in their raw format? Consider that there could be millions of those, for the "coolest" companies, and each one would on average require a few kilobytes (assuming we store media as links or don't store them at all). Even with just a hundred companies, it could be on the order of a few gigabytes.

Likewise, consider how an application like Facebook would work. When you try to access your wall, an algorithm computes the best posts to show you, based on your friends' walls, your preferences, the pages you follow, and so on.

It's a pretty complex and resource-consuming algorithm, so you want to cache its results as much as possible, since you probably don't need to recompute the feed if the same user accesses their wall after one or five minutes (or maybe you have an incremental update mechanism that only surfaces new posts when they are published—but that's another story and slightly off the point).

Now consider this caching mechanism for a billion walls: even if we store just the top 50 posts per wall, and for each post we just store its ID (typically a few bytes), we still need a terabyte for the cache.

These examples show how we can easily reach a size, for the cache, that's hard or impossible to keep in the RAM. It would still be possible to use NoSQL databases, or distributed caches, such as Memcached, Redis, or Cassandra, to name a few, but even there, the more entries we store, the slower it will be checking the cache. This will be clearer when we discuss the implementation of a typical cache.

We can also imagine a situation where we keep receiving different inputs that would need new entries in the cache. As you can imagine, we can't add new entries indefinitely to a cache: being a finite system, there will always be a point when an infinite number of entries will saturate it.

Therefore, once we have filled the cache, if we want to add new entries, we need to start purging some of the existing ones.

The question is, of course, which entries should we purge? The somehow uncanny answer is that it would be ideal to remove the ones that won't be requested anymore, or at least those that will be requested fewer times.

Unfortunately, as much as we've gotten better at forecasting, despite the amazing progress in AI we have seen, even computers don't have any psychic superpower, so we can't predict *exactly* which elements we are going to need the most and which ones the least.[16]

Spoiler alert: there are some assumptions that we can use to try to make educated guesses. One reasonable assumption is that if an entry hasn't been accessed for a long time, it has less value than an entry that was recently accessed. Depending on the size of the cache and on the time elapsed until the entry was last accessed, we could infer that the oldest entry is somehow stale, and it's likely it won't be needed soon or ever again.

On the other hand, depending on the context, even the opposite could be true: that entries that haven't been accessed for a long time will be needed soon. In that case, though, removing the fresher items usually doesn't work very well, and some other criteria must be found.

If we only look at the timestamp of last access, though, we discard other useful information. For example, if an entry was accessed several times, but not for the last few minutes, then all newer entries, even if only accessed once, will be considered more valuable. If you think about it, if an entry is only required once, it means it has been computed but never read from the cache, so caching it has not yet brought any advantage. After some time, if that entry is not yet accessed, the utility of keeping it becomes questionable. So, a different approach could be assigning a value to entries based on how often they are accessed.

We will discuss these recipes in detail in the next few sections, while we also detail the implementation of these caches.

[16]Of course, there are many techniques, including machine learning, that can provide good predictions, but always with some degree of error—especially high in a field like this where the users' behavior can change quickly and unexpectedly.

7.4 Getting rid of stale data: LRU cache

The first type of cache, or rather of eviction policy, that we are going to describe is the LRU (least recently used) cache, purging the cache's *least recently used* entry each time.

What do we need to implement this data structure? The operations we want to optimize for are

- Storing an entry given the name of a company (obviously)
- Checking if there is an entry stored for a name
- Retrieving an entry by name
- Getting the number of elements stored
- Getting the oldest entry and purging it from the cache

As we explained in section 7.3, this data structure will only be able to store a certain number of elements at the same time. The actual size of the cache can be decided on creation and, depending on the implementation, can even be changed dynamically. We will denote with `N` the number of elements that can be stored in the cache. When the cache is already at its full capacity, if we need to add a new entry, we will have to remove one of the existing ones, and in this case we will remove the one that was least recently used (hence the name).

Let's now reason about which one, among the basic data structures we have seen so far, could guarantee us the best performance. Handling the size of the cache is easy; we can keep a variable for that and update it in constant time, so we won't mention it any further in this analysis.

Checking if an entry exists is based on finding an entry by name, so only the latter operation needs to be analyzed.

Storing and retrieving entries by name should ring a bell. It's clearly what an associative array does, so hash tables would be the obvious choice there. Hash tables, however, are not great when it comes to retrieving the minimum (or maximum) element they contain.[17]

In fact, removing the oldest element could take up to linear time and, unless the expected life of the cache is so short that, on average, we are not going to fill it completely, this could slow down every insertion of a new entry.

Using arrays doesn't seem like a good idea, because they would not speed up any of the operations, or at most just a single one, while requiring all the space for maximum capacity to be allocated from the start.

Linked lists seem promising for keeping the order of insertion, but they wouldn't be great when it comes to looking up entries.

If you read appendix C, you might remember that there is a data structure offering a compromise between all of these different operations: balanced trees! With a tree, we would be able to guarantee that all of these operations could be performed in logarithmic time in the worst-case scenario.

---

[17] See chapter 2 and appendix C for a refresher.

Table 7.1 Comparative analysis of performance vs implementation for cache with n elements

	Array (unsorted)	Array (sorted)	Linked list	Hash table	Balanced tree
Storing an entry	O(1)	O(n)	O(n)	O(1) [a]	O(log n)
Finding entry by name	O(n)	O(log n) [b]	O(n)	O(1) [a]	O(log n)
Removing oldest entry	O(n) [c]	O(n)	O(1)	O(n)	O(log n)

[a] Amortized.
[b] Using binary search.
[c] It requires O(1) time to locate the entry but, considering a static array, after removing its first element, the rest of the elements must be shifted one position.

So, from table 7.1, we could infer that

- The tree would look like the best compromise on the general case.
- The hash table would be the best choice if we know the size of the cache is big enough (and the insertion of new elements infrequent enough) to rarely require removal of the oldest entry.
- The linked list could be a valid option if removing old entries was more important than storing entries or finding cache elements: but in that case, the cache would basically be useless and adding it would provide no benefit.
- In all cases, the memory needed to store `n` entries is `O(n)`.

Now the question is, can we do any better?

7.4.1 *Sometimes you have to double down on problems*

As you can imagine, if the answer were no, we wouldn't really be asking the question in the first place.

But how can we do any better? There isn't any other data structure that allows us to optimize all three main operations at the same time.

And yet . . . . What if I told you that it is possible to design an LRU cache that takes `O(1)` amortized time[18] for all those operations?

Before you go on and read the solution to the riddle, please try for a couple of minutes to imagine how that could be possible.

Let me give you two hints (spoiler alert: you might want to try designing a solution before reading them):

1. You can use as much extra memory as you want (but staying within `O(n)` should be your target).
2. The fact that I mentioned linked lists should ring a bell, and make you think about a specific data structure we saw in appendix C. Nevertheless, we have seen that it's not enough if you take it alone.

[18] Technically, as we have seen, it's more correct to say that the amortized time for `n` operations is `O(n)`, so individual calls usually take constant time, but some of them might and will take longer, up to `O(n)`.

Both hints point to the same idea: a single data structure might not be enough to build the most efficient solution to the problem.

On the one hand, we have data structures that are particularly good for quickly storing and retrieving entries. Hash tables are pretty much impossible to beat if that's the game.

On the other hand, hash tables are terrible when it comes to maintaining an ordering of things, but we have other structures that handle this very well. Depending on the kind of ordering we would like to keep, we might need trees, or we might be fine with lists. We'll actually see both cases in the rest of the chapter.

In light of this new hint, pause for another minute and try to imagine how to make this work. Can you come up with an idea of how to combine a hash table and another data structure in order to optimize all operations on a cache?

7.4.2 Temporal ordering

It turns out that we have a very simple way to do so. Before delving into this section, you might want to look at appendix C if you can't exactly remember the running time for operations on arrays and lists, and the difference between singly- and doubly-linked lists.

So, imagine that you only have to keep an ordering on the cache entries, being able to go from the least to the most recently used. Since the order is only based on insertion time, new elements are not changing the order of the older elements; therefore, we don't need anything fancy: we only need a structure that supports FIFO. We could just use a list or a queue. As you should remember, a linked list is usually the best choice when we don't know in advance the number of elements we will have to store or the number can change dynamically, while a queue is usually implemented using an array (and so more static in dimension), but optimized for insertion on the head and removal on the tail.

Linked lists can also support fast insertion/removal at their ends. We need, however, a doubly-linked list, as shown in figure 7.5, where we insert elements on the front, and remove from the tail. By always keeping a pointer to the tail and links from each node to its predecessor, we can implement tail removal in `O(1)` time.

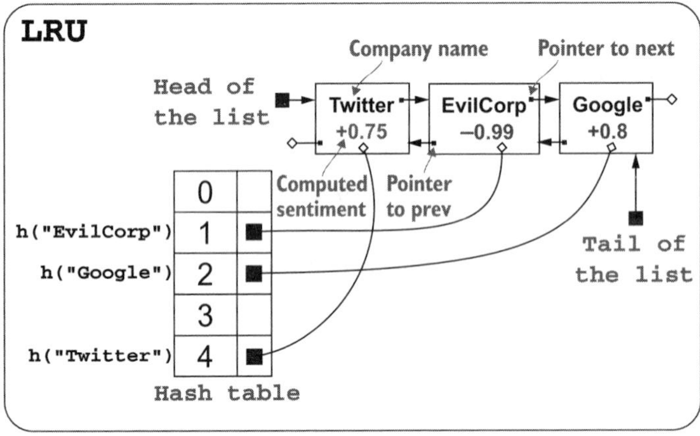
LRU
Company name
Pointer to next
Head of the list
Twitter
+0.75
EvilCorp
–0.99
Google
+0.8
Computed sentiment
Pointer to prev
0
h("EvilCorp") 1
h("Google") 2
3
h("Twitter") 4
Tail of the list
Hash table

Figure 7.5 Structure of an LRU cache. You can see the tree data elements that are stored for the cache and need to be updated after every operation: (1) The hash table. (2) The head of a doubly-linked list. (3) A pointer to the last element in the list. Notice how each element in the hash table points to a node in the list where all the data is stored. To get from a list entry to the corresponding hash entry, we have to hash the name of the company stored in the node, which is the key for the table. For the sake of simplicity, collision resolution is not considered in this and the following figures.

Listing 7.1 shows some pseudo-code implementing an LRU with linked lists.

Listing 7.1 LRU cache construction

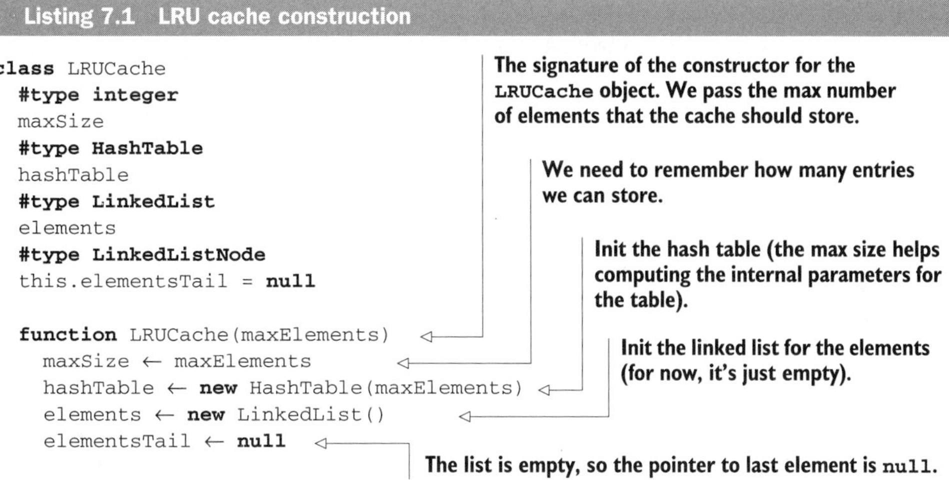
The signature of the constructor for the LRUCache object. We pass the max number of elements that the cache should store.
We need to remember how many entries we can store.
Init the hash table (the max size helps computing the internal parameters for the table).
Init the linked list for the elements (for now, it's just empty).
The list is empty, so the pointer to last element is null.

```
class LRUCache
  #type integer
  maxSize
  #type HashTable
  hashTable
  #type LinkedList
  elements
  #type LinkedListNode
  this.elementsTail = null

  function LRUCache(maxElements)
    maxSize ← maxElements
    hashTable ← new HashTable(maxElements)
    elements ← new LinkedList()
    elementsTail ← null
```

When static queues are implemented using arrays, we can save some extra memory in comparison to linked lists, which would use it for pointers to other nodes and for the node object itself. This is an implementation detail, though, that depends on the language used and doesn't change the order of magnitude of the memory used: it's `O(n)` in both cases.

So, in the end, how do we choose between lists and queues? Well, we need to reason a bit more about our design. So far, we have only considered the hash table and the linked list separately, but we need to make them work together in synchrony.

We might store very large objects in the cache, and we definitely don't want to duplicate them in both data structures. One way to avoid duplication is storing the entries only in one of the structures and referencing them from the other one. We could either add the entries to the hash table and store in the other DS the key to the hash table, or vice versa.

Both linked lists and queues could support either way. But we are going to use a linked list instead; the reason will be clear in a few lines.

We also need to decide which data structure should hold the values and which one should be left with the reference. Here, we are arguing that the best choice is having hash table entries store pointers to linked list nodes, and have the latter store the actual values, and the main reason for that is the same as for choosing lists over queues.[19]

This reason stems from a situation we haven't considered yet.

[19]There is also more to the story. If we do the opposite, then the way we link from a linked list node to the hash table entry will be tied to the implementation of the hash table. It could be an index for open addressing or a pointer if we use chaining. This coupling to an implementation is neither good design nor, often, possible, as you usually can't access standard library internals (for good reason!).

This cache is called *least recently used*. It's not least recently *added*. This means the ordering is not just based on the time we first add an element to cache, but on the last time it was accessed (which can be the same, for unlucky entries that are never reused after they have been saved, although it usually shouldn't be).

So, considering the set method to add a new entry to the cache (implemented in listing 7.2), when we have a *cache miss*, trying to access an element that is not on the cache, we just add a new entry to the front of our linked list, as shown in figure 7.6.

Listing 7.2 LRU cache set

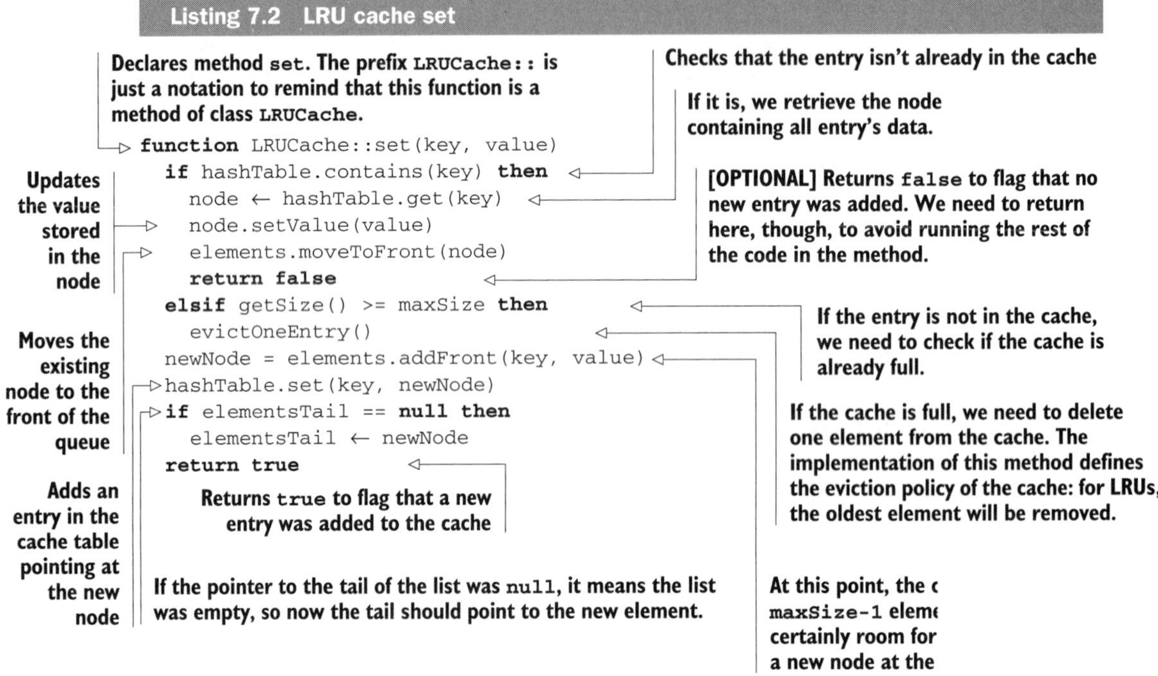

```
function LRUCache::set(key, value)
  if hashTable.contains(key) then
    node ← hashTable.get(key)
    node.setValue(value)
    elements.moveToFront(node)
    return false
  elsif getSize() >= maxSize then
    evictOneEntry()
  newNode = elements.addFront(key, value)
  hashTable.set(key, newNode)
  if elementsTail == null then
    elementsTail ← newNode
  return true
```

Declares method set. The prefix LRUCache:: is just a notation to remind that this function is a method of class LRUCache.
Checks that the entry isn't already in the cache
If it is, we retrieve the node containing all entry's data.
[OPTIONAL] Returns false to flag that no new entry was added. We need to return here, though, to avoid running the rest of the code in the method.
Updates the value stored in the node
Moves the existing node to the front of the queue
If the entry is not in the cache, we need to check if the cache is already full.
If the cache is full, we need to delete one element from the cache. The implementation of this method defines the eviction policy of the cache: for LRUs, the oldest element will be removed.
Returns true to flag that a new entry was added to the cache
Adds an entry in the cache table pointing at the new node
If the pointer to the tail of the list was null, it means the list was empty, so now the tail should point to the new element.
At this point, the
maxSize-1
certainly room for
a new node at the

But when we run into a *cache hit*, as shown in figure 7.7, accessing an element that is indeed stored on the cache, we need to move an existing list element to the front of the list, and we can only do that efficiently if we can both retrieve in constant(-ish[20]) time a pointer to the linked list node for the existing entry (which could be anywhere in the list, for what we know), and remove an element from the list in constant time (again, we need a doubly-linked list for this; with an array-based implementation of a queue, removal in the middle of the queue takes linear time).

If the cache is full, we need to remove the least-recently-used entry before we can add a new one. In this case, the method to remove the oldest entry, described in listing 7.3 and illustrated in figure 7.8, can access the tail of the linked list in constant time, from which we recover the entry to delete. To locate it on the hash table and

[20] Remember we still need to include the time for computing each hash value for the entry we look up. See appendix C for more on this topic.

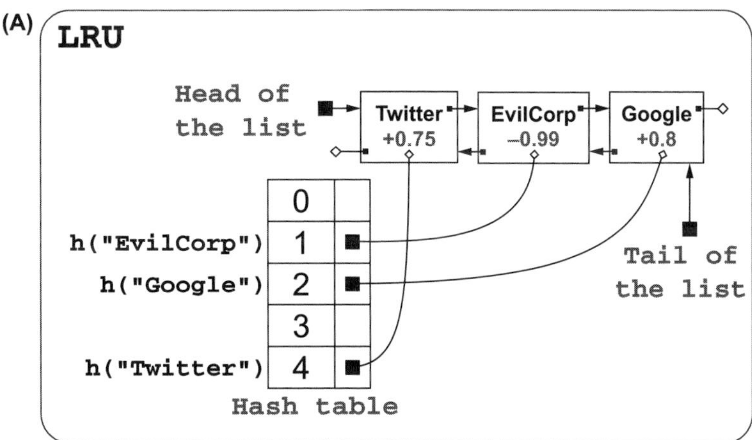
(A)
LRU
Head of the list
Twitter +0.75
EvilCorp –0.99
Google +0.8
0
h("EvilCorp") 1
h("Google") 2
3
h("Twitter") 4
Hash table
Tail of the list

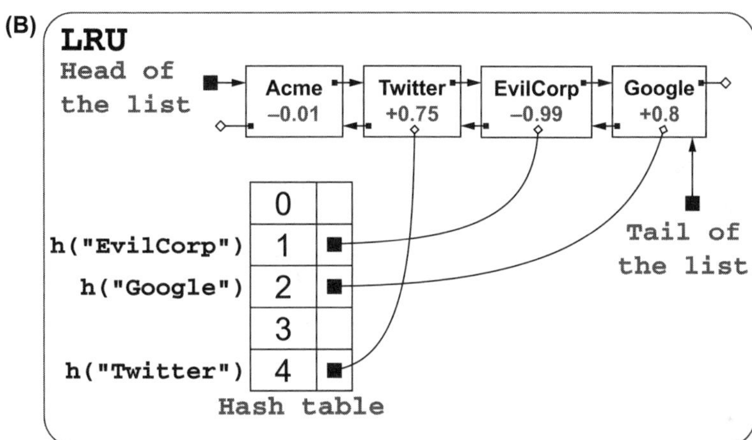
(B)
LRU
Head of the list
Acme –0.01
Twitter +0.75
EvilCorp –0.99
Google +0.8
0
h("EvilCorp") 1
h("Google") 2
3
h("Twitter") 4
Hash table
Tail of the list

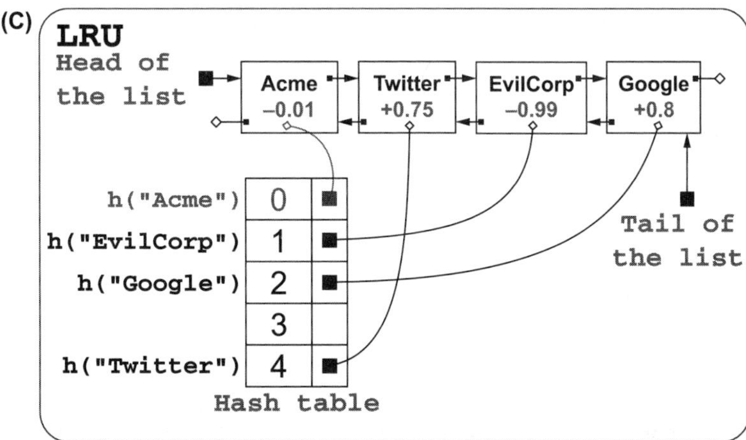
(C)
LRU
Head of the list
Acme –0.01
Twitter +0.75
EvilCorp –0.99
Google +0.8
h("Acme") 0
h("EvilCorp") 1
h("Google") 2
3
h("Twitter") 4
Hash table
Tail of the list

Figure 7.6 Add on a cache miss. (A) The cache before adding a new element. At this point, we look up "Acme" and get a cache miss. (B) We add to the front of the list a new node for "Acme." (C) We create a new entry in the hash table and update the pointer to the new head of the list.

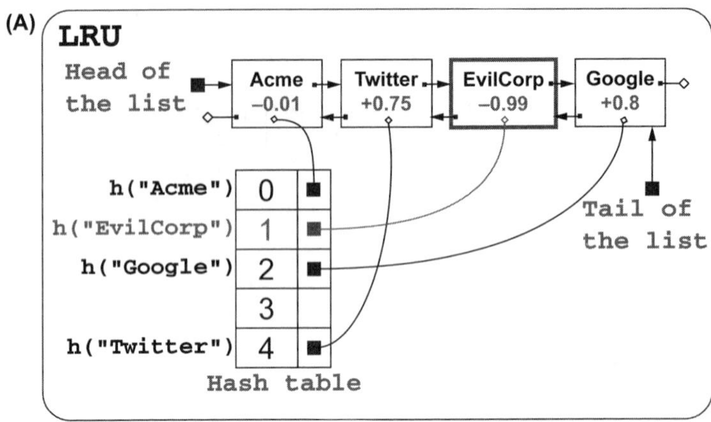
(A)
LRU
Head of the list
Acme -0.01
Twitter +0.75
EvilCorp -0.99
Google +0.8
h("Acme") 0
h("EvilCorp") 1
h("Google") 2
3
h("Twitter") 4
Tail of the list
Hash table

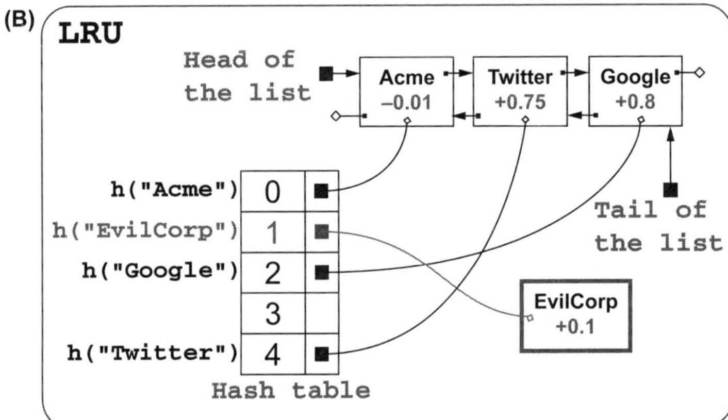
(B)
LRU
Head of the list
Acme -0.01
Twitter +0.75
Google +0.8
h("Acme") 0
h("EvilCorp") 1
h("Google") 2
3
h("Twitter") 4
Tail of the list
EvilCorp +0.1
Hash table

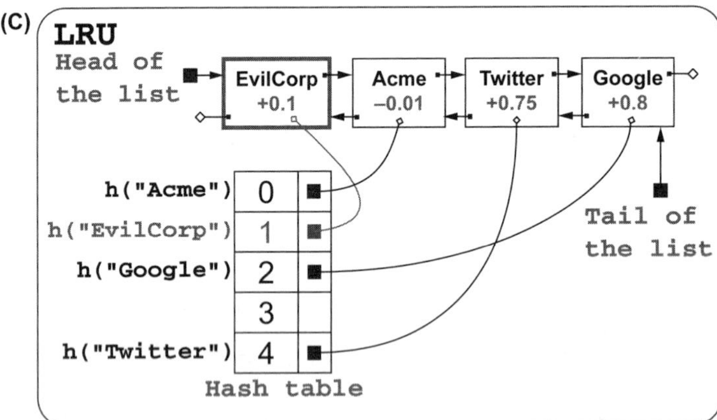
(C)
LRU
Head of the list
EvilCorp +0.1
Acme -0.01
Twitter +0.75
Google +0.8
h("Acme") 0
h("EvilCorp") 1
h("Google") 2
3
h("Twitter") 4
Tail of the list
Hash table

Figure 7.7 Update of a cache entry on cache hit. (A) The initial state of the cache. At this stage, the entry to update, "EvilCorp," has been looked up and we had a cache hit. The lookup happens on the hash table; hence, the EvilCorp entry and link are highlighted. (B) The list node for EvilCorp is updated with the new data (looks like EvilCorp spent some cash to turn around its reputation!) and it's also removed from the list, whose links are updated. (C) The node is now added to the front of the list. No update is necessary for the hash table.

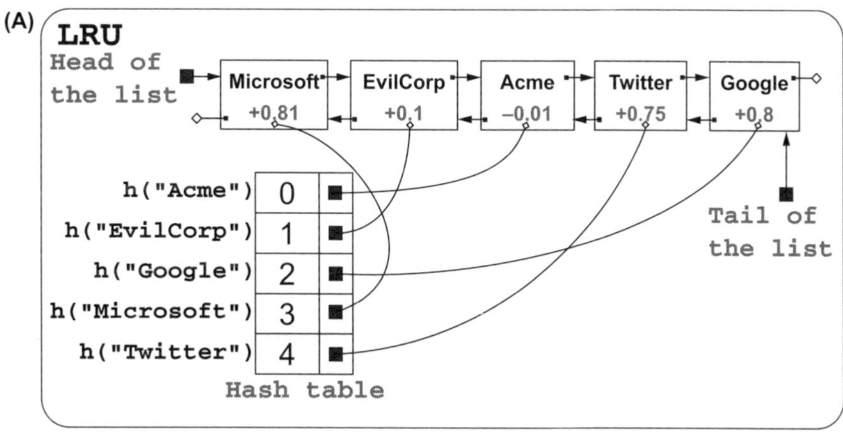
(A)
LRU
Head of the list
Microsoft +0.81
EvilCorp +0.1
Acme −0.01
Twitter +0.75
Google +0.8
h("Acme") 0
h("EvilCorp") 1
h("Google") 2
h("Microsoft") 3
h("Twitter") 4
Hash table
Tail of the list

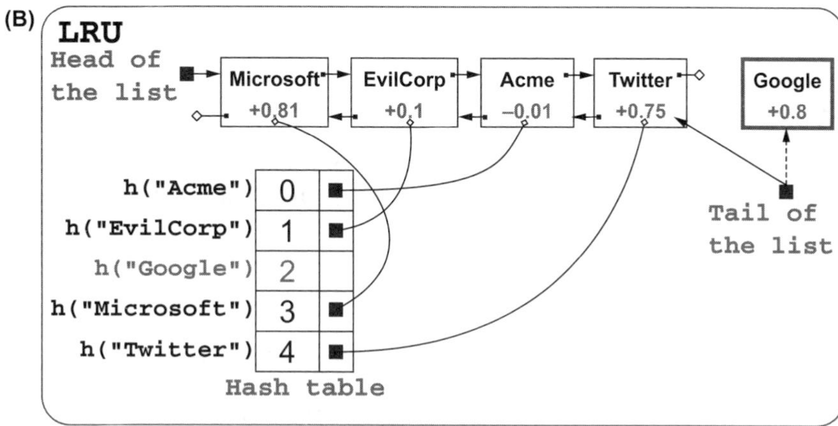
(B)
LRU
Head of the list
Microsoft +0.81
EvilCorp +0.1
Acme −0.01
Twitter +0.75
Google +0.8
h("Acme") 0
h("EvilCorp") 1
h("Google") 2
h("Microsoft") 3
h("Twitter") 4
Hash table
Tail of the list

Figure 7.8 Removal of the LRU entry (will be followed by an add on miss, like the one in figure 7.6). (A) The initial state of a full cache. (B) The pointer to the tail of the list is updated, as well as the links from/to the second-to-last node. The corresponding entry in the hash table is also removed, so the node for the entry is not referenced from the cache anymore (depending on the language, it might be garbage collected, or we need to manually destroy it and release the memory it uses).

delete from it, we will need to hash the entry (or its ID) at an extra cost (potentially non-constant: for strings, it will depend on the length of the string).

Listing 7.3 LRU cache `evictOneEntry` (private method)

```
function LRUCache::evictOneEntry()
  if hashTable.isEmpty() then
    return false
  node ← elementsTail
  elementsTail ← node.previous()
  if elementsTail != null then
    elementsTail.next ← null
  hashTable.delete(node.getKey())
  return true
```

- Checks that the cache is not empty
- If it is, returns `false` to flag failure
- Updates the pointer to the least recent element. Invariant: if the cache is not empty, the tail is not `null`
- If the new tail is not `null`, updates its pointer to the next element (that must be `null` now, being the new tail)
- Removes the entry from the hash table
- Returns `true` to flag success

There are still a couple of methods in the API that we haven't discussed yet: `get(key)` and `getSize()`. Their implementation, though, is trivial, because they are just wrappers for the homonymous methods in hash tables, at least if we keep values in the hash table directly. If, instead, we keep values in the linked list, and the hash table has pointers to list nodes, then in `get` we need to resolve this further indirection, as shown in listing 7.4.

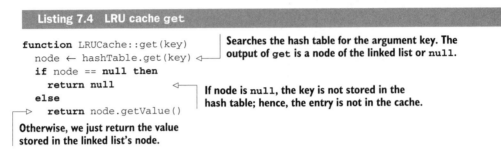

Listing 7.4 LRU cache get

```
function LRUCache::get(key)
  node ← hashTable.get(key)
  if node == null then
    return null
  else
    return node.getValue()
```

Searches the hash table for the argument key. The output of `get` is a node of the linked list or `null`.

If node is `null`, the key is not stored in the hash table; hence, the entry is not in the cache.

Otherwise, we just return the value stored in the linked list's node.

7.4.3 Performance

So, if you look at all the previous listings, they only contain operations that are either constant-time or amortized constant-time (for the hash table). That gives us the boost in performance that we were looking for!

Table 7.2 shows an updated version of table 7.1, including an entry for the LRU cache.

Table 7.2 Comparative analysis of performance vs implementation for cache with n elements

	Array (unsorted)	Linked list	Hash table	Balanced tree	LRU cache
Storing an entry	O(1)	O(n)	O(1) [a]	O(log n)	O(1) [a]
Finding entry by name	O(n)	O(n)	O(1) [a]	O(log n)	O(1) [a]
Eviction	O(n)	O(1)	O(n)	O(log n)	O(1) [a]

[a] Amortized time

7.5 When fresher data is more valuable: LFU

We have hinted at this in the previous sections: sometimes the least recently used entries are the ones less likely to be requested again . . . but that is not necessarily true in all contexts.

It may happen that some data was popular in the past and currently becomes temporarily irrelevant, but then it will likely be accessed again in the near future.

Think about an online retailer that operates worldwide. If a product is particularly popular in one or just a few countries, it will hit high peaks of requests during busy hours for that country, while it will hardly be accessed at all during the low peaks of activity for that same area.[21]

Another example could simply be a spurious peak of requests for certain items, as shown in figure 7.9.

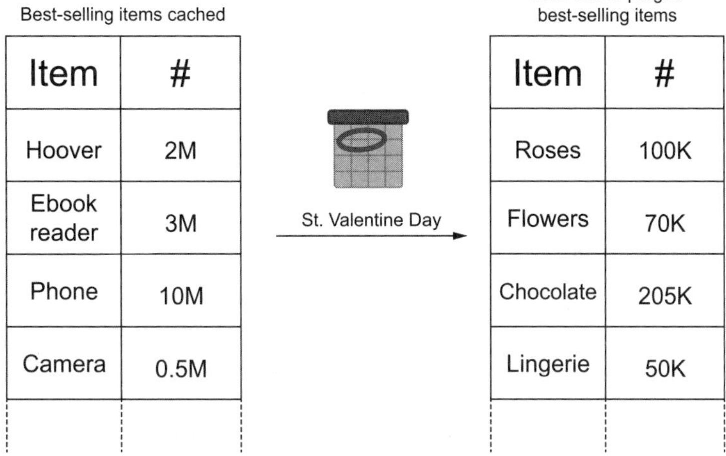
Best-selling items cached
Item
#
Hoover
2M
Ebook reader
3M
Phone
10M
Camera
0.5M
St. Valentine Day
LRU cache purges best-selling items
Item
#
Roses
100K
Flowers
70K
Chocolate
205K
Lingerie
50K

Figure 7.9 An example of a possible situation where LRU eviction policy would purge most "best-selling" items from a cache, in favor of the more recently viewed ones which become popular during a peak of requests. In the figure, items are ordered according to their most recent view; the number of views is shown only to display how most recent views during a peak can wipe out normal best-selling products. While LRU policy never guarantees that best-selling items will stay in the cache, the higher frequency with which they are accessed makes it more likely that they will stay in the cache (because it is likely they will go to the head of the queue before being purged). During a peak, if the number of items that suddenly become popular is large enough, they could fill the cache and force the usual items to be purged. This would be a temporary side effect that will regress after the peak. In some situations, this could also be desirable, because items popular during a peak should be accessed faster than the regular best-selling ones. LRU has a more dynamic turnaround than LFU, as we will see.

Either way, we might end up purging from the cache data that on average is used frequently over time, because there might be fresher data—entries that have been accessed more recently, but perhaps will never ever (or for a long time, longer than the average life of a cache entry) be accessed again.

If that's a possibility, an alternative policy could be based on counting how many times an entry has been accessed since it was added to the cache, and always retaining those items that are accessed the most.

This purging strategy is called *LFU* for *Least Frequently Used* (sometimes also referred to as *MFU, Most Frequently Used*) and comes with the advantage that items that are stored in the cache and never accessed again get purged out of the cache fairly quickly.[22]

[21]This example is purely for illustration. In all likelihood, cache, DBs, web servers, and so on for such a retailer will be sharded geographically exactly to exploit this locality of preferences.

[22]If implemented correctly. In particular, you need to be careful how you break ties when two entries have the same count—assigning higher value to newer entries is usually the best choice.

7.5.1 So how do we choose?

Those are not the only possible strategies for cache purging. A web cache, for instance, could also consider the cost of retrieving some information in terms of latency, compute time, and even actual costs when, as in our example, you need to pay an external service to retrieve some information.

And that's just one of many examples. The key point here is that you need to choose the best strategy for your context and for the characteristics of your application. Partly you can determine it during design, but to validate and fine tune your choice, you will likely have to run some profiling and collect statistics on the usage of your cache (don't be alarmed, though; there are several tools that can automatically do that for you).

7.5.2 What makes LFU different

To describe an LFU, we are not going to start from scratch; that would make no sense, as we already have a good basis to start with—our LRU cache.

We've said it over and again: the difference between two cache types is the eviction policy. Well, that's true for the most part, although not quite the whole story.

As shown in figure 7.10, we could implement our LFU from the code in section 7.4 by just changing the eviction policy and therefore the order of elements in the list.

When we add a new entry, we set its counter to 1, and we could insert it at the tail of the list, while on a cache hit we could increment the node's counter and move it toward the head of the list until we find another node with a larger counter.

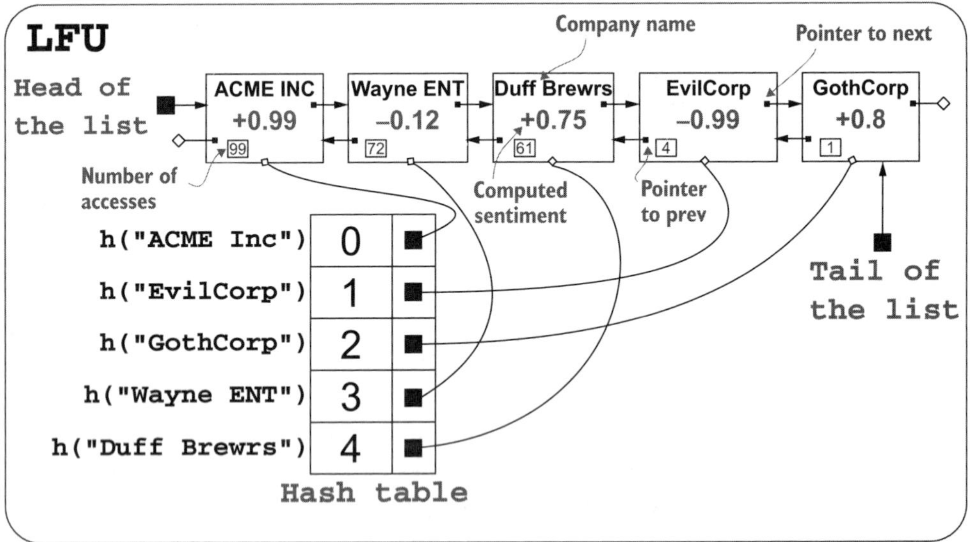
LFU
Company name
Pointer to next
Head of the list
ACME INC
+0.99
99
Wayne ENT
–0.12
72
Duff Brewrs
+0.75
61
EvilCorp
–0.99
4
GothCorp
+0.8
1
Number of accesses
Computed sentiment
Pointer to prev
h("ACME Inc") 0
h("EvilCorp") 1
h("GothCorp") 2
h("Wayne ENT") 3
h("Duff Brewrs") 4
Tail of the list
Hash table

Figure 7.10 An inefficient implementation of an LFU cache. When all elements of a list with `n` entries have the same value for counter, and one element at the end of the list is accessed, we will have to perform `n-1` node swaps to bubble up the updated entry to the front of the list.

That would certainly work correctly. But how efficient would it be? Would there be a way to improve the performance of our cache?

We can forget about constant-time insertion: that only works for the LRU. We can at least maintain constant-time lookup, and it's better than nothing.

But adding or updating a new element could take up to linear time in edge cases where most of the elements are used with the same frequency.

Can we do any better? Well, once again, at this point a bell should ring (if it doesn't, you might want to take a look at chapter 2 and appendix C before moving on).

We are no longer basing our eviction policy on a FIFO (first in, first out) queue.[23] The order of insertion doesn't matter anymore; instead, we have a priority associated with each node.

Now do you see where I am going? The best way to keep an order on entries based on their dynamically changing priority is, of course, a priority queue. It might be a heap, a Fibonacci heap, or any other implementation, but we will stick with the abstract data structure in the code, leaving to users the task of thinking about which implementation works best for them, depending on the programming language they use and, of course, the context in which they will use the cache.[24] For the performance analysis, though, we will consider a heap because it gives us reasonable-enough performance guarantees on all operations, combined with a clean, simple implementation.

Take a look at figure 7.11 to see how this changes our cache internals. Now we have only two things to change in our implementation to switch from an LRU to an LFU:

- The eviction policy (all the logic about choosing which element to remove)
- The data structure used to store elements

It's time to look at some more code. We highlighted the differences between the corresponding LRU's methods to make it easier for the readers to compare them.

The initialization of the cache, shown in listing 7.5, is almost identical to the LRU one; we just create an empty priority queue instead of a linked list.

Listing 7.5 LFU cache construction

```
function LFUCache(maxElements)
  maxSize ← maxElements
  hashTable ← new HashTable(maxElements)
  elements ← new PriorityQueue()
```

This time we need to create a priority queue. On the other hand, we don't need the pointer to the tail anymore. We assume that elements with lower values for priorities are towards the top of the queue (as it happens in a min-heap).

When it comes to adding an entry, things get a bit trickier. Remember that we mentioned how you need to be careful in order to implement the priority? We want to make sure that among the elements with the minimum number of entries, the oldest is removed first; otherwise, we could end up removing the latest entry over and over again, without giving it a chance to have its counter increased.

---

[23]One could say a FIFO+ queue, because elements can also be moved to the head of the queue at any time.

[24]Depending on the relative frequency of read/write, you might want to fine-tune one operation or the other.

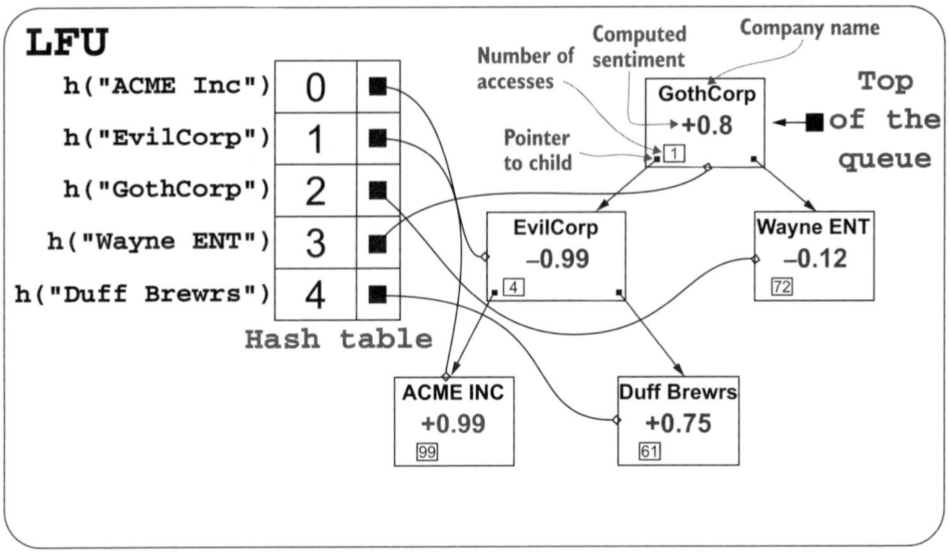
LFU
h("ACME Inc")
h("EvilCorp")
h("GothCorp")
h("Wayne ENT")
h("Duff Brewrs")
0
1
2
3
4
Hash table
Number of accesses
Computed sentiment
Company name
Pointer to child
Top of the queue
GothCorp
+0.8
1
EvilCorp
–0.99
4
Wayne ENT
–0.12
72
ACME INC
+0.99
99
Duff Brewrs
+0.75
61

Figure 7.11 As opposed to the example in figure 7.10, an efficient implementation of an LFU cache, using a priority queue to keep track of which elements should be evicted next. Here the `PriorityQueue`, which is an abstract data type, is represented as a binary heap. Note that we don't need to keep separate pointers for the points of insertion and eviction like for the linked list.

The solution is described in listing 7.6, where we use a tuple, `<counter, timestamp>` as priority, where the timestamp is the time of last access to an entry, and it's used to break ties on the counter; here, higher frequency and larger timestamps mean higher priority.

Listing 7.6 LFU cache set

```
function LFUCache::set(key, value)
  if hashTable.contains(key) then
    node ← this.hashTable.get(key)
    node.setValue(value)
    node.updatePriority(new Tuple(node.getCounter() + 1, time()))
    return false
  elsif getSize() >= maxSize then
    evictOneEntry()
  newNode ← elements.add(key, value, new Tuple(1, time()))
  hashTable.set(key, newNode)
  return true
```

Checks that the entry isn't already in the cache (we get a different kind of object here).

Instead of just moving the node to the front of the list, here we have to increment the counter by one, update the time of last access, and trickle the entry down towards the end of the queue.

Adds a new entry to the priority queue. Here the counter is I, being a new entry.

Finally, we have the method to evict one of the entries, which is implemented in listing 7.7. Using a priority queue makes its implementation even easier, because all the details of removing the element and updating the queue are encapsulated in the priority queue itself.

Listing 7.7 LFU cache evictOneEntry (private method)

```
function LFUCache::evictOneEntry()
  if hashTable.isEmpty() then
    return false
  node ← elements.pop()
  hashTable.delete(node.getKey())
  return true
```

Instead of handling removal from the tail of a linked list, we just remove the top element from a priority queue. Invariant: if the hash table is not empty, the queue must not be empty.

7.5.3 Performance

Let's once again update our table with the performance for LFU. As shown in table 7.4, since all writing operations for an LFU involve modifying a heap, we can't have the constant time guarantee anymore, except for the lookup.

It's worth noting that with a Fibonacci heap, insertion and update of priority in the heap would run in amortized constant time, but deleting the top element would still require logarithmic time, so we couldn't improve the asymptotic running time needed for storing an entry (because it uses delete).

Table 7.3 Comparative analysis of performance vs implementation for cache with n elements

	Array	List	Hash table	Tree	LRU cache	LFU cache
Storing an entry	O(1)	O(n)	O(1) [a]	O(log n)	O(1) [a]	O(log n) [a]
Finding entry by name	O(n)	O(n)	O(1) [a]	O(log n)	O(1) [a]	O(1) [a]
Eviction	O(n)	O(1)	O(n)	O(log n)	O(1) [a]	O(log n) [a]

[a]Amortized time.

7.5.4 Problems with LFU

Of course, no policy is always perfect, and even LFU has some cons. Most notably, if the cache runs for long, the turnaround time for older entries that are not popular anymore could be very long.

Let's consider an example: if you have a cache with at most `n` entries, and the most frequently used one, `X`, has been requested `m` times before, but at some point isn't being accessed anymore (for example, it goes out of stock), then for a set of `n` new entries to cause the eviction of `X`, they will have to be requested `n*m` times at least.

Plugging in some numbers, if your cache holds a thousand elements and `X` was requested a thousand times, it will take at least one million accesses to a thousand brand-new entries before `X` is evicted after it becomes useless. Obviously, if more accesses are made to other entries already in the cache, then this number goes down, but on average it should be in that order of magnitude.

To solve this issue, some possible solutions are

- Limiting the maximum value for the counter of an entry

- Resetting or halving the counter of entries over time (for instance, every few hours)
- Computing the weighted frequency based on the time of last access (this would also solve our issue with ties on the counter, and we could avoid storing tuples as priorities)

LRU and LFU are not the only type of cache available. Starting from an LFU cache, and just (this time for real) changing the eviction policy by choosing a different metric for entries priority, custom types can be created to adapt to specific contexts.

For instance, we could decide that certain companies are more important than others, or we might want to weight the number of accesses with the age of the data, halving it every 30 minutes from the last access.

As complicated as it may sound so far, that's not all of it. You have choices about how to run a cache, but you also have more choices when it comes to how to use it.

7.6 How to use cache is just as important

That's right, the cache type is only part of the story. To make it work properly, you also need to use it in the best possible way for your application.

For instance, if you place a cache in front of a database, on writing operations you could decide to write values only to the cache and only update the DB if another client requests the same entry; or, on the other hand, you could decide to always update the DB.

Even more, you could decide to write on the DB only and update the cache just when data is requested for read, or update the cache on writes.

These policies described above all have names, because they are widely used in software design and engineering.

Write-Behind (or *Write-Back*), our first example, is a storage policy where data is written into cache on every change while it's written into the corresponding location on the main storage (memory, DB, and so on) only at specified intervals of time or under certain conditions (for instance, on reads).

In this case, the data on cache is always fresh, while data on the DB (or other support) might be stale. This policy helps keep latency low and also reduces the load on the DB, but it might lead to data loss; for instance, when we write back only on reads, and an entry stored in cache is never read after write. In some applications this data loss is fine, and in those cases write back is the preferred policy.

Write-Through (or *Write-Ahead*), always writes entries both on cache and on the main storage at the same time. This way the database will usually have only one write and will (almost) never be hit by the application for read. This is slower than Write-Behind, but reduces the risk of data loss, bringing it down to zero, with only the exception of edge cases and malfunctions. Write-Through strategy doesn't improve writing performance at all (but caching would still improve reading performance); instead, it is particularly useful for read-intensive applications when data is written once (or seldom) and read many times (usually in a short time). Session data is a good example of usage for this strategy.

Write-Around refers to the policy of writing data only to the main storage, and not to cache. This is good for write-and-forget applications, those ones that seldom or never reread recently written data. The cost of reading recently written data in this configuration is high because they will result in a cache miss.

Read-Through refers to the overall strategy of writing entries on the cache only when they are read, so they are already written on another, slower, memory support. The writing policy that's used for this purpose can be any of Write-Back or Write-Around. The peculiarity of this policy is that in Read-Through, the application only interfaces to cache for reading, and the *cache store* will be delegated to read data from the main storage on a cache miss.

Refresh-Ahead is a caching strategy used in caches where elements can go stale, and they would be considered expired after a certain time.[25] In this approach, cache entries with high requests that are about to expire are proactively (and asynchronously) read and updated from the main source. This means that the application will not feel the pain of a slow DB read and cache store.

Cache-Aside has the cache sitting on the side of the application, and only talking to the application. It's different from Read-Through because in this case the responsibility of checking the cache or the DB is on the application, which will first check the cache and, in case of miss, do some extra work to also check the DB and store the value read on the cache.

Choosing the best strategy can be as important as acing the cache implementation, because choosing unwisely can overload and crash your database (or whatever the main storage is, in your case).

7.7 Introducing synchronization

So far, we have always assumed that our cache objects were used in a single-threaded environment.

What do you think would happen if we used code in listing 7.6 in a concurrent environment? If you are familiar with concurrent code, you can already imagine that we might have issues with race conditions.

Let's take another look at that code, copied over to listing 7.8 for your convenience, with some minimal simplifications.

Listing 7.8 Simplified version of LFU cache set

```
function LFUCache::set(key, value)
  if (this.hashTable.contains(key)) then                              #1
    node ← this.hashTable.get(key)                                    #2
    node.setValue(value)                                              #3
```

[25]This kind of cache is particularly useful in *eventually consistent* systems. Eventual consistency relaxes the consistency constraint, allowing for instance data in the cache to be slightly off-sync with respect to the most recent version of the same entry stored in a database. This can be useful if we are fine with some information being slightly off-sync. For instance, for a shopping cart, we can probably handle the availability of an entry being off-sync for a 100ms or even a second.

```
    return node.updatePriority(node.getCounter())                      #4
  elsif getSize() >= this.maxSize                                      #5
    evictOneEntry()                                                    #6
  newNode ← this.elements.add(key, value, 1)                           #7
  hashTable.set(key, newNode)                                          #8
  return true
```

Let's imagine we have two concurrent calls to add two new entries (neither of them is in the cache yet) and our cache already contains `maxSize-1` elements. In other words, the next element will fill the cache to its maximum capacity.

Now those two requests will proceed in parallel and suppose call A is the first one to get to line 5 in listing 7.8. The condition is `false`; then it moves to line 7. But before call A executes line 7, call B gets to line 5, and—guess what?—the `if` condition is still `false`, so call B will move on to line 7 as well and execute it and line 8.

As a result, the cache will hold one element more than allowed. Figure 7.12 shows this situation. The good news is that on line 5, we already do things the right way and check if current size is greater than or equal to the max allowed size. If we were just checking for equality, this race condition would have caused the cache to grow indefinitely, likely until it overflowed your system's heap.

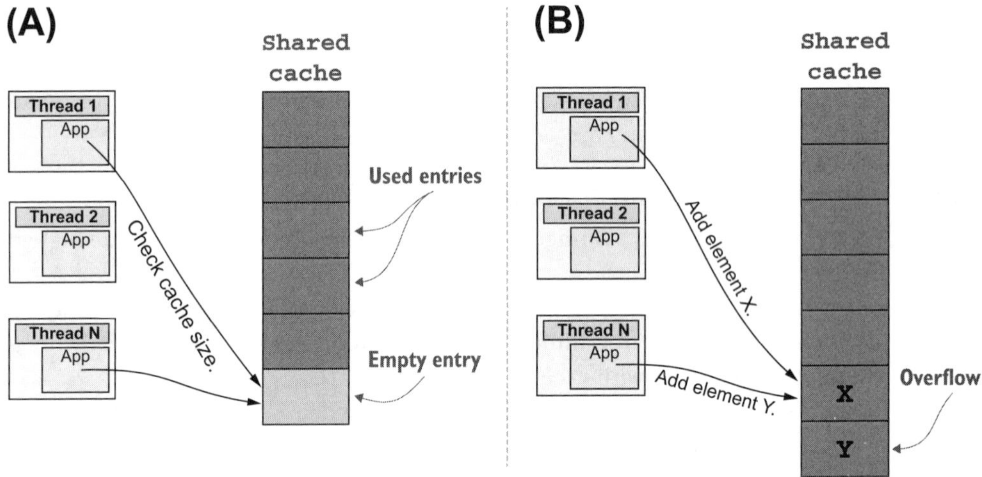
(A)
Shared cache
Thread 1
App
Thread 2
App
Thread N
App
Check cache size.
Used entries
Empty entry
(B)
Shared cache
Thread 1
App
Thread 2
App
Thread N
App
Add element X.
Add element Y.
X
Y
Overflow

Figure 7.12 A shared cache used in a multithreaded environment, without implementing synchronization. (A) Two threads concurrently try to add a new element to a cache with only one free spot. When the `LFUCache::set` method inside each thread concurrently checks for cache size (line 5 in listing 7.8), they both see it's not full. (B) Without synchronization, both threads add an element to the cache (line 7), without evicting. Depending on the implementation of the cache (and of `elements.add`), this could lead to overflow of the cache or just to one of the two values being overwritten by the other. It's important to understand that even if the cache handles purging internally, as it should be (the app should only worry about reading/writing elements; only the cache should decide when purging is necessary), if cache's methods are not synchronized, race conditions can and do happen inside those methods.

Likewise, line 1 could bring to race conditions if two parallel calls to set the same key happen simultaneously.

It also gets worse than this. For instance, think about how we might want to fix this problem. You might be tempted to add another check right before line 7, but would that work? It would somehow lower the odds that things might go berserk, but it wouldn't really solve the problem.

The issue here is that the set operation is not *atomic*: while we are in the process of setting a new entry (or updating an old one), at the same time we might be performing the same operation in another thread for another entry, the same operation for the same entry, or even an entirely different operation, such as evicting an element from the cache.

When we operate in a single-threaded environment, calling cache's methods synchronously, things go smoothly because each method call is completed before anyone else can change the cache, so we have the illusion of atomicity.

In a multi-threaded environment, we need to be careful and explicitly regulate the execution of these methods and access to the shared resources, so that all methods that mutate the state of an object are executed simulating full isolation (so no one else can modify the resource, and perhaps also no one else can read from it). Figure 7.13 can give you an idea of how we can correct the workflow to prevent the race conditions previously discussed.

For composite data structures such as caches, we need to be twice as careful, because we need to make sure that also the basic data structures upon which they're built are *thread-safe*.[26]

And thus, for LFU, we need to ensure that both the priority queue and the hash table support concurrent execution.

Modern programming languages provide plenty of mechanisms to ensure thread-safety, from locks to semaphores to latches.

An extensive covering of this topic would require a book on its own, so unfortunately we will have to make do with an example. We'll show how to solve this problem in Java, providing the full code for thread-safe LRU/LFU in our repo on GitHub.[27]

[26] Or, in other words, they can be safely run in a multi-threading environment, without leading to race conditions.

[27] See https://github.com/mlarocca/AlgorithmsAndDataStructuresInAction#cache.

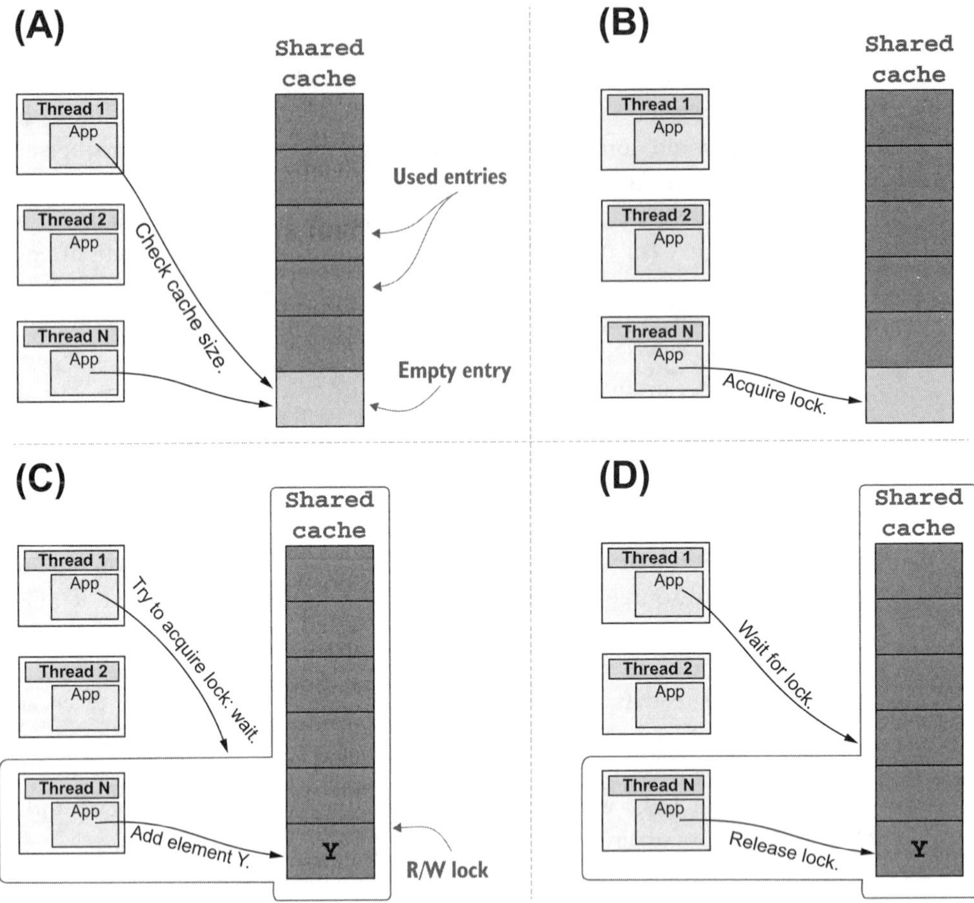
(A)
Shared cache
Thread 1
App
Thread 2
App
Thread N
App
Check cache size.
Used entries
Empty entry
(B)
Shared cache
Thread 1
App
Thread 2
App
Thread N
App
Acquire lock.
(C)
Shared cache
Thread 1
App
Thread 2
App
Thread N
App
Try to acquire lock: wait.
Add element Y.
Y
R/W lock
(D)
Shared cache
Thread 1
App
Thread 2
App
Thread N
App
Wait for lock.
Release lock.
Y

Figure 7.13 Using a synchronized implementation for the cache, we can avoid race conditions. In the example shown in figure 7.12, a synchronized data structure requires any thread to acquire a lock on it (B) before being able to write a value (C). If another thread tries to acquire the lock while it is still in use by thread N, it will be left waiting until the lock is released (D). After that (not shown in the figure), the waiting thread can acquire the lock, or possibly compete with other threads trying to acquire it.

7.7.1 Solving concurrency (in Java)

If we are making another exception in this chapter, showing some code in a specific programming language rather than pseudo-code, it's because we feel that these concepts can only by tackled effectively within the concrete context of a real language.

As many programming languages support the same concepts, it should be easy to port this logic to your favorite environment.

We actually need to start from the class constructor, implemented in listing 7.9, because there will be new elements to be added.

Listing 7.9 Java implementation, LFU cache constructor

```
LFUCache(int maxSize) {
  this.maxSize = maxSize;                                                  #1
  this.hashTable=new ConcurrentHashMap<Key, PriorityQueueNode >(maxSize);  #2
  this.elements = new ConcurrentHeap<Pair<Key, Value>, Integer>();         #3
  ReentrantReadWriteLock lock = new ReentrantReadWriteLock();              #4
  this.readLock = lock.readLock();                                         #5
  this.writeLock = lock.writeLock();
}
```

There are a few noticeable changes with respect to listing 7.5, besides, of course, switching to Java syntax.

At lines 2 and 3, notice how we used a `ConcurrentHashMap` instead of a simple `HashMap`, as you might have expected, and the same goes for the `ConcurrentHeap`[28] class. We want our internal data structures to be synchronized as well, to guarantee atomicity and isolation. Technically, if we handle the synchronization of `LRUCache's` methods correctly, there will be no concurrent access at all to its internal fields, so we could also be fine with the regular, single-thread data structures. If we use their concurrent versions, we need to be super-careful, because that could lead to bugs and deadlocks.[29]

7.7.2 Introducing locks

When we get to line 4, though, we see a new entry, a brand-new attribute for our class: an object of type `ReentrantReadWriteLock`. Before explaining what a reentrant lock is, we should make one thing clear: this is the mechanism that we are going to use to handle concurrent access to `LFUCache's` methods. Java provides several different ways to do so, from declaring methods as synchronized to using semaphores, latches, and so on of these mechanisms. Which one is the best depends—as always—on the context, and sometimes more than one method could work. In this case, I prefer using a reentrant *read/write* lock rather than declaring methods as synchronized, because it gives us more flexibility in deciding when we should use a lock on read and when on write. As we'll see, there might be a big impact on performance if we don't get this right.

But first things first: we still need to define what a lock is, not to mention what reentrant means.

A lock is a concurrency mechanism whose name is pretty self-explanatory. You probably have already heard of database locks, and the principle is exactly the same for code. If an object (an instance of class) has some code wrapped inside a lock, this means that for that instance, no matter how many calls are made to that method, the

[28]Java standard library doesn't provide an implementation of `PriorityQueue`, so you won't find this class natively in your JRE. We provide a version of a synchronized heap in our repo.

[29]A situation where all threads are blocked waiting for some shared resources, but none of them can acquire it. This causes the application to become unresponsive and stuck, and ultimately crash.

locked portion of code can only be executed by one call at a time—all the others will have to wait for their turn.

In our example, it means that of the two calls to `set`, while the first is executed, the second is left waiting.

As you can see, this is a powerful mechanism, but it's also dangerous, because failing to release a lock can leave all other calls hanging forever (*deadlock*) and even just using locks excessively can degrade performance sensibly, introducing unnecessarily long delays.

Locks basically move execution from parallel to synchronous (hence the term *synchronization*) by using waiting queues to regulate access to a shared resource.

Explaining in-depth how a lock works and how deadlocks can happen and can be prevented usually takes a couple of chapters in a book on operating systems, so it's out of our scope. We encourage interested readers to go on and read more on the subject[30] because it's becoming more and more important for modern programming and web applications, but also compute-intensive applications that run in parallel on GPUs.

Now, what does reentrant mean? As the word suggests, with a reentrant lock a thread can enter (or lock) a resource more than once, and every time it does, a counter is incremented by one, while when it unlocks the resource, the counter is decremented by one, and the lock is actually released when this counter gets to zero. Why is it important to have a reentrant lock? Because if the same thread tries to lock the same resource more than once, we could get into a deadlock.

No, seriously, why is it important to us? You will have to wait a few paragraphs until we will show you in practice.

7.7.3 Acquiring a lock

So, now that we have an idea of what a lock is, we are ready to take a look at the modified version of the `set` method in listing 7.10.

As you can see, as soon as we enter the method, we lock our resource (the whole cache) for writing. What does it mean? When a write lock is set on a resource, the thread holding the lock is the only one that can write to *and* read from that resource. It means that all other threads, either trying to read or write on the resource, are going to have to wait until the current lock holder releases it.

The second instruction here is a `try`, with a `finally` block at the end of the method (lines marked with 4 and 5), where we release the lock. This is necessary to prevent deadlock: if any of the operations inside the `try` fail, we still release the lock before exiting the function, so that other threads can acquire the lock and not be blocked anymore.

---

[30] A superb start is *C++ Concurrency in Action* (by Anthony Williams, Manning Publications, 2019), if you are familiar with C++, or would like to learn more about it. *Concurrency in .NET* (by Riccardo Terrell, Manning Publications, 2018) is your choice of election if functional programming is your way.

Listing 7.10 Java concurrent LFU cache set

```
public boolean set(Key key, Value value) {
  writeLock.lock();                                                    #1
  try {                                                                #2
    if (this.hashTable.contains(key)) {
      PriorityQueueNode node = this.hashTable.get(key);
      node.setValue(value);
      return node.updatePriority(node.getCounter());
    } else if (this.getSize() >= this.maxSize) {
      this.evictOneEntry();                                            #3
    }
    PriorityQueueNode newNode = this.elements.add(key, value, 1);
    this.hashTable.put(key, newNode);
    return true;
  } finally {                                                          #4
    writeLock.unlock();                                                #5
  }
}
```

In these examples, we are still using the hash table to store references to the priority queue nodes, the way we were storing references to the linked list nodes for LRU. While for LRU this makes sense, in order to keep the constant running time for all operations, as explained in section 7.4.2, for LFU cache we can store just values in the hash table. This makes implementation simpler, as shown on our repo, but possibly at the cost of changing the running time for the operation.

Take a minute to think about it before reading the explanation. The reason, as you may have figured out, is simple: both in `set` and `get` we call `updatePriority` on the priority queue. If we have a reference to the node to update, `pushdown` and `bubbleUp` will require logarithmic time, as shown in chapter 2, sections 2.6.1 and 2.6.2.

Finding an element in a heap, however, would normally require linear time. Alternatively, in section 2.6.8 we showed that it is possible to use an auxiliary hash table inside our priority queue and have search performed in amortized constant time, so that `updatePriority` would then run in amortized logarithmic time.

We previously hinted at the fact that we should go easy on using locks, so the question arises: Could we acquire the lock later in the function?

That depends. We need to make sure that while we check the hash table for `key`, no other thread is writing on it. If we use a concurrent structure for the hash table, we could move the write lock acquisition inside the first branch of the `if`, but then we would also need to change the rest of the function (because evicting one entry and adding the new one should all happen as an atomic operation) and be careful with how we use the hash table, since we introduce a second resource on which we lock, and that might lead to deadlock.[31]

[31] If thread A locks on the hash table and thread B acquires the write lock on the whole cache, and then both need the other thread to continue, we get to the equivalent of a Mexican standoff for threads. And that never ends well in movies.

So, the short answer is, let's keep it simple (also because we wouldn't have much of an advantage anyway).

7.7.4 Reentrant locks

Now we can finally explain how a reentrant lock prevents deadlock in our case. At the line marked with #3 in listing 7.10, the current thread calls `evictOneEntry` to remove one item from the cache. We decided to keep the method private in our example, for good reason, but let's now imagine that we need to have it as a public method, guaranteeing the option to clients to free space in the cache. (Maybe because of memory or garbage collection issues we need to shrink the cache dynamically—we certainly would rather not restart it altogether and lose all of its content.)

In that case, we need to make `evictOneEntry` synchronized as well, and hence acquire a write lock inside of it. With a non-reentrant lock, `evictOneEntry` would try to acquire the write lock, but `set` has already acquired it, and can't free it until `evictOneEntry` finishes. Long story short, our thread is stuck waiting for a resource that will never be freed, and all other threads will soon be stuck as well. That is basically a recipe for deadlock, and it's that easy to get yourself into such a situation. That's why you should be careful with synchronization mechanisms.

With reentrant locks instead, since both `evictOneEntry` and `set` belong to the same thread, `evictOneEntry` on line 1 is able to acquire the lock that is held by `set` and can go on with its execution. Deadlock avoided, at least this time!

7.7.5 Read locks

We haven't yet talked about read locks. We mentioned how important they are for performance, but why? Let's revisit the `get` method in listing 7.11.

We acquire a read lock before reading data from the cache's internal fields and release it as the very last step before exiting the function.

It seems exactly like what we do with `set`, right? The only change is that we use a read lock instead, so the difference must be there—and it actually is.

Listing 7.11 LFU cache `get`, Java version

```
public Value get(Key key) {
  readLock.lock();                                            #1
  try {
    PriorityQueueNode node = this.hashTable.get(key);
    if (node == null) {
      return null;
    } else {
      node.updatePriority(node.getCounter() + 1);             #2
      return node.getValue();
    }
  } finally {
    readLock.unlock();                                        #3
  }
}
```

Only one thread can hold a write lock at a single time, but a read lock can be held by many threads at the same time, provided no thread is holding a write lock.

When we read from a data structure (or a database) we don't modify it, so if 1, 2, 10, or a million threads are reading from the same resource at the same time, they will always get consistent results (if the invariant is implemented correctly, and we don't have side effects that mutate the resource).

When we write on a resource, we change it, and while the process is ongoing, all reads and writes will make no sense, because they will be based on inconsistent data. That leads to four possible combinations of locks (Read-Read, Read-Write, Write-Read, and Write-Write), as shown in table 7.4.

If any (other) thread is holding a read lock, we can acquire another read lock, but need to wait for a write lock until all the read locks are released.

If any thread is holding a write lock, all other threads need to wait to acquire either a write or a read lock.

Table 7.4 Combinations of locks requested and held

Lock requested/held	Read	Write
Read	Allowed	Need to wait
Write	Need to wait	Need to wait

So, the advantage of actually distinguishing between read and write locks for our cache is that all calls to `get` can be executed in parallel, and only calls to `set` will block. Had we not made this distinction, access to the cache would as a result have been entirely synchronous, with only one thread at a time being able to check the cache. This would have introduced an unnecessary latency in our application, reducing the advantage of using a cache and possibly even making it counterproductive.

7.7.6 *Other approaches to concurrency*

Using locking mechanisms is not the only way to deal with concurrency. Locking handles the access to a segment of code that mutates a resource, so that we are sure that these instructions applying modification will be executed by one thread, and one thread only, at each instant in time.

On the other end of the spectrum, there is a completely symmetrical approach championed by functional programming: remove mutability from your resources altogether.

One of the principles of functional programming is, in fact, that all objects should be immutable. This has several advantages; for instance, it makes it easier to reason about code because we can analyze a function to be sure that no other method will influence what it does, and it removes race conditions altogether. It also has some disadvantages; for instance, it makes some operations harder, like keeping a running state, and makes it more expensive to update state in large objects.

When we talk about concurrency, having immutable objects means that you can read your resource without worrying that someone else will change it while you are reading it, so you don't have to set a lock.

Writing remains a bit more complicated.[32] In the functional world, a method like `set` would return not a Boolean, but a new instance of the cache itself, where its content has been updated.

7.8 Cache applications

This section would definitely be shorter if we listed examples of systems that do *not* use cache! Cache is ubiquitous, at all levels, from processors to the highest-level applications you can imagine.

Low-level, hardware caches work slightly differently, though, so we'd better stick to software caches.

As mentioned, many single- and multi-thread applications employ ad hoc in-memory caches to avoid repeating expensive computations.

These caches are usually objects (in OO[33] languages), provided by libraries, and allocate dynamic memory in the heap of the same application that uses them. In the case of multi-thread applications, the cache might run in its own thread and be shared among several threads (as we saw in the previous section, this configuration requires special attention to prevent race conditions).

The next step is bringing the cache out of one application, into its own process, and communicating with it through a certain protocol; this can be HTTP, Thrift, or even RPC.

A typical case is the several layers of cache in a web application:

- A CDN to cache and deliver static content (and some dynamic content)
- A web cache that caches content from the web server (usually entire pages and might be the CDN itself)
- An application cache storing the result of expensive server computations
- A DB cache storing the most-used rows, tables, or pages from a database

Finally, for large applications with thousands of requests per second (or more), caches need to be scaled together with the rest of the web stack. This means that a single process might not be enough to hold all the entries that the application needs to cache in order to run smoothly. For instance, if we have a million accesses per second to a database, a cache in front of it that can only store a million elements is probably close to useless, because there would be too high a turnaround, and all requests would basically go ahead to the DB, crashing it to a halt in a few minutes.

---

[32]You can still have race conditions when two threads try to update the shared cache at the same time, but this case can be solved with *optimistic locks*, basically (in an extreme simplification) versioning your resource. For further insight into optimistic locks, you might take a look at the *Compare-and-swap (CAS) algorithm*. Using immutability plus optimistic locks, you can get a sensible performance boost in many common contexts/languages.

[33]Object-Oriented languages like Java where classes and objects are language basic building blocks.

For this reason, distributed caches have been introduced. These caches, such as Cassandra, use several processes called nodes, each one of them being a standalone cache, plus another process (sometimes a special node), called the orchestrator, that is in charge of routing requests to the right node. Distributed caches use a special hashing function, *consistent hashing*[34] (see figure 7.14), to decide which node should store an entry.

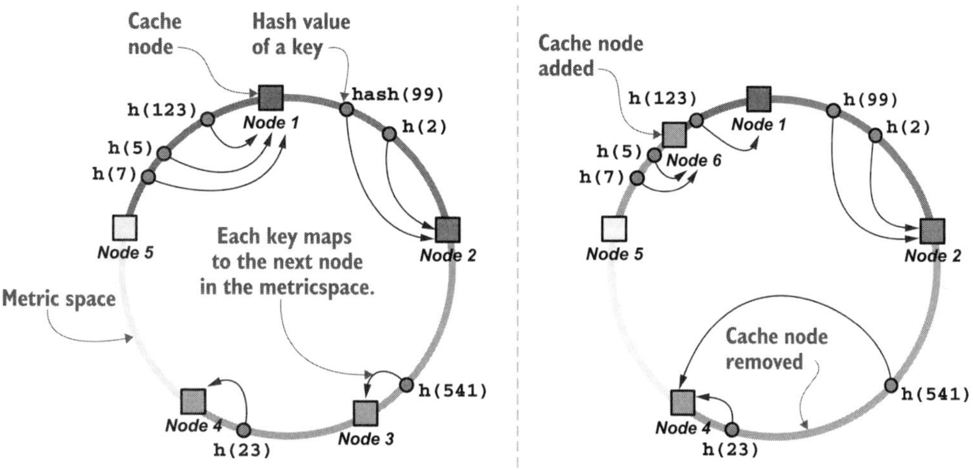
Cache node
Hash value of a key
hash(99)
h(123)
Node 1
h(2)
h(5)
h(7)
Node 5
Each key maps to the next node in the metricspace.
Node 2
Metric space
h(541)
Node 4
h(23)
Node 3
Cache node added
h(123)
Node 1
h(99)
h(2)
h(5)
Node 6
h(7)
Node 5
Node 2
Cache node removed
h(541)
Node 4
h(23)

Figure 7.14 An array of cache nodes using consistent hashing for distributing keys. On the left, the initial nodes array. Nodes and keys map to the same metric space (the IDs space), usually represented as a circle (which could be obtained even with just a modulo operation on the hash values). Keys are assigned to the next node in the circle—that is, the node whose value is the smallest node's ID larger than the key's hashing. On the right, we can see how, when a cache node is removed or added, only a fraction of the keys needs to be remapped.

Web clients also make extensive use of caching: browsers have their own caches (although those work slightly differently, storing content on your disk), but they also have a DNS cache to store the IP addresses corresponding to the domains you browse. Lately, more caching has been added with local and session storage, and perhaps the most promising of all, service worker caching.

[34]Consistent hashing is a special kind of hashing that guarantees that when one of the nodes is removed, only the keys hosted on that node need to be remapped. See figure 7.14 to get an idea of how it works. It's not just about caches: if applied to a hash table, consistent hashing guarantees that when a table with n slots is resized, only one n-th of the keys stored needs to be remapped. This is particularly important for distributed caches, where billions of elements might need to be remapped or possibly cause the whole cache to crash.

Summary

- Caches are ubiquitous at all levels of the computation stack, from hardware caches in your processor to distributed web caches on the internet.
- Whether you're running complex vector algebra on a GPU or connecting to an external subscription service, if it is reasonable to assume that the result you just computed might be used again in the near future, just store it in a cache.
- Caches are useful at all levels, but while you could probably ignore them in standalone applications running locally on a single computer, they are paramount to allow web applications to scale to billions of requests per day.
- There are different types of caches, and the distinction is based on their eviction policy. A cache usually has a fixed maximum size, and when reached, the eviction policy states which entries must be purged out of the cache to make room for the newer ones.
- There are also different ways to plug a cache into a system. We have seen the difference between Write-Ahead, Read-Ahead, Write-Through, Write-Behind, and Refresh-Ahead.
- When we share a resource (in this case, a cache) between multiple threads, we need to be very careful in designing it so that we won't end up with race conditions, inconsistent data, or—even worse—deadlocks.
- If we use functional programming, we might make our life easier when it comes to concurrency.

Part 2

Multidemensional queries

The common thread for the central part of this book is *nearest neighbor search.* It is first introduced as yet another special case in search, then used as a building block of more advanced algorithms.

This section opens with a description of the issues and challenges that are found when dealing with multi-dimensional data: indexing these data and performing spatial queries. We will once again show how ad hoc data structures can provide drastic improvements over using basic search algorithms.

Next, this section describes two advanced data structures that can be used to search multi-dimensional data.

In the second half of this part, we'll check out applications of nearest neighbor search, starting with some practical examples, and then focusing on clustering, which heavily leverages spatial queries. Talking about clustering also allows us to introduce distributed computing, in particular the *MapReduce* programming model, which can be used to process volumes of data that are too large to be handled by any single machine.

There is an important difference in the structure of part 2 in comparison to the first seven chapters. As we'll see, the discussion about these topics is particularly rich, and there is no way that we can cover them, or even just their crucial bits, in a single chapter. Therefore, while in part 1 each chapter followed a different pattern to explain topics, we'll have to follow a single pattern throughout part 2, where each chapter will cover only one piece of our usual discussion.

Chapter 8 introduces the nearest neighbor problem, discusses a few naïve approaches to multi-dimensional queries, and introduces the problem used as an example for most of part 2.

Chapter 9 describes *k-d trees*, a solution for efficient search in multi-dimensional data sets, focusing on the 2D case (for the sake of visualization).

Chapter 10 presents more advanced versions of these trees, *r-trees*, which are briefly illustrated, and *ss-trees*, for which we'll instead delve into specifications for each method. In the final sections of this chapter we also discuss the performance of ss-trees and how they can be improved further, and then compare them to k-d trees.

Chapter 11 focuses on the applications of nearest neighbor search, with a use case described in depth (finding the closest warehouse from which goods should be shipped to customers), but also introducing several problems that can benefit from the application of k-d trees or ss-trees.

Chapter 12 focuses on an interesting use case that leverages the efficient nearest neighbor search algorithms presented so far. It enters the machine-learning world and describes three clustering algorithms, *k-means*, *DBSCAN*, and *OPTICS*.

Chapter 13 concludes this part by introducing *MapReduce*, a powerful computational model for distributed computing, and applies it to the three clustering algorithms: *k-mean* and *DBSCAN*, discussed in chapter 12, and *canopy clustering*, introduced in this chapter.

8 Nearest neighbors search

This chapter covers

- Finding closest points in a multidimensional dataset
- Introducing data structures to index multidimensional space
- Understanding the issues with indexing high dimensional spaces
- Introducing efficient nearest neighbor search

So far in this book we have worked with containers that were holding unidimensional data: the entries that we stored in queues, trees, and hash tables were always assumed to be (or to be translatable to) numbers—simple values that could be compared in the most intuitive mathematical sense.

In this chapter, we will see how this simplification doesn't always hold true in real datasets, and we'll examine the issues connected to handling more complex, multidimensional data. Do not despair, though, because in the next chapters we will also describe data structures that can help handle this data and see real applications that leverage efficient nearest neighbor search as part of their workflow, such as *clustering*.

As we'll see, the discussion on this area is particularly rich, and there is no way that we can cover it, not even just its crucial bits, in a single chapter. Therefore, while in part 1 each chapter was following the same pattern to explain topics, we'll have to stretch this pattern to the whole part 2, where each chapter will cover only a single piece of our usual discussion:

- Chapter 8 contains an introduction to the problem and the real-world example we will tackle.
- Chapters 9-10 describe three data structures that can be used to implement nearest neighbor search efficiently.
- Chapter 11 applies those data structures to the problem described here and introduces more applications for them.
- Chapters 12-13 focus on a particular application of nearest neighbor search: clustering.

8.1 The nearest neighbors search problem

Let's start our journey for this chapter from figure 8.1: a map showing a few cities (taken from an alternate universe) and the locations of some warehouses in their area.

Imagine you are living in the 1990s, the dawn of the internet era, with e-commerce taking its very first steps.

You are running an online store where you sell locally produced products by collaborating with a few retailers. They sell to shops in the real world, and you provide them with the infrastructure to also sell online, for a small price.

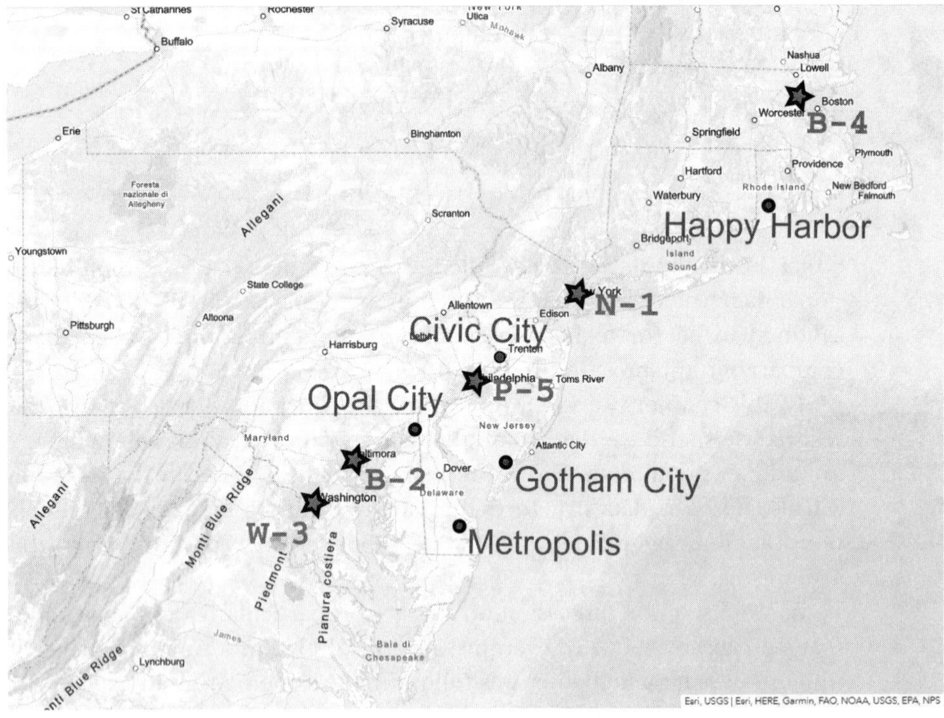

Buffalo
Syracuse
Utica
Albany
Nashua
Lowell
Boston
Worcester
B-4
Erie
Binghamton
Springfield
Plymouth
Providence
Hartford
Rhode Island
New Bedford
Falmouth
Waterbury
Allegani
Scranton
Happy Harbor
Youngstown
State College
N-1
Allentown
Edison
Pittsburgh
Altoona
Civic City
Harrisburg
Toms River
P-5
Opal City
New Jersey
Maryland
Atlantic City
Dover
B-2
Gotham City
Delaware
Allegani
Monti Blue Ridge
W-3
Metropolis
Piedmont
Pianura costiera
Baia di Chesapeake
Lynchburg
Esri, USGS | Esri, HERE, Garmin, FAO, NOAA, USGS, EPA, NPS

Figure 8.1 A hypothetical map of warehouses (marked with stars) next to the major cities on the coast (in an alternate universe)

Each warehouse will take care of deliveries for its orders, but to gain traction and have more retailers hop on board, you offer a special deal: for each delivery further than 10 km away, you will cut your commission proportionally to the distance.

Back to figure 8.1. You are the chief architect of this company and your main goal is finding a way, when a client orders a product, to come up with the closest warehouse that has the product in stock, and, if possible, keeping within a distance of 10 km.

Long story short, to keep your company in business and to keep your job, it's vital that you always redirect each user to the closest warehouse.

Imagine that someone from Gotham City tries to order some French cheese. You look at your list of warehouses, compute the distance between your customer's mailing address and each of them, and pick the closest one, P-5. Immediately after that, someone from Metropolis buys two wheels of the same cheese; unfortunately, you can't use any of the distances computed before, because the source point, the location of the customer, is completely different. So, you just go through that list of stores again, compute all the distances, and choose warehouse B-2. If the next request comes, say, from Civic City, off you go! You once again need to compute all N distances again, to all N warehouses.

8.2 Solutions

Now, I know, figure 8.1 only shows five warehouses, so it seems a trivial, quick operation to go through all warehouses for each user. You could even handle orders manually, choosing case by case based on your gut feeling and experience.

But suppose that after one year, since your business is working well, more stores have decided to sell on your website, and you have close to a hundred of them in that same area. That's challenging, and your customer care department can't cope with a thousand orders a day: manually selecting the closest place for each order doesn't work anymore.

So, you write a small piece of code that automatically performs the previous steps for each order and checks all the distances for each order.

After another year, however, the business is going so well that your CEO decides you are ready to go national after closing a deal that will see hundreds or thousands of medium and large stores (spread across the country) join your platform.

Computing millions of distances per user starts to seem a little overwhelming and inefficient—also, since you are only in the late '90s, servers are not that fast, server farms are a rarity, and data centers are something for large hardware companies such as IBM. They are not yet a thing for e-commerce.

8.2.1 First attempts

Your first proposal can be precomputing the closest warehouse for each user once and for all products, but that doesn't really work, because users can and will move, or sometimes they want to have stuff sent to their office or to the post office and not to their homes. Plus, the availability of goods will change over time, so the closest shop isn't always the best one. You would need to keep a list of shops, ordered by distance, for each customer (or at least each city). Haven't I already mentioned that data centers aren't yet a thing?

8.2.2 Sometimes caching is not the answer

So, this is one of those cases where cache doesn't really help us a lot. As we mentioned in chapter 7, there aren't many such situations, but sometimes they do happen.

Reasoning in 2-D, we might try a different approach, inspired by real maps: divide our map into tiles, using a regular grid. This way, we can easily find which tile contains a point from its coordinates (simply dividing the value of each coordinate by the size of a tile; see figure 8.2) and search the closest points in the same tile or in the neighboring tiles. This, indeed, seems to help reduce the number of points we need to compare; there is, however, a catch. This approach works if data is regularly spaced, which is usually not the case with real datasets, as shown in figure 8.2.

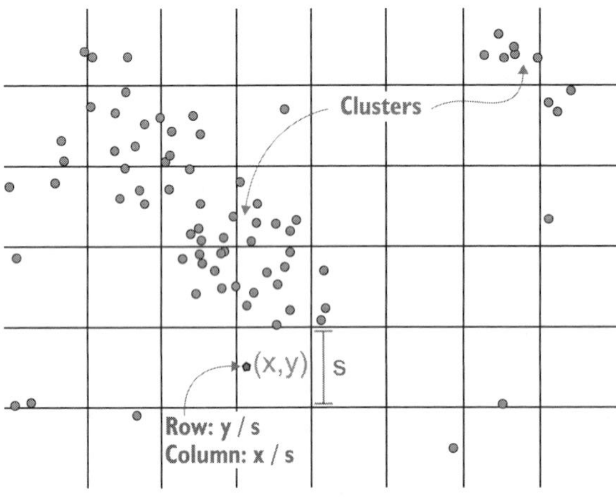
Clusters
(x,y)
s
Row: y / s
Column: x / s

Figure 8.2 Indexing 2-D space with regular, equal-sized tiles. While finding the tile where a point lies is easy, irregular distribution of points in a dataset causes, on average, many cells to be empty, while a few of them have high density.

Real data forms clusters, dense conglomerates that gather many points close to each other, alternated with sparse areas with few points. With a regularly spaced grid, the risk is having many empty tiles and a few tiles that gather hundreds or thousands of points, hence defying the purpose of this approach. We need something different, something more flexible.

8.2.3 Simplifying things to get a hint

The solution to this problem seems elusive. In these cases, it sometimes helps to solve a simplified version of the problem and then come up with a more general solution that works for our initial problem.

Suppose, for instance, that we were able to restrict our search to a 1-D search space. Say that we need to serve only customers on a single road that extends for miles and miles, and all our warehouses are also placed along this same road.

To simplify things even further, suppose that the road is perfectly straight, and that the total distance we cover is short enough that we don't have to worry about the earth's surface being curved, latitude, longitude, etc. Basically, we assume that an approximation with a 1-D segment is close enough to our space, and we can use Euclidean distance in 1-D as a proxy for the real distance between cities.

Figure 8.3 might help you picture the scenario. We have a line segment with a starting point marked as `0`, and the cities and warehouses that we saw in figure 8.1, but now all of them are on the same line.

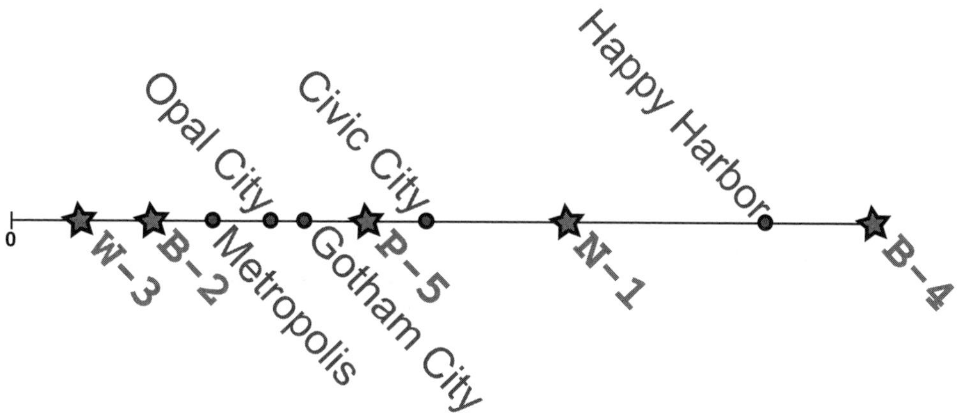
0
W-3
B-2
Opal City
Metropolis
Gotham City
Civic City
P-5
N-1
Happy Harbor
B-4

Figure 8.3 Cities and warehouses from figure 8.1, now projected on a 1-D space, a line segment

This is an approximation of the initial scenario, where those points belong to a 2-D plane, which in turn is an approximation of the reality, where the same points are on a 3-D curved surface. Depending on the use case, we might be fine with either approximation, or require a more precise model taking into account the curvature of the earth's surface.

Given a random point on the segment, we would like to know which one of the reference points is closer. Being in a 1-D case, this looks awfully similar to binary search, right? Check figure 8.4 to see how binary search can be used to find the closest 1-D point.

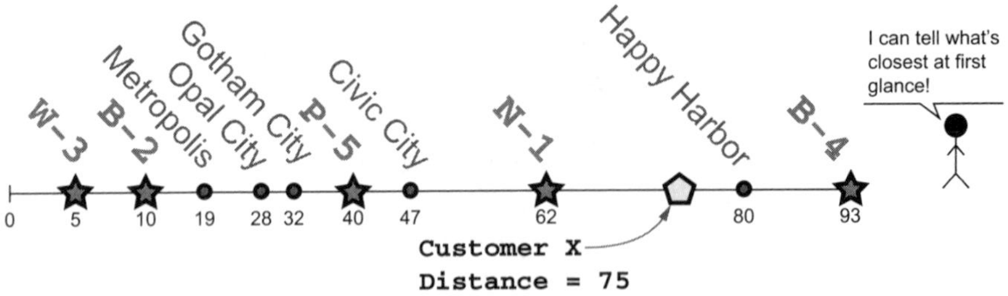
(A) How a human sees the problem
W-3
B-2
Metropolis
Opal City
Gotham City
P-5
Civic City
N-1
Happy Harbor
B-4
I can tell what's closest at first glance!
0
5
10
19
28
32
40
47
62
80
93
Customer X
Distance = 75

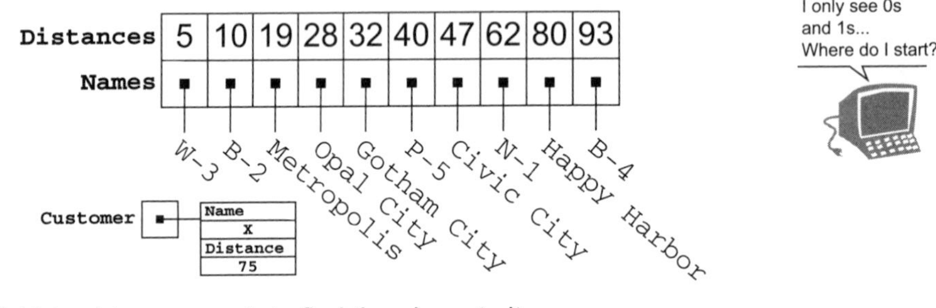
(B) How a computer sees the problem
Distances
5 10 19 28 32 40 47 62 80 93
Names
W-3
B-2
Metropolis
Opal City
Gotham City
P-5
Civic City
N-1
Happy Harbor
B-4
I only see 0s and 1s... Where do I start?
Customer
Name
X
Distance
75

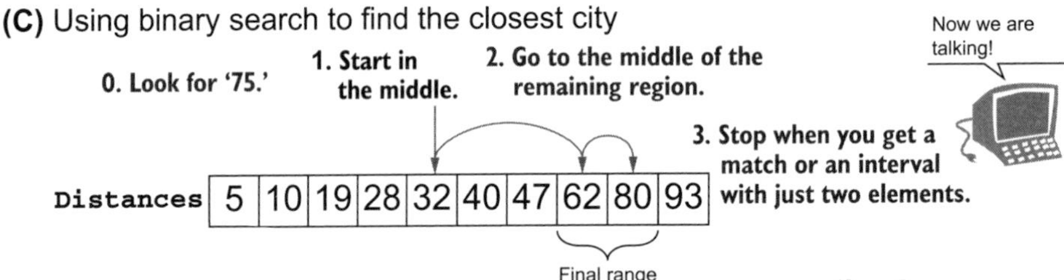
(C) Using binary search to find the closest city
0. Look for '75.'
1. Start in the middle.
2. Go to the middle of the remaining region.
3. Stop when you get a match or an interval with just two elements.
Now we are talking!
Distances
5 10 19 28 32 40 47 62 80 93
Final range
4. Compare the searched value with the elements in the range to find the closest one.

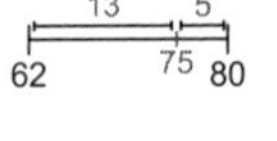
13
5
62
75
80

Figure 8.4 How the 1-D version of the search problem is solved by humans and computers. Each city, warehouse, and customer is defined in terms of a distance from a fixed point (the origin, whose distance is 0). (A) Humans can easily look at a 1-D map, place a point on it, and see the closest entry. (B) A computer, on the other hand, needs instructions to find a relation between a point and what it sees as just an ordered sequence of numbers. Linear scan of the sequence is an option, but (C) binary search is a better option. We start from the middle of the sequence, check whether our value (75) is equal to the element in the middle (32), and since it is not, we move to the right of 32, in the middle of the sub-sequence between 40 and 93. We keep doing so until we either find a perfect match (which would also be the closest entry), or we end up with a sub-sequence that has just two elements. If that's the case, we compare the two elements to our value, and see that 80 is closer than 62. So Happy Harbor is our winner.

8.2.4 *Carefully choose a data structure*

Binary search on an array is cool, but arrays are not really known for their flexibility (as we discuss in appendix C). If we would like to add another point between `W-3` and `B-2`, for instance, we would have to move all array entries points from `B-2` to `B-4`, and possibly reallocate the array if it's a static array.

Luckily, we do know a data structure that is more flexible than arrays and would allow us to perform a binary search efficiently. As its name suggests, a binary search tree (BST) is what we are looking for. In figure 8.5 we show a balanced binary search tree; remember that we need the tree to be balanced to guarantee logarithmic running time on the most common operations.

For this example, we show a tree that contains both cities and warehouses. You can imagine, for the sake of simplification, that each city has a big warehouse or distribution center, so our searches can just return the closest entry (either a city or a warehouse) to a customer (that is not in one of the cities in the tree).

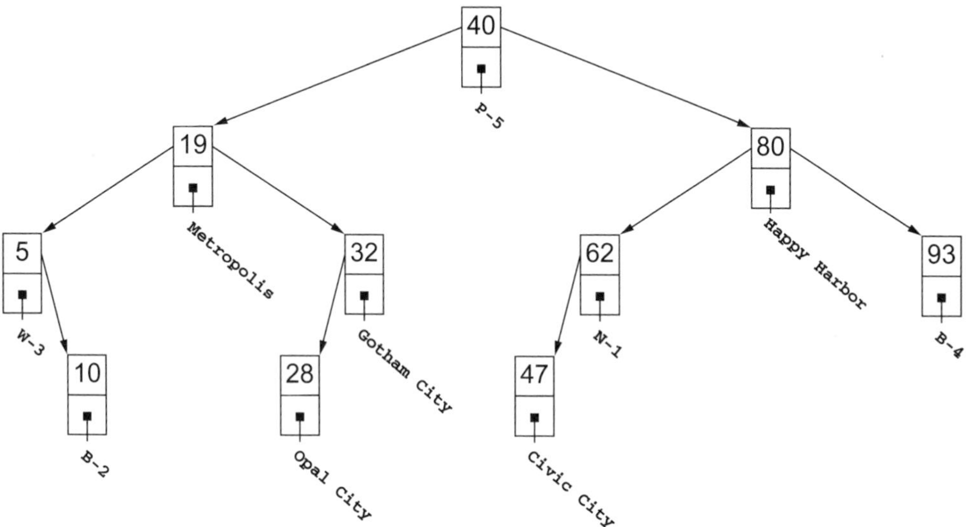
40
P-5
19
Metropolis
80
Happy Harbor
5
W-3
32
Gotham City
62
N-1
93
B-4
10
B-2
28
Opal City
47
Civic City

Figure 8.5 A balanced binary search tree containing cities and warehouses in our example. Note that this is only one of the possible balanced search trees for these values. For this set of values, there are at least 32 valid binary search trees that are also balanced. As an exercise, you can try to enumerate all of them (hint: Which internal nodes can be rotated[1] without changing the tree height?)

And indeed, insertion, removal, and search are guaranteed to be logarithmic on our balanced BST. This is much better than our initial linear time search, isn't it? A logarithmic running time grows amazingly slowly; just think that for a million points, we would go down from a million distances to be computed to just about 20!

Figure 8.6 shows how we would run binary search on the binary search tree shown in figure 8.5 to find the nearest neighbor of a point whose distance from the origin (aka its x coordinate) is 75. If we had an exact match, the nearest neighbor would be the result of binary search. When we don't have an exact match, which is the most common case, then the nearest neighbor will always be either the node where the binary search fails, or its parent.

[1] Here, rotation refers to the balancing operation performed, among others, on red-black trees.

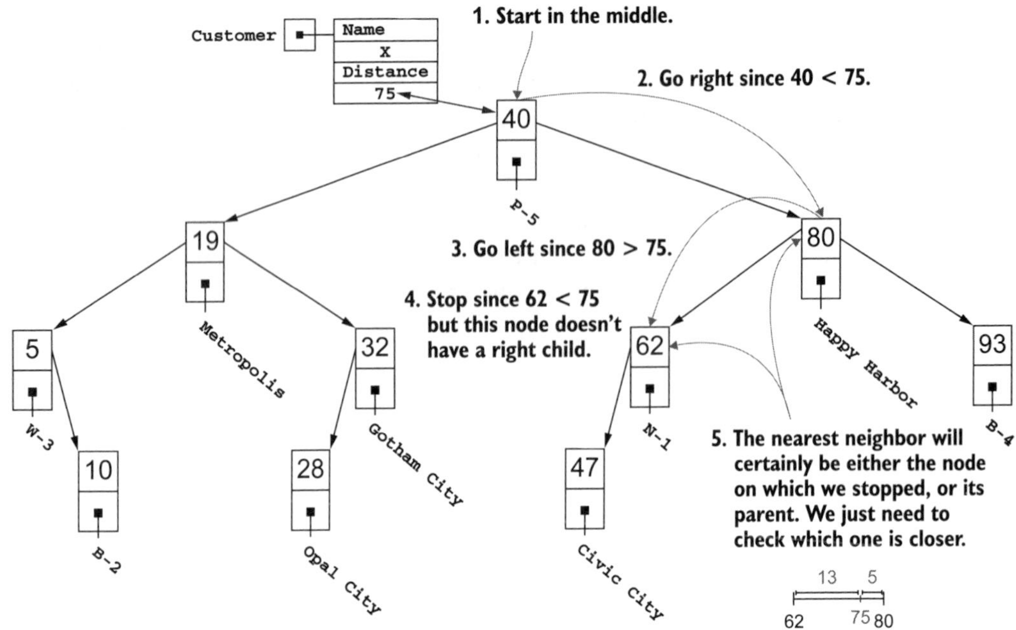

Customer
Name
X
Distance
75
1. Start in the middle.
2. Go right since 40 < 75.
3. Go left since 80 > 75.
4. Stop since 62 < 75 but this node doesn't have a right child.
5. The nearest neighbor will certainly be either the node on which we stopped, or its parent. We just need to check which one is closer.
40
P-5
19
Metropolis
80
Happy Harbor
5
W-3
32
Gotham City
62
N-1
93
B-4
10
B-2
28
Opal City
47
Civic City
13
5
62
75
80

Figure 8.6 Using search on a binary search tree to find the nearest neighbor (in 1-D) of a target point

So, what's the algorithm to find the nearest neighbor of a 1-D point, when our dataset is stored in a binary search tree?

1. Run search on the binary search tree.
2. If there is an exact match, the entry found is the nearest neighbor (with distance equal to `0`).
3. Otherwise, check which entry is closest to your target between the last entry visited (the one on which search stopped) and its parent.

Now that we have brilliantly solved the problem in 1-D, the question arises: Can we use a similar data structure to solve the problem in 2-D?

8.3 Description and API

Of course, the answer is yes. Probably the fact that we asked the question already led you to suspect it. But nonetheless, getting from 1-D to 2-D is a big leap. There is no easy way to imagine a tree that works in two dimensions. Worry not, though; we'll get into a detailed explanation in the next section. Once we have taken that leap, it will be easy to move to 3-D and in general to hyper-spaces with an arbitrary number of dimensions.

We also won't be limited to datasets that lie in 2-D or 3-D geometric space. The dimensions can be anything, as long as we can define a distance measure on them, with the caveat that the distance measure respects some requirements; namely, it needs to be Euclidian distance.[2] For example, we can have 2-D entries where the first coordinate is their price and the second coordinate is their rating, and then we can ask for the closest entry to a target tuple, like (100$, 4.5 rating). Even more, we will be able to ask for the `N` closest entries to that target.

In this and the following chapters we are going to describe three data structures, three containers, that allow for efficient nearest neighbor queries. But not just that—they will provide a few special operations:

- Retrieving the `N` closest points to a target point (not necessarily in the container)
- Retrieving all the points in the container within a certain distance from a target point (geometrically interpretable as all points within a hyper-sphere)
- Retrieving all the points in the container within a range (all points lying inside a hyper-rectangle, or a semi-hyperspace)

Let's now briefly introduce the three structures we will describe in these chapters:

- *K-d tree*—A k-d tree is a special binary tree in which every non-leaf node represents a splitting hyper-plane that divides the `k`-dimensional space into two half-spaces. Points on one side of this splitting hyper-plane are stored in the left subtree of the node and points in the other half-space created by the hyper-plane are stored in the right subtree. We'll focus on k-d trees in chapter 9.
- *R-tree*—The *R* here is for rectangle. An R-tree groups nearby points and defines the minimum bounding box (that is, hyper-rectangle) containing them. Points in the container are partitioned in a hierarchical sequence of minimum bounding boxes, one for each intermediate node, with the one at the root containing all the points, and the bounding box of each node fully containing all its children's bounding boxes. In chapter 10 we will give a brief description of how R-trees work.
- *SS-tree*—Similar to R-trees, but *Similarity Search Trees* use hyper-spheres as bounding regions. Hyper-spheres are constructed with a recursive structure: the leaves only contain points, while inner spheres' children are other hyper-spheres. Either way, a hyper-sphere can gather up to a certain number `n` of points (or spheres), within a certain distance from the sphere's center. When it gets more than `n` children or some of them are too far away with respect to the others, then the tree is rebalanced. We'll describe in detail how this is done in chapter 10, which is devoted to SS-trees.

And finally, let's define a generic interface, common to all concrete implementations.

---

[2] A Euclidean distance is the ordinary straight-line distance between two points in Euclidean space, like the Euclidean plane or 3-D Euclidean space, and their generalizations to k dimensions.

<table>
<tr><th colspan="2">Abstract data structure: <code>NearestNeighborContainer</code></th></tr>
<tr><td>API</td><td><pre>class NearestNeighborContainer {
 size(),
 isEmpty(),
 insert(point),
 remove(point),
 search(point),
 nearestNeighbor(point),
 pointsInRegion(targetRegion)
}</pre></td></tr>
<tr><td>Contract with client</td><td>The container allows inserting and removing points, and the following queries:
▪ Existence: Check if a point is in the container.
▪ Nearest Neighbor: Return the closest point (or optionally the closest <code>N</code> points, for any <code>N</code>) to a target point. The target point doesn't have to be in the container.
▪ Region: Return all the points in the container within a certain region, either a hyper-sphere or hyper-rectangle.</td></tr>
</table>

8.4 Moving to k-dimensional spaces

In section 8.2, we showed that it is possible to efficiently solve the nearest neighbor problem in 1-D by using a binary search tree. If you read through the book and the appendices on core data structures, you should be familiar with binary trees. (If you did skip appendix C, this is your clue: go check out binary trees!)

When we go from 1-D to 2-D, however, the situation becomes slightly more complicated, since at each node we don't have a clear fork between two paths, namely left and right children. We have seen the same concept in ternary trees, where at each node we have a fork with three paths (or more, in `n`-ary trees), and the direction we have to follow depends on the result of comparison with more than just `true`/`false` possible outcomes. But would an `n`-ary tree help us in this situation? Let's analyze what happens in 1-D and see if we can generalize.

8.4.1 Unidimensional binary search

To recap what was described in section 8.2, it's easy to perform binary search when our entries can lie on unidimensional space. Figure 8.7 exemplifies how the entries can be translated to points on a line (that's basically a unidimensional space) so that each point on that line implicitly defines a left and a right.

So, each node has a value that corresponds to a point on that line, and each point on the line defines a left and right. But wait—in a binary search tree we also have left and right paths for each of our nodes: that's why it's so easy to know what to do in binary trees search!

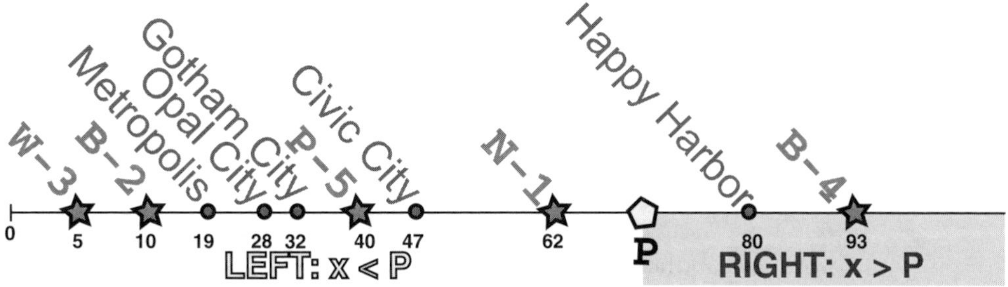
W-3
B-2
Metropolis
Gotham City
Opal City
P-5
Civic City
N-1
Happy Harbor
B-4
0
5
10
19
28
32
40
47
62
P
80
93
LEFT: x < P
RIGHT: x > P

Figure 8.7 Real numbers on $\mathbb{R}$. Given a point P, the continuous line is naturally partitioned into a left and a right subset.

8.4.2 Moving to higher dimensions

Now that we understand the mechanism for real numbers, what about $\mathbb{R}^2$? What about points in a Euclidean bidimensional space? What about $\mathbf{C}$ (the set of complex numbers)?

> **NOTE** Notice that $\mathbb{R}^2$ and $\mathbf{C}$ are bidimensional Euclidean spaces, and entries of these spaces can be represented with a pair of real numbers.

Well, if we move to higher dimensions, how to run binary search is not as clear as in the unidimensional case.

Binary search relies on recursively dividing a search space into halves, but if you consider a point P in the Cartesian plane, how can we partition the plane into two regions, left and right of P? Figure 8.8 shows a few possible ways to do so.

A visually intuitive approach could be splitting the plane along a vertical line passing through P, so that in our representation of the Cartesian plane, the two semi-spaces will actually be drawn on the left and on the right of P. See figure 8.8.

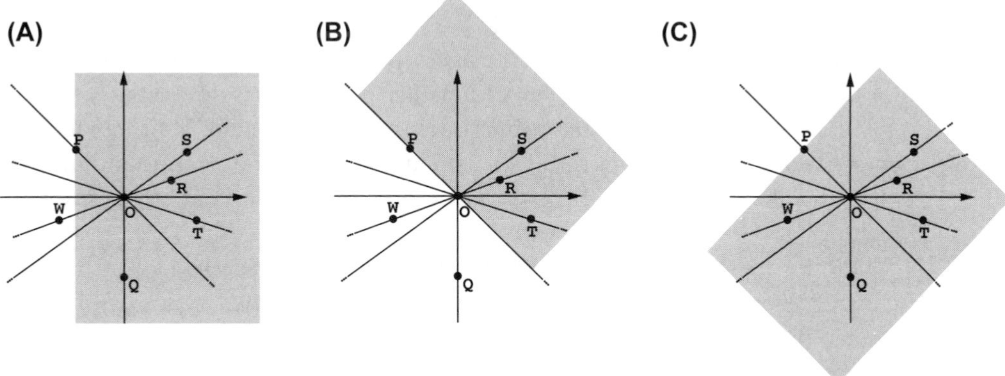
(A)
(B)
(C)
P
S
R
W
O
T
Q

Figure 8.8 Points in a Cartesian plane. Lines through the origin and each point are shown. A few possible partitionings into left and right of P are shown. (A) Splitting the plane with a vertical line passing through P. (B) Drawing a line passing through P and the origin will define two semi-spaces on the two sides of the line. (C) Using the same line as B but partitioning points whose projection on that line is left or right of P.

This solution can look fine while using `P` as a pivot, but if we take other points, a couple of drawbacks will emerge:

- Looking at point `R` in figure 8.9, if we draw a vertical line, parallel to the `y` axis, and use the `x` coordinate to partition points, we get `W`, `P`, `O`, `Q`, and `U` in the left partition, and `S` and `T` in the right one. This means that despite `U` and `S` being much closer than `U` and `O` or `S` and `T`, they end up in different partitions (while the other two pairs of points are in the same partition).
- If we consider `O`, in which partition will `Q` be? And what about any other point on the `y` axis? We can arbitrarily assign points with the same `x` coordinate of our pivot to the left or right partition, but we'll have to do so for all of them, no matter how far they are from `O` on the `y` axis.

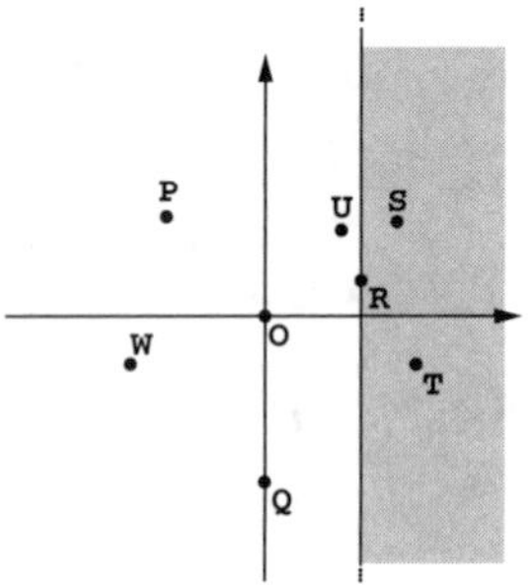
P
U
S
R
W
O
T
Q

Figure 8.9 Another example of partitioning $\mathbb{R}^2$ space using a line parallel to `y` axis and passing for a given point (`R`, in this case)

Both examples show issues that are derived from the same mistake: we are ignoring the points' `y` coordinates altogether. Using only a fraction of the available information can't be ideal; whenever we give up some info about a dataset, we are missing out on the opportunity to organize data more efficiently.

8.4.3 Modeling 2-D partitions with a data structure

Using the same, single-direction approach for all points doesn't really work, so maybe dividing a plane into four quadrants would be a better idea.

Indeed, figure 8.10 shows that this works better than our previous attempts. Of course, since there are four quadrants, left and right partitioning doesn't apply any more.

We can use a tree where each node has four children instead of two, one child for each possible quadrant. Points on the axes or on the lines passing by a point can be arbitrarily assigned to one of the quadrants (as long as this is done consistently).

This seems to work for $\mathbb{R}^2$, allowing us to overcome the main limit we identified for our previous attempt. Both `x` and `y` coordinates are taken into consideration to group points together (this would be even more apparent if you add more points to the diagram).

Now the question is whether we extend this solution to $\mathbb{R}^3$. To move to a 3-D space, we need to answer one question: Into how many sub-hyperplanes do we split the plane for each point? In 1-D, it was two segments for each point, in 2-D it was four quadrants, and similarly in 3-D we will need eight octants.[3]

[3] An octant is, by definition, one of the eight divisions of a Euclidean three-dimensional coordinate system. Usually octants refer to the eight hyper-cubes resulting from splitting $\mathbb{R}^3$ along the three Cartesian axes, so each octant is defined by the sign of the coordinates. For instance, (+++) is the octant where all coordinates are positive, (+-+) is the one where `x` and `z` are positive, and `y` is negative.

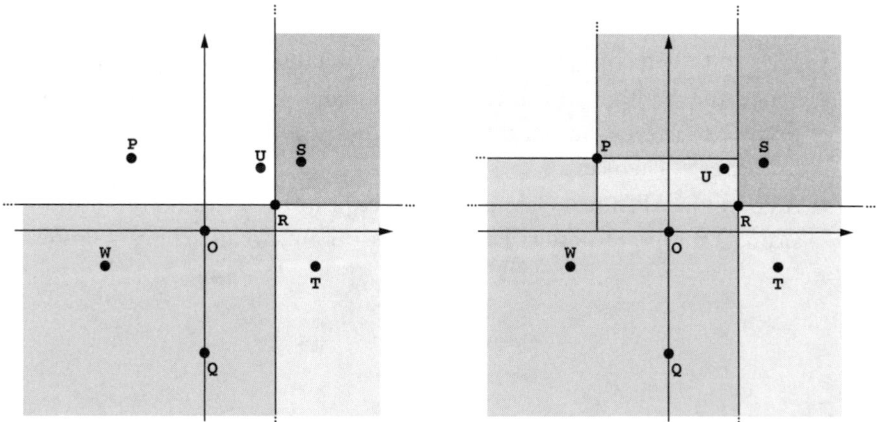
P
U
S
R
W
O
T
Q
P
S
U
R
W
O
T
Q

Figure 8.10 **Four-way partitioning of the plane. For each point, we split the area it belongs to in four quadrants using the lines passing through the point and parallel to the axes. For the first one, `R` in the example, we get four infinite quadrants (left). When we choose the next point, `P` (right), we have to further divide the upper-left quadrant into four parts: we get a finite rectangle, to which `U` belongs, and three infinite sections of the plane. For each further point, such as `U`, we further split the region it belongs to into four more smaller regions.**

Therefore, for each point in the dataset we will add a node with eight children, one for each octant resulting from splitting the 3-D space along lines parallel to the cartesian axes and passing through the point.

In general, for a `k`-dimensional space, we will need 2^k children for each node in the tree, because each point would partition the hyperspace in 2^k parts.

For real datasets, with the advent of big data, we will have to deal with high-dimensional spaces, meaning that `k` might easily be in the order of 10 to 30, or even 100. It's not unusual for datasets to have hundreds of features, and millions of points, and there are use cases where we need to perform nearest neighbor search on these datasets to make sense of them (clustering is one, as we will see in chapter 12).

Even with a smaller number of features, in the order of 10, each node would already have around a thousand children. As we saw in chapter 2 when talking about d-way heaps, when the branching factor of a tree grows too much, the tree flattens and becomes closer to a list.

But with 100-dimensional datasets, the number of children per node would be closer to 10^{30}, a number so large that it becomes challenging to store even a single node of such a tree. We certainly need to do better than that. But how?

As we will see in the next couple of chapters, computer scientists have found a few different ways to cope with these issues. In the next chapter, in particular, we introduce k-d trees, a data structure that uses a tiny variation on the approach in section 8.4.3 to avoid the exponential growth of the tree.

Summary

- We can't use a conventional container to handle multidimensional data.
- When the number of dimensions of a dataset grows, indexing with traditional methods becomes unfeasible due to the exponential growth of the number of branches at each step.
- A common API for a class of containers can hold multi-dimensional data, providing a method to query for the closest points to an arbitrary target.

9 K-d trees: Multidimensional data indexing

This chapter covers

- Indexing a 2-D (and in general k-D) dataset efficiently
- Implementing nearest neighbor search with k-d trees
- Discussing k-d trees' strengths and flaws

This chapter will be structured slightly differently from our book's standard, simply because we will continue here a discussion started in chapter 8. We introduced a problem: searching multidimensional data for the nearest neighbor(s) of a generic point (possibly not in the dataset itself).

In this chapter, we follow up on those topics, so we won't introduce a new problem, but pick up the "closest hub" example from chapter 8 and show a different option to solve it, using k-d trees.

9.1 Right where we left off

Let's recap where we left off in previous chapters. We are designing software for an e-commerce company, an application to find the closest warehouse selling a given product for any point on a very large map. See figure 9.1 to visualize. To have a ballpark idea of the kind of scale we need, we want to serve millions of clients per day across the country, taking products from thousands of warehouses, also spread across the map.

In section 8.2, we established that a brute-force solution where we skim through the whole list of points to compare differences can't work for a live solution.

We have also seen how the multidimensional structure of the data prevents us from using the basic solutions we saw in the first part of the book, from heaps to hash maps.

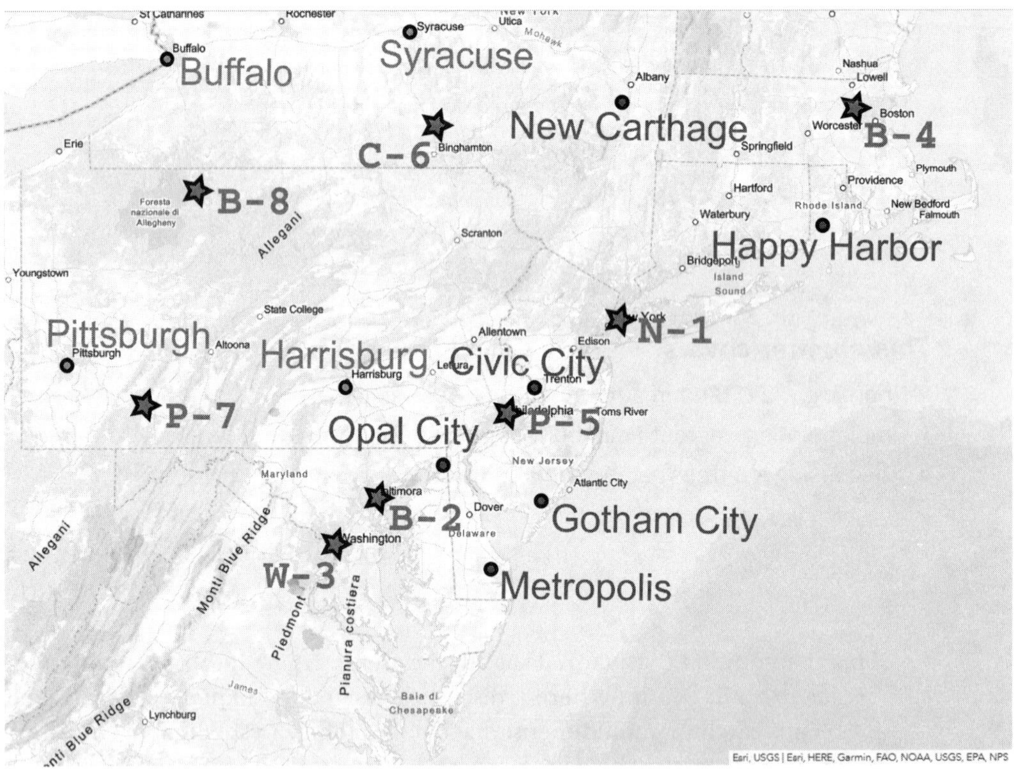

Buffalo
Syracuse
New Carthage
C-6
B-4
B-8
Happy Harbor
N-1
Pittsburgh
Harrisburg
Civic City
P-7
Opal City
P-5
B-2
Gotham City
W-3
Metropolis
Binghamton
Albany
Boston
Worcester
Springfield
Hartford
Providence
Waterbury
Erie
Youngstown
Scranton
State College
Allentown
Edison
Trenton
Toms River
Altoona
New Jersey
Maryland
Atlantic City
Dover
Lynchburg
Esri, USGS | Esri, HERE, Garmin, FAO, NOAA, USGS, EPA, NPS

Figure 9.1 Our example map, showing cities (real and imaginary) and warehouses (all imaginary!) on the east coast. In a typical application for k-d trees, given a point on the map, we would like to find the closest warehouse or the closest city to that point. Map source: ArcGIS.

Viable solutions, however, do exist. In this chapter we will first explain the issues we face in moving to multi-dimensional spaces; then, in this and the next chapter, we will delve into a few alternatives to efficiently tackle those challenges.

9.2 Moving to k-D spaces: Cycle through dimensions

You might have the impression that we've hit a dead end, and even in the scientific community it certainly seemed so for a long time.

The answer came in the form of a heuristic, by the hand (and brain) of Jon Louis Bentley.[1]

The idea is as brilliant as it is simple and stems from the considerations that led us this far in chapter 8. If we restrict to 2-D spaces, instead of splitting each region into four sub-regions for each point, we can perform a 2-way split, but alternating splits along vertical lines to split along horizontal lines.

For each split, we partition the points in a region into two groups. Then, at the next split, when we choose the next pivot in each of the two sub-regions, we will use a perpendicular direction to do the next partitioning.

Figure 9.2 shows a few steps of this algorithm. You can see how for the first pivot chosen we draw a vertical line passing through the point, then for the second one we draw a horizontal semi-line (we are splitting a semi-plane now, not the whole plane again!), and then a vertical (semi)line again.

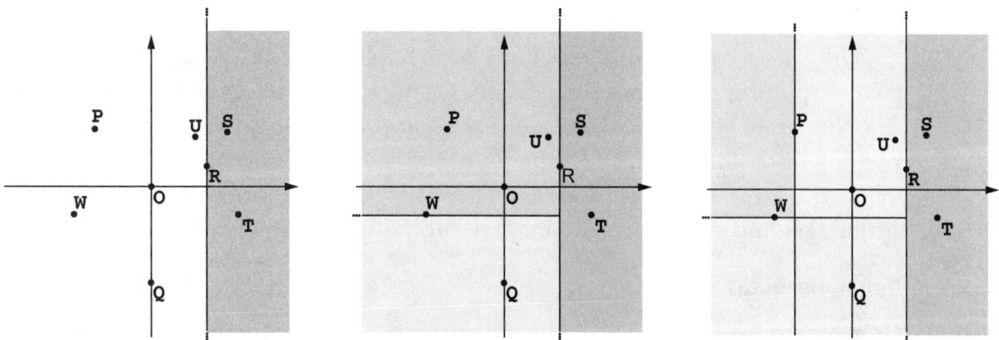
P
U
S
R
W
O
T
Q
P
U
S
R
W
O
T
Q
P
U
S
R
W
O
T
Q

Figure 9.2 Partitioning points in the 2-D Cartesian space by cycling through the directions along which we split. For the first split (left) we choose point `R` and draw a vertical line (parallel to `y` axis, `x` coordinate is constant) passing through it. We have thus created two half-spaces, a lighter-shaded one on the left and a darker-shaded one on the right of this line, grouping points `W`, `P`, `O`, `Q`, `U` on one side, and `S`, `T` on the other. Point `R` is the pivot of this partitioning. Next, we choose point `W` in the lighter shade partition. This time, we draw a horizontal line (parallel to `x` axis, `y` coordinate is constant). It splits the lighter shade partition into two new partitions, one in the top-left area of the plane, containing `P`, `O` and `U`, and one in the bottom-left area, with just `Q`. If we further split the top-left area at point `P`, we again need to use a vertical line, as shown in the right-most part of the figure.

Notice that in the Cartesian plane, a vertical line through a point $P=(P_x, P_y)$ has a peculiar characteristic: it is parallel to the y axis, and all points on the line have the same value for their x coordinate, P_x. Likewise, a horizontal line passing through P is made of all the points in the plane for which $y=P_y$.

[1] "Multidimensional binary search trees used for associative searching." *Communications of the ACM*, 1975, Vol. 18, Issue 9, pp. 509-517

So, when we split the plane along a vertical line through `P=(Px,Py)`, what we really mean is that we create two partitions, one for the points `L` in the plane for which $L_x<P_x$, and one for those points `R` for which $R_x>P_x$. And similarly, for horizontal lines, using the `y` coordinates of the points.

This binary partitioning allows us to use binary trees to index our points. Each node in the tree is the pivot we chose to partition the remaining region of space, and its left and right subtrees gather all points in the two partitions, and represent the two sub-regions resulting from the split we perform along the pivot (check out figures 9.2 and 9.5).

Can this algorithm be generalized to higher dimensions? Yes, it naturally allows a generalization to higher dimensions, because we split on a single coordinate for each point, but we can do a round-robin through all the coordinates of a `k`-dimensional space, and the `i`-th level of the binary tree we build will correspond to a split along the `(i mod k)`-th dimension.

This means that in a 2-D space, the root will split the plane along the `x` axis, its children will split each of the two semi-planes along the `y` axis, and then their children will split again along the `x` axis and so on. In a `k`-dimensional space, with `k > 2`, we start with the first coordinate at level `0` (the root), and then move to the second at height `1`, the third at height `2`, and so on.

This way, we partition the plane into rectangular areas. With respect to our initial idea of splitting points with vertical lines only, we have fewer areas extending to infinity (while if we always used the same coordinate all areas would be infinite!) and avoid keeping distant points in the same partition.

At the same time, each node has just two children, and we can maintain all the advantages and guarantees of binary partitioning and binary search.

9.2.1 Constructing the BST

So far, we have just hinted at the construction of a binary search tree, implying that there is a direct translation of the partitions, or rather the pivots we choose, into a BST.

We have also implied that the BST we are going to construct is an important part of the k-d tree. Let's give a more formal definition to clarify the relation between these two data structures.

> **DEFINITION** A k-d tree is a binary search tree whose elements are points taken from a `k`-dimensional space, that is, tuples with `k` elements, whose coordinates can be compared. (To simplify, let's assume that each coordinate's values can be translated into real numbers.) In addition to that, in a k-d tree, at each level `i`, we only compare the `i`-th (modulo `k`) coordinate of points to decide which branch of the tree will be traversed.

In fewer words, a k-d tree can be described in terms of a binary search tree with a fancy comparison method on its keys. The added value is given by the algorithms for search that can be performed on this kind of tree much more efficiently than on other simpler data structures.

Figure 9.3 shows the construction of an example tree for the unidimensional case. This is an edge case, because singletons (tuples with dimension 1) will result in always using the x coordinate in points (that is, the whole singleton).

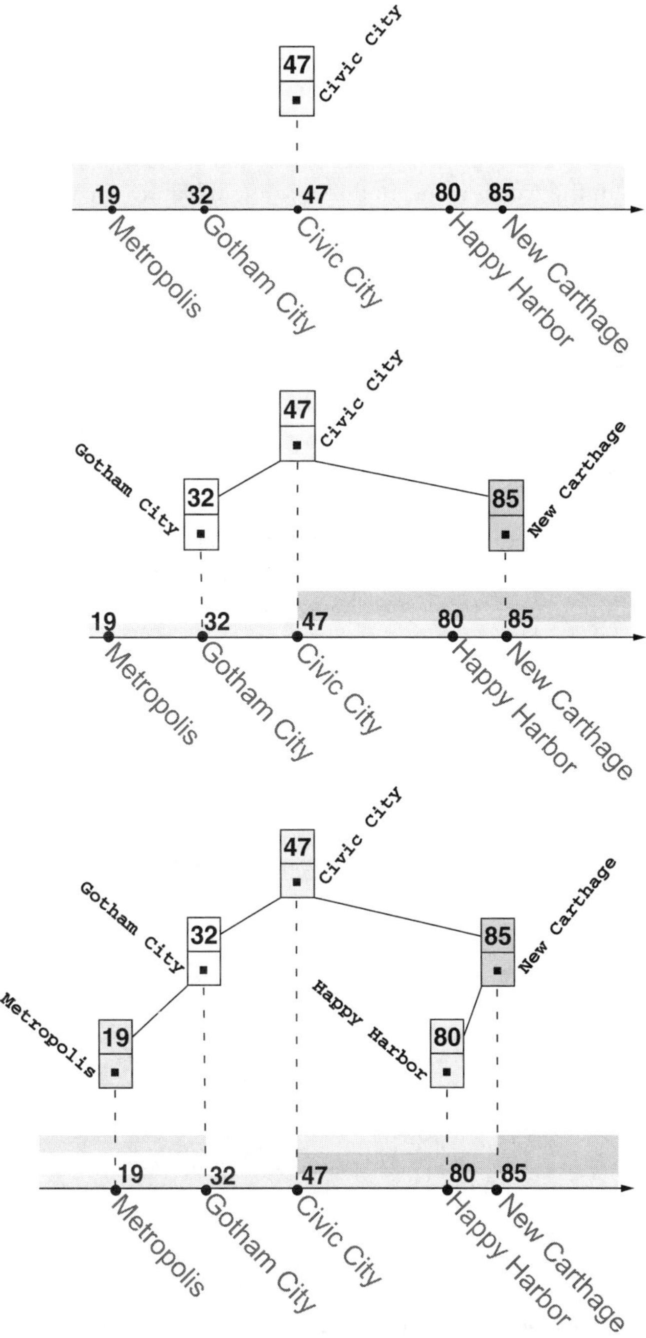
47
Civic City
19
32
47
80
85
Metropolis
Gotham City
Civic City
Happy Harbor
New Carthage
47
Civic City
Gotham City
32
85
New Carthage
19
32
47
80
85
Metropolis
Gotham City
Civic City
Happy Harbor
New Carthage
47
Civic City
Gotham City
32
85
New Carthage
Metropolis
19
Happy Harbor
80
19
32
47
80
85
Metropolis
Gotham City
Civic City
Happy Harbor
New Carthage

Figure 9.3 Constructing a BST from the pivots of a 1-D dataset. (Left) We add the first pivot, which is going to be the root of the tree. The pivot creates an implicit divide along the x axis, partitioning the remaining points into left and right subsets. The region covered by a node is the union of the partitions its pivot creates, so the root covers the whole subset. (Center) Each of the two sub-regions implied by the root is further partitioned by selecting a point in each region as a pivot. As shown by the highlighting above the horizontal axis, each of these nodes at level 1 now covers half of the space (while the root still covers the whole space). (Right) Level 2 nodes are added, further partitioning the space. Notice how some regions are still only covered by nodes at level 1 because these intermediate nodes only have one child.

Notice how each node of the tree "covers" a region of the dataset in a hierarchical way: the root covers the whole dataset, level 1 nodes cover the left and right partitions created using the root as a pivot, and level 2 nodes cover the even smaller partitions created using level 1 nodes as pivots.

Here, when we use the term "cover," we mean that given an entry `X` in the search space (in 1-D, given a real number `X`), and if we query the tree (as a binary search tree) for `X`, then all nodes we traverse during the search for `X` (which form a path from the root to a node `N`) cover `X`. In particular, the node on which the search stops is the one covering the smallest region for `X`.

In other words, each node in the tree is associated to a range of values for which it will be traversed when searching the tree; that range is the region covered by the node.

Make sure to go through the example in figure 9.3 and understand every step; maybe even try to run an example yourself (for instance, by just changing the pivots or their order and checking how the tree changes). It is important to understand the unidimensional case because it will make it simpler to understand the 2-d tree construction.

In order to better show the steps of the construction of a 2-d tree and highlight the advantages of cycling through the dimensions used to partition, we add a few cities to figure 9.1 in order to have a more uniform 2-D spatial distribution. In figure 9.4 we have also added a coordinate system: both the origin and the scale are arbitrary, and completely marginal for the results of the algorithm. We can always apply any translation and scale operation, since they preserve the Euclidean distances.

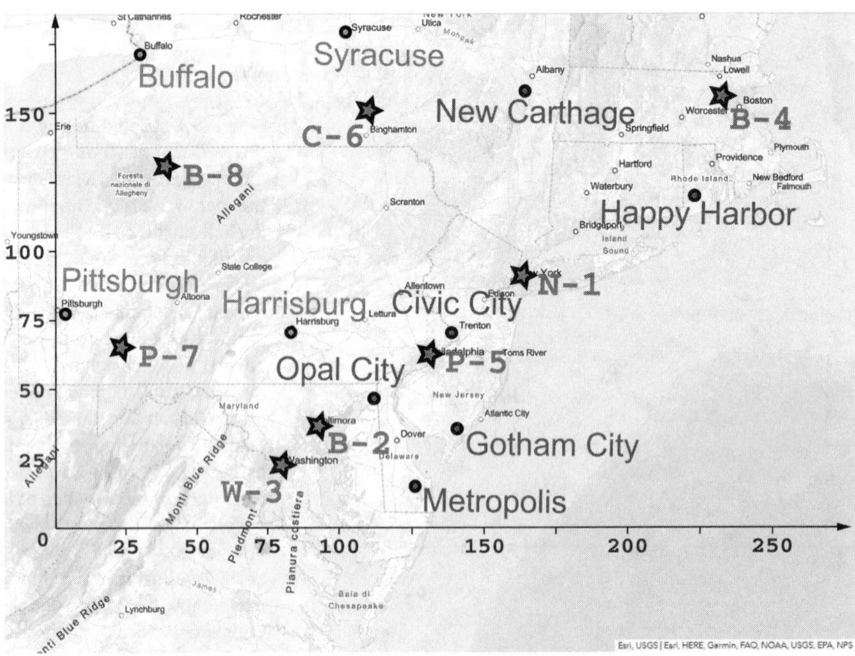
Syracuse
Buffalo
New Carthage
B-4
C-6
B-8
Happy Harbor
Pittsburgh
Harrisburg
Civic City
N-1
P-7
Opal City
P-5
B-2
Gotham City
W-3
Metropolis
150
100
75
50
25
0
25
50
75
100
150
200
250
Utica
Albany
Nashua
Lowell
Boston
Worcester
Springfield
Binghamton
Plymouth
Providence
Hartford
Rhode Island
New Bedford
Falmouth
Waterbury
Scranton
Erie
State College
Allentown
Altoona
Trenton
Toms River
New Jersey
Maryland
Atlantic City
Dover
Delaware
Lynchburg
Esri, USGS | Esri, HERE, Garmin, FAO, NOAA, USGS, EPA, NPS

Figure 9.4 A richer version of the map in figure 9.1, with a coordinate system. Map source: ArcGIS.

Figure 9.5 shows the results of the first couple of steps of the algorithm that builds the tree. In this figure you can see a different scale than in the previous picture. While the other one was more realistic, with distances between points closer to the real distances in miles between cities, it could also generate some unnecessary confusion in the drawings; moreover, as we mentioned, the coordinate system is not really important for the algorithm, as long as it's consistent.

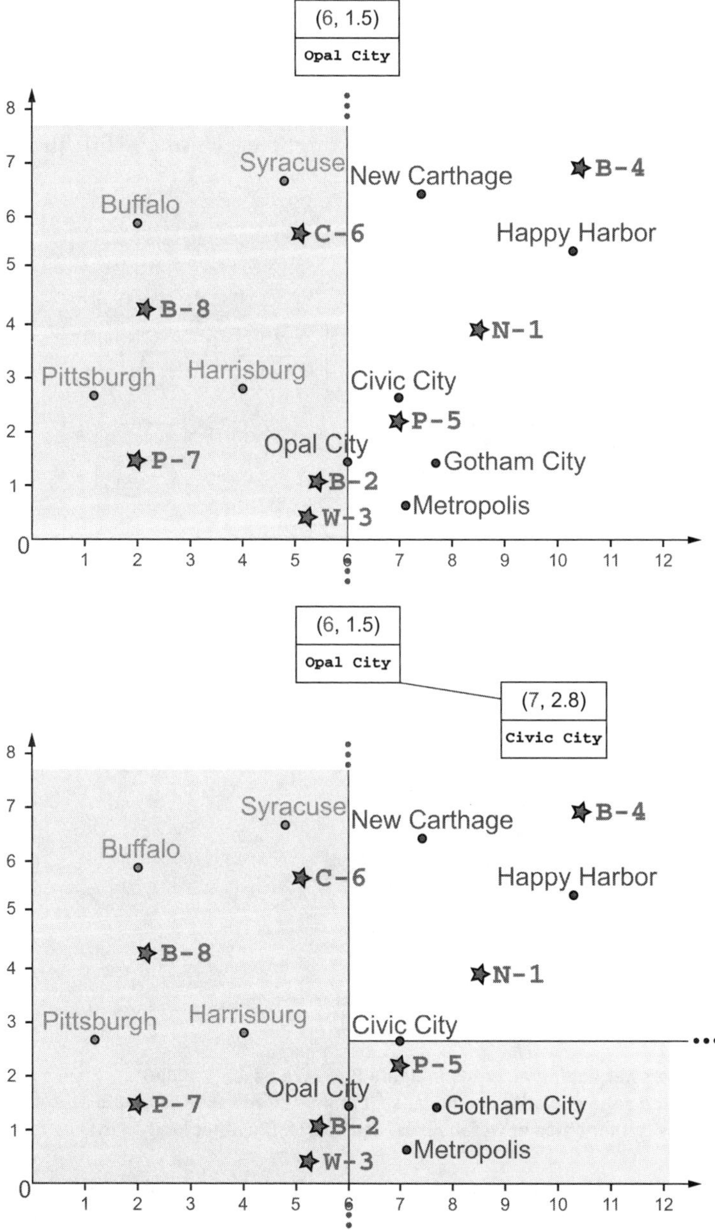
(6, 1.5)
Opal City
Syracuse
New Carthage
B-4
Buffalo
C-6
Happy Harbor
B-8
N-1
Pittsburgh
Harrisburg
Civic City
P-5
Opal City
P-7
Gotham City
B-2
Metropolis
W-3
(6, 1.5)
Opal City
(7, 2.8)
Civic City
Syracuse
New Carthage
B-4
Buffalo
C-6
Happy Harbor
B-8
N-1
Pittsburgh
Harrisburg
Civic City
P-5
Opal City
P-7
Gotham City
B-2
Metropolis
W-3

Figure 9.5 The first two steps of constructing a k-d tree for our map of DC cities. (Left) First we split vertically with pivot "Opal City," which becomes the root of the k-d tree. (Right) The right partition (created by the root) is further split along a horizontal line passing through our second pivot, "Civic City," so in the BST we add a right child to the root. This node corresponds to another split into a top and bottom sub-region.

The first point we choose as pivot is "Opal City."[2] Since we first split using x coordinates, all cities on its left will go into one partition, and all cities on its right will go to the other partition. Then, as a second step, let's focus on the right partition. We choose, for instance, "Civic City" as a pivot, and this time we have to use y coordinates to split, so all points in the top-right region will go in a sub-partition of the right one, and all points in the bottom-right region will go into the other. We now have three partitions, and we can further split any of them.

In figure 9.6, we show the resulting tree after inserting all the cities (without the warehouses). The edges have the same vertical or horizontal split on each level, and both vertical and horizontal edges are alternated in any path.

Splits now define 10 clearly separated regions, and if you look at how warehouses are distributed, you can get an idea of what city they might be close to with just a glance at the region they are in.

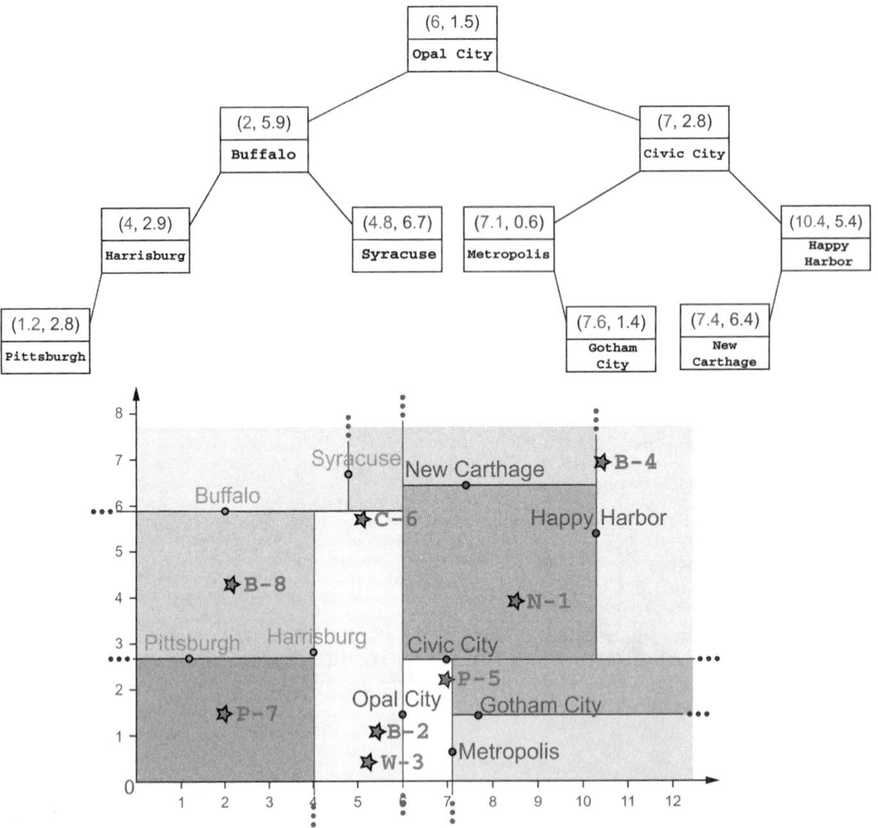
(6, 1.5)
Opal City
(2, 5.9)
Buffalo
(7, 2.8)
Civic City
(4, 2.9)
Harrisburg
(4.8, 6.7)
Syracuse
(7.1, 0.6)
Metropolis
(10.4, 5.4)
Happy Harbor
(1.2, 2.8)
Pittsburgh
(7.6, 1.4)
Gotham City
(7.4, 6.4)
New Carthage
Syracuse
New Carthage
B-4
Buffalo
C-6
Happy Harbor
B-8
N-1
Pittsburgh
Harrisburg
Civic City
P-5
P-7
Opal City
Gotham City
B-2
W-3
Metropolis

Figure 9.6 The k-d tree resulting after adding all cities in figure 9.4. (We haven't added warehouses to the tree, both for the sake of clarity and because it makes more sense to create a tree with just one kind of entries, either cities or warehouses, and search the other kind on it.)

[2] Here we choose points arbitrarily to obtain a clearer visualization. In section 9.3.3 we will explain how to make this choice programmatically to obtain a balanced tree.

There is not, however, a direct match, and looking at regions is not enough to determine the closest point. For instance, if you look at B-8 in the picture, it's not clear if Buffalo, Pittsburgh, or Harrisburg is the closest city, and C-6 looks closer to Syracuse than Harrisburg, despite being "covered" by the latter and not the former.

Determining the closest point(s) requires a few more steps than in regular binary search trees (the unidimensional case), and we will defer the description of the full algorithm to the next section.

As mentioned, this construction method for k-d trees naturally generalizes to higher dimensions, although it becomes more difficult to visualize the trees and the spaces itself.

For k=3, we can still imagine $\mathbb{R}^3$ divided in parallelepipeds, as shown in figure 9.7, but for 4-D and further, we lack an immediate geometric interpretation. That said, as long as we treat k-D points as tuples, it is possible to follow the same steps we have seen for a 2d-tree without any change.

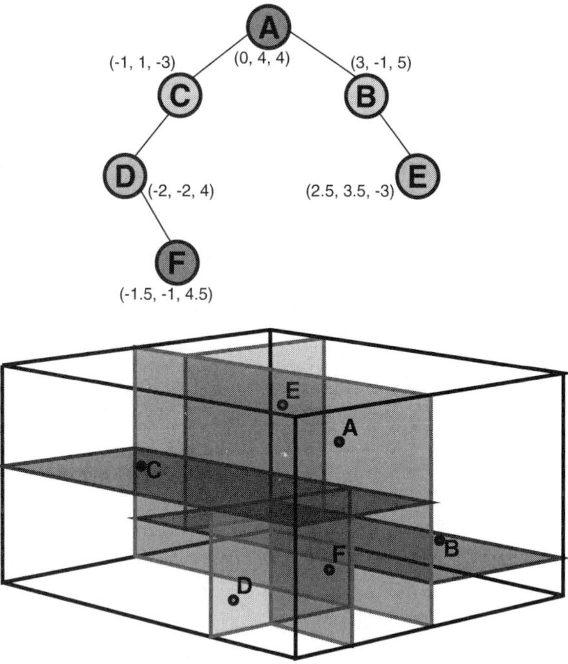
A
(0, 4, 4)
C
(-1, 1, -3)
B
(3, -1, 5)
D
(-2, -2, 4)
E
(2.5, 3.5, -3)
F
(-1.5, -1, 4.5)
E
A
C
B
F
D

Figure 9.7 An example of a 3-D tree (aka k-d tree with dimension 3). For the sake of clarity, regions are not highlighted, and nodes are filled with the same color of their split planes.

9.2.2 *Invariants*

We could sum up the definition of k-d trees in a few invariants. A k-d tree is defined as a binary search tree, whose elements are k-dimensional points, and that abides by the following invariants:

- All points in the tree have dimension k.
- Each level has a *split coordinate* index j, such that 0 ≤ j < k.

- If a node `N`'s split coordinate index is `j`, then `N`'s children have a split coordinate equal to `(j+1) mod k`.
- For each node `N`, with split coordinate index `j`, all nodes `L` in its left subtree have a smaller value for `N`'s split coordinate, `L[j] < N[j]`, and all nodes `R` on `N`'s right subtree have a larger or equal value for `N`'s split coordinate, `R[j] ≥ N[j]`.

9.2.3 The importance of being balanced

So far in this section we've consciously ignored a detail, a special characteristic we look for when it comes to binary search trees: whether the tree is balanced or not. As for the regular BST, you might have already figured out that the order in which we insert elements in our k-d tree determines the shape of the tree. Even having finite areas is not a synonym of having small areas, or good partitioning. If you look at the example in figure 9.6, we have carefully chosen points "by hand" in order to create a balanced tree, but it is easy to provide an example of a terrible insertion sequence that would create an imbalanced tree (just insert points starting from the top-left going in order toward the bottom-right corner, for instance).

Here we also consider a binary partitioning "good" only if it manages to split the whole set being partitioned into two subsets approximately of the same size.

If we manage to obtain a good partitioning at each step, we will have a balanced tree with logarithmic height. Given a sequence of points, it is possible, however, to choose an order of insertion for the points that will produce a skewed tree with linear height.

We'll see in a few pages how we can prevent this from happening under certain conditions. Rebalancing on insertion is not, unfortunately, as viable an option for k-d trees as it was for binary search trees.

Before worrying about balancing trees, let's see in detail the way methods such as `insert`, `remove`, and all the queries work for k-d trees.

9.3 Methods

We have now seen a few examples of k-d trees and how we can construct them. By now, it should be clear what a k-d tree looks like, the main ideas behind this data structure, and how we can leverage it.

It's time to delve into the main methods for k-d trees and see how they work and how they can be implemented. In this section we will present pseudo-code for these methods, and you can find an actual implementation on our repo on GitHub.[3]

Figure 9.8 shows a pre-constructed k-d tree that we are going to use as a starting point for this section. In order to focus on the details of the algorithm, we are going to use a simplified view, showing points on a Cartesian plane where axes are omitted. Points are denoted with capital letters (we are leaving out city names for now) to abstract out the context and focus on the algorithms. Vertical and horizontal splits are

[3] See https://github.com/mlarocca/AlgorithmsAndDataStructuresInAction#k-d-tree.

still shown, but we won't highlight the regions as we did in figures 9.6; as a consequence, we can fill tree nodes (instead of edges) with shading to show that vertical or horizontal splits will be used at a certain level.

While in figure 9.8 coordinates are shown next to both nodes and points, we might sometimes omit them for the sake of neatness, as shown in figure 9.8.

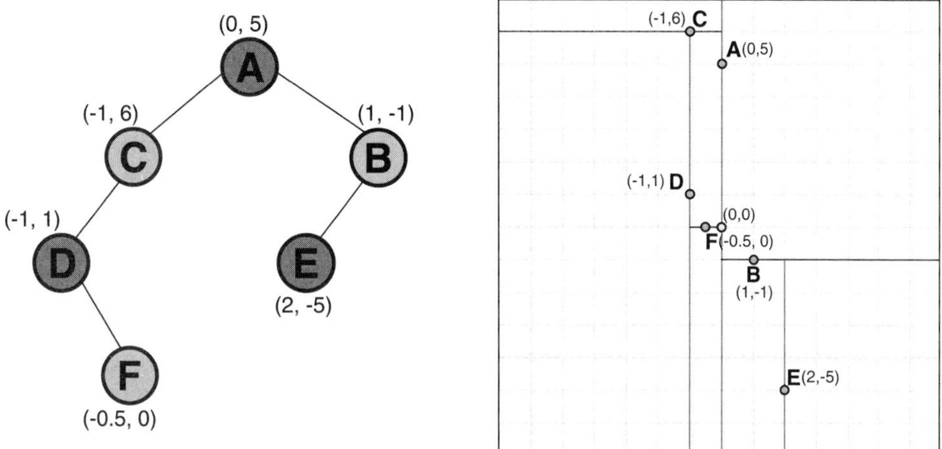
(0, 5)
A
(-1, 6)
C
(1, -1)
B
(-1, 1)
D
E
(2, -5)
F
(-0.5, 0)
(-1,6) C
A(0,5)
(-1,1) D
(0,0)
F(-0.5, 0)
B
(1,-1)
E(2,-5)

Figure 9.8 An example k-d tree for a 2-D dataset. On the left, the tree representation. On the right, a visualization of (a portion of) the 2-D Cartesian plane, where the origin is at the center of the square. The vertical lines pass through nodes A, D, and E and correspond to splits along the `x` coordinate. The horizontal lines are drawn through nodes B, C, and F, and correspond to splits along the `y` coordinate.

We will start with the "easy" methods first: `search` and `insert` work almost exactly as in basic BSTs; we will still describe them and provide their pseudo-code, but if you are already familiar with binary search trees, feel free to skim through the next few sub-sections.

But before that, we need to define a model for the k-d tree and its nodes; see listing 9.1.

Listing 9.1 The `KdTree` class

```
class KdNode
  #type tuple(k)
  point
  #type KdNode
  left
  #type KdNode
  right
  #type integer
  level
  function KdNode(point, left, right, level)

class KdTree
```

```
#type KdNode
root
#type integer
k
function KdTree(points=[])
```

A `KdTree` just contains a root node and a constructor method, taking an optional array of points as input. We'll take a look at how a k-d tree can be constructed later, after we introduce the insertion method. For now, suffice it to say that it will set the root to either a void entry (be it `null`, a special instance of `KdNode`, or whatever is more appropriate for the language used).

For the sake of convenience, let's assume a tree also stores the value `k`, the dimension of the space on which the tree is defined.

The root is, as said, an instance of `KdNode`. This data structure models a node of a BST, with its left and right children, and its value, a point in the `k`-dimensional space. We will use the special value `null` to model an empty node (and thus an empty tree).

9.3.1 Search

In section 9.2 we have implicitly described how search works on k-d trees. There is nothing fancy in this algorithm; it's just a regular search on binary search trees storing tuples, with the caveat that instead of comparing the whole tuple at each step, we only use one coordinate. At level `i`, we compare the `i`-th coordinate (or `i mod k, if i ≥ k`).

Listing 9.2 shows a few helper functions that will help us keeping our code clean. We encapsulate in these functions the logic of cycling through split coordinates while traversing the tree, instead of duplicating it across all the methods. This way the other methods will be more readable, and if we ever have to change the way this comparison is done (for instance, because we find a bug or we want to implement a fancier algorithm), we just need to touch one single place in the code base.

Listing 9.2 Helper functions

```
function getNodeKey(node)
  return getPointKey(node.point, node.level)

function getPointKey(point, level)
  j ← level % k
  return point[j]

function compare(point, node)
  return sign(getPointKey(point, node.level) - getNodeKey(node))
```

Given a tree node, returns the value of the coordinate that needs to be used, given the level at which the node is stored

In turn, it calls the function extracting this value from the node point.

Given a point (a tuple with `k` values) and an index for the level, returns the tuple entry that should be used in comparisons for nodes at that level

Just returns the correct tuple entry

We assume the method has access to `k`, the dimension of the tree. At level `i`, we need to extract the tuple value at index `i mod k` (0-based indexing).

Compares a point to a node, returning 0 if the node's point matches the first argument, a value lower than 0 if the point is on the "left" of the node, greater than 0 otherwise

The `sign` function returns the sign of a numeric value: -1 for negative values, +1 for positive ones, or 0.

Computes the distance between a point and its projection on the split line passing through a node

This distance is nothing other than the absolute value of the difference between the `j`-th coordinates of the two points, where `j = node.level mod k`.

```
function splitDistance(point, node)
  return abs(getPointKey(point, node.level) - getNodeKey(node))
```

Listing 9.3 shows the pseudo-code for the search method. The pseudo-code for all these methods will assume that we are providing an internal version that takes a `KdNode` as argument. The public API for `KdTree` will provide adapter methods that will call the internal ones; for instance `KdTree::search(target)` will call `search(root, target)`.

Listing 9.3 The `search` method

Search returns the tree node that contains a target point, if the point is stored in the tree; it returns `null` otherwise. We explicitly pass the root of the (sub)tree we want to search so we can reuse this function for subtrees.

If the `node` is already `null`, we are traversing an empty tree, and by definition it does not contain any point.

If the target point matches this node's point, then we have found what we are looking for.

```
function search(node, target)
  if node == null then
    return null
  elsif node.point == target then
    return node
  elsif compare(target, node) < 0 then
    return search(node.left, target)
  else
    return search(node.right, target)
```

Otherwise, we need to compare the appropriate coordinates of target and node's point. We use the helper method previously defined, and check if it is lower than 0, which would mean that we have to take a left turn during tree traversal, and therefore we run the method recursively on the left or right branch.

This way we have more flexibility in reusing these methods (for instance, we can run search on just a subtree, not the whole tree).

Notice that this recursive implementation is eligible for tail-recursion optimization on those languages and compilers supporting it (check appendix E for an explanation of tail-recursion).

Let's follow the example in figure 9.9 step by step.

We start by calling `search(A, (-1.5, -2))`, where node `A` is the root of the k-d tree, as shown in the figure. Since `A` is not `null`, at line #2 the condition fails, and we can compare `A.point`, which is the tuple `(0, 5)`, to our target at line #4. They obviously don't match, so we move on to line #6 and use the `compare` helper function to check which direction we should take. `A.level` will evaluate to `0`, so we compare the first value in each of the tuples: `-1.5 < 0`, so we traverse the left subtree and call `search(C, (-1.5, -2))`.

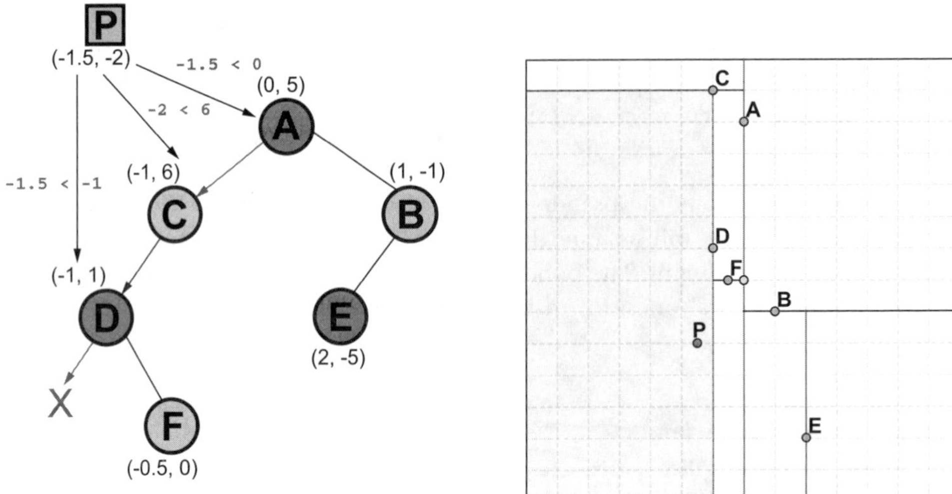
P
(-1.5, -2)
-1.5 < 0
-2 < 6
-1.5 < -1
(0, 5)
A
(-1, 6)
C
(1, -1)
B
(-1, 1)
D
E
(2, -5)
X
F
(-0.5, 0)
C
A
D
F
B
P
E

Figure 9.9 An example of an unsuccessful search on a k-d tree (2-D). The searched point, `P`, would ideally lie in the region highlighted on the bottom left, which corresponds to the left subtree of node `D`.

For this call, we repeat more or less the same steps, except this time `C.level` is equal to 1, so we compare the second value in each tuple. `-2 < 6` so we still go left, calling `search(D, (-1.5, -2))`.

Once again, we go through lines #2, #4, and #6, and we take a left turn; only this time, `D.left == null`, so we call `search(null, (-1.5, -2))`, which will return `null` at line #2. The execution backtracks through the call stack, and our original call will also return `null`, stating that the target point was not found on the k-d tree.

Figure 9.10 shows another example, calling `search(A, (2, -5))`. On the first call, conditions at lines #2 and #4 are false, as well as the condition at line #6, since `2 > 0`. This time, therefore, we take a right turn at node `A`, and recursively call `search(B, (2, -5))`, then in turn `search(E, (2, -5))`, for which the condition at line #4 is true (`E.point` matches target), and thus we finally return node `E` as the result of the original call.

How fast is `search` on a k-d tree? Like for regular BSTs, its running time is proportional to the height of the tree. If we keep the tree balanced, therefore, the running time will be `O(log(n))` for a tree holding `n` points.

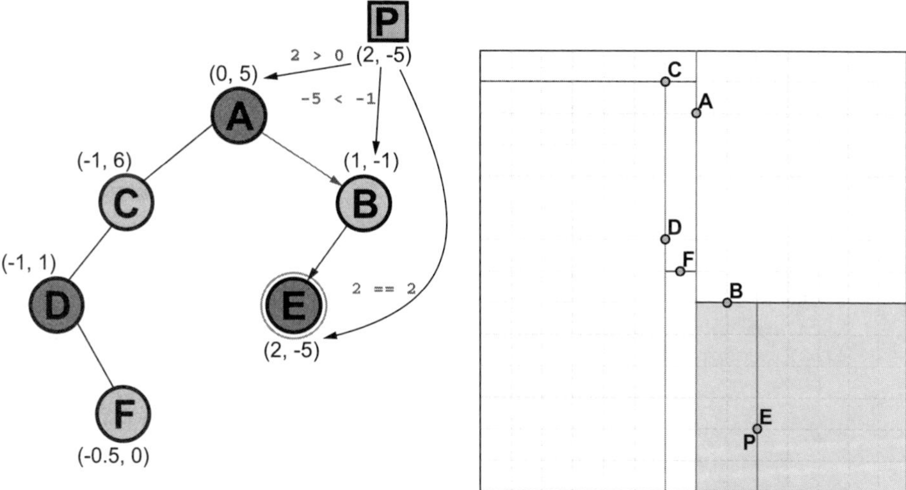
P
2 > 0 (2, -5)
(0, 5)
-5 < -1
A
(-1, 6)
(1, -1)
C
B
(-1, 1)
D
E
2 == 2
(2, -5)
F
(-0.5, 0)
C
A
D
F
B
E
P

Figure 9.10 An example of a successful search on a k-d tree (2-D). Here points `P` and `E` are coincident, and the highlighted region corresponds to the subtree rooted at node `E`.

9.3.2 *Insert*

As we have seen on BSTs, insertion can be implemented in two steps. The first step is running a search for the point to add, which will either find that the point is already in the tree, or stop at its parent-to-be, the node to which the new point should be added as a child. If the point is already in the tree, then what we do next depends on the policy we adopt on duplicates. If duplicates are not allowed, we might ignore the new point or fail; otherwise we have a wide range of solutions, from using a counter on nodes to keep track of how many times a point was added, up to consistently adding duplicates to either branch of a node—for instance, always in the left sub-branch, although as we have seen in appendix C, this leads to slightly unbalanced trees on average.

If, instead, the point was not on the tree, search will fail on the node that should have the new point as its child, and the second step will consist of creating a new node for the point and adding it in the correct branch of its parent.

Listing 9.4 shows an approach that doesn't reuse the `search` method. This approach, while not DRY,[4] allows us to simplify both methods. To be reusable in `insert`, `search` should also return the parent of the node found (and even more importantly, the last node traversed, when the target is not found), which is not of any particular use for `search`, whose implementation would thus become unnecessarily complicated. Moreover, this way we can write insert in a more elegant way, using a pattern that naturally supports immutability.[5]

---

[4] Don't Repeat Yourself. In this case we have some code duplication that makes the code slightly less maintainable.

[5] Immutability of data structures is a key point of functional programming. It has several advantages, from being intrinsically thread-safe to easier debugging. While this code doesn't implement an immutable data structure, it can be easily changed to adhere to that pattern.

Listing 9.4 The insert method

Inserts a point on the tree. The method will return a pointer to the root of the (sub)tree containing the new point. The level to which the node is added is set to 0 by default.

If node is null, we are traversing an empty tree, so we have performed an unsuccessful search. We can therefore create a new node and return it, so the caller can store a reference to it. Notice how this also works when the tree is empty, creating and returning a new root.

```
function insert(node, newPoint, level=0)
  if node == null then
    return new KdNode(newPoint, null, null, level)
  elsif node.point == newPoint then
    return node
  elsif compare(newPoint, node) < 0 then
    node.left ← insert(node.left, newPoint, node.level + 1)
    return node
  else
    node.right ← insert(node.right, newPoint, node.level + 1)
    return node
```

If the new point matches this node's point, we ran a successful search and we have a duplicate. Here, we will just ignore duplicates, but you can handle it by changing these lines.

Otherwise, we need to compare the coordinates of `target` and `node`'s point: we use the helper method previously defined, and check if it is lower than 0, which would mean we have to take a left turn during tree traversal, and therefore we run the method recursively on the left branch, setting the result as the new left (or right) child of the current node.

Figures 9.11 and 9.12 show two examples of insertion of new points on the k-d tree in figure 9.10.

Let's follow the first example step by step. It starts with a call to `insert(A, (-1.5, 2))`, where we don't pass any value for `level`, thus defaulting it to the right value for root (as defined in the function signature, this value is `0`).

`A <> null`, so the condition at line #2 won't match; `A.point <> (-1.5, 2)`, and also at line #4 the condition is `false`. When we get to line #6, `-1.5 < 0`, so `compare` will return `-1`, and we traverse the left subtree and call `insert(C, (-1.5, -2), 1)`.

The next few calls will proceed similarly (like we have seen for `search`), and in turn we call `insert(D, (-1.5, -2), 2)`, `insert(null, (-1.5, -2), 3)`. For the latter, the condition at line #2 will be true, so we create a new node, `KdNode((-1.5, -2), null, null, 3)`, and return it to the previous call in the stack trace. There, at line #7, we set `.left` to this new `KdNode` we created, and then return `D`.

Notice how at line #6 we are breaking ties by partitioning coordinates with the same value as the current node on its right. This decision might seem of little importance, but we will see that it's a big deal when it comes to deleting nodes.

If we take a look at the stack trace for the example in figure 9.12, we can see how it is entirely similar to the one for the previous case:

```
insert(A, (2.5, -3))
  insert(B, (-1.5, 2), 1)
    insert(E, (-1.5, 2), 2)
     insert(null, (-1.5, 2), 3)
     return new KdNode((-1.5, 2), null, null, 3)
    return E
  return B
return A
```

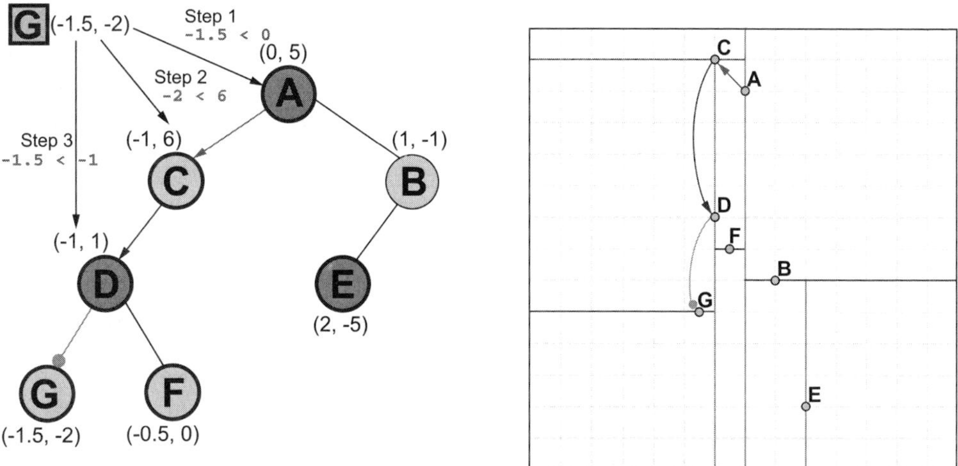
G (-1.5, -2)
Step 1
-1.5 < 0
(0, 5)
Step 2
-2 < 6
Step 3
-1.5 < -1
(-1, 6)
(1, -1)
(-1, 1)
(2, -5)
(-1.5, -2)
(-0.5, 0)
A
B
C
D
E
F
G

Figure 9.11 Inserting a new point on a k-d tree (2-D). To the k-d tree in figure 9.10 we add a new point G. Insertion, like for BSTs, consists of a (unsuccessful) search, after which we can identify the node that will be the parent of the node to add. If the new point already exists on the tree, your conflict resolution policy might lead you to ignore the duplicate or handle it properly.

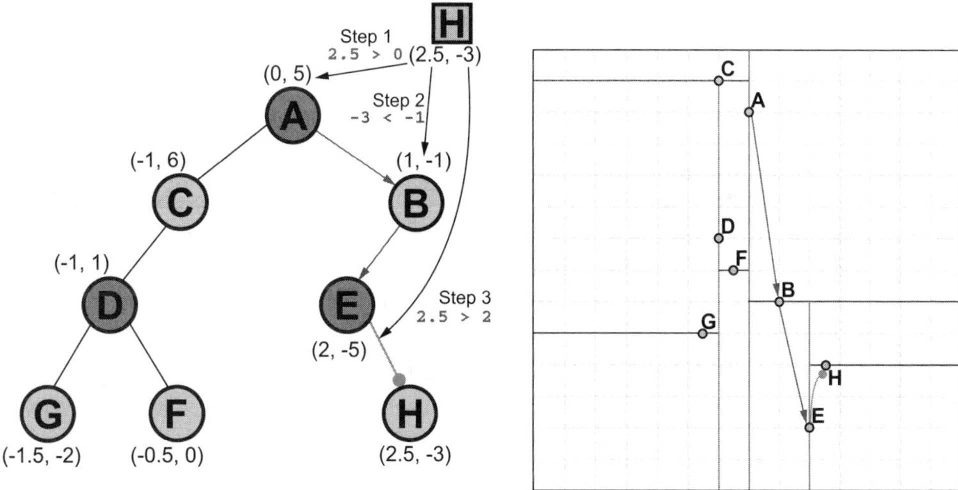
H
Step 1
2.5 > 0
(2.5, -3)
(0, 5)
Step 2
-3 < -1
(-1, 6)
(1, -1)
(-1, 1)
Step 3
2.5 > 2
(2, -5)
(-1.5, -2)
(-0.5, 0)
(2.5, -3)
A
B
C
D
E
F
G
H

Figure 9.12 Another example of inserting a new point on a k-d tree (2-D). The starting point is the k-d tree resulting after the insertion in figure 9.11.

9.3.3 *Balanced tree*

Before moving on to the most advanced methods designed for k-d trees, let's take a step back. In section 9.2.3 we have already described one key point of k-d trees. We need our tree to be balanced. In the previous sections we saw how search and insertion have running time `O(h)` proportional to the height of the tree, and thus having a balanced tree will mean that `h = log(n)`, and in turn that all these methods will run in logarithmic time.

Unfortunately, a k-d tree is not a self-balancing tree, like RB-trees or 2-3-trees, for example. This means that if we perform a large number of insertions and deletions on a tree, on average the tree will be tendentially balanced, but we have no guarantee of that. Moreover, if we resolve ties on coordinate comparison by always going to the same side, then it is proven that we will break the balance over many operations.

To solve this problem, we can slightly change the `compare` method that we defined in listing 9.2 so that it will never return 0. Whenever we have a match, half of the time it will return -1, and half of the time +1, thereby achieving a better balance for the tree. The choice needs to be consistent, so we can't use randomness and have a perfect balance; instead, a possible solution to implement this correction, as shown in listing 9.5, is to return -1 when the node's level is even, and +1 when it's odd (or vice versa; it doesn't really matter, as long as it's consistent).

Listing 9.5 Revised compare

```
function compare(point, node)
  s ← sign(getPointKey(point, node.level) - getNodeKey(node))
  if s == 0 then
    return node.level % 2 == 0 ? -1 : +1
  else
    return s
```

- The signature of the method remains unchanged.
- We store the value of the sign of the difference between the components, that is, what was computed by the old method.
- If this value is 0, meaning that the value of the coordinate compared is the same, then we go left half of the time, and right the other half. Otherwise, we just return the sign that will be either 1 or -1.

This helps us to achieve a better-balanced tree on average, but still doesn't provide any guarantee. To date, there is not a solution to easily keep a k-d tree balanced while maintaining `O(h)` running time for insertion.

Nevertheless, if we know the set of points to insert in advance (when we create the k-d tree), then we can find an optimal order of insertion that allows us to construct a balanced tree. If the tree is not changed after construction, or if the number of elements inserted/deleted is negligible in comparison to the size of the tree, then we can have a worst-case balanced k-d tree, and `insert` and `search` will run in worst-case logarithmic time.

Listing 9.6 shows the algorithm to create a balanced k-d tree from a set of points.

Listing 9.6 Balanced construction

```
function constructKdTree(points, level=0)
  if size(points) == 0 then
```

- Constructs a k-d tree from a set of `points`. We also pass the level, so we can recursively call this method for subtrees.
- If `points` is empty, we need to create an empty node, so we just return `null`.

If `points` has just one element, we can create a leaf, a node without children, so recursion stops here.

Otherwise, we first find the median of the set of points and its left and right partitions. We use a method, not shown here for the sake of space, similar to quicksort's partition—just operating on one of the coordinates at a time (the coordinate whose index is given by level).

```
    return null
  elsif size(points) == 1 then
    return new KdNode(points[0], null, null, level)
  else
    (median, left, right) ← partition(points, level)
    leftTree ← constructKdTree(left, level + 1)
    rightTree ← constructKdTree(right, level + 1)
    return new KdNode(median, leftTree, rightTree, level)
```

Recursively constructs k-d trees for the left and right partitions

Finally, the root of this tree is created, assigning the left and right subtrees previously created.

The principle is simple: the tree has to hold all the points in the set and, ideally, we would like left and right subtrees of the root to have the same number of elements. To achieve that, we can find the median in the set of points with respect to the first coordinate of the points, and use it as a pivot for the root, having half of the remaining points that will end up on the root's left branch, and half on its right branch. But each of the branches of the root is a k-d tree itself, so it is possible to repeat the same step for the root's left and right subtrees, with the caveat that we need to find the medians comparing the second coordinates for each point, instead. And so on for each level of the tree; we just need to keep track of the depth of the recursion, which tells us in what level of the tree we currently are.

The key point in listing 9.6 is the call to the `partition` method at line #7. We need to pass `level` as an argument because it will tell us which coordinate we need to use to compare points. The result of this call will be a tuple with the median of the `points` array and two new arrays with `(n-1)/2` elements each, if `size(points) == n`.

Each point in `left` will be "smaller" (with respect to the coordinate at index `level % k`) than `median`, and each point in `right` will be "larger" than `median`; therefore, we can recursively construct both (balanced) subtrees using these two sets.

Notice that we can't just sort the array once and chunk it up into halves recursively, because at each level the sorting criteria change!

To understand how this works, let's consider a call to `constructKdTree([(0,5),(1,-1),(-1,6),(-0.5,0),(2,5),(2.5,3),(-1, 1),(-1.5,-2)])`.

The median for this set (with regard to the first coordinate, the median of all the first values of the tuples) is either `-0.5` or `0`: there is an even number of elements, so there are technically two medians. You can double-check the values by sorting the array.

Say we choose `-0.5` as the median; then we have

```
(median, left, right) ← (-0.5,0), [(-1, 1),(-1.5,-2),(-1,6)], [(1,-1),
➥ (2.5,3),(2,5)(0,5)]
```

So, at line #8 we call `constructKdTree([(-1, 1),(-1.5,-2),(-1,6)], 1)` to create the root's left subtree. This in turn will partition the sub-array, but comparing the second coordinates of each tuple, the median of `y` coordinates is 1, so we have

```
(median, left, right) ← (-1, 1), [(-1.5,-2)], [(-1,6)]
```

And so on; the method would similarly run on the other partitions created on the initial array.

What's the running time of method `constructKdTree`? We will use $T_k(n)$ to denote the running time for a k-d tree of dimension `k`, on an array with `n` elements. Let's check the method step by step: lines #2–5 only require a constant amount of time, as does line #10, which is just creating a new node. Lines #8 and #9 are recursive calls, and they will be called on sets of points with at most `n/2` elements, so we know they will take $T_k(n/2)$ steps each.

Finally, line #7, where we call `partition`: it's possible to find a median in linear time, and we can also partition an array of `n` elements around a pivot with `O(n)` swaps (or create two new arrays, also with `O(n)` total assignments).

So, summing up, we have this formula for the running time:

$$T_k(n) = 2 * T_k(n/2) + O(n)$$

There are a few ways to solve this equation—for example, the substitution method or telescoping—but the easiest is probably using master theorem.[6] All of these methods are beyond the scope for this book, so we will just provide you with the solution, leaving it to the curious reader to work out the details:

$$T_k(n) = O(n * \log(n))$$

In other words, the balanced construction method takes *linearithmic*[7] time.

To complete our analysis, if we look at the extra memory needed by this method, it will require `O(n)` memory for the tree. However, there is more. If we don't partition the array in place and create a copy for each left and right sub-array, then each call to a partition will use `O(n)` extra memory. Deriving a similar formula to the one for the running time, we could find out that also `M(n) = O(n * log(n))`.

Conversely, by partitioning the array in place, we can obtain the best possible result:

$$M_k(n) = O(n)$$

That's because we only need a constant amount of memory for the internals of the function, plus the `O(n)` memory needed for the tree.

---

[6] See https://en.wikipedia.org/wiki/Master_theorem_(analysis_of_algorithms).

[7] `n*log(n)` is often referred to as linearithmic, as a *crasis* of linear and logarithmic.

9.3.4 Remove

After search and insert, we can continue with the third basic operation on a container: remove. This is despite the fact that on a k-d tree, delete is not such a common operation, and some implementations don't even offer this method. As we discussed in the previous section, k-d trees are not self-balancing, so they perform best when they are created with a static set of points, avoiding frequent insertion and removal.

Nevertheless, in any real-world application you'll likely need to be able to update your dataset, so we are going to describe how to remove elements. Figures 9.13 and 9.14 show the remove method in action on our example k-d tree, and the result of removing point D from it.

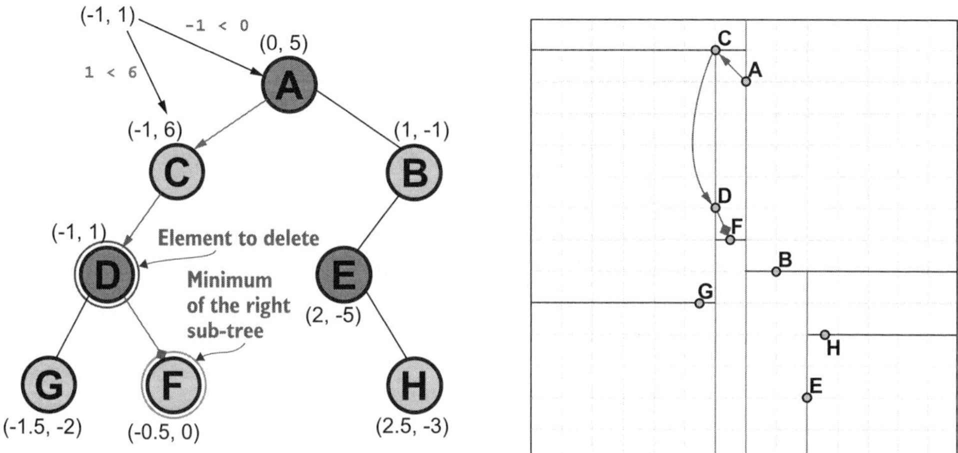
(-1, 1)
-1 < 0
(0, 5)
1 < 6
A
(-1, 6)
(1, -1)
C
B
(-1, 1)
Element to delete
D
E
Minimum
of the right
sub-tree
(2, -5)
G
F
H
(-1.5, -2)
(-0.5, 0)
(2.5, -3)
C
A
D
F
B
G
H
E

Figure 9.13 Deleting point D from our example k-d tree. Method remove, like for BSTs, consists of a (successful) search to find the node to remove, followed, if the node to remove is an internal node with at least one subtree, by a traversal to find an element with which it can be replaced. In this example, an internal node is removed.

Similarly to insert and search, this method is based on binary search tree removal. There are, however, two issues that make k-d tree's version sensibly more complicated, and they are both connected to how we find a replacement in the tree for the node we are going to remove.

To see what these issues are, we need to take a step back. In binary search trees, when we delete a node, we can face one of three situations (see figure 9.15).

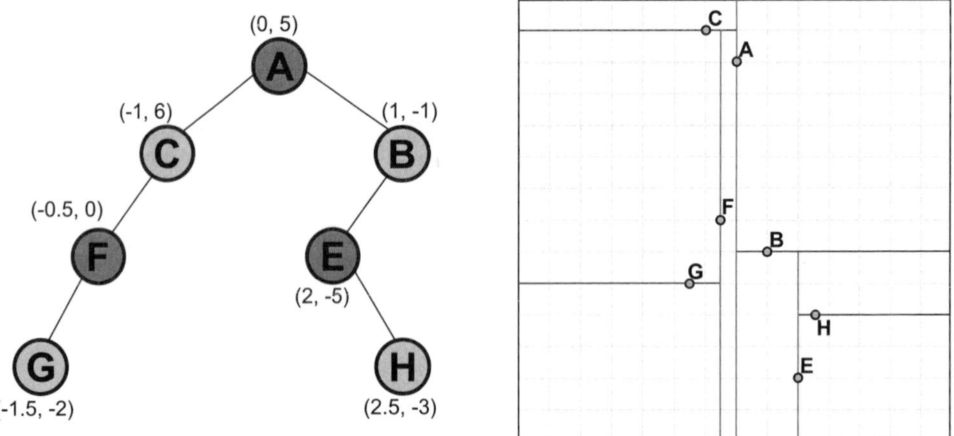
(0, 5)
A
(-1, 6)
C
(1, -1)
B
(-0.5, 0)
F
E
(2, -5)
G
H
(-1.5, -2)
(2.5, -3)
C
A
F
B
G
H
E

Figure 9.14 The k-d tree resulting after deleting point D

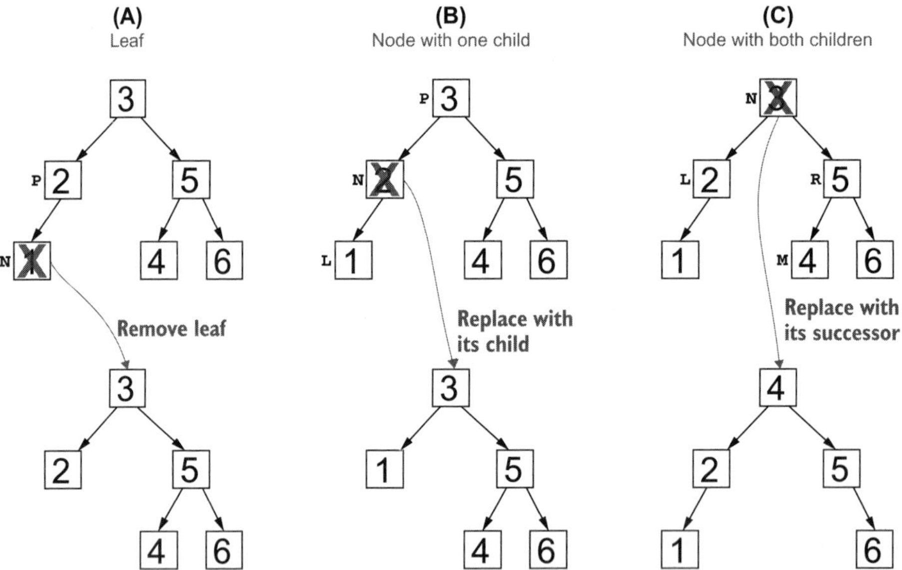
(A)
Leaf
(B)
Node with one child
(C)
Node with both children
Remove leaf
Replace with its child
Replace with its successor

Figure 9.15 Possible cases when deleting a node from a binary search tree. (A) Deleting a leaf. (B) Deleting a node with a single child. (Works symmetrically if the child is in the right branch). (C) Deleting a node with both children.

1 The node we need to remove is a leaf. In this situation, we can just safely remove the node from the tree, and we are done.

2 The node `N` to-be-removed has only one child. Here simply removing the node would disconnect the tree, but we can instead bypass it by connecting `N`'s parent to its children (independently of it being in the left or right subtree of `N`). This won't violate any invariant for the BST. For instance, in the case shown in figure 9.15B, `N` is a left child of its parent `P`, so it's smaller than or equal to `P`, but likewise, all elements in the subtree rooted at `N` will be smaller than or equal to `P`, including `N`'s child `L`.

3 If the node `N` that we need to remove has both children, we can't just replace it with one of its children (for instance, if we were to replace the root in figure 9.15C with its right child `R`, then we would have to merge `R`'s left child with `N`'s, and that would require worst-case linear time (and also be a waste).

   Instead, we can find the successor[8] of `N`. By construction, it will be the minimum node in its right subtree, let's call it `M`, which in turn means the leftmost node of its right subtree. Once we have found it, we can delete `M` and replace `N`'s value with `M`'s value. No invariant will be violated, because `M` was no smaller than `N`, and `N` in turn was no smaller than any node in its left subtree.

   Moreover, `M` will certainly configure as either case (A) or case (B), because being the left-most node, it won't have a left child. This means that deleting `M` will be easy and recursion stops at `M`.

When we move from regular BSTs to k-d trees, the first difference is caused by the fact that at each level we only use a single coordinate to partition points in the two branches. If we have to replace a node `N` at level `i`, at that level we are using coordinate `j = i mod k`, so we know its successor (for coordinate `j`) will be in `N`'s right subtree. However, when we move to `N`'s child, that node will use another coordinate, j_1 = `(i+1) mod k`, to partition its children. As you can see in figure 9.16, that means that the successor of `N` doesn't have to be in `R`'s left subtree.

That's bad news, because it means that while for BSTs we could quickly traverse `N`'s right subtree to its leftmost node in order to find `N`'s successor, now we can only do that for level `l` where `l mod k == i mod k`. In all the other levels, we will have to traverse both subtrees to look for the minimum.

Listing 9.7 shows the pseudo-code for the `findMin` method. The first difference you can see with respect to BST's version is that we need to pass the index of the coordinate for which we look for the minimum. For instance, we could call `findMin(root, 2)` to search the node in the whole tree with the minimum value for the third coordinate—assuming `k>=3`.

[8] Note that we could also use `N`'s predecessor in a symmetrical way.

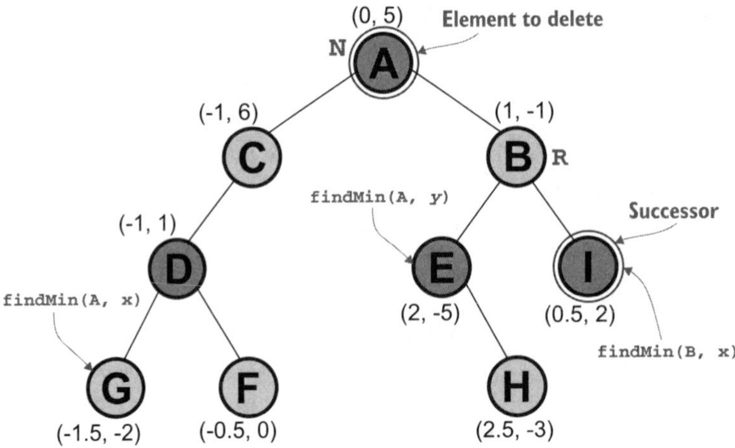

(0, 5)
Element to delete
N
A
(-1, 6)
C
(1, -1)
B
R
findMin(A, y)
Successor
(-1, 1)
D
E
I
findMin(A, x)
(2, -5)
(0.5, 2)
findMin(B, x)
G
F
H
(-1.5, -2)
(-0.5, 0)
(2.5, -3)

Figure 9.16 An example of how the successor of a node, or more generally the minimum of a subtree with respect to a certain coordinate, can lie anywhere in the subtree. The results of a few calls to `findMin` on the whole tree and on node `B` are explicitly shown.

Listing 9.7 The `findMin` method

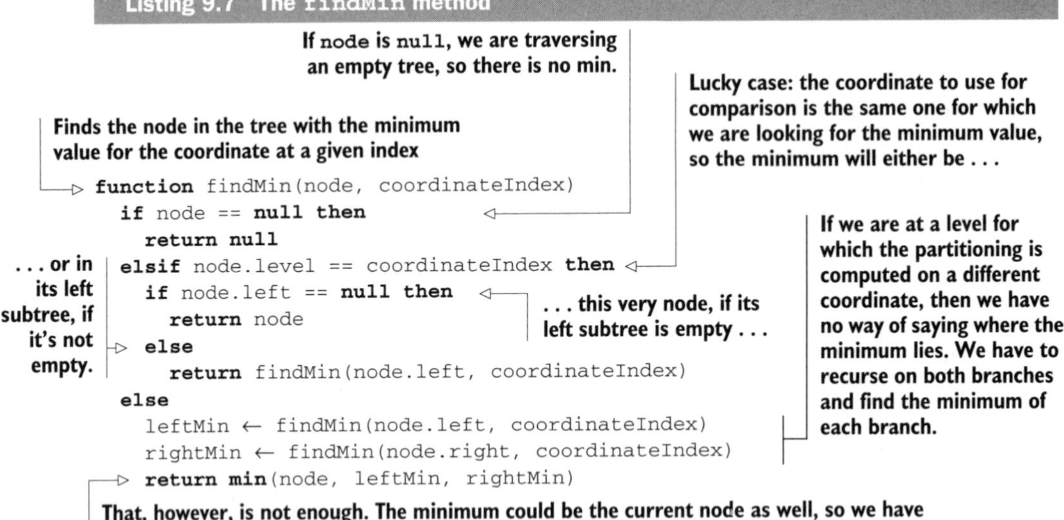

```
function findMin(node, coordinateIndex)
  if node == null then
    return null
  elsif node.level == coordinateIndex then
    if node.left == null then
      return node
    else
      return findMin(node.left, coordinateIndex)
  else
    leftMin ← findMin(node.left, coordinateIndex)
    rightMin ← findMin(node.right, coordinateIndex)
    return min(node, leftMin, rightMin)
```


Finds the node in the tree with the minimum value for the coordinate at a given index
If node is null, we are traversing an empty tree, so there is no min.
Lucky case: the coordinate to use for comparison is the same one for which we are looking for the minimum value, so the minimum will either be . . .
. . . this very node, if its left subtree is empty . . .
. . . or in its left subtree, if it's not empty.
If we are at a level for which the partitioning is computed on a different coordinate, then we have no way of saying where the minimum lies. We have to recurse on both branches and find the minimum of each branch.
That, however, is not enough. The minimum could be the current node as well, so we have to compare these three values. We assume that function min here is an overload that takes nodes as input and handles null by considering it to be larger than any non-null node.

This greater complexity in the `findMin` method unfortunately reflects on its running time. It can't be logarithmic as with BSTs because we are traversing all branches for all levels except the ones matching `coordinateIndex`, so in `(k-1)/k` cases.

And, in fact, it turns out that the running time for `findMin` is `O(n^((k-1)/k))`. If `k==2`, this means `O(n^(1/2)) = O(√n)`, which is not as good as logarithmic, but still sensibly better than a full scan. As `k` grows, though, this value gets closer and closer to `O(n)`.

The enhanced version of `findMin` solves the issue with the coordinates. Now you might hope that plugging it into the regular BST's `remove` is enough, but that's unfortunately not the case. There is another issue that complicates things a bit further.

If you go back to figure 9.15 (B), for BSTs there were two lucky cases for which deleting a node was easy: deleting a leaf and deleting a node with only one child.

For k-d trees, only leaves can be deleted easily. Unfortunately, even if the node `N` to be deleted has only one child `C`, we can't just replace `N` with its child, because this would change the direction of the splits for `C` and its entire subtree, as shown in figure 9.17.

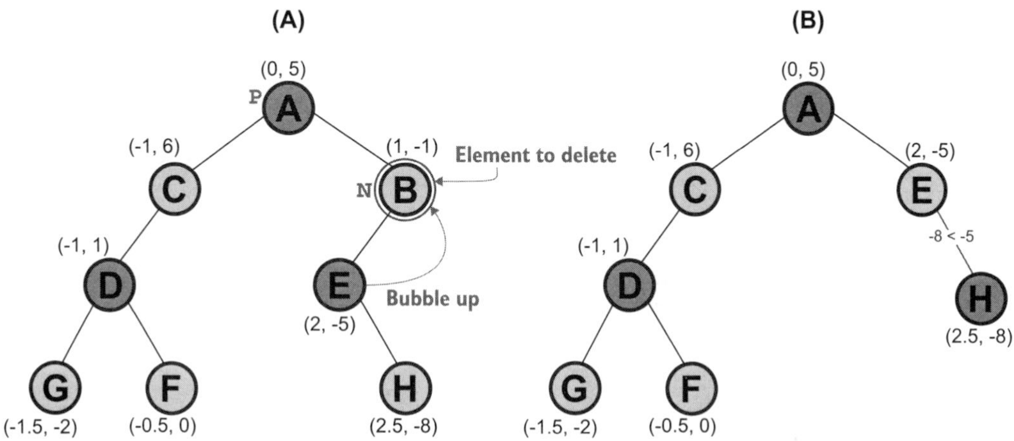
(A)
(B)
(0, 5)
P
A
(-1, 6)
C
(1, -1)
Element to delete
N
B
(-1, 1)
D
E
Bubble up
(2, -5)
G
F
H
(-1.5, -2)
(-0.5, 0)
(2.5, -8)
(0, 5)
A
(-1, 6)
C
(2, -5)
E
-8 < -5
(-1, 1)
D
H
(2.5, -8)
G
F
(-1.5, -2)
(-0.5, 0)

Figure 9.17 An example of a k-d tree deletion for which replacing the deleted node with its only child wouldn't work. (A) The initial tree, from which we remove node B. This node has only one child, so in a BST it would just be replaced by its child. (B) However, in a k-d tree this might cause violation of the k-d tree invariants, because moving a node one level up changes the coordinate on which the split is performed, when using it as a pivot.

In that example, we attempt to remove node `B`, which only has one child and no right branch (it works similarly in the symmetric case). If we tried to simply replace `B` with its children `E`, this node would appear one level up in the tree, and likewise all its children.

So, before node `E` was using `x` coordinates to partition nodes in its subtree, so that node `H` was on the right of `E` because `H`'s `x` coordinate `(2.5)` is larger than `E`'s `(2)`.

After we move `E` and its subtree up, we would need to use `y` coordinates to partition nodes in `E`'s subtree. But `H`'s `y` coordinate `(-8)` is larger than `E`'s `(-5)`, so node `H` doesn't belong to `E`'s right branch anymore, and the k-d tree invariants are violated.

In this case it might look like something easy to fix, but we would need to reevaluate every single node in `E`'s subtree and rebuild it.

This would certainly require `O(n)` time, where `n` is the number of nodes in the subtree rooted at the node we remove.

A better solution would be to replace the node `N` that we want to remove with its successor or its predecessor. If `N` only has a right child, we can just find its successor using `findMin`, as we described in the example in figure 9.16.

When node `N` only has a left child, can we replace it with its predecessor? As much as you might be tempted to think so, in this situation another issue comes up.

We mentioned when we described the `insert` method that the way we break ties on `insert` has an influence on the `remove` method as well.

And indeed, figure 9.18 shows an example where this becomes relevant. The problem is that when we break ties on `insert` and `search` by going right, we implicitly assume an invariant:[9] that for any internal node `N`, no node in its left branch will have the same value for the coordinate used to partition `N`'s subtree. In figure 9.18, this means that no node in the left branch of node `B` has a `y` coordinate equal to `N`'s.

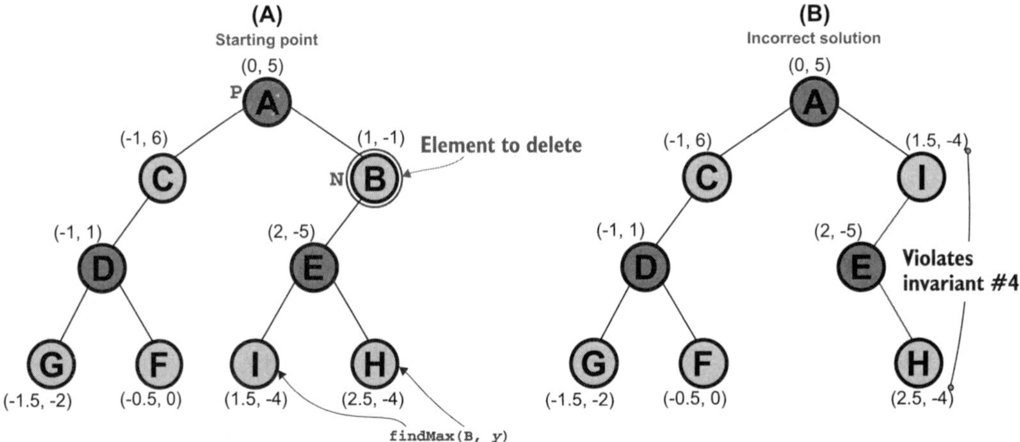
(A)
Starting point
(0, 5)
P
A
(-1, 6)
C
(1, -1)
Element to delete
N
B
(-1, 1)
D
(2, -5)
E
G
F
I
H
(-1.5, -2)
(-0.5, 0)
(1.5, -4)
(2.5, -4)
findMax(B, y)
(B)
Incorrect solution
(0, 5)
A
(-1, 6)
C
(1.5, -4)
I
(-1, 1)
D
(2, -5)
E
Violates invariant #4
G
F
H
(-1.5, -2)
(-0.5, 0)
(2.5, -4)

Figure 9.18 An example showing why, when we delete a node with only a left child, we can't replace the current node with the minimum of the left branch. On the right, we can see how `H` causes the fourth invariant of k-d trees to be violated, because it is on the left branch of node `I`, but has the same value for `I`'s split coordinate.

If we replace `N` with the max of its left branch, however, it is possible that in `N`'s old left branch there was another node with the same `y` coordinate. In our example, that would be the case since there are two nodes with the same maximal value for `y`, node `I` and node `H`.

By moving node `I` to replace `B`, we would therefore break search, because node `H` would never be found by the `search` method in listing 9.3.

Luckily the solution is not too complicated. We can instead run `findMin` on the left branch, replace `N`'s point with the node `M` found by `findMin`, and set `N`'s old left branch as the right branch of this new node we are creating, as shown in figure 9.19.

[9] This is implied by invariant 4 as described in section 9.2.2

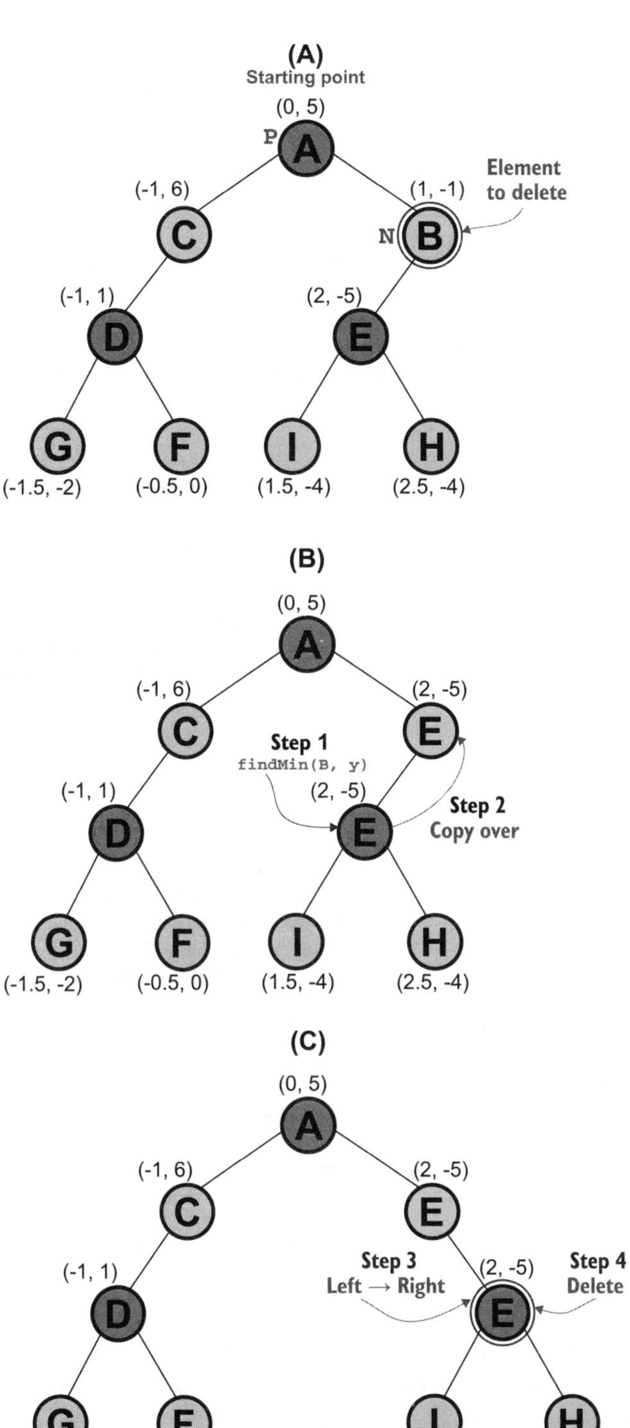
(A)
Starting point
(0, 5)
P
A
(-1, 6)
(1, -1)
Element to delete
C
N
B
(-1, 1)
(2, -5)
D
E
G
F
I
H
(-1.5, -2)
(-0.5, 0)
(1.5, -4)
(2.5, -4)
(B)
(0, 5)
A
(-1, 6)
(2, -5)
C
E
Step 1
findMin(B, y)
(-1, 1)
(2, -5)
Step 2
Copy over
D
E
G
F
I
H
(-1.5, -2)
(-0.5, 0)
(1.5, -4)
(2.5, -4)
(C)
(0, 5)
A
(-1, 6)
(2, -5)
C
E
Step 3
Left → Right
(2, -5)
Step 4
Delete
(-1, 1)
D
E
G
F
I
H
(-1.5, -2)
(-0.5, 0)
(1.5, -4)
(2.5, -4)

Figure 9.19 Correct steps for deleting a node `N` with only a left child. In figure 9.18, we saw that finding the max of the left branch won't work. Instead, we need to find the min `M`, use it to replace the deleted node, and then set `N`'s old left branch as the new node's right branch. Then we only need to remove `M` from the left branch, which requires a new call to remove. (As you can see, unfortunately we can make no assumptions on this call; it might cascade and require more recursive calls to remove.)

Then we just need to remove the old node M from that right branch. Notice that unlike what happened with binary search trees, we can make no assumptions on M here, so we might need to repeat these steps in the recursive call deleting M.

Listing 9.8 sums up all these considerations into a pseudo-code implementation for method remove.

Listing 9.8 The remove method

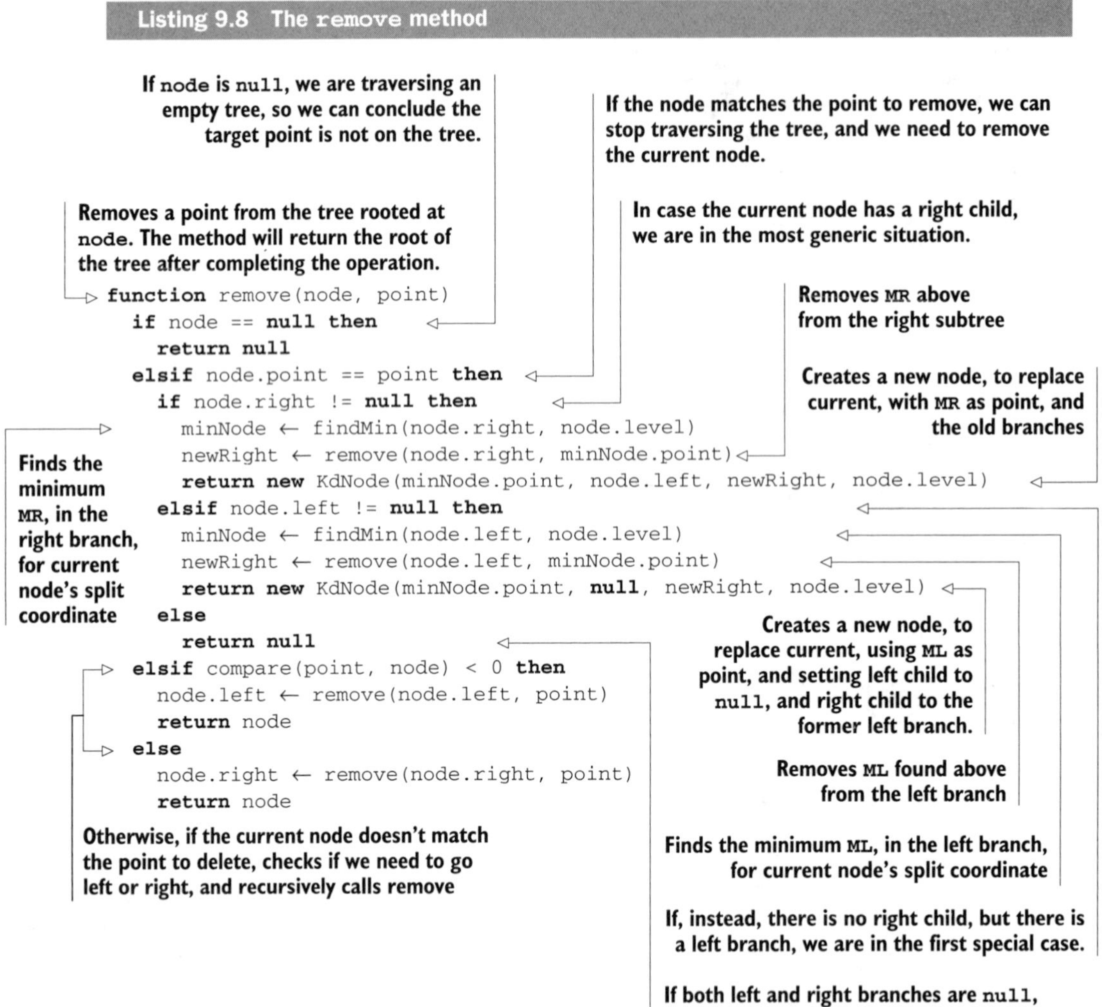
If node is null, we are traversing an empty tree, so we can conclude the target point is not on the tree.
If the node matches the point to remove, we can stop traversing the tree, and we need to remove the current node.
Removes a point from the tree rooted at node. The method will return the root of the tree after completing the operation.
In case the current node has a right child, we are in the most generic situation.
Removes MR above from the right subtree
Creates a new node, to replace current, with MR as point, and the old branches
Finds the minimum MR, in the right branch, for current node's split coordinate
Creates a new node, to replace current, using ML as point, and setting left child to null, and right child to the former left branch.
Removes ML found above from the left branch
Otherwise, if the current node doesn't match the point to delete, checks if we need to go left or right, and recursively calls remove
Finds the minimum ML, in the left branch, for current node's split coordinate
If, instead, there is no right child, but there is a left branch, we are in the first special case.
If both left and right branches are null, we are at a leaf, so we can just remove it.

```
function remove(node, point)
  if node == null then
    return null
  elsif node.point == point then
    if node.right != null then
      minNode ← findMin(node.right, node.level)
      newRight ← remove(node.right, minNode.point)
      return new KdNode(minNode.point, node.left, newRight, node.level)
    elsif node.left != null then
      minNode ← findMin(node.left, node.level)
      newRight ← remove(node.left, minNode.point)
      return new KdNode(minNode.point, null, newRight, node.level)
    else
      return null
  elsif compare(point, node) < 0 then
    node.left ← remove(node.left, point)
    return node
  else
    node.right ← remove(node.right, point)
    return node
```

If we look at the running time for remove, the cost of the calls to findMin drives up the total cost, which thus can't be logarithmic anymore (as it was for BSTs). To perform a more rigorous analysis, let's again denote as $T_k(n)$ the running time for this method, where k is the dimensionality of the points' space and n is the number of nodes in the tree. When we look more closely at each conditional fork, if we assume that we are working on a balanced tree, then

- Each branch of the conditional at line #15 would trigger a recursive call on approximately half the nodes, and so require time $T_k(n/2)$.
- If we enter the code blocks after conditionals at lines #2 or #13, those only require constant time.
- Conditionals at lines #5 and #9 both will run code blocks that requires creating a new node, $O(1)$, running `findMin`, $O(n^{1-1/k})$, and recursively calls `remove`.

The worst case here is the latter: we don't know where the minimum node will be in its branch. It could be far down the tree or just the root of the branch; thus, if we end up in a case similar to figure 9.17 (either with a missing left or right branch, indifferently), we might have to call `remove` recursively on `n-1` nodes, in the absolute worst case.

However, we assumed that our k-d tree is balanced. Under this assumption, left and right branches should have more or less the same number of nodes, and therefore if the right branch of a node is empty, the probability that the left branch has one node is still high, that it has two nodes is less likely, and it goes down with three nodes, and so on. For a certain constant, for example 5, we can say that in a situation like the one in figure 9.17, where a node has a single branch, then it is highly unlikely that branch has more than a constant number of nodes (say five). And we can thus assume that in a balanced tree, such an imbalanced case can happen at most a constant number of times during a call to `remove`. Or, more precisely, on a large number of removals, we can assume that the amortized cost of running the code blocks starting at lines #5 and #9 would be $T_k(n/2)$.

Our recurrence would therefore become

$$T_k(n) = T_k(n/2) + O(n^{1-1/k})$$

Using the master theorem's third case, since $1-1/k > \log_2(1)=0$, and $(n/2)^{1-1/k} \leq n^{1-1/k}$, we can then conclude that the amortized time required by `remove` on a balanced k-d tree is

$$T_k(n) = O(n^{1-1/k})$$

In other words, `remove`'s running time is dominated by `findMin`; this also means that in a 2-D space, the amortized running time for `remove` would be $O(\sqrt{n})$.

9.3.5 Nearest neighbor

We are now ready to study the most interesting operation provided by k-d trees, the nearest neighbor (NN) search. First, we are going to restrict to the case where we search for the single closest point in the dataset with respect to a target point (which, in general, doesn't have to be contained in the same dataset). Later we will generalize this operation to return an arbitrary number `m`[10] of points such that no other point in the dataset is closer to the target.

[10]This method is usually denoted as a k-nearest-neighbor search, but the use of `k` here could cause confusion with the dimension of the tree; hence we will just use `m` or `n` to indicate the number of points we look for.

In a brute-force scenario, we would have to compare each point in the dataset to our target, compute their relative distances, and keep track of the smallest one, exactly the way we search for an element in an unsorted array.

However, a k-d tree, much like a sorted array, has structural information about the relative distance and position of its elements, and we can leverage that information to perform our search more efficiently.

Listing 9.9 shows the pseudo-code implementing nearest neighbor search. To understand this code, however, we first need to ask, how does nearest neighbor search work?

Listing 9.9 The `nearestNeighbor` method

```
function nearestNeighbor(node, target, (nnDist, nn)=(inf, null))
  if node == null then
    return (nnDist, nn)
  else
    dist ← distance(node.point, target)
    if dist < nnDist then
      (nnDist, nn) ← (dist, node.point)
    if compare(target, node) < 0 then
      closeBranch ← node.left
      farBranch ← node.right
    else
      closeBranch ← node.right
      farBranch ← node.left
    (nnDist, nn) ← nearestNeighbor(closeBranch, target, (nnDist, nn))
    if splitDistance(target, node) < nnDist then
      (nnDist, nn) ← nearestNeighbor(farBranch, target, (nnDist, nn))
    return (nnDist, nn)
```

- Finds the closest point to a given target. We also pass the best values found so far for nearest neighbor (NN) and its distance to help pruning. These values default to `null`, `infinity` for a call on the tree root.
- If the `node` is `null`, we are traversing an empty tree, so the nearest neighbor can't change with respect to what we have already found.
- Otherwise, we have three tasks: check if the current node is closer than previously found NN, traverse the branch on the same side of the split with respect to the target point, and check if we can prune the other branch (or traverse it as well).
- We compute the distance between the current node's point and `target`.
- If that distance is less than the current NN's distance, we have to update the values stored for the NN and its distance.
- Checks if the target point is on the left branch of the split. If it is, the left branch is the closest to the target point, otherwise it is the furthest.
- We certainly need to traverse the closest branch in search of the nearest neighbor. It is important to do so first and update the mementos for NN's distance, to improve pruning.
- Using one of the helper functions defined in listing 9.2, we compute the distance between the split line passing through the current node and the target point. If this distance is closer than the distance to current nearest neighbor, then the furthest branch might contain points closer than the current nearest neighbor (see figure 9.21).
- Traverses the furthest branch and updates the current values for NN and its distance
- Returns the closest point found so far

We start from the consideration that each tree node covers one of the rectangular regions in which the space was partitioned, as we have shown in figures 9.5 and 9.6. So first we want to find which region contains our target point `P`. That's a good starting point for our search, because it's likely that the point stored in the leaf covering that region, `G` in this example, will be among the closest points to `P`.

Can we be sure that G will be the closest point to P, though? That would have been ideal, but unfortunately that's not the case. Figure 9.20 shows this first step in the algorithm, traversing a path in the tree from the root to a leaf, to find the smallest region containing P.

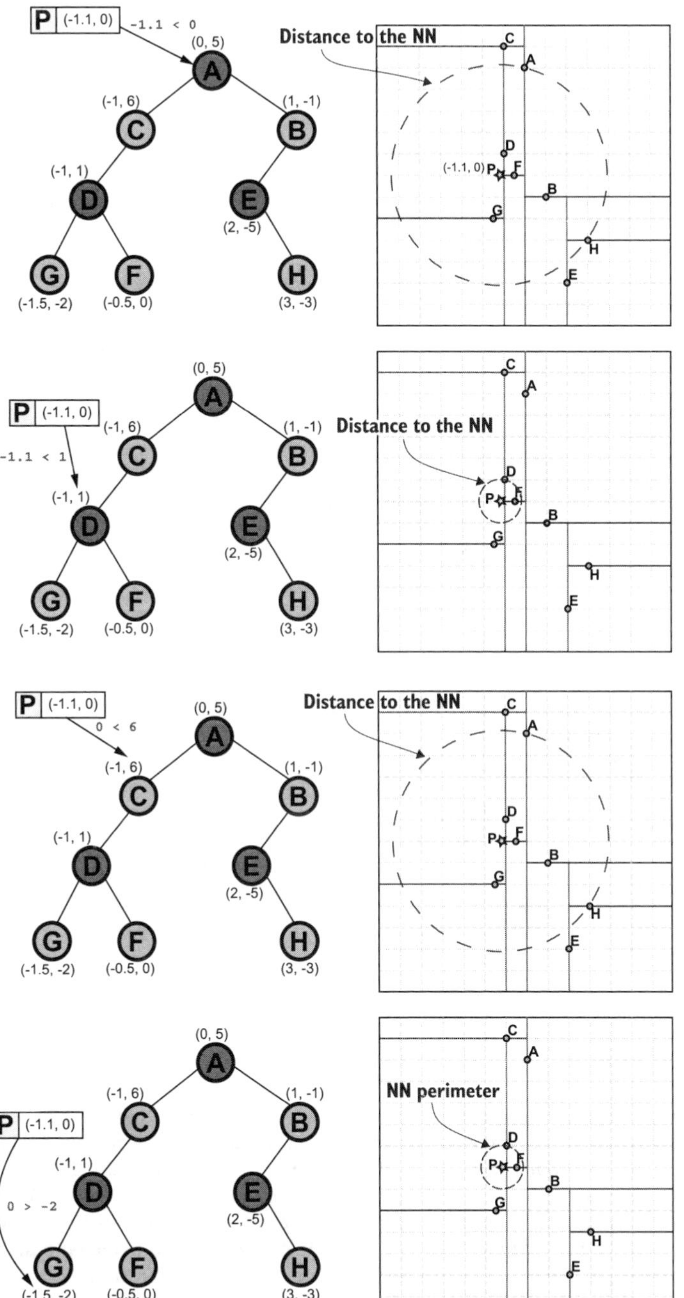
P (-1.1, 0)
-1.1 < 0
(0, 5)
A
(-1, 6)
C
(1, -1)
B
(-1, 1)
D
E
(2, -5)
G
F
H
(-1.5, -2)
(-0.5, 0)
(3, -3)
Distance to the NN
(-1.1, 0)
-1.1 < 1
0 < 6
NN perimeter
0 > -2

Figure 9.20 The first few steps of nearest neighbor search. The first phase of nearest neighbor search consists of a search on the tree, during which we keep track of the distance of each node (aka point) we traverse: more precisely, if we need to find N nearest neighbors for P, we need to keep track of the N smallest distances we find. In this case we are showing the query for N=1. Thus, if the search is successful, then we definitely have the nearest neighbor, at distance 0. Otherwise, when search ends, we are not yet sure we have found the actual nearest neighbor. In this example, the point at the minimum distance we have found during traversal is D but, as you can see from the figure, we can't be sure that another branch of the tree doesn't have a point within the radius given by dist(D).

As you can see, we check the distance of every intermediate point along the path, because any of them can be closer than the leaf. Even if intermediate points cover larger regions than leaves, inside each region we don't have any indication of where dataset points might lie. If we refer to figure 9.20, if point `A` had been at `(0,0)`, the tree would have had the same shape, but `P` would have been closer to `A` (the root) than `G` (a leaf).

But even that is not enough. After finding the region containing `P`, we can't be sure that in neighboring regions there aren't one or more points even closer than the closest point we found during this first traversal.

Figure 9.21 exemplifies this situation perfectly. So far, we have found that `D` is the closest point (among those visited) to `P`, so the real nearest neighbor can't be at a

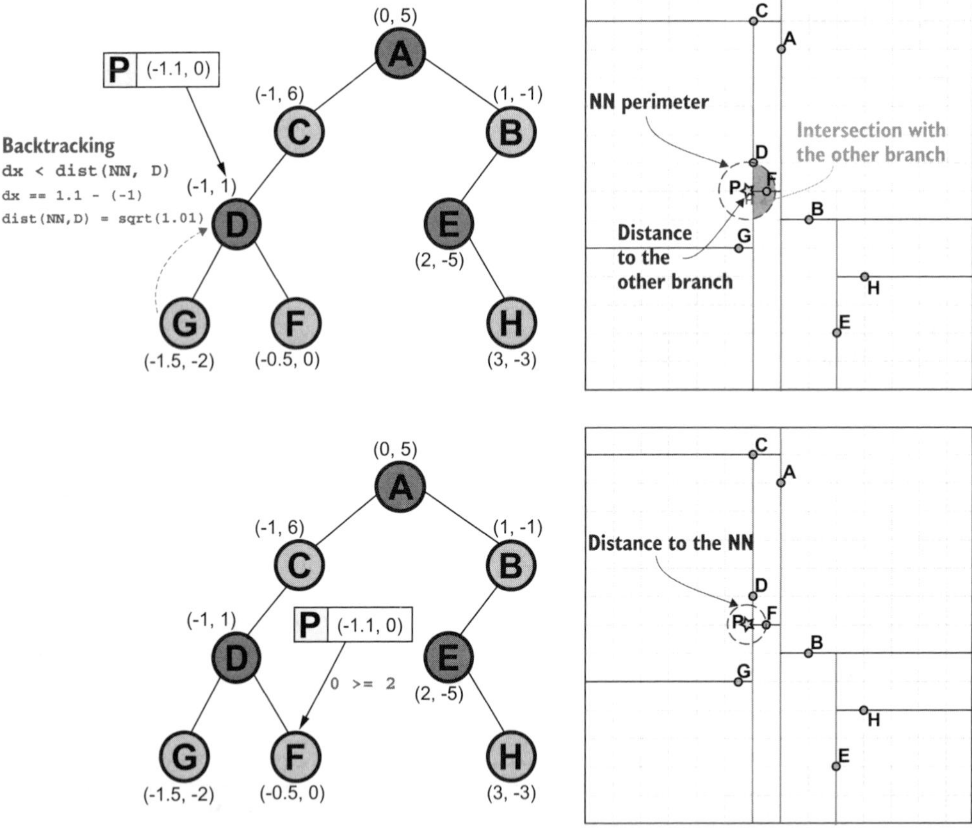

(0, 5)
A
P (-1.1, 0)
(-1, 6)
(1, -1)
C
B
Backtracking
dx < dist(NN, D)
dx == 1.1 - (-1)
dist(NN,D) = sqrt(1.01)
(-1, 1)
D
E
(2, -5)
G
F
H
(-1.5, -2)
(-0.5, 0)
(3, -3)
NN perimeter
Intersection with the other branch
Distance to the other branch
0 >= 2
Distance to the NN

Figure 9.21 The second step, after an unsuccessful search, is to backtrack to check other branches of the tree for closer points. It is possible to have such points because when we traverse the tree, we cycle through the coordinates that we compare at each level, so we don't always go in the direction of the closest point, but we are forced to go on one side of the pivot, depending only on a single coordinate. This means it is possible that the nearest neighbor is on the wrong side of the pivot with respect to our target point `P`. In this example, when we reached `D`, since it creates a vertical split, we needed to move to the left, as shown in figure 9.20. Unfortunately, the target point `P` and its nearest neighbor lie on opposite sides of the split line for `D`. So, once we reach the end of the path, we need to backtrack to check other branches.

distance larger than the one between D and P. We can thus trace a circle (a hyper-sphere, in higher dimensions) centered at P and with a radius equal to `dist(D, P)`. If this circle intersects other partitions, then those regions might contain a point closer than D, and we need to get to them.

How do we know if a region intersects our current nearest neighbor's hyper-sphere? That's simple: each region stems by the partitioning created by split lines. When traversing a path, we go on one side of the split (the one on the same side as P), but if the distance between a split line and P is less than the distance to our current nearest neighbor, then the hyper-sphere intersects the other partition as well.

To make sure we visit all partitions still intersecting the NN hyper-sphere, we need to backtrack our traversal of the tree. In our example, we go back to node D, then check the distance between P and the vertical split line passing through D (which, in turn, is just the difference of the x coordinates of the two points). Since this is smaller than the distance to D, our current NN, then we need to visit the other branch of D as well. When we say visit, we mean traversing the tree in a path from D to the closest leaf to P. While we do so, we visit node F and discover that it's closer than D, so we update our current NN (and its distance: you can see that we shrink the radius of our nearest neighbor perimeter, the circle marking the region where possible nearest neighbors can be found).

Are we done now? Not yet; we need to keep backtracking to the root. We go back to node C, but its split line is further away than our NN perimeter (and it doesn't have a right branch, anyway), so we go back to node A, as shown in figure 9.22.

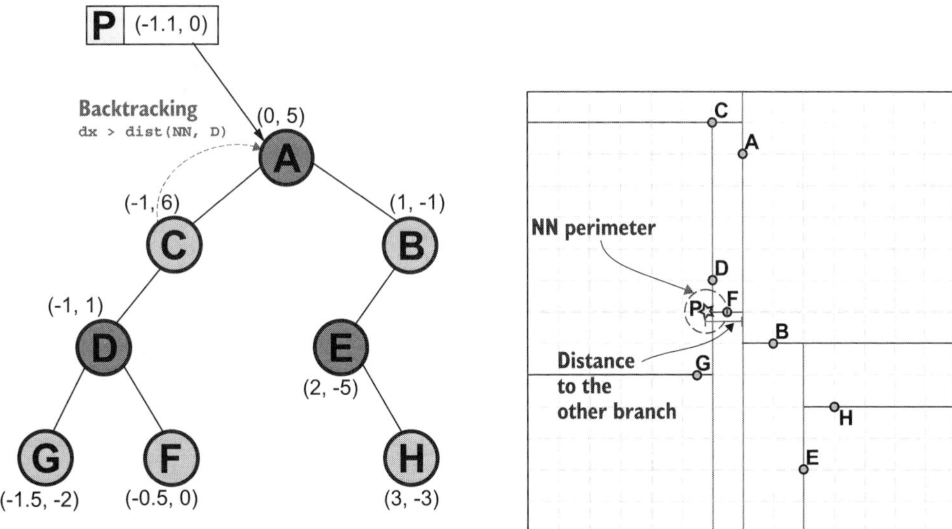
P (-1.1, 0)
Backtracking
dx > dist(NN, D)
(0, 5)
A
(-1, 6)
C
(1, -1)
B
(-1, 1)
D
E
(2, -5)
G
F
H
(-1.5, -2)
(-0.5, 0)
(3, -3)
NN perimeter
Distance to the other branch
C
A
D
P
F
B
G
H
E

Figure 9.22 We need to backtrack toward the root. If we had to check every possible branch of the tree, however, this would be no better than scanning the whole list of points. Instead, we can use all the information we have to prune the search. In the geometric representation on the right, we show a visual hint of why it would be useless to check A's right sub-branch. If you look back at figure 9.21, you can see that we knew that we couldn't rule out D's right sub-branch without traversing it.

At node `A` we took the left branch during search, meaning `P` is on the left semi-plane. If we were to traverse the right subtree of `A`, all the points in that subtree would have their `x` coordinate greater than or equal to `A`'s. Therefore, the minimum distance between `P` and any point in the right sub-tree of `A` is at least the distance between `P` and its projection on the vertical line passing through `A` (i.e., `A`'s split line). In other words, the minimum distance for any point right of `A` will at least be the absolute value of the difference between `P`'s and `A`'s `x` coordinates.

We can therefore prune search on `A`'s right branch, and since it was the root, we are finally done. Notice how the more we climb back on the tree, the larger are the branches (and the regions) that we can prune—and the larger the saving.

We can generalize this method to find an arbitrary large set of the closest points in the dataset, also known as the n-nearest-neighbor[11] search method.

The only differences are

- Instead of the distance of a single point, we need to keep track of the `m` shortest distances if we want the `m` closest points.
- At each step, we use the distance of the `m`-th closest point to draw our NN perimeter and prune search.
- To keep track of these `m` distances, we can use a bounded priority queue. We described something similar in chapter 2, section 2.7.3, when we described a method to find the `m` largest values in a stream of numbers.

Listing 9.10 details the pseudo-code for the `nNearestNeighbor` method.

Listing 9.10 The `nNearestNeighbor` method

```
function nNearestNeighbor(node, target, n)
  pq ← new BoundedPriorityQueue(n)
  pq.insert((inf, null))
  pq ← nNearestNeighbor(node, target, pq)
  (nnnDist, _) ← pq.peek()
  if nnnDist == inf then
    pq.top()
  return pq

function nNearestNeighbor(node, target, pq)
```

Finds the n points in the k-d tree that are closest to a given target

Initializes a max-heap (or any other (max) priority queue), bounded in its size, so that it will only contain the n smallest elements added to it. Refer to chapter 2, section 2.7.3, to see how insertion in such a queue works.

Before starting our search, we need to initialize the priority queue by adding a "guard": a tuple containing infinity as distance, a value that will be larger than any other distance computed, and so it will be the first tuple removed from the queue if we find at least n points in the tree.

We start the search on the root, using a recursive internal function.

We take a peek at the queue produced by the call at line #4, and . . .

. . . if its top element is still at an infinite distance, we need to remove it, because it means we have added less than n elements to the queue.

Once that's taken care of, we can just return to the caller the queue with the elements we found.

Internal version of the function taking an already initialized priority queue. The queue will encapsulate the logic about keeping track of the n-th closest neighbors and their distances, which we'll use to prune search.

[11]As mentioned, this is also referred to as k-nearest-neighbor in literature.

Once we are sure the current node is not `null` it's likely that we can compute the distance between the current node's point and target.

If `node` is `null` it's likely that we are traversing an empty tree, so the nearest neighbors can't change with respect to what we have already found.

We try to insert the tuple (current distance, current point) into the bounded (max) priority queue. This helper data structure takes care of keeping only the smallest `n` tuples, so that current point will only be added if its distance is among the `n` smallest distances found so far.

Checks if the target point is on the left branch of the split. If it is, the left branch is the closest to the target point; otherwise it is the furthest.

```
if node == null then
  return pq
else
  dist ← distance(node.point, target)
  pq.insert((dist, node.point))
  if compare(target, node) < 0 then
    closeBranch ← node.left
    farBranch ← node.right
  else
    closeBranch ← node.right
    farBranch ← node.left
  pq ← nNearestNeighbor(closeBranch, target, pq)
  (nnnDist, _) ← pq.peek()
  if splitDistance(target, node) < nnnDist then
    pq ← nNearestNeighbor(farBranch, target, pq)
  return pq
```

We certainly need to traverse the closest branch in search of the nearest neighbor. It is important to do so first and update the priority queue, and so the distance to the `n`-th closest neighbor, to improve pruning.

We need to retrieve the distance to the `n`-th closest neighbor, and we can do so by peeking at the tuple at the top of the bounded priority queue. Notice that this works if the queue has less than `n` elements. Since at line #3 we added a tuple with distance equal to infinity, that tuple will be at the top of the heap until we add `n` points, and so `nnnDist` will be set to infinity here, as long as we haven't yet added at least `n` points to the queue. Note: Underscore here is a placeholder, meaning that we are not interested in the value of the second element of the pair.

Returns the priority queue with the points found so far

Traverses furthest branch and updates current values for NNs and their distance

Using one of the helper functions defined in listing 9.2, we compute the distance between the split line passing through the current node and the target point. If this distance is closer than the distance to the current `n`-th nearest neighbor, as it's stored in the queue, then the furthest branch might contain closer points.

What's the running time for nearest neighbor search? Let's start with the bad news: in the worst-case scenario, even for a balanced tree, we might have to traverse the whole tree before finding a point's nearest neighbor(s).

Figure 9.23 shows a couple of examples of such a degenerate case. While the second example is artificially constructed as a literal edge case with all the points lying on a circle, the one in figure 9.23 (A) shows the same tree we used in our previous examples and demonstrates how even on random, balanced trees it is possible to find counter-examples where the method behaves poorly by just carefully choosing the target point for the search.

So, unfortunately there isn't much to do: the worst-case running time for this kind of query is `O(n)`.

That's the bad news. Luckily, there is also a silver lining.

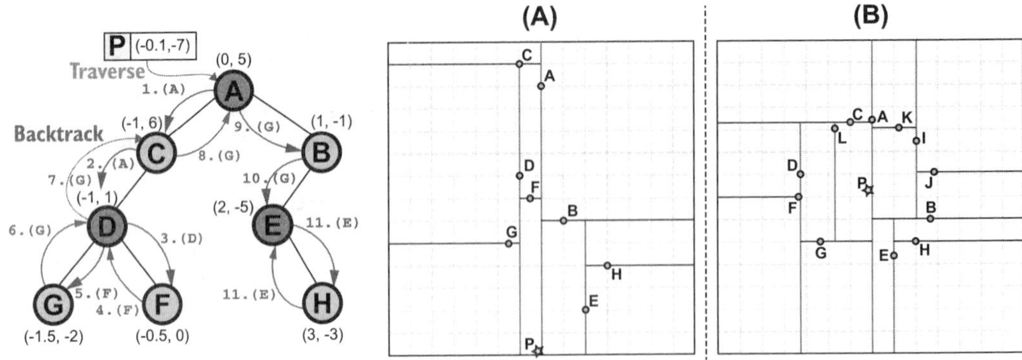
(A)
(B)
P (-0.1,-7)
Traverse
Backtrack
(0, 5)
(1, -1)
(-1, 6)
(-1, 1)
(2, -5)
(-1.5, -2)
(-0.5, 0)
(3, -3)
1. (A)
2. (A)
3. (D)
4. (F)
5. (F)
6. (G)
7. (G)
8. (G)
9. (G)
10. (G)
11. (E)
11. (E)

Figure 9.23 Edge cases for nearest neighbor search, which require traversing the whole tree. (A) An example built on the k-d tree from figures 9.20–9.22. By carefully choosing the target point, we can force the algorithm to search the whole tree, as shown on the tree representation. (B) We show the spatial representation only of an edge case where all the points lie in a circle, and we choose the center of the circle as target of the search. Notice how the distance from `P` to a split line will always be shorter than the radius of the circle (which, in turn, is the distance to the nearest neighbor).

Turns out that the average running time for nearest neighbor search on a balanced k-d tree is `O(2^k + log(n))`. The proof for this probabilistic bound is particularly complex and would require too much space to properly cover it here. You can find it in the original paper by Jon Bentley that first introduced k-d trees.

Nevertheless, to give you an intuition about why it works this way, consider a two-dimensional space: one point divides it into two halves, two points info three regions, three points will create four regions, and so on, and in general `n` points will create `n+1` regions. If the tree is balanced and `n` is sufficiently big, we can assume these regions are approximately equally sized.

Now suppose the dataset covers a unitary area.[12] When we run a nearest neighbor search we first traverse the tree from the root to the closest leaf,[13] and this, for a balanced tree, means traversing `O(log(n))` nodes. Since we hypothesized that each region is approximately the same size, and we have `n+1` of them, the area covered by the closest leaf will also be a rectangular region of area approximately equal to `1/n`. That means that there is a reasonably high probability that the distance between the target point and the nearest neighbor we have found during this traversal is no larger than half the diagonal of the region, which in turn is smaller than the square root of the region's area, or in other words, $\sqrt{1/n}$.

The next step in the algorithm is backtracking to visit all the regions that are within that distance from the target point. If all the regions are equally-sized and regularly shaped, this means that any region within distance must be in one of the neighboring rectangles (with respect to our leaf's region), and from geometry we know that

---

[12]Since we can define an ad-hoc unit measure for the area, it is always possible to imagine so.

[13]The one leaf that is closest to the target point, as shown in listing 9.9.

in such a situation, with regular equally sized rectangles that can be approximated to a rectangular grid, each rectangle has eight neighbors. From figure 9.24, however, it is possible to see how, on average, even if potentially we would have to traverse at most eight more branches, it's likely we only have to check four of them, because only the ones adjacent to the current region's sides will be within distance $\sqrt{1/n}$. Hence, this makes the total average running time `O(4*log(n))`.

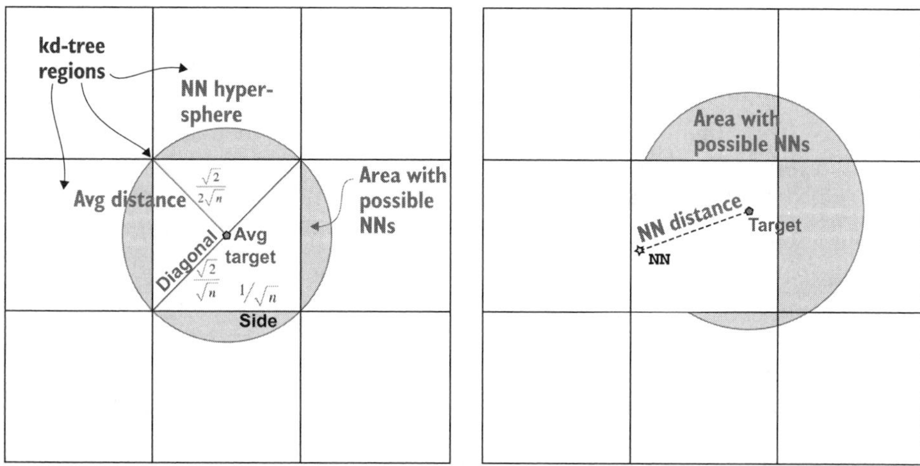
kd-tree regions
NN hyper-sphere
Avg distance
Area with possible NNs
Diagonal
Avg target
Side
Area with possible NNs
NN distance
Target
NN

Figure 9.24 A perfectly regular k-d tree partitioning with square cells. On the left, we show what can be considered the average case, with the tree's leaf point at the center of the region. Then the furthest the target could be, inside the region, is at half the distance of the square's diagonal. If we draw the circle circumscribed to the square, it intersects just the four regions adjacent to the sides of the current one. On the right is an example of another more generic and less optimistic case. Even if the distance is larger than the average, the hypersphere centered at the target node only intersects four other regions. Of course, in the worst-case scenario, it might intersect up to eight other regions.

If we move to $\mathbb{R}^3$, then the possible neighbors for each cube are 26, but the minimum distance will be $\sqrt[3]{1/n}$. With similar considerations we can infer that only less than eight regions will be close enough to have points within the minimum distance found so far; likewise, if we move to $\mathbb{R}^4$, and so on.

So, in summary, after finding the region where the target point of our search lies, we need to examine another `O(2`^{k}`)` points, making total running time `O(2`^{k} `+ log(n))`. While `k` is a constant for a given dataset, and we could in theory ignore it in big-O analysis, in the general case `k` is considered a parameter, as we measure the performance of this method with respect to both size and dimension of the k-d tree changes. It's also apparent that for large values of `k`, 2^k becomes so big that it dominates the running time, since

$$\log(n) > 2^k \Leftrightarrow n > 2^{2^k}$$

and in practice for $k \geq 7$ there is already no chance of having a dataset big enough to satisfy the inequality. For `n > 2`^{k}, however, this method still has an advantage over the brute-force search.

A final consideration: Pruning heavily depends on the "quality" of the nearest neighbor we have found so far. The shorter the distance to the current nearest neighbor, the more branches we can prune, and in turn the higher speed-up we can get. Therefore, it is important to update this value as soon as possible (we do this in our code for each node on the first time we visit it) and to traverse the most promising branches first. Of course, it is not easy to determine what the most promising branch is at any point. A good, although imperfect, indicator could be the distance between the target point and split line for a branch. The closer the target, the larger should be the intersection between the nearest neighbor perimeter (the hyper-sphere within which it's still possible to find a closer point to the target), and the region on the other side of the split line. That's the reason why we traverse the tree using a depth-first search: we backtrack on the smallest branches first, so hopefully when we reach larger branches close to the top of the tree, we can prune them.

9.3.6 Region search

While k-d trees were mainly designed to perform nearest neighbor search, they turned out to be particularly efficient for another kind of operation: querying the intersection of our dataset with a given region in the `k`-dimensional space.

In theory this region could be of any shape, but this operation becomes meaningful only if we can efficiently prune the branches we traverse during the query, and this heavily depends on the region's morphology.

In practice, there are two main cases we are interested in:

- Hyper-spherical regions, as shown in figure 9.25; the geometric interpretation is to query points within a certain distance from a certain point of interest.
- Hyper-rectangular regions, as shown in figure 9.26; here, the geometric interpretation is to query points whose values are in certain ranges.

When we deal with spherical regions, we are in a similar situation as the nearest neighbor search: we need to include all the points within a certain distance from a given point. It's like performing a NN-search, where we never update the distance to the nearest neighbor, and instead of keeping track of only one point (the NN), we gather all points closer than that distance.

In figure 9.25 you can see how we are going to prune branches. When we are at a split, we will certainly have to traverse the branch on the same side of the center of the search region `P`. For the other branch, we check the distance between `P` and its projection on the split line. If that distance is lower than or equal to the search region's radius, it means that there is still an area of intersection between that branch and the search region, and so we need to traverse the branch; otherwise, we can prune it.

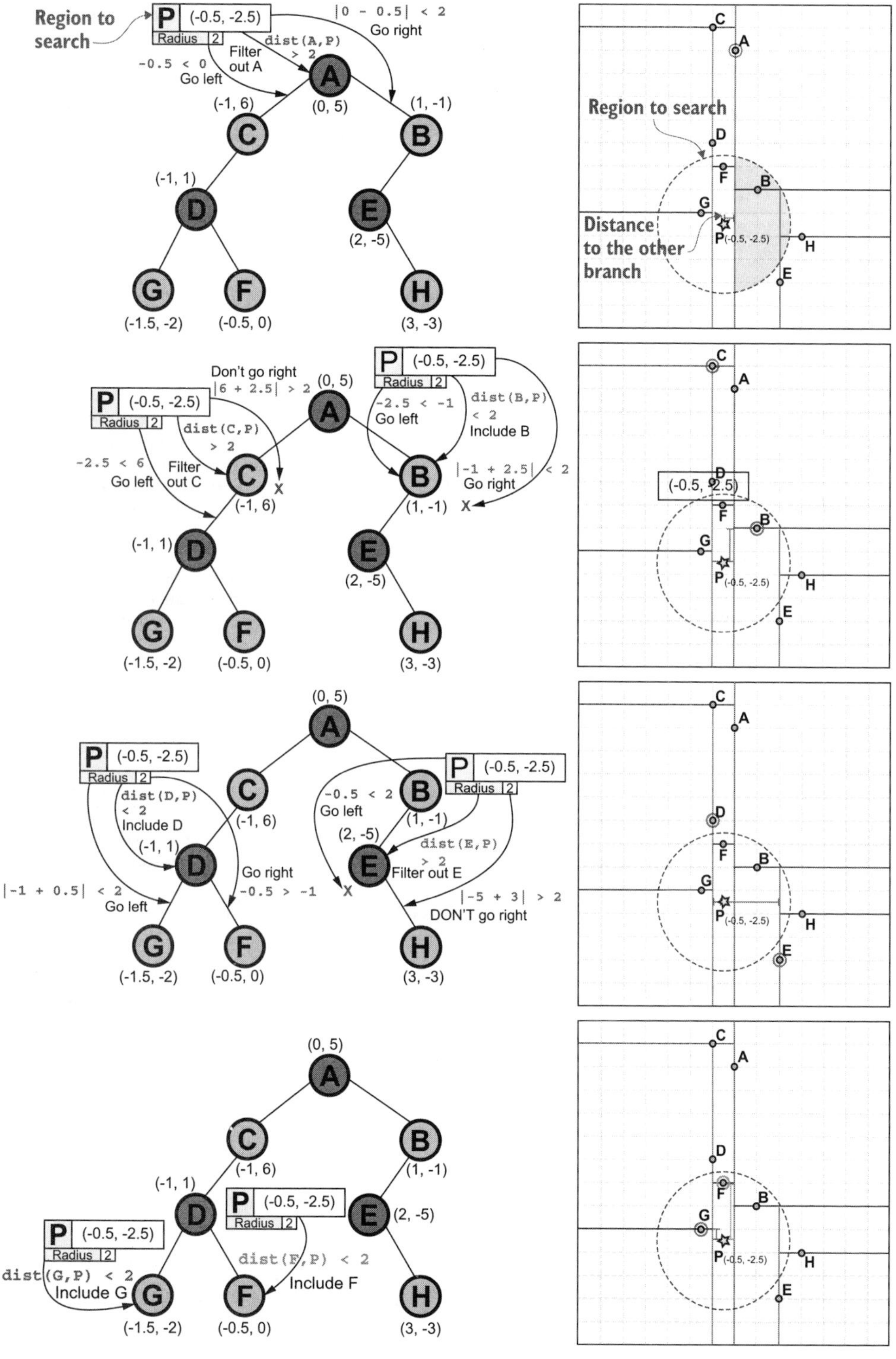
Region to search
P (-0.5, -2.5)
Radius 2
|0 - 0.5| < 2
Go right
dist(A,P) > 2
Filter out A
-0.5 < 0
Go left
A (0, 5)
C (-1, 6)
B (1, -1)
D (-1, 1)
E (2, -5)
G (-1.5, -2)
F (-0.5, 0)
H (3, -3)
Region to search
Distance to the other branch
P(-0.5, -2.5)
Don't go right
|6 + 2.5| > 2
-2.5 < -1
Go left
dist(B,P) < 2
Include B
dist(C,P) > 2
-2.5 < 6
Go left
Filter out C
|-1 + 2.5| < 2
Go right
dist(D,P) < 2
Include D
-0.5 < 2
Go left
dist(E,P) > 2
Filter out E
Go right
-0.5 > -1
|-1 + 0.5| < 2
Go left
|-5 + 3| > 2
DON'T go right
dist(F,P) < 2
Include F
dist(G,P) < 2
Include G

Figure 9.25 Region search on a k-d tree returns all the points in a k-d tree within a given hyper-sphere. This means looking for points within a given Euclidean distance from the sphere's center. We start our search from the root: it's not within the sphere. The point is on A's left branch, so we need to traverse it, but even if A is not within the sphere, the split line through it intersects the sphere, so there is a portion of the sphere intersecting the right branch of A as well (highlighted in the top-left figure). For the following steps, we are showing in parallel the execution on all branches at a given level, for the sake of space. (This is also a good hint that these processes could be executed in parallel.)

Listing 9.11 shows the pseudo-code for this method. As you can see, it's pretty similar to the regular NN-search.

Listing 9.11 The `pointsInSphere` method

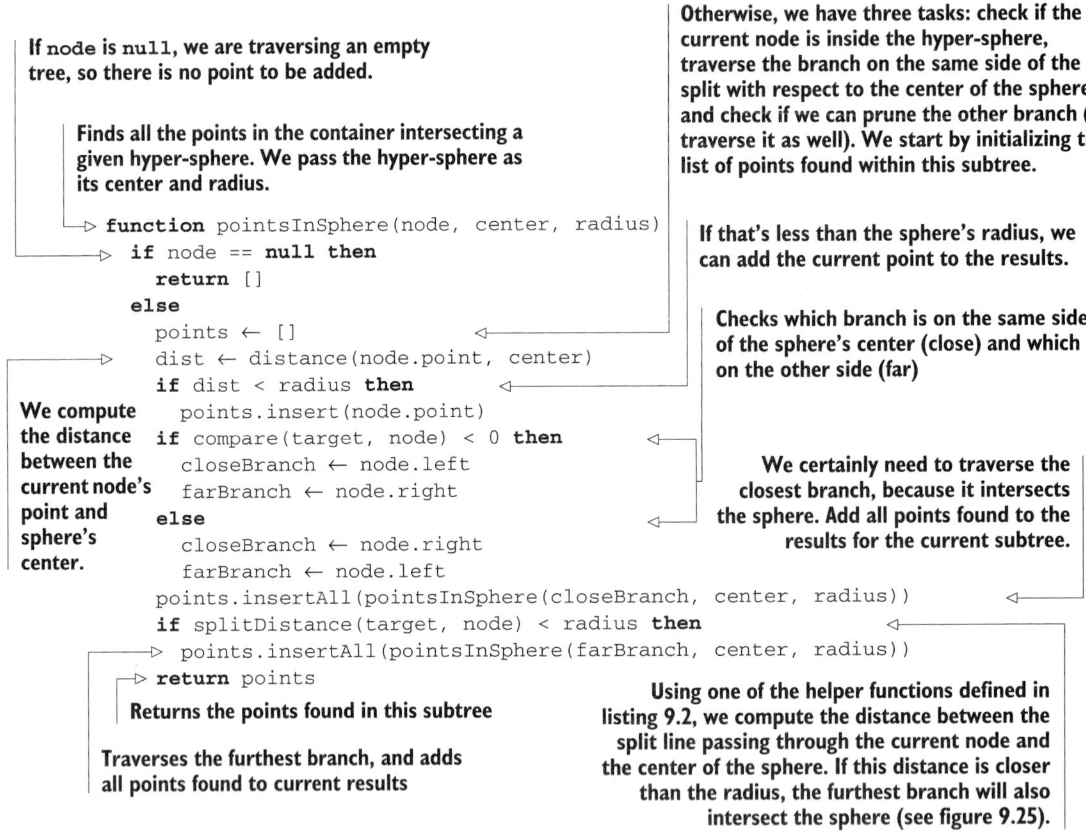

```
function pointsInSphere(node, center, radius)
  if node == null then
    return []
  else
    points ← []
    dist ← distance(node.point, center)
    if dist < radius then
      points.insert(node.point)
    if compare(target, node) < 0 then
      closeBranch ← node.left
      farBranch ← node.right
    else
      closeBranch ← node.right
      farBranch ← node.left
    points.insertAll(pointsInSphere(closeBranch, center, radius))
    if splitDistance(target, node) < radius then
      points.insertAll(pointsInSphere(farBranch, center, radius))
    return points
```


Finds all the points in the container intersecting a given hyper-sphere. We pass the hyper-sphere as its center and radius.
If node is null, we are traversing an empty tree, so there is no point to be added.
Otherwise, we have three tasks: check if the current node is inside the hyper-sphere, traverse the branch on the same side of the split with respect to the center of the sphere, and check if we can prune the other branch (or traverse it as well). We start by initializing the list of points found within this subtree.
We compute the distance between the current node's point and sphere's center.
If that's less than the sphere's radius, we can add the current point to the results.
Checks which branch is on the same side of the sphere's center (close) and which on the other side (far)
We certainly need to traverse the closest branch, because it intersects the sphere. Add all points found to the results for the current subtree.
Using one of the helper functions defined in listing 9.2, we compute the distance between the split line passing through the current node and the center of the sphere. If this distance is closer than the radius, the furthest branch will also intersect the sphere (see figure 9.25).
Traverses the furthest branch, and adds all points found to current results
Returns the points found in this subtree

The other region we are going to use for these queries is a rectangular shape. As you can imagine, the only difference with respect to `pointsinSphere` is the way we check whether we have to prune a branch. If we assume that the rectangle is oriented along the Cartesian axes used for splits, then pruning might even be considered easier, as shown in figure 9.26. But suppose we are at a horizontal split; then we need to understand if the split line intersects the search region, and in this case we will traverse both branches, or if it's above or below the region, which tells us which branch we can prune. This can be checked by simply comparing the `y` coordinate current node's point—call it N_y—with top (R_t) and bottom (R_b) `y` coordinates of the rectangular region, as we can have three cases:

- $R_b \leq N_y \leq R_t$—We need to traverse both branches.
- $N_y > R_t$—We can prune the left branch.
- $R_b > N_y$—We can prune the right branch.

And similarly for vertical splits, by checking the `x` coordinates instead of the `y` coordinates, it can also be generalized for `k`-dimensional spaces, cycling through dimensions.

This method is particularly useful when we need to search values within simple boundaries for each feature in data. For instance, if we have a dataset containing the tenures and salaries of employees, we might want to search all employees who worked for the company between two and four years and have salaries between 40K and 80K . . . and give them a raise![14]

This search, implemented in listing 9.12, translates into a rectangle with boundaries parallel to the dataset feature axes, meaning that in our boundaries each feature is independent of any other feature. If, instead, we had conditions that would mix more than one feature (for instance, a salary lower than 15K for each year of tenure), then the boundaries of the search region would be segments of generic lines, not parallel to any axis.

[14]In a perfect world . . .

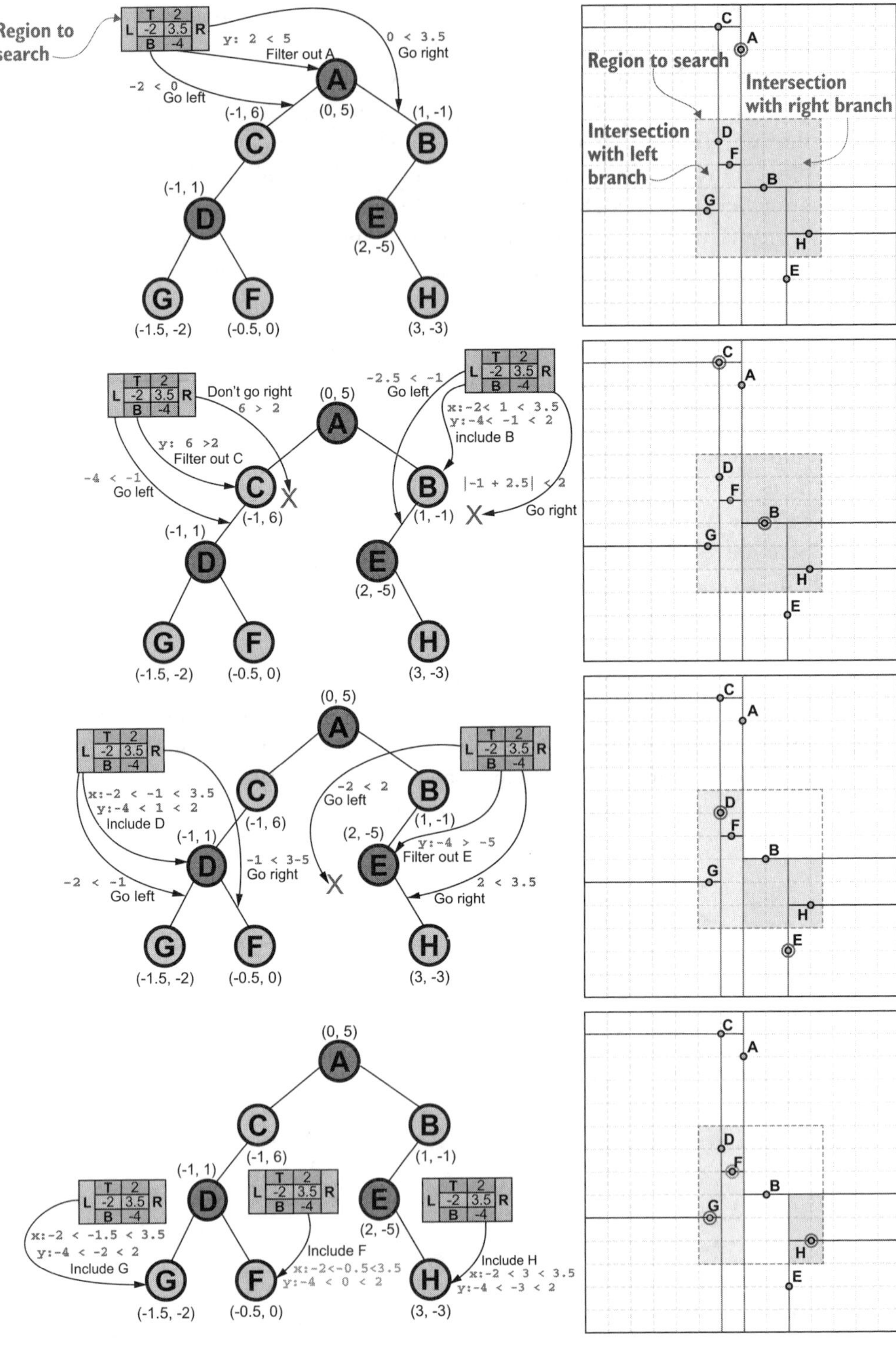
Region to search
y: 2 < 5
Filter out A
0 < 3.5
Go right
-2 < 0
Go left
Region to search
Intersection with right branch
Intersection with left branch
Don't go right
6 > 2
y: 6 >2
Filter out C
-4 < -1
Go left
-2.5 < -1
Go left
x:-2< 1 < 3.5
y:-4< -1 < 2
include B
|-1 + 2.5| < 2
Go right
x:-2 < -1 < 3.5
y:-4 < 1 < 2
Include D
-2 < -1
Go left
-1 < 3-5
Go right
-2 < 2
Go left
y:-4 > -5
Filter out E
2 < 3.5
Go right
x:-2 < -1.5 < 3.5
y:-4 < -2 < 2
Include G
Include F
x:-2<-0.5<3.5
y:-4 < 0 < 2
Include H
x:-2 < 3 < 3.5
y:-4 < -3 < 2

Figure 9.26 Region search on a k-d tree returns all the points in a k-d tree within a given hyper-rectangle. This means looking for points that, for each coordinate, satisfy two inequalities: each coordinate must be within a range. For instance, in this 2-D example, the points' `x` coordinates need to be between `-2` and `3.5`, and `y` coordinates between `-4` and `2`.

In that case, the problem becomes harder to solve, and we might need something more complex, such as the simplex algorithm,[15] to search the points satisfying our range query.

Listing 9.12 The `pointsInRectangle` method

```
function pointsInRectangle(node, rectangle)
  if node == null then
    return []
  else
    points ← []
      if (rectangle[i].min ≤ node.point[i] ≤ rectangle[i].max
            ∀ 0≤i<k) then
      points.insert(node.point)
    if intersectLeft(rectangle, node) then
      points.insertAll(pointsInRectangle(node.left, rectangle))
    if intersectRight(rectangle, node) then
      points.insertAll(pointsInRectangle(node.right, rectangle))
    return points
```

Annotations:

- **Finds all the points in the container intersecting a given hyper-sphere. We pass the hyper-rectangle as an argument, so we can assume it is a list of named tuples, each containing the boundaries for a dimension of the rectangle, as a range (min-max values).** (function)
- **If the `node` is `null`, we are traversing an empty tree, so there is no point to be added.** (if node == null)
- **Otherwise, we have three tasks: check if the current node is inside the hyper-rectangle, check if the left and right branches intersect the rectangle (at least one of them will), and traverse any that do intersect.** (else)
- **We start by initializing the list of points found within this subtree.** (points ← [])
- **If, for each dimension `i`, the `i`-th coordinate of the current node's point is within the rectangle's boundaries for that coordinate, then we can add the current point to the results.**
- **If the rectangle boundaries intersect the left branch, either being on the left of the current node's split line, or intersecting it, then we need to traverse the left branch and add all points found to the current results. For the sake of space, we won't provide this helper function, but you can easily write it using figure 9.26 as a reference.**
- **If the rectangular search region intersects the right branch, we can symmetrically recurse on the right child.**
- **Finally, we return all points found in this subtree.**

What's the performance of both region-searches? Well, as you can imagine, it heavily depends on the regions we search. We go on a full range from two edge cases:

[15] The simplex algorithm is an ingenious optimization method. It is not related to or helped by k-d trees and, as such, is out of scope for this chapter, but it's interesting reading, and you can read more here: https://en.wikipedia.org/wiki/Simplex_algorithm.

- For very small regions intersecting only a single branch corresponding to a leaf, we will prune every other branch, and just follow a path to the leaf, so the running time will be `O(h)`, where `h` is the height of the tree – `O(log(n))` for a balanced tree with `n` points.
- When the region is large enough to intersect all points, we will have to traverse the whole tree, and the running time will be `O(n)`.

Therefore, we can only say that the worst-case running time is `O(n)`, even if the methods will efficiently prune the tree whenever possible.

9.3.7 A recap of all methods

As we have seen, k-d trees provide a speed-up over brute-force search on the whole dataset; table 9.1 summarizes the performance of the methods described in this chapter. While the worst-case running time for nearest neighbor search (and removal) is still linear (exactly as for brute-force), in practice the amortized performance on balanced k-d trees is slightly to consistently better. The improvement is higher in low dimensional spaces and still consistent in medium-dimensional spaces.

In high-dimensional spaces, the exponential term on `k` for nearest neighbor becomes dominant and makes supporting the extra complexity of such a data structure not worth it.

Table 9.1 Operations provided by k-d tree, and their cost on a balanced k-d tree with `n` elements

Operation	Running time	Extra space
`search`	`O(log(n))`	`O(1)`
`insert`	`O(log(n))`	`O(1)`
`remove`	$O(n^{1-1/k})$ [a]	`O(1)`
`findMin`	$O(n^{1-1/k})$ [a]	`O(1)`
`nearestNeighbor`	$O(2^k + \log(n))$ [a]	`O(m)` [b]
`pointsInRegion`	`O(n)`	`O(n)`

[a]Amortized, for a k-d tree holding `k`-dimensional points.
[b]When searching for the `m` nearest neighbors, with `m` constant (not a function of `n`).

9.4 Limits and possible improvements

If we look back at our "find the closest hub" problem, we started this chapter with basically nothing better than brute-force search to find the nearest neighbor of a point in a multi-dimensional dataset. Then, going through a few less-than-ideal attempts, we built our understanding of the traps and challenges in such a task and finally introduced k-d trees.

K-d trees are great because they offer a major speed-up over linear search; yet, they still have potential issues:

- K-d trees might be hard to implement efficiently.
- K-d trees are not self-balancing, so they perform best when they are constructed from a stable set of points, and the number of inserts and removes are limited with respect to the total number of elements. Unfortunately, static datasets are not the norm in the big-data era.
- When we deal with high-dimensional spaces, k-d trees become inefficient. As we have seen, the time needed for removal and nearest neighbor search is exponential in `k`, the dimension of the dataset. But for sufficiently large values of `k`, this can hinder any performance benefits over brute-force search. We have seen that nearest neighbor searches perform better than naïve search if $n > 2^k$, so starting at $k \approx 30$, we would need an ideal dataset (one with a regular distribution of points) with billions of elements in order for k-d tree to overperform brute-force.
- K-d trees don't work well with paged memory; they are not memory-efficient with respect to the locality of reference because points are stored in tree nodes, so close-by points won't lie close by memory areas.
- While they handle points well, k-d trees can't handle non-punctiform objects, such as shapes or any object with a non-zero measure.

The inefficiency of high-dimensional datasets stems from the fact that in these datasets, data becomes very sparse. At the same time, when we traverse a k-d tree during NN-search, we can only prune a branch when it doesn't intersect the hyper-sphere centered in the target point and with a radius equal to the minimum distance found so far. It is highly likely that this sphere will intersect many of the branches' hyper-cubes in at least one dimension.

To overcome these limitations, we could try a few approaches:

- We could use different criteria to decide where to partition the `k`-dimensional space, using different heuristics:
  - Don't use a splitting line passing through points, but just divide a region into two balanced halves (either with respect to the number of points or the sub-regions' size; basically, choose the mean instead of the median).
  - Instead of cycling through dimensions, choose at every step the dimension with the greatest spread or variance, and store the choice in the tree node.
- Instead of storing points in nodes, each node could describe a region of space and link (directly or indirectly) to an array containing the actual elements.
- We could approximate nearest neighbor search. For instance, we could use *locality sensitive hashing*.
- Or we could find new ways to partition the `k`-dimensional space, ideally trying to reduce sparsity.

Heuristics help on some datasets, but in general won't solve the issue with higher dimensional spaces.

The approximate approach doesn't produce an exact solution, but there are many cases where we can settle with a sub-optimal result, or we can't even define a perfect metric. For example, think about retrieving the closest document to an article or the closest item to something you want to buy, but is out of stock. We won't go on this path for now. Instead, in the next chapter we will delve into the latter approach with SS-trees. We will also defer to chapter 11 the discussion about applications of nearest neighbor search.

Summary

- When the number of dimensions of a dataset grows, this usually brings an exponential increase in either the complexity or memory needed.
- We need to carefully design our data structures to avoid or limit this exponential burst, but we can't remove it altogether. When the number of dimensions is large, it's hard, if even possible, to maintain good performance.
- K-d trees are an advanced data structure that helps perform spatial queries (nearest neighbor search and intersections with spherical or rectangular regions) more efficiently.
- K-d trees are great with low- and medium-dimensional spaces, but suffer sparsity with high-dimensional spaces.
- K-d trees work better on static datasets because we can build balanced trees on construction, but `insert` and `remove` are not self-balancing operations.

10 Similarity Search Trees: Approximate nearest neighbors search for image retrieval

This chapter covers

- Discussing the limits of k-d trees
- Describing image retrieval as a use case where k-d trees would struggle
- Introducing a new data structure, the R-tree
- Presenting SS-trees, a scalable variant of R-trees
- Comparing SS-trees and k-d trees
- Introducing approximate similarity search

This chapter will be structured slightly differently from our book's standard, because we will continue here a discussion started in chapter 8. There, we introduced the problem of searching multidimensional data for the nearest neighbor(s) of a generic point (possibly not in the dataset itself). In chapter 9, we introduce k-d trees, a data structure specifically invented to solve this problem.

K-d trees are the best solution to date for indexing low- to medium-dimensional datasets that will completely fit in memory. When we have to operate on high-dimensional data or with big datasets that won't fit in memory, k-d trees are not enough, and we will need to use more advanced data structures.

In this chapter we first present a new problem, one that will push our indexing data structure beyond its limits, and then introduce two new data structures, R-trees and SS-trees, that can help us solve this category of problems efficiently.

Brace yourself—this is going to be a long journey (and a long chapter!) through some of the most advanced material we have presented so far. We'll try to make it through this journey step by step, section by section, so don't let the length of this chapter intimidate you!

10.1 Right where we left off

Let's briefly recap where we left off in previous chapters. We were designing software for an e-commerce company, an application to find the closest warehouse selling a given product for any point on a very large map. Check out figure 9.4 to visualize it. To have a ballpark idea of the kind of scale we need, we want to serve millions of clients per day across the country, taking products from thousands of warehouses also spread across the map.

In section 8.2, we have already established that a brute-force approach is not practical for applications at scale, and we need to resort to a brand-new data structure designed to handle multi-dimensional indexing. Chapter 9 described k-d trees, a milestone in multidimensional data indexing and a true game changer, which worked perfectly with the example we used in chapters 8 and 9 where we only needed to work with 2-D data. The only issue we faced is the fact that our dataset was dynamic and thus insertion/removal would produce an imbalanced tree, but we could rebuild the tree every so often (for instance, after 1% of its elements had been changed because of insertions or removals), and amortize the cost of the operation by running it in a background process (keeping the old version of the tree in the meantime, and either putting insert/delete on hold, or reapplying these operations to the new tree once it had been created and "promoted" to current).

While in that case we could find workarounds, in other applications we won't necessarily be so lucky. There are, in fact, intrinsic limitations that k-d trees can't overcome:

- K-d trees are not self-balancing, so they perform best when they are constructed from a stable set of points, and when the number of inserts and removes is limited with respect to the total number of elements.
- The curse of dimensionality: When we deal with high-dimensional spaces, k-d trees become inefficient, because running time for search is exponential in the

dimension of the dataset. For points in the k-dimensional space, when `k ≈ 30`, k-d trees can't give any advantage over brute-force search.

- K-d trees don't work well with paged memory, because they are not memory-efficient with respect to the locality of reference, as points are stored in tree nodes, so nearby points won't lie close to memory areas.

10.1.1 A new (more complex) example

To illustrate a practical situation where k-d trees are not the recommended solution, let's pivot on our warehouse search and imagine a different scenario, where we fast-forward 10 years. Our e-commerce company has evolved and doesn't sell just groceries anymore, but also electronics and clothes. It's almost 2010, and customers expect valuable recommendations when they browse our catalog; but even more importantly, the company's marketing department expects that you, as CTO, make sure to increase sales by showing customers suggestions they actually like.

For instance, if customers are browsing smartphones (the hottest product in the catalog, ramping up to rule the world of electronics, back in the day!), your application is supposed to show them more smartphones in a similar price/feature range. If they are looking at a cocktail dress, they should see more dresses that look similar to the one they (possibly) like.

Now, these two problems look (and partially are) quite different, but they both boil down to the same core issue: given a product with a list of features, find one or more products with similar features. Obviously, the way we extract these feature lists from a consumer electronics product and a dress is very different!

Let's focus on the latter, illustrated in figure 10.1. Given an image of a dress, find other products in your catalog that look similar—this is a very stimulating problem, even today!

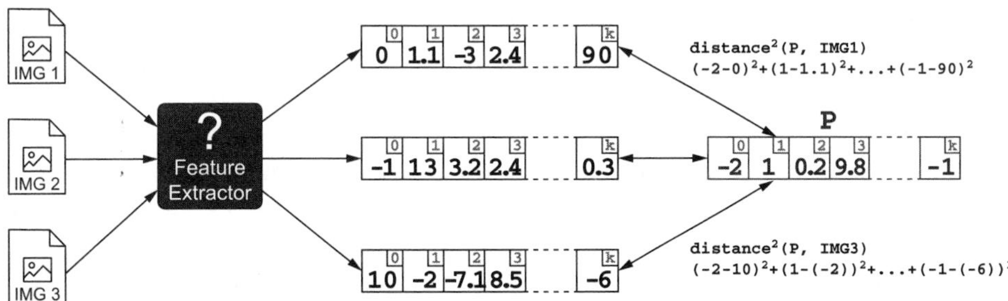
IMG 1
IMG 2
IMG 3
?
Feature
Extractor
0 1 2 3 k
0 1.1 -3 2.4 90
-1 13 3.2 2.4 0.3
10 -2 -7.1 8.5 -6
P
-2 1 0.2 9.8 -1
distance²(P, IMG1)
(-2-0)²+(1-1.1)²+...+(-1-90)²
distance²(P, IMG3)
(-2-10)²+(1-(-2))²+...+(-1-(-6))²

Figure 10.1 Feature extraction on an image dataset. Each image is translated into a feature vector (through what's represented as a "black box" feature extractor, because we are not interested in the algorithm that creates this vectors). Then, if we have to search an entry `P`, we compare `P`'s feature vector to each of the images' vectors, computing their mutual distance based on some metric. (In the figure, Euclidean distance. Notice that when looking for the minimum of these Euclidean distances, we can sometimes compute the squared distances, avoiding applying a square root operation for each entry.)

The way we extract features from images completely changed in the last 10 years. In 2009, we used to extract edges, corners, and other geometrical features from the images, using dozens of algorithms specialized for the single feature, and then build higher-level features by hand (quite literally).

Today, instead, we use deep learning for the task, training a CNN[1] on a larger dataset and then applying it to all the images in our catalog to generate their feature vectors.

Once we have these feature vectors, though, the same question arises now as then: How do we efficiently search the most similar vectors to a given one?

This is exactly the same problem we illustrated in chapter 8 for 2-D data, applied to a huge dataset (with tens of thousands of images/feature vectors), and where tuples have hundreds of features.

Contrary to the feature extraction, the search algorithms haven't changed much in the last 10 years, and the data structures that we introduce in this chapter, invented between the late 1990s and the early 2000s, are still cutting-edge choices for efficient search in the vector space.

10.1.2 Overcoming k-d trees' flaws

Back in chapter 9, we also mentioned a couple of possible structural solutions to cope with the problems discussed in the previous section:

- Instead of partitioning points using a splitting line passing through a dataset's points, we can divide a region into two balanced halves with respect to the number of points or the sub-region's size.
- Instead of cycling through dimensions, we can choose at every step the dimension with the greatest spread or variance and store the choice made in each tree node.
- Instead of storing points in nodes, each node could describe a region of space and link (directly or indirectly) to an array containing the actual elements.

These solutions are the basis of the data structures we will discuss in this chapter, R-trees and SS-trees.

10.2 R-tree

The first evolution of k-d trees we will discuss are R-trees. Although we won't delve into the details of their implementation, we are going to discuss the idea behind this solution, why they work, and their high-level mechanism.

R-trees were introduced in 1984 by Antonin Guttman in the paper "R-Trees. A Dynamic Index Structure For Spatial Searching."

They are inspired by B-trees,[2] balanced trees with a hierarchical structure. In particular, Guttman used as a starting point B+ trees, a variant where only leaf nodes contain data, while inner nodes only contain keys and serve the purpose of hierarchically partitioning data.

---

[1] Convolutional Neural Network, a type of deep neural network that is particularly well-suited to process images.

[2] A B-tree is a self-balancing tree optimized for efficiently storing large datasets on disk.

10.2.1 A step back: Introducing B-trees

Figure 10.2 shows an example of a B-tree, in particular a B+tree. These data structures were meant to index unidimensional data, partitioning it into pages,[3] providing efficient storage on disk and fast search (minimizing the number of pages loaded, and so the number of disk accesses).

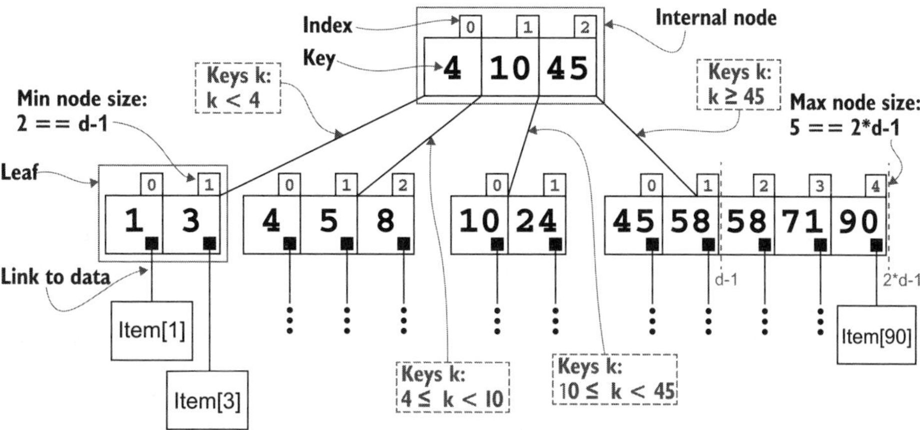
Index
Key
Internal node
Keys k: k < 4
Keys k: k ≥ 45
Min node size: 2 == d-1
Max node size: 5 == 2*d-1
Leaf
Link to data
1 3
4 5 8
10 24
45 58 58 71 90
4 10 45
d-1
2*d-1
Item[1]
Item[3]
Item[90]
Keys k: 4 ≤ k < 10
Keys k: 10 ≤ k < 45

Figure 10.2 B+ tree explained. The example shows a B+ tree with a branching factor of `d == 3`.

Each node (both internal nodes and leaves) in a B-tree contains between `d-1` and `2*d-1` keys, where `d` is a fixed parameter for each tree, its branching factor:[4] the (minimum, in this case) number of children for each node. The only exception can be the root, which can possibly contain fewer than `d-1` keys. Keys are stored in an ordered list; this is fundamental to have a fast (logarithmic) search. In fact, each internal node with `m` keys, k_0, k_1, ..., k_{m-1}, $d-1 \le m \le 2*d*-1$, also has exactly `m+1` children, C_0, C_1, ..., C_{m-1}, C_m, such that $k < k_0$ for each key `k` in the subtree rooted in C_0; $k_0 \le k < k_1$ for each key `k` in the subtree rooted in C_1; and so on.

In a B-tree, keys and items are stored in the nodes, each key/item is stored exactly once in a single node, and the whole tree stores exactly `n` keys if the dataset has `n` items. In a B+ tree, internal nodes only contains keys, and only leaves contain pairs, each with keys and links to the items. This means that a B+tree storing `n` items has `n` leaves, and that keys in internal nodes are also stored in all its descendants (see how, in the example in figure 10.2, the keys `4`, `10`, and `45` are also stored in leaves).

Storing links to items in the leaves, instead of having the actual items hosted in the tree, serves a double purpose:

- Nodes are more lightweight and easier to allocate/garbage collect.
- It allows storing all items in an array, or in a contiguous block of memory, exploiting the memory locality of neighboring items.

[3] A *memory page*, or just *page*.

[4] An attentive reader will remember that we already discussed the branching factor in chapter 2 for d-ary heaps.

When these trees are used to store huge collections of large items, these properties allow us to use memory paging efficiently. By having lightweight nodes, it is more likely the whole tree will fit in memory, while items can be stored on disk, and leaves can be loaded on a need-to basis. Because it is also likely that after accessing an item `X`, applications will need to access one of its contiguous items, by loading in memory the whole B-tree leaf containing `X`, we can reduce the disk reads as much as possible.

Not surprisingly, for these reasons B-trees have been the core of many SQL database engines since their invention[5]—and even today they are still the data structure of choice for storing indices.

10.2.2 From B-Tree to R-tree

R-trees extend the main ideas behind B+trees to the multidimensional case. While for unidimensional data each node corresponds to an interval (the range from the left-most and right-most keys in its sub-tree, which are in turn its minimum and maximum keys), in R-trees each node `N` covers a rectangle (or a hyper-rectangle in the most generic case), whose corners are defined by the minimum and maximum of each coordinate over all the points in the subtree rooted at `N`.

Similarly to B-trees, R-trees are also parametric. Instead of a branching factor `d` controlling the minimum number of entries per node, R-trees require their clients to provide two parameters on creation:

- `M`, the maximum number of entries in a node; this value is usually set so that a full node will fit in a page of memory.
- `m`, such that `m ≤ M/2`, the minimum number of entries in a node. This parameter indirectly controls the minimum height of the tree, as we'll see.

Given values for these two parameters, R-trees abide by a few invariants:

1. Every leaf contains between `m` and `M` points (except for the root, which can possibly have less than `m` points).
2. Each leaf node `L` has associated a hyper-rectangle R_L, such that R_L is the smallest rectangle containing all the points in the leaf.
3. Every internal node has between `m` and `M` children (except for the root, which can possibly have less than `m` children).
4. Each internal node `N` has associated a bounding (hyper-)rectangle R_N, such that R_N is the smallest rectangle, whose edges are parallel to the Cartesian axes, entirely containing all the bounding rectangles of `N`'s children.
5. The root node has at least two children, unless it is a leaf.
6. All leaves are at the same level.

---

[5] See, for instance, https://sqlity.net/en/2445/b-plus-tree/.

Property number 6 tells us that R-trees are balanced, while from properties 1 and 3 we can infer that the maximum height of an R-tree containing `n` points is $\log_m(n)$.

On insertion, if any node on the path from the root to the leaf holding the new point becomes larger than `M` entries, we will have to split it, creating two nodes, each with half the elements.

On removal, if any node becomes smaller than `m` entries, we will have to merge it with one of its adjacent siblings.

Invariants 2 and 4 require some extra work to be maintained true, but these bounding rectangles defined for each node are needed to allow fast search on the tree.

Before describing how the search methods work, let's take a closer look at an example of an R-tree in figures 10.3 and 10.4. We will stick to the 2-D case because it is easier to visualize, but as always, you have to imagine that real trees can hold 3-D, 4-D, or even 100-D points.

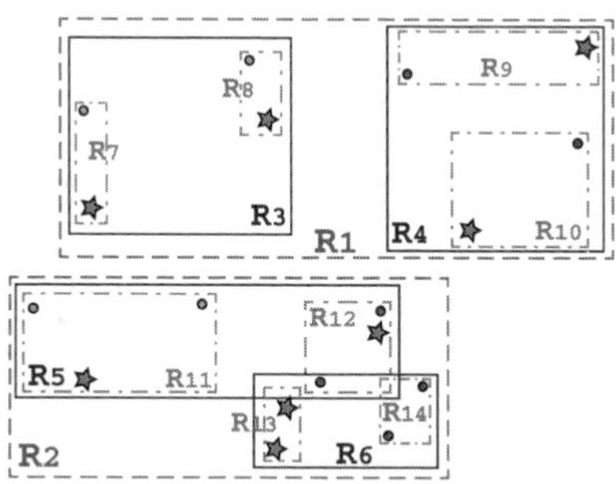
R9
R8
R7
R3
R1
R4
R10
R12
R5
R11
R13
R14
R2
R6

Figure 10.3 Cartesian plane representation of a (possible) R-tree for our city maps as presented in the example of figure 9.4 (the names of the cities are omitted to avoid confusion). This R-tree contains 12 bounding rectangles, from R_1 to R_{12}, organized in a hierarchical structure. Notice that rectangles can and do overlap, as shown in the bottom half.

If we compare figure 10.3 to figure 9.6, showing how a k-d tree organizes the same dataset, it is immediately apparent how the two partitionings are completely different:

- R-trees create regions in the Cartesian plane in the shape of rectangles, while k-d trees split the plane along lines.
- While k-d trees alternate the dimension along which the split is done, R-trees don't cycle through dimensions. Rather, at each level the sub-rectangles created can partition their bounding box in any or even all dimensions at the same time.

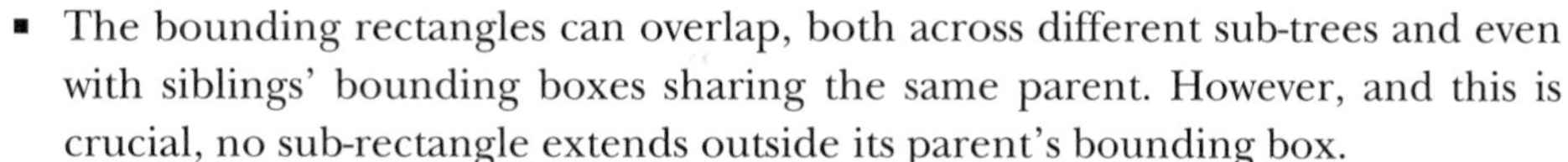

- The bounding rectangles can overlap, both across different sub-trees and even with siblings' bounding boxes sharing the same parent. However, and this is crucial, no sub-rectangle extends outside its parent's bounding box.
- Each internal node defines a so-called *bounding envelope*, that for R-trees is the smallest rectangle containing all the bounding envelopes of the node's children.

Figure 10.4 shows how these properties translate into a tree data structure; here the difference with k-d trees is even more evident!

Each internal node is a list of rectangles (between `m` and `M` of them, as mentioned), while leaves are lists of (again, between `m` and `M`) points. Each rectangle is effectively determined by its children and could indeed be defined iteratively in terms of its children. For practical reasons such as improving the running time of the search methods, in practice we store the bounding box for each rectangle.

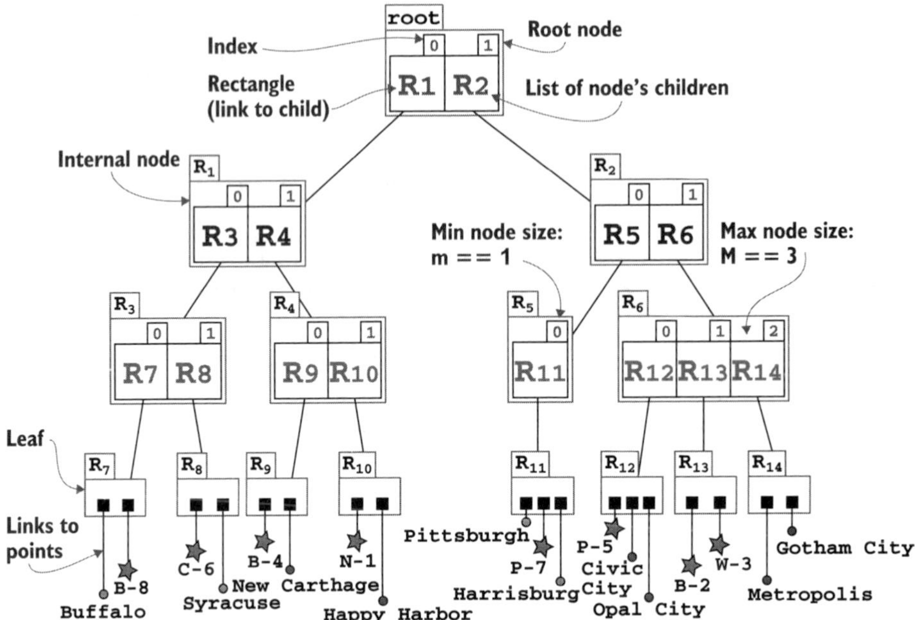
root
Index
Root node
Rectangle
(link to child)
List of node's children
Internal node
Min node size:
m == 1
Max node size:
M == 3
Leaf
Links to
points
Pittsburgh
P-5
P-7
Civic
City
Harrisburg
Opal City
B-8
Buffalo
C-6
Syracuse
B-4
New Carthage
N-1
Happy Harbor
W-3
B-2
Gotham City
Metropolis

Figure 10.4 The tree representation for the R-tree from figure 10.3. The parameters for this R-tree are `m==1` and `M==3`. Internal nodes only hold bounding boxes, while leaves hold the actual points (or, in general, `k`-dimensional entries). In the rest of the chapter we will use a more compact representation, for each node drawing just the list of its children.

Because the rectangles can only be parallel to the Cartesian axes, they are defined by two of their vertices: two tuples with `k` coordinates, one tuple for the minimum values of each coordinate, and one for the maximum value of each coordinate.

Notice how unlike k-d trees, an R-tree could handle a non-zero-measure object by simply considering its bounding boxes as special cases of rectangles, as illustrated in figure 10.5.

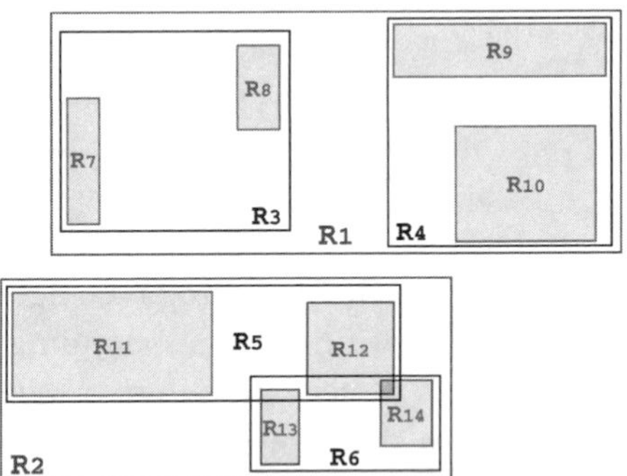
R9
R8
R7
R10
R3
R1
R4
R11
R5
R12
R14
R13
R6
R2

Figure 10.5 R-trees entries, besides points, can also be rectangles or non-zero-measure entities. In this example, entities R_7 to R_{14} are the tree's entries, while R_3 to R_6 are the tree's leaves.

10.2.3 Inserting points in an R-tree

Now, of course, you might legitimately wonder how you get from a raw dataset to the R-tree in figure 10.5. After all, we just presented it and asked you to take it as a given.

Insertion for R-trees is similar to B-trees and has many steps in common with SS-trees, so we won't duplicate the learning effort with a detailed description here.

At a high level, to insert a new point you will need to follow the following steps:

1. Find the leaf that should host the new point `P`. There are three possible cases:
   a. `P` lies exactly within one of the leaves' rectangles, `R`. Then just add `P` to `R` and move to the next step.
   b. `P` lies within the overlapping region between two or more leaves' bounding rectangles. For example, referring to figure 10.6, it might lie in the intersection of R_{12} and R_{14}. In this case, we need to decide where to add `P`; the heuristic used to make these decisions will determine the shape of the tree (as an example, one heuristic could be just adding it to the rectangle with fewer elements).
   c. If P lies outside of all rectangles at the leaves' level, then we need to find the closest leaf `L` and add `P` to it (again, we can use more complex heuristics than just the Euclidean distance to decide).
2. Add the points to the leaf's rectangle `R`, and check how many points it contains afterward:
   a. If, after the new point is added, the leaf still has at most `M` points, then we are done.
   b. Otherwise, we need to split `R` into two new rectangles, R_1 and R_2, and go to step 3.
3. Remove `R` from its parent R_P and add R_1 and R_2 to R_P. If R_P now has more than `M` children, split it and repeat this step recursively.
   a. If `R` was the root, we obviously can't remove it from its parent; we just create a new root and set R_1 and R_2 as children.

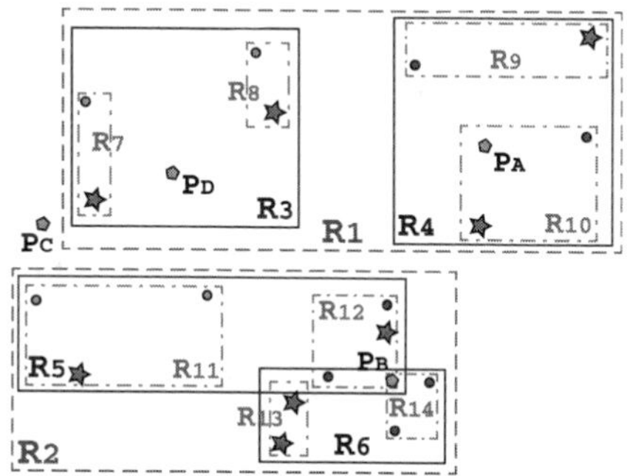
R1
R2
R3
R4
R5
R6
R7
R8
R9
R10
R11
R12
R13
R14
PA
PB
PC
PD

Figure 10.6 Choosing the R-tree leaf's rectangle to which a point should be added: the new point can lie within a leaf rectangle (P_A), within the intersection of two or more leaves' rectangles (P_B), or outside any of the leaves (P_C and P_D).

To complete the insertion algorithm outlined here, we need to provide a few heuristics to break ties for overlapping rectangles and to choose the closest rectangle, but even more importantly, we haven't said anything about how we are going to split a rectangle at points 2 and 3.

This choice, together with the heuristic for choosing the insertion subtree, determines the behavior and shape (not to mention performance) of the R-tree.

Several heuristics have been studied over the years, each one aiming to optimize one or more usages of the tree. The split heuristics can be particularly complicated for internal nodes because we don't just partition points, but `k`-dimensional shapes. Figure 10.7 shows how easily a naïve choice could lead to inefficient splits.

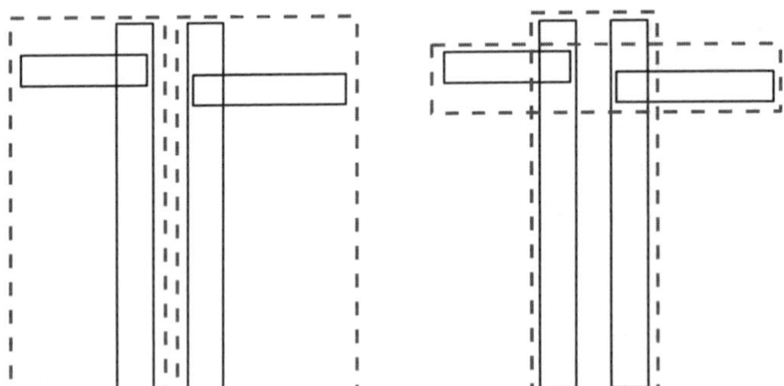
Bad split
Good split

Figure 10.7 An example of bad and good splits of an internal node's rectangle, taken from the original paper by Antonin Guttman

Delving into these heuristics is out of the scope of this section; we refer the curious reader to the original paper by Antonin Guttman for a proper description. At this point, though, we can already reveal that the complexity of handling hyper-rectangles and obtaining good splits (and merges, after removals) is one of the main reasons that led to the introduction of SS-trees.

10.2.4 Search

Searching for a point or for the nearest neighbor (*NN*) of a point in R-trees is very similar to what happens in k-d trees. We need to traverse the tree, pruning branches that can't contain a point, or, for NN search, are certainly further away than the current minimum distance.

Figure 10.8 shows an example of an (unsuccessful) point search on our example R-tree. Remember that an unsuccessful search is the first step for inserting a new point, through which we can find the rectangle (or rectangles, in this case) where we should add the new point.

The search starts at the root, where we compare point P's coordinates with the boundaries of each rectangle, R_1 and R_2; P can only be within R_2, so this is the only branch we traverse.

At the next step, we go through R_2's children, R_5 and R_6. Both can contain P, so we need to traverse both branches at this level (as shown by the two curved arrows, leaving R_2 in the bottom half of figure 10.8).

This means we need to go through the children of both rectangles R_5 and R_6, checking from R_{11} to R_{14}. Of these, only R_{12} and R_{14} can contain P, so those are the only rectangles whose points we will check at the last step. Neither contains P, so the search method can return `false`, and optionally the two leaves' rectangles that could host P, if inserted.

Nearest neighbor search works similarly, but instead of checking whether a point belongs to each rectangle, it keeps the distance of the current nearest neighbor and checks to see if each rectangle is closer than that (otherwise, it can prune it). This is similar to the rectangular region search in k-d trees, as described in section 9.3.6.

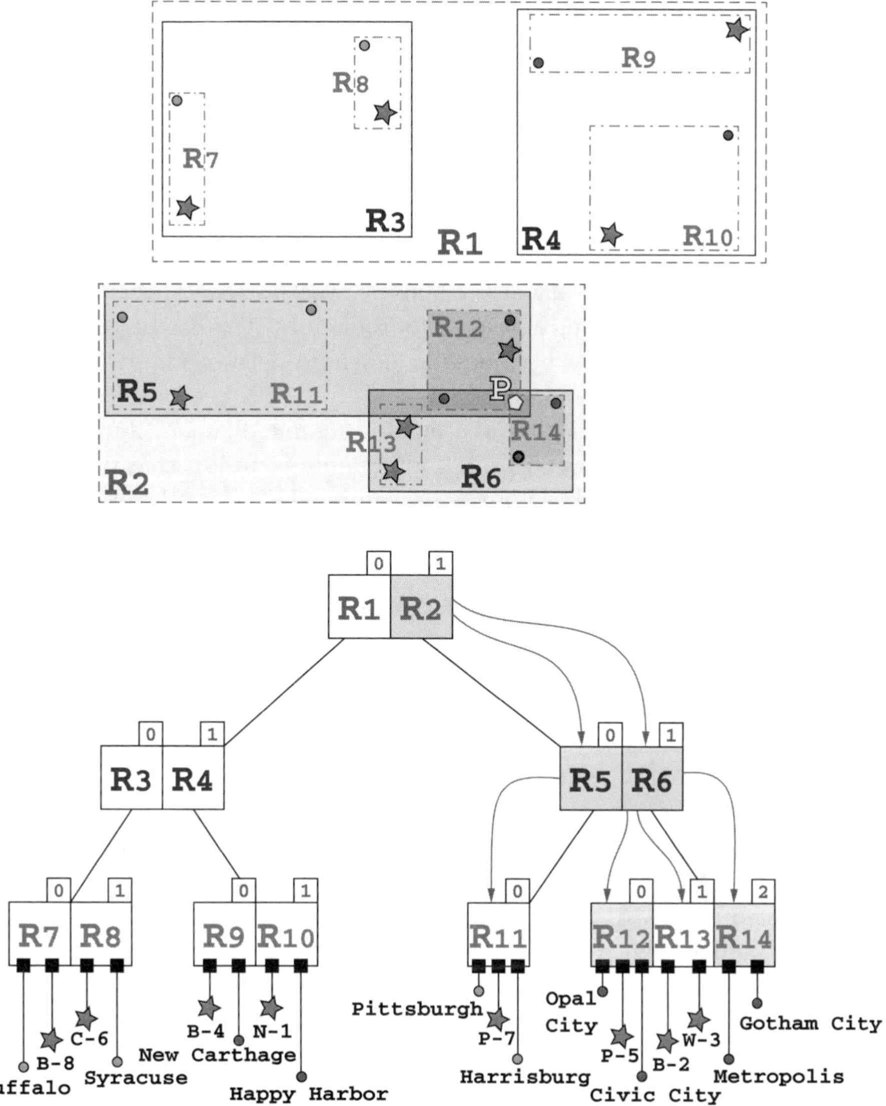
R1
R2
R3
R4
R5
R6
R7
R8
R9
R10
R11
R12
R13
R14
P
Pittsburgh
P-7
Harrisburg
Opal City
P-5
Civic City
B-2
W-3
Gotham City
Metropolis
B-8
Buffalo
C-6
Syracuse
B-4
N-1
New Carthage
Happy Harbor

Figure 10.8 Unsuccessful search on the R-tree in figures 10.4 and 10.5. The path of the search is highlighted in both the Cartesian and tree views, and curved arrows show the branches traversed in the tree. Notice the compact representation of the tree, compared to figure 10.5.

We won't delve into NN-search for R-trees. Now that you should have a high-level understanding of this data structure, we are ready to move on to its evolution, the SS-tree.

It's also worth mentioning that R-trees do not guarantee good worst-case performance, but in practice they usually perform better than k-d trees, so they were for a long time the de facto standard for similarity search and indexing of multidimensional datasets.

10.3 Similarity search tree

In section 10.2, we saw some of the key properties that influence the shape and performance of R-trees. Let's recap them here:

- The splitting heuristic
- The criteria used to choose the sub-tree to add new points (if more than one overlaps)
- The distance metric

For R-trees, we assumed that aligned boxes, hyper-rectangles parallel to the Cartesian axes, are used as bounding envelopes for the nodes. If we lift this constraint, the shape of the bounding envelope becomes the fourth property of a more general class of similarity search trees.

And, indeed, at their core, the main difference between R-trees and SS-trees in their most basic versions, is the shape of bounding envelopes. As shown in figure 10.9, this variant (built on R-trees) uses spheres instead of rectangles.

Although it might seem like a small change, there is strong theoric and practical evidence that suggest using spheres reduces the average number of leaves touched by a similarity (nearest neighbor or region) query. We will discuss this point in more depth in section 10.5.1.

Each internal node `N` is therefore a sphere with a center and a radius. Those two properties are uniquely and completely determined by `N`'s children. `N`'s center is, in fact, the centroid of `N`'s children,[6] and the radius is the maximum distance between the centroid and `N`'s points.

To be fair, when we said that the only difference between R-trees and SS-trees was the shape of the bounding envelopes, we were guilty of omission. The choice of a different shape for the bounding envelopes also forces us to adopt a different splitting heuristic. In the case of SS-trees, instead of trying to reduce the spheres' overlap on split, we aim to reduce the variance of each of the newly created nodes; therefore, the original splitting heuristic chooses the dimension with the highest variance and then splits the sorted list of children to reduce variance along that dimension (we'll see this in more detail in the discussion about insertion in section 10.3.2).

As for R-trees, SS-trees have two parameters, `m` and `M`, respectively the minimum and maximum number of children each node (except the root) is allowed to have.

And like R-trees, bounding envelopes in an SS-tree might overlap. To reduce the overlap, some variants like *SS⁺-trees* introduce a fifth property (also used in R-tree's variants like *R*-trees*), another heuristic used on insert that performs major changes to restructure the tree; we will talk about SS⁺-trees later in this chapter, but for now we will focus on the implementation of plain SS-trees.

---

[6] The centroid is defined as the center of mass of a set of points, whose coordinates are the weighted sum of the points' coordinates. If `N` is a leaf, its center is the centroid of the points belonging to `N`; if `N` is an internal node, then we consider the center of mass of the centroids of its children nodes.

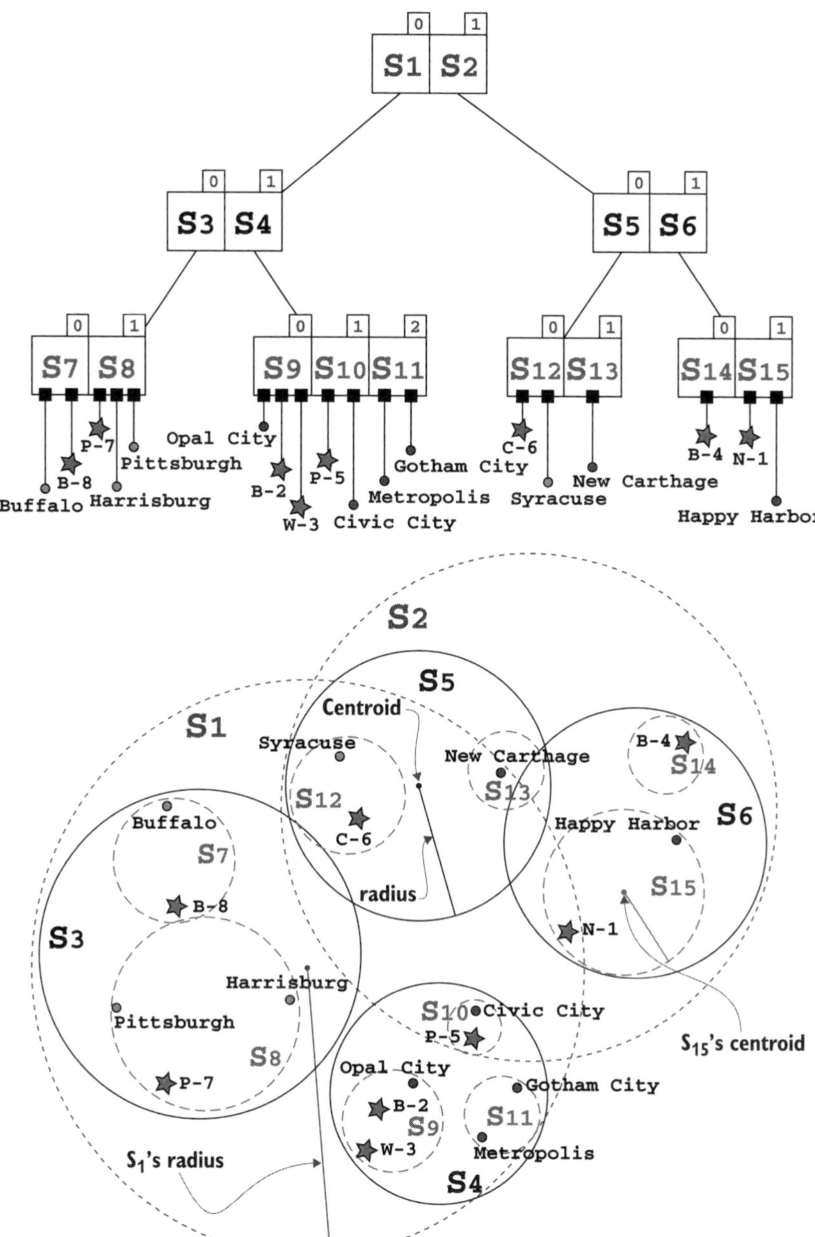
S1
S2
S3
S4
S5
S6
S7
S8
S9
S10
S11
S12
S13
S14
S15
Opal City
Pittsburgh
Harrisburg
Buffalo
B-8
P-7
B-2
P-5
W-3
Civic City
Metropolis
Gotham City
C-6
Syracuse
New Carthage
B-4
N-1
Happy Harbor
Centroid
radius
S$_1$'s radius
S$_{15}$'s centroid

Figure 10.9 Representation of a possible SS-tree covering the same dataset of figures 10.4 and 10.5, with parameters `m==1` and `M==3`. As you can see, the tree structure is similar to R-trees'. For the sake of avoiding clutter, only a few spheres' centroids and radii are shown. For the tree, we use the compact representation (as shown in figures 10.5 and 10.8).

The first step toward a pseudo-implementation for our data structures is, as always, presenting a pseudo-class that models it. In this case, to model an SS-tree we are going to need a class modeling tree nodes. Once we build an SS-tree through its nodes, to access it we just need a pointer to the tree's root. For convenience, as shown in listing 10.1, we will include this link and the values for parameters `m` and `M` in the `SsTree` class, as well as the dimensionality `k` of each data entry, and assume all these values are available from each of the tree nodes.

As we have seen, SS-trees (like R-trees) have two different kind of nodes, leaves and internal nodes, that are structurally and behaviorally different. The former stores `k`-dimensional tuples (references to the points in our dataset), and the latter only has links to its children (which are also nodes of the tree).

To keep things simple and as language-agnostic as possible, we will store both an array of children and an array of points into each node, and a Boolean flag will tell apart leaves from internal nodes. The `children` array will be empty for leaves and the `points` array will be empty for internal nodes.

Listing 10.1 The `SsTree` and `SsNode` classes

```
class SsNode
  #type tuple(k)
  centroid
  #type float
  radius

  #type SsNode[]
  children

  #type tuple(k)[]
  points

  #type boolean
  Leaf

  function SsNode(leaf, points=[], children=[])

class SsTree
  #type SsNode
  root
  #type integer
  m
  #type integer
  M
  #type integer
  k

  function SsTree(k, m, M)
```

Notice how in figure 10.9 we represented our tree nodes as a list of spheres, each of which has a link to a child. We could, of course, add a type `SsSphere` and keep a link to each sphere's only child node as a field of this new type. It wouldn't make a great design, though, and would lead to data duplication (because then both `SsNode` and `SsSphere` would hold fields for centroids and radius) and create an unnecessary level of indirection. Just keep in mind that when you look at the diagrams of SS-trees in these pages, what are shown as components of a tree node are actually its children.

One effective alternative to translate this into code in object-oriented programming is to use inheritance, defining a common abstract class (a class that can't be instantiated to an actual object) or an interface, and two derived classes (one for leaves and one for internal nodes) that share a common data and behavior (defined in the base, abstract class), but are implemented differently. Listing 10.2 shows a possible pseudo-code description of this pattern.

Listing 10.2 Alternative Implementation for SsNode: SsNodeOO

```
abstract class SsNodeOO
  #type tuple(k)
  centroid
  #type float
  radius

class SsInnerNode: SsNodeOO
  #type SsNode[]
  children
  function SsInnerNode(children=[])

class SsLeaf: SsNodeOO
  #type tuple(k)[]
  points
  function SsLeaf(points=[])
```

Although the implementation using inheritance might result in some code duplication and greater effort being required to understand the code, it arguably provides a cleaner solution, removing the logic to choose the type of node that would otherwise be needed in each method of the class.

Although we won't adopt this example in the rest of the chapter, the zealous reader might use it as a starting point to experiment with implementing SS-trees using this pattern.

10.3.1 SS-tree search

Now we are ready to start describing `SsNode's` methods. Although it would feel natural to start with insertion (we need to build a tree before searching it, after all), it is also true that as for many tree-based data structures, the first step to insert (or delete) an entry is searching the node where it should be inserted.

Hence, we will need the `search` method (meant as *exact element search*) before we can insert a new item. While we will see how this step in the `insert` method is slightly different from plain `search`, it will still be easier to describe insertion after we have discussed traversing the tree.

Figures 10.10 and 10.11 show the steps of a call to `search` on our example SS-tree. To be fair, the SS-tree we'll use in the rest of the chapter is derived from the one in figure 10.9. You might notice that there are a few more points (the orange stars), a few of the old points have been slightly moved, and we stripped all the points' labels, replacing them with letters from `A` to `W`, in order to remove clutter and have cleaner diagrams. For the same reason, we'll identify the point to search/insert/delete, in this and the following sections, as `Z` (to avoid clashes with points already in the tree).

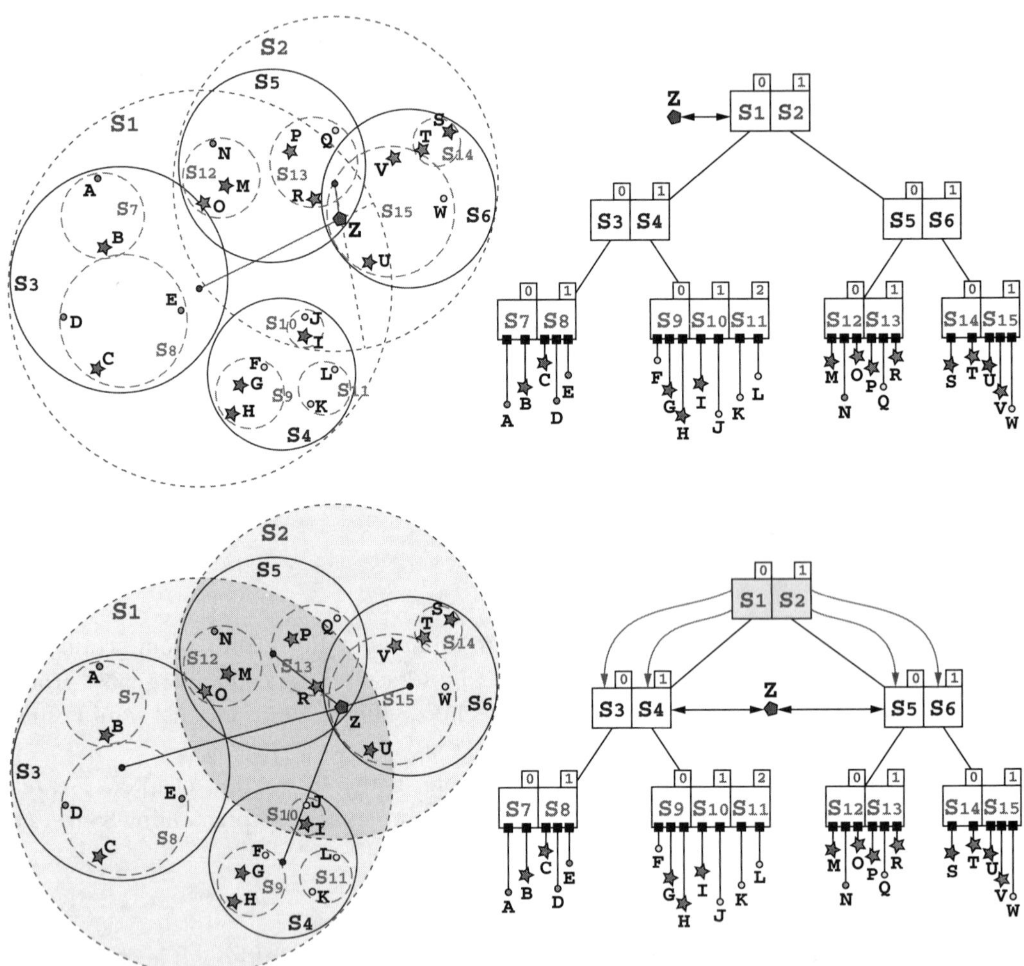
S1 S2
S3 S4
S5 S6
S7 S8
S9 S10 S11
S12 S13
S14 S15
Z
A B C D E F G H I J K L M N O P Q R S T U V W
0 1 2

Figure 10.10 Search on a SS-tree: the first few steps of searching for point Z. The SS-tree shown is derived from the one in figure 10.9, with a few minor changes; the name of the entries have been removed here and letters from `A` to `W` are used to reduce clutter. (Top) The first step of the search is comparing `Z` to the spheres in the tree's root: for each of them, computes the distance between `Z` and its centroid, and checks if it's smaller than the sphere's radius. (Bottom) Since both S_1 and S_2 intersect `Z`, we need to traverse both branches and check spheres S_3 to S_6 for intersection with `Z`.

To continue with our image dataset example, suppose that we now would like to check to see if a specific image `Z` is in our dataset. One option would be comparing `Z` to all images in the dataset. Comparing two images might require some time (especially if, for instance, all images have the same size, and we can't do a quick check on any other trivial image property to rule out obviously different pairs). Recalling that our dataset supposedly has tens of thousands of images, if we go this way, we should be prepared to take a long coffee break (or, depending on our hardware, leave our machine working for the night).

But, of course, by now readers must have learned that we shouldn't despair, because this is the time we provide a better alternative!

And indeed, as we mentioned at the beginning of the chapter, we can create a collection of feature vectors for the images in our dataset, extract the feature vector for `Z`—let's call it F_Z—and perform a search in the feature vectors space instead of directly searching the image dataset.

Now, comparing F_Z to tens or hundreds of thousands of other vectors could also be slow and expensive in terms of time, memory, and disk accesses.

If each memory page stored on disk can hold `M` feature vectors, we would have to perform `n/M` disk accesses and read `n*k` float values from disk.

And that's exactly where an SS-tree comes into play. By using an SS-tree with at most `M` entries per node, and at least `m≤M/2`, we can reduce the number of pages loaded from disk to[7] $2*\log_M(n)$, and the number of float values read to $\sim k*M*\log_M(n)$.

Listing 10.3 shows the pseudo-code for SS-tree's `search` method. We can follow the steps from figures 10.10 and 10.11. Initially `node` will be the root of our example tree, so not a leaf; we'll then go directly to line #7 and start cycling through `node`'s children, in this case S_1 and S_2.

Listing 10.3 The `search` method

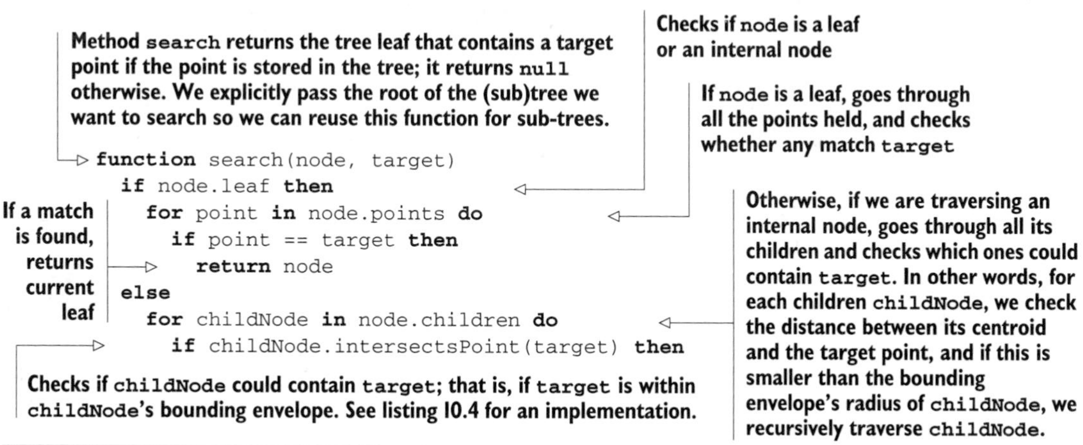
Method search returns the tree leaf that contains a target point if the point is stored in the tree; it returns null otherwise. We explicitly pass the root of the (sub)tree we want to search so we can reuse this function for sub-trees.
Checks if node is a leaf or an internal node
If node is a leaf, goes through all the points held, and checks whether any match target
function search(node, target)
  if node.leaf then
    for point in node.points do
      if point == target then
        return node
  else
    for childNode in node.children do
      if childNode.intersectsPoint(target) then
If a match is found, returns current leaf
Otherwise, if we are traversing an internal node, goes through all its children and checks which ones could contain target. In other words, for each children childNode, we check the distance between its centroid and the target point, and if this is smaller than the bounding envelope's radius of childNode, we recursively traverse childNode.
Checks if childNode could contain target; that is, if target is within childNode's bounding envelope. See listing 10.4 for an implementation.

[7] Since the height of the tree is at most $\log_m(n)$, if `m==M/2` (the choice with the largest height) $\log_{M/2}(n) \sim= \log_M(n)$.

If no child of current node could contain the `target`, or if we are at a leaf and no point matches `target`, then we end up at this line and just return `null` as the result of an unsuccessful search.

If that's the case, performs a recursive search on `childNode`'s branch, and if the result is an actual node (and not `null`), we have found what we were looking for and we can return.

```
      result ← search(childNode, target)
      if result != null then
        return result
  return null
```

For each of them, we compute the distance between `target` (point `Z` in the figure) and the spheres' centroids, as shown in listing 10.4, describing the pseudo-code implementation of method `SsNode::intersectsPoint`. Since for both the spheres the computed (Euclidean) distance is smaller than their radii, this means that either (or both) could contain our target point, and therefore we need to traverse both S_1 and S_2 branches.

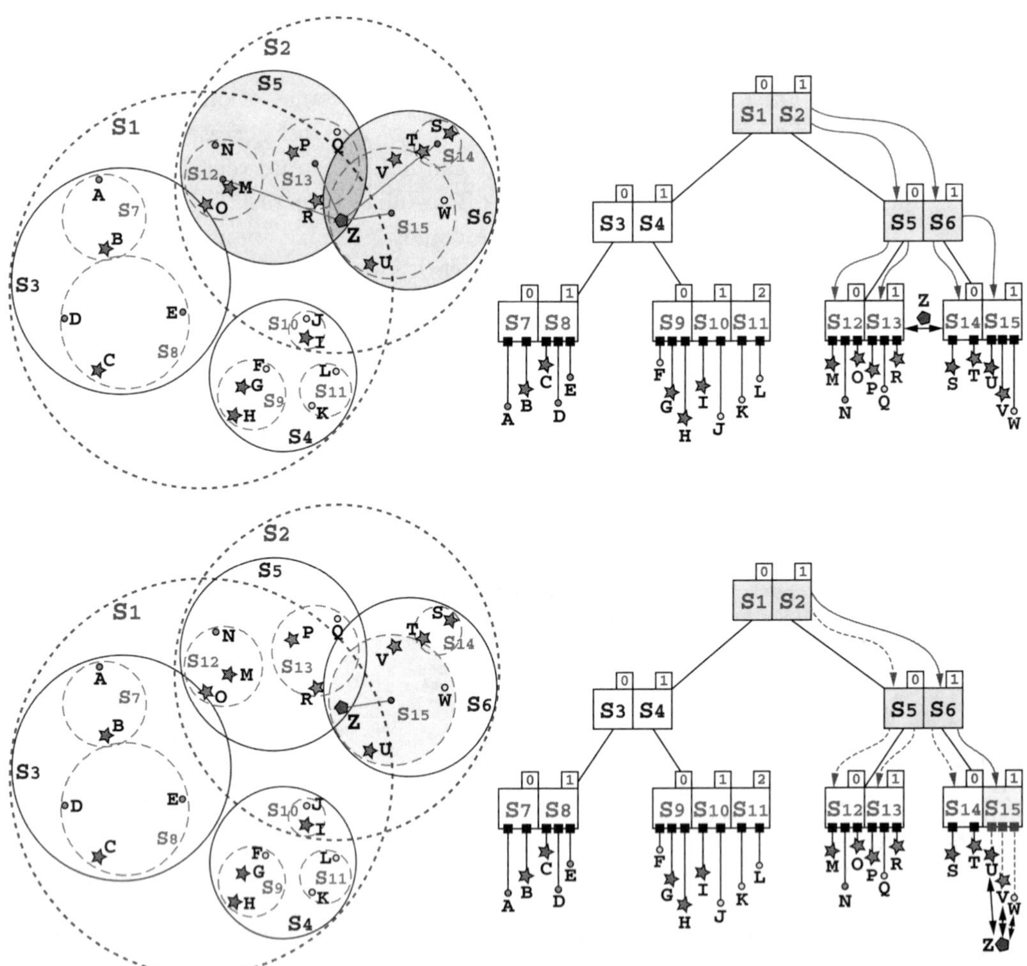

S1
S2
S3
S4
S5
S6
S7
S8
S9
S10
S11
S12
S13
S14
S15
A
B
C
D
E
F
G
H
I
J
K
L
M
N
O
P
Q
R
S
T
U
V
W
Z
0
1
2

Figure 10.11 Search on an SS-tree: Continuing from figure 10.10, we traverse the tree up to leaves. At each step, the spheres highlighted are the ones whose children are being currently traversed (in other words, at each step the union of the highlighted spheres is the smallest area where the searched point could lie).

This is also apparent in figure 10.10, where point Z clearly lies in the intersection of spheres S_1 and S_2.

The next couple of steps in figures 10.10 (bottom half) and 10.11 execute the same lines of code, cycling through node's children until we get to a leaf. It's worth noting that this implementation will perform a depth-first traversal of the node: it will sequentially follow down to leaves, getting to leaves as fast as possible, back-tracking when needed. For the sake of space, these figures show these paths as they were traversed in parallel, which is totally possible with some modifications to the code (that would, however, be dependent on the programming language of an actual implementation, so we will stick with the simpler and less resource-intensive sequential version).

The method will sometime traverse branches where none of the children might contain the target. That's the case, for instance, with the node containing S_3 and S_4. The execution will just end up at line #12 of listing 10.3, returning `null` and back-tracking to the caller. It had initially traversed branch S_1; now the `for-each` loop at line #7 will just move on to branch S_2.

When we finally get to leaves S_{12}-S_{14}, the execution will run the cycle at line #3, where we scan a leaf's points searching for an exact match. If we find one, we can return the current leaf as the result of the search (we assume the tree doesn't contain duplicates, of course).

Listing 10.4 shows a simple implementation for the method checking whether a point is within a node's bounding envelope. As you can see, the implementation is very simple, because it just uses some basic geometry. Notice, however, that the `distance` function is a structural parameter of the SS-tree; it can be the Euclidean distance in a k-dimensional space, but it can also be a different metric.[8]

Listing 10.4 Method `SsNode::intersectsPoint`

Since the bounding envelope is a hyper-sphere, it just needs to check that the distance between the node's centroid and the argument point is within the node's radius. Here, `distance` can be any valid metric function, including (by default) the Euclidean distance in R^k.

Method `intersectsPoint` is defined on `SsNode`. It takes a point and returns `true` if the point is within the bounding envelope of the node.

```
function SsNode:: intersectsPoint(point)
  return distance(this.centroid, point) <= this.radius
```

10.3.2 Insert

As mentioned, insertion starts with a search step. While for more basic trees, such as *binary search trees*, an unsuccessful search returns the one and only node where the new item can be added, for SS-trees we have the same issue we briefly discussed in section 10.2 for R-trees: since nodes can and do overlap, there could be more than one leaf where the new point could be added.

This is such a big deal that we mentioned it as the second property determining the SS-tree's shape. We need to choose a heuristic method to select which branch to traverse, or to select one of the leaves that would already contain the new point.

[8] As long as it satisfies the requirements for a valid metric: being always non-negative, being `null` only between a point and itself, being symmetrical, and abiding by the triangular inequality.

SS-trees originally used a simple heuristic: at each step, they would select the one branch whose centroid is closest to the point that is being inserted (those rare ties that will be faced can be broken arbitrarily).

This is not always ideal, because it might lead to a situation like the one shown in figure 10.12, where a new point z could be added to a leaf already covering it, and instead ends up in another leaf whose envelope becomes larger to accept Z, and ends up overlapping the other leaf. It is also possible, although unlikely, that the leaf selected is not actually the closest one to the target. Since at each level we traverse only the closest node, if the tree is not well balanced, it might happen that at some point during traversal the method bumps into a skewed sphere, with the center of mass far away from a small leaf—something like S_6 in figure 10.12, whose child S_{14} lies far away from its center of mass.

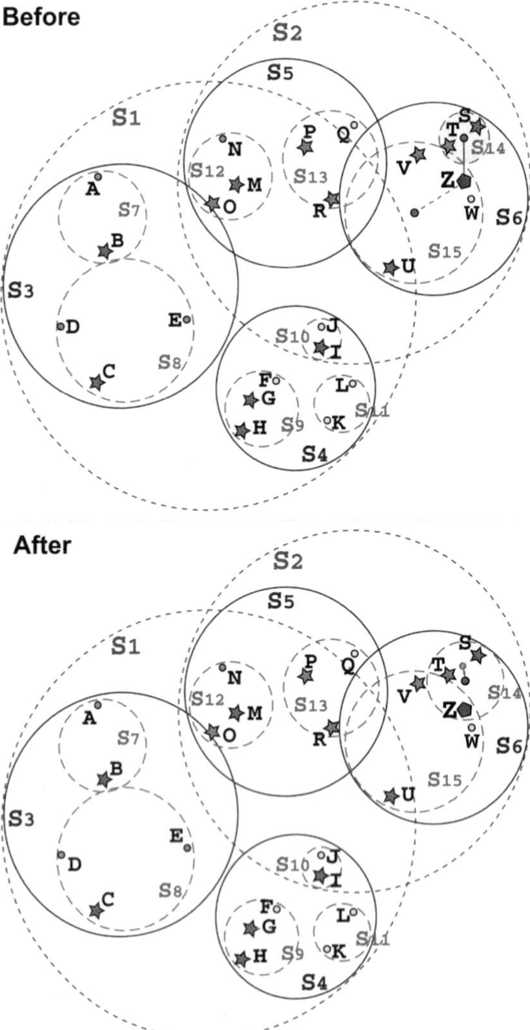
Before
S2
S5
S1
N
P
Q
S
T
S14
V
S12
M
S13
Z
A
O
R
W
S6
S7
B
S15
U
S3
D
E
S10
J
I
C
S8
F
L
G
S11
H
S9
K
S4
After
S2
S5
S1
N
P
Q
S
T
V
S14
S12
M
S13
Z
A
O
R
W
S6
S7
B
S15
U
S3
E
D
S10
J
I
C
S8
F
L
G
S11
H
S9
K
S4

Figure 10.12 An example where the point z, which will be inserted into the tree, is added to the closest leaf, S_{14}, whose bounding envelope becomes larger as a result, and overlaps another existing leaf, S_{15}, which could have held z within its bounding envelope. In the bottom half, notice how S_{14}'s centroid moves as a result of adding the new point to the sphere.

On the other hand, using this heuristic greatly simplifies the code and improves the running time. This way, we have a worst-case bound (for this operation) of $O(\log_m(n))$, because we only follow one path from the root to a leaf. If we were to traverse all branches intersecting Z, in the worst case we could be forced to visit all leaves.

Moreover, the code would also become more complicated because we might have to handle differently the cases where no leaf, exactly one leaf, or more than one leaf intersecting Z are found.

So, we will use here the original heuristic described in the SS-tree first paper, shown in listing 10.5. It can be considered a simpler version of the search method described in section 10.3.1, since it will only traverse a single path in the tree. Figure 10.13 shows the difference with a call to the search method for the same tree and point (refer to figures 10.10 and 10.11 for a comparison).

Listing 10.5 The `searchParentLeaf` method

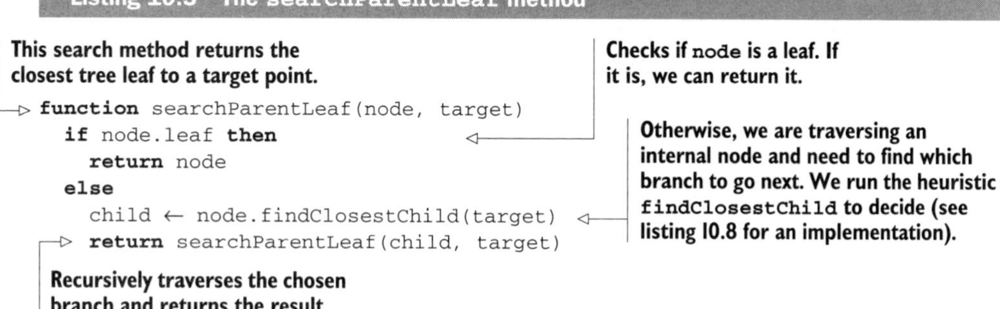
This search method returns the closest tree leaf to a target point.
Checks if node is a leaf. If it is, we can return it.
Otherwise, we are traversing an internal node and need to find which branch to go next. We run the heuristic findClosestChild to decide (see listing 10.8 for an implementation).
Recursively traverses the chosen branch and returns the result

```
function searchParentLeaf(node, target)
  if node.leaf then
    return node
  else
    child ← node.findClosestChild(target)
    return searchParentLeaf(child, target)
```

However, listing 10.5 is just meant to illustrate how this traversal works. In the actual `insert` method, we won't call it as a separate step, but rather integrate it. That's because finding the closest leaf is just the first step; we are far from being done with insertion yet, and we might need to backtrack our steps. That's why we are implementing `insert` as a recursive function, and each time a sub-call returns, we backtrack on the path from the root to current node.

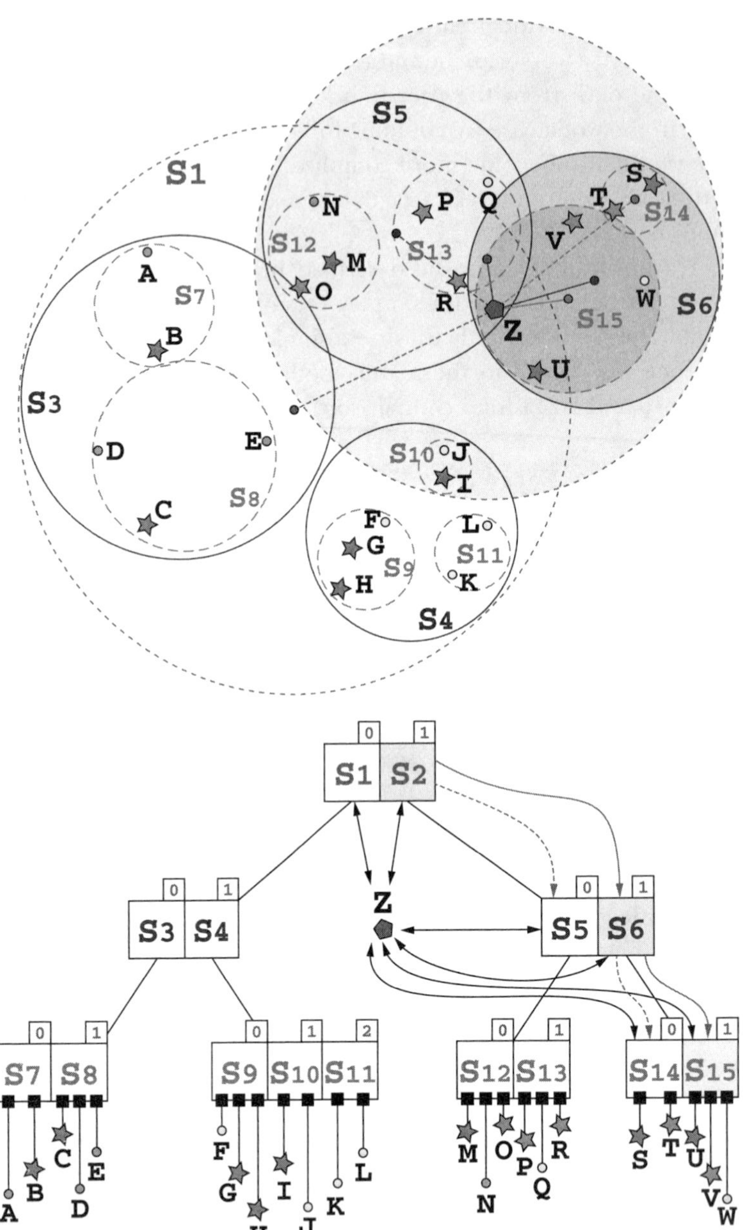
S5
S1
S12
S13
S14
S6
S15
S7
S3
S8
S10
S9
S11
S4
A
B
C
D
E
F
G
H
I
J
K
L
M
N
O
P
Q
R
S
T
U
V
W
Z
S1 S2
S3 S4
S5 S6
S7 S8
S9 S10 S11
S12 S13
S14 S15

Figure 10.13 An example of the tree traversing for method `searchParentLeaf`. In contrast with figures 10.10 and 10.11, here the steps are condensed into a single diagram for the sake of space. The fact that only one path is traversed allows this compact representation. Notice how at each step the distance between `Z` and the centroids in the current node are computed (in this figure, we used for distances the same level-based color code as for spheres, and the segments drawn for distances have one end in the center of the sphere they are computed from, so it's easy to spot the distance to the root node, and to spheres at level 1, and so on), and only the branch with the shortest distance (drawn as a thicker, solid line) is chosen. The spheres' branches traversed are highlighted on both representations.

Suppose, in fact, that we have found that we should add `Z` to some leaf `L`, that already contains `j` points. We know that `j ≥ m > 1`, so the leaf is not empty, but there could be three very different situations:

1. If `L` already contains `Z`, we don't do anything, assuming we don't support duplicates (otherwise, we can refer to the remaining two cases).
2. `j < M`—In this case, we add `Z` to the list of `L`'s children, recompute the centroid and radius for `L`, and we are done. This case is shown in figure 10.12, where `L==S`$_{14}$. On the left side of the figure, you can see how the centroid and radius of the bounding envelopes are updated as a result of adding `Z` to `S`$_{14}$.
3. `j == M`—This is the most complicated case, because if we add another point to `L`, it will violate the invariant requiring that a leaf holds no more than `M` points. The only way to solve this is by splitting the leaf's point into two sets and creating two new leaves that will be added to `L`'s parent, `N`. Unfortunately, by doing this we can end up in the same situation as if `N` already had `M` children. Again, the only way we can cope with this is by splitting `N`'s children into two sets (defining two spheres), removing `N` from its parent `P`, and adding the two new spheres to `P`. Obviously, `P` could also now have `M+1` children! Long story short, we need to backtrack to the root, and we can only stop if we get to a node that has less than `M` children, or if we do get to the root. If we have to split the root, then we will create a new root with just two children, and the height of the tree will grow by 1 (and that's the only case where this can happen).

Listing 10.6 shows an implementation of the `insert` method using the cases just described:

- The tree traversal, equivalent to the `searchParentLeaf` method, appears at lines #10 and #11.
- Case 1 is handled at line #3, where we return `null` to let the caller know there is no further action required.
- Case 2 corresponds to lines #6 and #18 in the pseudo-code, also resulting in the method returning `null`.
- Case 3, which clearly is the most complicated option, is coded in lines #19 and #20.
- Backtracking is handled at lines #12 to #21.

Figures 10.14 and 10.15 illustrate the third case, where we insert a point in a leaf that already contains `M` points. At a high level, insertion in SS-trees follows B-tree's algorithm for `insert`. The only difference is in the way we split nodes (in B-trees the list of elements is just split into two halves). Of course, in B-trees links to children and ordering are also handled differently, as we saw in section 10.2.

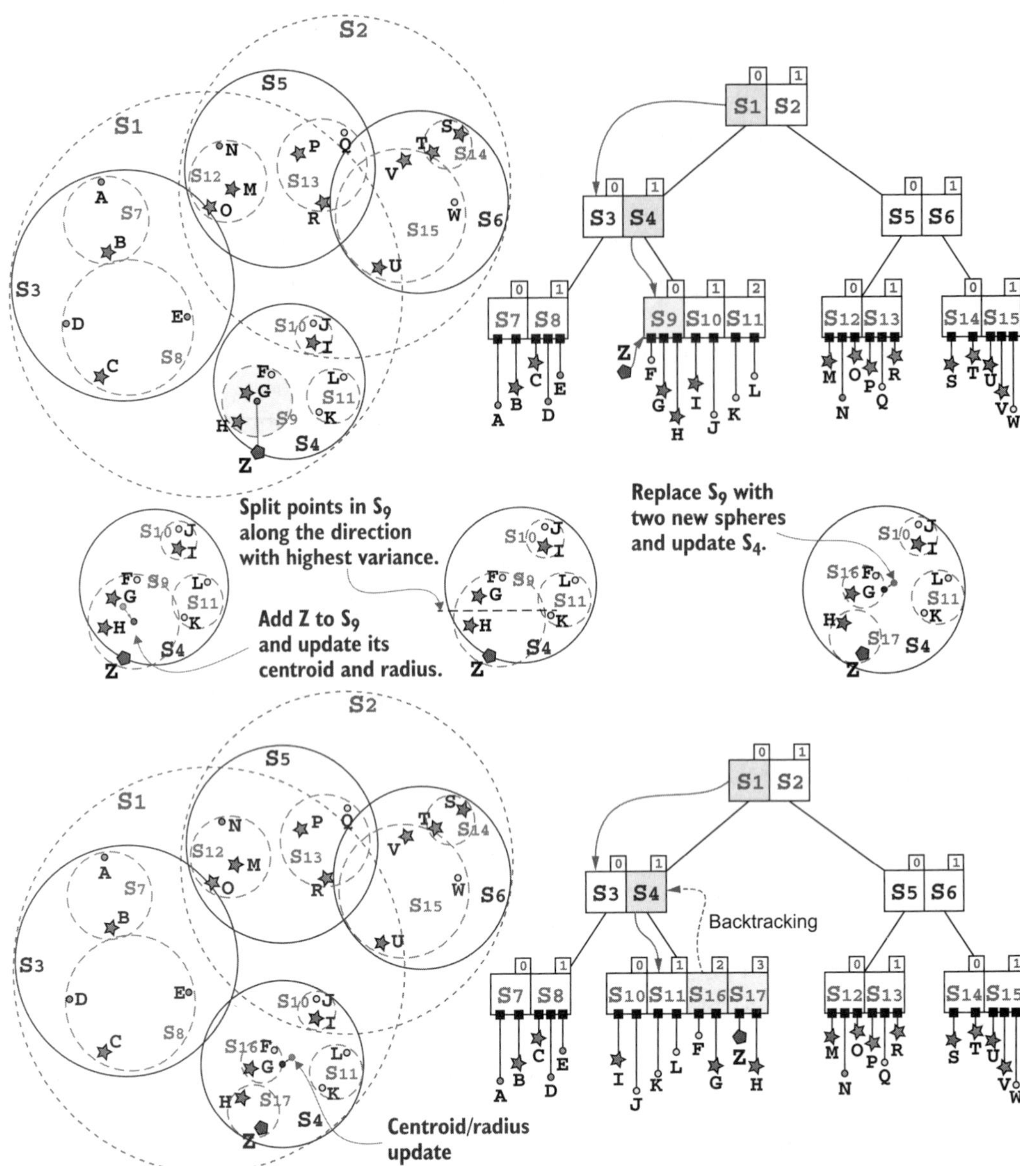
Split points in S_9 along the direction with highest variance.
Add Z to S_9 and update its centroid and radius.
Replace S_9 with two new spheres and update S_4.
Backtracking
Centroid/radius update

Figure 10.14 Inserting a point in a full leaf. (Top) The search step to find the right leaf. (Center) A closeup of the area involved. S_9 needs to be updated, recomputing its centroid and radius. Then we can find the direction along which points have the highest variance (y, in the example) and split the points so that the variance of the two new point sets is minimal. Finally, we remove S_9 from its parent S_4 and add two new leaves containing the two point sets resulting from the split. (Bottom) The final result is that we now need to update S_4's centroid and radius and backtrack.

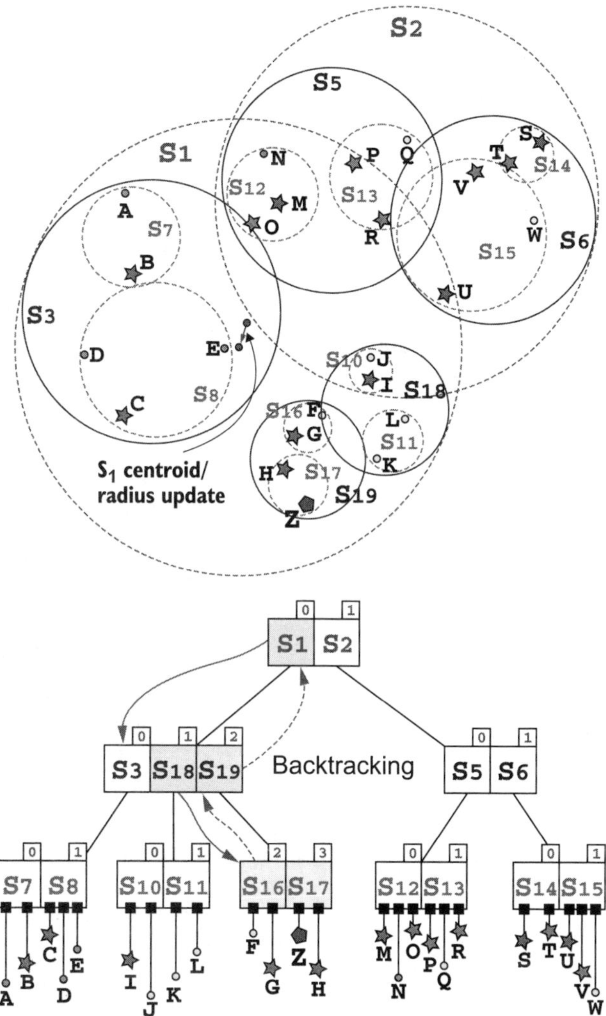
S2
S5
S1
S12
S13
S14
S15
S6
S3
S7
S8
S10
S18
S16
S11
S17
S19
S_1 centroid/
radius update
S1 S2
S3 S18 S19
Backtracking
S5 S6
S7 S8
S10 S11
S16 S17
S12 S13
S14 S15
A B C D E
I J K L
F G Z H
M N O P Q R
S T U V W

Figure 10.15 Backtracking in method `insert` after splitting a leaf. Continuing from figure 10.14, after we split leaf S_9 into nodes S_{16} and S_{17}, we backtrack to S_9's parent S_4, and add these two new leaves to it, as shown at the end of figure 10.14. S_4 now has four children, one too many. We need to split it as well. Here we show the result of splitting S_4 into two new nodes, S_{18} and S_{19}, that will be added to S_4's parent, S_1, to which, in turn, we will backtrack. Since it now has only three children (and `M==3`) we just recompute centroid and radius for S_1's bounding envelope, and we can stop backtracking.

In listing 10.6 we used several helper functions[9] to perform insertion; however, there is still one case that is not handled. What happens when we get to the root and we need to split it?

[9] Remember: one of the golden rules of clean code is breaking up long, complex methods into smaller ones, so that each method is focused on one goal only.

The reason for not handling this case as part of the method in listing 10.6 is that we would need to update the root of the tree, and this is an operation that needs to be performed on the tree's class, where we do have access to the root.

Listing 10.6 The insert method

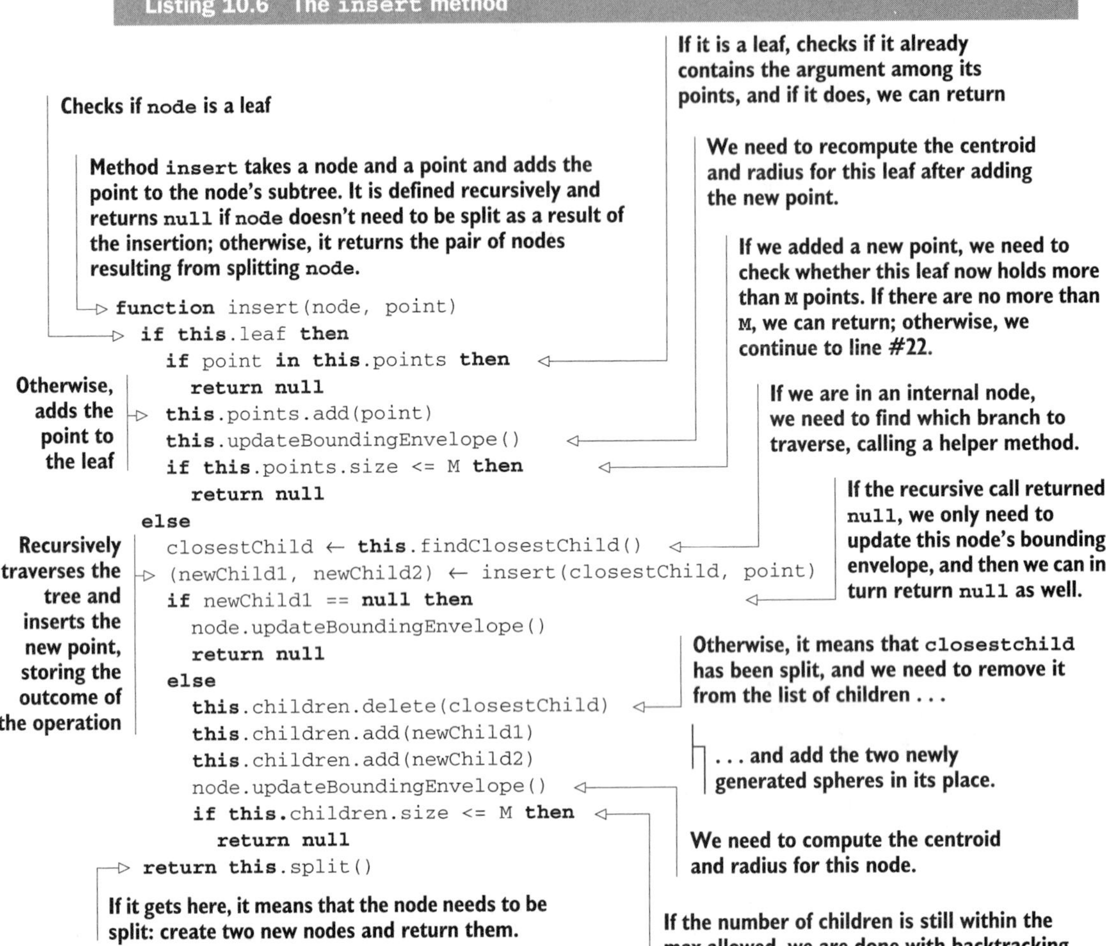

```
function insert(node, point)
  if this.leaf then
    if point in this.points then
      return null
    this.points.add(point)
    this.updateBoundingEnvelope()
    if this.points.size <= M then
      return null
  else
    closestChild ← this.findClosestChild()
    (newChild1, newChild2) ← insert(closestChild, point)
    if newChild1 == null then
      node.updateBoundingEnvelope()
      return null
    else
      this.children.delete(closestChild)
      this.children.add(newChild1)
      this.children.add(newChild2)
      node.updateBoundingEnvelope()
      if this.children.size <= M then
        return null
  return this.split()
```

Method insert takes a node and a point and adds the point to the node's subtree. It is defined recursively and returns null if node doesn't need to be split as a result of the insertion; otherwise, it returns the pair of nodes resulting from splitting node.
Checks if node is a leaf
If it is a leaf, checks if it already contains the argument among its points, and if it does, we can return
Otherwise, adds the point to the leaf
We need to recompute the centroid and radius for this leaf after adding the new point.
If we added a new point, we need to check whether this leaf now holds more than M points. If there are no more than M, we can return; otherwise, we continue to line #22.
If we are in an internal node, we need to find which branch to traverse, calling a helper method.
Recursively traverses the tree and inserts the new point, storing the outcome of the operation
If the recursive call returned null, we only need to update this node's bounding envelope, and then we can in turn return null as well.
Otherwise, it means that closestchild has been split, and we need to remove it from the list of children . . .
. . . and add the two newly generated spheres in its place.
We need to compute the centroid and radius for this node.
If the number of children is still within the max allowed, we are done with backtracking.
If it gets here, it means that the node needs to be split: create two new nodes and return them.

Therefore, we will give an explicit implementation of the tree's method for `insert`. Remember, we will actually only expose methods defined on the data structure classes (`KdTree`, `SsTree`, and so on) and not on the nodes' classes (such as `SsNode`), but we usually omit the former's when they are just wrappers around the nodes' methods. Look at listing 10.7 to check out how we can handle root splits. Also, let me highlight this again: this code snippet is the only point where our tree's height grows.

Listing 10.7 The `SsTree::insert` method

```
function SsTree::insert(point)
  (newChild1, newChild2) ← insert(this.root, point)
  if newChild1 != null then
    this.root = new SsNode(false, children=[newChild1, newChild2])
```

- Method `insert` is defined on `SsTree`. It takes a point and doesn't return anything.
- Calls the `insert` function on the root and stores the result
- If, and only if, the result of `insert` is not `null`, it needs to replace the old tree root with a newly created node, which will have as its children the two nodes resulting from splitting the old root.

10.3.3 Insertion: Variance, means, and projections

Now let's get into the details of the (many) helper methods we call in listing 10.6, starting with the heuristic method, described in listing 10.8, to find a node's closest child to a point `Z`. As mentioned, we will just cycle through a node's children, compute the distance between their centroids and `Z`, and choose the bounding envelope that minimizes it.

Listing 10.8 The `SsNode::findClosestChild` method

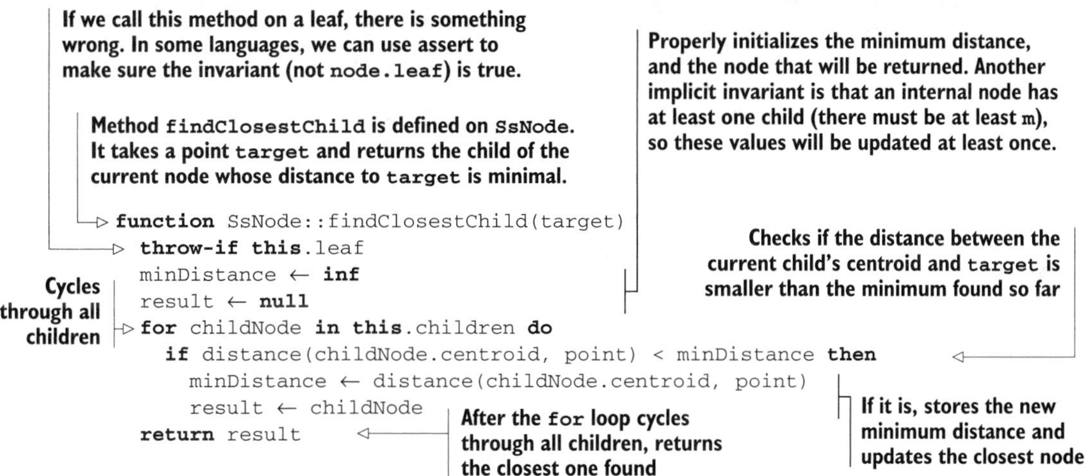
If we call this method on a leaf, there is something wrong. In some languages, we can use assert to make sure the invariant (not node.leaf) is true.
Method findClosestChild is defined on SsNode. It takes a point target and returns the child of the current node whose distance to target is minimal.
Properly initializes the minimum distance, and the node that will be returned. Another implicit invariant is that an internal node has at least one child (there must be at least m), so these values will be updated at least once.
Checks if the distance between the current child's centroid and target is smaller than the minimum found so far
Cycles through all children
If it is, stores the new minimum distance and updates the closest node
After the for loop cycles through all children, returns the closest one found

```
function SsNode::findClosestChild(target)
  throw-if this.leaf
  minDistance ← inf
  result ← null
  for childNode in this.children do
    if distance(childNode.centroid, point) < minDistance then
      minDistance ← distance(childNode.centroid, point)
      result ← childNode
  return result
```

Figure 10.16 shows what happens when we need to split a leaf. First we recompute the radius and centroid of the leaf after including the new point, and then we also compute the variance of the `M+1` points' coordinates along the `k` directions of the axis in order to find the direction with the highest variance; this is particularly useful with skewed sets of points, like S_9 in the example, and helps to reduce spheres volume and, in turn, overlap.

If you refer to figure 10.16, you can see how a split along the `x` axis would have produced two sets with points `G` and `H` on one side, and `F` and `Z` on the other. Comparing the result with figure 10.14, there is no doubt about which is the best final result!

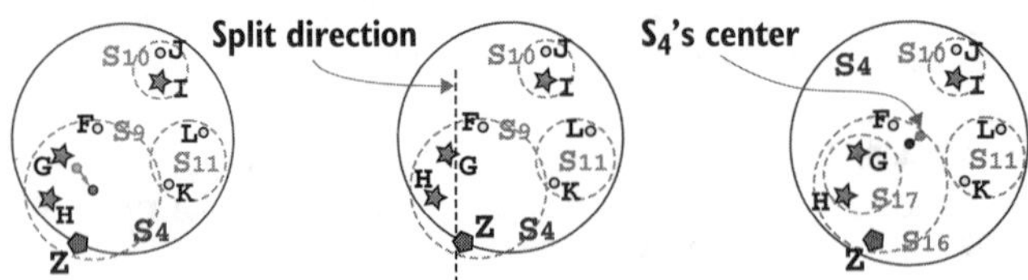
Split direction
S4's center
S10
S9
S11
S4
S17
S16
F
G
H
I
J
K
L
Z

Figure 10.16 Splitting a leaf along a non-optimal direction. In this case, the `x` axis is the direction with minimal variance. Comparing the final result to figure 10.14, although `S4`'s shape doesn't change significantly, S_{16} has more than doubled in size and completely overlaps S_{17}; this means that any search targeted within S_{17} will also have to traverse S_{16}.

Of course, the outcome is not always so neat. If the direction of maximum variance is rotated at some angle with respect to the x axis (imagine, for instance, the same points rotated 45° clockwise WRT the leaf's centroid), then neither axis direction will produce the optimal result. On average, however, this simpler solution does help.

So, how do we perform the split? We start with listing 10.9, which describes the method to find the direction with maximum variance. It's a simple method performing a global maximum search in a linear space.

Listing 10.9 The `SsNode::directionOfMaxVariance` method

```
function SsNode::directionOfMaxVariance()
  maxVariance ← 0
  directionIndex ← 0
  centroids ← this.getEntriesCentroids()
  for i in {0..k-1} do
    if varianceAlongDirection(centroids, i) > maxVariance then
      maxVariance ← varianceAlongDirection(centroids, i)
      directionIndex ← i
  return directionIndex
```

- Method `directionOfMaxVariance` is defined on `SsNode`. It returns the index of the direction along which the children of a node have maximum variance.
- Properly initializes the maximum variance and the index of the direction with max variance
- Gets the centroids of the items inside the node's bounding envelope. For a leaf, those are the points held by the leaf, while for an internal node, the centroids of the node's children.
- Cycles through all directions: their indices, in a `k`-dimensional space, go from `0` to `k-1`.
- Checks whether the variance along the `i`-th axis is larger than the maximum found so far
- If it is, stores the new maximum variance and updates the direction's index
- After the `for` loop cycles through all axis' directions, returns the index of the direction for which we have found the largest variance

We need, of course, to compute the variance at each step of the `for` loop at line #5. Perhaps this is the right time to remind you what variance is and how it is computed. Given a set S of real values, we define its mean μ as the ratio between the sum of the values and their multiplicities:

$$\mu = \frac{1}{|S|}\sum_{s \in S} s$$

Once we've defined the mean, we can then define the variance (usually denoted as σ^2) as the mean of the squares of the differences between `S`'s mean and each of its elements:

$$\sigma^2 = \frac{1}{|S|}\sum_{s \in S}(s-\mu)^2$$

So, given a set of n points $P_0..P_{n-1}$, each P_j with coordinates $(P_{(j,0)}, P_{(j,1)}, \ldots, P_{(j,k-1)})$, the formulas for mean and variance along the direction of the `i`-th axis are

$$\mu_i = \frac{1}{n}\sum_{j=0}^{n-1} P_{j,i}$$

$$\sigma_i^2 = \frac{1}{n}\sum_{j=0}^{n-1}(P_{j,i}-\mu_i)^2$$

These formulas are easily translatable into code, and in most programming languages you will find an implementation of the method computing variance in core libraries; therefore, we won't show the pseudo-code here. Instead, let's see how both functions for variance and mean are used in the `updateBoundingEnvelope` method (listing 10.10) that computes a node centroid and radius.

Listing 10.10 The `SsNode::updateBoundingEnvelope` method

```
function SsNode::updateBoundingEnvelope()
  points ← this.getCentroids()
  for i in {0..k-1} do
    this.centroid[i] ← mean{point[i] for point in points}
  this.radius ←
    max{distance(this.centroid, entry)+entry.radius for entry in points}
```

Gets the centroids of the items inside the node's bounding envelope. For a leaf, those are the points held by the leaf, while for an internal node, the centroids of the node's children.

Method `updateBoundingEnvelope` is defined on `SsNode`. It updates the centroid and radius for the current node.

Cycles through the `k` coordinates of the (`k`-dimensional) space

For each coordinate, computes the centroid's value as mean of the points' values for that coordinate. For instance, for the `x` axis, computes the mean of all `x` coordinates over all points/children in the node.

The radius is the maximum distance between the node's centroid and its children's envelope. This distance includes the (Euclidean) distance between the two centroids, plus the radius of the children. We assume that points here have radius equal to `0`.

This method computes the centroid for a node as the center of mass of its children's centroids. Remember, for leaves, their children are just the points it contains, while for internal nodes, their children are other nodes.

The center of mass is a k-dimensional point, each of whose coordinates is the mean of the coordinates of all the other children's centroids.[10]

Once we have the new centroid, we need to update the radius of the node's bounding envelope. This is defined as the minimum radius for which the bounding envelope includes all the bounding envelopes for the current node's children; in turn, we can define it as the maximum distance between the current node's centroid and any point in its children. Figure 10.17 shows how and why these distances are computed for each child: it's the sum of the distance between the two centroids and the child's radius (as long as we assume that points have `radius==0`, this definition also works for leaves).

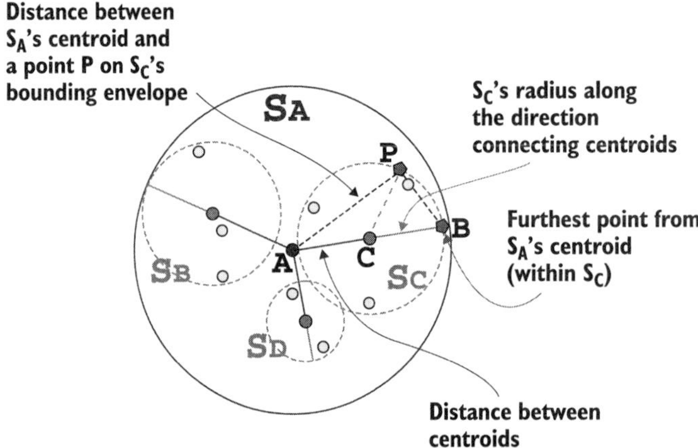
Distance between
S_A's centroid and
a point P on S_C's
bounding envelope
SA
P
S_C's radius along
the direction
connecting centroids
B
Furthest point from
S_A's centroid
(within S_C)
SB
A
C
SC
SD
Distance between
centroids

Figure 10.17 Computing the radius of an internal node. The point in S_C that is further away from S_A's centroid A is the point on the bounding envelope that's furthest from C along the opposite direction WRT S_A's centroid, and its distance is therefore the sum of the distance A-C between the two centroids, plus S_C's radius. If we choose another point P on the bounding envelope, its distance from A must be smaller than the distance A-B, because metrics by definition need to obey the triangular inequality, and the other two edges of triangle ACP are AC and CP, which is S_C's radius. You can check that this is also true for any of the other envelopes in the figure.

10.3.4 Insertion: Split nodes

We can now move to the implementation of the `split` method in listing 10.11.

Listing 10.11 The `SsNode::split` method

Method `split` is defined on `SsNode`. It returns the two new nodes resulting from the split.

```
function SsNode::split()
  splitIndex ← this.findSplitIndex(coordinateIndex)
  if this.leaf then
```

Finds the best "split index" for the list of points (leaves) or children (internal nodes)

[10]Assuming a point's centroid is the point itself. We will also assume points have a radius equal to 0.

If this is a leaf, the new nodes resulting from the split will be two leaves, each with part of the points of the current leaf. Given `splitIndex`, the first leaf will have all points from the beginning of the list to `splitIndex` (not included), and the other leaf will have the rest of the `points` list.

If this node is internal, then we create two new internal nodes, each with one of the partitions of the `children` list.

```
    newNode1 ← new SsNode(true, points=this.points[0..splitIndex-1])
    newNode2 ← new SsNode(true, points=this.points[splitIndex..])
  else
    newNode1 ← new SsNode(false, children=this.children[0.. index-1])
    newNode2 ← new SsNode(false, children=this.children [index..])
  return (newNode1, newNode2)
```

Returns the pair of new `SsNodes` created

This method looks relatively simple, because most of the leg work is performed by the auxiliary method `findSplitIndex`, described in listing 10.12.

Listing 10.12 The `SsNode::findSplitIndex` method

Method `findSplitIndex` is defined on `SsNode`. It returns the optimal index for a node split. For a leaf, the index refers to the list of points, while for an internal node it refers to the children's list. Either list will be sorted as a side effect of this method.

Finds along which axes the coordinates of the entries' centroids have the highest variance

We need to sort the node's entries (either points or children) by the chosen coordinate.

Gets a list of the centroids of this node's entries: a list of points for a leaf, and a list of the children's centroids, in case we are at an internal node. Then, for each centroid, extract only the coordinate given by `coordinateIndex`.

```
function SsNode::findSplitIndex()
  coordinateIndex ← this.directionOfMaxVariance()
  this.sortEntriesByCoordinate(coordinateIndex)
  points ← {point[coordinateIndex] for point in this.getCentroids()}
  return minVarianceSplit(points, coordinateIndex)
```

Finds and returns which index will result in a partitioning with the minimum total variance

After finding the direction with maximum variance, we sort[11] points or children (depending on if a node is a leaf or an internal node) based on their coordinates for that same direction, and then, after getting the list of centroids for the node's entries, we split this list, again along the direction of max variance. We'll see how to do that in a moment.

Before that, we again ran into the method returning the centroids of the entries within the node's bounding envelope, so it's probably the right time to define it! As we mentioned before, the logic of the method is dichotomic:

- If the node is a leaf, this means that it returns the points contained in it.
- Otherwise it will return the centroids of the node's children.

[11] Disclaimer: A function that returns a value and has a side effect is far from ideal and not the cleanest design. Using indirect sorting would be a better solution. Here, we used the simplest solution because of limited space, but be advised.

Listing 10.13 puts this definition into pseudo-code.

Listing 10.13 The SsNode::getEntriesCentroids method

Method `getEntriesCentroids` is defined on `SsNode`. It returns the centroids of the entries within the node's bounding envelope.

```
function SsNode::getEntriesCentroids()
  if this.leaf then
    return this.points
  else
    return {child.centroid for child in this.children}
```

If the node is a leaf, we can just return its points.

Otherwise, we need to return a list of all the centroids of this node's children. We use a construct typically called list-comprehension to denote this list (see appendix A).

After retrieving the index of the split point, we can actually split the node entries. Now we need two different conditional branches to handle leaves and internal nodes differently: we need to provide to the node constructors the right arguments, depending on the type of node we want to create. Once we have the new nodes constructed, all we need to do is return them.

Hang tight; we aren't done yet. I know we have been going through this section for a while now, but we're still missing one piece of the puzzle to finish our implementation of the `insert` method: the `splitPoints` helper function.

This method might seem trivial, but it's actually a bit tricky to get it right. Let's say it needs at least some thought.

So, let's first go through an example, and then write some pseudo-code for it! Figure 10.18 illustrates the steps we need to perform such a split. We start with a node containing eight points. We don't know, and don't need to know, if those are dataset points or nodes' centroids; it is irrelevant for this method.

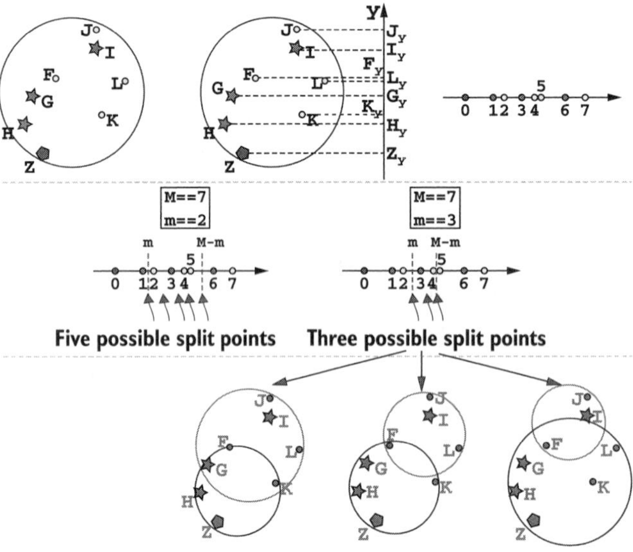
Five possible split points
Three possible split points
M==7
m==2
M==7
m==3
m
M-m

Figure 10.18 Splitting a set of points along the direction of maximum variance. (Top) The bounding envelope and its points to split; the direction of maximum variance is along the y axis (center), so we project all points on this axis. On the right, we rotate the axis for convenience and replace the point labels with indices. (Middle) Given that there are 8 points, we can infer `M` must be equal to `7`. Then `m` can be any value ≤`3`. Since the algorithm chooses a single split index, partitioning the points on its two sides, and each partition needs to have at least `m` points, depending on the actual value of `m`, we can have a different number of choices for the split index. (Bottom) We show the three possible resulting splits for the case where `m==3`: the split index can be `3`, `4`, or `5`. We will choose the option for which the sum of the variances for the two sets is minimal.

Suppose we have computed the direction of maximum variance and that it is along the `y` axis; we then need to project the points along this axis, which is equivalent to only considering the `y` coordinate of the points because of the definition of our coordinate system.

In the diagram we show the projection of the points, since it's visually more intuitive. For the same reason, we then rotate the axis and the projections 90° clockwise, remove the points' labels, and index the projected points from left to right. In our code, we would have to sort our points according to the `y` coordinate (as we saw in listing 10.12), and then we can just consider their indices; an alternative could be using indirect sorting and keeping a table of sorted/unsorted indices, but this would substantially complicate the remaining code.

As shown, we have eight points to split. We can deduce that the parameter `M`, the maximum number of leaves/children for a tree node, is equal to 7, and thus `m`, the minimum number of entries, can only be equal to 2 or 3 (technically it could also be 1, but that's a choice that would produce skewed trees, and usually it's not even worth implementing these trees if we use `m==1`).

It's worth mentioning again that the value for `m` *must* be chosen at the time of creation of our SS-Tree, and therefore it is fixed when we call `split`. Here we are just reasoning about how this choice influences how the splits are performed, and ultimately the structure of the tree.

And indeed, this value is crucial to the `split` method, because each of the two partitions created will need to have at least `m` points; therefore, since we are using a single index split,[12] the possible values for this split index go from `m` to `M-m`. In our example, as shown in the middle section of figure 10.18, this means

- If `m==2`, then we can choose any index between 2 and 6 (5 choices).
- If `m==3`, then the alternatives are between 3 and 5 (3 choices).

Now suppose we had chosen `m==3`. The bottom section of figure 10.18 shows the resulting split for each of the three alternative choices we have for the split index. We will have to choose the one that minimizes variance for both nodes (usually, we minimize the sum of the variances), but we only minimize variance along the direction we perform the split, so in the example we will only compute the variance of the y coordinates of the two sets of points. Unlike with R-trees, we won't try to minimize the bounding envelopes' overlap at this stage, although it turns out that reducing variance along the direction that had the highest variance brings us, as an indirect consequence, a reduction of the average overlap of the new nodes.

Also, with SS^+-trees, we will tackle the issue of overlapping bounding envelopes separately.

[12]For SS-trees we partition the ordered list of points by selecting the split index for the list, and then each point on the left of the index goes in one partition, and each point on the right in the other partition.

For now, to finish with the insertion method, please look at listing 10.14 for an implementation of the `minVarianceSplit` method. As mentioned, it's just a linear search among `M - 2*(m-1)` possible options for the split index of the points.

Listing 10.14 The `minVarianceSplit` method

```
function minVarianceSplit(values)
  minVariance ← inf
  splitIndex ← m
  for i in {m, |values|-m} do
    variance1 ← variance(values[0..i-1])
    variance2 ← variance(values[i..|values|-1])
    if variance1 + variance2 < minVariance then
      minVariance ← variance1 + variance2
      splitIndex ← i
  return splitIndex
```

- Method `minVarianceSplit` takes a list of real values. The method returns the optimal index for a node split of the values. In particular, it returns the index of the first element of the second partition; the split is optimal with respect to the variance of the two sets. The method assumes the input is already sorted.
- Initializes temporary variables for the minimum variance and the index where to split the list
- Goes through all the possible values for the split index. One constraint is that both sets need to have at least `m` points, so we can exclude all choices for which the first set has less than `m` elements, as well as those where the second set is too small.
- For each possible value `i` for the split index, selects the points before and after the split, and computes the variances of the two sets
- If the sum of the variances just computed is better than the best result so far, updates the temporary variables
- Returns the best option found

And with this, we can finally close this section about `SsTree::insert`. You might feel this was a very long road to get here, and you'd be right: this is probably the most complicated code we've described so far. Take your time to read the last few sub-sections multiple times, if it helps, and then brace yourself: we are going to delve into the `delete` method next, which is likely even more complicated.

10.3.5 Delete

Like `insert`, `delete` in SS-trees is also heavily based on B-tree's `delete`. The former is normally considered so complicated that many textbooks skip it altogether (for the sake of space), and implementing it is usually avoided as long as possible. The SS-tree version, of course, is even more complicated than the original one.

But one of the aspects where R-trees and SS-trees overcome k-d trees is that while the latter is guaranteed to be balanced only if initialized on a static dataset, both can remain balanced even when supporting dynamic datasets, with a large volume of insertions and removals. Giving up on `delete` would therefore mean turning down one of the main reasons we need this data structure.

The first (and easiest) step is finding the point we would like to delete, or better said, finding the leaf that holds that point. While for `insert` we would only traverse one path to the closest leaf, for `delete` we are back at the search algorithm described in section 10.3.1; however, as for `insert`, we will need to perform some backtracking, and hence rather than calling search, we will have to implement the same traversal in this new method.[13]

Once we have found the right leaf `L`, assuming we do find the point `Z` in the tree (otherwise, we wouldn't need to perform any change), we have a few possible situations—an easy one, a complicated one, and a seriously complicated one:

1. If the leaf contains more than `m` points, we just delete `Z` from `L`, and update its bounding envelope.
2. Otherwise, after deleting `Z`, `L` will have only `m-1` points, and therefore it would violate one of the SS-tree's invariants. We have a few options to cope with this:
   a. If `L` is the root, we are good, and we don't have to do anything.
   b. If `L` has at least one sibling `S` with more than `m` points, we can move one point from `S` to `L`. Although we will be careful to choose the closest point to `L` (among all its siblings with at least `m+1` points), this operation can potentially cause `L`'s bounding envelope to expand significantly (if only siblings far away from `L` have enough points) and unbalance the tree.
   c. If no sibling of `L` can "lend" it a point, then we will have to merge `L` with one of its siblings. Again, we would then have to choose which sibling to merge it with and we might choose different strategies:
      i. Choosing the closest sibling
      ii. Choosing the sibling with larger overlap with `L`
      iii. Choosing the sibling that minimizes the coordinates variance (over all axes)

Case 2(c) is clearly the hardest to handle. Case 2(b), however, is relatively easy because, luckily, one difference with B-trees is that the node's children don't have to be sorted, so we don't need to perform rotations when we move one point from `S` to `L`. In the middle-bottom sections of figure 10.19 you can see the result of node S_3 "borrowing" one of the S_4 children, S_9—it's just as easy as that. Of course, the hardest part is deciding which sibling to borrow from and which of its children should be moved.

For case 2(b), merging two nodes will cause their parent to have one less child; we thus have to backtrack and verify that this node still has at least `m` children. This is shown in the top and middle sections of figure 10.19. The good news is that we can handle internal nodes exactly as we handle leaves, so we can reuse the same logic (and mostly the same code) for leaves and internal nodes.

Cases 1 (at the bottom of figure 10.19) and 2(a) are trivial, and we can easily implement them; the fact that when we get to the root we don't have to do any extra action (like we have to for insert) makes the `SsTree::delete` wrapper method trivial.

[13]We could reuse `search` as the first call in `delete` (and `searchClosestLeaf` in `insert`) if we store a pointer to its parent in each node, so that we can climb up the tree when needed.

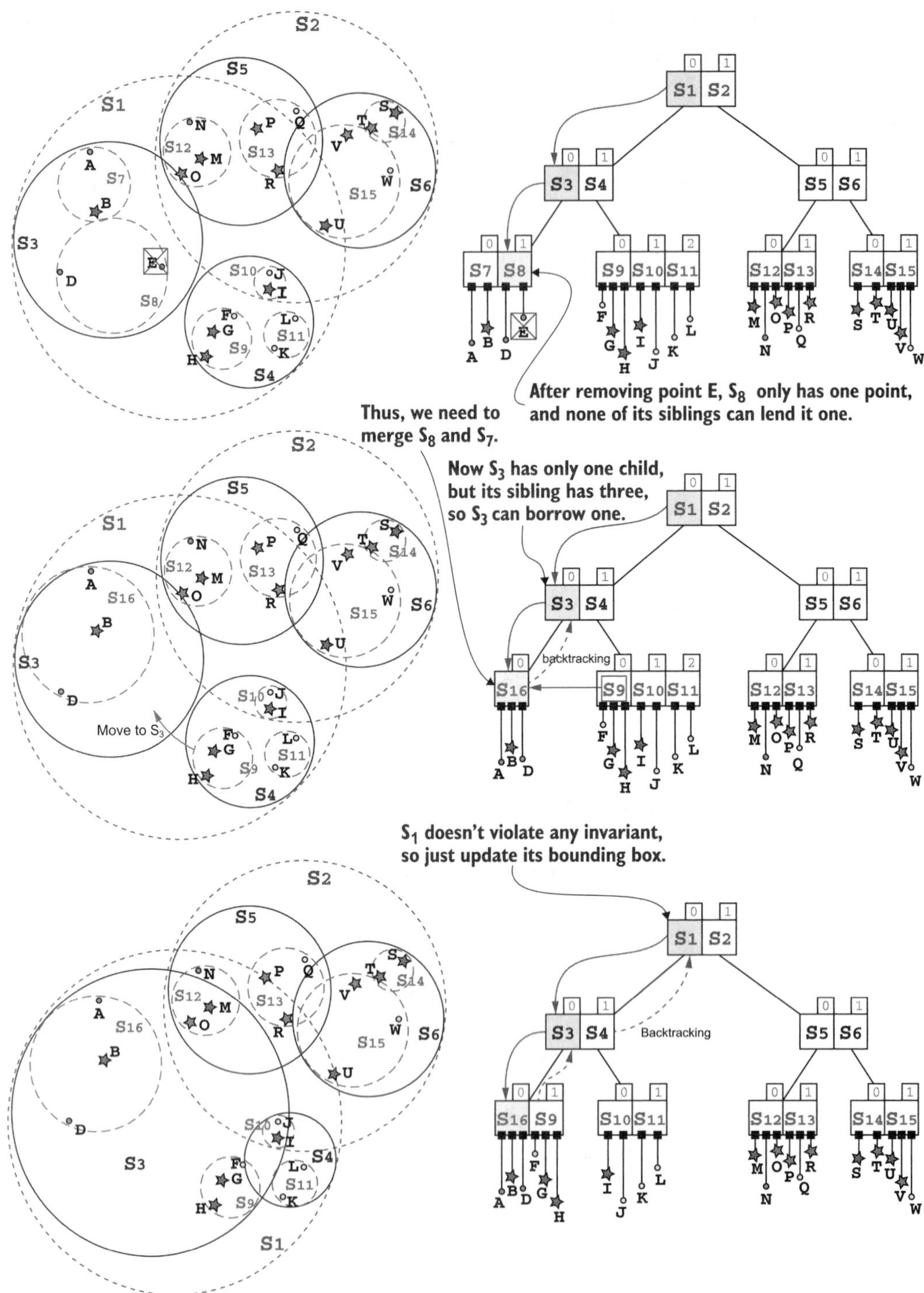
After removing point E, S_8 only has one point, and none of its siblings can lend it one.
Thus, we need to merge S_8 and S_7.
Now S_3 has only one child, but its sibling has three, so S_3 can borrow one.
backtracking
Move to S_3
S_1 doesn't violate any invariant, so just update its bounding box.
Backtracking

Figure 10.19 Deleting a point. This example shows, in order, cases 2(c), 2(b), and 1 described in this section.

Enough with the examples; it's time to write the body of the delete method, shown in listing 10.15.

Listing 10.15 The delete method

```
function delete(node, target)
  if node.leaf then
    if node.points.contains(target) then
      node.points.delete(target)
      return (true, node.points.size() < m)
    else
     return (false, false)
  else
    nodeToFix ← null
    deleted ← false
    for childNode in node.children do
      if childNode.intersectsPoint(target) then
        (deleted, violatesInvariants) ← delete(childNode, target)
        if violatesInvariants == true then
          nodeToFix ← childNode
        if deleted then
          break
  if nodeToFix == null then
    if deleted then
      node.updateBoundingEnvelope()
    return (deleted, false)
```

Method delete takes a node and a point to delete from the node's subtree. It is defined recursively and returns a pair of values: the first one tells if a point has been deleted in current subtree, and the second one is true if current node now violates SS-tree's invariants. We assume both node and target are non-null.

If the current node is a leaf, checks that it does contain the point to delete and . . .

. . . removes the point . . .

. . . and returns (true, true) if the node now contains fewer than m points, to let the caller know that it violates SS-tree invariants and needs fixing, or (true, false) otherwise, because the point was deleted in this subtree.

Otherwise, if this leaf doesn't contain target, we need to backtrack the search and traverse the next unexplored branch (the execution will return to line #13 of the call handling node's parent, unless node is the root of the tree), but so far no change has been made, so it can return (false, false).

If node is not a leaf, we need to continue the tree traversal by exploring node's branches. We start by initializing a couple of temporary variables to keep track of the outcome of recursive calls on node's children.

Cycles through all of node's children that intersect the target point to be deleted

Recursively traverses the next branch (one of the children that intersects target), searching for the point and trying to delete it

If the recursive call returns true for violatesInvariants, it means that the point has been found and deleted in this branch, and that childNode currently violates the SS-tree's invariants, so its parent needs to do some fixing.

To that extent, we save current child in the temporary variable we had previously initialized.

If a point has been deleted in the current node's subtree, then exit the for loop (we assume there are no duplicates in the tree, so a point can be in one and one branch only).

Check if none of node's children violates SS-tree's invariants. In that case, we won't need to do any fix for the current node.

However, if the point was deleted in this subtree, we still need to recompute the bounding envelope.

Then we can return, letting the caller know if the point was deleted as part of this call, and that this node doesn't violate any invariant.

If, instead, one of the current node's children does violate an invariant as the result of calling `delete` on it, the first thing we need to do is retrieve a list of the siblings of that child (stored in `nodeToFix`) but filtering in only those that in turn have more than `m` children/points. We will try to move one of those entries (either children or points, for internal nodes and leaves respectively) from one of the siblings to the one child from which we deleted `target`, and that now has too few children.

Checks if there is any sibling of `nodeToFix` that meets the criteria

If `nodeToFix` has at least one sibling with more than `m` entries, moves one entry from one of the siblings to `nodeTofix` (which will now be fixed, because it will have exactly `m` points/children).

```
    else
      siblings ← node.siblingsToBorrowFrom(nodeToFix)
      if not siblings.isEmpty() then
        nodeToFix.borrowFromSibling(siblings)
      else
        node.mergeChildren(
          nodeToFix, node.findSiblingToMergeTo(nodeToFix))
      node.updateBoundingEnvelope()
    return (true, node.children.size() < m)
```

Otherwise, if there is no sibling with more than `m` elements, we will have to merge the node violating invariants with one of its siblings.

If it gets here, we are at an internal node and the point has been deleted in `node`'s subtree; checks also if `node` now violates the invariant about the minimum number of children.

Before we return, we still need to recompute the bounding envelope for the current node.

As you can see, this method is as complicated as `insert` (possibly even more complicated!); thus, similarly to what we did for `insert`, we broke down the `delete` method using several helper functions to keep it leaner and cleaner.

This time, however, we won't describe in detail all of the helper methods. All the methods involving finding something "closest to" a node, such as function `findSiblingToMergeTo` in listing 10.15, are heuristics that depend on the definition of "closer" that we adopt. As mentioned when describing how `delete` works, we have a few choices, from shortest distance (which is also easy to implement) to lower overlap.

For the sake of space, we need to leave these implementations (including the choice of the proximity function) to the reader. If you refer to the material presented in this and the previous section, you should be able to easily implement the versions using Euclidean distance as a proximity criterion

So, to complete our description of the `delete` method, we can start from `findClosestEntryInNodesList`. Listing 10.16 shows the pseudo-code for the method that is just another linear search within a list of nodes with the goal of finding the closest entry contained in any of the nodes in the list. Notice that we also return the parent node because it will be needed by the caller.

Listing 10.16 The `findClosestEntryInNodesList` method

Function `findClosestEntryInNodesList` takes a list of nodes and a target node and returns the closest entry to the target and the node in the list that contains it. An entry here is, again, meant as either a point (if `nodes` are leaves) or a child node (if `nodes` contains internal nodes). The definition of "closest" is encapsulated in the two auxiliary methods called at lines #5 and #6.

Initializes the results to `null`; it is assumed that at line #6 function `closerThan` will return the first argument, when `closestEntry` is null.

```
function findClosestEntryInNodesList(nodes, targetNode)
  closestEntry ← null
```

For each node, gets its closest entry to targetNode. By default, closest can be meant as "with minimal Euclidean distance."

Cycles through all the nodes in the input list

Compares the entry just computed to the best result found so far

```
closestNode ← null
for node in nodes do
  closestEntryInNode ← node.getClosestCentroidTo(targetNode)
  if closerThan(closestEntryInNode, closestEntry, targetNode) then
    closestEntry ← closestEntryInNode
    closestNode ← node
return (closestEntry, closestNode)
```

If the new entry is closer (by whatever definition of "closer" is assumed) then updates the temporary variables, with the results

Returns a pair with the closest entry and the node containing it for the caller's benefit

Next, listing 10.17 describes the borrowFromSibling method, which moves an entry (respectively, a point, for leaves, or a child node, for internal nodes) to the node that currently violates the minimum points/children invariant, taking it from one of its siblings. Obviously, we need to choose a sibling that has more than m entries to avoid moving the issue around (the sibling will have one less entry afterward, and we don't want it to violate the invariant itself!). For this implementation, we will assume that all elements of the list siblings, passed in input, are non-null nodes with at least m+1 entries, and also that siblings is not empty. If you are implementing this code in a language that supports assertions, you might want to add an assert to verify these conditions.[14]

Listing 10.17 The SsNode::borrowFromSibling method

Method borrowFromSibling is defined in class SsNode. It takes a non-empty list of siblings of the current node and moves the closest entry with regard to the current node from one of the siblings to the current node.

Searches the list of siblings for the closest entry to the current node. Here the definition of "closest" must be decided when designing the data structure. The helper function will return both the closest entry to be moved and the sibling that currently contains it.

```
function borrowFromSibling(siblings)
  (closestEntry, closestSibling) ←
      findClosestEntryInNodesList(siblings, this)
  closestSibling.deleteEntry(closestEntry)
  closestSibling.updateBoundingEnvelope()
  this.addEntry(closestEntry)
  this.updateBoundingEnvelope()
```

Deletes the chosen entry from the node that currently contains it and updates its bounding envelope

Adds the chosen entry to the current node and re-computes its bounding envelope

If this condition is met, we want to find the best entry to "steal," and usually this means the closest one to the destination node, but as mentioned, other criteria can be used. Once we find it, we just need to move the closest entry from the source to the destination of this transaction and update them accordingly.

[14]Assuming you implement this method as a private method. Assertions should never be used to check input, because they can be (and often are, in production) disabled. Checking arguments in private methods is not ideal and must be avoided when they are forwarded from user input. Ideally, you would only use assertions on invariants.

If, instead, this condition is not met, and there is no sibling of the child violating invariants from which we can borrow an entry, it can mean one of two things:

1. There are no siblings: assuming `m≥2`, this can only happen if we are at the root, and it only has one child. In this case, there is nothing to do.
2. There are siblings, but all of them have exactly `m` entries. In this case, since `m≤M/2`, if we merge the invalid node with any of its siblings, we get a new node with `2*m-1<M` entries—in other words, a valid node that doesn't violate any invariant.

Listing 10.18 shows how to handle both situations: we check whether the second argument is `null` to understand if we are in the former or latter case, and if we do need to perform a merge, we also clean up the parent's node (which is the one node on which the `mergeChildren` method is called).

Listing 10.18 The `SsNode::mergeChildren` method

```
function mergeChildren(firstChild, secondChild)
  if secondChild != null then
    newChild ← merge(firstChild, secondChild)
    this.children.delete(firstChild)
    this.children.delete(secondChild)
    this.children.add(newChild)

function merge(firstNode, secondNode)
  assert(firstNode.leaf == secondNode.leaf)
  if firstNode.leaf then
    return new SsNode(true,
      points=firstNode.points + secondNode.points)
  else
    return new SsNode(false,
      children=firstNode.children + secondNode.children)
```

- **We assume the first argument is always non-null (we can add an `assert` to check it, in those languages supporting assertions). If the second argument is `null`, it means this method has been called on the root and it currently has just one child, so we don't have to do anything. If we assume `m≥2`, in fact, this is only possible when `node` is tree's root node (but still possible).**
- **Method `mergeChildren` is defined in class `SsNode`. It takes two children of the current node and merges them in a single node.**
- **Performs the merge, creating a new node**
- **Adds the result of the call to merge to the list of this node's children**
- **Deletes the two former children from the current node**
- **Auxiliary function `merge` takes two nodes and returns a node that has the entries of both inputs**
- **Verifies that either both nodes are leaves or neither is**
- **If the nodes are leaves, returns a new node whose points are the union of the nodes' sets of points**
- **If the nodes are internal, creates a new node with children from both inputs**

This was the last piece of pseudo-code we were missing for `delete`. Before wrapping up this section, though, I'd like to exhort the reader to take another look at figure 10.19. The final result is a valid SS-tree that doesn't violate any of its invariants, but let's be honest, the result is not that great, right? Now we have one huge sphere, S_3, that is taking up almost all the space in its parent's bounding envelope and significantly overlapping not just its sibling, but also its parent's other branch.

If you remember, this was mentioned as a risk of handling merges in case 2(b) in the description for `delete`. It is, unfortunately, a common side effect of both node merges and moving nodes/points among siblings; especially when the choice of the entry to move is constrained, a far entry can be picked up for merge/move, and—as in the example in figure 10.19—in the long run, after many deletions, this can make the tree unbalanced.

We need to do better if we would like to keep our tree balanced and its performance acceptable, and in section 10.6 we will see a possible solution: SS⁺-trees.

10.4 Similarity Search

Before discussing how to improve the balancing of SS-trees, we can finish our discussion of their methods. So far, we have seen how to construct such a tree, but what can we use it for? Not surprisingly, nearest neighbor search is one of the main applications of this data structure; you probably guessed that. Range search, like for k-d trees, is another important application for SS-trees; both NN and range searches fall into the category of similarity search, queries on large, multi-dimensional spaces where our only criterion is the similarity between a pair of objects.

As we discussed for k-d trees in chapter 9, SS-trees can also (more easily) be extended to support approximated similarity search. If you remember, in section 9.4, we mentioned that approximate queries are a possible solution to k-d tree performance issues. We'll talk in more depth about these methods in section 10.4.2.

10.4.1 Nearest neighbor search

The nearest neighbor search algorithm is similar to what we saw for k-d trees; obviously, the tree structure is different, but the main change in the algorithm's logic is the formula we need to use to check whether a branch intersects the NN query region (the sphere centered at the query point and with a radius equal to the distance to the current guess for the nearest neighbor)—that is, if a branch is close enough to the target point to be traversed. Also, while in k-d trees we check and update distance at every node, SS-trees (and R-trees) only host points in their leaves, so we will only update the initial distance after we traverse the tree to the first leaf.

To improve search performance, it's important to traverse branches in the right order. While it is not obvious what this order is, a good starting point is sorting nodes based on their minimum distance from the query point. It is not guaranteed that the node that *potentially* has the closest point (meaning its bounding envelope is closest to the target point) will *actually* have a point so close to our target, and so we can't be sure that this heuristic will produce the best ordering possible; however, on average it helps, compared to following a random order.

To remind you why this is important, we discussed in section 9.3.5 how getting to a better guess of the nearest neighbor distance helps us prune more branches, and thus improve search performance. In fact, if we know that there is a point within distance `D` from our query point, we can prune all branches whose bounding envelopes are further than `D`.

Listing 10.19 shows the code for the `nearestNeighbor` method, and figures 10.20 and 10.21 show examples of a call to the method on our example tree. As you can see, the code is quite compact: we just need to traverse all branches that intersect the sphere centered at the search points and whose radius is the distance to the current nearest neighbor, and update the best value found in the process.

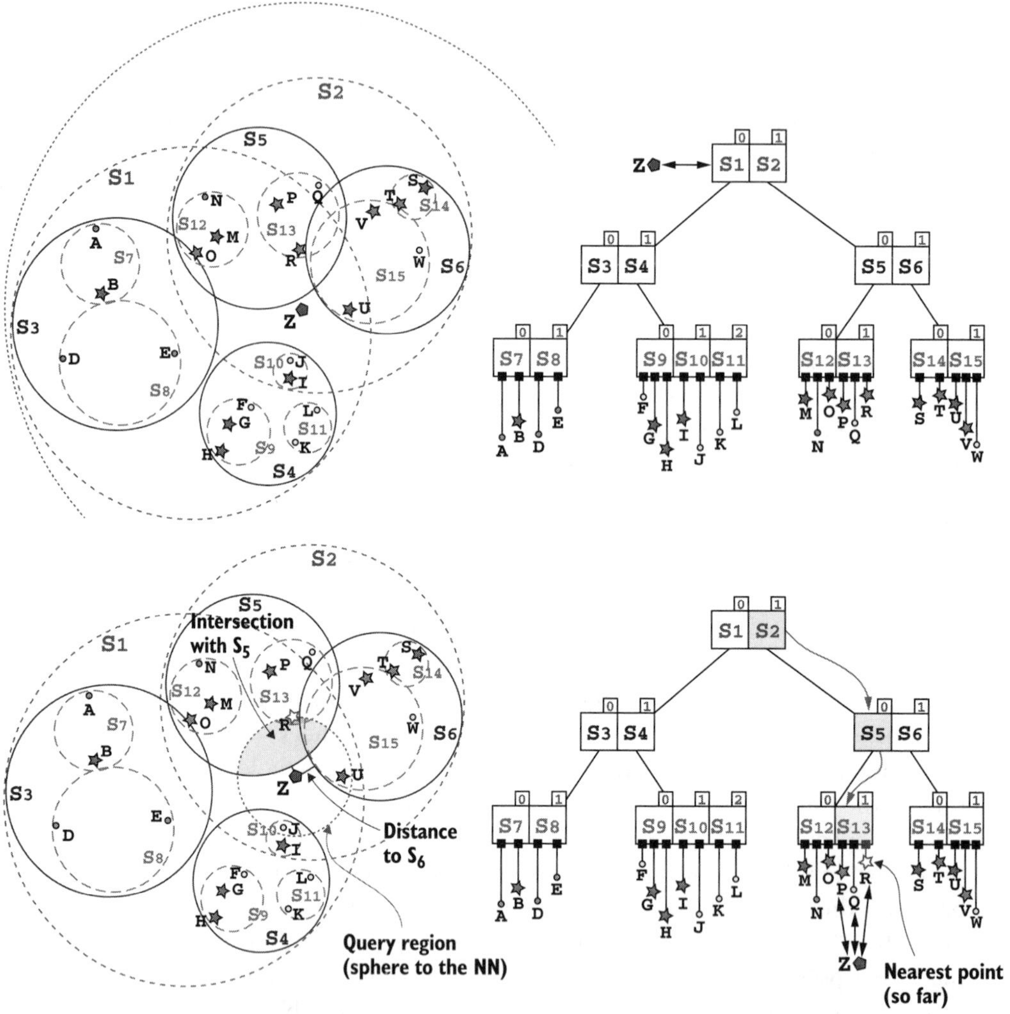
Intersection with S_5
Distance to S_6
Query region (sphere to the NN)
Nearest point (so far)

Figure 10.20 Nearest neighbor search. This figure shows the first steps of the call on the root of the tree. (Top) Initially, the search area is a sphere centered at the query point Z, and with infinite radius (although here it's shown as a circle that includes the whole tree, for consistency). (Bottom) The search traverses the tree, choosing first the closest branches. S_5's border is closer than S_6's, so we visit the former first (although, as you can see, the opposite choice would be the best, but the algorithm can't know that yet). Normally the distance is computed from a node's bounding envelope, but since Z intersects both S_1 and S_2, it first chooses the one whose centroid is closer. The algorithm goes in depth as much as possible, traversing a path to a leaf before back-tracking. Here we show the path to the first leaf: once there, we can update the query region that now is the sphere centered at Z with radius equal to the distance to R, the closest point in S_{13}, which is therefore saved as the best guess for the nearest neighbor.

This simplicity and cleanness are not unexpected. We have done the hard work of the design and creation of the data structure, and now we can enjoy the benefits!

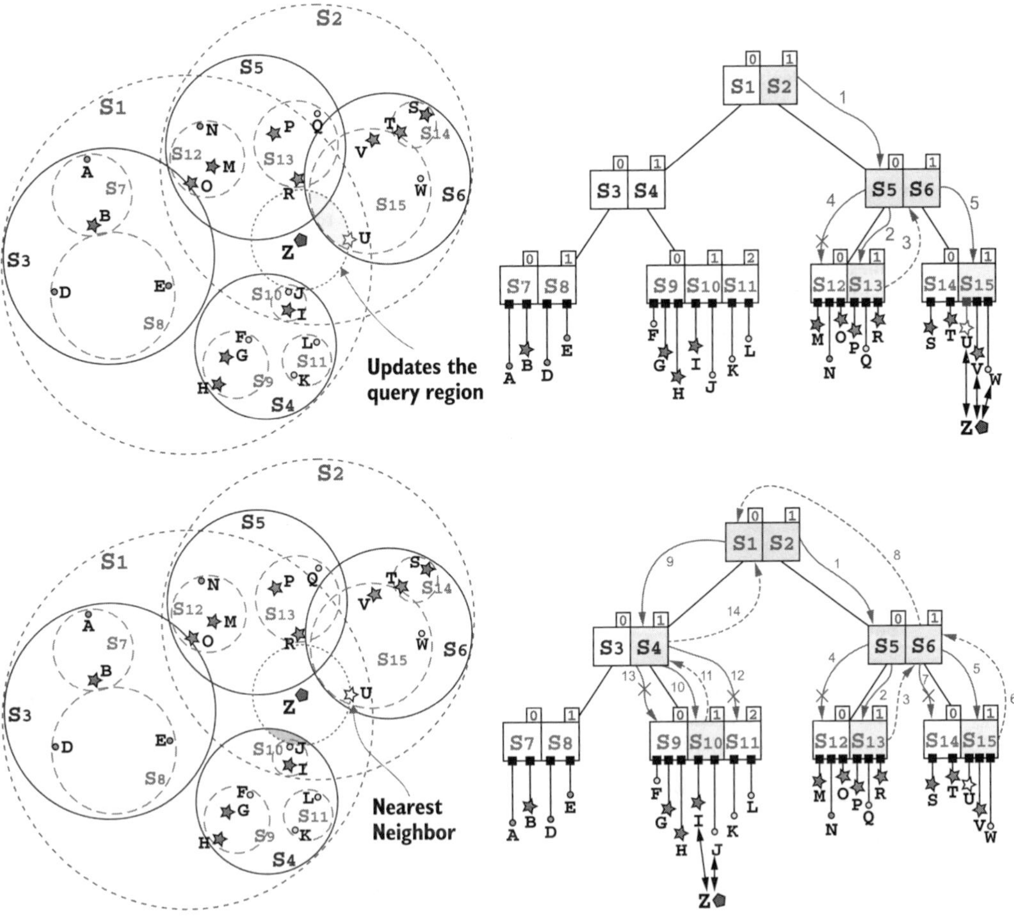

Updates the query region
Nearest Neighbor

Figure 10.21 Nearest neighbor search. A summary of the next steps in the traversal. Arrows are numbered to reflect the order of the recursive calls. (Top) After visiting S_{13} and finding R as the best guess for the nearest neighbor, S_{12} is skipped because it's outside the update search region. Then the execution backtracks, and we get to S_5's sibling, S_6, which still has a non-null intersection with the search region. (Bottom) Fast-forward to the end of the traversal. We need to traverse S_1's branch as well, because Z lies within it. As a matter of fact, the search region intersects another leaf, S_{10}, so we need to traverse a path to it. As you can see, point J is close to being Z's nearest neighbor, so it's not unlikely that we would find the true NN in a later call.

Listing 10.19 The nearestNeighbor method for SS-tree

```
function nearestNeighbor(node, target, (nnDist, nn)=(inf, null))
  if node.leaf then
    for point in node.points do
      dist ← distance(point, target)
      if dist < nnDist then
        (nnDist, nn) ← (dist, point)
  else
    sortedChildren ← sortNodesByDistance(node.children, target)
    for child in sortedChildren do
      if nodeDistance(child, target) < nnDist then
        (nnDist, nn) ← nearestNeighbor(child, target, (nnDist, nn))
  return (nnDist, nn)
```

Annotations:

- **function nearestNeighbor:** Function nearestNeighbor returns the closest point to a given target. It takes the node to search and the query point. We also (optionally) pass the best values found so far for nearest neighbor (NN) and its distance to help pruning. These values default to null and infinity for a call on the tree root, unless we want to limit the search inside a spherical region (in that case, just pass the sphere's radius as the initial value for nnDist).
- **if node.leaf then:** Checks if node is a leaf. Leaves are the only nodes containing points, and so are the only nodes where we can possibly update the nearest neighbor found.
- **for point in node.points do:** Cycles through all points in this leaf
- **dist ← distance(point, target):** Computes the distance between current point and target
- **if dist < nnDist then:** If that distance is less than the current NN's distance, we have to update the values stored for the NN and its distance.
- **sortedChildren ← …:** If, instead, node is an internal node, we need to cycle through all its children and possibly traverse their subtrees. We start by sorting node's children from the closest to the furthest with respect to target. As mentioned, a different heuristic than the distance to the bounding envelope can be used here.
- **for child in sortedChildren do:** Cycles through all children in the order we sorted them
- **if nodeDistance(child, target) < nnDist then:** Checks if their bounding envelope intersects with the NN bounding sphere. In other words, if the distance from target to the closest point within child's bounding envelope is smaller than the pruning distance (nnDist).
- **(nnDist, nn) ← nearestNeighbor(…):** If the distance between target and child is smaller than the pruning distance, then it traverses the subtree rooted at child, updating the result.
- **return (nnDist, nn):** All that remains is to return the updated values for the best result found so far.

Of the helper methods in listing 10.19, it's important to spend some time explaining function nodeDistance. If we refer to figure 10.22, you can see why the minimum distance between a node and a bounding envelope is equal to the distance between the centroids minus the envelope's radius: we just used the formula for the distance between a point and a sphere, taken from geometry.

We can easily extend the nearest neighbor search algorithm to return the n-th nearest neighbor. Similar to what we did in chapter 9 for k-d trees, we just need to use a bounded priority queue that keeps at most n elements, and use the furthest of those n points as a reference, computing the pruning distance as the distance from this point to the search target (as long as we have found fewer than n points, the pruning distance will be infinity).

Likewise, we can add a threshold argument to the search function, which becomes the initial pruning distance (instead of passing infinity as the default value for nnDist), to also support search in spherical regions. Since these implementations can

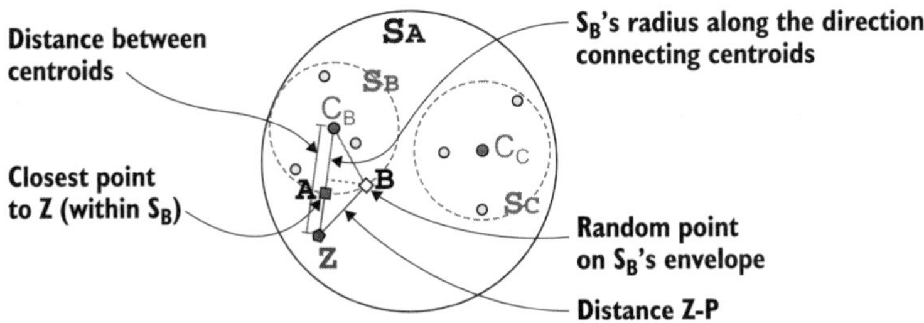
Distance between centroids
Closest point to Z (within S_B)
S_B's radius along the direction connecting centroids
Random point on S_B's envelope
Distance Z-P
SA
SB
CB
Cc
Sc
A
B
Z

Figure 10.22 Minimum distance to a bounding envelope. Consider the triangle ZBC_B. Then, for the triangular inequality, $|C_BB|+|BZ|>|ZC_B|$, but $|ZC_B|==|ZA|+|AC_B|$ and $|AC_B|==|C_BB|$ (they are both radii), so ultimately $|C_BB|+|BZ|>|ZA|+|AC_B| \Rightarrow |BZ|>|ZA|$. Therefore, the minimum distance is the length of segment from Z to S_B's sphere, along the direction connecting its centroid to Z.

be trivially obtained, referring to chapter 9 for guidance, we leave them to the readers (for a hint, check the implementation on the book's repo on GitHub[15]).

10.4.2 Region search

Region search will be similar to what we have described for k-d trees—the only difference being how we need to compute the intersection between each node and the search region, besides the structural change due to the fact that points are only stored in leaves.

Listing 10.20 shows a generic implementation of this method for SS-trees that assumes the region passed as argument includes a method to check whether the region itself intersects a hyper-sphere (a node's bounding envelope). Please refer to section 9.3.6 for a detailed explanation and examples about search on the most common types of regions, and their algebraic meaning.

Listing 10.20 The `pointsWithinRegion` method for SS-tree

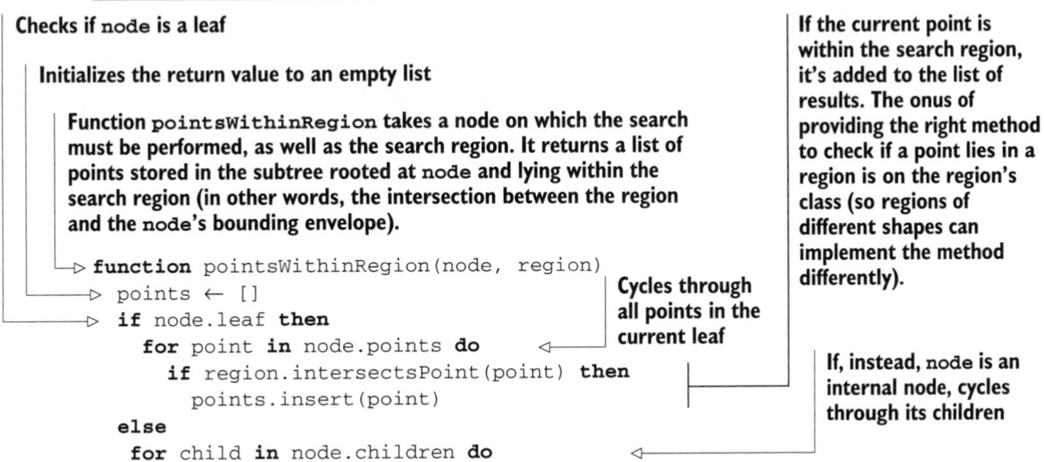
Checks if node is a leaf
Initializes the return value to an empty list
Function pointsWithinRegion takes a node on which the search must be performed, as well as the search region. It returns a list of points stored in the subtree rooted at node and lying within the search region (in other words, the intersection between the region and the node's bounding envelope).
If the current point is within the search region, it's added to the list of results. The onus of providing the right method to check if a point lies in a region is on the region's class (so regions of different shapes can implement the method differently).
Cycles through all points in the current leaf
If, instead, node is an internal node, cycles through its children

```
function pointsWithinRegion(node, region)
  points ← []
  if node.leaf then
    for point in node.points do
      if region.intersectsPoint(point) then
        points.insert(point)
  else
   for child in node.children do
```

[15] See https://github.com/mlarocca/AlgorithmsAndDataStructuresInAction#ss-tree.

Checks to see if the search region intersects the current child. Again, the region's class will have to implement this check.

If there is any intersection (so there might be points in common), we should call this method recursively on the current child, and then add all the results found, if any, to the list of points returned by this method call.

```
    if region.intersectsNode(child) then
      points.insertAll(pointsWithinRegion(child, region))
return points
```

At this point, we can just return all the points we collected in this method call.

10.4.3 Approximated similarity search

As mentioned, similarity search in k-d trees, as well as R-trees and SS-trees, suffers from what is called the *curse of dimensionality*: the methods on these data structures become exponentially slower with the growth of the number of dimensions of the search space. K-d trees also suffer from additional sparsity issues that become more relevant in higher dimensions.

While using R-trees and SS-trees can improve the balance of the trees and result in better trees and faster construction, there is still something more we can do to improve the performance of the similarity search methods.

These approximate search methods are indeed a tradeoff between accuracy and performance; there are a few different (and sometimes complementary) strategies that can be used to have faster approximate queries:

- *Reduce the dimensionality of the objects*—Using algorithms such as PCA or Discrete Fourier Transform, it is possible to project the dataset's object into a different, lower-dimensional space. The idea is that this space will maintain only the essential information to distinguish between different points in the dataset. With dynamic datasets, this method is obviously less effective.
- *Reduce the number of branches traversed*—As we have seen in the previous section, our pruning strategy is quite conservative, meaning that we traverse a branch if there is any chance (even the slightest) that we can find a point in that branch closer than our current nearest neighbor. By using a more aggressive pruning strategy, we can reduce the number of branches (and ultimately dataset points) touched, as long as we accept that our results might not be the most accurate possible.
- *Use an early termination strategy*—In this case, the search is stopped when the current result is judged good enough. The criterion to decide what's "good enough" can be a threshold (for instance, when a NN closer than some distance is found), or a stop condition connected to the probability of finding a better match (for instance, if branches are visited from closer to further with regard to the query point, this probability decreases with the number of leaves visited).

We will focus on the second strategy, the pruning criterion. In particular, we can provide a method that, given a parameter ϵ, called the *approximation error*, with $0.0 \leq \epsilon \leq 0.5$, guarantees that in an approximated n-nearest neighbor search, the n-th nearest neighbor returned will be within a factor (1+ϵ) from the true n-th nearest neighbor.

To explain this, let's restrict[16] to the case where n==1, just plain NN search. Assume the approximated NN-search method, called on a point P, returns a point Q, while the real nearest neighbor of P would be another point N≠Q. Then, if the distance between P and its true nearest neighbor N is d, the approximated search distance between P and Q will be at most (1+ϵ)*d.

Guaranteeing this condition is easy. When we prune a branch, instead of checking to see if the distance between the target point and the branch's bounding envelope is smaller than the current NN distance, we prune unless it is smaller than 1/(1+ϵ) times the NN's distance.

If we denote with Z the query point, with C current nearest neighbor, and with A the closest point to Z in the branch pruned (see figure 10.21), we have, in fact

$$d(Z, A) \geq \frac{1}{1+\epsilon} \cdot d(Z, C) \Rightarrow \frac{d(Z, C)}{d(Z, A)} \leq 1 + \epsilon$$

So, if the distance of the closest point in the branch is higher than the current NN's distance over the reciprocal of (1+ϵ), we are guaranteed that the possible nearest neighbor held in the branch is no further than an epsilon factor from our current nearest neighbor.

Of course, there could be several points in the dataset that are within a factor (1+ϵ) from the true nearest neighbor, so we are not guaranteed that we get the second-closest point, or the third, and so on.

However, the probability that these points exist is proportional to the size of the ring region with radii nnDist and nnDist/(1+ϵ), so the smaller we set ϵ, the lower the chances we are missing closer points.

A more accurate estimate of the probability is given by the area of the intersection of the aforementioned ring with the bounding envelope of the node we skip. Figure 10.23 illustrates this idea, and shows the difference between SS-trees, k-d trees, and R-trees: the probability is maximum when the inner radius is just tangent to the area, and a sphere has a smaller intersection, with respect to any rectangle.

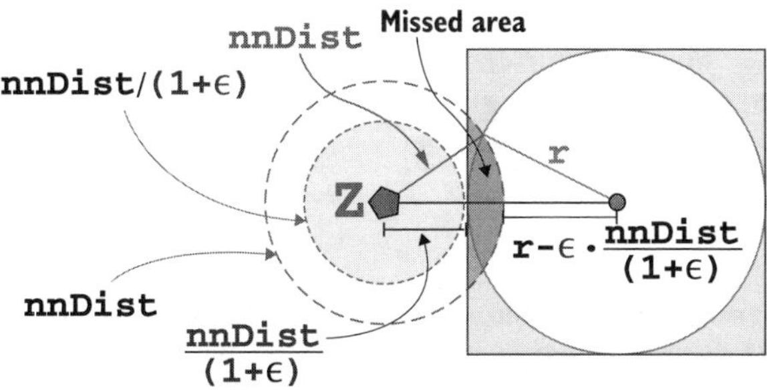

nnDist
Missed area
nnDist/(1+ϵ)
r
Z
r-ϵ · nnDist/(1+ϵ)
nnDist
nnDist/(1+ϵ)

Figure 10.23 The probability of missing j points by using an approximation error is proportional to the intersection of the pruned search area (the ring with radius (ϵ /(1+ϵ))*nnDist) and the bounding envelope of the node intersecting this region, but not the internal sphere with reduced radius. The maximum probability corresponds to a region tangent to the internal sphere. The figure shows how the intersection is smaller for spherical bounding envelopes than for rectangular ones.

[16]This can easily be extended to n-nearest neighbor by considering the distance of the n-th NN instead.

If we set ϵ==0.0, then we get back the exact search algorithm as a special case, because `nnDist/(1+epsilon)` becomes just `nnDist`.

When ϵ>0.0, a traversal might look like figure 10.24, where we use an example slightly different from the one in figures 10.20 and 10.21 to show how approximate NN search could miss the nearest neighbor.

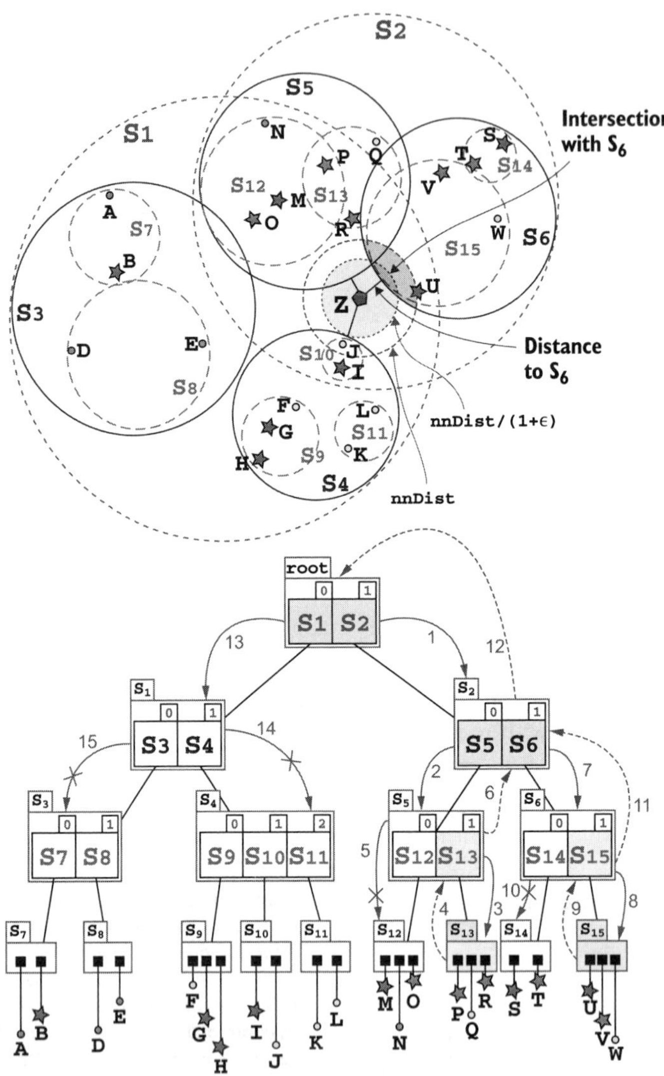
S2
S5
S1
Intersection with S_6
Distance to S_6
nnDist/(1+ϵ)
nnDist
root
S1 S2
S3 S4
S5 S6
S7 S8
S9 S10 S11
S12 S13
S14 S15

Figure 10.24 Approximated nearest neighbor search. The example is similar (almost identical) to the one in figures 10.20 and 10.21, to allow a close comparison. We show the verbose representation of the tree to make clearer the path followed in traversal. Node S_4 contains J, the true NN, whose bit is further away from the query point Z than S_5 and S_6, and outside the approximated query region (ϵ has been chosen ad hoc, obviously, to cause this condition, in this example, ϵ~=0.25). Arrows are numbered in the order in which they are traversed.

In many domains we can be not just fine, but even happy, with approximate search. Take our example of the search through a dataset of images: Can we really be sure that an exact match is better than an approximate one? If we were working with geographic coordinates—say, on a map—then a factor ϵ difference could have dire consequences (at the very best, taking a longer route would be expensive, but it might get as bad as safety issues). But when the task is finding the dresses that most closely resemble a purchase, then we can't even guarantee the precision of our metric. Maybe a couple of feature vectors are slightly closer than another pair, but in the end, to the human eye, the latter images look more similar!

So, as long as the approximation error ϵ is not too large, chances are that an approximated result for "most similar image" will be as good as, or maybe better, than the exact result.

The interested reader can find plenty of literature on the topic of approximated similarity search and delve deeper into the concepts that we could only superficially examine here. As a starting point I suggest the remarkable work of Giuseppe Amato.[17]

10.5 SS⁺-tree[18]

So far, we have used the original SS-tree structure, as described in the original paper by White and Jain[19]; SS-trees have been developed to reduce the nodes overlapping, and in turn the number of leaves traversed by a search on the tree, with respect to R-trees and k-d trees.

10.5.1 Are SS-trees better?

With respect to k-d trees, the main advantage of this new data structure is that it is self-balancing, so much so that all leaves are at the same height. Also, using bounding envelopes instead of splits parallel to a single axis mitigates the curse of dimensionality because unidimensional splits only allow partitioning the search space along one direction at a time.

R-trees also use bounding envelops, but with a different shape: hyper-rectangles instead of hyper-spheres. While hyper-spheres can be stored more efficiently and allow for faster computation of their exact distance, hyper-rectangles can grow asymmetrically in different directions: this allows us to cover a node with a smaller volume, while hyper-spheres, being symmetrical in all directions, generally waste more space, with large regions without any point. And indeed, if you compare figure 10.4 to figure 10.8, you can see that rectangular bounding envelopes fit the data more tightly than the spherical ones of the SS-tree.

---

[17]See Amato, Giuseppe. "Approximate similarity search in metric spaces." Diss. Technical University of Dortmund, Germany, 2002.

[18]This section includes advanced material focused on theory.

[19]See White, David A., and Ramesh Jain. "Similarity indexing with the SS-tree." Proceedings of the Twelfth International Conference on Data Engineering. IEEE, 1996.

On the other hand, it can be proved that the decomposition in spherical regions minimizes the number of leaves traversed.[20]

If we compare the growth of the volume of spheres and cubes in a k-dimensional spaces, for different values of k, given by these formulas

$$V_{Cube} = r^k, V_{Sphere} = \frac{r^k \pi^{k/2}}{(k/2)!}$$

we can see that spheres grow more slowly than cubes, as also shown in figure 10.25.

And if a group of points is uniformly distributed along all directions and shaped as a spherical cluster, then a hyper-sphere is the type of bounding envelope that wastes the lowest volume, as you can see also for a 2-D space in figure 10.23, where a circle of radius r is inscribed in a square of side 2r. If the points are distributed in a circular cluster, then all the areas between the circle and its circumscribed square (highlighted in figure 10.23) are potentially empty, and so wasted.

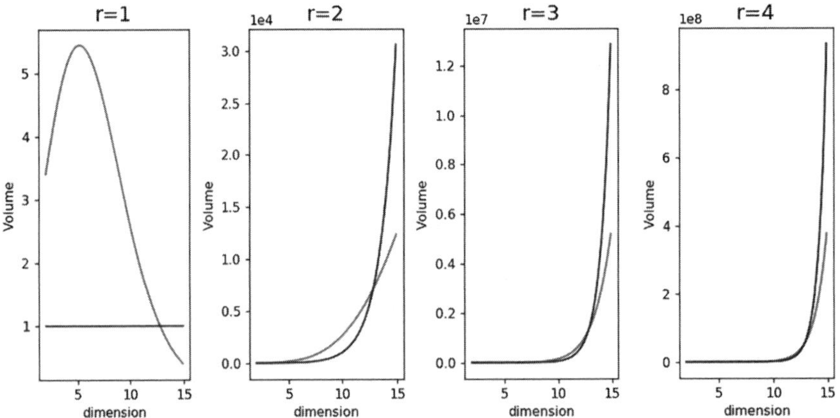
r=1
r=2
r=3
r=4
1e4
1e7
1e8
Volume
dimension

Figure 10.25 Volume of spheres (lighter line) and cubes (darker line) for various radii, as a function of the number of dimensions of the search space

Experiments have confirmed that SS-trees using spherical bounding envelopes perform better on datasets uniformly distributed along all directions, while rectangular envelopes work better with skewed datasets.

Neither R-trees nor SS-trees can offer logarithmic worst-case upper bounds for their methods. In the (unlikely, but possible) worst case, all leaves of the tree will be traversed, and there are at most n/m of them. This means that each of the main operations on these data structures can take up to linear time in the size of the dataset. Table 10.1 summarizes their running time, comparing them to k-d trees.

[20]See Cleary, John Gerald. "Analysis of an algorithm for finding nearest neighbors in Euclidean space." ACM Transactions on Mathematical Software (TOMS) 5.2 (1979): 183-192.

Table 10.1 Operations provided by k-d tree, and their cost on a balanced k-d tree with `n` elements

Operation	k-d tree	R-tree	SS-tree
`Search`	`O(log(n))`	`O(n)`	`O(n)`
`Insert`	`O(log(n))`	`O(n)`	`O(n)`
`Remove`	$O(n^{1-1/k})$ [a]	`O(n)`	`O(n)`
`nearestNeighbor`	$O(2^k + \log(n))$ [a]	`O(n)`	`O(n)`
`pointsInRegion`	`O(n)`	`O(n)`	`O(n)`

[a] Amortized, for a k-d tree holding k-dimensional points.

10.5.2 *Mitigating hyper-sphere limitations*

Now this question arises: Is there anything we can do to limit the cons of using spherical bounding envelopes so that we can reap the advantages when we have symmetrical datasets, and limit the disadvantages with skewed ones?

To cope with skewed datasets, we could use ellipsoids instead of spheres, so that the clusters can grow in each direction independently. However, this would complicate search, because we would want to compute the radius along the direction connecting the centroid to the query point, which in the general case won't lie on any of the axes.

A different approach to reduce the wasted area attempts to reduce the volume of the bounding spheres used. So far we have always used spheres whose center was a group of points' center of mass, and whose radius was the distance to the furthest point, so that the sphere would cover all points in the cluster. This, however, is not the smallest possible sphere that covers all the points. Figure 10.26 shows an example of such a difference.

Computing this smallest enclosing sphere in higher dimensions is, however, not feasible, because the algorithm to compute the exact values for its center (and radius) is exponential in the number of dimensions.

What can be done, however, is computing an approximation of the smallest enclosing sphere, starting with the center of mass of the cluster as an initial guess. At the very high level, the approximation algorithm tries at each iteration to move the center toward the farthest point in the dataset. After each iteration, the maximum distance the point can move is shortened, limited by the span of the previous update, thus ensuring convergence.

We won't delve deeper into this algorithm in this context; the interested readers can read more about this method, starting, for instance, with this article[21] by Fischer et al. For now, we will move to another way we could improve the balancing of the tree: reducing the node overlap.

[21] See Fischer, Kaspar, Bernd Gärtner, and Martin Kutz. "Fast smallest-enclosing-ball computation in high dimensions." European Symposium on Algorithms. Springer, Berlin, Heidelberg, 2003.

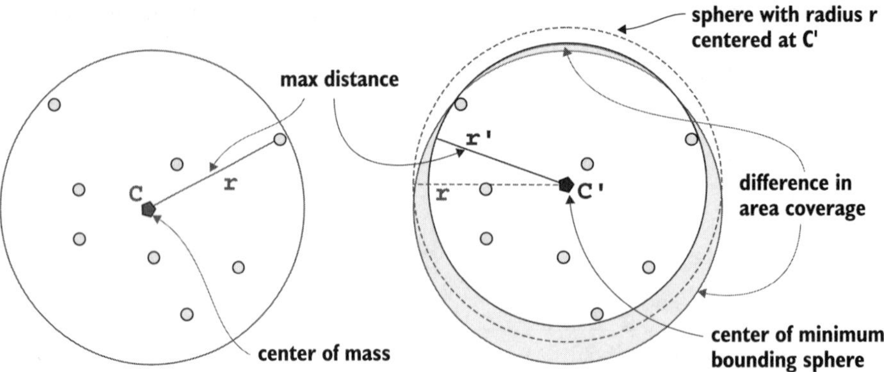
sphere with radius r
centered at C'
max distance
r'
r
C
r
C'
difference in
area coverage
center of mass
center of minimum
bounding sphere

Figure 10.26 Difference between the spheres with minimum radius centered at the cluster centroid (left), and the minimum covering sphere (right) for an example set of points.

10.5.3 Improved split heuristic

We saw in section 10.3 that splitting and merging nodes, as well as "borrowing" points/children from siblings, can result in skewed clusters that require bounding envelopes larger than necessary, and increase node overlap.

To counteract this effect, Kurniawati et al., in their work[22] on SS$^+$-trees, introduce a new split heuristic that, instead of only partitioning points along the direction of maximum variance, tries to find the two groups such that each of them will collect the closest nearby points.

To achieve this result, a variant of the k-means clustering algorithm will be used, with two constraints:

- The number of clusters will be fixed and equal to `2`.
- The maximum number of points per cluster is bound to `M`.

We will talk in more depth about clustering and k-means in chapter 12, so please refer to section 12.2 to see the details of its implementation.

The running time for k-means, with at most `j` iterations on a dataset with `n` points, is `O(jkn)`,[23] where, of course, `k` is the number of centroids.

Since for the split heuristic we have `k==2`, and the number of points in the node to split is `M+1`, the running time becomes `O(jdM)`, compared to `O(dM)` we had for the original split heuristic described in section 10.3. We can therefore trade off the quality of the result for performance by controlling the maximum number of iterations `j`.

[22] "SS+ tree: an improved index structure for similarity searches in a high-dimensional feature space." *Storage and Retrieval for Image and Video Databases V.* Vol. 3022. International Society for Optics and Photonics, 1997.

[23] To be thorough, we should also consider that computing each distance requires `O(d)` steps, so the running time, if `d` can vary, becomes `O(djkn)`. While for SS-trees we have seen that it becomes important to keep in mind how algorithms perform when the dimension of the space grows, a linear dependency is definitely good news, and we can afford to omit it (as it is done by convention, considering the dimension fixed) without distorting our result.

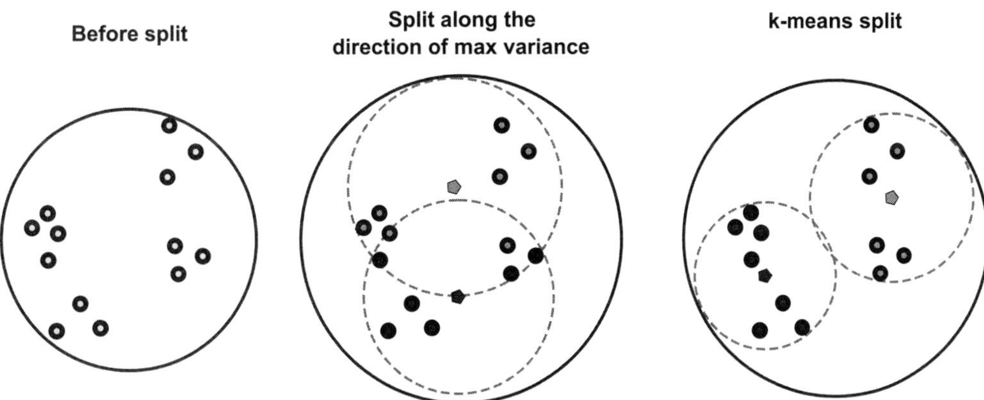
Before split
Split along the direction of max variance
k-means split

Figure 10.27 An example of the different partitions produced by the split heuristic in the original SS-tree version (center) and the k-means split heuristic (left). For the original heuristic, the direction of maximum variance was along the `y` axis. For this example, we assume `M==12` and `m==6`.

Figure 10.27 shows an example of how impactful this heuristic can be, and why the increase in running time is well worth it.

Although newer, more complex clustering algorithms have been developed during the years (as we'll see in chapter 12, where we'll also describe DBSCAN and OPTICS), k-means is still a perfect match for SS-trees, because it naturally produces spherical clusters, each with a centroid equal to the center of mass of the points in the cluster.

10.5.4 Reducing overlap

The k-means split heuristic is a powerful tool to reduce node overlapping and keep the tree balanced and search fast, as we were reminded at the beginning of last section; however, we can unbalance a node while also deleting points, in particular during merge or when we move a point/child across siblings. Moreover, sometimes the overlapping can be the result of several operations on the tree and involve more than just two nodes, or even more than a single level.

Finally, the k-means split heuristic doesn't have overlap minimization as a criterion, and because of the intrinsic behavior of k-means, the heuristic could produce results where a node with larger variance might completely overlap a smaller node.

To illustrate these situations, the top half of figure 10.28 shows several nodes and their parents, with a significant overlap.

To solve such a situation, SS+-trees introduce two new elements:

1. A check to discover such situations.
2. A new heuristic that applies k-means to all grandchildren of a node `N` (no matter whether they are points or other nodes; in the latter case their centroids will be used for clustering). The clusters created will replace `N`'s children.

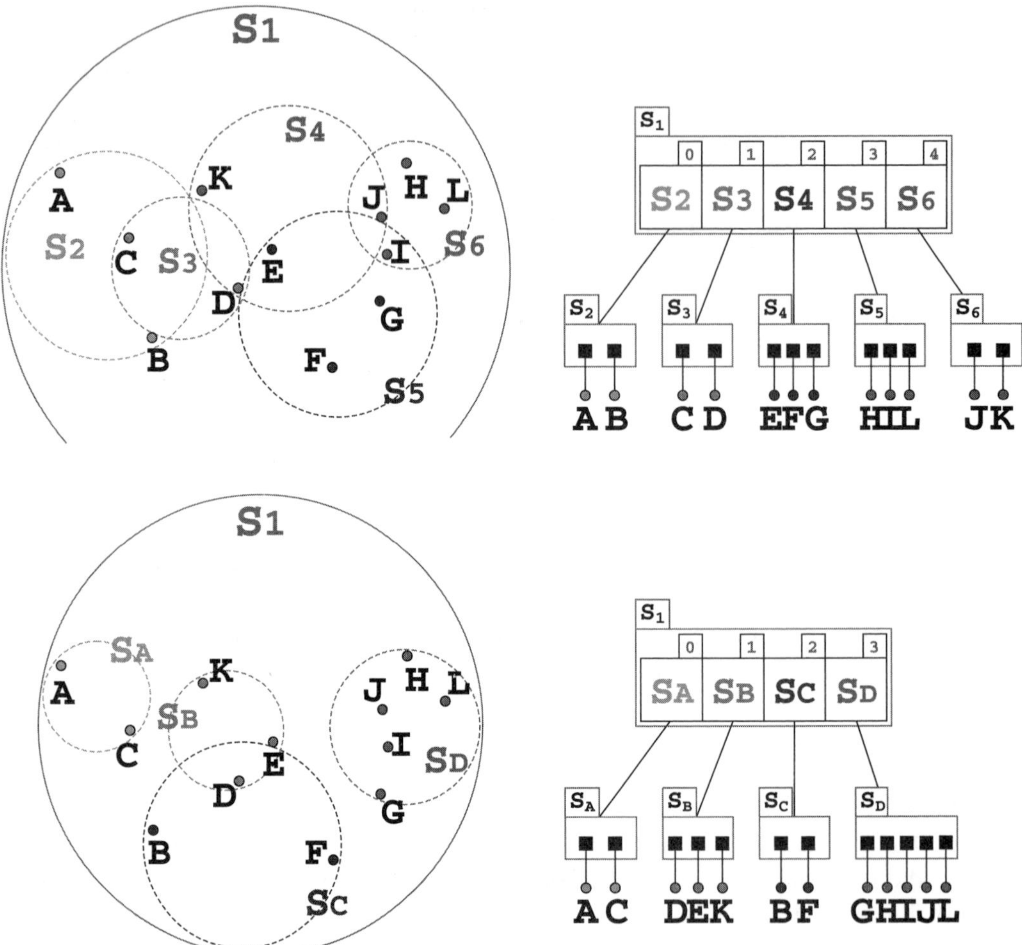
S1
S4
S2
S3
S5
S6
A
B
C
D
E
F
G
H
I
J
K
L
0
1
2
3
4
S2 S3 S4 S5 S6
AB
CD
EFG
HIL
JK
SA
SB
SC
SD
SA SB SC SD
AC
DEK
BF
GHIJL

Figure 10.28 An example where the grandchildren-split heuristic could be triggered and would lower the nodes overlap. The SS-tree in the example has `m==2` and `M>=5`. The k-means split heuristic is run on the points `A-L`, with `k==5`. Notice how k-means can (and sometimes will) output fewer clusters than the initial number of centroids. In this case, only four clusters were returned.

To check the overlap, the first thing we need is the formula to compute the volume of intersections of two spheres. Unfortunately, computing the exact overlap of two hyperspheres, in the generic k-dimensional case, requires not just substantial work and good calculus skills to derive the formulas, but also robust computing resources, as it results in a formula that includes an integral whose computation is clearly expensive enough to cause you to question its usefulness in a heuristic.

An alternative approach is to check whether one of the two bounding envelopes is completely included in the other. Check that the center of one sphere is contained in the other one, and that the distance of the centroid of the smaller sphere is closer than R-r to the centroid of the larger one, where R is the radius of the larger sphere and, as you might expect, r is the radius of the smaller one.

Variants of this check can set a threshold for the ratio between the actual distance of the two centroids and R-r, using it for an approximation of the overlapping volume as this ratio gets closer to 1.

The reorganization heuristic is then applied if the check's condition is satisfied. A good understanding of k-means is needed to get into the details of this heuristic, so we'll skip it in this context, and we encourage readers to refer to chapter 12 for a description of this clustering algorithm. Here, we will use an example to illustrate how the heuristic works.

In the example, the heuristic is called on node S_1 and the clustering is run on its grandchildren, points A-L. As mentioned, these could also be centroids of other internal nodes, and the algorithm wouldn't change.

The result is shown in the bottom half of figure 10.28. You might wonder why there are now only four children in node S_1: even if k-means was called with k, the number of initial clusters, equal to five (the number of S_1's children), this clustering algorithm could output fewer than k clusters. If at any time during its second step, points assignment, one of the centroids doesn't get any point assigned, that centroid just gets removed and the algorithm continues with one less cluster.

Both the check and the reorganization heuristic are resource-consuming; the latter in particular requires O(jMk) comparisons/assignments, if j is the number of maximum iterations we use in k-means. Therefore, in the original paper it was recommended to check the overlap situation after splitting nodes, but to apply the reorganization infrequently.

We can also easily run the check when an entry is moved across siblings, while it becomes less intuitive when we merge two nodes. In that case, we could always check all pairs of the merged node's sibling, or—to limit the cost—just sample some pairs.

To limit the number of times we run the reorganization heuristic and avoid running it again on nodes that were recently re-clustered, we can introduce a threshold for the minimum number of points added/removed on the subtree rooted at each node, and only reorganize a node's children when this threshold is passed. These methods prove to be effective in reducing the variance of the tree, producing more compact nodes.

But I'd like to conclude the discussion about these variants with a piece of advice: start implementing basic SS-trees (at this point, you should be ready to implement your own version), then profile them within your application (like we did for heaps in chapter 2), and only if SS-trees appear to be a bottleneck and improving their running time would reduce your application running time by at least 5-10%, try to implement one or more of the SS^+-tree heuristics presented in this section.

Summary

- To overcome the issues with k-d trees, alternative data structures such as R-trees and SS-trees have been introduced.
- The best data structure depends on the characteristics of the dataset and on how it needs to be used, the dimension of the dataset, the distribution (shape) of the data, whether the dataset is static or dynamic, and whether your application is search-intensive.
- Although R-trees and SS-trees don't have any guarantee on the worst-case running time, in practice they perform better than k-d trees in many situations, and especially for higher-dimensional data.
- SS^+-trees improve the structure of these trees by using heuristics that reduce the number of nodes overlapping.
- You can trade the quality of search results for performance by using approximated similarity searches.
- There are many domains where exact results for these searches are not important, because either we can accept a certain error margin, or we don't have a strong similarity measure that can guarantee that the exact result will be the best choice.
- An example of such a domain is similarity search in an image dataset.

11 Applications of nearest neighbor search

This chapter covers

- Adapting abstract algorithms to the complexity of real systems
- Designing a solution for the "closest hub" problem using NN search
- Adding filtering to NN search to support business logic and dynamic supply
- Dealing with faulty networks and failure, and deploying to the real world
- Applying NN search to other domains, such as physics and computer graphics

It's time to harvest what we've sown and to start solving the problems we have discussed in the last few chapters. As always, after a deep dive into theory, we try to give you a "real-life" angle, and in this chapter, we will incrementally build a solution for the "closest hub" problem, one that takes into account many of the issues a real application would face. But make no mistake—we can't tackle all the possible issues here, and this chapter doesn't aim to be an exhaustive description of all the possible problems you could face;

neither it is a runbook about how to operate your e-commerce application. Only practice, rolling up your sleeves, and getting burned while trying can teach you that. What you can find in this chapter, besides a few examples of real-world technical challenges, is a hands-on example of the analysis process that brings you from a solution "on paper" for your use case, to a working application coping with the complex facets of reality.

11.1 An application: Find nearest hub

Now that we have seen how to implement k-d trees (in chapter 9) and SS-trees (chapter 10), we can focus on the problems we are able to solve by using these structures. And we can go back to our initial example: writing an application to find the closest warehouse/shop/retailer to customers, in real time. Figure 11.1 shows yet another variation of the map first introduced in figure 8.1, where we show a few (real) cities and some imaginary shops in the area around them. In our example, we need to find the closest shop that is able to deliver a certain item to customers after they purchase that item on our website. For this reason, we only show the kind of goods sold for each shop, rather than the shop's name or brand.

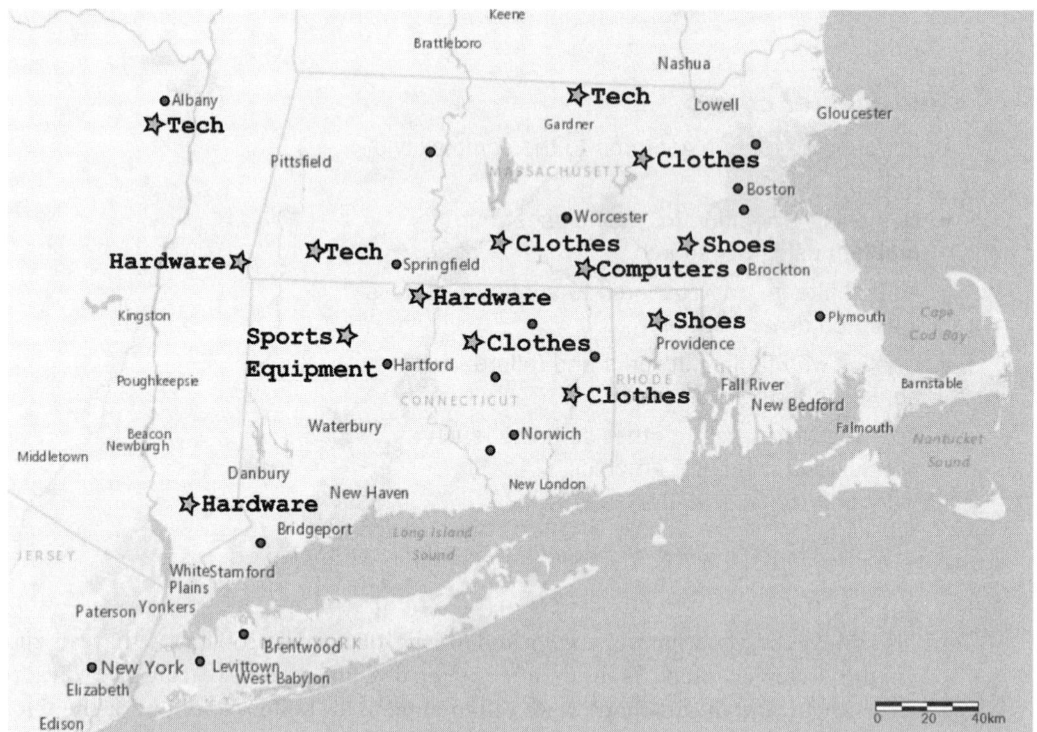

Keene
Brattleboro
Nashua
Albany
Tech
Tech
Lowell
Gardner
Gloucester
Pittsfield
Clothes
Boston
Worcester
Hardware
Tech
Clothes
Shoes
Springfield
Computers
Brockton
Hardware
Kingston
Sports Equipment
Shoes
Plymouth
Clothes
Providence
Hartford
Poughkeepsie
Fall River
Barnstable
Clothes
New Bedford
Waterbury
Falmouth
Beacon
Newburgh
Norwich
Middletown
Danbury
New London
Hardware
New Haven
Bridgeport
White Plains
Stamford
Paterson
Yonkers
Brentwood
New York
Levittown
West Babylon
Elizabeth
Edison
0
20
40km

Figure 11.1 A map[1] with cities and hypothetical distribution centers (in this chapter we will often use retailer/shop as synonyms), and customers (dots). For these shops, on the map we only indicate what they sell for the sake of clarity.

[1] Sources: Esri, DeLorme; HERE; and MapmyIndia.

Given all the work done in the previous chapters, in this chapter we could actually get away without even writing any code. k-d tree, SS-tree, or another similar data structure can take care of all the operations we need; just create a container with the full list of warehouses, and then, for each customer's request, query it to find the closest hub.

If, however, the retailer's stock is dynamic, and items can go out of stock in one place or be restocked in another, then our current model won't work, and we need to make a tiny change to our tree nodes and our search method. We will talk about these details later in this chapter. First, let's see how we can write a solution to the basic version of our e-commerce problem.

11.1.1 Sketching a solution

Initially we will make some assumptions to simplify our scenario. Assume all the shops have all the products in stock at all times. Figure 11.2 shows a possible workflow for order processing under this scenario; of course, this is not what would happen in real life, but simplifying a problem usually helps us sketch a first solution upon which we can iterate, introducing one by one the constraints found in real situations and reasoning about how they influence our applications and how we can cope with them:

- Shops have dynamic inventory, so we need to check whether the closest shop to a customer actually sells an item and has it in stock.
- Delivery costs and other considerations might cause us to prefer a further shop to the closest one.
- If we need to make HTTP calls as part of our workflow, we need to take extra care to avoid network pitfalls, and we might have to carefully select our algorithm to cope with issues such as fault tolerance and timeouts.

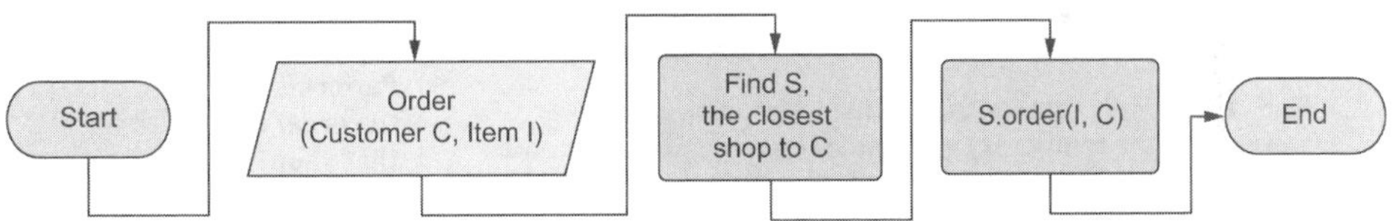
Start
Order
(Customer C, Item I)
Find S,
the closest
shop to C
S.order(I, C)
End

Figure 11.2 Simplified workflow for an order on the e-commerce site. After receiving the order from the customer, look up the closest retailer (assuming there will be always one selling the item ordered) and then place the order with it. Since we assume everything always works, we have a very linear (and unrealistic) workflow.

The core of the problem, in this setting, is to keep an updated list of stores and retrieve the closest one to a customer each time an order is placed on the website.

Listing 11.2 shows these trivial operations; we also define an auxiliary type for shops in listing 11.1.

Listing 11.1 The Shop class

```
class Shop
  #type string
  shopName
  #type Array<Item>
  items
  #type tuple(k)
  point

  function Shop(shopName, location, items)     <-- The constructor for the class
  function order(item, customer)               <-- Performs the actual purchase.
```

The constructor for the class

Performs the actual purchase. (Details of this method can't be generalized, and they are not relevant to our discussion. Just imagine that this will update stock and start the process of actually shipping the goods to the customer.)

It encapsulates the information associated with a retailer. It will become even more useful later in the chapter as we develop our final solution. We store the location of the shop in the field point, for the sake of consistency with what we have seen in the previous chapters.

Listing 11.2 The addShop and BuyItem methods

The addShop method takes the root of our container tree, the name of the shop and its location (a 2-D point), and optionally a list of items.

```
function addShop(treeRoot, shopName, shopLocation, items=[])
  shop ← new Shop(shopName, shopLocation, items)
  if treeRoot == null then
    return new Node(shop, null, null, 0)
  else
      return insert(treeRoot, shop, treeNode.level + 1)

function buyItem(treeRoot, customerLocation, item)
  closestShop ← nearestNeighbor(treeRoot, customerLocation)
  closestShop.order(item, customerLocation)
```

Creates a new instance of Shop

If the tree is empty . . .

. . . just creates a new root

Otherwise, inserts the new shop in the tree (insert will create a new Node for it)

Defines a method to call when a customer buys an item

Finds the closest retailer to the customer and stores it to the temporary variable closestShop

Performs the order on that shop

From the previous snippets, however, it's apparent that we'll need to make some adjustments to the node objects and to the API of the methods we have defined in the previous chapters.

For example, the Node class could hold a reference to the shop, as shown in listing 11.3, rather than directly to a point, and methods like insert, likewise, would take an instance of Shop as an argument and not just a point, so that the new signature would look something like

```
function insert(node, newShop, level=0)
```
[2]

[2] We omit the implementation here that will differ from what is shown in chapters 9 and 10 for replacing every occurrence of newPoint with newShop.point and using newShop instead of newPoint as argument to the Node constructor.

Listing 11.3 Redefining Node

```
class Node
  #type Shop
  shop
  #type Node
  left
  #type Node
  right
  #type integer
  level

  function Node(shop, left, right, level)
```

The application code looks so simple, but do not let it fool you: the complexity is all hidden in the `order` function that performs all the operations involved in actually placing an order to a real shop. This likely means that you have to interact with each shop's own web applications,[3] so first of all, you have to imagine that you need a common API by which all the shops' services need to abide.[4]

11.1.2 Trouble in paradise

Now we've finally have defined a simple method that we can use to find the closest retailer to our customer and let them know about the purchase so that they can ship goods to users.

Notice how simple listing 11.2 is. Simplicity, in IT as in life, is often a good thing. Simple code usually means maintainable and flexible code. The problem is that sometimes things look great on paper, but when you deploy your application and open it to real traffic, you often find issues you hadn't thought of or even imagined. For example, in the real world, you have to deal with dynamic inventory for each shop and, even worse, race conditions.[5]

The first issue we have overlooked is that not all the retailers have all the goods in stock. So, it's not enough to find the closest shop to a customer; we need to find the closest retailer that can actually sell and deliver the product bought by our user. If the user buys more than one item and we need to deliver them all in one go (to save on shipping or just to reduce user churn), we likely want to filter shops that have all the items at the same time, whenever possible. But then another question arises. If the user buys products A and B, and there is one shop that could ship both, but it's 100 miles away from the customer, and two shops each have only one of the items, but

[3] Unless, of course, you also provide IT infrastructure to all the shops as part of the service, which is possible, although obviously more challenging both technically and financially.

[4] That's probably the easy part, because each shop can write an adapter to bridge the gap between their internal software and your interface.

[5] A race condition is a situation that occurs when a system attempts to perform two or more operations at the same time, but the outcome of the operations depends on them being executed in a specific order. In other words, a race condition happens when operations A and B are executed at the same time, but we get a correct result if, for example, A finishes before B, while we get an error if B finishes before A.

they're within 10 miles of the customer, which solution should we choose? What about choosing between a closer shop that has a longer delivery time or higher cost, and another one that is further away, but cheaper and ultimately better for the customer?

Even more issues come up if we lay down the architecture of the system (see figure 11.3). So far, we have treated shop datasets as if they were local, but that's not necessarily the case; each retailer can have their own system with which we need to interact:

- They can sell items offline, for instance. If that happens, our information about their stock can become stale. Similarly, we can get out of sync if a shop's items are restocked.
- In listing 11.2 and figure 11.3, we assume that a call to `shop.order` will succeed, but since it's likely to be a remote call over HTTP, there are many reasons why it could fail independently of the item availability in the shop's inventory: the call could time out, the shop's application could crash and be unreachable, and so on. If we don't check their response, we will never know if the order was successfully placed. And if we do check, but never get a response, what should we do?

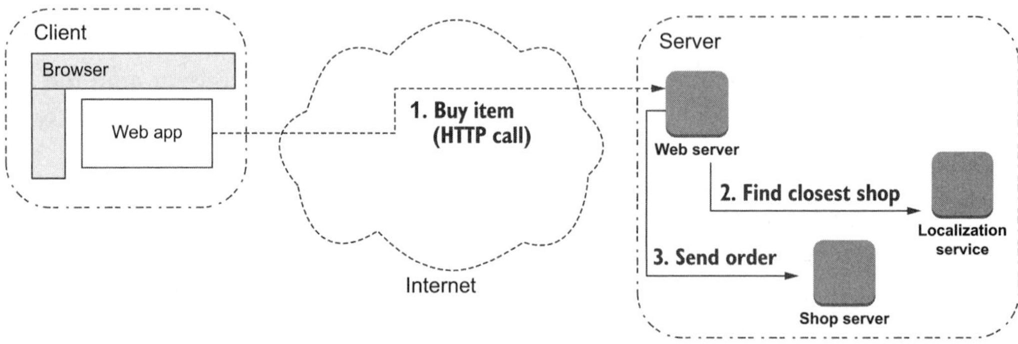
Client
Browser
Web app
1. Buy item
(HTTP call)
Internet
Server
Web server
2. Find closest shop
Localization service
3. Send order
Shop server

Figure 11.3 Simplified architecture for the e-commerce application described in chapter 8 and here in section 11.1

These are extremely challenging issues, that we'll try to solve in the next sections.

11.2 Centralized application

Let's set architectural questions aside for the moment, assume we handle in-house (within the same virtual machine running our web application) all orders for retailers, and focus on the first round of questions. At some point, we asked how we should choose which shop or combination of shops is best in order to serve a customer. Neither k-d trees, nor SS-trees, nor any other data structure can (or should) answer this question. This is a business-related decision that changes from company to company, and perhaps over time or with other variables within the same company.

What we can do, though, is provide our containers with a way to filter points in a NN search by some conditions that we can pass into our code, thus allowing whoever uses the container to reason about the business rules, customize them, and pass them as arguments to the search method.

11.2.1 Filtering points

By creating hooks through which clients can customize business logic, we provide a *template* method that can be effectively customized depending on the business needs.

Listing 11.4 shows the code for k-d tree's nearest neighbor search, modified to allow filtering of points.

As you can see, we pass an extra argument (with respect to the regular method in listing 9.9), a predicate that is evaluated on the current node before accepting this point as a nearest neighbor.

The only difference with the basic version, besides boilerplate to pass around this new argument, is at line #5, where the predicate is actually evaluated on the current node.

This version of the method allows us to filter single points and solve the first of the issues mentioned in the previous section, making sure that we choose a shop that actually has the item(s) a customer ordered.

Listing 11.4 The `filteredNearestNeighbor` method

If the node is `null`, we are traversing an empty tree, so the nearest neighbor can't be found in this branch of the tree. It is still possible that by backtracking, another branch is visited when it is found.

Otherwise, we have three tasks: check if the current node is closer than the previously found NN, traverse the branch on the same side of the split with respect to the target point, and check if we can prune the other branch (or traverse it as well).

Finds the closest point to a given target, among those satisfying a predicate. We also pass the best values found so far for NN and its distance to help pruning. These values default to `null`, `infinity` for a call on the tree root.

```
function fNN(node, location, predicate, (nnDist, nn)=(inf, null))
  if node == null then
    return (nnDist, nn)
  else
    dist ← distance(node.shop.point, location)
    if predicate(node) and dist < nnDist then
      (nnDist, nn) ← (dist, node.shop)
    if compare(location, node) < 0 then
      closeBranch ← node.left
      farBranch ← node.right
    else
      closeBranch ← node.right
      farBranch ← node.left
    (nnDist, nn) ← fNN(closeBranch, location, predicate, (nnDist, nn))
    if splitDistance(location, node) < nnDist then
```

We compute the distance between the current node's point and the target location.

If the current node satisfies the predicate provided and its distance to target is less than the current NN's distance, we have to update the values stored for the NN and its distance.

Checks if the target point is on the left branch of the split. If it is, the left branch is the closest to the target point; otherwise it is the furthest.

We certainly need to traverse the closest branch in search of the nearest neighbor. It is important to do so first and update the mementos for NN's distance, to improve pruning.

Using one of the helper functions defined in listing 9.2, we compute the distance between the split line passing through the current node and the target point. If this distance is closer than the distance to the current nearest neighbor, then the furthest branch might contain points closer than the current nearest neighbor (see figure 9.21).

```
    (nnDist, nn) ← fNN(farBranch, location, predicate, (nnDist, nn))
  return (nnDist, nn)
```

Traverses the furthest branch and updates the current values for NN and its distance

Returns the closest point found so far

For instance, we could redefine nodes as shown in listing 11.3, and pass to `fNN` the predicate `hasItemX()` defined in listing 11.5. We can also define a more generic version, `hasItem()`, that takes two arguments, an item and a shop, and uses currying[6] to create a unary predicate checking a single fixed item in the shop, and pass it as shown in listing 11.6.

Listing 11.5 Method `hasItemX`

Defines a function taking a node as argument to check if it has a certain item X (fixed)

```
function hasItemX(node)
  return X in node.shop.items
```

Just checks whether the list of items associated with a shop contains the item X

To find the nearest shop that can ship Pinot noir, we can call our `fNN` method with something like

```
fNN(treeRoot, customerPosition, hasItem("Pinot noir"))
```

Listing 11.6 A curried version of `hasItemX`

A generic version for `hasItem` takes the item as well as the node as arguments.

```
function hasItem(item, node)
  return item in node.shop.items

nn = fNN(root, customerLocation, hasItem(X))
```

Checks if the list of items associated with a shop contains `item`

We pass a curried instance of `hasItem` to the `fNN` method to find the closest point whose shop has item `x` in the inventory (here `x` is supposed to be a variable containing the item we look for).

Unfortunately, while this filtering mechanism allows us to filter out retailers that don't have the items we need, it isn't powerful enough to let us decide that it is best to choose a closer retailer with higher shipment costs over a cheaper one that is twice as far away, and in general it can't deal with complex conditions comparing different solutions.

[6] Currying is a functional programming technique that allows us to transform the execution of a function with `n` arguments in a sequence of `n` executions of unary functions. It allows, for instance, defining a generic function, such as `add(a,b)` which adds numbers `a` and `b`, and then creates new functions by fixing the first argument: `add5 = add(5)`. Or we could just as easily call the original function like this to add 4 and 3: `add(4)(3)`. Not all programming languages natively allow currying, but many allow workarounds to achieve it.

11.2.2 Complex decisions

If what we really need is not just filtering shops according to some criteria, but also choosing the best options among them, then we have to seek a more powerful mechanism.

We have two main choices:

- Use n-nearest neighbor to retrieve a list of n shops that satisfy our criteria, and then process this list to decide which one, among the possible solutions, is the actual best choice.
- Or we can replace the predicate passed to our nearest neighbor method, as shown in listing 11.7, which instead of a unary predicate is using a binary function that takes as arguments the current node and the best solution found so far, and returns which one is the best.

And, of course, we can also use a combination of the two methods.

The first solution doesn't ask for any change to our container, so we won't need to develop it any further. You can use sorting, a priority queue, or any selector algorithm you like in order to decide which solution is the best, according to your business rules. This mechanism has an advantage: it also allows you to try solutions where you order different items at different shops and see if that works better than the best "all-at-one-place" solution.

Listing 11.7 Another version of the `filteredNearestNeighbor` method

```
function fNN(node, location, cmpShops, (nnDist, nn)=(inf, null))
  if node == null then
    return (nnDist, nn)
  else
    dist ← distance(node.shop.point, location)
    if cmpShops((dist, node.shop), (nnDist, nn)) < 0 then
      (nnDist, nn) ← (dist, node.shop)
    if compare(location, node) < 0 then
      closeBranch ← node.left
      farBranch ← node.right
    else
      closeBranch ← node.right
      farBranch ← node.left
```

Annotations:

- Finds the closest point to a given target. In this case, we pass `cmpShops` method to compare two shops and return which one is best. We assume the return value follows the standard conventions for the compare functions: `-1` means the first argument is smaller, `1` the second is smaller, and `0` they are equal.
- If the node is `null`, we are traversing an empty tree, so the nearest neighbor can't change with respect to what we have already found.
- Otherwise, we have three tasks: check if the current node is better than the previously found NN, traverse the branch on the same side of the split with respect to the target point, and check if we can prune the other branch (or traverse it as well).
- We compute the distance between the current node's point and the target location.
- We use the `cmpShops` method to decide which of the shops better satisfies our needs.
- Checks if the target point is on the left branch of the split. If it is, the left branch is the closest to the target point; otherwise, it is the furthest.

Using one of the helper functions defined in listing 9.2, we compute the distance between the split line passing through current node and the target point. If this distance is closer than the distance to current nearest neighbor, then the furthest branch might contain points closer than the current nearest neighbor (see figure 9.21).

We certainly need to traverse the closest branch in search of the NN. It is important to do so first and update the mementos for NN's distance to improve pruning.

```
    (nnDist, nn) ← fNN(closeBranch, location, cmpShops, (nnDist, nn))
    if splitDistance(location, node) < nnDist then
      (nnDist, nn) ← fNN(farBranch, location, cmpShops, (nnDist, nn))
    return (nnDist, nn)
```

Returns the closest point found so far

Traverses the furthest branch and updates the current values for NN and its distance

When we pass a compare function to fNN, instead, this flexibility is not going to be possible, and we will only examine solutions where all items are shipped by the same shop.

If that's fine, because we have guarantees that we can always find such a shop (or we handle separately the case where we fail to find one), the "compare function" mechanism has the advantage of requiring less extra memory and being overall faster.

As mentioned, the idea is that we can encapsulate all the business logic in a binary function that will compare the node currently being traversed in nearest neighbor search with the best solution found at that point of the traversal. We also assume that this predicate will perform any necessary filtering, for example, making sure that the current node's retailer has all items in stock. The changes needed to our search method are minimal, as shown in listing 11.7. We simply gather together two steps (filtering shops and comparing the current solution with the best one found so far), and instead of just checking distances during our NN search, we use a function passed as an argument to fNN, function cmpShops,[7] to decide which entry is *nearer*.

So, now the heart of the business logic lies in this method, which in turn will decide which shops are filtered in and how we choose the our best option.

There are a couple of edge cases that we should always address in this function:

- If the current node is filtered out, always choose the current NN.
- If the best solution found so far is empty (that is, nn == null), then the current node should always be chosen, unless it is filtered out (at point 1).

Listing 11.8 provides a possible generic implementation of this comparison method, including filtering out shops that don't have all items in stock, and checking distances by using an unspecified heuristic method to decide which shop is the best.

Listing 11.8 A possible comparison method

A comparison method to decide which shop is preferable in our search. It takes both shops (the current node's and the nearest neighbor's found so far) as well as their distances.

```
function compareShops(boughtItems, (dist, shop), (nnDist, nnShop))
  if shop==null or not (item in shop.items ∀ item in boughtItems) then
    return 1
```

If shop is null, or it doesn't have all the items in the purchase list (boughtItems), then we return 1 to let the caller know that the current nearest neighbor is still the best solution.

[7] Stands for compareShops; the abbreviation was forced to better fit code lines onto the page.

Otherwise, if we haven't yet stored a NN, return -1: the current node is better than nothing.

If the distance of the current node is not worse than what we had already found, we can compare the two shops using a heuristic and see which one is better. Here this heuristic encapsulates any business logic; for instance, if a shop has lower shipment costs, if they sell the goods at lower price, or any other domain-specific condition.

```
    else if nnShop == null then
      return -1
    else if dist <= nnDist and heuristic(shop, nnShop) then
      return -1
    else
      return 1
```

If everything else fails, we just stick with what we have currently saved as nearest neighbor.

```
fNN(root, customerPosition, compareShops(["Cheddar", "Gravy", "Salad"]))
```

An example of a call to the (filtered) nearest neighbor method, searching for the most convenient shop that sells all three items in the list

Figure 11.4 summarizes the method logic in a flow chart.

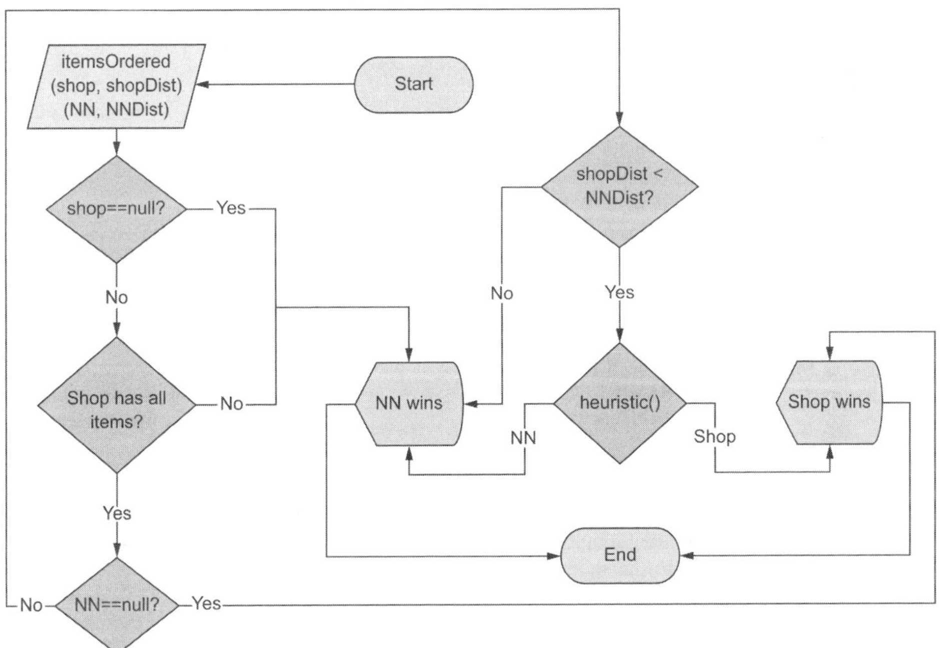
itemsOrdered
(shop, shopDist)
(NN, NNDist)
Start
shop==null?
Yes
No
Shop has all items?
No
Yes
NN==null?
No
Yes
shopDist < NNDist?
No
Yes
NN wins
heuristic()
NN
Shop
Shop wins
End

Figure 11.4 Flow chart describing the logic of the compare function defined in listing 11.8

It's worth clarifying once again that the choice of the heuristic is not connected to any of the data structures we have seen, and, vice versa, those algorithms don't depend on this function. It's just a heuristic method that encapsulates all the domain-specific logic, and so it changes from application to application. Depending on how you write it, and how you model the `Shop` class, you can customize the behavior of the search method to solve your instance of the problem.

11.3 Moving to a distributed application

So far, so good: we have solved the "closest hub" problem assuming we are in control of all the pieces of the applications, and we can be sure that the systems registering the order and starting the process to send goods to customers are always available and never fail.

If only the world worked this way! Unfortunately, not only do systems (applications, computers, networks, and so on) fail, but there is also a good chance that, for an e-commerce web application like the one we described, some crucial pieces are not even under our control. That is, we are likely dealing with a distributed application that includes different services, running on different machines (possibly located far away from each other), and communicating through remote calls over a network. Figure 11.5 builds upon the simplified architecture in figure 11.3, depicting a more realistic situation, where the retailers' servers live on their separate machines, and thus in a different addressing space, only accessible through remote calls (over HTTP, or any other communication protocol, such as *IPFS*[8]).

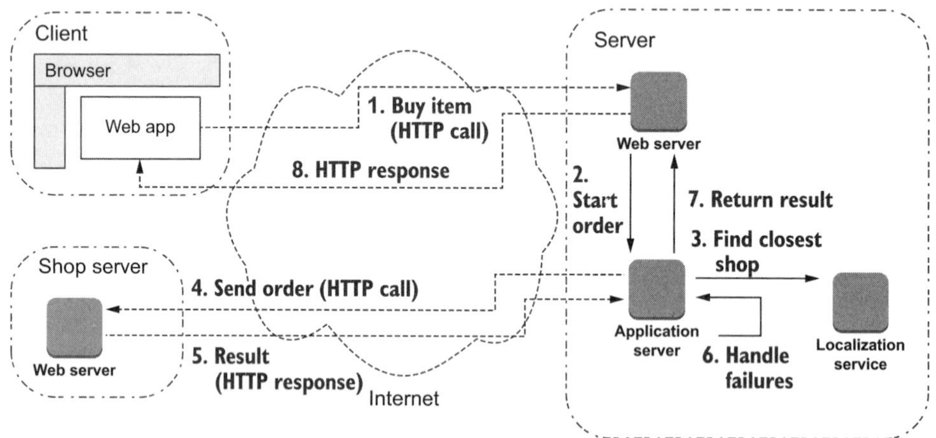
Client
Browser
Web app
1. Buy item (HTTP call)
8. HTTP response
Server
Web server
2. Start order
7. Return result
3. Find closest shop
Shop server
Web server
4. Send order (HTTP call)
5. Result (HTTP response)
Internet
Application server
6. Handle failures
Localization service

Figure 11.5 A more realistic design for the e-commerce application, taking into account the complexity of a distributed architecture and introducing a separate application server to deal with failures of HTTP calls to the shops' servers

As you can imagine, this changes the rules of the game. While we can have tight control of what runs on our machine (virtual or physical), once we introduce remote calls, we also introduce additional failure points, and we also need to deal with latency. For instance, if we synchronously call a method in our application, we know it can fail, and hopefully we also know why it would fail. We know it can take some time to compute (or, possibly, even loop forever), but we are also sure that the method was called and started doing its job.

[8] IPFS is a peer-to-peer hypermedia protocol; see https://ipfs.io. It's worth checking it out.

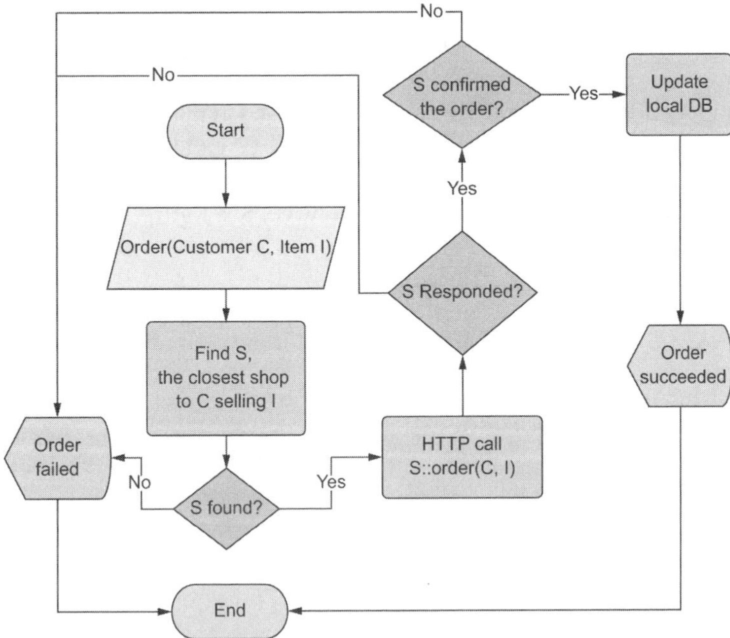
No
No
S confirmed the order?
Yes
Update local DB
Start
Yes
Order(Customer C, Item I)
S Responded?
Find S, the closest shop to C selling I
Order succeeded
Order failed
HTTP call S::order(C, I)
No
Yes
S found?
End

Figure 11.6 A workflow for order processing that takes into account some possible sources of failure. As a result, the execution is not linear anymore, and the logic of handling an order is more complex.

Processing an order, when we take all these factors into consideration, becomes sensibly more complicated, as shown in figure 11.6.

11.3.1 Issues handling HTTP communication

When we move to distributed systems, communication over the network is an additional source of uncertainty. We know that we sent an HTTP request, but if we don't get an answer, we have no way of knowing if the message arrived, if the network is broken, if the server is broken, or if it is hanging on a time-consuming task.[9]

We therefore have to decide how to handle this uncertainty. First of all, are we going to wait until we get a response (synchronous layout); send a request and do something else while we wait for an answer; or "fire and forget"—that is, send a request and not wait for any answer from the remote server?

This communication channel is part of a workflow of user interaction, with users waiting for a response, and their patience is usually limited. Who would wait 10 minutes (or just two!) before hitting reload on the page?

[9] Obviously, if we do get an answer, we can check the HTTP code and see if there is a network error or, assuming the callee correctly implements rules on the HTTP code to send back in case of an error, why the remote service is failing.

And indeed, for an ecommerce page, where the user expects to see a live update within a reasonable time, usually web servers have short timeouts on the calls they receive, meaning they would respond with a 5XX error after a few seconds, usually less than 10.

This introduces additional challenges, because if we keep a longer timeout for our call to the shop's server, there is a chance that the HTTP call from the customer fails, but our call to the shop succeeds afterward,[10] and we introduce a discrepancy, possibly even causing the customer to buy the same item twice. See figure 11.7 illustrating this case with sequence diagrams.

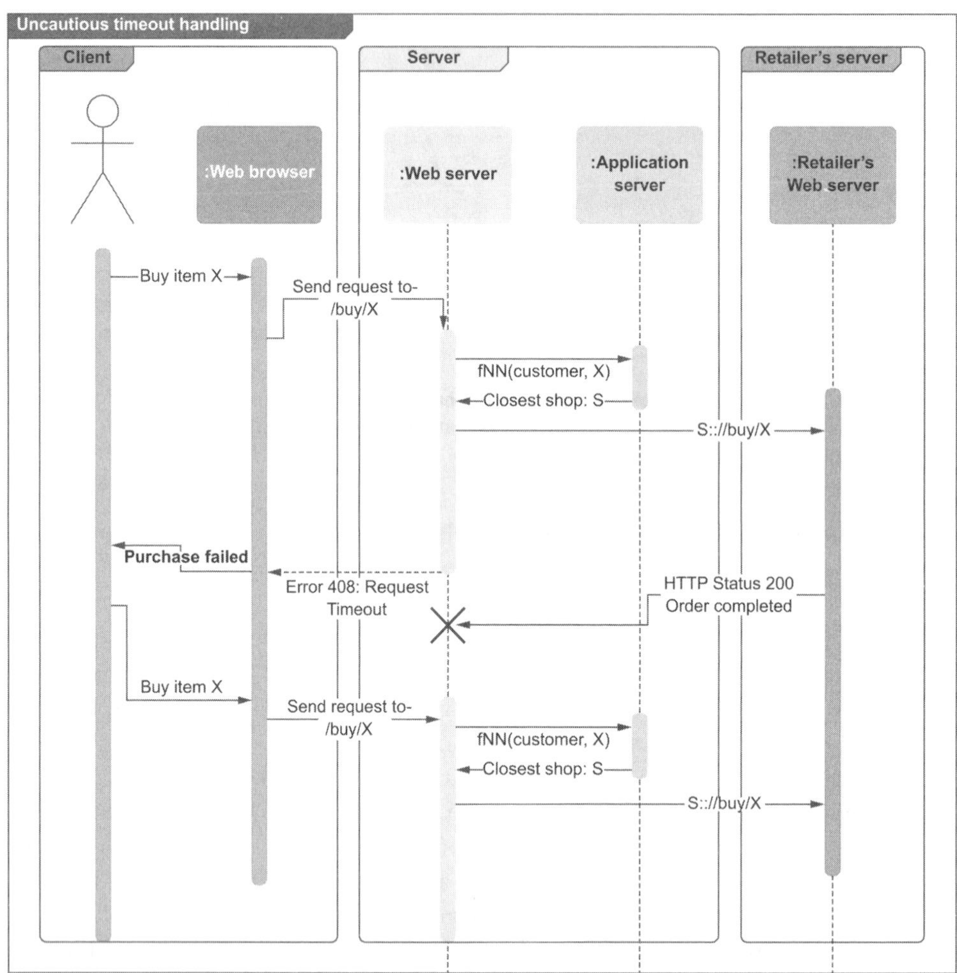
Uncautious timeout handling
Client
Server
Retailer's server
:Web browser
:Web server
:Application server
:Retailer's Web server
Buy item X
Send request to- /buy/X
fNN(customer, X)
Closest shop: S
S::/buy/X
Purchase failed
Error 408: Request Timeout
HTTP Status 200 Order completed
Buy item X
Send request to- /buy/X
fNN(customer, X)
Closest shop: S
S::/buy/X

Figure 11.7 A sequence diagram showing how an improper handling of timeouts, when calls to external services are involved, could cause dire consequences. The application's web server times out before receiving an answer from the external service, so the user sees that the order didn't go through, while the retailer's service has registered it. If the user tries to order the item again, there will be a duplicate.

[10] This is the case with HTTP/1.1, where requests cannot be canceled by the caller. HTTP/2 specification, on the other hand, introduces the possibility of canceling requests sent.

If the shops' servers have a timeout set to 8 seconds[11] we need to complete all the remaining operations within 2 seconds, which likely leaves us less than a second to run the nearest neighbor search.

In short, when we move to distributed architectures, there are lot more factors we need to be careful about that go beyond the mere use of algorithms. Nevertheless, the choice of the search algorithm is even more important. A bad choice can have dire consequences for our web application.

That means we need to be careful about the algorithm we implement:

- Different data structures have different levels of performance for the average and worst case. You can decide to go with the algorithm that is the fastest on average to serve as many requests as possible in the shortest time, or to go with the algorithm that has the best worst-case performance to be sure that all requests will complete within the allotted time (even if, on average, it will be slower).
- If the dataset to search through constantly grows past a certain point, it will probably become too large to allow you to run a NN search in the time available. At that point, you need to think about other ways to scale your application—for example, with a geographical sharding of the data; or if that doesn't make sense for your business, with an approximate algorithm leveraging a random sharding with parallelization, and then choosing the best of the solutions returned for each shard.
- If you are using an approximated algorithm, then usually you have a trade-off between performance and accuracy. In that case, you need to make sure you can compromise on the quality of the results to obtain an answer within the time you can afford to wait.

11.3.2 Keeping the inventory in sync

If the situation doesn't already look complicated enough to you, there is another troubling issue that we haven't considered yet: Where do we get the information about the availability of items?

So far, we have assumed that this information is in the node of our k-d tree (or SS-tree), but that might not be the case. If you think about it, when we place an order to a retailer, their inventory goes down, but the inventory in our container does not necessarily reflect that.

There are a number of issues to take into account: the retailer could sell goods through other channels (either another e-commerce site or a brick-and-mortar shop), and we need to update our copy of the inventory when that happens. We need to communicate over a network, so we need to be careful about race conditions to avoid placing orders twice or missing them.

---

[11]Unfortunately, as mentioned, with HTTP/1.1 we can't decide this timeout that is set on the servers. We have to adjust to the settings of shops' servers, and in particular to the longest of those timeouts. So, in the example, assume that 8 seconds is the longest time after which a request to one of these servers is guaranteed to fail.

While we could think of workarounds for both issues, it is best to switch to a different approach. Figure 11.8 shows an ever more complex architecture for our app that includes a DB (which could be something like Memcached, a SQL DB, or a combination of both) and another service whose goal is just running (as a daemon, independently on the main app) and periodically asking the retailers' servers for an updated inventory. Once a response is received asynchronously, the service will update the local DB with the fresh values.

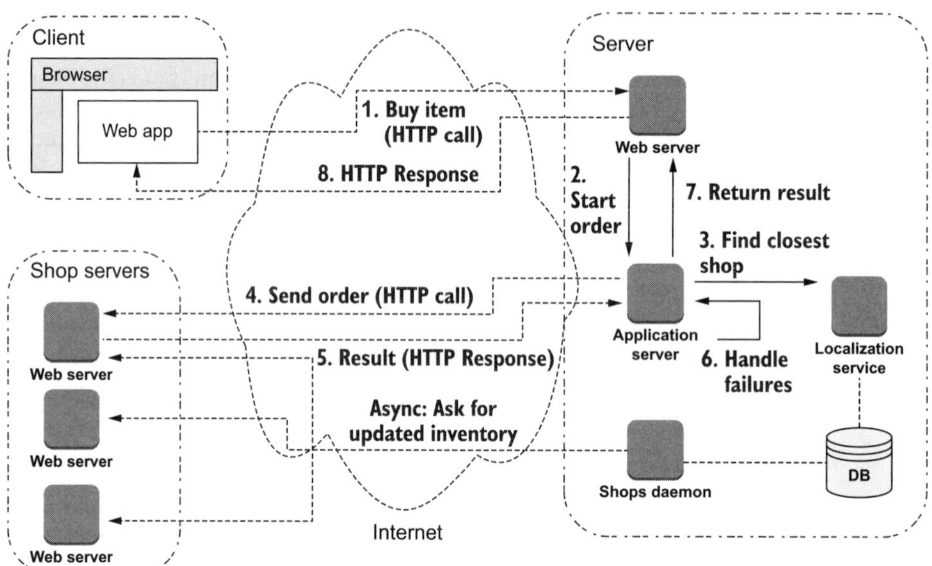
Client
Browser
Web app
Server
1. Buy item (HTTP call)
8. HTTP Response
Web server
2. Start order
7. Return result
3. Find closest shop
Shop servers
4. Send order (HTTP call)
Application server
6. Handle failures
Localization service
5. Result (HTTP Response)
Web server
Async: Ask for updated inventory
Web server
Shops daemon
DB
Internet
Web server

Figure 11.8 An even more advanced design, including a daemon that asynchronously polls shops' servers to sync the local DB to their inventories

This also means that when we run the nearest neighbor search, we need to make sure that our in-memory copy of the inventory for the shops is up-to-date. Here we will also have to compromise between performance and accuracy, because making one DB call (even if mediated through a fast cache) is likely going to be too slow. So we probably want to have another daemon running on our server's machine on a thread in the application server that gets the diff from the database, only for the values changed from the last update, goes through the list of shops (kept in some shared memory area), and updates those values.

11.3.3 Lessons learned

We have delved into our e-commerce application, iterating from a coarse-grained design for a centralized application to the smallest details of a distributed system.

While this discussion can't be exhaustive, and isn't meant to be, I hope it was useful to provide you with an idea of how you can structure the design process that leads from an algorithm to a full, production-ready application that leverages it. Hopefully, it also provided useful pointers to the possible issues you could face in the development of a web application and what you could look for if you'd like to keep learning in this area.

Now it's time to move on and present you with a few more problems, in completely different contexts, that can be solved using nearest neighbor search.

11.4 Other applications

Maps aren't the only field of application for nearest neighbor search. They were not even the application for which k-d trees were originally invented; k-d trees just happened to work very well on this domain, but these containers were meant to solve problems in higher dimensional spaces, rather than in 2-D or 3-D space.

To give you an idea of the vast number of fields that can leverage these algorithms, we'll briefly go through a few examples on very different domains.

11.4.1 Color reduction

The problem is simple: you have an RGB bitmap image using a certain palette; for example, the usual 16 million RGB, where each pixel of the image has three channels associated with it—red, green, and blue—and each of these colors has an associated intensity value between 0 and 255. Figure 11.9 shows an example of how a bitmap image is encoded. For instance, if a pixel is meant to be completely red, it will be associate with the tuple (R=255, G=0, B=0),[12] a darker blue pixel with something like (0, 0, 146), and a yellow one with (255, 255, 0); black is (0, 0, 0), and white is (255, 255, 255).

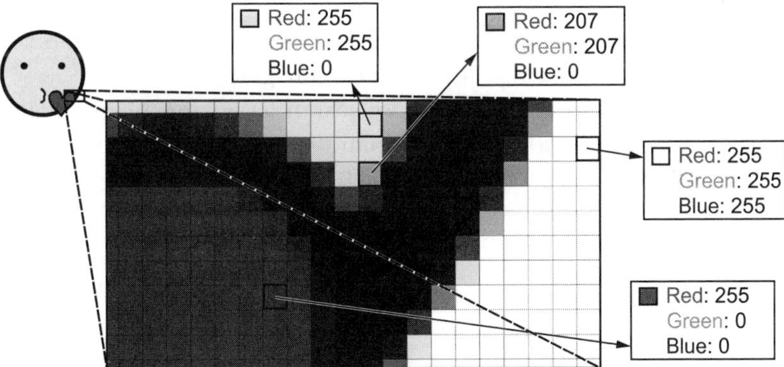
Red: 255
Green: 255
Blue: 0
Red: 207
Green: 207
Blue: 0
Red: 255
Green: 255
Blue: 255
Red: 255
Green: 0
Blue: 0

Figure 11.9 RGB bitmap format. An image is made of tiny points, its pixels, and for each of them its color is determined by the combination of three primary colors: red, green, and blue, each of which can have an intensity between 0 and 255.

[12]Meaning that the intensity will be maximum for the red channel and minimum for the other two channels.

To store such an image, we need 3 bytes per pixel.[13] For an image with a resolution of 1280 x 720 pixels,[14] this means 2.7649.800 bytes, more than 2 MBs; and 1920 × 1080 pixels[15] images require almost 6 MBs at 16M colors.

To save space, you could either use a compressed format, which could cause a loss of information or transform the data to a different space,[16] or reduce the number of colors you use for each pixel. Suppose that you are storing images for a specific purpose, such as images of road signs to be fed to a machine learning model for training.

If you don't care about the background, road signs themselves use a very limited set of colors, so you can decide that it is fine to down-sample the colors you use to a 256-color scale.[17] This will allow a factor of 3 savings for your storage, which means 4 GBs for every thousand pictures stored (if you are storing or processing them on the cloud, this likely means a huge savings of time and money).

So the problem is this: How do you transform each image from one color scale to the other by keeping the highest fidelity?

You will have to choose 256 colors and "bin" each of the 16M original colors into these 256 buckets. The key is how you choose the destination colors scale. There are, of course, many ways to do that; you could choose the same 256 colors for all images, perhaps by sampling uniformly the original 16M scale, but you could also decide for each image the best scale to reduce the loss of information.

How you choose this scale was actually the subject of an interview question I was asked by one of the best engineers with whom I had the pleasure to work. We'll leave it as an exercise for the reader to think about how this problem can be best solved, so we avoid spoiling the question.

But once you somehow come up with the best choice for the 256 colors to use, how do you transform each pixel from one scale to the other?

Here is where nearest neighbor search comes into play: we create a k-d tree, or SS-tree, containing each of the 256 selected colors for the destination scale; the dimension of the search space will be, as you can imagine, 3.

For each pixel in the original image, we search its nearest neighbor in the tree, and store the index of the color in the destination scale closest to the original color of the pixel. Listing 11.9 shows pseudo-code for these operations, using an SS-tree.

---

[13]If we store it uncompressed. Formats such as JPG or WEBM store a compressed version of the image with a slight loss in quality but using sensibly less memory—at least one order of magnitude less.

[14]An image at 720p resolution, also known as HD. Today this is even considered poor quality.

[15]Resolution 1080p or full HD. Still, far from the 4K resolution that's the standard these days.

[16]JPG algorithm transforms the image from pixel space to frequency space.

[17]Although this is unlikely to be the case if you are trying to train a robust model, bear with me just for the sake of illustrating this.

Listing 11.9 Down-sampling image colors using NN-search

Creates an SS-tree starting from the list of 256 sampled colors. Here we explicitly pass the dimension of the search space, 3, just for clarity (it can be inferred from the points in the list, of course). We assume that each of the sampled colors in the container will be associated with its index in the destination color scale.

Goes through each pixel in the source image

In the most generic case, pixels could be modeled as objects with more fields than just color; for instance, their position in the image. If that's so, we just need the RGB components for the NN search.

```
tree ← SsTree(sampledColors, 3)
for pixel in sourceImage do
  (r, g, b) ← pixel.color
  sampled_color ← tree.nearestNeighborSearch(r, g, b)
  destIndex[pixel.index].color_index ← sampled_color.index
```

Finds the nearest neighbor of current color

In the destination image, sets the color index for the transformed pixel based on the index in the destination color scale of the sampled color that is closest to the original pixel's color.

You can see how simple it is to perform such advanced tasks when you have the right data structure! That's because all the complexity is encapsulated in the implementation of the SS-tree (or k-d tree or equivalent), and that's also why the main goal of this book is helping readers to recognize the situations where they can use these data structures—that alone will make you stand out as a developer, producing faster and more reliable code.

11.4.2 Particle interaction

In particle physics simulations, scientists need to model systems where a high number of atoms, molecules, or sub-atomic particles interact in a closed environment. For instance, you could simulate the evolution of a gas when the temperature changes, or a laser beam hits the gas, and so on.

Figure 11.10 shows a simplification of what such a simulation could look like. Considering that at an average 25°C room temperature there are approximately 10^{22} molecules in a square meter of air, you can imagine that even with small boxes and rarefied gases, your simulation should handle billions of billions of items for each step of the simulation.

These particle simulations are all about computing the interaction between particles, but with such numbers, checking how each particle interacts with any other particle is simply not feasible. There would be ~10^{40} pairs to check, and that number is just too big for any traditional computer.[18]

Moreover, it doesn't always even make sense: electrical force and gravity have a limited range of action, and so outside of a certain radius the magnitude of the interaction between two particles would be negligible.

You see where I'm going, right? This is the perfect use case for either a `n`-nearest neighbor search, where we approximate the simulation by assuming that each particle

[18] Quantum computers could come to the rescue, though, in these situations: check out *Learn Quantum Computing with Python and Q#*, by Sarah C. Kaiser and Christopher E. Granade (Manning Publications, 2021).

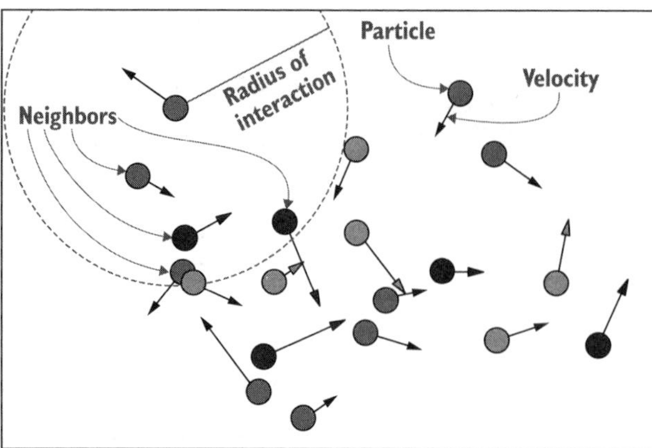
Particle
Radius of interaction
Velocity
Neighbors

Figure 11.10 A simplified representation of particle interaction. Several particles of different types interact in closed environment (for instance, gas particles in a sealed box). Each particle has a an associated velocity. For each particle, we compute the interaction only with the closest neighbors, to save computational resources.

is only influenced by the `n` closest particles to it (and by tuning `n` we can trade-off precision for speed), or alternatively we can only check the interaction of each particle with the ones inside the radius of action of the four fundamental forces (or a subset of them, depending on the type of particles).

Listing 11.10 describes a possible implementation of such a simulation leveraging an SS-tree to perform range-based queries and filter, for each particle, the surrounding particles with which it is relevant to compute the interaction. The catch is that the k-d tree (or equivalent DS) used needs to be updated after every step of the simulation (since the position of each particle changes), but even so, the speedup that can be obtained is impressive.

Listing 11.10 Particle interaction with range search

```
function simulation(numParticles, simulationComplete)
  particles ← initParticles(numParticles)
  while (not simulationComplete)
    tree ← SsTree(particles, 3)
    forces = {ō for particle in particles}
    for particle in particles do
```

- First we need to initialize our `n` particles: depending on the simulation we could desire a random initialization or setting a specific configuration.
- Defines a function to run the simulation, to which we pass the number of particles and a predicate that becomes true once the simulation is complete (might be based on number of iterations or other conditions; for instance, the system getting into a stable state)
- Runs a loop until the simulation completes
- At each step of the simulation, we need to initialize an SS-tree (or similar DS) with the current configuration of the system. Since the position of the particles changes at each step, we need to update the tree or create a new one every time. We assume the simulation is in a 3-D environment, but there are special cases where the dimension of the tuples could be different.
- Initialize an array holding, for each particle, the resultant force operating on it. Each entry is a 3-D vector (for the assumption made above), holding the vector sum of all forces acting on a particle. Initially we set elements to ō, the `null` vector.
- Iterates over each particle

For a particle, find its neighbors, that is, the other particles whose effects will be more relevant on the current one. In this example, we use a spherical range search within a certain radius, for instance, a threshold at which interaction is not relevant anymore. This value depends on the problem, obviously. Alternatively, we could also decide to only compute the interaction with the `m` closest points, for some `m`.

For each of the selected "neighbors," computes the force resulting from the interaction of the two particles

```
    neighbors ← tree.pointsInSphere(particle.position, radius)
    for neighbor in neighbors do
      forces[particle] += computeInteraction(particle, neighbor)
  for particle in particles do
    update(particle, forces[particle])
```

Once all forces are computed, cycles through all particles again and updates their position and velocity. We should also take into account interaction with the box boundaries; for instance, inverting the velocity if the particle hits the walls, assuming an elastic collision (or more complex interaction in case of inelastic collision).

In this configuration, we compute the force between particles `A` and `B` twice: once when `particle==A` and `neighbor==B`, and once when `particle==B` and `neighbor==A`. This is harmless, though inefficient. With a small change we can keep track of the pairs updated and make sure to compute the interaction only once.

11.4.3 Multidimensional DB queries optimization

As we saw in chapter 9, k-d trees support multidimensional range queries (MDRQ), searches that select intervals in two or more dimensions of a multidimensional search space. (For instance, as we suggested in chapter 9, a query that searches every employee between thirty and sixty years old and that earns between 40 and 100 thousand dollars per year).

These queries are common in business applications, and many databases support optimized techniques to speed them up. While you won't find it in MySQL, PostgreSQL has supported NN search indexes since version 9, and Oracle implements them in Extensible Indexing.

When indexing tables with a single key field (and many non-key fields), we can use a binary search tree to provide fast (logarithmic) lookup in searches based on the indexed field.

K-d trees provide a natural extension of that use case when we need to index tables with composite keys. While traversing the tree, we will cycle through all the fields in the composite key. Moreover, k-d trees provide methods for exact match, best match (the nearest neighbor search), and range search; partial match queries could also be supported.

Partial queries on k-d trees

Although we haven't included partial queries in our containers' API, implementing them is straightforward—we perform a regular exact match traversal on the fields in the query, while we follow both branches in levels corresponding to fields of the keys that are not filtered in the query.

For instance, if we use a k-d tree for geospatial data, and we look for all the points on a line parallel to the `x` axis, such that `x==C`, we would traverse both branches in the nodes at odd levels (where we split on `y`), while at even levels (corresponding to `x` coordinate splits), we would only traverse the branch containing `C`.

(continued)
Figures 11.11 and 11.12 show how a partial range search works on a k-d tree.

Alternatively, we can also use the existing `pointsInRectangle` method, passing a range spanning from the minimum possible to the maximum possible value for those fields we are not going to put restrictions on. For instance, in this example, we would set these criteria:

```
{x: {min:C, max:C}, y:{min=-inf, max=inf}}
```

Figures 11.11 and 11.12 show an example of how a partial query can be run on a k-d tree.

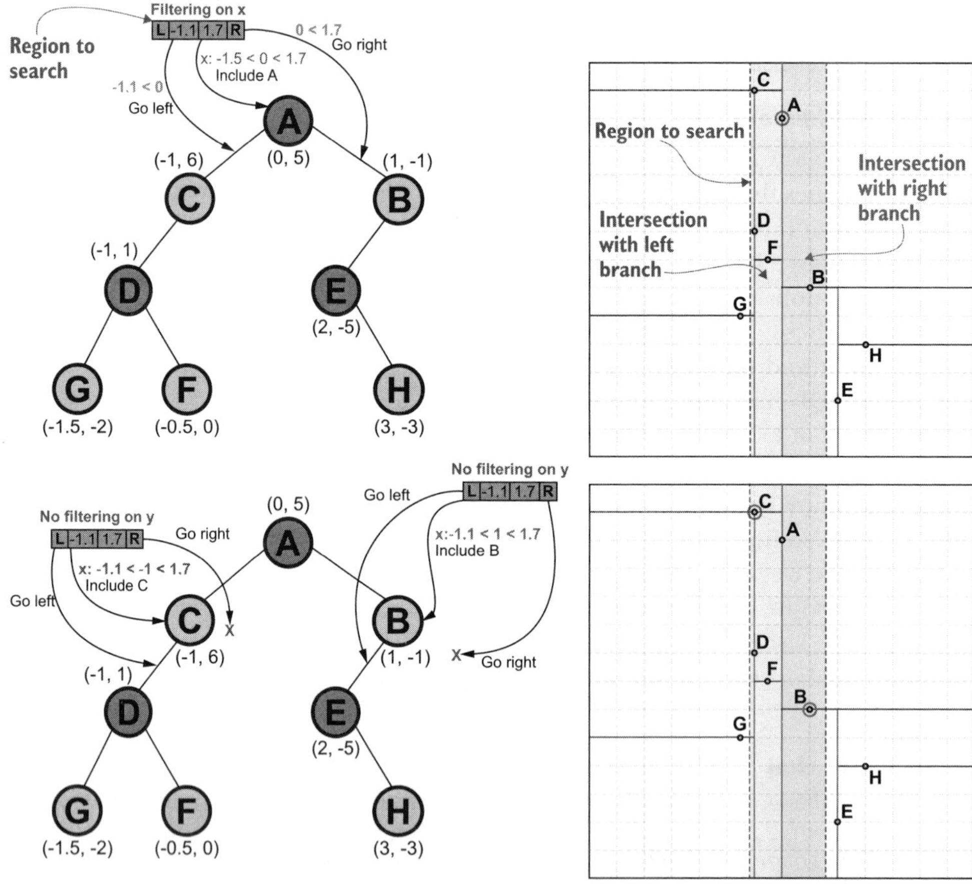
Filtering on x
L -1.1 1.7 R
Region to search
0 < 1.7
Go right
x: -1.5 < 0 < 1.7
Include A
-1.1 < 0
Go left
A (0, 5)
C (-1, 6)
B (1, -1)
D (-1, 1)
E (2, -5)
G (-1.5, -2)
F (-0.5, 0)
H (3, -3)
Region to search
Intersection with right branch
Intersection with left branch
No filtering on y
L -1.1 1.7 R
Go right
x: -1.1 < -1 < 1.7
Include C
Go left
No filtering on y
L -1.1 1.7 R
Go left
x:-1.1 < 1 < 1.7
Include B
Go right

Figure 11.11 An example of running a partial query on a k-d tree. The example shows a partial range query on a 2-D tree with fields x and y, where the search specifies a criterion only on x. Take all points whose x value is between -1.1 and 1.7, regardless of the value of y. In the first step, filtering is applied on the x coordinates of the root, since the first split is on the x coordinate. The second step, on nodes C and B, doesn't perform any filtering, because the split on those nodes is on the y coordinates, while the partial search is only about an x range. The x coordinates of nodes C and B are checked to determine if they should be included in the results.

Many SQL queries can be directly translated into calls to our data structure's methods. Let's see a few examples of how that is possible.

First, let's set the context. Imagine we have a SQL table with three fields: name, birthdate, and salary. The first two could be enough for a primary key,[19] but we also want to create an index on salary, because for some reason we run a lot of queries on salary. Thus, our index will use a 3-D tree with the same fields.

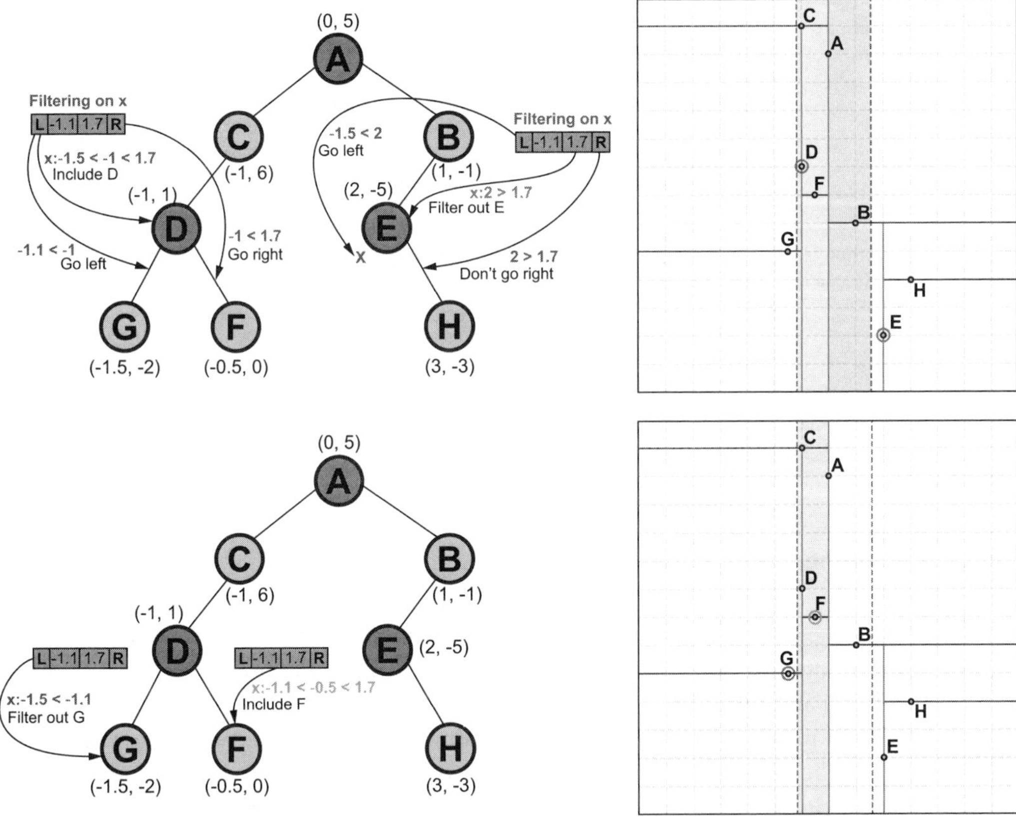
(0, 5)
Filtering on x
L -1.1 1.7 R
x:-1.5 < -1 < 1.7
Include D
(-1, 1)
(-1, 6)
-1.1 < -1
Go left
-1 < 1.7
Go right
-1.5 < 2
Go left
(1, -1)
(2, -5)
x:2 > 1.7
Filter out E
2 > 1.7
Don't go right
(-1.5, -2)
(-0.5, 0)
(3, -3)
x:-1.5 < -1.1
Filter out G
x:-1.1 < -0.5 < 1.7
Include F

Figure 11.12 Continuing the example in figure 11.11 about running a partial query on a k-d tree. The third step, in the top part, shows another filtering step: nodes `D` and `E`'s split-coordinate is again `x`, so we can prune the branches on which we will search. On the last step, since we are at the leaf level, we only check whether nodes `G` and `F` should be added to the results (only `F` will).

Table 11.1 shows a few examples of SQL snippets translated into calls to k-d tree's methods.

[19]Of course, especially if we have a lot of data, we have no guarantee that these two fields will be unique, because two people can share the same birthdate and name. Let's assume, just to keep our example simple, that this is not the case.

Table 11.1 Translating SQL queries into calls to k-d tree methods (assuming a k-d tree is used to implement multi-indexing on the table described in this section)

Operation	Exact match search
SQL[20]	`SELECT * FROM people WHERE name="Bruce Wayne" AND birthdate="1939/03/30" AND salary=150M`
k-d tree	`tree.search(("Bruce Wayne", "1939/03/30", 150M))`
Operation	**Range search**
SQL	`SELECT * FROM people WHERE name>="Bruce" AND birthdate>"1950" AND birthdate<"1980" AND salary>=1500 AND salary<=10000`
k-d tree[21]	`tree.pointsInRectangle({name:{min:"Bruce", max: inf}, birthdate:{min:"1950", max:"1980"}, salary:{min: 1500, max:10000}})`
Operation	**Partial search**
SQL	`SELECT * FROM people WHERE birthdate>"1950" AND birthdate<"1980" AND salary>=1500 AND salary<=10000`
k-d tree	`tree.partialRangeQuery({birthdate:{min:"1950", max:"1980"}, salary:{min: 1500, max:10000}})`
k-d tree[22]	`tree.pointsInRectangle({name:{min:-inf, max: inf}, birthdate:{min:"1950", max:"1980"}, salary:{min: 1500, max:10000}})`

11.4.4 Clustering

Finally, we get to one of the most important applications of nearest neighbor search: clustering. This application is so important that we will pledge a whole chapter, the next chapter, to explaining two clustering algorithms that use NN search at their core: DBSCAN and OPTICS.

We'll provide a proper description of what clustering is in the next chapter. For now, suffice it to say that clustering is an unsupervised learning method, where a machine learning model is fed with a set of unlabeled points, and it outputs a possible grouping of these points in meaningful categories. For instance, we could develop a clustering algorithm that, given a dataset of people (with age, education, financial situation, and so on), groups them in categories that share similar interests. The algorithm won't be able to tell us what these categories are, though. It's a data scientist's job to study the algorithm output and see, for instance, that one category matches middle-class teenagers, another seems to fit college-graduated baby boomers, and so on. This kind of algorithm is often used to target online advertisement.

---

[20]Select * is usually frowned upon, and for good reason. We'll use it here to keep code simple, but you should only select the fields you actually need to use.

[21]In our example implementation in listing 9.12, we passed a tuple of min-max objects

[22]As an alternative to implementing explicitly the partial match query, we can use the `pointsInRectangle` method by carefully choosing the ranges for the fields that have no restrictions.

Clustering is also used as a preliminary step for other more sophisticated algorithms, because it provides a cheap way to break down large datasets into coherent groups. We'll see this and lot more in the next chapter.

Summary

- Nearest neighbor search can be used to improve geographical matching of physical resources; for example, finding the closest shop to a customer.
- When we move from theory to real-world applications, we have to take many factors into account and adjust our NN search algorithm to take into account business logic; for instance, allowing filtering of the resources among which we search or weighting the results according to some business rules.
- We also have to deal with the limitations of physical IT systems, including memory restrictions, CPU availability, and network constraints.
- Distributed web applications impose new issues that need to be taken into account when designing a system. It's not enough to come up with a good algorithm; we need to choose/design one that also works in the real system we are building.
- NN search is useful in a number of other areas, from simulations in particle physics to machine learning.

12 Clustering

This chapter covers

- Classifying different types of clustering
- Partitioning clustering
- Understanding and implementing k-means
- Density-based clustering
- Understanding and implementing DBSCAN
- OPTICS: Refining DBSCAN as hierarchical clustering
- Evaluating clustering results

In the previous chapters we have described, implemented, and applied three data structures designed to efficiently solve nearest neighbor search. When we moved to their applications, we mentioned that clustering was one of the main areas where an efficient nearest neighbor search could make a difference. We had to delay this discussion, but now it's finally time to put the icing on the cake and get the most out of our hard work. In this chapter, we will first briefly introduce clustering, explaining what it is and how it relates to machine learning and AI. We'll see that there are different types of clustering, with radically different approaches, and then we will present and discuss in detail three algorithms that use different approaches. By going through the whole chapter, readers will be exposed to the theoretical foundations for this topic, learn about algorithms that can be implemented or just applied to break down datasets into smaller homogeneous groups, and also, in the process, get a deeper understanding of nearest neighbor search and multi-dimensional indexing.

But before we start, let's quickly introduce an example of a problem that motivates the use of clustering. Throughout the previous chapters in part 2 of this book, we have developed this example of an e-commerce site, starting from the early days when the internet became mainstream. Now it's time to bring our company into the 2010s and add a data science team. In fact, for sales to thrive, we will need to perform customer segmentation in order to understand our customers' behavior and categorize customers based on what we know about them:[1] their purchasing habits and financial situation, as well as their demographics, age, level of education, and country or state where they live, which are all factors that influence people's taste and spending capacity.

Customer segmentation partitions customers into homogeneous groups sharing similar purchasing power, purchase history, or expected behavior. Clustering is one step of this process, where the groups are formed from raw, unlabeled data. Clustering algorithms don't output a description of the groups; they just return a partitioning of the whole customer base, and then data scientists need to perform further analysis of the different morphotypes to understand how these groups are composed. Once this knowledge is derived, it can be used by marketing teams to tailor targeted campaigns toward each of these groups (or some of them, if some of the groups are crucial to the company's wealth). For instance, on a video streaming website (such as Netflix), data scientists might be able to identify a group of users that will likely watch comedies, another group more interested in action movies, and so on.

In real-world examples, customers have hundreds of features that are considered for marketing segmentation; here, for the sake of visualization and to make explanations easier, we will use a simplified example, with just two features: annual income and average monthly expenses on our e-commerce site. We will pick up this example again later in the chapter, but first, we will give you some more context and the tools to perform clustering analysis.

12.1 Intro to clustering

In recent years, especially from the second half of the first decade of this century, a single branch of AI got so much momentum that now it's often considered in the media and public opinion as synonymous to AI. I'm talking, of course, about *machine learning* (*ML*), which in turn has been lately (since ~2015) increasingly identified with *deep learning* (*DL*).

The truth is that deep learning constitutes just a part of machine learning, gathering all those models built with *deep* (intended as "with many layers") neural networks, and machine learning, in turn, is just a branch of artificial intelligence.

[1] That's also the reason why every company, online or offline, tries to discover as much information about you as possible: data is paramount in this era.

In particular, machine learning is the branch that is focused on developing mathematical models that describe a system after learning its characteristics from data.

ML and deep DL can achieve impressive, eye-catching, and sometimes incredible results (at the time of writing you can think of, for instance, life-like artificially generated faces, landscapes, and even movies created by GANs[2]), but they can't, and neither do they aim to, build an "intelligent" agent—something closer to the romantic idea of an artificial consciousness that cult movies like *Short Circuit* or *War Games* gave us. That is rather the goal of *general artificial intelligence.*

12.1.1 Types of learning

The main classification of machine learning models is based on the type of "learning" they perform, in particular focusing on the way we provide feedback to the model during training:

- Supervised learning—These models are trained on labeled data; that is, for each entry in the training set, there is a label (for *classification* algorithms) or a value (*regression* algorithms) that is associated to that entry. Training will tune models' parameters in order to increase the accuracy of the model in associating the correct class or value to new entries. Examples of SL are object detection (classification) or predictive models to estimate goods' prices (regression).
- Reinforcement learning—Rather than providing explicit labels associated to the data, the model performs some kind of task, and only at the end does it receive feedback about the outcome (stating either success or failure). This is one of the most interesting areas of research at the time of writing, and some examples include game theory (for instance, an agent learning to play chess or Go) and many areas of robotics (such as teaching a robotic arm to juggle).
- Unsupervised learning—This category differs from the first two because in this case the algorithms are not presented with any feedback on data, but their goal is rather to make sense of data by extrapolating its inner (and often hidden) structure. Clustering is the main form of unsupervised learning.

We will obviously focus on unsupervised learning in the rest of the chapter. Clustering algorithms, in fact, take an unlabeled dataset and try to gather as much information as possible about its structure, grouping together similar data points while setting apart dissimilar ones.

Although at first it might seem less intuitive than supervised or reinforcement learning, clustering has several natural applications, and possibly the best way to describe clustering is by exemplifying a few of them:

[2] Generative Adversarial Networks are a particular type of deep neural networks, where two competing models are trained to generate artificial content (based on a training set) and to discriminate artificial from real content. Their co-evolution increases the lifelikeness of the content generated.

1 *Market segmentation*—Take purchase data and find groups of similar customers. Since they behave in the same way, it's likely that a marketing strategy would work (or fail) consistently across a group (if segmentation is done properly).

   An algorithm won't output labels for the groups; it won't tell us if a group is "students under 25" and another "mid-aged book writers, with a passion for comics." It will only gather similar people together, and then data analysts can further examine the groups to understand more about their composition.

2 *Finding outliers*—Find data that stands out. Depending on the context, it could be noise in a signal, a new species of flowers in a rain forest, or even a new pattern or behavior in customer analytics.

3 *Preprocessing*—Find clusters in the data and process each cluster separately (and possibly in parallel). This obviously provides a speedup, but it also has another side-effect. Since it reduces the max amount of space needed at any single time, when a huge dataset is broken up into smaller pieces, each piece can fit in memory or be processed on a single machine, while the whole dataset can't. Sometimes you can even use a fast clustering algorithm (for instance, *canopy clustering*) as a preprocessor step for a slower clustering algorithm.

12.1.2 Types of clustering

Clustering is an NP-Hard[3] problem, and as such it is computationally difficult (impossible for today's real datasets) to solve it exactly. Moreover, it is hard to even define objective metrics that can assess the quality of a solution! Figure 12.1 explains this concept. For some cluster shapes, our intuition tells us that the two rings should be in different clusters, but it's hard to come up with a metric function that objectively states so (minimum distance, for instance, wouldn't work). And this becomes even harder for high-dimensional datasets (where our intuition can't even help us validate these metrics, because it's hard to represent and interpret anything beyond 3-D spaces).

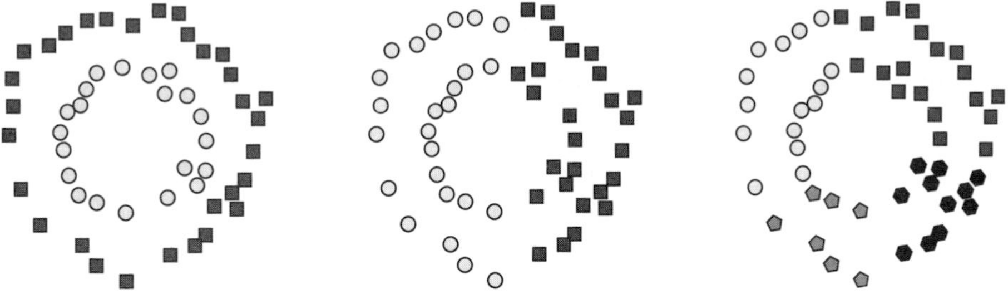

Figure 12.1 A dataset that's challenging to cluster. On the left, the ideal clustering that matches our intuition. Next to it, non-optimal results produced by metrics like proximity or affinity propagation.

[3] The `NP-Hard` class of problems includes those problems that are at least as hard as the hardest problems in `NP`; as we have already seen in chapter 2, the `NP` class contains those problems that can be solved in polynomial time on a non-deterministic machine, and in particular, the problems that are in `NP` but not in class `P` can't be solved in polynomial time on a deterministic machine. To date, determining if there is any problem in `NP-P` is one of greatest challenges in computer science.

For these reasons, all clustering algorithms are heuristics that converge more or less quickly to a locally-optimal solution.

Under the category labeled "clustering," we group several data-partitioning algorithms, using approaches completely different from each other. All these approaches can be applied to the problems described in the previous section almost transparently, although, obviously, each approach has strengths and flaws, and we should select the best-fitting algorithms based on our requirements.

A first relevant distinction is made between hard and soft clustering, as also shown in figure 12.2:

- In hard clustering, to every point the output assigns a single cluster, one and only one (or at most one, if the clustering algorithm can also detect noise).
- In soft clustering, for each point `P` and each group `G`, the output provides a probability that `P` belongs to `G`.

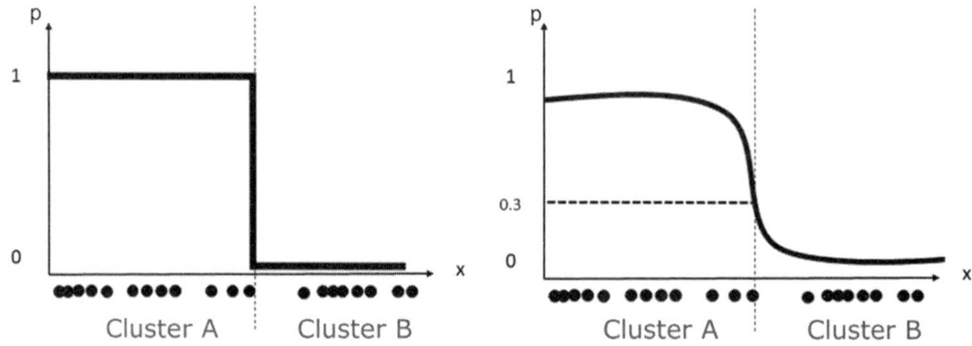
P
1
0
X
Cluster A
Cluster B
P
1
0.3
0
X
Cluster A
Cluster B

Figure 12.2 The difference between hard and soft clustering can be explained in terms of the membership function they adopt. Hard clustering's outputs are either 0 or 1 for each point and each cluster, with the constraint that it can be 1 for only one of the point-cluster combinations. Soft clustering's membership function outputs a probability between 0 and 1 (any value in-between) and for each point, it can be non-zero for multiple clusters.

The other main criterion to classify clustering algorithms differentiates *partitioning clustering* from *hierarchical clustering*:

- Partitioning clustering, aka *flat clustering*, outputs a division of the input dataset into partitions, so no cluster is the subset of another, nor does it intersect any other cluster.
- Hierarchical clustering produces a hierarchy of clusters that can be then interpreted and "sliced" at any given point, depending on parameters set for the algorithm.

Obviously these two criteria are orthogonal; for instance, you can have hard partitioning clustering algorithms (such as k-means) or soft hierarchical ones (such as OPTICS).

Other criteria often used to classify these algorithms are centroid-based versus density-based, and randomized versus deterministic.

In the next section, we'll first describe an algorithm for partitioning clustering: k-means, the progenitor of all clustering algorithms. Then we'll move to a different type of flat clustering, DBSCAN, and finally we'll pick up the discussion on hierarchical clustering and introduce OPTICS, which is also density-based. Table 12.1 summarizes the "identity card" for the three algorithms presented in this chapter.

Table 12.1 Summary of the characteristics of clustering algorithms presented in this chapter

Categories	k-means	DBSCAN	OPTICS
Membership	Hard	Hard	Soft
Structure	Flat	Flat	Hierarchical
Strategy	Centroid-based	Density-based	Density-based
Determinism	Randomized	Deterministic	Deterministic
Outliers detection	No	Yes	Yes

Don't worry; in the next sections for each of these properties we will explain in detail what it means and provide examples to make the distinction clearer.

12.2 K-means

Let's start our discussion with a classic algorithm, one with a history of success going back to the 1950s: k-means, a partitioning algorithm that gathers data in a predetermined number of spherical clusters.

Figure 12.3 illustrates how k-means works. We can break down the algorithm in three high-level steps:

1. *Initialization*—Create `k` random *centroids*, random points that can or cannot belong to the dataset and will be the centers of the spherical clusters.
2. *Classification*—For each point in the dataset, compute the distance to each centroid, and assign the aforementioned point to the closest among the centroids.
3. *Recentering*—The points assigned to a centroid form a cluster. For each cluster, compute its center of mass (as described in section 10.3), and then move the cluster's centroid to the center of mass computed.
4. Repeat steps *classification* and *recentering* until no point, at step 2, switches to a different cluster, or the maximum number of iterations is reached.

Steps 2–4 of this algorithm are a deterministic heuristic that computes exact distances between points and centroids, and then updates the centroids to the center of mass of each cluster. However, the algorithm qualifies as a Monte Carlo randomized algorithm because of its first step, where we use random initialization. Turns out this step is crucial for the algorithm. The final result, in fact, is heavily influenced by the initial choice of the centroids. A bad choice can slow down convergence, which, in turn, given that the maximum number of iterations is bounded, will likely lead to an early

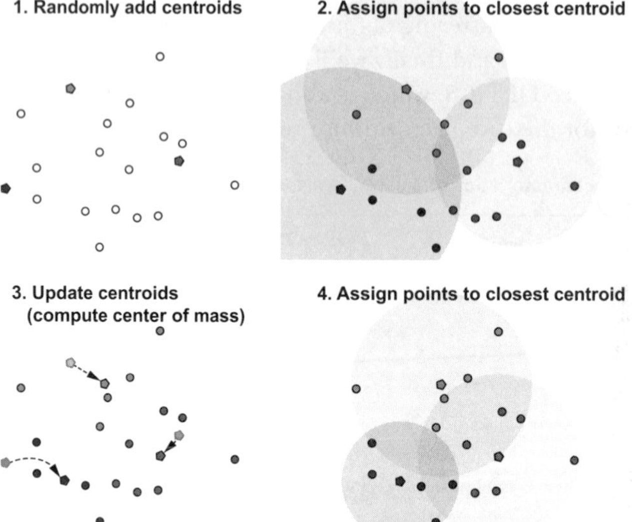
1. Randomly add centroids
2. Assign points to closest centroid
3. Update centroids
(compute center of mass)
4. Assign points to closest centroid

Figure 12.3 An example of the k-means algorithm with `k==3`. Dataset points are initially lightly shaded. Step 1: `k` centroids (shaped as pentagons) are randomly created. Each centroid is assigned a different color: RGB. Step 2: For each point, measure the distance to all centroids, and assign the point to the closest one. At the end, each centroid `C` will define a cluster, a sphere centered at `C` and whose radius is the distance to the furthest point assigned to `C`. The clusters are highlighted in the same color as their centroids. Step 3: Update the centroids: for each cluster, compute its center of mass. Step 4: Repeat steps 2 and 3 `j` times. Some points will switch to a different cluster.

stop and a poor result. And because the algorithm will remove centroids to which no points are assigned—a very bad initial choice with several centroids close to each other—this could lead to an unwanted reduction of the number of centroids in the early stages of the heuristic (see figure 12.4).

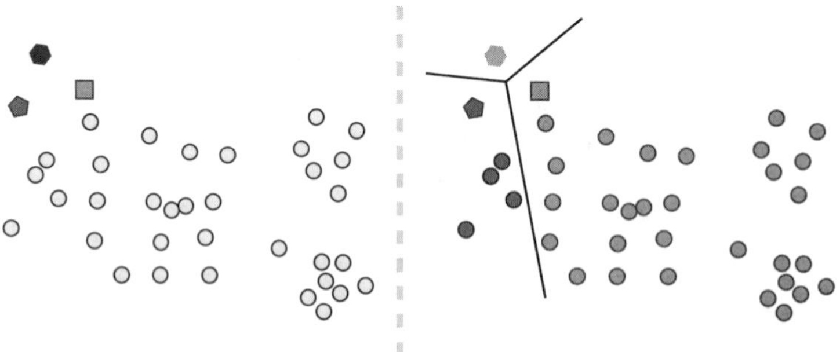

Figure 12.4 A very unlucky choice of initial centroids (shown as polygons). All centroids are gathered together in one corner of the dataset. The black line shows an approximation of the border between the regions determined by each centroid (on each line, ideally, the distance between the centroids it separates is the same). Since the centroid represented with a hexagon is further away than the other two, no point will be assigned to it, so it will be removed from the list of centroids. The choice appears also unbalanced for the other two centroids, although the next update steps will (slowly) rebalance the situation, moving the square toward the center of the cluster on the right.

To mitigate this issue, in practice k-means is always used with a random-restart strategy: the algorithm is run several times on a dataset, each time with a different random initialization of the centroids, and then results are compared to choose the best clustering (more about this in the last section of the chapter).

Listing 12.1 shows the code for the main method performing k-means clustering. We broke down the main steps into separate functions to get cleaner, more easily maintainable code and we'll delve into each step in the next pages. You can also check out implementations of the method on the book's repo on GitHub.[4]

Listing 12.1 k-means clustering

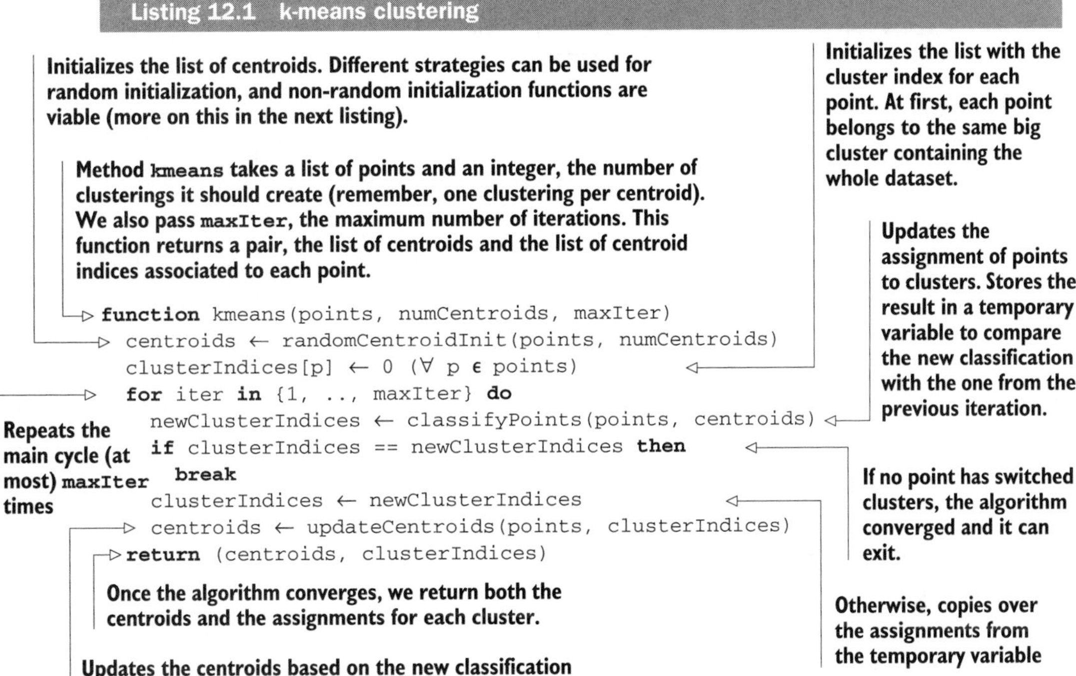

```
function kmeans(points, numCentroids, maxIter)
  centroids ← randomCentroidInit(points, numCentroids)
  clusterIndices[p] ← 0 (∀ p ∈ points)
  for iter in {1, .., maxIter} do
    newClusterIndices ← classifyPoints(points, centroids)
    if clusterIndices == newClusterIndices then
      break
    clusterIndices ← newClusterIndices
    centroids ← updateCentroids(points, clusterIndices)
  return (centroids, clusterIndices)
```

Initializes the list of centroids. Different strategies can be used for random initialization, and non-random initialization functions are viable (more on this in the next listing).
Method kmeans takes a list of points and an integer, the number of clusterings it should create (remember, one clustering per centroid). We also pass maxIter, the maximum number of iterations. This function returns a pair, the list of centroids and the list of centroid indices associated to each point.
Initializes the list with the cluster index for each point. At first, each point belongs to the same big cluster containing the whole dataset.
Updates the assignment of points to clusters. Stores the result in a temporary variable to compare the new classification with the one from the previous iteration.
Repeats the main cycle (at most) maxIter times
If no point has switched clusters, the algorithm converged and it can exit.
Otherwise, copies over the assignments from the temporary variable
Once the algorithm converges, we return both the centroids and the assignments for each cluster.
Updates the centroids based on the new classification

The algorithm can be seen as a search heuristic converging to a (local) optimum, with slightly more complex than normal functions to compute the score and the gradient step. At line #6, we have a stop condition that checks if the algorithm converged. If the classification hasn't changed in the last step, then the centroids will be the same as in the previous step, so any further iteration will be futile. Since these functions are quite expensive to compute at each step, and convergence is not guaranteed, we add another stop condition by capping the execution to a maximum number of iterations. As mentioned, we abstracted away the logic of the update and score functions in separate methods. But before looking at those, it's interesting to check out the random initialization step, which is often underestimated. Listing 12.2 shows the implementation we suggest for this function.

[4] See https://github.com/mlarocca/AlgorithmsAndDataStructuresInAction#k-means.

Listing 12.2 randomCentroidInit

```
function randomCentroidInit(points, numCentroids)
  centroids ← sample(points, numCentroids)
  for i in {0, .., numCentroids-1} do
    for j in {0, .., dim-1} do
      centroids[i][j] ← centroids[i][j] + randomNoise()
  return centroids
```

- Method randomCentroidInit takes the list of points in the dataset and the number of centroids it should create. It returns the list of centroids generated.
- Initializes the list of centroids by randomly sampling (without replacement) numCentroids points from the dataset
- Cycles through the list of centroids (their indices)
- For each centroid, cycles through its coordinates (assuming dim, the number of coordinates, is, for instance, a class variable; otherwise, you could use |centroids[i]|).
- Updates the current coordinate by adding some random noise
- Returns the list of centroids

While there are several viable alternatives (for instance, randomly drawing each coordinate from the domain's boundaries, or using actual dataset's points), a solution that gets us several advantages is randomly perturbating `k` points casually drawn from the dataset:

- First, we don't have to worry about the domain's boundaries. If each centroid's coordinate was generated completely at random, we would have to first scan the dataset to find the acceptable range for each coordinate.
- Even paying attention to the dataset's boundaries, sampled points could end up in sparse or empty regions, and as such they could later be removed. Instead, by uniformly drawing points from the dataset, the centroids will be close to points in the data and . . .
- . . . centroids will be drawn with higher probability in areas with higher density of points.
- Randomly perturbating the points, however, helps reduce the risk that all the points will be concentrated in the denser areas.

The code in listing 12.2 is also intuitive, though there are a couple of interesting points to raise.

At line #2 we use a generic sampling function that draws `n` elements from a set without repetition; the details of this method are not important here, and you don't need to worry about them. Most programming languages will provide such a function in their core libraries,[5] so it's unlikely you will have to implement it.[6]

We can move to the classification step, described in listing 12.3. Method `classifyPoints` is a brute-force search of all the point-centroid pairs, whose goal is finding the closest centroid to each pair. If you've read the book thus far, you should by now feel

[5] For instance, in Python you can import `sample` from module `random`, or in JavaScript you can use underscore library's `sample` method.

[6] But if you do, then you should check out chapter 11 of *Practical Probabilistic Programming* by Stuart Russell (Manning Publications, 2016), where it is neatly explained.

goose bumps when you hear "brute-force" and, as a conditional reflex, think, can we do any better? We'll talk about this question a couple of sections down the road.

Listing 12.3 classifyPoints

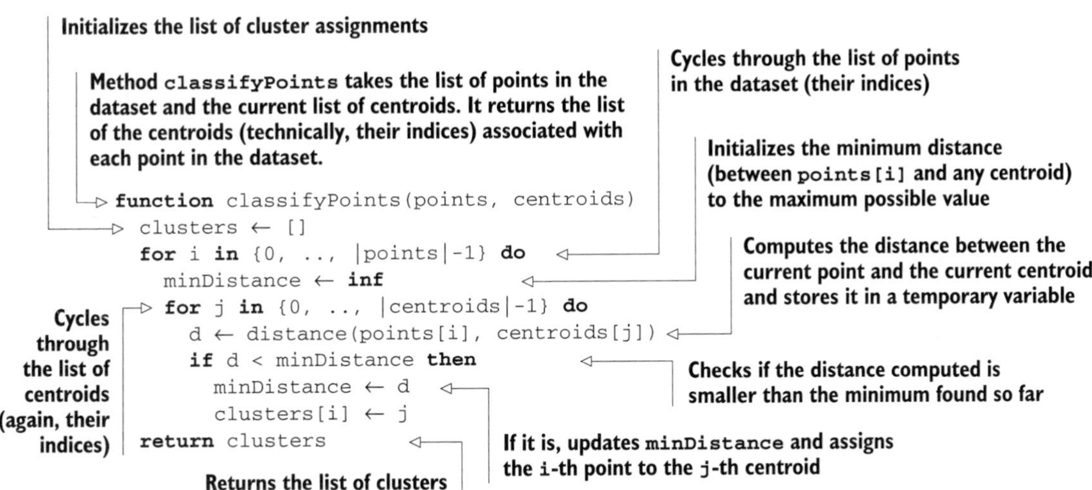
Initializes the list of cluster assignments
Method classifyPoints takes the list of points in the dataset and the current list of centroids. It returns the list of the centroids (technically, their indices) associated with each point in the dataset.
Cycles through the list of points in the dataset (their indices)
Initializes the minimum distance (between points[i] and any centroid) to the maximum possible value
Computes the distance between the current point and the current centroid and stores it in a temporary variable
Cycles through the list of centroids (again, their indices)
Checks if the distance computed is smaller than the minimum found so far
If it is, updates minDistance and assigns the i-th point to the j-th centroid
Returns the list of clusters
function classifyPoints(points, centroids)
  clusters ← []
  for i in {0, .., |points|-1} do
    minDistance ← inf
    for j in {0, .., |centroids|-1} do
      d ← distance(points[i], centroids[j])
      if d < minDistance then
        minDistance ← d
        clusters[i] ← j
  return clusters

For the moment, let's see the last helper method we need to implement to complete the k-means algorithm, the one updating centroids, described in listing 12.4.

Listing 12.4 updateCentroids

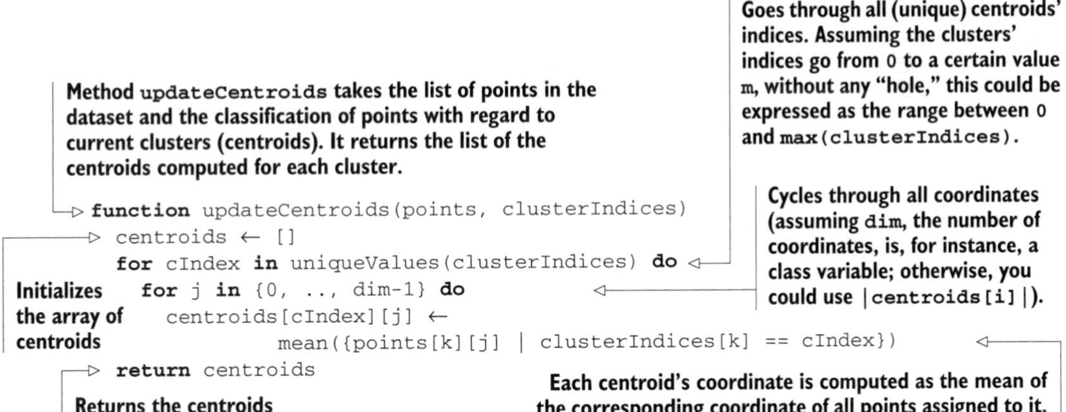
Goes through all (unique) centroids' indices. Assuming the clusters' indices go from 0 to a certain value m, without any "hole," this could be expressed as the range between 0 and max(clusterIndices).
Method updateCentroids takes the list of points in the dataset and the classification of points with regard to current clusters (centroids). It returns the list of the centroids computed for each cluster.
Cycles through all coordinates (assuming dim, the number of coordinates, is, for instance, a class variable; otherwise, you could use |centroids[i]|).
Initializes the array of centroids
Each centroid's coordinate is computed as the mean of the corresponding coordinate of all points assigned to it.
Returns the centroids
function updateCentroids(points, clusterIndices)
  centroids ← []
  for cIndex in uniqueValues(clusterIndices) do
    for j in {0, .., dim-1} do
      centroids[cIndex][j] ←
              mean({points[k][j] | clusterIndices[k] == cIndex})
  return centroids

To update centroids, as we've mentioned, we will just compute the center of mass for each cluster. This means that we need to group all points by the centroid they are assigned to, and then for each group, compute the mean of the points' coordinates.

This pseudo-code implementation doesn't apply any correction to remove centroids that have no point assigned to them—they are just ignored. The issue with the centroids array is also not tackled; the array is simply initialized to the empty one, assuming it will be resized dynamically while adding new elements to it. But of course, in a real implementation, both issues should be taken care of, according to what each language allows for initialization and resizing of arrays.

If you'd like to take a look at real implementations of k-means, you can find a Python version on the book's repo on GitHub. At https://github.com/andreaferretti/kmeans you can also find a nice resource (unrelated to the book) that, like a Rosetta Stone, contains implementations of this algorithm in many programming languages (you can find a version for most of the mainstream languages).

Now that we have described how k-means is implemented, let's take another look at how it works.

12.2.1 Issues with k-means

Figure 12.5 shows the result of applying k-means to an artificial dataset. The dataset has been carefully crafted to represent the ideal situation where k-means excels. The clusters are easily (and linearly[7]) separable, and they all are approximately spherical.

First, let's start with a positive note about k-means. Figure 12.5 shows how it manages to correctly identify clusters with different density; for instance, the two clusters in the bottom-left corner have a larger average distance between points (and hence a lower density) than the cluster in the top-right corner. This might seem like something to take for granted, but not all clustering algorithms will deal so well with heterogeneous distributions. In the next section, we'll see why this is a problem for DBSCAN.

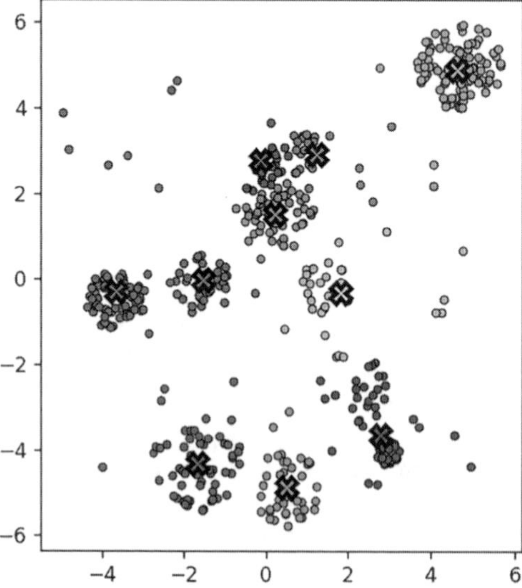
6
4
2
0
−2
−4
−6
−4
−2
0
2
4
6

Figure 12.5 A typical clustering produced by k-means. Dataset's points are plotted as circles, and centroids are shown as thick-edged Xs.

[7] In a `d`-dimensional space, two sets S_1 and S_2 are linearly separable if there exists at least one `(d-1)`-dimensional hyperplane that divides the space such that all points of S_1 are on one side of the hyperplane, and all points of S_2 are on the other side of it.

That's all for the good news: you can also see that there are a few points that are not close to any of the spherical clusters. We added some noise to the dataset as well to show one of k-means' critical issues: it can't detect outliers, and in fact, as shown in figure 12.5, outlier points are added to the closest clusters. Since centroids are computed as centers of the mass of the clusters, and the mean function is sensitive to outliers, if we don't filter out outliers before running k-means, the undesirable consequence is that the centroids of the clusters will be "attracted" by outliers away from the best position they could hold. You can see this phenomenon in several clusters in figure 12.5.

The issue with outliers, however, is not the worst problem with k-means. As mentioned, this algorithm can only produce spherical clusters, but unfortunately, in real datasets not all clusters are spherical! Figure 12.6 shows three examples where k-means clustering fails to recognize the best clustering.

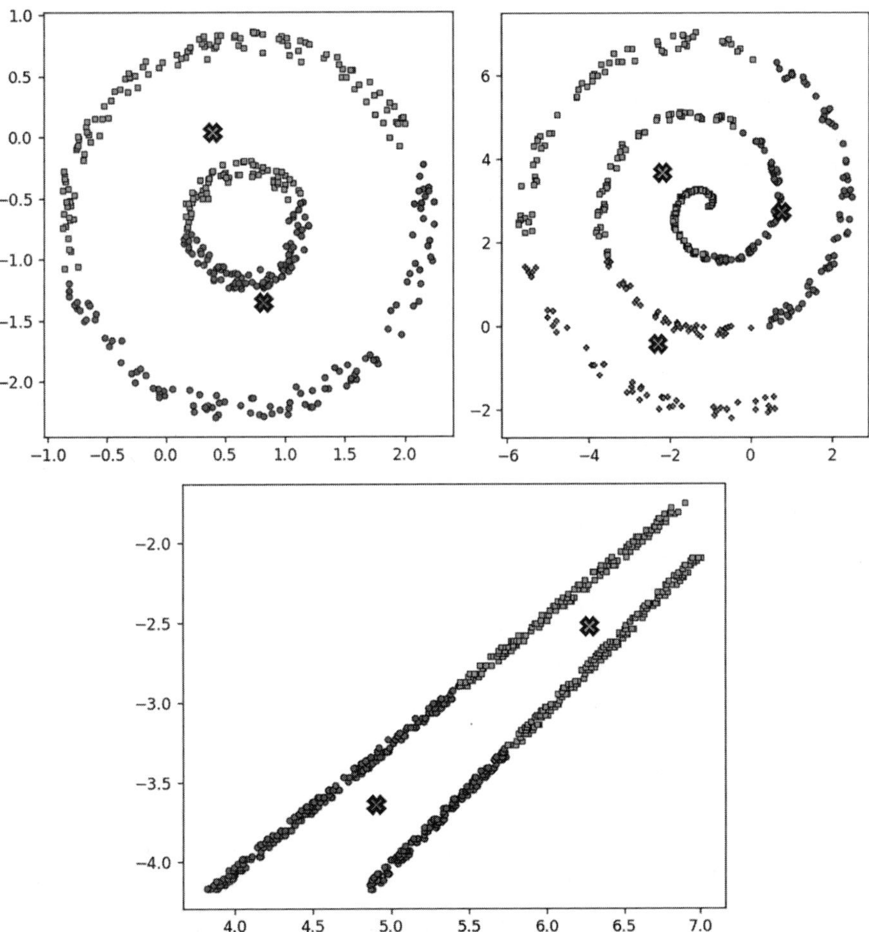
1.0
0.5
0.0
−0.5
−1.0
−1.5
−2.0
−1.0
−0.5
0.0
0.5
1.0
1.5
2.0
6
4
2
0
−2
−6
−4
−2
0
2
−2.0
−2.5
−3.0
−3.5
−4.0
4.0
4.5
5.0
5.5
6.0
6.5
7.0

Figure 12.6 Three examples where the clustering result produced by k-means can never be optimal. (Left) Two concentric rings (two centroids). (Right) A spiral (three centroids: the optimal solution here would be to have a single cluster). (Bottom) Two linear clusters close to each other.

Not-linearly separable clusters can't be approximated with spherical clusters, and as such, k-means can't separate non-convex clusters like clusters shaped as two concentric rings. Moreover, in all those situations where the clusters' shape is not spherical and the points can't be separated correctly using minimum distance from a centroid, k-means will struggle to find good solutions.

Another issue with k-means is that the number of clusters is a hyper-parameter, meaning that the algorithm is not able to determine the right number of clusters automatically,[8] and instead it takes the number of centroids as an argument. This means that unless we have some insight deriving from domain knowledge and suggesting to us the right number of categories into which we should cluster the dataset, then to find the right number of clusters for a dataset, we will need to run the algorithm multiple times, trying different values for the number of centroids, and comparing the results using some kind of metric (visual comparison is only possible for 2D and 3D datasets). We'll talk about this in section 12.5.

These issues are certainly limiting, although there are domains in which we can assume or even prove that data can be modeled well with spherical clusters. But even in the best-case scenario or in intermediate situations where a spherical cluster is still a good approximation, there is another issue that can limit the application of this clustering algorithm: the curse of dimensionality.

12.2.2 The curse of dimensionality strikes again

We already bumped into the curse of dimensionality when we described k-d trees in chapter 9: a data structure that works well for low-to-medium-dimensional spaces but behaves poorly in high-dimensional spaces.

It's not a coincidence that we find this issue again for k-means. This algorithm is a search heuristic that minimizes the Euclidean distance of points to cluster's centroid. In high-dimensions, however

- The ratio between volume and surface grows exponentially.
- Most points of a uniformly distributed dataset are not close to the center of mass, but rather far away toward the surface of the cluster.
- If data is uniformly distributed in a hypercube (a domain where each feature is uniformly distributed in a fixed range), then in high dimensions most points are close to the faces of the hypercube.
- Approximating a hypercube with its subscribed hypersphere will leave out most of the points.
- To include all the points, we need the hypersphere superscribed to the hypercube, and as we saw in section 10.5.1, the amount of volume wasted grows exponentially with the number of dimensions.

---

[8] As we have seen, k-means can discard some centroids, but this effect is very limited and unpredictable.

- In a `d`-dimensional space, with `d >> 10`, under certain reasonable assumptions for data distribution, the nearest neighbor problem becomes ill-defined,[9] because in high dimensions the ratio between the distance from a target to the nearest and farthest neighbor becomes almost 1. For instance, if points are equally spaced (for example, placed on a grid), then the `2d` closest points to any centroid are all at the same distance from it. This means that the nearest neighbor of a point becomes ambiguously defined.

In simple terms, for higher-dimensional datasets, unless the distribution of clusters is exactly spherical, the spheres needed to include all points are so large that they will likely overlap each other for a significant portion of their volume; moreover, for close-to-uniformly distributed datasets and when many centroids are used, the search for the nearest centroid can be inaccurate. This, in turn, leads to slower convergence, because some points can be assigned back and forth to different, almost equally close centroids.

In summary, we need to keep in mind that k-means is a good option only for low-to-medium-dimensional (with at most around 20 dimensions) datasets where we know that clusters can be accurately approximated with hyperspheres.

12.2.3 K-means performance analysis

When we do know that a dataset meets the pre-conditions to apply k-means, however, this algorithm is a viable option and produces good results quickly. How quickly? That's what we are going to ascertain in this section.

Let's assume we have a dataset with `n` points, each point belonging to a `d`-dimensional space (hence each point can be represented as a tuple of `d` real numbers), and that we would like to partition the points into `k` different clusters.

If we examine each sub-step in listing 12.1, we can conclude that

- The random initialization step takes `O(n*d)` assignments (`d` coordinates for each of the `n` points).
- Initializing cluster indices takes `O(n)` assignments.
- The main cycle is repeated `m` times, where `m` is the maximum number of iterations allowed.
- Assigning points to centroids takes `O(k*n*d)` operations, since for each point, we need to compute `k` `d`-dimensional (squared) distances, and each requires `O(d)` operations to be computed.
- Comparing two points classifications requires `O(n)` time, but this can be amortized inside the method doing the partitioning, with a careful implementation.

[9] Beyer, Kevin, et al. "When is "nearest neighbor" meaningful?" International conference on database theory. Springer, Berlin, Heidelberg, 1999.

- Updating the centroids requires computing, for each centroid, d times (one for each coordinate[10]) a mean over at most n points, and so a total of `O(k*n*d)` operations. If we can assume that the points are distributed evenly among clusters, each cluster will at most contain `n/k` points, and therefore the average worst-case running time becomes `O(k*(n/k)*d) = O(n*d)`.

The running time for the algorithm is therefore `O(m*k*n*d)`, with `O(n+k)` extra memory needed to store the points classification and the list of centroids.

12.2.4 Boosting k-means with k-d trees

When we described the code for k-means, we saw that the partitioning step, where we assign each point to exactly one of the centroids, is a brute-force search among all combinations of points and centroids. Now we wonder, can we speed it up in any way?

In section 10.5.3 we saw how k-means can help SS+-trees' performance by making them more balanced when used in split heuristics. But is it possible that the opposite is also true? You might see where I'm going with this: Is it possible to replace brute-force search with something more efficient?

If you think about it, for each point we are looking for its nearest neighbor among the set of centroids, and we already know a data structure or two to speed up this search!

But rather than SS+-trees, in this case the context would suggest we could try k-d trees for three reasons. Before reading them, try to pause for a minute and think about why we could prefer k-d trees. If you can't think of all three reasons, or if you don't have a completely clear idea about why these reasons hold, you can look at sections 9.4 and 10.1 that explain these concepts in more detail.

The reasons why k-d trees would be better suited than SS+-trees for the nearest centroid search are

- The size of the dataset (the centroids) is small: hence there is a very large probability that it will fit into memory. In this case, k-d trees are the best choice if the other two conditions also hold.
- The dimension of the search space goes from low to medium. We know this is the case (if we have done our homework!) because k-means also suffer from the curse of dimensionality, and shouldn't be applied to high-dimensional datasets.
- K-d trees can offer a theoretical worst-case upper bound that is better than brute-force search: $O(2^d + d*\log(k))$ for k d-dimensional centroids. SS+-trees, however, can't offer better-than-linear worst-case running time.

Moreover, the data structure used will have to be recreated from scratch at each iteration of k-means' main cycle, so we won't be dealing with a dynamic dataset that would cause a k-d tree to become imbalanced over time.

The fact that we have to create a new dataset at each iteration, at the same time, is one of the biggest cons of using this approach, because we will have to pay this extra

[10] On GPUs and processors designed for vector computing, operations can be executed simultaneously on all coordinates of the d-dimensional tuples with higher efficiency.

price. Also, we will need `O(k)` extra memory to store it. It won't change the asymptotic memory print of the algorithm, but in practice it will be relevant, especially if `k`, the number of centroids, is high.

In most applications, though, it is reasonable to expect to have `k << n`. In other words, the number of centroids will be several orders of magnitude smaller than the number of points.

Listing 12.5 shows how we can change the pseudo-code for method `classifyPoints` to use a k-d tree in place of brute-force search.

As you can see, the code is much shorter than the version in listing 12.3, because most of the complexity of the search is now encapsulated in the `KdTree` class.

Listing 12.5 `classifyPoints` using k-d trees

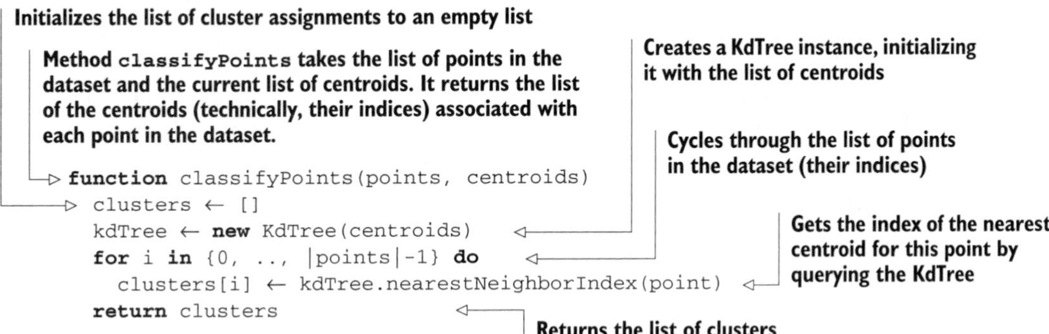
Initializes the list of cluster assignments to an empty list
Method classifyPoints takes the list of points in the dataset and the current list of centroids. It returns the list of the centroids (technically, their indices) associated with each point in the dataset.
Creates a KdTree instance, initializing it with the list of centroids
Cycles through the list of points in the dataset (their indices)
Gets the index of the nearest centroid for this point by querying the KdTree
Returns the list of clusters

```
function classifyPoints(points, centroids)
  clusters ← []
  kdTree ← new KdTree(centroids)
  for i in {0, .., |points|-1} do
    clusters[i] ← kdTree.nearestNeighborIndex(point)
  return clusters
```

Notice that since we would like to find out the index of the centroid closer to each point, we assume that the `KdTree` object can keep track of the indices of its points in the initialization array, and that we have a query method that returns the index of the closest point, rather than the point itself. It's not hard to find a workaround if this is not the case. We can keep a hash table associating centroids to their indices and add an extra step to retrieve the index of the centroid returned by the `KdTree`.

Performance-wise, since creating a k-d tree for the centroids will require `O(k*log(k))` steps, each of which can require up to `O(d)` operations (because we are dealing with `d`-dimensional points), then the whole classification step will require $O(d*k*log(k) + n*2^d + n*d*log(k)) = O(n*2^d + d*(n+k)*log(k))$ steps, instead of `O(n*k*d)` operations.

Formally, we can work out the exact conditions for which $O(n*2^d + d*(n+k)*log(k)) < O(n*k*d)$; for our purpose, however, we can just informally use some intuition to see that

- $n*2^d < n*k*d \Leftrightarrow d << k$
- `d*(n+k)*log(k) < n*k*d ⇔ (n+k)*log(k) < n*k ⇔ n < n*k/log(k)-k` This can be shown to hold for `n > k`, but plotting the difference between the two sides shows that for a fixed `n`, the difference grows as `k` grows, so the savings are more noticeable when there are many centroids.

The whole algorithm, assuming that clusters are evenly distributed with approximately `n/k` points each, would then run in `O(m*(n*2`^{d} `+ d*(n+k)*log(k) + n*d)) = O(m*(n*2`^{d} `+ d*(n+k)*log(k)))` and so, in theory, and net of the constant multipliers and implementation details, it seems that it could be a good idea to use a data structure such as k-d trees to improve nearest neighbor search.

As we have seen, however, if the theoretical margin is small, sometimes a more complex implementation only beats asymptotically worse solutions for large, or at times very large, inputs. To double-check if, in practice, it is worth it to go through the trouble of creating and searching a k-d tree at each iteration, we ran some profiling that you can check out on the book's repo.[11]

Once again, we used a Python implementation to do the comparison. By now it should go without saying, but these results are obviously only significant for this language and this particular implementation. Nevertheless, they do prove something.

For k-d trees, we used SciPy's implementation[12] provided in module `scipy.spatial`. If you have read this book's earlier chapters, you probably remember one of the golden rules we mentioned. Before implementing something yourself from scratch, look to see if there is something trustworthy already available. In this case, SciPy's implementation is not only likely more reliable and efficient than the version we could write ourselves (since SciPy's code has been already tested and tuned at length), but it also implements the `query` method, performing NN search, by returning the index (relative to the order of insertion) of the point returned. That's exactly what we need for our k-means method, and it will save us from storing extra data to get from points to indices.

Figure 12.7 shows the result of profiling for the Python method `cluster_points` implemented with brute-force search, and k-d tree's nearest neighbor.

If you look closely at the four charts in figure 12.7, you can see how the line for the k-d tree implementation is more stable through the various values of `k`, while the slope of the upper line for the brute-force search algorithm becomes steeper as `k` grows.

This trend is even more apparent if we look at the data from a different angle, by keeping `n` fixed and plotting the running time as a function of `k`, as we do in figure 12.8.

So, we can say that at least in Python, implementing the points partitioning subroutine by using k-d trees provides an advantage over the naïve brute-force search.

[11]See http://mng.bz/A0x7.

[12]See http://mng.bz/KM5g.

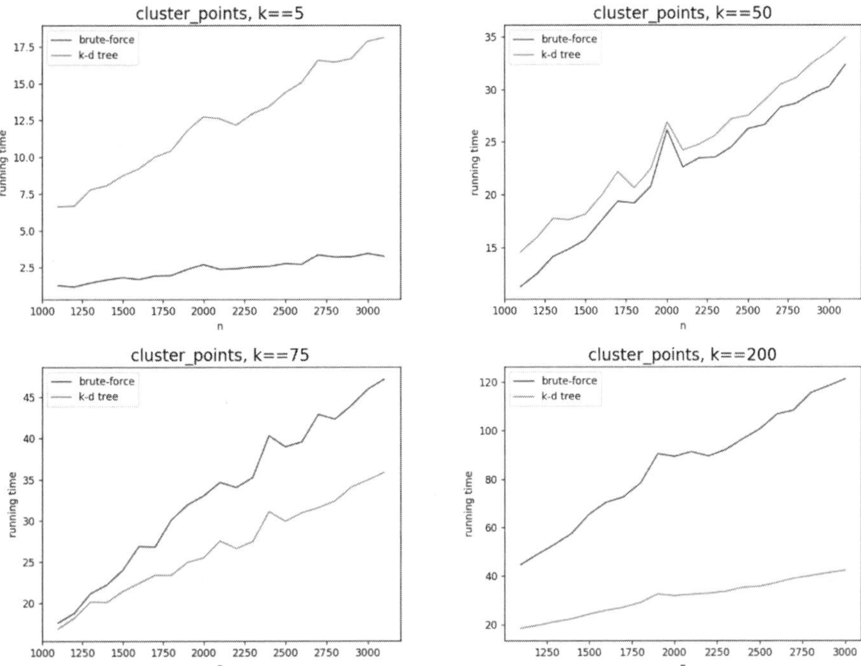

cluster_points, k==5
brute-force
k-d tree
running time
n
cluster_points, k==50
brute-force
k-d tree
running time
n
cluster_points, k==75
brute-force
k-d tree
running time
n
cluster_points, k==200
brute-force
k-d tree
running time
n

Figure 12.7 Running time comparison between `classifyPoints` implementations using brute-force search (darker line) and k-d tree's nearest neighbor (lighter). The running times are shown as functions of `n`, the number of points, for fixed values of `k`, the number of centroids. (Top left) `k==5`, the method using k-d tree, is always slower, and its running time grows faster. (Top Right) `k == 50`, the method using a k-d tree, is still slower, but its growth is similar to the brute-force one. (Bottom Left) `k==75`, the method using brute force, is initially taking a similar amount of time, but as `n` grows, the curves for the two running times diverge and k-d tree implementation grows more slowly. (Bottom Right) `k==200`, the k-d tree implementation, takes half the time of the brute-force approach even for small values of `n`, and it grows much more slowly.

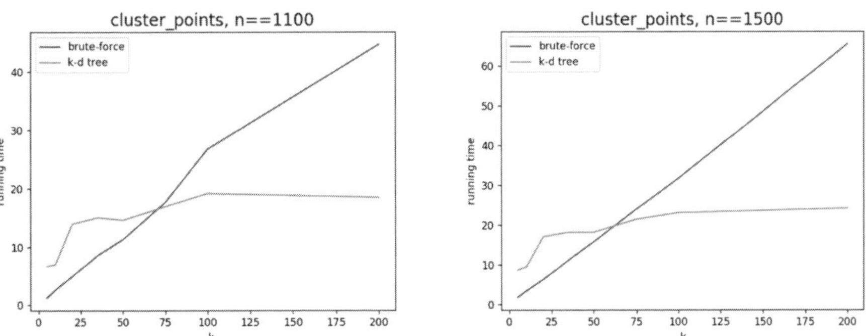

cluster_points, n==1100
brute-force
k-d tree
running time
k
cluster_points, n==1500
brute-force
k-d tree
running time
k

Figure 12.8 Running time comparison between `classifyPoints` (left) and `k_means` (right) implementations using brute-force search and k-d tree's nearest neighbor. The running times are shown as functions of `k`, the number of centroids, for fixed values of `n`, the size of the dataset. The charts are plotted for `n==1500`, but they show the same trend for all tested values of `n > 1000`. When comparing the two plots, it's also evident how the `classifyPoints` method accounts for most of the running time of this k-means implementation.

12.2.5 Final remarks on k-means

To conclude this section on k-means, let's summarize our conclusions:

- K-means is a centroid-based hard-clustering method.
- If implemented with an auxiliary k-d tree, the running time for the algorithm is `O(m*(n*2^d + d*(n+k)*log(k)))`.
- K-means works well on low-to-medium-dimensional data, when cluster shapes are spherical and the number of clusters can be estimated *a priori*, but works well even if the dataset doesn't have a homogeneous distribution.
- K-means works poorly on high-dimensional data, and when clusters can't be approximated with hyperspheres.

Now that we have described the progenitor of all clustering algorithms, we need to fast-forward 40 years to the invention of the next algorithm we are going to present.

12.3 DBSCAN

The paper introducing *DBSCAN* was published in 1996, presenting a novel approach to address the problem.[13] DBSCAN is an acronym for "Density-based spatial clustering of applications with noise," and the main difference in the approach with respect to k-means is already clear from its name. While k-means is a centroid-based algorithm, and as such builds clusters as convex sets around points elected as centroids, a density-based algorithm defines clusters as sets of points that are close to each other, close enough that the density of points in any area of a cluster is above a certain threshold. The natural extension of this definition, by the way, introduces the concept of noise (also referred to as *outliers*) for those points that are in low-density regions. We will formally define both categories in a few lines, but first, we still have a few high-level considerations on the algorithm.

Like k-means, DBSCAN is a flat hard-clustering algorithm, meaning that each point is assigned to (at most) one cluster (or no cluster, for outliers) with 100% confidence, and that all clusters are objects at the same level, no hierarchy of these groups is kept.

In k-means, random initialization of the centroids has a major role in the algorithm (with good choices speeding up convergence), so much so that often several random restarts of the algorithm are compared before choosing the best clustering. This isn't true for DBSCAN, where points are cycled through somewhat randomly. But this has a lower influence, if any, on the final result; therefore, this algorithm can be considered deterministic.[14]

---

[13]Ester, Martin, et al. "A density-based algorithm for discovering clusters in large spatial databases with noise." Kdd. Vol. 96. No. 34. 1996. The approach used is closely related to another paper from 1972: Ling, Robert F. "On the theory and construction of k-clusters." *The Computer Journal* 15.4 (1972): 326-332.

[14]Technically, if two runs of DBSCAN cycle through the points in the same order, then the final result will be exactly the same. For k-means to be considered deterministic, we should instead replace the random initialization with a deterministic one.

DBSCAN, finally, extends the concept of *single-linkage clustering*[15] (*SLC*) by introducing a minimum points-density required to consider two points connected to each other. This reduces the *single-link chain effect*, the worst side effect of SLC, causing independent clusters connected by a thin line of (noise) points to be mistakenly classified as a single cluster.

12.3.1 Directly vs density-reachable

To understand how DBSCAN works, we need to start with a few definitions. Please use figure 12.9 as a reference while going through them to help check your understanding:

- Point `p`, in figure 12.9, is said to be a core point because there are at least `minPoints` points (including `p` itself) within distance ϵ from it (where, in the example, `minPoints==3`).
- Point `q` is *directly reachable* from `p` because point `q` is within distance ϵ from `p`, which is a core point. A point can only be directly reachable from a core point.
- A point `w` is *reachable* (or, equivalently, *density-reachable*) from a core point (such as `p`) through a path of core points $p=w_1, \ldots, w_n=w$, if each w_{i+1} is directly reachable from w_i. From the previous definition of direct-reachability, it follows that all points in the path, except `w`, need to be core points.
- Any two points that are density-reachable from each other are, by definition, in the same cluster.
- If there is any point `r` that is not reachable from any other point in the dataset, then `r` (and all the points like `r`) is marked as an outlier (or, equivalently, as noise).

The algorithm is built around the concept of core points: each of them has at least a certain number of neighbors within a specific distance. This can be seen from a different angle as well: core points are points in areas with at least a minimum density.

Core points (such as `p`, `q`, and so on in figure 12.9) that are reachable (meaning, adjacent) to each other belong to the same cluster. Why? Because we conjecture that high-density areas (as opposed to the low-density majority of the domain) define clusters. But all points that are within a distance ϵ from a core point `p` belong to the same cluster as `p`'s too.

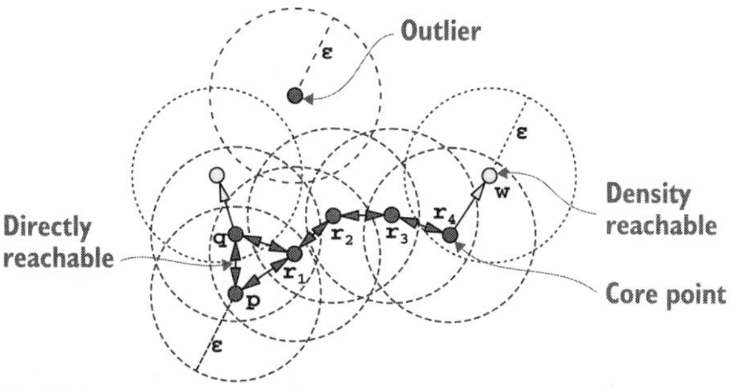
Outlier
ε
ε
Density
reachable
Directly
reachable
q
w
r4
r2
r3
r1
p
Core point
ε

Figure 12.9 Core points, directly reachable points, and reachable points, given a radius ϵ and a threshold `minPoints` (the minimum number of points in a core region) equal to 3; hence, core points need to have at least two neighbors within distance ϵ.

[15] Single-linkage clustering (SLC) is a class of bottom-up hierarchical clustering algorithms where, at each step, the pair of clusters at minimum distance is merged (initially every point is in its own cluster).

12.3.2 From definitions to an algorithm

Moving from the definitions in the previous section to an algorithm is surprisingly simple.

For a given point p, we need to check how many of its neighbors lie within a radius ε. If there are more than a certain number m, then we mark p as a core point and add its neighbors to the same cluster; otherwise, never mind; we do nothing. Figure 12.10 illustrates this step that is going to be repeated for every point in the dataset, with the help of a set to keep track of the points that we want to process next (in any order) for the current cluster.

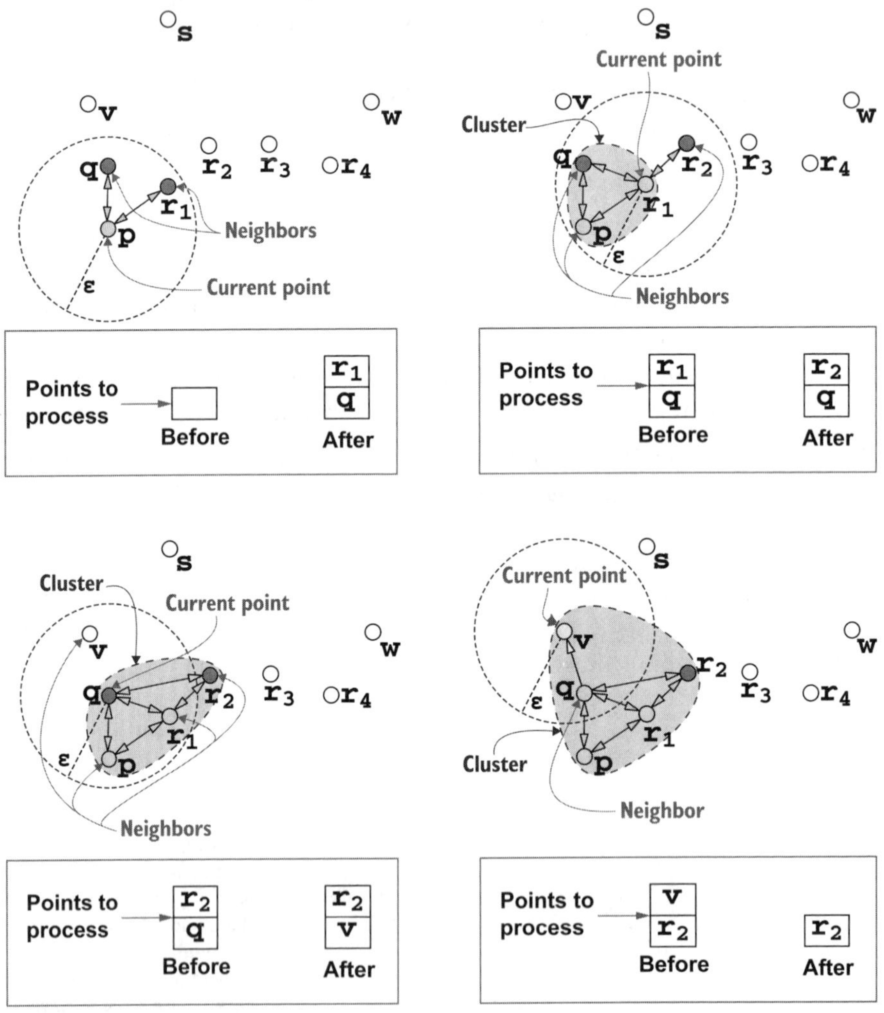
s
v
w
q
r2
r3
r4
r1
p
Neighbors
ε
Current point
Points to process
Before
After
Cluster
Neighbor

Figure 12.10 A few steps of the main loop of DBSCAN. When core points are processed (the first three steps in the figure) all their undiscovered neighbors are added to current cluster and to a set (`not` a queue) of points to be processed. Conversely, when the current point being processed is not a core point, like `v` in the last step, then no further action is taken.

Now we have to ask ourselves what happens when we process a point w that is not a core point, but is directly reachable from a core point p. Is it okay if we don't take any action while processing w?

As you can see from figures 12.9 and 12.10, if p is a core point and w is directly reachable from it, then the distance between w and p must be at most ϵ; therefore, when we check p, we will add all of p's neighbors within radius ϵ to the same cluster as p, and hence w will end up in the same cluster as p.

What if there are two core points p and q that are density-reachable from each other, and are both reachable from w? Well, by definition, there will be a chain of core points w_1, ..., w_n between q and p, so in turn each core point in the path will be added to the same cluster as q, and finally so will p as well when it's w_n's turn.

What if p and q are core points that are not reachable from each other, but are both reachable from a point w? Can w be a core point?

Let's reason *ad absurdum*:[16] suppose that w is reachable from p, a core point, that it is processed before w. Hence, there is a chain of core points p_1, ..., p_n, each reachable from the previous one, that connects p to w.

Suppose also that w, by the time p_n is processed, has already been added to another cluster, different from p's. This means that there is a core point q, for which w is reachable from q (and hence there is a chain of core points q_1, ..., q_k, and so on), but p is not reachable from q because they are in different clusters.

Now, w can be a core point, or not a core point.

If w was a core point, then there would be a chain made of the core points q, q_1, ..., q_k, w, p_1, ..., p_n, p, where all points are reachable from each other; therefore, by definition p would be reachable from q, and this goes against our initial hypothesis.

It follows that w can't be a core point. It must be a non-core point reachable from at least two different core points, a situation illustrated in figure 12.11.

In these cases, reachable points can be added to either cluster, but the difference will be just about a single point. It also means that the two clusters are separated by an area with lower-than-threshold density (although not completely empty).

The final result won't be influenced by the order in which points are processed, because sooner or later we will discover that all density-reachable points belong to the same cluster. Nevertheless, there is an efficient way and a bad way to process the points. Depending on the order we follow, we might be forced to use different methods to keep track of the clusters.

The bad way is this: If we processed points in a completely random order, then we would need to keep track of the cluster assigned to each point (initially each point being in its own cluster), but we would also need to keep track of which clusters need to be merged (every time we process a core point, we'll have to try[17] to merge at least `minPoints-1` clusters); this becomes complicated to handle and requires an ad hoc data structure, the disjoint set we described in chapter 5.

---

[16] *Reductio ad absurdum*, from Latin "reduction to absurdity" is a logical argument that proves a statement by showing that, if false, it would lead to an impossible result.

[17] Some of the neighbors of the core point could have already been merged.

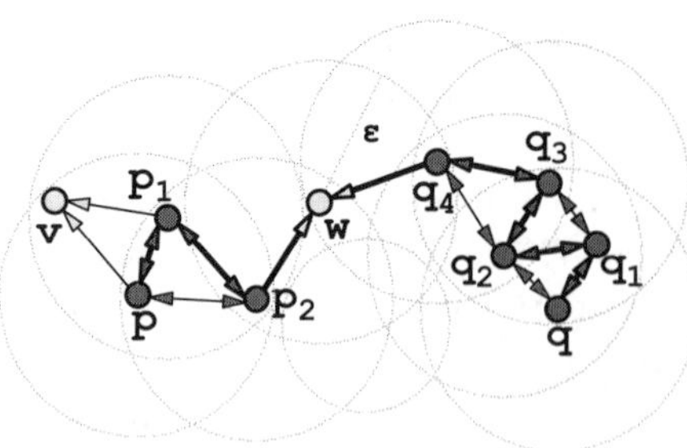

ε
q3
p1
v
w
q4
q2
q1
p
p2
q

Figure 12.11 An edge point w is directly reachable from at least two different clusters. In this example, minPoints is set to 4; the path from q to p is highlighted with thicker arrows.

If, instead, we process the neighbors of each core point p right after finishing with p, as shown in figure 12.10, then we can just build clusters in a sequence, growing each cluster point by point until no further point can be added to it, without any need of merging clusters or keeping track of the history of merges.

By following this order, points like q and p in figure 12.11 will never be added to the same cluster, and it doesn't really matter to which of them a (so-called) edge point like w is merged. As a matter of fact, edge points are the only points for which DBSCAN is not entirely deterministic, because they can be added to any of the clusters from which they are reachable, and the one cluster to which they are eventually added depends on the order used to process the dataset's points.

There is one last question we need to ask: How many times do we need to iterate DBSCAN's main loop? That will be exactly once per point. This is completely different from k-means, where we had many iterations of a few steps on the whole dataset. While k-means is a search heuristic adjusting some parameters to move to a local minimum,[18] DBSCAN is a one-pass deterministic algorithm computing the best partitioning (and at the same time identifying outliers) based on the points' density in different areas.

12.3.3 And finally, an implementation

Once we have outlined how the algorithm works at a high level, we are ready to write an implementation of DBSCAN, shown in listing 12.6. A Python implementation is also available on the book's repo on GitHub.[19]

Listing 12.6 DBSCAN clustering

Method dbscan takes a list of points, the radius of the dense area defining core points, and the minimum number of points needed in the dense area for a point to be a core point. This function returns an array of the cluster indices associated with the points (or, equivalently, a dictionary associating points to cluster indices).

Initializes the current cluster's index to 0. We will use the special value 0 to mark a point as unprocessed, while the other special value -1 will be used to flag outliers. Valid cluster indices start from 1.

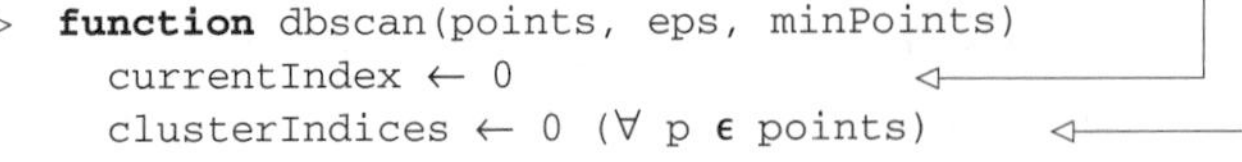

```
function dbscan(points, eps, minPoints)
  currentIndex ← 0
  clusterIndices ← 0 (∀ p ∈ points)
```

Initializes a list with the cluster index for each point. At first, each point is marked as unprocessed.

[18] As we have seen in the previous sections, the cost function that k-means minimizes is the Euclidean distance to centroids (and, indirectly, the in-cluster Euclidean distance).

[19] See https://github.com/mlarocca/AlgorithmsAndDataStructuresInAction#dbscan.

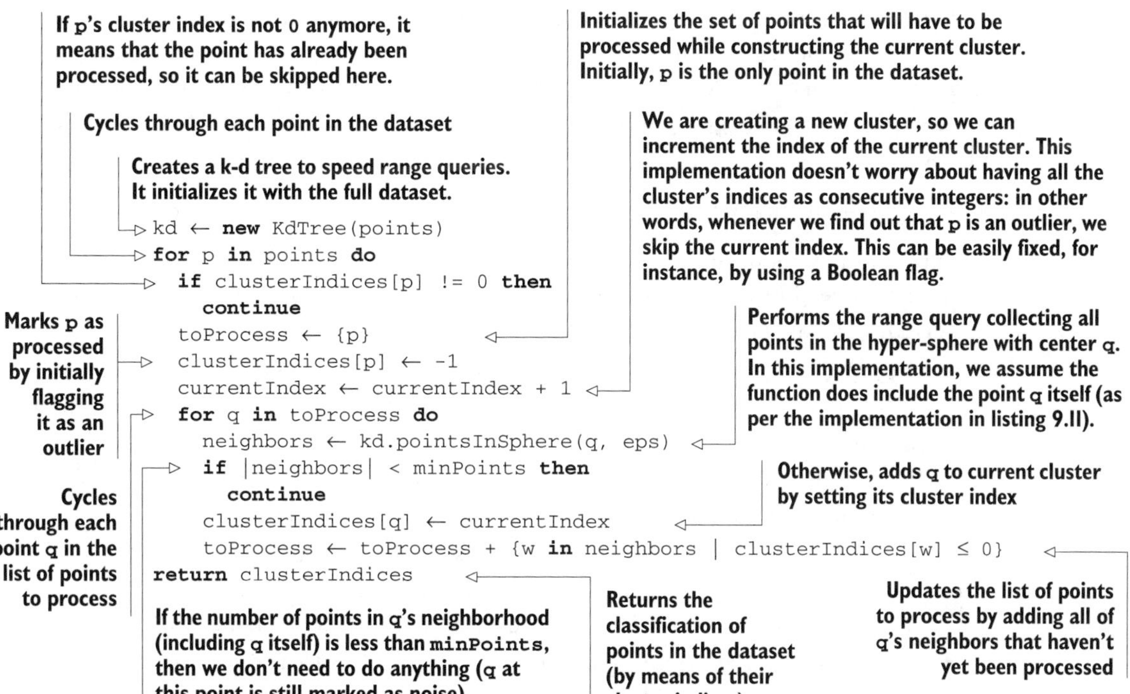
If p's cluster index is not 0 anymore, it means that the point has already been processed, so it can be skipped here.
Initializes the set of points that will have to be processed while constructing the current cluster. Initially, p is the only point in the dataset.
Cycles through each point in the dataset
We are creating a new cluster, so we can increment the index of the current cluster. This implementation doesn't worry about having all the cluster's indices as consecutive integers: in other words, whenever we find out that p is an outlier, we skip the current index. This can be easily fixed, for instance, by using a Boolean flag.
Creates a k-d tree to speed range queries. It initializes it with the full dataset.
Marks p as processed by initially flagging it as an outlier
Performs the range query collecting all points in the hyper-sphere with center q. In this implementation, we assume the function does include the point q itself (as per the implementation in listing 9.11).
Cycles through each point q in the list of points to process
Otherwise, adds q to current cluster by setting its cluster index
Updates the list of points to process by adding all of q's neighbors that haven't yet been processed
Returns the classification of points in the dataset (by means of their cluster indices)
If the number of points in q's neighborhood (including q itself) is less than minPoints, then we don't need to do anything (q at this point is still marked as noise).

```
kd ← new KdTree(points)
for p in points do
  if clusterIndices[p] != 0 then
    continue
  toProcess ← {p}
  clusterIndices[p] ← -1
  currentIndex ← currentIndex + 1
  for q in toProcess do
    neighbors ← kd.pointsInSphere(q, eps)
    if |neighbors| < minPoints then
      continue
    clusterIndices[q] ← currentIndex
    toProcess ← toProcess + {w in neighbors | clusterIndices[w] ≤ 0}
return clusterIndices
```

If you recall, we mentioned in chapter 11 that data structures such as k-d trees and SS-trees are often used in clustering. For k-means and DBSCAN, a multidimensional indexing structure is used to speed up range queries. You might have figured this out from the definition of *core points*, given that to decide whether a point `p` is a core point, we need to check how many dataset points there are in its neighborhood within a certain radius from `p`.

And while for k-means we need to perform nearest neighbors queries, for DBSCAN we will instead run range queries, looking for all the points within a hypersphere.

You can also find a Python implementation on the book's repo,[20] as well as a Jupyter Notebook[21] to experiment with the algorithm.

Obviously, for DBSCAN as well as for k-means, it is possible to use brute-force linear search to find each point's neighborhood. For k-means, however, the speedup is nice but not vital (usually k-means implementations don't bother about this), for DBSCAN the performance gain would be dramatic. Can you guess why? Before going further and reading the explanation, try to think about it for a minute.

The difference with DBSCAN is that the search extends on the whole dataset, while for k-means we only look for the closest among `k` centroids (and usually `k << n`).

---

[20]See http://mng.bz/ZPza.

[21]See http://mng.bz/RXEO.

If we have `n` points in the input dataset, then the difference, given the running time of the whole algorithm, is between `O(n`^{2}`)` and `O(n*log(n))`, assuming that the range queries take each `O(log(n))`.[22] Just as a reminder, with one million points in our dataset, this means going down from ~`10`^{12} (a trillion) operations to ~`6*10`^{6} (six million).

12.3.4 Pros and cons of DBSCAN

We have already mentioned a few characteristics peculiar to DBSCAN that help us overcome some limits of other clustering algorithms like k-means or single-linkage clustering. Let's quickly review them here:

- DBSCAN is able to determine the number of clusters (given the hyper-parameters with which it is called), while k-means needs this number to be provided as a parameter.
- It only takes two parameters, that can also be derived by the domain (possibly through a preliminary scan to collect statistics on the dataset).
- DBSCAN can handle noise in the datasets by identifying outliers.
- It can find arbitrarily shaped clusters and can partition non-linearly separable clusters (see figure 12.12 and compare it to figure 12.6 for k-means).
- By tuning the `minPoints` parameter, it is possible to reduce the single-link effect.
- The algorithm is almost entirely deterministic and the order in which points are processed is mostly irrelevant. A different order can only change the assignment of points on the edge of clusters when they are equally close to more than one cluster (as we have seen in figure 12.11).

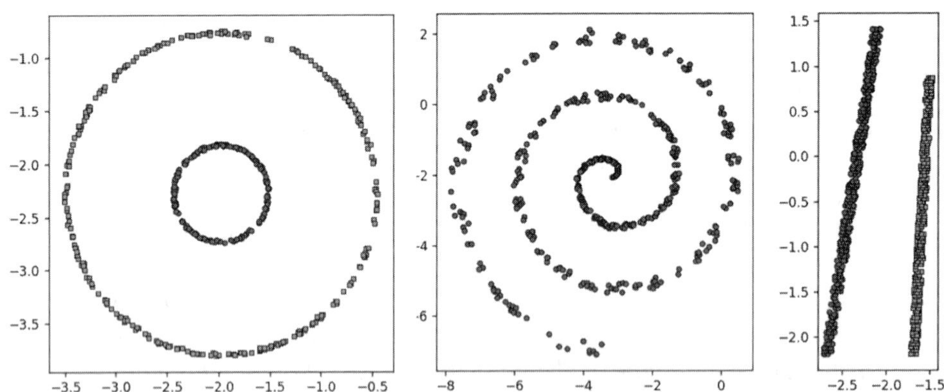
-1.0
-1.5
-2.0
-2.5
-3.0
-3.5
-3.5 -3.0 -2.5 -2.0 -1.5 -1.0 -0.5
2
0
-2
-4
-6
-8 -6 -4 -2 0
1.5
1.0
0.5
0.0
-0.5
-1.0
-1.5
-2.0
-2.5 -2.0 -1.5

Figure 12.12 The three example datasets in figure 12.6, where k-means was failing: processing them with DBSCAN, and with the right choice of parameters, we can obtain a proper clustering for each of them.

[22] The running time of these queries, as we saw in chapter 9, can't be upper-bounded by anything better than `O(n)` in the worst case. However, the running time of range queries on hyper-spheres depends on the radius of the sphere, and under certain assumptions on the value of ϵ, `O(log(n))` can be an accurate estimate for the average running time.

So much for the good news. As you can imagine, every rose has its thorns, and DBSCAN has some shortcomings as well:

- DBSCAN is *almost* entirely deterministic, but not completely. For some applications, it might be a problem if points at the border of two or more clusters are aleatorily assigned to one or another.
- DBSCAN also suffers from the curse of dimensionality. If the metric used is the Euclidean distance, then as we saw in section 12.2.2, in high-dimensional spaces all neighbors of a point are at the same distance, and the distance function becomes basically useless. Luckily, other metrics can also be used with DBSCAN.
- If a dataset has areas with different densities, it becomes challenging, or sometimes impossible, to choose parameters ε and `minPoints` such that all clusters will be partitioned correctly. Figure 12.13 shows an example illustrating how the result produced by DBSCAN is sensitive to the choice of parameters, and figure 12.14 shows another example with areas of different density that make it impossible to choose a value for epsilon that will cluster both areas properly.
- Related to this aspect, one of the problems with successfully running this algorithm is that it can be challenging to find the best values for its parameters when there is no previous knowledge of the dataset.

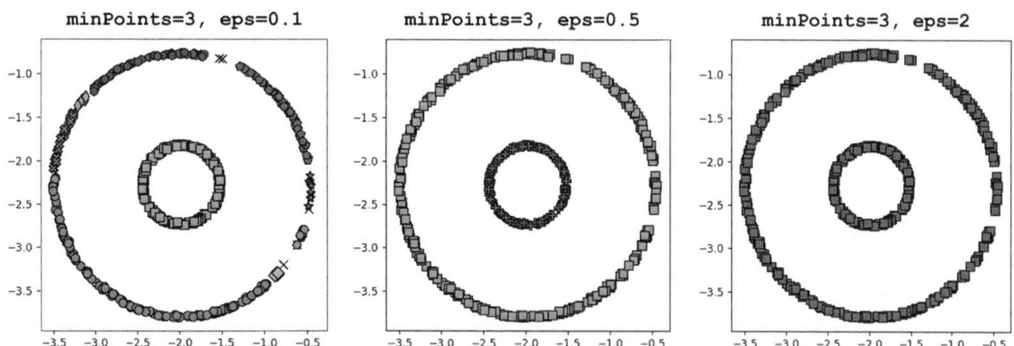
minPoints=3, eps=0.1
minPoints=3, eps=0.5
minPoints=3, eps=2
-1.0
-1.5
-2.0
-2.5
-3.0
-3.5
-3.5 -3.0 -2.5 -2.0 -1.5 -1.0 -0.5

Figure 12.13 Using the first example dataset in figure 12.12, we can see how sensitive to the choice of parameters (in particular of ϵ) the result of DBSCAN is. All the examples ran DBSCAN on the same dataset with parameter `minPoints` set to 3 (the dimension of the domain plus 1). (Left) Using a value too small for ϵ causes the dense area to be too small, so data is partitioned into too many small clusters. A few points, plotted with X-shaped markers, are even marked as outliers. (Center) When the right value for the domain is chosen, the result is that DBSCAN partitions data perfectly into two concentric rings. (Right) When the radius ϵ is set to a value so big that the dense area of inner points extends to points of the outer ring, then the whole dataset is mistakenly assigned to the same cluster.

Hyperparameter[23] tuning, as it often happens in machine learning, is crucial and not always easy. Setting `minPoints` is usually straightforward. As a rule of thumb, for

[23] In machine learning, the parameters passed to an algorithm, and fixed before learning starts, are often called hyperparameters to distinguish them from the parameters of the model (for instance, the weights of a neural network) produced by the algorithm.

d-dimensional datasets, you choose `minPoints > d`, and values around `2*d` are often ideal. For particularly noisy datasets it is also recommended to use larger values of this parameter to strengthen the noise filtering. Conversely, determining the right value for ϵ is often challenging and requires either deep domain knowledge, or extensive tuning. Figure 12.13 shows, by keeping fixed `minPoints`, how values of ϵ that are too small (for a given dataset) cause an excessive fragmentation of the dataset into small clusters, while values that are too large have the opposite effect, reducing the ability of the algorithm to spot different clusters.

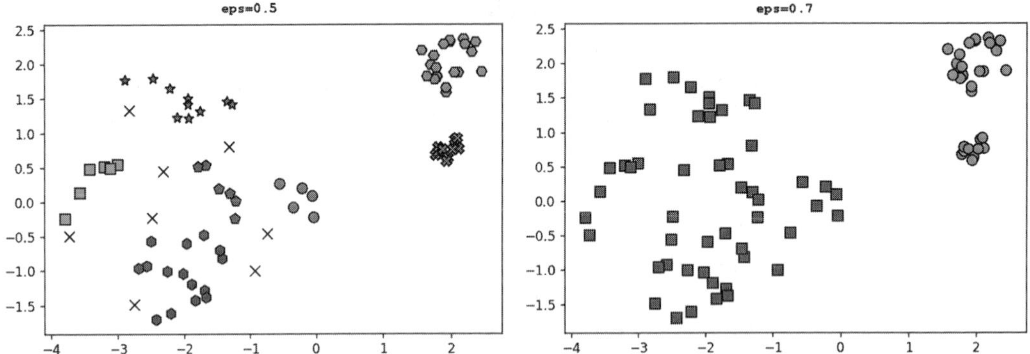
eps=0.5
eps=0.7
2.5
2.0
1.5
1.0
0.5
0.0
−0.5
−1.0
−1.5
−4
−3
−2
−1
0
1
2

Figure 12.14 An example of a dataset with areas of heterogeneous density for which it's not possible to find a single value of ϵ that fits all areas. The dataset has a low-density cluster in the left area and two high-density clusters, close to each other, in the top-right corner. (Left) With a low value of ϵ, the low-density cluster is broken into many small clusters surrounded by noise. (Right) With higher values, the two clusters on the right are merged. There is no value for which these clusters are correctly separated and at the same time the one on the left is recognized as a single cluster.

Clearly, the need for such a tuning would bring us back to a situation similar to using k-means, where we needed to know in advance how many clusters we wanted. And while in this two-dimensional example it might seem easy to find what the "right" number of clusters should be, when we move to higher-dimensional spaces, we lose the possibility of using our intuition, and determining the right values of the algorithm hyperparameters based on the number of clusters becomes impossible.

In the next couple of sections, we will examine two different ways to cope with hyperparameters and address their issues.

12.4 OPTICS

As we saw in the last section, DBSCAN is a powerful algorithm that is able to identify non-linearly separable clusters of any shape; however, it has a weak spot connected to the parameters regulating the density thresholds. In particular, it is hard to find the best value for epsilon, the radius of the core-region determining what points are reachable from each other. When a dataset has areas with different densities, then it becomes even more impossible to find a value that works equally well for the whole dataset (as shown in figure 12.14).

It doesn't matter if we try to search for this value manually or semi-automatically (see section 12.5). If we stick with the DBSCAN algorithm alone, the algorithm is not enough to handle non-uniform datasets.

It didn't take too long until computer scientists came up with a new idea that could help in these situations: the key step missing was "Ordering Points To Identify the Clustering Structure," which the authors turned into an acronym, *OPTICS*,[24] to name the algorithm they had invented.

When we were discussing DBSCAN, we talked about the order in which points are processed. For DBSCAN, the only thing that matters is that points in the same cluster (that is, core points reachable from each other) are processed together; however, as we have seen, this is more a matter of optimization so that we don't have to keep a disjoint set and merge clusters when we find a pair of directly reachable points, because the order of processing may only influence the assignment of non-core points on the edge of clusters.

The idea behind OPTICS is that, instead, this order does matter, and in particular it can make sense to keep expanding a "frontier" for the current cluster by adding the unprocessed point that is closest to the cluster (if it is reachable from the cluster).

Figure 12.15 illustrates this concept in a simplified scenario. In order to choose the right point, it's obviously necessary to keep track of the distances of all undiscovered neighbors of a cluster,[25] and for this purpose, the authors of the paper introduced two definitions: to each point, they associated a core distance and a reachability distance.

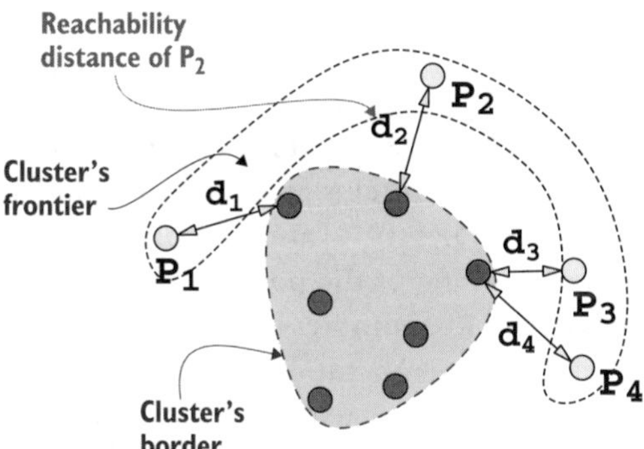
Reachability distance of P_2
Cluster's frontier
Cluster's border
d_1
d_2
d_3
d_4
P_1
P_2
P_3
P_4

Figure 12.15 Considering the distance of undiscovered points (P_1 to P_4) from (points within) a certain cluster. The key idea in OPTICS is "discovering" these points from the closest to the furthest; in the example, P_3 would be the next one to be processed.

12.4.1 Definitions

The core distance of a point `p` is the minimum distance for that point to be considered a core point. Since the definition of a core point, given in section 12.3 for DBSCAN, depends on the parameters ϵ, the radius of dense regions, and `minPoints`

---

[24]Ankerst, Mihael, et al. "OPTICS: ordering points to identify the clustering structure." ACM Sigmod record. Vol. 28. No. 2. ACM, 1999.

[25]Here we adopt the definition of "neighbor of a cluster" meaning a point that is a neighbor (and hence reachable) of any point currently in the cluster.

(M for short, in the following formulas), the minimum number of points needed to define a dense region, these definitions also depend on those hyperparameters:

$$\text{core-distance}_{\varepsilon, M}(p) = \begin{cases} Undefined & \text{if} |N_\varepsilon(p)| < M \\ M-\text{th smallest distance in } |N_\varepsilon(p)| & \text{otherwise} \end{cases}$$

Naturally, if a point is not a core point (and so less than M points are in its ϵ-neighborhood), its core distance is undefined. Conversely, its core distance will be the distance of its M-th nearest neighbor:[26] if this happens, core distance can be interpreted as the minimum value that we can assign to the parameter ϵ for p to be a core point (given a fixed value for minPoints).

Once we have defined the core distance, we can use it to define a new kind of metric, the reachability distance between two points:

$$\text{reachability-distance}_{\varepsilon, M}(p, q) = \begin{cases} Undefined & \text{if} |N_\varepsilon(p)| < M \\ max(\text{core-distance}_{\varepsilon, M}(q), distance(q, p)) & \text{otherwise} \end{cases}$$

Reachability distance is not symmetric. Given a point q, the reachability distance of p from q can be interpreted as the minimum value of ϵ for which p is density-reachable from q; therefore, it must be at least p's core distance (for the closest minPoints to p), or the actual distance between p and q. Moreover, if p and q are nearest neighbors (in particular if there is no point closer to p than q), then this value is the smallest value we can assign to ϵ in order for p and q to belong to the same cluster.

12.4.2 OPTICS algorithm

Once given these two definitions, we can easily describe the algorithm. Its core idea is similar to DBSCAN, adding points to the current cluster only if they are reachable from points already in the cluster. However, OPTICS is also completely different. For starters, it doesn't produce just a flat partitioning of the points, but instead it builds a hierarchical clustering. We'll get back to this in a minute.

OPTICS takes the same parameters as DBSCAN, but ϵ, in this case, has a different meaning. It's the largest radius that will be considered to determine the core and reachability distance. For this reason (and for disambiguation, as we'll see), in the rest of the chapter we will refer to this parameter for OPTICS as ϵ_{MAX}. By using this approach, the algorithm simultaneously constructs density-based clusterings for an infinite number of values of ϵ (all values between 0 and ϵ_{MAX}), and hence for an infinite number of densities.

In the formulas in the previous sub-section we have seen that these distances are set to undefined if the ϵ-neighborhood of a point doesn't have enough neighbors. This also means that the reachability distance from a point q (to any other core point) will be undefined if it's not a core point, with M-1 neighbors within a radius ϵ_{MAX}.

[26]Assuming we consider p as its own neighbor . . . technically, since we agreed that for p to be a core point there needs to be M points within a radius ϵ from p, to compute the core distance we take the distance of its (M-1)-th neighbor.

Therefore, if we set ϵ_{MAX} to a large value, then we will have fewer points marked as noise and, in a way, we will leave more open options because we will allow larger values for the core distance, and we will have more points with a defined value for reachability distance.

However, a larger radius for the core density areas means that these areas will contain more points, and this makes the algorithm slower.

In the main section of the algorithm, in fact, for each point processed we need to update the reachability distance of all undiscovered points in its ϵ-neighborhood. The more points it contains, the slower the algorithm will be.

As we briefly mentioned, OPTICS' main cycle grows the current cluster[27] `C` by adding the closest point to the cluster's frontier, which is the point with the smallest reachability distance from any point already in `C`. The cluster is formed in a way similar to DBSCAN's because all points reachable from the cluster's seed (the first point processed for a new cluster) are added to it. However, forming these clusters is not the direct objective of OPTICS.

When a new point is "discovered" and processed, its reachability distance from the cluster is set in stone. This cluster-to-point distance is not to be confused with the reachability distance between two points. For a point `q` and a cluster `C`, we define the reachability distance of `q` from `C` as the minimum of the reachability distance from `p` to `q`, for all points `p` in `C`:

$$\text{reachability-distance}_{\varepsilon, M}(q, C) = max\{\text{reachability-distance}_{\varepsilon, M}(q, p) \forall p | p \varepsilon C\}$$

If when we process a point `p`, we update the reachability distances of all points in its ε-neighborhood, and we keep a priority queue with all the undiscovered points in the neighborhoods of any point in `C`, then we can be sure that

1. The reachability distance of all the points at the frontier of the cluster (all the points that are neighbors to at least one point in the cluster) is correctly stored.
2. The value stored is the smallest of the reachability distances from any of the points already processed to `q` (although we only care about the current cluster's).
3. The top of the queue holds the closest point to cluster `C`:
   a. Technically, at the top of the queue we have the point `q` with an associated value ϵ_q (the smallest value for ε for which `q` would still be reachable from `C`) such that, considering any other points `w` in `C`'s frontier, $\epsilon_q \leq \epsilon_w$.
4. Therefore, any of the points still to be processed will have at least the same reachability distance from `C`, or higher.

[27] Technically, as we have noted, it simultaneously grows an infinite number of clusters for all the possible values of density allowed, but for the sake of simplicity, we will focus on a single cluster in the description, the one that would be obtained with $\epsilon=\epsilon_{MAX}$.

Listings 12.7 and 12.8 describe the main OPTICS algorithm, while on the book's repo on GitHub,[28] you can find a Python implementation of the algorithm and this Jupyter Notebook to experiment with it.

Listing 12.7 OPTICS Clustering

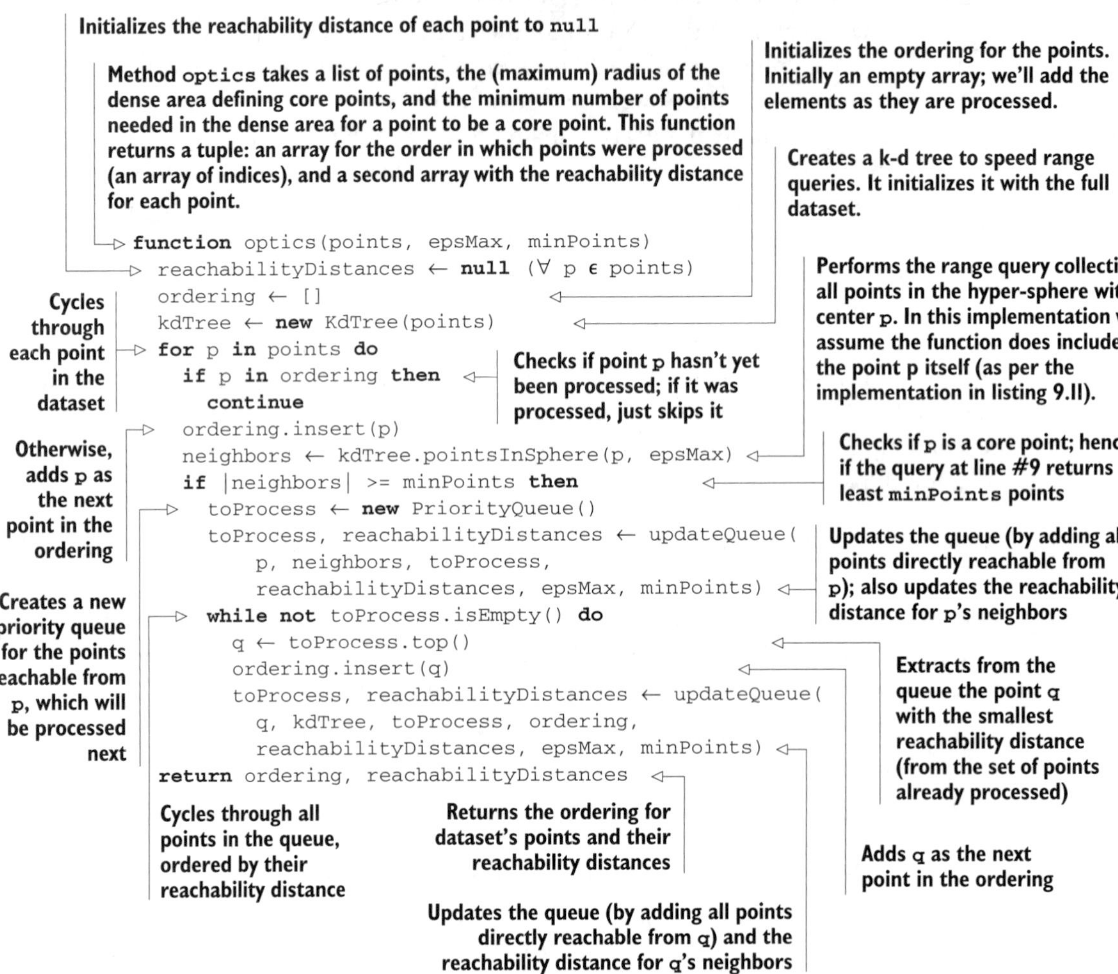

```
function optics(points, epsMax, minPoints)
  reachabilityDistances ← null (∀ p ϵ points)
  ordering ← []
  kdTree ← new KdTree(points)
  for p in points do
    if p in ordering then
      continue
    ordering.insert(p)
    neighbors ← kdTree.pointsInSphere(p, epsMax)
    if |neighbors| >= minPoints then
      toProcess ← new PriorityQueue()
      toProcess, reachabilityDistances ← updateQueue(
          p, neighbors, toProcess,
          reachabilityDistances, epsMax, minPoints)
      while not toProcess.isEmpty() do
        q ← toProcess.top()
        ordering.insert(q)
        toProcess, reachabilityDistances ← updateQueue(
          q, kdTree, toProcess, ordering,
          reachabilityDistances, epsMax, minPoints)
  return ordering, reachabilityDistances
```

Initializes the reachability distance of each point to null
Method optics takes a list of points, the (maximum) radius of the dense area defining core points, and the minimum number of points needed in the dense area for a point to be a core point. This function returns a tuple: an array for the order in which points were processed (an array of indices), and a second array with the reachability distance for each point.
Initializes the ordering for the points. Initially an empty array; we'll add the elements as they are processed.
Creates a k-d tree to speed range queries. It initializes it with the full dataset.
Performs the range query collecting all points in the hyper-sphere with center p. In this implementation we assume the function does include the point p itself (as per the implementation in listing 9.11).
Cycles through each point in the dataset
Checks if point p hasn't yet been processed; if it was processed, just skips it
Otherwise, adds p as the next point in the ordering
Checks if p is a core point; hence, if the query at line #9 returns at least minPoints points
Creates a new priority queue for the points reachable from p, which will be processed next
Updates the queue (by adding all points directly reachable from p); also updates the reachability distance for p's neighbors
Extracts from the queue the point q with the smallest reachability distance (from the set of points already processed)
Cycles through all points in the queue, ordered by their reachability distance
Returns the ordering for dataset's points and their reachability distances
Adds q as the next point in the ordering
Updates the queue (by adding all points directly reachable from q) and the reachability distance for q's neighbors

The algorithm's core (also illustrated in figure 12.16 on a simplified example) consists of a cycle through each point in the dataset. Entries are processed in chunks of contiguous, reachable points (the starting point is chosen either randomly or according to its position in the dataset), and non-core points are "skipped" (similar to what happened in DBSCAN).

[28]See http://mng.bz/j4V8.

The points that are reachable from the ones already processed are kept in a priority queue and extracted according to their reachability distance (the smallest reachability distance from any of the processed points is on top of the queue, as we have already seen).

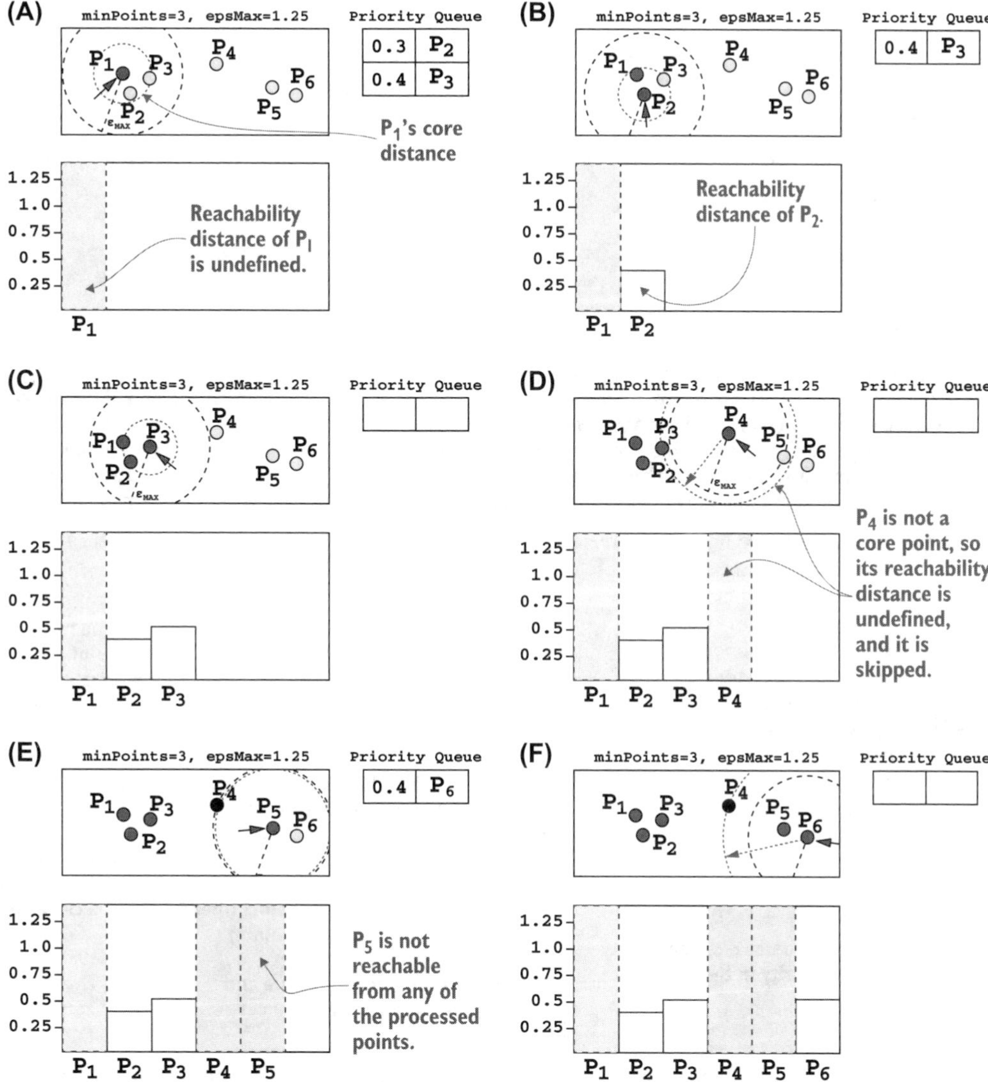
(A)
minPoints=3, epsMax=1.25
Priority Queue
0.3 P2
0.4 P3
P1's core distance
Reachability distance of P1 is undefined.
(B)
minPoints=3, epsMax=1.25
Priority Queue
0.4 P3
Reachability distance of P2.
(C)
minPoints=3, epsMax=1.25
Priority Queue
(D)
minPoints=3, epsMax=1.25
Priority Queue
P4 is not a core point, so its reachability distance is undefined, and it is skipped.
(E)
minPoints=3, epsMax=1.25
Priority Queue
0.4 P6
P5 is not reachable from any of the processed points.
(F)
minPoints=3, epsMax=1.25
Priority Queue
1.25
1.0
0.75
0.5
0.25
P1 P2 P3 P4 P5 P6

Figure 12.16 An example of how OPTICS constructs the ordering and list of reachability distances. Notice that the choice of the first point is completely arbitrary; it can even be random. Here we chose to start from P_1 just for convenience, to present a cleaner example. Likewise, at step (E) we could have chosen P_6 instead of P_5: if that happened, we wouldn't have been able to compute its reachability distance from P_5 (or vice versa). Choosing a larger value for ϵ_{MAX} would help avoid these situations.

There is a key piece of code still missing, the `updateQueue` method. That's where the reachability distances are actually updated (together with the priority queue). Listing 12.8 bridges this gap. The main purpose of this method is to go through all points `q` in the ϵ-neighborhood of a point `p` (the point that is currently being processed) and update `q`'s reachability distances by checking to see if `p` is closer to it than any of the other points previously processed.

As you can see from figure 12.16, we use the priority queue to keep track of the (intermediate) reachability distances for points and set these distances in stone only when a point is processed. Moreover, we can see that the reachability distance of the first point to be processed for each of the clusters will certainly be either undefined or larger than ϵ_{MAX}.

Listing 12.8 OPTICS `updateQueue`

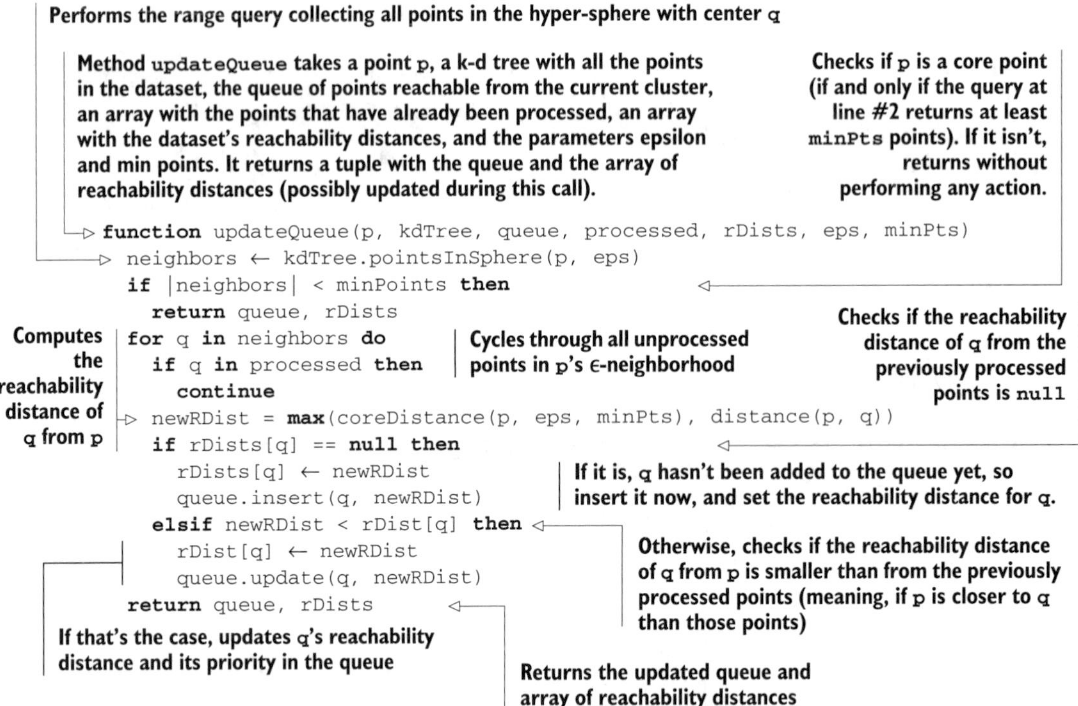
Performs the range query collecting all points in the hyper-sphere with center q
Method updateQueue takes a point p, a k-d tree with all the points in the dataset, the queue of points reachable from the current cluster, an array with the points that have already been processed, an array with the dataset's reachability distances, and the parameters epsilon and min points. It returns a tuple with the queue and the array of reachability distances (possibly updated during this call).
Checks if p is a core point (if and only if the query at line #2 returns at least minPts points). If it isn't, returns without performing any action.
Computes the reachability distance of q from p
Cycles through all unprocessed points in p's ϵ-neighborhood
Checks if the reachability distance of q from the previously processed points is null
If it is, q hasn't been added to the queue yet, so insert it now, and set the reachability distance for q.
Otherwise, checks if the reachability distance of q from p is smaller than from the previously processed points (meaning, if p is closer to q than those points)
If that's the case, updates q's reachability distance and its priority in the queue
Returns the updated queue and array of reachability distances

```
function updateQueue(p, kdTree, queue, processed, rDists, eps, minPts)
  neighbors ← kdTree.pointsInSphere(p, eps)
  if |neighbors| < minPoints then
    return queue, rDists
  for q in neighbors do
    if q in processed then
      continue
    newRDist = max(coreDistance(p, eps, minPts), distance(p, q))
    if rDists[q] == null then
      rDists[q] ← newRDist
      queue.insert(q, newRDist)
    elsif newRDist < rDist[q] then
      rDist[q] ← newRDist
      queue.update(q, newRDist)
  return queue, rDists
```

I realize that the discussion so far has been quite abstract. To understand the real purpose of computing these values for the reachability distance and the ordering of processing for the dataset, and how they can be used to build a hierarchical clustering, we need to get ahead of ourselves and take a look at figure 12.17, which shows a reachability plot that can be considered the output of OPTICS (and also requires a further step after the main algorithm, as we'll see in the next section).

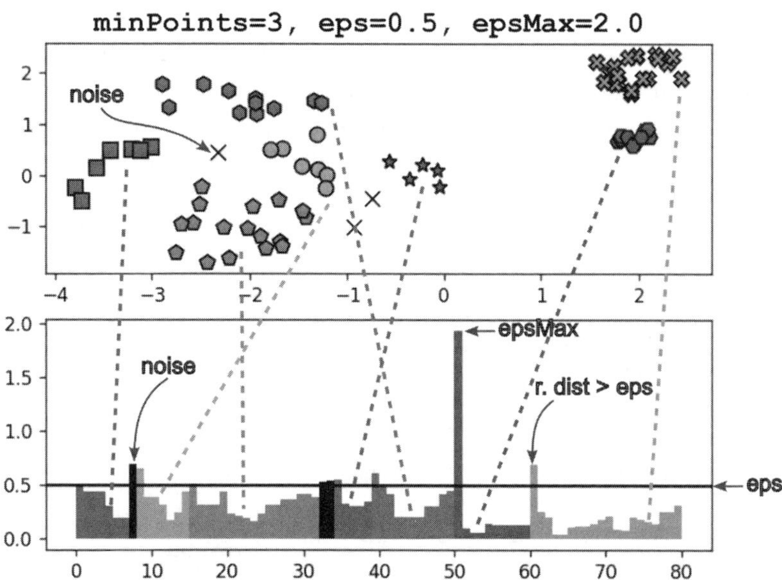
OPTICS
minPoints=3, eps=0.5, epsMax=2.0
noise
noise
epsMax
r. dist > eps
eps

Figure 12.17 A reachability plot. The top chart shows the clustered dataset, the bottom half the reachability distances of points in the dataset, in the same order as points are processed by OPTICS. Outliers are shown in black (with an X marker in the top plot); clusters are assigned the same shade (or color, if you are reading the digital version) in both charts (dashed lines link clusters across the charts). The reachability distances are computed by OPTICS given parameters `minPoints` and ϵ_{MAX}. Further, there is a parameter ϵ that determines the cutoff point for reachability distances and therefore the actual partitioning into clusters.

12.4.3 From reachability distance to clustering

The first thing you should notice in figure 12.17 is that the plot is determined by three parameters: `minPoints` and ϵ_{MAX} are the arguments passed to OPTICS, but there is also another value ε that is used as a threshold for the reachability distance. Obviously, as you can imagine, $\epsilon \leq \epsilon_{MAX}$; this threshold is used in a step that is performed separately on OPTICS' results (we'll describe it in a few lines).

Setting a threshold ϵ for the reachability distance means deciding that the radius of the core region around points is equal to ϵ. This is equivalent to running DBSCAN with that particular value as radius.

The reachability plot shown in figure 12.17 is a special plot composed of two interconnected charts. The top one simply shows the final (flat) clustering that we obtain by setting the threshold to ϵ, while the bottom one shows the ordered sequence of reachability distances and explains how the clustering was derived. Clusters and reachability distances are filled with matching colors, so it's easier to see what points in the top half match the sections in the bottom half (outliers are marked using black, and for the sake of convenience and to properly plot all values, we assign ε_{MAX} instead of `undefined` to the reachability distance of outliers). By doing so we are, in practice, loosening the requirements for the reachability criterion for these points, but since it's already the largest possible value that we can assign to the threshold ϵ, it won't change anything in the following steps.

So, how do we form these clusters, given $\epsilon \leq \epsilon_{MAX}$? Figure 12.18 illustrates the idea behind this algorithm (at a high level, combining it with elements of OPTICS). We start looking at reachability distances, following the ordering in which points were processed by OPTICS, so that we know that the reachability distance of the next point is the smallest possible among all undiscovered points (keep in mind that the reachability distances stored are points-to-cluster distances, and that's also why ordering is important!).

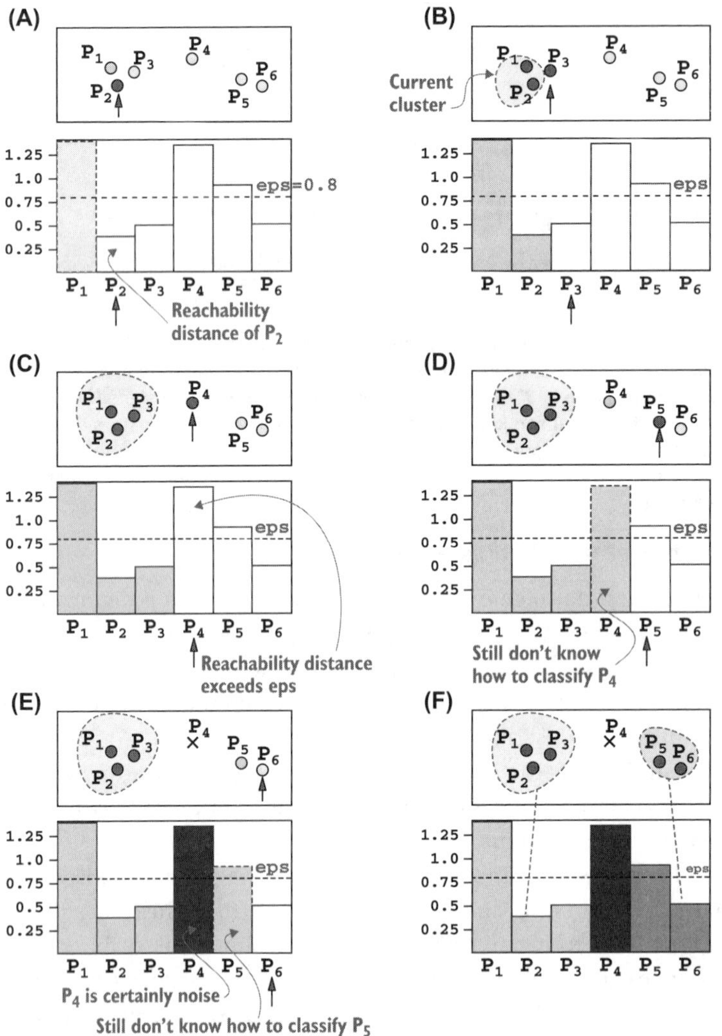

(A)
eps=0.8
Reachability distance of P_2
(B)
Current cluster
eps
(C)
Reachability distance exceeds eps
(D)
Still don't know how to classify P_4
(E)
P_4 is certainly noise
Still don't know how to classify P_5
(F)

Figure 12.18 An example of the algorithm to derive a flat clustering from OPTICS' reachability distances. Notice that while the reachability distances are built on the chart left-to-right, points are examined in order of their reachability distance, starting from a randomly chosen entry (so this particular order for the points was chosen, in this example, just for convenience).

We start from the first point processed—call it P_1—and create a new cluster C_1; being the first point of a new cluster, P_1's reachability distance is undefined, so we still don't know if P_1 is an outlier or part of a cluster. We can only tell after the next step, shown in part (A) of figure 12.18, by checking the reachability distance (from C_1) of the next point P_2.

Since this value is smaller than ϵ (in the example, 0.8), then we add P_2 to C_1 and move to the next point P_3, also added to C_1 as shown in (B) and (C). From a visual point of view, in the reachability chart you can see that the reachability distance for P_2 is below the threshold line (parallel to the horizontal axis) for ϵ=0.8.

When we get to P_4, we realize that its reachability distance from C_1 (or technically from any of the points processed before P_4) is larger than ϵ, and hence P_4 is not reachable from C_1. Since the points are processed in order of reachability distance from the current cluster, this means that there is no point still to be processed that can be reachable from points in C_1 if the radius of core regions is equal to ϵ; hence, we "close" the current cluster and start a new one.

We start a new cluster for P_4, but we don't know how to classify it yet. When we check `P5`'s reachability distance (D), we discover that it is also larger than ϵ, and this means that the algorithm has detected that `P4` is an outlier (because it's not reachable by any point in the dataset, given parameters `minPoints` and ϵ). Notice that the radius that matters here is ϵ. By using a higher value for ϵ_{MAX}, we have simply instructed OPTICS to filter out as noise only those points with a reachability distance larger than ϵ_{MAX}, while for points with a reachability distance at most ϵ_{MAX}, we simply defer the decision to this second step. In practice, this allows us to compute reachability distances only once, and try several values for ϵ (up to ϵ_{MAX}) in this second step with minimal computational effort.

We repeat the process one more time (E) for P_6, and since its reachability distance (from P_5) is smaller than ϵ, we know that it's reachable from P_5 and we can add both to the same cluster (F). If there were more points to process, we would have continued in the same way.

One final remark before moving to the implementation, shown in listing 12.9. Notice that if we run OPTICS twice starting with the same point, the dataset will be processed in the same order, and the results will be identical (net of possible ties on reachability distance). Therefore, OPTICS can be considered as completely deterministic.

Listing 12.9 OPTICS `opticsCluster`

```
function opticsCluster(ordering, reachabilityDistances, eps)
  currentClusterIndex ← 0
  incrementCurrentIndex ← false
  clusterIndices ← -1 (∀ p ∈ points)
```

- **Method `opticsCluster` takes the ordering and reachability distances produced by `optics`, and a parameter `eps<=epsMax`, used to extract a flat clustering from the (infinitely many) possible clusterings computed by OPTICS. It returns an array of the cluster indices associated with the points (or, equivalently, a dictionary associating points to cluster indices).**
- **Initializes the index of the current cluster**
- **Initializes a flag that is used to keep track of when a previous cluster ended**
- **Initializes the indices of the cluster assignments. Initially all points are marked as outliers.**

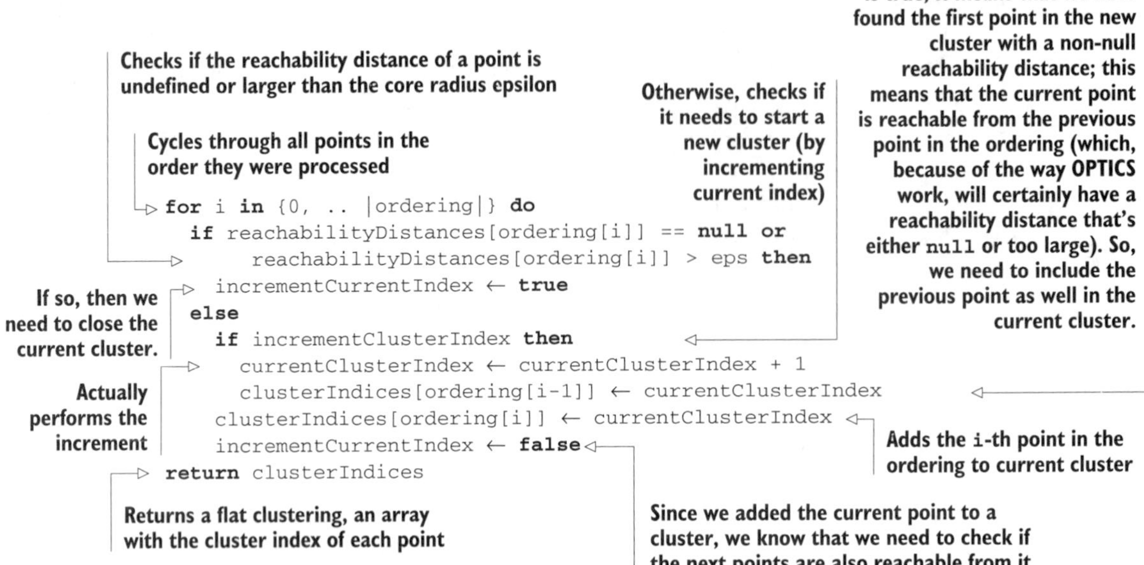
Checks if the reachability distance of a point is undefined or larger than the core radius epsilon
Cycles through all points in the order they were processed
Otherwise, checks if it needs to start a new cluster (by incrementing current index)
If incrementClusterIndex is true, it means that we have found the first point in the new cluster with a non-null reachability distance; this means that the current point is reachable from the previous point in the ordering (which, because of the way OPTICS work, will certainly have a reachability distance that's either null or too large). So, we need to include the previous point as well in the current cluster.
If so, then we need to close the current cluster.
Actually performs the increment
Adds the i-th point in the ordering to current cluster
Returns a flat clustering, an array with the cluster index of each point
Since we added the current point to a cluster, we know that we need to check if the next points are also reachable from it.

```
for i in {0, .. |ordering|} do
  if reachabilityDistances[ordering[i]] == null or
       reachabilityDistances[ordering[i]] > eps then
    incrementCurrentIndex ← true
  else
    if incrementClusterIndex then
      currentClusterIndex ← currentClusterIndex + 1
      clusterIndices[ordering[i-1]] ← currentClusterIndex
    clusterIndices[ordering[i]] ← currentClusterIndex
    incrementCurrentIndex ← false
return clusterIndices
```

One note on the method `opticsCluster`: In the original paper, the authors presented a slightly different method using points' core distance to decide if a new cluster should be started. The version presented here stems from the consideration that if the reachability of a point q is undefined or above the threshold ϵ, while point p, the successor to q in the processing order, has a reachability distance that's below ϵ, then q must be a core point. p's reachability distance from the set of points processed before q, in fact, must also be undefined or greater than q's; otherwise p would have been processed before q. Consequently, p's reachability distance in the plot is the reachability distance between p and q, and according to section 12.4.1, that's only defined if q is a core point.

12.4.4 Hierarchical clustering

Now that we have learned how to produce a flat clustering from OPTICS results, we are in good shape to proficiently use the algorithm. We had mentioned, though, that OPTICS is a hierarchical clustering algorithm. What does that mean and how does it work with OPTICS?

Hierarchical clustering algorithms produce a multi-layer partitioning of a dataset. This result is often represented with a dendrogram, a tree-like structure that holds a stratified structure. I like to think of exploring dendrograms as analogous to coring: we can take a section of the dendrogram and see what the flat clustering associated with that section looks like.

But enough with the abstract analogies; let's delve into an example to clarify how this works!

Figure 12.19 shows a reachability plot obtained from the same reachability distances and ordering as the one in figure 12.17, but with a different value for ϵ. Using a larger value for this radius, obviously the reachability areas around points are larger and fewer clusters are formed.

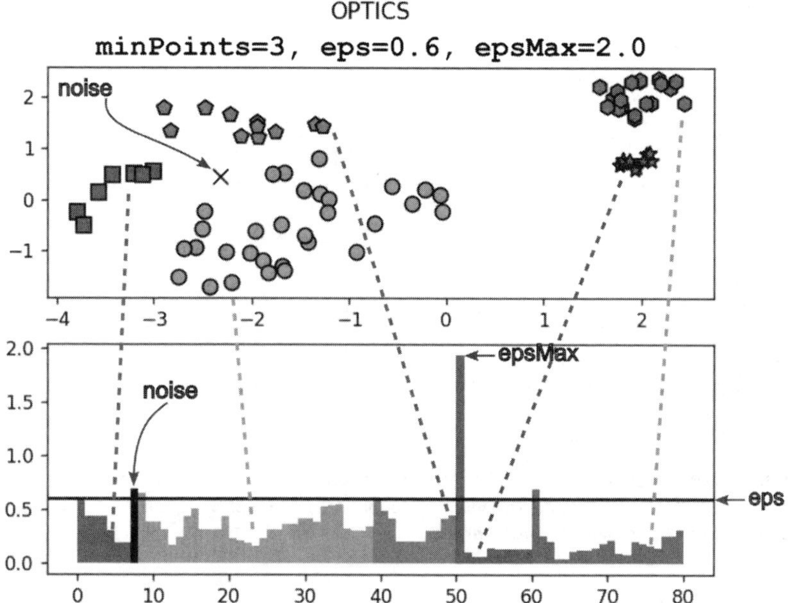
OPTICS
minPoints=3, eps=0.6, epsMax=2.0
noise
noise
epsMax
eps

Figure 12.19 A reachability plot similar to the one in figure 12.17, but with a different choice for ϵ. With a larger value, fewer clusters are formed.

Does this clustering make more sense than the one shown in figure 12.17? It's hard to say just by looking at it; answering the question would probably require some domain knowledge or the tools that we will present in the next section. But since there is now just a single noise point surrounded by three clusters, we might think it makes sense that the points on the left half of the dataset all form a single cluster. To obtain that, we can try a larger value for ϵ, as shown in figure 12.20.

With `ϵ==0.7` the goal is reached, but there is a catch: the two clusters on the right are also merged into a single one! This happens because the two peaks in the reachability distance plot, highlighted in figure 12.20, that mark the edges of clusters C1 and C3 in the same figure, have values smaller than 0.7, so these two small clusters are reachable from the biggest ones next to them.

Is there a way to keep C_3 separated from C_4, but C_1 merged to C_2? For DBSCAN, we have seen in figure 12.14 that this is not possible. For OPTICS, a flat clustering separating one but not the other would only be possible if there was a value of ϵ smaller than C_3's threshold but larger than C_1's. As figure 12.21 illustrates, this is not the case.

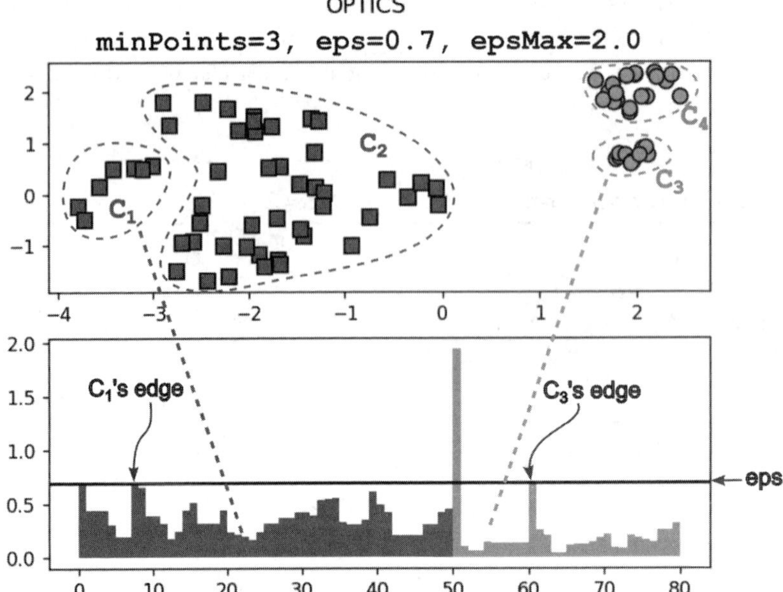
OPTICS
minPoints=3, eps=0.7, epsMax=2.0
C1
C2
C3
C4
C1's edge
C3's edge
eps

Figure 12.20 Another reachability plot from the same results for OPTICS with a larger value for ϵ: 0.7. Unfortunately, the value is too large, and clusters C_3 and C_4, that we would like to keep distinct, are merged.

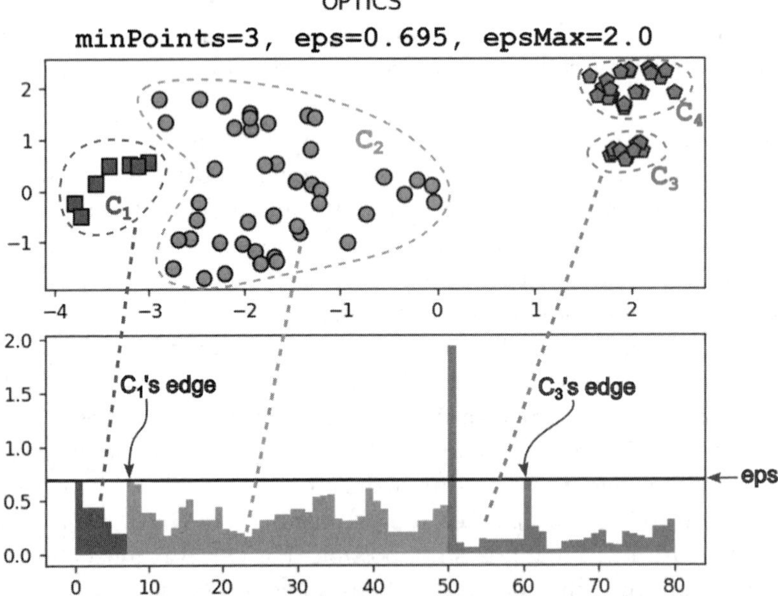
OPTICS
minPoints=3, eps=0.695, epsMax=2.0
C1
C2
C3
C4
C1's edge
C3's edge
eps

Figure 12.21 Yet another reachability plot with `ϵ==0.695`**. This value is smaller than the reachability distance between clusters C_1 and C_2, but it's not small enough to keep clusters C_3 and C_4 separated.**

We seem to be back to the old issue with DBSCAN: it is not possible to find a single value of ϵ that works for the whole dataset, since there is one "half" of it (where x<0) that has a sensibly lower density than the rest of the dataset. (You can also see this from the reachability distances: the area, originally in green, on the right, [starting at index 50 on the lower graph] has a dramatically lower average for the reachability distance.) This is where the hierarchical clustering's added value comes into play; when we run the main OPTICS algorithm, we produce an ordering and a reachability plot. These don't provide a clustering immediately, but they are (or rather imply) a set of flat clusterings that we can obtain by "cutting" the reachability plot with a specific value of ϵ taken from [0, ϵ_{MAX}].

If we try all possible values of epsilon and keep track of the resulting clustering, we can analyze how the partitioning evolves. The best way to perform this analysis is through a dendrogram, a tree-like structure shown in figure 12.22, where—for the sake of clarity—the x axis only shows as lowest-level entries the eight clusters (plus some noise) in figure 12.17, while it would normally have one entry per point in the dataset. Notice how the clusters and noise points are ordered along the x axis of the

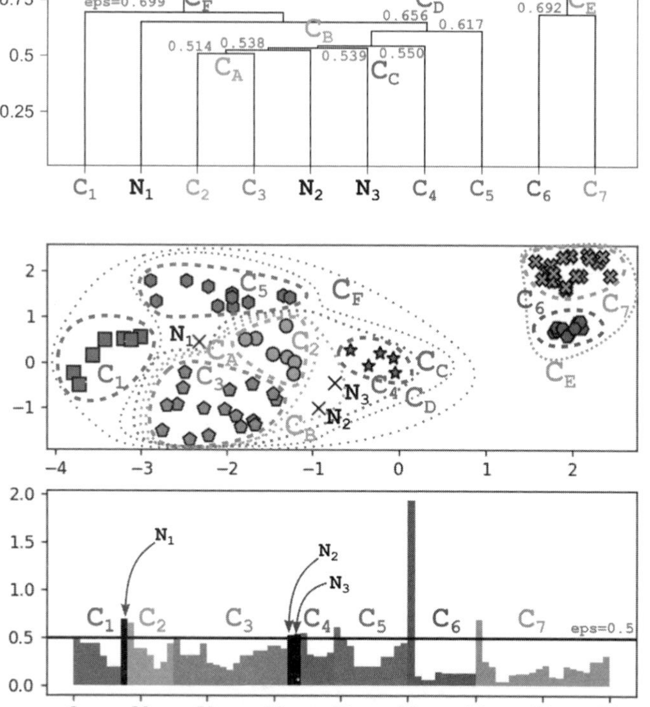
eps=1.94
eps=0.699
0.514
0.538
0.539
0.550
0.656
0.617
0.692
C_A C_B C_C C_D C_E C_F
C_1 N_1 C_2 C_3 N_2 N_3 C_4 C_5 C_6 C_7
eps=0.5

Figure 12.22 The dendrogram built from the result produced by OPTICS, on our example dataset, with parameters ϵ_{MAX}=2.0 and minPoints=3. For the sake of clarity, we omit the bottom portion of the dendrogram for ϵ<0.5. The clusters formed for ϵ==0.5 are named from C_1 to C_7, and are considered the basic units in this plot (normally we would start from the single points). Super-clusters merged from them are named C_A to C_F.

dendrogram: all points in this plot must follow the same order as in the reachability plot (which, in turn, is the same order points are processed by OPTICS).

Now, looking at a dendrogram you can see why this is called hierarchical clustering: it keeps track of a hierarchy of clusters going (top to bottom) from a single cluster containing the whole dataset, to `N` singletons, which are proto-clusters with a single dataset point in them. Moving from the top of the dendrogram to its bottom means virtually exploring all the possible values for ϵ, and the flat clusterings associated with those values: when, in figures 12.17, 12.19, and so on, we chose `ϵ=0.5` or `ϵ=0.6`. We were figuratively cutting a section of the dendrogram and taking a peak at the clusters formed at that level. As we have seen, though, cutting such a section with a line perpendicular to the ϵ axis (meaning a line where ϵ is constant through the whole dataset) doesn't work for our non-uniform dataset.

The great thing about having a hierarchy of clusters, though, is that we don't have to cut this dendrogram at the same height for the whole dataset! In other words, we can use different values of ϵ in different branches of the dendrogram. How do we decide which branches and what values? Well, with 2-D datasets, we can be guided by our intuition, but in higher dimensions, it can stem from domain knowledge or be derived by some metric. For instance, in our example, we can consider the partitioning after the first split in the dendrogram, C_E and C_F, and compare their average density. Since density is clearly very different between the two branches, we can come up with two different values for ϵ in each of them, based on the statistics of each subset: higher where density is lower (or, equivalently, where the average reachability distance is higher).

If the result is not yet satisfactory, we can keep traversing each branch of the dendrogram repeating this step, until one of the following happens:

- We reach a point were both branches have similar characteristics.
- We get the desired number of clusters (if we have an idea from domain knowledge).
- We are satisfied by the result of some metric we have defined (see the next section).
- Or we chose a threshold for the max depth we can traverse the tree, and we reach it.

Figure 12.23 shows how this would work for our example, assuming we are satisfied with traversing the dendrogram only up to the first split. You can see that now, instead of a segment, we have a step function cutting through the reachability plot and the dendrogram. In figure 12.23, while we only retain three clusters, C_F, C_6, and C_7, we have left the border of all C_F's sub-clusters visible in the chart.

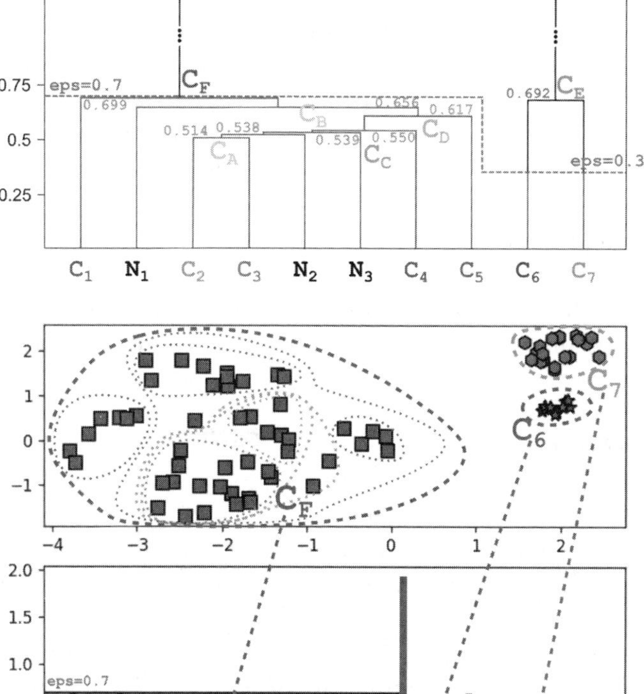
eps=1.94
eps=0.7
0.699
0.514
0.538
0.656
0.617
0.539
0.550
0.692
eps=0.32
C1 N1 C2 C3 N2 N3 C4 C5 C6 C7
eps=0.7
eps=0.32

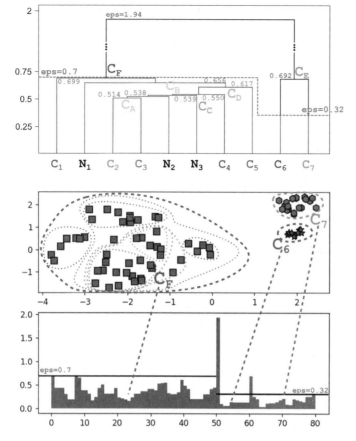

Figure 12.23 The dendrogram built from the result produced by OPTICS, on our example dataset, with parameters ϵ_{MAX}=`2.0` and `minPoints=3`. For the sake of clarity, we omit the bottom portion of the dendrogram for ϵ<`0.5`. Here we apply two different thresholds in two branches of the dendrogram.

12.4.5 Performance analysis and final considerations

Hierarchical clustering is powerful, but also resource-consuming, compared to flat clustering. While it is estimated in the original paper that the core OPTICS algorithm runs approximately 1.6 times slower than DBSCAN (on the same datasets), keeping the hierarchical clustering and building and exploring the dendrogram obviously also require extra memory and computation.

For the core algorithm, a quick glance at listing 12.6 and 12.7 shows us that the code processes each point exactly once (because each point is added to and removed from the priority queue once), and runs one region-query for each point processed; however, entries in the priority queue can be updated multiple times, potentially each time a point is processed. The size of the priority queue depends on the size of the dense regions, and the larger ϵ_{MAX}, the more points will be in the queue. Potentially, the queue could contain all the points starting from iteration 1 (if $\epsilon_{MAX} \geq$ max pairwise distance), and all points in the queue could be updated each time a new point is processed. Likewise, the time needed for nearest neighbor searches, even if using worst-case bounded structures such as k-d trees, depends on ϵ_{MAX}, and if the radius of the region searched is large enough, these queries become linear scans of the dataset.

For these reasons, the worst-case running time of the algorithm is quadratic! Nevertheless, it can be shown that with an appropriate choice for ϵ_{MAX}, the nearest neighbor search can be performed in amortized logarithmic time, and similarly the size of the priority queue can be bound.[29] Therefore, with a wise choice of ϵ_{MAX}, the average running time can be as low as `O(n*log(n))` for a dataset with `n` points.

The original paper contains a more formal description of the algorithm and the theory behind it, and an automated procedure to build a hierarchical clustering structure from the reachability plot. It's a good starting point if you'd like to deepen your understanding of this algorithm.

For more interesting reading, see the paper on *DeLiClu*,[30] an advanced algorithm that extends OPTICS with ideas from single-linkage clustering, allowing us to avoid the parameter ϵ_{MAX} altogether, and at the same time optimizing the algorithm and improving its running time.

12.5 Evaluating clustering results: Evaluation metrics

At this point in the chapter, we have learned about three different (and increasingly complex and effective) clustering algorithms, their strengths, and their weaknesses. Despite being so different from one another, there is one thing that all of these algorithms have in common: they require a human to set one or more hyper-parameters in order to achieve the best result.

Setting these parameters manually can be beyond challenging: while with 2-D datasets it's possible to take a look at the resulting clustering and decide if it looks good or not, with higher-dimensional datasets we don't have the luxury of using our intuition.

It is time to define a more formal way to assess the quality of a clustering. It's finally time to talk about evaluation metrics.

To best develop this discussion, we'll revive our initial example: customer segmentation for our e-commerce site, based on two features, annual income and average monthly bill on the platform. Figure 12.24 shows a synthetic dataset with a realistic distribution (based on data from a real website). The dataset has been preprocessed, normalizing the points. Data massaging is a standard step in data science; it helps make sure that features with larger values have the same weight on the final decision. For instance, in our example, we can reasonably assume that the annual salary is in the range $100K–200K, while the average monthly expenses on the website are somewhere between $500–1,000. If that was the case, one feature would have values three orders of magnitude larger than the other, and the dataset would be completely skewed. In other words, if we used Euclidean distance to measure how close two points are, the difference in annual salary would contribute overwhelmingly more

[29] Also, by using a Fibonacci heap, the "update priority" method, lowering priorities, would only require an amortized `O(1)` running time, so even a linearithmic number of calls would at most require `O(n*log(n))` total time.

[30] Achtert, Elke, Christian Böhm, and Peer Kröger. "DeLi-Clu: boosting robustness, completeness, usability, and efficiency of hierarchical clustering by a closest pair ranking." Pacific-Asia Conference on Knowledge Discovery and Data Mining. Springer, Berlin, Heidelberg, 2006.

than the difference in monthly expenses to the final distance between two customers, making the second feature irrelevant.

To avoid this effect, we perform a normalization step by subtracting the mean of each feature to every single point, and then dividing by the feature's standard deviation.[31]

On the left side of figure 12.24, we show a possible clustering for the dataset. You don't need to be a domain expert to see that this appears to be a bad choice for the number of clusters.

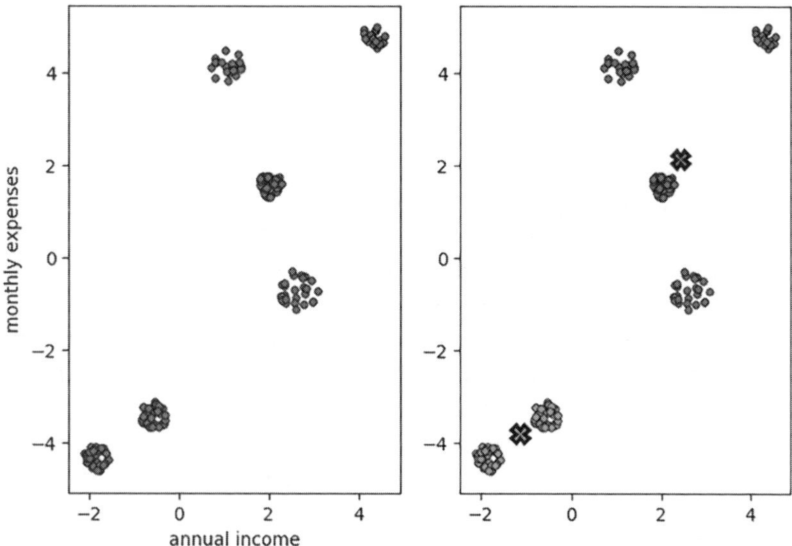
monthly expenses
annual income
4
2
0
−2
−4
−2
0
2
4

Figure 12.24 A synthetic dataset showing customers of a hypothetic e-commerce website after feature scaling. On the right, a possible (bad) clustering for the dataset.

Can we write a method or a mathematical formula to express the (poor) quality of this choice?

Let's start from a consideration: What are the consequences of a bad clustering? Looking at the picture, we can see that points that should belong to different clusters (for example the four clusters in the top-right quadrant) are instead grouped together. As a result, points that are far away from each other are all in the same cluster. And if we think about the very definition of k-means, its target is minimizing the squared Euclidean distance of the points to their centroids. When too few centroids are created (as in the example), this will force many points to be assigned to a single centroid, even if far away. Therefore, the average distance of points in each cluster from their centroid will be higher than if we chose the right number of centroids!

---

[31]This is called z-score normalization and has the advantage of producing data with zero-mean and unit-variance. There are other ways to perform feature scaling; to learn more take a look, for instance, at chapter 2 of *Machine Learning in Action,* by Peter Harrington (Manning Publications, 2012).

If we run the algorithm several times, with different values for the number of centroids, we can compute the average (or median) distance of points from their centroids, and choose the lower value. Is that good enough?

Well, we are close, but not quite there. If you think about it, whatever the value of `k` (the number of centroids) that we tested last, if we choose `k+1`, with one more centroid the average distance will drop a little further because each centroid will have fewer and closer points in its cluster. If we take this to an extreme, by choosing `k=n` (one centroid per point in the dataset) we will obtain an average distance-to-centroid equal to zero (because each point will have its own centroid).

How can we counter-balance this? The truth is that we can't really balance it easily, but there is an easy empiric method that helps us choose the best value. We'll see that in a minute.

First, let's make another important point clear: the distance of points from centroids is only one of many possible metrics. Incidentally, this metric only works for centroid-based clustering algorithms; it wouldn't be applicable to OPTICS or DBSCAN. A similar metric that would also work for those algorithms is the intra-cluster distance: the average pair-wise distance between points in the same cluster. Another interesting measure, useful when dealing with categorical features, is the total cohesion (similar to the distance to cluster center, but using the cosine distance instead of the Euclidean distance).

In the rest of this section, we'll adopt the intra-cluster average distance as our metric. Now, however, it's time to reveal the *elbow method*, an empirical tool that's used in clustering as well as across machine learning to spot the best value for hyper-parameters.

Figure 12.25 shows an example of applying the elbow method to our customers dataset to determine the best number of clusters based on intra-cluster average distance. But it would also be possible to use the same method to decide on the best value for ϵ or `minPoints` if we were using DBSCAN instead.

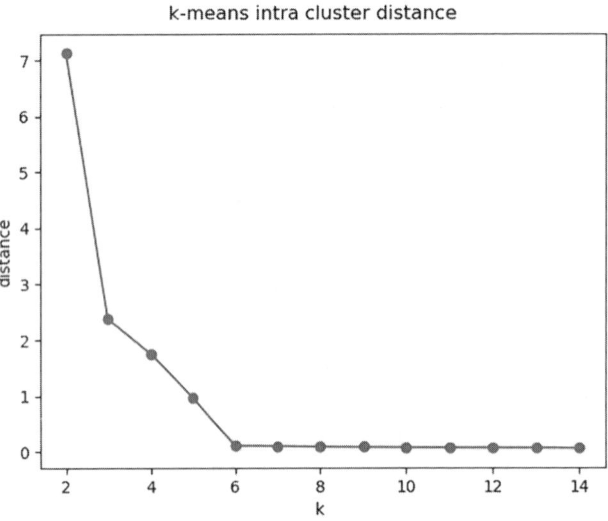
k-means intra cluster distance
distance
k
0
1
2
3
4
5
6
7
2
4
6
8
10
12
14

Figure 12.25 The elbow method used to determine the best value for the number of clusters into which the dataset in figure 12.24 should be split. You can guess where the name comes from.

From figure 12.25 you can guess where the name of this method comes from: the plot looks like a bent arm, and we want to choose the value corresponding to the elbow, the point where the growth of the function changes drastically.

For our example, that value is `k=6`. After that, the metric value improves very little. For real datasets, the transition can be less neat (in this case, clusters are very compact and far from each other, so once we reach the optimal number of clusters, the improvement with adding another centroid is almost null), but there is often a point that's like a watershed: on its left, the slope of the curve is closer to (or larger than) -45°; on its right, it's closer to 0°.

There are, of course, a few details to take into account to successfully implement this method. First, since k-means is a randomized method, it's important to run it several times per value of k. Then you can pick the best value among all the runs (and also store the clustering produced, as we do in the Notebook on the book's repo), or the average or median value for the metric, depending on your goal.[32] Moreover, you need to carefully choose the best metric for your problem. You might want to minimize the distance of points inside one cluster to make sure clusters are as homogeneous as possible, or, for instance, maximize the distance between different clusters to make sure you have a neat separation between different groups.

Listing 12.10 summarizes the steps that should be performed to successfully apply the elbow method (up to the plotting, not included for obvious reasons). As mentioned, you can check it out in the Notebook on the book's repo.

Listing 12.10 The elbow method

Method `kmeansElbow` takes a list of points, a list of values to test for `k` (aka `numCentroids`), the number of clusterings it should create, `maxIter`, the maximum number of iterations for k-means, and how many runs of the algorithm are needed for each value of `k` tested. This function returns an associative array with the best value for the intra-cluster distance metric obtained for each number of centroids tested.

```
function kmeansElbow(points, ksToTest, maxIter, runsPerK)
  results ← {}
  for k in ksToTest do
    M ← []
    for i in {1,..,runsPerK} do
      (centroids, clusters) ← kmeans(points, k, maxIter)
      M[i] ← intraClusterDistance(points, centroids, clusters)
    results[k] ← min(M)
  return results
```

Initializes the associative array with the results

Cycles through all the values for `k` to test

Initializes an array to keep track of the results (because we are running the algorithm several times for each value of `k`)

Repeats `runsPerK` times

Runs k-means with the given input and hyper-parameters

Computes the intra-cluster distance metric on the output of the algorithm

Chooses the best result of the intra-cluster distance metric among all runs with the current value for the number of centroids

Returns the results (optionally you could save the clustering corresponding to the best metric value for each value of `k` and return the list of clusterings as well)

---

[32]If you are optimizing the choice for the current dataset, picking the best result makes sense. If you'll have to run the algorithm on several datasets with similar characteristics, then you might need to find a value that can generalize well, and using the median could be your best bet.

12.5.1 Interpreting the results

To check whether the elbow method works, we have stored the results producing the best metric values for each value of k tested (the ones that are plotted in figure 12.25), and we can take a look at some of them in figure 12.26 to verify that our choice makes sense. And indeed, with k=5 we would have too few centroids, and two clusters would be assigned to the same centroid (left chart, bottom-left corner), while with k=7, a single "natural" cluster gets split by two centroids (right chart, middle).

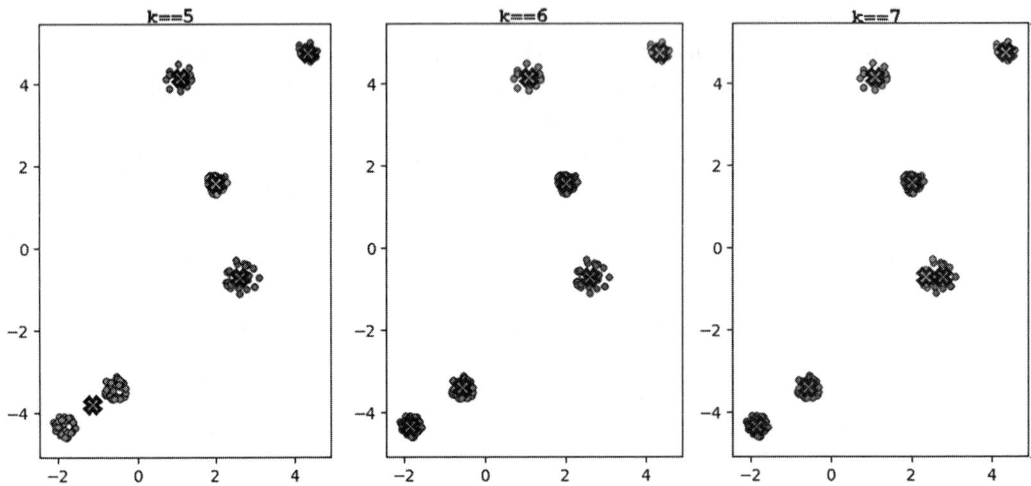
k==5
k==6
k==7
4
2
0
−2
−4
−2
0
2
4

Figure 12.26 Best k-means clustering for our example dataset with k equals 5, 6, and 7. You can notice that 6 is indeed the ideal value, and the smallest value that has enough centroids for the dataset natural clusters.

Once we have established that six clusters are the best choice for our dataset, we can try to interpret the result of the clustering. We can see the top-right corner, for instance, that is made of customers with high annual income and who spend generously on the website. A bit to the right of these clusters, there is another interesting group: people who, despite a lower income, spend almost as much in monthly purchases as the wealthiest cluster. In the lower left corner, we can see two clusters of people with low incomes that also don't spend a lot of money on e-commerce. These two groups can either be marketed to together, or further analysis can be performed to understand the differences and target products more appropriately to each group. Considering that they are bringing in limited income, though, the marketing section could rather ask the data science team to focus on the two clusters toward the center of the chart: middle-class customers that could be encouraged with targeted campaigns, and that can be asked to fill out surveys that will help the marketing team improve customers' satisfaction.

We have seen just one example in action of how clustering can help your company thrive, but there are many, many more. Now it's your turn to apply these powerful techniques to your data!

Summary

- Clustering is the main application of unsupervised learning, used to make sense of unlabeled data, discovering patterns in raw data.
- Some applications of clustering are marketing segmentation, noise detection (for instance, in signals), and data preprocessing.
- The oldest clustering algorithm, k-means, is the easiest to implement, but also has limitations in the shape of the clusters. It can only spot convex clusters and can't handle non-linearly separable data.
- A different approach to clustering, DBSCAN is about identifying groups based on the density of the points. It can handle any shape and non-linearly separable data, but it doesn't work well with datasets with areas of heterogenous density. Moreover, it's hard and unintuitive to choose the best values for the algorithm hyper-parameters.
- OPTICS, a newer method based on DBSCAN, builds a hierarchical clustering and allows us to handle datasets with varying density. It also makes it easier to choose the values of the parameters.
- To assess the quality of a clustering for a dataset, we can use evaluation metrics such as intra-cluster distance, inter-cluster distance, or total cohesion.
- The elbow method is a tool that provides graphical feedback to choose the best values for the algorithms' hyper-parameters.

13 Parallel clustering: MapReduce and canopy clustering

This chapter covers

- Understanding parallel and distributed computing
- Canopy clustering
- Parallelizing k-means by leveraging canopy clustering
- Using the MapReduce computational model
- Using MapReduce to write a distributed version of k-means
- Leveraging MapReduce canopy clustering
- Working with MR-DBSCAN

In the previous chapter we introduced clustering and described three different approaches to data partitioning: k-means, DBSCAN, and OPTICS.

All these algorithms use a single-thread approach, where all the operations are executed sequentially in the same thread.[1] This is the point where we should question our design: Is it really necessary to run these algorithms sequentially?

During the course of this chapter, we will answer this question, and present you with alternatives, design patterns, and examples that will give you the tools to spot opportunities for code parallelization and use the best practices in the industry to easily achieve major speedups.

After going through this chapter, readers will understand the difference between parallel and distributed computing, discover canopy clustering, learn about MapReduce, a computational model for distributed computing, and finally be able to rewrite the clustering we saw in the previous chapter to operate in a distributed environment.

13.1 Parallelization

Although the RAM model (presented in appendix B) is traditionally single-threaded and algorithm analysis usually focuses on sequential execution and improving the running time of single-process applications, parallelization, when applicable, can allow for tremendous speed-ups, and it should be in the tool belt of every software engineer.

Multi-threading in coding interviews

When it comes to algorithm analysis in coding interviews, you might find that there are diverging opinions on this point. As a personal anecdote, during a round of interviews, I found two interviewers with opposite positions, one considering parallelization "cheating" to solve the problem we were discussing, and another expecting the interviewee to suggest parallelization to solve it. Keep this in mind during your next interview. Of course, it also depends on the specific problems and on where the interviewer wants to lead you, but asking the interviewer about your options for multi-threading and parallelization is often a good idea (provided you know what you are talking about!)

To give you an idea of the kind of speed-up we are talking about, I saw an application's running time go down from 2 hours to less than 5 minutes by leveraging Kubernetes and Airflow to distribute data download and processing into small chunks, instead of processing the same data sequentially. Of course, splitting data and processing each chunk separately is not always possible; it depends on the domain and on the algorithm.

So, this is the point where we ask ourselves, is clustering a domain where we can parallelize execution and get away with it?

Can we break down our datasets and apply the algorithms we discussed in chapter 12 to each partition independently?

[1] Multi-processor machines can, however, apply optimizations where some operations are executed in parallel across different cores. This level of parallelization, however, is limited by the number of cores on a chip—currently at most in the order of a hundred, for the most powerful servers.

13.1.1 Parallel vs distributed

Before we get to the point, a disclaimer is due: usually with the term *parallel computing* we only address computations that run on multiple CPUs on the same system—multi-threading, in synthesis. When we think about using multiple CPUs across several machines communicating through a network, then we are instead referring to what's called *distributed computing*. Figure 13.1 shows a diagram that illustrates this difference.

Parallel computing is limited by the number of CPUs on a single machine, while distributed computing is a better approach for scaling out systems and processing

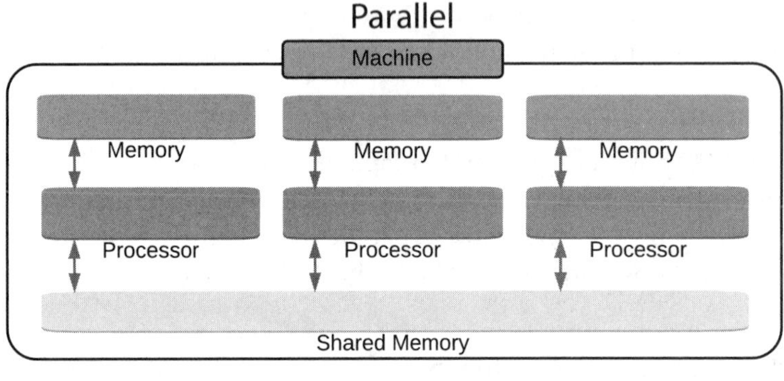
Parallel
Machine
Memory
Memory
Memory
Processor
Processor
Processor
Shared Memory

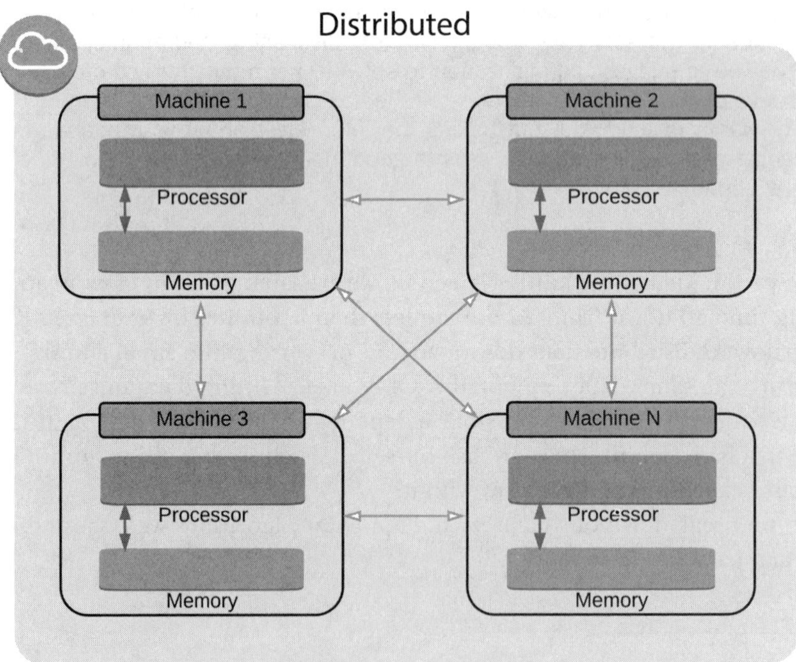
Distributed
Machine 1
Processor
Memory
Machine 2
Processor
Memory
Machine 3
Processor
Memory
Machine N
Processor
Memory

Figure 13.1 A schematic view of the difference between parallel and distributed computing models

huge datasets. On the other hand, if a dataset can fit into a single machine's memory, the parallel computing approach results are sensibly faster, since the processes can communicate through shared memory, while nodes in distributed systems need to exchange information through a network (at the time of writing, the latency[2] is 100ns vs 150ms,[3] so a factor of 10^6).

In this chapter, we'll often use the term parallel computer to refer to both. The computational models we present are software abstractions that could run seamlessly on threads on a single machine or on a distributed system, and the only discriminant would be the size of the input and the resources needed, not the algorithms we use.

13.1.2 Parallelizing k-means

Let's now get more specific in order to answer this question: Can we make k-means a parallel algorithm?

Looking at each step of the algorithm separately will help us "divide and conquer" the problem. Please refer to section 12.2 for the description and implementation of k-means.

The first step is *initialization*, creating an initial guess for the centroids. If this is done completely at random, this step is independent of the dataset and its running time is only proportional to the number `k` of clusters; therefore, the fully randomized version is not worth parallelizing. Parallelization could be necessary when points are drawn independently from a distribution without replacement. We'll see how to distribute this step in section 13.3.2.

Step 3, *re-centering*, computes the center of mass for each cluster. We will tackle this first because each cluster is processed independently and computing the center of mass for a cluster only needs the points in it. We can definitely parallelize this step, with one process for each cluster, so that the execution time will be one of the longest running threads. If the sequential version needs `n*d` sums and `k*d` divisions, where `n` is the number of points in the dataset and `d` its dimension (the cardinality of each point), assuming a uniform split to clusters (best-case scenario, of course) each process will perform `d*n/k` additions and `d` divisions. If all threads finished at the same time and ran at the same speed as the original sequential algorithm, we would obtain a `k`-fold speed-up.

Step 2, *classification*, is more complicated to parallelize. In theory, we would need to check all points' distances in order to assign them to the right centroid. Thinking about this more carefully, though, do we really need all points? If you refer to figure 12.3 in chapter 12, it seems apparent that a point will only switch to a cluster adjacent to its current assignment, and never to one far away. Also, if a centroid `c'` moved further away from a second cluster `C` (assuming the centroid of the second cluster didn't move), it would be impossible for a point in C to be assigned to `c'`. We would need to be very careful, though, with the assumptions we made, so this step would be somewhat more complicated to parallelize.

---

[2] References: http://mng.bz/Wdql and http://norvig.com/21-days.html#answers.

[3] Considering a WAN or high-performance cloud service. Local clusters in datacenters, when properly configured, can lower this latency by two orders of magnitude, down to 1ms.

Even by just parallelizing step 3 of the k-means algorithm, we can obtain a nice speed-up with respect to the sequential version.

Can we do better? Yes, we can, in at least two different ways; to see how, we will need first to introduce a new algorithm and then a game-changing programming model.

13.1.3 Canopy clustering

What if we could run a quick, coarse-grained pseudo-clustering, before running any real clustering algorithm, to get an idea of the distribution of data?

Canopy clustering is normally used for this purpose. It groups points into spherical regions (circles in our 2-D examples), like k-means, but unlike it, these regions can overlap, and most points are assigned to more than one region.

The canopy clustering algorithm is faster and simpler than k-means, because it runs in a single pass, doesn't have to compute the centroids for the canopies (spherical pseudo-clusters), and doesn't compare each point to each centroid; instead, it elects one point in the dataset as the center of each canopy and adds points around it to the canopy.

The algorithm can be made even faster if, instead of the exact distance metric for points in k-dimensional space, a fast approximate metric is used. This gives a less precise result that can be refined by using a proper clustering algorithm as a next step. As we'll see in the next section, using canopy clustering to bootstrap other algorithms can both speed up convergence and reduce the running time.[4]

Figure 13.2 shows how canopy clustering works through an example, while listing 13.1 describes its pseudo-code.

Listing 13.1 Canopy clustering

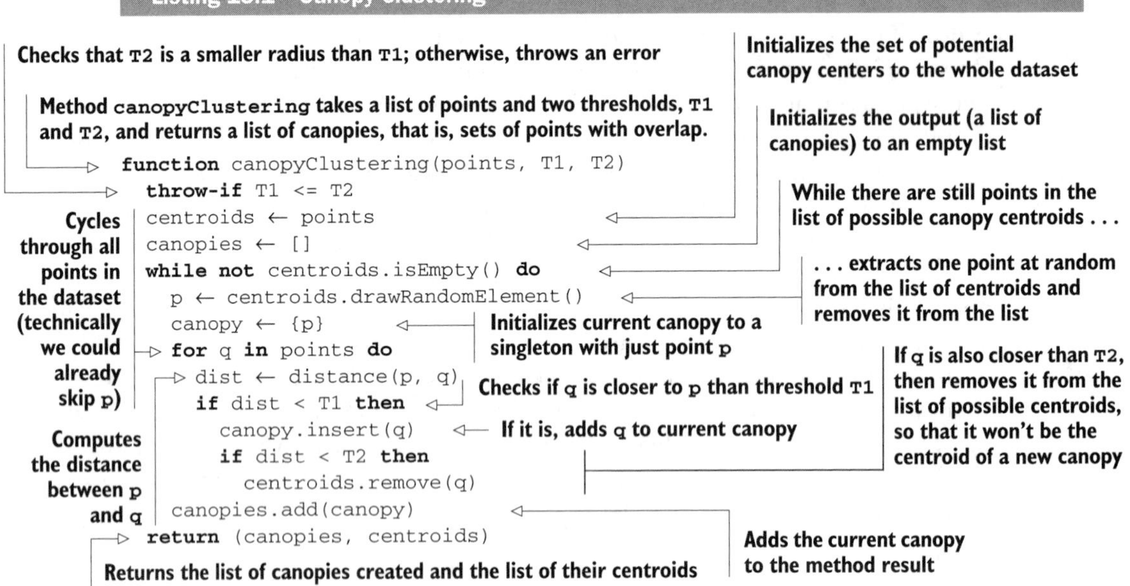

```
function canopyClustering(points, T1, T2)
  throw-if T1 <= T2
  centroids ← points
  canopies ← []
  while not centroids.isEmpty() do
    p ← centroids.drawRandomElement()
    canopy ← {p}
    for q in points do
      dist ← distance(p, q)
      if dist < T1 then
        canopy.insert(q)
        if dist < T2 then
          centroids.remove(q)
    canopies.add(canopy)
  return (canopies, centroids)
```

Checks that T2 is a smaller radius than T1; otherwise, throws an error
Method canopyClustering takes a list of points and two thresholds, T1 and T2, and returns a list of canopies, that is, sets of points with overlap.
Initializes the set of potential canopy centers to the whole dataset
Initializes the output (a list of canopies) to an empty list
While there are still points in the list of possible canopy centroids . . .
. . . extracts one point at random from the list of centroids and removes it from the list
Initializes current canopy to a singleton with just point p
Cycles through all points in the dataset (technically we could already skip p)
Computes the distance between p and q
Checks if q is closer to p than threshold T1
If it is, adds q to current canopy
If q is also closer than T2, then removes it from the list of possible centroids, so that it won't be the centroid of a new canopy
Adds the current canopy to the method result
Returns the list of canopies created and the list of their centroids

[4] It can both reduce the number of iterations needed and reduce the number of operations performed in each iteration.

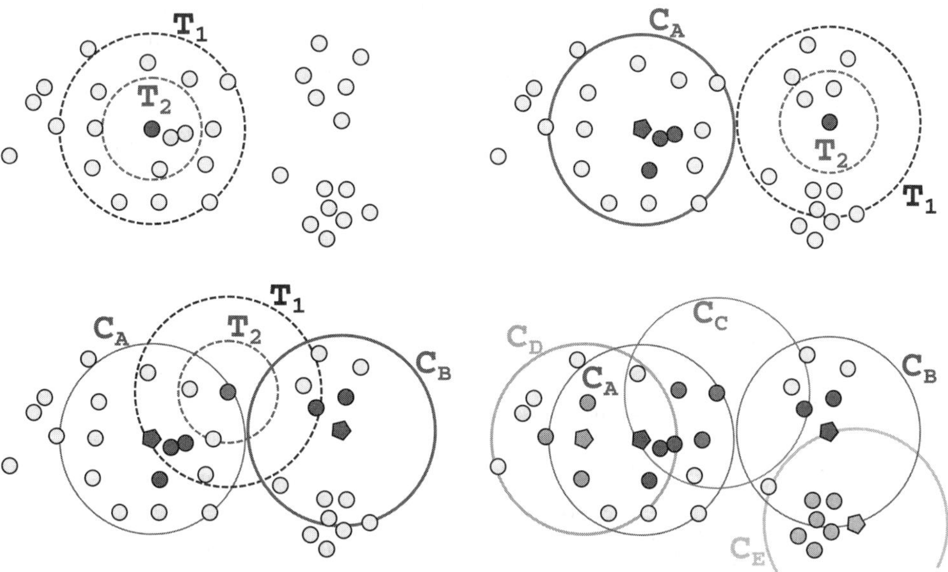
T1
T2
CA
T1
T2
T1
CA
T2
CB
CC
CD
CA
CB
CE

Figure 13.2 An example of canopy clustering running on a dataset. The first three sub-figures show the creation of tree canopies, starting from randomly chosen points. Circles filled with a solid color other than the lightest shading are points removed from the list of possible centroids, while pentagons are the centroids of canopies. The solid-color points are removed from the list because they lie within the inner radius (T_2) from the centroids (as shown in the first three steps). The last sub-figure shows the clusters created after a few more steps. Note that there are still some lightly shaded points, so at least three more canopies (that will partially overlap the five shown) will be created to include those points.

At a high level, the algorithm can be described by a few simple steps:

1. Select and remove a random point `p` from the dataset and initialize a new canopy with it (lines #6–7).
2. For each remaining point `q`, check if the distance between `p` and `q` is smaller than a threshold T_1 (lines #8–10); if it is, add `q` to current canopy (line #11).
3. If said distance is also smaller than a second threshold T_2, remove `q` from the list of possible canopy centroids (lines #12–13) so it won't be the center of a new canopy.
4. Repeat steps 1–3 until no point is left (line #5).

This process produces spherical agglomerates with radius (at most) T_1; the inner radius T_2 identifies the critical distance within which points can be confidently considered to be related to each other (or equivalently, in same cluster). While a point `q` (at steps 2–3) could have already been added to a different canopy, if it's within the inner radius of current canopy's centroid `c`, we are confident the pair `(q, c)`, is maximally correlated, and even if we chose `q` as a centroid, we couldn't form a canopy that better fits `q`.

If you are wondering why we can rely on these distances and how we can come up with a good value for T_2 (and T_1), you are on top of the main issue: these parameters usually need to be tuned (trying a few different ones and checking the number/quality of the canopies), and sometimes good initial estimates for these distances come from experience and domain knowledge. For instance, if you were clustering geographical data about cellphone cells and you knew that no two cells are further away than a few kilometers, you would have a hint about T_1.

Deciding these values is not as big deal as it may seem; it is not important to come up with the best possible value, but rather to find an acceptable one for both parameters. As we mentioned, this algorithm only provides a coarse-grain clustering.

13.1.4 Applying canopy clustering

Canopy clustering is often used as a pre-processing step for k-means, but it can also be used for DBSCAN and OPTICS. As a matter of fact, for those algorithms it has one further advantage. But we'll get to that in a moment. First, let's talk about how to combine canopy clustering and k-means.

The easiest way is quite intuitive. We can take the coarse-grained clusters (with overlap) output by canopy clustering, and for each of them compute their center of mass. Because these clusters can overlap each other, some points will belong to more than one of them; therefore, we can't just treat these canopies as the result of an iteration of k-means! However, we can use their centroids to bootstrap k-means, replacing the default (random) initialization step with a more balanced choice.

Alternatively, we could run canopy clustering with coarse values of T_1 and T_2, and improve the initialization step by making sure to draw a fraction of the initial centroids from each of these areas. If the canopy clustering returned `m<=k` pseudo-clusters, draw `k/m` centroids from each of them. In practical experiments, this bootstrapping provided a relevant speed-up in convergence for k-means.

If you remember what we discussed in chapter 12, DBSCAN (section 12.3) has a weak spot when applied to datasets with non-uniform density, and OPTICS (section 12.4) can partially remedy this issue, at the cost of a heavier computational load and some experimenting with its parameters. Ideally, what we would need is to run DBSCAN independently on areas with different density and tune its parameters (or just the value for ϵ) for each of these areas separately.

Using canopy clustering as a first step can help us with this issue. If we run DBSCAN on each pseudo-cluster separately, we can expect smaller regions to have a more uniform density, and regions with different density to be—likely—assigned to different pre-clusters.

After computing all the clusters for these areas, however, we still aren't done. Because the pseudo-clusters were (possibly) overlapping, the local clusters might also overlap. Besides checking to see if we should merge clusters that overlap, there is a more subtle effect: as shown in figure 13.3, two non-overlapping clusters could have points that are in each other's ϵ-neighborhood! So, we need to also check those pseudo-clusters whose hyperspheres are closer to each other than the larger of the values of ϵ used for those areas (in case DBSCAN was called on them with different values for its hyper-parameters).

The good news is that for such canopies, we don't have to check every combination of points drawn from their Cartesian product,[5] but only the points in the external ring of each of them, at a distance from the canopy's center greater or equal to $T_2-\epsilon$.

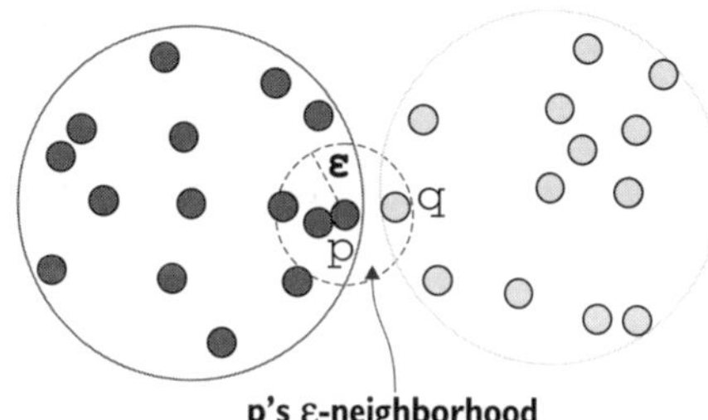
ε
p
q
p's ε-neighborhood

Figure 13.3 Non-overlapping canopy pseudo-clusters could still be considered as belonging to the same cluster by DBSCAN, if both have points close to their border, and the closest points are within each other's ϵ-distance.

Now the issue is that we can parallelize the execution of DBSCAN on each pseudo-cluster, but to put together all the results, we need to check all the pairs of clusters produced by each parallel run, and all the (filtered) pairs of points in the Cartesian product between the external rings of these clusters. Do we need to run these checks in a single thread on a single machine, hence going back to sequential execution?

13.2 MapReduce

For a long time, engineers have struggled to efficiently parallelize execution of algorithms like DBSCAN, at least from a practical point of view, because of both hardware limits and lack of software infrastructure. The most used distributed programming model was GRID computing, until it was realized that a different approach would make computation not just faster, but potentially more robust. That's when the MapReduce programming model was adopted on a large scale, after being patented and used by Google in the early 2000s.

Although there are several implementations of MapReduce, (or we should say there are several products leveraging MapReduce to provide tools that orchestrate distributed resources to solve tasks, such as Apache Hadoop, Hive, or CloudDB), I believe its main value is in the model it provides, which can be applied to a plethora of tasks.

For this reason, we'll try to explain how it works through an example.

13.2.1 Imagine you are Donald Duck . . .

Imagine Donald Duck dozing on his hammock—as always—on a lazy afternoon, when suddenly a phone ringing louder than normal (and more annoyingly than normal!) wakes him up. He knows before even answering that he is being gently summoned by his lovely uncle Scrooge McDuck, and he needs to rush to the Money Bin—a kind request to which he gladly responds, in order to avoid being disowned (and overwhelmed by debt).

Long story short: as always, his good old Uncle Scrooge has a long, boring task for Donald to attend to. This time, since he is securing the Money Bin main room and has to move all the coins to a different, giant, safe, he wants to take advantage of the situa-

---

[5] The Cartesian Product between two sets is the multiplication of the two sets to form a new set, containing all the ordered pairs such that the first element belongs to the first set and the second element belongs to the second set.

tion (surprise, surprise!) and count and catalog all the coins in his Money Bin . . . by the next morning.

We are talking about millions of coins, so it would be humanly impossible to do this on one's own. When Donald Duck regains his senses (he understandably fainted when Uncle Scrooge broke the news), he figures out that he'll need all the help he can get, so he runs to Gyro Gearloose's and convinces him to create a hoard of robo-clones that will be able to learn how to recognize different coins and catalog them.

This step is the "classical" parallelization step: you break the work down (into piles of coins) to several copies of your software (the counting/catalogue routine), and write down, for each pile, what coins you found and how many of them there are. For instance, a machine could produce a list like this:

```
£1: 1034 pieces
50¢: 53982 pieces
20p: 679 pieces
$1: 11823 pieces
1¢: 321 pieces
```

So, problem solved? Well . . . not really. Robo-clones are expensive and take time to build, so even a genius like Gyro could only provide a hundred of them by quickly rewiring some not-so-well-behaved robo-waiters he created in one of his experiments. Now they became quite fast at counting money, but each of them has a huge pile of coins, resulting in a long list of coin types with their quantities. Figure 13.4 illustrates the situation: once they're finished, it's up to Donald to add up the hundreds of entries in all those hundreds of lists.

After fainting again and being woken up using Uncle Scrooge's ammonia (he'll be charged for it, it goes without saying), good old Donald crawls to Gyro's lab with a desperate cry for more help.

Unfortunately, Gyro can't afford to build more counting machines! But he wouldn't be a genius if he couldn't solve this problem.

And to do so, he won't have to build anything; just getting some help and using a different algorithm will do. After doing a quick computation in his head, he estimates that there are about two hundred different types of coins. So he rounds up the whole family and gives a task to each of them: they will have to handle five types of coins each, but they won't have to count them. They will receive a few lists (well, a hundred of them) from the counting machines, but each list will only have five entries for the same five types of coins, together with how many of them the individual counting machine found.

To achieve this, he provides each counting machine with an address to locate each member of the McDuck family—for instance, an email address such as `huey.mcduck@duckmail.com`—and a dictionary that is the same for each machine and that lists the types of coins handled by each member of the family. To simplify things, we can imagine that each member is assigned all the coins from a single country. For instance, as shown in figure 13.5, Huey could get all US dollars, Dewey all UK sterling pounds, Louie all Euros, and so on. But in a real application, each of them could get any combination of coin denominations.

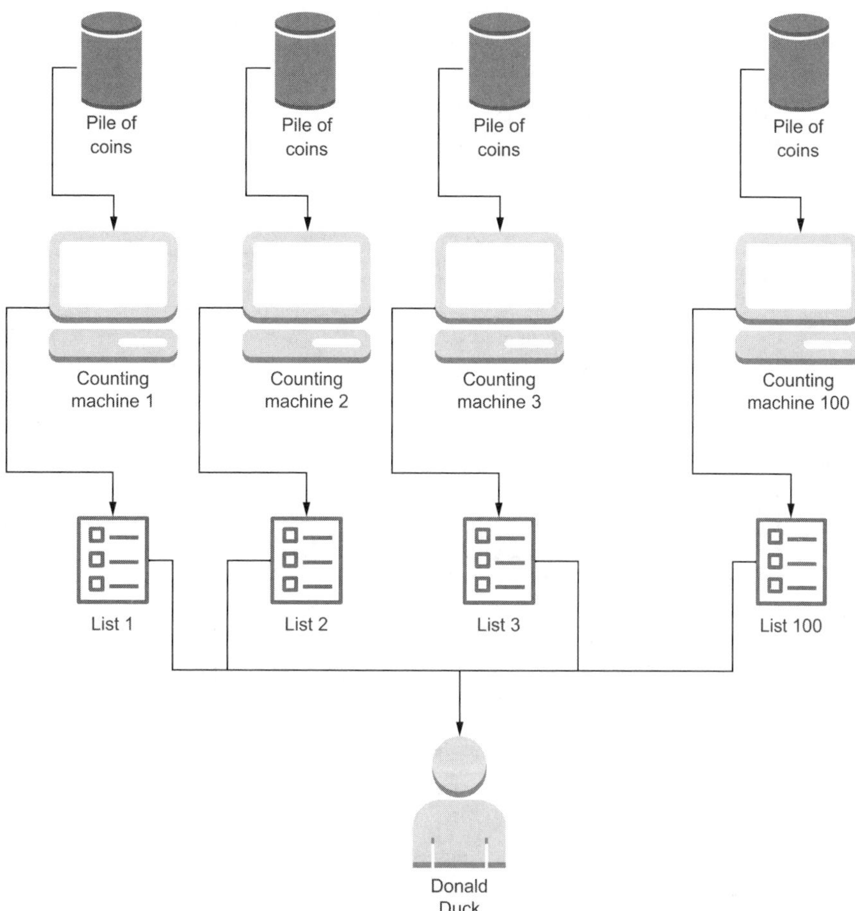
Pile of coins
Pile of coins
Pile of coins
Pile of coins
Counting machine 1
Counting machine 2
Counting machine 3
Counting machine 100
List 1
List 2
List 3
List 100
Donald Duck

Figure 13.4 A first attempt to parallelize coin counting. In this configuration, poor Donald still has to sum hundreds of lists with hundreds of entries each.

Once a machine is done counting, it goes through the members of the family and sends them each an email with the total number of coins found for each of the types they are responsible for. Then each family member will have to sum the values in each list, for each type of coin, and send the final result to Uncle Scrooge—just a few hundred integer additions per duck; a tedious job, maybe, but one that shouldn't take too long (just make sure not to let Fethry anywhere near a computer!).

For instance, if Daisy Duck is assigned the $1, 50¢, 25¢, and 1¢ coins, then all the machines will send her a short list that looks like this:

```
25¢: 1.034 pieces
$1: 11823 pieces
50¢: 53982 pieces
1¢: 321 pieces
```

Figure 13.5 shows the shift in paradigm. While before the person who had to make sense of all the lists was the bottleneck of the computation, now, introducing a new

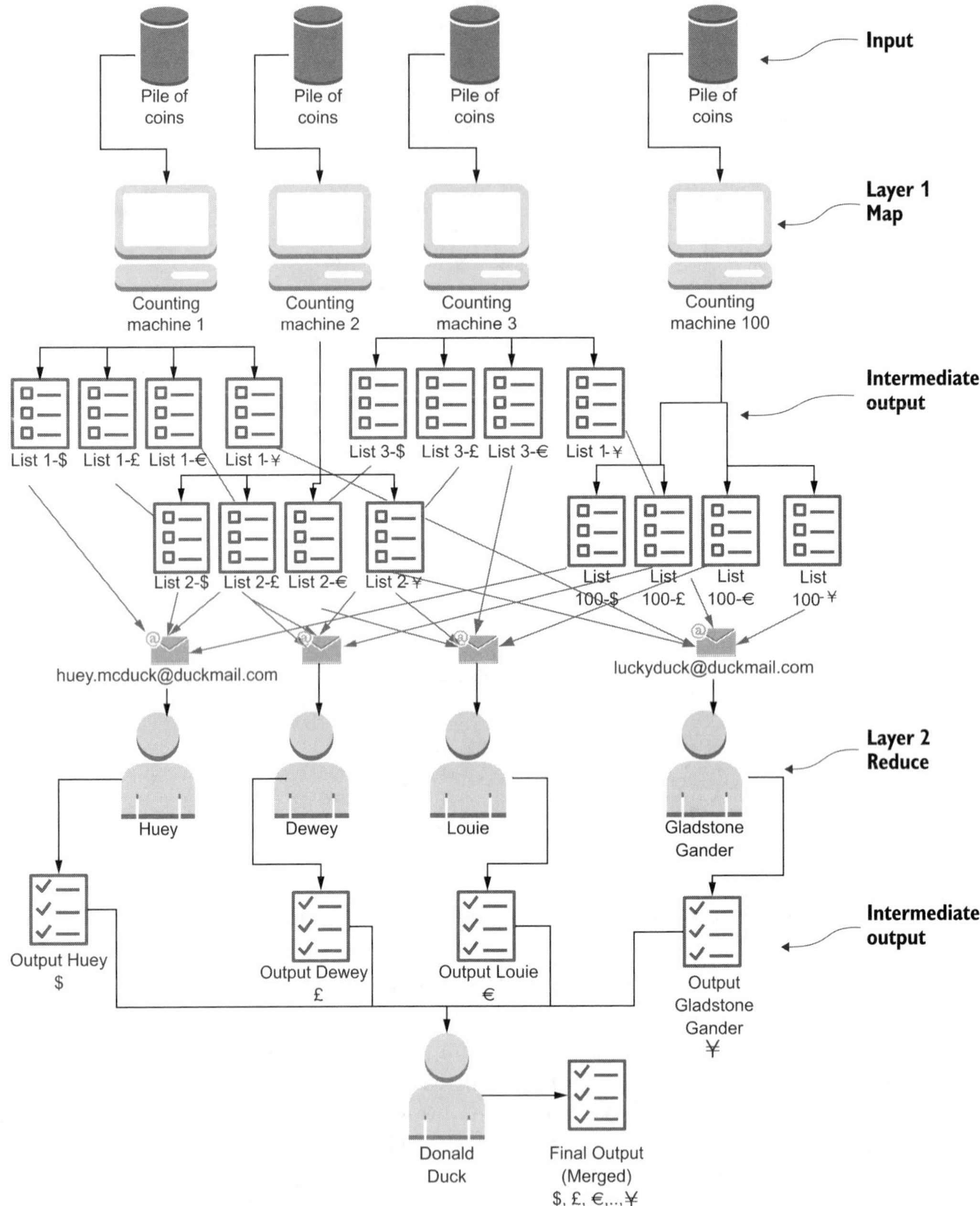
Input
Pile of coins
Pile of coins
Pile of coins
Pile of coins
Layer 1
Map
Counting machine 1
Counting machine 2
Counting machine 3
Counting machine 100
Intermediate output
List 1-$
List 1-£
List 1-€
List 1-¥
List 3-$
List 3-£
List 3-€
List 1-¥
List 2-$
List 2-£
List 2-€
List 2-¥
List 100-$
List 100-£
List 100-€
List 100-¥
huey.mcduck@duckmail.com
luckyduck@duckmail.com
Layer 2
Reduce
Huey
Dewey
Louie
Gladstone Gander
Intermediate output
Output Huey $
Output Dewey £
Output Louie €
Output Gladstone Gander ¥
Donald Duck
Final Output (Merged) $, £, €,..,¥

Figure 13.5 Revised coin counting process, using MapReduce and a little help. Now, each counting machine produces several lists, one for each member of the McDuck family at level 2. They, in turn, will have to check a hundred lists, but each with just a few entries, and sum up the values in each list by entry.

intermediate level in the workflow, and breaking down the work so that each entity at this level has a limited amount of work to do makes the difference.

The key, though, is that the results outputted at level 1 can be partitioned in groups and each of these groups can then be handled separately at level 2.

13.2.2 First map, then reduce

Time to abandon our cartoon heroes for a more life-like example, where both levels of this parallel computation would be performed by machines. The operation at level 1 is called *Map*, because it *maps* each entry in the input dataset (more precisely, in the portion of the dataset handled by a machine) into something else, extracting the information that's relevant for computing the final result. The mappers in our example could likely just run a "coin-recognition" software, without keeping a count,[6] and send lists containing unsorted occurrences of coins to the machines at level 2. Something like this:

```
$100: 1
50¢: 1
$100: 1
$1: 1
25¢: 1
...
```

Here, the info extracted by mappers is just the presence of a coin.

Then the machines at level 2 would specialize in counting. Every machine at level 2 would receive all the entries for occurrences of a certain group of coins, and do something with them (counting them, for example, but it could also sum up their values or filter them). This step is therefore called *Reduce*, because it takes info limited to a homogeneous group of entries and combines (aka *reduces*) them to get our final result.

As mentioned, the key disadvantage of the classic, "flat" parallel computation is that composing the results of all the parallel threads/processes/machines would be the bottleneck of the whole process. If a single process has to spawn the threads and then get their results and combine them, it will still have to sequentially access the entire dataset at least once, and even if it also parallelizes the process that combines the intermediate results, it still remains a bottleneck, as shown in figure 13.6. On the left half, you can see that for basic parallelism, the "intermediate output" is all sent to the orchestrator that has to gather it and sort it to the machines in layer 2.

In MapReduce, however, every step is intrinsically parallel. Data is already broken down into pieces that can be processed independently and results are routed to the reducers by each mapper on its own, without passing through a central orchestrator.

[6] Typically a per-key count on mappers' output would be done by a third abstraction, the combiners, that are sort of like mini-reducers operating on the same machines as mappers, and only on the output of individual mappers. Instead of a list with a ton of entries with value 1, the mapper would send out a list with just a few entries, reducing both bandwidth and the workload for reducers.

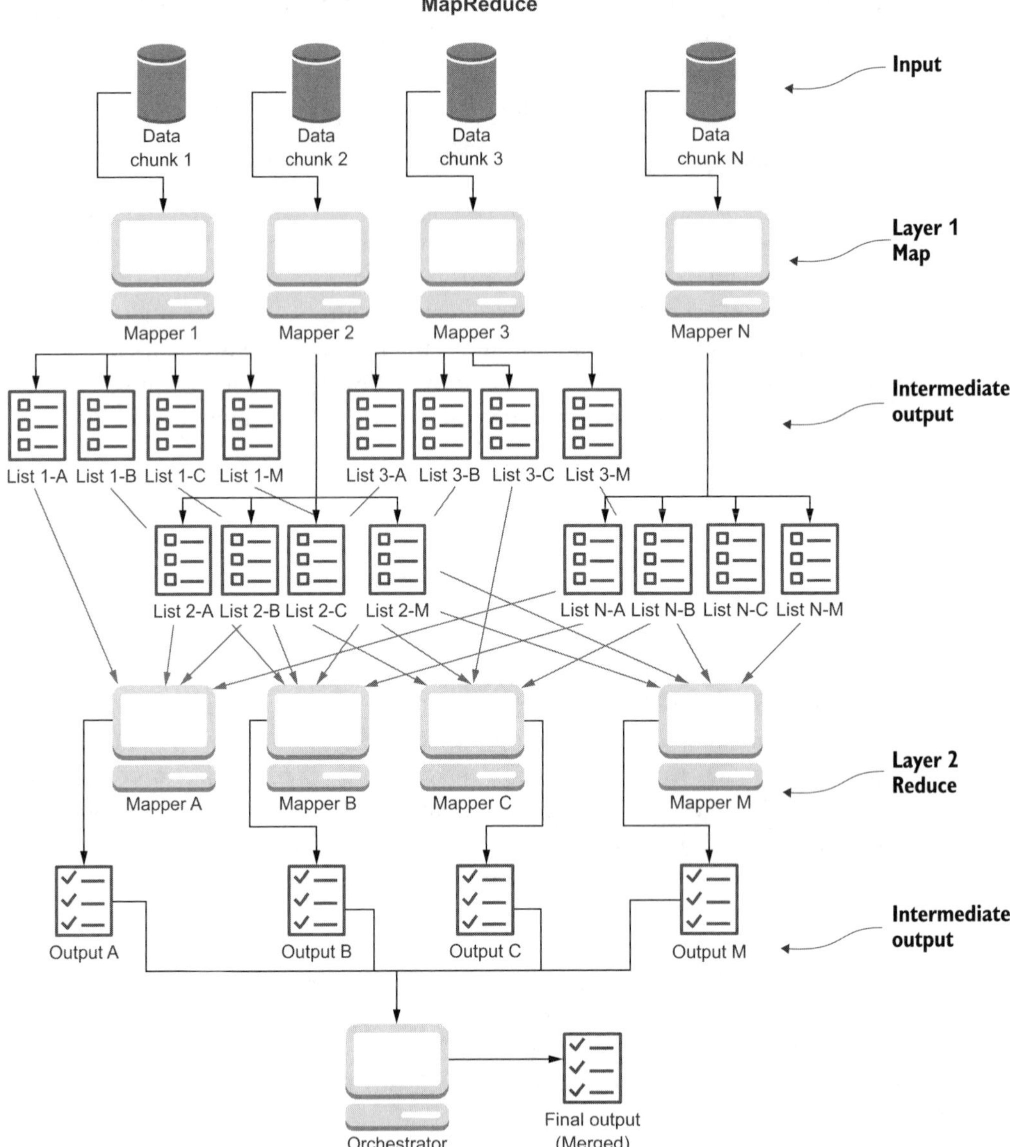
MapReduce
Input
Data chunk 1
Data chunk 2
Data chunk 3
Data chunk N
Layer 1 Map
Mapper 1
Mapper 2
Mapper 3
Mapper N
Intermediate output
List 1-A List 1-B List 1-C List 1-M
List 3-A List 3-B List 3-C List 3-M
List 2-A List 2-B List 2-C List 2-M
List N-A List N-B List N-C List N-M
Layer 2 Reduce
Mapper A
Mapper B
Mapper C
Mapper M
Intermediate output
Output A
Output B
Output C
Output M
Orchestrator
Final output (Merged)

Figure 13.6A Comparing the classical approach to parallel computing to MapReduce. We assume that in both cases, data is already broken down into chunks and can be passed by location, that is, by providing something like a file handle without the need for the orchestrator to read the data. In the basic parallel approach, using processes (either running on threads or on different machines), the orchestrator needs to spin up the threads and make sense of their results. It can either combine these results itself, or spawn more processes to combine them (as shown in the figure), but it will be the bottleneck either way.

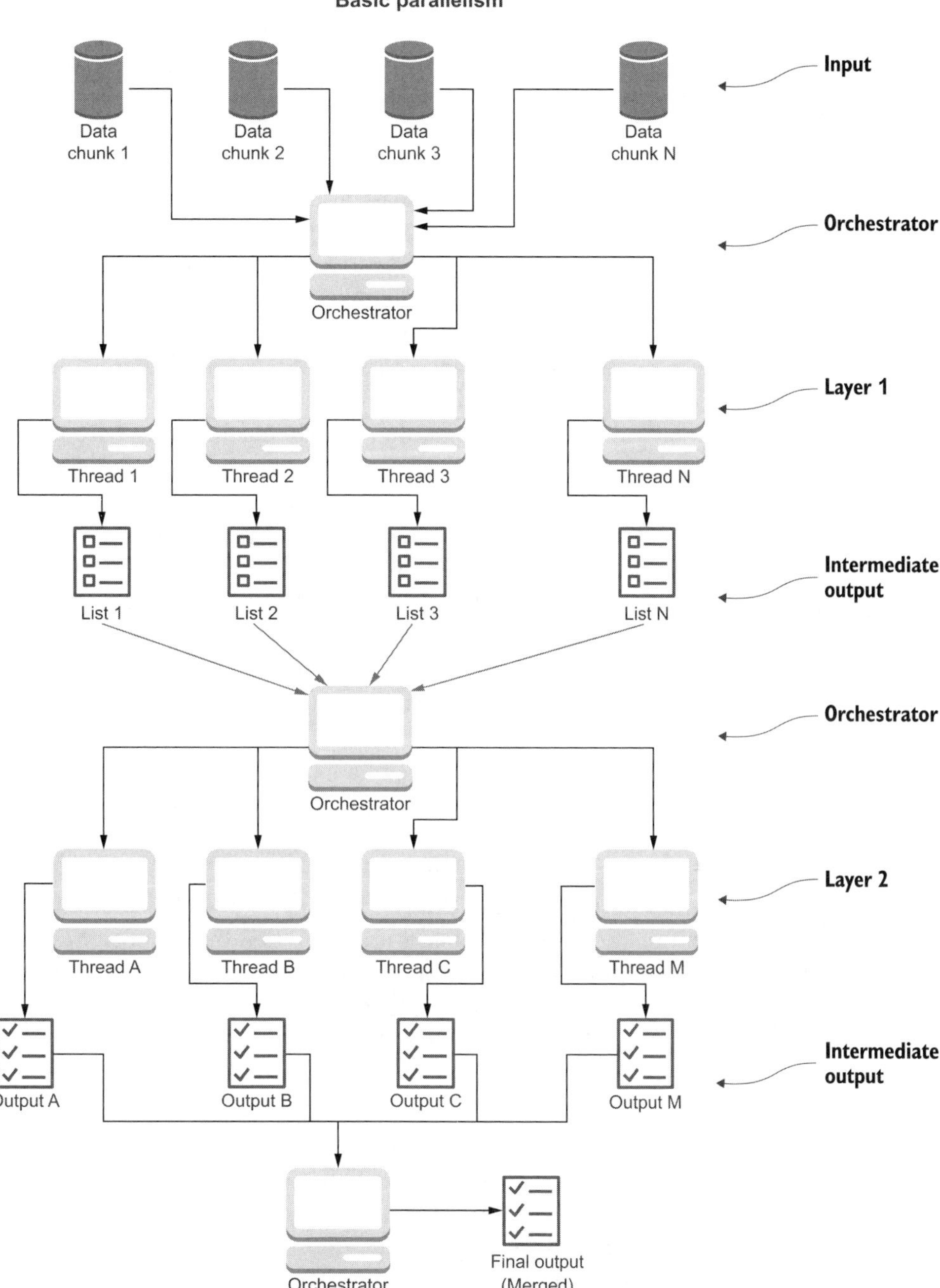
Basic parallelism
Data chunk 1
Data chunk 2
Data chunk 3
Data chunk N
Input
Orchestrator
Orchestrator
Thread 1
Thread 2
Thread 3
Thread N
Layer 1
List 1
List 2
List 3
List N
Intermediate output
Orchestrator
Orchestrator
Thread A
Thread B
Thread C
Thread M
Layer 2
Output A
Output B
Output C
Output M
Intermediate output
Orchestrator
Final output (Merged)

Figure 13.6B Continues from figure 13.6A

Technically, the reducers are the ones that read the information from each mapper, while the mappers' task is to create temporary files for each reducer in a specific location (different for each reducer—imagine, for instance, that each mapper creates a different folder or a dedicated virtual disk for each reducer).

Besides speed, the MapReduce approach has another advantage: if a machine crashes, that single machine can be replaced without having to restart the whole computation. This, in turn, can help us increase availability and reduce latency by allocating redundant resources to preventively cope with malfunctions.

One thing needs to be clear. In MapReduce there is also an orchestrator, a leader node that controls the computation (spinning up the computational nodes, or requesting existing resources, assigning the input chunks to the mappers, planning how to route intermediate results to reducers, and handling/recovering from errors). The difference from canonical parallelism, though, is that this special node doesn't actually read the input or compute it, and that intermediate results don't have to pass through it, so it's not a bottleneck for computation. An objection could be that the primary node is still a bottleneck for availability, because if the leader node crashes, the computation can't be completed; however, using replicas (either live copies or primary-replica), we could get availability guarantees through (limited) redundancy.

There are catches, of course. The first one is that not all computations are suitable for the MapReduce model (or for parallel execution altogether). In general, if data entries are somehow connected, and scattered pieces of data influence each other's contribution to the final result, then parallelization could be impossible: time series are a good example of data that normally needs to be processed sequentially, because the final result depends on the sequence of adjacent data.

For MapReduce, requirements are even higher. In order to gain an advantage from applying it, we need data that can be grouped by some attributes/fields, and that can be reduced for each of these groups separately.

The operation performed in reducers, moreover, must be associative, so that the order in which the intermediate sub-lists are outputted by mappers must not matter.

It's worth noting that if, instead of cataloging all the coins, we would like to just count how many of them there are (without distinguishing their type) or compute the total value, we wouldn't need reducers. Each parallel process would just output its total, and then they could be added by a single central process.

The second catch is that there is no centralized entity that splits the work and distributes it evenly to the reducers, so one can get very busy while another waits without anything to do. Going back to our story, for instance, while Daisy Duck will have to worry about US currency, Gladstone Gander is assigned all rare coins from small countries (lucky him), and thus the lists he gets are almost all empty, and he has to perform just a few additions.

13.2.3 There is more under the hood

We have seen a few advantages of the MapReduce model, but there is also more to its success that can't be seen at a high level. In chapter 7, when talking about caches and multi-threading, we discussed locks and synchronization. Every parallel computation with a shared state will need synchronization, be it to aggregate results, break down data, and assign it to computing units (threads or machines), or just check that the processing is complete.

The key advantage of MapReduce is that it intrinsically limits shared state to a minimum (by embracing functional programming concepts such as immutability[7] and pure functions[8]), providing a programming paradigm, a way to specify the problem, that forces us to state a problem in such a way so as to eliminate shared state[9] and handle the synchronization still needed under the hood.

13.3 MapReduce k-means

To efficiently parallelize any algorithm, we first need to answer two questions: How do datapoints influence computation, and what data do we really need at any time to perform a certain step?

In the case of both k-means and canopy clustering, the way we compute the various steps dictates a MapReduce implementation. Let's examine each step of k-means separately:[10]

- In the *classification step*, when we assign points to canopies/clusters, for each point the operation is computed independently, and the only thing that matters is the list of centroids. So, we can shard the data however we like, as long as we pass all the centroids to each mapper.
- In the *re-centering* step, to update k-means' centroids, for each centroid we only need the data assigned to it, and each point is assigned to a single centroid, so we can partition the dataset and process each group separately.
- *Initialization* is trickier for k-means; we would need to draw points randomly from the full dataset, and this would seem to hinder parallelization. We can, however, employ a few possible strategies to distribute the computational load:
  - Randomly shard the dataset and then independently draw centroids at random from each shard (although it can be tricky to obtain an overall uniform distribution of samples).
  - Run canopy clustering first and feed those canopy centroids to k-means as the initial choice of centroids. Then the question becomes, can we also distribute canopy clustering? Although a little trickier, it turns out that we can do that.

---

[7] Methods of an immutable data structure, rather than changing the object `A` on which they are called, create a new object `B` whose state is the result of applying the called method to `A`. For instance, the method that appends an element to a list `L1` would create a brand-new list `L2` with `|L1| + 1` elements and leave `L1` unchanged.

[8] A pure function is any function that doesn't have a side effect: it takes 0, 1, or more inputs, and returns an output (possibly in the form of a tuple), without relying on any change to the input or to the global state. In a sense, a pure function is exactly like a mathematical function.

[9] That's also the reason why, as discussed in the previous sub-sections, it can't be applied to all those problems that cannot be formulated in a way that eliminates shared state.

[10] Notice that here we will list k-means steps from the easiest to the hardest to parallelize.

It follows that parallelizing canopy clustering is the key step here, and also the trickiest part. We'll worry about it later in this chapter. Before delving into this step, let's give a high-level description of the full algorithm for distributed k-means:

- Initialize the centroids using canopy clustering.
- Iterate (at most `m` times).
  - Points classification:
    - Shard the dataset and send the shards, together with the list of centroids, to mappers.
    - Each mapper assigns points to one of the centroids. Send the data to the reducers, aggregated by the centroid chosen (ideally there will be one reducer per centroid).
  - Centroids update:
    - Each reducer will compute the center of mass of its cluster and return the new centroid.

This is also summarized[11] in listing 13.2 and shown in the example in figure 13.7.

Listing 13.2 MapReduce k-means

```
function MRkmeans(points, numShards, numClusters, maxIter, T1, T2)
  shards ← randomShard(points, numShards)
  centroids ← MRcanopyCentroids(points, numClusters, T1, T2)
  mappers ← initMappers(numShards, classifyPoints, shards)
  reducers ← initReducers(numClusters, centerOfMass)
  for i in {0, .., maxIter-1} do
    newCentroids ← mapReduce(centroids, mappers, reducers)
```

Annotations:

- Method `MRkmeans` takes a list of points, the number of desired chunks in which the dataset should be sharded, the number of desired clusters, and two thresholds, `T1` and `T2`, to be used for the canopy clustering initialization step.
- Breaks down the dataset into `numShards` random shards. This is usually done automatically by the primary node of MapReduce, but in this case, we will use a customized version.
- Initializes the centroids by using a distributed version of canopy clustering
- Initializes `numShards` mappers; each will run the `classifyPoints` method and will hold a copy of one of the dataset's shards. The mappers will be alive (and hold the same copy of the input) for the whole lifetime of this method.
- Initializes `numClusters` reducers, one per centroid. The reducers will run the `centerOfMass` method (computing the center of mass of a set of points) and will be alive for the whole method's lifetime, but they won't hold any data.
- Repeats the main cycle at most `maxIter` times
- Runs one iteration of MapReduce, using the mappers and reducers already created. Mappers will receive the current list of centroids as input (in addition, each mapper already holds one shard of the dataset points). Reducers will read their input (points in one of the clusters) from the mappers. Each reducer will output the coordinates of a centroid, and the results produced by all reducers will be combined in a list, assigned to a temporary variable.

[11] Keep in mind that this is not a real implementation, so we can take some shortcuts to try and explain the fundamental ideas more clearly. A Hadoop MapReduce job, for instance, would look different.

```
    if centroids == newCentroids then
      break
    else
      centroids ← newCentroids
  return combine(mappers, centroids)
```

If no centroid has changed, the algorithm converged so it can exit the main cycle

Otherwise, copies over the assignments from the temporary variable

Uses combiners or run mappers a last time to get the final classification of points, given current centroids

The first thing you should know is that we are not talking about good old plain MapReduce in this case. The base model of computation is MapReduce, but since the k-means heuristic consists of repeating some steps `m` times, we will need to start the computation several times. This is illustrated by the workflow in figure 13.7: the output of each MapReduce job, a list of centroids, is also the input of the next job, and moreover sharding the dataset and distributing it to the mappers is a step that doesn't need to be repeated for each job, because there is no reason why the shard assigned to a mapper should change.

For these reasons, rather than running `m` times MapReduce separately, we can use a more efficient (in this context) evolution of this programming model, *Iterative MapReduce*.[12]

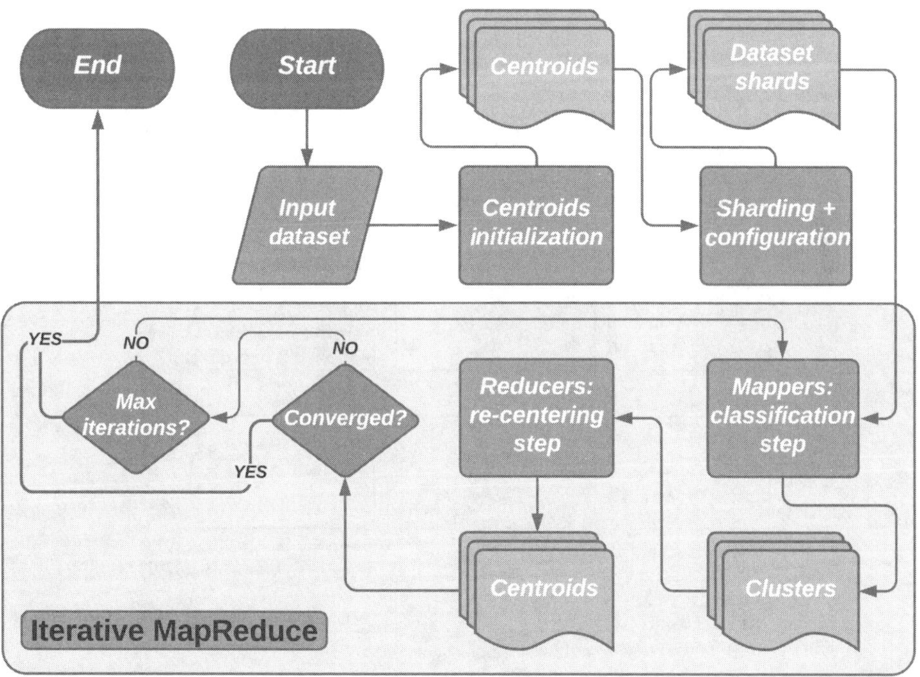
End
Start
Centroids
Dataset shards
Input dataset
Centroids initialization
Sharding + configuration
YES
NO
NO
Max iterations?
Converged?
YES
Reducers: re-centering step
Mappers: classification step
Centroids
Clusters
Iterative MapReduce

Figure 13.7 A flowchart describing the workflow of k-means, implemented with iterative MapReduce

[12] A good starting point to delve into Iterative MapReduce is http://mng.bz/8NG5.

The idea is that we spin up mappers and reducers once, sharding data during the configuration of the mappers and assigning point shards to each mapper only once. Then we iterate the classic MapReduce cycle until needed, passing only the current list of centroids as input to all the mappers. Thus, the amount of data per job to be passed to each mapper is going to be several orders of magnitude smaller than the dataset size, and ideally it will also be significantly smaller than the size of each shard. We can pass the number of mappers to create an argument to our enhanced k-means method, and tune this parameter based on the size of the dataset and the capacity of each mapper.

Figure 13.8 illustrates well how the computation proceeds from this point. Each mapper performs the classification step on the fraction of points assigned to it. Then reducers (ideally one per cluster) will read data from each mapper: the `i`-th reducer will only get the points assigned to the `i`-th centroid (or to the centroids assigned to the reducer, if more than one).

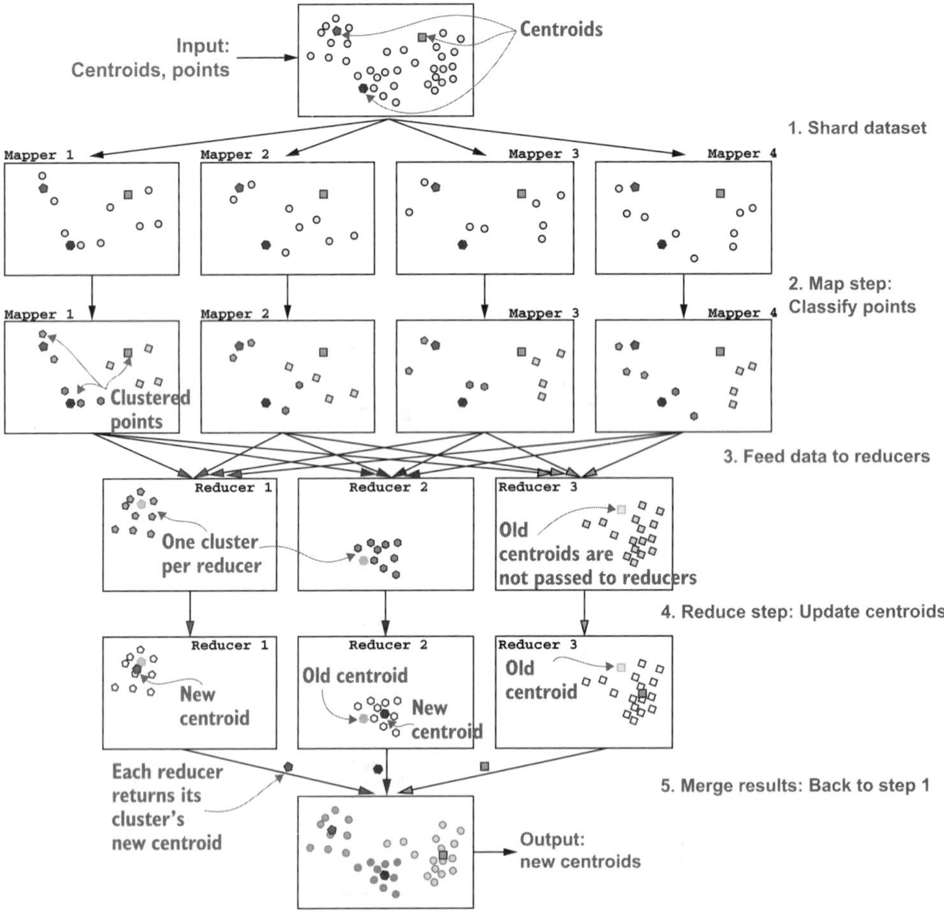
Input:
Centroids, points
Centroids
1. Shard dataset
Mapper 1
Mapper 2
Mapper 3
Mapper 4
2. Map step:
Classify points
Clustered
points
3. Feed data to reducers
Reducer 1
Reducer 2
Reducer 3
One cluster
per reducer
Old
centroids are
not passed to reducers
4. Reduce step: Update centroids
New
centroid
Old centroid
New
centroid
Old
centroid
5. Merge results: Back to step 1
Each reducer
returns its
cluster's
new centroid
Output:
new centroids

Figure 13.8 An iteration of k-means main cycle implemented with iterative MapReduce. With respect to figure 13.7, the first step shown here is the sharding + configuration, while the rest of the figure shows a single iteration of "Iterative MapReduce."

Notice how reducers don't get any information about current centroids (in the illustration, in fact, in the reducer steps old centroids are shown as semi-transparent polygons) because each reducer only needs all the points[13] that belong to a cluster, in order to compute its center of mass.

Each reducer eventually outputs the centroid computed (and just that; no points returned, to save bandwidth and ultimately time) and the MapReduce primary will combine the `k` results (where `k` is the number of centroids/reducers) into a single list, that will be fed again to the mappers in the next iteration of the cycle!

Once the cycle is over, we only get centroids as result. We can run the mappers one last time outside of the cycle to get the points assigned to each cluster (in this step, at line #12 of listing 13.2, we can imagine a new set of reducers will be used: dummy pass-through nodes, just returning their input).

This implementation of k-means only uses canopy clustering to bootstrap convergence with a better-than-random initial choice of centroids. Distributing the classification and re-centering steps is already a great improvement, and there is a good chance that the improvement you get is already enough to satisfy your requirements.

Still, even if canopy clustering is faster than an iteration of k-means and can be made even faster by using a cheap approximated metric instead of Euclidean distance, for huge datasets the risk is that you can waste most of the gain obtained by distributing the implementation of k-means through MapReduce if you run canopy clustering on a single machine. Moreover, sometimes this option isn't even available for huge datasets that won't fit on any machine.

Luckily for us, we can apply MapReduce to canopy clustering as well!

13.3.1 Parallelizing canopy clustering

Canopy clustering is a bit trickier to redesign as a distributed algorithm because it has only one step: drawing canopy centroids from the dataset and filtering out points within a certain distance from them so that they won't later be selected as centroids. The issue is that in this step, for each centroid drawn from the dataset, we need to go through the whole dataset for the filtering part. In theory, for each centroid we would just need to process those points in its canopy, but we can't identify them in advance!

To get to a good solution, it can be useful to think about the real goal for canopy clustering: we want to get a set of canopy centroids that are no closer to each other than some distance T_2. The key point is that between any two of these canopy's centers, the distance must be above a minimum value, so that the canopies won't overlap too much. As we mentioned, this distance is similar to the "core distance" in DBSCAN, and points within a radius T_2 can be assumed to belong to the same cluster with high probability.

[13]Technically, computing the mean of a set of values could also be distributed: a combiner would need to take as input the shards' centroids and the number of points in each shard to compute the overall center of mass.

Suppose we shard our initial dataset, as shown in the top step of figure 13.9. If we then apply canopy clustering to each shard independently, we'll get a certain number of centroids, probably different from mapper to mapper. If we recombine these centroids together, however, we have no guarantee that they will respect the requirement of being not closer than T_2 from each other, because centroids from different shards haven't been compared to each other.

It's not time to give up yet, though! Luckily, there is an easy solution to this issue, and the solution is still . . . canopy clustering!

In fact, if we gather all the centroids from each mapper together, we can apply the canopy clustering algorithm again to this new (smaller) dataset, refining the selection, and this time guaranteeing that no two points in the output from this second pass will be at a closer distance than T_2. Check the last row in figure 13.9 to get an idea of how this second pass works. The solution is also efficient because the size of the new data-

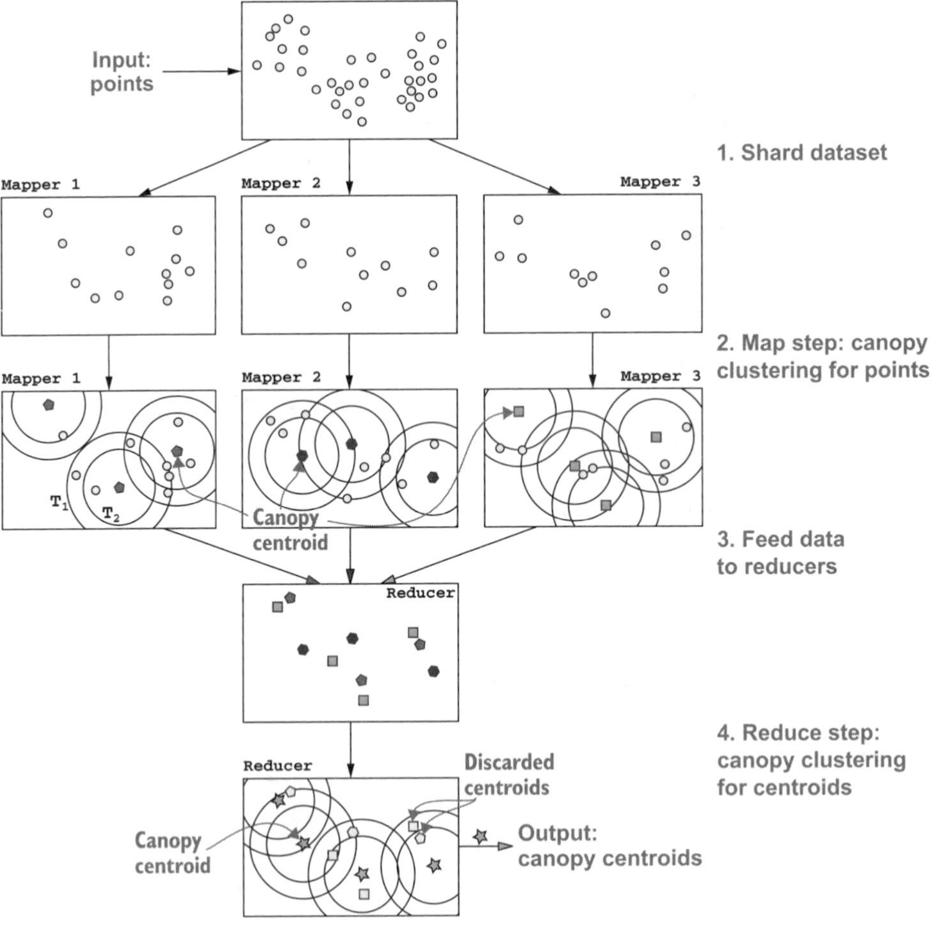
Input:
points
1. Shard dataset
Mapper 1
Mapper 2
Mapper 3
2. Map step: canopy
clustering for points
T1
T2
Canopy
centroid
3. Feed data
to reducers
Reducer
4. Reduce step:
canopy clustering
for centroids
Discarded
centroids
Canopy
centroid
Output:
canopy centroids

Figure 13.9 Canopy clustering implemented with MapReduce

set (containing only the centroids produced by the mappers) is orders of magnitude smaller than the original dataset (assuming the distances T_1 and T_2 have been chosen properly), and therefore in step 2 we can spin up a single reducer and run canopy clustering on a single machine and on all the centroids from step 1.

At this point, we need to make a consideration. When used as a preliminary step for k-means, the algorithm has a slightly different goal (and different output) than when used as a standalone coarse-grained clustering algorithm:

- To k-means, we only have to return a list of centroids.
- The standalone algorithm will also need to return, for each canopy, the points belonging to it.

Therefore, we need to treat these two cases separately.

13.3.2 Centroid initialization with canopy clustering

Let's start with canopy clustering as the initialization step for k-means. Listing 13.3 summarizes a possible implementation for the MR job performing this task. At first glance, we don't need to do anything other than what we have shown in the previous section: we just return the output of the reducer, the list of centroids.

But there is a catch (there always is!): How do we decide how many centroids should be returned by canopy clustering?

The answer is that we can't control it directly, but only through the values of the two distance thresholds passed to the algorithm, and only to some extent. In the end, the algorithm is a randomized heuristic and the number of canopies created can vary at each run, even with the same values for the hyper-parameters.

Listing 13.3 MapReduce canopy centroids generation

```
function MRcanopyCentroids(points, numCentroids, T1, T2, numShards)
  shards ← randomShard(points, numShards)
  mappers ← initMappers(numShards, canopyClustering, shards)
  reducers ← initReducers(1, canopyClustering)
  while true do
```

Annotations:

- Method `MRcanopyCentroids` takes a list of points, the number of desired centroids, and two thresholds, `T1` and `T2`, to be used for the canopy clustering initialization step. It also takes the number of shards.
- Breaks down the dataset into `numShards` random shards. This is usually done automatically by the primary node of MapReduce, but in this case, we will use a customized version.
- Initializes `numShards` mappers; each will run the `canopyClustering` method and will hold a copy of one of the dataset's shards. The mappers will be alive (and hold the same copy of the input) for the whole lifetime of this method.
- Initializes a single reducer that will run `canopyClustering` on the set of all centroids returned by all mappers. This node also will be alive for the whole method's lifetime, but it won't hold any data.
- Repeats until convergence (it might be a good idea to set a max number of iterations, and also save the closest result found)

```
  centroids ← mapReduce(T1, T2, mappers, reducers)
  if |centroids| == numCentroids then
    break
  elsif |centroids| > numCentroids then
    delta ← random(T2)
    T2 ← T2 + delta
    T1 ← T1 + delta
  else
    T2 ← T2 - random(T2)
return addRandomNoise(centroids)
```

We need to get fewer centroids, so we can try raising the threshold so canopies will be larger and each will hold more points in their inner perimeter. Since `T1` must be larger than `T2`, we need to increment that value as well to be sure. The random value added needs to be some function of `T2`, to be sure that the delta is meaningful.

Runs MapReduce, using the mappers and reducers already created. Mappers will receive the current values for the thresholds (in addition, each mapper already hold one shard of the dataset points). The single reducer will read their input (the canopy centroids selected for each shard) from the mappers and return a refined list of centroids.

If the number of centroids matches the desired result, breaks out of the cycle

Otherwise, checks if the algorithm returned more centroids than needed

If, instead, we need more centroids, we can try making the inner threshold smaller.

Returns the centroids after adding some random noise to them (as described in chapter 12, for k-means we might want to select centroids close to the dataset points, but not exactly the ones in the dataset)

So, we need to think outside the box to handle this. Because there is a strong random component that influences the result of each run, we can run canopy clustering several times and take the result that is closer to our expectation. This might not be enough, though, because the variance between different runs is limited, and if we start with the "wrong" values for the thresholds, the algorithm could always output too many (or too few) centroids.

To solve this issue, we have two options: either manually tuning these thresholds after each run, or, alternatively, performing some kind of search in the domain of the thresholds, trying different values for them, either by adding at each run a random value to our initial choice for T_1 and T_2, or by tuning the thresholds depending on the number of canopies returned (lowering T_2 when too few centroids are selected in the last run, and raising it when we get too many). If we'd like to get really fancy, we can even use ML to find the best values.

While the former idea is a brute-force, fully randomized search, a better targeted solution seems more promising, because we could direct the search toward values that should work better for our goal. We can use the same idea behind *gradient descent*,[14] although with a simpler algorithm that just decides the direction of the update, without worrying about slopes and gradients. For instance, we could run a cycle where we adjust the value for the inner threshold (and, when needed, also the one for the outer

[14]Gradient descent is an optimization algorithm for finding local minimums of a function `F`. It explores the function's domain in a systematic way, taking steps proportional to the gradient of `F` at current point `X`, which (simplifying) can be geometrically interpreted as the direction of greatest change for `F` at `X`.

threshold) depending on the difference between the result we get from canopy clustering and the number of centroids we need.

Considering the random factor in this algorithm, however, this is clearly still a naïve search over the possible values of T_2, and it could possibly lead to an infinite loop. To correct this situation, we could add a stop condition (and an argument) checking that a maximum number of iterations is not exceeded. At the same time, we could also store the result that is closest to our request in a temporary variable that we update at each run, and return this result whenever the maximum number of iterations is reached without finding a set of canopies with exactly `numCentroids` entries. Most of the time it can be acceptable if we return, for instance, 101 centroids instead of 100 (the point being, the caller will have the chance to check the result and decide).

We leave it to the readers, as an exercise, to extend listing 13.3 in order to handle the thresholds choice automatically, and we'll instead move on to describe the distributed version of the full canopy clustering distributed algorithm, the one returning not only the canopy centroids, but also the overlapping sets of points that are associated with each canopy.

13.3.3 MapReduce canopy clustering

The *classification* step, assigning each point to one or more canopies, can be implemented in a few different ways:

- As a follow-up of the method described in listing 13.3. However, because classification will involve all points, if we don't distribute this step, we will lose most of the advantage of running the algorithm to choose centroids in parallel.
- In the same method as centroids initialization, but with a different MapReduce job.
- In the same MapReduce job we described in the previous section, with the reducer that is in charge of also performing classification at the same time that it chooses which centroids should be kept. In particular, the reducer would get from mappers all the lists of points assigned to each centroid, so rather than cycling through all dataset points again, it could reuse these lists (we'll see later in this section how it will need to combine them).

The first option is rather easier, but naïve. Implementing the classification step at least in the same method as the choice of centroids gives us two main advantages:

- We can, in theory, reuse the same mappers, which already hold onto their shards of data, by just passing them the list of canopy centroids.
- When we perform classification, there is an issue with the centroids filtering we perform in the reducers. So far, we have been able to ignore it, but running centroid filtering and classification together allows us to solve this issue efficiently.

Figure 13.10 shows what might happen when we filter out one or more centroids during the reduce step in our previous algorithm. We haven't mentioned this issue until now because it only affects the algorithm when we assign points to canopies, while it is irrelevant when we only care about centroids, as in the k-means initialization steps.

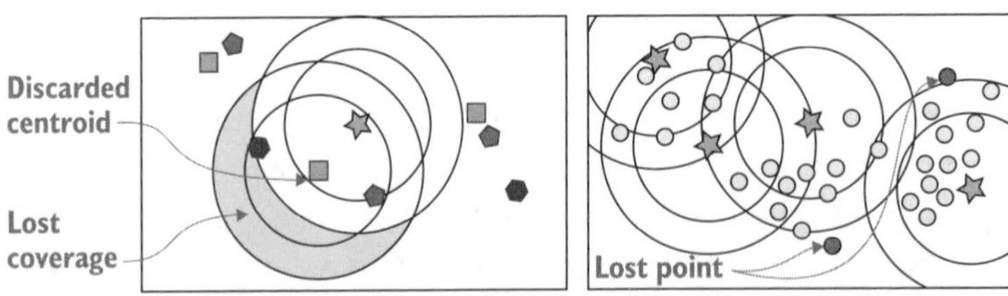
Discarded centroid
Lost coverage
Lost point

Figure 13.10 How filtering out centroids in the reducer step of MapReduce canopy clustering influences the dataset coverage by canopies. (Left) When a centroid C is discarded because it is too close to one that has been chosen, part of the area covered by C's canopy becomes uncovered. (Right) This can result in some points lying outside of any canopy.

The problem is that when we filter out any one of the centroids selected during the map step, a fraction of the points in its canopy might not be covered anymore, not even by the centroid that was chosen in its place. See the left side of figure 13.10, where the centroid marked as a star is drawn from the list of centroids, and as a result, the other centroid within the inner radius T_2 from the selected one is filtered out; however, the shaded area (highlighted by shading) is not covered by the canopy centered at the other centroid (the star).

While sometimes the lost coverage is made up for by other canopies, this isn't always the case: the right side of the same figure shows an example where a few points remain uncovered after a specific choice of centroids to keep.

There are several options for solving this issue:

- Consider the "lost" points as outliers (this is not really reliable, though, because they might lie in the middle of some big cluster that can't be covered by a single canopy).
- Enlarge canopies: the discarded centroids can be appropriately marked during a run of canopy clustering every time one of the centroids is chosen. During this phase, it is possible to keep track of the outer radius associated with each canopy, and make it large enough to cover all points in the canopy of the removed point. The cheapest way to do so is to set the radius of all canopies to T_1+T_2, but this would obviously be increasing the overlapping between canopies.
- Go through unassigned points (those that are not within a distance T_1 from any of the survived centroids) at the end of the classification step and assign them to the closest centroid. This solution will limit to the minimum the overlapping of canopies (each canopy's radius will be at most T_1+T_2, but as small as the distance to the furthest of these new points), but it will be more costly.
- If we perform classification in the same MapReduce job as the choice of centroids, we can find an efficient solution. Mappers will also have to produce a list with the sets of points associated to each centroid and pass these sets to the reducer along with the list of centroids for each shard. In the reducer, an ad hoc variant of canopy clustering is run, and when a centroid c is drawn, the sets assigned to all centroids within a radius T_2 from c are merged and assigned to

c's canopy. This is the best solution in terms of performance, because it saves one iteration over all points in all shards and only requires a single reducer. The downside is that it needs many lists of canopies to be transferred to the reducer, and a custom version of the canopy clustering algorithm that handles merging centroids.

Listing 13.4 summarizes a high-level implementation of canopy clustering leveraging MapReduce, with classification performed in the same method, but in a second MapReduce job with respect to the choice of centroids. Lines #2–5 run the same algorithm that in listing 13.3 performs the distributed computation of canopy's centroids. Lines #6–9, on the other hand, run the code specific to this version, performing the assignment of each point `p` to all the canopies for which `p` is within a distance T_1+T_2 from the canopy's center. As we have mentioned, choosing a larger radius ensures that no points will remain uncovered.

Listing 13.4 MapReduce canopy clustering

Initializes `numShards` mappers; each will run the `canopyClustering` method and will hold a copy of one of the dataset's shards. The mappers will be alive (and hold the same copy of the input) for the whole lifetime of this method.

Breaks down the dataset into `numShards` random shards. This is usually done automatically by the primary node of MapReduce, but in this case, we will use a customized version.

Method `MRcanopyCentroids` takes a list of points, the number of desired centroids, and two thresholds, `T1` and `T2`, to be used for the canopy clustering initialization step. It also takes the number of shards.

Initializes a single reducer that will run `canopyClustering` on the set of all centroids returned by all mappers. This node will also be alive for the whole method's lifetime, but it won't hold any data.

```
function MRcanopyClustering(points, T1, T2, numShards)
  shards ← randomShard(points, numShards)
  mappers ← initMappers(numShards, canopyClustering, shards)
  reducers ← initReducers(1, canopyClustering)
  centroids ← mapReduce(T1, T2, mappers, reducers)
  mappers.setMethod(classifyPoints)
  reducers ← initReducers(|centroids|, join)
  canopies ← mapReduce(T1+T2, mappers, reducers)
  return (canopies, centroids)
```

Initializes a set of reducers, one for each canopy created from the first MapReduce job. Each reducer will get the points assigned to a single specific canopy (centroid) and will return the list of all points assigned to that canopy.

Updates the method run in the mapper nodes. Ideally, the same machines can be reused, so we don't need to shard the dataset again or transfer the shards to new machines (this, however, might not be possible in all MapReduce implementations). The new method to run is a simple classification step going through all points, and for each point checking which centroids are within distance `T1+T2`. Each mapper will take the list of canopy centroids as input (plus its shard of the initial dataset).

Runs the new MapReduce job and gets the final list of canopies (following the same order as `centroids`)

Returns both the list of centroids and the list of canopies

Runs MapReduce, using the mappers and reducers already created. Mappers will receive the current values for the thresholds (in addition, each mapper already holds one shard of the dataset points). The single reducer will read their input (the canopy centroids selected for each shard) from the mappers and return a refined list of centroids.

The method performing these assignments, `classifyPoints`,[15] is run in the mappers for each shard separately. As for k-means, this step can be performed independently on each point, as long as the mapper has the full list of centroids.

The output of each mapper will be a list of lists with one entry per centroid: the list of points associated with that centroid. Notice that each point can be associated with at least one, but potentially many centroids. Each mapper will have entries for several centroids, and each centroid will have points assigned to it across several mappers: that's why in this MR job we also need one reducer per canopy (that is, per centroid).

Each reducer will then work on a single canopy, merging the lists for that canopy produced by each mapper; the final result will be the list of canopies produced by each reducer.

This subroutine described in lines #6–8 is also illustrated in figure 13.11.

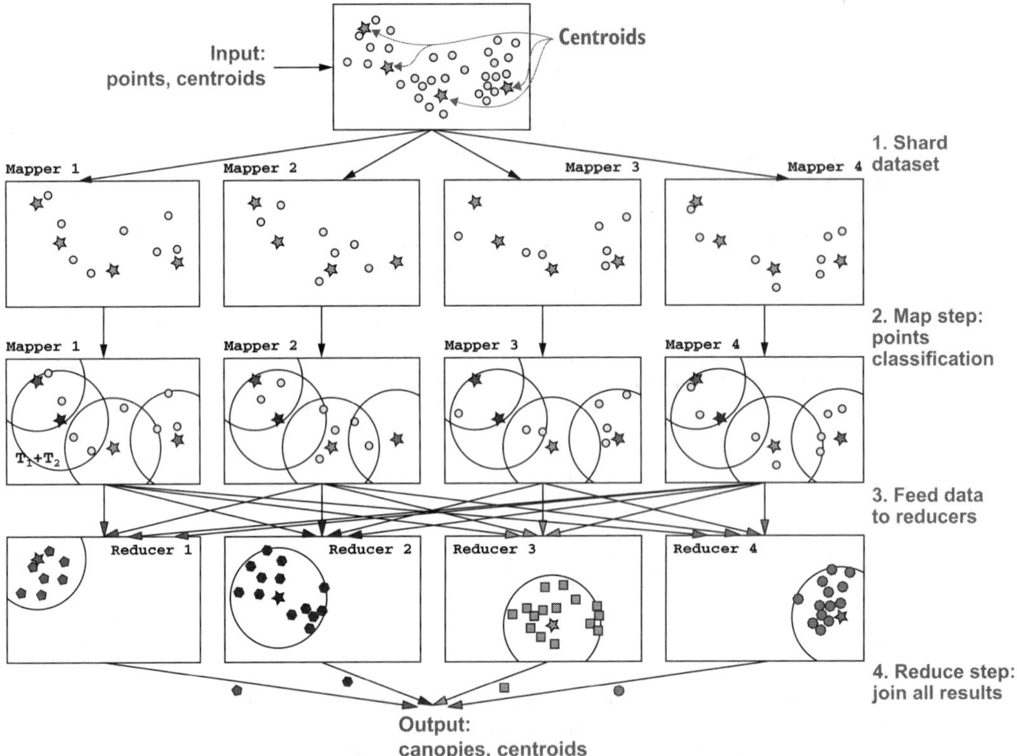
Input:
points, centroids
Centroids
1. Shard
dataset
Mapper 1
Mapper 2
Mapper 3
Mapper 4
2. Map step:
points
classification
Mapper 1
Mapper 2
Mapper 3
Mapper 4
T_1+T_2
3. Feed data
to reducers
Reducer 1
Reducer 2
Reducer 3
Reducer 4
4. Reduce step:
join all results
Output:
canopies, centroids

Figure 13.11 An example of a MapReduce job to classify points into canopies, given a list of centroids

[15] The implementation of `classifyPoints` is omitted. It can be derived from listing 12.3 by changing the condition checked, remembering that we don't look for the closest centroid in this case, but need all centroids within a certain distance. Also, this function would be the right point where the issue with unassigned points could be addressed; remember that the easiest, one-size-fits-all solution can be using a threshold distance equal to `T1+T2`.

This concludes our discussion on canopy clustering, and we encourage the reader to try to write down a job for this algorithm with one of the open source implementations of MapReduce, for instance, Hadoop, or check out Mahout, a distributed linear algebra framework by Apache foundation, that does implement a distributed version of canopy clustering.[16]

13.4 MapReduce DBSCAN

So far, so good. Our first attempt at distributed clustering was with k-means and we were in luck: we discovered that it can be easily rewritten as a distributed algorithm because its steps can be performed independently for each point (classification) or each cluster (re-centering). We applied MapReduce to canopy clustering as well, even if its first step, drawing the canopies centroids, was not immediately parallelizable and required a deeper reasoning to obtain the best clustering.

To close the circle and complete the topic, in this section we are going to discuss how to apply the MapReduce paradigm to a clustering algorithm that is intrinsically non-parallelizable, at least at first glance: DBSCAN.

As we saw in section 12.3, in DBSCAN the clustering is computed by exploring and leveraging the relations between points that are therefore interconnected. Sharding a dataset would change the ε-neighborhood of most points, and some of the core points might not be recognized as such because their ε-neighborhoods are scattered across several shards.

Although it is possible to think about a MapReduce job computing the size of the ε-neighborhood of each point with a distributed computing model, the core of DBSCAN relies on sequentially going through points and their neighbors, and thus it seems it would make more sense to explore different options.

We already discovered in section 13.1.4 that we could use canopy clustering as a first step, apply DBSCAN to each canopy separately, and then iteratively merge clusters in neighboring canopies when points close to their borders or in the overlapping regions are within each other's ε-neighborhood.

This approach becomes problematic for a few reasons:

- It's hard to keep track of the canopies that needs to be checked, and of the points inside the canopies to compare. All pairs of canopies need to be compared to check whether they overlap or their distance is smaller than ϵ, and then for each pair of canopies all points need to be compared to the other canopy.
- Given the shape of the envelopes (hyperspheres), it is complicated to compute the distance between points in a canopy's external rings and the other canopy (see section 10.4.3 and figure 10.23 to get an idea of the complicated geometric implication for the 2-D case, which gets even more complicated for hyperspheres in higher dimensions).

[16]See http://mng.bz/E2EX.

- Getting the thresholds passed to canopy clustering right is complicated; because of the spherical shape of canopies, we will have to use a larger-than-needed T_1 radius and a significant overlapping between canopies to capture the relations between clusters in different canopies.
- When the overlapping between canopies is large, points get assigned to several canopies, and thus they will need to be processed several times for each pair of canopies. This easily becomes a computational nightmare, making vain all the effort we did to parallelize.

This solution can therefore work limitedly in certain specific cases, in specific configurations, but doesn't work in high-dimensional datasets.

Nevertheless, the basic idea is valid, and we can make it work by simply changing the way we shard the dataset. Instead of relying on random sharding or spherical canopies, we can break the dataset into a regular grid, where each cell is of the same size. Cells are hyper-rectangles instead of hyper-spheres, and for each coordinate the domain can be split differently, causing the cells' (rectangles') sides to each be of a different length.

This is an improvement over dealing with canopies, because identifying points close to the borders becomes easy. We can just check that the absolute value of the difference between the point and the border along some coordinate is smaller than a threshold, instead of computing the distance between a point and a hyper-sphere; moreover, it's also easier and cheaper to shard the dataset into grid cells.

But it gets even better! Instead of having to compare points close to the borders of adjacent cells, we can define the cells to be slightly overlapping, and precisely to be overlapping, for each coordinate, over a rectangular area of side ϵ, as shown in figure 13.12.

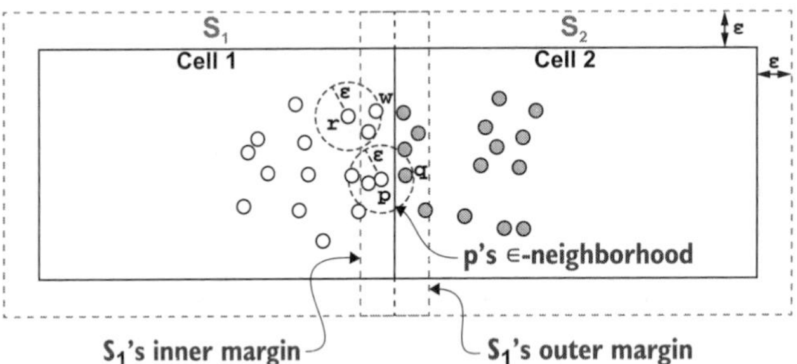

S_1
Cell 1
S_2
Cell 2
ε
ε
ε
r
w
ε
q
p
p's ϵ-neighborhood
S_1's inner margin
S_1's outer margin

Figure 13.12 Sharding data for MapReduce DBSCAN (MR-DBSCAN). After dividing the domain into equally sized cells, for each shard we need to include all points in one cell, plus all the points within a distance equal to ϵ from its borders. In practice, instead of the cells, we take a rectangle obtained by stretching the cell further in all directions, and each of the sides will measure like the corresponding cell's side plus 2ϵ. This way, core points close to the cells' borders will have their ϵ-neighborhood contained in either shard.

This way each adjacent cell overlaps the next one over a length of 2ϵ, and the ϵ-neighborhood of each point in the overlapping section will be part of at least one of the two adjacent cells (for instance, point `p` in the figure has its ϵ-neighborhood completely contained in S_1). The trick, therefore, is that if p is a core point in one of the shards, it will also be a core point in the union of the shards, and hence its neighbors on both sides of the cells' border should be directly-reachable[17] from p, and in turn end up in the same cluster. Therefore, if p is assigned to cluster C_1 for shard S_1, and to cluster C_2 for shard S_2, it follows that clusters C_1 and C_2 should be merged.

Vice versa, if we consider any point that is outside the shard's border, like r in figure 13.12, which is on the left of S_1's inner margin, then we know for sure that

- Its distance from the shard's border is larger than ϵ, and therefore its ϵ-neighborhood doesn't intersect S_1's outer margin.
- If there is a point z in S_2 that is reachable from r, then there must be a chain of core points that are directly reachable from z and r (for the definition of reachability, see section 12.3.1), and at least one of these points—call it w—must be in either S_1's inner or outer margin, because these areas extend exactly for a length equal to 2ϵ, which is exactly the diameter of the core points' ϵ-neighborhood.
- Therefore, we can ignore r, because we'll join its cluster to z's when we examine point w.

The consequence of what we informally proved[18] here is that, instead of comparing each point in a cell to all the points close to the border of the adjacent cells, we can just keep track of the core points within a distance ϵ from a cell's border (or 2ϵ from a shard's border), and merge those clusters that have a point in either that inner or outer margin that is a core point in either of the adjacent cells.

Figure 13.13 shows an example of how a MapReduce job would perform a distributed clustering of a 2D dataset using DBSCAN, and the reduction described in this section and listing 13.5 uses pseudocode to describe the step needed.

Listing 13.5 MapReduce DBSCAN

Breaks down the dataset into `numShards` regular cells; each cell will be extended for a length `eps` in all directions to define a shard, and all of these are saved into `shards`. Since we need grid-based sharding, we do need a customized sharding function. This method also needs to return the list of adjacent shards (better if a list of pairs of adjacent shards, without duplicates), and the list of points in the margin regions for each pair of adjacent shards.

Method `MRdbscan` takes a list of points, the number of desired cells in which the dataset should be sharded, and the parameters for DBSCAN algorithm, the radius and minimum number of points that define a dense zone.

Initializes `numShards` mappers; each will run the DBSCAN clustering method and will hold a copy of one of the dataset's shards. The mappers will be alive (and hold the same copy of the input) for the whole lifetime of this method.

```
function MRdbscan(points, numShards, eps, minPts)
  shards, adjList, marginPoints ← gridShard(points, numShards, eps)
  mappers ← initMappers(numShards, dbscan, shards, eps, minPts)
```

[17]See section 12.3.1 for a definition of reachability and some examples.

[18]For a formal proof and a detailed description of the algorithm, see He, Yaobin, et al. "MR-DBSCAN: A scalable MapReduce-based DBSCAN algorithm for heavily skewed data." *Frontiers of Computer Science* 8.1 (2014): 83-99.

Runs MapReduce using the mappers and reducers already created. Mappers will use the shards of data they already hold as input. Reducers will read their input (clusters and outliers local to shards) from the mappers (plus, they already hold info about which points are in the margin area between each pair of adjacent shards). Each reducer will output a list of clusters to merge, and a list of outlier points to keep for each pair of shards.

Initializes one reducer for each pair of shards in the adjacency list. The reducers will run the `mergeClusters` method and will be alive for the whole method's lifetime, and they will hold data about the adjacent shards they operate on, and the margin points between those two shards.

Before returning, we need to combine the results from reducers by merging clusters (possibly re-indexing clusters in a global way) and fixing the list of outliers.

```
reducers ← initReducers(adjList, mergeClusters, marginPoints)
clusters, noise, mergeList ← mapReduce(mappers, reducers)
return combine(clusters, noise, mergeList)
```

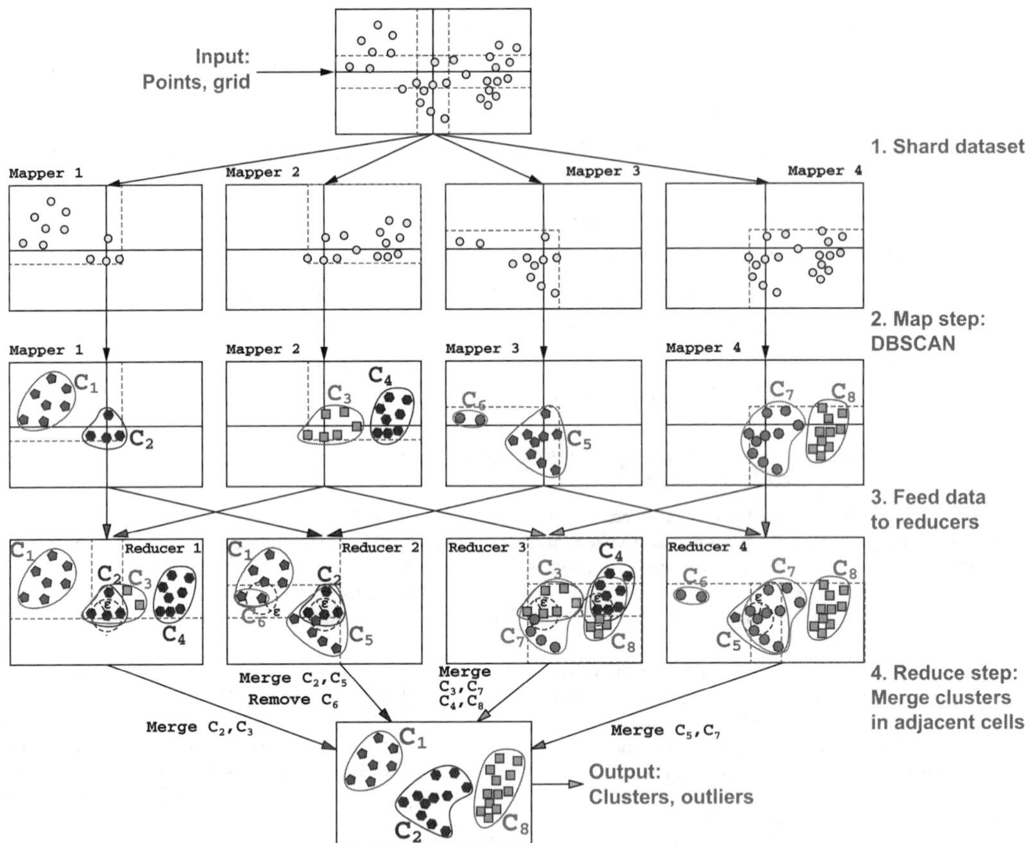

Input:
Points, grid
1. Shard dataset
Mapper 1
Mapper 2
Mapper 3
Mapper 4
2. Map step:
DBSCAN
3. Feed data
to reducers
Reducer 1
Reducer 2
Reducer 3
Reducer 4
4. Reduce step:
Merge clusters
in adjacent cells
Merge C2,C3
Merge C2,C5
Remove C6
Merge
C3,C7
C4,C8
Merge C5,C7
Output:
Clusters, outliers

Figure 13.13 An example of MapReduce DBSCAN running with four cells. We'll need one mapper for each (extended) cell, and one reducer for each pair of adjacent cells. Because the dataset in the example is small, and we use just four cells with a large value for ϵ, the fraction of points in the margin is unrealistically high. In real situations, there are relatively fewer points in the borders, and the savings obtained by distributing the algorithm is orders of magnitude higher.

The first step is sharding the dataset according to a regular grid. Each grid cell is then expanded in all directions with a further area of side ϵ, and shards are formed by filtering all points within these expanded rectangles (which, it's important to remember, overlap along their common edges with adjacent cells).

Each mapper performs DBSCAN clustering on its shard, and at the next step, a reducer is spun up for each pair of adjacent shards (in this example, we used a 2x2 grid, so there are four pairs of adjacent grid cells).

Reducers need to receive, from each mapper, the list of clusters found, the list of noise points (if any), and the list of points in the margin region between the two shards that the reducer will process.

The reducer then checks to see if there is a core point in the shared margin region, and if so, it merges the two clusters to which the points belong. In the example in figure 13.13, we deliberately used a global incremental indexing for clusters at this stage, but in reality, this global indexing is not easily achievable with a single pass! That's because we don't know in advance how many clusters a mapper will find. Merging clusters can also be handled locally, but at some point, an extra step will be needed to re-index all clusters globally.

If we suppose that clusters have global indexing, however, we can handle merging clusters using a data structure with which you should already be familiar: the disjoint set, which we described in chapter 5.

You might have noticed that there are some edge cases we should keep in mind. Clusters in one shard, for instance, can be subsets of a bigger cluster in another shard. In the example, reducer 2 gets clusters `C1` and `C6`, with the latter completely included in the former; in this case, even if no point in the margin regions is a core point, obviously[19] we need to merge the two clusters (or, equivalently, get rid of `C6`).

Likewise, if a point `p` is classified as a core point in one shard and noise in the other, there won't be clusters to merge: `p` will already be in the right cluster, but we also need to be careful, because it should be removed from the list of outliers.

The output of each reducer will be a list of local clusters to merge, or, alternatively, the disjoint set keeping track of the merges. A further brief composition step can take care of producing the list with the point assignments to the final clusters and the list of outliers, based on reducers' output.

The pseudo-code for this MapReduce job is simpler than any other job in this chapter, but don't be fooled—most of the complexity is hidden in the methods `gridShard`, `dbscan`, and `mergeClusters`.

Method `dbscan` is exactly the same method that we described in section 12.3. In most languages, we will be able to reuse it without any modification. `gridShard`, in its most naïve version, just iterates over points and computes the index of the cell by performing a modulo division (plus a few checks to see if the point is in the margin of

---

[19] C_6 doesn't qualify to merge with C_1, because none of its points in the margin region are core points; therefore, we need to explicitly perform some extra check (for instance, for each pair of clusters, verify if one is a subset of the other) to recognize these situations.

adjacent cells). We'll address some problems connected to this method later in this section, but we won't get into the details of its implementation.

Finally, method mergeClusters is a nice application of disjoint set, the data structure we described in chapter 5. Listing 13.6 shows a possible implementation of this method that treats argument clustersSet like an instance of disjoint set shared among all reducers. While this is not practically possible,[20] it is conceptually equivalent to having the reducers emitting a list of clusters to merge and perform the operations on the disjoint set in the combiner stage, after reducers finish their job. For this reason, we can consider clustersSet like a facade[21] simplifying the process of emitting a pair of clusters to merge and sending the pair to the combiner, where the actual disjoint set is created and merge operations are performed.

Listing 13.6 Method mergeClusters

```
function mergeClusters(shard1, shard2, marginPoints, clustersSet)
  for p in marginPoints.intersection(shard1, shard2) do
    if shard1.isCorePoint(p) or shard2.isCorePoint(p) then
      if shard1.isNoise(p) then
        shard1.markNoise(p, false)
      elsif shard2.isNoise(p) then
        shard2.markNoise(p, false)
      else
        clustersSet.merge(shard1.getCluster(p), shard2.getCluster(p))
  return clustersSet, shard1, shard2
```

Annotations:

- Method mergeClusters takes two shards, extending two adjacent cells, a set of margin points, and a disjoint set on the list of clusters. We assume that clusters have already been re-indexed globally, and that clustersSet is a facade emitting a pair of clusters to merge. (line 1)
- For each margin point in the intersection between the two shards, assume marginPoints is an instance of a class handling these kinds of operations, abstracting away the complexity that is not relevant to this method. (line 2)
- Checks if p is a core point in at least one of the two shards (also, we assume the shard objects created by mappers handle this kind of method). If it is not, we can ignore it. (line 3)
- Checks if p is classified as noise, as an outlier, in the first shard (line 4)
- If it is so, it will be in a cluster in shard2, and we only need to remove it from the list of outliers in shard1. (line 5)
- Same thing if it is an outlier in shard2 (also, remember it can only be an outlier in one of the shards, as it's a core point in at least one) (line 6)
- If p is not an outlier in either shard, it means it is assigned to a cluster in both; hence, we need to merge those clusters. (line 9)
- The relevant information we updated is all in the set of clusters and the two shards. Assuming we pass these structures by value (at least the shards), we can return them at the end of the method. (line 10)

The implementation goes through all points in the margin region between the two shards (use figure 13.12 as a reference) and checks if any of these points is a core point in at least one of the shards. Then we just need to make sure it's not a noise

[20] It wouldn't make sense to have a shared object in the MapReduce model! Can you explain why? (Hint: Besides technical challenges, do we really want to introduce shared state?)

[21] See https://en.wikipedia.org/wiki/Facade_pattern.

point in the other shard (handled as an edge case) and merge the two clusters (c_1 will be in `shard1` and c_2 will be in `shard2`). Optionally, we can check that c_1 and c_2 are not one subset of the other and handle that case differently.

There is one final detail we need to address before wrapping up the discussion on MapReduce DBSCAN: the sharding step. Before continuing reading, stop for a minute and think about how this case is different from what we have seen before, and what issues we could face in this step.

Do you see the problem? Deterministically sharding points according to a rectangular grid will not be as cheap as the random sharding we have seen so far! Before running and even configuring the MapReduce job to perform this sharding, in fact, we would need to run a single-thread process creating the grid and assigning each point to a shard, depending on the point's position. If the grid has `m` cells, and the dataset holds `n` points with `d` coordinates each, then this step will require, in the worst case, `O(n*d*m)` comparisons.

To speed things up, we can use an R-tree. As mentioned in chapter 10, R-trees can hold non-zero-measure objects, and in particular shapes like rectangles (see figure 10.5). We can therefore create an R-tree whose items are the grid cells, and for each point find the closest cell. Since R-trees have linear-time worst-case running time, however, we don't improve our asymptotic result (but in most cases R-trees will result, in practice, in faster than naïve search).

To seriously speed things up, however, what we really need is to distribute even the sharding step with a new MapReduce job. We know that each point can be compared to cells independently; therefore, if we split the dataset into random shards, each shard can be processed by a battery of mappers. Reducers, at the same time, will just group points by extended cell(s),[22] and finally produce (not randomly, this time) new shards that can then be used in the first step of the MR-DBSCAN job (the one illustrated in figure 13.13). As a further optimization, since reducers for this job (sharding) will already have all the data for a cell, we can repurpose the same machines to be the mappers in the MR-DBSCAN job.

It's also worth mentioning that the number of adjacent cells grows linearly with the dimension of the space, since the number of faces of a `d`-dimensional hypercube is equal to `2*d`. This means that the sharding algorithm can scale out to higher dimensions.

Finally, it's worth mentioning that because we are performing this sharding step as an independent MapReduce job, we are forced to use a regular grid. On the contrary, the article by He et al. presenting MR-DBSCAN[23] uses a different, more sophisticated approach, where statistics on the dataset are collected in a first pass through the dataset, splitting the domain into an irregular collection of parallel rectangles (see figure 13.14) each with ideally uniform density. Then, leveraging the statistics collected, we can also tune the parameters for DBSCAN to adapt to the different density found in different cells.

---

[22]Since cells are overlapping, a point can be assigned to more than one cell.

[23]He, Yaobin, et al. "MR-DBSCAN: A scalableMapReduce-based DBSCAN algorithm for heavily skewed data." *Frontiers of Computer Science* 8.1 (2014): 83-99.

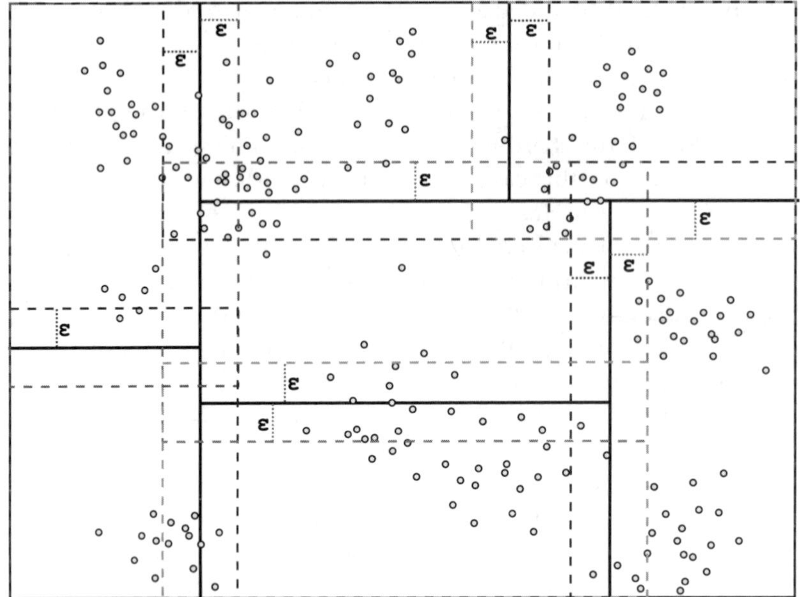
ε
ε
ε
ε
ε
ε
ε
ε
ε
ε
ε

Figure 13.14 An example of an irregularly shaped grid for sharding a dataset in MR-DBSCAN. Notice that shards (dashed-lines rectangles) are built by expanding cells in each direction for a distance equal to ϵ, the dense region's radius.

Summary

- Canopy clustering is an algorithm for computing a coarse-grained pseudo-clustering of a dataset, with the advantage of being very inexpensive compared to more accurate clustering algorithms such as k-means or DBSCAN.
- We distinguish between parallel computing, running some software in several threads on the same machine, and distributed computing, where several machines and possibly resources on the cloud are used to run software in a joint effort.
- MapReduce is a computational model that leverages the cloud to scale out processing of large datasets.
- k-means, canopy clustering, and DBSCAN can all be rewritten as distributed algorithms by using the MapReduce model.

Part 3

Planar graphs and minimum crossing number

The final part of this book has a single data structure as its main thread: *graphs*. They will be used, however, more as a touchstone to compare different techniques throughout chapters whose main focus will be on *optimization algorithms*.

We won't delve into the basics of graphs, but we still start this part with a brief introduction to their basic concepts and a few cornerstone algorithms to traverse graphs.

These are necessary to describe an interesting, often neglected problem that has broad application in our industry: displaying graphs in the two-dimensional plane. This is a difficult problem that can't be solved efficiently on classical computers. Nevertheless, it's one for which approximate solutions are often enough, and this gives us a good reason to introduce *optimization algorithms*, the real star of part 3.

The final chapters of this book will describe three optimization techniques that are widely used to tackle optimization problems and drive today's AI and big data effort: *gradient descent*, *simulated annealing*, and *genetic algorithms*.

Chapter 14 is a short introduction to *graphs*, condensing the basics of this fundamental data structure needed to understand part 3. It also illustrates *DFS*, *BFS*, *Dijkstra's*, and *A** algorithms, and describes how to use them to solve the "minimum-distance path" problem.

Chapter 15 introduces *graph embeddings*, planarity, and a couple of problems we will try to solve in the remaining chapters: finding the *minimum crossing number* (*MCN*), embedding a graph, and drawing a graph nicely.

Chapter 16 describes a fundamental algorithm in machine learning, *gradient descent*, and shows how it can be applied to graphs and embeddings.

Chapter 17 builds on the previous chapter and presents *simulated annealing*, a more powerful optimization technique that tries to overcome gradient descent shortcomings when we have to deal with non-differentiable functions or functions with multiple local minima.

Chapter 18, finally, describes *genetic algorithms*, an even more advanced optimization technique that helps with faster convergence.

14 An introduction to graphs: Finding paths of minimum distance

This chapter covers

- Introducing graphs from a theoretical point of view
- Learning strategies for implementing graphs
- Finding the best route for deliveries
- Introducing search algorithms on graphs: BFS and DFS
- Using BFS to find the route that traverses the fewest blocks
- Finding the shortest route with Dijkstra's minimum distance algorithm
- Finding the quickest route with A* algorithm for optimal search

We already described the basics of trees in appendix C and used several kinds of trees in the previous chapters: binary search trees, heaps, k-d trees, and so on. You should now be familiar with them. Graphs could be considered a generalization of trees, although in reality the opposite is true, and it is trees that are a special case of graphs. A tree, in fact, is a connected, acyclic undirected graph. Figure 14.1 shows an example of two graphs, only one of which is a tree. Don't worry if you are not sure which one, because in this chapter we'll take a closer look at the meaning of those properties in the definition of trees, and they will help us to better explain graphs' properties and make sense of these examples.

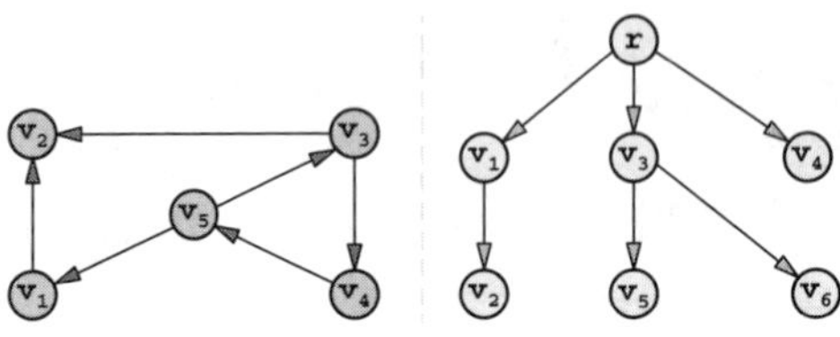

Figure 14.1 Two graphs, only one of which is also a tree. Can you tell which one?

But to do so we need to follow a meaningful order and so, we first need to give a formal definition of graphs and understand how we can represent them.

Once we have laid that foundation, we can start modeling interesting problems with graphs and developing algorithms to solve them.

In particular, here we will focus on the "shortest distance" problem. In chapters 8–11 we developed our example of an e-commerce platform by introducing k-d trees and nearest neighbor search to find the closest hub for deliveries, so that parcels need to travel the least possible distance. Nevertheless, there will still be some road to travel to get our orders to the customers, and our margin gets thinner if we waste time and gas for each delivery.

Conversely, if we were able to optimize the route fared, we could save some money for each parcel, and a lot of money at scale, on thousands or millions of deliveries.

In this chapter we will solve this problem, finding the best route to make a single delivery (from a warehouse to the customer's home), by using graphs; we will tackle the problem at different levels of abstraction, demonstrating how search algorithms such as BFS, Dijkstra, and A* (pronounced "A-star") work.

14.1 Definitions

A graph G is usually defined in terms of two sets:

- A set of *vertices* `V`: independent, distinct entities that can appear in any multiplicity. A graph can have 1, 2, 100, or any number of vertices but, in general, graphs don't support duplicate vertices.
- A set of *edges* `E` connecting vertices: an edge is defined by a pair of vertices, the first one usually denoted as the *source* vertex, and the second one called the *destination* vertex.

So, we write `G=(V,E)` to make it clear that the graph is made of certain sets of vertices and edges; for instance, the graph in figure 14.2 is formally written as

$$G = ([v_1, v_2, v_3, v_4], [(v_1,v_2),(v_1,v_3),(v_2,v_4)])$$

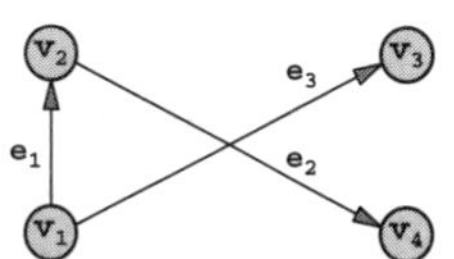

v2
v3
e3
e1
e2
v1
v4

Figure 14.2 An example of a (directed) graph

An edge whose source and destination are the same is called a *loop* (see figure 14.3). *Simple graphs* can't have any loops, nor can they have multiple edges between the same pair of nodes. Conversely, *multigraphs* can have any number of edges between two distinct vertices. Both simple graphs and multigraphs can be extended to permit loops.

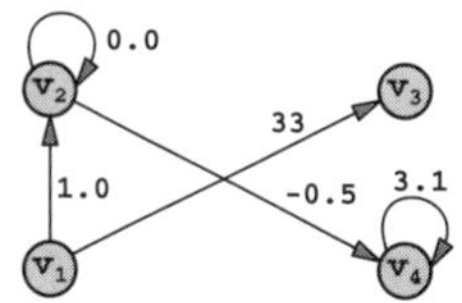

0.0
v2
v3
33
1.0
-0.5
3.1
v1
v4

Figure 14.3 A directed weighted graph, with loops. (Edge labels are omitted for the sake of clarity.)

We won't bother with multigraphs in this book; instead we'll focus on simple graphs, usually without loops.

We can express the previous definitions more formally. Given the set of edges E

- For simple graphs, $E \subseteq \{(x, y) \mid (x, y) \in V^2 \land x \neq y\}$
- For simple graphs supporting loops, $E \subseteq V^2$

It's also possible to associate a weight to each edge. In this case, the graph is called a *weighted graph* or, equivalently, a *network*, where each edge becomes a triplet, and the set of graph's edges becomes

- For simple graphs, $E \subseteq \{(x, y, w) \mid (x, y) \in V^2 \land w \in \mathbb{R} \land x \neq y\}$
- For simple graphs supporting loops, $E \subseteq V^2 \times \mathbb{R}$

Figure 14.3 shows an example of a weighted graph with loops.

14.1.1 Implementing graphs

The previous section formally defines graphs; however, when we move from theory to practice, we often have to face new issues and cope with constraints.

As much as mathematical notation makes it clear how we should represent graphs on paper, we need to decide, for instance, what's the best way to store them into a data structure.

There are several questions to answer, depending on the context: Should we store labels for vertices and edges, or should we just assign an index to vertices using natural numbers, and enumerate edges following the natural ordering of pairs of indices?

While storing vertices is relatively easy (using lists, and possibly a dictionary to associate each vertex to its label), there is also another question that goes beyond any context: How should we store edges?

That question is not as trivial as it might seem: the caveat is that at some point we will want to check to see if there is an edge between two vertices, or maybe find all outgoing edges of a certain vertex. If we just store all edges in a single list, either sorted or unsorted, then we will have to scan the whole list to find out our answers.

Even with a sorted list, that means accessing `O(log(|E|))` elements for the operations in the previous paragraph, and `O(|E|)` for listing all edges going into a vertex.

No surprise, it turns out we can do better. There are two main strategies to store a graph's edges:

- *Adjacency lists*—For each vertex `v`, we store a list of the edges `(v, u)`, where `v` is the source and `u`, the destination, is another vertex in `G`.
- *Adjacency matrix*—It's a `|V|×|V|` matrix, where the generic cell `(i,j)` contains the weight of the edge going from the `i`-th vertex to the `j`-th vertex (or `true/false`, or `1/0`, in case of un-weighted graphs, to state the presence/absence of an unweighted edge between those two vertices).

Before examining pros and cons of both strategies, let's illustrate them with an example. Given the graph in figure 14.2, its adjacency list representation is the following dictionary mapping vertices to lists of edges:

```
1 -> [(1,2), (1,3)]
2 -> [(2,4)]
3 -> []
4 -> []
```

The adjacency matrix representation is the following:

	v_1	v_2	v_3	v_4
v_1	0	1	1	0
v_2	0	0	0	1
v_3	0	0	0	0
v_4	0	0	0	0

As you can see, they are very different. One aspect that stands out immediately is that in the adjacency matrix, most cells are filled with 0s. This stems from the fact that the graph in figure 14.2 only has a few edges, of the many possible.

We know that because edges are pairs of vertices, in a simple graph the maximum number of edges is `O(|V|²)`. What's the minimum number, though?

It can be anything; a graph can even (hypothetically) have no edges at all. A connected graph, however, must have at least `|V|-1` edges.

Table 14.1 Weaknesses and strengths of graph representations

Operation	Adjacency list	Adjacency matrix
Edge insert	O(1)	O(1)
Edge delete	O(|V|)	O(1)
List of outgoing edges	O(|E|)	O(|V|)

Table 14.1 Weaknesses and strengths of graph representations

Operation	Adjacency list	Adjacency matrix
List of ingoing edges	O(|E|)	O(|V|)
Space needed	O(|E|+|V|)	O(|V|²)
Vertex insert	O(1)	O(|V|)[a]
Vertex delete	O(|V|+|E|)[b]	O(|V|)[a]

[a] This is an optimistic bound, assuming the adjacency matrix can be resized dynamically. Otherwise, a truer bound is O(|V|²).
[b] We need to check all edges to remove those whose destination has been deleted.

Keeping this in mind, we'll now provide a definition, one that will be handy later in this section:

A graph G=(V,E) is said to be *sparse* if |E|=O(|V|); G is said to be *dense* when |E|=O(|V|²).

In other words, sparse graphs have a number of edges comparable to the number of vertices, which are therefore loosely connected to each other, while in dense graphs, each vertex is connected to most of the other vertices.

Table 14.1 summarizes the pros and cons of the two different representations of graphs. In a few words, the adjacency list representation is better for sparse graphs because it requires a lot less memory, and because for sparse graphs |E|≈|V|, and thus most operations can be performed efficiently.

For dense graphs, conversely, since the number of edges is close to the maximum possible, the adjacency matrix representation is more compact and efficient. Moreover, this representation allows more efficient implementation of some algorithms on graphs, such as the search of connected components or transitive closure.

In general, when no assumption can be made on the graph, and unless it is otherwise required by the context, the adjacency list representation is preferred because it is more flexible and it supports adding new vertices more easily.

14.1.2 Graphs as algebraic types

There is another aspect of graph representation that is orthogonal to the way we store edges: consistency.

To be fair, inconsistencies are much more likely to happen with the adjacency list representation, but they are still possible in certain situations, even using the adjacency matrix.

The problem is the following. Regardless of its representation, consider the following graph: G=([1,2], [(1,2), (1,3), (2,2)]).

The graph G has two vertices, [1,2], but it has an edge whose destination is the vertex "3". This can happen for any reason; for instance, sloppiness in deleting vertex "3", or an error while adding edges.

Moreover, the graph has a loop, the edge (2,2). What if G was supposed to be a simple graph without loops?

Of course, we can add validation to our Graph class' methods to prevent these situations, but the data structure itself can't guarantee that these errors won't happen.

To overcome these limitations, we can define our graphs as an algebraic type;[1] this way, we define graphs as one of the following:

- The empty graphs.
- A singleton, a single vertex with no edges.
- The connection between two graphs G and G'. We define one or more edges whose source is in G and destination is in G'.
- The union of two graphs G=(V,E) and G'=(V',E'). We just compute the union of both the vertices and edges set to obtain G″=(V ∪ V', E ∪ E').

This representation prevents the inconsistencies we talked about and guarantees that we won't get malformed graphs, but also allows us to formally define algorithms as transformations on graphs and mathematically prove their correctness.

Trying to understand graphs as an algebraic type is a useful exercise to help you gain a deeper understanding of this data structure. At the same time, we need to acknowledge that considering the overhead for these operations, practical uses are limited and mostly relegated to functional languages providing pattern matching on types, such as Scala, Haskell, or Clojure.[2]

14.1.3 Pseudo-code

To complete the discussion, listing 14.1 provides an overview of the class that we'll use for graphs in this book. It uses adjacency lists and models edges and vertices as classes, allowing us to implement different types of graphs by changing the details of these models (for instance, allowing weighted edges).

Listing 14.1 The Graph class

```
class Vertex
  #type string
  label

class Edge
  #type Vertex
  source
  #type Vertex
  dest
```

[1] An algebraic data type is one particular kind of composite type, formed by combining other types, usually with a definition "by induction," with one or more base types, and operators to combine them. This presentation nicely explains how to define them in C++ and what the benefits are: https://www.youtube.com/watch?v=ojZbFIQSdl8

[2] For an example with Haskell, see: Mokhov, Andrey. "Algebraic graphs with class (functional pearl)." ACM SIGPLAN Notices. Vol. 52. No. 10. ACM, 2017. A Scala implementation (ongoing, at the time of writing) can be found here: https://github.com/algebraic-graphs/scala.

```
  #type double
  weight
  #type string
  label

class Graph
  #type List[Vertices]
  vertices
  #type HashTable[Vertex->List[Edge]]
  adjacencyList

  function Graph()
    adjacencyList ← new HashTable()

  function addVertex(v)
    throw-if v in vertices
    vertices.insert(v)
    adjacencyList[v] ← []

  function addEdge(v, u, weight=0, label="")
    throw-if not (v in vertices and u in vertices)
    if areAdjacent(v, u) then
      removeEdge(v, u)
    adjacencyList[v].insert(new Edge(v, u, weight, label))

  function areAdjacent(v, u)
    throw-if not (v in vertices and u in vertices)
    for e in adjacencyList[v] do
      if e.dest == u then
        return true
    return false
```

When we add a new vertex, provided it's not a duplicate, we first need to add it to the vertices list.

But we also want to initialize the adjacency list for the new vertex; it will simplify our lives later!

Checks if the vertices are adjacent, that is, if there is already an edge from `v` to `u`

If so, removes the old one first (this method is omitted, but can be derived from `areAdjacent`)

Adds a new edge, created based on the arguments, to the adjacency list for the source vertex

Iterates through all edges in the adjacency list for the source vertex

As soon as it finds an edge whose destination matches `u`, we can return `true`. If none matches, the vertices are not adjacent.

As for concrete implementation, a Java version can be found on the book repo on GitHub,[3] and a JavaScript version is provided by the JsGraphs library; the latter will also implement the algorithms described in the next sections.

14.2 Graph properties

As we mentioned, graphs are very similar to trees. They are both made of entities (vertices) connected by relations (edges), with a couple of differences:

- In trees, vertices are usually called nodes.
- In trees, edges are somewhat implicit. Since they can only go from a node to its children, it's more common to talk about parent/children relations than explicitly list edges. Also, because of this, trees are implicitly represented with adjacency lists.

[3] See https://github.com/mlarocca/AlgorithmsAndDataStructuresInAction#graph.

Furthermore, trees have other peculiar characteristics that make them a strict subset of the whole set of graphs. In particular, any tree is a simple, undirected, connected, and acyclic graph.

We have illustrated in the previous section what *simple graph* means. In fact, a tree cannot have multiple edges between two nodes, nor can it have loops; instead, only a single edge between a node and each of its children is allowed.

Let's now see what the other three properties mean.

14.2.1 Undirected

As we mentioned in section 1, a graph is directed when all its edges can be traversed in a single direction, from source (the first vertex in the edge's pair) to destination.

In undirected graphs, conversely, the edges can be traversed in both directions. The difference is shown in figure 14.4.

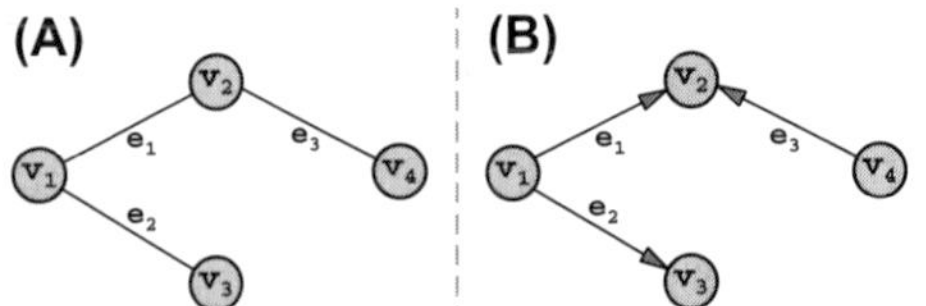
(A)
(B)
v1
v2
v3
v4
e1
e2
e3

Figure 14.4 An undirected graph (A) versus a directed graph with the same vertices (B). The two graphs are not equivalent; in particular, the latter can't be transformed into an equivalent undirected graph.

An undirected graph can easily be represented as a directed graph, by expanding each undirected edge `(u,v)` into a couple of directed edges `(u,v)` and `(v,u)`.

Vice versa is usually not true, and many directed graphs can't be transformed into their undirected isomorphic counterpart.[4]

So, unless the application context suggests otherwise, representing directed graphs is the least restricting choice.

It's also worth noting that if the adjacency matrix representation is used, undirected graphs can be represented using only half the matrix, because they always have a symmetrical adjacency matrix: `A[u,v] = A[v,u]` for every pair of vertices `u,v`.

14.2.2 Connected

A graph is *connected* if, given any pair of its vertices `(u,v)`, there is a sequence of vertices `u`, $(w_1, \ldots, w_K)$, `v`, with $k \geq 0$, such that there is an edge between any two adjacent vertices in the sequence.

For *undirected* graphs, this means that in a connected graph, any vertex can be reached by all other vertices, while for *directed* graphs, it means that each vertex has at least an in-going or an out-going edge.

For either kind, it means that the number of edges is at least `|V|-1`.

[4] Any directed graph where there is an edge (u,v), but not the inverse edge (v,u), can't be transformed into an isomorphic undirected graph (meaning an undirected graph with the same shape, that is, with the same set of vertices, connected in the same way).

Figure 14.5 shows a few examples of connected and disconnected undirected graphs. The notion of connected graph makes the most sense for undirected graphs, while for directed graphs we instead introduce the notion of *strongly connected components*, illustrated in figure 14.6.

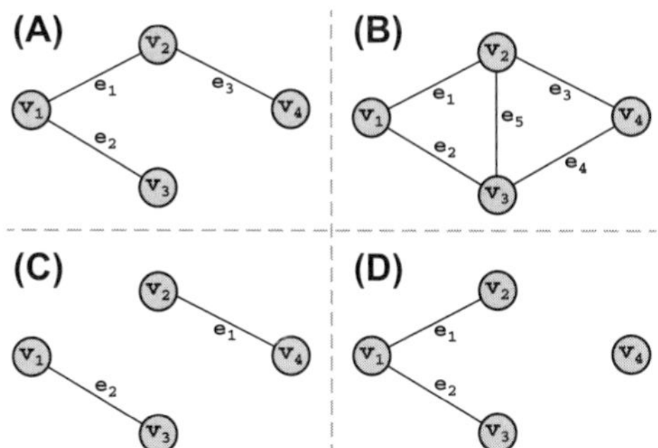
(A)
(B)
(C)
(D)

Figure 14.5 Connected graphs ((A), (B)) versus disconnected graphs ((C), (D))

In a *strongly connect component (*SCC*)*, every vertex is reachable from every other vertex; strongly connected components must therefore have cycles (see section 14.2.3).

The notion of strongly connected components is particularly important. It allows us to define a graph of the SCCs, which is going to be sensibly smaller than the original graph, and run many algorithms on this graph instead. We can gain a great increase in speed by first examining a graph at a high level, and then (possibly) studying the interaction within each SCC.

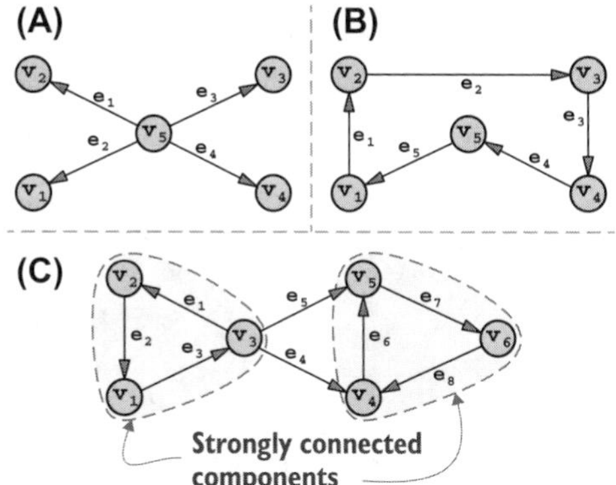
(A)
(B)
(C)
Strongly connected components

Figure 14.6 Only graph (B) is strongly connected, but graph (C) has two strongly connected components.

A tree is usually regarded as an undirected graph, at least in graph theory; but in implementations, each node usually stores the links to its children and only sometimes to its parent. If references to parents are not stored in children, then each edge is not traversable from child to parent, making it a de facto directed edge.

14.2.3 Acyclic

A *cycle*, in a graph, is a non-empty sequence of edges `(u,v₁), (v₁,v₂), …, (v_K,u)` that starts and ends at the same vertex.

An *acyclic graph* (shown in figure 14.7) is a graph that has no cycle.

Both directed and undirected graphs can have cycles, and as such there is a subset of acyclic graphs that is of special interest: *directed acyclic graphs* (*DAGs*).

A DAG has a few interesting properties: there must be at least one vertex that has no incoming edge (otherwise, there would be a cycle); moreover, since it's acyclic, the set of edges defines a partial ordering on its vertices.

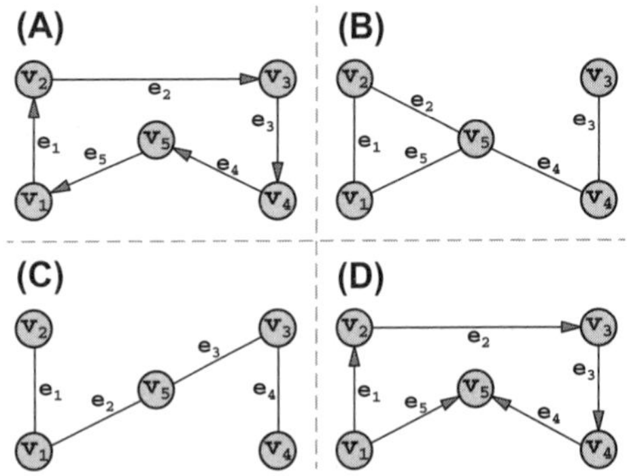
(A)
(B)
(C)
(D)

Figure 14.7 Cyclic graphs ((A) directed, (B) undirected) versus acyclic graphs ((C) and (D))

Given a directed acyclic graph `G=(V,E)`, in fact, a partial ordering is a relation ≤ such that for any couple of vertices `(u,v)`, exactly one of these three conditions will hold:

- u ≤ v, if there is a path of any number of edges starting from u and reaching v.
- v ≤ u, if there is a path of any number of edges starting from v and reaching u.
- u <> v; they are not comparable because there isn't any path from u to v or vice versa.

Figure 14.8 shows a couple of generic DAGs and a chain: the latter is the only kind of DAG defining a total ordering on its nodes.

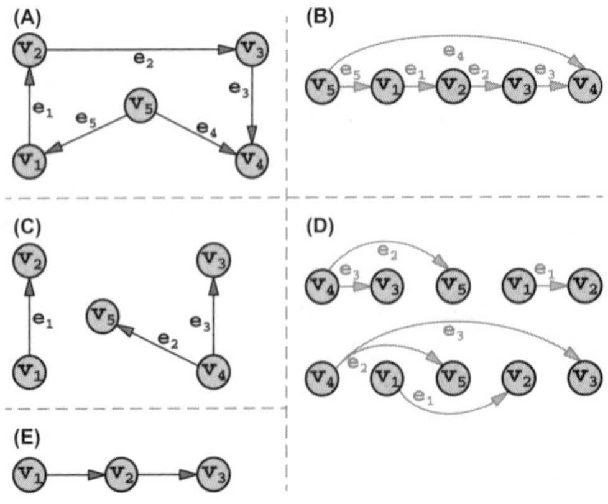
(A)
(B)
(C)
(D)
(E)

Figure 14.8 A few examples of DAGs. (A) A connected DAG. (B) A topological sorting for the graph; notice that the output of topological sorting is just a sequence of vertices, and that edges are not considered. Nevertheless, they are shown to demonstrate how they only go left-to-right, if vertices in the topological sorting are listed horizontally (from left to right). (C) A disconnected DAG. (D) A couple of possible topological sorting examples for the graph in (C). (E) A chain graph: for this DAG, there is only one possible topological sorting.

The partial ordering on DAGs provides a *topological sorting*, an ordering of the vertices such that, for any edge in the graph, the edge's starting point occurs before its ending point; usually each graph has several equivalent topological orderings. All chains, like the one in figure 14.8 (E), certainly have a single unique topological sorting, but it's also possible that a non-chain graph also has a single topological sorting (see figure 14.8 (A–B)).

DAGs and topological ordering have many fundamental applications in computer science, spanning from scheduling (at all levels) to resolving symbol dependencies in linkers.

14.3 Graph traversal: BFS and DFS

To perform searches on a graph, as well as to apply many other algorithms, it is necessary to traverse the graph following its edges.

As with trees, there are many possible ways to traverse a graph, depending on the order in which outgoing edges are traversed. In trees, however, it's always clear where to start the traversal: from the root. By starting from the root, we are always sure that we can traverse a tree and reach all its nodes. In graphs, however, there isn't a special vertex like a tree's root, and in general, depending on the vertex chosen the starting point, there might or might not be a sequence of edges that allows us to visit all vertices.

In this section, we will focus on simple directed graphs; no other assumption will be made. We are not restricting ourselves to strongly connected graphs, and in general, we don't have further domain knowledge to choose the vertex from which we should start the search. Consequently, we can't guarantee that a single traversal will cover all the vertices in the graph. On the contrary, several "restarts" from different starting points are normally needed to visit all the vertices in a graph: we'll show this while discussing DFS.

Initially, however, we will focus on a specific use case: considering the starting point as "given" (externally chosen, without the algorithm knowing much about it) and traversing the graph from it. Based on these assumptions, we will discuss the two most common traversal strategies used on graphs.

14.3.1 Optimizing delivery routes

It's time to go back to the problem with which we introduced this chapter: we have a single delivery to perform from a source point, the warehouse or factory where goods are stocked, to a single destination, the customer's address.

The hypothesis that we handle deliveries one by one is, obviously, already a simplification. In the general case, it would be too expensive, and delivery companies try to gather together orders from the same warehouse to nearby destinations to spread the costs (gas, the employee's time, and so on) over several orders.

Finding the best route passing through several points, however, is a computationally hard problem;[5] conversely, the best route for the single-source, single-destination case can be found efficiently.

---

[5] Have you ever heard of the "traveling salesman problem," or TSP? That's one of the most-studied hard problems.

We'll develop a generic solution for this problem incrementally, across this and the next few sections, starting with a further-simplified scenario and removing those simplifications step by step, while presenting more complex algorithms to solve these cases.

So, to start our discussion, we need to think about our goal: What's the "best" route? We can assume, for instance, that the best route is the shortest route, but we could also prefer to find the fastest route or the cheapest one, depending on our requirements.

For the moment, let's assume we want the shortest route. If we simplify the scenario and ignore factors such as traffic, road conditions, and speed limits, then we can hypothesize that the shorter the distance, the faster we can travel it.

But even this simplified scenario can be made simpler. Figure 14.9, for instance, shows a portion of a city where roads form a regular grid. This is a common situation in many cities in the United States, while elsewhere in the world it's not necessarily as common. In Europe, many city centers have a plan originally designed during the Middle Age or even earlier, and roads are far less regular.

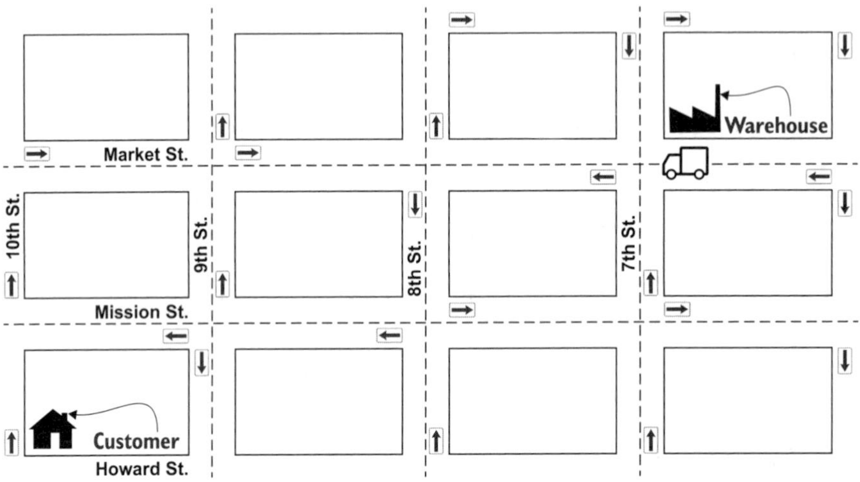
Warehouse
Market St.
10th St.
9th St.
8th St.
7th St.
Mission St.
Customer
Howard St.

Figure 14.9 An example map: a portion of San Francisco's downtown, where blocks form a regular grid

For the moment we can imagine restricting to this ideal situation, but why do that? Well, because it makes our job easier. If all blocks are the same, and can be approximated with squares (or rectangles whose sides' proportions are close to squares'), then we don't have to worry about real distances; we can just count the number of blocks traveled to compute the length of a route. The problem would be trivial to solve . . . if it wasn't for one-way streets! Once we have a minimum viable solution working for this simplified scenario, we can think about developing it to cover more life-like situations.

Figure 14.10 shows the graph that can be built over the map shown in figure 14.9, where we added a vertex at each road intersection, and an edge going from vertex v to vertex u means that from the intersection modeled with v to the one modeled with u, there is a road that can be traveled in that direction (and not necessarily in the opposite direction, from u to v).

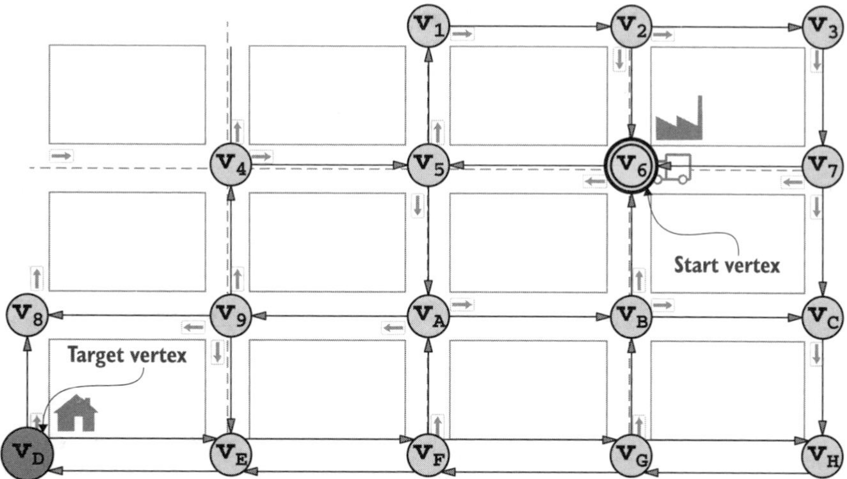
V1
V2
V3
V4
V5
V6
V7
Start vertex
V8
V9
VA
VB
VC
Target vertex
VD
VE
VF
VG
VH

Figure 14.10 Building a graph on the map in figure 14.8. We added a vertex to each road intersection (some vertices are, however, omitted for better readability) and edges connect adjacent intersections connected by a one-way street (two-way streets are modeled with a couple of edges).

If all roads could be traveled in both directions, we would just go west on Market from the warehouse until we crossed 10th St., and then south on 10th down to our destination.

Given the road signs in figure 14.9, however, this is not possible, and we need to take detours. In the next sub-section, we'll see how.

14.3.2 Breadth first search

Listing 14.2 shows the pseudo-code for *Breadth First Search (BFS)*, whose goal, as the name suggests, is to widen the search as much as possible, keeping a perimeter of already visited vertices, and expanding this perimeter to the neighboring vertices. This is shown in figure 14.11, where the graph in figure 14.6 (C) is used to demonstrate the first few steps of this algorithm.

Listing 14.2 The `bfs` method

```
function bfs(graph, start, isGoal)
  queue ← new Queue()
  queue.insert(start)
```

Method `bfs` takes a graph, a starting point vertex, and a predicate (`isGoal`) that takes a vertex and returns `true` if the goal of the search is reached. Method `bfs` returns a pair with the goal vertex, and a dictionary encoding the shortest paths.

Initializes a simple FIFO queue

Adds the starting point to the queue, so that it will be extracted on the first iteration

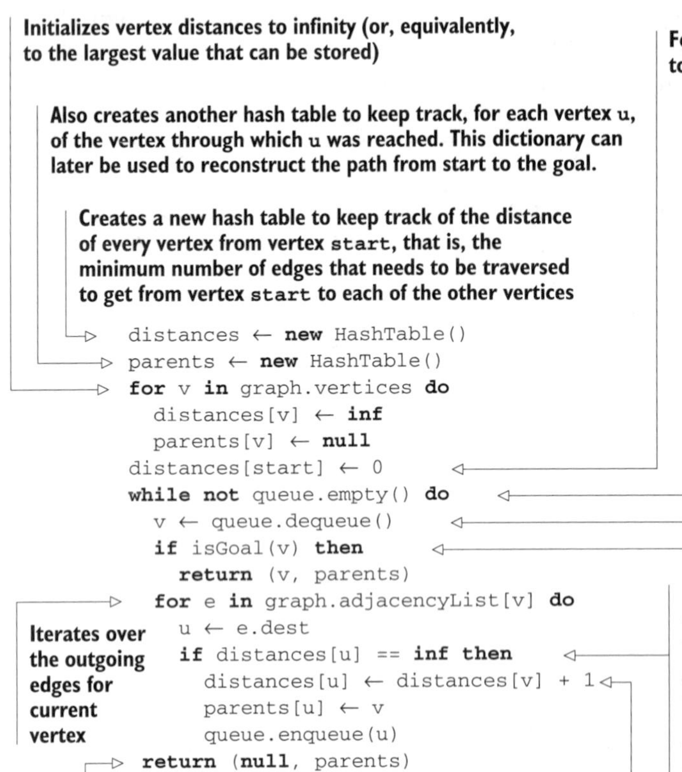
Initializes vertex distances to infinity (or, equivalently, to the largest value that can be stored)
Also creates another hash table to keep track, for each vertex u, of the vertex through which u was reached. This dictionary can later be used to reconstruct the path from start to the goal.
Creates a new hash table to keep track of the distance of every vertex from vertex start, that is, the minimum number of edges that needs to be traversed to get from vertex start to each of the other vertices
Iterates over the outgoing edges for current vertex
If the goal is never reached, we need to return null or, equivalently, another value that signals that the search failed.

```
distances ← new HashTable()
parents ← new HashTable()
for v in graph.vertices do
  distances[v] ← inf
  parents[v] ← null
distances[start] ← 0
while not queue.empty() do
  v ← queue.dequeue()
  if isGoal(v) then
    return (v, parents)
  for e in graph.adjacencyList[v] do
    u ← e.dest
    if distances[u] == inf then
      distances[u] ← distances[v] + 1
      parents[u] ← v
      queue.enqueue(u)
 return (null, parents)
```

For the starting point only, we need to set its distance (from itself) to 0.

Starts a loop, running until the queue is empty. It will run at least once, because of line #3.

Dequeues the head of the queue (equivalently, extracts the top of a priority queue). This will become the current vertex.

If we reached the goal, we are done; just return current vertex. The function isGoal can abstract the condition checked to find the goal vertices: it can be reaching one or more specific goal vertices, or getting to vertices that satisfy a certain condition.

If this vertex hasn't been discovered yet (its distance has never been set), then the path with fewer edges from start to u certainly passes through v (because of the way we are expanding the search frontier). Notice that because all edges are assigned distance 1, this condition is only true the first time we discover a vertex, reaching it in the least number of hops from the source.

Consequently, the first time a vertex is discovered, sets its distance, its parent, and then adds it to the queue so it can later be visited in a future iteration

At its core, this algorithm keeps a queue of vertices that will be visited next, the so-called *frontier*. Vertices are kept in a specific order, so that they are processed from the one closest to the source, to the ones furthest away. The container used to keep track of the vertices in the frontier could be a priority queue, but it would be overkill. Because the metric we use to compute the distance of each vertex from the source is just the number of edges traveled, it turns out that the algorithm naturally discovers vertices in the same order in which they need to be processed. Furthermore, each vertex's distance can be computed at the time of discovery (the first time each vertex is found while visiting another vertex adjacency list).

So, besides the initialization performed in lines #2–9, the core of the BFS algorithm is the loop at line #10: a vertex v is dequeued and visited. After (optionally) checking whether we reached the search's goal (if so, we can already return v), we start exploring v's neighborhood (aka its adjacency list, all its outgoing edges). If we find a vertex u that we hadn't discovered yet, then we know that its distance from the

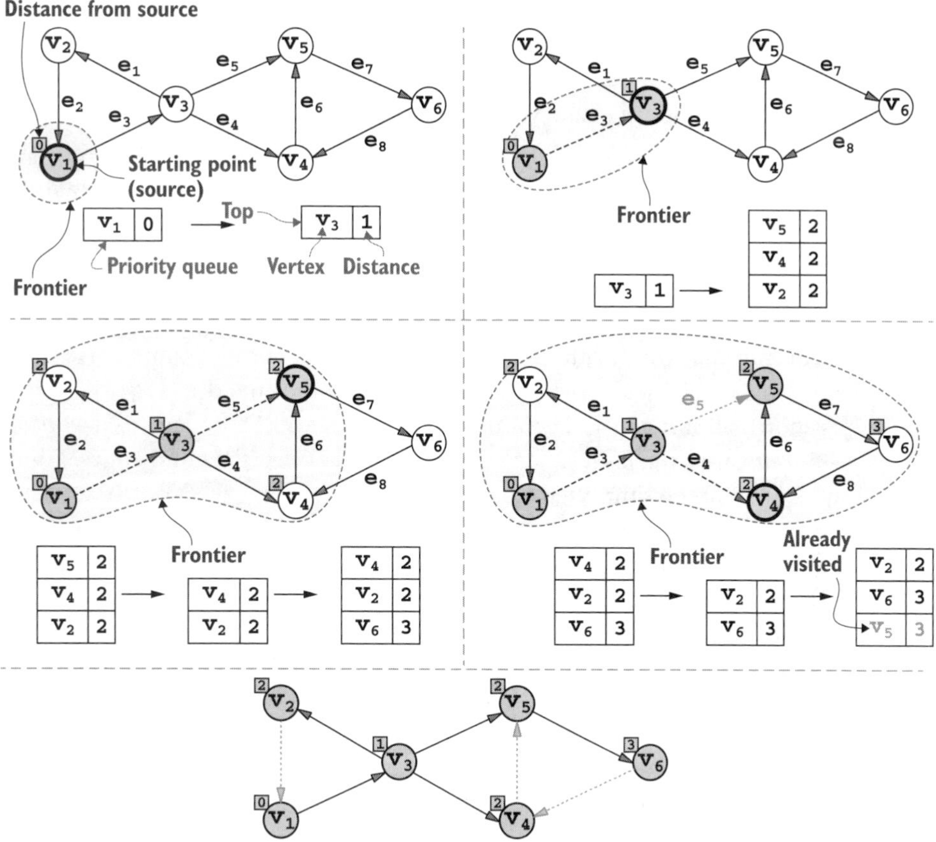
Distance from source
Starting point
(source)
Top
Priority queue
Vertex
Distance
Frontier
Already
visited

Figure 14.11 BFS in action. In this example, we show a single-source, all-vertices run computing the distance between a source and all vertices in the graph. The algorithm explicitly maintains a queue with the vertices in the frontier, which will be explored next. The vertices are naturally ordered by their distance from the source, so a regular queue can be used, though conceptually the algorithm behaves as if it was using a priority queue. Dashed edges in the first four sub-figures are those edges traversed from source to current vertex (the one at the top of the queue on the left), while the dotted, semi-transparent edges in the bottom figure are those edges that aren't included in the shortest paths from the source vertex to the rest of the graph.

source will be the distance to get to v plus 1; therefore we can set the distance for u and add u to the tail of the queue.

How can we be sure that u is going to be visited in the right order, that is, after all vertices closer to the source than u and before the ones further away than u?

This can be proved by induction on the distance of vertices. The base of the induction is the initial case. We add the source vertex with a distance 0. This vertex is the only one at distance 0, and so any other vertex added later can't be closer than (or as close as) the source.

For the inductive step, we assume that our hypothesis is true for all vertices at distance d-1, and we want to prove it for vertex v at distance d; therefore, v is extracted from the queue after all vertices at distance `d-1` and before all vertices at distance `d+1`. From this, it follows that none of the vertices in the queue can have distance `d+2`, because no vertex at distance `d+1` has been visited yet, and we only add vertices to the queue when examining each visited vertex's adjacency list (so, the distance of a vertex added can only grow by `1` unit with respect to its parent). In turn, this guarantees that `u` will be visited before any vertex at distance `d+2` (or further away) from the source.

For the inductive hypothesis, moreover, we are sure that all vertices at distance `d-1` are visited before `v`, so all vertices at distance `d` are already in the queue, and hence they will be visited before `u`.

This property allows us to use a simple queue instead of a priority queue. Not bad, considering that the former has a `O(1)` worst-case running time for enqueuing and dequeuing its elements (while heaps, for example, need `O(log(n))` steps for each operation), allowing us to keep the running time of BFS linear. It's a worst-case `O(|V| + |E|)`, linear in the largest between the number of vertices and edges. For connected graphs, this can be simplified to `O(|E|)`.

We mentioned that checking whether search has reached the goal (line #12) and the whole concept of goal vertex are optional. We can also use BFS to just compute the paths and distances from a single source to all the other vertices in the graph.[6] It's worth noting that as of today there is no known algorithm that can find the shortest path to a single destination more efficiently than BFS. In other words, it's asymptotically equivalently expensive to compute the single-source-single-destination shortest path, and the single-source-all-destinations shortest paths.[7]

If we were interested in all the distances between all the pairs of vertices, we would have better options than running BFS `|V|` times (but that's out of scope here).

14.3.3 Reconstructing the path to target

Quite often, besides computing the minimum distance of a certain vertex from a source vertex, we are also interested in discovering the shortest path to that vertex, meaning which edges should be followed, and in which sequence, to get from source to destination.

As shown in the bottom part of figure 14.11, we can obtain a tree considering the "parent" relation between visited and discovered vertices: each vertex `u` has exactly one parent, the vertex `v` that was being visited when `u` was discovered (line #15 in listing 14.2).

This tree contains all the shortest paths from the source vertex to the other vertices, but the output of the BFS algorithm is just a dictionary, so how can we reconstruct these paths from the `parents` container that is returned?

Listing 14.3 describes the algorithm. It starts from the goal vertex (the last vertex in the path) and reconstructs the path backward at each step, looking for the parent

[6] By either removing the checks for goal or passing a function that always returns `false` as the `isGoal` argument.

[7] Just to be clear, this is different than computing the optimal route through several or all vertices. Single-source-all-destinations only computes the optimal paths from the source to each other vertex taken individually.

of the current vertex. In simple graphs, since there is only one edge between an ordered pair of vertices, if we know that we moved from vertex v to vertex u, the edge traversed becomes implicit. In multigraphs, we would have to keep track of the actual edge chosen at each step.

Listing 14.3 The path reconstruction method

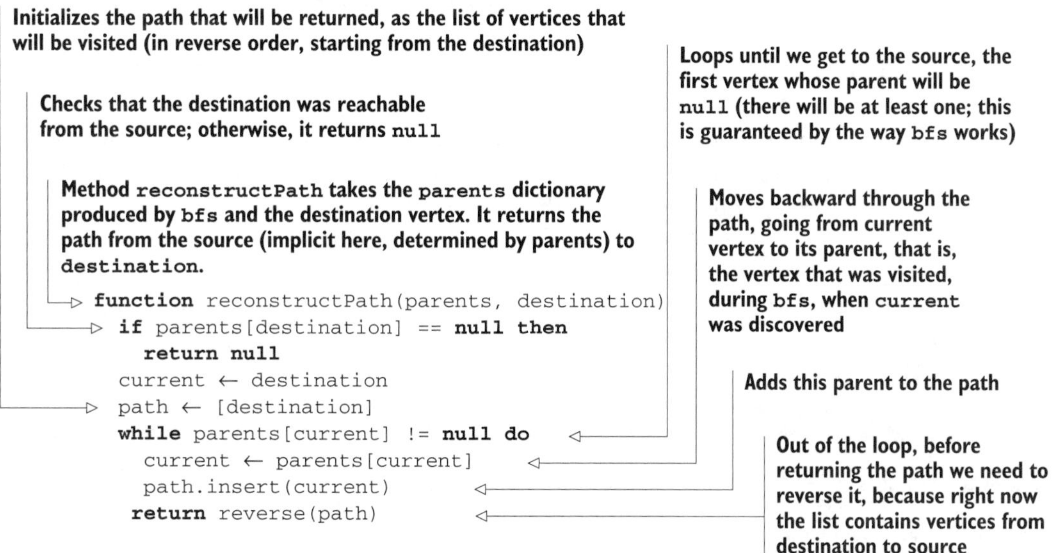
Initializes the path that will be returned, as the list of vertices that will be visited (in reverse order, starting from the destination)
Checks that the destination was reachable from the source; otherwise, it returns null
Method reconstructPath takes the parents dictionary produced by bfs and the destination vertex. It returns the path from the source (implicit here, determined by parents) to destination.
Loops until we get to the source, the first vertex whose parent will be null (there will be at least one; this is guaranteed by the way bfs works)
Moves backward through the path, going from current vertex to its parent, that is, the vertex that was visited, during bfs, when current was discovered
Adds this parent to the path
Out of the loop, before returning the path we need to reverse it, because right now the list contains vertices from destination to source

```
function reconstructPath(parents, destination)
  if parents[destination] == null then
    return null
  current ← destination
  path ← [destination]
  while parents[current] != null do
    current ← parents[current]
    path.insert(current)
   return reverse(path)
```

The code in listing 14.3 assumes that the parents dictionary is well formed, that the graph is connected, and that there is a path from source to destination. If all of that holds true, there are only two cases where the current vertex can have a null parent: either current is the destination vertex (and in that case, it means it wasn't reachable from the source), or current is the source vertex.

If parents[destination] != null, in fact, this means that the destination was reached by traversing a path from the source (because of the way BFS works), and it can be proven by induction that there must be a chain of vertices between those two vertices.

Let's see the algorithm in action on the result of the run shown in figure 14.11. bfs, on that graph, using v_1 as source, returned the following values for parents:

$$[v_1 \rightarrow \textbf{null},\ v_2 \rightarrow v_3,\ v_3 \rightarrow v_1,\ v_4 \rightarrow v_3,\ v_5 \rightarrow v_3,\ v_6 \rightarrow v_5].$$

If we start at v_5, for instance, we see that parents[v_5]== v_3, and this means that we need to add v_3 to path after v_5, and then look at its parent, and so on.

Right before line #9, we have path==[v_5, v_3, v_1], and reversing it, we get the sequence of vertices we were looking for.

14.3.4 Depth first search

BFS, as we have seen, uses a clear strategy to traverse a graph. It starts from the closest vertices to a source, and then it propagates in all directions like a wave, in concentric rings: first all the vertices at distance 1, then the next ring, with all the vertices at distance 2, and so on.

This strategy is, as we have seen, quite effective when we have to find the shortest paths from a source to the other vertices in a graph; at the same time, of course, this is not the only possible strategy to traverse a graph.

A different approach, for instance, is to traverse paths "in depth." It's like when you are in a maze looking for the exit: you keep going as far away from the source as possible, choosing your direction at each intersection, until you hit a dead end (in graph terms, until you get to a vertex without any untraveled outgoing edges). At that point, you retrace your steps up to the previous bifurcation (the previous vertex with at least an untraveled edge), and choose a different path.

This is the idea behind *Depth First Search (DFS)*, basically the opposite strategy from BFS. This algorithm, described in listing 14.4, can't be used to find shortest paths, but it has numerous important applications in graph theory, and also in practice.

Listing 14.4 The dfs visit of a vertex (and its neighborhood)

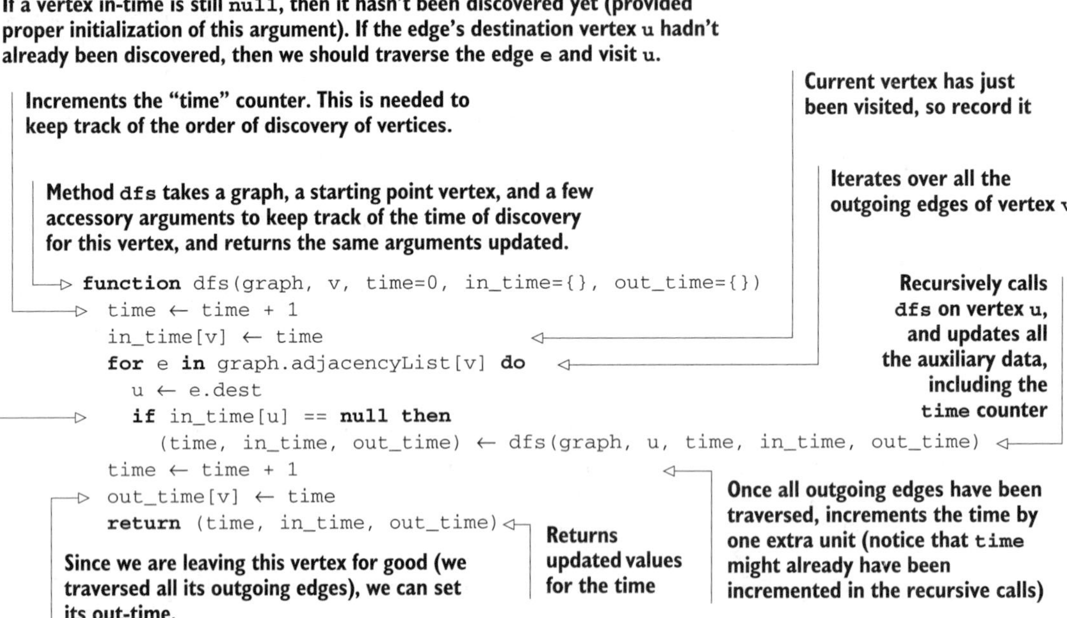
If a vertex in-time is still null, then it hasn't been discovered yet (provided proper initialization of this argument). If the edge's destination vertex u hadn't already been discovered, then we should traverse the edge e and visit u.
Increments the "time" counter. This is needed to keep track of the order of discovery of vertices.
Current vertex has just been visited, so record it
Method dfs takes a graph, a starting point vertex, and a few accessory arguments to keep track of the time of discovery for this vertex, and returns the same arguments updated.
Iterates over all the outgoing edges of vertex v
Recursively calls dfs on vertex u, and updates all the auxiliary data, including the time counter
function dfs(graph, v, time=0, in_time={}, out_time={})
  time ← time + 1
  in_time[v] ← time
  for e in graph.adjacencyList[v] do
    u ← e.dest
    if in_time[u] == null then
      (time, in_time, out_time) ← dfs(graph, u, time, in_time, out_time)
  time ← time + 1
  out_time[v] ← time
  return (time, in_time, out_time)
Once all outgoing edges have been traversed, increments the time by one extra unit (notice that time might already have been incremented in the recursive calls)
Returns updated values for the time
Since we are leaving this vertex for good (we traversed all its outgoing edges), we can set its out-time.

Figure 14.12 shows an example of DFS traversal on the same graph we used to illustrate BFS and using the same vertex, v_1, as a starting point. You can see how the sequence of vertices visited is completely different (and not just because of the way we break ties about which edge to traverse first). The most noticeable detail is, perhaps, that we use a stack instead of a queue to keep track of the next vertices to be visited.

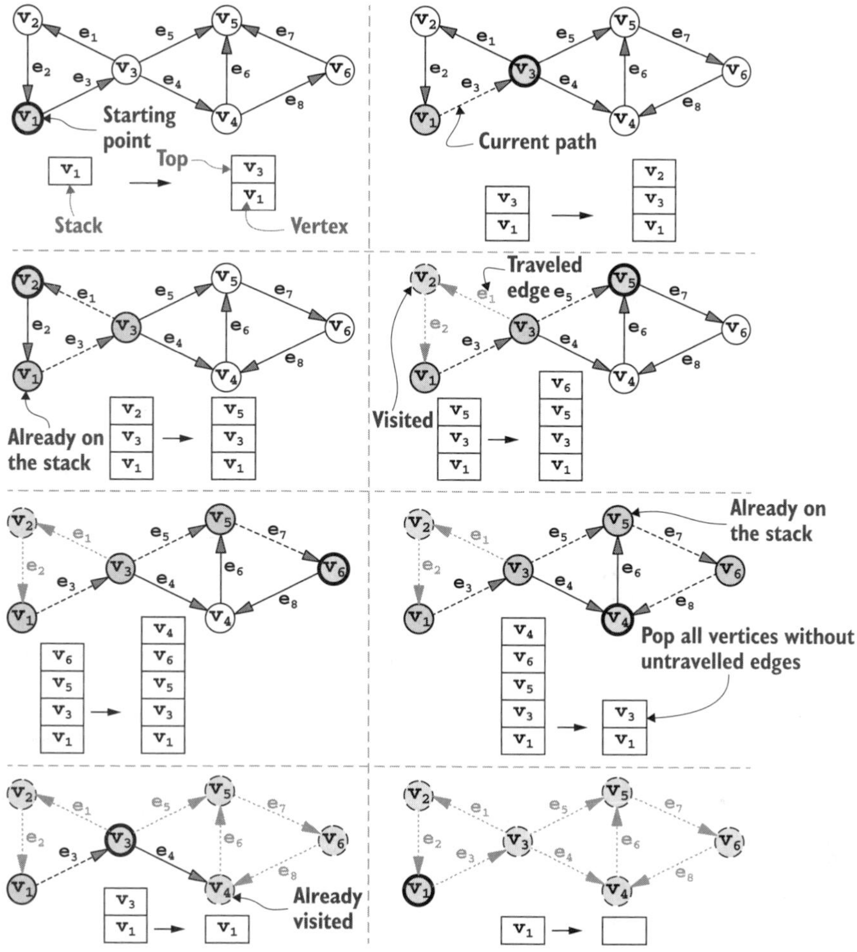
Starting point
Top
Stack
Vertex
Current path
Already on the stack
Traveled edge e_5
Visited
Already on the stack
Pop all vertices without untravelled edges
Already visited

Figure 14.12 DFS in action. The algorithm implicitly (usually, in recursive implementations—otherwise explicitly) maintains a stack with the next vertices to be traversed. If the stack is kept explicitly, it is also necessary to remember which edges have been travelled.

Similarly to BFS, there is no guarantee that a single run of a DFS traversal will visit all vertices in the graph. This is shown in figure 14.13, where instead of starting the traversal from v_1, we choose to start from v_4. Because the graph has two strongly connected components, and the first one can't be reached from v_4, this unavoidably means that vertices v_1 to v_3 can't be visited in this traversal.

To complete the traversal of the graph, we need to start another traversal in one of the remaining vertices, the ones that haven't been visited before: this is shown in

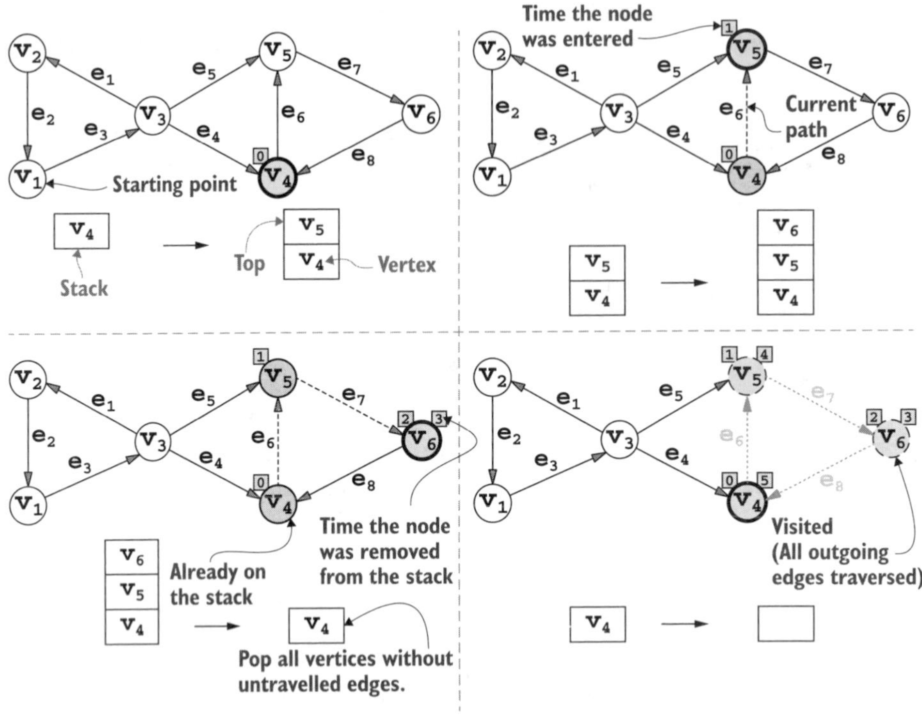

Starting point
Stack
Top
Vertex
Time the node was entered
Current path
Already on the stack
Time the node was removed from the stack
Pop all vertices without untravelled edges.
Visited (All outgoing edges traversed)

Figure 14.13 DFS in action. The starting point is crucial in the graph's traversal; both DFS and BFS couldn't reach all vertices, for instance, if the traversal started at vertex v_4 (or, for what is worth, v_5 or v_6). In this figure, vertices are also marked with the "time" they are processed, and the time they are removed from the stack. These values are relevant for several algorithms.

figure 14.14 where the new traversal starts from vertex v_3, and avoids the three vertices that hadn't already been visited in the first run.

To complete the discussion, listing 14.5 shows the code to perform a full DFS traversal of a graph, with restarts.

Listing 14.5 The dfs traversal of a graph

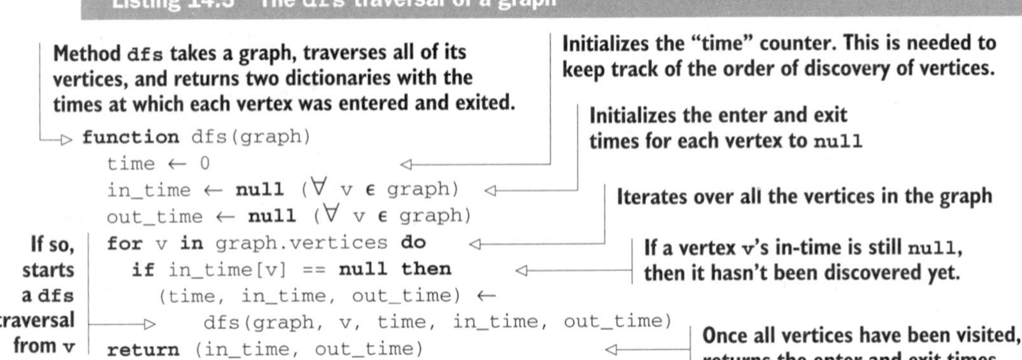

```
function dfs(graph)
  time ← 0
  in_time ← null (∀ v ∈ graph)
  out_time ← null (∀ v ∈ graph)
  for v in graph.vertices do
    if in_time[v] == null then
      (time, in_time, out_time) ←
          dfs(graph, v, time, in_time, out_time)
  return (in_time, out_time)
```


Method dfs takes a graph, traverses all of its vertices, and returns two dictionaries with the times at which each vertex was entered and exited.
Initializes the "time" counter. This is needed to keep track of the order of discovery of vertices.
Initializes the enter and exit times for each vertex to null
Iterates over all the vertices in the graph
If a vertex v's in-time is still null, then it hasn't been discovered yet.
If so, starts a dfs traversal from v
Once all vertices have been visited, returns the enter and exit times

It's also possible to pass a callback to method `dfs`, so that during traversal it can be called on each vertex visited. This can be used for a number of things, from updating the graph (changing vertices' labels or any other attribute associated), to computing certain arbitrary operations on graphs. All you need to do is pass the callback as an extra argument in listings 14.4 and 14.5 and call the callback as the first thing in listing 14.4.

You can also see that in figures 14.13 and 14.14, we also added the "times" at which vertices are visited and exited (after that their whole adjacency list has been traversed). These values are fundamental for several applications, such as computing the topological sorting (for DAGs: just order vertices by reversed out-time), finding cycles (if a neighbor of the currently visited vertex has an in-time, but not an out-time), or computing connected components.

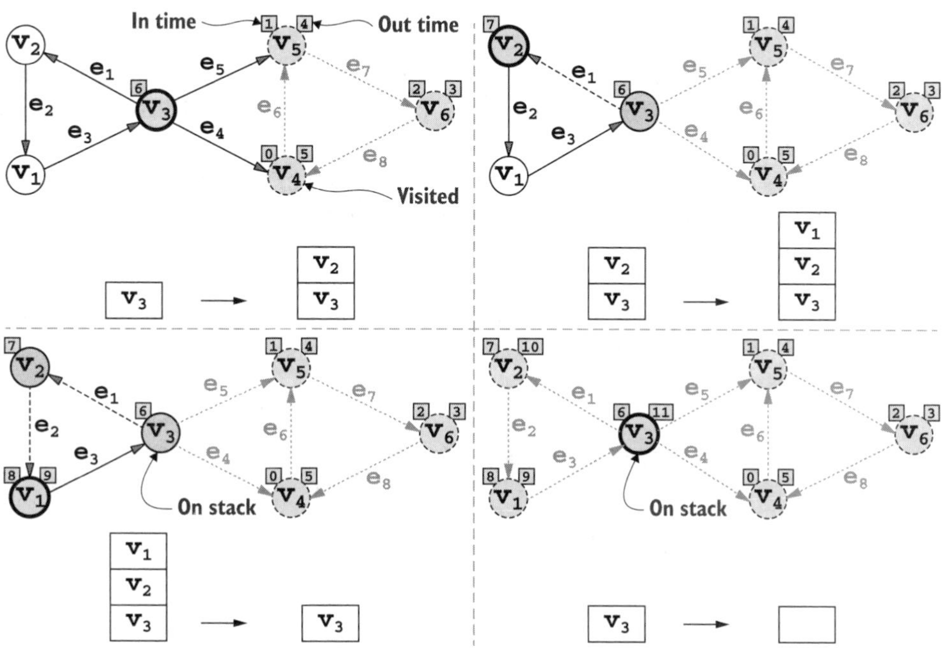
In time
Out time
Visited
On stack
On stack

Figure 14.14 DFS in action. Following up on the example in figure 14.13, we can resume the traversal and get to all the vertices by randomly selecting one of the vertices left, and restarting DFS from it.

A final note on performance: as for BFS, this algorithm also has a linear running time `O(|V| + |E|)` and requires `O(|V|)` recursive calls (or, equivalently, `O(|V|)` extra space for the stack).

14.3.5 *It's queue vs stack again*

When we look at these traversal algorithms, the first thing that should be clear is that their purposes, the contexts in which they are applied, are fundamentally different. BFS is used when the source vertex `s` is known, and we want to find the shortest path to a certain goal (a specific vertex, all vertices that can be reached from `s`, or a certain condition).

DFS, however, is mostly used when we need to touch all the vertices, and we don't care where we start. This algorithm provides great insight into a graph's structure, and it's used as a basis for several algorithms, including finding a topological sorting for DAGs, or computing the strongly connected components of a directed graph.

The interesting bit about these algorithms is that their basic version, performing only the traversal, can be rewritten as the same templated algorithm where newly discovered vertices are added to a container from which, at each iteration, we get the next element. For BFS, this container will be a queue and we'll process vertices in the order they are discovered, while for DFS, it will be a stack (implicit in the recursive version of this algorithm), and the traversal will try to go as far as possible before backtracking and visit all vertex's neighbors.

14.3.6 Best route to deliver a parcel

Now that we have seen how BFS works and how to reconstruct the path from a source to a destination, we can go back to our example and apply BFS to the graph in figure 14.10; the result is shown in figure 14.15.

In this case, the shortest path is pretty obvious—it's the closest possible path to the "straight-line distance" between the source and the destination, and it's also the path of minimum *Manhattan Distance*.[8]

And yet, by just removing the edge between vertices v_9 and v_E, the result would have to change completely. Try it out as an exercise to work out the solution for this modified case (manually or by writing your own version of BFS and running it).

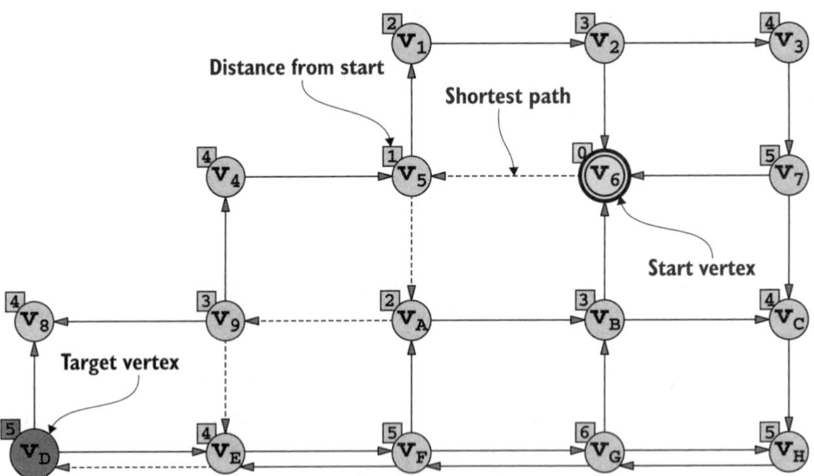
Distance from start
Shortest path
Start vertex
Target vertex
2 V1
3 V2
4 V3
4 V4
1 V5
0 V6
5 V7
4 V8
3 V9
2 VA
3 VB
4 VC
5 VD
4 VE
5 VF
6 VG
5 VH

Figure 14.15 The shortest path to destination, and shortest distances to all the vertices, computed using BFS on the graph in figure 14.10. The shortest path is shown with dashed arrows, while distances are shown next to each vertex.

[8] The Manhattan Distance, also known as block distance, is the sum of the absolute difference of the Cartesian coordinates of two points. The name comes from the fact that on the island of Manhattan, most streets have a grid layout, and so the shortest path between two intersections has a distance equal to the sum of the block's sides.

14.4 Shortest path in weighted graphs: Dijkstra

Simplifying our scenario allowed us to use a simple and fast algorithm, BFS, to obtain an approximated shortest path for our deliveries. While our simplification works well for modern city centers, such as for downtown San Francisco, it can't be applied to more generic scenarios. If we need to optimize deliveries for a wider area in San Francisco, or in other cities lacking this regular road structure, approximating distances with the number of blocks traveled doesn't work well anymore.

If we move from San Francisco (or Manhattan) to Dublin's center, for instance, as figure 14.16 shows, streets don't have a regular layout anymore, and blocks can greatly vary in size and shape, so we need to take into account the actual distance between each pair of intersections, which won't be their Manhattan distance anymore.

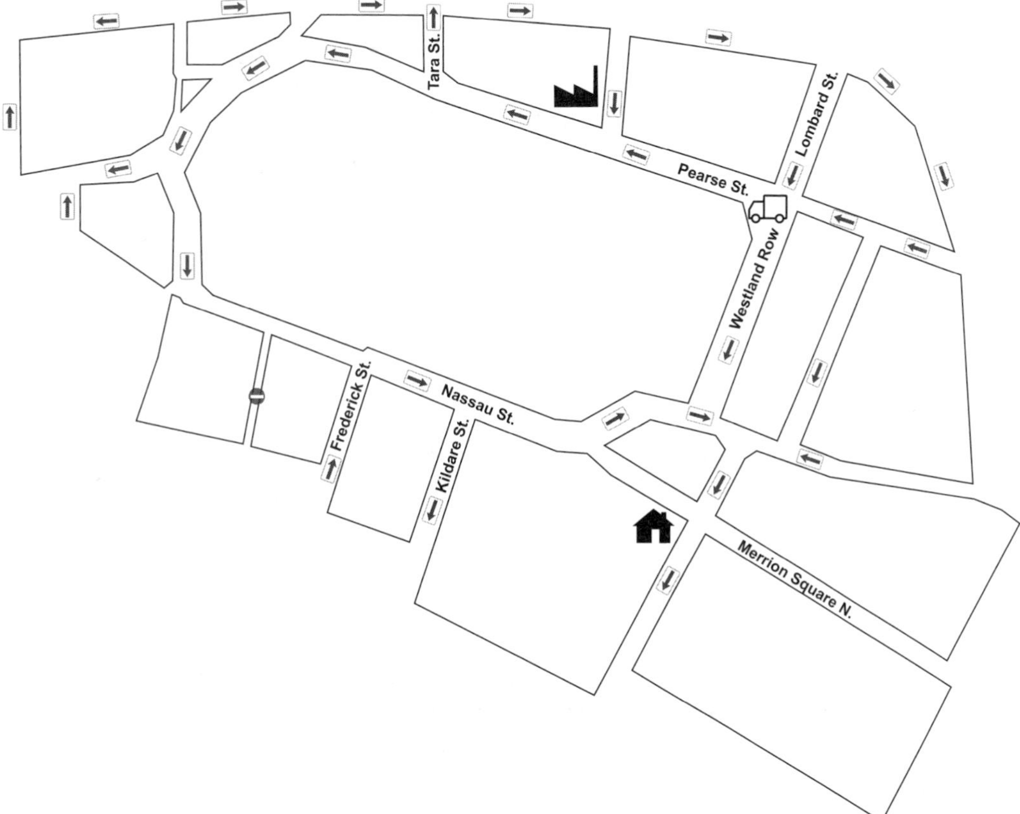
Tara St.
Lombard St.
Pearse St.
Westland Row
Frederick St.
Nassau St.
Kildare St.
Merrion Square N.

Figure 14.16 An example of city map (Dublin's city center), where the simplifications used to apply BFS for shortest paths wouldn't be possible

14.4.1 Differences with BFS

Like BFS, Dijkstra's algorithm takes a graph and a source vertex as input (optionally a goal vertex as well), and computes the minimum distance from the source to the goal (or equivalently, with the same asymptotic running time, to all the other vertices in the graph). Differently than for BFS, though, in Dijkstra's algorithm the distance between two vertices is measured in terms of edges' weight. Consider figure 14.17, which shows a directed, weighted graph that models the map shown in figure 14.16.

In this context, the minimum distance between two vertices u and v is the minimum sum, across all paths from u to v, of the weights of edges in the path. If there is no such path, that is, if there is no way to go from u to v, then the distance between them is considered to be infinite.

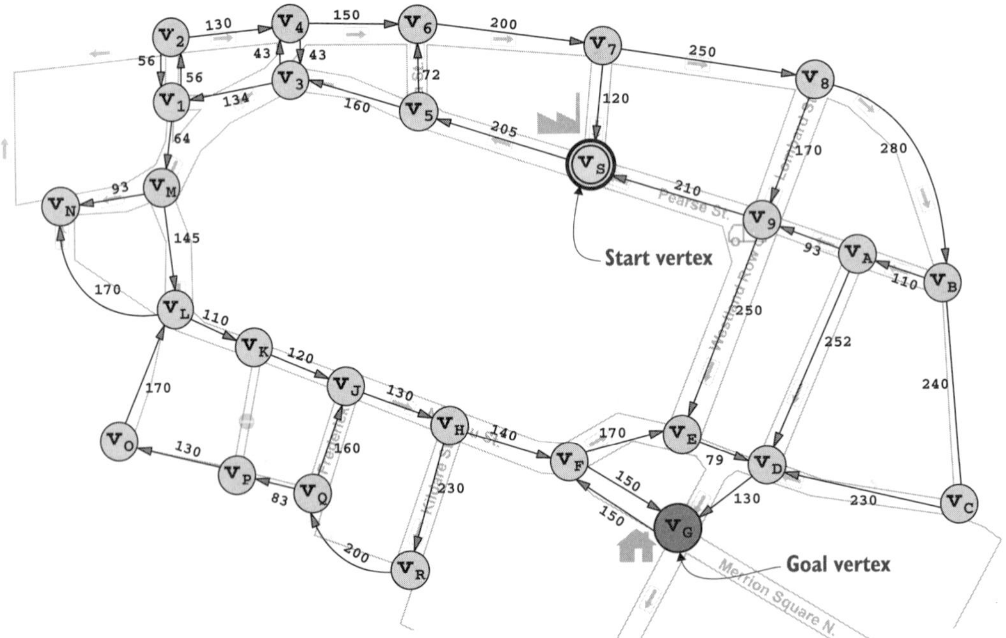

Start vertex
Goal vertex
Pearse St.
Westland Row
Merrion Square N.

Figure 14.17 Overlaying a directed weighted graph over the map in figure 14.16. Edges' weights are the distances (in meters) between the intersections modeled by the edge's vertices.

Figure 14.18 shows, on a simpler example graph, how Dijkstra's algorithm works. It is similar to BFS, with two main differences:

- The metric used is the sum of weights instead of path lengths.
- Consequently, the container needs to be used to keep track of the next vertices to be visited: we can't make do with a plain queue anymore; we need a priority queue.

Everything else, the logic of the algorithm and the auxiliary data used, is similar to BFS. That's very convenient for us because we can rewrite this algorithm from listing 14.2 with minimal changes. If you think that this similarity is a coincidence, though, hold your breath untill section 14.5.[9]

14.4.2 Implementation

Listing 14.6 describes Dijkstra's algorithm in detail. Comparing it to listing 14.2, you can see how it resembles the BFS algorithm, so much so that we can use the same algorithm shown in listing 14.3 to reconstruct the shortest path for Dijkstra's as well. Nonetheless, we need to be even more careful about performance in this case.

Listing 14.6 Dijkstra's algorithm

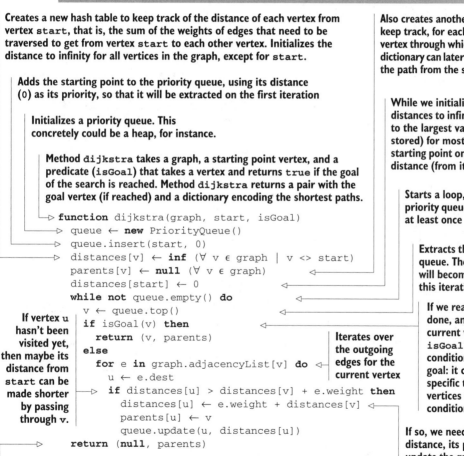

Creates a new hash table to keep track of the distance of each vertex from vertex `start`, that is, the sum of the weights of edges that need to be traversed to get from vertex `start` to each other vertex. Initializes the distance to infinity for all vertices in the graph, except for `start`.

Adds the starting point to the priority queue, using its distance (`0`) as its priority, so that it will be extracted on the first iteration

Initializes a priority queue. This concretely could be a heap, for instance.

Method `dijkstra` takes a graph, a starting point vertex, and a predicate (`isGoal`) that takes a vertex and returns `true` if the goal of the search is reached. Method `dijkstra` returns a pair with the goal vertex (if reached) and a dictionary encoding the shortest paths.

Also creates another hash table to keep track, for each vertex `u`, of the vertex through which `u` was reached. This dictionary can later be used to reconstruct the path from the start to the goal.

While we initialized the vertex distances to infinity (or, equivalently, to the largest value that can be stored) for most vertices, for the starting point only, we need to set its distance (from itself) to `0`.

Starts a loop, running until the priority queue is empty. It will run at least once because of line #3.

Extracts the top of the priority queue. The vertex extracted will become current vertex for this iteration, `v`.

If we reached the goal, we are done, and it just returns the current vertex. The function `isGoal` can abstract the condition checked to find the goal: it can reach one or more specific target vertices or get to vertices that satisfy a certain condition.

```
function dijkstra(graph, start, isGoal)
  queue ← new PriorityQueue()
  queue.insert(start, 0)
  distances[v] ← inf (∀ v ϵ graph | v <> start)
  parents[v] ← null (∀ v ϵ graph)
  distances[start] ← 0
  while not queue.empty() do
    v ← queue.top()
    if isGoal(v) then
      return (v, parents)
    else
      for e in graph.adjacencyList[v] do
        u ← e.dest
        if distances[u] > distances[v] + e.weight then
          distances[u] ← e.weight + distances[v]
          parents[u] ← v
          queue.update(u, distances[u])
  return (null, parents)
```

Iterates over the outgoing edges for the current vertex

If vertex `u` hasn't been visited yet, then maybe its distance from `start` can be made shorter by passing through `v`.

If so, we need to update `u`'s distance, its parent, and then update the queue, so that `u` will be popped from it at the right time (that is, when it becomes the closest vertex to the frontier of visited vertices).

If the goal is never reached, we need to return `null` or, equivalently, another value that signals that search failed. We can still return the `parents` dictionary to reconstruct the shortest paths to all the vertices that were reachable from `start`.

[9] Please do not literally hold your breath! And no, not even if you are speed-reading.

14.4.3 Analysis

While in BFS each vertex was added to the (plain) queue and never updated, Dijkstra's algorithm uses a priority queue to keep track of the closest discovered vertices, and it's possible that the priority[10] of a vertex changes after it has already been added to the queue.

This is due to a fundamental difference. BFS only uses the number of edges traversed as a metric, and if we use the edge's weight instead, then it's possible that a path including more edges has a lower weight than another path including fewer edges. For instance, looking at figure 14.18, there are two paths between v_1 and v_2; the path $v_1 \rightarrow v_3 \rightarrow v_2$ only traverses 2 edges, but its total weight is 8, while the other path, $v_1 \rightarrow v_3 \rightarrow v_5 \rightarrow v_2$ has length 3, but its total weight is just 5. The second path is longer, and visits one more vertex between v_3 and v_2, so the distance to v_2 will be initially set to 8 (when v_3 is visited), and then updated to 5 when it's v_5's turn to be visited.

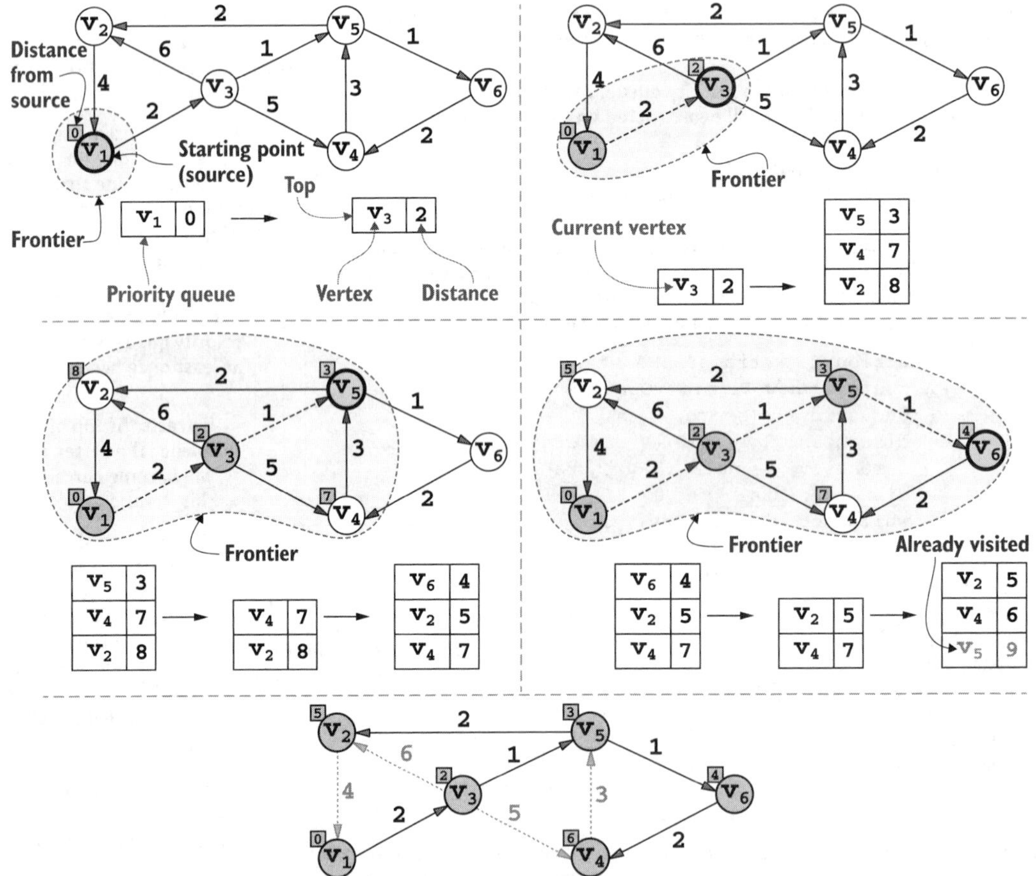
Distance from source
Starting point (source)
Frontier
Top
Priority queue
Vertex
Distance
Current vertex
Already visited

Figure 14.18 Running Dijkstra's algorithm on a directed graph (derived from the example in figure 14.10)

[10] We'll use a min-heap to store vertices in the frontier, and their distance from source is used as priority.

Because of this behavior, every time a new vertex is visited, potentially all its neighbors' priorities can be updated.

In turn, this influences the asymptotic performance of Dijkstra's algorithm, which depends on how efficiently this "update priority" operation can be implemented. In detail, for Dijkstra's algorithm, we can implement the priority queue as

- An array (sorted or unsorted, as described in appendix C)
- A heap
- A Fibonacci heap

The running time using an array for the priority queue is going to be `O(|E|*|V|)`, because each vertex will require `O(|V|)` operations to update priority or to adjust the queue after extraction.

With the remaining two choices, the running time is `O(|V|*log(|V|) + |E|*DQ(|V|))` where

- `|V|` is the number of vertices on the graph.
- `|E|` is the number of edges.
- `DQ(|V|)` is the (average) running time of each "priority update" operation.

Table 14.2 summarizes the running time of Dijkstra's algorithm, relating it to the implementation of priority queue used.

Table 14.2 Running time of Dijkstra's algorithm, on a connected graph `G=(V,E)`

	Array	Heap	Fibonacci Heap
`Running Time`	`O(|E|*|V|)`	`O(|E|*log(|V|))`	`O(|V|*log(|V|) + |E|)`[a]

[a]Amortized.

The best theoretical result is obtained with a Fibonacci heap, for which the amortized time to decrease the priority of an element is `O(1)`. However, this data structure is complicated to implement and inefficient in practice, so our best bet is using heaps. As we saw in section 2.9, d-way heaps allow us to have a more efficient implementation in practice.

14.4.4 Shortest route for deliveries

So far in this section, we've discussed how Dijkstra's algorithm works, how we can implement it, and its performance.

Now there is only one thing left to tackle: how we apply this algorithm to our example and find the shortest route to deliver an order to a customer.

The good news is that it's actually straightforward. Once we have created the graph in figure 14.17, we can just apply the algorithm to it (or to the example in figure 14.10, exactly how we did for BFS) and reconstruct the shortest path.

The result for this section's example is shown in figure 14.19, where we computed and showed the shortest distance from the source vertex (v_S) to every other vertex.

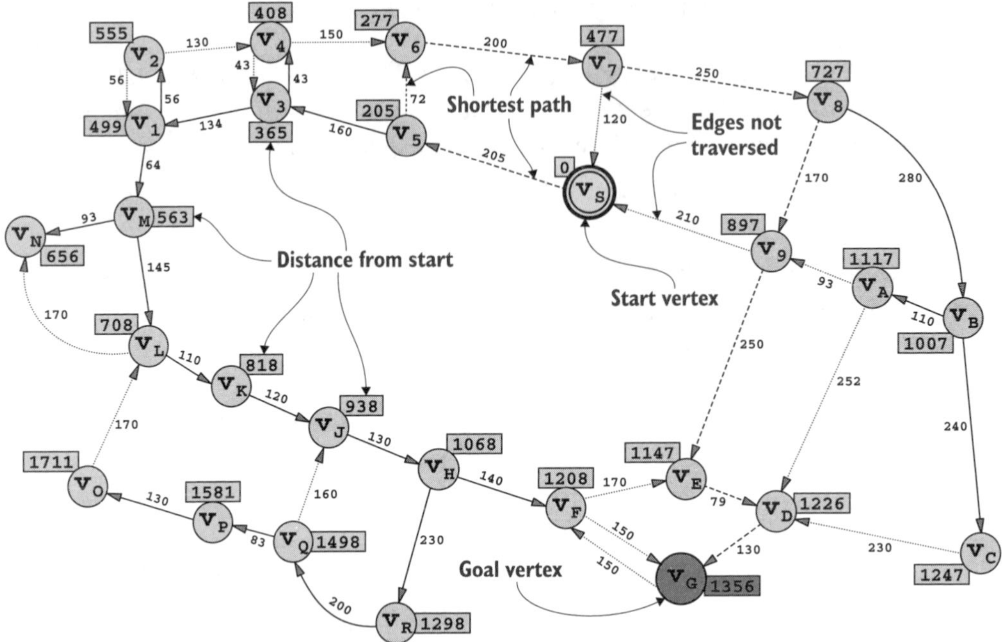
Shortest path
Edges not traversed
Distance from start
Start vertex
Goal vertex

Figure 14.19 The result of running Dijkstra's algorithm on the example in figure 14.17. Notice that there are two paths from source (v_S) to destination (v_G) whose length is very close; see how hard it would be to spot the shortest (and yet counterintuitive) one. Dashed lines are used for edges in the shortest path, solid lines are used for edges that are traversed, but don't end up in the shortest path, and finally dotted lines are used for those edges that aren't even traversed (because, at some point, it's clear that any path including them would be longer than the shortest path found).

Notice that there are some edges, drawn with a thin dotted line, that don't belong to any shortest path, while the shortest path to our destination, v_G, is highlighted with thick dashed lines.

This example is perfect to illustrate the need of algorithms such as Dijkstra's because there are two paths between v_S and v_G that add up almost to the same distance, and our intuition would likely go for the longest one, because it looks more linear.

One final consideration: As we mentioned, applying the algorithm was straightforward, but only because of one property of this graph. It doesn't have any edge with negative weight. Any such edge would, in fact, violate the assumption behind the algorithm: that if we expand the frontier of visited vertices by choosing the closest unvisited vertex at each iteration, then at the time a vertex is visited, we know its minimum distance from start.

This happens because Dijkstra's algorithm (like BFS) is a *greedy* algorithm, a kind of algorithm that can find the solution to a problem by making locally optimal choices. In fact, to decide which vertex to visit next, we only need to take into account the outgoing edges of the vertices we've already visited. Greedy algorithms can only be applied to certain problems: having negative edges makes a problem unfit to be solved with any greedy algorithm, because locally-optimal choices won't be possible anymore.

Negative-weight edges might seem counterintuitive, but they are actually quite common. If we measure distances using the gas consumed to travel between two vertices, and the goal is to not end up with an empty tank, then an edge corresponding to a road with a gas station could have a negative weight. Likewise, if we associate a cost to the gas, then an edge that allows us to perform a second delivery or a pick-up could have negative cost because we could earn extra money if we travel it.

To cope with negative edges, we need to use *Bellman-Ford*'s algorithm, an ingenious algorithm that uses the dynamic programming technique to derive a solution that takes into account negative-weight edges. Bellman-Ford's algorithm is more expensive to run than Dijkstra's; its running time is `O(|V|*|E|)`. Although it can be applied to a broader set of graphs, it too has some limitations: it can't work with graphs with negative-weight cycles[11] (at the same time, though, it can be used as a test to find such cycles).

14.5 Beyond Dijkstra's algorithm: A*

As we have seen, BFS and Dijkstra's algorithms are very similar to each other; it turns out that they both are a particular case of the A* (pronounced "A-star") algorithm.

This algorithm, shown in listing 14.7, is not just more generic; it improves the performance of Dijkstra's algorithm in at least two different situations. Before delving into those scenarios, though, let's focus on the differences between these algorithms and A*.

Listing 14.7 The A* algorithm

```
function aStar(graph, start, isGoal, distance, heuristic)
  queue ← new PriorityQueue()
  queue.insert(start, 0)
  distances[v] ← inf (∀ v ∊ graph | v <> start)
  fScore[v] ← inf (∀ v ∊ graph | v <> start)
  parents[v] ← null ( v ∊ graph)
```

Method `aStar` takes: a graph; a vertex; the starting point; a predicate (`isGoal`) that takes a vertex and returns `true` if the goal of the search is reached; a function (`distance`) that takes an edge and returns a float, the distance between its two vertices; a function (`heuristic`) that takes a vertex `v` and returns a float, an estimate of the distance between `v` and the goal. Method `aStar` returns a pair with the goal vertex (if reached), and a dictionary encoding the shortest paths.

Initializes a priority queue. This could be concretely, for instance, a heap.

Adds the starting point to the priority queue, using its distance (`0`) as its priority, so that it will be extracted on the first iteration

Creates a new hash table to keep track of the distance of each vertex from vertex `start`, that is, the sum of the weight of edges that needs to be traversed to get from vertex `start` to each other vertex. Initializes these distances to infinity for all vertices but vertex `start`.

Also creates a new hash table for the f-score of a vertex, capturing the estimated cost to be sustained to reach the goal from `start` in a path passing through a certain vertex. Initializes these values to infinity for all vertices but vertex `start`.

Finally, creates another hash table to keep track, for each vertex `u`, of the vertex through which `u` was reached. This dictionary can later be used to reconstruct the path from `start` to the goal.

[11] If a graph has a negative-weight cycle, defined as a cycle for which the sum of edges' weights is negative, then discussing shortest paths could be meaningless. By repeatedly traversing the cycle, in fact, one could get to an arbitrarily low total cost.

If we reached the goal, we are done, and just return the current vertex. The function `isGoal` can abstract the goal condition checked: it can be reaching one or more specific goal vertices or getting to vertices that satisfy a certain condition.

Extracts the top of the priority queue. The vertex extracted will become the current vertex for this iteration, `v`.

Starts a loop, running until the priority queue is empty. It will run at least once, because of line #3.

If so, we need to update its distance and its parent, and then update the queue, so that `u` will be popped from it at the right time (that is, when it becomes the closest vertex to the frontier of visited vertices).

While we initialized the vertex distances to infinity (or, equivalently, to the largest value that can be stored) for most vertices, for the starting point only, we need to set its distance (from itself) to `0`.

```
  distances [start] ← 0
  fScore[start] ← heuristic(start)
  while not queue.empty() do
    v ← queue.top()
    if isGoal(v) then
      return (v, parents)
    else
      for e in graph.adjacencyList[v] do
        u ← e.dest
        if distances[u] > distances[v] + distance(e) then
          distances[u] ← distance(e) + distances[v]
          fScore[u] ← distances[u] + heuristic(u)
          parents[u] ← v
          queue.update(u, fScore[u])
  return (null, parents)
```

If vertex `u` hasn't been visited yet, then maybe its distance from start can be made shorter by passing through `v`.

Iterates over the outgoing edges for current vertex

Updates the f-score for `u` combining the distance between `start` and `u` (for which we already have its exact value) and an estimate of the cost of reaching the goal from `u`

If the goal is never reached, we need to return `null` or, equivalently, another value that signals that search failed. We can still return the `parents` dictionary to reconstruct the shortest paths to all the vertices that were reachable from `start`.

As we can see at line #1 of listing 14.7, this generic definition of A* takes two extra arguments, a distance function, and a heuristic. They both contribute to the computation of the so-called f-score at line #18. This value is a mix of the cost of reaching the current node `u` from the source and the expected cost needed in order to reach the goal from `u`.

By controlling these two arguments, we can obtain either BFS or Dijkstra's algorithm (or neither). For both of them, the heuristic will need to be a function that is identically equal to `0`, something we could write like `lambda(v) → 0`. Both of these algorithms, in fact, completely disregard any notion of or information about the distance of vertices to goal.

For the distance metrics, the situation is different:

- Dijkstra's algorithm uses the edge's weight as a distance function, so we need to pass something like `distance = lambda(e) → e.weight`.
- BFS only takes into account the number of edges traversed, which is equivalent to considering all edges to have the same weight, identically equal to `1`! And thus, we can pass `distance = lambda(e) → 1`.

In practice, 99.9% of the times, you'd better directly implement Dijkstra's algorithm or BFS, and not as a special case of A*. This brings us to a golden rule about keeping things simple that I learned from a great engineer I worked with.

> **NOTE** Do not make your code more generic than needed. You shouldn't consider writing a generic version of something until you have at least three different variants that could be implemented as minor changes of the same generic code.[12]

General purpose code, such as the generic version of A* shown in listing 14.7, usually carries some overhead, for instance, to call methods or lambdas like `distance`, instead of just retrieving an edge's length, or for BFS, using a priority queue instead of a faster plain queue. It also becomes increasingly hard to maintain and reason about.

So, from these considerations, it should be clear that A* hasn't been developed to provide a generic method to be parameterized. And yet, it can be extremely useful.

As we mentioned, in fact, there are at least two good reasons to implement A*, two contexts in which A* provides an advantage over Dijkstra's.

Let's be clear from the beginning: this is not always true; in the general case, Dijkstra's algorithm is asymptotically as fast as A* (or the latter might not even be meaningfully applicable).

A* gains an advantage only in some contexts where we have extra information that we can somehow use.

The first case where we can use A* to drive search faster to the goal is when we have information about the distance from all or some vertices to the goal(s). Figure 14.20 explains this situation better than a thousand words! Notice that in this particular case, the key factor is that the vertices, modeling physical places in the real world, carry extra information with them (their position, which is fixed) that can help estimate their distance to the final goal. This isn't always true and is usually not the case for generic graphs.

To put it differently, the extra information here doesn't come from the graph, but from domain knowledge.

The good news is somewhat limited though, because there is no a priori guarantee that A* will perform better than Dijkstra's algorithm. On the contrary, it's easy to craft an example where A* will always do as badly as Dijkstra's algorithm. Check out figure 14.21 to get an idea how we can tweak our previous example to fool A*! The key, here and always, is the quality of the extra information captured by the heuristic function: the more reliable and closer to real distance the estimate, the better A* performs.

---

[12]Of course, using patterns like template or strategy will help keep your codebase DRY and easier to maintain, but the point is that implementing general purpose methods or classes will make your code less clean and maintainable, so you need to balance out both aspects.

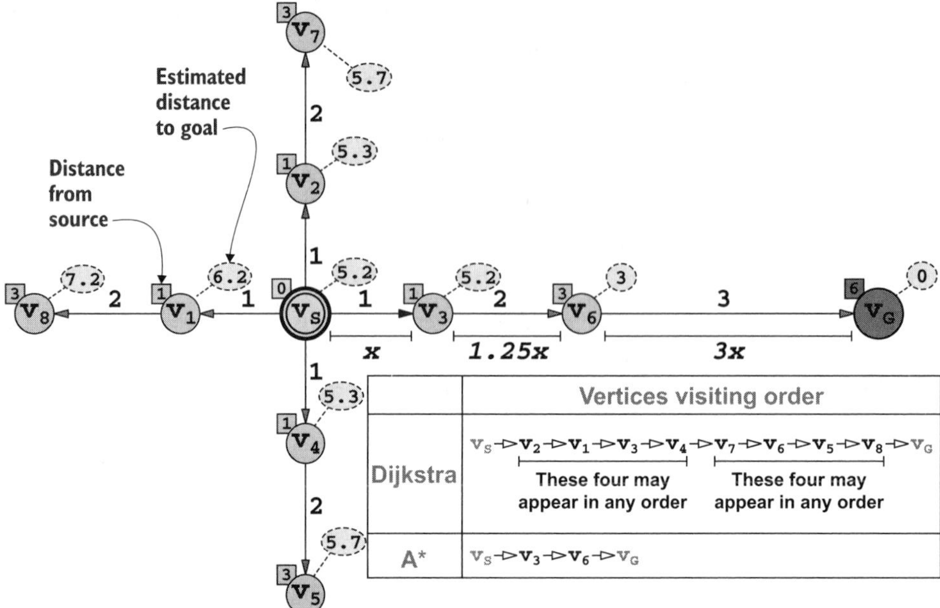

Estimated distance to goal
Distance from source
x
1.25x
3x
Vertices visiting order
Dijkstra
These four may appear in any order
These four may appear in any order
A*

Figure 14.20 An example graph where A* provides a significant speedup over Dijkstra's algorithm. While this is an edge case, in many situations we have some domain knowledge that A* can leverage to prune search branches and get a significant speedup. Notice that here the straight-line distance between vertices, used as a heuristic, as well as the edge weights, are expressed in multiples of a generic unit denoted by x (it could be meters, or miles, and so on). The numbers in the squares next to each vertex are the distance of that vertex from source, while the numbers in the dashed ellipses are the estimated distance to goal for each vertex, computed as the straight-line distance from that vertex to vertex v_G.

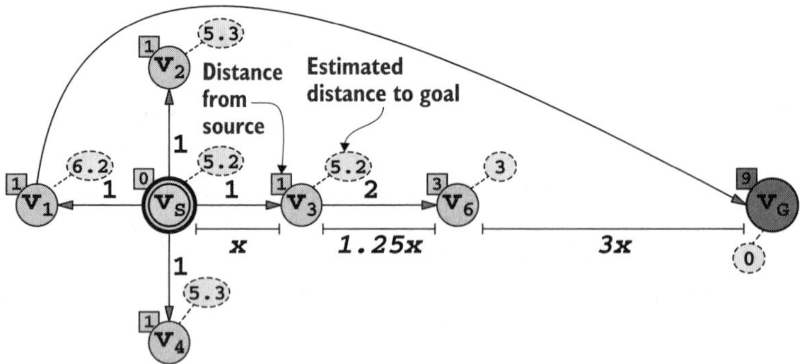

Distance from source
Estimated distance to goal
x
1.25x
3x

Figure 14.21 An edge case where A* certainly can't outperform Dijkstra's algorithm. Both algorithms will visit all vertices (A* always in the same order, Dijkstra's in a partially random order), before eventually travelling the edge from v_1 to v_G.

14.5.1 *How good is A* search?*

If we were in a class and this was a live presentation, this should be your follow-up question: Can we craft an example where A* performs consistently worse than Dijkstra's algorithm?

It turns out we can, easily: if we take the example of figure 14.21 and change just the weight of the edge from v_1 to v_G, setting it to any value smaller than 2, and at the same time we keep the same estimates, then we would be sure that A* would visit every other vertex before getting to the goal, while Dijkstra's would never visit v_6 and, depending on the order it processes edges out of v_S, it might also skip vertices v_2 to v_4.

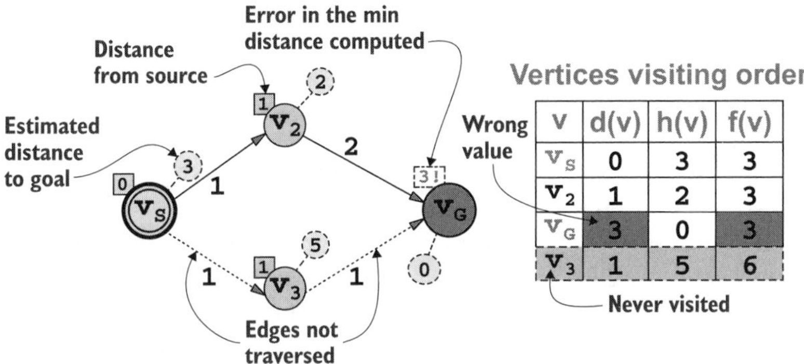
Error in the min
distance computed
Distance
from source
Estimated
distance
to goal
Edges not
traversed
Wrong
value
Vertices visiting order
Never visited

v	d(v)	h(v)	f(v)
v_S	0	3	3
v_2	1	2	3
v_G	3	0	3
v_3	1	5	6

Figure 14.22 Another edge case for A*, where the algorithm returns a non-optimal solution. Because the estimate for vertex v_3 is bloated, the goal is reached through a different path before even visiting v_3; once the goal is reached, the search stops and the wrong (non-optimal) path is returned.

The key for this example is that the heuristic overestimates the distance to goal for v_1 (and a few more vertices): A*, it turns out, minimizes the estimated cost, which can be different from the actual cost, and whenever this estimate is pessimistic, we get into trouble.

The previous example, in fact, shows how using the wrong estimates can make the search unnecessarily slower, which is inconvenient but sometimes acceptable. Things could be much worse, however, because we could also find examples where A* returns a solution whose cost is not optimal. In figure 14.22, the estimate for vertex v_3 is bloated, and consequently vertex v_G is reached through a different path before even visiting v_3. Remember that once the goal is reached, the search stops and so the wrong (non-optimal) path is returned.

While sometimes this can be considered acceptable, in practice, we usually want to avoid it, and we luckily have a way to guarantee this.

It can be proved, in fact, that A* is *complete*[13] and *optimal* when the heuristic function satisfies two conditions: it must be *admissible* and *consistent.*

[13]Completeness guarantees that only a finite number of nodes will have to be visited before reaching the goal.

- *Admissible (aka optimistic)*—Such a heuristic never overestimates the cost to reach the goal.
- *Consistent*—A heuristic is consistent if, given a vertex v and any of its successor u, the estimated cost for u is at most the estimated cost for v, plus the cost of getting from v to u. In formula, `heuristic(u) ≤ distance(v, u) + heuristic(v)`.

As one of our reviewers of this book suggested, there is an even clearer way to remember the difference between these two conditions: *admissible* means it's not overestimating the cost of a path, and *consistent* means it's not overestimating the cost of an edge.

When we plan to use A* search, the first thing we need to ensure is that we have a heuristic function that is both admissible and consistent. This condition is necessary and sufficient to ensure the optimal solution will be found.[14]

What does all of this mean for our problem—delivering goods to customers? Well, to speed up the search for the best route, we can use the "straight-line distance to the customer's address" as the heuristic. This will guide search, favoring paths that get closer to the goal over those that are directed away from it; in turn, it will require us to visit fewer vertices before reaching the goal.

Figure 14.23 shows how A* would find the best route for our previous example, the one to which we applied Dijkstra's algorithm in figure 14.19. While running Dijkstra's algorithm, we would have had to visit all vertices whose distance from the source is smaller than `1356` (the total distance of the shortest path from source to goal). A* can reach the goal faster and, although it still visits some vertices not on the shortest path, it doesn't go through vertices v_A, v_B, v_C, v_F, v_N, v_R, which are instead visited by Dijkstra's.

In this particular example, with A* we can save traversing 6 edges over 23, which is quite good (a 25% save), especially considering that there are two paths with a very close weight, differing by just 2 meters.

Considering road distance as edges' weight and straight-line distance as the heuristic, we can see that straight-line distance is certainly optimistic, because the road distance can never be shorter; at best it can be the same.

Straight-line distance is also a consistent heuristic. In fact, if we apply our choices to the condition for consistency, we get

```
straight_line(u, goal) ≤ road_distance(v, u) + straight_distance(v)
```

which is certainly true, since `straight_line(v,u)≤road_distance(v,u)`, and straight-line distance, being a Euclidean distance, certainly abides by triangle inequality.[15]

While this condition always holds, the value of the heuristic for a vertex u can be larger than the value assigned to its parent v. For example, in figure 14.23, consider vertices v_E and v_D: the straight-line distance between vertex v_D and the goal is larger

[14] For trees, admissibility alone is a sufficient condition. Can you explain why? Hint: In a tree, how many paths from root to a goal vertex pass through a given node u?

[15] Given three points A, B, and C belonging to a Euclidean space, it always holds true that `distance(A,C) ≤ distance(A,B) + distance(B,C)`.

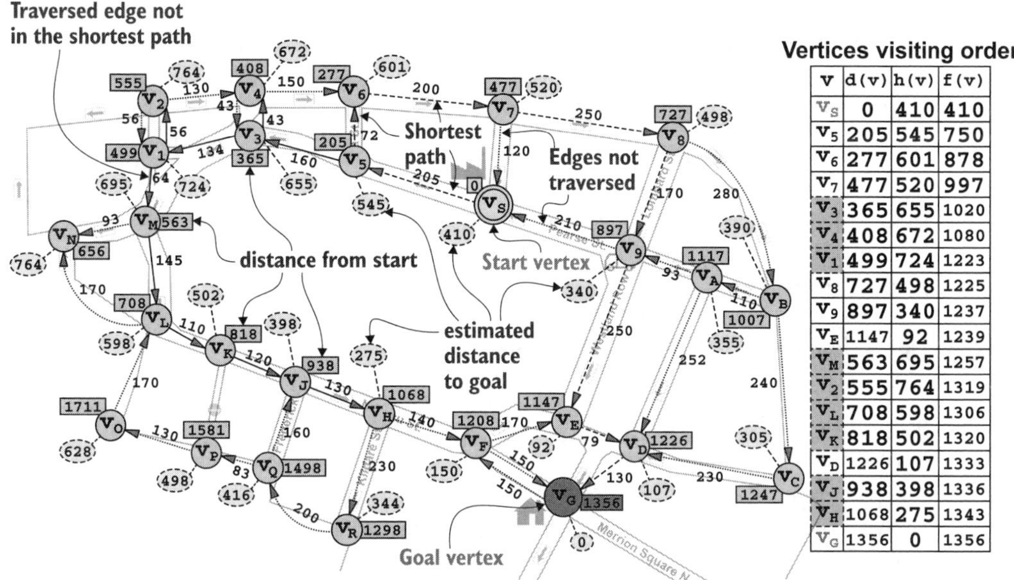
Traversed edge not in the shortest path
Shortest path
Edges not traversed
distance from start
Start vertex
estimated distance to goal
Goal vertex
Vertices visiting order

v	d(v)	h(v)	f(v)
v_S	0	410	410
v_5	205	545	750
v_6	277	601	878
v_7	477	520	997
v_3	365	655	1020
v_4	408	672	1080
v_1	499	724	1223
v_8	727	498	1225
v_9	897	340	1237
v_E	1147	92	1239
v_M	563	695	1257
v_2	555	764	1319
v_L	708	598	1306
v_K	818	502	1320
v_D	1226	107	1333
v_J	938	398	1336
v_H	1068	275	1343
v_G	1356	0	1356

Figure 14.23 Applying A* to the example graph in figure 14.19: while with Dijkstra we would have had to visit all vertices whose distance from source is smaller than `1356`, A* reaches the goal faster, and although it still visits some vertices not in the shortest path (highlighted with a shaded background in the table on the right), we can avoid paying a visit to vertices v_A, v_B, v_C, v_F, v_N, v_R.

than its parents', v_E's. This happens because not all vertices are connected by an edge (or rather, two directional edges), and so, for example, from v_E (which is the closest vertex to the goal), you can reach v_G only with a detour, by first going through v_D.

It can be proved that if, instead, the graph was fully connected, we would also visit vertices according to their straight-line distance from the goal. In other words, the value of the heuristic would monotonically decrease during the traversal.

Then again, most useful graphs are not fully connected, and luckily we don't need this strict condition for A* to be able to find the optimal solution, but we can make do with a consistent and admissible heuristic.

These properties can guarantee that the best solution will be found, but should we also aim to get the most accurate estimate possible? There might be many admissible and consistent heuristics, but does the algorithm find the best route faster if we choose one with a more precise estimate?

Needless to say, when we have to compute thousands of routes per hour, using a more efficient search can save a lot of computation, allowing shipments to leave the factory faster and ultimately saving money.

Once again, we can get a theoretical guarantee about A* performance: if we fix the heuristic and distance, then for any consistent heuristic, A* will not just be optimal, but also optimally-efficient. This means that no other algorithm is guaranteed to expand fewer nodes than A*.

That being said, the closer the estimate is to the actual distance of a vertex to the goal, the faster the algorithm will reach the goal. As an example, try to come up with a better heuristic for the graph in figure 14.23. (Hint: What could be more precise than straight-line distance?)

While we are happy to have a way to guarantee that A* will find the optimal solution, we also mentioned that sometimes it is acceptable to settle for a sub-optimal one. Especially when the cost of traversal is high, or there are constraints on the response time, we might want to choose a non-admissible heuristic that guarantees faster convergence.

14.5.2 Heuristics as a way to balance real-time data

That concludes our discussion about optimality of search. We also mentioned there is at least one other scenario where A* can prove itself particularly useful. Let's briefly explore it.

The great power of having this heuristic function is that we can use a different metric with respect to the distance and convey more information about the domain. Heuristics could even combine several data, as long as the value returned by a heuristic is scaled appropriately to make sense when compared to the edge's distance. For instance, it would make little sense (and cause terrible performance) to use meters for edges' weights and seconds (or even millimeters) for the heuristic's estimates; however, we can always scale millimeters to meters or, if the heuristic conveys information about the average time needed to reach the goal from each vertex, then we could multiply it for the roads' average or minimum speed to obtain a quantity that could then be added to any edge's weight.

But we can also take this to the next level by decoupling even more the purposes of the distance and of the heuristic. Imagine that we are computing the best route on the go, instead of a priori, like a car navigator does.

First, we switch our metric from distance to travelling time, and the time needed to traverse a road changes depending on traffic, weather, areas closed to transit during certain hours, and so on.

However, the average time needed when following a certain route is known in advance, and we can use that as a compass to balance our live decisions.

Suppose, for instance, that now you are also planning deliveries on a larger scale, and you need to ship some goods from Naples to Florence. When you get to Rome, the faster route would be through the motorway passing east of the city, and it usually would take slightly less than three hours. However, your navigator realizes that for the next 10 miles on that route there is heavy traffic, while going around Rome on the west side, the traffic is all clear. If the navigator just used Dijkstra's algorithm, the next edge to expand would be the shorter time for the next 10 miles, and it would lead you west.

Unfortunately, that would add at least one hour to your trip. A* can come to the rescue and balance the short-term advantage of a traffic-free motorway section with the long-term gain of a shorter and usually faster route.

Although this example is extremely simplified, you get the point. A* can better balance long-term costs with local choices, and that's why it has been the state-of-the-art in AI, for example, for pathfinding in video games.[16]

The next step to improve these navigation algorithms would be considering how requests for shortest path are handled in a vacuum. Especially during rush hours, when many users will request the shortest path between similar locations, suggesting the same route to all of them could lead to unnecessarily high traffic on some roads, and very low traffic on others. Wouldn't it be great if a more balanced routing system could take into consideration all requests involving the same segments, spread the traffic over several routes, and minimize the congestion due to vehicles sharing the same road?

That goal is ambitious, out of scope for this book, and out of reach of classic computers. That's why quantum developers[17] are working on it, with encouraging results.

Summary

- Graph is a data structure that can model many problems, and in general it works well when there are entities connected by some kind of proximity relation.
- While usually the adjacency list representation works better for most problems, for some problems with dense graphs the adjacency matrix is preferable.
- There are many possible ways to explore a graph, but the most common are Breadth First Search (BFS) and Depth First Search (DFS).
- Dijkstra's algorithm extends BFS when the shortest path needs to be computed in terms of the minimum edges' weight, not just the minimum number of edges.
- A* provides an improvement on Dijkstra's when we have extra information besides the edges' weight, information that can be conveyed into a heuristic estimating the distance from each vertex to the goal.

---

[16]Other applications of A*, Dijkstra's and BFS range from IP routing to graph theory and even garbage collection.

[17]You can read the details here: http://mng.bz/w99B. Graph theory is one of those fields that can be revolutionized by quantum computing; for an introduction to practical quantum computing, check out *Quantum Computing for Developers*, by Johan Vos (Manning Publications, 2021), and *Learn Quantum Computing with Python and Q#*, by Sarah C. Kaiser and Christopher E. Granade (Manning Publications, 2021).

15 Graph embeddings and planarity: Drawing graphs with minimal edge intersections

This chapter covers

- Embedding graphs on a 2-D plane
- Defining graph planarity
- Introducing complete and bipartite complete graphs
- Discussing algorithms to find out if a graph is planar
- Defining minimum crossing number for non-planar graphs
- Implementing algorithms to detect crossing edges

Now that we have introduced graphs properly in chapter 14, we are ready to take the next step: drawing a graph. So far we've talked about graphs in abstract terms, yet we had to visualize them in a certain way to describe how shortest path algorithms work. In chapter 14 we did it manually and took it for granted, but what about an automated approach to embed these data structures in a Euclidean space, and in particular in the 2-D plane?

This is not always needed for all graph applications, nor it is always possible; there are, however, many applications where the way we lay a graph's vertices and edges on a surface is crucial. Take, for instance, *printed circuits board (PCB)* design, shown in figure 15.1. The way electronic components (vertices) and conductive tracks (edges) are positioned on the board is crucial not just to the good functioning of the circuit, but also to optimizing the manufacturing process and reducing the amount of copper used, as well as the overall costs.

In this chapter, we are going to gradually introduce the main concepts about graph embeddings, focusing on 2-D planes, planar graphs, and how to minimize the intersections of the edges when a graph is not planar.

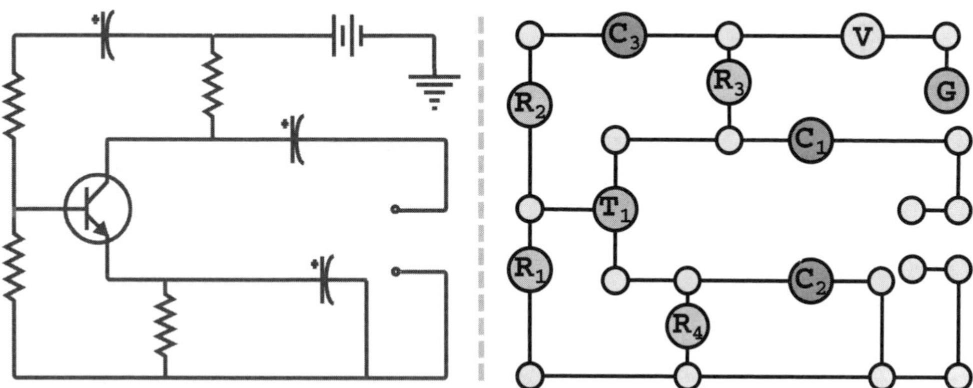
C3
V
R3
G
R2
C1
T1
R1
C2
R4

Figure 15.1 An example of an electronic circuit, and a graph embedding from which the circuit's layout may have been derived. Looking at the graph, all electronic components have a vertex dual (with different shaded colors by type), and the joints have been modeled with vertices on the graph (to cope with the fact that we need to restrict to horizontal and vertical segments for conductive tracks).

While we explain these concepts, we'll also lay the groundwork to build an application that takes a graph and displays it nicely on the screen (or, equivalently, on paper).

15.1 Graph embeddings

Graphs are an amazing data structure. In chapter 14 we just scratched the surface, talking about Dijkstra's and A*, and there are many other cool applications for graphs. You must have heard of knowledge graphs,[1] or graph databases[2] such as Neo4J, just to name a few that are hyped these days.

---

[1] A knowledge graph is an extremely advanced data structure that organizes data in the form of a graph providing in a single DS the data itself and a way to understand it. Google's knowledge graph, for example, is used to refine searches through semantics.

[2] Graph databases leverage the fact that modern data is highly interconnected, to allow organizing and querying information in a semantic way, using the graph's edges to model dynamic relations between pieces of data (the graph's vertices). This can be thought of as taking a relational DB, like a classical SQL DB, and making it more flexible and even more powerful. Take a look, for instance, at Neo4J in action, or Fullstack GraphQL.

But graphs are also used to model more tangible applications; for example, a printed circuit board can be represented as a graph, where electronic components are the vertices, and conductive tracks on the board (usually made out of copper) are the edges.[3] Besides that, we as humans often need to visualize a graph for better comprehension. Consider, for instance, a flow chart (which, not surprisingly, is a graph), like the one shown in figure 15.2.

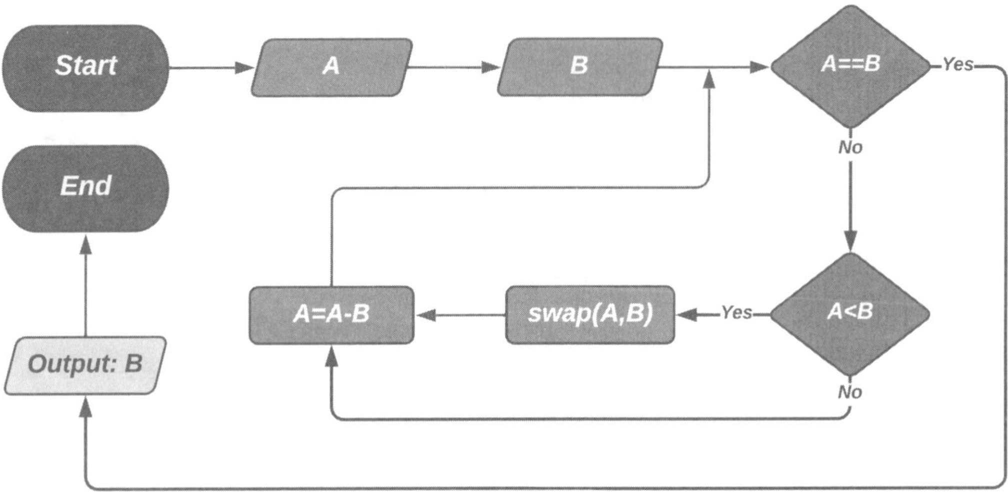
Start
A
B
A==B
Yes
No
End
A=A-B
swap(A,B)
Yes
A<B
Output: B
No

Figure 15.2 A flow chart (in this example, one for the algorithm computing the greatest common divisor (GCD) of two numbers) is a special type of graph.

When we can visualize it, it's easy both to follow the flow and to get a high-level idea of its overall structure. Check out its formal definition, in terms of graph's vertices and edges:

```
G = (
V = [Start, A, B, A==B, A<B, swap(A,B), A=A-B, Output: B, End],
E = [Start -> A, A -> B, A==B -[Yes]-> Output: B, A==B -[No]-> Output: B,
➥ A<B -[Yes]-> swap(A,B), A<B -[No]-> A=A-B, swap(A,B) -> A=A-B, A=A-B ->
➥ A==B, Output: B -> End]
)
```

Was it as easy to understand as looking at its drawing?

I think that we can agree there is fundamental value in drawing graphs, at least when we are supposed to understand and manually process them. Although this is not always the case,[4] there are many examples where we do want to visualize graphs, for instance in flow charts, UML diagrams, PERT charts, and so on.

[3] In this case, for PCBs, the edges are limited to polylines made of perpendicular segments.

[4] For instance, nobody would be expected to understand Google's knowledge graph by taking a glance at it (especially considering that it has a humongous number of vertices and edges): that graph, or graph databases, is not meant to be processed by the human mind, but through algorithms.

The next thing we need to agree (or not) upon is that not all visualizations are equally useful. Look at figure 15.3 and compare it to figure 15.2. I don't know about you, but rather than using the diagram in figure 15.3, I might as well look at the definition of the graph: that's how confusing it feels.

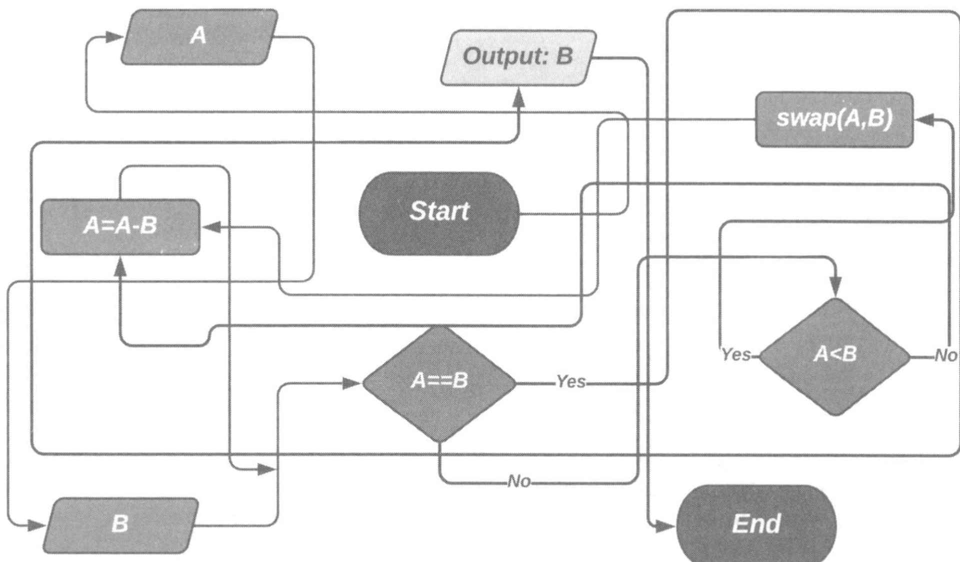
A
Output: B
swap(A,B)
Start
A=A-B
Yes
A<B
No
A==B
Yes
No
B
End

Figure 15.3 The same flow chart as in figure 15.2, but with a different layout. Can you still make sense of it?

The key difference between the two layouts is that in figure 15.3, edges cross each other multiple times, making it difficult to follow them. In figure 15.2, no edges were crossing—this is a *planar embedding* for a *planar graph*! Don't worry, we'll define those in a minute. Before that, there is one further consideration: the drawing could get even worse, if you think about it—at least in figure 15.3, edges don't overlap with vertices.

15.1.1 Some basic definitions

In the previous section, we saw how drawing a graph without intersections between its edges makes the visualization a lot clearer. But is it always possible to do so to avoid these intersections?

Hold on to this question; we'll come back to it. Meanwhile, we can look at a couple of definitions that we'll use during this and later chapters.

Drawing a graph on a plane can be thought of as placing vertices on a 2-D Euclidean space. Informally, we can imagine each vertex as a point in $\mathbb{R}^2$ (the set of all pairs of real numbers), and each edge as an arc (or a polyline) between two vertices.

More formally, we can define a planar embedding as an isomorphism (a 1:1 mapping) between an abstract graph `G` and a plane graph `G'`.

A plane graph, in turn, is defined as a pair of finite sets `(V, E)`, denoted as vertices and edges respectively, such that

- `V` is a subset of $\mathbb{R}^2$.
- Every edge `e ∈ E` is a section of a *Jordan curve* passing through two vertices.
- No two edges have the same pair of endpoints.
- No edge intersects a vertex (other than its endpoints) or any other edge.

We still owe you a definition: a Jordan curve is a planar, simple and closed curve, a non-self-intersecting continuous loop in the plane. See figure 15.4 for a few examples.

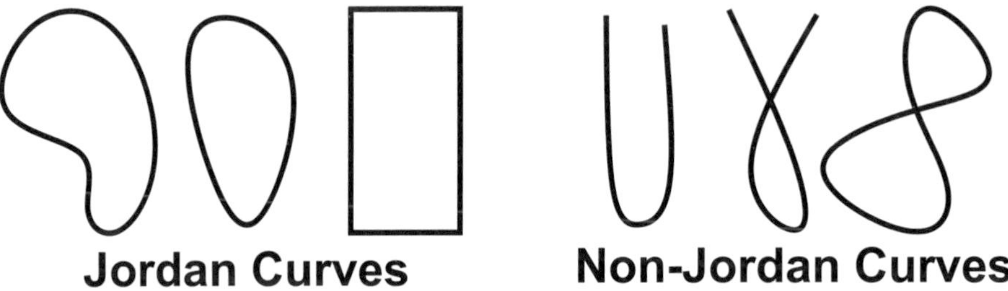
Jordan Curves
Non-Jordan Curves

Figure 15.4 Examples of Jordan and non-Jordan curves. A Jordan curve is a closed curve whose border doesn't have intersection points (it's not "twisted" like the last two examples). Notice how a rectangle (or any polygon's perimeter) is a valid Jordan curve. For graphs' edges we'll use sections of Jordan curves, so the only restriction will be that it must not self-intersect in any point.

A planar graph is thus defined as an abstract graph `G` for which there exists a planar embedding.

Now back to our question, which we can reformulate using our definitions: Are all graphs planar?

The answer is, unfortunately, no, not all graphs are planar. The first algorithm to check whether a graph is planar was given by the Polish mathematician Kazimierz Kuratowski; his theorem characterizes planarity in terms of *forbidden graphs*. It states, in fact, that for a graph to be planar, it can't contain two specific non-planar graphs as its subgraphs.

These two graphs are the simplest non-planar graphs: the complete graph K_5 and the complete bipartite graph $K_{3,3}$; Kuratowski's theorem states that "a graph is planar if and only if it doesn't contain as a subgraph neither K_5 nor $K_{3,3}$, nor any *subdivision* of those two graphs."

This was an amazing result, but to appreciate it better, we should first consider a few more definitions.

15.1.2 Complete and bipartite graphs

A *complete graph* is a graph where each vertex is connected by an edge to each other vertex in the graph. In these graphs, the number of edges is maximal for simple graphs, being quadratic with respect to the number of vertices: $|E| = O(|V|^2)$.

Notice, however, that a complete graph doesn't contain loops; therefore, the exact number of edges of a complete graph with `n` vertices is `n * (n-1) / 2`, where `|V| == n`.

Complete graphs are denoted with the letter `K`, from Kuratowski's initials, and a subscript that indicates the number of vertices in the graph; therefore, K_5 (figure 15.5) denotes the complete graph with 5 vertices, and in general, K_n is the complete graph with `n` vertices.

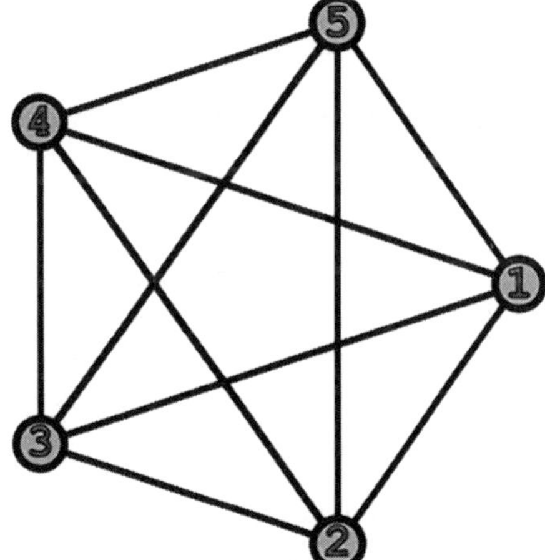
5
4
1
3
2

Figure 15.5 An embedding of a complete graph with 5 vertices. Is this the best way to draw it?

A *bipartite graph* is a connected graph where vertices can be partitioned into two groups, let's call them `A` and `B`, such that vertices in group `A` are only connected to vertices in group `B` (in other words, each vertex in group `A` can't have any edge to another vertex within group `A`, and likewise for group `B`).

A *complete bipartite graph* just has all the possible edges between the two groups of vertices—again, loops are not allowed.

$K_{n,m}$ is the generic complete bipartite graph with two partitions of `n` and `m` vertices each, and $K_{3,3}$ (figure 15.6) is the complete bipartite graph with two partitions having 3 vertices each.

A complete bipartite graph whose partitions have size `n` and `m` has exactly `n * m` edges.

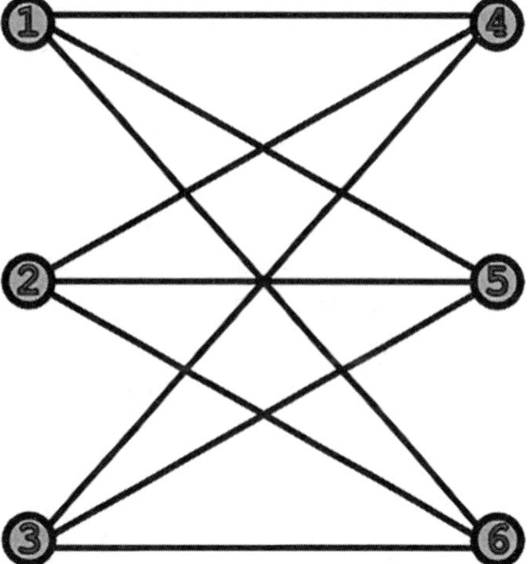
1
4
2
5
3
6

Figure 15.6 An embedding of `K3,3`. Again, do you think there could be a more convenient embedding for this graph?

The generic *embedding* (not necessarily planar) is defined similarly to what we did in the previous section; it's an isomorphism Γ between a graph `G` and a subset `G'=(V,E)` of $\mathbb{R}^2$, such that:

1. `V` is a subset of $\mathbb{R}^2$
2. Every edge `e ϵ E` is a section of a Jordan curve[5] between two vertices.
3. No two edges have the same pair of endpoints.
4. No edge intersects a vertex (other than its endpoints).

[5] A Jordan curve is a planar, simple and closed curve, a non-self-intersecting continuous loop in the plane.

Basically, with respect to the definition of a plane graph and planar embedding given in section 15.1.1, we only waive the requirement that no edges can ever cross.

15.2 Planar graphs

Kuratowski's theorem might seem counterintuitive, defining a planar graph in terms of what it can't contain. It was, however, an important tool to

1. Recognize that two categories of graphs (complete and complete bipartite) are non-planar (except for their smallest specimens), and there's no need to try to find ways to avoid intersections when drawing them.
2. Mathematically prove when a graph isn't planar.

Although it was a great tool for mathematical proofs, using it for an algorithm that automatically checks if a graph is planar was another story.

We'll see how to implement a planarity testing algorithm later in this section. First, let's finish our discussion of Kuratowski's graphs.

If we look at figure 15.5, that embedding of K_5 has 5 points where edges cross; for each abstract graph G, however, there are infinitely many possible embeddings. As you can imagine, there are infinitely many ways you can draw G, moving each vertex a little bit (or a large bit) in any direction, and even using a different curve for the edges (for instance, infinitely many curves instead of segments).

This holds true for K_5 as well, obviously. Now the point is, are all these embeddings equivalent, with respect to the way edges cross each other?

Well, we already know a way to draw K_5 so that 5 pairs of edges cross, so if we can find another way where its edges cross more, or less, we have evidence that not all embeddings are the same.

Long story short, figure 15.7 shows an embedding for K_5 with just a single cross-point between two edges.

Therefore, we can say that the answer to this question is no, they aren't all equivalent. As a matter of fact, working to find the "best"[6] possible embedding for graphs will be our quest for the rest of this book.[7]

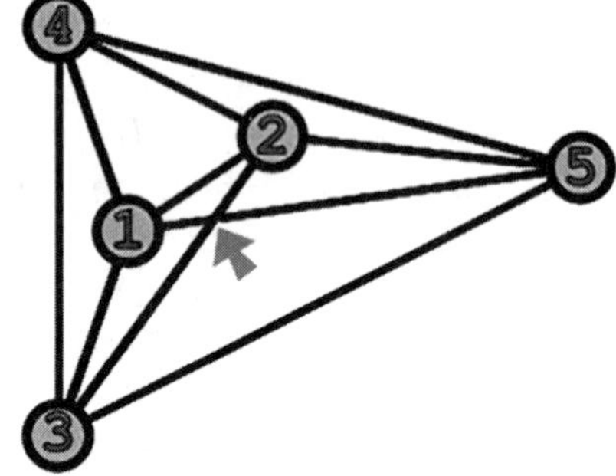
4
2
5
1
3

Figure 15.7 A better embedding for K_5. In this case we have only one crossing point, indicated by the fat arrow. Notice that there are still infinitely many embeddings equivalent to this one.

[6] We'll also have to discuss what makes an embedding the best or at least better: "having fewer intersections" is a good starting point, though.

[7] While we present ways to solve this problem, we'll introduce new algorithms and techniques that can also be applied to other areas besides graphs.

15.2.1 Using Kuratowski's theorem in practice

Kuratowski's theorem states that K_5 and $K_{3,3}$ are the "simplest" graphs that don't have a planar embedding. What did he mean by "simplest"? Well, in this case it means that that there isn't any smaller graph (meaning with fewer vertices or edges) that isn't planar, and so every sub-graph of either K_5 or $K_{3,3}$ has a planar embedding.

I've always found it curious that there are two base cases. It wasn't possible to find a single base graph because these two are fundamentally anisomorphic, but at the same time, it's quite remarkable that any other non-planar graph can be reconducted just to these two.

You might wonder how we know both that there is no way to draw these graphs without intersections, and that there isn't any simpler graph that's not planar. Well, Kuratowski proved it, so we can trust his theorem.

But in case you still have doubts, you can also try to scramble the vertices in figure 15.7 and see if you can find a planar embedding; make yourself comfortable, because it might take a while, until you realize it's not possible!

The other half of the claim, that there isn't any smaller non-planar graph, is easier to show. Let's focus on K_5 and first look at a graph with fewer vertices, in particular K_4, shown in figure 15.8.

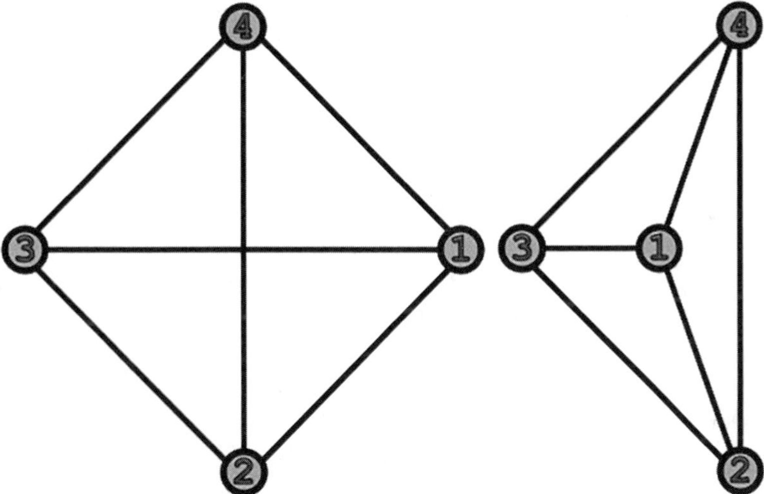
4
3
1
2
4
3
1
2

Figure 15.8 Two embeddings for K_4. Although it would seem like a good candidate for non-planarity, it's enough to move one vertex around to find a planar embedding, as shown on the right.

At first sight, if we draw this graph naively, it seems like it has a pair of crossing edges. It's easy, however, to move one of the vertices past the crossing point to obtain a planar embedding.

The other possibility to rule out is that there is a non-planar graph with fewer edges than K_5; however, if we look at figure 15.7, it's immediately obvious that if we remove either edge 1->5 or edge 2->3, then we also get rid of the one intersection in the drawing, as shown in figure 15.9. Since a complete graph is symmetrical and relabeling-invariant,[8] we can obtain an equivalent embedding (ignoring the labels) regardless of which edge we remove from K_5.

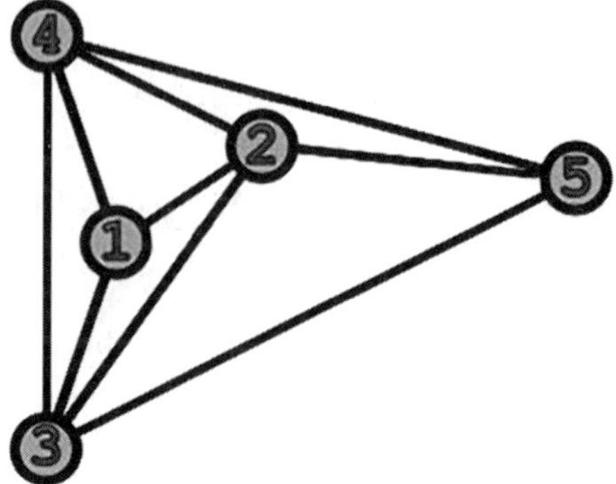
4
2
5
1
3

Figure 15.9 Any graph obtained by removing an edge from K_5 can be embedded in the plane without any intersection.

In conclusion, the largest sub-graphs of K_5 are planar, and hence any other graph with 5 or less vertices and less than 9 edges is planar.

The same thing can be shown for $K_{3,3}$; investigating its sub-graphs can be a good exercise to gain a better understanding of bipartite graphs and embeddings.

15.2.2 Planarity testing

Checking to see if a graph is planar is trickier than you might think. Even checking whether an embedding is planar isn't that easy: that's one of the tasks our brain performs easily, but it's not that simple to replicate with an algorithm. If we want to avoid resorting to computer vision (and we usually do, for this kind of task[9]) we need to restrict the way we draw edges, for instance, limiting to straight-line segments or Bézier curves, so that we can use math formulas to compute if they intersect. Still, the computational effort needed to check the number of intersections on a large graph remains considerable.

And this is just for a single embedding. Determining if a graph is non-planar means proving that for any possible embedding we can come up with, there is at least an intersection.

We already introduced Kuratowski's work on planar graphs, providing the first method to determine if a graph is planar.

Planarity, however, had already been studied for a long time, and in fact Euler, in the 18th century, came up with an invariant (proved only in 1811 by Cauchy) providing necessary conditions for a graph to be planar.

Although these conditions are not sufficient, so they can't be used to prove planarity, they are cheap to compute and, when violated, they rule out planarity.

[8] It doesn't matter how we label the vertices, because vertices are isomorphic: equivalent one to another, and each adjacent to all the other vertices.

[9] Besides being computationally heavy, state-of-the-art computer vision needs a large dataset and a long time to train, and obviously it doesn't provide a deterministic algorithm.

The two conditions we can more easily implement in our tests are

- Given a simple, connected graph `G=(V,E)` with at least 3 vertices, `G` is planar only if `|E| ≤ 3|V| - 6`.
- If `|V| > 3` and `G` doesn't have any cycle with length 3, then `G` is planar only if `|E| ≤ 2|V| - 4`.

So, as a first step in a planarity test algorithm, we can check, in linear time `O(V+E)`, both conditions:[10] if either doesn't hold, we already know that the answer is "non-planar".

There are several algorithms to test for planarity. While none of them is particularly easy to implement, many are also inefficient: the first efficient algorithm, running in worst-case linear time, was derived only in 1974 by Hopcroft and Tarjan.

The inefficient algorithms that had been developed before would take up to `O(|V|³)`, or even worse, as we'll see.

One way to try to improve the situation is by using the divide-and-conquer strategy to break down the original graphs into smaller subgraphs that can be tested separately.

This is possible thanks to the following two lemmas:

- A graph is planar if and only if all its connected components are planar.
- A graph is planar if and only if all its biconnected components are planar.

In chapter 14 we have already given the definition of *connected graph*: `G` is connected when from any vertex `v ∈ G` it is possible to find a path to any other vertex `u ∈ G`. If a graph is not connected, we can define its connected components as the maximal disjoint subgraphs of `G` that are connected.

A *biconnected graph* is a connected graph with the additional property that there is not a single vertex `v ∈ G` such that removing `v` from `G` will disconnect the graph. An equivalent definition of a biconnected graph can be given: `G` is biconnected if for any pair of vertices `u, v ∈ G` there exist two disjoint paths between them. These two paths, therefore, can't have any edge in common or any vertex except for `u` and `v`.

The proof of the first lemma is trivial. For a disconnected graph, because there are no edges between its connected components, it's sufficient to draw each component such that it won't overlap with the others.

As a consequence of the two lemmas, we can split any graph `G` into its biconnected components and apply the planarity testing of choice to each of them separately.

15.2.3 A naïve algorithm for planarity testing

Since we have mentioned more than once that there is an (inefficient) algorithm based on Kuratowski's theorem that is fairly straightforward to implement, let's actually start from there. Listing 15.1 shows a template method that wraps any planarity testing algorithm, making sure we break down a graph into its connected (or, even better, biconnected) components and running the testing on each of them.

---

[10]The first condition can be checked in constant time if we have the information about the size of the graph.

In chapter 14 we have seen how we can find the connected components of a graph using DFS; finding biconnected components is slightly more complicated, but it can still be done using a modified version of DFS.[11]

Listing 15.1 Planarity testing template algorithm

```
function planarityTesting(graph, isPlanar)
  components ← biconnectedComponents(graph)
  for G in components do
    if not isPlanar(G) then
      return false
  return true
```

- Method `planarityTesting` is a template meta-function taking a graph and a planarity testing algorithm, and applying the algorithm passed to all the biconnected components of the graph. If any fails the planarity testing, the graph is non-planar.
- Breaks down the graph into its biconnected components (you could use connected components to keep it simple)
- Cycles through the graph's components
- If any component isn't planar, the whole graph is non-planar.
- If all components are planar, we can return `true`.

Now we need to define the actual method performing planarity testing on each biconnected (or connected) component. Listing 15.2 shows the method based on Kuratowski's theorem.

The algorithm leverages the inductive definition of a graph. While trees can be defined by induction on the number of vertices (we construct larger trees by adding children to a root), given a graph `G=(V,E)`, it can be inductively grown in two different ways.

As we have seen in chapter 14, in fact, it could be

- `G'=(V+{v}, E)`: we add a new vertex to `G`.
- `G'=(V, E+{(u,v)}) | u, v ∈ V`: we add a new edge to `G`.

Listing 15.2 Planarity testing based on KK's theorem

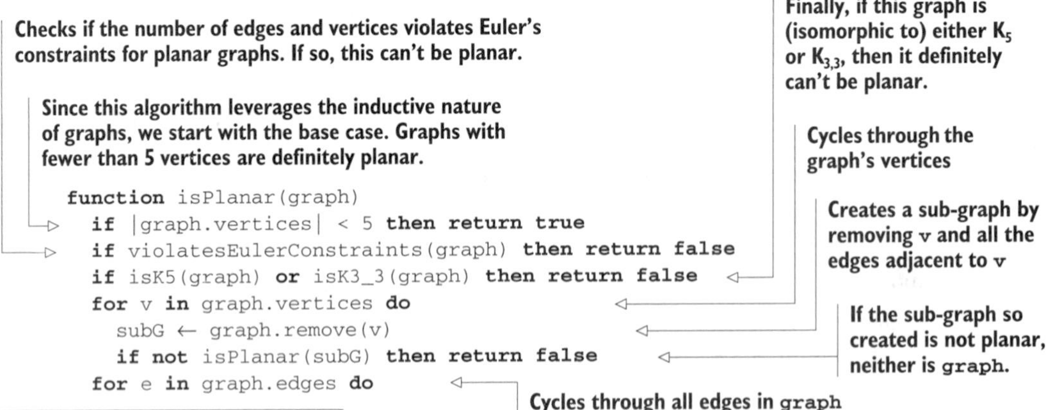

```
function isPlanar(graph)
  if |graph.vertices| < 5 then return true
  if violatesEulerConstraints(graph) then return false
  if isK5(graph) or isK3_3(graph) then return false
  for v in graph.vertices do
    subG ← graph.remove(v)
    if not isPlanar(subG) then return false
  for e in graph.edges do
```

- Checks if the number of edges and vertices violates Euler's constraints for planar graphs. If so, this can't be planar.
- Since this algorithm leverages the inductive nature of graphs, we start with the base case. Graphs with fewer than 5 vertices are definitely planar.
- Finally, if this graph is (isomorphic to) either K_5 or $K_{3,3}$, then it definitely can't be planar.
- Cycles through the graph's vertices
- Creates a sub-graph by removing `v` and all the edges adjacent to `v`
- If the sub-graph so created is not planar, neither is `graph`.
- Cycles through all edges in `graph`

[11] We won't have the space here to describe this algorithm, but you can find a description online at https://en.wikipedia.org/wiki/Biconnected_component.

```
    subG ← graph.remove(e)
    if not isPlanar(subG) return false
  return true
```

This time creates a sub-graph by just removing the current edge.

If the resulting sub-graph isn't planar, neither is `graph`.

If we made it all the way to this line, then the graph is planar.

When it comes to decomposing `G`, therefore, we need to consider two sets of subgraphs:

- *Induced subgraphs*—All the graphs that could be obtained by individually removing each vertex of `G` (induction rule 1), and all the edges in turn touching the vertex removed.
- *Spanning subgraphs*—All the graphs that could be obtained by individually removing each edge of `G` (induction rule 2).

These two sets of graphs are recursively checked at lines #5–7 and #8–10, respectively. Since the algorithm is recursive, we need a base case: we could use the empty graph, trivially, but since we know that all graphs with 4 or fewer vertices are planar, we can stop our recursion earlier (see line #2) and save computational resources.

The only thing remaining is checking if the current input is a non-planar graph. Normally we would just use another base case (actually, 2), at line #4, where we check to see if recursion brought us either K_5 or $K_{3,3}$ (for Kuratowski's theorem, we know that this means non-planar). In this case, though, we added another check at line #3, using Euler's inequalities to our advantage: as we saw in section 15.2.2, if the graph we are examining has too many edges for its vertices, it must be non-planar.

To see how the utility methods performing these checks work, let's take a look at listings 15.3, 15.4, and 15.5.

Listing 15.3 Planarity testing utility methods: Euler's invariants

Checks Euler's invariants on a graph

```
function violatesEulerConstraints(graph)
  (n,m) ← (|graph.vertices|, |graph.edges|)
  if m > 3 * n - 6 then
    return true
  if not hasCycleOfLength3(graph) and m > 2 * n - 4 then
    return true
  return false
```

Temporary variables for number of vertices and edges in graph

First constraint: If a graph is planar then $|E| \leq 3|V| - 6$.

Second (stricter) constraint: If a graph is planar and doesn't have any cycle of length 3, then $|E| \leq 2|V| - 4$.

The method to check Euler's constraints, shown in listing 15.3, is directly derived from the formulas in section 15.2.2. The hardest part is verifying that a graph doesn't have any cycle of length 3: this can be done using a modified version of DFS that returns all cycles, and runs in linear `O(V+E)` time. Since this is quite expensive and requires a non-trivial effort to write and maintain the code, the benefit of including this second check is debatable and—especially on your first try—it might not be worth it: you can start with checking the first constraint only, and remove the `if` at line #5.

Listing 15.4 Planarity testing utility methods: K5 testing

```
function isK5(graph)
  if |graph.vertices| == 5 and |graph.simpleEdges| == 10 then
    return true
  return false
```

Method `isK5` takes a graph and checks if it is the complete graph with 5 vertices.

Graph K_5 has 5 vertices and exactly 10 edges (not counting loops). Here we assume that `graph.simpleEdges` returns all edges in a graph except for possible loops.

Listing 15.4 shows the method to check if a graph is (isomorphic to) K_5. Obviously it needs to have 5 vertices (!), but we also know how many edges it should have, exactly 10. Notice that here we are talking about simple edges, where source and destination are distinct (so, no loops).

Listing 15.5 Planarity testing utility methods: K3,3 testing

Method `isK3_3` takes a graph and checks if it is the complete bipartite graph with two partitions of three vertices each.

```
function isK3_3(graph)
  (n,m) ← (|graph.vertices|, |graph.simpleEdges|)
  if n == 6 and m == 9 then
    if isBipartite(graph) and partitionsSize(graph) == (3,3) then
      return true
  return false
```

Temporary variables for number of vertices and edges in graph

Graph $K_{3,3}$ has 6 vertices and exactly 9 edges (not counting loops): here we assume that `graph.simpleEdges` returns all edges in a graph excluding loops.

That's not enough, though. We also need to check that the graph is bipartite and the two partitions have the right size.

Listing 15.5 shows the method to check if a graph is (isomorphic to) $K_{3,3}$. This is a bit more complicated because it's not enough to check that the count of vertices (6) and edges (9) is right. We also need to check that the graph is bipartite and that both partitions have size 3.

This brings us to the last step we need to implement: finding out if a graph is bipartite, and retrieving the two partitions.

To do so, we exploit a property of bipartite graphs: a graph is bipartite if and only if it's possible to color its vertices with exactly two different colors, such that there isn't any pair of adjacent vertices with the same color. Figure 15.10 shows a few examples to clarify this definition.

We can perform graph coloring easily by modifying the `BFS` algorithm:

1. We represent the source vertex as a red hexagon.
2. Once we extract a vertex from the queue, we color all its neighbors with the opposite color: for example, blue squares (as shown in figure 15.10) if the current vertex is a red hexagon, and vice versa.
3. If any of the adjacent vertices is already colored with the same color as the current vertex, then the graph is not bipartite.

Listing 15.6 shows the pseudo-code for a method returning the two partitions while it checks if the graph is bipartite. You can also take a look at a Java implementation on

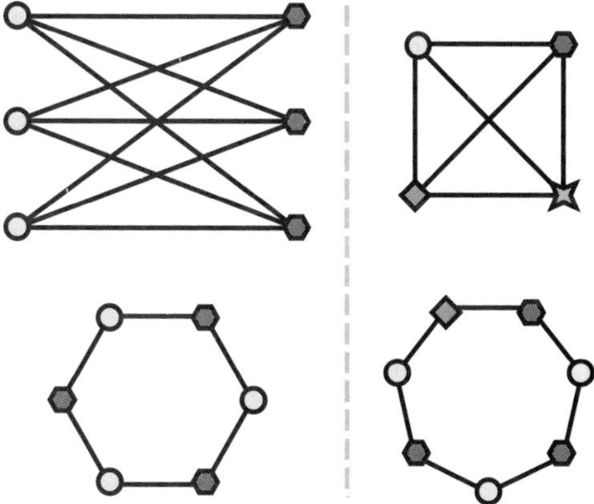

Figure 15.10 Bipartite graphs and coloring. All graphs are colored with the minimum possible number of colors. On the left, two examples of bipartite graphs; on the right, non-bipartite graphs. As you can see, two colors are not enough for these graphs (we also use different shapes, along with shading, for the vertices to help with visualizing the difference).

the book's repo on GitHub[12] or a JavaScript implementation provided by JsGraph, the JavaScript library that has been used to draw most of the examples of embeddings in this chapter.

Listing 15.6 Checking if a connected graph is bipartite

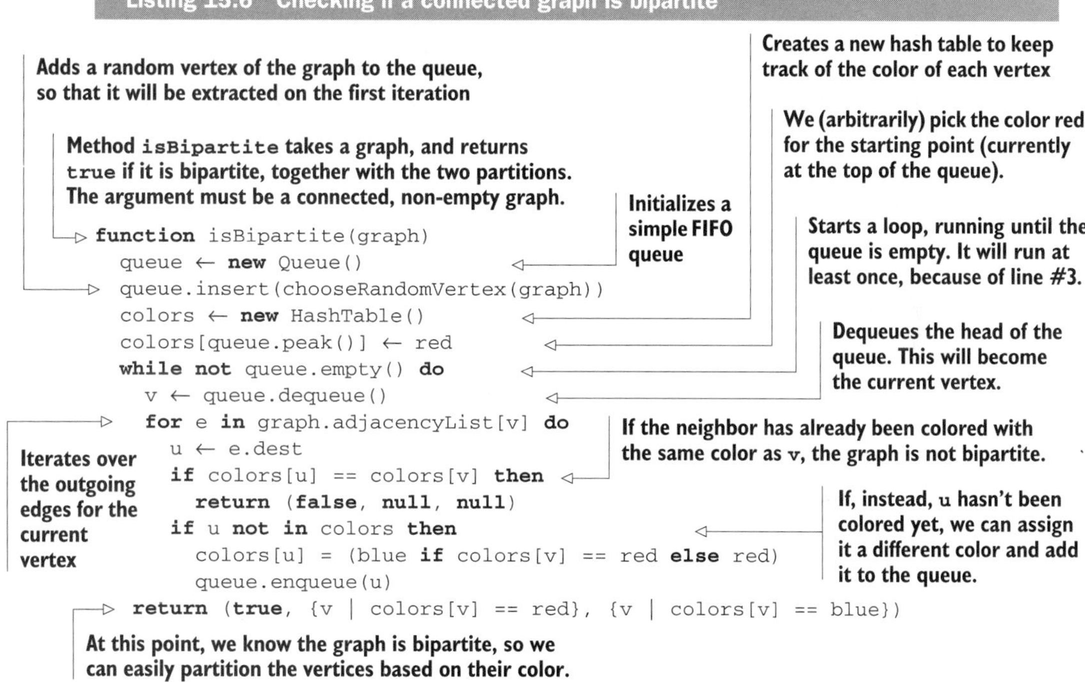
Adds a random vertex of the graph to the queue, so that it will be extracted on the first iteration
Method isBipartite takes a graph, and returns true if it is bipartite, together with the two partitions. The argument must be a connected, non-empty graph.
Creates a new hash table to keep track of the color of each vertex
We (arbitrarily) pick the color red for the starting point (currently at the top of the queue).
Initializes a simple FIFO queue
Starts a loop, running until the queue is empty. It will run at least once, because of line #3.
Dequeues the head of the queue. This will become the current vertex.
Iterates over the outgoing edges for the current vertex
If the neighbor has already been colored with the same color as v, the graph is not bipartite.
If, instead, u hasn't been colored yet, we can assign it a different color and add it to the queue.
At this point, we know the graph is bipartite, so we can easily partition the vertices based on their color.

```
function isBipartite(graph)
  queue ← new Queue()
  queue.insert(chooseRandomVertex(graph))
  colors ← new HashTable()
  colors[queue.peak()] ← red
  while not queue.empty() do
    v ← queue.dequeue()
    for e in graph.adjacencyList[v] do
      u ← e.dest
      if colors[u] == colors[v] then
        return (false, null, null)
      if u not in colors then
        colors[u] = (blue if colors[v] == red else red)
        queue.enqueue(u)
  return (true, {v | colors[v] == red}, {v | colors[v] == blue})
```

[12] See https://github.com/mlarocca/AlgorithmsAndDataStructuresInAction#graph

15.2.4 Improving performance

This is the bulk of the simplest algorithm we have to test graph planarity. We know it's inefficient, but exactly how inefficient?

It's a recursive algorithm, where from each call to the method can stem several recursive calls; the depth of the recursion is already linear in the size of the original graph `G=(V,E)`, because we remove one vertex or one edge at a time.

The breadth of the recursion tree (the number of recursive calls) is also linear, although in the size of the graph that is currently run on, let's call it `G'=(V', E')`. This is because the two `for` loops cycle through all vertices and all edges in `G'`.

We can write a formula for the running time. If `|V'|=n, |E'|=m`, then

```
T(n,m) = n * T(n-1, m) + m * T(n, m-1)
T(0,0) = 1
T(0,*)=1
T(*,0)=1
```

For a recurrence relation[13] of the form `T(n) = n * T(n-1)`, the solution depends on the value of the base term. If as in this case, `T(0) = 1`, then `T(n) = n!` – this, at least, when we have a single variable. Our specific case, where we have two variables, grows even faster.

The last thing we want in a formula for an algorithm's running time is a factorial—a function that grows faster than the exponential function. This means that the algorithm, as presented in listing 15.2, can only be used for small graphs.

When you see a factorial pop up in your calculations, it will likely mean that you are computing the same thing over and over again, multiple times.

This is the case for our algorithm as well; let's see an example, with a small graph with just three vertices. Let `G=({1,2,3}, E)` be our initial graph. For the sake of our example, we won't bother with its edges, but focus on the recursion on vertices.

The `for` loop at line #4 of listing 15.2 will issue three calls[14] for the following graphs:[15]

```
(V',E')=({2,3}, E-{1}), ({1,3}, E-{2}), ({1,2}, E-{3})
```

Each of those graphs will in turn produce two calls:

```
({3}, E-{1,2}), ({2}, E-{1,3}),
({3}, E-{1,2}), ({1}, E-{2,3}),
({2}, E-{1,3}), ({1}, E-{2,3})
```

[13] A recurrence relation is an equation that recursively defines a sequence of values, where each term of the sequence is defined as a function of the preceding terms. Check out appendix B for more on how to solve recurrence relations.

[14] Imagine, for the sake of providing a simple example, that at line #2 we are using the empty graph as a base to halt the recursion.

[15] We write `E-{1}` as a shortened notation for `E-{(1,v) | v∈{2,3}, (1,v) ∈E}`, and similarly for the other vertices.

As you can see, in the second round of calls, each graph appears twice. If we also consider the recursion on the edges, it gets much worse.

Usually this kind of expansion ends up in a memory crash long before the recursion gets closer to the base cases.

The most common strategy for coping with this is to avoid the duplicates by one of the following:

- Define a better recursion that avoids the duplicates (not always possible).
- Prune the search tree avoiding duplicated work (*branch and bound* algorithms).
- Compute and store the results for the smaller cases and read them when needed while computing larger problems (*dynamic programming* algorithms).

For this problem, we can reasonably go for the third option and use *memoization*[16] to provide a sort of cache of the results of the algorithm for smaller problems.

This will give us some improvement, but as we'll see, the most efficient algorithms developed for planarity testing, instead, order the edges to be added or removed at each step in such a way to guarantee a linear number of steps (therefore using the first of the strategies in the list).

By avoiding computing things twice, we guarantee that we will examine each distinct subgraph at most once, so that the number of steps becomes bounded by the number of possible subgraphs. For a graph with `n` vertices and `m` edges, there are 2^n *induced subgraphs* (because there are 2^n subset of vertices) and 2^m spanning subgraphs (considering the subset of edges). The total number of possible subgraphs is thus bounded by 2^{n+m}, which is better than factorial, but still too large to consider the algorithm usable for graphs with more than ~20 vertices.

There are other small improvements that we can add; although not as impactful as avoiding duplicates, they all contribute to speeding up the algorithm. For instance, we can improve our halting condition. We don't need to wait until we get down to K_5 or $K_{3,3}$; any complete graph with 5 or more vertices, or any complete bipartite graph with both partitions having 3 or more vertices, is certainly non-planar.

Most of these cases, however, are already caught by Euler's invariants.

Listing 15.7 shows the pseudo-code for the improved method; you can find a Java implementation on the book's repo[17] or a JavaScript implementation provided by JsGraph.

Listing 15.7 Planarity testing with cache

```
function isPlanar(graph, cache={})
  if graph in cache then return (cache[graph], cache)
  if |graph.vertices| < 5 then return (true, cache)
  if violatesEulerConstraints(graph) then
```

First, we check if the graph is in our cache. The cache can be as simple as a dictionary, as long as graphs are serializable.

If the number of edges and vertices violates Euler's constraints for planar graphs, we know the graph is not planar. Before returning, we need to update the cache so this graph won't be checked again in another branch of the computation.

[16] See appendix E on recursion and the use of memoization to prevent stack overflow.

[17] See https://github.com/mlarocca/AlgorithmsAndDataStructuresInAction#graph

Instead of looking for K_5 or $K_{3,3}$ only, we check whether it is complete (since the graph has at least 5 vertices, it's definitely non-planar) or complete bipartite (in this case, we also need to check that the smallest of the two partitions has size 3).

```
    cache[graph] ← false
    return (false, cache)
  if isComplete(graph) or isNonPlanarCompleteBipartite(graph) then
    cache[graph] ← false
    return (false, cache)
  for v in graph.vertices do
    subG ← graph.remove(v)
    (planar, cache) ← isPlanar(subG, cache)
    if not planar then
      cache[graph] ← false
      return (false, cache)
  for e in graph.edges do
    subG ← graph.remove(e)
    (planar, cache) ← isPlanar(subG, cache)
    if not planar then
      cache[graph] ← false
      return (false, cache)
  cache[graph] ← true
  return (true, cache)
```

Cycles through the graph's vertices

When we perform a recursive call, we need to update the cache as well. Besides the cache, the algorithm stays the same.

Cycles through all edges in graph. Follows the same pattern as for vertices.

If we made it all the way to this line, then the graph is planar; we need to update the cache and return `true`.

15.2.5 *Efficient algorithms*

The algorithm presented in listing 15.7 is still too slow to be affordable on large graphs. Still, it can be a feasible, low-cost[18] option that can work on small graphs.

There are far better algorithms that have been developed for planarity testing. While they take different approaches to provide an answer (and a planar embedding) in linear time, they all have something in common: they are fairly complicated.

As in, "research papers spanning dozens of pages" complicated. Describing them in detail goes beyond the scope of this chapter, but we'll briefly describe a few prominent ones and provide pointers for the interested readers.[19]

Be aware that the effort to implement these algorithms might be consistent. Also keep in mind that if your constraints can be relaxed, and you can accept an algorithm that provides a reasonable embedding, even without guarantees that it will be planar, you can use simpler heuristics to generate embeddings (more on this later).

As we mentioned, the first linear-time algorithm for planarity testing was developed in 1974 by Hopcroft and Tarjan,[20] improving a previously-developed[21] `O(|V|²)` variant. Their idea is based on vertex addition, so the algorithm starts bottom-up,

[18]In terms of effort to write and maintain the code.

[19]For a comprehensive summary, check out Patrignani, Maurizio. "Planarity Testing and Embedding," in *Handbook of Graph Drawing and Visualization*, (Chapman and Hall/CRC, 2013), 1–42.

[20]Hopcroft, John; Tarjan, Robert E. (1974), "Efficient planarity testing," *Journal of the Association for Computing Machinery*, 21 (4): 549–568

[21]Tarjan, R. E. "Implementation of an efficient algorithm for planarity testing of graphs." unpublished implementation, Dec (1969).

keeping the possible planar embeddings for each incrementally-built induced subgraph[22] of the original one.

As we previously mentioned, this strategy defines a different approach to recursion: bottom-up rather than top-down, incremental and not divide-and-conquer, but above all, by carefully reconstructing the original graph one vertex at the time, it avoids analyzing all sub-graphs, and only performs a linear number of steps.

The key is that while adding vertices, the algorithm keeps track of the possible embeddings of the sub-graph.

Fast-forward to 2004, when a brand-new approach[23] was developed by Boyer and Myrvold: it's an edge-addition method, so it incrementally adds edges instead of vertices. It's still linear, `O(|V|+|E|)`, but it has the great advantage of avoiding any requirement for specific data structures to store the candidate embeddings. This algorithm is currently one of the state-of-the-art solutions to find planar embeddings for planar graphs; the best part is that you can find an open source implementation online on boost.org: http://mng.bz/5jj7.

The last algorithm we are going to mention is the planarity testing algorithm[24] by Fraysseix, de Mendes, and Rosenstiehl, which is the other state-of-the-art algorithm in this area. It characterizes planar graphs in terms of a left-right ordering of the edges in a depth-first search tree, and its implementation is DFS-based, although obviously the DFS method needs to be modified accordingly, and it uses *Trémaux trees*, special spanning trees produced by a DFS visit of a graph.

15.3 Non-planar graphs

Now that we have at least one planarity testing algorithm in our tool belt, we can look at our task, visualizing graphs nicely on screen, with more confidence. Some of the planarity testing algorithms also output a planar embedding, and that gives us a good starting point.

And yet, we have a long way to go.

Let's start with two considerations:

- Is reducing the number of crossing edges the only criterion we should follow?
- We know not all graphs are planar . . . should we just give up on non-planar graphs?

Let's focus on the first question. What do you think? Take a minute to imagine what other characteristics make a good visualization and, vice versa, what could go wrong with this.

Then take a look at figure 15.11 to corroborate your thoughts.

---

[22]As we have already seen, an induced subgraph is obtained by removing one or more vertices from the original graph.

[23]Boyer, John M.; Myrvold, Wendy J. (2004), "On the cutting edge: simplified O(n) planarity by edge addition" (PDF), *Journal of Graph Algorithms and Applications*, 8 (3): 241–273

[24]de Fraysseix, Hubert; Ossona de Mendez, Patrice; Rosenstiehl, Pierre (2006), "Trémaux trees and planarity," *International Journal of Foundations of Computer Science*, 17 (5): 1017–1029.

Looking at it, we can see that there are at least three different aspects that contribute to the poor look and comprehensibility of the visualization:

1. The most evident effect is that it's impossible to read any text. This is because elements are unnecessarily far from each other, and we need to zoom out to see the whole chart.
2. Some edges are all twisted and windy, making it harder to follow them.
3. Compared to figure 15.1, the relative position of the elements fails to suggest the direction of flow. Adjacent nodes are far from each other, with nodes modeling other unrelated steps in between.

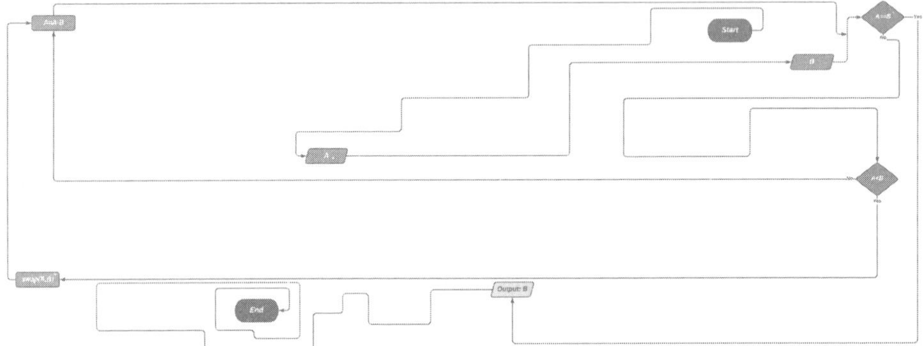
Start
End
Output: B

Figure 15.11 Another embedding gone berserk for the flow chart in figure 15.1

OK, this is what's wrong with the chart in figure 15.11. Can we transform these considerations into requirements to have a better visualization? Let's try this:

1. Adjacent vertices (aka vertices connected by an edge) must be placed as close as possible in the plane. Of course, we need some sort of a compromise because we don't want vertices to get too close (otherwise they would overlap with each other or hide the edge between them), and also if a vertex v is adjacent to many others, we can't afford too many of these vertices to cluster around v.
2. Draw edges in the simplest possible way: either segments or arcs of ellipses should work.
3. Reduce the number of edges crossing. Aim for no intersections if a graph is planar or as few as possible for non-planar ones.

In the next chapters, we will see how these requirements can be translated into mathematical expressions to model a *cost function* that can reflect how good a graph is.

We'll use the rest of this chapter to talk in more depth about the third point.

As we have seen, there are graphs for which it's not possible to find an embedding without any edge crossing.

Edge intersections in higher dimensional spaces

Interestingly enough, if we move from the plane to 3-D space, it becomes trivial to find an embedding to $\mathbb{R}^3$ such that no edges cross. If we consider the following Jordan curve `C(t)`, a surface defined as

$$C(t) = \begin{cases} x = t \\ y = t^2 \ , t \geq 0 \\ z = t^3 \end{cases}$$

then we can map each vertex to a distinct point on the curve and draw edges as segments between the vertices. It can then be proven that there is no way to choose a set of four points from `C(t)` such that they all lie on the same plane, and therefore the segments between pairs of points can't cross each other.

For non-planar graphs `G`, however, we can define a value, called a *crossing number*, that is the smallest possible number of edge crossings of all the possible embeddings of `G` to $\mathbb{R}^2$.

Planar graphs, obviously, have a crossing number equal to 0; both non-planar graphs we saw earlier in the chapter, K_5 and $K_{3,3}$, have a crossing number equal to 1.

15.3.1 Finding the crossing number

Kuratowski's theorem tells us the necessary and sufficient condition for a graph to be planar, but it doesn't help much with computing the minimum crossing number of non-planar graphs. The problem of finding the crossing number for a non-planar graph has been investigated far less than planarity testing/embedding. While there are several efficient algorithms that provide planar embeddings for planar graphs, to date there isn't an efficient algorithm that can find the minimum crossing number for generic graphs.

As a matter of fact, it has been proven that determining the crossing number of a generic graphs is an *NP-complete* problem.

There are, however, notable exceptions[25] if we narrow the field; for example, it has been recently proven[26] that there is a simple algorithm to check if a non-planar graph has crossing number 1.

Assuming that `G` is a non-planar graph (and hence it has at least 5 vertices, as a consequence of Kuratowski's theorem), for each pair of non-adjacent[27] edges `a→b`, `c→d`, we remove both edges, and add a new vertex `v`, and 4 new edges `a→v`, `v→b`, `c→v`, `v→d`.

---

[25] Clancy, Kieran, Michael Haythorpe, and Alex Newcombe. "A survey of graphs with known or bounded crossing numbers." arXiv preprint arXiv:1901.05155 (2019).

[26] Haythorpe, M. "QuickCross–Crossing Number Problem".

[27] Two edges are adjacent if they have at least one vertex in common; in a pair of non-adjacent edges, therefore, all the four vertices are distinct.

If the new graph obtained is planar, then the crossing number of the original graph is exactly 1.

Some of the most interesting results in this area focus on complete and complete bipartite graphs. Guy's and Zarankiewicz' conjectures postulate a formula for the crossing number of these graphs, but they haven't been proven so far.

Guy's conjecture hypothesizes that the minimum crossing number of the generic complete graph with n vertices is given by

$$Z(K_n) = \frac{1}{4} \cdot \left\lfloor \frac{n}{2} \right\rfloor \cdot \left\lfloor \frac{n-1}{2} \right\rfloor \cdot \left\lfloor \frac{n-2}{2} \right\rfloor \cdot \left\lfloor \frac{n-3}{2} \right\rfloor$$

Zarankiewicz' conjecture, however, provides an estimate for complete bipartite graphs with two partitions having n and m vertices, respectively:

$$Z(K_{n,\,m}) = \frac{1}{4} \cdot \left\lfloor \frac{n}{2} \right\rfloor \cdot \left\lfloor \frac{n-1}{2} \right\rfloor \cdot \left\lfloor \frac{m}{2} \right\rfloor \cdot \left\lfloor \frac{m-1}{2} \right\rfloor$$

As of today, both formulas have been proven to hold as upper bounds, meaning that the crossing number for these graphs is not larger than the value computed using the formulas, and they have not yet been disproved as lower bounds.

If we try to apply these results to the two graphs we have already introduced, we get

$$Z(K_5) = \frac{1}{4} \cdot \left\lfloor \frac{5}{2} \right\rfloor \cdot \left\lfloor \frac{4}{2} \right\rfloor \cdot \left\lfloor \frac{3}{2} \right\rfloor \cdot \left\lfloor \frac{2}{2} \right\rfloor = 1$$

$$Z(K_{3,\,3}) = \left\lfloor \frac{3}{2} \right\rfloor \cdot \left\lfloor \frac{2}{2} \right\rfloor \cdot \left\lfloor \frac{3}{2} \right\rfloor \cdot \left\lfloor \frac{2}{2} \right\rfloor = 1$$

So, for K_5 and $K_{3,3}$ the expectation is consistent with what we have mentioned and with our experience. As a matter of fact, Guy's conjecture has been proven to hold true as an exact value for $n \leq 12$, while Zarankiewicz' for $n,m \leq 7$.

If we consider, for instance, graph K_6, shown in figure 15.12, the expected (and proven) crossing number is 3.

And yet, it's significantly harder to obtain an embedding with minimal crossings between edges. An example embedding is shown in figure 15.13.

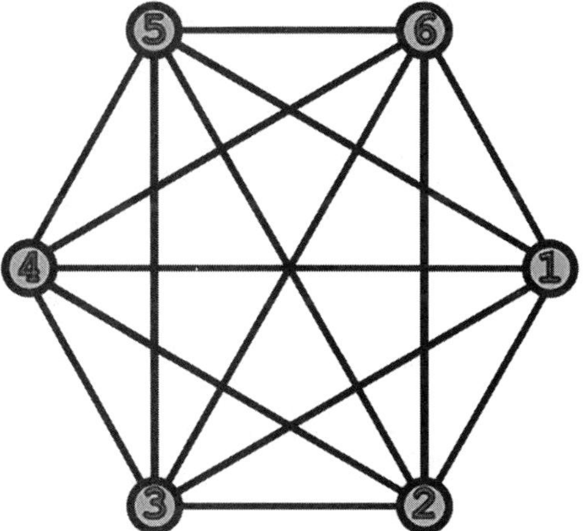
5
6
4
1
3
2

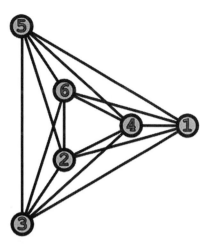

Figure 15.12 A naïve embedding for K_6: there are 15 crossing pairs of edges with this layout.

Figure 15.13 A minimum crossing embedding for K_6, with just 3 intersections.

15.3.2 Rectilinear crossing number

Have you noticed that so far, we've only drawn graphs using segments? While this has served our purpose well, and we've always been able to draw graphs with the minimum number of intersections, this is not always true.

In fact, we need to introduce a new definition: the *rectilinear crossing number* of a graph `G` is the minimum number of edges crossing in a straight-line drawing of `G`; that is, an embedding on the plane for `G` where edges are drawn as straight-line segments.

When we restrict to straight-line segments for the edges, we are using a fraction of the possible embeddings. It shouldn't be surprising, therefore, that the rectilinear crossing number of a graph is never smaller than its crossing number.

Now, can it be larger? It has been proven that for any graph `G` with a crossing number smaller than or equal to 3, it's possible to come up with a straight-line drawing with minimal crossings: in other words, whenever the crossing number **`cr`**`(G)` is 3 or less, it matches the rectilinear crossing number, **`rcr`**`(G)`.

Although this is great, because it means that planar graphs can indifferently be drawn as straight-line or curve-line drawings, the result can't be generalized. There exist, in fact, graphs for which **`cr`**`(G) = 4 <` **`rcr`**`(G)`. Figure 15.14 shows the original example used for the proof in a paper[28] from 1993. In the left half of the figure, you can see a straight-line drawing of the graph, with 12 edge intersections. This is also the rectilinear crossing number of the graphs, and no matter how much you move vertices around, you can't get fewer intersections, as long as you only draw edges with straight line segments.

[28]Bienstock, Daniel, and Nathaniel Dean. "Bounds for rectilinear crossing numbers." *Journal of Graph Theory* 17.3 (1993): 333-348.

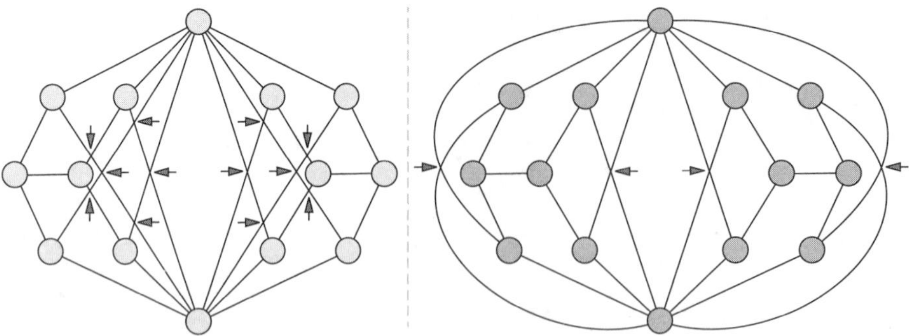

Figure 15.14 The simplest graph for which the rectilinear crossing number is larger than the crossing number. Intersections are highlighted by the little arrows.

On the other hand, the right half of figure 15.14 shows that by using cubic Bézier curves and moving a few edges to the external face of the first embedding, we can reduce the number of intersections to just 4; this is also the crossing number for this graph.

The interesting part is that by using this graph as a starting point, it is possible to construct graphs with a crossing number equal to 4, but with a rectilinear crossing number arbitrarily large (potentially up to infinity). For the proof and the construction rules, please refer to the original article.

For complete graphs, it's known that for `n≥10`, `rcr(Kn)>cr(Kn)`; unfortunately, we can't do any better for our examples for K_5 and K_6: even using generic Jordan curves, the best embedding we can get for K_6 is the one shown in figure 15.15, which still has three intersections.

Nevertheless, using arcs allows us to choose a simpler and more regular layout for the vertices.

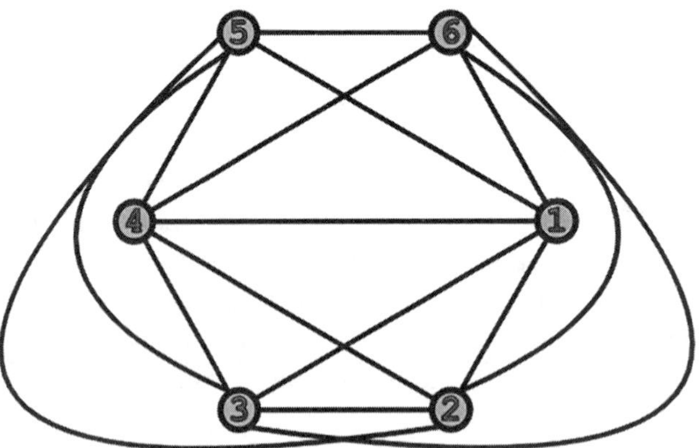
5
6
4
1
3
2

Figure 15.15 An alternative minimum crossing embedding for K_6: using curves for the edges allows us to keep a more regular layout for the vertices.

So, long story short, if we draw large graphs using only straight-line segments, chances are that we have to accept a larger number of edge intersections than is actually possible, because the rectilinear crossing number is larger than the crossing number for many graphs. Does that mean we have to dismiss this way of drawing graphs? Not at all!

First, as we have seen, for all planar graphs and all graphs whose crossing number is smaller than 4, we can use the straight-line drawing without any loss; not all the other graphs with `cr(G) ≥ 4`, moreover, have a worse `rcr(G)` than their `cr(G)`.

It turns out that for practical purposes, we are often more interested in drawing planar or almost-planar graphs, because flow-charts, PERT diagrams, workflows, and so on are usually fairly sparse graphs, which in turn are less likely to have a high crossing number. After all, from Euler's invariants we know that planar graphs must be sparse (because the number of edges is linear in the number of vertices).

Second, even if curve-line embeddings can lead to fewer crossing points, it doesn't mean that it's easy to find one. As a matter of fact, these drawings are much harder to find with an algorithm because we have to optimize many more parameters. Besides the position of the vertices, we also have to find the ideal curves that reduce the number of intersections. This will add at least one or two parameters per edge, if Bézier's quadratic or cubic curves are used, making the search space much larger and harder to search. The number of parameters, in fact, goes from `O(V)` to `O(V+E)`, which in turn is $O(V^2)$ in the worst case.

Third, using curves requires a larger computational power. The algorithm to check if two segments intersect is significantly easier than checking if two curves do (and it can be made even easier with some restrictions on the position of the vertices). This means that even computing the number of intersections in a candidate solution is more expensive with curve-line drawings.

In the next chapters, we will focus on straight-line drawings, but we'll also show how to extend them to curve-line graphs.

15.4 Edge intersections

The last bit of code we need to make our initial fully randomized algorithm for minimal-crossing embeddings is the method that checks if two edges intersect.

In this section we'll start discussing the variant for straight-line drawings; since edges are drawn as segments, it's easier to check if they intersect.

Then we'll move to Bézier curves, briefly explaining how they work, the subset of curves we'll allow, and how to check for intersections for elements of this subset.

15.4.1 Straight-line segments

Let's start with the intersection between two segments. After all, we have also said that we decided to focus on straight-line drawings, so we'll devote more space to discussing this case.

An initial strategy to cheaply screen pairs that are not intersecting is shown in figure 15.16. If we draw a box, parallel to the axes, around each of the two segments, then obviously the two segments can't cross if the boxes do not intersect. In turn, the two boxes can't intersect if the projections of the two segments over the Cartesian axes don't intersect on both the `x` and `y` axes.

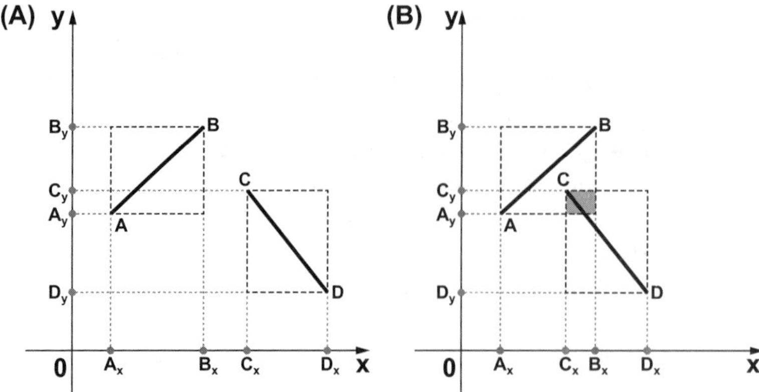
(A)
y
B
C
A
D
0
x
(B)
y
B
C
A
D
0
x

Figure 15.16 Examples of non-intersecting segments: the bounding-box check can only rule out an intersection, but cannot confirm it.

This condition, having the projected segments not intersecting, is sufficient, but not necessary for establishing that two segments do not cross. Figure 15.16 (B) shows how there can be segments whose boxes intersect, but that don't cross.

So, we have an asymmetric situation:

- If we find out that the projections of the segments do not intersect over one of the two axes, we can conclude that the segments do not intersect.
- Otherwise, we can't make any assumptions, and we need to further investigate.

We can do that in many ways, for instance, by verifying that the extremes of a segment fall on the opposite sides of the line passing through the other segment, as shown in figure 15.17.

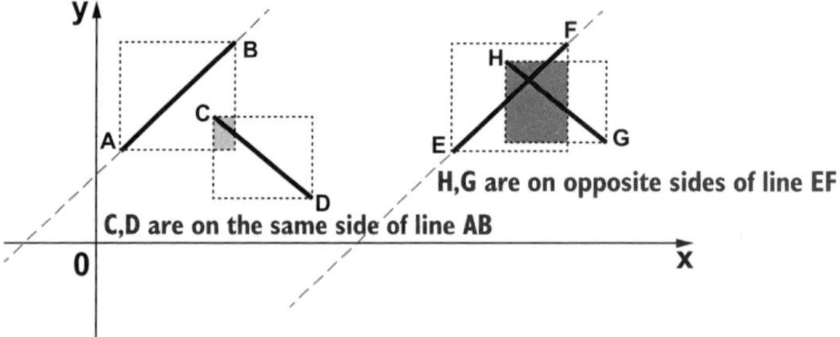
y
B
C
A
D
F
H
E
G
H,G are on opposite sides of line EF
C,D are on the same side of line AB
0
x

Figure 15.17 Segment intersection: if bounding boxes have a non-null intersection, the discriminant becomes whether or not the vertices of segment `CD` (or `HG`) are on opposite sides of the line passing through the segment `AB` (`EF`), and vice versa.

This, however, requires a bit too much fiddling with edge cases (for instance, parallel segments), so I prefer a different, more elegant, method I recently discovered.

The gist of it is shown in figure 15.18. It doesn't involve bounding boxes; rather, we want to find the intersection point of the lines passing through the segments and then check that it lies within both segments. There are, actually, three possible cases:

- The intersection of the two lines, point `P`, lie outside of both segments.
- `P` lies inside one of the two segments, but not both.
- `P` lies within both segments.

The third case is the only one where we have an intersection.

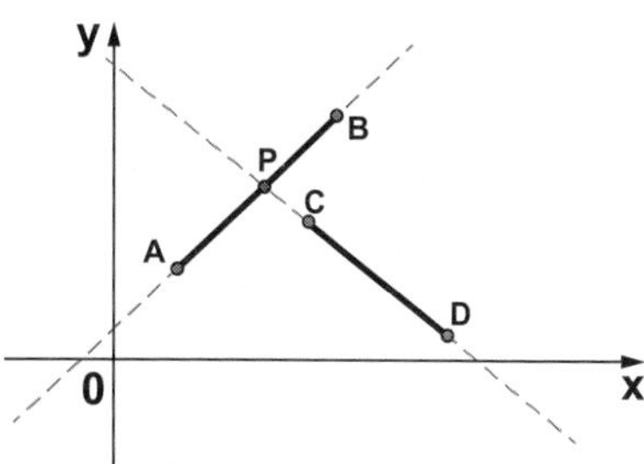
y
B
P
C
A
D
0
x

Figure 15.18 Checking whether the point of intersection of the two lines falls within both segments

How do we find `P`? Well, first, more precisely, we will use vectors and semi-lines rather than just lines.

We define vectors **v**=BA=(B_x-A_x,B_y-A_y) and **w**=DC=(D_x-C_x,D_y-C_y). These vectors start from the second point in the segment and end at the first one. Now, remember that vectors can be translated seamlessly, so, for instance, we can move the **v** so that it starts where **w** ends, or vice versa, and compute their sum or product. For instance, considering the vector **u** that is shown in figure 15.19 (A) (and that we'll define in a few lines), we show it sharing point `A` with **v** out of convenience, so that it's apparent how the two vectors are orthogonal.

Assuming that vectors **v** and **w** aren't parallel (which we can easily check by taking their cross product), the lines passing through them will cross at one point `P`, that might or might not lie inside the segments. Either way, there must be two real numbers, `h` and `g`, such that the scaled vectors `h*`**v** and `g*`**w**, when their start point is set to `B` and `D` respectively, both end exactly at point `P`, as shown in figure 15.19 (B).

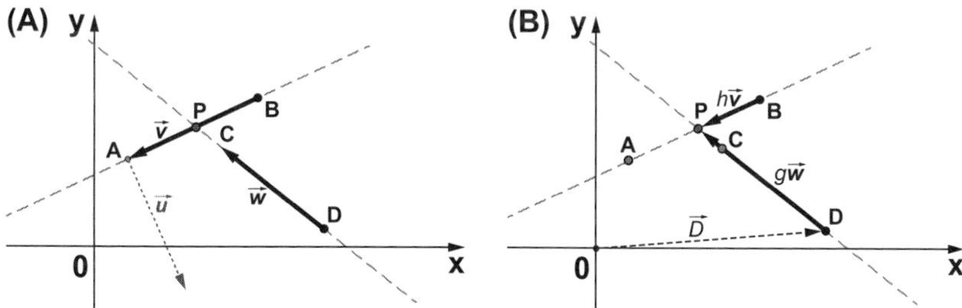
(A) y
P
B
v
A
C
u
w
D
0
x
(B) y
hv
P
B
A
C
gw
D
D
0
x

Figure 15.19 A vector approach to check whether the point of intersection of the two lines falls within both segments

In other words, the coordinates of point `P` can be expressed in terms of both vectors, and the following equation must hold:

```
B + h*v = D + g*w                                    (1)
```

Notice that B and D can also be considered vectors: in particular, the vectors that go from the origin to those two points.

We had mentioned we would define a new vector u. Well, now is the time to consider it:

$$\mathbf{u} = (-v_y, v_x) = (A_y - B_y, B_x - A_x)$$

This vector has a special property; its dot product with vector **v** is zero:

$$\mathbf{u} \cdot \mathbf{v} = \mathbf{v} \cdot \mathbf{u} = v_x v_y - v_y v_x = 0$$

Going back to equation (1), we can multiply both sides by u, which is not null (as long as A and B are distinct points, which we assume as a hypothesis, because distinct vertices can't be assigned to the same point). Doing so we get

$$B \cdot \mathbf{u} + h * \mathbf{v} \cdot \mathbf{u} = D \cdot \mathbf{u} + g * w \cdot \mathbf{u} \Rightarrow B \cdot \mathbf{u} = D \cdot \mathbf{u} + g * w \cdot \mathbf{u}$$

As such we eliminate the unknown h and solve the equation for g:

$$g = \frac{(B-D) \cdot \vec{u}}{\vec{w} \cdot \vec{u}} = \frac{(B_x - D_x, B_y - D_y) \cdot (A_y - B_y, B_x - A_x)}{(D_x - C_x, D_y - C_y) \cdot (A_y - B_y, B_x - A_x)} =$$

$$= \frac{B_x A_y - B_x B_y - D_x A_y + D_x B_y + B_y B_x - B_y A_x - D_y B_x + D_y A_x}{D_x A_y - D_x B_y - C_x A_y + C_x B_y + D_y B_x - D_y A_x - C_y B_x + C_y A_x} =$$

$$= \frac{D_x(B_y - A_y) + D_y(A_x - B_x)}{(D_x - C_x)(A_y - B_y) + (D_y - C_y)(B_x - A_x)}$$

Similarly, we can define vector $\mathbf{z} = (-w_y, w_x)$, such that $\mathbf{z} \cdot \mathbf{w} = 0$, and derive a formula for h:

$$h = \frac{(D-B) \cdot \vec{z}}{\vec{v} \cdot \vec{z}} = \frac{B_x(D_y - C_y) + B_y(C_x - D_x)}{(B_x - A_x)(C_y - D_y) + (B_y - A_y)(D_x - C_x)} =$$

All that's left is reasoning about the meaning of these two solutions. Looking at figure 15.19, can you tell which one, between h and g is, for this example, larger than 1?

If you notice, in this particular example vector, BP is smaller than vector BA, and as such, h must have a value between 0 and 1. The scalar g must be larger than 1, because vector DP is longer than DC.

For the former situation, clearly P is within the segment BA, while for the latter, it's clearly outside DC.

When either value is 0 or 1, it means that P coincides with one of the segment's endpoints. If both h and g are equal to either 0 or 1, then we have an edge case where the two segments have a vertex in common. These two edge cases are shown in figure 15.20.

In conclusion, if we assume that all 4 vertices are distinct, then the two segments intersect if and only if both $0 \le h \le 1$ and $0 \le g \le 1$ (but only at most one of them is either 0 or 1).

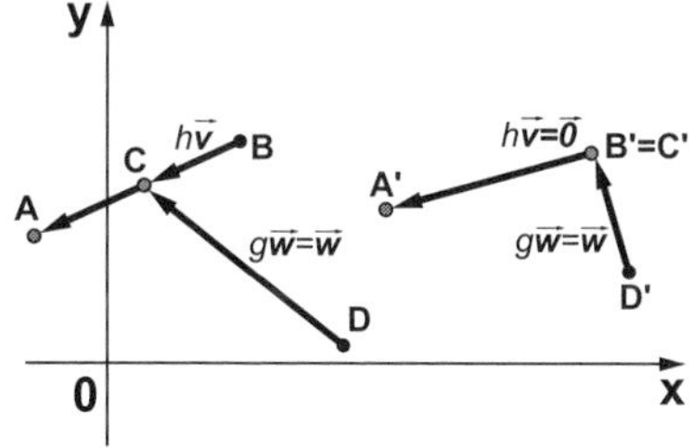
y
hv
B
C
A
gw=w
D
0
x
hv=0
B'=C'
A'
gw=w
D'

Figure 15.20 Two edge cases for the vectorial method. In the first case, segments `AB` and `CD`, we have `0≤h≤1` and `g==1`. Therefore, vertex `C` lies on the segment `AB`. The second example, segments `A'B'` and `C'D'`, has `h==0` and `g==1`. In this case, two of the endpoints must be the same, and in fact `B'==C'`.

Listing 15.8 shows the code to compute the scaling coefficient (either of `h` or `g`; which one depends on the order of the points we pass) for one segment with respect to the other.

Listing 15.8 Method `vectorScalingFactor`

```
function vectorScalingFactor(A, B, C, D)
  v = (B.x-A.x, B.y-A.y)
  w = (D.x-C.x, D.y-C.y)
  u = (-v.y, v.x)
  return ((B.x-D.x) * u.x + (B.y-D.y) * u.y) / (w.x * u.x + w.y * u.y)
```

Method `vectorScalingFactor` takes four points, assuming they are the endpoints of segments `AB` and `CD`, and returns the scaling factor that needs to be applied to vector `CD` in order to end exactly on segment `AB`.

We reuse this coefficient in listing 15.9, where we check the intersection between two graph edges.

Listing 15.9 Method `edgesIntersection`

```
function edgesIntersection(e1, e2)
  h = vectorScalingFactor(
      e1.source, e1.destination, e2.source, e2.destination)
  g = vectorScalingFactor(
      e2.source, e2.destination, e1.source, e1.destination)
  return 0 ≤ h ≤ 1 and 0 ≤ g ≤ 1 and not (h in {0,1} and g in {0,1})
```

We assume, for the sake of space, that the edge's properties `source` and `destination` return points, which in turn have `x` and `y` fields for their coordinates.

Method `edgesIntersection` takes two edges and returns `true` if and only if the segment representations of the edges intersect.

As we have seen, there is an intersection if both `h` and `g` are between `0` and `1`, but if both are exactly `0` or `1`, then the edges are just adjacent.

15.4.2 Polylines

In our examples in chapter 15 we have drawn a few flowcharts by using polylines for edges, and specifically a subset of all polylines where the only segments allowed are parallel to the Cartesian axes. In this configuration, checking for intersections becomes somewhat easier, because while it's true that for each edge we need to consider the segments composing it, checking the intersections of two segments that can either be vertical or horizontal becomes much easier and boils down to checking their endings' coordinates.

One important difference with this representation is that the number of intersections between two edges is not just `0` or `1` anymore; they can intersect multiple times—one more reason to prefer other styles over polylines.

15.4.3 Bézier curves

An interesting and flexible alternative to polylines is provided by Bézier curves. These curves are a valuable solution because they can be drawn with a variable degree of precision, depending on the computational resources available. Bézier curves have a beautiful mathematical formula and are both flexible and precise. Going into the details of how they work is beyond the scope of this book, but we'll try to give a quick introduction that should be enough to get you started. To the interested reader that would like to delve into this topic, we have two freely available online resources:

- Sederberg, Thomas W. "Computer aided geometric design" (2012).
- "A Primer on Bézier Curves", https://pomax.github.io/bezierinfo/.

Let's start building our intuition with the geometric definition of Bézier curves, shown in figure 15.21 for a quadratic curve.

A quadratic curve requires three points: two endpoints (`S` and `E` in figure 15.21) and a control point (C_1). First, we have to draw the two segments between the endpoints and C_1. Then we need to choose two points on those segments, under the constraint that if the point on SC_1 (call it `A`) is such that $SA/SC=t$, then `B`, the endpoint on EC_1, must satisfy $EB/EC_1=(1-t)$. These two points, `A` and `B`, will be the endpoints of another segment, `AB`, on which we choose a point P_t such that $AP_t/AB=t$.

If `t==0`, then P_t==A, while when `t==1` then P_t==B. The collection of all these points P_t, for all values of `t` between `0` and `1`, makes a quadratic Bézier curve between `A` and `B`.

Notice how the segment A_tB_t is always tangent to the curve.

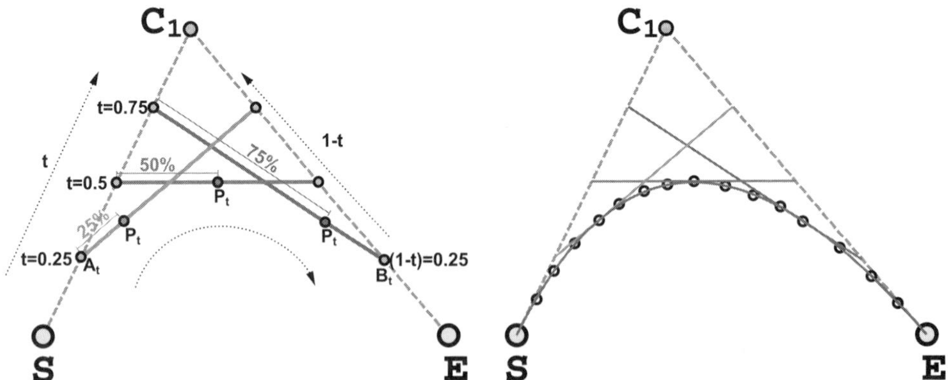
C1
t=0.75
1-t
t
50%
75%
t=0.5
Pt
25%
Pt
Pt
t=0.25
At
(1-t)=0.25
Bt
S
E
C1
S
E

Figure 15.21 How a quadratic Bézier curve is drawn. A quadratic curve requires three points: two endpoints (`S`, `E`) and a control point (C_1, or just `C` for the sake of clarity here henceforth). First we have to draw the two segments between the endpoints and `C`. Then, we can draw segments whose endpoints are on `SC` and `EC`, under the constraint that if the endpoint on the former, call it `A`, is such that `SA/SC=t`, then `B`, the remaining endpoint, must satisfy `EB/EC=(1-t)`. Finally, on segment `AB`, we choose a point `P` such that `AP/AB=t`.

For cubic Bézier curves the procedure becomes a bit more involved, as shown in figure 15.22. There are two control points, C_1 and C_2, and we first have to draw the segments C_1C_2 and select a point C_t on this segment. We'll have to note the ratio between the two subsegments created by this point, $t=C_1C_t/C_1C_2$.

Then we select two points A_t and B_t on the segments between the endpoints and the closest control point, such that $SA_t/SC_1=t$ and $C_2B_t/C_2E=t$.

Finally, for the three points A_t, B_t and C_t, we need to go through the same steps we performed for a quadratic curve, and select a point P_t.

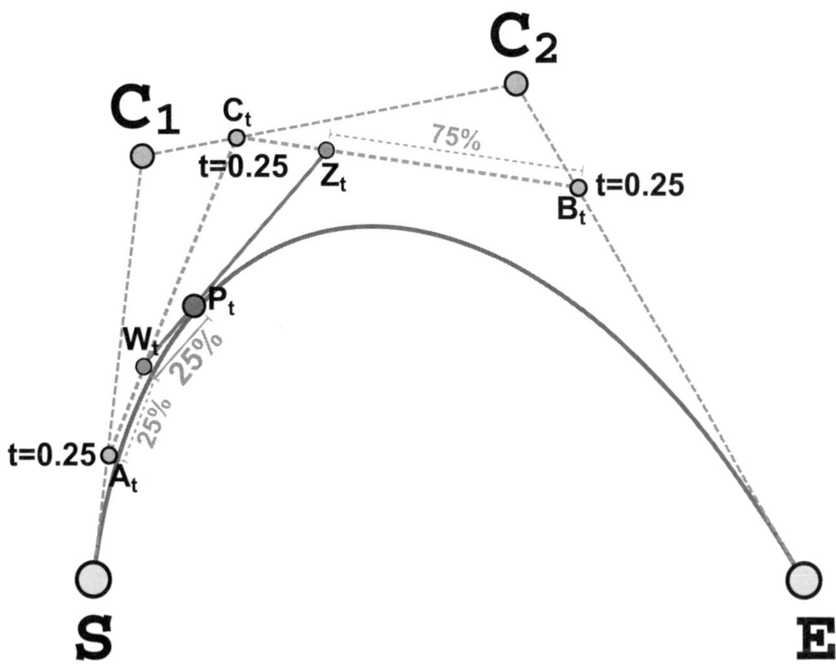
C2
C1
Ct
75%
t=0.25
Zt
t=0.25
Bt
Pt
Wt
25%
25%
t=0.25
At
S
E

Figure 15.22 Drawing a cubic Bézier curve. You can appreciate the increased complexity compared to quadratic curves.

Technically a Bézier curve is an iterative linear interpolation. When we select points A_t, B_t, (and C_t) we apply linear interpolation (varying the ratio `t`), and likewise we can do this for the segments between the generated points.

So, if we start with two segments (quadratic curve), we can apply linear interpolation twice to find the curve's points. With three initial segments (cubic curve), we pick three points, which in turn define two new segments, and so on; we thus apply linear interpolation three times.

Following this definition, even a straight-line segment can be expressed as a Bézier curve. It has no control points and just 1 segment, so we apply linear interpolation once.

In this edge case, it's easy to see that the generic point P_t is given by the vectorial equation:

$$P_L(t) = E \cdot t + S \cdot (1-t),\ t \in [0, 1]$$

We won't derive it for a quadratic curve, but here is how it will look:

$$P_Q(t) = E \cdot t^2 + C_1 \cdot 2 \cdot t \cdot (1-t) + S \cdot (1-t)^2,\ t \in [0, 1]$$

In general, for a Bézier curve with n-2 control points, we can express its generic point as

$$P(t) = \sum_{i=0}^{n} Q_i \cdot \binom{n}{i} \cdot t^i \cdot (1-t)^{n-1},\ t \in [0, 1]$$

using the conventions: $S=Q_0$, $E=Q_n$ and $C_i=Q_i$ ∀ i=1,..,n-1.

15.4.4 Intersections between quadratic Bézier curves

In our examples, we are only going to use a subset of the set of Bézier curves—*symmetric quadratic Bézier curves* where the control point lies at exactly the same distance between the two endpoints. This way, we can simplify the way we reason about the curve and the way we look for intersections.

Looking at figure 15.23, we can see a few interesting facts:

- The curve is always going to be a section of a parabola.
- We can store point C by using a single real value (the distance from the line passing through the endpoints).
- The tangent to the curve that's parallel to segment SE is exactly halfway between the same segment and point C.

We'll see later why the third point is especially important for us.

First, we need to give a brief overview of the methods that can be used to check intersections between Bézier curves:

- *Bézier subdivision* is a method based on *convex hull*[29]—For a Bézier curve with n-2 control points, its convex hull is the polygon with n sides whose vertices are the endpoints and control points. Figure 15.24 illustrates how it's possible to compute the intersection of

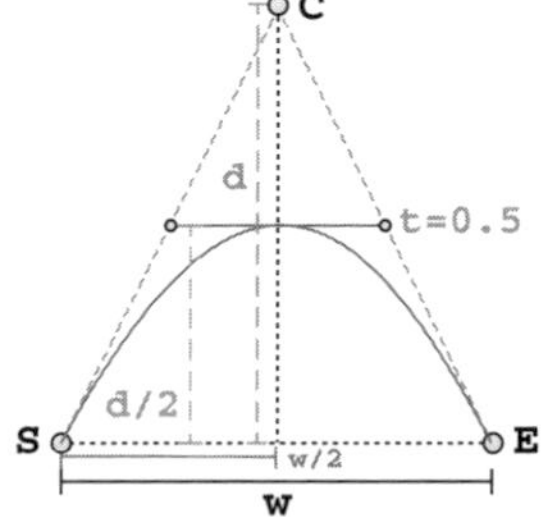
C
d
t=0.5
d/2
S
E
w/2
w

Figure 15.23 A quadratic Bézier curve where the control point lies at the same distance from the endpoints. The tangent to the curve parallel to the segment SE is at a distance of d/2 from that segment, where d is the distance of point C from segment SE.

[29]The convex hull of a shape is the smallest convex set that contains it.

two curves by comparing their convex hulls. If they do not overlap, the curves do not intersect; otherwise, the curves are each split in half and the two halves of one curve are checked for overlap against the two halves of the other curve. This step can be iterated until either there is no overlap between any pair of sections, or the curves are split into sections so small that they can be approximated with segments (within a certain acceptable error). Then, we can just use the algorithm in section 15.4.1 to check that no pairs of segments intersect.

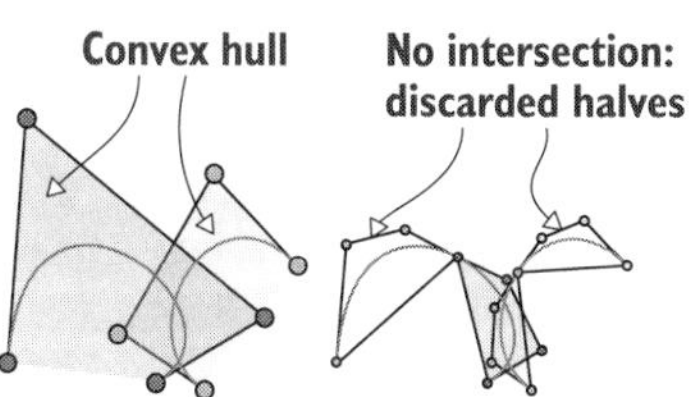
Convex hull
No intersection: discarded halves

Figure 15.24 The Bézier subdivision method in action (first iteration). The points shown are the actual control points of cubic curves. This method can obviously also be applied to quadratic, quartic, or generic curves.

- *Bézier clipping*—For generic Bézier curves, this is the most efficient method, but also the most complicated. We won't get into the details for this one.
- *Interval subdivision*—This is similar to Bézier clipping, but it adapts better to our stricter requirements. The difference is that in this case, we first find the vertical and horizontal tangents to the curve. By splitting the curve, making sure that the points where its tangent is parallel to one of the axes are at the extremes of each segment, we guarantee that in each segment the curve is monotone (because a function can change its trend only in such points), and that for each value point on the x axes, there is only one point belonging to the curve in each one of these sections. Figure 15.25 illustrates how it works for a generic Bézier curve. In turn, we can use these properties to further split the curve by halving each segment along the x axis and computing the exact point on the curve. This point will be one of the corners of each section's bounding box, and we can easily compare the bounding boxes of two curves. They will all be parallel to the Cartesian axis, so we just need to check a few inequalities to find out if they intersect.

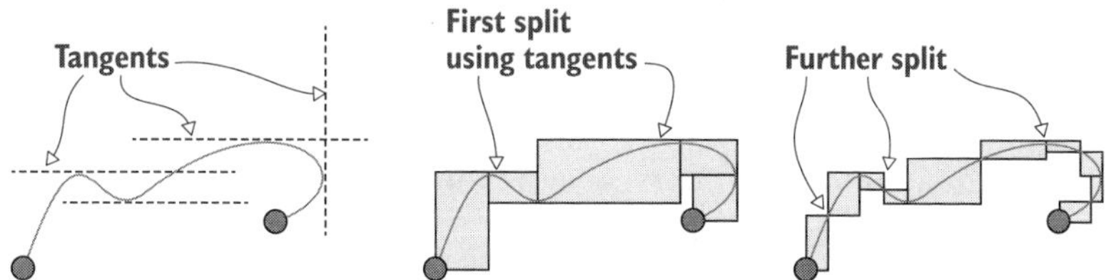
Tangents
First split using tangents
Further split

Figure 15.25 The interval subdivision method in action on a generic Bézier curve

Applying the interval subdivision method to symmetric quadratic Bézier curves is even simpler, because these curves have at most two points where its tangent is parallel to one of the axes. Moreover, we can easily compute an initial, coarse-grained bounding box for each of these curves. As shown in figure 15.26, they all lie within the rectangle delimited by the line passing through its endpoints, the parallel to the former tangent

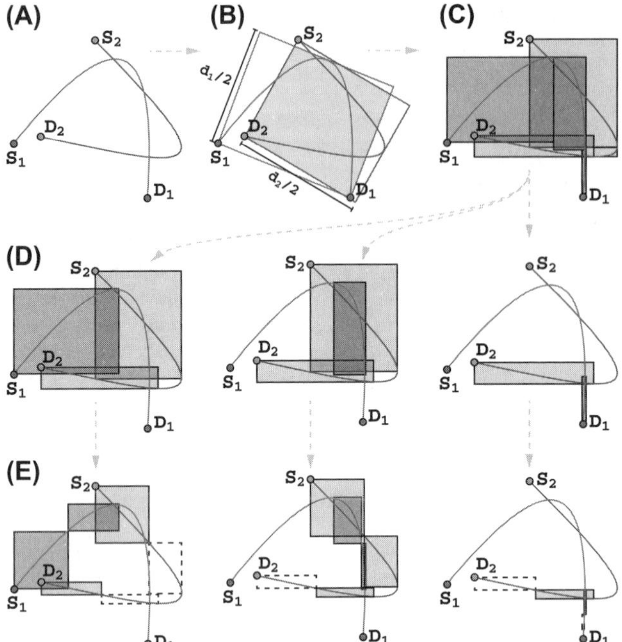
(A)
(B)
(C)
(D)
(E)
$d_1/2$
$d_2/2$
S_1
S_2
D_1
D_2

Figure 15.26 The interval subdivision method used to check intersections between two symmetric, quadratic Bézier curves (A). (B) Compute the bounding boxes using what we know about the curve's tangents at apex. Here, they overlap. (C) We thus need to move forward, computing the tangents to the curve parallel to the axes, and use them as pivot points at which we can split the curves. Each section is now monotonic and can be interpolated with a segment. Each pair of sections from the two curves will at most cross in one point. (D) For each section in curve C_1, compute the intersections using only the overlapping sections in curve C_2 (then sum the results for each of the three cases). (E) We can split each section further by halving it. Only some sub-sections will still overlap, and we can iterate steps (D-E) until they become small enough that the error in approximating a curve with a segment is within a given threshold.

to the apex of the curve (at distance `d/2` from segment `SE`, as we have previously mentioned), and the perpendicular lines to `SE` passing to those endpoints.

Therefore, we can informally define the algorithm to check for intersection of two symmetric quadratic Bézier curves as the following steps:

1. Compute the bounding boxes of the two curves, as shown in figure 15.26 (A).
2. If the bounding boxes do not intersect, return 0; if they do, continue.
3. Compute the vertical and horizontal tangents to each curve, and use them to split the curve into two or three sections (depending on if they have both tangents or just one).
4. Recursively
   a. For each of the sections of curve c_1, check which sections in curve c_2 it overlaps.
   b. If no two sections overlap, return 0.

c Otherwise, return the sum[30] of the intersections for the remote calls among the overlapping pairs:
   i For each pair of overlapping sections.
   ii Split each of the overlapping sections in half.
   iii If the sections are small enough to be approximated with segments, compute the segments' intersection.
   iv Otherwise, recursively check the four sections resulting from the split.

If we compare this algorithm to the one in section 15.4.1 for segment intersection, the main difference that stands out is that this algorithm is recursive (or equivalently iterative), while for segments we only need to perform a constant number of operations.

This means that if we use curves instead of segments, computing the edge crossing at each iteration of an optimization algorithm is going to be much more expensive.

Moreover, with quadratic curves we already have four possible intersections for each pair of edges, and for cubic curves it's obviously even worse: we have more parameters to optimize, and each change can make a greater difference.

That's why we are focusing on straight-line drawings. One should really double-check the requirements and discuss the benefits and costs, before deciding to embark on the more challenging enterprise of curve-line embeddings.

15.4.5 Vertex-vertex and edge-vertex intersections

So far, we have delayed the discussion about validating an embedding by checking that no pair of vertices share the same position, and that no edge crosses a vertex.

There are many ways to draw edges, as we have seen, but there are also many ways to draw vertices: they can be punctiform, they can be drawn as circles, but they can also be drawn as squares, octagons, or any kind of polygon, really. Depending on these choices, we'll need a different algorithm.

Here, we'll assume that vertices are drawn with circles (punctiform vertices being an edge-case, a circle with a radius close to zero), and edges are drawn with segments. This will give you the tools to handle the simplest solution and a basis to build more complex ones, if needed.

For vertices, in particular, if you choose to use squares or regular polygons, you can always consider the *circumscribed circle*[31] or *minimum bounding circle*[32] of the polygon and change the constraints considering these circles instead of the actual shape of the vertices.

Using circles makes our lives a lot easier; it allows us to just check the distance between two vertices (between their centers) or between a vertex and an edge.

---

[30]Remember that while two segments only cross at most in one point, two parabolas can cross in up to four points. Once we split both curves along the tangent points, each section can only cross another section at most once.

[31]The circumscribed circle is a circle passing through all vertices of a polygon.

[32]The minimum bounding circle is the smallest circle covering all points in a set.

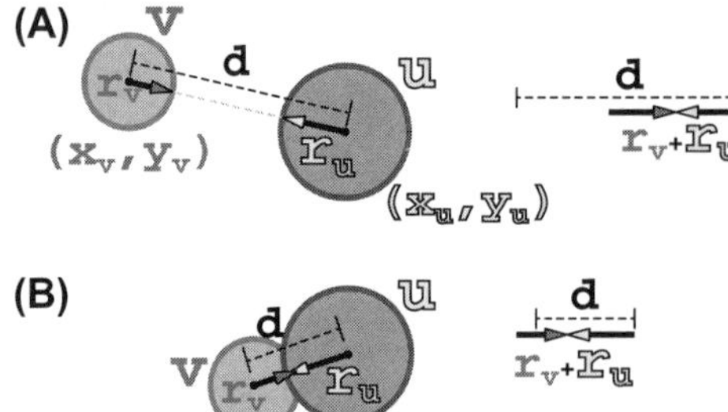
(A)
v
d
u
d
(x_v, y_v)
r_v+r_u
(x_u, y_u)
(B)
u
d
d
v
r_v+r_u

Figure 15.1 Vertex intersection with another vertex. For two circles to overlap, the distance d between their centers must be smaller than the sum of the circles' radii. If $d > r_v + r_u$, as in (A), we are clear; when $d \leq r_v + r_u$, as in (B), the two circles overlap.

For two vertices, the algorithm is trivial: we just need to check that the distance between their centers is larger than the sum of their radii. Figure 15.27 shows why.

To make sure an edge doesn't overlap with a vertex (which is not an endpoint for the edge), we need to make sure that the distance between the edge and the vertex is larger than the vertex's radius.

In turn, when edges are drawn with straight-line segments, this forces us to check three distances. If the distances between the two segment's endpoints (S, E in figure 15.28) and the vertex's center (let's call it C) are smaller than the vertex radius, then we certainly have an intersection. Even if these distances are larger, though, the vertex could intersect the edge somewhere in the middle, so we need to check the distance between the line passing through the segment and the vertex's center, and that the point of minimum distance between the vertex and the line falls inside the segment.

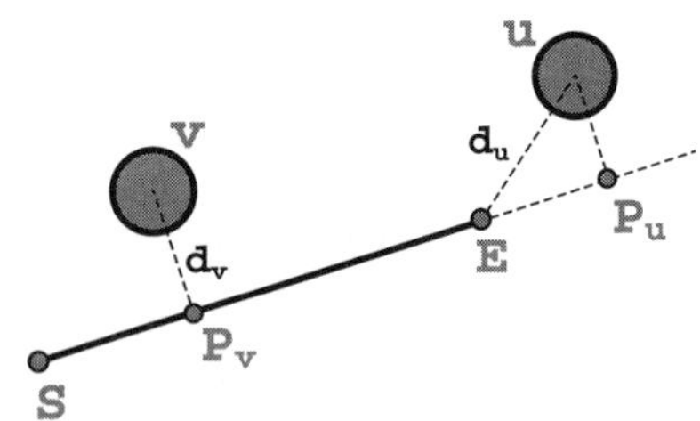
u
v
d_u
P_u
E
d_v
P_v
S

Figure 15.28 Vertex intersection with a segment. When considering the distance between a segment and a vertex, there are cases (v in the figure) where we need to use the line-point distance, and others where the distance to an extreme is what matters.

To find the point-to-segment distance, we can use the following formula (which we won't derive here):

$$dist(\overline{SE}, C) = \frac{|(E_y - S_y)C_x - (E_x - S_x)C_y + E_x S_y - E_y S_x|}{\sqrt{(E_x - S_x)^2 + (E_y - S_y)^2}}$$

And finally, to check if the intersection between the line passing through the segment and the line of minimum distance to a vertex (a line perpendicular to the segment passing through a vertex) falls within or outside a segment, we can use the same algorithm we developed for segment intersection, using points S and E on one side, and v and P_v (or u and P_u) on the other side. We just need to check that the multiplicator factor is between 0 and 1.

Summary

- Graphs are abstract algebraic structures; to visualize them, it's possible to embed a graph to a geometrical space.
- An embedding is a mapping between vertices and points in a Euclidean space, and between edges and (Jordan) curves in the same space.
- If an embedding maps a graph to the plane, and none of the edges intersect another edge or a vertex (besides its endpoints), then the embedding is called a planar embedding.
- While it's possible to embed all graphs in the 3-D Euclidean space without edge intersections, not all graphs are planar.
- If we restrict the shape of the edges to straight-line segments, instead of generic Jordan curves, for some graphs it's not possible to find a straight-line drawing with the minimum possible number of intersections.
- Computing if and how edges cross is not easy. In straight-line drawings it's less expensive because checking two segments only requires a constant number of operations on vectors. When moving to curves, recursive algorithms (or their iterative counterparts) are needed.

16 Gradient descent: Optimization problems (not just) on graphs

This chapter covers

- Developing a randomized heuristic to find the minimum crossing number
- Introducing cost functions to show how the heuristic works
- Explaining gradient descent and implementing a generic version
- Discussing strengths and pitfalls of gradient descent
- Applying gradient descent to the graph embedding problem

If I mention a technique called *gradient descent*, does it ring a bell? You might not have heard of it, or maybe you recognize the name but can't quite recall how it works. If so, that's fine. If, however, I ask you about machine learning, classification problems, or neural networks, chances are that you know exactly what I'm talking about; and I bet these terms also sparked your interest much more.

Well, gradient descent (or a variation on the theme) is the optimization technique that is used behind the scenes by many machine-learning algorithms. But did you know that long before being used as the backbone of supervised learning, this technique was designed to solve optimization problems, like some of the ones we have seen on graphs?

If you didn't, or if you'd like to delve into this topic and learn more about how gradient descent works, this should be the perfect chapter for you.

Remember that in chapter 15 we discovered that while for planar graphs there are efficient algorithms that find a planar embedding in linear time, not all graphs are planar, and it's not always possible to draw a graph's edges in the plane without them intersecting.

What's worse, each non-planar graph has a minimum number of intersections when drawn in the plane, but there is not (and there cannot be[1]) any efficient algorithm that can find this number (or an embedding with as few intersections as possible) for any generic graph.

The minimum edge crossing problem is NP-hard, and as of today, verifying crossing numbers is unfeasible for many categories of non-planar graphs with more than ~20 vertices.

Well, it seems there is not much we can do . . . or is there?

In this chapter, we are going to introduce heuristics to embed graphs with as few intersections as possible, approaching their crossing number. If you refer to figure 16.1, the goal of these heuristics, when applied, for instance, to graph K_4, is to find the embedding on the right or an equivalent one with no edges crossing. We'll start with naïve, brute-force-style algorithms, and then refine them to obtain better results (fewer intersections) faster,[2] and we'll talk about optimization.

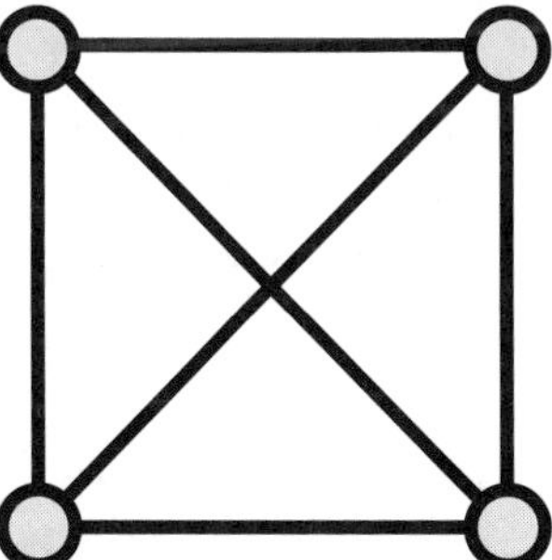

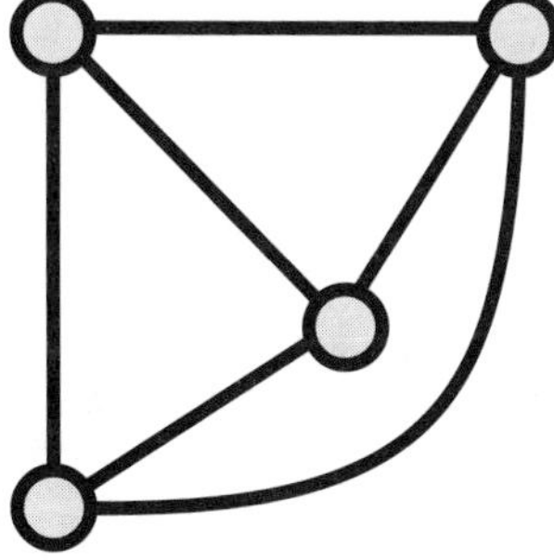

Figure 16.1 Two embeddings for the complete graph K_4. The one on the left is not optimal because there is a pair of edges crossing.

[1] Unless somebody proves that P=NP, which is still unknown, but is considered unlikely.

[2] This refinement process will also continue in the next few chapters, where we introduce new categories of optimization algorithms.

Throughout the following sections, we'll define the category of optimization problems, which has deep implications for our daily lives: network routing, delivery schedules, circuit board printing, and component design. These problems can all be expressed in terms of graphs, a cost function, and an optimization algorithm whose goal is to find the minimum cost configuration. We'll discuss three different optimization techniques to find approximate solutions for them: *random sampling*, *hill climbing*, and *gradient descent*.

16.1 Heuristics for the crossing number

In the introduction to the chapter, we were wondering if there was anything we could do to get us out of this tight spot with crossing number analysis. The truth is that to the best of current knowledge, we can't do much, at least unless we relax the requirement for a deterministic algorithm to guarantee the correct answer and return an embedding with a graph's *minimum crossing number* (or *minimum rectilinear*[3] *crossing number*).

A common strategy to deal with *NP-hard* problems, in fact, is to use heuristics. These algorithms, often operating non-deterministically, are able to provide a sub-optimal answer in a reasonable amount of time.

NOTE We have already met randomized algorithms throughout this book, for instance, in chapters 3 and 4, but if you could use a refresher, feel free to take a look at appendix F, which provides a brief summary of randomized algorithms.

16.1.1 Did you just say heuristics?

I realize the concept of heuristics might be confusing: Why would we accept an algorithm that doesn't return the correct answer? Sometimes we can't. There are problems for which we absolutely need to get the right answer, even if we need to wait longer; for instance, if you are running a nuclear power plant or designing a new drug, you don't want to settle for a sub-optimal solution before trying all the possible (and reasonable) configurations.

At other times, getting to the right answer might not even be possible. An exponential algorithm becomes unfeasible for inputs larger than a few dozen elements, and we would not even be able to see the program output an answer for larger inputs.

Can't we just make computers faster?

Even a supercomputer that can perform ~10^{16} operations per second to run an exponential algorithm that performs `O(2^n)` steps, for an input size 100 will need `O(10^14)` seconds, which is, give or take, 3 million years!

---

[3] As we saw in chapter 15, if we only draw edges as straight-line segments, for some graphs we won't be able to obtain an embedding with as few intersections as possible. That's why the rectilinear crossing number has been introduced: the minimum number of edge intersections across all possible graph's straight-line drawings.

> And if we were able to make our computers a million times faster (which, even when Moore's law was holding, would have taken 30 years), then we would only increase our ability to solve the problem a tiny bit: our computation would still require 3 years for 100 elements, 3 thousand years for 110, and again 3 million years for 120!

For easier problems, even if the time to wait would not be longer than human history, it could still be too long. Think about live events or forecasting—there won't be much use for tomorrow's weather forecast if it's delivered in three days!

So, in all these cases, we might be willing to accept a sub-optimal answer, provided we can get it within a reasonable time—but that's not the whole story.

Another important consideration in favor of heuristics is that despite not being able to guarantee the optimal solution on all inputs, some heuristics are able to return the optimal result in a reasonable time for a subset of the whole problem space, and in some cases they prove to work quite well in practice on real-world data.

How is this possible? It's because the theory of NP-hardness is about *worst-case performance*, and for some problems there are a minority of edge cases that turn out to be hard to solve; but for practical applications we are often interested in *average-case hardness*, aka how difficult on average it is to solve a problem on the instances of the problem that we see in real scenarios.

There are many heuristics that have been developed for graph algorithms, for example, to solve the traveling salesman problem[4] or find a clique on a graph.[5] Not all the heuristics are the same, of course. Usually they are a compromise between performance and accuracy, and for some of these algorithms it's possible to prove bounds on their precision, such as proving that the solution they output will be within a certain margin from the optimal solution.

So, what kind of heuristic could we use to find a good (or at least decent) graph embedding?

Now, I'd like you to keep in mind what we said a few lines previously: there can be many different approximate algorithms for each problem, and not all of them are equally good.

We'll start easy, with a simple heuristic that's far from ideal. It will serve a purpose, let us understand the problem scenario, and then we can (and will) iterate over it to improve its performance.

Before we start with our first attempt, I encourage you to think about this before moving on, and try to develop your idea. Who knows, you might have a breakthrough and come up with a new solution!

---

[4] Given a list of cities and the distances between each pair of cities, find the shortest possible route that visits each city exactly once and returns to the origin city. This is, needless to say, an NP-complete problem.

[5] Find the largest subset of vertices in a graph such that each vertex in the subset is adjacent to all the other vertices in the same subset. In other words, find the largest complete subgraph of a given graph.

Whenever you are ready, let's go. We will reuse an algorithm that we saw in previous chapters, specifically a helper method we used in clustering.

Remember k-means?[6] We had this problem of initializing the centroids: come up with an initial choice for `k` points in a `n`-dimensional space. It looked easier than it actually was, didn't it? And yet we saw how important it is to make a good choice for the initial points, so you can get a fast convergence and a good result.

Take a look at section 12.2, and in particular at listings 12.1 and 12.2, to see how we implemented the random initialization of points for the centroids.

Here, with the graph embedding, we have a similar problem. We need to choose a certain number of 2-D points, and the way we chose them will directly determine the result (this time, there isn't an optimization algorithm running after the choice).

One important difference is that with k-means we had an underlying distribution and choosing the points such that they were uniformly distributed with respect to this distribution was harder and needed particular caution.

For graph embedding, we can draw our points from a finite portion of the plane, typically a rectangle,[7] and those points will determine the number of edge intersections.

Let's define the problem more formally now:

Given a simple graph `G=(V,E)` with `n=|V|` vertices and `m=|E|` edges, we need to draw `n` random points from a finite rectangle whose corners[8] are `(0,0)` and `(W,H)`, so that

- Each point `(x,y)` is such that `0≤x<W, 0≤y<H`.
- Edges will be drawn as straight-line segments.
- Vertices will be drawn as points (or circles) centered at those `n` points.
- No two vertices can be assigned to the same center, so given two points `(x1, y1)` and `(x2,y2)`, either `x1≠x2` or `y1≠y2`.
- No vertex can lie on the path of an edge.
- We assume `G` has no loops.[9] If it did, we could always draw loops without intersecting any other edge.

Figure 16.2 shows a few examples of valid and invalid choices of vertex centers, given our constraints; in particular, we will have to check the conditions at points 4 and 5 once we have chosen all the points, but we'll defer the discussion about checking these issues. For now, we can assume we have helper methods for these checks, and if we find that any of these constraints are violated, then we have two strategies to make it right:

- Correct the vertices position, for example slightly perturbating, at random, those points that coincide or intersect an edge.
- Discard the solution violating a constraint and start over.

---

[6] Check out chapters 12 and 13.

[7] It is useful to have some flexibility about the region from which points are drawn, because this way we can get better results depending on the size of the graph, avoiding too dense and too sparse embeddings.

[8] Top-left and bottom-right, following the way we index the screen's rows and columns in most programming languages.

[9] If you remember chapter 14, a loop is an edge that starts and ends at the same vertex.

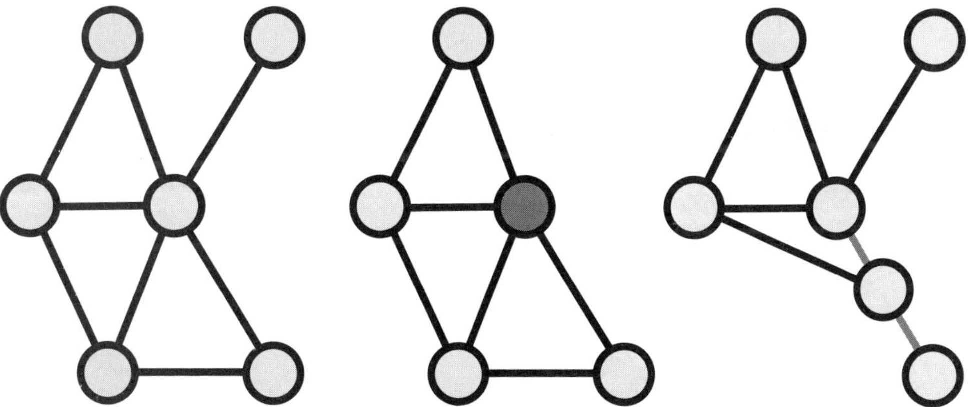

Figure 16.2 Three embeddings for the same graph. On the left, a valid embedding. The embedding in the middle is not valid because two vertices are assigned the same position, while the one on the right has a vertex intersecting an edge (one for which it's not an endpoint).

Notice that if we draw vertices as circles (as in figure 16.2) and not just points, we will have to make the requirement on vertices stronger, requiring that the two circles don't intersect.

Now, as we saw for k-means, when we count on random methods, we can be lucky, but more often than not we won't be. Figure 16.3 shows a particularly unlucky assignment for the K_6 graph. As we know from chapter 15, it's possible to draw this complete graph in the plane with three intersections between its edges.

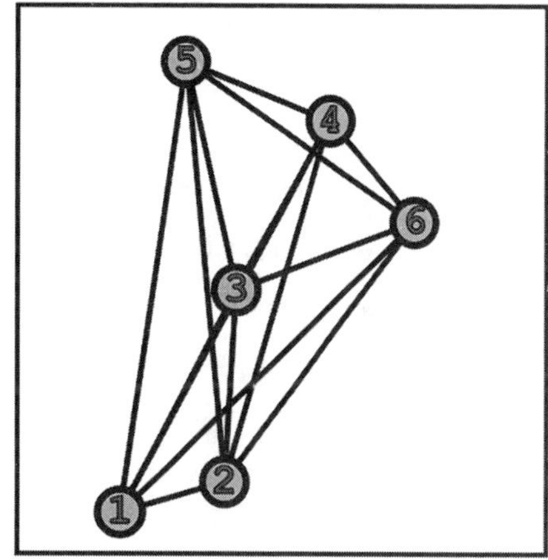

5
4
6
3
2
1

Figure 16.3 A random embedding for the K_6 complete graph. Notice how particularly bad the choice of positions turned out to be.

A way to raise our chances with k-means was to use the random-restart technique, basically running the algorithm (and in turn the random initialization) several times, and then saving the best solution found across all those runs.

This strategy looks interesting for our problem as well:

1. Randomly generate the positions of the vertices.
2. Check that the assignment abides by the constraints for edges and vertices (and discard the current assignments if it doesn't).
3. Compute the number of edge intersections.
4. If it's the best result so far, keep it; otherwise, discard it.
5. Restart from 1.

This workflow is shown in figure 16.4 and implemented in listing 16.1. This heuristic is called ***random sampling***.

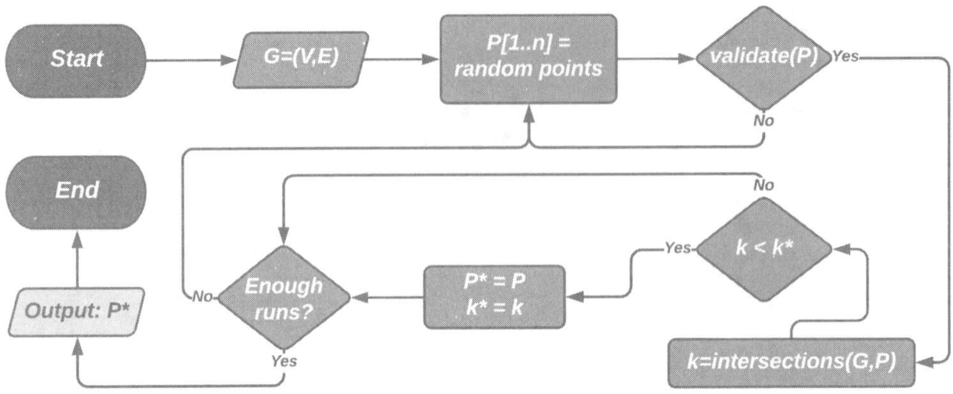
Start
G=(V,E)
P[1..n] =
random points
validate(P)
Yes
No
End
No
k < k*
Yes
Enough
runs?
No
P* = P
k* = k
Output: P*
Yes
k=intersections(G,P)

Figure 16.4 A flowchart for the algorithm generating random embeddings and selecting the one with the fewest edge intersections

Listing 16.1 Random sampling for minimum crossing number embedding

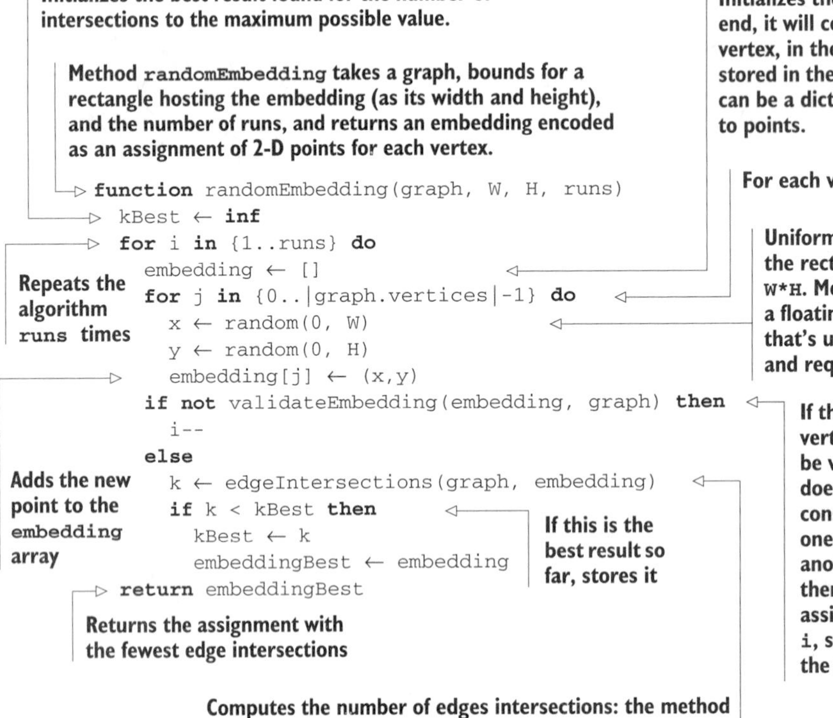

```
function randomEmbedding(graph, W, H, runs)
  kBest ← inf
  for i in {1..runs} do
    embedding ← []
    for j in {0..|graph.vertices|-1} do
      x ← random(0, W)
      y ← random(0, H)
      embedding[j] ← (x,y)
    if not validateEmbedding(embedding, graph) then
      i--
    else
      k ← edgeIntersections(graph, embedding)
      if k < kBest then
        kBest ← k
        embeddingBest ← embedding
  return embeddingBest
```

Initializes the best result found for the number of intersections to the maximum possible value.

Method `randomEmbedding` takes a graph, bounds for a rectangle hosting the embedding (as its width and height), and the number of runs, and returns an embedding encoded as an assignment of 2-D points for each vertex.

Repeats the algorithm `runs` times

Initializes the array of points. In the end, it will contain one point per vertex, in the same order they are stored in the graph. Alternatively, this can be a dictionary, mapping vertices to points.

For each vertex in the graph . . .

Uniformly draws a 2-D point from the rectangular region of size `W*H`. Method `random` can return a floating point or just an integer; that's up to your implementation and requirements.

Adds the new point to the `embedding` array

If the assignment of vertices coordinates can't be validated (that is, if it doesn't abide by the constraints, and at least one vertex intersects another vertex or an edge), then it discards this assignment (decrementing `i`, so that this iteration in the loop will be repeated).

If this is the best result so far, stores it

Returns the assignment with the fewest edge intersections

Computes the number of edges intersections: the method is generic, so it can support straight and curve edges, although in this case we assume the former.

One last word of caution: we don't need to assume the graph is connected, but breaking it down into connected components before applying the heuristic can improve the final result.

In listing 16.1 we abstract two important helper methods: `validate` and `edgeIntersections`. Both can be implemented separately and adapted to the actual context we decide to operate in.

For both, however, it's possible to give a generic definition that in turn abstracts over more specific methods: listings 16.2 and 16.3 shows these definitions.

Listing 16.2 Method `validateEmbedding`

```
function validateEmbedding(graph, embedding)
  n ← |graph.vertices|
  for i in {0..n-2} do
    for j in {i+1..n-1} do
      if vertexIntersectsVertex(embedding[i], embedding[j]) then
        return false
  for edge in graph.edges do
    for vertex in graph.vertices do
      if vertex <> edge.source and vertex <> edge.destination and
          edgeIntersectsVertex(
            embedding[indexOf(edge.source)],
            embedding[indexOf(edge.destination)],
            embedding[indexOf(vertex)]) then
        return false
  return true
```

- **Method `validateEmbedding` takes a graph and an embedding to validate, and returns `true` if the embedding passed the check, or `false` if it needs to be rejected.**
- **Cycles through all pair of vertices**
- **Checks that the two vertices don't intersect each other. This check is context-dependent; it can be just making sure the two points aren't the same, or checking that the circles used to draw the vertices have no intersection. If the check fails, the embedding is to be rejected.**
- **Cycles through all `graph's` edges**
- **For each edge, cycles through all vertices to make sure `vertex` is not drawn in such a way that it crosses the edge**
- **If `vertex` is not one of the edge's endpoints, we need to make sure that the edge is not drawn over `vertex` (otherwise, it might look like two edges adjacent to this vertex). If this happens for any vertex/edge, we need to reject the embedding.**

The implementation of the helper methods used in listings 16.2 and 16.3 was discussed in the last chapter, in section 15.4.

Notice that the helper methods checking if a vertex intersects another vertex or an edge are context-dependent, based on how we draw vertices. If they are drawn with circles, we need to make sure that the circles used to draw every pair of vertices have no intersection, and that no edge is drawn over the vertex's circle (otherwise, it might seem like it's two edges adjacent to this vertex).

Listing 16.3 Method `edgeIntersections`

```
function edgeIntersections(graph, embedding)
  m ← |graph.edges|
  k ← 0
```

- **Method `edgeIntersections` takes a graph and an embedding to validate, and returns the number of intersections between the graph's edges when drawn with current embedding.**
- **Some basic initialization**

```
for i in {0..m-2} do                    <-- Cycles through every pair of edges
  edge1 ← graph.edges[i]
    for j in {i+1..m-1} do
      edge2 ← graph.edges[j]
      if edgeIntersection(edge1, edge2) then   <-- If this pair of edges intersects
        k ← k + 1                                  when drawn, increases the
return k                                           intersections counter by 1
```

Like the previous method, we abstracted away the actual algorithm checking the edges. This way, depending on the context, you can use one assuming edges are drawn using straight-line segments, or Bézier curves, and so on.

16.1.2 Extending to curve-line edges

In the previous section, we added as a constraint that edges were to be drawn as straight-line segments. As a consequence, we were optimizing the embeddings to reduce the intersections of a straight-line drawing, and the total number of intersections could only be as low as the rectilinear crossing number of a graph. As we saw in chapter 15, there are many graphs for which the rectilinear crossing number is larger than the crossing number (which, in turn, is the absolute minimum for the number of intersections in any planar embedding of a graph).

The restriction to straight-line drawings was not explicitly required in the code, which was kept as abstract as possible. However, if we would like to use curves for the edges, we need to apply at least one change to listing 16.1: we also have to decide how each edge is modeled. This can be done in several ways, the simplest being randomly choosing some parameters that determine how each edge is drawn—up to, possibly, running some optimization on these parameters to minimize the intersections.

First, however, we need to decide which parameters we are talking about. To keep things simple, we restrict this to Bézier curves: quadratic Bézier curves can be described with three parameters (the two endpoints, plus a control point), while the cubic version, which (as shown in figure 16.5) is more flexible, needs two control points, for a total of four 2-D points (which make eight scalar parameters).

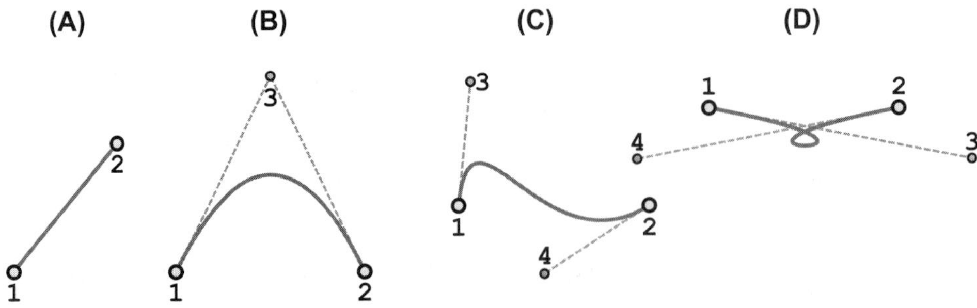
(A)
(B)
(C)
(D)
1
2
1
2
3
1
2
3
4
1
2
3
4

Figure 16.5 Examples of Bézier curves. Segment (A) can be considered an edge case with 0 control points, while quadratic curves (B) have one control point, and cubic ones (C, D), the most flexible variant, have two control points (plus the two endpoints, of course).

We have discussed the details of these representations in section 15.4.3. By setting in stone the choice of a subcategory of these curves (the quadratic, symmetric Bézier curves, as shown in figure 16.6), we can already describe how to extend the algorithm in listing 16.1 to deal with the extra parameters.

In particular, to stay true to the choice of a fully randomized algorithm, we could just randomly choose each edge's control point(s); however, so much freedom in the choice could lead to weird shapes for the edges, making the convergence of the algorithm to a good solution slower.

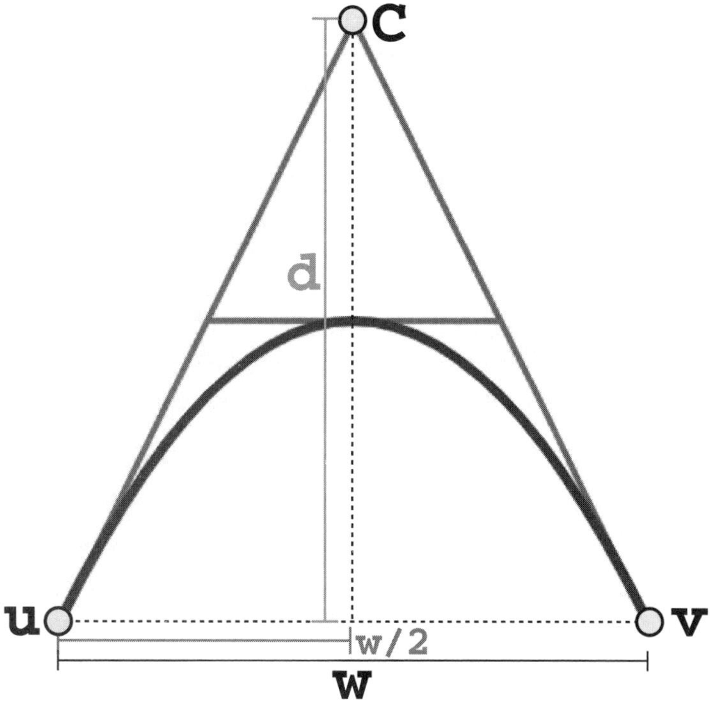
C
d
u
v
w/2
w

Figure 16.6 A quadratic Bézier curve used to draw an edge between vertices `u` and `v`. The point `C` is the curve's control point. For this example, we restrict to a subset of all the possible quadratic Bézier curves between two points, and in particular to just those curves where the control point lies on the line perpendicular to the segment `uv`, and passing through the middle of the segment (in other words, the line made by points in the plane that are at the same distance to `u` and `v`).

A more feasible alternative could be restricting even more the curves that can be used, for example, using quadratic curves whose control point is at the same distance from both edge's endpoints. This choice, explained in figure 16.6, allows us to balance flexibility and complexity so that we only need to add a single real number to the model of each edge, the distance of the control point from the segment between the endpoints (denoted with `d` in the figure). It's also advisable (but not strictly necessary) to restrict the possible values of `d` so that its absolute value will be in the order of magnitude of `w`, the distance between the endpoints; negative values of d will cause the convexity of the edge to flip (in figure 16.6, with a negative value for d, the curve would be drawn below the segment uv passing through the vertices).

16.2 How optimization works

So, random sampling seems to work. If you try the version implemented in the JsGraphs library,[10] you can see that (on average) the crossing number provided by the random algorithm with restart is better than the one returned by the one-pass random version. Intuitively, we can understand why: if we toss a coin 100 times, it's easier to get at least one head than if we toss the same coin just once.

To see how this operates in a more formal framework, we could use a visualization of how the optimization proceeds. This is not trivial, because what we are optimizing here is a function of 2n parameters, when a graph has n vertices. For each vertex, we can change its x and y coordinates.

Now, humans are really good at visualizing functions of 1 parameter in a 2-D plot: the x axis is usually the parameter, and the y axis shows the value of the function; with 2 parameters, we can still visualize things meaningfully. Until AR/VR goes mainstream, we have to make do with a 2-D projection of a 3-D plot, which is not ideal, but still feasible (as you'll see in figure 16.8).

The issue becomes harder when we get to 3 parameters. One workaround is to introduce "time" as the fourth dimension, and as such, the plot can be shown as a 3-D wave that changes depending on the third parameter.

Besides being hard to make sense of, this solution doesn't solve the problem when we have 4 or more parameters. What we can usually do in these cases is lock k-2 parameters, out of k total variables, and see how the function behaves as the other 2 variables change.

We'll do something similar with our graph embedding problem to show you how this works, and to better understand our problem.

But first of all, what function are we talking about in this case?

16.2.1 Cost functions

We call the target of our optimization a ***cost function***: it expresses well the idea that our solution (each solution we try) has a cost, and that we are trying to minimize it.

There is a vast category of problems called ***optimization problems*** for which finding a solution is equivalent to exploring the problem space and eventually picking the solution with the lowest cost. For these problems, usually there are many possible definitions of cost functions that can be used. Some are better than others (we'll see why), and when we do have a choice, it's important to spend time and choose wisely, because it can have a great impact on how fast we can find an optimal solution, or sometimes even on whether we can find one at all. In general, however, most optimization problems are proven to be NP-hard, regardless of the specific choice of cost function.

[10] See http://mng.bz/w9na.

The cost function we have chosen for our graph embedding problem is simply the number of edge intersections for a given embedding. Spoiler alert: this choice is problematic with some optimization algorithms, as we'll see later.

So, in figure 16.7 we can see the complete graph K_4, an embedding that has 8 degrees of freedom: let's agree to lock 7 of them, and only allow the horizontal position of vertex v_4 to change.

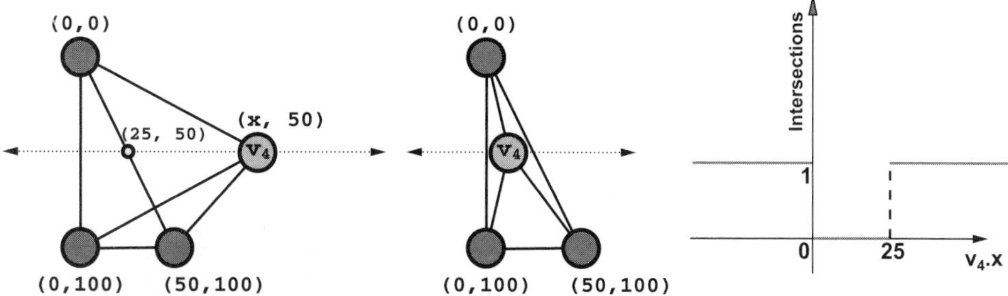
(0,0)
(25, 50)
(x, 50)
V4
(0,100)
(50,100)
(0,0)
V4
(0,100)
(50,100)
Intersections
1
0
25
V4.X

Figure 16.7 The cost function for "number of intersections" for a specific embedding of K_4. The position of 3 out of 4 vertices is locked, and for the last one, v_4 in the graphic, we can only change its horizontal position. Under these assumptions, the cost as a function of v_4's x position is a discontinuous function, equal to 0 when `0 < x < 25`, and equal to 1 when `x < 0` or `x > 25`. Notice how at `x==0` and `x==25` we have two discontinuity points, and in particular, we assume the cost is infinite at those points, because the vertex is exactly lying on one of the edges between the other vertices.

The cost function looks like a *step function*, with its value going abruptly from `1` to `0` when the vertex enters the internal face of the sub-graph induced by the other three vertices (the triangle marked by the unnamed vertices in figure 16.7).

If we had allowed vertex v_4 to move both vertically and horizontally, we would have had, instead, a 3-D chart showing a surface.

This is shown in figure 16.8 for the complete graph K_5, or to be more precise, for one of the possible embeddings for this graph.

Notice that here we have *surfaces* of discontinuity, where the cost function changes its value: when `|x|==|y|` (`v` lying on a line passing through the diagonals of the square), and when `x` or `y` are equal to `0` or `100` (lines lying on the perimeter of the square). For any point on these surfaces, the cost will be infinite, because as shown in the third example in the figure, vertex `v` will lie on one of the edges between the other vertices (and our constraints assign an infinite cost to these invalid configurations).

Moreover, as you can see, no matter how hard we try, we can't find a position for vertex `v` that will guarantee us an embedding with the minimum possible crossing number; this is because the position of the other 4 vertices is not optimal for a straight-line drawing of K_5.

In turn, the underlying reason is that if we consider the larger problem of finding the best embedding (with none of the vertices locked), we hit a ***local minimum*** of the cost function: a point or region in the n-dimensional problem space where the cost function has a lower value than in the surrounding area, but not the lowest possible overall.

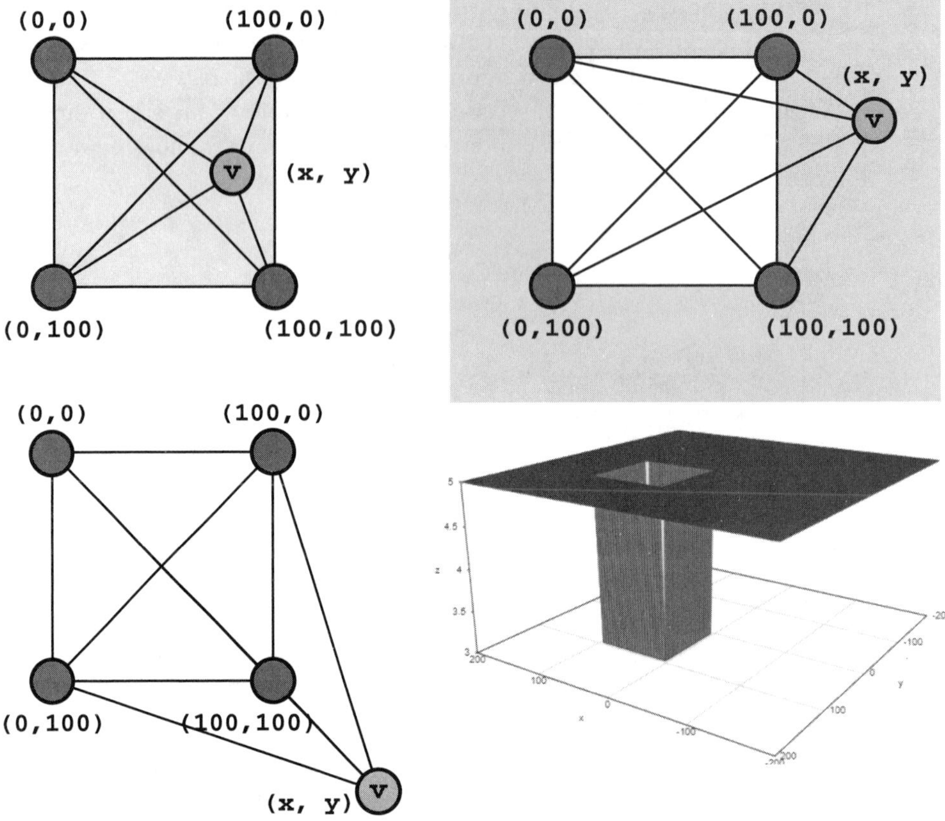

(0,0)
(100,0)
v
(x, y)
(0,100)
(100,100)

Figure 16.8 The cost function for "number of intersections" for a specific embedding of K_{45}. The position of 4 vertices is locked, and only vertex v can be moved freely. If we move v inside the perimeter of the square created by the other vertices, the number of intersections is consistently 3; outside the square, it becomes 5. Notice that here we have surfaces of discontinuity!

If we could take a 2-D projection of the cost function on a generic configuration of the graph (not specifically the embedding in figure 16.8), it might hypothetically look somewhat similar to figure 16.9.

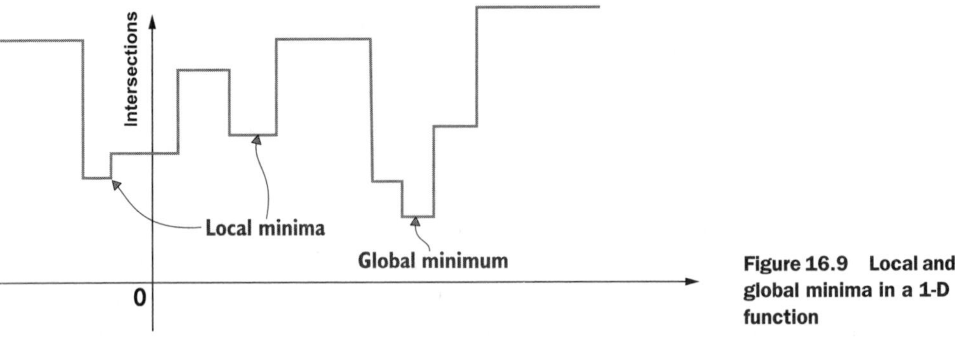

Intersections
Local minima
Global minimum
0

Figure 16.9 Local and global minima in a 1-D function

16.2.2 Step functions and local minima

Local minima aren't really good news. Ideally, we would like to have a single global minimum and a cost function that smoothly converges toward it.

A bowl-shaped function, for example, like the section of conic curve shown in figure 16.9, would suit us particularly well and work fine with most learning algorithms.

Why is that? Well, you can imagine an optimization algorithm like a marble that is left rolling on the surface of the cost function. There are, of course, marbles of different weights and friction, and some marbles on some surfaces get stuck and need to be pushed around; likewise, there are different learning algorithms.

If you release a marble on a surface like the cost function in figure 16.9, there is a good chance that it will just stay on the plateau where it lands. If you give it a little push, it might end up in a pit corresponding to a local minimum, and be stuck there, unless you pick it up and release it elsewhere.

Conversely, if you release a marble on a smooth surface like figure 16.10, like when you toss it into a bowl, then it will roll down to the bottom of the bowl, maybe oscillate a little, and in the end settle down in the lowest point, where gravity can't pull it down any further.

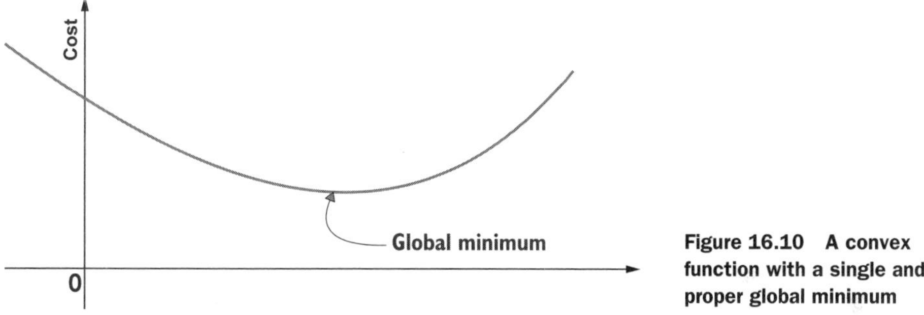
Cost
Global minimum
0

Figure 16.10 A convex function with a single and proper global minimum

16.2.3 Optimizing random sampling

Using this "marble" analogy, an optimization problem can be seen as two things:

- The cost function is analogous to the marble track: the smoother its path to the optimal cost, the better algorithms can (in theory) work. Notice that we can build several "tracks" between a starting point and a finish line—engineering the best possible track is part of the solution.
- An optimization algorithm is like a marble rolling down the path. For the analogy to be more accurate, though, we need to say that both the marble and the way that it's tossed and interacts with the track are part of the analogy of the optimization algorithm.

What about our *random sampling* algorithm? How can we express it in our analogy? Regardless of the cost function, the algorithm does the same thing. Imagine the track is made of sand or mud, so when a marble is tossed onto the track, it digs a small hole in the sand or mud and stops where it lands. This mechanism is independent of the shape of the cost function, and it works the same even with a smooth, bowl-shaped function like the one in figure 16.10.

Figure 16.11 is an attempt at capturing how random sampling (which doesn't perform any optimization after initialization) works.

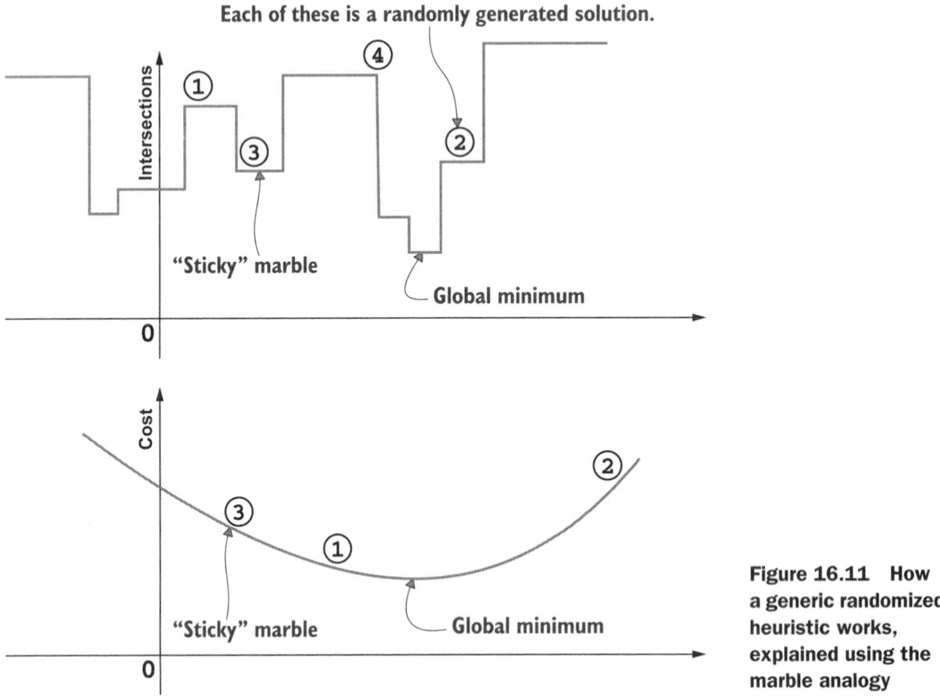
Each of these is a randomly generated solution.
Intersections
1
2
3
4
"Sticky" marble
Global minimum
0
Cost
"Sticky" marble
Global minimum
0

Figure 16.11 How a generic randomized heuristic works, explained using the marble analogy

A randomized heuristic is like tossing dozens, hundreds, or thousands of marbles at our muddy track (without being able to see where the finish line is). They stay exactly where they land, and in the end, we just choose the one that landed the closest to the finish line. The key is doing many attempts, hoping that at least one will land close enough to the optimal solution. Of course, the track could be so long that no matter how many times we try, we won't be able to get any closer to a good solution: that's the case with exponential problems, where the number of possible solutions is huge, when the input is large enough.

Moreover, we need to be careful when using a completely randomized algorithm. We might toss several marbles in the same position, and we could generate the same solution more than once.

If there is a good thing about this approach (besides being extremely cheap), it's that the shape of the cost function doesn't matter. We don't need to engineer a good "track," because there isn't going to be any "marble rolling" after initialization.

At the same time, this is also the worst part—we can't take advantage if we have a good cost function that smoothly degrades towards a global minimum.

If we think about marbles races, we can perhaps find a workaround for that. If you've ever played with marble on the beach, you probably know what to do when one is stuck in a pit on the sand track—you give the marble a nudge to get it out of there and start rolling again.

The analogy with randomized algorithms is *local optimization*. We can have sub-heuristics performing a local optimization; for example, trying to move vertices around one by one within a short distance from the randomly assigned initial position and checking to see if the crossing number improves.

This algorithm is called *hill climbing*, or in our case, since we try to minimize a function instead of maximizing it, we can call it *hill descent*.

Figure 16.12 visualizes the analogy. In our case, despite the nudge, the marble only travels a short distance (well, it's a muddy track, isn't it?), but we might still get some improvement. What we really do is explore the cost function in a small area around each solution, and if we find a position for which the cost is lower, we move our "marble" there.

If you look closely at figure 16.12, you can see that in this case, the shape of the cost function does matter. While with a differentiable, bowl-shaped function we always get an improvement, with a step function (like our example, "minimum number of intersections"), sometimes the marbles are stuck in local minima and sometimes they are on large plateaus, so moving them around won't get us anywhere better.

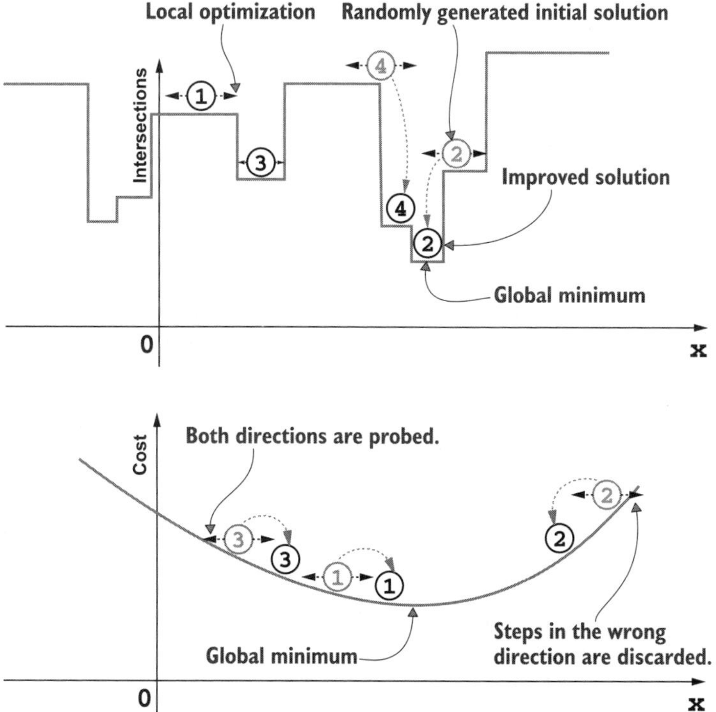
Local optimization
Randomly generated initial solution
Intersections
1
3
4
2
Improved solution
Global minimum
0
x
Cost
Both directions are probed.
Global minimum
Steps in the wrong direction are discarded.

Figure 16.12 How a generic randomized heuristic with local optimization works, explained using the marble analogy. Notice that we need to try to update x in both directions and check if we get an improvement.

Another thing that we must note is that with this algorithm, we have to try moving in both directions. By randomly exploring the area surrounding a solution, we are blindly poking similar solutions, but without any rationale. For instance, in the bottom example in figure 16.12, by looking at the marbles and the shape of the cost function, we would know that in order to get an improvement, we should increase the value of the only parameter for solutions 1 and 3, and decrease it for solution 2. Using hill descent, we would try to both increase and decrease it for all solutions, and just see what happens. For functions of more than a single parameter, we would either search the surrounding area around the current solution, or probe a random direction, and move if we can get a better value.

Applying this to our graph problem, this means we would move a vertex in all directions, and each time compute the edge intersections of the new embedding.

And if this looks bad with a 2-D cost function, remember that as the dimensionality of the search space grows, we face the curse of dimensionality (see chapters 9–11), and we will have `2n` parameters to tune for a graph with `n` vertices.

So, we might want to try a more efficient approach.

16.3 Gradient descent

Why do we have to play "go fish" when we try local optimization? Remember that for a graph with `n` vertices, it means we are in `2n`-dimensional space, so trying to move in every direction[11] randomly . . . is a lot!

Looking at our 2-D example, where the cost function depends on a single variable, the direction we should explore seems pretty obvious!

But in a multidimensional space, where we can't visualize the shape of the surface, how do we know which parameters should be tuned and in which direction?

The mathematical solution to this quest is called *gradient descent*. Gradient descent is an optimization technique that, under certain conditions, can be applied to different categories of optimization problems.

The idea is simple: we can look at the slope of a function at a given point and move toward the direction in which the function decreases the fastest. The name stems from the fact that for a differentiable function, the direction of the steepest slope is given by its gradient.

This is illustrated in figure 16.13 for a single-variable, differentiable function.

Before discussing it a bit more formally, let's see how we could frame it in our marbles example: it's like we are allowed to push marbles with a nudge, and they can travel a short distance before stopping again in the sand. Similar to what happens when you play with marbles in the sand, you need several nudges to reach the goal, and they only move a short distance. If you give them a nudge in the right direction,

[11] Here we are not talking about moving our imaginary marble on the surface of the cost function: this is a generic description fitting this entire category of optimization problems. For the particular problem of the minimum intersection embedding, the way we explore the surrounding area of the cost function is, indeed, moving each vertex around.

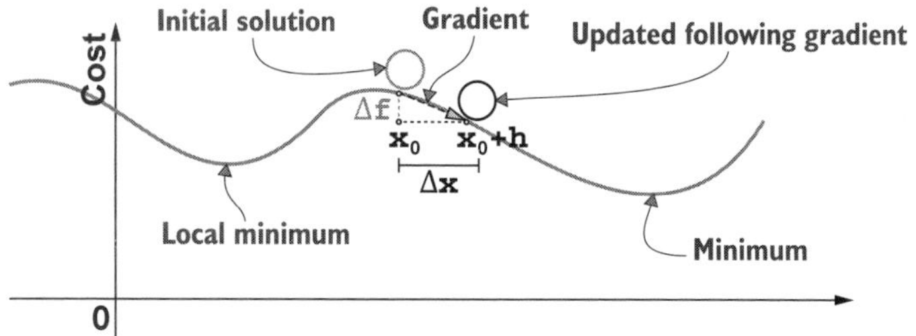
Initial solution
Gradient
Updated following gradient
Cost
Δf
x0
x0+h
Δx
Local minimum
Minimum
0

Figure 16.13 Gradient descent: `Δf` is the change in the cost function caused by a variation `Δx` in its parameter.

they move a little further toward the finish line (or your goal). But to make things more interesting, in our game you can only see a short portion of the track next to your current position, as if you were playing in the fog or with lens distortion.

Gradient descent is formally described using calculus. Don't worry if you haven't had an introduction to calculus, because you are not going to need it to apply gradient descent: there are many great libraries that already implement it for you. Actually, thinking about writing your own version is a bad idea, because this algorithm needs to be fine-tuned and highly optimized to exploit a GPU's power.

16.3.1 The math of gradient descent

If you did take a calculus class, you probably remember the notion of a derivative: given a single-variable, continuous function `f(x)`, we define its derivative as the ratio between how `f` changes in response to a small change in its argument `x`. Formally, we write

$$f'(x) = \frac{\partial f}{\partial x} = \lim_{\Delta x \to 0} \frac{\Delta f}{\Delta x} = \lim_{h \to 0} \frac{f(x+h) - f(x)}{h}$$

This value can be finite, infinite, or even not defined for a given function and a specific value of `x`; if for a function `f` its first derivative is always defined, we call `f` a differentiable function.

For differentiable functions, there are formulas that allow us to find the exact mathematical definition of their derivatives, which in turn are going to be a function themselves. For instance, if `f(x)=x, then f'(x)=1` (the constant function). The derivative of the quadratic function $f(x)=x^2$ is $f'(x)=2x$, and the derivative of the exponential function $f(x)=e^x$ is $f'(x)=e^x$ (yes, it's the exponential function itself!)

There are many interesting results from the geometric interpretation of function derivates,[12] but we can't go through them all here.

The most important result, from our point of view, is that if we compute the value of the first derivative of a function in a given point, it tells us if the function is growing in that point, and how much. In other words, and as a simplification, it tells us if by slightly increasing the value of `x, f(x)` also increases, or decreases, or stays the same.

[12] Note that there are higher-order derivates too, although here we'll stop at the first-order derivative.

We can apply this to our optimization algorithm. For instance, in figure 16.13, if we computed the first derivative of the cost function at point x_0, we'd get a negative value that would tell us that f grows when x becomes smaller. Since we want to move toward smaller values of f, we know that we should update x by assigning it a larger value.

We can repeat this step over and over, thus following a downhill path along the cost function's surface.

If this looks easy to compute, however, in multidimensional spaces this gets far more complicated: for a n-dimensional function g, the gradient of the function at a given point is a vector whose components are the partial derivatives of the function, computed in that point.

For instance, with a 2-D domain (see figure 16.15 to visualize it), we define the partial derivative of g(x,y) along x as

$$g_x'(x, y) = \frac{\partial g}{\partial x} = \lim_{h \to 0} \frac{g(x+h, y) - g(x, y)}{h}$$

And we define the gradient of g in a point $P_0=(x_0,y_0)$ as a vector with one column and two rows, whose components are the partial derivates of function g with respect to x and y, computed at point P_0

$$\nabla g(P_0) = \begin{bmatrix} \frac{\partial g}{\partial x}(P_0) \\ \frac{\partial g}{\partial y}(P_0) \end{bmatrix}$$

The geometrical interpretation of the gradient of a function is that it's a vector pointing in the direction of fastest growth of the function. That's why gradient descent actually uses the *negative gradient*, $-\nabla g$, which is simply the opposite of the gradient.

16.3.2 Geometrical interpretation

Listing 16.4 gives a summarized description of the gradient descent algorithm.

Listing 16.4 Method gradientDescent

Method gradientDescent takes a function f, a starting point P0, a learning rate alpha, and the maximum number of steps to perform, maxSteps. It returns a point in the domain—ideally the point where f has the smallest value (either locally or globally).

```
function gradientDescent(f, P0, alpha, maxSteps)
  for _ in {1..maxSteps} do
    for i in {1.. |P0|} do
```

Starts the iteration, running the main cycle at most maxSteps times

Cycles through the coordinates of point P0

Creates a new point P, where each coordinate of P is assigned the corresponding coordinate of P0, with a small delta computed from f's gradient: in particular we need to compute the partial derivative of f with respect to its i-th coordinate, and then the value this derivative has at point P0. The value of the gradient is multiplied by a learning rate alpha.

If all the derivatives were 0, we are either in a plateau region, or in a minimum point, and so gradient descent can't improve any further. In reality, we should check that the norm of the difference is not smaller than some precision, both because computer arithmetic has finite precision, and because when the gradient is very small, the possible improvement can be negligible, and not worth the computational resources.

```
      P[i] ← P0[i] - alpha * derivative(f, P0, i)
    if P == P0 then
      break
    P0 ← P
  return P0
```

At the end of each step, updates the current point

It's important to understand that we don't have the full view of the cost function when we run gradient descent, and we don't "move" over the surface; rather, at each step we only compute how much we should change the input variables, depending on the slope of the surface at that point. See figure 16.14 to get an idea of the steps, and figure 16.15 to get an idea of how it looks like with a 2-D function's domain.

In our marble-race analogy, it's as if the track is swathed in a dense fog, and we can only see a few feet away: enough to see where to aim for a cautious next step, because if we push the marble too hard, we risk sending it off of the track, or in the wrong direction.

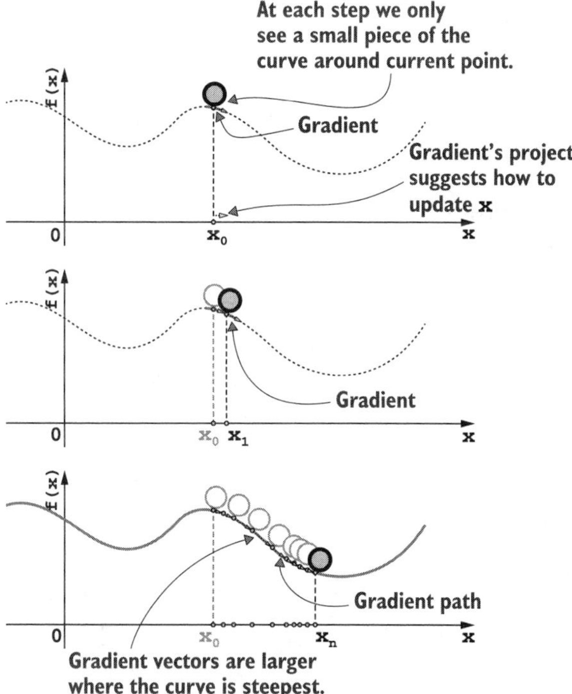
At each step we only see a small piece of the curve around current point.
Gradient
Gradient's projection suggests how to update x
f(x)
0
x0
x
Gradient
x1
Gradient path
xn
Gradient vectors are larger where the curve is steepest.

Figure 16.14 A few steps of gradient descent: notice the path made by concatenating the gradient vectors after each update; larger vectors mean the gradient was larger (and the curve slope steeper), so in turn Δx the step update for our variable will also be larger.

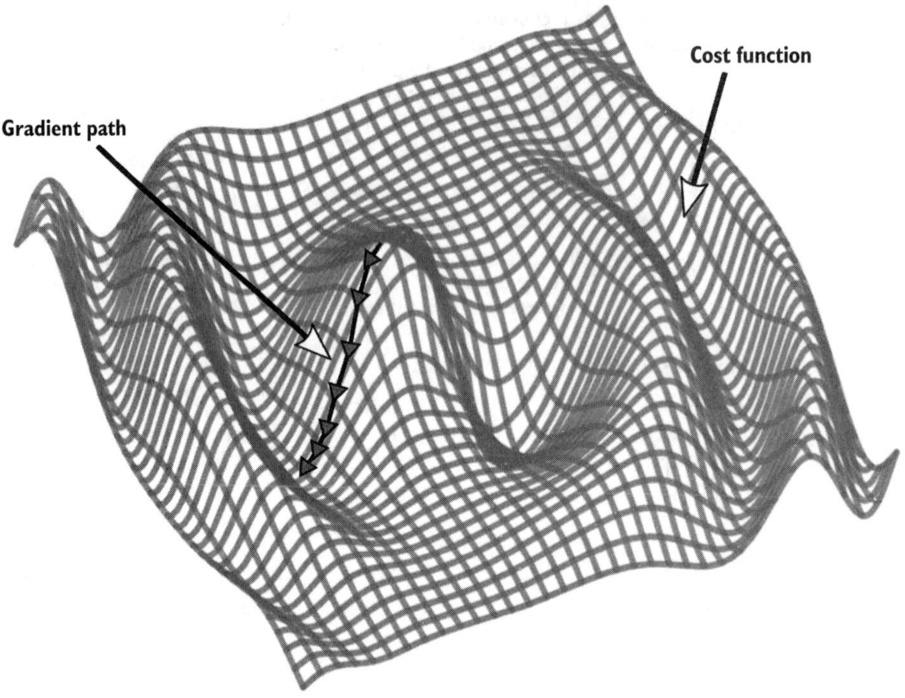
Cost function
Gradient path

Figure 16.15 Gradient descent applied to a function of two variables. The cost function defines a surface.

The method itself is actually surprisingly short and simple, isn't it? It's an iterative optimization algorithm, so we have a loop to perform, and we pass an argument with the maximum number of steps allowed, just to be sure it won't loop forever (we'll see that there are situations where this is possible).

We repeat the same update step until we get to a minimum of the function, or at most a certain number of times. The step itself is also basic: we compute the gradient of the input function coordinate by coordinate, by computing the first-order partial derivative of `f` along each of the directions of `f`'s domain (the problem space).

As mentioned, we can stop when we reach a minimum. One of the most important results in calculus is Fermat's theorem[13] that proves a point in the domain of a differentiable function is a minimum or a maximum if and only if the derivative of that function is zero at that point; therefore, we can just check that all the partial derivatives are zero (or, more realistically, that their value is below some precision).

By using the gradient of a function `f` to decide how much (and in what direction) we should move, we naturally take big steps when `f` changes fast, and small steps when `f` changes slowly. Transferred to our marble-race example, the marble would travel

[13]Not the most famous one! Although one might argue that this particular theorem is even more important.

fast in a steep, straight section, while we would need to be careful when a turn is near to avoid going off-track.

As for the starting point P_0, you might wonder how we choose it. There are different ways, but unless you have domain knowledge telling you otherwise, it's best to choose it randomly and possibly run the optimization several times, starting each time from a new, randomly chosen point and keeping track of the best overall result.

Can you see it? We are back to random sampling, but applying a sophisticated local optimization heuristic after each sample is taken.

16.3.3 When is gradient descent appliable?

To be able to apply gradient descent, we need the cost function to be differentiable, at least in the neighborhood of the points where we compute the gradient.

Moreover, it helps if we already know the exact formula for the function we would like to optimize, so that we can also express the partial derivatives with mathematical formulas and compute gradients exactly. If we don't have the definition for the function to optimize, however, we can always resort to the formal definition of derivatives as mathematical limits, and compute the gradient numerically by explicitly evaluating the ratio between Δf and Δx_i for increasingly small increments of each of the coordinates of the problem space.

One question you might want to ask this: If we do have the definition of `f`, and it is differentiable, why do we have to run an iterative optimization? Can't we just find its exact minimum using calculus?

Well, that's of course possible, in theory; it is also doable, at least for low-dimensional spaces and for some kinds of functions.

However, finding exact solutions becomes hard to automate, and even to compute, in high-dimensional spaces. The number of equations needed to analytically find the global minimum grows exponentially with the problem's size. Moreover, these functions can have hundreds, thousands, or even an infinite number of local minima (think, for example, about `sin(x+y)` or even `x*sin(y))`, and to automate the search of a global optimum, we'd need to have all those points checked.

In general, gradient descent works well when we have a chance to design a cost function that has either a global minimum or, at most, a few local minima (better if they are of approximately the same cost). As we'll see in section 16.4, that's why it works perfectly with the kind of cost functions we design for supervised learning.

16.3.4 Problems with gradient descent

One important thing to note in listing 16.4 is that we provide a learning rate `alpha`. This is a hyper-parameter of the algorithm, regulating how big the steps are that we take. As in the marble analogy, when we don't have a clear view of the track, taking large steps can speed us up, but it can also send the marble off-course; similarly, in gradient descent, large steps can miss minima (figure 16.16 (A)) or even worse, in some situations they can cause loops or even get far away from the best solution, in situations like the one shown in figure 16.16 (B).

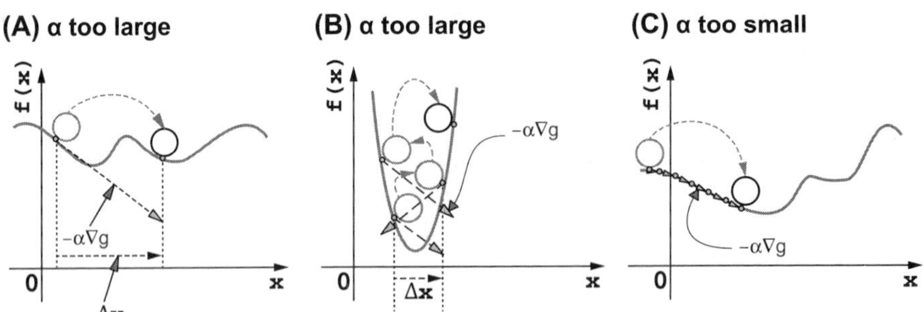
(A) α too large
(B) α too large
(C) α too small
f(x)
-α∇g
Δx
0
x

Figure 16.16 Gradient descent: Δf is the change in the cost function caused by a variation Δx in its parameter.

Vice versa, when alpha is too small (figure 16.16 (C)), convergence can be far too slow and the optimization algorithm will never get to a minimum within a reasonable time (or within the maximum number of iterations allowed).

Which values of alpha are too big or too small also depends on the context, and in particular on the specific function we are trying to optimize.

If we didn't have the chance to pass this learning parameter, then for cost functions such as the one in figure 16.16 (B), where the slope of the curve is steep, the optimization would not converge to the minimum (but rather diverge), and at the same time, for examples like 16.14 (C), convergence would be too slow, or the algorithm could get stuck in local minima.

By using a learning rate, we can tune[14] this `alpha` hyper-parameter and adapt the optimization algorithm to the function we need to optimize.

An even better solution, however, is to use a variable `alpha`; for example, a value that decreases as the steps progress. Initially, it's large enough to let the optimization quickly explore a wide area and possibly get out of local minima, and then it gets smaller and smaller, so that in the end, fine-tuning can be done and oscillation around stationary points (minima) is avoided.

Another great option is to introduce the concept of momentum. Instead of basing the next step on just the last gradient, gradient descent with momentum smooths the update by computing the delta as a linear combination of the last few gradients (with older gradients having a lower weight on the final result than newer ones).

As the term suggests, having a momentum (the way it happens in kinematics) means that if the algorithm speed was high, and so it was updating a coordinate with large steps, then when the slope of the curve changes, the speed will smooth out, but not abruptly.

[14]Tuning an algorithm's hyper-parameters, as we'll see, is one of the challenges of using heuristics. There is no single value for these parameters that works with all problems and instances, and the tuning is usually hard to automate. It's an area where the experience of the algorithmist really makes the difference.

The easiest formula to add momentum into our update rule for points can look like this

```
Pt+1 ← β*Pt - α*(1-β)*∇g(Pt)
```

where P_t is a point in the problem space, specifically the point reached by the algorithm at time `t`. The higher is beta, the smoother (and slower) the update will be:

```
P2 ← β*P1 - α*(1-β)*∇g(P1) = β²*P0 - α*β*(1-β)*∇g(P0) - α*(1-β)*∇g(β*P1 -
➥ α*(1-β)*∇g(P1))
```

So, after 2 steps, if `β=0.99`, then `98%` of the value of P_2 is given by P_0; conversely, if `β=0.1`, P_0 directly influences P_2 only for 1%.

16.4 Applications of gradient descent

As mentioned earlier, gradient descent is an optimization technique that, given a cost function, helps find a solution (a point in the problem space) that has an optimal (or nearly optimal) cost.

As such, it is only a piece of the process of solving a problem, and at the same time, it can be applied to several different problems and techniques.

The overall algorithm depends first, as we have seen, on the cost function used, but also on the goal of the optimization.

We have already discussed optimizing a cost function to find the cheapest solution to a well-defined problem, and this is a category of algorithms that greatly benefits from the application of gradient descent, whenever we can describe a differentiable cost function.

Lately, though, a different category of algorithms using gradient descent has gained popularity: learning algorithms.

> **NOTE** I've always found the name machine learning a bit deceptive, because it somehow suggests this branch involves machines that can learn in the same way humans do, which unfortunately is not the case, although there are some similarities.

When we apply gradient descent to solving a problem such as traveling salesman or graph embedding, we have a static (usually huge) domain, and our goal is to find a point in that domain. In machine learning, instead, we have a dataset, and we want to make sense of it by "learning" a model that describes the dataset and (more importantly) generalizes to inputs that were not in the dataset.

Take, for instance, supervised learning (whose most prominent examples are shown in figure 16.17); this is a field where gradient descent is widely applied!

The goal of supervised learning is to develop a mathematical model[15] that can succinctly describe the dataset, and is able to predict the output for new, never-seen

---

[15]Nothing more than a function from a domain to a range, really. No matter how complex this function can be, it's still a deterministic mapping between an input (possibly multidimensional) and an output.

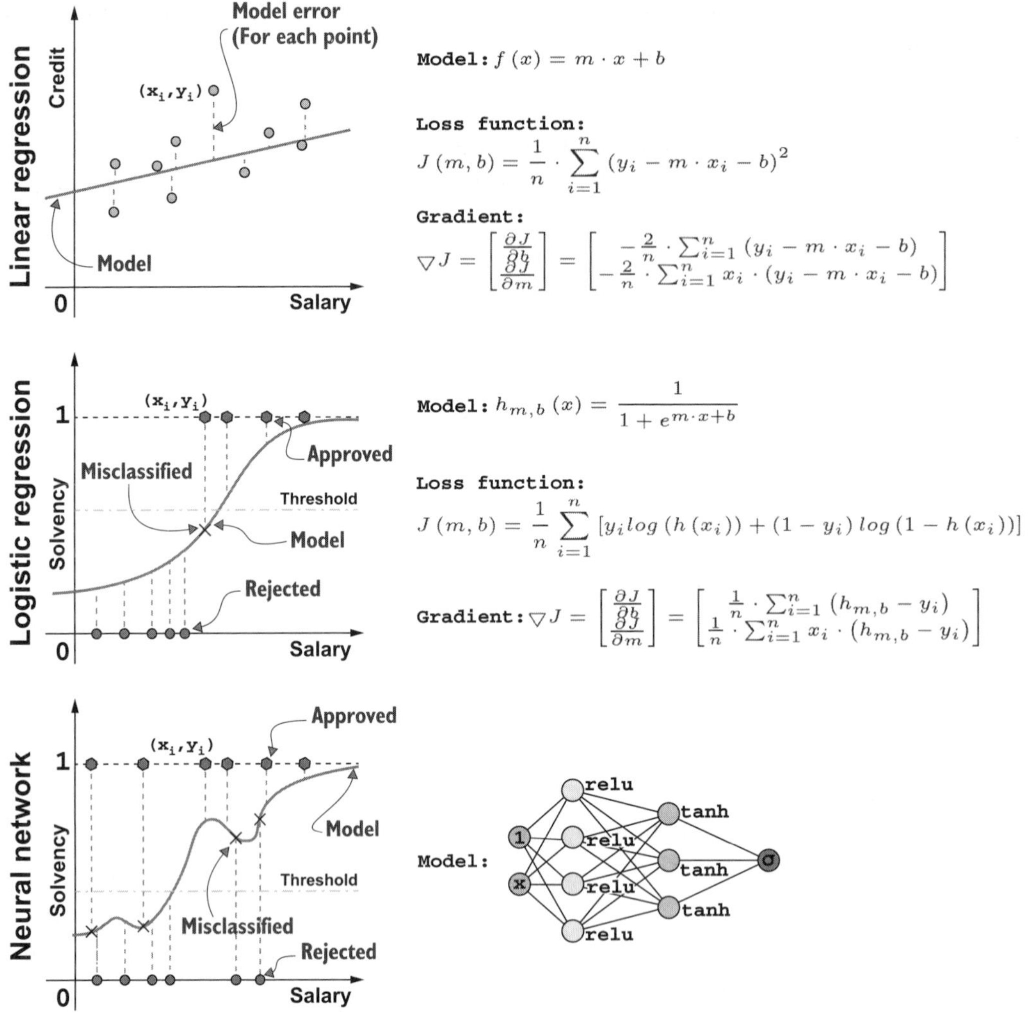
Linear regression
Model error
(For each point)
Credit
(x_i, y_i)
Model
0
Salary
Model: $f(x) = m \cdot x + b$
Loss function:
$J(m,b) = \frac{1}{n} \cdot \sum_{i=1}^{n} (y_i - m \cdot x_i - b)^2$
Gradient:
$\nabla J = \begin{bmatrix} \frac{\partial J}{\partial b} \\ \frac{\partial J}{\partial m} \end{bmatrix} = \begin{bmatrix} -\frac{2}{n} \cdot \sum_{i=1}^{n} (y_i - m \cdot x_i - b) \\ -\frac{2}{n} \cdot \sum_{i=1}^{n} x_i \cdot (y_i - m \cdot x_i - b) \end{bmatrix}$
Logistic regression
1
(x_i, y_i)
Approved
Misclassified
Threshold
Solvency
Model
Rejected
0
Salary
Model: $h_{m,b}(x) = \frac{1}{1 + e^{m \cdot x + b}}$
Loss function:
$J(m,b) = \frac{1}{n} \sum_{i=1}^{n} [y_i log(h(x_i)) + (1 - y_i) log(1 - h(x_i))]$
Gradient: $\nabla J = \begin{bmatrix} \frac{\partial J}{\partial b} \\ \frac{\partial J}{\partial m} \end{bmatrix} = \begin{bmatrix} \frac{1}{n} \cdot \sum_{i=1}^{n} (h_{m,b} - y_i) \\ \frac{1}{n} \cdot \sum_{i=1}^{n} x_i \cdot (h_{m,b} - y_i) \end{bmatrix}$
Neural network
Approved
1
(x_i, y_i)
Model
Solvency
Threshold
Misclassified
Rejected
0
Salary
Model:
1
x
relu
relu
relu
relu
tanh
tanh
tanh
σ

Figure 16.17 A few approaches used in supervised machine learning. All of them use gradient descent for learning. Note that the models are arbitrarily chosen, and also for the loss functions there are other possible choices. Gradients and loss functions for neural networks are omitted for the sake of brevity. While only supervised learning is shown here, there are also clustering algorithms that leverage gradient descent.

inputs, be they a real value (linear regression), a category (logistic regression), or a label (clustering).

For all these types of learning, there is one extra step that we haven't had in the optimization problems we've seen so far in this chapter when we were simply exploring a problem's space. Now we also have to choose which model we want to use, which is actually the first thing we need to do.

To better explain this, we'll go into some details of linear regression.

16.4.1 An example: Linear regression

Speaking of deceptive names, we couldn't avoid mentioning linear regression. The story of the origin of the name of this learning technique is also fascinating, and it's worth Googling it. Hopefully, we stimulated your curiosity about it.

But what is really important for us is that linear regression ultimately is about finding a model that describes the relation between one or more inputs (aka *independent variables*) and a real number outputted by the model (the *dependent variable*).

We've mentioned this "model" a few times now, and you can also see it in figure 16.17, so you might be asking what it is.

The model is a category of mathematical functions that we choose to approximate the true relation between dependent and independent variables in our dataset.

For instance, we might have a dataset associating some characteristics of cars (the year they were built, their engine, how many miles they've traveled, and so on) to their market price, and we would like to learn the relation between the former and the latter so that we can input the description (in terms of the same independent variables we had in the dataset) of a car we spotted at the dealer's, and see if the price they are asking is fair (and hopefully avoid being tricked into paying too much for a wreck).

We need to choose the model we think could best fit the data.[16] To keep it simple, let's restrict to functions with a single parameter (it could be the engine power). As shown in figure 16.18, we can choose a constant function (`y = m`, a line parallel to the x axis), a generic line of the form `y = mx + b`, a quadratic curve ($m_1*x^2 + m_2 * x + b$), or even more complicated models.

The simpler the model, in general, the fewest data points are needed to "learn it," because after we choose the complexity of the model, we have a category of functions, and we still have to learn the parameters that tell us which specific function in that category is the best for our dataset.

For example, if we choose a generic line, then we still have to decide the values for the parameters `m` and `b`: it could be `y = x + 1` or `y = -0.5*x +42`.

The way we choose those is through *training*, which is nothing other than applying gradient descent.

In linear regression, in fact, we define a cost function (usually referred to as a *loss function* in machine learning) that measures the distance between the value predicted by the model for the dependent variable associated to each point in the dataset,[17] and the actual value from the data.

This function is generally the sum of least square errors, or some variant of it. As shown in figure 16.17 and 16.19, we minimize the squared distance, along the `y` axis, between each point and the model line, and this gives us a convex, bowl-shaped function with a global minimum—as we have seen, that's pure gold for gradient descent!

---

[16]Usually we try different models and automate the choice based on how well they perform, but this is far beyond the scope of this discussion.

[17]Actually, a subset of the dataset called a training set. This is not the place to go into the details of how and why we choose it; just remember it's quite important to leave some dataset points out for later testing to assess the quality of the model.

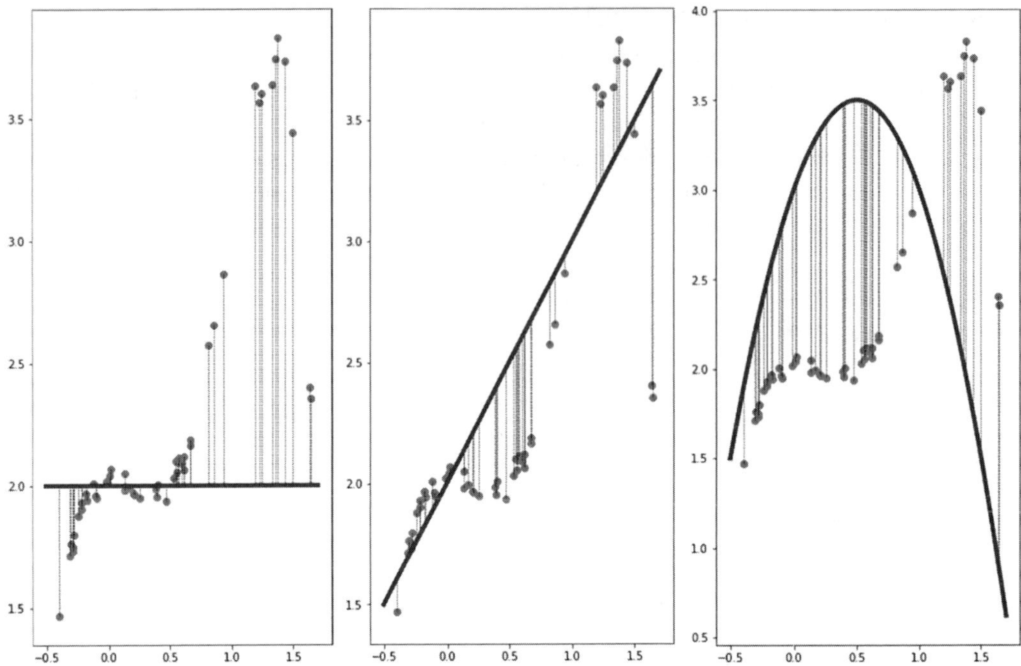
3.5
3.0
2.5
2.0
1.5
−0.5
0.0
0.5
1.0
1.5
4.0
1.0
0.5

Figure 16.18 Linear regression on a dataset (points shown as dots) using increasingly complex models: a constant, a line, and a quadratic curve. You can see that a higher-order model doesn't necessarily fit the data better.

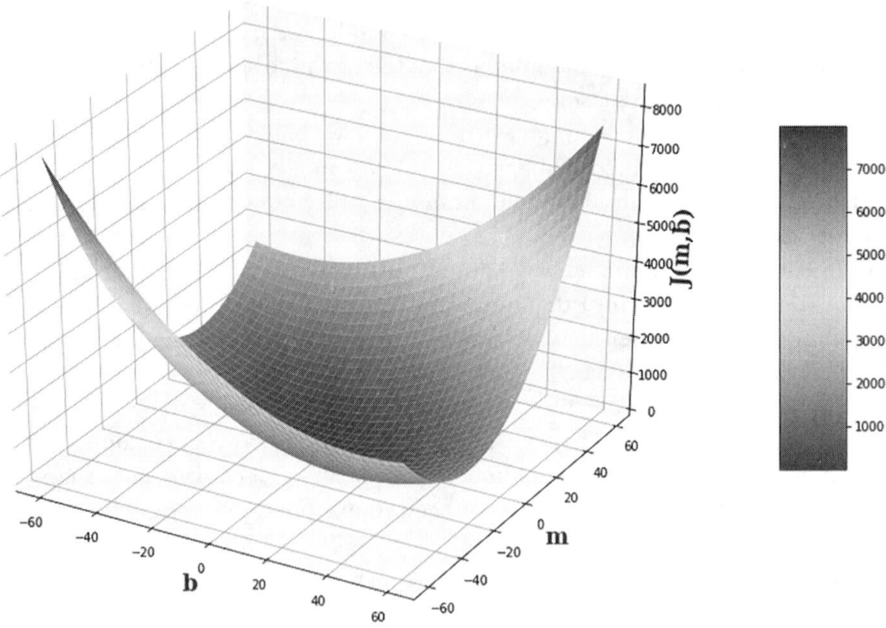
J(m,b)
8000
7000
6000
5000
4000
3000
2000
1000
0
b
−60
−40
−20
0
20
40
60
m

Figure 16.19 The cost function of the example in figure 16.18 (B). Using the sum of squared errors, the cost is a function of m and b.

One important fact to highlight in both figures 16.17 and 16.19 is that the loss function depends on parameters `m` and `b`,[18] not on the points of the dataset; therefore, when we compute its partial derivates, they are computed with respect to the model parameters, which are then updated by gradient descent.

There is so much more to say about linear regression and supervised learning that it would take another full book!

And, in fact, there are so many books you can check, if you'd like to delve into machine learning. Here there are a few suggestions that I've personally found extremely useful:

- *Grokking Machine Learning*, a nice starting point for beginners, written by Luis Serrano (Manning Publications, 2019). You couldn't ask for a better guide.
- *Grokking Deep Learning*, by DeepMind's Andrew W. Trask (Manning Publications, 2019), an excellent introduction, ideal for approaching the world of deep learning.
- *Deep Learning with Python*, written by François Chollet, the author of the Keras library (Manning Publications, 2017); you'll learn how to use it to build image and text classification models and generators.
- *Deep Learning with JavaScript*, by Shanquing Cai, et al. (Manning Publications, 2020), in case you'd like to build models for the web that run in the browser, using Tensorflow.js and written by its main authors.

There are, of course, many more great books out there. It's impossible to list them all here, but these are a good starting point.

16.5 Gradient descent for graph embedding

So, now that we have discussed at length how gradient descent works and its (many) strengths and flaws, you should be able to figure out how to apply it to our case study, a heuristic to find a straight-line drawing for graphs, with the minimum number of intersections between edges.

And your answer should be . . . that gradient descent can't really help. If we look at figures 16.7–16.12, it's clear that the cost function for "minimum number of intersections" is step-shaped, with large plateau regions (where the gradient is null) and sudden drops.

You might be wondering, then, why we've introduced gradient descent. Some readers could guess the next step, but if you haven't take a minute to mentally go over what we've learned in the last couple of chapters, and then let's delve into our next challenge.

Before revealing it, let me also highlight that the discussion in sections 16.3 and 16.4 allowed us to develop a better intuition about cost functions and provided a semiformal characterization: even if the reward was just that, we wouldn't have wasted our time, because the framework we have established will help us describe and understand the algorithms presented here and in the next two chapters.

---

[18] When we use a linear model: in general, we denote with `W` or Θ the vector of parameters for the model; remember, these parameters are actually the objective of the learning algorithm.

But there is more. If you went through chapter 15, in section 15.3 we reasoned about what it means for an embedding to be good, or just better than another. Edge intersections are a part of this, even an important one, but there are other considerations, for instance, that adjacent vertices should be close to each other. When there is no edge between a pair of vertices, they can and should be drawn far away from each other.

Drawing a graph in an aesthetically-pleasing way can be as or more important than just reducing the number of edges crossing.

It can make the graph look cleaner and more easily understandable, and it can help you use available space better (especially on dynamic websites) or make more meaningful charts.

And last but not least, an aesthetically pleasing appearance can be expressed with a better cost function, a smoother one for which we can use optimization algorithms like gradient descent.

16.5.1 A different criterion

When using straight-line drawings, we can imagine vertices as ions, electrically charged particles. When there is an edge between two vertices, the particles attract each other (as if they had opposite charges), while a pair of vertices not connected by edges repel each other.

Then we can try to find an equilibrium point for the system, a disposition of the particles such that all the forces balance each other and the system can maintain a stable condition. Sometimes, instead of explicitly computing[19] the point of equilibrium, we can try to approximate it by simulating the evolution of the system using a heuristic.

It turns out that there is a whole class of graph embedding algorithms that adopt this principle: the so-called *force-directed graph drawing* algorithms.

The goal of these algorithms is to lay down a graph's vertices in the 2-D space so that adjacent vertices are more or less at the same distance, and as such, all edges are of the same length in the plane, and, of course, there are as few edge intersections as possible. This is done by computing forces among the adjacent vertices (attractive forces), and among all non-adjacent vertices (repulsive), based on their relative positions, and then updating the system (that is, those positions) based on the forces computed and some parameters, trying to minimize the energy of the whole system.

To further refine our initial analogy, we can use springs (or gravity) as the physics counterpart of edges, and a fainter electrical repulsion[20] among all pair of vertices. Note that all these forces depend on the distance between the vertices—you can replace them with different formulas, as long as you keep this characteristic. Figure 16.20 gives you an idea of how such systems can work.

---

[19] The mathematical solution involves finding the zeroes of the differential equations describing a system.

[20] In reality, electrical forces between particles are orders of magnitude stronger than gravity, of course. But the purpose of the analogy is not to be exact, just to be lifelike and intuitive, and to reuse a well-studied framework.

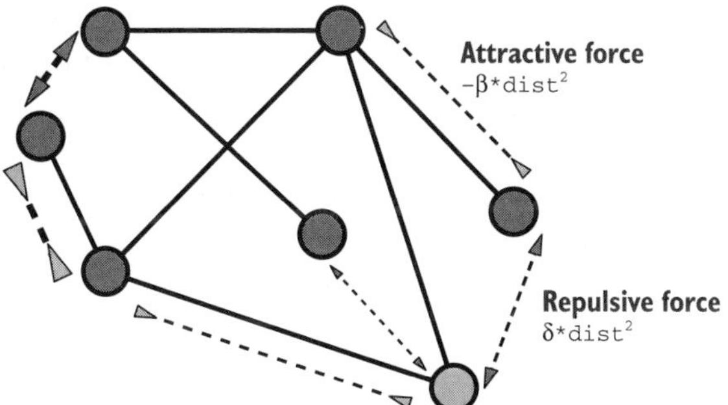
Attractive force
-β*dist²
Repulsive force
δ*dist²

Figure 16.20 A force-directed drawing algorithm using a physics simulation, with attractive and repulsive forces acting on vertices to provide an aesthetically pleasing embedding. Notice how forces are larger (thicker lines) when vertices are closer. For the sake of clarity, we don't show all the forces acting on all pairs of vertices, just a few examples.

The next thing we need is to formalize these criteria into a formula for the cost function. That will describe the landscape of the problem, which we can then try to explore by using gradient descent, or one of the other categories of algorithms we'll discuss later in the book:

$$J(V) = \delta \cdot \sum_{v \in V} \sum_{u \in V/\{v\}} \|u-v\|_2^2 - \beta \cdot \sum_{v \in V} \sum_{u \in \mathrm{adj}(v)} \|u-v\|_2^2$$

where the term inside the summations is the squared 2-norm, that when computed on the (vector) difference of the two points, gives us the square of the distance between the two points.

$$\|u-v\|_2^2 = (u_x - v_x)^2 + (u_y - v_y)^2$$

If you are wondering why we use the squared distance, it's not just because it's cheaper to compute.[21] The main reason is that the derivative of a square root is a pain. And, of course, the shape of the function's surface would also be different.

Now, that's a big improvement with respect to a step function. This function is at least differentiable, and that's pretty good. Partial derivatives with respect to x and y coordinates of a generic vertex w can be precisely computed:

$$\frac{\partial}{\partial w_x} J(V) = -4 \cdot \delta \cdot \sum_{u \in V/\{w\}} (u_x - w_x) + 4 \cdot \beta \cdot \sum_{u \in \mathrm{adj}(w)} (u_x - w_x)$$

$$\frac{\partial}{\partial w_y} J(V) = -4 \cdot \delta \cdot \sum_{u \in V/\{w\}} (u_y - w_y) + 4 \cdot \beta \cdot \sum_{u \in \mathrm{adj}(w)} (u_y - w_y)$$

Scalars β and δ are so-called hyper-parameters of the algorithm. They balance the importance of the attractive and repulsive force, and we need to adjust their values to get the result we want; this can be done manually or automatically.

[21] Square roots are notoriously expensive operations to perform.

This isn't always easy, of course. For instance, a large value for the attractive force parameter will work well for sparse graphs, keeping vertices from drifting apart, but for a dense graph, if β>δ, then all the vertices will end up converging to the center of the graph.

A possible alternative is deciding, based on the vertices/edges in the graph and on the size of the canvas where we embed the graph, the ideal length for an edge (or an ideal range for such length). This way, optimization will move away from solutions where all the vertices are clustered too closely:

$$\overline{J}(V) = \delta \cdot \sum_{v \in V} \sum_{u \in V/\{v\}} \|u-v\|_2^2 - \delta \cdot \sum_{v \in V} \sum_{u \in \mathrm{adj}(v)} [\|u-v\|_2 - (\text{ideal edge length})]^2$$

Neither of these cost functions aims to directly reduce the number of intersections, but as you can imagine, having shorter edges and keeping adjacent vertices close to each other indirectly help drive that number down. And neither function is ideal, because they are not bowl-shaped, so they will have several local minima. While we can't easily correct this shortcoming, we still have a workaround. We can use a random-restart algorithm, randomly selecting an initial position for the vertices, and surf the cost function downhill with gradient descent.

16.5.2 Implementation

Perseverance is the key, so if we repeat a gradient descent step a few times (or maybe a lot of times—it really depends on the context!), starting from different positions and perhaps even with different learning rates, the final result might not be that bad.

In the next chapter, we'll see a more sophisticated technique to make our optimization more flexible and raise our chances of landing a good result.

For now, let's implement the single-iteration gradient descent solution, starting with listing 16.5.

Listing 16.5 Method `forceDirectedEmbedding`

For each vertex, updates its `x` and `y` coordinates by using gradient descent rules. We must use a new variable to hold these new values, because for gradient descent to work, we need to compute all the gradients using the coordinates at current iteration before the update.

Method `forceDirectedEmbedding` takes a graph, a learning rate `alpha`, and the maximum number of steps to perform, `maxSteps`. It returns a point in the domain: an assignment for the coordinates of each vertex.

Cycles through each vertex, assigning its position randomly

Starts the iteration, running the main cycle at most `maxSteps` times

Cycles, again, through all vertices in the graph

```
function forceDirectedEmbedding(graph, alpha, maxSteps)
  for v in graph.vertices do
    (x[v], y[v]) ← randomVertexPosition()
  for _ in {1..maxSteps} do
    for v in graph.vertices do
      x1[v] ← x[v] - alpha * derivative(graph, v, x)
      y1[v] ← y[v] - alpha * derivative(graph, v, y)
```

```
    if x == x1 and y == y1 then
      break
    (x,y) ← (x1, y1)
  return (x,y)
```

This way we can check if we've reached a minimum point, where the gradient is zero and no update is performed (likely, here we want to pass some tolerance `epsilon`, and stop when the sum of the differences between the old and new positions is smaller than `epsilon`).

At the end of each iteration, updates the current coordinates

The code in listing 16.5 is a duplicate of the body of the general-purpose gradient descent method we previously saw in listing 16.4. While it's still possible to use that method, in this case we have a more specific domain that can allow us some optimization, and overall, I believe, to express more clearly how this algorithm works internally.

For instance, you can see that we never use the cost function, but we only need to be able to compute its partial derivatives. (Now it should make more sense why, as we had mentioned, we prefer to use the squared distance in the cost function to avoid square roots.)

Speaking of the gradient, the partial derivates can easily be computed using the formula we have provided (or a similar one, if you use a different cost function). It only requires running two `for` loops over the vertices, so explicit code is not shown here.

It's easy to use this method for a random-restart algorithm: just decide how many attempts you'd like to perform, and run a loop calling method `forceDirectedEmbedding`.

The caveat is that in this case, we do need an explicit definition of the cost function, because (as shown in listing 16.6) after each call to `forceDirectedEmbedding`, we will have to check the cost of the solution returned and compare it to the best result so far.

Listing 16.6 Method `forceDirectedEmbeddingWithRestart`

```
function forceDirectedEmbeddingWithRestart(graph, alpha, runs, maxSteps)
  bestCost ← inf
  for _ in {1..runs} do
    (x,y) ← forceDirectedEmbedding(graph, alpha, maxSteps)
    if cost(graph, x, y) < bestCost then
      (bestX, bestY, bestCost) ← (x, y, cost(graph, x, y))
  return (bestX,bestY)
```

This concludes our discussion of gradient descent. In the next chapters, we will explore alternative algorithms for optimization of cost-based solutions.

Summary

- Many problems, including many in machine learning, are based on defining a proper cost function that measures how good a solution is, and then running an optimization algorithm to try to find the solution with minimal cost.
- Gradient descent is based on the geometric interpretation of cost functions. For differentiable functions, we assume that each solution to the problem can be interpreted as a point in an n-dimensional space, and a single step of gradient descent is performed by computing the gradient of the cost function at the current point.
- These points, where the cost function takes a locally-optimal value, are the nemesis of optimization algorithms in general, and gradient descent in particular. The algorithm would get stuck in local minima and we would never find the globally-optimal solution.
- The crossing number doesn't play well as a cost function, because it makes a step function with plenty of local minima plateaus.
- As an alternative, we can map our problem into a so-called force-directed graph drawing simulation, which focuses on drawing a graph nicely, and optimizes the crossing number only indirectly.

17 Simulated annealing: Optimization beyond local minima

This chapter covers

- Introducing simulated annealing
- Using simulated annealing to improve delivery schedules
- Presenting a primer on the traveling salesman problem
- Using simulated annealing for minimum crossing embeddings
- Using an algorithm based on simulated annealing to draw graphs nicely

If you have read chapters 15 and 16, you should by now be familiar with graph embeddings and optimization problems. In the previous chapter, in particular, we explained how to reformulate graph embedding as an optimization problem, and we introduced gradient descent, an optimization technique that can be used to find (near-)optimal solutions to this category of problems. In particular, we discussed two solutions to the problem, seen as crossing-number optimization and as a force-directed graph drawing; gradient descent is particularly suitable for the latter, while particularly bad for the former.

One issue we have seen with gradient descent is that it tends to get stuck in local minima, which is pretty much the last thing we would want, considering that we often have to deal with cost functions having lots of local peaks.

We have already discussed one workaround for this issue, running gradient descent several times using random-restart to choose a different starting point each time.

Still, even with this technique, each iteration of gradient descent is pretty much doomed (in the best-case scenario) to end in the closest local minimum along the steepest path from the starting point. It would be great, instead, if even a single run could have some non-null[1] probability to move over a local minimum and find a better solution.

In this chapter, we'll discuss an algorithm that does exactly that, and more. It also overcomes some of the constraints that limit the applicability of gradient descent. After reading this chapter, you will have learned about *simulated annealing*, a powerful optimization technique, how to apply it to some of the hardest problems on graphs, and how to weigh pros and cons of choosing it over other optimization techniques.

Simulated annealing is quite powerful as is: among the algorithms we have described, it's the only one that's able to balance narrow and broad search, exploring a large portion of the problem space and managing to make local progresses.

Moreover, it's been around since the 1970s, and that explains why it's one of the favorite heuristics used in optimization. During the last 20–30 years, new optimization techniques have been developed, such as *genetic algorithms* (which we'll discuss in the next chapter), and *artificial immune systems (AIS)*, which use different biology-inspired approaches to speed up convergence, but the adoption ratio for simulated annealing remains high, and recently it has also been revived with *quantum annealing*.

Last but not least, you'll improve your ability to plan deliveries over several destinations by learning about the *traveling salesman problem* (*TSP* for short) and how to find near-optimal solutions in a reasonable time. Continuing our discussion on optimizing logistics for our imaginary e-commerce company, we will move from planning a single trip for each delivery to optimizing the route of a delivery truck across several cities, so that it can be loaded once at the company's warehouse and make several deliveries without going back.

[1] Technically, even gradient descent can move past a local minimum, depending on the shape of the function around it and on the learning rate; see figure 16.16.

17.1 Simulated annealing

In chapter 16 we introduced local optimization techniques as a way to improve over mere random sampling algorithms. We discussed gradient descent at length and alluded to a randomized optimization technique. If you remember our analogy to marble races, gradient descent would always move a marble (our solution) along the steepest path on the track (the landscape produced by the cost function), but stop in valleys. Figure 17.1 contrasts the gradient descent approach with the random search local optimization called *hill descent*.[2] In this case, the algorithm picks a direction randomly and checks if by making a short (possibly random) step in that direction we get to an improvement. If so, it moves to the new solution; otherwise, no change is made, and another attempt is performed at the next iteration. As we also saw in chapter 16, for gradient descent it is, in theory, possible to step over local minima, if the learning rate is large enough; however, this is also unlikely to happen.

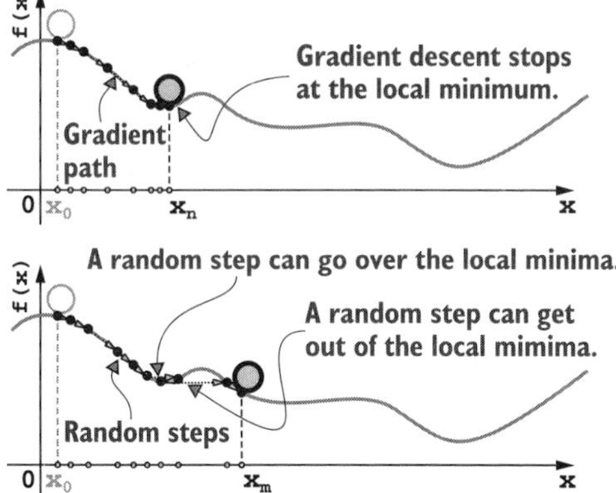
f(x)
Gradient descent stops
at the local minimum.
Gradient
path
0
x0
xn
x
A random step can go over the local minima.
f(x)
A random step can get
out of the local mimima.
Random steps
0
x0
xm
x

Figure 17.1 Gradient descent versus local random optimization. While for gradient descent, steps are proportional to the curve's steepness, the random steps are . . . just random (within a reasonable radius). That's why it's easier for the random algorithm to step over a local minimum, or even get out of it (technically, both are possible for gradient descent as well, as we saw in chapter 16, depending on the learning rate and shape of the cost function).

Be warned, though, that in figure 17.1 we are not showing all the failed attempts where local random optimization tried the wrong direction: overall, getting to the same point will need more steps than gradient descent, because instead of going in the direction of maximum change, we are wandering around randomly. This is more apparent looking at a 2-D domain/3-D surface, like the one shown in figure 17.2.

As it is, this approach shares some of the same issues we discussed in chapter 16 about gradient descent. It is likely to get stuck in local minima and plateaus. And, even worse, it's taking a slower way to get there.

On the plus side, it also has some advantages. First and foremost, we can release the constraint about the cost function being differentiable, and can actually even ignore the definition of the function, as long as we have a way to compute it.[3] This is

---

[2] The original name would be *hill climbing*, when the goal of the optimization is maximization; since we aim to reduce cost, though, that would be confusing.

[3] Not having a static formula can be helpful with dynamic cost functions like externally computed metrics or simulations (for instance, in reinforcement learning, the cost is determined by running a simulation).

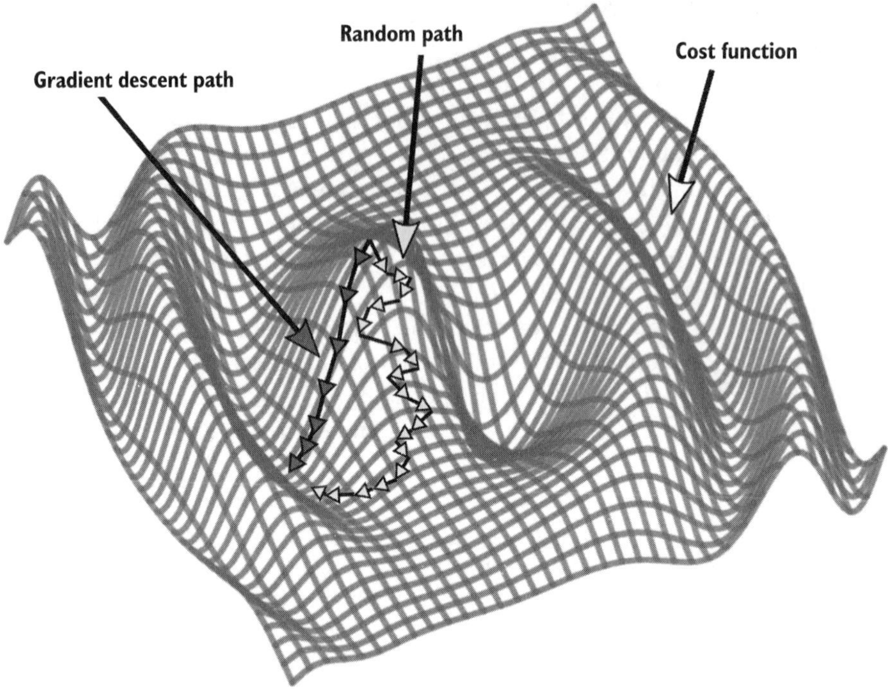
Random path
Cost function
Gradient descent path

Figure 17.2 Gradient descent versus local random optimization on a cost function of two parameters. Can you guess which one is going to take more steps?

especially useful with functions such as the edge crossing of an embedding, a step function which is not differentiable in the points where its value abruptly changes and has a derivative identically equal to zero elsewhere.

The obvious downside, as shown in figure 17.2, is that the random optimization is going to require many more steps than gradient descent, because it will take long detours. Even worse, since it will not take the direction where the function decreases faster, it will likely end up in a different spot than gradient descent. It's impossible to predict where, and whether it will find a better or worse final value. To cope with this, the only strategy is perseverance: increasing the number of runs and storing the best result across them is likely to bring to a satisfying result (the more runs, the better the expected solution).

Finally, there are issues faced in gradient descent that not even the randomized method can shake off.

For instance, while it's possible that the random optimization algorithm gets out of a local minimum, it's not guaranteed. Since both algorithms are greedy,[4] they only move from the current position when they find a domain point to which a lower cost

[4] Greedy algorithms make locally-optimal choices (for instance, they only go to positions with a lower cost). Unfortunately, this doesn't always translate into getting to optimal results.

corresponds; it's possible that the range of the random steps is not wide enough to get it out of a pit. You can see this in figure 17.1, where the "leap" the algorithm has to make to get itself out of a local minimum is pretty large compared to the other updates. If such a large delta is even allowed (depending on how the algorithm is configured through its hyper-parameters), it will likely take a lot of random attempts before it generates a step that is both in the right direction and sufficiently far away.

17.1.1 Sometimes you need to climb up to get to the bottom

An example of an even more troubling configuration for the local optimization algorithm is shown in figure 17.3. The gap between the current minimum where the randomized algorithm is stuck and the next point in the cost function's landscape with a lower value (the closest improvement) is way too far away to get there in a single step. What we would need is for the algorithm to be able to say, fine, it doesn't matter if I'm in a minimum; I'll climb over this hill and see if the next valley (or the one after the next) is deeper.

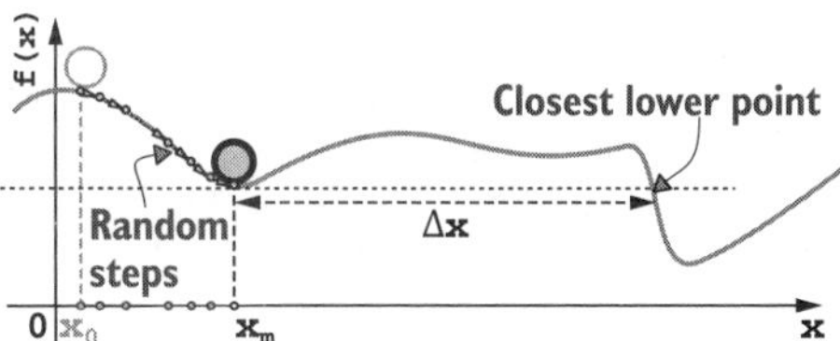
f(x)
Closest lower point
Random
steps
Δx
0
x0
xm
x

Figure 17.3 A limitation that the random local optimization algorithm shares with gradient descent is that it only moves downhill. If the next position with a better value for the cost function is too far, the algorithm won't be able to reach it in a single step, and so it will be stuck.

Of course, there are many ways to do that. For instance, we could store somewhere the best solution we have found and keep exploring, moving past a local minimum. Another option could be deciding that sometimes a step uphill is fine. We can plan it systematically, every few steps, or probabilistically, accepting a step uphill with a certain probability.

Simulated annealing uses the latter approach; while in its original formulation it doesn't keep track of the best solutions found, this can be easily added.

This heuristic[5] takes its name from a technique used in metallurgy, *annealing*, that consists of repeated cycles where a material is heated up and then controllably cooled to improve its strength: something like a blacksmith forging an iron sword by quenching it in cold water, but in a more controlled way (and without water!).

Simulated annealing does something quite similar. In its simplest version it consists of a single cooling phase, but variants exist that alternate phases where the temperature has risen, with others when the system has cooled.

The system's temperature, in turn, is directly connected to the energy of the simulated system and the probability that it is allowed to transition to a higher-energy state (in other words, to a solution for which the cost function takes higher values).

[5] We can consider simulated annealing a category of heuristics, aka *meta-heuristic*: each algorithm using simulated annealing to solve a specific problem is going to be a heuristic.

Figure 17.4 shows a possible path on a 3-D surface that resembles the progress of simulated annealing optimization. This time, the algorithm is capable of getting itself out of a local minimum, even by taking a counter intuitive step uphill: that's the difference compared to greedy algorithms (including the ones summarized in section 17.1) and the true advantage of this technique.

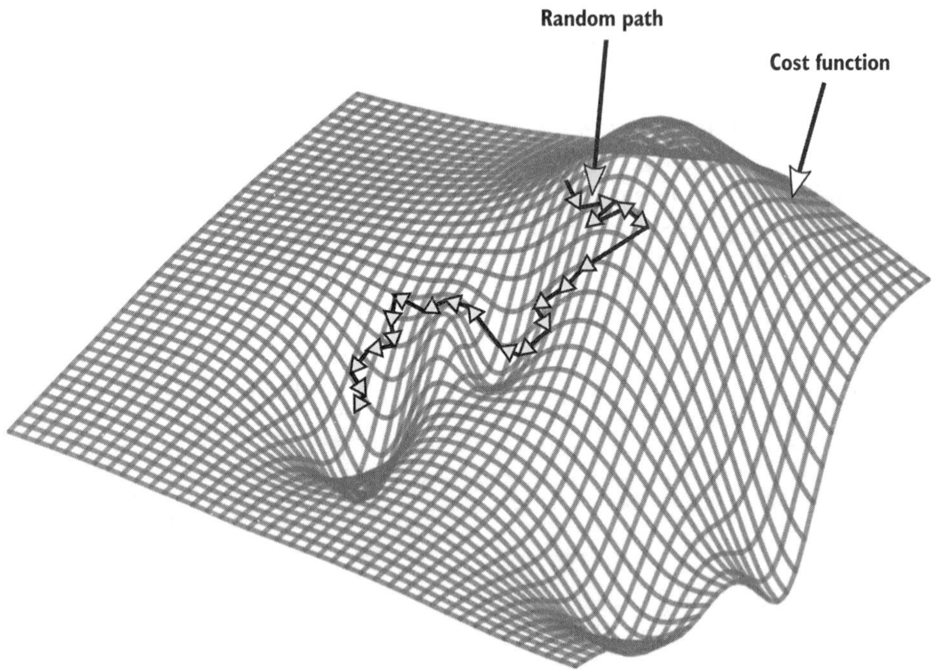
Random path
Cost function

Figure 17.4 The ups and downs of a possible path followed by simulated annealing optimization. Be warned, this is an artificial example. It's likely that in real runs, in the initial phases, the algorithm would move all over the place, while later, when the temperature drops, it will converge toward one of the minima.

The path shown in figure 17.4, however, though possible,[6] is not typical of simulated annealing. A more common path would be much more chaotic, and would have made the figure a bit too messy.

The algorithm, in real applications, is more likely to initially jump back and forth, exploring several areas of the landscape, and often moving uphill. Then, as cooling progresses, it will be less likely to transition to higher positions, and at the same time we can directly or indirectly reduce the length of the random steps. Overall, after the initial exploration phase, it should enter a fine-tuning phase.

An example of the whole process is shown in figure 17.5. As you can see, I was not exaggerating about how chaotic it looks!

---

[6] With the right configuration, and, as we'll see, with a small-range transition function.

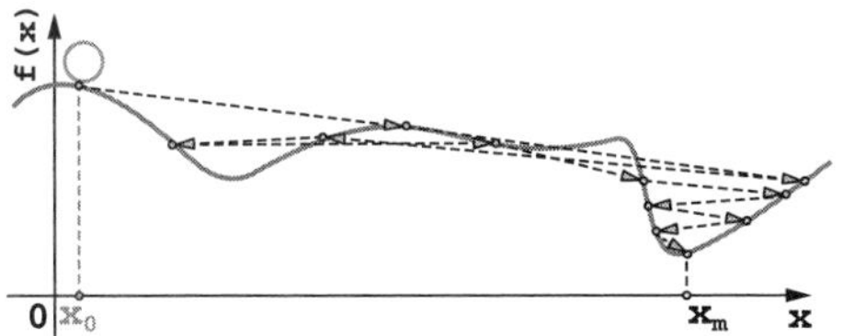
f(x)
0
x_0
x_m
x

Figure 17.5 A more realistic example of a possible simulated annealing path to the minimum for a function of a single parameter. Initially steps are larger and the probability of accepting a worse result is higher. As the cooling progresses, fine-tuning kicks-in, with smaller steps only (or mostly) towards better results.

17.1.2 Implementation

So, enough talking about how cool this algorithm is; let's look at some pseudo-code. Listing 17.1 presents the algorithm, and a JavaScript implementation, provided as part of the JsGraphs library, is linked on the book's repo on GitHub.[7]

Listing 17.1 A generic implementation of simulated annealing

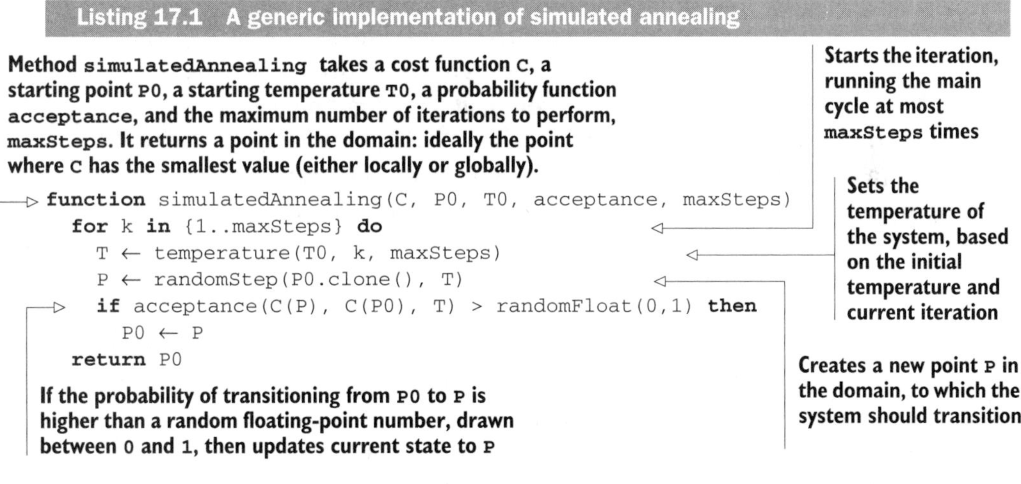

```
function simulatedAnnealing(C, P0, T0, acceptance, maxSteps)
  for k in {1..maxSteps} do
    T ← temperature(T0, k, maxSteps)
    P ← randomStep(P0.clone(), T)
    if acceptance(C(P), C(P0), T) > randomFloat(0,1) then
      P0 ← P
  return P0
```

Method simulatedAnnealing takes a cost function C, a starting point P0, a starting temperature T0, a probability function acceptance, and the maximum number of iterations to perform, maxSteps. It returns a point in the domain: ideally the point where C has the smallest value (either locally or globally).
Starts the iteration, running the main cycle at most maxSteps times
Sets the temperature of the system, based on the initial temperature and current iteration
Creates a new point P in the domain, to which the system should transition
If the probability of transitioning from P0 to P is higher than a random floating-point number, drawn between 0 and 1, then updates current state to P

The algorithm looks beautifully simple, doesn't it? And quite concise, although, as always, we try to present generic methods as templates, and when possible, we abstract as many sub-routines as possible into helper methods that can later be implemented according to the context.

In this case, there are three of them; in the next section we'll discuss both the function computing how the temperature evolves and the one giving the probability of acceptance of a transition. Now, let's discuss function `randomStep`, which allows us to build the next tentative solution to which the algorithm could transition.

This function needs, obviously, to be domain-dependent: the size of the problem space and the type of solutions will determine how we can change the current solution (a point in the problem space). For the graph-embedding problem, for instance, we can randomly move each vertex along both axes, within the maximum area in which the graph must be embedded.

[7] https://github.com/mlarocca/AlgorithmsAndDataStructuresInAction#simulated-annealing.

But as you can see at line #4, we added a dependency on the temperature for this function!

We mentioned in the previous section that you can adjust the length of the random step directly or indirectly. The short answer is that you want to be careful if you do it directly, but it's an option. To see why, we first have to better explain in detail the other two functions and understand why simulated annealing works.

17.1.3 Why simulated annealing works

If you feel that the way simulated annealing works is slightly counterintuitive, well, you are not alone. After all, if the algorithm can make large steps, and it can also move to worse positions without making any use of any knowledge of the cost function (either previous or acquired while running), how do we know it will end up in the area of the global minimum and not get stuck in some sort of funnel to a local minimum when we start reducing temperature? Well, we don't. But with most landscapes, if we run the algorithm long enough and find the right configuration, in practice it will get pretty close to the global optimum and outmatch gradient descent.

There are lots of "ifs" in that proposition. The truth is that, like most heuristic algorithms, it works well in practice when it's in the hands of someone who knows how to tune it properly and has enough computing time to make it run for lots of iterations.

Still, if that's the case, then simulated annealing is a great alternative for scenarios where gradient descent would suffer. It's not that one is better than the other; like all tools, there are problems for which gradient descent works better, and others where it would be hard or impossible to apply it. But let's see in detail why it does work.

The key to the algorithm is the probabilistic mechanism that allows the algorithm to move uphill (lines #2–5), toward worse values for the cost function, and in particular the function that spits out the probability of accepting a positive delta, depending on temperature and on the magnitude of this delta.

Assuming that at a given iteration, when temperature has the value `T`, the algorithm attempts to transition from current point P_0 to a point `P`, then we can express this probability function $A(P_0, P, T)$ as

$$A(P, P_0, T) = \begin{cases} e^{-\frac{C(P_0) - C(P)}{k \cdot T}} & \text{if } C(P) \geq C(P_0) \\ 1 & \text{otherwise} \end{cases}$$

where `C(P)` is the cost of solution `P` (similarly for P_0), and `k` is a constant that must be calibrated on the initial temperature and max delta in the cost function, so that in the initial phase of the algorithm (when the system's temperature is close to the initial temperature), the probability of acceptance of a positive delta is close to 1 for any two states.

Typically, the probability of transitioning to a lower-energy state is set to 1, so that such a transition is always allowed in any phase of the simulation.

But of course, this is not the only way to define this function. It is, however, a typical definition for the acceptance probability, because it stems directly from the metallurgic analogy: this formula is directly inspired by the Boltzmann distribution that measures the probability that a system is in a state with a certain energy and temperature.[8] But instead of an absolute value for the energy, for simulated annealing we consider a variation from a lower to a higher energy state.

Now, what's the effect of this probability distribution on the single step of the algorithm? Let's consider the case where the amplitude of the update step in the problem space is not constrained (so we could even move between opposite corners of the domain) and take a look at figure 17.6.

Initially, when the temperature of the system is high (figure 17.6 (A)), and by construction the probability distribution should allow almost any update (no matter how bad it seems), the algorithm can move all over the landscape and even get out of local minima, even if this means that it might abandon an optimal position for one of the worst negative peaks. Actually, at this stage, it is even easy for the algorithm to walk away from good solutions.

This mimics high-energy systems, where particles (or molecules) move chaotically in all directions.

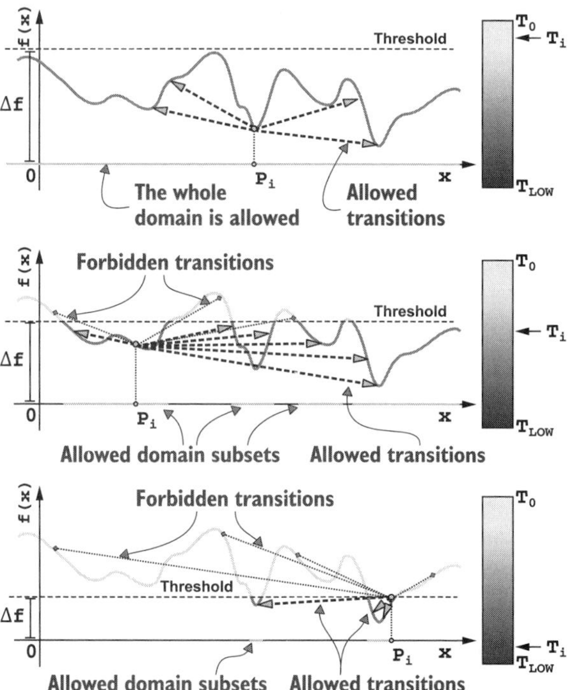
f(x)
Threshold
Δf
0
P_i
x
The whole domain is allowed
Allowed transitions
T_0
T_i
T_{LOW}
Forbidden transitions
Allowed domain subsets
Allowed transitions

Figure 17.6 The effect of temperature on the probability of transitioning to a higher-energy state, and in turn on the annealing algorithm. (A) Initially, the temperature is high enough that any transition is allowed. At this stage, the algorithm behaves like random sampling (without storing the best result) and explores a large section of the domain. (B) When the system cools down, transitions to higher states become unlikely, and above some threshold they become so unlikely as to be considered forbidden. Transitions to lower states are always allowed. (C) When we are close to the end of the annealing simulation, the probability of moving to higher-energy states is so slim as to be negligible; the system can only move to better solutions.

[8] Accordingly, the constant k is called Boltzmann's constant.

As the system cools down, the distribution changes (figure 17.7 (B)). Going uphill becomes less likely, and some positions above a certain delta (with respect to their cost) become completely unreachable.

Finally, when temperature gets close to the T_{LOW}, the halting temperature (or equivalently, as we'll see, when we are close to the maximum number of iterations), going uphill becomes so unlikely as to be basically forbidden, and the algorithm can only transition to lower-energy states. It behaves like *hill descent*.[9] Looking at figure 17.6 (C), however, you can see that there is a difference, and transitions to points far away in the domain are allowed if they correspond to a lower cost. This means the algorithm can still get out of local minima (and it's hopefully even probable that it will!) and converge to a local optimum.

Notice that the acceptance or rejection of a transition to a new state is not related to the distance of the new state from the current one in the problem space. It's only based on the energy levels of the two states, which in turn are given by (or at least proportional to) the value of the cost function in those states.

Even more importantly, after the very initial stages where basically all transitions are allowed, then the further uphill a new state is, the less likely it becomes for the transition to be accepted. This is why the algorithm works well, because it progressively encourages transitions toward areas where cost is lower (see figure 17.6 (B–C)), while not limiting the search to the neighborhood of the current position in the problem space.

Why do transitions uphill work? Because when going uphill, it might be able to go over a cliff and reach a deeper valley. While it might seem counterintuitive on a 2-D chart, this becomes even more relevant in high-dimensional space.

Similar to the metallurgic process, however, cooling down the system with the right pace is instrumental to the quality of the final result.

And, of course, being a merely stochastic process, it also needs some "luck"; especially toward the end, many random steps will produce transitions uphill, and as such will be rejected. But if we try hard enough, for many iterations, chances are that a positive change will be randomly found.

And that's the strength of the algorithm, and, at the same time, its weakness. We can reach an improvement, but since we discard progressively more and more attempted updates, we'll need several iterations (technically: a lot of them!) and, of course, a good function for the random steps to probe the problem space.

This makes the algorithm particularly slow and resource-consuming, especially if iterations (generating a random point and evaluating the cost function) are expensive to compute.

[9] We described hill descent in chapter 16.

17.1.4 Short-range vs long-range transitions

Now, again, the question arises: Do we want to progressively limit the range of transitions, and in turn how far the algorithm can move at each step in the domain space?

We could make the length of the maximum update step dependent on the temperature parameter `T`, and as such, it would shrink in time.

But the interesting part is that even if we keep the same maximum step length for the whole process, there is some kind of indirect reduction while the temperature cools. As shown in figure 17.6, the filtering actually happens on the co-domain of the cost function, but the indirect effect is limiting the domain to a subset of the original problem space; and, in turn, the effect is the same as water running down funnels—it gets channeled and velocity slows down (as pressure builds up).

If we further restrict the acceptable transitions based on proximity along the problem space, on one hand we get a greater number of attempted updates in the area surrounding the current point, which could be good if we are close to the global minimum, because it would speed up convergence.

On the other hand, we would likely lose the ability to get out of local minima, which is the best reason to use simulated annealing in the first place.

Therefore, one "safe" solution is to implement the `randomStep` method as pure, random sampling; however, this means that we will need a lot of iterations to find a transition downhill, and the algorithm will keep bouncing between valleys without focusing on fine-tuning. An interesting compromise could be increasing the probability of small steps, but still allowing far-reaching updates, and even trying them every few iterations. This can be done in combination with shrinking the range of the local-search (the small steps) as the temperature cools down.

The last thing we need to discuss is how to update the temperature. Similar to the acceptance probability, there are several possible viable options for this function—there are no restrictions on it.

Typically, however, geometric (aka exponential) decay is used, with the temperature value updated not every iteration, but after some interval (for instance, every 1000 iterations or so).

The mathematical formula for this function is

$$T_i = \alpha T_{i-1}, 0 < \alpha < 1$$

The temperature at iteration `i` is a fraction of the temperature at iteration `i-1;` α, which must be between `0` and `1`, controls how much cooler the temperature gets between two iterations.

Now, you might have to fiddle a bit with the value of α and the interval between temperature updates to tune them and get the best results. In general, exponential decay slows down quickly at the beginning and slowly from halfway to the end. Figure 17.7 shows a few examples of how the ease of the slowdown depend on the choice of α.

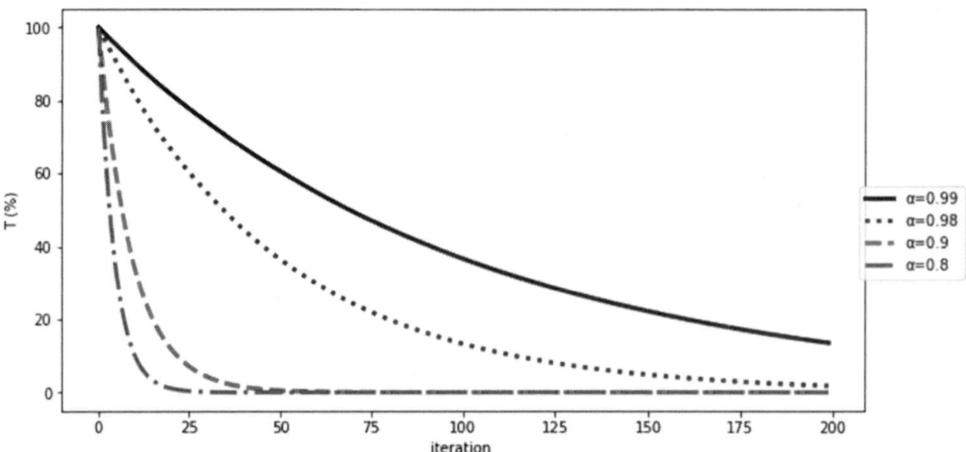
100
80
60
40
20
0
T (%)
0
25
50
75
100
125
150
175
200
iteration
α=0.99
α=0.98
α=0.9
α=0.8

Figure 17.7 To understand how the parameter α controls cooling in simulated annealing, let's look at the *exponential decay* function: `f(i)=`T_i`= α*f(i-1),∀i>0`. In this chart, we set `f(0)=`T_0`=100` and show how the function's shape changes with the rate α, which controls how fast the function goes to zero. Why is it called exponential decay, you ask? Because $T_1 = \alpha T_0$, $T_2 = \alpha T_1 = \alpha^2 T_0$, and in general $T_n = \alpha^n T_0$. If α is between 0 and 1, α^n and in turn T_n get progressively (exponentially) smaller.

In practice, α≈`0.98` is usually a safe bet for an initial choice (then, you can take it from there and tune it).

17.1.5 Variants

As we have seen, simulated annealing—despite being an indisputably powerful tool—also has some flaws, the most concerning of which is its slow speed in converging due to its stochastic nature.

And so, like for all algorithms, over time many variants have been studied to remedy its shortcomings and make it even better.

We already alluded to a trivial modification that we could add: storing the best solution found across all iterations. It might happen, in fact, especially on large, multidimensional problem spaces, that during the initial high-energy phase we serendipitously land in proximity to a global minimum, then move uphill afterward, and never manage to get back to such a good result again. How likely this is to happen depends on many factors, such as the shape of the landscape (the cost function) and whether the right configuration for the parameters was found. In any case, remembering the best result ever can be an easy win.

Pushing this consideration a little further, *simulated annealing with restart* stores one or a few of the best results found across iterations, and when it gets stuck, it moves to one of these previous (and advantageous) positions, resetting the descent or just moving to a different area of the problem space.

We have mentioned, if you remember, that despite being lower with respect to greedy algorithms, the probability of getting stuck in local minima is still not `null`.

In particular, this event can be concurrently caused by a few factors:

- Non-optimal choice of the algorithm's parameters. Cooling becomes, for instance, too fast, and the algorithm gets stuck away from global minimum.
- Bad luck. As we said, it's a stochastic algorithm, after all, and it might reach the optimum too soon and never be able to go back once the system cools down.
- The update step (more likely so). While we saw that random sampling causes the fewest constraints toward other areas in the problem space with lower energy, it will slow down local convergence (possibly too much to be acceptable).
- Sometimes it's possible to have update rules that allow long steps, while other times (as we'll see), it might be easier to implement only small steps, which means that those long leaps to different areas that could bring the algorithm outside of local minima are more rare.

When some or all of these happen, using random restart could save the day.

Another issue with simulated annealing is that tuning its parameters can be tricky and annoying. In *adaptive simulated annealing* the algorithm parameters, `k` and α, are automatically adjusted as the algorithm progresses, or depending on the trend in the energy level. The latter uses mechanisms borrowed from thermodynamics, allowing even increases in temperature (simulating cycles of cooling down and warming up).

17.1.6 Simulated annealing vs gradient descent: Which one should I use?

We have seen that simulated annealing is slower than gradient descent to get to minima: the latter takes the fastest route, so it's hard to beat on a clear course.

The caveat is that gradient descent requires a differentiable cost function and gets easily stuck in local minima.

Whenever the cost function is not differentiable or step-shaped, as with the minimum-crossing-embedding problem, or the problem space is discrete (for problems like the TSP, which we'll describe later in this chapter), then simulated annealing is preferred over gradient descent.

Likewise, for problems where we have flexible requirements about running time and the quality of the solution, simulated annealing might still be preferable to gradient descent. Keep in mind that simulated annealing is a *Monte Carlo algorithm,* and so (as we discuss in appendix F) it returns a sub-optimal solution, whose quality increases with the quantity of time we allot for the algorithm to run.

When, instead, we have guarantees about the differentiability and shape of the function (for instance, if we are sure we have a bowl-shaped function, as with linear/logistic regression, and so on), then we want to take advantage of the superpowers of gradient descent.

Are there cases where simulation annealing is best avoided?

Obviously, as we have discussed, if a problem doesn't admit near-optimal solutions, but rather demands the best possible one, then simulated annealing is not the best tool in our belt.

The shape of the cost function matters as well. When the cost function has narrow valleys, the algorithm will have a low probability of finding them, and if they hold the global minima, it's unlikely simulated annealing will converge to a near-optimal solution.

Finally, as we will see in our examples, an important requirement is that the cost function should be easily calculated for a new candidate solution (possibly allowing us to directly compute the delta based only on the difference with the current solution). Since this cost is computed at each iteration, a computationally intensive cost function will slow down the optimization, forcing us to run the algorithm for fewer iterations.

17.2 Simulated annealing + traveling salesman

I hope you have found the discussion about simulated annealing interesting so far. We learned about a tremendously useful tool, and now it's time to put it into practice; luckily, we have just the perfect application for it!

Do you remember our e-commerce company? We left it in chapter 14 dealing with deliveries, optimizing routes for single-destination deliveries inside town.

As we mentioned, planning individual deliveries from a warehouse to customers for each order is uneconomic and unrealistic.

This doesn't mean that what we learned in chapter 14 about optimizing routes with Dijkstra's and $A*$ algorithms was useless. It's quite the opposite: that's some fine-grained optimization that we can always perform for a single delivery, going from the generic `i`-th destination to the next one. Since we will have to compute these routes on the fly, it's even more important to use an efficient algorithm.

And yet, since to amortize delivery costs and stay on the market we need to load each truck with several shipments (and possibly load each truck to maximum capacity) and have it go out on daily tours with several deliveries, finding the optimum path from a source to a destination is not enough anymore.

In this section, we'll focus on optimizing the route of a delivery truck, assuming its load (and in turn its destinations) are already fixed. Once we have improved this phase, we still have another, higher-level optimization in front of us: assigning the deliveries to the trucks to minimize the distance (or travel time, or, more likely, cost) across all trucks and all deliveries. But we need to take one step at a time, so in this chapter we'll focus on the following problem: given a list of cities, each connected to each other by roads, find the optimal tour, aka a sequence of the cities such that we move from each city to the next one, at some cost (for instance, the distance between the two cities) and eventually return to the first city while keeping the total cost minimal.

Figure 17.8 illustrates this situation: you can see 10 real and DC Universe cities, the connections between each pair of cities, and—highlighted—the shortest tour touching each city exactly once.

Now, we are considering a single delivery per city just to make the example clearer, with all steps being at the same scale. Nothing changes, however, if instead we have multiple deliveries in each city. Because the intra-city distances will be smaller than the ones between different cities, deliveries in the same city will be naturally clustered together. It is also likely possible for the problem to be optimized at different levels in two steps: first, find the best order in which cities should be visited, and then, within each city, compute the best route, using the same algorithm.[10] But these are just low-level details.

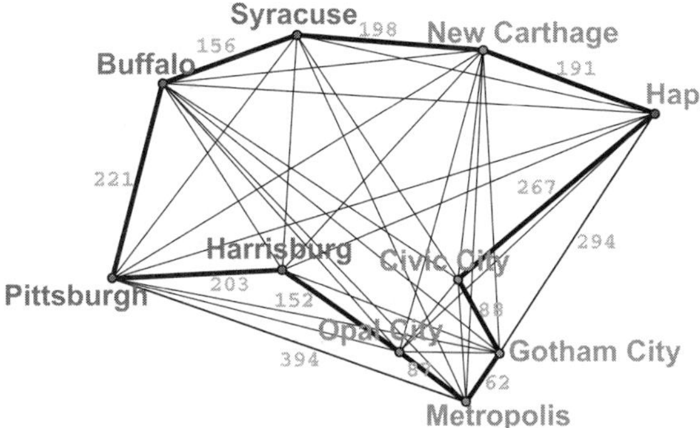
Syracuse
198
New Carthage
156
Buffalo
191
Happy Harbor
221
267
294
Harrisburg
Civic City
Pittsburgh
203
152
88
Opal City
394
Gotham City
62
Metropolis

Figure 17.8 An example map, mixing the DC Universe's cities and other real ones, with some distances: because this is a complete graph with close to fifty edges, we are only showing a few numbers, almost only for the edges in the best tour (the thicker edges).

The abstract formulation of this riddle is a well-known computer science problem known as the *traveling salesman problem (TSP)*. As you might have guessed, it's a difficult puzzle to solve, in particular a *NP-complete* problem; this implies it's both *NP-Hard* and in *NP*—the former meaning that there is no known deterministic algorithm that can solve it in polynomial time, while the latter means that if we have a candidate solution, we can check it in polynomial time.

Informally, we can say that we expect any deterministic algorithm that solves the TSP will need exponential time (although we can't be sure, because we don't have an answer to the *P vs NP* problem).

The first consequence for us of the TSP being NP-Hard is that we can't assume we'll be able to solve an instance of this problem on the fly, on a driver's mobile phone, or even a laptop computer (unless the number of cities to deliver to is small; but for the 10 cities in figure 17.8, there are already 10! ~ 3.6 million possible sequences). We need computer power, and planning ahead, and possibly even computing ahead, to reuse the results as much as possible.

Even with a supercomputer at our service, in fact, the running time of an exact algorithm just grows too fast. With 15 cities, there are ~1.3 trillion possible solutions, which becomes `2.4e18` (2 billion of billions) with 20 cities. Even assuming that we can find an algorithm running in exponential time (which is asymptotically better than factorial), we couldn't handle more than ~40 different deliveries (probably far fewer).

[10] We would have to constrain the first and last delivery in each city to be the closest to the connections to the previous and the next city in the tour. Even so, it's possible that the solution found in two steps is not the best possible. If the connections to other cities starts in different areas of town, this could influence the choice of the best sequence for the cities; the influence, however, could be small enough to be considered acceptable.

17.2.1 Exact vs approximated solutions

The last consideration we make is that we can afford to compromise on the optimal solution. We can be fine using a near-optimal solution; we don't need the best possible. For instance, if we add a few miles over a total of 1,000 miles per trip, it feels acceptable, while doubling the total distance of the tour would be quite expensive, and making it 10 times costlier would be a disaster.

This is not true for every context, and there are situations where we need the absolute best because even a small difference is translated into a large cost, or maybe it could help save lives. In surgery simulations, for instance, a small error can have dire consequences, as you can imagine.

But since we are okay with sub-optimal solutions, this means we can use a heuristic to get an acceptable solution within a reasonable time.

Several heuristics have been developed specifically for TSP. For instance, for graphs whose distances obey the triangle inequality (like ours), a class of algorithms using the *minimum spanning tree* of a graph (see section 2.8.2) and running in *linearithmic* time, `O(n*log(n))`, can guarantee a solution whose cost is at most twice the minimum cost, and on average[11] between just 15 and 20% higher than the shortest tour.

We want to try a different way, though. This is clearly an optimization problem, so why not try to tackle it with our new shining tool, simulated annealing?

> **Is using simulated annealing the right choice for my project?**
>
> A word of caution is necessary here. We have mentioned Maslow's hammer law a few times throughout this book, and this configures like a case where we need to think carefully before choosing which tool to employ. The risk, as you know by now, is being tempted to use a hammer (simulated annealing) when a screwdriver could work better.
>
> So, before deciding if simulated annealing is worth implementing, we need to ask ourselves a few questions, such as these: Do we have the skills inside our team/company to develop and tune this algorithm? Would we have better skills for another solution? What's the difference in effort needed between these solutions? What's the benefit of one versus the other?

Simulated annealing can potentially bring us a better solution than the average provided by the MST heuristic; it can even lead us to global optimum. Moreover, let's assume we don't have expertise on the specific problem inside the company: overall, it might be worth trying simulated annealing, which is high-level and potentially could be reused for other optimization problems in the future.

When it comes to the cost function, we are in luck. It naturally stems from the problem's very definition: it's the sum of the edges between adjacent vertices in the sequence (including between its last and first entries, of course).

[11] As we discussed in chapter 16, NP-hardness is based on the worst-case scenarios; many problems, however, are difficult only for a minority of edge cases, while many real-world scenarios can be tackled more efficiently.

17.2.2 Visualizing cost

One nice thing about the solutions to the TSP is that the problem space is the set of all the possible permutations of a graph's vertices, and since each sequence can be mapped to an integer, we have a way to show a nice 2-D chart for the cost function, and even see how the algorithm progresses. The problem space, of course, is huge when the number of vertices grows, as it appears clearly in figure 17.9, where we have to zoom in on a small portion of the domain to be able to distinguish the landscape of the cost function.

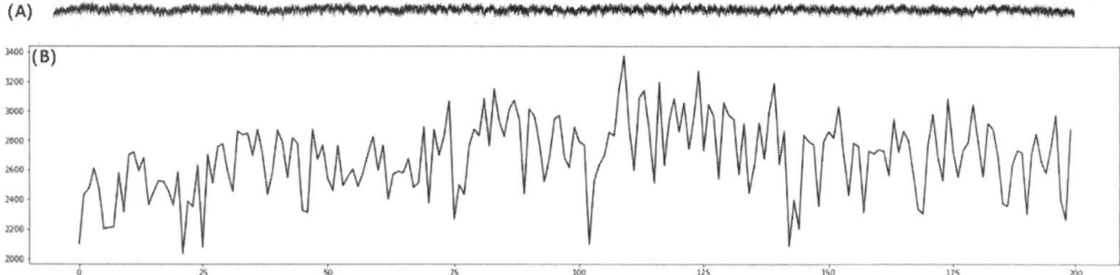

(A)
(B)
3400
3200
3000
2800
2600
2400
2200
2000
0
25
50
75
100
125
150
175
200

Figure 17.9 The cost landscape for the TSP applied to the graph in figure 17.8 (A). The cost function is displayed for the whole domain; it's hard to make sense of it! 17.8 (B) Zooming in on the first few hundreds of permutations, we can see that there are several local minima.

To provide a clearer view and description of the process, we need to keep the set of cities small: for instance, we can restrict to the six DC Universe cities in figure 17.8, obtaining the graph shown in figure 17.10, for which there are just 720 possible permutations of the vertices. This produces the landscape shown in figure 17.11, which is far less clogged than what we saw in figure 17.9.

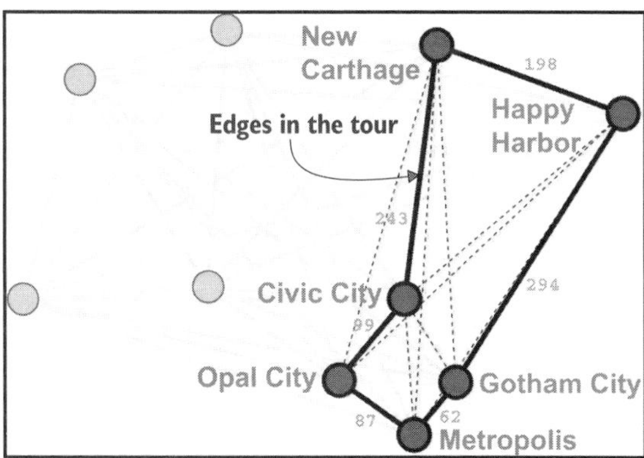

New Carthage
198
Happy Harbor
Edges in the tour
243
294
Civic City
89
Opal City
Gotham City
87
62
Metropolis

Figure 17.10 Solving TSP for a subgraph of the K_{10} graph shown in figure 17.8. The figure highlights the K_6 complete graph formed by the cities belonging to the DC Universe, and the best solution found. The rest of the vertices/edges of the original graph are grayed out for clarity.

Now, since we have the full landscape, you might point out that we could just brute-force search it and find the best solution, and you'd be right; we have evaluated the cost of each single permutation to draw the chart in figure 17.11, so we can just extract its minimum. As shown in the figure, the best solution is the sequence:

```
[New Carthage, Happy Harbor, Gotham City, Metropolis, Opal City, Civic City]
```

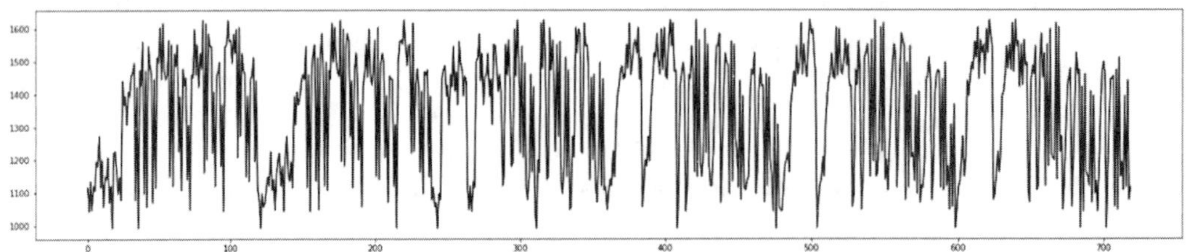
1600
1500
1400
1300
1200
1100
1000
0
100
200
300
400
500
600
700

Figure 17.11 The cost landscape for TSP applied to the complete graph K_6 as shown in figure 17.10. Besides the actual values, notice some patterns repeating.

The point is that we wouldn't be able to do that for larger instances. With the full graph in figure 17.8, for example, it already takes several minutes to generate all 3.6 million possible permutations!

17.2.3 Pruning the domain

The reason we wanted to show you the cost function on the full domain of the subproblem with six vertices is because this chart can teach us a lot. For instance, we can see there are many local minima that appear to have the same cost. Can you guess why that is?

As always, take a couple of minutes (if you'd like) to think about the answer, before moving on to the solution.

To answer the question, consider these permutations of the cities in the graph:

```
[Opal City, Civic City, New Carthage, Happy Harbor, Gotham City, Metropolis]
[New Carthage, Happy Harbor, Gotham City, Metropolis, Opal City, Civic City]
```

What's the difference between these two permutations, in terms of solutions? Since we are considering closed tours (from the first city, through all other cities, and then back to the start), they are completely identical, except the second one is shifted left by two cities. In fact, the cost of the two tours is the same (because they involve the same edges).

There are six equivalent sequences that can be derived from the one we gave as a solution, one for each city used as a starting point.

We can therefore fix in advance the city from which the tour starts, knowing that this won't affect the result, but it will cut the number of permutations we need to examine. From 720 we go down to only 120—not bad, and it will be an even better gain for larger graphs.

Moreover, consider that this will work well with the specific instance of the problem we need to solve for our e-commerce company. We always need to start (and end) our tours at the warehouse, where the goods to deliver are loaded on the trucks.

If we set, for instance, `New Carthage` as the starting point, there might still be several equally good solutions (if multiple sub-paths have the same total cost), but if the graph is undirected there will only be, at most, two equivalent solutions:

```
[New Carthage, Happy Harbor, Gotham City, Metropolis, Opal City, Civic City]
[New Carthage, Civic City, Opal City, Metropolis, Gotham City, Happy Harbor]
```

That's because if edges have the same cost in both directions, we can travel through a simple cycle (a tour) in either direction (in figure 17.10, clockwise or counter-clockwise).

But we don't mind having two possible global solutions, so there is no further action we should take here.

17.2.4 State transitions

Now it's time to translate this constraint into code. Luckily for us, that's not too difficult, given how we designed the simulated annealing algorithm in listing 17.1. We need to pass the definition of the function that computes the transition to the next state, and right there, we can always set the first vertex of the sequence to the same value. We also have the cost function figured out, so we are ready to implement all the missing pieces.

Listing 17.2 starts by exploring the cost function, which, as we have discussed, is the sum of the weights of the edges between two adjacent vertices in the permutation. Still, while computing this value we need to be careful about a couple of details. First and foremost, we assume that the input graph has an edge between every pair of vertices. If this isn't true, we need to check for it and return a special value (for instance, infinity, or any large-enough weight) to basically guarantee any solution including missing edges will be naturally discarded. Another alternative could be checking the solutions when transitions are computed and making sure that those with missing edges between adjacent vertices will be discarded early.

Listing 17.2 Cost function for TSP

Method `tspTourCost` takes a graph and a candidate solution `P` (a point in the problem space, that is, a permutation of the list of vertices in the graph) and computes the cost of the solution as the sum of the weight of all edges in the candidate tour. It's assumed the graph has an edge between every pair of vertices (or, alternatively, that the methods return a special value, like `inf`, if there isn't one).

```
function tspTourCost(graph, P)
  cost ← 0
  for k in {0..|P|} do
    cost ← cost + graph.edgeBetween(P[k], P[(k+1)%|P|]).weight
  return cost
```

Cycles through the sequence

Checks the edge between `k`-th vertex in the sequence and its successor, the one at position (`k+1`) modulo the length of the sequence (so that when it gets to the last element of the list, it will circle back and its successor will be the first vertex)

The other detail we would like to highlight is that we need to wrap around the array, because we have to add the cost of the edge between the last and first vertices in the sequence (the edge that closes the tour). This can be handled in many ways, using modulo being the most succinct, while the most efficient would be treating this last edge as a separate case outside the `for` loop.

When it comes to the transitions to a new solution, we have a few options:

- *Swapping adjacent vertices*—After selecting a random position in the sequence, we would swap the vertex at the given index with its successor. For instance, the solution `[1,2,3,4]` could change into `[2,1,3,4]` or `[1,3,2,4]`, and so on. This transition corresponds to a local search, where only the immediate neighborhood of the current solution is explored; this raises the probability that fine tuning leads to improvement, but makes leaps and getting out of local minima harder.
- *Swapping any pair of vertices*—Both positions for the vertices to swap are chosen at random, and they are simply swapped: `[1,2,3,4]` can also become `[3,2,1,4]`, which was not allowed by the previous operator. These kinds of transitions allow medium-range search, although the two solutions are still quite close to each other.
- *Generating a new sequence at random*—This allows us to leap across the whole domain at any stage of the algorithm, making it less likely to lead to fine-grain improvements toward a local minimum in the final stage of the simulation, because relatively few attempts will be made in the neighborhood of current solutions. At the same time, it will also leave the door open for distant leaps to any area of the domain, whenever a better solution is (randomly) found.

And, of course, many more intermediate options are available, such as doing a fixed or random number of swaps per transition or moving a whole segment of the solution elsewhere.

Which one of these works best? That's a good question, which is hard to answer from a theoretical point. Let's try them out on our K_{10} graph, as shown in figure 17.8, and see which one gives the best average result. We will perform 1,000 simulations, each running for the same number of steps and with the same values for `k` and α, and compare the average cost for the solutions. We'll also assume that each sequence starts with `"New Carthage"`, so that we cut duplicate solutions by a factor 10. Results are summed up in table 17.1.

Of course, the domain this time is still huge, ~3.6 million permutations, but not so large that we can't afford brute-force (armed with some patience; it takes a while); therefore, we know that the best possible solution has cost `1625` (as shown in figure 17.8):

```
["New Carthage", "Syracuse", "Buffalo", "Pittsburgh", "Harrisburg",
➥ "Opal City", "Metropolis", "Gotham City", "Civic City"]
```

Table 17.1 Average cost for the best solution found by simulated annealing with different algorithms for transitions

Operation	Mean cost (α=0.98, T_0=200 and k=1000)
Adjacent Swaps	1937.291
Random Swaps	1683.563
Random Permutation	1831.886

It's interesting that the best result is obtained with the medium-range search, while the worst one is given by the local search. This means that with the configuration used, the local search gets stuck in local optima, while the random permutation is too erratic and fails to obtain local convergence in the final stage of the algorithm, when the temperature gets low.

We must stress that with different parameters, this could change completely. Take, for instance, α, the decaying factor: with a difference choice, the cooling process would be slower, so we wonder, could this allow the local search to work better? Let's try it out; the results are in table 17.2.

Table 17.2 Average cost, with different temperature decay rate

Operation	Mean cost (α=0.97)	Mean cost (α=0.98)	Mean cost (α=0.99)
Adjacent Swaps	1972.502	1937.291	1868.701
Random Swaps	1692.044	1683.563	1668.248
Random Permutation	1816.658	1831.886	1913.416

Increasing the temperature decay rate from 0.97 to 0.99 means that the cooling is performed more slowly and uniformly (you can refer to figure 17.7 to visualize the decay curves). In turn, this seems to help when we use only local search around the current solution, while making thing worse when used for full-domain searches. The medium-range search performed through random vertex swaps gets even closer to the best cost, on average.

These results show a couple more things that are worth highlighting:

- Even on a small case (10 vertices) and running thousands of iterations, we get arbitrarily close to the best solution, but we don't always get the best result. That's a calculated risk with heuristics.
- Finding the best configuration for an optimization algorithm requires time, experience, and sometimes a bit of luck.

We also tried larger values for alpha, such as α=0.995, which are not shown in the table, partly because they lead to poor results. Probably the cooling becomes too slow and the algorithm gets closer to random sampling (this suspicion is corroborated by the fact that with a smaller value for k, the normalizing Boltzmann constant, the deterioration in the results smoothens).

To conclude this section on TSP, listing 17.3 shows a method that implements a random transition from current state to the next one, by combining all three methods discussed so far. An implementation of these methods for library JsGraphs can be found on GitHub.

Listing 17.3 Random transition function for TSP

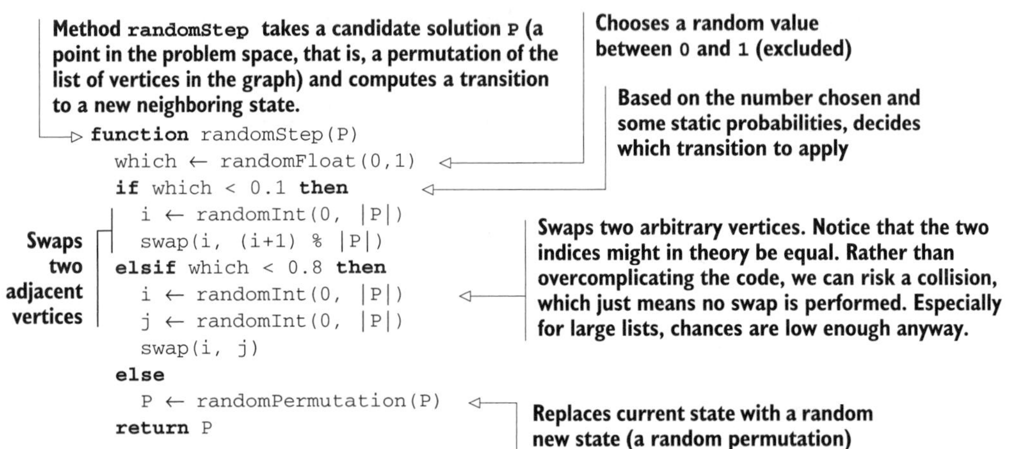
Method randomStep takes a candidate solution P (a point in the problem space, that is, a permutation of the list of vertices in the graph) and computes a transition to a new neighboring state.
Chooses a random value between 0 and 1 (excluded)
Based on the number chosen and some static probabilities, decides which transition to apply
Swaps two adjacent vertices
Swaps two arbitrary vertices. Notice that the two indices might in theory be equal. Rather than overcomplicating the code, we can risk a collision, which just means no swap is performed. Especially for large lists, chances are low enough anyway.
Replaces current state with a random new state (a random permutation)

```
function randomStep(P)
  which ← randomFloat(0,1)
  if which < 0.1 then
    i ← randomInt(0, |P|)
    swap(i, (i+1) % |P|)
  elsif which < 0.8 then
    i ← randomInt(0, |P|)
    j ← randomInt(0, |P|)
    swap(i, j)
  else
    P ← randomPermutation(P)
  return P
```

How does this method comparatively perform? Table 17.3 compares it to the three "pure" solutions: it manages to get the best of all the possible strategies and drives the average cost down with all choices for α.

Table 17.3 Comparing average solution cost found using an ensemble of original methods

Operation	Mean cost (α=0.97)	Mean cost (α=0.98)	Mean cost (α=0.99)
Adjacent Swaps	1972.502	1937.291	1868.701
Random Swaps	1692.044	1683.563	1668.248
Random Permutation	1816.658	1831.886	1913.416
Ensemble Step	1683.966	1672.494	1660.904

This seems to suggest that an ensemble method, with the right ratio between the long and distant local searches, can leverage the strengths of both types of transition heuristics.

The best result, with the ensemble method, is obtained with a larger decay rate, so with a more uniform cooling process.

Figure 17.12 shows the algorithm in action: how cost evolves while cooling the system. While initially the cost is fluctuating, the oscillation becomes progressively

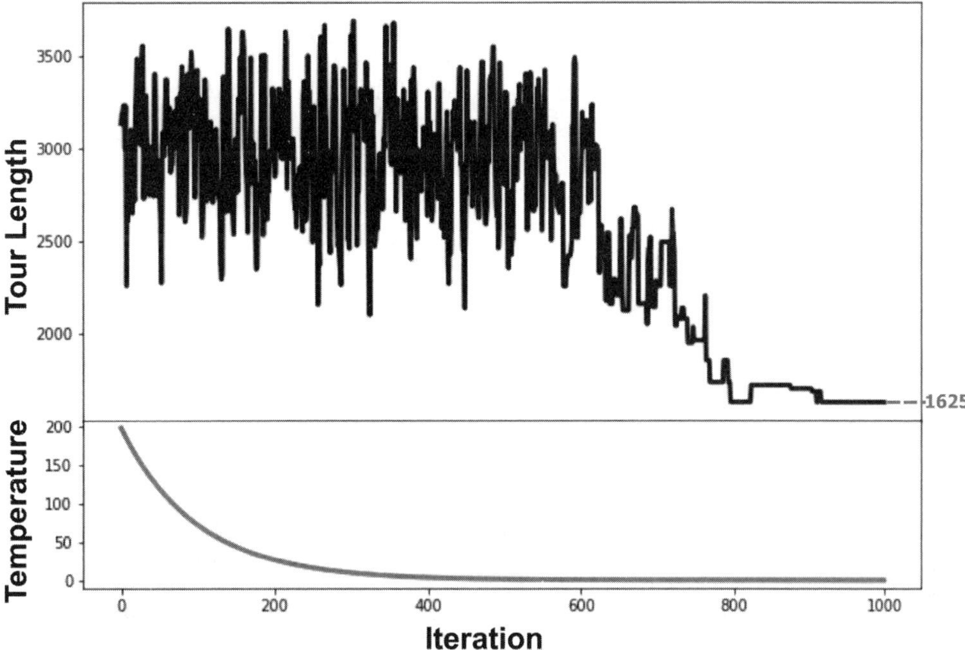
Tour Length
3500
3000
2500
2000
1625
Temperature
200
150
100
50
0
0
200
400
600
800
1000
Iteration

Figure 17.12 A run of simulated annealing for K_{10} TSP. It takes a while, but finally finds the path to global minimum.

narrower and, once the temperature is low enough, search is channeled toward the global minimum.

We haven't explored all the possible values for α, `k`, T_0, and even the relative probabilities of applying each of the three transition operators within the ensemble method could be further tuned. To be more systematic, we should build a few more examples with different graphs, and then write a small piece of code that changes one parameter at a time and records the mean or median cost found. Try it out using the code included in JsGraph library as a starting point; it could be a nice exercise.

17.2.5 Adjacent vs random swaps

The last point I'd like to briefly discuss is why it seems that swapping random vertices works better than swapping adjacent pairs.

One factor that contributes to this can be seen with the following example, illustrated in figure 17.13: it shows a case where the local-search transition heuristic, swapping only adjacent pairs, might struggle. First, we have an example of a swap between two random vertices (17.13 (A)) that grants a good improvement in the cost function. This transition will be always accepted, regardless of the temperature of the system.

When only swaps between adjacent pairs are allowed (17.13 (B)), in this example several pejorative moves (two, in this case, but it can be made an arbitrarily long sequence) must be accepted before getting to the same final configuration shown in

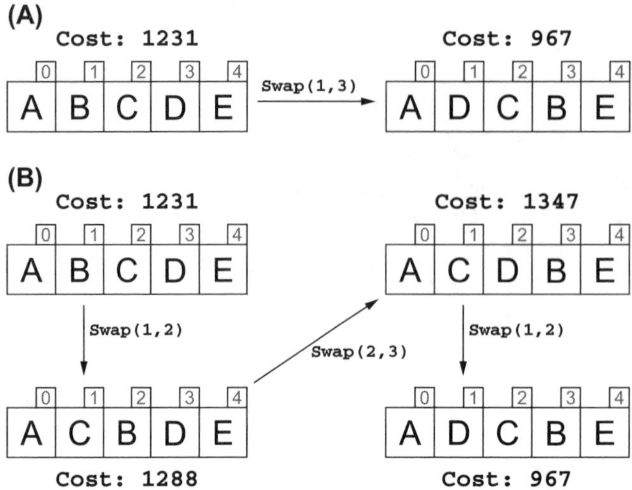
(A)
Cost: 1231
0 1 2 3 4
A B C D E
Swap(1,3)
Cost: 967
0 1 2 3 4
A D C B E
(B)
Cost: 1231
0 1 2 3 4
A B C D E
Swap(1,2)
0 1 2 3 4
A C B D E
Cost: 1288
Swap(2,3)
Cost: 1347
0 1 2 3 4
A C D B E
Swap(1,2)
0 1 2 3 4
A D C B E
Cost: 967

Figure 17.13 An example of why the local search transition heuristic, swapping only adjacent pairs, might struggle. In the top half, a swap between two random vertices (A) is performed. There is a good improvement in the cost function, so this transition will be always accepted. When only swaps between adjacent pairs are allowed (B), several pejorative moves (two, in this case, but it can be made an arbitrarily long sequence) must be accepted before getting to the same configuration as (A). This might happen in the early stages of the cooling process, but as we get to the end of the cooling cycle it becomes unlikely.

figure 17.13 (A). Accepting a sequence of transitions uphill might happen in the early stages of the cooling process, but as we get to the end of the cooling cycle, it becomes progressively less likely for a sequence of bad moves to be accepted. Hence, by using only narrow search, the algorithm might find it impossible to improve an intermediate result.

The consideration that the acceptance rate for sequences of moves exponentially decays with the temperature can also suggests a different approach for our `randomStep` method—passing the temperature along, and making narrow search more likely to happen in the early stages (when the temperature is higher), while applying an inverse dependence for long search probability, which could then be more likely in late stages.

I encourage you to try it out by changing the code[12] cloned from JsGraphs's GitHub repo. Getting your hands dirty is a great way to become familiar with simulated annealing.

17.2.6 Applications of TSP

Besides our issue with delivery routes, efficient TSP approximation algorithms can benefit a lot of real-world scenarios.

The story goes that one of the pioneers of research about the TSP was motivated, in the 1940s, by the need to optimize bus routes to pick children up for school.

[12]See http://mng.bz/PPWv.

Later, this problem was applied pervasively to the logistic of most services that involve planning tours, from mail delivery to farming.

In time, cable companies started to use it to improve scheduling of service calls, and more recently (and more relevantly to our field), it has become a must to make the automated process of drilling holes in and soldering printed circuit boards (*PCB*) more efficient, and even to aid some processes in genome sequencing.

17.3 Simulated annealing and graph embedding

To solve the TSP, we were dealing with a graph while ignoring its embedding,[13] the only thing that mattered was the distance between pair of vertices.

In the last couple of chapters, we focused on abstract graphs and finding meaningful ways to embed them in the plane.

If you recall, when we presented simulated annealing, we said it could work well with discrete cost functions, and even step-shaped cost functions. Those, as we have seen, are some of the situations where it's advisable to prefer simulated annealing over gradient descent.

Therefore, how could we close this chapter without trying to use simulated annealing to crack the *minimum edge crossing* problem?

17.3.1 Minimum edge crossing

As always, to apply our template for simulated annealing (shown in listing 17.1) to a concrete problem, we need to specify two functions: the cost function and the update step.

The former is often implied by the problem, and so it is here, for the basic version of the problem: we just count how many edges intersect.

The latter, the update step, leaves more leeway to the algorithm designer. Should we just move a single vertex randomly? By how much? Should we swap the positions of two vertices? Should edges be taken into consideration during the update?

The one advice I can give in these situations is to start small, get something simple working, and then try to add new ideas and validate them by measuring whether or not they help convergence. This is what we have done with the TSP by first developing the methods performing a single action, measuring their effectiveness, and then combining them in a random ensemble.

To make things more concrete, we'll focus on finding an embedding close to the rectilinear crossing number (rcn) for complete graph K_8. If you remember Guy's conjecture, which we provided in chapter 15, it gives us an exact formula for this graph's crossing number, which is 18. In that same chapter, however, we also learned that the rectilinear crossing number for complete graphs can be and usually is larger than its crossing number;[14] in this case, `rcn(K8)` is `19`.

---

[13]Or, equivalently, we could say that we were dealing with precisely one embedding on the graph.

[14]Because we are restricted to using straight-line segments, that are a sub-set of all possible curves for edges.

So, let's start with a simple step that takes a vertex and slightly moves it within a certain range. After fiddling with the range of updates for vertices, we chose to update both `x` and `y` separately, by choosing two random deltas within 10% of the drawing area's width and height respectively. Smaller ranges made the algorithm too slow, while with larger values the algorithm behaved erratically. Then, running simulated annealing with `k=0.1, α=0.97,` T_0`=200` and `maxSteps=500`, the average `rcn` over 100 runs was `21.904`. Not bad, but not particularly good.

Two considerations must be made. First, we kept the number of steps low (if you recall, we used up to 10,000 for TSP in the last section). The second consideration is that for the same reasons (which we'll discuss in a second), we had to go down from 1,000 runs to just 100.

Both changes are due to the fact that computing the cost function and the transitions (by cloning a graph embedding) were particularly computationally heavy. Of course, this is partly due to using a general-purpose version of simulated annealing; it could be optimized by writing an ad hoc version that doesn't need to clone the whole embedding, but just remember what was changed, and what the cost of the current solution was (and maybe also computing the delta based on the changes, not the whole solutions: for instance, just compute the number of intersections for the vertex moved before and after the change).

I would like to avoid focusing on these optimizations here. Don't get me wrong; optimization is crucial, especially for production-ready code, but early optimization can also get in the way of improving your algorithm or learning process. Premature optimization is still the source of all evil (well, maybe not all of it, but a good chunk!).

In this case, I preferred providing simple, clean, non-optimized code rather than more obscure (though better-performing) routines.

The next step was adding a larger-range search: swapping two vertices' positions in 10% of the iterations, so that 90% of the time we apply the short-range transition. How do you think it went? Well, just poorly; the average number of intersections grew to `22.89`. This, however, wasn't unexpected. If you think about it, a complete graph is completely symmetrical, so that swapping two vertices is totally useless! Even worse, it was detrimental because we were wasting 10% of the iterations, hence the poorer result.

Nevertheless, this transition can be useful for other types of graphs that aren't symmetrical, so we'll leave it in. (While we are using complete graphs for our examples, the algorithm can and will be applied to any graph. We'll see in the next section some examples where swapping vertices becomes crucial to getting a good result.)

Yet, we still need to do something different to improve our algorithm. What about choosing a single vertex and moving it randomly anywhere in the drawing area?

We applied this transition 10% of the time, and the average crossing number went down to 19.17, meaning that the algorithm was almost always finding the best solution. Speaking of which, figure 17.14 compares two solutions for the embedding of K_8. The one on the left was found by the random sampling algorithm provided in chapter 16, and the other one is the result of the simulated annealing-based method.

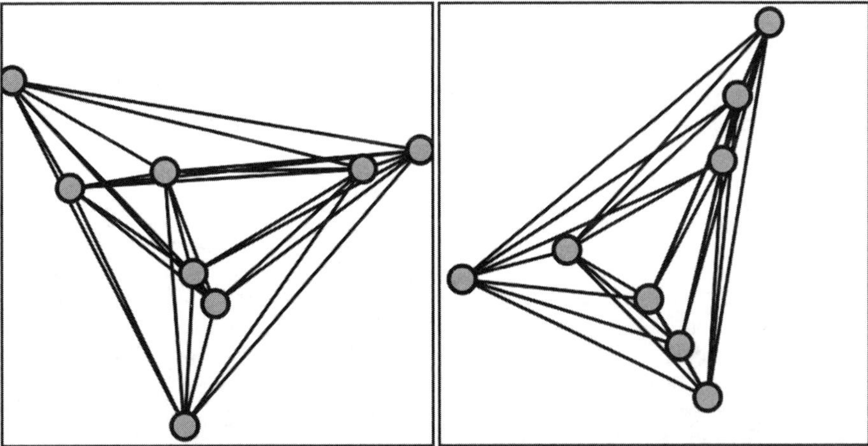

Figure 17.14 Two embeddings of complete graph K_8. On the left, one was computed by the random sampling algorithm; on the right is the result of simulated annealing. Both algorithms were run for 500 iterations: random sampling could only get as low as 27 intersections, but simulated annealing produced an optimal embedding with 19 crossing points.

It goes without saying that there could be a lot more work to do to improve the algorithm by fine-tuning the parameters and perhaps coming up with better operators to tweak the solutions.

Last but not least, the algorithm should be tried and optimized on a diverse set of graphs to be sure to avoid overfitting it to complete graphs. (Alternatively, when faced with a specific problem, you can tune parameters on small instances of the graphs you expect to see, and once ready, apply the tuned version to your real instances.)

From what we could see, scaling up to K_{10} (figure 17.15), for instance, the configuration we used seems to work well with larger complete graphs.

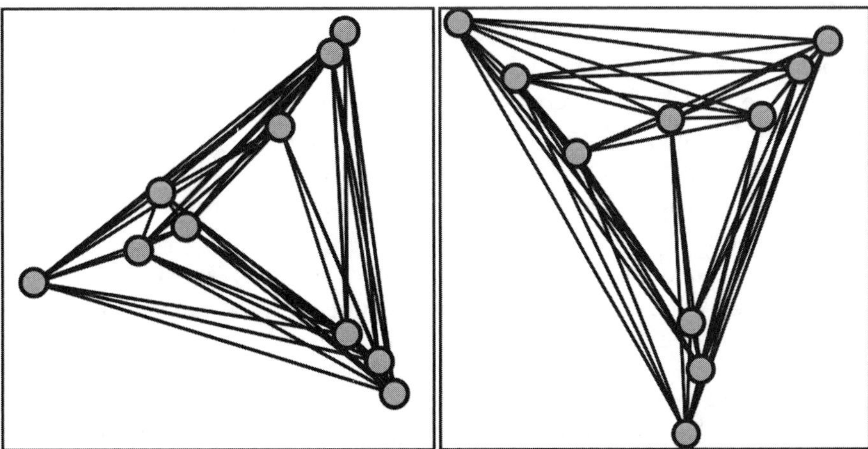

Figure 17.15 Two embeddings of complete graph K_{10}. Simulated annealing (right) produced an optimal embedding with 62 intersections, while the one output by random sampling has 81 intersections.

17.3.2 Force-directed drawing

In section 16.5 we described a class of graph drawing algorithms called force-directed drawing that use a physics-based approach to compute aesthetically-pleasing embeddings of graphs. Figure 17.16 reminds us why a nice embedding is important when graphs need to be visualized.

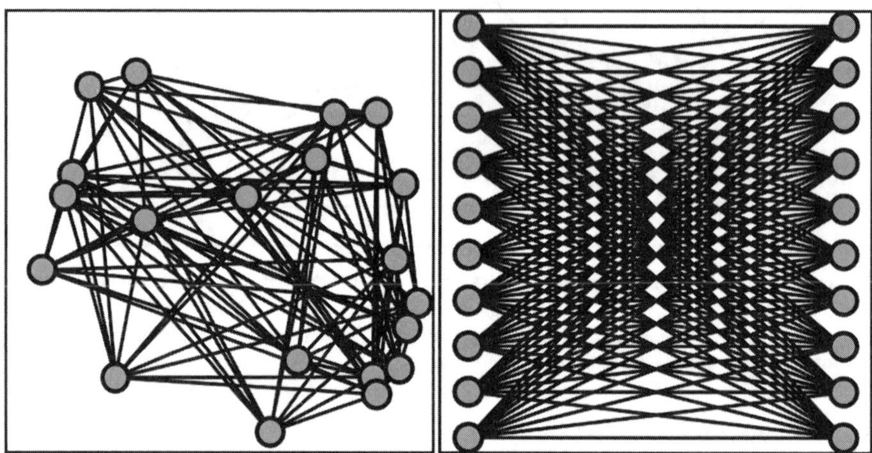

Figure 17.16 A nice embedding can make the difference in understanding a graph: complete bipartite graphs $K_{10,10}$ is drawn randomly (left) and symmetrically (right). Which one better shows the structure of this graph?

The spring embedder model for drawing undirected graphs was first introduced[15] by Peter Eades in the late 1980s, then refined[16] by Kamada and Kawai, who introduced the idea of optimal edge length and sequential vertex update (by moving only one vertex at each step).

The algorithm is evolved into a state of minimum energy by using gradient-descent. Often, though, by using a deterministic learning technique like gradient descent, we are bound to remain stuck in local minima, reaching an equilibrium for the system, but not the state with the minimum possible energy.

It's no surprise that simulated annealing can help in this case as well. Davidson and Harel first used this technique[17] to converge to optimal embeddings while staying out of local pitfalls.

The problem with using standard simulated annealing is that random search makes convergence too slow. To work around this limitation, several authors suggested using

---

[15]P. Eades. "A Heuristic for Graph Drawing." *Congressus Numerantium*, 42:149-160, 1984.

[16]T. Kamada and S. Kawai. "An algorithm for drawing general undirected graphs." *Information Processing Letters*, 31, 1989.

[17]Ron Davidson and David Harel. "Drawing graphs nicely using simulated annealing." *ACM Transactions on Graphics,* 15(4):301–331, 1996.

hybrid solutions that leverage the strengths of both approaches. GEM[18] algorithm stands out among them for its innovative approach and impressive results.

GEM doesn't use simulated annealing, but it borrows the concept of temperature from it. There is no cooling cycle; rather the temperature (which is still expressing the degree of "chaos" in the system) is used to control the range of movement for vertices on update, is computed for each vertex after an update, and is scaled down to smooth vertices' oscillation.

Since GEM algorithm is not directly appliable as an instance of simulated annealing, we'll stick with the algorithm developed by Davidson and Harel, which produces results of comparable quality.

As we mentioned in the previous chapters, the first step with graph drawing algorithms is stating the criteria that will be used to judge the quality of an embedding; the crossing number is not the only key to drawing graphs nicely. Davidson and Harel's approach uses five criteria:

- Distributing nodes evenly to spread the vertices uniformly in the canvas
- Keeping vertices away from borders
- Making edge-lengths uniform
- Minimizing edge-crossings
- Avoiding vertex-edges overlap by keeping vertices from coming too close to edges

We must also clarify that the algorithm assumes the edges will be drawn as straight-line segments. Now, let's see how these five criteria translate to formulas by writing five components of the cost function.

For the first component, the algorithm uses a formula derived from electric potential energy; given two vertices `v_i` and `v_j`, we compute

$$\frac{\lambda_1}{d_{ij}^2}$$

where `d_ij` is the distance between the two vertices, and λ_1 is a parameter we pass to the algorithm to control the weight of this component, a normalizing factor that defines the relative importance of this criterion compared to the others. This term behaves like a repulsive force, so higher values push the algorithm to prefer embeddings with larger distances between the vertices.

To keep vertices away from borders, we add another component. For each vertex `v_i` we compute

$$\lambda_2\left(\frac{1}{r_i^2} + \frac{1}{l_i^2} + \frac{1}{t_i^2} + \frac{1}{b_i^2}\right)$$

[18]Frick, Arne, Andreas Ludwig, and Heiko Mehldau. "A fast adaptive layout algorithm for undirected graphs (extended abstract and system demonstration)." International Symposium on Graph Drawing. Springer, Berlin, Heidelberg, 1994.

Here the values r_i, l_i, t_i, and b_i, are the distances between v_i and the margins of the rectangular canvas where the graph is embedded; λ_2 is another normalization factor, to weight this term. Higher values of λ_2 will cause embeddings with vertices close to the borders to be penalized more.

Now let's talk about edges. For each edge $e_k = u \rightarrow v$, we compute

$$\lambda_3 d_k^2$$

where d_k = `distance(u,v)` is the length of the edge and λ_3 is the usual normalization parameter. This behaves like an attractive force, so larger values for λ_3 favor smaller distances between adjacent vertices.

For edge intersections, we can just count them and multiply the numbers of intersections by a normalization factor λ_4.

Finally, to keep vertices away from edges (if you remember, this was one of the key criteria we gave in chapter 16 to validate embeddings) we can add this term for each vertex-edge pair:

$$\frac{\lambda_5}{{g_{kl}}^2}$$

where g_{kl} = `distance(e_k,v_l)` and λ_5 is another normalization factor.

This term (another repulsive force) is quite expensive to compute (the edge-vertex distance is computationally heavy, as we saw in chapter 15), and even in the original paper is not used in the default settings of the algorithm. We'll leave it out for now, while encouraging the reader to implement it as an exercise and then experiment with it on the examples we will show.

Listing 17.4 shows an implementation of the full cost function (with all five components), although the examples shown were run without the edge-vertex distance term.

As the next step, we would need the methods to compute transitions to new solutions; luckily, though, we can reuse the same methods we defined in the last section. After all, the problem space is the same; the only thing that we need to change is the cost function because we are changing our criteria to decide what a good embedding is.

Listing 17.4 Cost function for Davidson and Harel's algorithm

```
function cost(P, w, h, lambda1, lambda2, lambda3, lambda4, lambda5)
  total ← 0
  for v in P.vertices do
    total ← total + lambda2 * ((1/x²) + (1/y²) + (1/(w-x)²) + (1/(h-y)²))
    for u in P.vertices-{v} do
```

Method `cost` takes the current solution, `P` (a graph embedding, and also a point in the problem space), width (`w`) and height (`h`) of the canvas, and the normalizing factors for the components.

Cycles through the vertices in the graph.

Adds the second component of the objective function, corresponding to the repulsive force between vertices and the canvas' borders

Cycles through all vertices except `v`

```
      total ← total + lambda1 / distance(u, v)^2
  for e=(u,v) in P.edges do
    total ← total + lambda3 * distance(u, v)^2
    for z in P.vertices-{u,v} do
      total ← total + lambda5 / distance(e, z)^2
  total ← total + lambda4 * P.intersections()
  return total
```

- Adds the first component of the cost function, the repulsive force between vertices
- Cycles through edges, for each edge e between vertices u and v …
- Adds the third component, the attractive force between adjacent vertices
- Cycles through all vertices except the edge's endpoints
- Adds the fifth component, the repulsive force between edges and vertices (except for each edge's endpoints, of course)
- At last, adds the fourth component, proportional to the number of edge intersections in the embedding

The algorithm in the paper was only using the vertex local update heuristic, but not with a constant range, rather making the neighborhood in which a vertex can be moved smaller with the progressing of the algorithm.

You can also find the working code implemented for the JsGraphs library on GitHub.[19]

Speaking of good embeddings, in this case it makes little sense to check the quality of the results by looking at the average numbers over many repetitions: we want graphs to be drawn nicely, and there is no magic formula to measure "niceness." The only way to judge the results is by presenting them to the human eye.

Figure 17.17 is, I think, the perfect summary to explain what we have been building in these last couple of sections. We are trying to come up with a nice embedding for the square grid graph with side 4, a graph with 16 vertices arranged like a square mesh.

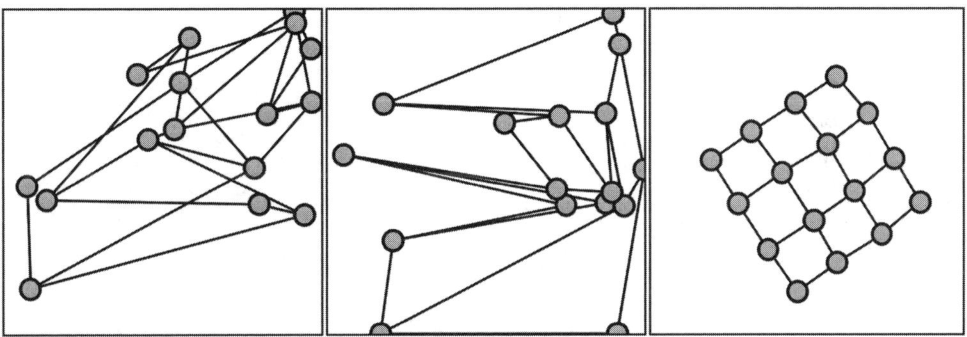

Figure 17.17 The square mesh graph with 16 vertices embedded by random sampling (left), minimum crossing simulated annealing (center), and Davidson and Harel's algorithm (right)

Random sampling struggles to even find an embedding without intersections, a goal that is reached by the algorithm presented in section 17.3.1, which, however, doesn't do a particularly good job of making the structure of the graph clear to us.

The drawing on the right, instead, looks almost perfectly symmetrical. Would you have been able to understand the shape of this graph from the other two embeddings?

[19] See http://mng.bz/JD1a.

For the record, this embedding was obtained by using the values summarized in table 17.4.

Table 17.4 Parameter values for Davidson and Harel's drawing algorithm, used to draw the square grid in figure 17.17

Parameter	Meaning	Value
T_0	Initial temperature	1000
k	(pseudo) Boltzmann constant	1e+8
α	Temperature decay	0.95
Max Steps		10000
λ_1	Distance to border	10
λ_2	Distance between vertices	0.01
λ_3	Edge length	2e-8
λ_4	Edge intersections	100

Figure 17.18 shows a couple more examples, with a larger grid and a different kind of graph, the triangular grid. They both look pretty nicely drawn, after some parameter tuning.

Before getting too excited and assuming this is the perfect algorithm for all graphs, we obviously need to try it on other kinds of graphs.

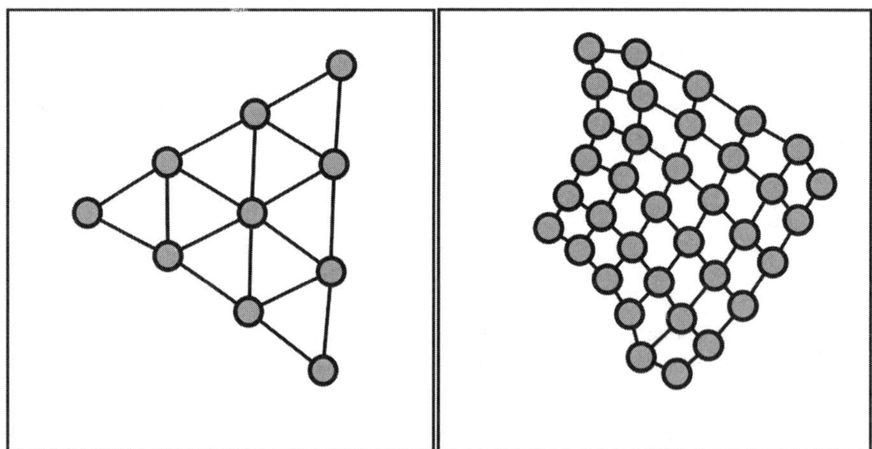

Figure 17.18 The triangular graph with 4 vertices per side and the square mesh graph with 36 vertices embedded by Davidson and Harel's algorithm.

Figure 17.19 shows the results for K_5 and K_7. For both graphs, the embedding found has the minimum possible number of intersections, and vertices look well-spread but, as you can see, these embeddings are not perfect, because some vertices are too close to non-adjacent edges, and thus some edges overlap.

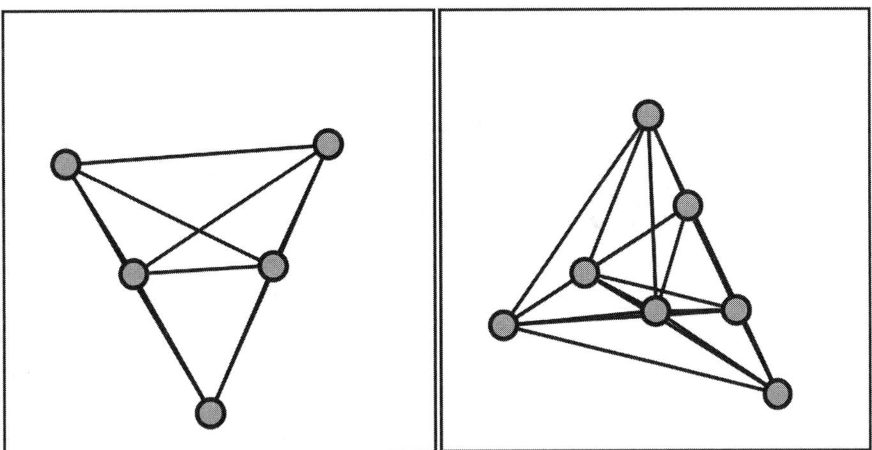

Figure 17.19 Complete graphs K_5 and K_7 embedded by Davidson and Harel's algorithm. Here we could use that fifth component of the cost function keeping vertices away from edges.

These situations can be corrected by adding the fifth component of the cost function, the one discouraging short distances between vertices and edges.

So, to close this chapter, here is a bit of homework for you: extend the cost function and find better embeddings for these graphs.

Summary

- Simulated annealing is a stochastic alternative to gradient descent that uses concepts from physics to provide a dynamic technique, focusing on large-range search in the initial phases, and fine-tuning towards the end.
- Pros: it should be preferred when the domain of the cost function is discrete, the cost function is not differentiable or step-shaped, and there are many local minima.
- Cons: it should be avoided when local minima are in narrow "valleys," because it becomes unlikely that the algorithm will find them.
- Compared to gradient descent, which takes the steepest path to minima, simulated annealing will need many more iterations to get to the same point.
- Simulated annealing can't be guaranteed to return the optimal solution. If suboptimal solutions are not admissible, then a different algorithm should be used.
- Finding the right configuration requires time and needs to be done for each problem.
- The traveling salesman problem is a difficult problem to solve, but it is ubiquitous in logistics, planning, and electronics (for circuit boards).

18 Genetic algorithms: Biologically inspired, fast-converging optimization

This chapter covers

- Introducing the genetic algorithm
- Exploring whether genetic algorithms are better than simulated annealing
- Solving the "Packing to Mars" problem with genetic algorithms
- Solving TSP and assigning deliveries to trucks with genetic algorithms
- Creating a genetic algorithm to solve minimum vertex cover
- Discussing applications of genetic algorithms

While *gradient descent* and *simulated annealing* are great optimization techniques, they both have shortcomings: the former is fast but has a tendency to get stuck in local minima and needs the cost function to be differentiable, while the latter can be quite slow in converging.

In this chapter we are going to learn about the *genetic algorithm*, yet another optimization technique that uses an approach inspired by nature to overcome both issues, providing more resilience to local minima by evolving a pool of solutions and at the same time speeding up convergence.

We will apply this technique to a few hard problems that can't be solved efficiently with deterministic algorithms. We'll start by using 0–1 knapsack, which we discovered in chapter 1, to explain the theory behind genetic algorithms. Then we'll briefly discuss a genetic algorithm for *TSP*,[1] and show how (and why) it converges faster than simulated annealing; finally, we will also introduce two new problems:

- *Vertex cover*, which is useful in many areas, from network security to bioinformatics
- *Maximum flow*, fundamental to network connectivity, compiler optimization, and much more

18.1 Genetic algorithms

When it comes to optimization algorithms, the gist is that we are trying to replace a brute-force search over the whole problem space with a local search that filters out as many points in the problem space as possible: finding the same result by searching a much smaller domain.

Optimization algorithms explore the neighborhood of current solutions, which are points in the search space, and do this either deterministically or randomly, trying to spot areas of interest, promising regions where we expect to find better solutions than what the search has previously found.

The way we perform this filtering, the range of the search and how "local" it actually is, if we move randomly or in a deterministic way: these are the key factors that characterize the different techniques we have described in chapters 16 and 17.

In the previous chapter we discovered simulated annealing and discussed how it converges to near-optimal solutions by allowing transitions uphill, while gradient descent only moves downhill, toward better solutions, and as such it gets easily stuck in local minima. Simulated annealing can therefore work better than gradient descent when the cost function has many local (sub-)minima.

While powerful, simulated annealing can't be perfect, and indeed we have also seen that there are two main drawbacks to consider:

- The algorithm is slow to converge. While gradient descent, which is deterministic, takes the fastest route downhill,[2] simulated annealing (which instead is stochastic) randomly wanders across the cost function's landscape, and as such it might require many attempts before finding the right direction.

[1] We discussed the travelling salesman problem at length in section 17.2.

[2] Technically, it follows the path of steepest descent, with a *locally-optimal*, greedy choice at each step. These choices usually aren't *globally optimal*, and hence gradient descent is not guaranteed to reach global optimum, unless the cost function has a particular, convex shape with a single minimum point.

- With certain shapes for the cost functions, where local/global minima are in narrow valleys, the probability that simulated annealing randomly "walks" into those valleys can be low, so low that it can fail to reach a near-optimal solution altogether.

In section 17.1 we analyzed in some depth why simulated annealing works well, and how it creates this sort of dynamic filtering, indirectly restricting (based on their cost) the domain points that can be reached at a given stage. If you remember, initially the algorithm jumps from point to point, as likely to go uphill as downhill, exploring the landscape at large.

We have also seen how it can happen that the optimization finds a near-optimal solution in the early stages, and then moves away from it, because in the initial phase it's likely to accept transitions uphill. The problem is that simulated annealing has no memory, it doesn't keep track of the past solutions, and—especially if we allow long-range transitions—there is a concrete risk that the algorithm will never get back to a solution that was as good.

An even more probable risk is that the algorithm does find the valley containing global minimum at some early-ish stage, not necessarily getting any closer to the end of the valley (perhaps landing just somewhere close to the entrance of the valley), and then moves away and never manages to enter it again.

Figure 18.1 illustrates these situations. In section 17.1 we also discussed how simulated annealing with restart can keep track of past solutions and—when stuck—randomly restart from one of these past positions, to check if a solution better than the current best is found.

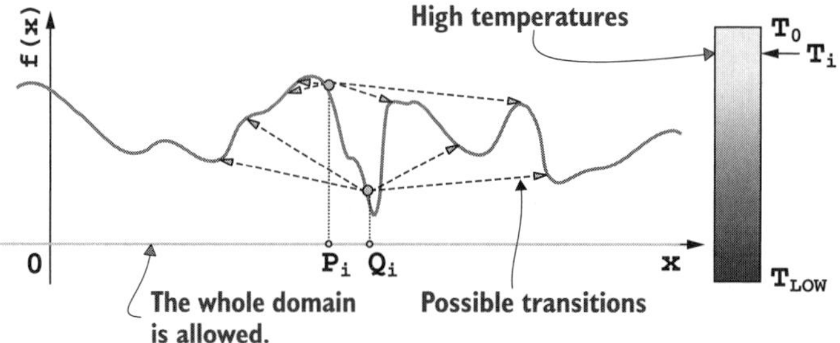
f(x)
High temperatures
T0
Ti
0
Pi Qi
x
TLOW
The whole domain is allowed.
Possible transitions

Figure 18.1 An example of a scenario where simulated annealing would find a promising (P_i), or even good (Q_i) solution in an early stage (as suggested by the temperature of the system, T_i, still close to T_0): since all transitions, even uphill, are likely accepted when the temperature is high, the algorithm might move away from the sweet spot in the cost function landscape, and possibly never find its way back.

This workaround can help somewhat with the former situation, where we get to a great solution early, but it's unlikely to improve the latter (just finding a promising position at the entrance of a valley), because we only save at most a small number of the best previously found solutions. As such, even if the optimization had managed to find the beginning of a path to global minimum, we would forget about it, unless we were lucky enough to land close to the bottom of the valley.

18.1.1 Inspired by nature

Simulated annealing was inspired by metallurgy, mimicking its cooling process to drive a system from chaotic to ordered behavior. Nature, as a matter of fact, has often been a great source of inspiration for mathematics and computer science. Just think about neural networks, probably the most pervasive of these examples, at the time of writing.

For biological processes, such as neural networks, it's not hard to imagine why. They have been adapted and perfected over millions of years, and since their efficiency is tightly connected to organisms' survival, we can find clever and efficient solutions everywhere in nature.

Genetic algorithms are yet another example of biologically inspired algorithms and, even more, they are based on this very principle of evolution in response to stimuli from the environment.

As shown in figure 18.2, a genetic algorithm is an optimization algorithm that maintains a pool of solutions at each iteration. Compared to simulated annealing, this allows maintaining a larger degree of diversity, probing different areas of the cost function's landscape at the same time.

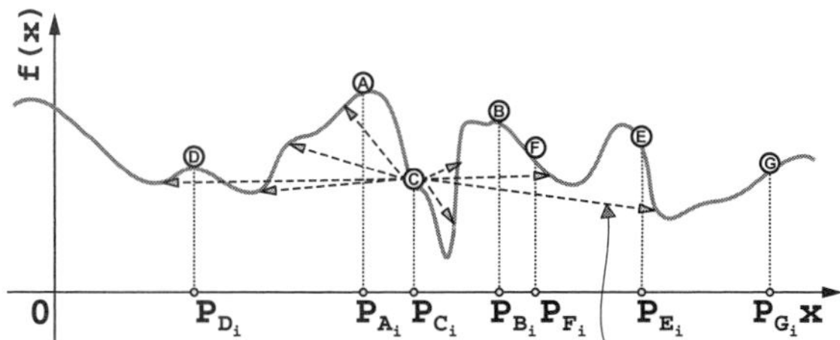
f(x)
A
B
C
D
E
F
G
0
P_{D_i}
P_{A_i} P_{C_i}
P_{B_i} P_{F_i}
P_{E_i}
P_{G_i} x
The whole domain is allowed at all times (unless thresholding is used).
Possible transitions

Figure 18.2 An example of how genetic algorithms would tackle the scenario in figure 18.1. At a generic iteration (in the figure, we assume we are at the i-th iteration), which could indifferently be toward the beginning or the end of the simulation, the algorithm maintains a pool of possible solutions. At the next iteration, the pool (as a whole) will transition to a new set of candidate solutions (based on the current ones—we'll see how later in this section). Usually the new solutions can be anywhere in the domain.

One thing that can't be shown in this "cost function" kind of graphic is that genetic algorithms also evolve the solutions by recombining them: this allows us to take the strengths of different solutions and merge them into a better one. Take, for instance, the TSP problem, which we described in section 17.2 (we'll also talk about it again in the next section). Imagine that we have two poor solutions, each having the best possible sequence for a different half of the vertices, but each with terrible solutions for the remaining half. By combining these two solutions in the right[3] way, we can take the good halves from each and get a great candidate solution, possibly (if you are lucky!) even the best possible.

This idea of combining solutions is something that we don't find either in gradient descent (obviously!) or in simulated annealing, where a single solution is kept and "studied" at any time.

We'll see that this new idea is embodied in a new operator, the *crossover operator*, that derives from the biological analogy used for this technique. But to avoid getting ahead of ourselves, we still need to reveal what inspired genetic algorithms; in doing so, we will also make clear where the name comes from.

A genetic algorithm is an optimization meta-heuristic based on the principles of genetics and natural selection. We mentioned that this optimization technique maintains a pool of solutions; what we hadn't said is that these solutions will mimic a population that has evolved through several generations—each organism in the population is defined by a chromosome (or, sometimes, a pair of chromosomes), that encodes a single solution to the problem that's optimized.

Biologically inspired algorithms

Most living organisms on this planet are made up of cells,[4] each of which carries the same[5] genetic material in a set of chromosomes (usually more than one, for advanced organisms such as animals or plants). Each chromosome is a *DNA* (*deoxyribonucleic acid*) molecule that can be broken down into a sequence of nucleotides, each of which is, in turn, a sequence of *nitrogen-containing nucleobases* encoding information. The information contained in each cell's DNA is used by cells to drive their behavior and synthesize proteins. Figure 18.3 succinctly illustrate these concepts.

So, in a nutshell, chromosomes encode information determining an organism's behavior (*genetics*), and in turn how well an organism can adapt to its environment, survive, and generate offspring (*natural selection*).

Computer scientist John Holland, inspired by this mechanism, in the early 1970s devised[6] a way to use these two principles to evolve artificial systems. One of his students, David Goldberg (considered for a long time the expert of reference on this topic), popularized this approach through his research and his book at the end of the 1980s.[7]

---

[3] We'll talk about this in detail in section 18.2.

[4] With the notable exception of viruses, which are just DNA or RNA encapsulated in a protein coat.

[5] Approximately the same, as there can be small local variations, for various reasons including copy errors.

[6] Holland's book was originally published in 1975. You can currently find the 1992 MIT press edition: *Adaptation in natural and artificial systems: an introductory analysis with applications to biology, control, and artificial intelligence*, MIT Press, 1992.

[7] *Genetic Algorithms in Search, Optimization, and Machine Learning*, Addison-Wesley Professional, 1988.

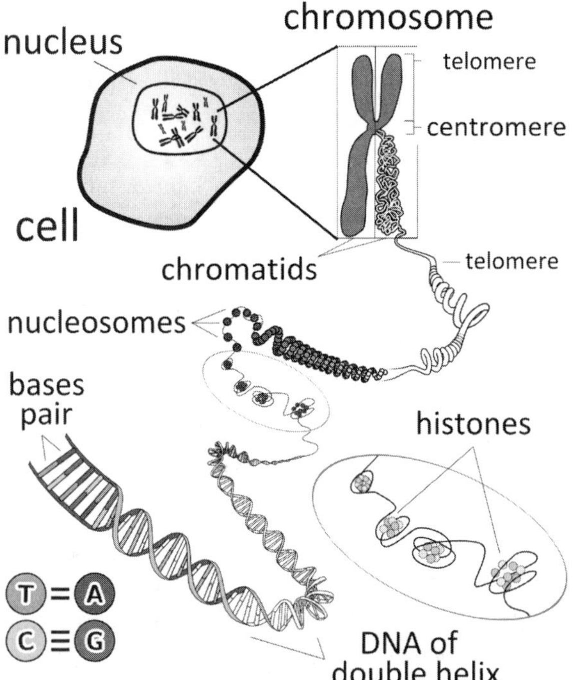
chromosome
nucleus
telomere
centromere
cell
chromatids
telomere
nucleosomes
bases
pair
histones
T = A
C ≡ G
DNA of
double helix

Figure 18.3 From cells to DNA: A cell's genome is contained in its nucleus, inside structures called chromosomes, whose telomeres, when unraveled, reveal double helixes of DNA, a sequence made of just four nucleobases (hence we can consider DNA a base-4 encoding). Source: https://commons.wikimedia.org/w/index.php?curid=10856406, author: KES47.

The core idea, shown in figure 18.4 in the next section, is to encode a solution as a chromosome and assign each chromosome to an organism. Then, naturally, it follows that based on how good a solution is, we derive how fit the corresponding organism is for its environment. Fitness, in turn, is a proxy for the chances of an organism to reproduce and pass its genetic material to the next generation through its offspring. As in nature, the alpha-individuals of a population, the stronger (or faster, or smarter) ones, tend to have a higher chance of surviving longer and finding a mate.

But perhaps the best way to understand genetic algorithms is by seeing them in action. To that extent, and to keep things concrete, while we describe all the building blocks of this meta-algorithm, we'll develop an example along the way to help readers visualize how each component works. Do you remember the 0–1 knapsack problem? We are going all the way back to chapter 1, when we introduced this problem to model our "packing to Mars" situation. Back then, we mentioned there is a pseudo-polynomial dynamic algorithm that can provide the absolute best solution, but it can be too slow when the capacity of the knapsack is large. Branch-and-bound approximated algorithms exist that can compute near-optimal solutions (with some guarantees on the upper bound and in reasonable time), although the efficient ones are usually quite complex.[8]

To get a fast, clear, simple optimization algorithm, we will implement a genetic algorithm that can find approximated, near-optimal solutions to the knapsack problem.

Before we delve into the details of genetic algorithms, I suppose you could use a refresher. Let's quickly review the problem definition, and the instance we were using.

> **NOTE** In the generic 0–1 knapsack problem, we have a container with a limited capacity `M`, and a set of goods, each characterized by a weight (or any other measure of capacity) `w`, and a value `v`. If we add an item to our knapsack (or any generic container we decide to use!) it must be all of it; we can't add fractions of items. The sum of the weights of all available items exceeds the capacity of the knapsack, so we need to choose a subset of items, and the goal, therefore, is to choose the particular subset that maximizes the value of the goods carried.

In section 1.4.1, we tackle a more concrete problem: given the list of goods shown (for your convenience) in table 18.1, we'd like to fill a crate that can carry at most 1 ton, not with as much food as possible, but with the largest total calorie count possible.

As such, we could easily check that wheat flour, rice, and tomatoes could sum up to the maximum carriable weight, but they wouldn't give the maximum number of calories.

In chapter 1, we briefly described the key consideration that is used by the branch-and-bound heuristics to approximate this problem. It computes the value by weight (in this case, calories by weight) for each of the goods, and prefers food with higher ratios; although that's used as a starting point by the Martello-Toth algorithm, just choosing products in descending order of per-kilo values won't give us the best possible solution.

And, in fact, the dynamic programming algorithm that exactly solves the 0–1 knapsack problem won't even compute this ratio; we will not use it here either, so it's not even shown in table 18.1.

Table 18.1 A recap of the available goods for the mission to Mars, with their weight and calories

Food	Weight (kgs)	Total calories
Potatoes	800	1,502,000
Wheat Flour	400	1,444,000
Rice	300	1,122,000

[8] For example, the Martello-Toth algorithm which is one of the state-of-the-art solutions: Martello, Silvano, and Paolo Toth. "A bound and bound algorithm for the zero-one multiple knapsack problem." *Discrete Applied Mathematics* 3.4 (1981): 275-288.

Table 18.1 A recap of the available goods for the mission to Mars, with their weight and calories

Food	Weight (kgs)	Total calories
Beans (can)	300	690,000
Tomatoes (can)	300	237,000
Strawberry jam	50	130,000
Peanut butter	20	117,800

If you'd like to have a closer look at the problem, please feel free to skim through section 1.4; let's now move on to discussing the main components of genetic algorithms (*GA*).

To completely define an optimization algorithm, we need to specify the following components:

- *How to encode a solution*—Chromosomes, for GA
- *Transitional operators*—Crossover and mutations
- *A way to measure cost*—Fitness function
- *How system evolves*—Generations and natural selection

18.1.2 Chromosomes

As we mentioned, chromosomes encode a solution to the problem we need to solve. In the original work by Holland, chromosomes were only supposed to be strings of bits, sequences of zeros and ones. Not all problems can be encoded with a binary string (we'll see an example in section 18.2 with TSP), and so a more generic version was derived later, allowing *genes* (each of the values in a chromosome) to be continuous, real values.

Conceptually, those versions can be considered equivalent, but whenever we don't use binary strings for the chromosomes, we will likely require restrictions on the possible values they can store: the operators acting on organisms will have to be adjusted in order to check and maintain these constraints.

Luckily for us, the 0–1 knapsack is the perfect example to discuss the original genetic algorithm, because a solution to this problem can be encoded exactly as a binary string. For each item, a zero means we leave it on Earth, while a 1 means we add it to the crate going to Mars.

Figure 18.4 shows a bit-string representation for a chromosome that can be used in our example. Two different solutions (or *phenotypes*, in biological terms) can be represented by two chromosomes (or *genotypes*): their difference boils down to the difference between the two bit-strings.

It's worth noting that for this example we have a 1:1 mapping between genotype and phenotype: a solution (the phenotype) is uniquely identified by its representation (the genotype) and so two organisms with the same genotype will translate to the same solution and in turn to the same fitness value (as we'll discuss in a few sections).

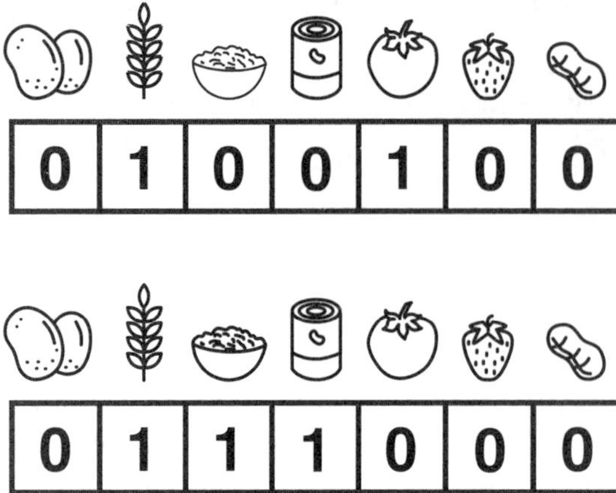
0 1 0 0 1 0 0
0 1 1 1 0 0 0

Figure 18.4 Examples of encoding chromosomes for the knapsack problem (the specific instance described in section 1.4). Two figures are shown: the differences in the genotypes (the two strings) are reflected in the phenotypes (the goods taken to Mars: wheat flour and tomatoes versus wheat flour, rice, and beans). The latter chromosome encodes the best solution for the instance of the problem summed up in table 18.1.

In the context of our 0–1 knapsack example, if two organisms have the same genotype, both solutions will add the same set of goods to the crate to Mars.

The equivalence between genotype and phenotype is, however, not observed in nature, where the difference between them is clear, because the genome only encodes developmental rules, not precise outcomes, and an organism is also determined by its interaction with the environment.[9]

Likewise, in some simulated problems fitness is not always fully determined by genotype. One of the first examples of an application of genetic algorithms I studied was the work[10] of Floreano and Mondada at EPFL, where they evolved the neural networks of small two-wheel robots, simulating the evolution of gatherers, and later of predator and prey populations (in a sort of hide and seek game).

In this experiment, the genotype was the set of weights for a robot's neural network, which, incidentally, also completely identify the phenotype. Each organism's fitness, though, was later determined by its interaction with the environment and with other robots.

If we were to extend their original work by allowing online learning for the robots (today, it wouldn't be hard to imagine applying stochastic or mini-batch backpropagation to evolve the NN's weights based on the input from the environment), then neither would the phenotype be completely determined by the genotype, at least not after the first update, because after that, the way weights change is heavily influenced by the interaction of the robot with the environment.

With respect to figure 18.4, we also need to make one more thing clear: the actual representation of chromosomes depends on the actual, specific problem we are

[9] Consider, for example, a couple of twins, who share their DNA, but each of them is a different and unique being.

[10] For example, check out "Evolutionary neurocontrollers for autonomous mobile robots," N*eural Networks* Volume 11, Issues 7–8, October–November 1998, pages 1461-1478

solving. In this case, it depends on the specific instance of the 0–1 knapsack (although a generic representation for all 0–1 knapsacks can and should be designed).

If we want to design code for the genetic algorithm main method, instead, we should be concerned with designing organisms, for example, modeling them with a class that will be provided the actual chromosome (and as we'll see, the methods doing modifications on them) whether at runtime through composition, as arguments (using the strategy design pattern), or at compile time through inheritance (the template design pattern).

> **NOTE** The genetic algorithm is a meta-algorithm, a template that is completed by the code specific to each problem tackled. As such, there is part of the code that is generic—the structural code defining the optimization technique—and another part that is specific to the problem. At this point, while describing the components of genetic algorithms, we'll provide the pseudocode for the template, and since we are using the knapsack problem as an example, we'll also provide some pseudocode to implement examples of the specific methods for the 0–1 knapsack, with these snippets clearly marked.

Listing 18.1 shows a possible implementation of the `Individual` class, modeling each individual organism in the population evolved.

Listing 18.1 Class Individual

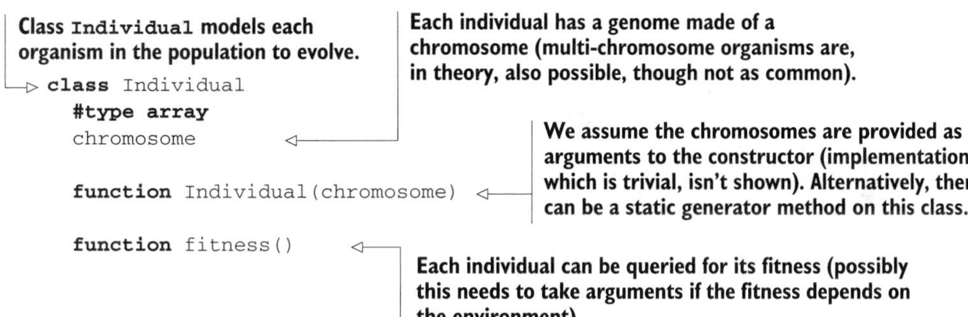
Class Individual models each organism in the population to evolve.
class Individual
#type array
chromosome
Each individual has a genome made of a chromosome (multi-chromosome organisms are, in theory, also possible, though not as common).
function Individual(chromosome)
We assume the chromosomes are provided as arguments to the constructor (implementation, which is trivial, isn't shown). Alternatively, there can be a static generator method on this class.
function fitness()
Each individual can be queried for its fitness (possibly this needs to take arguments if the fitness depends on the environment).

18.1.3 Population

The most apparent difference between simulated annealing and genetic algorithms is that instead of tuning a single solution, genetic algorithms will evolve a population of individuals.

Listing 18.2 shows a possible implementation for a method that initializes the population that will be used for the genetic algorithm. This is also a templated method, since it will have to be provided with the actual code for initializing the single chromosomes (which, again, will depend on the actual problem tackled).

Listing 18.2 Method initPopulation

```
function initPopulation(size, chromosomeInitializer)
  population ← []
  for i in {1,…,size} do
    population.add(new Individual(chromosomeInitializer()))
  return population
```

Method `initPopulation` takes the size of the population to create (assumed, or checked, to be positive) and a function to initialize individual chromosomes. It returns the newly created population.

Init `population` as an empty list

Adds as many new individuals as necessary, each with a newly created genome

There are a few different strategies that can be used for initialization. You can rely on random initialization to provide diversity in your initial population. This is the original and still most common approach, but in certain situations you might also add constraints on the chromosomes (to avoid invalid solutions) or even decide to provide an initial population (that can, for instance, be the output of a different algorithm or of a previous iteration).

For a generic instance of the 0–1 knapsack problem, since chromosomes are just bit strings, we are good with a random generator, as shown in listing 18.3.

Listing 18.3 0–1 knapsack: chromosome generation

```
function knapsackChromosomeInitializer(genesNumber)
  chromosome ← []
  for i in {0,…,genesNumber-1} do
    chromosome[i] ← randomBool().toInt()
  return chromosome
```

Method `knapsackChromosomeInitializer` takes the size of the chromosome to create (assumed, or checked, to be positive) and returns a random bit string (or, in this case, a bit array for the sake of simplicity).

Init `chromosome` as an empty list

Generates as many random bits as necessary. Here we used a Java-like pattern, but it's also possible to directly use a method that returns random integers between `0` and `1`.

There is a caveat: not all randomly generated strings are acceptable solutions for a given instance of the knapsack problem. For example, a string with all values set to 1 would certainly mean (for a non-trivial instance) that the weight constraint has been violated. As we'll see next, we can assign a low fitness to solutions that violate this constraint; alternatively, when we generate chromosomes, we can add a check to avoid violating it in the first place.

18.1.4 Fitness

Connected to the definitions of chromosome and organism, there is the notion of *fitness* of an individual. As you can see in listing 18.1, the `Individual` class has a `fitness` method returning a value that measures how well an organism adapts to its environment.

The term *fitness* naturally implies a maximization problem, because higher fitness is usually associated with better performance in an environment. Conversely, for many problems we usually want to express our problems' goals as *cost functions* to be minimized, so we have two choices: either implement the genetic algorithm template in such a way that a lower value for fitness means better performance, or reformulate our cost functions according to the choice we made. For instance, if we need to find the point of highest elevation on a map, we can either implement a maximization algorithm or set the fitness function to `f(P)=-elevation(P)`, for any given point on the map, and stick with our usual minimization strategy (as we saw in chapters 16 and 17 for `gradient descent` and `simulated annealing`).

Consider our example with the 0-1 knapsack problem: the goal is naturally expressed by a value function that we want to maximize, the sum of the nutritional values of the goods added to the crate.

The first chromosome in figure 18.4, for example, is `0100100`, which means we sum the calories of rice and tomatoes, for a total of `1,359,000` calories. What happens when we exceed the weight that the crate can carry, for instance, with the chromosome `1111111`? To spot these edge cases, we need to check the total weight while computing the fitness and assign a special value (for instance, in this case, `0`) to those solutions that violate the constraint on the weight.

An alternative can be making sure that this situation never occurs by carefully checking it in the operators that create and modify individuals (initialization, crossover, and mutations, as we'll see). This solution, however, may have consequences on the optimization process, artificially reducing the plurality of features in the population.

At this point, if the template method that we have implemented for our genetic algorithms tries to maximize the fitness of individuals, we are golden. What if, instead, our implementation strives for lower fitness? For this particular case, we might have an easy solution: we sum the values of the goods discarded, corresponding to zeroes in a chromosome. For any given solution, the lower this sum is, the higher will be the sum of the calories of the goods in the crate. Of course, if we go this way, we have to assign a very high value (even infinity) to the solutions where the weight threshold is exceeded.

18.1.5 Natural selection

We now have the tools to create a single organism, generate a whole population, and check individual fitness. In turn, this allows us to mimic a basic natural process that guides the evolution of populations in the wild: *natural selection.*

In nature, we see it everywhere: the strongest, fastest individuals, the ones that are best at hunting or at hiding, tend to survive longer, and in turn (or in addition to that) they have greater chances of mating and transmitting their genes to the next generation.

The goal of genetic algorithms is to use a similar mechanism to have the population converge toward good solutions. In this analogy, the genes of individuals with high fitness[11] encode features that give them an advantage over the competitors.

In our knapsack example, a good feature could be including food with high calories-per-weight ratio. Solutions including potatoes will be individuals with low fitness, and that therefore will struggle to survive to the next generations. As an example, in the

[11]In the rest of the chapter, we'll talk about "high fitness" as a generic term, decoupling it from the actual implementation. It will mean large values for those problems maximizing a function and small values when the goal of the optimization is to minimize a cost.

predator-prey simulation mentioned in section 18.1.2, the prey that developed a strategy to hide behind objects were more efficient in escaping predators.

Listing 18.4 shows, through some pseudocode, how natural selection (in genetic algorithms) works. This method regulates how a population transitions between the current generation and the next one, taking the old population as input, and returning a new population, randomly created from the original organisms through a set of operators.

Listing 18.4 Natural selection

The first thing to do is to initialize the new population. This can be done by simply creating a new, empty list. A more generic alternative, however, is to allow passing a method for this initialization, which could, for instance, be used to include elitism.

Select two individuals from the old population. The selection method is passed as an argument (equivalently, as for the others, it can be provided through inheritance).

Method `naturalSelection` takes the current population and returns a new population evolved from the input one. The function also needs to be provided the operators that will change the population, either in the arguments list or, for instance, through inheritance.

Add new individuals, one by one, until the new population matches the old one in size.

```
function naturalSelection(
    population, elitism, selectForMating, crossover, mutations)
  newPopulation ← elitism(population)
  while |newPopulation| < |population| do
    p1 ← selectForMating(population)
    p2 ← selectForMating(population)
    newIndividual ← crossover.apply(p1, p2)
    for mutation in mutations do
      mutation.apply(newIndividual)
    newPopulation.add(newIndividual)
  return newPopulation
```

Combines the two organisms using crossover; details of this and the other operators are, as discussed, for the most part specific to the problem, and will be discussed later in this section. In order for this template to work, however, we require that crossovers and mutations abide by a common interface, and that they are implemented as objects providing an `apply` method (we'll also discuss wrappers, to make this easy).

Adds the newly generated individual to the output list

For each possible mutation, apply it to the result of crossover (as we'll see, each mutation is characterized by a probability of happening, so it will be randomly decided if any mutation is applied to organisms).

This natural selection process is applied at each iteration of the algorithm. When the algorithm starts, it's always with a fully formed population outputted by the initialization method (its size is determined at runtime through a method argument, as we have seen). Individuals in the input population are evaluated for their fitness and then go through a process of selection that determines which ones are going to either pass to the next generation unaltered or propagate their genes through mating.

In the genetic algorithm's simplest form, the new population is just initialized as an empty list (line #2), a list which is then *populated* (pun intended) with the new individuals resulting from selection and mating (#3–#6).

For mating, there are, obviously, differences with respect to the biological analogy. First and foremost, in genetic algorithms sexual reproduction between two *asexual* organisms is generally[12] used: moreover, the recombination of genetic material between the two parents doesn't follow any biologically meaningful rules and the actual details of how crossover is performed are for the most part left to the specific problem that is solved.

Finally, we add mutations to the genetic material after crossover, modeling crossover and mutations as separate phases.

Figure 18.5 illustrates the general mechanism with an analogy to the biological process.

We start with an initial population where individuals have a common basis, but also some peculiar characteristics. The diversity and variance in the population largely depends on which stage of the simulated evolution we are in. As we'll see, our aim is having greater diversity at the beginning of the simulation and then have the population converge toward a few homogenous, high-fitness groups.

In our example, our population of ducks shows a few unique features, from the shapes of their beak, to their colors/patterns, to the shape of wings and tails. If you look closely, you should be able to spot them and to figure out how these changes are encoded in their chromosomes.

This is because, as we have discussed, each feature in an individuals' phenotype is determined by a difference in their genotype, a `1` that becomes a `0`, or vice versa (or maybe a few bits that need to flip together, or even, if we move past binary strings, a gene assigned with a different real number).

In order to perform selection, we need to evaluate each duck's fitness. This can be as easy as feeding each chromosome to a function or as complicated as running a simulation for hours (as in the predator-prey setting we described) and seeing which individuals survive longer or perform a real-world task better.

We'll only talk about selection for mating in the next subsection, but one thing is generally true regardless of the details of the selection mechanism chosen: organisms with higher fitness will have greater chances of being chosen to pass their genes to the next generation. This is crucial, maybe the only really crucial part, because without this "meritocracy," no optimization would be performed.

Once we have selected two individuals, we need to recombine their genetic material. We'll also tackle crossover and mutations in their own section, but one thing that we have already mentioned is that these operators, acting on chromosomes, are largely determined by the specific problem that is being solved.

In our example in figure 18.5, our little duckling takes its feathering pattern and color from one parent and its tail shape from the other. Then a further mutation kicks in changing the feathering again from a checkerboard pattern to a polka dot pattern.

[12] It is possible, and it has been attempted, to include the notions of sex-specific chromosomes and sexual subgroups, but, to the best of my knowledge, the possible improvements in the efficiency or effectiveness of the algorithm are in the order of magnitude of optimization. As an example, the dedicated reader can check Zhang, Ming-ming, Shu-guang Zhao, and Xu Wang. "Sexual Reproduction Adaptive Genetic Algorithm Based on Baldwin Effect and Simulation Study [J]." *Journal of System Simulation* 10 (2010).

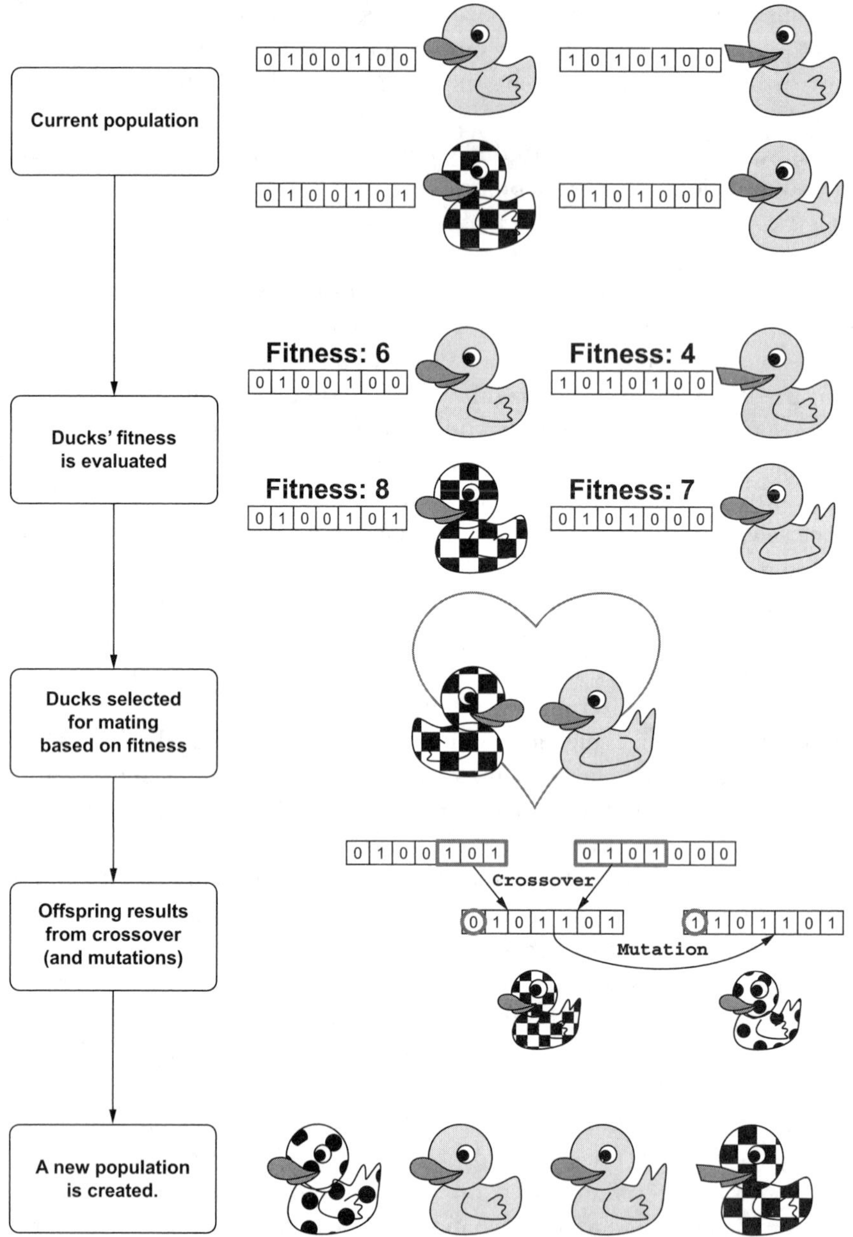
Current population
0 1 0 0 1 0 0
1 0 1 0 1 0 0
0 1 0 0 1 0 1
0 1 0 1 0 0 0
Ducks' fitness is evaluated
Fitness: 6
0 1 0 0 1 0 0
Fitness: 4
1 0 1 0 1 0 0
Fitness: 8
0 1 0 0 1 0 1
Fitness: 7
0 1 0 1 0 0 0
Ducks selected for mating based on fitness
0 1 0 0 1 0 1
0 1 0 1 0 0 0
Crossover
Offspring results from crossover (and mutations)
0 1 0 1 1 0 1
1 1 0 1 1 0 1
Mutation
A new population is created.

Figure 18.5 Natural selection in genetic algorithms, in an analogy with the biological process.

The new population, formed by repeating this process many times, should show a larger presence of those genes/features associated with high-fitness individuals in the initial population.

Now that we have seen how the broad natural selection process works, it's time to dive into the specifics of its steps.

18.1.6 Selecting individuals for mating

Let's start with selection: we'll go back to our knapsack problem example to better explain it.

There are several techniques that can possibly be used for selecting, at each iteration, the individuals that will mate or progress; some of the most successful alternatives are

- Elitism
- Thresholding
- Tournament selection
- Roulette wheel selection

But there are also many other possible techniques used. Considering our restricted list, the first two techniques are filters on the old population, while the remaining two are methods to select organisms for mating.

Elitism and thresholding, illustrated in figure 18.6, are used to decide what organisms can or can't transmit their genomes to the next generation.

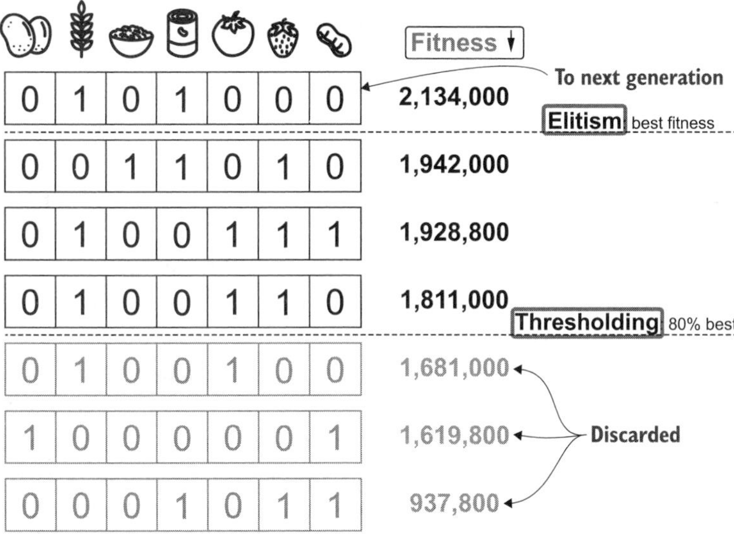
Fitness
0 1 0 1 0 0 0
2,134,000
To next generation
Elitism
best fitness
0 0 1 1 0 1 0
1,942,000
0 1 0 0 1 1 1
1,928,800
0 1 0 0 1 1 0
1,811,000
Thresholding
80% best
0 1 0 0 1 0 0
1,681,000
1 0 0 0 0 0 1
1,619,800
Discarded
0 0 0 1 0 1 1
937,800

Figure 18.6 Elitism and thresholding illustrated with an example (0-1 knapsack problem). Elitism takes the best individual(s) (one or a few of the highest-fitness entries) and directly brings them to the next generation without mating or mutations. Thresholding takes care of the opposite problem: it's a hard barrier that stops low-fitness individuals from passing their genes to the next generation. It's possible to discard a certain fixed number of individuals, or all individuals below some threshold. For instance, in this example (where we maximize fitness value), all individuals below 80% of the fitness value of the best individual will be discarded and never selected for mating.

Elitism allows the best individuals to pass completely unaltered to the next generation. Whether or not to apply this principle is up to the algorithm designer; as always, it might work better with some problems and worse with others.

Without elitism, all organisms in the current iteration would be replaced in the next one, so that all organisms would "live" exactly one generation; with this workaround, we can instead simulate a longer lifespan for particularly well-fitting individuals—the better their fitness in comparison to the average population's, the longer they will be kept.

In turn, this will also ensure that the genes of the *alpha organisms* will be present, untouched, in the next generation too (although it's not certain they will still be the top-fitness individuals in the next generation).

One notable effect of using elitism is that the fitness of the best element in the population is monotonically improving over generations (that, however, might not be true for the average fitness).

Thresholding has the opposite goal: it will prevent the lowest-fitness organisms from transmitting their genes to the next generations, which in turn reduces the probability that the algorithm explores less-promising areas of the fitness function's landscape.

The way it works is simple. We set a threshold for the fitness of the individuals that are allowed to be selected for mating and ignore the ones outside the requirements. We can discard a fixed number of organisms, such as the five individuals with the worst fitness value, or discard a variable number of individuals based on their fitness value.

In the latter scenario, the threshold on the fitness value is usually set dynamically (changing each generation) and based on the fitness value of the best individual for that generation. With a static, absolute value (which would require domain knowledge to be set), the risk is that it would be ineffective (resulting in the whole population being filtered in) or even worse, fatal for the simulation when it's too stringent, resulting in all, or almost all, individuals being filtered out in the early stages.

In the example in figure 18.6 we suggested setting the threshold to 80% of the best individual's fitness value.[13] Whether or not thresholding should be applied and what the threshold ratio should be completely depend on the actual problem to be solved.

After filtering the initial population, and possibly escorting the best individuals to the next generation, we are still tasked with recreating the remaining individuals in the new population. To do so, we implement *crossover*, which will be discussed in the next sub-section, as a way to generate a new organism from two parents, and *mutations*, to provide genetic diversity to the new generations. The necessary step before being able to apply crossover is, therefore, selecting those two parents. As you can see in listing 18.4, we are going to perform this selection several times at each iteration.

There are many possible ways to select individuals for mating—we are going to discuss two of the most common here.

---

[13]Because we are trying to maximize the fitness function for the 0-1 knapsack; otherwise, with a function to be minimized, we could have set it to 120%, or 105%, and so on.

Tournament selection is one of the simplest (and easiest-to-implement) selection techniques used in genetic algorithms; it's illustrated through an example in figure 18.7. Conceptually, we randomly select a handful of organisms and then have them "compete" in a tournament where only the winner gets the right to mate. This is similar to what we see everywhere in wildlife, where (usually) male adults fight for the right to mate with females (ever watched a documentary on deer crossing horns during mating season?).

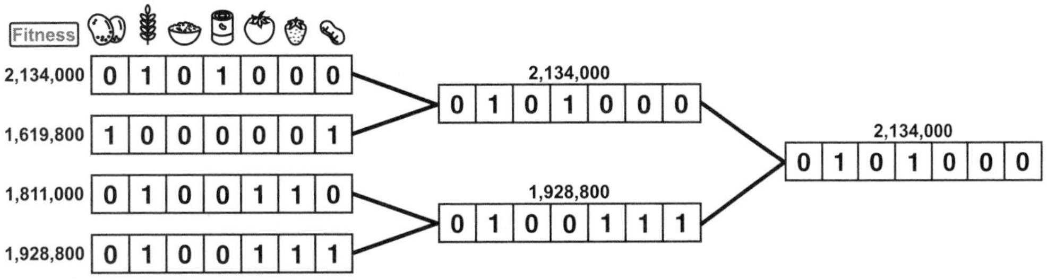
Fitness
2,134,000 0 1 0 1 0 0 0
1,619,800 1 0 0 0 0 0 1
1,811,000 0 1 0 0 1 1 0
1,928,800 0 1 0 0 1 1 1
2,134,000 0 1 0 1 0 0 0
1,928,800 0 1 0 0 1 1 1
2,134,000 0 1 0 1 0 0 0

Figure 18.7 Tournament selection applied to our instance of the 0-1 knapsack problem

Now, in reality we don't actually code a tournament, unless we are running a tournament simulation![14] As shown in listing 18.5, we just randomly select k individuals and take the one with the best fitness. The exact number, k, can vary depending on the problem and on the size of the population, but usually somewhere around 3 to 5 elements could be a good choice. Consider that the larger the pool of individuals participating in the tournaments, the lower the chance for low-fitness individuals to be chosen.

Listing 18.5 Tournament selection

```
function tournamentSelection(population, k)
  bestFitness ← lowestPossibleFitness()
  for i in {1,..,k} do
    j ← randomInt(|population|)
    if isHigher(population[j].fitness, bestFitness) then
      bestElement ← population[j]
      bestFitness ← bestElement.fitness
  return bestElement
```

- Method `tournamentSelection` takes current population and the number of elements that should participate in each tourney, and returns an individual, the best among the ones selected for the "tournament."
- Init the temporary variable storing the best fitness found. Since this is a generic method and we don't know if, in concrete problems, the best fitness will mean highest or lowest values, we use a helper function returning the "lowest" possible fitness, 0 for functions that will be maximized, infinity for the ones to be minimized.
- Repeat k times
- Randomly selects an index between 0 and the population's size. Indirectly, this selects an individual. In this implementation there are no measures to avoid duplicated selections, which can be fine when the population size is large (and consequently probability of duplicates is low), but still, you need to be aware of this.
- Checks if this element is better than the current best; again, we use a helper function to abstract on the meaning of good/high fitness
- If we found a new best, just updates the temporary variables

[14] For the predator-prey robots example, for instance, or for any setup where we evolve systems that run tasks in the physical world, we might actually do that and score individuals based on how they perform on a real task.

For instance, for the third-highest individual to be chosen, neither the best nor the second-best fitness organisms can be chosen (and, of course, the third-best must be), so the probability this happens with a pool of `k` individuals is[15]

$$1/n * [(n-2)/n]^{k-1}$$

assuming `n` is the size of the population.

For the lowest fitness individual (after, possibly, applying thresholding), it becomes

$$1/n * [1/n]^{k-1} = 1/n^k$$

The generic formula for the `m`-th best fitness becomes

$$1/n * [(n-m+1)/n]^{k-1}$$

As you can see, beyond the details and the actual exact probability, the chances of any individual (except the first) are decreasing exponentially with `k` (while polynomially with `m`).

It goes without saying that we need to apply tournament selection twice to get the pair of parents we need to generate a single element in the new population.

Roulette wheel selection is definitely more complicated to implement than tournament selection, but the high-level idea is the same: higher-fitness individuals must have more chances to be selected.

As we have seen, in tournament selection the probability that an element with low fitness is chosen decreases polynomially with the rank of the element (its position in the list of organisms sorted by fitness); in particular, since the probability will be $O([(n-m)/n]^k)$, the decrease will be super-linear, because `k` is certainly greater than `1`.

If, instead, we would like for lower-fitness elements to get a real chance of being selected, we could resort to a fairer selection method. One option is assigning the same probability to all organisms, but then we wouldn't really reward high-fitness individuals anymore.[16] A good balance would be, for example, making sure that the probability of selecting each individual is proportional to its fitness.

If we decide on the latter, we can use the roulette wheel selection. Each organism is assigned a section on a "roulette wheel" whose angle (and in turn the length of the arc subtended) is proportional to the fitness of the organism.

One way to obtain this is to compute the sum of the fitness of all individuals and then, for each one, see the percentage of the cumulative fitness for the whole population it accounts for.[17] For instance, figure 18.8 shows how to apply this to our example

---

[15] Approximately, with a few simplifications: the actual value depends on coding details like if the same individual can be chosen multiple times. This is fine, though, because we are not really interested in the exact values for these probabilities, but in understanding its order of magnitude and getting an idea of how it changes with `k`.

[16] For some problems, however, using elitism aggressively can compensate pure randomness in selection.

[17] This works when higher fitness means larger values, of course. It can be adapted to the other case by using the inverse of the fitness values, for example.

population for the knapsack problem. The angles of each organism's sector are computed with the formula `θ=2ϖ*f`, where `f` is the normalized fitness of the given individual, aka the fraction of the individual's fitness over the total sum for the whole population.

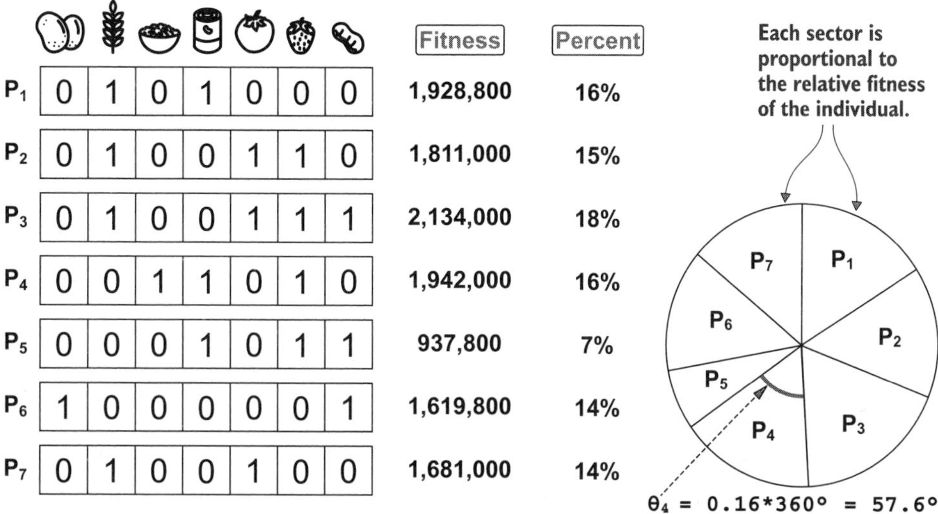
Fitness
Percent
P1 0 1 0 1 0 0 0 1,928,800 16%
P2 0 1 0 0 1 1 0 1,811,000 15%
P3 0 1 0 0 1 1 1 2,134,000 18%
P4 0 0 1 1 0 1 0 1,942,000 16%
P5 0 0 0 1 0 1 1 937,800 7%
P6 1 0 0 0 0 0 1 1,619,800 14%
P7 0 1 0 0 1 0 0 1,681,000 14%
Each sector is proportional to the relative fitness of the individual.
P7
P1
P6
P2
P5
P4
P3
θ4 = 0.16*360° = 57.6°

Figure 18.8 Roulette wheel selection once again applied to the example of 0-1 knapsack problem we are discussing in this section

Then each time we need to select a new parent for mating, we spin the wheel and see where it stops: higher fitness will have a larger probability of being picked, but lower ones still have a shot.

> **NOTE** Notice that if we choose to use rank instead of fitness, we'll need to sort the population first (time required: `O(n*log(n))`). Sticking to fitness, we only need a linear number of operations to compute the total and the percentages, and since this is computed at each iteration, for large populations we can have a relevant savings. Likewise, tournament selection also doesn't require prior sorting of the population.

When it comes to implementing this technique, however, we are clearly not going to bother with building an actual wheel (or even a simulated one)!

The easiest way we can achieve the same result is by building an array like the one shown in figure 18.9, where the `i`-th element contains the sum of the normalized[18] fitness of the first `i` individuals in the current population (taken in the order they are stored in the population array).

[18]For each individual, we normalize its fitness by dividing its value by the total sum of the population's fitness. This way, each normalized fitness is between 0 and 1, and their sum across the whole population is 1.

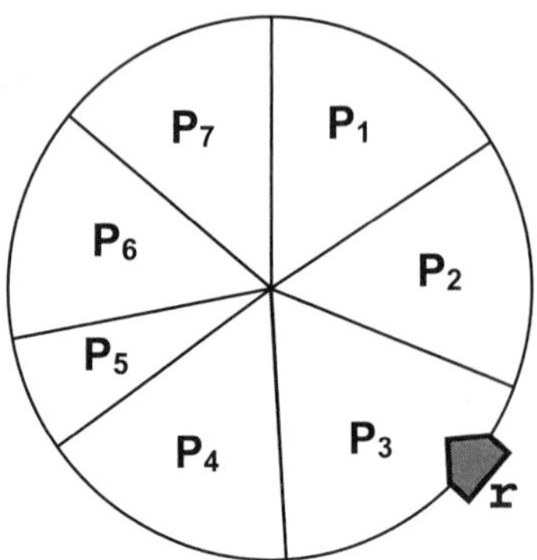
P7
P1
P6
P2
P5
P4
P3
r

After choosing a random number **r**, find out to which array element it corresponds: it's the one with the smaller value larger than **r**.

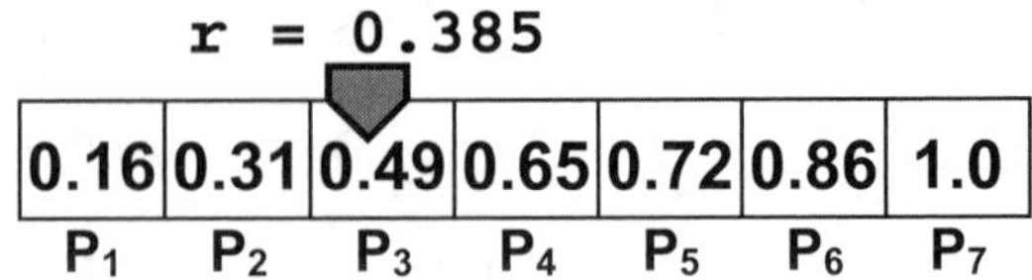
r = 0.385
0.16 0.31 0.49 0.65 0.72 0.86 1.0
P1 P2 P3 P4 P5 P6 P7

Figure 18.9 Roulette wheel selection in practice. We use an array with cumulative percentages; the difference between `A[i]` and `A[i-1]` is exactly the ratio between the `i`-th element's fitness and the sum of all elements' fitness.

For example, if we refer to the population shown in figure 18.8, the first element of the wheel-array holds the `population[0].normalizedFitness = 0.16`, the second element holds `population[0].normalizedFitness + population[1].normalizedFitness = 0.16 + 0.15`, and so on, as summarized in figure 18.9. Notice that the last element sums up exactly to 1. Ideally, we can imagine a hidden first element, not shown in the figure, whose value is 0 (we'll see that this helps with writing cleaner, succinct code).

To select an element, we draw a random number `r` from a regular distribution of real numbers between `0` and `1` (not included). Equivalently, in the wheel analogy, we would draw a random angle θ between 0° and 360° (not included) to find how much we should spin the wheel. The relation between the two numbers would be `θ=r*360`.

Listing 18.6 shows the method to generate a wheel-array like the one in figure 18.9.

To find where our wheel's pin is pointing, we need to run a search on the array. We look for the smallest element that's larger than `r`, the random number drawn by the selection routine. We can modify the binary search algorithm to perform this task and limit the runtime to `O(log(n))` for each element selected; therefore, for each iteration, we will have to perform `O(n*log(n))` operations to select parents and apply crossover.

Alternatively, a linear search is also possible. It's a lot easier to write and less likely to be buggy, but that makes the running times grow to `O(n)` and $O(n^2)$ respectively.

Listing 18.6 Creating a selection roulette wheel

```
function createWheel(population)
  totalFitness ← sum({population[i].fitness, i=0,…,|population|-1})
  wheel ← [0]
```

- Computes the total sum of all individuals' fitness values (here we use the simplified notation discussed in appendix A)
- Method `createWheel` takes current population and returns an array whose generic `i`-th elements is the cumulative fitness of all population's individuals, from the first to the `i`-th
- Initializes the array for the "roulette wheel." We set the first element to `0` for convenience, so that we don't have to handle a special case for the first individual outside the next `for` loop.

Each element in the roulette wheel's array is the sum of the normalized fitness of all individuals before it (already stored in `wheel[i-1]`) plus the ratio between the current individual's fitness and the sum of all organisms' fitness.

Cycles through all individuals in the population

```
    for i in {1,..,|population|} do
      wheel[i] ← wheel[i-1] + population[i-1].fitness / totalFitness
    pop(wheel, 0)
    return wheel
```

Optionally, we can now drop the first element of the array, containing a `0`. In many languages, this operation requires `O(n)` assignments, so we might want to avoid it. If we keep the first value, the search method can easily take that into account, for instance, by starting search from the element at index `1` and subtracting one from the index found before returning.

Choose wisely depending on the time constraints you have, as well as your domain knowledge. We leave the implementation of your preferred method of search as an exercise, and I strongly suggest you start with the simplest method, test it thoroughly, and then, if you really need the speedup, attempt to write the binary search method and compare their results.

18.1.7 Crossover

Once we have selected a pair of parents, we are ready for the next step: as we outlined in listing 18.4, it's time for crossover.

We mentioned this already, but just to give you a quick recap: crossover simulates mating and sexual reproduction of animal[19] populations in nature, stimulating diversity in the offspring by allowing the recombination of subsets of features from both parents in each child.

In the analogous algorithmic process, crossover corresponds to wide-range search of the fitness function landscape, since we generally recombine large sections of the genome (and hence of the solutions) carried by each of the parents. This is equivalent to a long leap in the problem space (and cost function landscape).

For instance, take our example problem: the 0-1 knapsack and packing goods for a journey in space. Figure 18.10 shows a possible definition for the crossover method for this problem: we choose a single crossover point, an index at which we cut both chromosomes; then one part of each chromosome (at the opposite sides of the crossover point) will be used for recombination. In this case, we just glue the two parts together.

Randomness is and should be a huge part of crossover. In our example, we can see it in the choice of the crossover point. Some choices (as in figure 18.10 (A)) will lead to improvements in the child's fitness, while other crossover points (as in figure 18.10 (B)) will lead to poorer or sometimes even disastrous results.

This single-crossover-point technique, if you noticed, actually produces two pairs of opposite sub-sequences (left-right and right-left of the crossover point). While in our example we only used one of the pairs and discarded the other, some implementations

[19]Some flowering plants also adopt sexual reproduction through pollination.

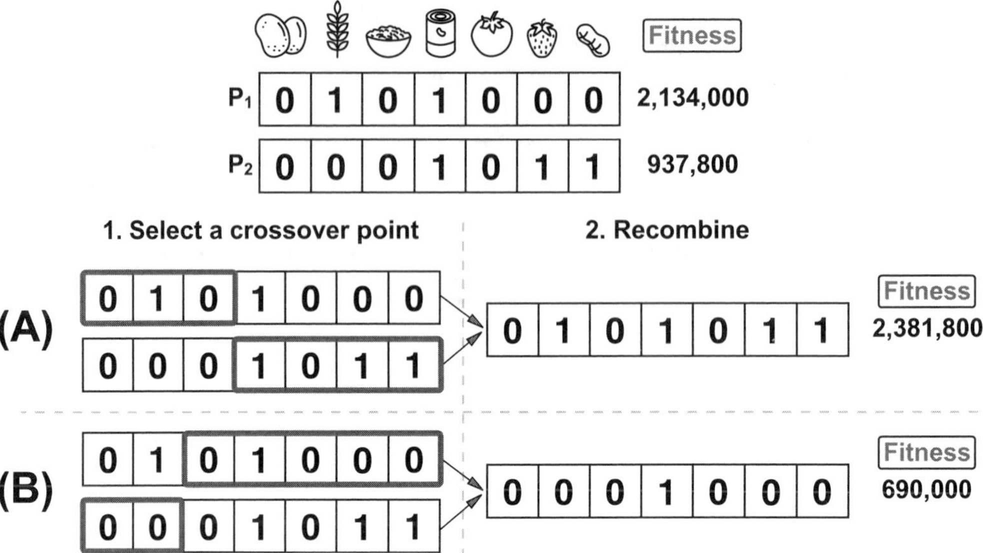

Fitness
P1 0 1 0 1 0 0 0 2,134,000
P2 0 0 0 1 0 1 1 937,800
1. Select a crossover point
2. Recombine
(A)
0 1 0 1 0 0 0
0 0 0 1 0 1 1
0 1 0 1 0 1 1
Fitness
2,381,800
(B)
0 1 0 1 0 0 0
0 0 0 1 0 1 1
0 0 0 1 0 0 0
Fitness
690,000

Figure 18.10 Examples of crossover for the knapsack problem. Once the two parents are selected, we need to choose a crossover point, and then recombine the two genomes. Depending on this choice, we can have an improvement (A) or a worsening (B) in fitness for the children.

of the genetic algorithm use both pairs to produce two children with all the possible combinations[20] (either keeping them both or just keeping the one with better fitness).

But nobody says we need to stick with the single-point crossover; that's just one of many alternatives. For instance, we could have a two-point crossover, selecting a segment of the first chromosome (and, implicitly, one or two remaining segments of the other), or we could even randomly select each value from one of the parents' chromosomes. Both examples are shown in figure 18.11.

And many more alternatives are possible: as we said before, crossover can only be defined on the actual chromosomes, and depending on their structure and constraints (it ultimately depends on the structure of the candidate solution), different ways of recombining chromosomes are possible. We'll see plenty of examples later in this chapter.

One last thing: it is customary to associate a *crossover chance*, aka crossover ratio, to our crossover operators. This represents the probability that crossover/mating actually happens between the selected individuals. For instance, with a crossover ratio of 0.7, there is a 70% chance that crossover does happen for any pair of organisms selected for mating.

As shown in listing 18.7, every time we apply crossover, we randomly decide what to do, based on the crossover chance. If the choice is not to apply crossover, then there

[20]The process is conceptually similar to early phases of ***meiosis***, the mechanism used by cells for sexual reproduction.

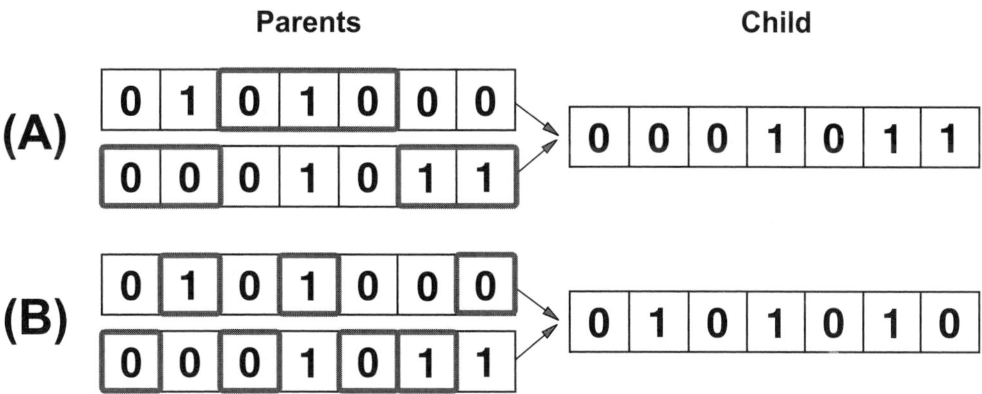
Parents
Child
(A)
0 1 0 1 0 0 0
0 0 0 1 0 1 1
0 0 0 1 0 1 1
(B)
0 1 0 1 0 0 0
0 0 0 1 0 1 1
0 1 0 1 0 1 0

Figure 18.11 More examples of crossover for the knapsack problem. (A) Two-point recombination: select a segment from the first chromosome, and the rest from the other. (B) For each gene (aka value), randomly decide from which parent it will be copied.

are a few alternatives; most commonly, we randomly select one of the parents that move to the next step. Notice that this is different from *elitism* because the organism outputted by crossover will still undergo mutations, while any individual selected by elitism will be copied completely unaltered to the new population.

Listing 18.7 A wrapper class for crossover operator

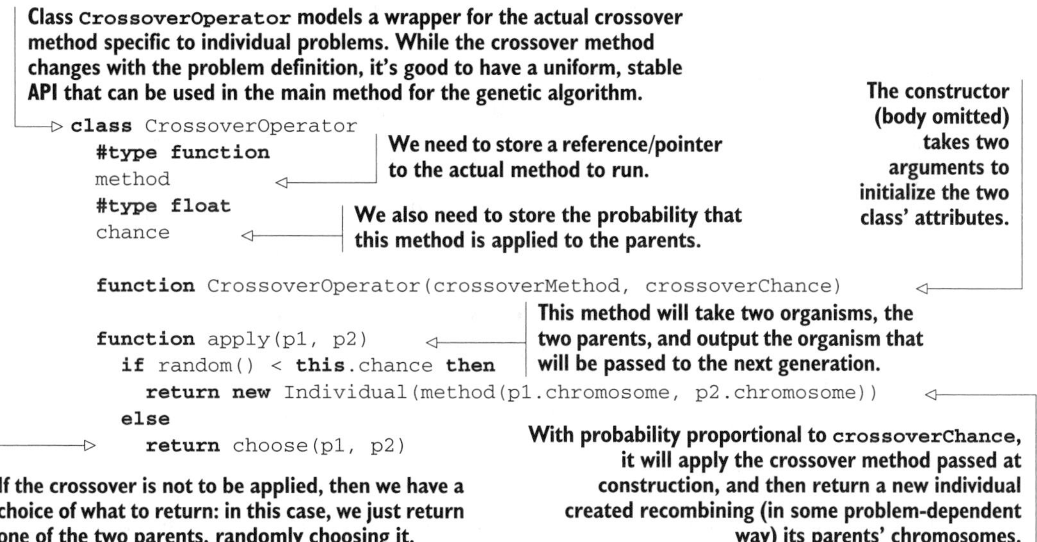

```
class CrossoverOperator
  #type function
  method
  #type float
  chance

  function CrossoverOperator(crossoverMethod, crossoverChance)

  function apply(p1, p2)
    if random() < this.chance then
      return new Individual(method(p1.chromosome, p2.chromosome))
    else
      return choose(p1, p2)
```

Class `CrossoverOperator` models a wrapper for the actual crossover method specific to individual problems. While the crossover method changes with the problem definition, it's good to have a uniform, stable API that can be used in the main method for the genetic algorithm.
We need to store a reference/pointer to the actual method to run.
We also need to store the probability that this method is applied to the parents.
The constructor (body omitted) takes two arguments to initialize the two class' attributes.
This method will take two organisms, the two parents, and output the organism that will be passed to the next generation.
With probability proportional to `crossoverChance`, it will apply the crossover method passed at construction, and then return a new individual created recombining (in some problem-dependent way) its parents' chromosomes.
If the crossover is not to be applied, then we have a choice of what to return: in this case, we just return one of the two parents, randomly choosing it.

Remember that listing 18.7 shows a wrapper for the actual crossover operator, compatible with the template we provided in listing 18.4 for natural selection's generic template. The actual method will be crafted and passed every time a specific problem instance is addressed.

Listing 18.8 shows the single-point crossover operator that we discussed for the 0-1 knapsack problem.

Listing 18.8 0-1 Knapsack: crossover

```
function knapsackCossover(chromosome1, chromosome2)
  i ← randomInt(1, |chromosome1|-1)
  return chromosome1[0:i] + chromosome2[i:|chromosome2|]
```

Method `knapsackCossover` takes two chromosomes (as bit strings) and returns a new chromosome obtained by recombining the head of the first one, with the tail of the second one.

Chooses a cut point, making sure at least one gene is taken from each parent

Returns the combination of the head of `chromosome1` (up to index `i`, excluded) and the tail of `chromosome2` (from the index `i` to the end)

18.1.8 Mutations

After a new organism is created through crossover, the genetic algorithm applies mutations to its newly recombined genome. In nature, as we have seen, the recombination of parents' genomes and mutations happens simultaneously[21] during sexual reproduction. Conceptually, this works analogously in genetic algorithms, although the two operators are implemented separately. If crossover is regarded as wide-range search, mutations are often used for small-range, local search.

We have seen that crossover promotes diversity in the new population, so why do we need mutations?

The answer is simple and best provided with an example (shown in figure 18.12). The population considered in this example shares the same values for three of the genes. This means that no matter how you recombine the organisms' genes during crossover, the resulting children will all have beans and strawberries included in the solution and potatoes excluded from it. This is a real risk for problems where chromosomes are large (carrying a lot of information), especially if the length of the chromosome is larger or comparable to the size of the population. The danger is that no matter how long we run our simulation, or how many iterations and crossovers we perform, we won't be able to flip the values for some genes, which in turn means that the areas of the problem spaces that we can explore are limited by the choice of the initial population. And this, of course, would be a terrible limitation.

To prevent this issue and increase the diversity in the genomic pool of our population, we add a mechanism that can change each gene independently and for any organism.

In Holland's original work, as we had mentioned, chromosomes were bit strings, and the mutation was also conceived as domain-agnostic. The mutation operator would be applied to each organism's chromosome, and for each gene (that is, each

[21] Mutations also happen spontaneously, with on-null probability, during *mitosis*, the mechanism used for asexual reproduction of all cells (*gametes* and *somatic cells*). These mutations can be key to the evolution of the organisms and species, when they happen in gametes, the cells involved in sexual reproduction.

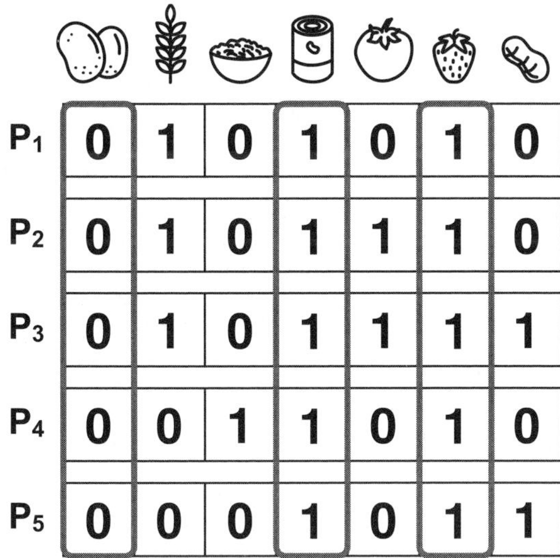
P1 0 1 0 1 0 1 0
P2 0 1 0 1 1 1 0
P3 0 1 0 1 1 1 1
P4 0 0 1 1 0 1 0
P5 0 0 0 1 0 1 1

Figure 18.12 An example of a population where, without mutations, there wouldn't be enough genetic diversity. All individuals have the same value for three of their genes.

bit) it would toss a coin[22] and decide if the bit should be flipped. This is shown in figure 18.13.

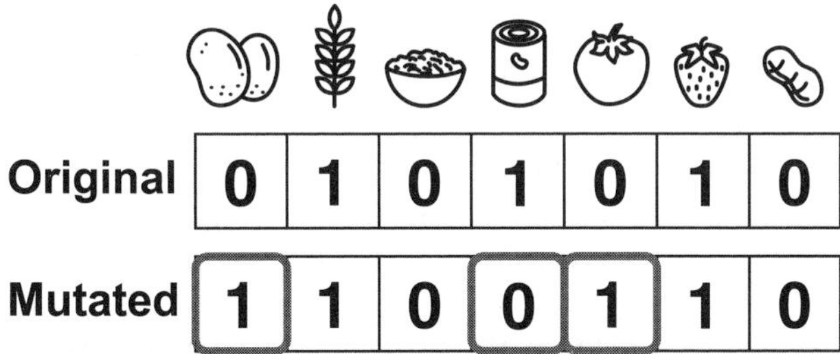
Original 0 1 0 1 0 1 0
Mutated 1 1 0 0 1 1 0

Figure 18.13 An example of mutation for the 0-1 knapsack problem. The mutation rate here is overly boosted (for the sake of presentation). In a real scenario it would likely be set somewhere between 1% and 0.1% (also depending on the size of the chromosomes). A too-large mutation ratio can hinder the stability of the algorithm's convergence toward the minimum, voiding the benefits of crossover and selection.

In modern genetic algorithms, however, chromosomes can take different shapes and have constraints, so mutations can become much more complex or be applied to the chromosome as a whole, rather than to single genes. As we'll see for TSP, for instance, a mutation operator can be applied (with a certain probability) just once to the whole chromosome (instead of to each of its genes) and swap two vertices in the tour.

The wrapper class for the mutation operator is identical to the one for crossover shown in listing 18.7, apart from minor differences in handling arguments, especially the ones to the wrapped methods: we only have one organism to pass, but it's a good

[22]An *unfair* coin, where the probability of applying a mutation would be far smaller than ½.

idea to also forward the mutation chance to the wrapped method. This is necessary for bit-wise mutations, such as the one we discussed for the knapsack problem, implemented in listing 18.9.

Listing 18.9 0-1 knapsack: Bit-wise mutation

Method `knapsackMutation` takes a chromosome (as a bit string) and a probability of mutation (as a real number between 0 and 1) and applies mutations to the chromosome. The method, in this implementation, alters the argument, but it's possible and often cleaner to clone the input and return a new object as output, unless this cloning becomes a bottleneck. Weigh the pros and cons and run some profiling before making a choice.

```
function knapsackMutation(chromosome, mutationChance)
  for i in {0,..,|chromosome|} do
    if random() < mutationChance then
      chromosome[i] ← 1 - chromosome[i]
  return chromosome
```

Cycles through each gene (that is, bit) in the chromosome

With probability `mutationChance(*100)`, flip current bit

18.1.9 The genetic algorithm template

Listing 18.10 provides an implementation of the main method for the genetic algorithm template, and also concludes our discussion of the 0-1 knapsack problem. We have all we need now to actually run the algorithm on our instance and find out that the best possible solution is bringing wheat flour, rice, and beans. To see a solution in action, and possibly apply it to larger problem instances with hundreds of possible items to pack, you can use the implementation of the genetic algorithm provided by JsGraphs on GitHub[23] and implement the methods for crossover, mutations, and random initialization that we discussed in this section. It will be a great exercise to test your understanding of this technique and delve deeper into its details.

Listing 18.10 A generic implementation of the genetic algorithm

Method `geneticAlgorithm` is a template method that implements the backbone of a genetic algorithm and can be adapted to run on several problems by passing the specialized methods for the concrete problems' instances.

```
function geneticAlgorithm(
➥ populationSize, chromosomeInitilizer, elitism, selectForMating,
➥ crossover, mutations, maxSteps)
  population ← initPopulation(populationSize, chromosomeInitilizer)
  for k in {1..maxSteps} do
    population ← naturalSelection(
    ➥ population, elitism, selectForMating, crossover, mutations)
  return findBest(population).chromosome
```

Repeats `maxSteps` times. Each iteration is a new generation in the simulation.

Initializes the population

Let natural selection take its course . . .

Finally, finds the best individual in the population and returns its chromosome (which is the best solution found). Method `findBest` can also be supplied as a parameter, if needed.

[23] See http://mng.bz/nMMd.

18.1.10 When does the genetic algorithm work best?

To recap what we have discussed so far, in chapters 16 and 17, we have presented a few techniques that can be used in optimization problems to find near-optimal solutions without exploring the whole problem space. Each of them comes with some strengths and some pain points:

- *Gradient descent* (chapter 16) converges fast but tends to get stuck in local minima. It also requires the cost function to be differentiable (as such, it couldn't be used in experimental settings or game theory, for instance in the predator-prey robotic evolution experiment described earlier in this section).
- *Random sampling* (chapter 16) overcomes the need for differentiability and the issue with local minima, but it's (unbearably) slow in converging (*when* it manages to converge).
- *Simulated annealing* (chapter 17) has the same advantages of random sampling, but evolves in a more controlled and steady way toward minima. Nevertheless, convergence can still be slow, and it has a hard time finding minima when they lie in narrow valleys.

At the beginning of the chapter, we discussed how the genetic algorithm can overcome many of the issues of these heuristics; for instance, it can speed up convergence, compared to simulated annealing, by keeping a pool of solutions and evolving them together.

To conclude this section, I'd like to provide yet another criterion that can help you choose which optimization technique you should use. It involves another term, *epistasis*, that is borrowed from biology: its mean is *gene interaction*, and in our algorithmic analogy, it expresses the presence of dependent variables—in other words, variables whose values depend on other variables.

Let's first go through an example to better explain this.

Each gene on a chromosome can be considered a separate variable that can assume values within a certain domain. For the 0-1 knapsack problem, each gene is an independent variable, because the value it assumes won't directly influence other variables. (If we enforce the constraint on the weight of each solution, however, flipping a gene to `1` might force us to flip one or more other genes to `0`. That's a loose indirect dependency, anyway.)

For the TSP, as we'll see, we assign a vertex to each gene with the constraint that there can't be any duplicate. As such, assigning a variable will impose constraints on all other variables (that won't be able to be assigned the same value), so we have a more direct, although still loose, dependency.

If our problem was optimizing the energy efficiency of a house that was being designed, and some variables were its area, the number of rooms, and the amount of wood needed for the floors, the latter would be dependent on the other two, because the area to cover with wood flooring would depend on the square feet and rooms of the house. Changing the size of the house would immediately force us to change the amount of wood used if the floor's thickness remains fixed (the possibility of changing its thickness makes it meaningful having a separate variable for this).

For 0-1 knapsack, we say that the problem has low variable interaction, and so low epistasis; the house optimization has high epistasis, while for the TSP, its epistasis is somewhere in the middle.

Now, the interesting thing is that the degree of variable interaction contributes to the shape of the landscape of the objective function that we want to optimize: the higher the epistasis, the wavier the landscape will likely look.

But above all, when the degree of interaction is high, varying one variable also changes the value of other variables, and this means making a bigger leap in the cost function's landscape and problem domain, making it harder to explore the surroundings of solutions and fine-tune the algorithm's results.

Knowing the epistasis of a problem can guide our choice of the best algorithm to apply:

- With low epistasis, minimum-seeking algorithms like gradient-descent work best.
- With high epistasis, it's best to prefer random search, so simulated annealing, or for very high variables interaction, random sampling.
- What about genetic algorithms? It turns out that they work best in a wide range of medium to high epistasis.

Therefore, when we design the cost/fitness function for a problem (which, let me state this clearly once again, is one of the most crucial steps to a good solution), we need to be careful about the degree of interaction in order to choose the best technique that we can apply.

During the design phase, we can also try to reduce the dependent variables, whenever possible. This will allow us to use more powerful techniques and ultimately get better solutions.

Now that we have concluded our discussion of the components and theory of genetic algorithms, we are ready to delve into a couple of practical applications to see how powerful this technique is.

18.2 TSP

We described the travelling salesman problem (or TSP for short) in chapter 17, where we also provided a solution based on simulated annealing.

Figure 18.14 shows the same example we produced in the previous chapter, an instance of the problem with 10 cities for which the best solution has cost `1625` (miles), the total length of the following path:

```
["New Carthage", "Syracuse", "Buffalo", "Pittsburgh", "Harrisburg",
➥ "Opal City", "Metropolis", "Gotham City", "Civic City" ]
```

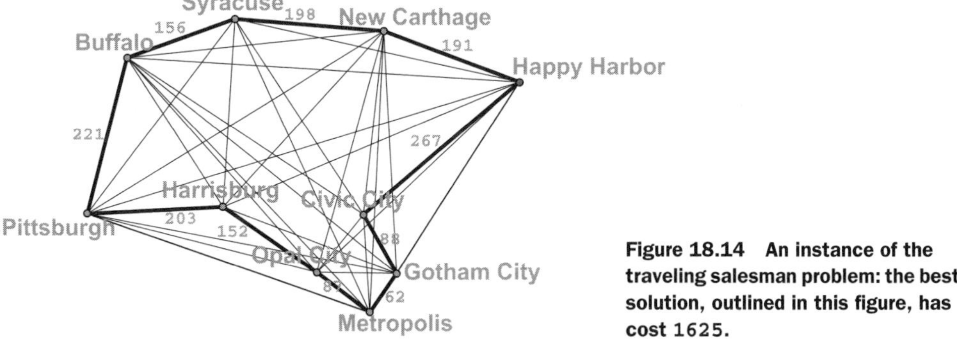
Syracuse
198
New Carthage
156
Buffalo
191
Happy Harbor
221
267
Harrisburg
Civic City
Pittsburgh
203
152
88
Opal City
Gotham City
62
Metropolis

Figure 18.14 An instance of the traveling salesman problem: the best solution, outlined in this figure, has cost `1625`.

Now we would like to tackle the same problem with a genetic algorithm and see if we can speed up convergence to a good solution (and possibly improve the average solution: remember that these optimization algorithms output near-optimal solutions, and so they provide no guarantee of always finding the best possible one).

18.2.1 Fitness, chromosomes, and initialization

A good starting point, in general, for all problems, is the design of how solutions are encoded and of the cost function. While with the 0-1 knapsack we wanted to maximize a quantity—the total value of the entries added to the knapsack—TSP is a minimization problem, so we'll assume the use of a minimization algorithm (as mentioned, otherwise we can just maximize the opposite or inverse of the cost).

Therefore, we can use the same definition for the fitness function of the genetic algorithm as the cost function we saw in section 17.2, and in particular in listing 17.2: that is, just the sum of the distances between adjacent vertices, as shown in figure 18.14.

We can even reuse the same encoding for solutions: they are permutations of the graph's vertices. This can easily be translated into chromosomes that won't be bit strings anymore in this case; we need each gene to be an integer value (the index of one of the vertices), with the implicit constraint that there can't be two genes holding the same value.

We can initialize any solution as a random permutation of the indices between `0` and `n-1`, where `n` is the number of vertices in the graph, just like we did for simulated annealing. We can even pass the same method as the `chromosomeInitializer` argument to method `initPopulation` in listing 18.2.

18.2.2 Mutations

Even for mutations, our job can be (at least for an initial assessment) pretty much limited to reusing methods developed in chapter 17 for local search, and if we'd like to compare to the performance of simulated annealing, we also shouldn't add new kinds of mutations.

There are, however, a few differences. First, while in listing 17.3 we implement an ensemble method, where with some probability one of the transitions will be applied, in genetic algorithms, this ensemble mechanism is already implicit for mutations, and thus we have to provide each mutation (aka local search) method separately.

Another difference is that for the genetic algorithm it doesn't really make sense to have a mutation that randomly recreates an individual from scratch. This goes against the principles of natural selection, and we have seen that genome diversity in the population is already supported by crossover and local mutations.

Therefore, we can extract two methods from listing 17.3, one for swapping adjacent vertices, and one for swapping random vertices, and in turn create two mutation operators from them. (Both are shown in listing 18.11. Warning: These methods, for the sake of simplicity, alter their inputs—while this is usually fine for GA mutations, you should be aware of that and state it clearly in the method's documentation.) To see these methods in action, see figure 17.13 in the previous chapter.

Listing 18.11 TSP mutations

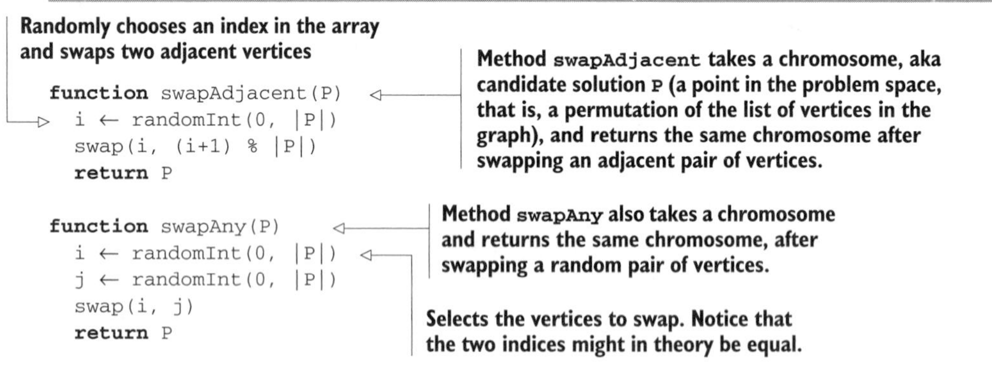

```
function swapAdjacent(P)
  i ← randomInt(0, |P|)
  swap(i, (i+1) % |P|)
  return P

function swapAny(P)
  i ← randomInt(0, |P|)
  j ← randomInt(0, |P|)
  swap(i, j)
  return P
```

Randomly chooses an index in the array and swaps two adjacent vertices
Method swapAdjacent takes a chromosome, aka candidate solution P (a point in the problem space, that is, a permutation of the list of vertices in the graph), and returns the same chromosome after swapping an adjacent pair of vertices.
Method swapAny also takes a chromosome and returns the same chromosome, after swapping a random pair of vertices.
Selects the vertices to swap. Notice that the two indices might in theory be equal.

A final, though important, consideration: the mutation chance in GAs will typically be much smaller than the ratios we used for the same methods in simulated annealing (because, obviously, for simulated annealing these "mutations" were the only way to explore the problem domain at any iteration).

As a first attempt, however, we tried to use the same probabilities to try and make a fairer comparison. A couple of sections later, we'll discuss how it went.

18.2.3 Crossover

In crossover lies the real novelty we are adding, with respect to simulated annealing: the latter had no way to combine two good solutions. Truth be told, there wasn't even a way to keep multiple solutions in the first place!

There are many ways in which we can combine two permutations of the same sequence. OK, perhaps not that many, but there is definitely more than one. Since we don't need to make things even more complicated, let's go for the simplest way—or at least the simplest I can think of.

We are still going to choose a single cutoff point, like for 0-1 knapsack, but then things get interesting. Let's see an example to help us understand. Figure 18.15 shows this crossover method in action for the example we have used since chapter 17, a graph with 10 vertices.

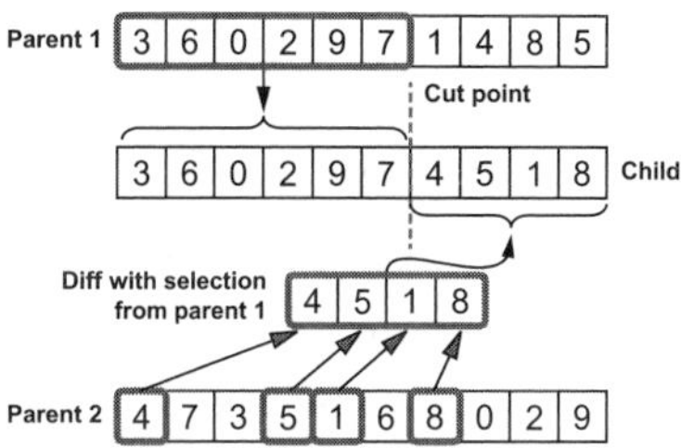
Parent 1
3 6 0 2 9 7 1 4 8 5
Cut point
3 6 0 2 9 7 4 5 1 8
Child
Diff with selection from parent 1
4 5 1 8
Parent 2
4 7 3 5 1 6 8 0 2 9

Figure 18.15 Crossover method for TSP. While the first half of the new chromosome can be directly copied from the first parent, deriving the second half from the second parent requires a lot more effort.

After randomly choosing a cut point, we copy all the genes in the first parent's chromosome to the child's genome, from the gene at index `0` to the one at the point of cut.

Now we need to fill the rest of the child's chromosome, but we can't just copy the sequence after the cut point (like we did for the knapsack's bit strings), because the last four genes in the second organism's chromosome contain vertices `0`, `2`, and `9`, which have already been assigned as values to genes in the first half of the new chromosome.

What we can do, instead, is go through the whole second chromosome from start to finish, and each time we find one of the vertices that was not copied from chromosome 1 to the child (vertices 1, 4, 8, and 5), we add this vertex to the new chromosome. This way, the net result is that the first part of the new chromosome, from its beginning to the cut point, is identical to its first parent's, while the vertices in the second part, after the cut point, appear in the same order as they do in the second parent (where, however, they might not have been adjacent to each other).

Listing 18.12 provides a possible implementation for this method.

Listing 18.12 TSP: crossover

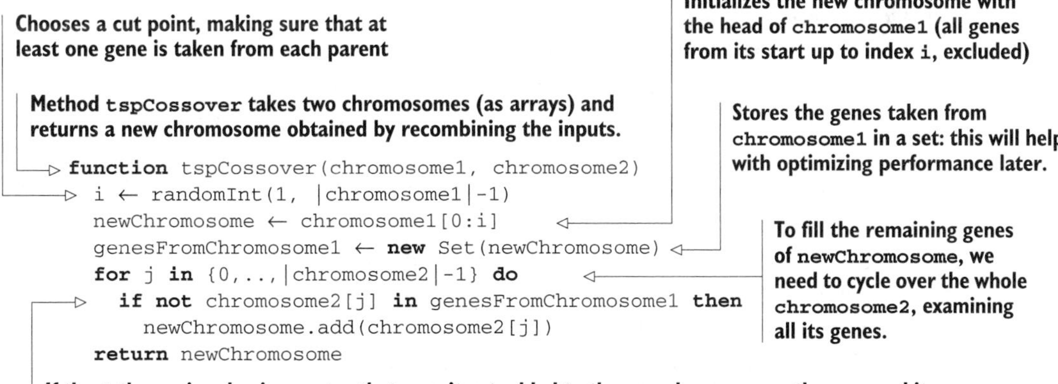
Chooses a cut point, making sure that at least one gene is taken from each parent
Method tspCossover takes two chromosomes (as arrays) and returns a new chromosome obtained by recombining the inputs.
Initializes the new chromosome with the head of chromosome1 (all genes from its start up to index i, excluded)
Stores the genes taken from chromosome1 in a set: this will help with optimizing performance later.
To fill the remaining genes of newChromosome, we need to cycle over the whole chromosome2, examining all its genes.
If the j-th gene's value is a vertex that wasn't yet added to the new chromosome, then append it to the end of it. For greater efficiency, we use a set to perform search in amortized constant time. Also, notice that we don't need to update the set, because there are no duplicates.

```
function tspCossover(chromosome1, chromosome2)
  i ← randomInt(1, |chromosome1|-1)
  newChromosome ← chromosome1[0:i]
  genesFromChromosome1 ← new Set(newChromosome)
  for j in {0,..,|chromosome2|-1} do
    if not chromosome2[j] in genesFromChromosome1 then
      newChromosome.add(chromosome2[j])
  return newChromosome
```

18.2.4 Results and parameters tuning

Now that we have all the pieces of the genetic algorithm defined and implemented, there are a couple of questions that we would like to answer:

- Do we get any improvement over simulated annealing?
- How much do crossover and mutations influence the performance of the algorithm?

You might have guessed it: now it's profiling time!

The former question is easier to answer. Simulated annealing, in our tests in section 17.2.4, based on JsGraphs' implementation, required approximately 600 iterations to converge to the best solution, and we were able to obtain an average cost equal to `1668.248` (remember, Monte Carlo algorithms, like simulated annealing and the genetic algorithm, don't always return the best result—there is no guarantee of that).

You can also take a look on JsGraphs' GitHub at the implementation[24] of a genetic algorithm to solve TSP. Running this algorithm with a population of 10 individuals, with the same mutations rates we used for simulated annealing, and a crossover chance of 0.7, the algorithm takes on average 10 generations to converge to the optimal solution (cost: `1625`). For a fair comparison we need to compare the iterations of simulated annealing (where a single solution is kept) to the product of the number of iterations of GA by the population size. Still, we go down from 600 to 100, a nice improvement.

But where we really understand the advantage we get is by computing the average cost on the same number of "total" iterations, for instance 1,000 iterations of simulated annealing versus a population of 25 individuals evolved for 40 iterations (or any combination whose product is 1,000). Without too much effort spent tuning the parameters, we were able to obtain an average cost equal to `1652.84`, using high chances for both crossover and random vertex swap mutation. With a population of 100 elements, the average goes down to `1636.8`.

Another interesting factor we would like to understand is this: How do crossover and mutations chances influence the evolution of the population?

To answer that, let's try to run the algorithm with only one of these operators enabled and draw a curve of the best organism's fitness. In order to get a better understanding and clearer charts, we'll use a more complicated instance of the problem: a complete graph with 50 vertices (and random weights for the edges).

Figure 18.16 shows a chart with the plots of the optimization trend for three runs of the algorithm on a population with 100 organisms for 100 generations. The first thing you are likely to notice is that the crossover operator plateaus at some (early) point, but this shouldn't be a surprise, right? We have already discussed the role of crossover and its limitations. In particular, it can recombine the genomes of the initial

[24]See https://github.com/mlarocca/jsgraphs/blob/master/src/graph/algo/genetic/tsp.mjs.

population, but if none of the organisms shows a certain feature,[25] then crossover can only improve fitness so much.

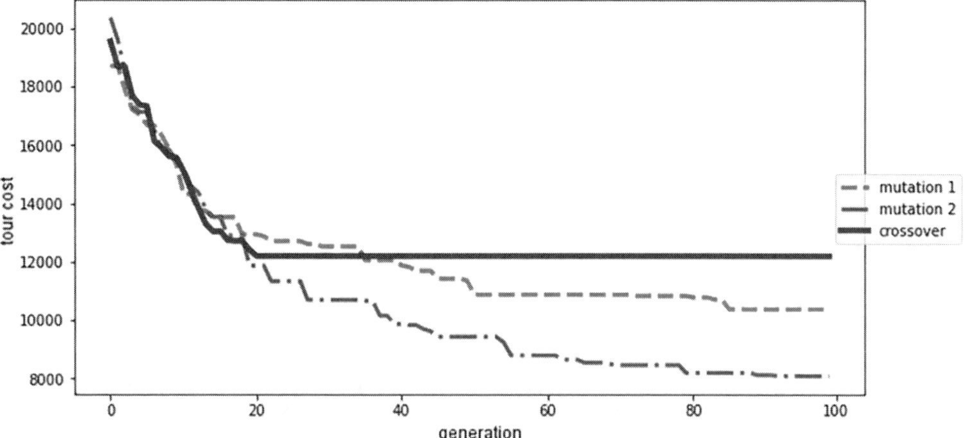
20000
18000
16000
14000
12000
10000
8000
tour cost
0
20
40
60
80
100
generation
mutation 1
mutation 2
crossover

Figure 18.16 How TSP population evolves when only mutations versus only crossover are enabled. Crossover-only evolution plateaus soon enough, while the mutation operator swapping random pairs is the most successful. On the x axis, there is the number of generations, while on the y axis is the cost of the tour.

We can also see that mutation 2 is more effective than mutation 1, which also plateaus at some point: here as well, it shouldn't be surprising. If you read chapter 17 about simulated annealing, where we introduced both these mutations, you saw that swapping only adjacent vertices is a small-range local search, which makes it more difficult to get out of local minima.

So far, so good, but what would happen if we were to increase the population size? This would increase the genome diversity in the initial population, so it's legitimate to expect crossover will be more effective, drawing from a larger pool.

Figure 18.17 confirms this idea. Crossover makes the algorithm evolve faster in the initial phases and manages to get as good a solution as the one obtained using only the most effective mutation.

This was a particularly happy case, though. Running the crossover-only version a few more times, as in figure 18.18, shows that the quality of the best solution found depends on the diversity and quality of the initial population. If we are lucky during initialization, the algorithm will get to an optimal solution; otherwise—as expected—using only the crossover, the algorithm will plateau to a sub-optimal solution. When

[25]For bit string representations, as we have discussed, this means that none of chromosomes has a certain value for a specific gene; for TSP, which has a different representation, it means that there is no chromosome with a certain subsequence of vertices. For instance, if no chromosomes have vertex `1` before vertex `0`, crossover won't be able to add this feature. Considering there is a quadratic number of pairs of vertices, it's unlikely that both possible orderings for all of the pairs appear in the initial population.

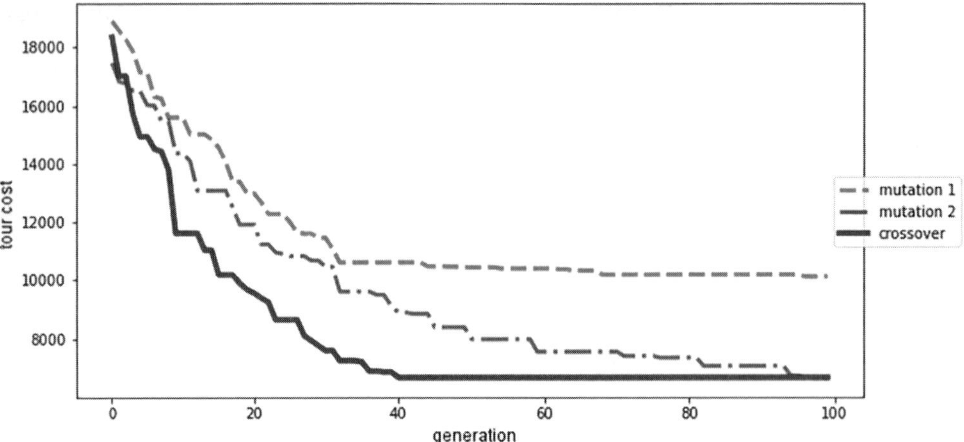
18000
16000
14000
12000
10000
8000
tour cost
0
20
40
60
80
100
generation
mutation 1
mutation 2
crossover

Figure 18.17 Same analysis as figure 18.16, but with a 10-fold population. With a larger population, crossover produces better results in earlier generations, and even gets to a result comparable to the mutations.

enabling only the mutations, the final result (not shown on the chart) has less variance across different runs, and the evolution plots of various attempts look similar.

Yet another consideration to make is that both charts in figures 18.16 and 18.17 also confirm that the "adjacent pairs swap" mutation is less relevant to the algorithm and can be put aside in favor of the "all pairs swap" one.

So, do we get any advantage in using crossover *and* mutations at the same time? To understand that, we need to abandon our charts (which provide an idea for the trend

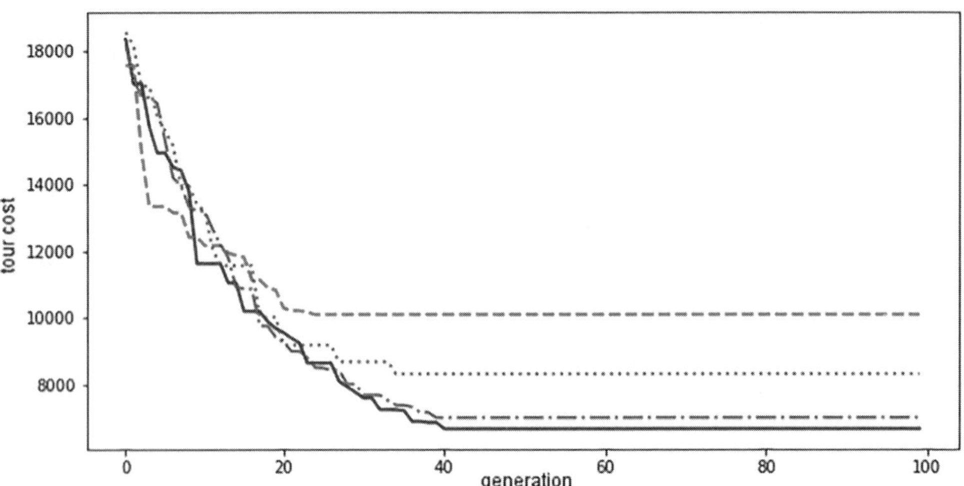
18000
16000
14000
12000
10000
8000
tour cost
0
20
40
60
80
100
generation

Figure 18.18 Using the same setup as for figure 18.17, we ran a few experiments using crossover-only (all with the same crossover chance, 0.7). This chart shows how there is a huge variance in the final results that depends entirely on the initial choice of the population (because there is no mutation).

of the simulation, but are not statistically relevant, because they are based on just a few runs), and run a more thorough analysis, summarized in table 18.2.

Table 18.2 Average best solution for the TSP genetic algorithm, varying the operators' chance. The results are sorted by tour cost, and we highlighted the most significant rows.

Crossover	Adjacent swap	Random swap	Average tour cost
0.2	0	0.5	6326.447
0.3	0.002	0.5	6379.628
0.2	0.02	0.5	6409.664
0.1	0.002	0.5	6428.103
0.2	0	0.2	6555.593
0.2	0.2	0.5	6753.441
0.2	0.2	0.2	6823.971
0.2	0	0.7	7016.033
0	0	0.2	7110.798
0	0	0.7	7143.873
0.7	0	0.7	7818.061
0	0.7	0	10428.917
0.7	0	0	11655.949
0.2	0	0	15210.800

As you can see, the best results have been found using a mix of crossover and mutations. Using random swaps mutation is more important than using crossover, while the adjacent swaps mutation is not only less important, but can even become detrimental when its chance is too high—the same way it happens for crossover. This might feel puzzling—after all, the worst you'd have expected was, maybe, that a mutation proved useless. How can we explain the fact that a higher chance for crossover and mutation 1 translates into worse solutions, on average? Well, the point is that even if we use elitism, when the other organisms in the new generations are affected by many changes, there is a higher chance that their fitness will get worse, and this effect becomes stronger with each generation, as the average fitness becomes better. If a solution is close to the optimal one, it's much easier for a random change's result to be pejorative than ameliorative.

That's because, unlike simulated annealing, where we reject pejorative changes in the final stages of the simulation, GAs accept them without questioning. Besides the small fraction of high-fitness elements potentially guaranteed by elitism, the rest of the population can drive the average fitness down when too many random changes happen at the same time.

One final word of caution: these results are still to be taken with a grain of salt, because the average is computed on "only" a thousand runs, and because we haven't explored extensively the domain of parameter values.

NOTE To do parameter fine-tuning in a systematic way, there is an effective protocol often used in machine learning. We start with a set of coarse-grained, heterogeneously spaced values to find the order of magnitude for the best solution (for instance, for the mutation chance, we could choose [0.01, 0.05, 0.1, 0.2, 0.5, 0.8, 1]), and then refine our search by repeating (one or more times) the process around the most promising values. (For instance, assuming the best results were obtained with 0.2 and 0.5, then we test [0.15, 0.2, 0.25, 0.3, ..., 0.45, 0.5, 0.55, 0.6].) Since we have multiple parameters, and we need to measure the results for all the combinations for the three of them (as shown in table 18.2), we really want to keep these lists as short as possible and refine them in several steps.

18.2.5 Beyond TSP: Optimizing the routes of the whole fleet

As we mentioned in chapter 17, solving TSP is nice, but only allows us to optimize the route of a single truck. With the business thriving, it's natural to have several trucks taking care of shipments from each warehouse (or possibly from more than one warehouse at the same time).

Each truck has a limited capacity, so we need to take parcel size into account (rings a bell?) and, moreover, each parcel's destination can significantly change the route needed to deliver all packages assigned to a truck.

This is an extremely complicated problem to optimize, because for each assignment of parcels to the available trucks, we need to optimize the trucks' routes one by one.

To simplify the problem, what's often done is splitting the area covered by a warehouse into zones and finding an a priori optimal assignment of these zones to trucks. This, however, forces us to settle for sub-optimal solutions and to include some redundancy in the trucks' capacity to cope with the fluctuations in demand.

An alternative is running a TSP optimization for each truck after assigning the deliveries to all vehicles, as part of the fitness function computation, and then sum whatever metric is used (miles run, or time spent, or gasoline consumed) across all of them.

As you can imagine, optimizing the larger problem is not easy, because for any change in the assignments of parcels to vehicles, we need to rerun at least two TSP optimizations.

In terms of *epistasis* (as defined in section 18.1.9), the fitness function has a high degree of dependence between its variables, so a genetic algorithm could be effective, but a random search could also be a viable alternative.

18.3 Minimum vertex cover

Now we can be quite satisfied with our genetic algorithm for TSP, and we can move on to new, interesting, and of course *NP-Hard* problems on graphs.

There is a rich body of literature on this kind of problem; some writings are milestones and benchmarks in computer science and some appear in many practical applications throughout engineering.

Minimum vertex cover is important both theoretically and practically, so we couldn't close this book without discussing it!

Given a graph `G=(V,E)`, a *vertex cover* for `G` is any set of its vertices that covers all of its edges; an edge `e=(u,v)` $\in$ `E` is covered by a subset of vertices `S` $\subseteq$ `V` if at least one of the edge's endpoints, either `u` or `v`, belongs to `S`.

Every graph has a trivial vertex cover: the set `V` of all vertices. What we are really interested in, though, is finding a minimum vertex cover, the smallest possible subset of vertices that covers all edges. Figure 18.19 shows a few examples of simple graphs and their vertex covers.

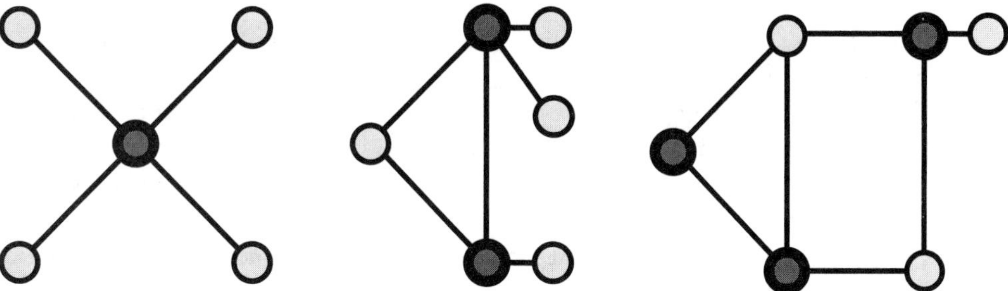

Figure 18.19 Three examples of minimum vertex covers on graphs. The thicker circles (red vertices) are the only ones needed to cover all edges for these graphs.

Notice that some graphs have a single solution (like the first one on the left), while others have multiple minima vertex covers. Can you find the alternative solution for the graph on the right?

Figure 18.20, instead, shows examples of what is *not* a minimum vertex cover.

The decision problem for the minimum vertex cover ("Given a subset of vertices, is it a minimum vertex cover for `G`?") has been proved to be NP-Hard.

Since there are $2^{|V|}$ possible subsets of `V`, a brute-force search seems out of the question.

There are polynomial-time approximation algorithms for minimum vertex cover, but they can only guarantee a result that is within an approximation factor in the order of magnitude of `2` (slightly lower than `2`) from the best solution.[26] This problem, in fact, belongs to a computational subclass of NP called *APX-complete problems*, the set

[26] If an algorithm has an approximation factor `a`, it means that on a problem with a solution whose value is `v`, the approximation algorithm will return a solution that is at most `a*v`.

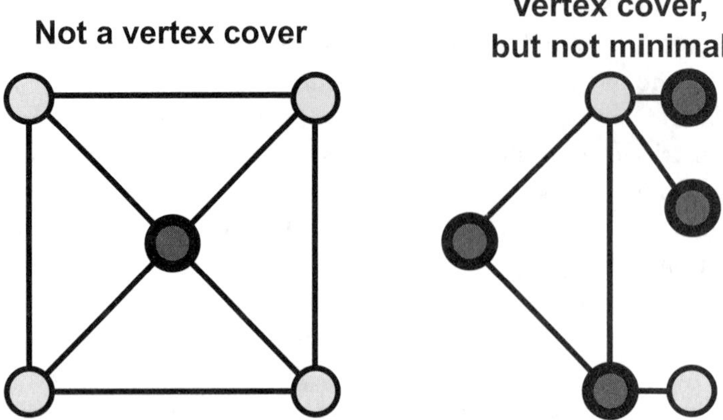
Not a vertex cover
Vertex cover,
but not minimal

Figure 18.20 Examples of subsets that are not a minimum vertex cover on these graphs. On the left, not all edges are covered by the vertex in the center of the graph, so that vertex by itself is not a vertex cover. On the right, an example of a vertex cover that, however, is not minimal (see figure 18.19).

of NP optimization problems for which there exists a polynomial-time constant-factor approximation algorithm.

For some categories of graphs, like bipartite graphs and trees, there exist worst-case polynomial-time algorithms to solve minimum vertex cover exactly, but besides these happy cases, we either accept an approximated (non-optimal) solution, or we need an exponential-time algorithm.

It goes without saying that we are going for the former by using a genetic algorithm. But first, let's talk about applications of this problem.

18.3.1 Applications of vertex cover

Back to our e-commerce company: as the business grows, so do warehouses. To protect the company from thefts and to guarantee the employees' safety, we need to install cameras that cover all the alleys. Suppose that our warehouses are shaped like the graphs in figure 18.20, where edges are alleys, and vertices are placed at cross points and dead ends; also suppose that cameras have special wide lenses (or motors, or both) and can cover up to 180° or even 360°. Then, the minimum number of cameras we need is given by the minimum vertex cover for those graphs.

Although oversimplified, this is a real, recurring application of the problem, the easiest to adapt to our example scenario, but definitely not the only one.

Another field where efficient vertex cover algorithms make a difference is bioinformatics, in particular computational biochemistry. It often happens that DNA sequences in samples present conflicts (the exact definition of conflict depends on the context) that we need to resolve: graphs come to our aid. We can define a conflict graph where vertices are sequences and edges are added when there is a conflict between any pair of sequences. Notice that this graph is potentially disconnected.

Since the goal is to resolve all conflicts by removing as few sequences as possible, what we are looking for is the minimum vertex cover of the conflict graph.

Going back to computer science applications, vertex cover can be used to aid network security. It has been employed[27] to design optimal strategies, in terms of combinatorial topology of routers, against the diffusion of stealth worms in large computer networks.

Finally, among the many other fields where we can find this problem, we'd like to mention one that we have already discussed in this book: minimum vertex cover has been used[28] to develop an efficient nearest neighbor classifier for general metric spaces (not limited to Euclidean spaces or to Hilbert spaces).

18.3.2 Implementing a genetic algorithm

Now it's time to roll up our sleeves and write a decent optimizer for this problem; the good news is that we can reuse most of the work we had done for the 0-1 knapsack!

The solutions to the minimum vertex cover problem, in fact, are subsets of the vertices, just like for the knapsack they were subsets of the items available. We can therefore implement chromosomes as bit strings and reuse the same crossover and mutation operators!

The only thing that changes, obviously, is the definition of the fitness function. Here the quality of the solution is given by the number of vertices in the chosen subset (the smaller, the better) under the constraint that all edges are covered. We could implement the constraint separately and discard all subsets that are not vertex covers or assign a huge value to their fitness. This way, however, a minimal solution that covers all edges but one would be penalized even with respect to the trivial solution containing all vertices (which is a valid vertex cover). It is important, instead, to keep the former solution in the population, as it could be turned into a valid vertex cover by adding a single vertex.

To work around this issue, I suggest we integrate the number of uncovered edges into the fitness function, with a certain multiplicator (by default, we can use `2`).

Considering the first example in figure 18.20, let's compare two possible solutions in figure 18.21. The graph on the left has one uncovered edge, so its fitness is `5`, the same as the trivial solution (on the right) which is a vertex cover. This example also shows how important it is that the multiplicator for the uncovered edges is greater than 1. If we just added the number of uncovered edges to the number of vertices, the solution on the left would have fitness equal to `4`, but any subset with 4 vertices would be a better, and valid, solution.

At the same time, using this fitness function, we don't discard a promising solution that is only two mutations away from the minimum vertex cover (which uses only 3 vertices).

---

[27]Filiol, Eric, et al. "Combinatorial optimization of worm propagation on an unknown network." *International Journal of Computer Science* 2.2 (2007): 124-130.

[28]Gottlieb, Lee-Ad, Aryeh Kontorovich, and Robert Krauthgamer. "Efficient classification for metric data." *IEEE Transactions on Information Theory* 60.9 (2014): 5750-5759.

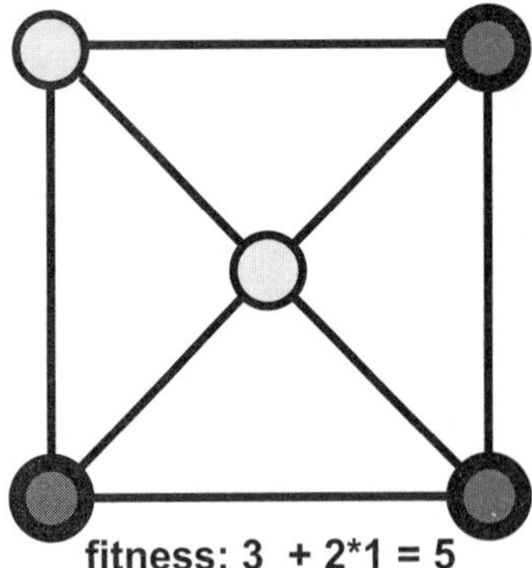
fitness: 3 + 2*1 = 5

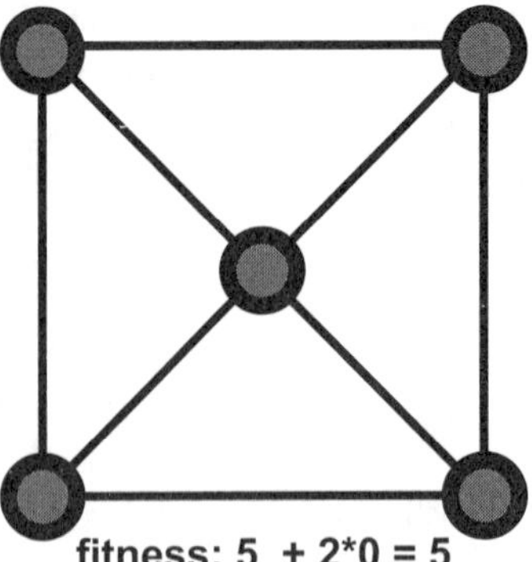
fitness: 5 + 2*0 = 5

Figure 18.21 Evaluating fitness of possible solutions. We combine the number of vertices with the number of edges not covered, to avoid discarding promising solutions which are not valid vertex covers, like the one on the left.

Listing 18.13 shows an implementation of the fitness function for this method. The caveat, with respect to the knapsack problem, is that we also need to pass an instance of the graph to this method, because it's needed in order to check which edges are covered by the solution. In many languages, this can be obtained without changing the template for the genetic algorithm (shown in listings 18.10 and 18.4) by currying the fitness function and bounding it to an instance of the graph before passing it to the genetic algorithm main method.

JavaScript, for instance, is one of the languages that allows this: check out the implementation provided with JsGraphs on GitHub.[29]

Listing 18.13 Vertex cover: fitness function

```
function vertexCoverFitness(graph, chromosome)
  fitness ← 0
  for gene in chromosome do
    if gene == 1 then
      fitness ← fitness + 1
  for edge in graph.edges do
    if chromosome[edge.source] == 0
      and chromosome[edge.destination] == 0 then
        fitness ← fitness + 2
  return fitness
```

- Method `vertexCoverFitness` takes a chromosome (a bit string) and returns the fitness value associated with the solution it's encoding.
- Initializes the fitness value to 0
- Cycles through all genes (all bits) in the chromosome
- If a gene is set to 1, it means we are using that vertex in the solution, so we have to account for it in the cost. Remember, the goal is minimizing the number of vertices used, while providing a valid vertex cover.
- Cycles through all edges in the graph
- If neither of the edge's endpoints are included in the solution, this edge is not covered (the solution in not a valid vertex cover). Rather than discarding it, we can add a penalty term to the fitness value. In this case, we add 2, but we could also pass the desired penalty as an argument instead and make this method more flexible.

[29] See https://github.com/mlarocca/jsgraphs/blob/master/src/graph/algo/genetic/vertex_cover.mjs.

And that was almost all the new code we need to write a solver for vertex cover. There is only a final word of caution.

To be certain to return a valid vertex cover, we will need to sort the final population by fitness and, starting from the one with the smallest fitness value, validate solutions: we can return the first one in the sorted list that is also covering all edges.

18.4 Other applications of the genetic algorithm

There are countless problems, both on graphs and on generic data structures, that can be formulated as optimization problems, for which a genetic algorithm could be an effective way to get to a near-optimal solution in a reasonable time.

We'll briefly discuss two of them that are particularly relevant for their applications: finding the maximum flow of a graph, and protein folding.

18.4.1 Maximum flow

The maximum flow problem is defined on a specific type of directed graphs called networks (see figure 18.22). A network `N=(V,E)` is a directed, weighted graph where there are two special nodes `s,t ∈ V: s` is called the source, and `t` is called the sink of the network. The peculiarity of these vertices is that the source only has outgoing edges, while the sink only has ingoing edges.

In networks, edges' weights are called *capacity*. The exact characterization of edges' capacity depends on the context. For instance, for a hydraulic network, edges model pipes, and their weight is the maximum volume of liquid that can go through the pipe at any time.

A network is used to model the flow through its vertices, starting from a source and arriving at a sink, where an edge's flow is the actual amount (for instance, of water) that goes through the edge. Each vertex `v` of the network has an inbound flow (for instance, the total amount of water through its ingoing edges) that can be redistributed to its outgoing edges, with the caveat that the total outbound flow must be equal to the inbound one. Referring to figure 18.22, showing an example of a network, node `D` can have a maximum inbound flow (the sum of its ingoing edges' capacity) of `5` units, and a maximum theoretical outbound flow of `6`. Therefore, the real flow through `D` can never be larger than `5`, and that only happens when its inbound flow is at max: if `D` at some point had an inbound flow of `4`, because some of the flow from `A` was diverted to `E` instead of `D`, its outbound flow would then be limited to `4`. When the maximum possible outbound flow is larger than the inbound flow, as in this case, it means that we need to make a choice about how to route the outgoing flow, because we can't use the capacity of outgoing edges to the fullest. For instance, considering that the max flow from `F` to the sink is `1`, it makes more sense to route flow from `D` toward vertex `G`, so that we maximize the total inbound flow of the sink `t`: this is also the goal of the maximum flow problem.

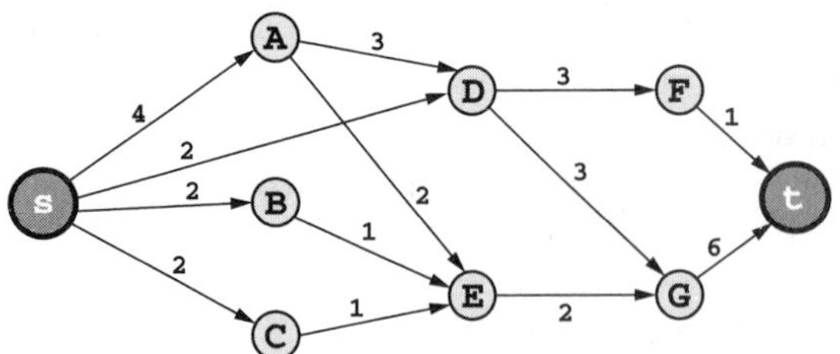
A
B
C
D
E
F
G
s
t
4
2
2
2
3
2
1
1
3
3
2
1
6

Figure 18.22 An example of a network, whose maximum flow is 6.

More formally, a flow for a network is defined as a mapping between edges and real numbers, an assignment to each edge, such that:

- The flow of an edge is smaller or equal to the edge's capacity.
- The total flow entering a vertex must be equal to the total flow exiting a vertex (except for `s` and `t`, which by definition have respectively *null inbound* and *null outbound* flows).

The value of the flow is defined as the sum of the flow exiting the source vertex `s` or, equivalently, the sum of the flow entering the sink vertex `t`.

A maximum flow for a network graph `G` is a valid flow whose value is the maximum possible for `G`.

Notice that a maximum flow problem is not NP-Hard, because there are several polynomial-time algorithms that can solve it exactly. These algorithms, however, are still at least $O(|V|^3)$, which makes them impractical for very large graphs; moreover, there are some variants of this problem that are NP-complete.

Now that the problem is clearly stated, how do we design a genetic algorithm for it?

First and foremost, as always, we need to decide about the fitness function and chromosome encoding. The latter is easy—we need one gene per edge, and each of them can be assigned any value between `0` and the edge's capacity.

This encoding (shown in figure 18.23) automatically validates the first constraint in the formal definition of flow, but it can't do anything for the second one. We still need to check each solution, because it will only be valid if the second constraint is abided by.

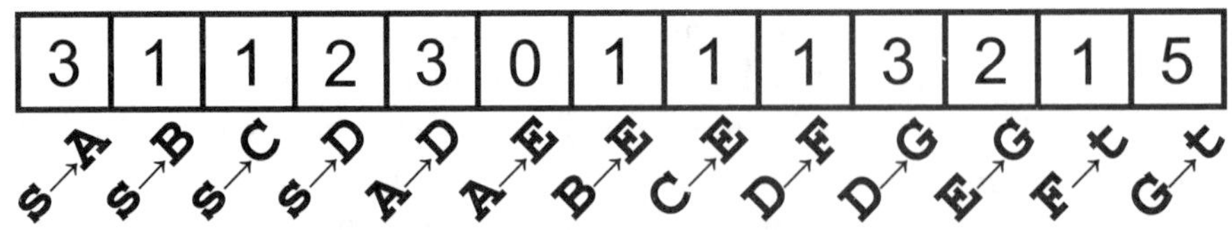
3 1 1 2 3 0 1 1 1 3 2 1 5
S→A S→B S→C S→D A→D A→E B→E C→E D→F D→G E→G F→t G→t

Figure 18.23 A solution (aka a chromosome) for the maximum flow of the network in figure 18.22. Is this a valid flow? Is it maximal?

We can do this in two ways: either we discard invalid flows (probably not a good choice, for the same reasons as it wasn't for vertex cover), or we add a term to the fitness function accounting for this.

For instance, we can compute the absolute value of the flow difference for all vertices (except `s` and `t`), and divide the solution's flow by the cumulative difference, if that's not zero.

Crossover and mutations are easier. We can use single point recombination and a punctiform mutation that randomly increases or decreases an edge's flow by 1 (within the edge's capacity).

If you've read through the chapter so far, you should have all the tools to not only implement this algorithm, but also to design more sophisticated, and possibly better, operators and try different definitions for the fitness function.

Instead of delving into the implementation, therefore, I'd like to spend a few words on why this is an important problem.

There are several practical applications of maximum flow in the physical world; for example, the scheduling of an airline's flight crew, or even more interesting to us, the *circulation-demand problem.* If you remember, our example e-commerce company was looking for ways to maximize the trucks' load and minimize the excess of capacity that is needed to face peaks in demand; it turns out that we could write that problem as a maximum flow problem!

In the circulation-demand problem, in fact, we have a source of goods, for instance, our warehouse, and a set of destinations where we need to deliver these goods. There are, however, also constraints. One is that the maximum capacity of each truck is an insurmountable limit, because we can't overload them. And if we have several warehouses/factories, the problem becomes even more challenging.

But, besides these practical issues, *maximum flow* is a classic problem in computer science and software engineering!

A few examples of problems that can be modeled as maximum flow optimization are image segmentation, scheduling, network connectivity, and compilers optimization.

18.4.2 Protein folding

In the last few chapters we have mostly discussed graph problems that can be solved through optimization (meta)heuristics. Before wrapping up our review of GAs' applications, I'd like to mention a different kind of problem, which is terribly important, as we've learned in these difficult times.

Proteins are large molecules, sequences of amino acids that are encoded in organisms' DNA and (once DNA is decoded by cells) produced by their cells to perform many different functions within each organism: regulating the response to stimuli, transporting simpler molecules within and across cells, catalyzing metabolic reactions, even DNA replication itself, and many more—they are instrumental to the functioning of any organism.

Among other things, the 3-D structure of surface proteins determines the ability of viruses to tie to receptors and infect certain types of cells—something that recently moved protein folding to the top of the list of the most pressing problems to solve.

Two proteins differ by their sequence of amino acids, which determines the 3-D structure of the protein, which in turn determines the protein's activity.

Protein folding is the physical process by which a linear protein chain (aka *polypeptide*) acquires its native 3-D conformation.

Now, the sequence of amino acids of a protein is determined by the DNA that encodes it, and is relatively easier to find out experimentally. It is the protein's 3-D structure, however, that determines its functionality, and that's much harder to determine in a lab (although new microimaging techniques are being developed).

One of the earliest and most successful applications of genetic algorithms was determining the most likely 3-D structure of proteins[30] whose sequence of amino acids was known. The idea is similar to what we discussed in chapters 16 and 17 for force-directed graph drawing (another reason why that was an important topic!). We can design a fitness function taking into account the attraction and repulsion forces between peptides (sequences of amino acids), amino acids, and even down to their atoms, and search for the 3-D configuration of minimal energy for the system.

Genetic algorithms and artificial immune systems have been the heuristics of choice for the protein folding problem. It's worth noting that at the time of writing, the current state of the art in this field is obtained by another biologically inspired algorithm, neural networks.[31]

18.4.3 Beyond genetic algorithms

Genetic algorithms are just a branch of the larger field of *evolutionary algorithms (EA)*, a category including all generic population-based meta-heuristic optimization algorithms.

I couldn't have chosen a better way to close this chapter, and the book, than with a summary of the most interesting EAs in computer science's literature. Consider it a starting point to deepening your understanding of optimization algorithms.

Memetic algorithm[32] is a class of optimization meta-heuristics directly derived from GA. Its peculiarity is that one or more of the mutation operators actually perform a local-search heuristics, something like random sampling over the current solution's neighborhood, driving each individual toward a local optimum at each iteration (for instance, trying to flip each bit in a chromosome individually, and retaining the best result), and making this algorithm a hybrid between GA and random sampling, or potentially even gradient descent. The key in either situation is leveraging additional domain knowledge for the problem to perform the local optimization.

---

[30] Schulze-Kremer, Steffen. "Genetic algorithms and protein folding." *Protein Structure Prediction*. Humana Press, 2000. 175-222.

[31] The AlphaFold project, developed by DeepMind: http://mng.bz/Qmm4.

[32] Moscato, Pablo. "On evolution, search, optimization, genetic algorithms and martial arts: Towards memetic algorithms." Caltech concurrent computation program, C3P Report 826 (1989): 1989.

Artificial immune system[33] *(AIS)* is a class of biologically inspired algorithms modeled after the immune system and its ability to learn and retain memory, that extends the work on genetic algorithms with operators like *clonal selection, affinity maturation,* and *negative selection.*

Particle swarm optimization,[34] which is instead better used on numerical optimization, uses flock dynamics to explore the cost function landscape. The mechanism is similar to genetic algorithms, with a population (swarm) of solutions that is maintained and moved around, only not through genetic operators, but simpler rules inspired by a mix of kinematics and biology.

Ant colony optimization[35] is a probabilistic technique inspired by the way ant colonies use pheromone-based communication to form paths to food sources. It's particularly well suited for problems on graphs and specifically for those that can be reduced to finding paths in a graph.

And these examples are just the tip of the iceberg; there are plenty of evolutionary algorithms inspired by different biological principles, so many that they deserve a book of their own.

18.4.4 Algorithms, beyond this book

We are at the end of this book, but this is not the end of your algorithmic journey!

First of all, if you enjoyed the topics in this book, here is a list of suggested readings that can help you delve further into some of them:

- *Grokking Machine Learning,* by Andrew Trask, talks extensively about machine learning and some of the training algorithms we have briefly described in chapters 12, 13, and 16. If you'd like to learn how gradient descent is used in linear regression and logistic regression, this book is a good starting point.
- *Grokking Artificial Intelligence Algorithms,* by Rishal Hurbans, delves into some of the topics we summarized in this book, such as search and optimization and evolutionary algorithms, and presents advanced concepts we have just mentioned, such as swarm intelligence.
- *Graph-Powered Machine Learning,* by Allesandro Nego, is a good choice if you'd like to put what you've learned about graphs to good use and tackle machine learning from a different angle.
- *Graph Databases in Action,* by Dave Bechberger and Josh Perryman, explores another recent application of graphs. With this book, you'll learn how graphs allow a better modeling of relations in data and why graph databases are the choice of election for highly-intercorrelated data.

---

[33]Kephart, Jeffrey O. "A biologically inspired immune system for computers." *In Proc. Of The Fourth International Workshop On Synthesis And Simulation Of Living Systems, Artificial Life IV.* 1994.

[34]Eberhart, Russell C., Yuhui Shi, and James Kennedy. *Swarm Intelligence.* Elsevier, 2001.

[35]Dorigo, Marco, and Luca Maria Gambardella. "Ant colony system: a cooperative learning approach to the traveling salesman problem." *IEEE Transactions on evolutionary computation 1.1* (1997): 53-66.

- *Algorithms and Data Structures for Massive Datasets,* by Dzejla Medjedovic et al., expands on the topics in this book, focusing on techniques to adapt data structures and algorithms to massive datasets and handle modern big data applications.

And then, if you'd like to test your understanding of the data structures we have discussed, here is my challenge for you: implement these algorithms in your favorite language, and add them to this repository[36] I created on GitHub! You'll find detailed instructions on the repo's README.[37]

Good luck for the next steps in your learning path, and I hope you will enjoy the coding challenge!

Summary

- As in populations dynamics, in a genetic algorithm the fitness of organisms is measured, and the ones that best adapt to their environment have a greater chance of surviving and passing their genome to the new generations.
- *Crossover* is a new concept, with respect to other optimization algorithms such as simulated annealing that allow the algorithm to randomly recombine features of several organisms.
- *Mutation* is the biological analogy to local-search optimization, just like the transition operators for simulated annealing.
- If in the cost function definition many variables are highly coupled, and changing one forces us to change one or more of the others, then the problem (as we modeled it) has high *epistasis.*
- When there is a high interdependence between variables, simulated annealing can perform better than genetic algorithms. It's worth trying both on smaller instances and deciding based on the actual data.
- *Vertex cover* is a problem with low epistasis where genetic algorithms shine.

---

[36]See https://github.com/mlarocca/AlgorithmsAndDataStructuresReadersContributions.
[37]See http://mng.bz/1rjn.

appendix A A quick guide to pseudo-code

For this book we decided to use pseudo-code to describe how algorithms work. This decision was mainly motivated by two considerations:

- We wanted to make the book accessible to readers with all kind of backgrounds, without being tied to a particular programming language or paradigm.
- By providing a generic description of the steps performed by the algorithm and abstracting away low-level details, we can focus on the essence of the algorithms without worrying about programming language quirks.

The whole point of pseudo-code should be to provide a generic, complete, and easy-to-understand description of algorithms; hence, if it is done properly, there should be no need to further explain it.

At the same time, even pseudo-code uses arbitrary conventions and needs to be consistent and well defined. Moreover, readers who are not familiar either with this approach or with the notations or conventions chosen might initially need some time to adjust and get up to speed.

For this reason, we decided to add a short guide explaining the notation we are going to use throughout the book. If you already feel comfortable with reading pseudo-code, you can safely skip this appendix, or just refer to it when you feel you need clarifications on notation.

A.1 Variables and basics

Like for every other programming language, the first fundamental step is being able to save values and recover them: as you all know, while low-level languages like `Assembly` uses *registers* as locations where you can park a value, higher-level languages introduced the concept of *variables.*

Variables are just named placeholders that can be created and to which values can be assigned and later read.

Some languages, the strongly typed ones, require each variable to accept only a certain type of value (for example, integers or strings) for the whole life of a variable. Other languages (loosely typed) will allow variables to hold any value without restricting them to a single type. The loosely typed approach also removes the need to declare variables before assigning them: a variable will be automatically created when it is first assigned (but note that using its value before assigning it will result in an error, in all loosely typed languages).

For pseudo-code, using a loosely typed approach is pretty natural; as mentioned, we would like to abstract as much as possible from implementation details.

Another open point for variables (and functions, and so on) is the naming convention used. This is not something that a programming language will force (usually), but rather a convention that stems from the community and from guidelines.

We will use *camelCase* for names, not for any technical reason or preference toward one programming language, but just because it uses fewer characters than *snake_case*, and that makes it easier to fit code on a book page.

So, for instance, we will use *doAction* rather than *do_action* for a function name, and something like *RedBox* for a class or object.

There are a few basic operations on variables that are needed to interact with them:

- *Assigning to a variable*—We use a left-pointing arrow; for instance, `index ← 1` assigns the value 1 to a variable named "index."
- *Reading a variable value*—We just use the variable name, and that becomes a placeholder for the value held by the variable when that line of code is executed: `index ← size` reads the value of the variable size and assigns it to `index`.
- *Comparing values*:
  - We use two equal characters to compare two variables or values[1] for equality: `index == size` or `index == 1` are two examples, the former comparing two variables, and the latter comparing a variable and a value.
  - To compare for inequality, we use either `<>` or `!=`: `index <> size`.

We adopt the standard operators for less than, greater than, and so on: `index <= size`, for instance, evaluates to `true` if index is less than or equal than `size`.

A.2 Arrays

Arrays can somewhat be considered a special case of variables, because you can assign/read the whole array or just its single elements. If you are not familiar with arrays and containers, check out appendix C.

[1] In the general case, we can compare two expressions composing both variables and values.

In our pseudo-code we will abstract over the details of the implementation of the arrays typical of individual programming languages. In particular, we will treat arrays as dynamic, without the need to explicitly allocate room for the elements before accessing them.

Some programming languages provide natively this concept of dynamic arrays; others provide something similar in their standard libraries, often with a data structure called `vector`.

Arrays can also either have a homogenous type, meaning that all their elements must have the same type, decided when the array is created, or can hold any value independently on the type. This is usually connected to a programming language being strongly or loosely typed.

As mentioned in the previous section, we will abstract over variable types in this book's pseudocode, so the latter approach will be naturally assumed. However, for most of our data structures we will only need arrays and containers that hold elements of the same type, and unless it's stated differently, you can safely assume this will be the case: just be aware that handling arrays with heterogeneous types is possible, but requires extra effort and care.

As for the nomenclature, to access an array element we use square brackets, like most programming languages do: `A[i]` denotes the value of the `i`-th element of array `A`, and similarly, to assign a value to that element, we use the regular syntax we have shown for variables, something like `A[j] ← b` (that assigns the value of the variable `b` to the `j`-th element of array `A`).

Whenever it's not stated otherwise, we will assume arrays use 0-based indexing, so the first element in array `A` will be `A[0]`, the second one `A[1]`, and so on.

We will also, occasionally, have to perform certain operations on arrays (and containers in general). For example, we might need to find the maximum value in an array of numbers, or the longest word in an array of strings, or the sum of values in a numeric array.

For these array-wide operations, we will use something closer to mathematical notation, for the sake of synthesis. For instance, given an array `A`

- `max{A}` stands for the maximum value of `A`.
- `sum{A}` is the sum of all element of `A`.
- `sum{x ∈ A | x > 0}` is the sum of positive elements of `A`.
- `A[i] ←` i^3 `(∀ i ∈ {0..|A|-1} | i % 3 ==0)` sets all elements of `A` whose indices are multiples of 3 to the cube of the index.

It goes without saying that depending on the programming language you choose, there might not be a direct translation into a single instruction, and you will need to use or write a helper method to perform the same operations.

A.3 Conditional instructions

The next fundamental concepts we need in order to write a meaningful program are conditional statements. Most programming languages implement conditionals with an *if-then-else* construction, and we will use a similar syntax.

For instance, to express a simple algorithm to compute the absolute value of a number x and store it in another variable y, we will use the following syntax:

```
if x < 0 then
  y ← -x
else
  y ← x
```

Conditions are not surrounded by parentheses, and we don't use curly braces for blocks (see section A.4). Also, notice that keywords will be in a **bold** font.

Sometimes, you won't need an else clause, specifically whenever you need to take action only if a condition is met and do nothing otherwise. For instance, figure A.1 shows an alternative version of the absolute value algorithm, assigning the absolute value of x to x itself; this allows us to simplify the initial code as

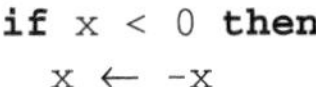

```
if x < 0 then
  x ← -x
```

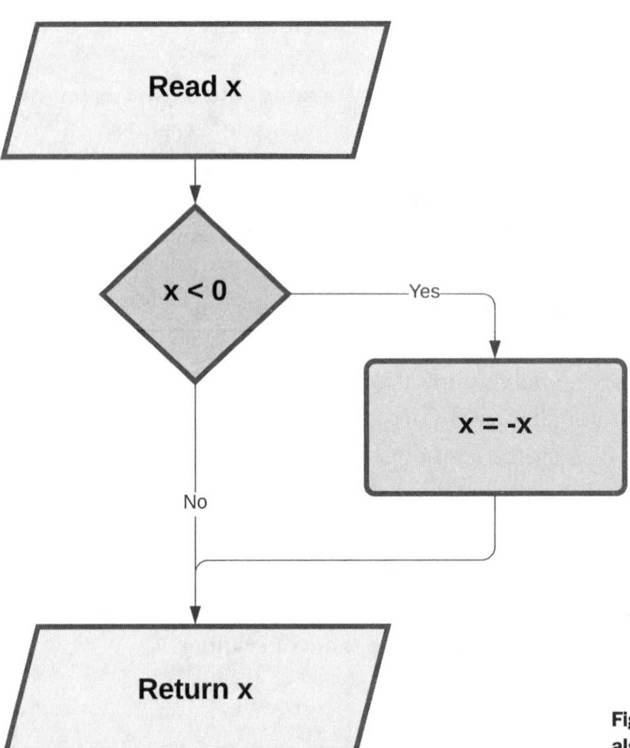
Read x
x < 0
Yes
x = -x
No
Return x

Figure A.1 Possible flowchart for an algorithm computing absolute value

A.3.1 Else-if

At other times we need to decide between more than two branches. In that case, while it is possible to implement the same logic using multiple nested if-then-else statements, it would make the code cumbersome and mangled (because of the indentation).

A more succinct approach uses the else-if variant, common in script languages such as Python and Ruby.

Here we decided to use the elsif keyword:

```
if x < 0 then
  y ← -1/x
elsif x > 0 then
  y ← 1/x
else
  y ← NaN
```

Incidentally, this code snippet computes the absolute value of the reciprocal of a number x, and NaN stands for "not a number," that's the best choice to express the fact that 1/0 is not defined.[2]

A.3.2 Switch

Many programming languages also offer a specialized instruction to be used when the condition we check can assume several discrete values. Usually this instruction is called switch and allows us to enumerate possible values that an expression can assume and perform a different case branch for each one of them (plus a default branch if the value doesn't match any of the other cases):

```
switch x² + y²
  case 0
    label ← "origin"
  case 1
    label ← "unit circle"
  default
    label ← "circle"
```

The code snippet evaluates the expression $x^2 + y^2$: each case statement corresponds to a different branch executed when the expression evaluates to whatever follows the keyword, so if $x^2 + y^2$ evaluates to 0, then the code after the first case is executed, and the variable label is set to "origin"; similarly, if the value is 1, label is set to "unit circle". For any other value, the branch after the keyword default is executed and the label is set to "circle".

We will use an extended version of this instruction, also allowing ranges to be specified in case statements:

[2] Another less mathematically precise alternative could have been assigning **inf** (which stands for infinity) to y, but since the sign of the limit depends on the direction we approach 0, neither +inf nor -inf would be correct.

```
switch x² + y²
  case 0
    label ← "origin"
  case [0,1]
    label ← "inside unit circle"
  case {1..10}
    label ← "multiple of unit circle"
  default
    label ← "outside unit circle"
```

In this code snippet, we use four different rule types for matching:

- The first one matches exactly one value (0).
- The second one matches all numbers between 0 and 1 included.
- The third rule matches all integers between 1 and 10 included.
- The last one matches all values (by default).

Notice that rules are evaluated from top to bottom, and the first clause matching will be selected, so, for instance, while the value 0 for $x^2 + y^2$ would match both the first and second (and fourth!) clause, only the top-most one will match.

Finally, we have shown examples evaluating numeric expressions, but we will allow all kind of values (for instance, strings) to be switched on.

A.4 Loops

The other fundamental constructs that are needed to control the workflow are loops.

Traditionally, programming languages provide at least two kinds of loops:

- for loops, where we iterate explicitly over some indices or the elements in a container
- while loops, which are somewhat more generic, where a predicate is given and the statements in the loop are executed until the predicate evaluates to true

There are several variations on both (for instance do-while, for-each, and repeat-until), but all loops can always be implemented in terms of the basic while loop.

We will use the for-each loop, and the basic while statement.

For both, we can further control the execution using keywords continue (that will force execution to skip to the next iteration in the loop) and break (that will force execution to immediately exit the loop without checking its predicate).

Providing a few examples should help to clarify this.

A.4.1 For loop

To exemplify the use of for loops, let's see how to sum all elements in an array A. There are at least three ways to do so.

The first one iterates over the length of the array:

```
n ← length(A)
total ← 0
for i in {0..n-1} do
  total ← total + A[i]
```

After the `for` keyword, we will specify the name of the variable (`i`) that will hold the values on which we iterate; then we need the `in` keyword, and after that the (ordered) list of values that `i` will assume (in this case, all integers from `0` to `n-1` included).

Since we only need the index `i` to access the current element in the array, we can obtain the same result in a more succinct way by iterating over `A`'s elements directly:

```
total ← 0
for a in A do
  total ← total + a
```

Finally, as we have shown in a previous section, whenever possible we will also use a mathematical notation instead of a `for` loop to be even more succinct, without hurting clarity:

```
total ← sum{A}
```

The last two options are, obviously, not always viable. For instance, if we need to write complex expressions using more than one element of an array at a time, then we might need to explicitly iterate over indices:

```
n ← length(A)
total ← A[0]
for i in {1..n-1} do
  total ← total + A[i] + A[i-1]²
```

A.4.2 While loop

As mentioned, `while` loops are intended to be more generic. As such, they can be used to implement the same logic of `for` loops, included in the examples in the previous section. This is an equivalent `for` loop to compute the sum of the elements in an array:

```
n ← length(A)
i ← 0
total ← 0
while i < n do
  total ← total + A[i]
  i ← i + 1
```

Clearly the `for-each` syntax is a way to express the same logic with less code (and also, as importantly, it encapsulates the logic of iterating through indices, making it less error-prone than the `while` loop, where we have to initialize and increment `i` explicitly).

With `while` loops, however, we can also write conditions that would be hard or impossible to express using `for` statements:

```
while not eof(file) do
  x ← read(file)
  total ← total + x
```

The code snippet abstracts the process of reading integers from a file and summing them, until we reach the end of the file (eof).

For a more concrete example, consider the algorithm to compute the *greatest common divisor (GCD)* of two integers, a and b:

```
while a <> b do
  if a > b then
    a ← a - b
  else
    b ← b - a
```

At the end of the loop, variable a will hold the GCD of a and b.

As you can see, both examples need to evaluate a predicate that is clearly harder to express with a for-each loop.

A.4.3 Break and continue

Sometimes you need to check multiple conditions or react to conditions that can only be evaluated inside the body of the loops. To cope with that, we can use break and continue. For instance, to refine the example summing numbers in a file, we might decide that we skip odd numbers and use 0 as a marker, which means that we stop summing numbers as soon as we read a 0:

```
while not eof(file) do
  x ← read(file)
  if x % 2 == 1 then
    continue
  elsif x == 0 then
    break
  total ← total + x
```

Whenever the next number read from the file is odd, then we skip to the next iteration of the loop (meaning we will again check the predicate, and find out if we are at the end of the file).

If, instead, the number is 0, we will exit the loop before incrementing our total.

Both keywords can also be used inside for loops.

A.5 Blocks and indent

So far, in most of our examples, loops and each branch of our conditionals consisted of exactly one instruction, and this made syntax particularly simple. However, that's not the case in general, and each branch of the if-then-else statement can execute an arbitrary number of instructions. To avoid ambiguity, we need to be able to group instructions into *blocks*.

In its simplest definition, a block of instructions is a sequence of instructions that is executed sequentially from top to bottom.

As always, different programming languages have different ways to specify blocks: some of them use curly braces to mark the beginning and ending of a block (for instance, C, Java, and so on), some use explicitly the begin and end keywords (for instance, Pascal), and others use indentation (Python).

Moreover, blocks can carry extra meaning in some programming languages, specifically if *block-scope* is used; then local variables defined inside a block can only be accessed inside that same block of code (including any nested block).

To simplify things, as mentioned, we won't bother with declaring variables, and we will instead assume *function-scope*, so variables can be accessed everywhere inside a function (see the following code snippet). We will also assume *lexical scope* (aka static scope), so the life of variables ends when a function execution is completed, and there will be no support for *closures*.

Finally, blocks will be defined by indentation only. You can see the previous examples are already indented, but the following example should clarify this even further:

```
for i in {0..n-1} do
  k ← i * 2
  j ← i * 2 + 1
  if i % 2 == 0 then
    A[k] ← 1
    A[j] ← 0
  else
    A[k] ← 0
    A[j] ← 1
A[2*n-1] ← 0
```

The `for` loop executes `n` times the eight lines below it (all but the very last line in the snippet) and each branch of the `if` statement has two instructions (that can be recognized because they are further indented).

The line containing `A[2*n-1] ← 0` does not have any indentation (it's at the same level of indentation of the first line) and that shows it is the next instruction to be executed after the `for` loop ends

A.6 Functions

To group and reuse code, we will use functions. A function defines a block of code where local variables are in scope. It also has a signature declaring its name and the arguments it expects: the variables that are the input to the function. Finally, a function also returns a value that is effectively the function's output.

Breaking code into functions allows writing reusable code that can be more easily understood and unit-tested, because (ideally) every function can (and should) only implement a single responsibility (or a single action/algorithm, if you prefer).

Take, for instance, the code in section A.4.2 that computes the GCD of two numbers. We can easily refactor it into a function:

```
function gcd(a, b)
  while a <> b do
    if a > b then
      a ← a - b
```

```
    else
      b ← b - a
  return a
```

Notice, among other things, how it is now immediately clear where the final result is stored—the best part is, the caller doesn't even have to worry about it, because the function takes care of returning the right value. Moreover, variables a and b only exist inside function gcd, and therefore anything happening inside the body of this function won't influence the rest of the code.

A.6.1 Overloading and default arguments

A function's arguments can have default values:

```
function f(a, b=2)
  return a * b²
```

For instance, a binary function f that has a default value for the second argument could be called with either two arguments, something like f(5,3), or just one. In that case, for example, f(5) is the same as calling f(5,2).

Default arguments allow a compact syntax for overloading functions and methods.

Because we are using a loosely-typed approach, this is the only kind of overloading we need or can even perform (while in strongly-typed languages like C++ or Java, we would need to overload functions for which an argument can be an integer or a string or . . .).

A.6.2 Tuples

Sometimes we need functions to return more than one value. To make things easy for us, we assume that functions can return tuples.

A tuple is similar to an array, although slightly different:

- It's a list of values with a fixed length (while arrays can grow or shrink).
- Its elements can have any type, and tuples can hold different types at the same time.

Tuples are denoted using parentheses: (1,2) is a tuple of length two (aka a *pair*) whose elements are numbers with values 1 and 2.

We can assign tuples of values to tuples of variables:

```
(x, y, z) ← (0, -1, 0.5)
```

is equivalent to

```
x ← 0
y ← -1
z ← 0.5
```

Likewise, we can write (name, age) ← ("Marc", 20).

This syntax can be extremely useful to implement functions returning multiple values. Suppose we have written a function `min_max` returning both the max and min values in an array; then we can assume it returns a pair of values and call it like this:

```
(a_min, a_max) ← min_max(A)
```

A.6.3 Tuples and destructuring objects

It is a good practice to avoid unnamed tuples, because the meaning of a field is not immediately apparent and is only determined by the position inside the tuple; therefore, objects are to be preferred (for instance, an object with a `min` and `max` field would be clearer in the example in the previous sub-section).

Tuples, however, provide a viable and synthetic alternative whenever the meaning of the fields is clear enough. To exploit this even further, we use a particular notation to assign all or part of the fields of an object to a tuple. Assume we have an object `Employee` with fields `name`, `surname`, `age`, `address`, and so on.

If `empl` is an instance of employee, we use the following syntax to extract any subset of fields from `empl` into *aliases*:[3]

```
(name, surname, age) ← empl
```

Of course, in this example, we extract only three fields.

This syntax is particularly convenient in combination with `for-each` loops, because we can iterate through a collection of employees and directly access aliases to the fields we need, without having to redundantly write something like `empl.name` each time we access a field of the `empl` object. Here is a comparative example to make the difference clear:

```
for empl in employees do
  user ← empl.surname + empl.age

for (surname, age) in employees do
  user ← surname + age
```

[3] An alias is just another name for a variable: it can be implemented by creating a new variable or just a reference to the original one.

appendix B *Big-O notation*

In this appendix, we provide a refresher about the RAM model and the renowned big-O mathematical notation, showing you it's not as bad as you might have heard. Don't worry; to go through the book you'll only need a high-level understanding, just the bare minimum to apply it in the algorithm analysis.

B.1 Algorithms and performance

Describing the performance of an algorithm is not a trivial exercise. You might be used to describing the performance of your code in term of benchmarks, and that might seem straightforward, but if you start thinking about how to describe it effectively, so that your findings can be shared and be meaningful to others, then it raises more issues than you initially thought of.

For example, what does performance even mean? It usually implies some kind of measure, so what will it be?

Your first answer might be that you measure the time interval needed to run the algorithm on a certain input. A step further might even be realizing that you might need to average over several inputs, and several runs on the same input, to account for external factors. This would still be a noisy measurement, especially with modern multicore architectures. It's going to be hard to sandbox your experiments, and both the operating system and background processes will influence the result.

But this is not even the worst part. This result will be largely influenced by the hardware you are running your experiments on, so it won't have any meaning as an absolute number. You might try to run a benchmark test and compare your algorithm performance to some other known algorithm. Sometimes this technique produces meaningful results, but it doesn't seem like the way to go, because there would still be too many variables to take into consideration, from the hardware and operating system it's running on to the type and size of input used in your tests.

Continuing in your reasoning, you can think about counting the instructions that are run. This is probably a good indicator of how much time will be needed to run the whole algorithm, and sufficiently generalizable, right?

Well . . . not quite.

1. Will you count machine instructions? If so, it will not be platform-agnostic.
2. If, instead, you count high-level instructions only, it will heavily depend on the programming language you choose. Scala or Nim can be much more succinct than Java, Pascal, or COBOL.
3. What can be considered an improvement? Is it relevant if your algorithm runs 99 instructions instead of 101?

We could keep going, but you should get the gist by now. The issue here is that we were focusing too much on details that have little importance. The key to get out of this impasse is to abstract out these details: this was obtained by defining a simplified computational model, the *RAM* model. The latter is a set of basic operations working on an internal *random access memory*.

B.2 The RAM model

Under the RAM model, a few assumptions hold:

- Each basic operation (arithmetic operations, `if`, or function call) takes exactly a single one-time step (henceforth just referred to as *step*).
- Loops and subroutines are not considered simple operations. Instead, they are the composition of many one-time-step operations and consume resources proportional to the number of times they run.
- Each memory access takes exactly one step.
- Memory is considered infinite.

The last point might seem a bit unrealistic, but notice that in this model we make no distinction between accesses to actual cache, RAM, hard drive, or data-center storage. In other words

- For most real-world applications, we can imagine providing the memory needed.
- With this assumption, we can abstract away the details of the memory implementation and focus on the logic.

Under the RAM model, the performance of an algorithm is measured as the number of steps it takes on a given input.

These simplifications allow us to abstract out the details of the platform. For some problems or some variants, we might be interested in bringing some details back. For instance, we can distinguish cache accesses from disk accesses. But in general, this generalization serves us well.

Now that we've established the model we'll use, let's discuss what we'll consider to be relevant improvement of an algorithm.

B.3 Order of magnitude

The other aspect we still need to simplify is the way we count instructions. We might decide to count only some kinds of operations like memory accesses. Or, when analyzing sorting algorithms, we can only take into account the number of element swaps.

Also, as suggested, small variations in the number of steps executed are hardly relevant. Rather, we could reason on order of magnitude changes: 2x, 10x, 100x, and so on.

But to really understand when an algorithm performs better than another one on a given problem instance, we need another epiphany: we need to express the number of steps performed as a function of the problem size.

Suppose we are comparing two sorting algorithms, and we state that "on a given test set, the first algorithm takes 100 steps to get to the solution while the second one takes 10." Does that really help us predict the performance of either algorithm on another problem instance?

Conversely, if we can prove that on an array with `n` elements, algorithm A needs `n * n` element swaps, while algorithm B only takes `n`, then we have a very good way to predict how each of them will perform on input of any size.

This is where big-O notation kicks in. But first, take a look at figure B.1 to get an idea of how the running times for these two algorithms would compare. This chart should make you realize why we would like to stick with algorithm B.

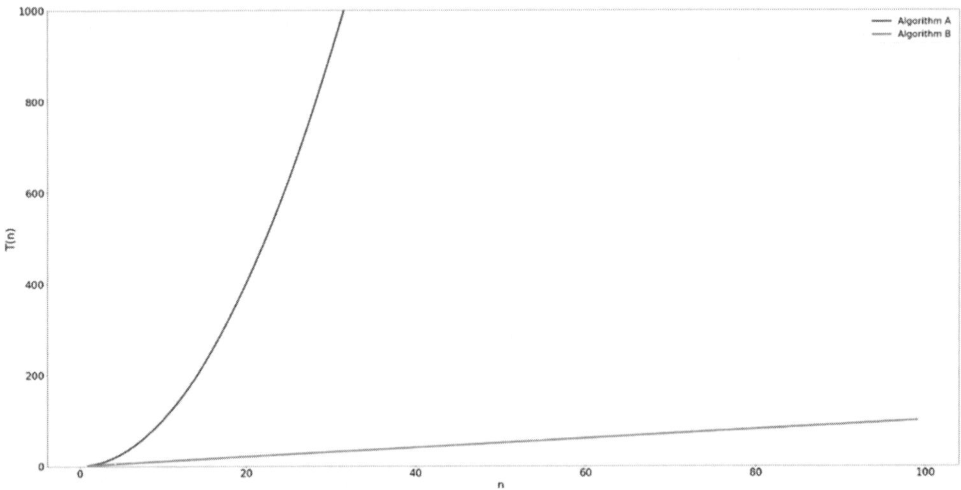

Algorithm A
Algorithm B
T(n)
n
1000
800
600
400
200
0
0
20
40
60
80
100

Figure B.1 Visual comparison of the running time of a quadratic algorithm (A) and a linear algorithm (B). The former grows so much faster that, although the `y` axes shows up to 10 times the max value reached by algorithm B, it only manages to show the plot for algorithm A (the curvy line) up to[1] `n~=30`.

[1] In this context, and for the rest of the book, ~= means "approximately equal to."

B.4 Notation

Big-O notation is a mathematical symbolization used to describe how certain quantities grow with the size of an input. Usually it takes the form of a capital `O`, enclosing an expression within parentheses: something like `O(f(n))`, hence the name big-O. `f(n)` here can be any function with input `n`; we only consider functions on integers, because `n` usually describes the size of some input.

We are not going to describe big-O notation in detail here; it's way out of our scope. But there are many textbooks available with in-depth dissertations on the topic.

The main concept you need to remember is that the notation `O(f(n))` expresses a bound.

Mathematically, saying `g(n) = O(f(n))` means that for any large enough input, there is a real value constant `c` (whose value does not depend on `n`), such that `g(n)` ≤ `c * f(n)` for every possible value of `n` (possibly larger than a certain value n_0).

For instance, if `f(n) = n` and `g(n) = 40 + 3*n`, we can choose `c = 4` and n_0 `= 40`.

Figure B.2 shows how these three functions grow with respect to each other. While `f(n)` is always smaller than `g(n)`, `c*f(n)` becomes larger than `g(n)` at some point. To better understand the turning point, we can evaluate the two formulas by substituting actual values for their parameter `n`. We use the following notation `f(1) -> 1` to assert that `f(1)` evaluates to `1` (in other words, the result of calling `f(1)` is equal to `1`).

For `n` lower than `40`, `g(n)` will be larger. For `n = 30, f(30) -> 120` and `g(n) -> 130`. Instead, we know that `f(40) -> 160` and `g(40) -> 160, f(41) -> 164` while `g(41) -> 163`. For any value greater than `41, 40 + 3 *n <= 4 * n`.

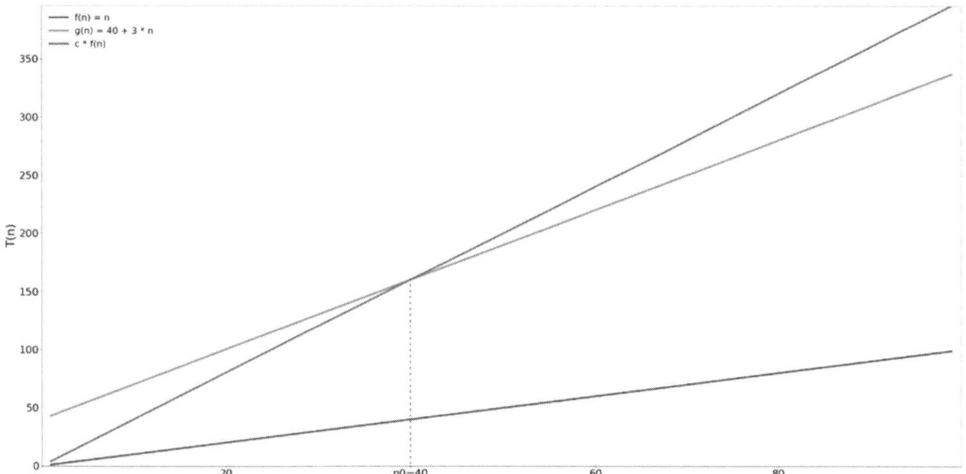
f(n) = n
g(n) = 40 + 3 * n
c * f(n)
T(n)
350
300
250
200
150
100
50
0
20
n0=40
60
80

Figure B.2 Visual comparison of functions: `f(n)=n`, `g(n) = 40 + 3*n`, `4*f(n)`. While `f(n)` is always smaller than `g(n)`, `4*f(n)` becomes larger than `g(n)` for sufficiently large values of `n`.

But don't forget that the condition g(n) ≤ c * f(n) must hold true for every n ≥ n_0. We can't rigorously prove that by plotting a chart or plugging in (a finite number of) values for n in the formula (see figure B.3 for a counter-example), but we would need to resort to some algebra; nevertheless, plotting the functions can help you get an idea of how they grow and whether you are going in the right direction.

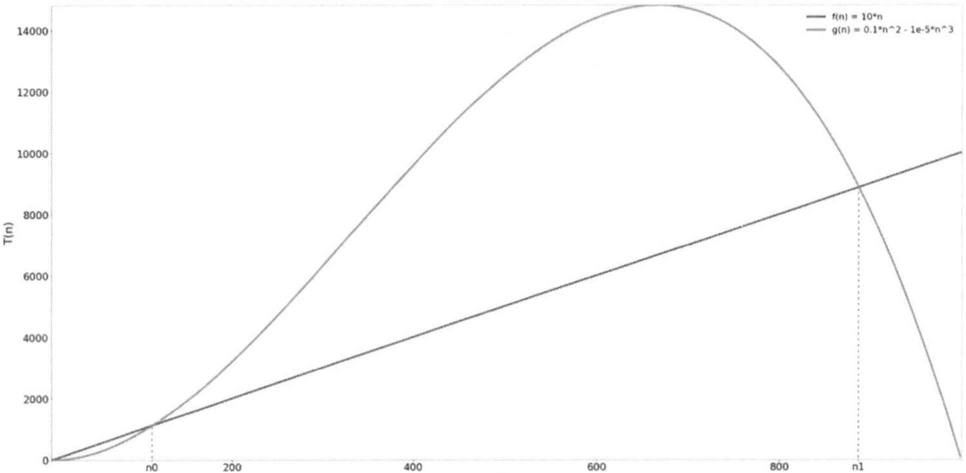
f(n) = 10*n
g(n) = 0.1*n^2 - 1e-5*n^3
T(n)
14000
12000
10000
8000
6000
4000
2000
0
n0
200
400
600
800
n1

Figure B.3 An example showing why we need to be careful when drawing conclusions. While g(n) is larger than f(n) at n_0~=112, this doesn't hold true for any value of n >n_0. In fact, at n_1~=887, we have another intersection between the two functions, and after that point f(n) again becomes larger than g(n).

Moving back to our example, if we say that algorithm A is O(n^2), it means that T(n) = O(n^2), where T(n) is the running time of the algorithm. Or, in other words, algorithm A will never require more than a quadratic number of steps.

The definition for O(n) has some consequences:

- "For any large enough input." This is a crucial piece. We are interested in how our functions behave when n gets (very) large and we don't care if for small values of n the inequalities don't hold. Think, for example, of the functions f(x) = e^x and g(x) = e * x. f(x) < g(x) when x is smaller than 1, but for larger values, f(x) grows much faster.
- Constant factors don't matter: O(n) = O(3 * n) = O(100 * n). You can prove this by choosing the right values for the constant in the previous inequality.
- Some problems require constant time: think about summing the first n integers. With the naïve algorithm, you would need n-1 sums, but with Gauss' method, you only need one sum, one multiplication and one division, independent of the output.

  To sum this up using a formula, we can write O(c) = O(1) for any positive constant c.

`O(1)` denotes a constant running time: in other words, one that does not depend on the input size.

- When summing big-O expressions, the biggest wins: `O(f(n) + g(n)) = O(f(n))` if `g(n) = O(f(n))`. So, if two algorithms are run in sequence, the total running time is dominated by the slowest.
- `O(f(n) * g(n))` can't be simplified unless either function is constant.

NOTE Often when we give an algorithm running time using big-O notation, we imply that the bound is both lower and upper—unless we explicitly say otherwise. Nevertheless, `Θ(f(n))` would be the correct notation for the class of functions whose upper and lower bound is `f(n)`.

Now we have all the tools we need to unequivocally describe algorithms' performance. You will see this notation in action a lot in the remaining sections of this appendix.

B.5 Examples

If it's the first time you have seen big-O notation, it's perfectly normal to feel slightly confused. It takes some time and lots of practice to get used to it.

Let's see a few examples and try to apply what we described in the previous section in mathematical terms.

Suppose you have 4 numbers you'd like to sum: `{1, 3, -1.4, 7}`. How many additions will you need? Let's see:

```
1 + 3 + (-1.4) + 7
```

It looks like you can do with three additions. What about if we have to sum 10 numbers? You can easily verify that we need nine. Can we generalize this number of operations for any size of the input? Yes, we can, as it's easy to prove that we always need `n-1` additions to sum up `n` numbers.

So, we can say that summing up the elements of a list of `n` numbers (asymptotically) requires `O(n)` operations. If we denote with `T(n)` the number of operations needed, we can say that `T(n) = O(n)`.

Let's consider two slight variations:

- We sum the first five elements of a list twice, and the other elements once.
- We sum the squares of the elements.

In the first case, if our list is `{1, 3, -1.4, 7, 4, 1, 2}`, we have

```
1 + 3 + (-1.4) + 7 + 4 + 1 + 2 + 1 + 3 + (-1.4) + 7 + 4
```

You can see the repeated elements underlined in this formula. So, for `n=7`, we need 11 operations.

In general, we will need `n+4` operations, and $T_1(n) = n+4$.

Is it true that $T_1(n) = O(n)$? Let's go back to our definition. We need to find two constants, an integer n_0 and a real number c, such that

$$T_1(n) \le c * n \text{ for each } n > n_0$$
$$\Leftrightarrow$$
$$n + 4 \le c * n \text{ for each } n > n_0$$
$$\Leftrightarrow$$
$$c \ge 1 + 4/n \text{ for each } n > n_0$$

Since 4/n decreases when n grows, we can choose c=2 and $n_0=4$, or, say, c=100 and $n_0=1$, and the inequality will be satisfied.

The same is true if we consider summing squares: for n numbers, we will need n multiplications (or squarings) and n-1 sums, so $T_2(n) = 2n-1$.

We can prove that $T_2(n) = O(n)$ by choosing c=2.5 and $n_0=1$.

Now, we could also say that $T_1(n) = O(n^2)$. We leave it as an exercise for you to find appropriate values for c and n_0. However, this bound would not be strict: in other words, there exist other functions of n such that $T_1(n) \le f(n) < O(n^2)$ for n large enough.

Likewise, we could also say that $T_1(n) = O(n^{1000})$. That would certainly be true, but how helpful would it be knowing that our algorithm takes less than the age of the universe on a small input?[2]

As you might suspect, we are usually interested in strict bounds. While this is true and expected, and for our summation examples it seems trivial to prove that the O(n) bound is strict, you might be surprised to learn that there are some algorithms for which we don't know what the stricter bound is, or at least we can't prove it.

As a final example, let's consider the task of enumerating all the couples of numbers in a list, regardless of their order. For instance, given the list {1, 2, 3}, we have the pairs (1,2), (1,3), (3,2).

It turns out that the number of unordered pairs for n elements is $T_3(n) = n * (n-1) / 2$:

$$T_3(n) = n * (n-1) / 2 \le 1*n^2 \text{ for } n > 1$$

Thus we can say $T_3(n) = O(n^2)$. This time, the quadratic bound is also a strict bound, as shown in figure B.4.

[2] This might be useful if we need to prove that an algorithm will actually run in finite time. But with real-world applications, it's usually of little practical use.

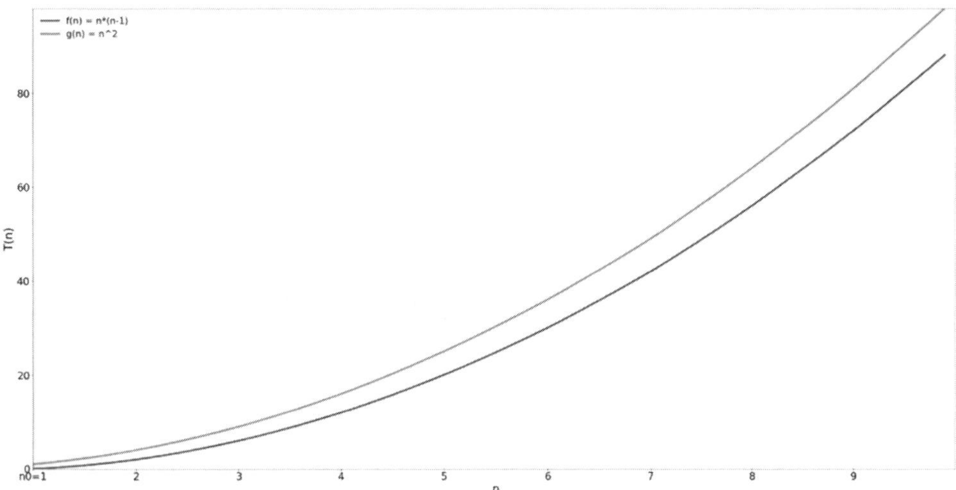
f(n) = n*(n-1)
g(n) = n^2
T(n)
80
60
40
20
0
n0=1
2
3
4
5
6
7
8
9
n

Figure B.4 Visual comparison of functions: `f(n)=n*(n-1)`, `g(n) = ` n^2. The latter is always larger for any positive value of `n`.

appendix C
Core data structures

You can't build a house from the roof down. Likewise, you can't build knowledge of advanced data structures if you don't master the basics first.

In this appendix, we provide an overview of core data structures and present some of the most widely used algorithms.

It starts with a refresher of the most basic data structures: *arrays*, *linked lists*, *trees*, and *hash tables*. We do expect readers to already be familiar with them; after all, these structures are the building blocks of the most advanced ones. But we'll provide a quick overview, just for your convenience.

In the last section, we briefly compare these data structures. For each of them, we will look at key features (like if they support ordering, and if they are *static* or *dynamic*) and sum them up in a table. This will help us decide, for each problem we might run into, which one of them would be more appropriate to support us in solving the problem.

C.1 Core data structures

Data structures (*DSs*) are one of the foundations of programming and have been progressively introduced since the very dawn of computer science.

In this section, we are going to explore the most basic ways to organize data items in memory so that those items can later be retrieved according to specific criteria. The nature of those criteria, together with the way storage is used and the performance of the basic operations (adding, removing, and searching elements) are what determine the characteristics of a data structure.

These core DSs are the building blocks for the implementations of countless advanced DSs.

C.2 Array

This is one of the simplest and yet most used data structures. It's provided natively by most programming languages: an *array* is a collection of homogeneous data. At a low level it is, roughly, a chunk of memory where elements are stored contiguously. Many programming languages only provide *static arrays*. Their sizes can't change and the number of elements they store needs to be decided when they are created (or at least at initialization). *Dynamic arrays*, however, can grow when new elements are added and shrink when elements are removed. Figure C.1 provides an example of how this works. It's not too hard to find dynamic arrays in mainstream languages: JavaScript arrays are intrinsically dynamic.

NOTE It can be proven that it's possible to implement dynamic arrays in such a way that, on aggregate,[1] insertion and removal are as fast as for static arrays.

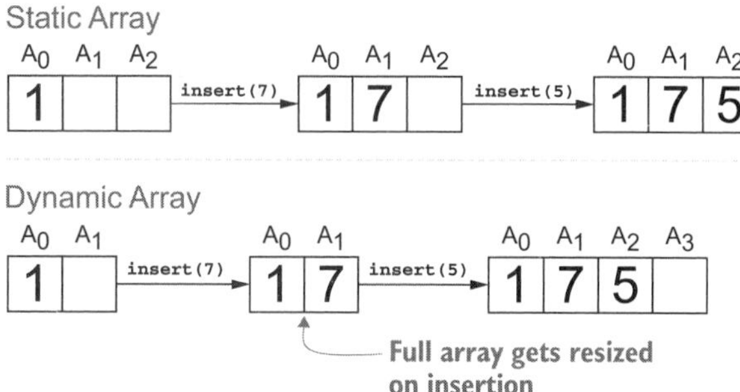
Static Array
A0 A1 A2
1
insert(7)
1 7
insert(5)
1 7 5
Dynamic Array
A0 A1
1
insert(7)
1 7
insert(5)
A0 A1 A2 A3
1 7 5
Full array gets resized on insertion

Figure C.1 An example of insertion into static (top) and dynamic arrays (bottom). Notice how the size of the static array in the upper half is constant (it always has three elements), while the dynamic array in the other half starts with size 2, its size is only increased (doubled, actually) when an element is added to a full array. In this example, the static array could not have any other element inserted unless we override another one.

Elements in arrays must all have the same type and require the same space to be stored.[2] When this specification is met, it makes it easier to move from one element to the next one by just adding to the former's memory address the size of array's elements.

NOTE Because they are allocated in a single block of memory, arrays are more likely to show the so-called locality of reference. When traversing an array, for example, data in the same page of memory is likely to be accessed in a short window of time. This can lead to several optimizations (see the original article[3] about the principle of locality).

[1] In big-O analysis, aggregate running time refers to the expected performance over a big enough number of operations. For instance, if we toss a (fair) coin once, we don't know if it's going to be heads or tails. If we toss it twice, it's possible that we get tails once and heads once, but it's far from being certain. If we repeat the experiment a million times, and the coin is fair and we don't do any tricks with it, then we will get heads and tails (very) close to 50% of the times. Likewise, for some algorithms, a single operation can take longer than expected, but if we run it on a high volume of data, the average running time will be predictable.

[2] At least in theory, low-level implementation may vary between different programming languages.

[3] Peter J. Denning, Stuart C. Schwartz, "Properties of the Working-Set Model," *Communications of the ACM*, Volume 15, Issue 3 (March 1972), pages 191-198.

The key advantage of arrays is that they have constant time access for all elements. It would be more accurate to say that every *position* in an array can be accessed in constant time. It's possible to retrieve or store the first element, or the last, or any intermediate element as long as its position is known. See figure C.2 as a reference.

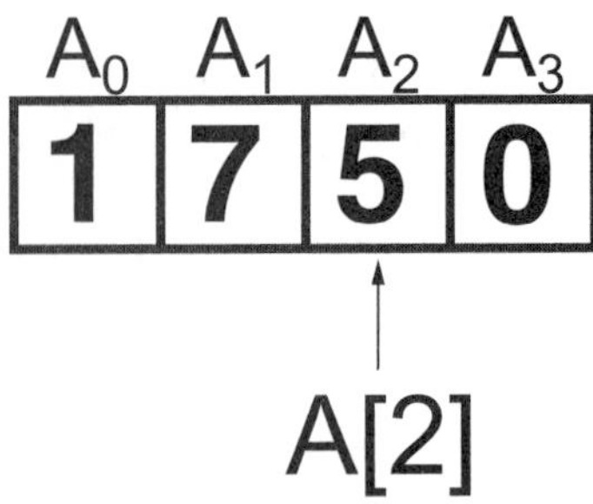
A0 A1 A2 A3
1 7 5 0
A[2]

Figure C.2 Retrieving the third element of an array. If the array is stored in a variable named `A`, then `A[2]` refers to the third element of the array. This is because on computers, both memory addresses and the indices of array elements start from 0.

While random access is one of the strengths of arrays, other operations are slower for them. As mentioned, you can't resize an array by just adding or removing an element at its tail. Every time such an operation is needed, you have to reallocate the array, unless you are using a dynamic array. In that case, you have to initially allocate a larger chunk of memory, keep track of the number of elements, and amortize the overhead for resizing on a larger number of operations.

As we'll see in the next section, lists can be optimal for insertions and deletions while they are slower for random access.

C.3 Linked List

A *linked list* stores a sequence of items by wrapping each item in an object, called a node.

As shown in figure C.3, each node holds a value and either one or two links (references) to other nodes.

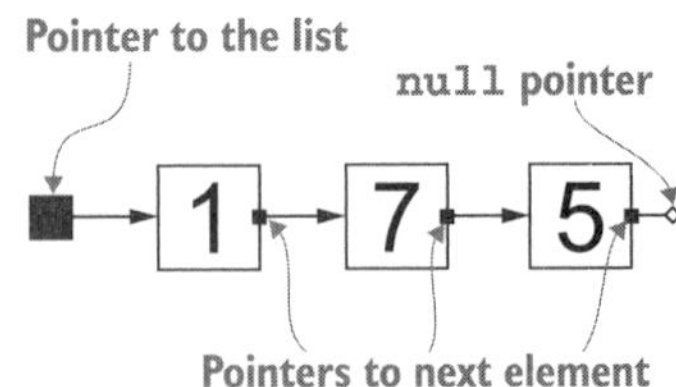
Pointer to the list
null pointer
1
7
5
Pointers to next element

Figure C.3 The graphic representation of a linked list. Here each element holds a pointer (aka reference or link) to the next node in the list. The reference to the first node is held by a special pointer, the head of the list. To go through the whole list, we need to follow the head pointer, and then traverse the list node by node.

A value can be a simple type, like a number, or a complex type, such as a string or an object. The order of the elements is determined exclusively by the list's links. Nodes don't need to be allocated contiguously and therefore lists are dynamic by nature. So, they can grow or shrink as needed.

More formally, a list can be defined recursively (see figure C.4). It can be either

- An empty list
- A node containing a value and a reference to a linked list

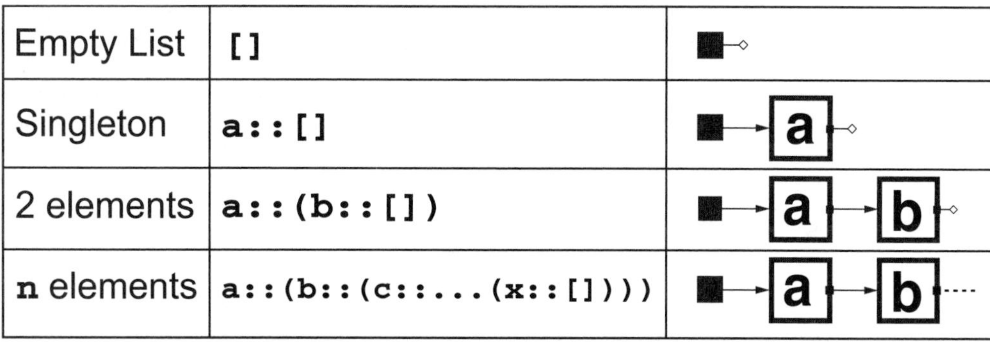

Empty List	`[]`	
Singleton	`a::[]`	a
2 elements	`a::(b::[])`	a b
n elements	`a::(b::(c::...(x::[])))`	a b ····

Figure C.4 Inductive definition of a list. The middle column uses a formal notation for the list, while the right column shows the graphical representation of the same list. In the formal representation, the recursive nature is more explicit, because it is indeed a recursive notation. The empty list is assumed as a primitive, a building block, and each non-empty list is recursively defined as its first element followed by its tail, a shorter, possibly empty list of the remaining elements.

Figure C.5 exemplifies another key feature of lists that can be either

- *Singly linked*—Every node has only a link (aka pointer or reference) to the next element.
- *Doubly linked*—Two links per node are stored: a link to the next element and one to the previous element.

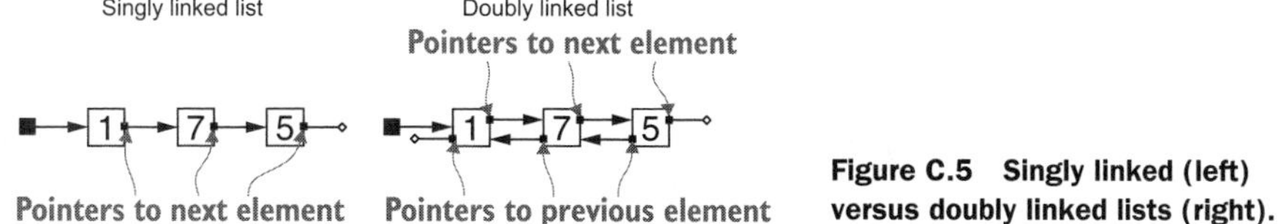
Singly linked list
Doubly linked list
Pointers to next element
1
7
5
1
7
5
Pointers to next element
Pointers to previous element

Figure C.5 Singly linked (left) versus doubly linked lists (right).

As mentioned before, the choice between singly and doubly linked is a trade-off. The former requires less space per node, and the latter allows for faster algorithms to delete an element, but needs a small overhead to keep the pointers updated.

In order to keep track of a linked list, the head of the list must be stored in a variable. When adding or removing elements from the list, we need to take extra care to update that reference to the head of the list as well: if we don't perform the update, it might end up pointing to an internal node, or even worse, to an invalid location.

Insertion in lists can happen

- *At the beginning*—That's the easiest place to add a node in constant time. Figure C.6 shows, in fact, that we only need to update the head reference with a new node and update the links for this new node and the old head (unless the list was empty).

Figure C.6 Insertion at the beginning of a linked list. (A) The original list. (B) Create a new node, whose next pointer is set to the previous head. (C) Correct the head pointer. (D) Final result.

- *At the end*—This is not a very practical solution, because we would need to traverse the whole list to find the last node; check figure C.7 to see why. We could think about keeping an extra pointer for the tail of the list, but this would cause an overhead because every method that changes the list would need to check if that reference needs to be updated.

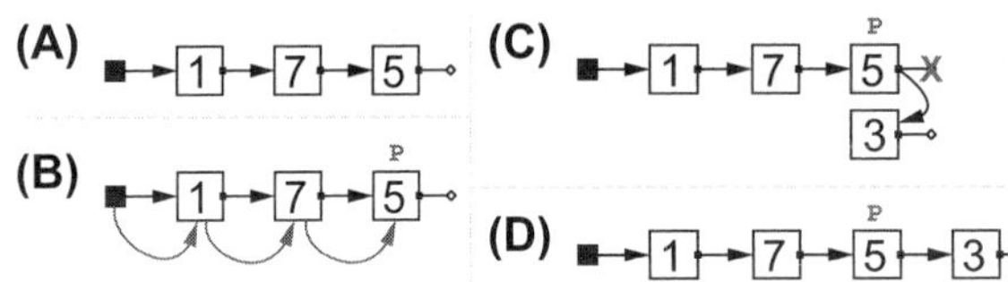
(A)
(B)
(C)
(D)
P

Figure C.7 Insertion at the end of a linked list. (A) The original list. (B) Walk the linked list until the last element: let's call it `P`. (C) Create a new node and update the next pointer for `P`. (D) Final result.

- *In any other position*—This is useful when keeping the list ordered. However, it's also expensive, requiring linear time in the worst case, as shown in figure C.8.

Figure C.8 Insertion in a linked list in any position. In this example, we show insertion on a sorted linked list (but sorting is not a requirement). (A) The original list. (B) Walk the linked list until we find the predecessor of the position where we want to insert the new element (being a singly linked list, we need to maintain a pointer to the predecessor during this search). Let's denote this predecessor with `P`. (C) Create a new node `N`, and update the next pointer for `P`. At the same time, set `N.next` to `P.next`. (D) Final result.

Similarly, we can double down on the same reasoning for node removal:

- *From the beginning*—It can be done in constant time by updating the head reference to the old head's successor (after checking that the list isn't empty). And we should make sure that the removed node is deallocated or made available for garbage collection.
- *From the end*—We need to find the second-to-last node and update its pointer to the next node. For a doubly linked list, we just get to the end of the list and then take its predecessor. For singly linked lists, we need to keep a reference

both to the current node and to its predecessor while we traverse the list. This is a linear-time operation.

- *From any other position*—Same considerations as for insertions, plus the concern about keeping a reference to the second-to-last element in the list.

Linked lists are recursive data structures. This stems out of their recursive definition, and it means that problems on lists can be reasoned about by induction. You can try to provide a solution for the base case (the empty list) as well as a way to combine some actions on the head of the list with solutions for its tail (which is a smaller list). For instance, if you have to develop an algorithm to search the max of a list of numbers, you can do the following:

- If the list is empty, return `null`.
- If the list has at least one element, take the list's head (call it `x`) and apply the algorithm to the list with the remaining `N - 1` elements obtaining a value `y`. Then the result is
  - `x` if `y` is `null` or `x >= y`
  - `y` otherwise.

C.4 Tree

Trees are another widely used abstract data type that provides a hierarchical structure, like lists, but in a branched shape. They can indeed be seen as a generalization of *linked lists*: each node has still a single predecessor, called its *parent*, but can have more than a single successor, here denoted as its *children*. Each tree node's *child* is itself a subtree (either empty or including a root and its subtrees).

A generic tree is illustrated in figure C.9, but a tree can also be formally defined as either

- An empty tree.
- A node with one or more references to its children, and (optionally) a reference to its parent

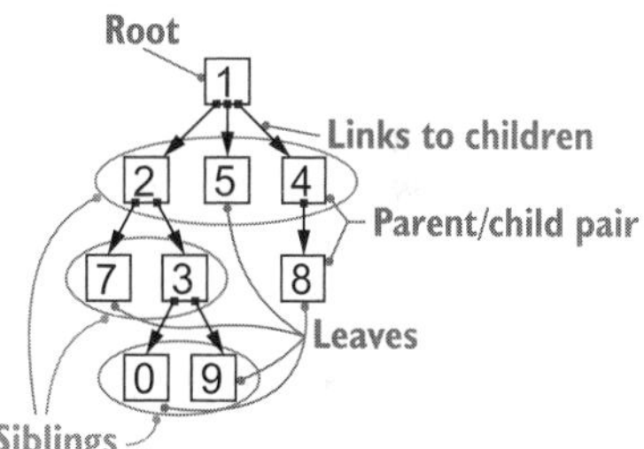
Root
1
Links to children
2
5
4
Parent/child pair
7
3
8
Leaves
0
9
Siblings

Figure C.9 An example of a tree. The top-to-bottom arrows represent the links between a node and its children; these arrows are always directed from parent to children. Every node has one and only one parent. Nodes that share the same parent are called siblings. There is no explicit link between siblings, but a node's siblings can only be reached through their common parent. Nodes with no children are called leaves.

Each tree node, like list's nodes, contains a value. Moreover, a node holds a list of references to other nodes, its children. There is a constraint: in a tree, each node is the child of just a single other node, except for the root, which has no parent (so no node in a tree points to its root). Therefore, we'll need to keep a reference (using a variable) to the root of the tree. This is the same as a singly linked list where the head of the list is not linked by other nodes. Moreover, trees define a "vertical" hierarchy, a parent-children relation, while there can be no relation between sibling nodes or between nodes in different subtrees.

Before moving on, let's review the terminology used when dealing with trees:

- If a node `x` has two children `y` and `z`, `x` is the *parent* of these nodes. So, the following is true: `parent(y) == parent(z) == x`. In figure C.9, the node labeled `1` is the parent of the nodes labeled `4`, `5`, and `2`.
- Being `x`, `y`, and `z` as defined here, `y` and `z` are called *siblings*.
- The *root* of a tree is the one and only node in a tree that has no parent.
- An *ancestor* of a node `x` is any node in the path from the tree's root to `x`. In other words, either `parent(x)`, `parent(parent(x))`, and so on. In figure C.9, `2` is an ancestor of `7`, `3`, `0`, and `9`.
- A *leaf* is any node that has no children. Another way to express this is that for a leaf, all the node's children are empty subtrees.
- A fundamental characteristic of a tree is its *height*, defined as the length of the longest path from the root to a leaf. The height of the tree in figure C.9 is `3` because the longest path is `1->2->3->0` (or equivalently `1->2->3->9`), and it traverses three parent-child links.

In the next section, we will focus on introducing binary search trees.

C.4.1 Binary search trees

A *binary tree* is a tree where the number of children for any node is at most 2, meaning that each node can have either 0, 1, or 2 children.

A *binary search tree (BST)* is a binary tree where each node has a key associated with it, and satisfies two conditions: if `key(x)` is the key associated with a node `x`, then

- `key(x) > key(y)` for every node `y` in the left subtree of `x`.
- `key(x) < key(z)` for every node `z` in the right subtree of `x`.

A node's key can also be its value, but in general, BST's nodes can store a key and a value, or any additional data, independently.

Let's continue with a few more definitions:

- A *balanced tree* is a tree where for each node, the height of its left and right subtrees differs at most by 1, *and* both its left and right subtrees are balanced.
- A tree is a *complete tree* if it has height `H` and every leaf node is either at level `H` or `H-1`.
- A *perfectly balanced tree* is a *balanced tree* in which, for each internal node, the heights of its left and right subtrees are the same.
- A *perfectly balanced* tree is also *complete*.

DEFINITIONS There are two definitions for tree *balancedness*: *height-balancedness*, which is the one used in the definitions provided, and *weight-balancedness*. They are independent characteristics of a tree, as neither of them implies the other. Both could lead to similar results, but the former is normally used, and we'll just refer to it in the rest of this book when we talk about balanced trees.

Binary search trees are recursive structures. Each BST, in fact, can be either

- An empty tree
- A node with a key and a left and right subtree

This recursive nature allows for intuitive recursive algorithms for all the basic operations on BSTs.

Binary search trees offer a compromise between the flexibility and performance of insertions in a linked list and the efficiency of search in an ordered array. All the basic operations (`insert`, `delete`, `search`, `minimum` and `maximum`, `successor` and `predecessor`) require examining a number of nodes proportional to the height of the tree.

Therefore, the shorter we manage to keep the height of a tree, the better performance on those operations will be.

What's the smallest possible height of a tree?

For a binary tree with `n` nodes, `log(n)` is the shortest possible height.

Let's consider a binary tree. There can be only one root, obviously. It can have at most 2 children, so there can be at most 2 nodes with height 1. Each of them can have 2 children, so there can be at most $4=2^2$ nodes with height 2. How many nodes with height 3 can a BST have? As you probably guessed, it's $2^3=8$. Going down the tree, at each level, we increase the height by one and double the number of nodes that the current level can hold.

So, at height `h`, we have 2^h nodes. But we also know that the total number of nodes for a complete tree with height `h` is $2^0 + 2^1 + 2^2 + 2^3 + ... + 2^h = 2^{h+1} - 1$.

To keep the height as small as possible, it is easy to see that we need to fill all the levels (except, possibly, the last one), because otherwise we could just move the nodes in the last level up the tree until we have no vacancies in the upper levels.

Therefore, if we have `n` nodes, $2^{h+1} - 1 \leq n$, and taking the log of both sides, $h \geq \log(n+1) - 1$.

BSTs are not balanced by nature: on the contrary, for the same set of elements, their shape and height can vary greatly depending on the sequence of insertions for those elements (see figure C.10).

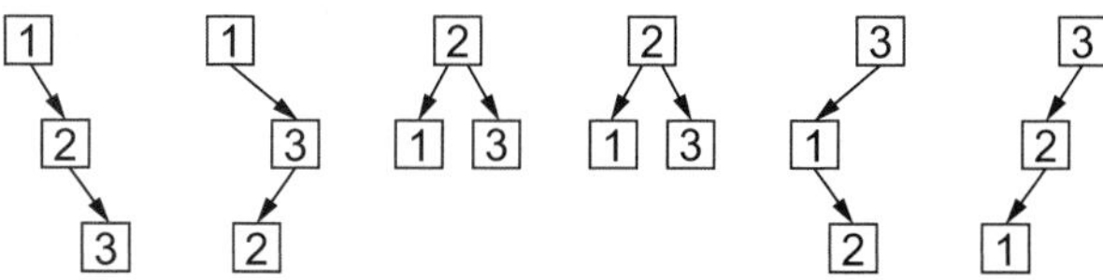

Figure C.10 All possible layouts for BSTs of size 3. The layout depends on the order in which elements are inserted. Notice how two sequences produce identical layouts for the insertion sequences `[2, 1, 3]` and `[2, 3, 1]`.

On average, after a high number of insertions, the probability of having a skewed tree is pretty low. It is worth mentioning, however, that the simplest algorithm for deleting a node tends to produce skewed trees. Many workarounds have been proposed for this problem but, as of today, there is no proof that they always produce a better result than the naïve version.

The silver lining is that there are several solutions that allows us to keep BSTs balanced without degrading performance for insert or delete. For instance

- 2-3 search trees
- red-black trees
- B-trees
- AVL trees

C.5 Hash table

Hashing is probably the most common way to represent symbol tables. If we need to associate each one of a set of keys to a value, then we are going to face a few problems.

C.5.1 Storing key-value pairs

We assume keys and values can be picked from different domains. Then, we need to decide if duplicate keys are allowed. For the sake of simplicity, we will consider only sets of unique keys: it is always possible to make a static group of keys unique.

The easiest case is when keys are non-negative integers. In theory, you can use an array to store the value associated with key `k` in the `k`-th element of the array. This, however, is only possible when the possible keys are limited in range. If, for example, any 32-bit positive integer was allowed, we would need an array with more than 3 billion elements—possibly larger than even the most modern machine's RAM. It gets even worse if for the possible values we consider "longs," aka 8-byte integers. We'd be talking about 18 billion of billions of elements. No, it's not a typo: we are talking about billions of billions.

The worst part is that by using arrays, even if we know that we'll store only a few thousands integer keys at a time, we'll still need an array with 2^{32} elements if any integer value is allowed for a key.

While there is little we can do to improve when we do have to store many elements, when we know that we might store only a handful of elements (say, a few hundreds or thousands), it's a whole different story. Even if we can still choose these elements from a large set (for example all the integers that can be represented with 32 bits, for a total of around 4 billion elements), but we'll only store a handful of them at the same time, then we can do better.

And that's precisely where hashing comes to the rescue.

C.5.2 Hashing

Hashing provides a compromise between key-indexed arrays and unsorted arrays in conjunction with sequential search. The former solution offers constant time search, but needs space proportional to the set of possible keys. The latter requires linear time for search, but space proportional to the number of actual keys.

Using hash tables, we fix the size of the array to, say, `M` elements. As we'll see, we might store more than `M` elements, though, depending on how we solve collisions. Then, we transform each key into an index between `0` and `M - 1`, using a hash function.

It's worth noting that introducing such a transformation relaxes the constraint about having only non-negative integers as keys. We can "serialize" any object into a string and transform any string into an integer modulo `M` as part of hashing. In the rest of the discussion, we'll assume keys are integers for the sake of brevity.

The exact hash function we need to use depends on the type of the keys, and it's correlated to the size of the array. The most notable examples include

- The *division method*—Given an integer key `k`, we define its hash `h(k)` as

$$h(k) = k\%M$$

where % represents the modulo operator.

For this method, `M`, the size of the table, should be a prime number that is not too close to a power of 2.

For instance, if `M=13`, we would have `h(0)=0, h(1)=1, h(2)=2,… h(13)=0, h(14)=1` and so on.

- *The multiplication method:*

$$h(k) = \lfloor M \cdot (k \cdot A\%1) \rfloor$$

where `0 < A < 1` is a real constant, and `(k*A % 1)` is the fractional part of `k*A`. In this case, `M` is usually chosen as a power of 2, but `A` has to be chosen carefully, depending on `M`.

For instance, say `M=16` and `A=0.25`; then

```
k = 0 => h(k) = 0
k = 1 => k * A = 0.25, k*A%1 = 0.25, h(k) = 4
k = 2 => k * A = 0.5, k*A%1 = 0.5, h(k) = 8
k = 3 => k * A = 0.75, k*A%1 = 0.75, h(k) = 12
k = 4 => k * A = 1, k*A%1 = 0, h(k) = 0
k = 5 => k * A = 1.25, k*A%1 = 0.25, h(k) = 4
…
```

and so on.

As you can see, 0.25 was not a great choice for `A`, because `h(k)` will only assume five different values. To this extent, however, it was a great choice to illustrate both the method itself and why you need to be careful choosing its parameters.

There are also more advanced methods to improve the quality of the hash function so that it gets closer and closer to uniform distribution.

C.5.3 Conflicts resolution in hashing

No matter how good or how uniform a hash function we can create, the number of keys, `m`, can grow until it becomes larger than the size of the table, `n`. At that point, the *pigeonhole principle* kicks in to rain on our parade.

DEFINITION The pigeonhole principle states that if the number of possible key values to store is larger than the available slots, at some point, we are bound to have two different keys mapped to the same slot. What happens if we try to add both keys to the table? In that case, we have a conflict. We therefore need a way to be able to resolve the conflict and make sure that it is possible to distinguish between the two different keys and find both of them in a search.

There are two main ways to solve conflicts due to different keys mapping to the same slot:

- *Chaining*—Each element in the array stores a link to another data structure, holding all the keys mapped to that element (see figure C.11). The secondary data structure can be a linked list (usually), a tree, or even another hash table (as in *perfect hashing*, a technique that allows the best possible hashing performance on a static set of keys, known in advance). In this case, there is no limit to the number of elements that can be stored in the hash table, but performance degrades as we add more and more elements, because at least some lists get longer and longer and require more steps to be traversed in order to find an element.

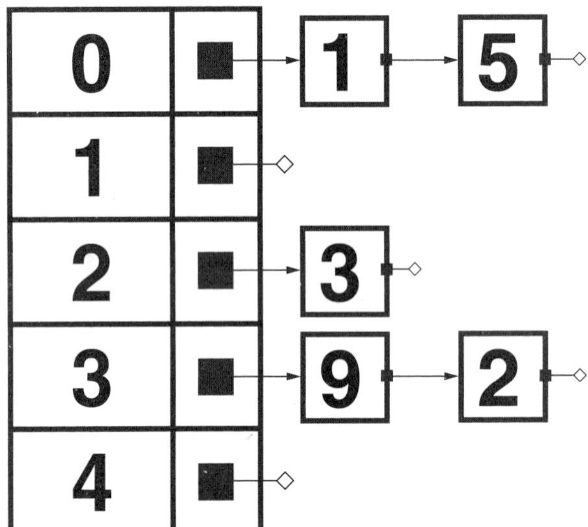
0
1
2
3
4
1
5
3
9
2

Figure C.11 Example of a hash table using chaining and a linked list for conflict resolution

- *Open addressing*—We store elements directly in the array, and on conflicts we generate (deterministically) another hash value for the next position to try. Figure C.12 shows an example of a hash table using open addressing for conflict resolution.
- Hash functions for open addressing look like

  $h(k, i) = (h'(k) + f(i, k)) \% M$

where `i` counts the number of positions already examined, and `f` is a function of the number of attempts, and possibly of the key as well. Open addressing allows us to save memory, because there are no secondary data structures, but has some problems that make it rarely the best choice. First and foremost, deleting elements becomes too complicated, and because the size of the hash table is limited and decided on creation, this means that these tables will fill up quickly and need to be reallocated. Even worse, elements tend to group in clusters and, when the table gets populated, many attempts are needed to find a free slot—basically there is a high probability that a linear number of attempts will already be needed when the table is nearly half-full.

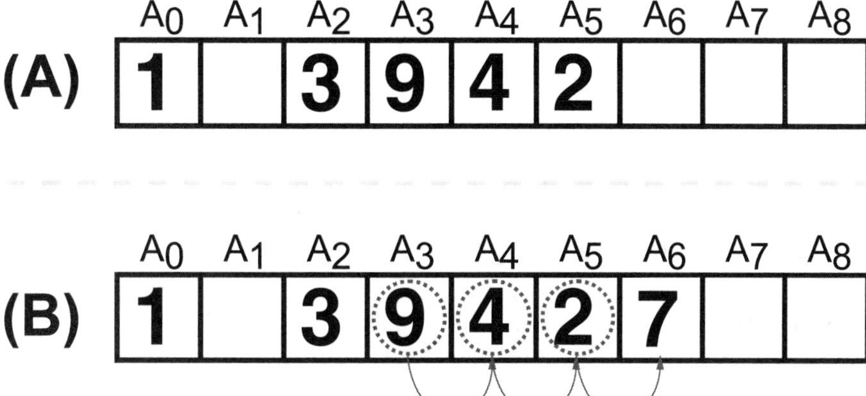
(A)
A0 A1 A2 A3 A4 A5 A6 A7 A8
1 3 9 4 2
(B)
A0 A1 A2 A3 A4 A5 A6 A7 A8
1 3 9 4 2 7

Figure C.12 A hash table using open addressing for conflict resolution. The assignment of the elements depends on the order of insertion. Assume that `f(i) = i` and that we have the same collisions as in figure C.11. (A) We can infer that 9 must have been inserted before 2 (otherwise, since we assume 9 and 2 would be mapped in the same spot, as in figure C.11, 2 would be stored in A_3). Also, 4 must have been added before 2, because when the algorithm finds out that A_3 is not empty, A_4 would be tried next (because `f(i) = i`, we do a linear scan of the positions following a collision). (B) We try to add 7, assuming `h(7) = 3`. Because of open addressing and the definition of function `f`, we try the elements in positions 3, 4, and 5, which are all already used. Then we finally try A_6, which is free, and we add the new key there.

Issues with scaling hash tables

Even with chaining hashing, the number of slots in the table is usually static, as changing the size of the table would change the hash function and therefore the target slot for potentially all elements already stored. This, in turn, would force us to delete every single element from the old table and then insert it into the new one. It's worth noting that this kind of situation often arises with distributed caches (such as Cassandra or Memcached) when a new node needs to be added, and—unless proper workarounds have been put in place in a website's architecture—this can cause bottlenecks or even crash a whole site.

In chapter 7, we describe *consistent hashing*, a way to mitigate this problem.

C.5.4 Performance

As mentioned, chaining is usually the method of choice to resolve collisions, because it gives several advantages in terms of running time and memory allocation. For a hash table using chaining and linked lists, where the table has size `m` and contains `n` elements, all operations require on average `O(n/m)` time.

> **NOTE** While most of the time it is fine to consider hash table operations to be `O(1)`, you should keep in mind that the worst-case time is `O(n)`. This happens if all elements are mapped to the same bucket (that is, the same chain) within the table. In such cases, the time needed to delete or search an element is `O(n)`. This is, however, a very unlikely event, at least when the hash functions used are properly designed.

The good news is that if the set of possible keys is static and known in advance, then it is possible to use *perfect hashing* and have a worst case `O(1)` time for all operations.

C.6 Comparative analysis of core data structures

Now that we have described all the core data structures, we'll try to sum up their characteristics by listing their properties and performance in table 2.1.

The properties we will include are

- *Order*—Whether a deterministic order for the elements can be maintained. It could be a natural order for the elements, or the insertion order.
- *Unique*—If duplicate elements/keys are forbidden.
- *Associative*—If elements can be indexed by a key.
- *Dynamic*—Whether the container can resize on insertion/removal, or its max size needs to be decided in advance.
- *Locality*—Locality of reference. If elements are all stored in a single, uninterrupted block of memory.

Table C.1 Comparative analysis of core data structures

Structure	Order	Unique	Associative	Dynamic	Locality
Array	yes	no	no	no [a]	yes
Singly-linked list	yes	no	no	yes	no
Doubly-linked list	yes	no	no	yes	no
Balanced tree (for example, BST)	yes	no	no	yes	no
Heap (see chapter 2)	no [b]	yes	key-priority	no	yes
Hash table	no	yes	key-value	yes [c]	no

a. Arrays are natively static in most languages, but dynamic arrays can be built from static ones with little performance overhead.

b. Heaps only define a partial order between their keys. They allow sorting keys based on their priority, but they don't keep any info on the order of insertion.

c. Hash tables are dynamic in size when conflict resolution is resolved with chaining.

As part of the comparison, we also have to take into account their relative performance. But what does performance really mean for a whole data structure, if we have only discussed the running time for their individual methods?

Usually the performance for a data structure, and even more for its implementation, is a trade-off between the individual performances of its methods. This is valid for all data structures: there is no ideal data structure that has optimal performance for all the operations it provides. For instance, arrays are faster for random, position-based access. But they are slow when their shape needs to be changed and very slow[4] when you need to look up an element by value. Lists allow for fast insertion of new elements, but lookup and access by position are slow. Hash tables have fast key-based lookup, but finding the successor of an element, or maximum and minimum, are very slow.

In practice, choosing the best data structure should be based on a careful analysis of your problem and the performance of the data structure, but it's more important to avoid using a bad data structure (which could cause a bottleneck) than to find the single best option available, just to gain a small savings on the average (and easier to implement) choice.

[4] Unsorted arrays are terribly slow for search and direct access. Sorted arrays can implement both in `O(log(n))`.

appendix D *Containers as priority queues*

One of the largest subsets of data structures, probably the largest (by far), is the set of containers. A *container* is a collection of objects, with operations for adding, removing, and retrieving them. The difference between each kind of container revolves around

1. The order in which the elements are extracted from the container
2. Whether the elements need to be unique, or multiple instances are allowed
3. Whether the container is associative, that is, if it stores plain elements or associates keys with values
4. How elements can be searched, and what operations can be performed on the stored data
5. Performance

Points 1-4 define an abstraction of a container, in other words, its behavior: in technical jargon, its API. Once the API is fixed, implementations can still differ, though.

But for now, let's focus on the abstract data structures: the caveat here is in the definition of priority. At a very high level, we have a black box, a *container*, that will hold our values, and remove and return a specific element every time we ask for one.

This description is generic enough that it can describe basically every type of container in data structures: it all boils down to consistently defining the priority of the elements. In mathematical terms, the priority is an univocal mapping between elements and a number, usually with the convention that lower values mean higher priority.

Some of these definitions for priority are so common that we categorize them as separate data structures. Let's look at a few of them.

D.1 Bag

A *bag*, shown in figure D.1, is a collection that only supports the `add` and `iterate` operations. It's not possible to remove items from a bag. After checking if the container is actually empty, clients can iterate through its elements; the actual order, however, is unspecified by definition, and clients must not rely on it.

Bags are useful when you need to collect objects and process them as a whole set rather than individually. For instance, you could collect samples and then, at a later point, compute statistics on them, such as average or standard deviation—the order is irrelevant in that case.

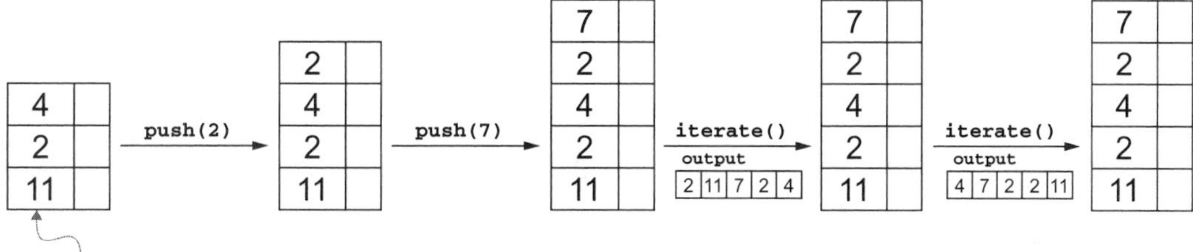
4
2
11
Element
push(2)
2
4
2
11
push(7)
7
2
4
2
11
iterate()
output
2 11 7 2 4
7
2
4
2
11
iterate()
output
4 7 2 2 11
7
2
4
2
11

Figure D.1 Operations on a bag. Insertion adds elements to the container but sets no index for them. The only other available operation is iterating through the bag's elements; that does not change the container, but the order in which elements are returned is not guaranteed, since it could be insertion order, but it could also be completely random each time the bag is iterated upon.

So, a bag can be described in terms of *priority queues (PQs)*: one for which element removal (method `top`) is disabled, it's possible to *peek* one element at a time, and the priority of each element is given by a random number from a uniform distribution. Priorities also change at every iteration.

D.2 Stack

A *stack* is a collection that returns its elements according to the *LIFO* (*Last In First Out*) policy. This means that the elements in the stack will be returned in the reverse order with respect to the order they were added to the stack. This makes stacks pretty useful when you need to reverse a sequence or access recently added elements first.

We can see a stack, like the one shown in figure D.2, as a specialized PQ where elements' priorities are given by the time at which they are inserted (most recently inserted elements have highest priority).

When comparing a stack to a bag, in fact, the first difference is that for stacks, order matters.

The second one is that while it is possible to iterate through the whole stack at once, it's also possible to remove elements from a stack. In particular, a stack is a limited access data structure, because it's only possible to add or remove elements to/from the top of the stack.

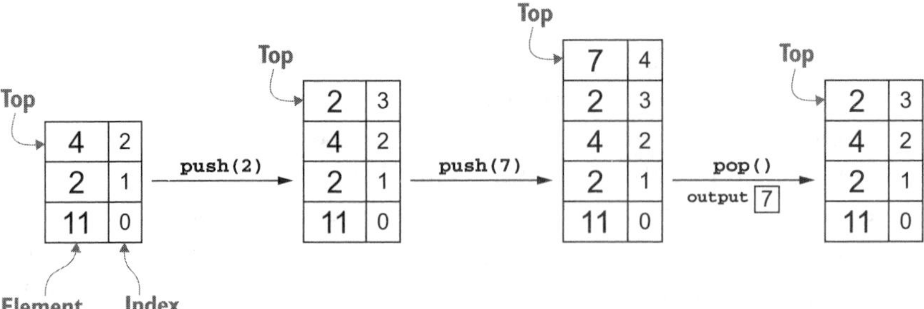
Top
4 2
2 1
11 0
Element
Index
push(2)
Top
2 3
4 2
2 1
11 0
push(7)
Top
7 4
2 3
4 2
2 1
11 0
pop()
output 7
Top
2 3
4 2
2 1
11 0

Figure D.2 Operations on a stack. Insertion (`push`) adds elements to the top of the stack. Delete (`pop`) removes the top element and returns it. For stacks (as well as for queues), a `peek` operation is also usually available, returning the top element without removing it from the container.

Typical real-world examples used to explain stacks usually include a pile of dirty dishes (you pick from the top of the pile, so you first wash the ones that have been added to the pile more recently). It is in computer science, however, that stacks find their largest and more crucial uses:

- *Memory management* allowing your programs to run (the call stack).
- *Implementation of the memento pattern* in turn allows you to undo actions in your editor or browse back and forth in your browser's history.
- *Enabling recursion* and being used as support for several algorithms.
- In the JavaScript world, you might have heard of *time-travel* in React.

And this list is by no means exhaustive.

D.3 Queue

A *queue* is a collection that is based on the FIFO (First In First Out) policy. Therefore, elements of a queue will be returned in the same order as they were added to it. While queues are also limited access data structures, elements are added to the front of the queue and removed from its back (which also means their implementation is slightly more complicated than stacks').

Figure D.3 shows an example of a queue.

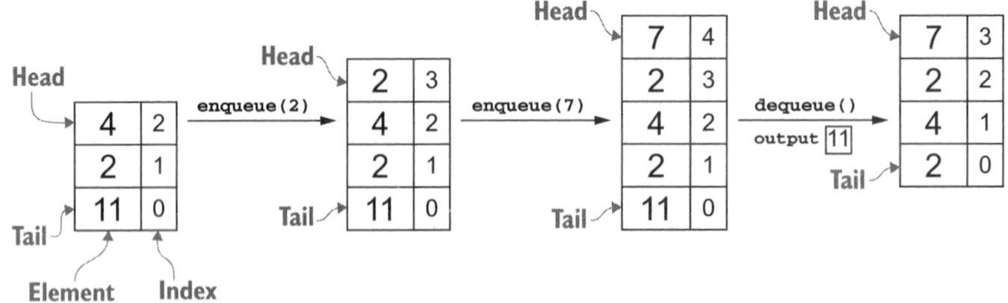
Head
4 2
2 1
11 0
Tail
Element
Index
enqueue(2)
Head
2 3
4 2
2 1
11 0
Tail
enqueue(7)
Head
7 4
2 3
4 2
2 1
11 0
Tail
dequeue()
output 11
Head
7 3
2 2
4 1
2 0
Tail

Figure D.3 Operations on a queue. Insertion (`enqueue`) adds elements to the front of the queue. Delete (`dequeue`) removes the element at the back of the queue and returns it.

A queue, as you can imagine at this point, is a particular case of priority queue where the priority of an element is its age: older elements have the highest priority.

The name, in this case, is quite revealing, and indeed in the real world this is the DS we (subconsciously) use every time we are waiting in a fair line: whoever has been waiting the longest is served first. Like stacks, queues are fundamental to computer science, and are used in many algorithms.

D.4 A comparative analysis of containers

In summary, we can partition the abstract structures discussed according to a few core characteristics: if keys are maintained in a certain order, if they need to be unique, and if the container is associative. In the analysis provided in table D.1, we include all containers shown in the previous sections, plus dictionaries (discussed in appendix C).

Table D.1 Comparison of Containers

Structure	Order	Unique	Associativity
`Bag`	No	No	None
`Stack`	Yes	No	None
`Queue`	Yes	No	None
`Priority Queue`	Yes	No [a]	None
`Dictionary`	No	Yes	key-value

a. As we mentioned in section 2.6.6, relaxing the uniqueness constraint for keys will require extra efforts on priority update.

appendix E Recursion

If you are reading this book, you are probably already familiar with loops. As discussed in appendix A, `for`, `while`, and `do-while` loops (and some more, depending on the language) all are examples of iteration.

Iterative loops are one straightforward way to repeatedly perform similar actions on a series of elements. Usually loops go hand in hand with certain data structures, for example, containers like lists and arrays.

Loops tend to work well when the data structure has a linear shape; sometimes, though, things are more complicated and a simple loop might not be enough to immediately solve the issue. We will see, for example, how trees and graphs are more challenging than lists. There are workarounds to use loops with these structures as well, but often a different approach works better.

In the rest of this book, we used pseudo-code to describe algorithms in a language-agnostic way. To better illustrate how recursion works, however, a real programming language works better than pseudo-code. So, for this appendix only, we will use JavaScript in code listings. The choice of JavaScript, out of many possible candidates, is motivated by two characteristics of this language:

- Full read/write closures
- Functions treated as first class citizens

These aspects allow us to illustrate an interesting technique called *memoization*, which can be used in specific contexts to improve the performance of recursive algorithms.

The same results could be obtained analogously in most functional programming languages. There are workarounds in OO languages too; for instance, in Java, memoization can be obtained through static class fields.

E.1 Simple recursion

The simplest case of recursion is when a function calls itself at a given point of its flow. The most used (and abused) examples of recursion are computing the factorial of a number and Fibonacci's numbers.

Listing E.1 shows a possible JavaScript implementation of a function computing Fibonacci's numbers.

Listing E.1 Fibonacci numbers, JavaScript

```
function fibonacci(n) {
    if (n < 0) {
      throw new Error('n can not be negative');
    } else if (n === 0 || n === 1) {
      return 1; // Base case
    } else {
      return fibonacci(n-1) + fibonacci(n-2);
    }
}
```

E.1.1 Pitfalls

Recursion is not free of risks. First, we need to make sure to define a base case that is always possible to reach. In the example in listing E.1, if we forgot to check that the argument n is non-negative, `fibonacci(-1)` would go through every single negative integer number that can be stored in JavaScript before hitting the base case for `n === 0`. But more likely, it would throw an `Error: Maximum call stack size exceeded` long before getting anywhere near the base case.

Of course, even using a loop, you'd need to get stopping conditions right; otherwise, you might end up with an infinite loop.

Even with that extra check, we are not safe yet. In weakly typed languages such as JavaScript, type-coercion will try to convert arguments passed to our function to numbers.

Try to call `fibonacci('a')` or `fibonacci(true)` instead. The method described previously doesn't check that n has the proper type; `'a' - 1` returns `NaN`,[1] as well as `NaN - 1`. Since `NaN` is not lower than 0, not equal to 0 or 1, the result is a (theoretically) infinite recursion call stack, that ends up once again in an `Error`.

Another possible downside is a waste of resources. If you look closely at listing E.1, you can understand why this is not the best use case for recursion. For instance, try to track down the recursive calls we make when we call `fibonacci(4)`:

---

[1] `NaN` is a special value in JavaScript, standing for *not a number*, and returned when there are issues parsing numbers or operating on numbers.

- fibonacci(4)
-   fibonacci(3)
-     fibonacci(2)
-       fibonacci(1)
-       fibonacci(0)
-     fibonacci(1)
-   fibonacci(2)
-     fibonacci(1)
-     fibonacci(0)

Indentation here is purely stylistic and meant to help you keep track of the hierarchy of the calls.

If you try with `fibonacci(5)`, it will be even more apparent that we compute the same value multiple times (at the cost of several function calls).

Computing sub-problems twice (or multiple times) is usually a *smell*, suggesting a different solution could be more efficient; and, in fact, in these cases usually *dynamic programming* could provide a better alternative.

In JavaScript, a similar approach to keep track of the result of recursive calls on sub-problems is memoization. With memoization, before making a recursive call, we check if we have cached the value, as shown in the implementation in listing E.2.

Listing E.2 Fibonacci using memoization

```
const fibonacci = (() => {            // We use IIFE to create a closure for memoization.
  let cache = [1, 1];                 // This is our "history." Initialized with return values for 1 and 0.
  const get = (n) => {                // This function (defined using lambda notation) takes care of memoization.
    if (n >= cache.length) {
      cache[n] = fibonacci(n);        // Updates history with a true recursive call
    }
    return cache[n];
  };
  return (n) => {                     // We return a function (which will be assigned to const fibonacci), effectively computing the n-th Fibonacci number, for input n.
    if (n < 0) {
      throw new Error('n can not be negative');
    } else if (n > 1) {
      return get(n - 1) + get(n - 2); // Computes f(n) by retrieving values for n-1 and n-2
    }
    return 1;                         // Covers the case n === 1 || n === 0
  };
})();                                 // Executes the IIFE so the result of the function call is assigned to the constant on the first line
```

Both using naïve recursion and memoization can lead to space issues and out-of-memory exceptions (more on this in a few sections).

E.1.2 Good recursion

The previous example shows that just using recursion didn't really improve the situation compared to an iterative algorithm. As a matter of fact, there are cases where recursion is the right choice, usually because either the very nature of the problem or its definition is recursive. Usually it's more a matter of clarity, of writing clean code, than it is of performance. In a couple of sections, however, we'll see how *tail recursion* combines both (at least in modern programming languages).

But for now, let's take a look at an elegant solution for the preorder traversal of a binary tree, shown in listing E.3.

Listing E.3 Binary tree preorder traversal

```
function preorder(node) {
  if (node === undefined || node === null) {
    console.log("leaf");
  } else {
    console.log(node.value);
    preorder(node.left);       <-- Recursive traversal of the left child
    preorder(node.right);      <-- Recursive traversal of the right child
  }
}
```

> **Tree traversal**
>
> Preorder traversal is a way of enumerating the keys stored in a tree. It creates a list starting with the key stored in the root, and then it recursively traverses its children's subtrees. When it gets to any node, it first adds the node's key to the list, and then goes to the children (in case of a binary tree, it starts from the left child, and then, only when that subtree is entirely traversed, goes to the right one).
>
> Other common traversals are inorder (the order is left subtree->node's key->right subtree) and postorder (left subtree -> right subtree -> node's key).

Of course, you can perform any action on the nodes, in addition to printing them. And yes, you can do the same with loops, as shown in listing E.4.

Listing E.4 Binary tree preorder traversal, iterative version

```
function preorderIterative(node) {
  if (node === undefined || node === null) {
    return;
  }
  let nodeStack = [node];      <-- We have to use an explicit stack to simulate the behavior of recursive calls (see the next section).
  while (nodeStack.length > 0) {
    node = nodeStack.pop();
    if (node === undefined) {
      console.log("leaf");
    } else {
```

```
        console.log(node.value);
        nodeStack.push(node.right);
        nodeStack.push(node.left);
      }
    }
  }
```

Pushing a node on the stack is equivalent to a recursive call in iterative terms.

The two methods are equivalent, but look at how elegant the first one is. Try to write both versions for post-order binary tree traversal, and you'll also realize that the iterative one is harder to get right.

E.2 Tail recursion

Every time we make a function call, we create a new entry in the program stack, a so-called *stack frame*. The stack frame consists of a few fields that are needed by our program or virtual machine to execute the called function, and then, when it's done, resume the execution of the caller function.

A (non-exhaustive) list of these fields includes

- The *program counter* (a pointer to the next instruction in the caller function to run after the new function finishes)
- All the arguments passed to the called function
- All the local variables
- A placeholder for the return value of the called function

Recursive calls are no exception, with the caveat that the first call to a recursive function might not return before the base case is hit. This means the call chain can get extremely long.

Take, for example, the factorial function, shown in listing E.5.

Listing E.5 Factorial function, JavaScript

```
function factorial(n) {
  if (n < 0) {
    throw new Error('n can not be negative');
  } else if (n === 0) {
    return 1;                      <-- Base case
  }
  let f = factorial(n - 1);
  return n * f;
}
```

Recursive call to `factorial`. We are using an explicit variable to make a point (see below).

A call to factorial with a positive integer n will require the creation of n stack frames. In figure E.1 we sketched the stack frame for a call to `factorial(3)`, where you can see three new stack frames are created. Since the stack area in memory is fixed and limited (and small compared to the heap), this is a recipe for disaster. Try to call this method with a sufficiently large value, and you are going to cause a segmentation fault.

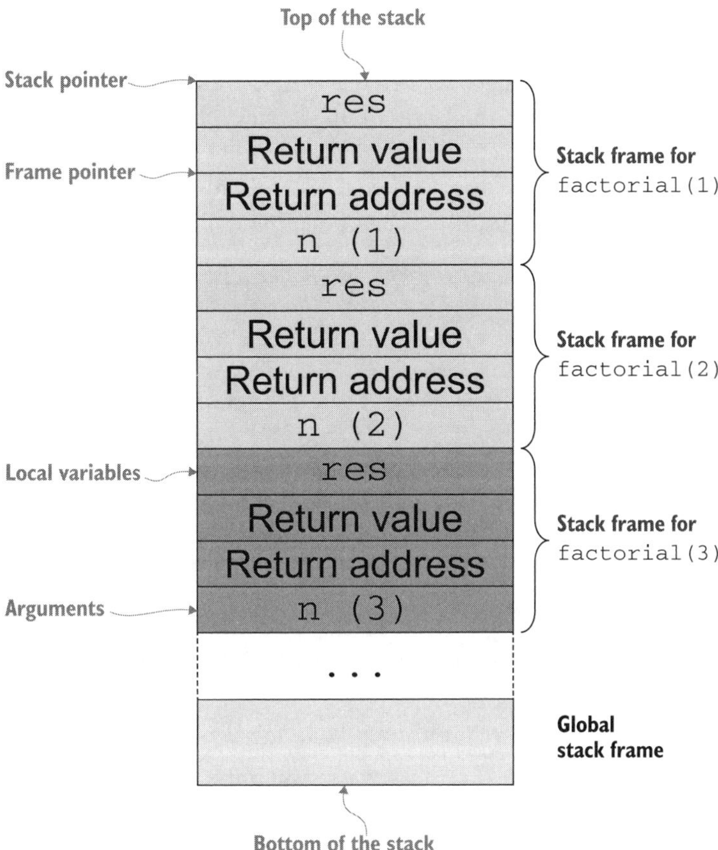
Top of the stack
Stack pointer
res
Return value
Frame pointer
Return address
n (1)
Stack frame for
factorial(1)
res
Return value
Return address
n (2)
Stack frame for
factorial(2)
Local variables
res
Return value
Return address
Arguments
n (3)
Stack frame for
factorial(3)
. . .
Global
stack frame
Bottom of the stack

Figure E.1 Example of a stack frame for a call to `factorial(3)`. Take the first definition of factorial as a reference.

A *segmentation fault*, aka *access violation*, is a failure condition, raised by hardware with memory protection, notifying an operating system that some software has attempted to access a restricted area of memory that had not been assigned to the software.

Luckily for us, modern compilers have a way to optimize certain kinds of recursive calls. A *tail call* is a function call that is performed as the last operation of a function. A function is *tail-recursive* if its recursive call(s) are in *tail position.* For more details about tail calls and recursion, see this excellent post on the 2ality blog.[2]

Most compilers optimize tail calls, by shortcutting the stack frame creation. With tail recursion, compilers can go even further, by rewriting the chain calls as a loop.

As for our example, in the case of JavaScript, support for tail call optimization was introduced with `ES2015`.

---

[2] See http://mng.bz/2ejm.

To make sure the compiler can optimize the machine code generated for our factorial function, however, we need to slightly change it to make sure the recursive call is the last operation before returning.

For some functions, however, this is particularly tricky. For instance, consider the factorial function: listing E.6 refactors it in such a way that it looks tail-recursive, but it's actually not! The last operation performed, in fact, is multiplying `n` by the result of the recursive call. No tail-call optimization can be applied in this case.

Listing E.6 Factorial function, refactored

```
function factorial(n) {
  if (n < 0) {
    throw new Error('n can not be negative');
  } else if (n === 0) {
    return 1;                <—— Base case
  }

  return n * factorial(n-1); <—— The recursive call is not the last instruction
}                                in this function; the multiplication is.
```

It seems like a dead end, but we shouldn't despair yet; everything is not lost. Listing E.7 shows how we can rewrite even a factorial as a tail-recursive method by adding an extra argument, an accumulator that keeps track of the multiplications already performed, allowing us to perform those operations before the final recursive call.

Listing E.7 Factorial function, tail-recursive

```
function factorial(n, acc=1) {       <—— The method now takes two arguments, the
  if (n < 0) {                           usual n, and an accumulator whose default
    throw new Error('n can not be negative');  value is 1 (so that calling factorial(n)
  } else if (n === 0) {                  is equivalent to factorial(n,1)).
    return acc;             <—— Base case: we return the accumulator with
  }                             the total product from previous calls.

  return factorial(n - 1, n * acc);  <—— Now, finally, the recursive call is the last
}                                        instruction in this function, as the multiplication
                                         is performed when the arguments are evaluated,
                                         before the recursive call.
```

What the compiler will do to optimize the tail call is simply translate it into a loop. In fact, tail recursion can always be easily written as a simple loop. For example, see listing E.8, where we use a `while` loop to compute factorial.

Listing E.8 Factorial function, iterative version

```
function factorial(n) {
  let acc = 1;            <—— Initializes the accumulator (base case)
  if (n < 0) {
```

```
    throw new Error('n can not be negative');
  }

  while (n > 1) {        <-- Simulates tail recursion with a loop
    acc *= n--;
  }
  return acc;
}
```

E.3 Mutual recursion

A function can call itself directly, but also through another function. If two or more functions call themselves in a cycle, then they are *mutual recursive.*

Mutual tail recursion can also be optimized in the same way as tail-call optimization does, but most compilers will only optimize simple tail recursion.

Listing E.9 gives an idea of how mutual recursion works.

Listing E.9 An example of mutual recursive functions

```
function f(n) {
  return n + g(n-1);      <-- Function f calls g.
}

function g(n) {
  if (n < 0) {
    return 1;
  } else if (n === 0) {
    return 2;
  } else {
    return n * f(n/3);      <-- And function g calls f back.
  }
}
```

We define a couple of methods, `f` and `g`, where function `f` never calls itself directly, and likewise in `g` there is no direct recursive call to itself.

However, check out the call stack for `f(7)`:

- `f(7)`
- `g(6)`
- `f(2)`
- `g(1)`
- `f(0.3333)`
- `g(-0.6666)`

A single call to `f` generates a chain of calls where the two functions alternate. Needless to say, mutual recursion is even trickier to track and optimize

appendix F Classification problems and randomnized algorithm metrics

To understand the performance analysis of data structures such as Treaps (chapter 3) and Bloom filters (chapter 4), we need to take a step back and first introduce a class of algorithms with which not every developer is familiar.

Most people, when prompted about algorithms, immediately think about deterministic algorithms. It's easy to mistake this subclass of algorithms for the whole group: our common sense makes us expect an algorithm to be a sequence of instructions that, when provided a specific input, applies the same steps to return a well-defined output.

That's indeed the common scenario. It is possible, however, to describe an algorithm as a sequence of well-defined steps that will produce a deterministic result but take an unpredictable (though finite) amount of time. Algorithms that behave this way are called *Las Vegas algorithms*.

Even less intuitively, it is possible to describe algorithms that might produce a different, unpredictable result for the same input in every execution, or might also not terminate in a finite amount of time. There is a name for this class of algorithms as well: they are called *Monte Carlo algorithms*.

There is some debate about whether the latter should be considered as algorithms or heuristics, but I lean toward including them, because the sequence of steps in Monte Carlo algorithms is deterministic and well-defined. In this book we do present a few Monte Carlo algorithms, so you will have a chance to form an educated opinion.

But before delving into these classes, we should define a particularly useful class of problems, *decision problems.*

F.1 Decision problems

When talking about algorithms that return either `true` or `false`, we fall into the class of problems called *binary decision problems.*

Binary classification algorithms assign one of two labels to the data. The two labels can actually be anything, but conceptually, this is equivalent to assigning a Boolean label to each point, so we'll use this notation in the rest of the book.

Considering only binary classification is not restrictive, since multiclass classifiers can be obtained by combining several binary classifiers.

One fundamental result in computer science, and in particular in the field of computability and complexity, is that any optimization problem can be expressed as a decision problem and vice versa.

For instance, if we are looking for the shortest path in a graph, we can define an equivalent decision problem by setting a threshold `T` and checking if there exists a path with length at most `T`. By solving this problem for different values of `T`, and by choosing these values using binary search, we can find a solution to the optimization problem by using an algorithm for the decision problem.[1]

F.2 Las Vegas algorithms

The class of so-called Las Vegas algorithms includes all randomized algorithms that

1. Always give as output the correct solution to the problem (or return a failure).
2. Can be run using a finite, but unpredictable (random) amount of resources. The key point is that how much resources are needed can't be predicted based on input.

The most notable example of a Las Vegas algorithm is probably randomized quicksort:[2] it always produces the correct solution, but the pivot is chosen randomly at every recursive step, and execution time swirls between `O(n*log n)` and $O(n^2)$, depending on the choices made.

F.3 Monte Carlo algorithms

We classify algorithms as Monte Carlo methods when the output of the algorithm can sometimes be incorrect. The probability of an incorrect answer is usually a trade-off with the resources employed, and practical algorithms manage to keep this probability small while using a reasonable amount of computing power and memory.

---

[1] If the threshold is guaranteed to be an integer or rational number, we can also guarantee that the solution will be in the same computational class as the solution to the decision problem, so if, for example, we have a polynomial solution to the decision problem, solving the optimization problem will also require polynomial time.

[2] See *Grokking Algorithms,* by Aditya Bhargava (Manning Publications, 2016), chapter 4, page 51.

For decision problems, when the answer to a Monte Carlo algorithm is just `true/false`, we have three possible situations:

- The algorithm is always correct when it returns `false` (so-called *false-biased* algorithm).
- The algorithm is always correct when it returns `true` (so-called *true-biased* algorithm).
- The algorithm might return the wrong answer indifferently for the two cases.

Monte Carlo algorithms are deterministic in the amount of resources needed, and they are used often as the dual of a Las Vegas algorithm.

Suppose we have an algorithm A that always return the correct solution, but whose resource consumption is not deterministic. If we have a limited amount of resources, we can run A until it outputs a solution or exhausts the allotted resources. For instance, we could stop randomized quicksort after `n*log n` swaps.

This way, we are trading accuracy (the guarantee of a correct result) for the certainty to have a (sub-optimal) answer within a certain time (or using at most a certain amount of space).

It's also worth noting that as we mentioned, for some randomized algorithms, we don't even know if they will eventually stop and find a solution (although this is usually not the case). Take, for example, the randomized version of Bogosort.

F.4 Classification metrics

When we analyze data structures such as Bloom filters or Treaps, examining the time and memory requirements of their methods is paramount, but not enough. Besides how fast they run, and how much memory they use, for Monte Carlo algorithms like these we also need to ask one more question: "How well does it work?"

To answer this question, we need to introduce *metrics*, functions that measure the distance between an approximated solution and the optimal one.

For classification algorithms, the quality of an algorithm is a measure of how well each input is assigned to its right class. For binary (that is, `true/false`) classification, therefore, it's about how accurately the algorithm outputs `true` for the input points.

F.4.1 Accuracy

One way of measuring the quality of a classification algorithm is to assess the rate of correct predictions. Suppose that over N_P points actually belonging to the `true` class:

- P_P are predicted as `true`.
- T_P, the so-called *true positives*, are both predicted as `true` and actually belong to the `true` class.

Likewise, let N_N be the number of points belonging to the `false` class:

- P_N is the total number of points for which our algorithm predicts the class `false`.

- T_N, the so-called *true negatives*, is the number of times both the predicted and the actual class of a point are `false`.

Then we can define *accuracy*:

$$accuracy = \frac{T_P + T_N}{N_P + N_N} = \frac{T_P + T_N}{N}$$

When the accuracy is 1, we have an algorithm that is always correct.

Unfortunately, except for that ideal case, accuracy is not always a good measure of the quality of our algorithms. Consider an edge case where 99% of the points in a database actually belongs to the `true` class. Then look at the following three classifiers:

- A classifier correctly labeling 100% of the false points and 98.98% of the true ones
- A classifier correctly labeling 0.5% of the false points and 99.49% of the true ones
- A classifier that always returns true as label

Astonishingly, the latter has better accuracy than the other two, even if it misses every single point in the false category.

> **TIP** If you'd like to double check this, plug in these numbers into the formula for accuracy.

In machine learning, if you were to use this metric on a training set skewed in a similar way,[3] you'd get a terrible model, or more precisely, a model that is likely to generalize poorly.

F.4.2 Precision and recall

To improve over bare accuracy, we need to keep track of the info about each category separately. To this end, we can define two new metrics:

- *Precision* (also called *positive predictive value*) defined as the ratio of correctly predicted true points (the *true positives*) over the total number of points for which `true` was predicted by the algorithm:

  $$precision = \frac{T_P}{P_P}$$

- *Recall* (also known as *sensitivity*) defined as the fraction of true positives over the total number of actual positives:

  $$recall = \frac{T_P}{N_P}$$

[3] For instance, a dataset where one of the classes is rare or difficult to get data for: this is often the case in medicine with rare diseases.

It is possible to give an alternate definition of precision and recall by introducing the number of *false positives* `Fp`, that is, points belonging to the `false` class for which `true` was incorrectly predicted, and the number of *false negatives* `Fn`:

$$precision = \frac{T_P}{T_P + F_P}$$

$$recall = \frac{T_P}{T_P + F_N}$$

Intuitively, while accuracy only measures how well we do on predictions, precision/recall metrics weigh our successes with our errors for the dual category. As a matter of fact, precision and recall are not independent, and one can be defined in terms of the other, so it's not possible to improve both indefinitely. In general, if you improve recall, you'll often get a slightly worse precision and vice versa.

For machine learning classifiers, every model can be associated with a precision/recall curve (see figure F.1), and the model's parameters can be tuned during training so that we can trade off the two characteristics.

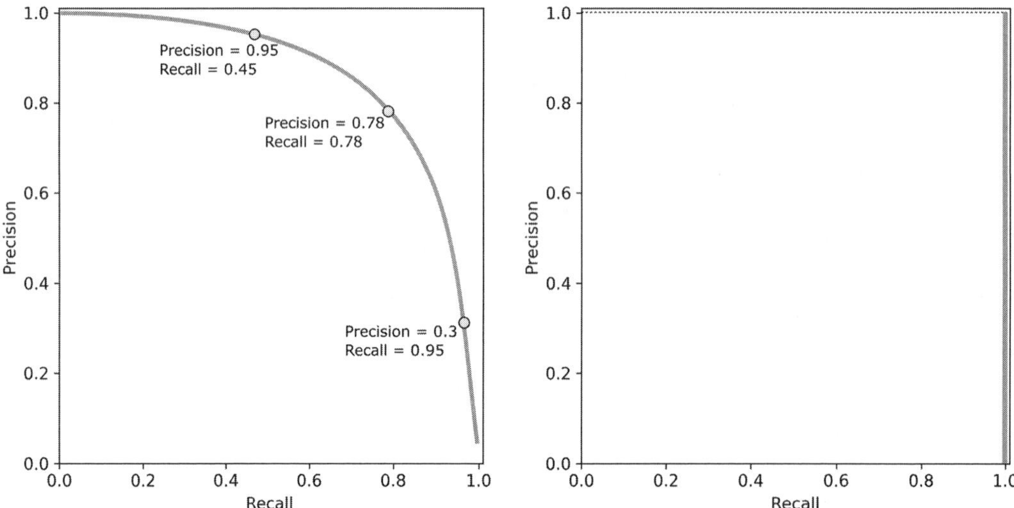
Precision = 0.95
Recall = 0.45
Precision = 0.78
Recall = 0.78
Precision = 0.3
Recall = 0.95
Precision
Recall
1.0
0.8
0.6
0.4
0.2
0.0
0.0
0.2
0.4
0.6
0.8
1.0
Precision
Recall

Figure F.1 Examples of precision-recall curve. The one on the left is a generic curve for a hypothetical algorithm. This is plotted by tuning the algorithm's parameters and recording the precision and recall obtained. After recording many attempts, we can get a drawing similar to this graphic. In general, when a given choice of the model's parameters improves precision, there will be a slight worsening of recall, and vice versa. On the right, a degenerate P-R curve for a false-biased algorithm, such as Bloom filters; its recall is always equal to 1, for any precision. True-biased algorithms have a symmetrical P-R curve.

So, for binary categorization, a perfect (100%) precision means that every point for which we output `true` actually belonged to the `true` category. Similarly, for recall, when it's 100%, we never have a false negative.

As an exercise, try to compute precision and recall for the examples in the previous sections and see how they give us more information about the quality of a model with respect to just its accuracy.

If we take Bloom filters (chapter 4) as an example, we explain in section 4.8 that when the output is `false`, we can be sure it's right, so Bloom filters have a 100% recall.

Their precision, unfortunately, is not as perfect. In section 4.10 we delve into the details of how to compute it. In this case, however, like for all false-biased algorithms, there is no trade-off with recall, and improving precision can only be done by increasing the resources used.

F.4.3 Other metrics and recap

There are, of course, other metrics that can be useful for classifiers. One of the most useful is the F-measure,[4] combining precision and recall into one formula. These alternative metrics, however, go beyond our scope.

If we continue with our parallel with Bloom filters, we can recap the meaning of the metrics we examined in that context:

- *Accuracy* answers the question, "What percentage of calls to `contains` are correct?"
- *Precision* answers the question, "What percentage of calls to `contains` returning `true` were correct?"
- *Recall* answers the question, "Among all calls to `contains` on elements actually contained in the filter, what percent of them returned `true`?" (This one, as we know, will always be 100% for Bloom filters).

[4] See https://en.wikipedia.org/wiki/F1_score.

index

Numerics

A

B

D

H

L

M

N

O

P

Q

R

S

T

U

V

W

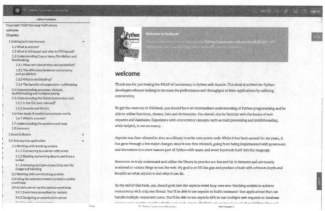